Contemporary Management

Management

Sixth Edition

Gareth R. Jones
Texas A&M University

Jennifer M. George
Rice University

McGraw-Hill Irwin

Boston   Burr Ridge, IL   Dubuque, IA   New York   San Francisco   St. Louis
Bangkok   Bogotá   Caracas   Kuala Lumpur   Lisbon   London   Madrid   Mexico City
Milan   Montreal   New Delhi   Santiago   Seoul   Singapore   Sydney   Taipei   Toronto

For Nicholas and Julia

McGraw-Hill
Irwin

CONTEMPORARY MANAGEMENT

Published by McGraw-Hill/Irwin, a business unit of The McGraw-Hill Companies, Inc., 1221 Avenue of the Americas, New York, NY, 10020. Copyright © 2009, 2008, 2006, 2003, 2000, 1998 by The McGraw-Hill Companies, Inc. All rights reserved. No part of this publication may be reproduced or distributed in any form or by any means, or stored in a database or retrieval system, without the prior written consent of The McGraw-Hill Companies, Inc., including, but not limited to, in any network or other electronic storage or transmission, or broadcast for distance learning.

Some ancillaries, including electronic and print components, may not be available to customers outside the United States.

This book is printed on acid-free paper.

1 2 3 4 5 6 7 8 9 0 WCK/WCK 0 9 8

ISBN   978-0-07-353043-7
MHID   0-07-353043-3

Vice president and editor-in-chief: *Brent Gordon*
Senior sponsoring editor: *Michael Ablassmeir*
Developmental editor II: *Laura Griffin*
Editorial assistant: *Kelly Pekelder*
Senior marketing manager: *Anke Braun Weekes*
Marketing coordinator: *Michael Gedatus*
Project manager: *Kathryn D. Mikulic*
Lead production supervisor: *Michael R. McCormick*
Designer: *JoAnne Schopler*
Senior photo research coordinator: *Lori Kramer*
Photo researcher: *Sarah Evertson*
Senior media project manager: *Greg Bates*
Cover design: *JoAnne Schopler*
Interior design: *Pam Verros*
Typeface: *10.25/12 Baskerville*
Compositor: *Laserwords Private Limited*
Printer: *Quebecor World Versailles Inc.*

Library of Congress Cataloging-in-Publication Data

Jones, Gareth R.
  Contemporary management / Gareth R. Jones, Jennifer M. George.–6th ed.
    p. cm.
  Includes index.
  ISBN-13: 978-0-07-353043-7 (alk. paper)
  ISBN-10: 0-07-353043-3 (alk. paper)
  1. Management. I. George, Jennifer M. II. Title.
HD31.J597 2009
658—dc22

                                    2008037273

www.mhhe.com

Brief Contents

PART ONE
Management

CHAPTER ONE
Managers and Managing 2

CHAPTER TWO
The Evolution
of Management Thought 38

CHAPTER THREE
Values, Attitudes, Emotions, and
Culture: The Manager as a Person 72

PART TWO
**The Environment of
Management**

CHAPTER FOUR
Ethics and Social Responsibility 108

CHAPTER FIVE
Managing Diverse Employees in a
Multicultural Environment 148

CHAPTER SIX
Managing in the Global Environment 186

PART THREE
**Decision Making, Planning,
and Strategy**

CHAPTER SEVEN
Decision Making, Learning, Creativity,
and Entrepreneurship 224

CHAPTER EIGHT
The Manager as a Planner and
Strategist 260

CHAPTER NINE
Value-Chain Management: Functional
Strategies for Competitive Advantage 302

PART FOUR
Organizing and Controlling

CHAPTER TEN
Managing Organizational Structure
and Culture 342

CHAPTER ELEVEN
Organizational Control and Change 384

CHAPTER TWELVE
Human Resource Management 420

PART FIVE
Leading Individuals and Groups

CHAPTER THIRTEEN
Motivation and Performance 460

CHAPTER FOURTEEN
Leadership 494

CHAPTER FIFTEEN
Effective Groups and Teams 526

PART SIX
**Managing Critical
Organizational Processes**

CHAPTER SIXTEEN
Promoting Effective Communication 564

CHAPTER SEVENTEEN
Managing Conflict, Politics,
and Negotiation 602

CHAPTER EIGHTEEN
Using Advanced Information
Technology to Increase Performance 632

GLOSSARY 667

CREDITS 679

INDEX 713

Contents

Part One Management

Chapter One — Managers and Managing 2

A Manager's Challenge
How Anne Mulcahy Created a New Xerox 3

Topics

Overview 5

What Is Management? 5

Achieving High Performance:
A Manager's Goal 5

Why Study Management? 7

Essential Managerial Tasks 8

Planning 8

Organizing 11

Leading 12

Controlling 12

Performing Managerial Tasks: Mintzberg's Typology 13

Levels and Skills of Managers 13

Levels of Management 15

Managerial Skills 16

Recent Changes in Management Practices 20

Restructuring and Outsourcing 20

Empowerment and Self-Managed Teams 21

Challenges for Management in a Global Environment 22

Building Competitive Advantage 23

Maintaining Ethical and Socially Responsible Standards 26

Managing a Diverse Workforce 28

Utilizing IT and E-Commerce 29

Practicing Global Crisis Management 30

Chapter Two — The Evolution of Management Thought 38

A Manager's Challenge
Finding Better Ways to Make Cars 39

Topics

Overview 41

Scientific Management Theory 42

Job Specialization and the Division of Labor 42

F. W. Taylor and Scientific Management 43

The Gilbreths 46

Administrative Management Theory 48

The Theory of Bureaucracy 49

Fayol's Principles of Management 50

Behavioral Management Theory 55

The Work of Mary Parker Follett 55

The Hawthorne Studies and Human Relations 56

Theory X and Theory Y 57

Management Science Theory 60

Organizational Environment Theory 61

The Open-Systems View 61

Contingency Theory 62

iv

Examples

Manager as a Person
Joe Coulombe Makes Trader
Joe's a Small Business
Success Story   10

Information Technology Byte
IBM Creates Global Self-
Managed Teams   22

Management Insight
Sharper Image Is No Longer
in Focus   25

Ethics in Action
How Not to Run a
Meatpacking Plant   27

Management in Action

Summary and Review   31

Management in Action   32
Topics for Discussion and Action   32
Building Management Skills   32
Managing Ethically   33
Small Group Breakout Exercise   33
Exploring the World Wide Web   34
Be the Manager   34
BusinessWeek Case in the News:
Howard Schultz's Starbucks
Challenge   34
BusinessWeek Case in the News:
Making Her Mark at Merck:
Margaret McGlynn Is on a
Fast Track   35

Examples

Ethics in Action
Fordism in Practice   45

Manager as a Person
Andrew Carnegie Creates the
New Industrial Company   47

Management Insight
Peters and Waterman's Excellent
Companies   54

Managing Globally
Teams, Teams, and More
Teams at Nokia   64

Management in Action

Summary and Review   65

Management in Action   66
Topics for Discussion and Action   66
Building Management Skills   66
Managing Ethically   67
Small Group Breakout Exercise   69
Exploring the World Wide Web   69
Be the Manager   69
BusinessWeek Case in the News:
Netflix: Flex to the Max   69
BusinessWeek Case in the News:
Oticon's No-Cubicle Culture   71

Contents

Chapter Three

Values, Attitudes, Emotions, and Culture: The Manager as a Person 72

A Manager's Challenge
Ryla Teleservices Stands Out
Among Telemarketers 73

Topics

Overview 75

Enduring Characteristics: Personality Traits 75

  The Big Five Personality Traits 75

  Other Personality Traits That Affect Managerial Behavior 80

Values, Attitudes, and Moods and Emotions 81

  Values: Terminal and Instrumental 82

  Attitudes 84

  Moods and Emotions 88

Emotional Intelligence 90

Organizational Culture 91

  Managers and Organizational Culture 92

  The Role of Values and Norms in Organizational Culture 94

  Culture and Managerial Action 99

Chapter Four

Ethics and Social Responsibility 108

A Manager's Challenge
The Ethics of the Global
Flower-Growing
Business 109

Topics

Overview 111

The Nature of Ethics 111

  Ethical Dilemmas 111

  Ethics and the Law 112

  Changes in Ethics over Time 113

Stakeholders and Ethics 114

  Stockholders 114

  Managers 115

  Employees 118

  Suppliers and Distributors 118

  Customers 120

  Community, Society, and Nation 122

  Rules for Ethical Decision Making 122

Why Should Managers Behave Ethically? 126

Ethics and Social Responsibility 129

  Societal Ethics 129

  Occupational Ethics 131

  Individual Ethics 132

  Organizational Ethics 133

Approaches to Social Responsibility 135

  Four Different Approaches 135

  Why Be Socially Responsible? 138

  The Role of Organizational Culture 138

Part Two The Environment of Management

Examples

Manager as a Person
Who Would Have Thought
Dirty Jobs Would Be a Hit?   79

Ethics in Action
Telling the Truth at Gentle Giant
Moving   83

Focus on Diversity
Changing Attitudes   85

Manager as a Person
PAETEC's Caring Culture   95

Management in Action

Summary and Review   101

Management in Action   102
Topics for Discussion and Action   102
Building Management Skills   102
Managing Ethically   103
Small Group Breakout Exercise   103
Exploring the World Wide Web   103
Be the Manager   104
BusinessWeek Case in the News:
The Blogging Czar of Moscow   104
BusinessWeek Case in the News:
Young and Impatient in India   105

Examples

Ethics in Action
The Ethics of Some Nonprofits
Are Not So Good   118

Ethics in Action
Whole Foods Market Practices
What It Preaches   120

Ethics in Action
Digital Piracy, Ethics, and Napster   125

Ethics in Action
Is It Right to Use Child Labor?   130

Ethics in Action
Jonathan Reckford Rebuilds
Goodwill at Habitat for Humanity   134

Ethics in Action
Apple Juice or Sugar Water?   137

Ethics in Action
Johnson & Johnson's Ethical
Culture   140

Management in Action

Summary and Review   141

Management in Action   142
Topics for Discussion and Action   142
Building Management Skills   142
Managing Ethically   143
Small Group Breakout Exercise   143
Exploring the World Wide Web   143
Be the Manager   144
BusinessWeek Case in the News:
Cleaning Up Boeing   144
BusinessWeek Case in the News:
Fixing Apple's "Sweatshop" Woes   145

Contents

Chapter Five

Managing Diverse Employees in a
Multicultural Environment 148

A Manager's Challenge
Reaping the Benefits of
Diversity 149

Topics

Overview 151

The Increasing Diversity
of the Workforce and the
Environment 151
  Age 152
  Gender 153
  Race and Ethnicity 154
  Religion 155
  Capabilities/Disabilities 155
  Socioeconomic
  Background 156
  Sexual Orientation 158
  Other Kinds of Diversity 159

Managers and the
Effective Management
of Diversity 159
  Critical Managerial Roles 159
  The Ethical Imperative
  to Manage Diversity
  Effectively 161
  Effectively Managing
  Diversity Makes Good
  Business Sense 162

Perception 164
  Factors That Influence
  Managerial Perception 164

Chapter Six

Managing in the Global Environment 186

A Manager's Challenge
Nestlé's Global Food Empire 187

Topics

Overview 188

What Is the Global
Environment? 189

The Task Environment 189
  Suppliers 189
  Distributors 193
  Customers 194
  Competitors 195

The General
Environment 198
  Economic Forces 199
  Technological Forces 199
  Sociocultural Forces 200
  Demographic Forces 201
  Political and Legal Forces 201

The Changing Global
Environment 202
  The Process of
  Globalization 204
  Declining Barriers to Trade
  and Investment 206
  Declining Barriers of
  Distance and Culture 207
  Effects of Free Trade on
  Managers 208

The Role of National
Culture 210
  Cultural Values and Norms 211
  Hofstede's Model of
  National Culture 211
  National Culture and
  Global Management 214

Examples

Perception as a Determinant
of Unfair Treatment 165

Overt Discrimination 169

How to Manage Diversity
Effectively 170

Steps in Managing Diversity
Effectively 170

Sexual Harassment 175

Forms of Sexual
Harassment 175

Steps Managers Can Take
to Eradicate Sexual
Harassment 176

Focus on Diversity
Preventing Discrimination
Based on Sexual Orientation 158

Ethics in Action
Disabled Employees Make
Valuable Contributions 166

Managing Globally
Women Struggle to Advance
in Their Careers in Japan 169

Management Insight
Top Execs Improve Their
Understanding of the Front Line 171

Management in Action

Summary and Review 177

Management in Action 178
Topics for Discussion and Action 178
Building Management Skills 179
Managing Ethically 179
Small Group Breakout Exercise 179
Exploring the World Wide Web 179
Be the Manager 180
BusinessWeek Case in the
News: What Works in Women's
Networks 180
BusinessWeek Case in the
News: The Best Places to
Launch a Career 182

Examples

Managing Globally
Global Supply Chain Management 192

Ethics in Action
Why Is Beer and Wine So
Expensive: Powerful Distributors 193

Managing Globally
American Rice Invades Japan 198

Managing Globally
Customizing Food to the Tastes
of Different Cultures 203

Managing Globally
IKEA Is on Top of the Furniture
World 205

Managing Globally
A *Gaijin* Works to Turn Around
Sony 212

Managing Globally
Nokia Makes a Big Bet
on Romania 215

Management in Action

Summary and Review 217

Management in Action 218
Topics for Discussion and Action 218
Building Management Skills 218
Managing Ethically 218
Small Group Breakout Exercise 219
Exploring the World Wide Web 219
Be the Manager 219
BusinessWeek Case in the News:
A Guide for Multinationals 220
BusinessWeek Case in the News:
Remade in the USA—Sony Global 221
BusinessWeek Case in the News:
Nokia Connects 223

Contents

Part Three Decision Making, Planning, and Strategy

Chapter Seven

Decision Making, Learning, Creativity, and Entrepreneurship 224

A Manager's Challenge
Making Good Decisions at
PUMA 225

Topics

Overview	227
The Nature of Managerial Decision Making	227
Programmed and Nonprogrammed Decision Making	228
The Classical Model	232
The Administrative Model	232
Steps in the Decision-Making Process	236
Recognize the Need for a Decision	236
Generate Alternatives	237
Assess Alternatives	238
Choose Among Alternatives	239

Implement the Chosen Alternative	239
Learn from Feedback	240
Cognitive Biases and Decision Making	241
Prior-Hypothesis Bias	241
Representativeness Bias	242
Illusion of Control	242
Escalating Commitment	242
Be Aware of Your Biases	243
Group Decision Making	243
The Perils of Groupthink	243
Devil's Advocacy and Dialectical Inquiry	244
Diversity Among Decision Makers	245

Chapter Eight

The Manager as a Planner and Strategist 260

A Manager's Challenge
Why Does Best Buy
Outperform Circuit City? 261

Topics

Overview	263
Planning and Strategy	263
The Nature of the Planning Process	264
Why Planning Is Important	264
Levels of Planning	265
Levels and Types of Planning	266
Time Horizons of Plans	268
Standing Plans and Single-Use Plans	268
Scenario Planning	269

Determining the Organization's Mission and Goals	270
Defining the Business	270
Establishing Major Goals	272
Formulating Strategy	273
SWOT Analysis	273
The Five Forces Model	276
Formulating Business-Level Strategies	277
Low-Cost Strategy	277
Differentiation Strategy	278

Examples

Management in Action

Organizational Learning and Creativity 245

Creating a Learning Organization 245

Promoting Individual Creativity 246

Promoting Group Creativity 247

Entrepreneurship and Creativity 248

Entrepreneurship and New Ventures 250

Intrapreneurship and Organizational Learning 251

Focus on Diversity
Programmed Decision Making at UPS 229

Manager as a Person
Curbing Overconfidence 231

Information Technology Byte
Revising Plans at Associated Business Systems 234

Management Insight
Decision Making and Learning from Feedback at GarageTek 240

Ethics in Action
Finding Funding to Do Good 249

Summary and Review 252
Management in Action 254
Topics for Discussion and Action 254
Building Management Skills 254
Managing Ethically 255
Small Group Breakout Exercise 255
Exploring the World Wide Web 255
Be the Manager 256
BusinessWeek Case in the News:
The Icelander Who Wants Saks 256
BusinessWeek Case in the News:
Bridging the Generation Gap 257

Examples

Management in Action

"Stuck in the Middle" 278
Focused Low-Cost and Focused Differentiation Strategies 279

Formulating Corporate-Level Strategies 281

Concentration on a Single Industry 282
Vertical Integration 282
Diversification 284
International Expansion 286

Planning and Implementing Strategy 292

Management Insight
Ups and Downs at Mattel 271

Manager as a Person
Douglas Conant Keeps Stirring Up Campbell Soup 274

Management Insight
Different Ways to Compete in the Soft-Drink Business 279

Management Insight
How to Make Related Diversification Work 285

Managing Globally
How DHL Entered the U.S. Package Delivery Business 290

Summary and Review 292
Management in Action 293
Topics for Discussion and Action 293
Building Management Skills 293
Managing Ethically 294
Small Group Breakout Exercise 294
Exploring the World Wide Web 294
Be the Manager 295
BusinessWeek Case in the News:
That Computer Is So You 295
BusinessWeek Case in the News:
Is the Bloom Off at FTD? 296
BusinessWeek Case in the News:
Swords to Plowshares and Back Again at Rockwell Collins 297
Appendix How to Develop a Business Plan 298
Developing a Business Plan 298
Writing a Detailed Business Plan 299
Developing Your Own Business Plan 300

Contents

Chapter Nine

Value-Chain Management: Functional Strategies for Competitive Advantage   302

A Manager's Challenge
Toyota's Approach to Building Competitive Advantage 303

Topics

Overview	305	Improving Quality	313
Functional Strategies, the Value Chain, and Competitive Advantage	305	Total Quality Management	314
		Improving Efficiency	318
Functional Strategies and Value-Chain Management	307	Facilities Layout, Flexible Manufacturing, and Efficiency	318
Improving Responsiveness to Customers	309	Just-in-Time Inventory and Efficiency	321
What Do Customers Want?	309	Self-Managed Work Teams and Efficiency	323
Managing the Value Chain to Increase Responsiveness to Customers	310	Process Reengineering and Efficiency	323
Customer Relationship Management	311	Information Systems, the Internet, and Efficiency	324

Chapter Ten

Managing Organizational Structure and Culture   342

A Manager's Challenge
Liz Claiborne Reorganizes Its Structure 343

Topics

Overview	345	The Job Characteristics Model	350
Designing Organizational Structure	345	Grouping Jobs into Functions and Divisions: Designing Organizational Structure	351
The Organizational Environment	346		
Strategy	347	Functional Structure	351
Technology	347	Divisional Structures: Product, Market, and Geographic	354
Human Resources	348		
Grouping Tasks into Jobs: Job Design	348	Matrix and Product Team Designs	358
Job Enlargement and Job Enrichment	349	Hybrid Structure	361

Part Four Organizing and Controlling

Examples

Management in Action

Improving Innovation — 324

Two Kinds of Innovation — 325

Strategies to Promote
Innovation and Speed
Product Development — 325

Managing the Value Chain:
Some Remaining Issues — 331

Boundary-Spanning Roles — 331

Value-Chain Management
Over Time — 333

Ethical Implications — 334

Information Technology Byte
How CRM Helped Empire
HealthChoice — 312

Management Insight
Starwood Uses Six Sigma to
Improve Hotel Performance — 316

Manager as a Person
Paddy Hopkirk Improves Facilities
Layout — 319

Management Insight
United Electric's Kanban System — 322

Management Insight
Google Encourages Innovation
and Product Development — 329

Management Insight
Toyota Is Not Perfect, But It
Continually Strives to Be — 333

Ethics in Action
The Human Cost of Improving
Productivity — 334

Summary and Review — 335

Management in Action — 337
Topics for Discussion and Action — 337
Building Management Skills — 337
Managing Ethically — 338
Small Group Breakout Exercise — 338
Exploring the World Wide Web — 338
Be the Manager — 339
BusinessWeek Case in the News:
Philips' Norelco — 339
BusinessWeek Case in the News:
No One Does Lean Like the
Japanese — 340

Examples

Management in Action

Coordinating Functions
and Divisions — 362

Allocating Authority — 362

Integrating and Coordinating
Mechanisms — 368

Organizational Culture — 370

Where Does Organizational
Culture Come From? — 372

Strong, Adaptive Cultures
versus Weak, Inert Cultures — 375

Managing Globally
Nokia's Geographic Structure
Helps It Conquer the World — 357

Managing Globally
How to Use Empowered Self-
Managed Teams — 365

Manager as a Person
Avon Is Calling for a New
Structure — 367

Manager as a Person
Sam Walton and Wal-Mart's
Culture — 371

Summary and Review — 377

Management in Action — 378
Topics for Discussion and Action — 378
Building Management Skills — 378
Managing Ethically — 379
Small Group Breakout Exercise — 379
Exploring the World Wide Web — 379
Be the Manager — 380
BusinessWeek Case in the News:
Information Technology: Stopping
the Sprawl at HP — 381
BusinessWeek Case in the News:
The Art of Motivation — 382

Contents

Chapter Eleven — Organizational Control and Change 384

A Manager's Challenge
What is the Best Way to Control People and Resources? 385

Topics

Overview 387

What Is Organizational Control? 387
- The Importance of Organizational Control 388
- Control Systems and IT 389
- The Control Process 390

Output Control 393
- Financial Measures of Performance 393
- Organizational Goals 396
- Operating Budgets 396
- Problems with Output Control 398

Behavior Control 399
- Direct Supervision 399
- Management by Objectives 400
- Bureaucratic Control 402
- Problems with Bureaucratic Control 404

Clan Control 406

Organizational Change 407
- Lewin's Force-Field Theory of Change 408
- Evolutionary and Revolutionary Change 409
- Managing Change 409

Chapter Twelve — Human Resource Management 420

A Manager's Challenge
Treating Employees Well Leads to Satisfied Customers 421

Topics

Overview 423

Strategic Human Resource Management 423
- Overview of the Components of HRM 424

The Legal Environment of HRM 427

Recruitment and Selection 429
- Human Resource Planning 430
- Job Analysis 431
- External and Internal Recruitment 432
- The Selection Process 434

Training and Development 438
- Types of Training 438

Types of Development 439
- Transfer of Training and Development 441

Performance Appraisal and Feedback 441
- Types of Performance Appraisal 441
- Who Appraises Performance? 444
- Effective Performance Feedback 445

Pay and Benefits 447
- Pay Level 447
- Pay Structure 447
- Benefits 448

Labor Relations 450
- Unions 450
- Collective Bargaining 451

Examples

Management Insight
Making the Financial Figures
Come Alive   395

Managing Globally
Wal-Mart Uses Output Control to
Expand Internationally   397

Management Insight
Microsoft Has Problems Controlling
and Evaluating Its Employees   401

Manager as a Person
Bob Iger's Big Changes at Walt
Disney   405

Management Insight
James Casey Creates a Culture
for UPS   407

Manager as a Person
Pfizer's Big Push to Create
Blockbuster Drugs   412

Management in Action

Summary and Review   413

Management in Action   415
Topics for Discussion and Action   415
Building Management Skills   415
Managing Ethically   416
Small Group Breakout Exercise   416
Exploring the World Wide Web   416
Be the Manager   417
BusinessWeek Case in the News:
Cracking the Whip at Wyeth   417
BusinessWeek Case in the News:
How Failure Breeds Success   418

Examples

Managing Globally
Managing Human Resources
at Semco   426

Focus on Diversity
Is It Age Discrimination?   428

Information Technology Byte
Fog Creek Software's Approach
to Recruiting   433

Focus on Diversity
Family-Friendly Benefits at
Guerra DeBerry Coody   449

Management in Action

Summary and Review   452

Management in Action   454
Topics for Discussion and Action   454
Building Management Skills   454
Managing Ethically   455
Small Group Breakout Exercise   455
Exploring the World Wide Web   455
Be the Manager   456
BusinessWeek Case in the News:
How to Make a Microserf Smile   456
BusinessWeek Case in the News:
Guess Who's Hiring in America   459

Contents

Part Five Leading Individuals and Groups

Chapter Thirteen — Motivation and Performance   460

A Manager's Challenge
Motivating Employees at Enterprise
Rent-A-Car 461

Topics

Overview 463

The Nature of Motivation 464

Expectancy Theory 467
  Expectancy 467
  Instrumentality 468
  Valence 469
  Bringing It All Together 470

Need Theories 471
  Maslow's Hierarchy of Needs 472
  Alderfer's ERG Theory 473

Herzberg's Motivator-Hygiene Theory 474
McClelland's Needs for Achievement, Affiliation, and Power 474
  Other Needs 475

Equity Theory 476
  Equity 476
  Inequity 477
  Ways to Restore Equity 477

Goal-Setting Theory 479

Chapter Fourteen — Leadership   494

A Manager's Challenge
Judy McGrath Leads
MTV Networks 495

Topics

Overview 497

The Nature of Leadership 497
  Personal Leadership Style and Managerial Tasks 497
  Leadership Styles Across Cultures 499
  Power: The Key to Leadership 500
  Empowerment: An Ingredient in Modern Management 503

Trait and Behavior Models of Leadership 504
  The Trait Model 504
  The Behavior Model 505

Contingency Models of Leadership 507
  Fiedler's Contingency Model 507

House's Path-Goal Theory 510
The Leader Substitutes Model 511
Bringing It All Together 512

Transformational Leadership 513
  Being a Charismatic Leader 514
  Stimulating Subordinates Intellectually 514
  Engaging in Developmental Consideration 514
  The Distinction Between Transformational and Transactional Leadership 515

Gender and Leadership 515

Emotional Intelligence and Leadership 516

Examples

Learning Theories 480
Operant Conditioning Theory 480
Social Learning Theory 483

Pay and Motivation 485
Basing Merit Pay on Individual, Group, or Organizational Performance 485
Salary Increase or Bonus? 486
Examples of Merit Pay Plans 487

Ethics in Action
McDonough Protects the Planet 465

Management Insight
Managing and Retaining Employees at the Container Store 469

Information Technology Byte
Boosting Motivation and Retention at Protus IP Solutions 471

Information Technology Byte
High Motivation Rules at the SAS Institute 475

Management in Action

Summary and Review 487
Management in Action 489
Topics for Discussion and Action 489
Building Management Skills 489
Managing Ethically 490
Small Group Breakout Exercise 490
Exploring the World Wide Web 490
Be the Manager 491
BusinessWeek Case in the News: Why Settle for Just One Line of Work? 491
BusinessWeek Case in the News: Nokia's New Home in Romania 492

Examples

Ethics in Action
Servant Leadership at Zingerman's 498

Manager as a Person
Liane Pelletier Uses Her Expert Power in Alaska 502

Ethics in Action
Consideration at Costco 505

Focus on Diversity
Admitting a Mistake Helps Small-Business Leader 517

Management in Action

Summary and Review 518
Management in Action 520
Topics for Discussion and Action 520
Building Management Skills 520
Managing Ethically 521
Small Group Breakout Exercise 521
Exploring the World Wide Web 522
Be the Manager 522
BusinessWeek Case in the News: Big Blue Goes for the Big Win 522
BusinessWeek Case in the News: When CEO's Aren't Leaders 523

Contents

Chapter Fifteen	**Effective Groups and Teams** 526

A Manager's Challenge
Employees Form Teams at
ICU Medical 527

Topics

Overview	529	Research and Development Teams	535
Groups, Teams, and Organizational Effectiveness	529	Command Groups	535
		Task Forces	536
Groups and Teams as Performance Enhancers	530	Self-Managed Work Teams	536
		Virtual Teams	538
Groups, Teams, and Responsiveness to Customers	532	Friendship Groups	539
		Interest Groups	540
Teams and Innovation	532	**Group Dynamics**	540
Groups and Teams as Motivators	534	Group Size, Tasks, and Roles	540
Types of Groups and Teams	534	Group Leadership	543
		Group Development over Time	543
The Top-Management Team	535	Group Norms	544
		Group Cohesiveness	548

Chapter Sixteen	**Promoting Effective Communication** 564

A Manager's Challenge
Managers Need Feedback
from Employees 565

Topics

Overview	567	Spoken Communication Electronically Transmitted	575
Communication and Management	567	Personally Addressed Written Communication	575
The Importance of Good Communication	567	Impersonal Written Communication	578
The Communication Process	569	**Communication Networks**	579
The Role of Perception in Communication	570	Communication Networks in Groups and Teams	579
The Dangers of Ineffective Communication	571	Organizational Communication Networks	580
Information Richness and Communication Media	572	External Networks	581
Face-to-Face Communication	573		

Part Six   **Managing Critical Organizational Processes**

Examples

Management in Action

Managing Groups and
Teams for High
Performance 551

Motivating Group Members
to Achieve Organizational
Goals 551

Reducing Social Loafing in
Groups 553

Helping Groups to Manage
Conflict Effectively 554

Information Technology Byte
Technology Helps Teams Achieve
Synergies by Identifying Expertise 531

Information Technology Byte
Pizza Teams Innovate at Amazon 533

Management Insight
Self-Managed Teams at Louis
Vuitton and Nucor Corporation 537

Management Insight
Teams Benefit from Deviance
and Conformity at IDEO 547

Summary and Review 554

Management in Action 556
Topics for Discussion and Action 556
Building Management Skills 556
Managing Ethically 557
Small Group Breakout Exercise 557
Exploring the World Wide Web 557
Be the Manager 558
BusinessWeek Case in the News:
Managing the New Workforce 558
BusinessWeek Case in the News:
International Isn't Just IBM's First
Name 560

Examples

Management in Action

Information Technology
and Communication 582

The Internet 582

Intranets 582

Groupware and
Collaboration Software 583

Communication Skills
for Managers 586

Communication Skills for
Managers as Senders 587

Communication Skills for
Managers as Receivers 589

Understanding Linguistic
Styles 590

Managing Globally
Global Communication Enables
Global Innovation 568

Management Insight
When Face-to-Face
Communication Is Called For 573

Ethics in Action
Monitoring E-mail and Internet
Usage 577

Information Technology Byte
Collaborating with Wikis 585

Summary and Review 593

Management in Action 595
Topics for Discussion and Action 595
Building Management Skills 595
Managing Ethically 596
Small Group Breakout Exercise 596
Exploring the World Wide Web 597
Be the Manager 597
BusinessWeek Case in the
News: The Water Cooler Is Now
on the Web 597
BusinessWeek Case in the News:
It's All About the Face-to-Face 599

Contents

Chapter Seventeen — Managing Conflict, Politics, and Negotiation 602

A Manager's Challenge
Ravi Kant Effectively Manages Conflict 603

Topics

Overview 604

Organizational Conflict 605
  Types of Conflict 605
  Sources of Conflict 607
  Conflict Management Strategies 609

Negotiation 613
  Distributive Negotiation and Integrative Bargaining 613

Strategies to Encourage Integrative Bargaining 613

Organizational Politics 615
  The Importance of Organizational Politics 616
  Political Strategies for Gaining and Maintaining Power 616
  Political Strategies for Exercising Power 619

Chapter Eighteen — Using Advanced Information Technology to Increase Performance 632

A Manager's Challenge
Now B&M Retailers Use IT to Attract Customers 633

Topics

Overview 635

Information and the Manager's Job 635
  Attributes of Useful Information 636
  What Is Information Technology? 637
  Information and Decisions 638
  Information and Control 638
  Information and Coordination 640

The IT Revolution 640
  The Effects of Advancing IT 641

IT and the Product Life Cycle 641
Computer Networks 643

Types of Management Information Systems 646
  The Organizational Hierarchy: The Traditional Information System 646
  Transaction-Processing Systems 647
  Operations Information Systems 647
  Decision Support Systems 648

Glossary 667

Credits 679

Index 713

Examples

Managing Globally
Xplane Integrates Operations
in Spain 610

Focus on Diversity
Indra Nooyi Builds Alliances 618

Ethics in Action
El Faro Benefits Multiple
Stakeholders 621

Management in Action

Summary and Review 622
Management in Action 624
Topics for Discussion and Action ... 624
Building Management Skills 624
Managing Ethically 625
Small Group Breakout Exercise 625
Exploring the World Wide Web 625
Be the Manager 626
BusinessWeek Case in the News:
My Way or the Highway at
Hyundai 626
BusinessWeek Case in the News:
A Town Torn Apart by Nestlé 628

Artificial Intelligence and
Expert Systems 649
Enterprise Resource
Planning Systems 650
E-Commerce Systems 653

The Impact and Limitations of Information Technology 654

Strategic Alliances, B2B
Network Structures, and IT 654
Flatter Structures and
Horizontal Information
Flows 656
Limitations of IT 659

Examples

Management Insight
Herman Miller's Office of the
Future 639

Management Insight
IBM's "Business-on-Demand" IT 644

Manager as a Person
How Judy Lewent Became One
of the Most Powerful Women in
Corporate America 648

Information Technology Byte
SAP's ERP System 651

Information Technology Byte
Information Flows at Tel Co.
and Soft Co. 657

Management Insight
The *Star Wars* Studio Reorganizes 659

Management in Action

Summary and Review 661
Management in Action 662
Topics for Discussion and Action ... 662
Building Management Skills 662
Managing Ethically 663
Small Group Breakout Exercise 663
Exploring the World Wide Web 663
Be the Manager 664
BusinessWeek Case in the News:
The Quickening at Nissan 664
BusinessWeek Case in the News:
FedEx: Taking Off Like "a Rocket
Ship" 665

Preface

In the sixth edition of our book, *Contemporary Management,* we keep to our theme of providing students with the most contemporary and up-to-date account of the changing environment of management and management practices. In revising our book, we have continued our focus on making our text relevent and interesting to students; something that we know from instructor and student feedback engages them and encourages them to make the effort necessary to assimilate the text material. We continue to mirror the changes taking place in management practices by incorporating recent developments in management theory and research into our text and by providing vivid, current examples of the way managers of companies large and small have responded to the changes taking place. Indeed, we have increased our focus on small businesses in the sixth edition; many more examples of the opportunities and challenges facing founders, managers, and employees in small businesses are integrated into the text.

The number and complexity of the strategic, organizational, and human resource challenges facing managers and all employees has continued to increase throughout the 2000s. In most companies, managers at all levels are playing "catch-up" as they work toward meeting these challenges by implementing new and improved management techniques and practices. Today, relatively small differences in performance between companies, for example, in the speed at which they can bring new products or services to market or in the ways they motivate their employees to find ways to reduce costs or improve performance, can combine to give one company a significant competitive advantage over another. Managers and companies that utilize proven management techniques and practices in their decision making and actions increase their effectiveness over time. Companies and managers that are slower to implement new management techniques and practices find themselves at a growing competitive disadvantage that makes it even more difficult to catch up. Thus, in many industries there is a widening gap between the most successful companies whose performance reaches new heights, and their weaker competitors because their managers have made better decisions about how to use a company's resources in the most efficient and effective ways.

The challenges facing managers continue to mount as changes in the global environment such as increasing global outsourcing and rising labor and commodity prices impact organizations, large and small. Moreover, the revolution in digital information technology has transformed the way managers make decisions across all levels of a company's hierarchy and across all its functions and global divisions. This edition of our book continues to address these emerging challenges. For example, we extend our treatment of global outsourcing and examine the many managerial issues that must be addressed when millions of functional jobs in information technology, customer service, and manufacturing are being sent to countries overseas. Similarly, increasing globalization means that managers must respond to the effects of major differences in the legal rules and regulations and ethical values and norms that prevail in countries around the globe. Many companies and their managers, for example, have been accused of ignoring "sweatshop" working conditions under which the products they sell are manufactured abroad.

Other major challenges we continue to expand on in the new edition include the impact of the steadily increasing diversity of the workforce on companies, and how this increasing diversity makes it imperative for managers to understand how and why people differ so that they can effectively manage and reap the performance benefits of diversity. Similarly, across all functions and levels, managers and employees must continuously search out ways to "work smarter" and increase performance. Using new information technology to improve all aspects of an organization's operations to improve efficiency and customer responsiveness is a vital part of this process. So too is the continuing need to innovate and improve the quality of goods and services, and the ways they are produced, to allow an organization to compete effectively. We have significantly revised the sixth edition of *Contemporary Management* to address these challenges to managers and their organizations

Major Content Changes

We have not altered the organization of our chapters in this edition; they follow the same sequence as the fifth edition. Instructors tell us they like the chapter changes we made last time and that they have improved the learning experience. For example, they approve of the way we integrated our coverage of entrepreneurship into Chapter 7, "Decision Making, Learning, Creativity, and Entrepreneurship," because it complements the discussion of creativity and allows us to discuss the many different issues involved in effective decision-making over time. At the same time, our two-chapter sequence on strategy—Chapter 8 discusses business- and corporate-level strategies, and Chapter 9 focuses on functional-level strategies—to improve competitive advantage was well received.

But once again, encouraged by the increasing number of instructors and students who are using our book with each new edition, and based on the reactions and suggestions of both users and reviewers, we have revised and updated our book in the following ways. First, just as we have included pertinent new research concepts in each chapter, so too we have been careful to eliminate outdated or marginal management concepts. As usual, our goal has been to streamline our presentation and keep the focus on the changes that have been taking place that have the most impact on managers and organizations. Our goal is to avoid presenting students with excessive content in too many and too long chapters just for the sake of including all outmoded management theory. In today's world of video downloads, sound bites, and text messaging, providing the best content is much more important than providing excessive amounts of content—especially when some of our students are often burdened by time pressures stemming from the need to work long hours at paying jobs and personal commitments and obligations.

Second, we have added significant new management content, and have reinforced its importance by using many new relevant small and large company examples that are described in new chapter opening cases entitled "A Manager's Challenge," in the many boxed examples featuring managers and employees in companies both large and small inside each chapter, and in the new (mainly from 2007–2008) "*BusinessWeek* Case in the News" closing cases.

Chapter 1, for example, includes a discussion of crisis decision making and the managerial implications of crises that are the result of natural causes, man-made causes, or geopolitical conflicts. Now, it includes additional material on crisis and turnaround management, which is especially relevant in today's economy for a variety of reasons, including the effects of the subprime mortgage crisis on many managers and companies. Turnaround management is also discussed in other chapters, such as Chapter 11. Chapter 1 also has an expanded discussion of ethics and diversity to prime students to consider the importance of understanding the implications of these complex, personal, and value-laden issues in later chapters. Chapter 2 has new coverage of the historical ethics of business, and how fortunes were made and lost by making management decisions that increased business performance but which eventually led to the passing of antitrust legislation to preserve fair competition and protect the public.

Chapter 3 has updated coverage of the manager as a person and how personal characteristics of managers (and all members of an organization) influence organizational culture and effectiveness as well as how they view and treat others. New and updated material on, for example, changing work attitudes, the importance of handling layoffs in a compassionate manner, and emotions and moods and their implications, highlight the contemporary landscape of management today.

Public concern over the ethical behavior of managers continues to increase as a result of the subprime mortgage problems that have led to huge crisis management issues in large financial companies, and that have subsequently affected many kinds of small businesses. We have expanded our coverage of the many issues involved in acting and managing ethically throughout the book and especially in Chapter 4, which focuses on "Ethics and Social Responsibility." For example, we discuss new issues in ethics and ethical dilemmas, and provide more conceptual tools to help students understand better how to make ethical decisions. We have expanded coverage of contemporary issues such as CEOs being convicted of rigging the time at which stock options are granted to managers to maximize the profits they can make when they sell those options. Also, we discuss new issues relating to the high pay of CEOs and the growing public concern that there need to be controls over how CEO pay is set—especially when compared to the way changes to the minimum wage low-paid workers receive are considered. New material on the effect of stock options on company performance that suggests that overuse of options can reduce performance is also described. As a final example, we have new coverage of the ethics of nonprofits, whose managers must also be scrutinized to ensure that they do not spend organizational resources on their own personal goals rather than those of the people and causes they are meant to help. Additionally, the ethical exercise at the end of every chapter continues to be a popular feature of our book.

Chapter 5, "Managing Diverse Employees in a Multicultural Environment," focuses on the effective management of the many faces of diversity in organizations for the good of all. Among the new issues we discuss are the increasing diversity of the population and workforce and ways to reap the benefits of diversity; how to ensure that all employees are treated fairly and are not discriminated against; and the implications of disabilities, sexual orientation, and religion in the workplace. To address current issues, in an era when many companies are facing discrimination lawsuits involving hundreds of millions of dollars, we discuss ways to effectively manage diversity and eliminate discrimination and sexual harassment.

Chapter 6, which contains an integrated account of forces in both the domestic and global environments, has also been revised to reflect continuing changes impacting organizations. For example, the chapter describes how increasing global competition and free trade as well as the growth of many global regional free trade associations, have changed the global value-creation process. At the same time, it describes how the rise of powerful new distributors, such as U.S. beer and wine distributors, can change competitive forces inside just one country. In addition, more coverage is given to the need for global customization, such as the need to customize food to suit the tastes of different cultures, and the way IKEA excells in making furniture to fit the needs of customers in different countries as it expands around the world.

Chapter 7, "Decision Making, Learning, Creativity, and Entrepreneurship," includes a discussion of new developments in these important areas. For example, we include a discussion of social entrepreneurs who seek to find creative ways to address social problems and needs in order to improve society and well-being by, for example, reducing poverty, increasing literacy, and protecting the natural environment. We discuss the challenges social entrepreneurs face in striving to achieve their social goals and how they can meet these challenges. More generally, we discuss how managers in organizations large and small can improve decision making, learning, and creativity in their organizations.

Reacting to reviewer comments, we have continued to refine our approach to our two strategy chapters. Chapter 8 has been rewritten and focuses on corporate-, global-, and business-level strategy. In Chapter 9, we have expanded our coverage of functional strategies for managing value-chain activities, incorporating the material on innovation from Chapter 19. These changes have allowed us to increase the links between the different levels of strategy making while still maintaining a strong focus on managing operations and processes.

In Chapter 8 we have an expanded focus on using strategies to build competitive advantage. We begin to discuss this issue in our new opening case, which contrasts the performance of electronics retailers Best Buy and Circuit City, and the chapter addresses the question of why different kinds of strategies result in different levels of company performance. We continue the theme with a new look at the changing fortunes of the toy industry, and why Mattel lost ground. Then we look at how Campbell Soup's dynamic CEO is reshaping the company into one with a new focus on health and nutritious foods to improve the company's competitive advantage. In Chapter 9, we continue to explore how companies can develop new functional-level strategies to improve efficiency, quality, innovation, and responsiveness to customers. We have more coverage of TQM, including the Six Sigma approach, which involves creating teams of expert change agents, known as "green belts and black belts," to take control of the problem finding-solving process and then train other employees in how to implement solutions. Then, in a new box we describe how the Starwood

Hotel chain is implementing Six Sigma to improve its hotels' performance. We also discuss new material on the need to maintain value-chain management over time and the problems involved in getting managers to commit to work toward continually increasing performance standards.

In Chapters 10 and 11, we offer new coverage of organizational structure and control and discuss the ways that companies are confronting the need to reorganize their hierarchies and way of doing business as the environment changes and competition increases. In Chapter 9, for example, we discuss how companies such as Liz Claiborne and Pier One have reorganized to improve their domestic performance—just as Nokia has reorganized its global operating structure to increase its global sales. In Chapter 11, we continue this theme by looking at how companies are changing their control systems to better motivate employees, such as how Microsoft and Walt Disney are working to find the right rewards and evaluation systems to maintain their global competitive edge.

We have updated and expanded our treatment of the many ways in which managers can effectively organize, manage, and lead employees in their companies. For example, Chapter 12 includes a discussion of how treating employees well can lead to satisfied customers, the steps small companies like Fog Creek Software take to recruit outstanding employees, the use of background checks, the role of mentoring in organizations, pay differentials, and family friendly benefits. As another example, Chapter 13 opens with the case of Enterprise Rent-A-Car, one of the largest employers of new college graduates, and the steps Enterprise takes to effectively train and motivate employees. This chapter also includes a discussion of prosocially motivated behavior and examples of people who are prosocially motivated to benefit others by a variety of factors, including protecting the natural environment and, more generally, includes an updated treatment of the many steps managers and organizations can take to have a highly motivated workforce.

Chapter 14 highlights the critical importance of effective leadership in organizations and factors that contribute to managers being effective leaders, includes a discussion of servant leadership with an example of servant leadership in action at Zingerman's, includes an updated discussion of transformational leadership illustrated with a running example of Sue Nokes's transformational leadership at T-Mobile, and includes a discussion of how emotional intelligence may help leaders respond appropriately when they realize they have made a mistake. Expanded and updated coverage of the effective management of teams, including virtual teams, is provided in Chapter 15. Chapter 16 includes updated coverage of effective communication and how, given the multitude of advances in information technology and the new ways in which they support and facilitate collaboration, managers and organizations can use these advances in ways that help, rather than inadvertently detract from, organizational effectiveness and innovation. Chapter 17 includes an updated discussion of the critical task of effectively managing conflict and politics in organizations and how to negotiate effectively on a global level.

We feel confident that the major changes we have made to the sixth edition of *Contemporary Management* reflect the changes that are occurring in management and the workplace; we also feel they offer an account of management that will stimulate and challenge students to think about their future in the world of organizations.

Unique Emphasis on Contemporary, Applied Management

In revising our book, we have kept at the forefront the fact that our users and reviewers are very supportive of our attempts to integrate contemporary management theories and issues into the analysis of management and organizations. As in previous editions, our goal has been to distill new and classic theorizing and research into a contemporary framework that is compatible with the traditional focus on management as planning, leading, organizing, and controlling but that transcends this traditional approach.

Users and reviewers report that students appreciate and enjoy our presentation of management, a presentation that makes its relevance obvious even to those who lack exposure to a real-life management context. Students like the book's content and the way we relate management theory to real-life examples to drive home the message that management matters both because it determines how well organizations perform and because managers and organizations affect the lives of people inside and outside the organization, such as customers and shareholders.

Our contemporary approach has led us to discuss many concepts and issues that are not addressed in other management textbooks and is also illustrated by the way we have chosen to organize and discuss these management issues. We have gone to great lengths to bring the manager back into the subject matter of management. That is, we have written our chapters from the perspective of current or future managers to illustrate, in a hands-on way, the problems and opportunities they face and how they can effectively meet them. For example, in Chapter 3 we provide an integrated treatment of personality, attitudes, emotions, and culture; in Chapter 4, a focus on ethics from a student's and a manager's perspective; and in Chapter 5, an in-depth treatment of effectively managing diversity and eradicating sexual harassment. In Chapters 8 and 9, our integrated treatment of strategy highlights the multitude of decisions managers must make as they go about performing their most important role—increasing organizational efficiency, effectiveness, and performance.

Our applied approach can also be clearly seen in the last three chapters of the book, which cover the topics of promoting effective communication; managing organizational conflict, politics, and negotiation; and using information technology in ways that increase organizational performance. These chapters provide a student-friendly, behavioral approach to understanding the management issues entailed in persuasive communication, negotiation, and implementation of advanced information systems to build competitive advantage.

Flexible Organization

Another factor of interest to instructors concerns the way we have designed the grouping of chapters to allow instructors to teach the chapter material in the order that best suits their needs. For example, the more micro-oriented instructor can follow Chapters 1 through 5 with Chapters 12 through 16 and then do the more macro chapters. The more macro-oriented professor can follow Chapters 1 and 2 with Chapters 6 through 11, jump to 16 through 18, and then do the micro chapters, 3 through 5 and 12 through 15. Our sequencing of parts and chapters gives instructors considerable freedom to design the course that best suits their needs. Instructors are not tied to the planning, organizing, leading, and controlling framework, even though our presentation remains consistent with this approach.

Acknowledgments

Finding a way to integrate and present the rapidly growing literature on contemporary management and make it interesting and meaningful for students is not an easy task. In writing and revising the various drafts of *Contemporary Management,* we have been fortunate to have the assistance of several people who have contributed greatly to the book's final form. First, we are grateful to Michael Ablassmeir, our senior sponsoring editor, for his ongoing support and commitment to our project and for always finding ways to provide the resources that we needed to continually improve and refine our book. Second, we are grateful to Laura Griffin, our developmental editor, for so ably coordinating the book's progress; and to her and Anke Braun Weekes, our senior marketing manager, for providing us with concise and timely feedback and information from professors and reviewers that have allowed us to shape the book to the needs of its intended market. We also thank JoAnne Schopler and Pam Verros for executing an awe-inspiring design; Kathryn Mikulic for coordinating the production process; Margaret Richardson de Sosa (Rice University) and Patsy Hartmangruber (Texas A&M University) for providing excellent word-processing and graphic support; and Iliya Atanasov (Rice University) for his assistance with research. We are also grateful to the many colleagues and reviewers who provided us with useful and detailed feedback and perceptive comments and valuable suggestions for improving the manuscript.

Producing any competitive work is a challenge. Producing a truly market-driven textbook requires tremendous effort beyond simply obtaining reviews of a draft manuscript. Our goal was simple with the development of *Contemporary Management:* to be the most customer-driven principles-of-management text and supplement package ever published! With the goal of exceeding the expectations of both faculty and students, we executed one of the most aggressive product development plans ever undertaken in textbook publishing. Hundreds of faculty have taken part in developmental activities ranging from regional focus groups to manuscript and supplement reviews and surveys. Consequently, we're confident in assuring you and your students, our customers, that every aspect of our text and support package reflects your advice and needs. As you review it, we're confident that your reaction will be, "They listened!"

We extend our special thanks to the faculty who gave us detailed chapter-by-chapter feedback during the development of the sixth edition:

Charley Braun, Marshall University

Brad Cox, Midlands Technical College

D. Harold Doty, University of Southern Mississippi

Scott Elston, Iowa State University

Robert C. Hoell, Georgia Southern University

Carol Larson Jones, Cal Poly Pomona, California

Gwen Jones, University of Akron

Don C. Mosley Jr., University of South Alabama

Sabine Turnley, Kansas State University

Isaiah O. Ugboro, North Carolina A&T State University

And our thanks also go to the faculty who contributed greatly to the fourth and fifth editions of *Contemporary Management:*

M. Ruhul Amin, Bloomsburg University of PA

Gerald Baumgardner, Pennsylvania College of Technology

James D. Bell, Texas State University

Danielle R. Blesi, Hudson Valley Community College

Barry Bunn, Valencia Community College

Gerald Calvasina, Southern Utah University

Bruce H. Charnov, Hofstra University

Jay Christensen-Szalanski, University of Iowa

Marian Cox Crawford, University of Arkansas-Little Rock

Teresa A. Daniel, Marshall University

Thomas W. Deckelman, Owens Community College

Richard S. DeFrank, University of Houston

Fred J. Dorn, University of Mississippi

Sandra Edwards, Northeastern State University

Kim Hester, Arkansas State University

Anne Kelly Hoel, University of Wisconsin-Stout

Gwendolyn Jones, University of Akron

Kathleen Jones, University of North Dakota

Joanne E. Kapp, Siena College

Nicholas Mathys, DePaul University

Daniel W. McAllister, University of Nevada–Las Vegas

Douglas L. Micklich, Illinois State University

Clive Muir, Stetson University

Karen Overton, Houston Community College

Gary Renz, Webster University L. Jeff Seaton, University of Tennessee–Martin

Fred Slack, Indiana University of Pennsylvania

M. James Smas, Kent State University

Please note the lists above do not include the more than 160 faculty members who reviewed or contributed to earlier editions of the text.

Finally, we are grateful to two incredibly wonderful children, Nicholas and Julia, for being all that they are and the joy they bring to all who know them.

Gareth R. Jones
Mays Business School
Texas A&M University

Jennifer M. George
Jesse H. Jones Graduate School of Management
Rice University

Guided Tour

Manager as a Person

Who Would Have Thought *Dirty Jobs* Would Be a Hit?

Mike Rowe is hardly the person you would have thought would have created a hit TV show like the Discovery Channel's *Dirty Jobs*.[25] Not the most ambitious of types, and as an actor in the business for over two decades who never made it big, his work experiences have ranged from performing with the Baltimore Opera to selling fake simulated diamonds on QVC on TV to appearing in Tylenol commercials.[26] While cohosting a local TV show on CBS-5 in San Francisco, Rowe hit upon the idea behind *Dirty Jobs*. Rowe did a segment on the show called "Somebody's Gotta Do It," viewers liked it, and it really struck a cord with him personally.[27]

Mike Rowe's openness to experience has given him a real appreciation of all kinds of work and jobs.

His openness to experience led him to try to develop a TV show featuring him working as an apprentice to men and women performing the kinds of hard, dirty work we all depend on and no one wants to do (think bat cave scavenger, worm dung farmer, roadkill cleaner, sewer inspector, pig farmer . . .).[28] As he puts it, his show features "men and women who do the kinds of jobs that make civilized life possible for the rest of us."[29] While he originally had a hard time finding a home for *Dirty Jobs* (the Discovery Channel turned him down twice before agreeing to air a pilot series in 2003), the show has become a bona fide hit, aired 700 times in 2007, and is the Discovery Channel's number-one show, according to David Zaslav, the CEO of Discovery Communications.[30]

Rowe's openness to experience enables him to get down and dirty with the best of them, try his hand at all sorts of dirty jobs, and thoroughly enjoy it. As would be expected, all sorts of mishaps occur and that is part of the fun. And, Rowe has come to appreciate the earnestness of the workers he profiles—"the celebration of work, and the mixing of pain and fun."[31] Interestingly enough, as one who never had embraced the value of too much hard work in the past, *Dirty Jobs* has instilled in Rowe a healthy respect and admiration for the people who perform all sorts of dirty jobs, work hard at them, and are happy when the work is done.[32]

Small Business

RICH AND RELEVANT EXAMPLES: Our reviewers were unanimous in their praise of the sheer range and depth of the rich, interesting, real-world examples we use to illustrate the chapter material and make it come alive. Moreover, unlike boxed material in other books, our boxes are seamlessly integrated into the text. They are an integral part of the learning experience and not tacked on or isolated from the text itself. This is central to our pedagogical approach.

NEW! 25 OF 37 *BUSINESSWEEK* CASE IN THE NEWS ARE NEW TO THIS EDITION: Each chapter contains two cases for analysis that are actual or shortened versions of BusinessWeek articles. The accompanying discussion questions encourage students to think about and analyze how real managers deal with real problems in the business world.

BusinessWeek **Case in the News** [LO 2, 5]

Young and Impatient in India

Ravikiran's parents took the safe route. In post-colonial India, even though they had college degrees, they chose low-paying but secure government jobs. Today, they live with their three sons in a modest concrete house in a working-class section of Bangalore. While colorful paintings of Hindu gods adorn their walls, the furniture is mostly plastic chairs and steel cots. For Ravikiran M.S., their eldest son, security and stability simply aren't enough. The 24-year-old programmer is brimming with ambition. He rides a motorbike to work and hopes to buy a car, And he expects quick promotions, dreaming of becoming a CEO. "I want the posh life," he declares.

Ravikiran is typical of India's in-a-hurry younger generation. With the tech-services boom, the country's college grads are coming of age in a time of economic optimism, and unlike their parents and grandparents, this group has vibrant job prospects and high hopes. The challenge for companies is to harness their energy while reining in inflated expectations. If these young people feel they're being short-changed in terms of either salary or advancement, the best and brightest will find work elsewhere, shift careers, or leave the country. "It's a very different generation," says S. Gopalakrishnan, chief executive of Indian tech giant Infosys Technologies. "They want immediate rewards."

Proving Ground

This pattern will be repeated in other emerging nations as prosperity spreads. So India is becoming a proving ground for managing the global workforce, with companies developing new schemes to keep the younger generation engaged. The likes of MindTree Consulting, Infosys, and IBM have revamped their orientation programs to better engage young people, tapped men and women under 30 to serve on management committees, and launched mini-MBA programs for eager young managers. "India is going to be a lab for lessons that we'll apply to other countries," says Lyndon Rego, manager of innovation at the Center for Creative Leadership in Greensboro, N.C., which develops leadership training programs in emerging markets.

The challenge for companies is to address both the desires and frustrations of the younger generation. These become abundantly evident in the cafés and bars of Bangalore. As the city has developed into India's Silicon Valley, it also has become the country's bar-hopping capital. "We need capitalism with a human face," says P.B. Devaiah, a 20-year-old industrial engineering major at a local college. Sitting with friends at Java City, a crowded coffee shop, he complains that much of the programming in India is the equivalent of sweatshop labor, where new hires are expected to spend as much as 12 hours a day writing code. "We're being used as machines," Devaiah says.

When the conversation turns to social issues, India's young people are likely to erupt in grousing about arranged marriage, the caste system, and interactions with Westerners—all of which should concern employers. Caste attitudes, for instance, clash with merit-based corporate values, and young techies sometimes feel

NEW! ALL A MANAGER'S CHALLENGE OPENING MINI CASES ARE NEW OR UPDATED: Challenge your students to think like real managers. Every chapter opens with "A Manager's Challenge" posing a chapter-related issue and a discussion on how managers in one or more organizations responded to that challenge. These challenges demonstrate the uncertainty and excitement surrounding the management process.

A MANAGER'S CHALLENGE

Making Good Decisions at PUMA

www.puma.com

Why is decision making of a paramount importance in organizations? When Jochen Zeitz took over as CEO of PUMA AG in 1993 at the age of 30, the company was facing major threats.[1] PUMA AG, based in the small German sneaker-producing town of Herzogenaurach,[2] had lost money for the past eight years and PUMA North America was facing imminent bankruptcy. The company's cash levels were very low and it was no match for major industry leaders like Adidas (Adidas and PUMA were both founded in Herzogenaurach by two brothers who have long competed with each other), Reebok, and Nike.[3]

Facing tough decisions about how to turnaround the company's fortunes, Zeitz decided that rather than trying to compete based on the performance capabilities of its athletic shoes and equipment, PUMA would focus more on style, colors, and lines of shoes. Essentially, Zeitz saw a potential opportunity in trying to start up a new division focus on experimental fashion and sport

Management Insight

Sharper Image Is No Longer in Focus

Sharper Image Corp. was started in 1977 by Richard Thalheimer to sell a lightweight watch for joggers. The store quickly became popular as a supplier of state-of-the-art innovative, quirky products that claimed to offer customers a better experience or higher quality. The specialty retailer grew to 183 stores, and in 2004 its sales had soared to over $776 million as customers proved willing to pay high prices for its innovative offerings. Things changed in 2005, however, as other companies such as Apple, Dell, and other specialty retailers began to offer state-of-the-art products. And, because Internet stores such as Amazon.com began to offer these products at

Struggling retail chain Sharper Image [...] major competition from Amazon.com [...] and Dell in providing niche-market [...] items. Can new CEO Ron Conway [...] the turnaround magic that he is kno[...]

NEW! EXPANDED AND UPDATED COVERAGE OF ETHICS, DIVERSITY, CULTURE, AND GLOBAL ISSUES: The authors have updated and, where necessary, expanded the coverage of ethics, diversity, and culture to support student understanding of these crucially important topics. See additional in-depth boxes throughout chapters–"Management Insight," "Ethics in Action," "Managing Globally," "Focus on Diversity," "Manager as a Person," and "Information Technology Byte."

Ethics in Action

Telling the Truth at Gentle Giant Moving

Gentle Giant Moving Company, based in Somerville, Massachusetts, was founded by Larry O'Toole in 1980 and now has over $28 million in revenues and offices in multiple states.[43] While moving is undoubtedly hard work and many people would never think about having a career in this industry, Gentle Giant's unique culture and approach to managing people have not only contributed to the company's success but also provided its employees with satisfying careers. For example, when Ryan Libby was in college, he worked for Gentle Giant during one of his summer vacations to make some extra money. Now the Assistant Manager for the Providence, Rhode Island, Gentle Giant Office, Libby is contemplating opening an office of his own. As he puts it, "First it was just a paycheck, and it kind of turned into a long-term career."[44]

Libby is just the kind of employee O'Toole seeks to hire–employees who start out driving moving trucks and eventually move into management positions running offices. While some moving companies hire a lot of temporary help in the summer to meet seasonal demand, 60% of Gentle Giant employees are employed full time.[45] Since the demand for moving services is lower in the winter, Gentle Giant uses this time to provide employees with training

At Gentle Giant Moving Co., employees are given leadership training, access to company outings, and the opportunity to advance to management positions.

A Wealth of Experiential Exercises The creative and flexible Management in Action end-of-chapter material provide instructors with a wealth of exercises that will challenge students to learn by doing. These activities and exercises are designed to be used in either large or small classes and each chapter include:

TOPICS FOR DISCUSSION AND ACTION: A set of chapter-related questions and points for reflection.

Management in Action

▶ Topics for Discussion and Action

DISCUSSION

1. Discuss why managers who have different types of personalities can be equally effective and successful. **[LO1]**

2. Can managers be too satisfied with their jobs? Can they be too committed to their organizations? Why or why not? **[LO2]**

3. Assume that you are a manager of a restaurant. Describe what it is like to work for you when you are in a negative mood. **[LO3]**

4. Why might managers be disadvantaged by low levels of emotional intelligence? **[LO4]**

ACTION

5. Interview a manager in a local organization. Ask the manager to describe situations in which he or she is especially likely to act in accordance with his or her values. Ask the manager to describe situations in which he or she is less likely to act in accordance with his or her values. **[LO2]**

6. Watch a popular television show, and as you watch it, try to determine the emotional intelligence levels of the characters the actors in the show portray. Rank the characters from highest to lowest in terms of emotional intelligence. As you watched the show, what factors influenced your assessments of emotional intelligence levels? **[LO4]**

7. Go to an upscale clothing store in your neighborhood, and go to a clothing store that is definitely not upscale. Observe the behavior of employees in each store as well as the store's environment. In what ways are the organizational cultures in each store similar? In what ways are they different? **[LO5]**

BUILDING MANAGEMENT SKILLS: Each chapter provides a number of activities specifically geared toward providing students the opportunity to gain important managerial skills.

MANAGING ETHICALLY: An exercise that presents students with an ethical scenario or dilemma and asks them, either individually or in a group, to think about the issue from an ethical perspective to better understand the challenges facing practicing managers today.

SMALL GROUP BREAKOUT EXERCISE: This feature ensures that students learn the importance of collaboration and teamwork in solving business challenges. It can be used in *small or large classes.*

EXPLORING THE WORLD WIDE WEB: requires students to actively search the Web to find the answers to a problem.

BE THE MANAGER: presents a realistic scenario in which a manager or organization faces some kind of challenge, problem, or opportunity. The student plays the role of a manager offering advice and recommending a course of action based on the chapter content.

CHOOSING EXERCISES: We offer a wide array of exercises so instructors can pick and choose from them over the course of the semester. Not only do they teach the meaning of management through different avenues but they further promote the learning experience. The Instructor's Manual provides guidance and solutions for implementing these activities in your classroom.

Building Management Skills [LO5]
Diagnosing Culture

Think about the culture of the last organization you worked for, your current university, or another organization or club to which you belong. Then, answer the following questions:

1. What values are emphasized in this culture?
2. What norms do members of this organization follow?
3. Who seems to have played an important role in creating the culture?
4. In what ways is the organizatio culture communicated to organizational members.

Managing Ethically [LO 1, 2]

Some organizations rely on personality and interest inventories to screen potential employees. Other organizations attempt to screen employees by using paper-and-pencil honesty tests.

Questions

1. Either individually or in a group, think about the ethical implications of using personality and interest inventories to screen potential employees. How might this practice be unfair to potential applicants? How might organizational members who are in charge of hiring misuse it?

2. Because of measurement error and validity problems, some relatively trustworthy pe "fail" an honesty test gi employer. What are the implications of trustwor people "failing" honesty and what obligations de think employers should when relying on honest for screening purposes

---

Small Group Breakout Exercise [LO 2, 3, 4, 5]
Making Difficult Decisions in Hard Times

Form groups of three or four people, and appoint one member as the spokesperson who will communicat findings to the whole class when called on by the instructor. Then discuss the following scenario:

You are on the top-management team of a medium-size company that manufactures cardboard boxes, containers, and other cardboard packaging materials. Your company is facing increasing levels of competition for major corporate customer accounts, and profits have declined significantly. You have tried everything you can to cut costs and remain competitive, with the exception of laying off employees. Your company has had a no layoff policy for the past 20 years, and you believe it is an important part of the organization's culture. However, you are experiencing mounting pressure to increase your firm's performance, and your no-layoff policy has been questioned by shareholders. Even though you haven't decided whether to lay off employees and thus break with a 20-year tradition for your company, rumors are rampant in your organization that something is afoot, and employees are worried. You are meeting today to address this problem.

1. Develop a list of options and potential courses of action to address the heighten competition and decline profitability that your co has been experiencing.

2. Choose your preferred action, and justify why take this route.

3. Describe how you will communicate your deci employees.

4. If your preferred option a layoff, justify why. If it involve a layoff, explain

---

Exploring the World Wide Web [LO 1, 2, 5]

Go to IDEO's Web site (www.ideo. com) and read about this company. Try to find indicators of IDEO's culture that are provided on the Web site. How does the design of the Web site itself, and the pictures and words it contains, communicate the nature of IDEO's organizational culture? What kinds of people do you th be attracted to IDEO? Wha people do you think would b be dissatisfied with a job at

---

Be the Manager [LO 1, 2, 3, 4, 5]

You have recently been hired as the vice president for human resources in an advertising agency. One of the problems that has been brought to your attention is the fact that in the creative departments at the agency, there are dysfunctionally high levels of conflict. You have spoken with members of each of these departments, and in each one it seems that there are a few members of the department who are creating all the problems. All of these individuals are valued contributors who have many creative ad campaigns to their credit. The very high levels of conflict are creating problems in the dep ments, and negative moods emotions are much more preva than positive feelings. What are going to do to both retain val employees and alleviate the exc sive conflict and negative feelin these departments?

For Instructors

Completely Updated Resources That Work Whether you are looking for new ways to engage your students and motivate them in your course, trying to ensure students are able to see the relevancy of the management concepts, or teaching critical thinking about the issues so they are able to apply them right away, McGraw-Hill Management has you covered! Jones/George is supported by a wealth of unique resources to support your on-campus, hybrid, and online courses. The accompanying Instructor's Resource CD-ROM (IRCD) includes the following, which are also available on the Online Learning Center (OLC).

POWERPOINT® PRESENTATION: 40 slides per chapter feature reproductions of key tables and figures from the text as well as original content—prepared by Brad Cox of Midlands Tech. Lecture enhancing additions such as additional examples, quick polling questions, and slides featuring "Movie Examples" from Video Cases and Management in the Movies can be used to generate discussion and to illustrate management concepts.

INSTRUCTOR'S MANUAL (IM): The IM supporting this text has been completely updated by Adrienne Hinds of Northern Virginia Community College and Kimberly Jaussi of SUNY Binghamton in order to save instructors time and support them in delivering the most effective course to their students. For each chapter, this manual provides chapter overview, lecture outline with integrated PowerPoint® slides, lecture enhancers, notes for end-of-chapter materials, video cases and teaching notes, and more.

Big Five Personality Traits

➢ **Openness to Experience**

≈ tendency to be original, have broad interests, be open to a wide range of stimuli, be daring and take risks

The **test bank** has been thoroughly revised, in response to customer feedback, by Eileen Hogan of Kutztown University. There are more than 100 questions per chapter, including true-false, multiple-choice, and essay, with particular expansion of scenario-based M/C questions requiring critical thought and application. Each question is tagged for the level of difficulty (corresponding to Bloom's taxonomy of educational objectives), AACSB standards, correct answer, page references, and whether the question is used anywhere else such as the OLC. The new AACSB tags allow instructors to sort questions by the various standards and create reports to help give assurance that they are including the recommended learning experiences in their curricula. Also, **EZ Test** is a flexible and easy-to-use electronic testing program that allows instructors to create tests from book-specific items. A downloadable desktop version can be found on the IRCD. And **EZ Test Online** (www.eztestonline.com) allows you to access the test bank from the OLC virtually anywhere and at anytime. EZ-Test-created exams and quizzes can be administered online, providing instant feedback for students.

Learning Objectives from chapter openers (1) are called out in the text margins (2), revisited in end-of-chapter material (3), and finally, tagged in the test bank (4) ensuring that students have mastered the important topics.

AACSB Statement

McGraw-Hill Companies is a proud corporate member of AACSB International. Understanding the importance and value of AACSB accreditation, the authors of Jones/George 6e have sought to recognize the curricula guidelines detailed in the AACSB standards for business accreditation by connecting selected questions in *Contemporary Management,* Sixth Edition or the test bank to the general knowledge and skill guidelines found in the AACSB standards.

The statements contained in *Contemporary Management,* Sixth Edition, are provided only as a guide for the users of this text. The AACSB leaves content coverage and assessment clearly within the realm and control of individual schools, the mission of the school, and the faculty. The AACSB does also charge schools with the obligation of doing assessment against their own content and learning goals. While *Contemporary Management,* Sixth Edition, and the teaching package make no claim of any specific AACSB qualification or evaluation, we have, within the sixth edition, labeled selected questions according to the six general knowledge and skills areas. The labels or tags within the book are as indicated. There are, of course, many more within the test bank, the text, and the teaching package that may be used as a standard for your course.

Assurance of Learning Ready

Educational institutions are often focused on the notion of assurance of learning, an important element of many accreditation standards. *Contemporary Management,* Sixth Edition, is designed specifically to support your assurance of learning initiatives with a simple, yet powerful, solution.

Each test bank question for the sixth edition maps to a specific chapter learning outcome/objective listed in the text. You can use our test bank software, *EZ Test,* to easily query for learning objectives that directly relate to the learning objectives for your course. You can use the reporting features of *EZ Test* to aggregate student results in a similar fashion, making the collection and presentation of assurance of learning data quick and easy.

Videos

McGraw-Hill Management provides you with the most diverse and comprehensive set of video material available for the principles of management course. Our unmatched set includes:

PRINCIPLES OF MANAGEMENT VIDEO DVD VOL. 1 (0073364142) AND NEW! VOL. 2 (0073364231): Now offering more than 70 video clips from sources such as BusinessWeek TV, PBS, NBC, BBC, CBS, and McGraw-Hill, are provided on 2 DVDs. These videos are organized by the four functions of management—planning, leading, organizing, and controlling—and feature 2 1/2 to 15 minute clips on companies such as Playstation, Panera Bread, Patagonia, Mini Cooper, and The Greater Chicago Food Depository as well as other topics including Employer-Subsidized Commuting, Grounded: Are U.S. Airlines Safe?, Using Facebook at Work, Adult Bullies, and Encore Careers. Corresponding Video Cases that tie the videos closely to the chapters can be found in the Instructor's Manual and online.

MANAGER'S HOT SEAT ONLINE! UPDATED AND EXPANDED: Now instructors can put students in the hot seat with access to an interactive program. Students are given an introduction to the situation, view a dossier of related management materials, and then watch 15 real managers apply their years of experience when confronting unscripted issues. As the scenario unfolds, questions about how the manager is handling the situation pop up, forcing the student to make decisions along with the manager. At the end of the scenario, students watch a post-interview with the manager, view how their responses matched up to the manager's decisions, and then submit a report critiquing the manager's choices while defending their own. Access to this online program is provided as part of the Premium Online Learning Access of this text. Access can also be purchased stand alone.

MANAGEMENT IN THE MOVIES DVD (0073317713): This faculty DVD makes it easy to bring that captivating power of big screen movies to your classroom! Each video clip illustrates a specific management topic in less than 2 1/2 minutes via a scene from major movies or TV show. For example, Groups–13 Going On 30, Ethics–John Q, Global Management–Gung Ho. The Management in the Movies DVD is available exclusively for current users of McGraw-Hill Principles of Management, OB and HRM texts and is supported by suggestions for usage of the clip, video summaries, and discussion questions for each segment!

MANAGEMENT IN THE MOVIES: TOPIC GRID

Book Concept	Movie Clip
Managers and Managing	Fast Times
Attitudes, Value, Culture	Hoosiers
Ethics	John Q
Diversity	Inside Man
Global Management	Gung Ho
Decision-Making	The Family Man
Manager as a Planner	Blackhawk Down
Value-Chain Management	The Killers
Organizational Structure	Apollo 13
Control and Change	Gung Ho
Human Resource Management	Double Indemnity
Motivation	American Pie
Leadership	Hoosiers
Groups	13 Going on 30
Communication	The Terminal
Conflict and Politics	Jaws
Information Technology	Agent Cody Banks
Innovation	The Terminal
Finance	Trading Places

For Students

PREMIUM ONLINE RESOURCES: Organized chapter by chapter, the online content is designed to reinforce and build on the text content. As students read the book, they can go online to take self-grading quizzes, review material, complete Video Cases, watch Destination CEO video clips, or work through interactive exercises like the Management History Timeline, Self-Assessments, or Test Your Knowledge Exercises. Chapter quizzes, narrated slides, and most videos are available for iPod download as premium content. The Premium Online Resources can be delivered multiple ways—professors and students can access them directly through the textbook Web site at www.mhhe.com/jonesgeorge6e, through PageOut, or within a course management system (i.e., WebCT, Blackboard, D2L, eCollege).

SELF-ASSESSMENTS: *McGraw-Hill Management* provides 23 interactive, self-scoring self-assessments so students can test their values, beliefs, skills, and interests in a wide variety of areas. This enables students to personally apply chapter content to their own lives and careers. Assessments provided include "What Is Your Guiding Ethical Principle?" and "What Is Your Decision-Making Style?". The self-assessments are organized by topic and are supported by an instructor manual and PowerPoint® presentation in the Group and Video Resource Manual.

TEST YOUR KNOWLEDGE EXERCISES: This interactive online application allows students to study 31 key concepts. After they review the key concept presented, students take quizzes in either practice or testing mode, to ensure comprehension. The application contains both knowledge and application questions.

BUSINESSWEEK EDITION: Your students can subscribe to *BusinessWeek* for a specially priced rate of $8.25 in addition to the price of the text. Students will receive a pass code card shrink-wrapped with their new text. The card directs students to a Web site where they enter the code and then gain access to *Business-Week*'s registration page to enter address information and set up their subscription. Students can now choose from receiving their subscription in print copy or digital format. To learn more about this option, please contact your McGraw-Hill representative.

Alternative & Cost Saving Options

e-Book Options

e-books are an innovative way for students to save money and to "go-green." McGraw-Hill's e-books are typically 55% of bookstore price. Students have the choice between McGraw-Hill's **two types of e-books:** CourseSmart (online e-book) and *VitalSource* (downloadable e-book).

Online e-book via *CourseSmart:*

CourseSmart is the online option for e-books. Through *CourseSmart,* students have the flexibility to access an exact replica of their textbook from any computer that has Internet service without plug-ins or special software. Access to the CourseSmart e-book is one year.

FEATURES: *CourseSmart* e-books allow students to highlight, take notes, organize notes, and share the notes with other *CourseSmart* users. Students can also search terms across all e-books in their purchased *CourseSmart* library. *CourseSmart* e-books can be printed (five pages at a time).

MORE INFO AND PURCHASE: Please visit www.coursesmart.com for more information and to purchase access to our online e-book. *CourseSmart* allows students to try one chapter of the e-book, free of charge, before purchase. Instructors should contact their McGraw-Hill representative for their one-year free access.

Downloadable e-book via *VitalSource*:

VitalSource is the downloadable option for e-books. When a student purchases a *VitalSource* e-book, it is theirs to keep *permanently* or until they delete from their computer. *VitalSource* e-books can be downloaded to up to two computers. Download and installation of the free "Bookshelf" application to the computer is required to access the e-book.

FEATURES: *VitalSource* e-books allow students to copy and paste e-book text into other documents (includes the citation information), students can highlight (with multiple colors), take notes, organize notes, and share notes with other *VitalSource* users. Pages are "reflowable," meaning students can customize views, fonts, and so forth. *VitalSource* includes a search feature that allows students to search across all *VitalSource* e-books within their purchased library. *VitalSource* e-books can be printed (two pages at a time).

MORE INFO AND PURCHASE: Students can purchase a *VitalSource* e-book and "Bookshelf" application at www.textbooks.VitalSource.com. *VitalSource* allows students and instructors to download the entire book free for a seven-day trial. Instructors should contact their McGraw-Hill representative for permanent access to their *VitalSource* textbook.

Custom Textbook Option

Offer your students a textbook that matches your course exactly in four simple steps! McGraw-Hill's Primis Online digital database offers the flexibility to customize your course including material from the largest online collection of textbooks, readings, and cases. Please visit www.primisonline.com for more information, or call (800) 962-9342.

Custom e-book Option

Primis leads the way in customized e-books with hundreds of titles available at prices that save students over 55% off the regular print purchase price. Additional information is available at (800) 962-9342, or by visiting www.wbooks.primisonline.com.

Authors

Gareth Jones is a Professor of Management in the Lowry Mays College and Graduate School of Business at Texas A&M University. He received his B.A. in Economics/Psychology and his Ph.D. in Management from the University of Lancaster, U.K. He previously held teaching and research appointments at the University of Warwick, Michigan State University, and the University of Illinois at Urbana-Champaign. He is a frequent visitor and speaker at universities in both the United Kingdom and the United States.

He specializes in strategic management and organizational theory and is well known for his research that applies transaction cost analysis to explain many forms of strategic and organizational behavior. He is currently interested in strategy process, competitive advantage, and information technology issues. He is also investigating the relationships between ethics, trust, and organizational culture and studying the role of affect in the strategic decision-making process.

He has published many articles in leading journals of the field, and his recent work has appeared in the *Academy of Management Review,* the *Journal of International Business Studies,* and *Human Relations.* An article on the role of information technology in many aspects of organizational functioning was published in the *Journal of Management.* One of his articles won the *Academy of Management Journal's* Best Paper Award, and he is one of the most prolific authors in the *Academy of Management Review.* He is or has served on the editorial boards of the *Academy of Management Review,* the *Journal of Management,* and *Management Inquiry.*

Gareth Jones has taken his academic knowledge and used it to craft leading textbooks in management and three other major areas in the management discipline: organizational behavior, organizational theory, and strategic management. His books are widely recognized for their innovative, contemporary content and for the clarity with which they communicate complex, real-world issues to students.

Jennifer George is the Mary Gibbs Jones Professor of Management and Professor of Psychology in the Jesse H. Jones Graduate School of Management at Rice University. She received her B.A. in Psychology/Sociology from Wesleyan University, her M.B.A. in Finance from New York University, and her Ph.D. in Management and Organizational Behavior from New York University. Prior to joining the faculty at Rice University, she was a Professor in the Department of Management at Texas A&M University.

Professor George specializes in organizational behavior and is well known for her research on mood and emotion in the workplace, their determinants, and their effects on various individual and group-level work outcomes. She is the author of many articles in leading peer-reviewed journals such as the *Academy of Management Journal,* the *Academy of Management Review,* the *Journal of Applied Psychology, Organizational Behavior and Human Decision Processes, Journal of Personality and Social Psychology,* and *Psychological Bulletin.* One of her papers won the Academy of Management's Organizational Behavior Division Outstanding Competitive Paper Award and another paper won the Human Relations Best Paper Award. She is, or has been, on the editorial review boards of the *Journal of Applied Psychology, Academy of Management Journal, Academy of Management Review, Administrative Science Quarterly, Journal of Management, Organizational Behavior and Human Decision Processes, Organization Science, International Journal of Selection and Assessment,* and *Journal of Managerial Issues,* was a consulting editor for the *Journal of Organizational Behavior,* and was a member of the SIOP *Organizational Frontiers Series* editorial board. She is a Fellow in the American Psychological Association, the American Psychological Society, and the Society for Industrial and Organizational Psychology and a member of the Society for Organizational Behavior. Professor George recently completed a six-year term as an Associate Editor for the *Journal of Applied Psychology.* She also has co-authored a widely used textbook titled *Understanding and Managing Organizational Behavior.*

Contemporary
Management

CHAPTER 1

Managers and Managing

After studying this chapter, you should be able to:

LO1 Describe what management is, why management is important, what managers do, and how managers utilize organizational resources efficiently and effectively to achieve organizational goals.

LO2 Distinguish among planning, organizing, leading, and controlling (the four principal managerial tasks), and explain how managers' ability to handle each one affects organizational performance.

LO3 Differentiate among three levels of management, and understand the tasks and responsibilities of managers at different levels in the organizational hierarchy.

LO4 Distinguish between three kinds of managerial skill, and explain why managers are divided into different departments to perform their tasks more efficiently and effectively.

LO5 Discuss some major changes in management practices today that have occurred as a result of globalization and the use of advanced information technology (IT).

LO6 Discuss the principal challenges managers face in today's increasingly competitive global environment.

Learning Objectives

A MANAGER'S CHALLENGE

How Anne Mulcahy Created a New Xerox

www.xerox.com

What is high-performance management? In 2001, Xerox, the well-known copier company, was near bankruptcy. The combination of aggressive Japanese competitors, which were selling low-price copiers, and a shift toward digital copying, which made Xerox's pioneering light-lens copying process obsolete, was resulting in plummeting sales. Losing billions of dollars, Xerox's board desperately searched for a new CEO who could revitalize the company's product line and change the way it operated.[1] The person they chose to plan the company's transformation was Anne Mulcahy, a 26-year Xerox veteran. Mulcahy began her career as a Xerox copier salesperson, transferred into human resource management, and then used her considerable leadership skills to work her way up the company's hierarchy to become its president.

As the new CEO, the biggest management challenge Mulcahy faced was deciding how to alter the company's structure and control systems to reduce Xerox's high operating costs to *save* billions of dollars. At the same time, however, she had to plan the best strategies for Xerox. Specifically, she had to decide how to best *invest* the company's remaining research dollars to innovate desperately needed new kinds of digital copiers that would attract customers back to the company and generate new revenues and profits. Simultaneously achieving both these objectives is one of the biggest challenges a manager can face, and how well

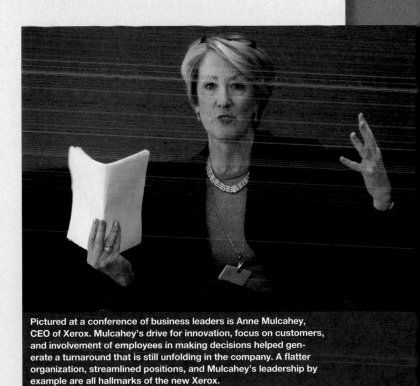

Pictured at a conference of business leaders is Anne Mulcahey, CEO of Xerox. Mulcahey's drive for innovation, focus on customers, and involvement of employees in making decisions helped generate a turnaround that is still unfolding in the company. A flatter organization, streamlined positions, and Mulcahey's leadership by example are all hallmarks of the new Xerox.

she performed these tasks would determine Xerox's fate, indeed its very survival.

To find a solution to this problem Mulcahy employed her substantial leadership skills. Known as an unassuming CEO who prefers to stay in the background and lead by example, she focused her efforts on involving and listening to Xerox's employees and customers. Mulcahy began a series of "town hall" meetings with Xerox employees, asked them for all kinds of creative input and their best efforts, but told them that tough times were ahead and that layoffs would be necessary.[2] At the same time, she emphasized that only their hard work to find ways to reduce costs could save the company. To help discover how the company should best invest its R&D budget, Mulcahy made reaching out to customers her other main priority. From the top down she insisted that managers and engineers at all levels should visit, meet, and talk to customers to uncover what they most wanted from new digital copiers—and from Xerox. One of her initiatives, called "Focus 500," requires that Xerox's top 200 managers go out into the field and visit Xerox's top 500 customers to develop an ongoing personal relationship with them. She reinforced this as a major priority by issuing standing orders that even if Xerox executives were in important meetings, they should immediately go to the phone and satisfy the needs of their assigned customers.

By listening closely to both employees and customers, Mulcahy and Xerox's managers and engineers gained new insights that led to the development of new strategies that have transformed the company's product line. Mulcahy's first strategy was to spend most of the R&D budget on developing two new kinds of digital copiers: a line of digital color copying machines for use by medium and large businesses and a line of low-end copiers offering a print quality, speed, and price that even Japanese competitors cannot match.[3] Her second strategy was to invest more resources to develop a new, efficient sales and service network to support Xerox's new copiers and improve customer service. Mulcahy also made major changes to Xerox's organizational structure by reducing the number of levels in the management hierarchy, which cut 26% from corporate overhead, and by streamlining its operating units, which reduced the number of employees from 95,000 to 55,000, to speed product development and reduce costs. By 2006 it was clear that Mulcahy and her managers had devised a successful turnaround plan to save Xerox; their strategy to focus on two new lines of copiers and a painful downsizing and reorganization paid off as the company's revenues and profits began to increase each year.[4]

Continuing to work closely with customers, Mulcahy and her managers have developed new strategies for Xerox based on innovating improved products and services. In talking to Xerox customers, it became clear they wanted a combination of copying software and hardware that would allow them to create highly customized documents for their *own* customers. Banks, retail stores, and small businesses need personalized software to create individual client statements, for example. Mulcahy decided to grow the customized services side of Xerox's business to meet these specialized needs. She also decided to replicate Xerox's sales and customer service operations around the globe and customize them to the needs of customers in each country.

The result was soaring profits. For example, in 2007 revenues increased by 11% compared to 2006 and profits almost doubled as more than half its revenues come from customers outside the U.S.[5] Similarly, a team of Xerox researchers came up with the idea for a dual-engine copier printer after customers in a focus group volunteered that they would be willing to pay extra for a copier that could continue to operate, if only at half speed, even when its primary engine broke down. The result was Xerox's Duel-Engine Nuvera 288 Digital Perfecting System in 2007, one of many new "customer-led innovations" that have resulted in two-thirds of its copier hardware profits coming from new products introduced since 2005![6] Small wonder Mulcahy is forecasting even better performance in 2008.[7]

Overview

The way in which Anne Mulcahy works to improve Xerox's performance illustrates many of the challenges facing people who become managers: Managing a company is a complex activity, and effective managers must possess many kinds of skills, knowledge, and abilities. Management is an unpredictable process. Making the right decision is difficult; even effective managers often make mistakes and the most effective managers are the ones, like Mulcahy, who continually strive to find ways to increase their companies' performance.

In this chapter, we look at what managers do and what skills and abilities they must develop if they are to manage their organizations successfully over time. We also identify the different kinds of managers that organizations need and the skills and abilities they must develop if they are to be successful. Finally, we identify some of the challenges that managers must address if their organizations are to grow and prosper.

What Is Management?

When you think of a manager, what kind of person comes to mind? Do you see someone who, like Anne Mulcahy or Michael Dell, can determine the future prosperity of a large for-profit company? Or do you see the administrator of a not-for-profit organization, such as a community college, library, or charity, or the person in charge of your local Wal-Mart store or McDonald's restaurant, or the person you answer to if you have a part-time job? What do all these people have in common? First, they all work in organizations. **Organizations** are collections of people who work together and coordinate their actions to achieve a wide variety of goals, or desired future outcomes.[8] Second, as managers, they are the people responsible for supervising and making the most of an organization's human and other resources to achieve its goals.

organizations Collections of people who work together and coordinate their actions to achieve a wide variety of goals or desired future outcomes.

management The planning, organizing, leading, and controlling of human and other resources to achieve organizational goals efficiently and effectively.

Management, then, is the planning, organizing, leading, and controlling of human and other resources to achieve organizational goals efficiently and effectively. An organization's *resources* include assets such as people and their skills, know-how, and experience; machinery; raw materials; computers and information technology; and patents, financial capital, and loyal customers and employees.

LO1 Describe what management is, why management is important, what managers do, and how managers utilize organizational resources efficiently and effectively to achieve organizational goals.

Achieving High Performance: A Manager's Goal

One of the most important goals that organizations and their members try to achieve is to provide some kind of good or service that customers value or desire. The principal goal of CEO Anne Mulcahy is to manage Xerox so that it creates a new stream of goods and services—such as more reliable speedy copiers, improved copier customer

Figure 1.1

Efficiency, Effectiveness, and Performance in an Organization

EFFICIENCY

	LOW	**HIGH**
HIGH	**Low efficiency/ High effectiveness** Manager chooses the right goals to pursue, but does a poor job of using resources to achieve these goals. Result: A product that customers want, but that is too expensive for them to buy.	**High efficiency/ High effectiveness** Manager chooses the right goals to pursue and makes good use of resources to achieve these goals. Result: A product that customers want at a quality and price that they can afford.
LOW	**Low efficiency/ Low effectiveness** Manager chooses wrong goals to pursue and makes poor use of resources. Result: A low-quality product that customers do not want.	**High efficiency/ Low effectiveness** Manager chooses inappropriate goals, but makes good use of resources to pursue these goals. Result: A high-quality product that customers do not want.

(vertical axis label: **EFFECTIVENESS**)

High-performing organizations are efficient *and* effective.

support, more versatile customized, color copiers—that customers are willing to buy. By 2008 Xerox led the field in many of these areas; it had achieved a leadership position in the global copying market.[9]

Similarly, the principal goal of doctors, nurses, and hospital administrators is to increase their hospital's ability to make sick people well—and to do so cost-effectively. Likewise, the principal goal of each McDonald's restaurant manager is to produce burgers, salads, fries, and shakes that people want to pay for and eat so that they become loyal, return customers.

Organizational performance is a measure of how efficiently and effectively managers use available resources to satisfy customers and achieve organizational goals. Organizational performance increases in direct proportion to increases in efficiency and effectiveness (see Figure 1.1).

Efficiency is a measure of how well or how productively resources are used to achieve a goal.[10] Organizations are efficient when managers minimize the amount of input resources (such as labor, raw materials, and component parts) or the amount of time needed to produce a given output of goods or services. For example, McDonald's continues to develop ever more efficient fat fryers that not only reduce the amount of oil used in cooking, but also speeds up the cooking of french fries; UPS continues to develop new work routines to reduce delivery time, such as instructing drivers to leave their truck doors open when going short distances. A manager's responsibility is to ensure that an organization and its members perform as efficiently as possible all the activities needed to provide goods and services to customers.

Effectiveness is a measure of the appropriateness of the goals that managers have selected for the organization to pursue and of the degree to which the organization achieves those goals. Organizations are effective when managers choose appropriate goals and then achieve them. Some years ago, for example, managers at McDonald's decided on the goal of providing breakfast service to attract more customers. The choice of this goal has proved very smart, for sales of breakfast food now account

organizational performance A measure of how efficiently and effectively a manager uses resources to satisfy customers and achieve organizational goals.

efficiency A measure of how well or how productively resources are used to achieve a goal.

effectiveness A measure of the appropriateness of the goals an organization is pursuing and of the degree to which the organization achieves those goals.

for more than 30% of McDonald's revenues and are still increasing—an important reason for its record profits in 2007. Mulcahy's goal is to create a constant flow of innovative copier hardware and software in order to provide customized services. High-performing organizations, such as Xerox, McDonald's, Wal-Mart, Intel, Home Depot, Accenture, and Habitat for Humanity are simultaneously efficient and effective (see Figure 1.1). Effective managers are those who choose the right organizational goals to pursue and have the skills to utilize resources efficiently.

Why Study Management?

Today, more students are competing for places in business courses than ever before; the number of people wishing to pursue Master of Business Administration (MBA) degrees—today's passport to an advanced management position—either on campus or from online universities and colleges is at an all-time high. Why is the study of management currently so popular?[11]

First, in any society or culture resources are valuable and scarce, so the more efficient and effective use that organizations can make of those resources, the greater the relative well-being and prosperity of people in that society. Because managers are the people who decide how to use many of a society's most valuable resources—its skilled employees, raw materials like oil and land, computers and information systems, and financial assets—they directly impact the well-being of a society and the people in it. Understanding what managers do and how they do it is of central importance to understanding how a society creates wealth and affluence for its citizens.

Second, although most people are not managers, and many may never intend to become managers, almost all of us encounter managers because most people have jobs and bosses. Moreover, many people today are working in groups and teams and have to deal with coworkers. Studying management helps people to deal with their bosses and their coworkers. It reveals how to understand other people at work and make decisions and take actions that win the attention and support of the boss and coworkers. Management teaches people not yet in positions of authority how to lead coworkers, solve conflicts between them, achieve team goals, and so increase performance.

Third, in any society, people are in competition for a very important resource—a job that pays well and provides an interesting and satisfying career—and understanding management is one important path toward obtaining this objective. In general, jobs become more interesting the more complex or responsible they are. Any person who desires a motivating job that changes over time might therefore do well to develop management skills and become promotable. A person who has been working for several years and then returns to school for an MBA can usually, after earning the degree, find a more interesting, satisfying job and one that pays significantly more than the previous job. Moreover, salaries increase rapidly as people move up the organizational hierarchy, whether it is a school system, a large for-profit business organization, or a not-for-profit charitable or medical institution.

Indeed, the salaries paid to top managers are enormous. For example, the CEOs and other top executives or managers of companies such as Xerox, Dell, Walt Disney, GE, and McDonald's receive millions in actual salary each year. However, even more staggering is the fact that many top executives also receive stock or shares in the company they manage, as well as stock options that give them the right to sell these shares at a certain time in the future.[12] If the value of the stock goes up, then the managers keep the difference between the price they obtained the stock option for (say, $10) and what it is worth later (say, $33). By the time Michael Eisner resigned as CEO of Disney in 2005 he had received over $1 billion from selling his stock options. When Steve Jobs became CEO of Apple again in 1997 he accepted a salary of only $1 a year. However, he was also awarded stock options that, with the fast rise in Apple's stock price in the 2000s, were worth several billions of dollars by 2008 and will continue to increase if Apple performs well (he was also given the free use of a $90 million jet).[13] These incredible amounts of money provide some indication

Figure 1.2
Four Tasks of Management

of both the responsibilities and the rewards that accompany the achievement of high management positions in major companies—and to anybody who successfully creates and manages a small business. What is it that managers actually do to receive such rewards?[14]

Essential Managerial Tasks

The job of management is to help an organization make the best use of its resources to achieve its goals. How do managers accomplish this objective? They do so by performing four essential managerial tasks: *planning, organizing, leading,* and *controlling* (see Figure 1.2). The arrows linking these tasks in Figure 1.2 suggest the sequence in which managers typically perform them. French manager Henri Fayol first outlined the nature of these managerial activities around the turn of the 20th century in *General and Industrial Management,* a book that remains the classic statement of what managers must do to create a high-performing organization.[15]

Managers at all levels and in all departments—whether in small or large companies, for-profit or not-for-profit organizations, or organizations that operate in one country or throughout the world—are responsible for performing these four tasks, which we look at next. How well managers perform these tasks determines how efficient and effective their organizations are.

Planning

LO2 Distinguish among planning, organizing, leading, and controlling (the four principal managerial tasks), and explain how managers' ability to handle each one affects organizational performance.

planning Identifying and selecting appropriate goals; one of the four principal tasks of management.

To perform the **planning** task, managers identify and select appropriate organizational goals and courses of action; they develop strategies about how to achieve high performance. The three steps involved in planning are (1) deciding which goals the organization will pursue, (2) deciding what strategies to adopt to attain those goals, and (3) deciding how to allocate organizational resources to pursue the strategies that attain those goals. How well managers plan and develop strategies determines how effective and efficient the organization is—its performance level.[16]

Michael Dell sits in the dorm room at the University of Texas, Austin, where he launched his personal computer company as a college freshman. When he visited, the room was occupied by freshmen Russell Smith (left) and Jacob Frith, both from Plano, Texas.

As an example of planning in action, consider the situation confronting Michael Dell, founder and CEO of Dell Computer, the largest seller of PCs in the U.S. in 2007. In 1984, the 19-year-old Dell saw an opportunity to enter the PC market by assembling PCs and then selling them directly to customers. Dell began to plan how to put his idea into practice. First, he decided that his goal was to sell an inexpensive PC, to undercut the prices of companies like IBM, Compaq, and Apple. Second, he had to decide on a course of action to achieve this goal. He decided to sell directly to customers by telephone and to bypass expensive computer stores that sold Compaq and Apple PCs. He also had to decide how to obtain low-cost components and how to tell potential customers about his products. Third, he had to decide how to allocate his limited funds (he had only $5,000) to buy labor and other resources. He chose to hire three people and work with them around a table to assemble his PCs.

Thus, to achieve his goal of making and selling low-price PCs, Dell had to plan, and as his organization grew, his plans changed and became progressively more complex. Dell and his managers are continually planning how to help the company maintain its position as the highest-performing PC maker. In 2003, Dell announced it would begin to sell printers and Internet music players, which brought it into direct competition with Hewlett-Packard (HP), the leading printer maker, and Apple, with its new PCs and iPod. It has since expanded the range of products it sells to include LCD screens of all sizes, digital cameras, TVs, and all kinds of broadband and other digital information services.

Dell's new plan has not worked very successfully, however. Apple remains the clear leader in the Internet music download and player business, and HP's printers far outsell Dell's. In fact, Dell's share of the global PC market fell sharply in 2006 and 2007, and it was forced to lower prices to compete with HP, which caught up and passed Dell in PC sales.[17] In 2007, HP became the largest global PC maker. In addition, in 2006 Apple announced it would begin using Intel chips, which allows Microsoft's Windows to work on Apple PCs, so Apple became a direct competitor with Dell. And, in 2007, a Taiwan PC maker, Acer, bought struggling Gateway to become the third largest global PC maker. To reverse Dell's declining performance and meet these challenges, Michael Dell decided to once again become its CEO and began to plan new strategies to better compete. Dell has fought back to once again become the largest U.S. PC maker, but it is still locked in a major battle with its competitors.

strategy A cluster of decisions about what goals to pursue, what actions to take, and how to use resources to achieve goals.

As the battle between Dell, HP, Acer, and Apple suggests, the outcome of planning is a **strategy,** a cluster of decisions concerning what organizational goals to pursue, what actions to take, and how to use resources to achieve these goals. The decisions that were the outcome of Michael Dell's original planning formed a *low-cost strategy.* A low-cost strategy is a way of obtaining customers by making decisions that allow an organization to produce goods or services more cheaply than its competitors so that it can charge lower prices than they do. Throughout its history, Dell has been constantly refining this strategy and exploring new strategies to reduce costs; Dell became the most profitable PC maker as a result of its low-cost strategy, but when HP and Acer also lowered their costs it lost its competitive advantage and its profits fell. By contrast, since its founding Apple's strategy has been to deliver new, exciting, and unique computer and digital products, such as its futuristic PCs, iPods, and iPhones, to customers—a strategy known as *differentiation.*[18] While this strategy almost ruined Apple in the 1990s when customers bought cheaper Dell PCs rather than Apple's higher-priced PCs, today its sales have increased as customers turn to its stylish PCs and Dell has been forced to offer more exciting, stylish products to fight back.

Planning is a complex, difficult activity because what goals an organization should pursue and how best to pursue them—which strategies to adopt—are almost always not immediately clear; planning is done under uncertainty. Managers take major risks when they commit organizational resources to pursue a particular strategy. Either success or failure is a possible outcome of the planning process. Dell succeeded spectacularly in the past with its low-cost strategy; but presently Apple is succeeding spectacularly with its differentiation strategy, and HP, after many problems, has enjoyed a turnaround because by lowering its costs it is now able to offer customers attractive PCs at similar prices to Dell's. So, managers at Dell and HP are continually planning how to outperform each other—and in 2008 Acer also became a major rival as its global market share increased sharply. In Chapter 8 we focus on the planning process and on the strategies organizations can select to respond to opportunities or threats in an industry. The way in which Joe Coulombe went about creating a successful management approach for his small business, a specialty, upscale supermarket illustrates well how important planning and strategy making are to a manager's career success.

Manager as a Person

Small Business

Joe Coulombe Makes Trader Joe's a Small Business Success Story

Trader Joe's, an upscale specialty supermarket chain, was started in 1967 by Joe Coulombe, who then owned a few convenience stores that were fighting an uphill battle against the growing 7-11 chain. 7-11 was able to offer customers a wider selection of lower-priced products, and Coulombe had to find a new way to manage his small business if it was going to survive. As he began planning new strategies to help grow his small business, he was struck by the fact that there might be a niche for supplying specialty products, such as wine, drinks, and gourmet foods, which were more profitable to sell; moreover, he would no longer be competing against giant 7-11. Coulombe changed the name of his stores to Trader Joe's and stocked them with every variety and brand of California wine that was then being produced. He also began to offer fine foods like bread, crackers, cheese, fruits, and vegetables to complement and encourage wine sales.

Trader Joe's first New York City store opened in 2006. Founder Joe Coulomb's intuitive move away from convenience store to specialty food and drink offerings won over customers bored with the usual supermarket fare and increasingly concerned about their health.

His planning paid off, customers loved his new upscale supermarket concept and the premium products he had chosen to stock sold quickly. Realizing that he quickly needed to capitalize on his success to protect his growing business, his strategy was to continually expand the variety of premium foods and drinks he sold and, taking advantage of the popularity of the name, he began to offer his own store label products. Today, over 80% of the products Trader Joe's sells sport its own label, so Coulombe's decision to reverse course and pursue a differentiation strategy within the premium-quality segment of the supermarket business has paid off.

From the beginning Coulombe realized that good planning was only the first step in successfully managing his small, growing company. He knew that to encourage customers to visit his stores and buy high-priced gourmet products he needed to provide them with excellent customer service, so he had to motivate his salespeople to perform at a high level. His approach to organizing was to decentralize authority, empowering salespeople to take responsibility for meeting customer needs. Rather than forcing employees to follow strict operating rules and to obtain the consent of their superior in the hierarchy of authority, employees were given autonomy to make decisions and provide personalized customer service. Coulombe's approach led employees to feel they "owned" their supermarkets, and he worked to develop a culture based on values and norms about providing excellent customer service and developing personalized relationships with customers, who are often on first-name terms.

Coulombe led by example and created a store environment in which employees were treated as individuals and felt valued as people. For example, the theme behind the design of his stores was to create the feeling of a Hawaiian resort: He and his employees wear loud Hawaiian shirts, store managers are called captains, and the store décor uses lots of wood and contains Tiki huts where employees provide customers with food and drink samples and interact with them. Once again, this helped to create strong values and norms that emphasize personalized customer service.

Finally, Joe Coulombe's approach to managing also was strongly influenced by the way he went about *controlling* salespeople. From the outset he created a policy of promotion from within the company so that the highest performing salespeople could rise to become store captains and beyond in the organization. And, from the beginning, he recognized the need to treat employees in a fair and equitable way to encourage them to develop the customer-oriented values and norms needed to provide personalized customer service. He decided that full-time employees should earn at least the median household income for their communities, which averaged $7,000 a year in the 1960s and is $48,000 today—an astonishingly high amount compared to the pay of employees of regular supermarkets such as Kroger's and Safeway. Moreover, store captains, who are vital in helping create and reinforce Trader Joe's store culture, are rewarded with salaries and bonuses that can exceed $100,000 a year. And, all salespeople know that as the store chain expands they may also be promoted to this level. In fact, in 2008, Trader Joe's has over 280 stores in 23 states and is still expanding because Coulombe's approach to managing his small business created the right foundation for an upscale specialty supermarket to grow and prosper.

Organizing

organizing Structuring working relationships in a way that allows organizational members to work together to achieve organizational goals, one of the four principal tasks of management.

organizational structure A formal system of task and reporting relationships that coordinates and motivates organizational members so that they work together to achieve organizational goals.

Organizing is the task managers perform to create a structure of working relationships that allow organizational members to interact and cooperate to achieve organizational goals. Organizing involves grouping people into departments according to the kinds of job-specific tasks they perform. In organizing, managers also lay out the lines of authority and responsibility between different individuals and groups, and they decide how best to coordinate organizational resources, particularly human resources.

The outcome of organizing is the creation of an **organizational structure,** a formal system of task and reporting relationships that coordinates and motivates members so that they work together to achieve organizational goals. Organizational structure determines how an organization's resources can be best used to create goods and services. As his company grew, for example, Michael Dell, just like Joe Coulombe, faced the issue of how to structure the organization. Early on he was hiring 100 new employees a week and deciding how to design his managerial hierarchy to best motivate and coordinate managers' activities. As his organization has grown to become the world's largest PC maker, he and his managers have created progressively more complex kinds of organizational structures to help it achieve its goals. We examine the organizing process in detail in Chapters 9 through 11.

Leading

leading Articulating a clear vision and energizing and enabling organizational members so that they understand the part they play in achieving organizational goals; one of the four principal tasks of management.

An organization's *vision* is a short, succinct, and inspiring statement of what the organization intends to become and the goals it is seeking to achieve—its desired future state. In **leading,** managers articulate a clear organizational vision for the organization's members to accomplish, and they energize and enable employees so that everyone understands the part he or she plays in achieving organizational goals. Leadership involves managers using their power, personality, influence, persuasion, and communication skills to coordinate people and groups so that their activities and efforts are in harmony. Leadership revolves around encouraging all employees to perform at a high level to help the organization achieve its vision and goals. Another outcome of leadership is a highly motivated and committed workforce. Employees responded well to Michael Dell's hands-on leadership style, which has resulted in a hardworking, committed workforce.

Ken Chenault, pictured here, is the President and CEO of American Express Company. Promoted in 1997, he climbed the ranks from their Travel Related Services Company, thanks to his "even temper and unrelenting drive." Respected by colleagues for his personality, most will say they can't remember him losing his temper or raising his voice. His open door policy for subordinates allows him to mentor AmEx managers and encourages all to enter and "speak their minds."

Salespeople at Trader Joe's appreciate how Joe Coulombe's leadership style, which is based on his willingness to delegate authority, give them the autonomy to provide high-quality personalized service. We discuss the issues involved in managing and leading individuals and groups in Chapters 13 through 16.

Controlling

controlling Evaluating how well an organization is achieving its goals and taking action to maintain or improve performance; one of the four principal tasks of management.

In **controlling,** the task of managers is to evaluate how well an organization has achieved its goals and to take any corrective actions needed to maintain or improve performance. For example, managers monitor the performance of individuals, departments, and the organization as a whole to see whether they are meeting desired performance standards. Michael Dell learned early in his career how important this is. If standards are not being met, managers seek ways to improve performance.

The outcome of the control process is the ability to measure performance accurately and regulate organizational efficiency and effectiveness. To exercise control, managers must decide which goals to measure—perhaps goals pertaining to productivity, quality, or responsiveness to customers—and then they must design control systems that will provide the information necessary to assess performance, that is, to determine to what degree the goals have been met. The controlling task also allows managers to evaluate how well they themselves are performing the other three tasks of management—planning, organizing, and leading—and to take corrective action.

Michael Dell had difficulty establishing effective control systems because his company was growing so rapidly and he lacked experienced managers. In the 1990s Dell's costs soared because no controls were in place to monitor inventory, which had built up rapidly, and in 1994 Dell's new line of laptop computers crashed because poor quality control resulted in defective products, some of which caught fire. To solve these and other control problems, Michael Dell hired hundreds of experienced managers from other companies to put the right control systems in place. As a result, by

1998 Dell was able to make computers for about 10% less than its competitors, which created a major source of competitive advantage it has enjoyed ever since. By 2001 Dell became so efficient it drove its competitors out of the market because it had a 20% cost advantage over them.[19] However, we noted earlier that in the 2000s Dell's rivals, such as HP, have learned to better control their activities and lower their costs, which has eroded Dell's competitive advantage. Controlling, like the other managerial tasks, is an ongoing, fluid, always-changing process that demands constant attention and action. We cover the most important aspects of the control task in Chapters 9, 11, 17, and 18.

The four managerial tasks—planning, organizing, leading, and controlling—are essential parts of a manager's job. At all levels in the managerial hierarchy, and across all jobs and departments in an organization, effective management means performing these four activities successfully—in ways that increase efficiency and effectiveness.

Performing Managerial Tasks: Mintzberg's Typology

Our discussion of managerial tasks may seem to suggest that a manager's job is highly orchestrated and that management is a logical, orderly process in which managers rationally calculate the best way to use resources to achieve organizational goals. In reality, being a manager often involves acting emotionally and relying on gut feelings. Quick, immediate reactions to situations, rather than deliberate thought and reflection, are an important aspect of managerial action.[20] Often, managers are overloaded with responsibilities, do not have time to spend on analyzing every nuance of a situation, and therefore make decisions in uncertain conditions without being sure which outcomes will be best.[21] Moreover, for top managers in particular, the current situation is constantly changing, and a decision that seems right today may prove to be wrong tomorrow. The range of problems that managers face is enormous *(high variety)*. Managers frequently must deal with many problems simultaneously *(fragmentation),* often must make snap decisions *(brevity),* and many times must rely on intuition and experience gained throughout their careers to do their jobs to the best of their abilities.[22]

Henry Mintzberg, by following managers around and observing what they actually *do*—hour by hour and day by day—identified 10 kinds of specific roles, or sets of job responsibilities, that capture the dynamic nature of managerial work.[23] He grouped these roles according to whether the responsibility was primarily decisional, interpersonal, or informational in nature; they are described in Table 1.1.

Given the many complex, difficult job responsibilities they have, it is no small wonder that many managers claim that they are performing their jobs well if they are right just half of the time.[24] And it is understandable that many experienced managers accept failure by their subordinates as a normal part of the learning experience and a rite of passage to becoming an effective manager. Managers and their subordinates learn both from their successes and from their failures.

Levels and Skills of Managers

department A group of people who work together and possess similar skills or use the same knowledge, tools, or techniques to perform their jobs.

To perform the four managerial tasks efficiently and effectively, organizations group or differentiate their managers in two main ways—by level in hierarchy and by type of skill. First, they differentiate managers according to their level or rank in the organization's hierarchy of authority. The three levels of managers are first-line managers, middle managers, and top managers—arranged in a hierarchy. Typically, first-line managers report to middle managers, and middle managers report to top managers.

Second, organizations group managers into different departments (or functions) according to their specific set of job-related skills, expertise, and experiences, such as a manager's engineering skills, marketing expertise, or sales experience. A **department,**

Table 1.1

Managerial Roles Identified by Mintzberg

Type of Role	Specific Role	Examples of Role Activities
DECISIONAL	Entrepreneur	Commit organizational resources to develop innovative goods and services; decide to expand internationally to obtain new customers for the organization's products.
	Disturbance Handler	Move quickly to take corrective action to deal with unexpected problems facing the organization from the external environment, such as a crisis like an oil spill, or from the internal environment, such as producing faulty goods or services.
	Resource Allocator	Allocate organizational resources among different tasks and departments of the organization; set budgets and salaries of middle and first-level managers.
	Negotiator	Work with suppliers, distributors, and labor unions to reach agreements about the quality and price of input, technical, and human resources; work with other organizations to establish agreements to pool resources to work on joint projects.
INTERPERSONAL	Figurehead	Outline future organizational goals to employees at company meetings; open a new corporate headquarters building; state the organization's ethical guidelines and the principles of behavior employees are to follow in their dealings with customers and suppliers.
	Leader	Provide an example for employees to follow; give direct commands and orders to subordinates; make decisions concerning the use of human and technical resources; mobilize employee support for specific organizational goals.
	Liaison	Coordinate the work of managers in different departments; establish alliances between different organizations to share resources to produce new goods and services.
INFORMATIONAL	Monitor	Evaluate the performance of managers in different tasks and take corrective action to improve their performance; watch for changes occurring in the external and internal environments that may affect the organization in the future.
	Disseminator	Inform employees about changes taking place in the external and internal environments that will affect them and the organization; communicate to employees the organization's vision and purpose.
	Spokesperson	Launch a national advertising campaign to promote new goods and services; give a speech to inform the local community about the organization's future intentions.

Figure 1.3
Levels of Managers

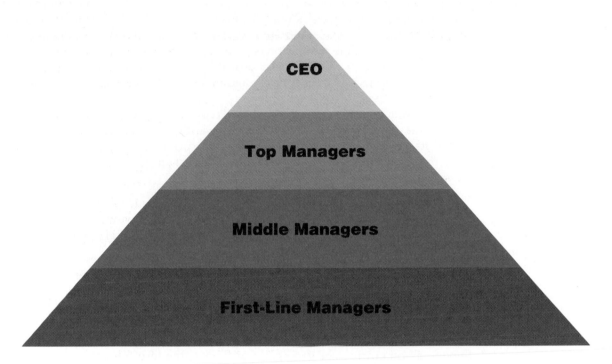

such as the manufacturing, accounting, engineering, or sales department, is a group of managers and employees who work together because they possess similar skills and experience or use the same kind of knowledge, tools, or techniques to perform their jobs. Within each department are all three levels of management. Next, we examine the reasons why organizations use a hierarchy of managers and group them, by the jobs they perform, into departments.

Levels of Management

LO3 Differentiate among three levels of management, and understand the tasks and responsibilities of managers at different levels in the organizational hierarchy.

As just discussed, organizations normally have three levels of management: first-line managers, middle managers, and top managers. (See Figure 1.3.) Managers at each level have different but related responsibilities for utilizing organizational resources to increase efficiency and effectiveness.

At the base of the managerial hierarchy are **first-line managers,** often called *supervisors*. They are responsible for the daily supervision of the nonmanagerial employees who perform many of the specific activities necessary to produce goods and services. First-line managers work in all departments or functions of an organization.

first-line manager
A manager who is responsible for the daily supervision of nonmanagerial employees.

Examples of first-line managers include the supervisor of a work team in the manufacturing department of a car plant, the head nurse in the obstetrics department of a hospital, and the chief mechanic overseeing a crew of mechanics in the service function of a new-car dealership. At Dell, first-line managers include the supervisors responsible for controlling the quality of its computers or the level of customer service provided by telephone salespeople. When Michael Dell started his company, he personally controlled the computer assembly process and thus performed as a first-line manager or supervisor.

middle manager
A manager who supervises first-line managers and is responsible for finding the best way to use resources to achieve organizational goals.

Supervising the first-line managers are **middle managers,** responsible for finding the best way to organize human and other resources to achieve organizational goals. To increase efficiency, middle managers find ways to help first-line managers and nonmanagerial employees better utilize resources to reduce manufacturing costs or improve customer service. To increase effectiveness, middle managers evaluate whether the goals that the organization is pursuing are appropriate and suggest to top managers ways in which goals should be changed. Very often, the suggestions that middle managers make to top managers can dramatically increase organizational performance. A major part of the middle manager's job is developing and fine-tuning skills and know-how, such as manufacturing or marketing expertise, that allow the organization to be efficient and effective. Middle managers make thousands of specific decisions about the production of goods and services: Which first-line supervisors should be chosen for this particular project? Where can we find the highest-quality resources? How should employees be organized to allow them to make the best use of resources?

Behind a first-class sales force, such as Trader Joe's, look for the middle managers responsible for training, motivating, and rewarding the salespeople. Behind a committed staff of high school teachers, look for the principal who energizes them to find ways to obtain the resources they need to do outstanding and innovative jobs in the classroom.

In contrast to middle managers, **top managers** are responsible for the performance of *all* departments.[25] They have *cross-departmental responsibility*. Top managers establish organizational goals, such as which goods and services the company should produce; they decide how the different departments should interact; and they monitor how well middle managers in each department utilize resources to achieve goals.[26] Top managers are ultimately responsible for the success or failure of an organization, and their performance (like that of Michael Dell and Anne Mulcahy) is continually scrutinized by people inside and outside the organization, such as other employees and investors.[27]

The *chief executive officer (CEO)* is a company's most senior and important manager, the one all other top managers report to. Today, the term *chief operating officer (COO)* is often used to refer to the top manager who is being groomed to take over as CEO when the current CEO retires or leaves the company. Together, the CEO and COO are responsible for developing good working relationships among the top managers of various departments (manufacturing and marketing, for example); usually top managers have the title "vice president." A central concern of the CEO is the creation of a smoothly functioning **top-management team,** a group composed of the CEO, the COO, the president, and the department heads most responsible for helping achieve organizational goals.[28]

The relative importance of planning, organizing, leading, and controlling—the four principal managerial tasks—to any particular manager depends on the manager's position in the managerial hierarchy.[29] The amount of time that managers spend planning and organizing resources to maintain and improve organizational performance increases as they ascend the hierarchy (see Figure 1.4).[30] Top managers devote most of their time to planning and organizing, the tasks so crucial to determining an organization's long-term performance. The lower that managers' positions are in the hierarchy, the more time the managers spend leading and controlling first-line managers or nonmanagerial employees.

Managerial Skills

Both education and experience enable managers to recognize and develop the personal skills they need to put organizational resources to their best use. Michael Dell realized from the start that he lacked sufficient experience and technical expertise in marketing, finance, and planning to guide his company alone. Thus, he recruited experienced managers from other IT companies, such as IBM and HP, to help him build his company. Research has shown that education and experience help managers acquire and develop three types of skills: *conceptual, human,* and *technical* or job-specific.[31]

Conceptual skills are demonstrated in the ability to analyze and diagnose a situation and to distinguish between cause and effect. Top managers require the best conceptual skills because their primary responsibilities are planning and organizing.[32]

---

top manager
A manager who establishes organizational goals, decides how departments should interact, and monitors the performance of middle managers.

top-management team
A group composed of the CEO, the COO, the president, and the heads of the most important departments.

LO4 Distinguish between three kinds of managerial skill, and explain why managers are divided into different departments to perform their tasks more efficiently and effectively.

conceptual skills The ability to analyze and diagnose a situation and to distinguish between cause and effect.

Figure 1.4
Relative Amount of Time That Managers Spend on the Four Managerial Tasks

By all accounts, Steve Jobs was chosen as CEO to transform Apple, just as Anne Mulcahy was chosen to revive Xerox, because of their ability to identify new opportunities and mobilize managers and other resources to take advantage of those opportunities.

Formal education and training are very important in helping managers develop conceptual skills. Business training at the undergraduate and graduate (MBA) levels provides many of the conceptual tools (theories and techniques in marketing, finance, and other areas) that managers need to perform their roles effectively. The study of management helps develop the skills that allow managers to understand the big picture confronting an organization. The ability to focus on the big picture lets managers see beyond the situation immediately at hand and consider choices while keeping in mind the organization's long-term goals.

Today, continuing management education and training, including training in advanced IT, are an integral step in building managerial skills because new theories and techniques are constantly being developed to improve organizational effectiveness, such as total quality management, benchmarking, and Web-based organization and business-to-business (B2B) networks. A quick scan through a magazine such as *BusinessWeek* or *Fortune* reveals a host of seminars on topics such as advanced marketing, finance, leadership, and human resources management that are offered to managers at many levels in the organization, from the most senior corporate executives to middle managers. Microsoft, IBM, Motorola, and many other organizations designate a portion of each manager's personal budget to be used at the manager's discretion to attend management development programs.

In addition, organizations may wish to develop a particular manager's abilities in a specific skill area—perhaps to learn an advanced component of departmental skills, such as international bond trading, or to learn the skills necessary to implement total quality management. The organization thus pays for managers to attend specialized programs to develop these skills. Indeed, one signal that a manager is performing well is an organization's willingness to invest in that manager's skill development. Similarly, many nonmanagerial employees who are performing at a high level (because they have studied management) are often sent to intensive management training programs to develop their management skills and to prepare them for promotion to first-level management positions.

human skills The ability to understand, alter, lead, and control the behavior of other individuals and groups.

Human skills include the ability to understand, alter, lead, and control the behavior of other individuals and groups. The ability to communicate, to coordinate, and to motivate people, and to mold individuals into a cohesive team, distinguishes effective from ineffective managers. By all accounts, Anne Mulcahy, Michael Dell, and Joe Coulombe all possess a high level of these human skills.

Like conceptual skills, human skills can be learned through education and training,[33] as well as be developed through experience. Organizations increasingly utilize advanced programs in leadership skills and team leadership as they seek to capitalize on the advantages of self-managed teams.[34] To manage personal interactions effectively, each person in an organization needs to learn how to empathize with other people—to understand their viewpoints and the problems they face. One way to help managers understand their personal strengths and weaknesses is to have their superiors, peers, and subordinates provide feedback about their job performance. Thorough and direct feedback allows managers to develop their human skills.

technical skills The job-specific knowledge and techniques required to perform an organizational role.

Technical skills are the job-specific skills required to perform a particular type of work or occupation at a high level. Examples include a manager's specific manufacturing, accounting, marketing, and increasingly, IT skills. Managers need a range of technical skills to be effective. The array of technical skills managers need depends on their position in their organizations. The manager of a restaurant, for example, may need cooking skills to fill in for an absent cook, accounting and bookkeeping skills to keep track of receipts and costs and to administer the payroll, and aesthetic skills to keep the restaurant looking attractive for customers.

As noted earlier, managers and employees who possess the same kinds of technical skills typically become members of a specific department and are known as, for example, marketing managers or manufacturing managers.[35] Managers are grouped into different departments because a major part of a manager's responsibility is to monitor, train, and supervise employees so that their job-specific skills and expertise increase. Obviously this is easier to do when employees with similar skills are grouped into the same department because they can learn from one another and become more skilled and productive at their particular jobs.

Figure 1.5 shows how an organization groups managers into departments on the basis of their job-specific skills. It also shows that inside each department, a managerial hierarchy of first-line, middle, and top managers emerges. At Dell, for example, Michael Dell hired experienced top managers to take charge of the marketing, sales, and manufacturing departments and to develop work procedures to help middle and first-line managers control the company's explosive sales growth. When the head of manufacturing found he had no time to supervise computer assembly, he recruited experienced manufacturing middle managers from other companies to assume this responsibility.

core competency The specific set of departmental skills, knowledge, and experience that allows one organization to outperform another.

Today, the term **core competency** is often used to refer to the specific set of departmental skills, knowledge, and experience that allows one organization to outperform its competitors. In other words, departmental skills that create a core competency give an organization a *competitive advantage*. Dell, for example, developed a core competency in materials management that allowed it to make PCs for less than its competitors—a major source of competitive advantage. Similarly, 3M is well known for its core competency in research and development that allows it to innovate new products at a faster rate than its competitors, and Trader Joe's has a competency in customer service that gives its loyal customers an attentive, personalized shopping experience.

Effective managers need all three kinds of skills—conceptual, human, and technical—to help their organizations perform more efficiently and effectively. The absence of even one type of managerial skill can lead to failure. One of the biggest problems

Figure 1.5

Types and Levels of Managers

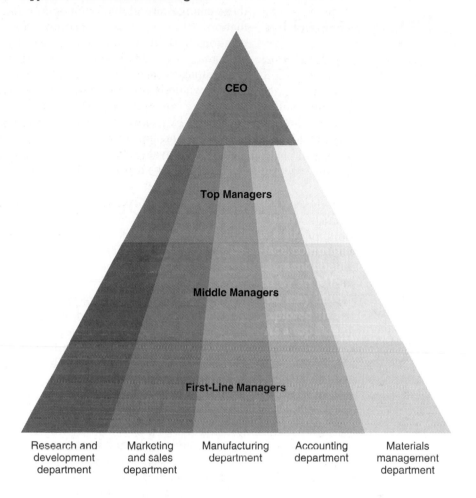

that people who start small businesses confront, for example, is their lack of appropriate conceptual and human skills. Someone who has the technical skills to start a new business does not necessarily know how to manage the venture successfully. Similarly, one of the biggest problems that scientists or engineers who switch careers from research to management confront is their lack of effective human skills. Ambitious managers or prospective managers are constantly in search of the latest educational contributions to help them develop the conceptual, human, and technical skills they need to perform at a high level in today's changing and increasingly competitive global environment.

Developing new and improved skills through education and training has become a major priority for both aspiring managers and the organizations they work for. As we discussed earlier, many people are enrolling in advanced management courses, but many companies, such as Microsoft, GE, and IBM, have established their own colleges to train and develop their employees and managers at all levels. Every year these companies put thousands of their employees through management programs designed to identify the employees who the company believes have superior competencies and whom it can develop to become its future top managers. In many organizations promotion is closely tied to a manager's ability to acquire the competencies that a particular company believes are important.[36] At 3M, for example, the ability to successfully lead a new product development team is viewed as a vital requirement for promotion; at IBM, the ability to attract and retain clients is viewed as a skill its consultants must possess. We discuss the various kinds of skills managers need to develop in most of the chapters of this book.

Recent Changes in Management Practices

The tasks and responsibilities of managers have been changing dramatically in recent years. Two major factors that have led to these changes are global competition and advances in new information technology (IT). Stiff competition for resources from organizations both at home and abroad has put increased pressure on all managers to improve efficiency and effectiveness. Increasingly, top managers are encouraging lower-level managers to look beyond the goals of their own departments and take a cross-departmental view to find new opportunities to improve organizational performance, as Michael Dell and Anne Mulcahy have done. Modern IT gives managers at all levels and in all areas access to more and better information and improves their ability to plan, organize, lead, and control. IT also provides employees with more job-related information and allows them to become more skilled, specialized, and productive.[37]

Restructuring and Outsourcing

To utilize IT to increase efficiency and effectiveness, CEOs and top-management teams have been restructuring organizations and outsourcing specific organizational activities to reduce the number of employees on the payroll and make more productive use of the remaining workforce.

restructuring Downsizing an organization by eliminating the jobs of large numbers of top, middle, and first-line managers and nonmanagerial employees.

Restructuring involves simplifying, shrinking, or downsizing an organization's operations to lower operating costs, as Xerox did. Restructuring can be done by eliminating departments and reducing levels in the hierarchy, both of which result in the loss of large numbers of jobs of top, middle, or first-line managers and nonmanagerial employees. Modern IT's ability to increase efficiency has increased the amount of downsizing in recent years. For example, IT makes it possible for fewer employees to perform a given task because it increases each person's ability to process information and make decisions more quickly and accurately. U.S. companies are spending over $50 billion a year on advanced IT that improves efficiency and effectiveness. We discuss IT's many dramatic effects on management in Chapter 18 and throughout this book.

Restructuring, however, can produce some powerful negative outcomes. It can reduce the morale of the remaining employees, who are worried about their own job security, something Anne Mulcahy had to deal with at Xerox. And top managers of many downsized organizations realize that they downsized too far when their employees complain they are overworked and when increasing numbers of customers complain about poor-quality service.[38] Dell faces this charge in the 2000s as it continues to reduce the number of its customer service reps and outsource their jobs to India to lower costs.

outsourcing Contracting with another company, usually abroad, to have it perform an activity the organization previously performed itself.

Outsourcing involves contracting with another company, usually in a low-cost country abroad, to have it perform a work activity the organization previously performed itself, such as manufacturing, marketing, or customer service. Outsourcing increases efficiency because it lowers operating costs, freeing up money and resources that can be used in more effective ways, for example, to develop new products.

The need to respond to low-cost global competition has speeded outsourcing dramatically in the 2000s. Over 3 million U.S. jobs in the manufacturing sector have been lost since 2000 as companies moved their operations to countries such as China, Taiwan, and Malaysia. Tens of thousands of high-paying jobs in IT have also moved abroad, to countries like India and Russia, where programmers work for one-third the salary of those in the United States. Dell currently employs over 15,000 customer service reps in India, for example.[39]

Large for-profit organizations today typically employ 10% to 20% fewer people than they did 10 years ago because of restructuring and outsourcing. Ford, IBM, AT&T, HP, Dell, and Du Pont are among the thousands of organizations that have streamlined their operations to increase efficiency and effectiveness. The argument is that the managers and employees who have lost their jobs will find employment in new and growing U.S. companies where their skills and experience will be better utilized. For example, the millions of manufacturing jobs that have been lost overseas will be replaced by higher-paying U.S. jobs in the service sector that are made possible because of the growth in global trade.

Empowerment and Self-Managed Teams

empowerment The expansion of employees' knowledge, tasks, and decision-making responsibilities.

The second principal way managers have sought to increase efficiency and effectiveness is by empowering lower-level employees and moving to self-managed teams. **Empowerment** is a management technique that involves giving employees more authority and responsibility over the way they perform their work activities, an approach Joe Coulombe followed at Trader Joe's. The way in which John Deere, the well-known manufacturer of tractors, empowered its employees illustrates how this technique can help raise performance. The employees who assemble Deere's vehicles possess detailed knowledge about how Deere products work. Deere's managers suddenly realized that these employees could become persuasive salespeople if they were given training. So groups of these employees were given intensive sales training and sent to visit Deere's customers and explain to them how to operate and service the company's new products. While speaking with customers, these newly empowered "salespeople" are also able to collect information that helps Deere develop new products that better meet customers' needs. The new sales jobs are only temporary; employees go on assignment but then return to the production line, where they use their new knowledge to find ways to improve efficiency and quality.

Often, companies find that empowering employees can lead to so many kinds of performance gains that they use their reward systems to promote empowerment. For example, Deere's moves to empower employees were so successful that the company negotiated a new labor agreement with its employees to promote empowerment. The agreement specifies that pay increases will be based on employees' learning new skills and completing college courses in areas such as computer programming that will help the company increase efficiency and quality. Deere has continued to make greater and greater use of teams throughout the 2000s, and its profits have soared because its competitors simply cannot match its user-friendly machines that are the result of its drive to be responsive to the needs of its customers.

Lonnie Love, an Illinois farmer, checks out the custom wiring job on his John Deere tractor. Technicians, such as the one working on Love's tractor, add irreplaceable know-how to help John Deere's sales force.

LO5 Discuss some major changes in management practices today that have occurred as a result of globalization and the use of advanced information technology (IT).

self-managed team A group of employees who assume responsibility for organizing, controlling, and supervising their own activities and monitoring the quality of the goods and services they provide.

LO6 Discuss the principal challenges managers face in today's increasingly competitive global environment.

Information technology is being increasingly used to empower employees because it expands employees' job knowledge and increases the scope of their job responsibilities. Frequently, IT allows one employee to perform a task that was previously performed by many employees. As a result, the employee has more autonomy and responsibility. IT also facilitates the use of a **self-managed team,** a group of employees who assume collective responsibility for organizing, controlling, and supervising their own work activities.[40] Using IT designed to provide team members with real-time information about each member's performance, a self-managed team can often find ways to accomplish a task more quickly and efficiently. Moreover, self-managed teams assume many of the tasks and responsibilities previously performed by first-line managers, so a company can better utilize its workforce.[41] First-line managers act as coaches or mentors whose job is not to tell employees what to do but to provide advice and guidance and help teams find new ways to perform their tasks more efficiently.[42] Using the same IT, middle managers can easily monitor what is happening in these teams and so make better resource allocation decisions as a result. The way in which IBM developed IT to take advantage of the performance-enhancing benefits of self-managed teams is discussed next.

IBM Creates Global Self-Managed Teams

IBM has been experiencing tough competition in the 2000s from IT-service companies around the world that are able to undercut IBM's prices because they have lower labor costs (recall that programmers in India earn one-third as much as U.S. programmers). Since IT services account for more than half of IBM's $90 billion annual revenues, it has been searching for ways to better utilize its talented workforce to both lower costs and offer customers unique, specialized kinds of services that its competitors cannot (and that it can charge a high price for). IBM has developed several kinds of techniques to accomplish this.

In the 2000s, IBM created "competency centers" around the world that are staffed by employees who share the same specific IT skill. In India, for example, IBM employs over 10,000 IT personnel who specialize in providing technical customer support for large U.S. companies. These employees work in self-managed teams and are responsible for managing all aspects of a particular client's specific needs. By using teams, IBM is now able to offer high-quality personalized service at a low price and compete effectively in the global marketplace.

Most of IBM's employees are concentrated in competency centers located in the countries in which IBM has the most clients and does the most business. These employees have a wide variety of skills, developed from their previous work experience, and the challenge facing IBM is to use these experts efficiently. To accomplish this, IBM used its own IT expertise to develop sophisticated software that allows it to create self-managed teams composed of IBM experts who have the optimum mix of skills to solve a client's particular problems. First, IBM programmers analyzed the skills and experience of its 70,000 global employees and inputted the results into the software program. Then they analyze and code the nature of a client's specific problem and input that information. IBM's program then matches each specific client problem to the skills of IBM's experts and identifies a list of "best fit" employees. One of IBM's senior managers then narrows down this list and decides on the actual composition of the self-managed team. Once selected, team members, from wherever they happen to be in the world, assemble as quickly as possible and go to work analyzing the client's problem. Together, team members then use their authority to develop the software and service package necessary to solve and manage the client's problem.

This new IT allows IBM to create an ever-changing set of global self-managed teams that form to solve the problems of IBM's global clients. At the same time, IBM's IT also optimizes the use of its whole talented workforce because each employee is being placed in his or her "most highly valued use," that is, in the team where the employee's skills can best increase efficiency and effectiveness. In addition, because each team inputs knowledge about its activities into IBM's internal information system, teams can watch and learn from one another—so their skills increase over time.

Challenges for Management in a Global Environment

Because the world has been changing more rapidly than ever before, managers and other employees throughout an organization must perform at higher and higher levels.[43] In the last 20 years, rivalry between organizations competing domestically (in the same country) and globally (in countries abroad) has increased dramatically. The rise of **global organizations,** organizations that operate and compete in more than one country, has put severe pressure on many organizations to identify better ways to use their resources and improve their performance. The successes of the German

global organizations
Organizations that operate and compete in more than one country.

chemical companies Schering and Hoechst, Italian furniture manufacturer Natuzzi, Korean electronics companies Samsung and LG, Brazilian plane maker Embraer, and Europe's Airbus Industries are putting pressure on companies in other countries to raise their level of performance to compete successfully against these global organizations.

Even in the not-for-profit sector, global competition is spurring change. Schools, universities, police forces, and government agencies are reexamining their operations because looking at the way activities are performed in other countries often reveals better ways to do them. For example, many curriculum and teaching changes in the United States have resulted from the study of methods that Japanese and European school systems use. Similarly, European and Asian hospital systems have learned much from the U.S. system—which may be the most effective, though not the most efficient, in the world.

Today, managers who make no attempt to learn from and adapt to changes in the global environment find themselves reacting rather than innovating, and their organizations often become uncompetitive and fail.[44] Five major challenges stand out for managers in today's world: building a competitive advantage, maintaining ethical standards, managing a diverse workforce, utilizing new information systems and technologies, and practicing global crisis management.

Building Competitive Advantage

competitive advantage
The ability of one organization to outperform other organizations because it produces desired goods or services more efficiently and effectively than they do.

What are the most important lessons for managers and organizations to learn if they are to reach and remain at the top of the competitive environment of business? The answer relates to the use of organizational resources to build a competitive advantage. **Competitive advantage** is the ability of one organization to outperform other organizations because it produces desired goods or services more efficiently and effectively than its competitors. The four building blocks of competitive advantage are superior *efficiency; quality; speed, flexibility,* and *innovation;* and *responsiveness to customers* (see Figure 1.6).

Organizations increase their efficiency when they reduce the quantity of resources (such as people and raw materials) they use to produce goods or services. In today's competitive environment, organizations continually search for new ways to use their resources to improve efficiency. Many organizations are training their workforces in the new skills and techniques needed to operate heavily computerized assembly

Figure 1.6

Building Blocks of Competitive Advantage

plants. Similarly, cross-training gives employees the range of skills they need to perform many different tasks, and organizing employees in new ways, such as in self-managed teams, allows them to make good use of their skills. These are important steps in the effort to improve productivity. Japanese and German companies invest far more in training employees than do American or Italian companies.

Managers must improve efficiency if their organizations are to compete successfully with companies operating in Mexico, China, Malaysia, and other countries where employees are paid comparatively low wages. New methods must be devised either to increase efficiency or to gain some other competitive advantage—higher-quality goods, for example—if outsourcing and the loss of jobs to low-cost countries are to be prevented.

The challenge from global organizations such as Korean electronics manufacturers, Mexican agricultural producers, and European marketing and financial firms also has increased pressure on companies to improve the skills and abilities of their workforces in order to improve the quality of their goods and services. One major thrust to improving quality has been to introduce the quality-enhancing techniques known as *total quality management (TQM)*. Employees involved in TQM are often organized into quality control teams and are responsible for finding new and better ways to perform their jobs; they also must monitor and evaluate the quality of the goods they produce. We discuss ways of managing TQM successfully in Chapter 9.

Today, companies can win or lose the competitive race depending on their *speed*—how fast they can bring new products to market—or their *flexibility*—how easily they can change or alter the way they perform their activities to respond to the actions of their competitors. Companies that have speed and flexibility are agile competitors: Their managers have superior planning and organizing abilities; they can think ahead, decide what to do, and then speedily mobilize their resources to respond to a changing environment. We examine how managers can build speed and flexibility in their organizations in later chapters. Both Michael Dell and Anne Mulcahy continuously strive to make Dell and Xerox agile companies that can react to the technological changes taking place in a digital world—now their problem is how to maintain their competitive advantage against HP, Apple, Kodak, and Canon!

innovation The process of creating new or improved goods and services or developing better ways to produce or provide them.

Innovation, the process of creating new or improved goods and services that customers want or developing better ways to produce or provide goods and services, poses a special challenge. Managers must create an organizational setting in which people are encouraged to be innovative. Typically, innovation takes place in small groups or teams; management decentralizes control of work activities to team members and creates an organizational culture that rewards risk taking. For example, in 2006 a team composed of Apple and Nike employees came up with the idea for a new model of iPod that would be able to record and measure the distance its owner had run, among other things, and the companies formed an alliance to make it.[45] Managing innovation and creating a work setting that encourages risk taking are among the most difficult managerial tasks. Innovation is discussed in depth in Chapter 9.

Organizations compete for customers with their products and services, so training employees to be responsive to customers' needs is vital for all organizations, but particularly for service organizations. Retail stores, banks, and hospitals, for example, depend entirely on their employees to perform behaviors that result in high-quality service at a reasonable cost.[46] As many countries (the United States, Canada, and Switzerland are just a few) move toward a more service-based economy (in part because of the loss of manufacturing jobs to China, Malaysia, and other countries with low labor costs), managing behavior in service organizations is becoming increasingly important. Many organizations are empowering their customer service employees and giving them the authority to take the lead in providing high-quality customer service. As noted previously, the empowering of nonmanagerial employees changes the role of first-line managers and often leads to the more efficient use of organizational resources.

Because of intense global competition, companies like Kodak, Xerox, Apple, GM, Ford, Levi Strauss, Heinz, and a host of others lost their competitive advantage. For example, technological change and the move toward digital imaging led demand for Kodak's film and light-based Xerox copiers to plunge. Others like GM and Levi Strauss have suffered because low-cost competitors undercut their prices. The managers of these companies face the challenge of turning around the performance of their companies by finding ways to restore competitive advantage—as Anne Mulcahy has done for Xerox.

turnaround management
The creation of a new vision for a struggling company based on a new approach to planning and organizing to make better use of a company's resources to allow it to survive and prosper.

Sometimes the best efforts of managers to revitalize their organization's fortunes fail, and faced with bankruptcy, the directors of these companies are forced to appoint a new CEO who has a history of success in rebuilding a company. **Turnaround management** is the creation of a new vision for a struggling company using a new approach to planning and organizing to make better use of a company's resources to allow it to survive, and eventually prosper. It involves developing radical new strategies such as reducing the number of products sold, changing how they are made and sold, and major closings of corporate and manufacturing operations. Organizations that appoint turnaround CEOs are generally experiencing a crisis because they have become inefficient or ineffective; sometimes this is because of poor management over a continuing period such as had occurred at Xerox, sometimes it occurs because a competitor introduces a new product or technology that makes their own products unattractive to customers. For example, when Apple introduced the iPhone in 2007, sales of the former best-selling mobile phone, Motorola's Razr, plummeted because customers want the state-of-the-art products and Motorola's profits tumbled. It appointed a new turnaround CEO to try to find a new way to compete in a changed market. Similarly, in 2008 The Sharper Image experienced its own crisis.

Management Insight

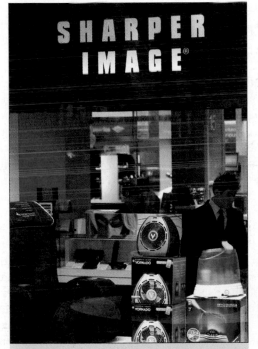

Struggling retail chain Sharper Image faces major competition from Amazon.com, Apple, and Dell in providing niche-market specialty items. Can new CEO Ron Conway execute the turnaround magic that he is known for?

Sharper Image Is No Longer in Focus

Sharper Image Corp. was started in 1977 by Richard Thalheimer to sell a lightweight watch for joggers. The store quickly became popular as a supplier of state-of-the-art innovative, quirky products that claimed to offer customers a better experience or higher quality. The specialty retailer grew to 183 stores, and in 2004 its sales had soared to over $776 million as customers proved willing to pay high prices for its innovative offerings. Things changed in 2005, however, as other companies such as Apple, Dell, and other specialty retailers began to offer state-of-the-art products. And, because Internet stores such as Amazon. com began to offer these products at much lower prices than Sharper Image's, its sales plummeted from $776 million to $400 million by 2007, a 26% drop, and profits turned to losses.

Managers realized problems were mounting in 2006 and a new CEO,

Steven Lightman, a direct marketing veteran, was brought in to restructure the company and revamp its product line. By February 2008 it was clear his turnaround was going too slowly and the company was in crisis. Lightman was replaced as CEO by Ron Conway, the head of a New York turnaround management company, and a person experienced in salvaging a company's resources and repairing broken businesses. Conway has over 25-years experience at turnaround management, and he brought with him a team of experts from his company to attempt to revitalize Sharper Image's product line and once again make it the trendy, hip place to shop. How well he succeeds remains to be seen; by February 2008 the company's stock price had dropped by 85%, so Conway and his turnaround team need to work fast to develop new strategies to sharpen his company's image.

Turnaround management is a particularly difficult and complex management task because it is done under conditions of great uncertainty. Customers, employees, and investors are unsure about the future; for example, will customer service be available, will employees retain their jobs, will investors get their money back? The risk of failure is greater for a troubled company, and usually a more radical restructuring and company reorganization are necessary to turn around its performance. Few companies stay on top all the time—and the only place left is "down"—and this is why it is so important that managers continually monitor how well their company is performing compared to its rivals, as we discuss in Chapters 8 and 9.

Achieving a competitive advantage requires that managers use all their skills and expertise, as well as their companies' other resources, to improve efficiency, quality, innovation, and responsiveness to customers. We revisit this theme often as we examine the ways managers plan strategies, organize resources and activities, and lead and control people and groups to increase efficiency and effectiveness.

Maintaining Ethical and Socially Responsible Standards

Managers at all levels are under considerable pressure to make the best use of resources to increase the level at which their organizations perform.[47] For example, top managers feel pressure from shareholders to increase the performance of the entire organization to boost its stock price, improve profits, or raise dividends. In turn, top managers may then pressure middle managers to find new ways to use organizational resources to increase efficiency or quality and thus attract new customers and earn more revenues—and then middle managers hit on their department's supervisors.

Pressure to increase performance can be healthy for an organization because it leads managers to question the way the organization is working and it encourages them to find new and better ways to plan, organize, lead, and control. However, too much pressure to perform can be harmful.[48] It may induce managers to behave unethically, and even illegally, when dealing with people and groups inside and outside the organization.[49] For example, a purchasing manager for a nationwide retail chain might buy inferior clothing as a cost-cutting measure; or to secure a large foreign contract, a sales manager in a large defense company might offer bribes to foreign officials. These issues faced the managers of companies that make footwear and clothing in the 1990s, when customers learned about the sweatshop conditions in which garment and shoe workers around the world labored. Companies such as Nike and Wal-Mart have made major efforts to stop sweatshop practices and prevent managers abroad from adopting work practices that harm their workers. They now employ hundreds of inspectors who police the factories overseas that make the products they sell and who can terminate contracts with suppliers when they behave in an unethical or illegal way.

The issue of social responsibility, discussed in Chapter 5, centers on deciding what, if any, obligations a company has toward the people and groups affected by its activities—such as employees, customers, or the communities in which it operates. Some companies have strong views about social responsibility; their managers believe they should protect the interests of others. But some managers may decide to act in an unethical way and put their own interests, or their company's, first, hurting others in the process. For example, Metabolife and NVE Pharmaceuticals used to make ephedra, a widely used dietary supplement. To protect their business, they did not reveal serious complaints about ephedra until forced to do so by lawsuits brought by people harmed by the drug. In 2003 Metabolife finally released over 16,000 customer reports about its ephedra products that listed nearly 2,000 adverse reactions, including 3 deaths.[50]

In 2004 the Food and Drug Administration (FDA) obtained the legal power to demand information from all the makers of ephedra pills. This revealed over 16,000 adverse-report events experienced by users, including at least 36 deaths. In 2004, it became illegal to make or sell ephedra in the United States.[51]

However, in their attempt to protect the $18 billion-a-year dietary supplement business, some pill makers continue to behave unethically. In particular, they have begun to use other chemical compounds that have ephedra-like effects in new varieties of pills. The FDA has issued warnings about these pills and has received new powers to police dietary supplement makers; however, the old saying *Caveat emptor* remains true: "Buyer beware."[52] A recent example showing why companies, managers, and customers must always keep the need to act in an ethical and socially responsible way at the forefront of their decision making is profiled in the following "Ethics in Action."

Ethics in Action

Small Business

How Not to Run a Meatpacking Plant

By all appearances the Westland/Hallmark Meat Co., owned by its CEO Steven Mendell, was considered to be one of the most efficient, sanitary, and state-of-the-art meatpacking companies in the United States. Based in Chico, California, its meatpacking plant, which regularly passed inspections by the United States Department of Agriculture (USDA), employed over 200 workers who slaughtered and then prepared the beef for shipment to fast-food restaurants such as Burger King and Taco Bell. Most of the millions of pounds of meat the plant prepared yearly, however, was delivered under contract to one of the federal government's most coveted accounts: the National School Lunch Program. In 2005 the plant was named supplier of the year by the National School Lunch Program.[53]

So, when at the end of 2007 the Humane Society turned over a videotape, secretly filmed by one of its investigators who had taken a job as a plant employee, to the San Bernardino County District Attorney that showed major violations of safety procedures, this caused an uproar. The videotape showed two workers dragging sick cows up the ramp that led to the slaughterhouse using metal chains and forklifts, and shocking them with electric prods and shooting streams of water in their noses and faces. Not only did the tape show inhumane treatment of animals, it also provided evidence that the company was flaunting the ban on allowing sick animals to enter the food supply chain—something that federal regulations explicitly outlawed for fear of human health and disease issues.

By February 2008 the USDA, concerned that contaminated beef had entered the supply chain, especially the one to the nation's schools, issued a notice for the recall of 143 million pounds of beef processed in the plant over the last two years, the largest recall in history. In addition, the plant was shut down as the

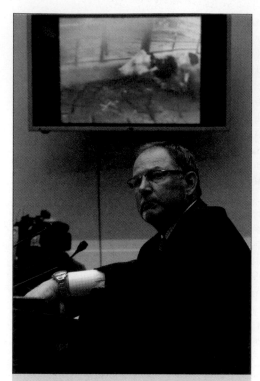

Westland/Hallmark Meat Company CEO Steven Mendell on the stand before Congress. Behind him plays the secretly-taken video of cattle being driven into the meatpacking plant. Mendell's company, putting profits before ethical accountability, is responsible for the largest ground beef recall ever to take place in the United States.

investigation proceeded. In March 2008, CEO Steven Mendell was subpoenaed to appear before the House Panel on Energy and Commerce Committee. He denied that these violations had taken place and that any diseased cows had entered the food chain. However, when panel members demanded that he view the videotape that he claimed he had not seen even though it was widely available, he was forced to acknowledge that "two cows" had in fact entered the plant and that inhumane treatment of animals had taken place.[54] Moreover, federal investigators turned up evidence that as early as 1996 the plant had been cited for overuse of electric prods to speed cattle through the plant and had been cited for other violations since, suggesting that these abuses had been going on for a long period. This view gained strength when one of the workers shown in the videotape claimed that he had just been "following orders from his supervisor" and that workers were pressured to ensure 500 cows a day were slaughtered and processed so the plant could meet its quota and make the high profits the meatpacking business provides.

These unethical, and often illegal, business practices caused major fears that over the years thousands of sick cows have entered the food chain and most of the 143 million pounds of beef recalled has already been consumed. Not only consumers and schoolchildren have been harmed by these unethical actions—it seems likely that the plant will be permanently shut down and that all 220 workers will lose their jobs. In addition, the employees directly implicated in the video have already been prosecuted and one, who pleaded guilty to animal abuse, was convicted and sentenced to six months imprisonment in March 2008.[55] Whether or not the company's managers will experience the same fate remains to be seen, but clearly all stakeholders have been hurt by the unethical and inhumane practices that, as the Humane Society had suspected for years, were commonplace in the plant.

Managing a Diverse Workforce

A major challenge for managers everywhere is to recognize the ethical need and legal requirement to treat human resources in a fair and equitable manner. Today, the age, gender, race, ethnicity, religion, sexual preference, and socioeconomic makeup of the workforce present new challenges for managers. To create a highly trained and motivated workforce, as well as to avoid major class-action lawsuits, managers must establish human resource management (HRM) procedures and practices that are legal, are fair, and do not discriminate against any organizational members.[56]

In the past, white male employees dominated the ranks of management. Today increasing numbers of organizations are realizing that to motivate effectively and take advantage of the talents of a diverse workforce, they must make promotion opportunities available to all employees, including women and minorities.[57] Managers must recognize the performance-enhancing possibilities of a diverse workforce, such as the ability to take advantage of the skills and experiences of different kinds of people.[58] Union Bank of California, one of the 30 largest banks in the United States, is a good example of a company that has utilized the potential of its diverse employees.[59]

Based in San Francisco, Union Bank operates in one of the most diverse states in the nation, California, where more than half the population is Asian, black, Hispanic, or gay. Recognizing this fact, the bank always had a policy of hiring diverse employees. However, the bank did not realize the potential of its diverse employees to create a competitive advantage until 1996 when George Ramirez, a vice president at Union

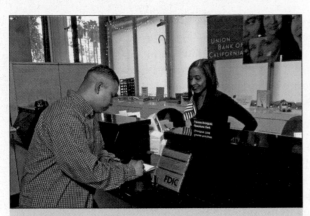

Union Bank's customer service representatives, such as the employee pictured here, are well known for building relationships with their diverse customer groups to improve the level of customer service. The diverse nature of Union Bank's employees reflects the diverse customer groups the bank serves.

Bank, proposed that the bank create a marketing group to attract Hispanic customers. His idea was so successful that a group of African-American employees, and later Asian-American and gay and lesbian employees, proposed similar marketing campaigns.

After these groups' considerable success in recruiting new customers, it was clear to Union Bank's managers that they could use employee diversity to improve not only customer service (e.g., by staffing banks in Latino neighborhoods with Latino employees)[60] but also the quality of decision making inside the organization.[61] Furthermore, the bank's reputation of being a good place for minorities to work has attracted highly skilled and motivated minority job candidates.

As its former CEO Takahiro Moriguchi said when accepting a national diversity award for the company, "By searching for talent from among the disabled, both genders, veterans, gay, all ethnic groups and all nationalities, we gain access to a pool of ideas, energy, and creativity as wide and varied as the human race itself. I expect diversity will become even more important as the world gradually becomes a truly global marketplace."[62] Union Bank's diversity practices have become a model for many other companies seeking to emulate its success.[63]

Managers who value their diverse employees not only invest in developing these employees' skills and capabilities but also succeed best in promoting performance over the long run. Today, more and more organizations are realizing that people are their most important resource and that developing and protecting human resources is an important challenge for management in a competitive global environment. We discuss the many issues surrounding the management of a diverse workforce in Chapter 5. Dell CEO Kevin Rollins made the following comments about the way a diverse workforce can help promote competitive advantage: "I've seen firsthand the power of a diverse workforce. Leveraging the similarities and differences of all team members enables Dell to develop the best products, provide a superior customer experience, and contribute in meaningful ways to the communities where we do business."[64]

Utilizing IT and E-Commerce

As we discussed above, another important challenge for managers is the efficient utilization of new information technology.[65] New technologies such as computer-controlled manufacturing and Web-based IT that link and enable employees in new ways are continually being developed. One interesting example of how IT is changing the jobs of people at all organizational levels comes from UPS where, until 2006, its drivers relied upon maps, note cards, and their own experience to plan the fastest way to deliver hundreds of parcels each day. This changed in 2006 after UPS invested over $600 million to develop a computerized route optimization system that each evening plans out each of its 56,000 drivers' routes for the next day in the most efficient way by, for example, minimizing the number of left turns that wastes both time and gas. The program has been incredibly successful; UPS drivers now drive millions of fewer miles each month, even as they deliver an increased number of packages at a faster rate.

Increasingly, new kinds of IT enable not just individual employees but also self-managed teams, by providing them with more and more important information and allowing

UPS Dispatch Coordinator Jim McCauley shows driver Muamer Pleh how many stops he will be making in his next delivery run—all made possible by the company's new software that allows each driver to plan the most efficient delivery route each day which saves the company time and money.

for virtual interactions around the globe by using the Internet. Increased global coordination helps to improve quality and increase the pace of innovation. Microsoft, Hitachi, IBM, and most companies now search for new IT that can help them to build a competitive advantage. The importance of IT is discussed in detail in Chapters 16 and 18, and throughout the text you will find icons that alert you to examples of how IT is changing the way companies operate.

Practicing Global Crisis Management

Today, another challenge facing managers and organizations is global crisis management. The causes of global crises or disasters fall into three main categories: natural causes, man-made causes, and international terrorism and geopolitical conflicts. Crises that arise because of natural causes include the hurricanes, tsunamis, earthquakes, famines, and diseases that have devastated so many countries in the 2000s; hardly any country has been left untouched by their effects. Java, for example, which was inundated by the huge Pacific tsunami of 2004, experienced a devastating earthquake in 2006 that also killed thousands of people and left tens of thousands more homeless.

Man-made crises are the result of factors such as global warming, pollution, and the destruction of the natural habitat or environment. Pollution, for example, has become an increasingly significant problem for companies and countries to deal with. Companies in heavy industries such as coal and steel have polluted millions of acres of land around major cities in eastern Europe and Asia; billion-dollar cleanups are necessary. Disasters such as the 1986 Chernobyl nuclear power plant meltdown released over 1,540 times as much radiation into the air as occurred at Hiroshima; over 50,000 people died as a result, while hundreds of thousands more have been affected.

Man-made crises, such as global warming due to emissions of carbon dioxide and other gases, may have made the effects of natural disasters more serious. For example, increasing global temperatures and acid rain may have increased the intensity of hurricanes, led to unusually strong rains, and contributed to lengthy droughts. Scientists are convinced that global warming is responsible for the destruction of coral reefs (which are disappearing at a fast rate), forests, animal species, and the natural habitat in many parts of the world. The shrinking polar ice caps are expected to raise the sea level by a few, but vital, inches.

Finally, increasing geopolitical tensions, which are partly the result of the speed of the globalization process itself, have upset the balance of world power as different countries and geographic regions attempt to protect their own economic and political interests. Rising oil prices, for example, have strengthened the bargaining power of major oil-supplying countries. This has led the United States to adopt global political strategies, including its war on terrorism, to secure the supply of oil vital to protect the national interest. In a similar way, countries in Europe have been forming contracts and allying with Russia to obtain its supply of natural gas, and Japan and China have been negotiating with Iran and Saudi Arabia. The rise of global terrorism and terrorist groups is to a large degree the result of changing political, social, and economic conditions that have made it easier for extremists to influence whole countries and cultures.

Management has an important role to play in helping people, organizations, and countries respond to global crises because it provides lessons on how to plan, organize, lead, and control the resources needed to both forestall and respond effectively to a crisis. Crisis management involves making important choices about how to (1) create teams to facilitate rapid decision making and communication, (2) establish the organizational chain of command and reporting relationships necessary to mobilize a fast response, (3) recruit and select the right people to lead and work in such teams, and (4) develop bargaining and negotiating strategies to manage the conflicts that arise whenever people and groups have different interests and objectives. How well managers make such decisions determines how quickly an effective response to a crisis can be implemented, and it sometimes can prevent or reduce the severity of the crisis itself.

Summary and Review

LO1 **WHAT IS MANAGEMENT?** A manager is a person responsible for supervising the use of an organization's resources to meet its goals. An organization is a collection of people who work together and coordinate their actions to achieve a wide variety of goals. Management is the process of using organizational resources to achieve organizational goals effectively and efficiently through planning, organizing, leading, and controlling. An efficient organization makes the most productive use of its resources. An effective organization pursues appropriate goals and achieves these goals by using its resources to create the goods or services that customers want.

LO2 **MANAGERIAL TASKS** The four principal managerial tasks are planning, organizing, leading, and controlling. Managers at all levels of the organization and in all departments perform these tasks. Effective management means managing these activities successfully.

LO 3, 4 **LEVELS AND SKILLS OF MANAGERS** Organizations typically have three levels of management. First-line managers are responsible for the day-to-day supervision of nonmanagerial employees. Middle managers are responsible for developing and utilizing organizational resources efficiently and effectively. Top managers have cross-departmental responsibility. Three main kinds of managerial skills are conceptual, human, and technical. The need to develop and build technical skills leads organizations to divide managers up into departments according to their job-specific responsibilities. Top managers must establish appropriate goals for the entire organization and verify that department managers are utilizing resources to achieve those goals.

LO5 **RECENT CHANGES IN MANAGEMENT PRACTICES** To increase efficiency and effectiveness, many organizations have altered the way they operate. Managers have restructured and downsized operations and outsourced activities to reduce costs. Companies are also empowering their workforces and utilizing self-managed teams to increase efficiency and effectiveness. Managers are increasingly utilizing IT to achieve these objectives.

LO6 **CHALLENGES FOR MANAGEMENT IN A GLOBAL ENVIRONMENT** Today's competitive global environment presents many interesting challenges to managers. One of the main challenges is building a competitive advantage by increasing efficiency; quality; speed, flexibility, and innovation; and customer responsiveness. Others are behaving in an ethical and socially responsible way toward people inside and outside the organization; managing a diverse workforce; utilizing new IT; and practicing global crisis management.

Management in Action

Topics for Discussion and Action

DISCUSSION

1. Describe the difference between efficiency and effectiveness, and identify real organizations that you think are, or are not, efficient and effective. **[LO1]**

2. In what ways can managers at each of the three levels of management contribute to organizational efficiency and effectiveness? **[LO3]**

3. Identify an organization that you believe is high-performing and one that you believe is low-performing. Give five reasons why you think the performance levels of the two organizations differ so much. **[LO 2, 4]**

4. What are the building blocks of competitive advantage?

Why is obtaining a competitive advantage important to managers? **[LO5]**

5. In what ways do you think managers' jobs have changed the most over the last 10 years? Why have these changes occurred? **[LO6]**

ACTION

6. Choose an organization such as a school or a bank; visit it; then list the different organizational resources it uses. How do managers use these resources to maintain and improve its performance? **[LO 2, 4]**

7. Visit an organization, and talk to first-line, middle, and top managers about their respective management roles in the

organization and what they do to help the organization be efficient and effective. **[LO 3, 4]**

8. Ask a middle or top manager, perhaps someone you already know, to give examples of how he or she performs the managerial tasks of planning, organizing, leading, and controlling. How much time does he or she spend in performing each task? **[LO3]**

9. Like Mintzberg, try to find a cooperative manager who will allow you to follow him or her around for a day. List the roles the manager plays, and indicate how much time he or she spends performing them. **[LO 3, 4]**

Building Management Skills
Thinking About Managers and Management [LO 2, 3, 4]

Think of an organization that has provided you with work experience and of the manager to whom you reported (or talk to someone who has had extensive work experience); then answer these questions.

1. Think of your direct supervisor. Of what department is he or she a member, and at what level of management is this person?

2. How do you characterize your supervisor's approach to

management? For example, which particular management tasks and roles does this person perform most often? What kinds of management skills does this manager have?

3. Do you think the tasks, roles, and skills of your supervisor are appropriate for the particular job he or she performs? How could this manager improve his or her task performance? How can IT affect this?

4. How did your supervisor's approach to management affect

your attitudes and behavior? For example, how well did you perform as a subordinate, and how motivated were you?

5. Think of the organization and its resources. Do its managers utilize organizational resources effectively? Which resources contribute most to the organization's performance?

6. Describe the way the organization treats its human resources. How does this treatment affect the attitudes and behaviors of the workforce?

7. If you could give your manager one piece of advice or change one management practice in the organization, what would it be?

8. How attuned are the managers in the organization to the need to increase efficiency, quality, innovation, or responsiveness to customers? How well do you think the organization performs its prime goals of providing the goods or services that customers want or need the most?

Managing Ethically [LO 1, 3]

Think about an example of unethical behavior that you observed in the past. The incident could be something you experienced as an employee or a customer or something you observed informally.

1. Either by yourself or in a group, give three reasons why you think the behavior was unethical. For example, what rules or norms were broken? Who benefited or was harmed by what took place? What was the outcome for the people involved?

2. What steps might you take to prevent such unethical behavior and encourage people to behave in an ethical way?

Small Group Breakout Exercise [LO 2, 3, 4]
Opening a New Restaurant

Form groups of three or four people, and appoint one group member as the spokesperson who will communicate your findings to the entire class when called on by the instructor. Then discuss the following scenario.

You and your partners have decided to open a large, full-service restaurant in your local community; it will be open from 7 a.m. to 10 p.m. to serve breakfast, lunch, and dinner. Each of you is investing $50,000 in the venture, and together you have secured a bank loan for $300,000 more to begin operations. You and your partners have little experience in managing a restaurant beyond serving meals or eating in restaurants, and you now face the task of deciding how you will manage the restaurant and what your respective roles will be.

1. Decide what each partner's managerial role in the restaurant will be. For example, who will be responsible for the necessary departments and specific activities? Describe your managerial hierarchy.

2. Which building blocks of competitive advantage do you need to establish to help your restaurant succeed? What criteria will you use to evaluate how successfully you are managing the restaurant?

3. Discuss the most important decisions that must be made about (a) planning, (b) organizing, (c) leading, and (d) controlling, to allow you and your partners to utilize organizational resources effectively and build a competitive advantage.

4. For each managerial task, list the issues to solve, and decide which roles will contribute the most to your restaurant's success.

Exploring the World Wide Web [LO2]

Go to the General Electric (GE) Web site at www.ge.com, click on "Our Company," then "company information," and then "Jeffrey Immelt," GE's CEO. You will see a list of articles that discuss his management style; click on articles such as "The Immelt Revolution, 2005" in *BusinessWeek* and the *Financial Times* article titled "Man of the Year 2003."

Search these articles or others for information that describes Immelt's approach to planning, organizing, leading, and controlling GE. What is his approach to managing? What effects has this approach had on GE's performance?

Be the Manager [LO 2, 5]

Problems at Achieva

You have just been called in to help managers at Achieva, a fast-growing Internet software company that specializes in B2B network software. Your job is to help Achieva solve some management problems that have arisen because of its rapid growth.

Customer demand to license Achieva's software has boomed so much in just two years that more than 50 new software programmers have been added to help develop a new range of software products. Achieva's growth has been so swift that the company still operates informally, its organizational structure is loose and flexible, and programmers are encouraged to find solutions to problems as they go along. Although this structure worked well in the past, you have been told that problems are arising.

There have been increasing complaints from employees that good performance is not being recognized in the organization and that they do not feel equitably treated. Moreover, there have been complaints about getting managers to listen to their new ideas and to act on them. A bad atmosphere is developing in the company, and recently several talented employees left. Your job is to help Achieva's managers solve these problems quickly and keep the company on the fast track.

Questions

1. What kinds of organizing and controlling problems is Achieva suffering from?

2. What kinds of management changes need to be made to solve them?

BusinessWeek Case in the News [LO 1, 2, 6]

Howard Schultz's Starbucks Challenge

There was joy in coffeeville when Howard Schultz returned as CEO of Starbucks (SBUX) on Jan. 7. "Uncle Howie to the rescue!" wrote one visitor to Starbucksgossip.com, a blog popular with the coffee chain's baristas. Wall Street echoed the sentiment. After a year of declines, shares rose by more than 8%, to $19.86, on Jan. 8.

It's a favorite business world fairy tale: the company in distress saved by the return of a visionary founder. The key, of course, is whether the leader's vision is the right one. Steve Jobs' triumphant return to Apple (AAPL) may be the dream, but there's also the story of Ted Waitt, the pony-tailed Gateway founder who took back the CEO job in 2001 only to see his baby eventually gobbled up by competitors after sticking to old ways of doing business. While many Starbucks watchers think Schultz is the right choice, some wonder whether he has a strategy that will jump-start growth.

That's a pertinent question, given that Schultz never entirely left. A vocal chairman since 2000, Schultz chimed in on earnings calls, penned memos to top managers, and regularly appeared on CNBC to talk coffee. Meanwhile the company's stock is down by 44% over the past year, and though overall sales are up, Starbucks has had trouble boosting business in its existing stores. Through it all, Schultz continued to occupy the same spacious office he held as CEO. Schultz declined to comment.

Familiar Strategy

No surprise, then, that much of the strategy Schultz outlined to analysts on Jan. 7 sounded familiar. Among his plans: to slow new store openings in the U.S. while investing overseas and focusing on "reigniting" the connection with consumers through new products and better store design.

Starbucks has already signaled that it plans to add fewer U.S. stores. International expansion has long been a priority. In a famous Feb. 14, 2007, memo, Schultz urged the company to restore the romantic coffee shop atmosphere of Starbucks' early days. The biggest news in his Jan. 7 conference call was his vow to shutter some struggling stores and to streamline management. He promised to give more details when the company announces earnings on Jan. 30.

A returning founder has more freedom to play with the formula than a hired CEO. Schultz, after all, has shown he can leverage the Starbucks brand in new ways, such as his idea to use the stores to introduce new music to customers. But founders' memories of the early days also can hinder change. Nostalgia can be dangerous,

says Jeffrey Sonnenfeld, senior associate dean at Yale University's School of Management. "[A company] is not a museum. It's not a religion."

Big Macs and Baristas

The challenges Starbucks faces today are much steeper, too. McDonald's (MCD) plans to add coffee bars and baristas throughout the U.S. (BusinessWeek.com, 1/10/08). And it's not easy being romantic when you're a $9.4 billion chain with 15,011 outlets.

At least one analyst thinks that Schultz's plans are wrongheaded. "Their business model still appears to be building stores to grow, and if they just [build more slowly and] become more relevant to consumers, everything will work itself out—I think those are all dangerous premises," says Marc Greenberg, a Deutsche Bank

(DB) analyst. "The runup in shares on Jan. 8 was a 'Hooray, Howard' rally, but does it say anything to the fundamental prospects of next year? No."

Questions for Discussion

1. What kinds of management challenges face Howard Schultz at Starbuck's?

2. What kinds of skills do you think that he has that will help him to perform effectively as Starbuck's new CEO?

Source: Burt Helm, Jena McGregor, and Brian Hindo, "Howard Schultz's Grande Challenge." Reprinted from the January 9, 2008, issue of *BusinessWeek* Online by special permission. Copyright © 2008 by The McGraw-Hill Companies, Inc.

BusinessWeek | Case in the News [LO 4, 6]

Making Her Mark at Merck: Margaret McGlynn Is on a Fast Track

For Merck's Margaret G. McGlynn, developing drugs is a deeply personal pursuit. As a child growing up in Buffalo, she learned early about the ravages of disease after three of her seven brothers and sisters died in childhood—one of measles before McGlynn was born and two of a rare genetic disorder. She was four years old when the measles vaccine was introduced, and as her mother drove her to a mass-immunization clinic, she reminded her of the child they'd lost. "I was a real believer that vaccines have a critically important role," says McGlynn.

Today vaccines have a critical role in Merck & Co.'s (MRK) turnaround effort, and McGlynn is right in the thick of it. The drug giant has launched four new vaccines since McGlynn took over as president of Merck Vaccines in September, 2005. Among them is Gardasil, hailed as a breakthrough

because it prevents some forms of human papilloma virus (HPV), a leading cause of cervical cancer. Merck rolled out Gardasil in June for females aged 9 to 26, with marketing focused on educating patients about the link between HPV and cancer. The product brought in $80 million in three months—a debut that CEO Richard T. Clark says beat expectations. When asked if McGlynn, 47, could be a CEO candidate one day, Clark says: "Absolutely. She's definitely CEO material."

McGlynn, a pharmacist who started at Merck as an intern in 1981, is helping restore some luster to the company's tarnished record. After its $2.5 billion-a-year arthritis medication Vioxx was yanked from the market in late 2004 because of cardiovascular side effects, Merck set out to slash costs and improve the way it develops and markets drugs. Merck expects to report 2006 earnings of at least $5.4 billion before special charges—slightly exceeding the estimate Clark gave at the beginning of the year—on sales of $22 billion. Investors pushed

Merck's stock up 36% in 2006, to 43. Analysts are counting on McGlynn to drive much of Merck's growth: Some predict revenues from her division will triple by 2010, to $6 billion.

Early on, McGlynn proved that she could churn out hits. As a product manager in the late 1980s, she turned Merck's treatment for high blood pressure, Vasotec, into the company's first $1 billion product. Her strategy stressed that the drug was also approved to treat congestive heart failure—an advantage competitors couldn't yet match. When McGlynn spotted rivals working on next generation blood pressure remedies, she spearheaded an effort to license one from DuPont (DD), because she knew this would be a faster way into the market than starting from scratch. That drug, Cozaar, and a follow-up are still among Merck's biggest successes, bringing in $3 billion a year.

An ability to argue her case in a "relentlessly logical and wonderfully intense way," as ex-boss David Anstice puts it, helped McGlynn rise rapidly. She worked in consumer marketing, managed care, and business development. She held top posts in U.S. marketing during the time Merck came under fire and then withdrew Vioxx. But most of the juries that have heard cases against the company have ruled in favor of Merck, and Mc-Glynn has emerged unscathed.

McGlynn's powers of persuasion have also helped her achieve results on Capitol Hill. Last summer, after Merck won approval to market a vaccine for shingles—a painful disease that strikes the elderly—she started knocking on doors all over Capitol Hill. Turned out that the new Medicare Part D drug plan prevented doctors from getting fully paid to administer vaccines. "I explained to [policymakers] that shingles is a debilitating illness that causes a major impact on quality of life," she says. They seem to have listened: On Dec. 9, Congress passed a bill that fixes the Medicare payment shortfall, which the President signed on Dec. 20.

Leading Merck's charge into the world of vaccines with the likes of Gardasil presents McGlynn with a new set of challenges. She has spent most of her career working on traditional pharmaceuticals, where success hinged almost entirely on the strength of Merck's marketing muscle. Vaccines, on the other hand, are heavily influenced by a range of powerful organizations, including the Centers for Disease Control and the American Academy of Pediatrics, which issue guidelines for physicians.

In Gardasil's case, Merck has been lobbying state legislators to mandate the vaccine for all young girls. The idea at first generated resistance from some conservative groups, who feared it would sanction promiscuous behavior, since HPV is sexually transmitted. McGlynn sent members of her team out to talk to the groups: "We meet with anyone, whether they share our viewpoint or not."

A People Person

In the end, McGlynn's skill at navigating political mazes could make the difference between a success and a multi-billion-dollar blockbuster. Kris Jenner, a health-care portfolio manager at T. Rowe Price Group Inc. (TROW), estimates Gardasil sales will peak at $2 billion a year, but could go as high as $4 billion if the states require it. Four states are weighing laws to mandate Gardasil.

A talent for marketing and connecting with customers was apparent back in McGlynn's teenage years, when she clerked at her father's community pharmacy. "She got to know all the personalities," says her brother Ed Hempling. "It was like Mayberry." Her admiration for her father's role as neighborhood medical expert led her to follow in his footsteps. Hempling describes her as "one of those kids with a 10-year plan."

A likely item in McGlynn's plan: fending off GlaxoSmithKline (GSK), which could launch an HPV vaccine in 2007. Glaxo's record of fierce price competition has some analysts worried that Merck might have to slash Gardasil's $360 price tag. To expand the potential market, Merck is testing it in older women and in men, who can be carriers. Taking a page from her Vasotec playbook, McGlynn plans to promote Gardasil's prime advantage: It protects against four HPV strains, whereas Glaxo's drug guards against only two. "That's a fair price for offering the broadest possible public health benefit," she says. Spoken like a real believer.

Questions for Discussion

1. What do you think are McGlynn's greatest skills as a manager?

2. In what way do these skills help her perform her management role at Merck?

Source: Arlene Weintraub, "Making Her Mark at Merck." Reprinted from the January 8, 2008, issue of *BusinessWeek* Online by special permission. Copyright © 2008 by The McGraw-Hill Companies, Inc.

CHAPTER 2

The Evolution of Management Thought

Learning Objectives

After studying this chapter, you should be able to:

LO1 Describe how the need to increase organizational efficiency and effectiveness has guided the evolution of management theory.

LO2 Explain the principle of job specialization and division of labor, and tell why the study of person-task relationships is central to the pursuit of increased efficiency.

LO3 Identify the principles of administration and organization that underlie effective organizations.

LO4 Trace the changes in theories about how managers should behave to motivate and control employees.

LO5 Explain the contributions of management science to the efficient use of organizational resources.

LO6 Explain why the study of the external environment and its impact on an organization has become a central issue in management thought.

A MANAGER'S CHALLENGE

Finding Better Ways to Make Cars

1900's 16 hrs a day (handwritten)

What is the best way to manage the work process? Car production has changed dramatically over the years as managers have applied different principles of management to organize and control work activities. Prior to 1900, small groups of skilled workers cooperated to hand-build cars with parts that often had to be altered and modified to fit together. This system, a type of *small-batch production,* was very expensive; assembling just one car took considerable time and effort; and skilled workers could produce only a few cars in a day. Although these cars were of high quality, they were too expensive. Managers of early car companies needed better techniques to increase efficiency, reduce costs, and sell more cars.

Henry Ford revolutionized the car industry. In 1913, Ford opened the Highland Park car plant in Detroit to produce the Model T Ford, and his team of manufacturing managers pioneered the development of *mass-production manufacturing,* a system that made the small-batch system almost obsolete overnight. In mass production, moving conveyor belts bring the cars to the workers. Each worker performs a single assigned task along a production line, and the speed of the conveyor belt is the primary means of controlling workers' activities. Ford experimented to discover the

(a) The photo on top, taken in 1904 inside a Daimler Motor Company factory, is an example of the use of small-batch production, a production system in which small groups of people work together and perform all the tasks needed to assemble a product. (b) In 1913, Henry Ford revolutionized the production process of a car by pioneering mass-production manufacturing, a production system in which a conveyor belt brings each car to the workers and each individual worker performs a single task along the production line. Even today cars are still built using this system, as evidenced in the photo of workers along a modern-day computerized automobile assembly line.

most efficient way for each worker to perform an assigned task. The result was that each worker performed one narrow, specialized task, such as bolting on the door or attaching the door handle, and jobs in the Ford car plant became very repetitive. They required little use of a worker's skills.[1] Ford's management approach increased efficiency and reduced costs by so much that by 1920 he was able to reduce the price of a car by two-thirds and to sell more than 2 million cars a year.[2] Ford became the leading car company in the world, and competitors rushed to adopt the new mass-production techniques.

The next change in management thinking about car assembly occurred in Japan when Ohno Taiichi, a Toyota production engineer, pioneered the development of *lean manufacturing* in the 1960s after touring the U.S. plants of the Big Three car companies. The management philosophy behind lean manufacturing is to continuously find methods to improve the efficiency of the production process in order to reduce costs, increase quality, and reduce car assembly time. Lean production is based on the idea that if workers have input and can participate continually in the decision-making process, their skills and knowledge can be used to increase efficiency.

In lean manufacturing, workers work on a moving production line, but they are organized into small teams, each of which is responsible for a particular phase of car assembly, such as installing the car's transmission or electrical wiring system. Each team member is expected to learn the tasks of all members of that team, and each work group is responsible not only for assembling cars but also for continuously finding ways to increase quality and reduce costs. By 1970, Japanese managers had applied the new lean-production system so efficiently that they were producing higher-quality cars at lower prices than their U.S. counterparts. By 1980 Japanese companies dominated the global car market.

To compete with the Japanese, managers of U.S. carmakers visited Japan to learn the new management principles of lean production. As a result, General Motors (GM) established the Saturn plant to experiment with this new way of involving workers; GM also established a joint venture with Toyota called New United Motor Manufacturing Inc. (NUMMI) to learn how to achieve the benefits of lean production. Meanwhile, Ford and Chrysler began to change their work processes to take advantage of employees' skills and knowledge.

In the 1990s global car companies increased the number of robots used on the production line and began to use advanced IT to build and track the quality of cars being produced. Indeed, for a time it seemed that robots rather than employees would be building cars in the future. However, Toyota discovered something interesting at its first fully roboticized car plant. When only robots build cars, efficiency does not continually increase because, unlike people, robots cannot provide input to improve the work process. The crucial thing is to find the right balance between using people, machinery, computers, and IT.

In the 2000s, global car companies are continuing to compete fiercely to improve and perfect better ways of making cars. Toyota is constantly pioneering new ways to manage its assembly lines to increase efficiency, and other Japanese carmakers such as Honda and Nissan are catching up fast. Ford, Chrysler, and GM have also made great strides in the last decade, and they are closing the quality gap with Toyota and Nissan. In the 2000s, however, U.S. carmakers have been saddled with high overhead costs because of such factors as employee pensions and health benefits that add over $1,000 to the cost of every car they make. In addition, Japanese carmakers introduced popular new car models at a faster pace and established U.S. plants to make them efficiently. Ford and GM are finding it hard to compete. In 2006 Ford and then GM announced plans to reduce their carmaking capacity by over 20% as they continued to lose market share. Their managers are racing to develop the cars customers want to buy today (be effective) and to make them reliably and cost-effectively (be efficient), something especially important as Toyota overtook GM to become the largest global carmaker in 2008.

Overview

As this sketch of the evolution of management thinking in global car manufacturing suggests, changes in management practices occur as managers, theorists, researchers, and consultants seek new ways to increase organizational efficiency and effectiveness. The driving force behind the evolution of management theory is the search for better ways to utilize organizational resources. Advances in management thought typically occur as managers and researchers find better ways to perform the principal management tasks: planning, organizing, leading, and controlling human and other organizational resources.

In this chapter, we examine how management thought has evolved in modern times and the central concerns that have guided ongoing advances in management theory. First, we examine the so-called classical management theories that emerged around the turn of the 20th century. These include scientific management, which focuses on matching people and tasks to maximize efficiency, and administrative management, which focuses on identifying the principles that will lead to the creation of the most efficient system of organization and management. Next, we consider behavioral management theories developed both before and after World War II; these focus on how managers should lead and control their workforces to increase performance. Then we discuss management science theory, which developed during World War II and has become increasingly important as researchers have developed rigorous analytical and quantitative techniques to help managers measure and control organizational performance. Finally, we discuss changes in management practices from the mid to the late 1900s and focus on the theories developed to help explain how the external environment affects the way organizations and managers operate.

By the end of this chapter you will understand the ways in which management thought and theory have evolved over time. You will also understand how economic, political, and cultural forces have affected the development of these theories and the ways in which managers and their organizations behave. In Figure 2.1 we summarize the chronology of the management theories discussed in this chapter.

Figure 2.1
The Evolution of Management Theory

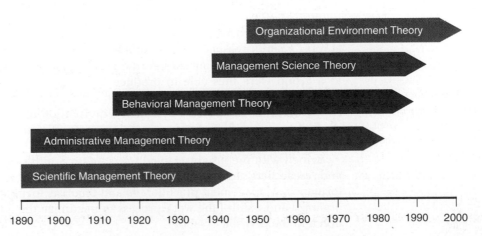

Scientific Management Theory

The evolution of modern management began in the closing decades of the 19th century, after the industrial revolution had swept through Europe and America. In the new economic climate, managers of all types of organizations—political, educational, and economic—were increasingly trying to find better ways to satisfy customers' needs. Many major economic, technical, and cultural changes were taking place at this time. The introduction of steam power and the development of sophisticated machinery and equipment changed the way goods were produced, particularly in the weaving and clothing industries. Small workshops run by skilled workers who produced hand-manufactured products (a system called *crafts production*) were being replaced by large factories in which sophisticated machines controlled by hundreds or even thousands of unskilled or semiskilled workers made products. For example, raw cotton and wool, which in the past had been spun into yarn by families or whole villages working together, were now shipped to factories where workers operated machines that spun and wove large quantities of yarn into cloth.

Owners and managers of the new factories found themselves unprepared for the challenges accompanying the change from small-scale crafts production to large-scale mechanized manufacturing. Moreover, many of the managers and supervisors in these workshops and factories were engineers who had only a technical orientation. They were unprepared for the social problems that occur when people work together in large groups in a factory or shop system. Managers began to search for new techniques to manage their organizations' resources, and soon they began to focus on ways to increase the efficiency of the worker-task mix.

Job Specialization and the Division of Labor

Initially, management theorists were interested in the subject of why the new machine shops and factory system were more efficient and produced greater quantities of goods and services than older, crafts-style production operations. Nearly 200 years before, Adam Smith had been one of the first writers to investigate the advantages associated with producing goods and services in factories. A famous economist, Smith journeyed around England in the 1700s studying the effects of the industrial revolution.[3] In a study of factories that produced various pins or nails, Smith identified two different manufacturing methods. The first was similar to crafts-style production, in which each worker was responsible for all of the 18 tasks involved in producing a pin. The other had each worker performing only 1 or a few of the 18 tasks that go into making a complete pin.

In a comparison of the relative performance of these different ways of organizing production, Smith found that the performance of the factories in which workers specialized in only one or a few tasks was much greater than the performance of the factory in which each worker performed all 18 pin-making tasks. In fact, Smith found that 10 workers specializing in a particular task could make 48,000 pins a day, whereas those workers who performed all the tasks could make only a few thousand at most.[4] Smith reasoned that this difference in performance was due to the fact that the workers who specialized became much more skilled at their specific tasks and as a group were thus able to produce a product faster than the group of workers who each performed many tasks. Smith concluded that increasing the level of **job specialization**—the process by which a division of labor occurs as different workers specialize in specific tasks over time—increases efficiency and leads to higher organizational performance.[5]

Armed with the insights gained from Adam Smith's observations, other managers and researchers began to investigate how to improve job specialization to increase performance. Management practitioners and theorists focused on how managers should organize and control the work process to maximize the advantages of job specialization and the division of labor.

LO1 Describe how the need to increase organizational efficiency and effectiveness has guided the evolution of management theory.

LO2 Explain the principle of job specialization and division of labor, and tell why the study of person-task relationships is central to the pursuit of increased efficiency.

job specialization The process by which a division of labor occurs as different workers specialize in different tasks over time.

F. W. Taylor and Scientific Management

Frederick W. Taylor (1856–1915) is best known for defining the techniques of **scientific management,** the systematic study of relationships between people and tasks for the purpose of redesigning the work process to increase efficiency. Taylor was a manufacturing manager who eventually became a consultant and taught other managers how to apply his scientific management techniques. Taylor believed that if the amount of time and effort that each worker expends to produce a unit of output (a finished good or service) can be reduced by increasing specialization and the division of labor, the production process will become more efficient. According to Taylor, the way to create the most efficient division of labor could best be determined by scientific management techniques, rather than intuitive or informal rule-of-thumb knowledge. Based on his experiments and observations as a manufacturing manager in a variety of settings, he developed four principles to increase efficiency in the workplace:

- Principle 1: *Study the way workers perform their tasks, gather all the informal job knowledge that workers possess, and experiment with ways of improving how tasks are performed.*

Frederick W. Taylor, founder of Scientific Management, and one of the first people to study the behavior and performance of people at work.

To discover the most efficient method of performing specific tasks, Taylor studied in great detail and measured the ways different workers went about performing their tasks. One of the main tools he used was a *time-and-motion study,* which involves the careful timing and recording of the actions taken to perform a particular task. Once Taylor understood the existing method of performing a task, he then experimented to increase specialization. He tried different methods of dividing and coordinating the various tasks necessary to produce a finished product. Usually this meant simplifying jobs and having each worker perform fewer, more routine tasks, as at the pin factory or on Ford's car assembly line. Taylor also sought to find ways to improve each worker's ability to perform a particular task—for example, by reducing the number of motions workers made to complete the task, by changing the layout of the work area or the type of tools workers used, or by experimenting with tools of different sizes.

- Principle 2: *Codify the new methods of performing tasks into written rules and standard operating procedures.*

Once the best method of performing a particular task was determined, Taylor specified that it should be recorded so that this procedure could be taught to all workers performing the same task. These new methods further standardized and simplified jobs—essentially making jobs even more routine. In this way efficiency could be increased throughout an organization.

- Principle 3: *Carefully select workers who possess skills and abilities that match the needs of the task, and train them to perform the task according to the established rules and procedures.*

To increase specialization, Taylor believed workers had to understand the tasks that were required and be thoroughly trained to perform the tasks at the required level. Workers who could not be trained to this level were to be transferred to a job where they were able to reach the minimum required level of proficiency.[6]

- Principle 4: *Establish a fair or acceptable level of performance for a task, and then develop a pay system that provides a reward for performance above the acceptable level.*

To encourage workers to perform at a high level of efficiency, and to provide them with an incentive to reveal the most efficient techniques for performing a task, Taylor advocated that workers benefit from any gains in performance. They should be paid a bonus and receive some percentage of the performance gains achieved through the more efficient work process.[7]

By 1910 Taylor's system of scientific management had become nationally known and in many instances was faithfully and fully practiced.[8] However, managers in many organizations chose to implement the new principles of scientific management selectively. This decision ultimately resulted in problems. For example, some managers using scientific management obtained increases in performance, but rather than sharing performance gains with workers through bonuses as Taylor had advocated, they simply increased the amount of work that each worker was expected to do. Many workers experiencing the reorganized work system found that as their performance increased, managers required that they do more work for the same pay. Workers also learned that increases in performance often meant fewer jobs and a greater threat of layoffs because fewer workers were needed. In addition, the specialized, simplified jobs were often monotonous and repetitive, and many workers became dissatisfied with their jobs.

Scientific management brought many workers more hardship than gain and a distrust of managers who did not seem to care about workers' well-being.[9] These dissatisfied workers resisted attempts to use the new scientific management techniques and at times even withheld their job knowledge from managers to protect their jobs and pay. It is not difficult for workers to conceal the true potential efficiency of a work system to protect their interests. Experienced machine operators, for example, can slow their machines in undetectable ways by adjusting the tension in the belts or by misaligning the gears. Workers sometimes even develop informal work rules that discourage high performance and encourage shirking as work groups attempt to identify an acceptable or fair performance level (a tactic discussed in the next section).

Unable to inspire workers to accept the new scientific management techniques for performing tasks, some organizations increased the mechanization of the work process. For example, one reason why Henry Ford introduced moving conveyor belts in his factory was the realization that when a conveyor belt controls the pace of work (instead of workers setting their own pace), workers can be pushed to perform at higher levels–levels that they may have thought were beyond their reach. Charlie Chaplin captured this aspect of mass production in one of the opening scenes of his famous movie *Modern Times* (1936). In the film, Chaplin caricatured a new factory employee fighting to work at the machine-imposed pace but losing the battle to the machine. Henry Ford also used the principles of scientific management to identify the tasks that each worker should perform on the production line and thus to determine the most effective way to create a division of labor to suit the needs of a mechanized production system.

From a performance perspective, the combination of the two management practices–(1) achieving the right mix of worker-task specialization and (2) linking people and tasks by the speed of the production line–makes sense. It produces the huge savings in cost and huge increases in output that occur in large, organized work settings. For example, in 1908 managers at the Franklin Motor Company using scientific management principles redesigned the work process, and the output of cars increased from 100 cars a *month* to 45 cars a *day;* workers' wages, however, increased by only 90%.[10] From other perspectives, however, scientific management practices raise many concerns. The definition of workers' rights, not by the workers themselves but by the owners or managers as a result of the introduction of the new management practices, raised an ethical issue, which we examine in the following "Ethics in Action."

Charlie Chaplin tries to extricate a fellow employee from the machinery of mass production in this scene from *Modern Times.* The complex machinery is meant to represent the power that machinery has over the worker in the new work system.

Ethics in Action

Fordism in Practice

From 1908 to 1914, through trial and error, Henry Ford's talented team of production managers pioneered the development of the moving conveyor belt and thus changed manufacturing practices forever. Although the technical aspects of the move to mass production were a dramatic financial success for Ford and for the millions of Americans who could now afford cars, for the workers who actually produced the cars many human and social problems resulted.

With simplification of the work process, workers grew to hate the monotony of the moving conveyor belt. By 1914 Ford's car plants were experiencing huge employee turnover—often reaching levels as high as 300% or 400% per year as workers left because they could not handle the work-induced stress.[11] Henry Ford recognized these problems and made an announcement: From that point on, to motivate his workforce, he would reduce the length of the workday from nine hours to eight hours, and the company would *double* the basic wage from $2.50 to $5.00 per day. This was a dramatic increase, similar to an announcement today of an overnight doubling of the minimum wage. Ford became an internationally famous figure, and the word *Fordism* was coined for his new approach.[12]

Henry Ford sits in an early model Ford outside a showroom in Detroit, Michigan, shortly after the corporation was formed in 1903. By 1914 Ford's car plants were experiencing huge employee turnover—as workers left because they could not handle the work-induced stress.

Ford's apparent generosity, however, was matched by an intense effort to control the resources—both human and material—with which his empire was built. He employed hundreds of inspectors to check up on employees, both inside and outside his factories. In the factory supervision was close and confining. Employees were not allowed to leave their places at the production line, and they were not permitted to talk to one another. Their job was to concentrate fully on the task at hand. Few employees could adapt to this system, and they developed ways of talking out of the sides of their mouths, like ventriloquists, and invented a form of speech that became known as the "Ford Lisp."[13] Ford's obsession with control brought him into greater and greater conflict with managers, who often were fired when they disagreed with him. As a result, many talented people left Ford to join a growing number of rival car companies.

Outside the workplace, Ford went so far as to establish what he called the "Sociological Department" to check up on how his employees lived and the ways they spent their time. Inspectors from this department visited the homes of employees and investigated their habits and problems. Employees who exhibited behaviors contrary to Ford's standards (for instance, if they drank too much or were always in debt) were likely to be fired. Clearly, Ford's efforts to control his employees led him and his managers to behave in ways that today would be considered unacceptable and unethical and in the long run would impair an organization's ability to prosper.

Despite the problems of worker turnover, absenteeism, and discontent at Ford Motor Company, managers of the other car companies watched Ford reap huge gains in efficiency from the application of the new management principles. They believed that their companies would have to imitate Ford if they were to survive. They followed Taylor and used many of his followers as consultants to teach them how to adopt the techniques of scientific management.

In addition, Taylor elaborated his principles in several books, including *Shop Management* (1903) and *The Principles of Scientific Management* (1911), which explain in detail how to apply the principles of scientific management to reorganize the work system.[14]

Taylor's work has had an enduring effect on the management of production systems. Managers in every organization, whether it produces goods or services, now carefully analyze the basic tasks that must be performed and try to devise the work systems that allow their organizations to operate most efficiently.

The Gilbreths

Two prominent followers of Taylor were Frank Gilbreth (1868–1924) and Lillian Gilbreth (1878–1972), who refined Taylor's analysis of work movements and made many contributions to time-and-motion study.[15] Their aims were to (1) break up and analyze every individual action necessary to perform a particular task into each of its component actions, (2) find better ways to perform each component action, and (3) reorganize each of the component actions so that the action as a whole could be performed more efficiently—at less cost in time and effort.

The Gilbreths often filmed a worker performing a particular task and then separated the task actions, frame by frame, into their component movements. Their goal was to maximize the efficiency with which each individual task was performed so that gains across tasks would add up to enormous savings of time and effort. Their attempts to develop improved management principles were captured—at times quite humorously—in the movie *Cheaper by the Dozen,* a new version of which appeared in 2004, which depicts how the Gilbreths (with their 12 children) tried to live their own lives according to these efficiency principles and apply them to daily actions such as shaving, cooking, and even raising a family.[16]

This scene from *Cheaper by the Dozen* illustrates how "efficient families," such as the Gilbreths, use formal family courts to solve problems of assigning chores to different family members and to solve disputes when they arise.

Eventually, the Gilbreths became increasingly interested in the study of fatigue. They studied how the physical characteristics of the workplace contribute to job stress that often leads to fatigue and thus poor performance. They isolated factors that result in worker fatigue, such as lighting, heating, the color of walls, and the design of tools and machines. Their pioneering studies paved the way for new advances in management theory.

In workshops and factories, the work of the Gilbreths, Taylor, and many others had a major effect on the practice of management. In comparison with the old crafts system, jobs in the new system were more repetitive, boring, and monotonous as a result of the application of scientific management principles, and workers became increasingly dissatisfied. Frequently, the management of work settings became a game between workers and managers: Managers tried to initiate work practices to increase performance, and workers tried to hide the true potential efficiency of the work setting to protect their own well-being.[17] The story of the way Andrew Carnegie created the most successful industrial company of his day, Carnegie Steel, illustrates the kind of management thinking that was sweeping through the United States at that time, the looming battles between management and workers, and the growing number of trade unions that were springing up to represent workers' interests.

Manager as a Person

Andrew Carnegie Creates the New Industrial Company

Andrew Carnegie, born in Scotland in 1835, was the son of a master handloom weaver who, at that time, employed four apprentices to weave fine linen table-cloths. His family was well-to-do, yet 10 years later they were living in poverty. Why? Advances in weaving technology had led to the invention of steam-powered weaving looms that could produce large quantities of cotton cloth at a much lower price than was possible through handloom weaving. Handloom weavers could not compete at such low prices, and Carnegie's father was put out of business.

In 1848 Carnegie's family, like hundreds of thousands of other families in Europe at the time, emigrated to the United States to find work and survive. They settled near Pittsburgh, where they had relatives, and Carnegie's father continued to weave tablecloths and sell them door-to-door for around $6 a week. Carnegie found a job as a "bobbin boy," replacing spools of thread on power looms in a textile factory. He took home $1.20 for working a 60-hour week.

Once his employer found out he could read and write, a rare skill at that time, Carnegie became a bookkeeper for the factory. In his spare time he became a telegraph messenger and learned telegraphy. He began to deliver telegrams to Tom Scott, a top manager at the Pennsylvania Railroad, who came to appreciate Carnegie's drive and talents. Scott made him his personal telegrapher for an astonishing sum of $35 a week. Carnegie was now 17; only seven years later, when he was 24, he was promoted to Scott's job, superintendent of the railroad's western division. At 30, he was offered the top job of superintendent of the *whole* railroad! Carnegie had made his name by continually finding ways to use resources more productively to reduce costs and increase profitability. Under his oversight of the western division, his company's stock price had shot up—which explains why he was offered the railroad's top job. He had also invested cleverly in railroad stock and was now a wealthy man with an income of $48,000 a year, of which only $2,800 came from his railroad salary.

Carnegie had ambitions other than remaining in his top railroad job, however. He had noticed U.S. railroads' growing demand for steel rails as they expanded rapidly across the country. At that time, steel was made by the method of small-batch production, a labor-intensive process in which small groups of employees worked together to produce quite small quantities of steel. This method was

Andrew Carnegie, depicted here in later life. His legacy is a complicated one of hard work as an immigrant, a rise to power and wealth through hardnosed management, accusations of monopolic business practices, and a committed dedication to philanthropy that caused him to avow that 'no one should die rich.'

expensive, and the steel produced cost $135 a ton. As he searched for ways to reduce the cost of steelmaking, Carnegie was struck by the fact that many different companies performed each of the different operations necessary to convert iron ore into finished steel products. One company smelted iron ore into "pig iron." Another company then transported the pig iron to other companies that rolled the pig iron into bars or slabs. Many other companies then bought these bars and slabs and made them into finished products such as steel rails, nails, wire, and so on. Intermediaries that bought the products of one company and then sold them to another connected the activities of these different companies. The many exchanges or "hand-offs" involved in converting iron ore into finished products greatly increased operating costs. At each stage of the production process, steel had to be shipped to the next company and reheated until it became soft enough to work on. Moreover, these intermediaries were earning large profits for providing this service, something that also raised the cost of the finished products.

The second thing that Carnegie noticed was that the steel produced by British steel mills was of a higher quality than that made in U.S. mills. The British had made major advances in steelmaking technology, and U.S. railroads preferred to buy their steel rails. On one of his frequent trips to Britain Carnegie saw a demonstration of Sir Henry Bessemer's new "hot blasting" method for making steel. Bessemer's famous process made it possible to produce great quantities of higher-quality steel *continuously,* as a process, not in small batches. Carnegie instantly realized the enormous cost-saving potential of the new technology. He rushed to become the first steelmaker in the United States to adopt it.

Carnegie subsequently sold all his railroad stock and used the proceeds to create the Carnegie Steel Company, the first low-cost Bessemer steelmaking plant in the United States. Determined to retain the profit that intermediaries were making in his business, he decided his company would perform *all* the steelmaking operations necessary to convert iron ore into finished products. For example, he constructed rolling mills to make steel rails *next* to his blast furnace so that iron ore could be converted into finished steel products in one continuous process. Carnegie's innovations led to a dramatic fall in steelmaking costs and revolutionized the U.S. steel industry. His new production methods reduced the price of U.S. steel from $135 a ton to $12 a ton! Despite the cheaper price, his company was still enormously profitable, and he ploughed back all his profits into building his steel business and constructed many new low-cost steel plants. By 1900, most of his competitors had been driven out of business because of his low prices; his company was the leading U.S. steelmaker, and he was one of the richest men in the world.

Although the story of Carnegie's new approach to management might seem like "business as usual," there is another side to Carnegie's management style. Critics say he increased profitability "on the backs" of his workers. Despite the enormous increase in productivity he had achieved by using the new mass-production steelmaking technology, he was continually driven by the need to find every way possible to reduce operating costs. To increase productivity, Carnegie gradually increased the normal workday from an already long 10 hours to 12 hours, six days a week. He also paid his workers the lowest wage rate possible even though their increasing skills in mastering the new technology were contributing to the huge increase in productivity. He also paid no attention to improving the safety of his mills, where workers toiled in dangerous conditions and thousands of workers were injured each year because of spills of molten steel. Any attempts by workers to improve their work conditions were uniformly rejected, and Carnegie routinely crushed any of the workers' attempts to unionize. Carnegie, in implementing new management techniques and creating the modern industrial company, also created the need for new administrative management theory—theory that could help managers find better ways of organizing and controlling resources to increase performance, as well as find new strategies for negotiating with and managing the increasingly unionized workforce that modern methods of production had brought into being.

Administrative Management Theory

Side by side with scientific managers like Carnegie studying the person-technology mix to increase efficiency, other managers and researchers were focusing on **administrative management,** the study of how to create an organizational structure and control system that leads to high efficiency and effectiveness. *Organizational structure* is the system of task and authority relationships that control

Figure 2.2
Weber's Principles of Bureaucracy

how employees use resources to achieve the organization's goals. Two of the most influential early views regarding the creation of efficient systems of organizational administration were developed in Europe: Max Weber, a German professor of sociology, developed one theory; Henri Fayol, the French manager who developed the model of management introduced in Chapter 1, developed the other.

The Theory of Bureaucracy

Max Weber (1864–1920) wrote at the turn of the 20th century, when Germany was undergoing its industrial revolution.[18] To help Germany manage its growing industrial enterprises at a time when it was striving to become a world power, Weber developed the principles of **bureaucracy**—a formal system of organization and administration designed to ensure efficiency and effectiveness. A bureaucratic system of administration is based on the five principles summarized in Figure 2.2.

- Principle 1: *In a bureaucracy, a manager's formal authority derives from the position he or she holds in the organization.*

Authority is the power to hold people accountable for their actions and to make decisions concerning the use of organizational resources. Authority gives managers the right to direct and control their subordinates' behavior to achieve organizational goals. In a bureaucratic system of administration, obedience is owed to a manager, not because of any personal qualities—such as personality, wealth, or social status—but because the manager occupies a position that is associated with a certain level of authority and responsibility.[19]

- Principle 2: *In a bureaucracy, people should occupy positions because of their performance, not because of their social standing or personal contacts.*

This principle was not always followed in Weber's time and is often ignored today. Some organizations and industries are still affected by social networks in which personal contacts and relations, not job-related skills, influence hiring and promotional decisions.

LO3 Identify the principles of administration and organization that underlie effective organizations.

administrative management The study of how to create an organizational structure and control system that leads to high efficiency and effectiveness.

bureaucracy A formal system of organization and administration designed to ensure efficiency and effectiveness.

authority The power to hold people accountable for their actions and to make decisions concerning the use of organizational resources.

- Principle 3: *The extent of each position's formal authority and task responsibilities, and its relationship to other positions in an organization, should be clearly specified.*

When the tasks and authority associated with various positions in the organization are clearly specified, managers and workers know what is expected of them and what to expect from each other. Moreover, an organization can hold all its employees strictly accountable for their actions when they know their exact responsibilities.

Max Weber developed the principles of bureaucracy during Germany's burgeoning industrial revolution to help organizations increase their efficiency and effectiveness.

- Principle 4: *Authority can be exercised effectively in an organization when positions are arranged hierarchically, so employees know whom to report to and who reports to them.*[20]

Managers must create an organizational hierarchy of authority that makes it clear who reports to whom and to whom managers and workers should go if conflicts or problems arise. This principle is especially important in the armed forces, FBI, CIA, and other organizations that deal with sensitive issues involving possible major repercussions. It is vital that managers at high levels of the hierarchy be able to hold subordinates accountable for their actions.

- Principle 5: *Managers must create a well-defined system of rules, standard operating procedures, and norms so that they can effectively control behavior within an organization.*

Rules are formal written instructions that specify actions to be taken under different circumstances to achieve specific goals (for example, if A happens, do B). **Standard operating procedures (SOPs)** are specific sets of written instructions about how to perform a certain aspect of a task. A rule might state that at the end of the workday employees are to leave their machines in good order, and a set of SOPs would specify exactly how they should do so, itemizing which machine parts must be oiled or replaced. **Norms** are unwritten, informal codes of conduct that prescribe how people should act in particular situations and are considered important by most members of a group or organization. For example, an organizational norm in a restaurant might be that waiters should help each other if time permits.

rules Formal written instructions that specify actions to be taken under different circumstances to achieve specific goals.

standard operating procedures (SOPs) Specific sets of written instructions about how to perform a certain aspect of a task.

norms Unwritten, informal codes of conduct that prescribe how people should act in particular situations and are considered important by most members of a group or organization.

Rules, SOPs, and norms provide behavioral guidelines that increase the performance of a bureaucratic system because they specify the best ways to accomplish organizational tasks. Companies such as McDonald's and Wal-Mart have developed extensive rules and procedures to specify the behaviors required of their employees, such as "Always greet the customer with a smile."

Weber believed that organizations that implement all five principles establish a bureaucratic system that improves organizational performance. The specification of positions and the use of rules and SOPs to regulate how tasks are performed make it easier for managers to organize and control the work of subordinates. Similarly, fair and equitable selection and promotion systems improve managers' feelings of security, reduce stress, and encourage organizational members to act ethically and further promote the interests of the organization.[21]

If bureaucracies are not managed well, however, many problems can result. Sometimes, managers allow rules and SOPs, "bureaucratic red tape," to become so cumbersome that decision making is slow and inefficient and organizations are unable to change. When managers rely too much on rules to solve problems and not enough on their own skills and judgment, their behavior becomes inflexible. A key challenge for managers is to use bureaucratic principles to benefit, rather than harm, an organization.

Fayol's Principles of Management

Henri Fayol (1841–1925) was the CEO of Comambault Mining. Working at the same time as, but independently from, Weber, Fayol identified 14 principles (summarized in Table 2.1 that he believed essential to increase the efficiency of the management

Table 2.1
Fayol's 14 Principles of Management

Division of Labor Job specialization and the division of labor should increase efficiency, especially if managers take steps to lessen workers' boredom.

Authority and Responsibility Managers have the right to give orders and the power to exhort subordinates for obedience.

Unity of Command An employee should receive orders from only one superior.

Line of Authority The length of the chain of command that extends from the top to the bottom of an organization should be limited.

Centralization Authority should not be concentrated at the top of the chain of command.

Unity of Direction The organization should have a single plan of action to guide managers and workers.

Equity All organizational members are entitled to be treated with justice and respect.

Order The arrangement of organizational positions should maximize organizational efficiency and provide employees with satisfying career opportunities.

Initiative Managers should allow employees to be innovative and creative.

Discipline Managers need to create a workforce that strives to achieve organizational goals.

Remuneration of Personnel The system that managers use to reward employees should be equitable for both employees and the organization.

Stability of Tenure of Personnel Long-term employees develop skills that can improve organizational efficiency.

Subordination of Individual Interests to the Common Interest Employees should understand how their performance affects the performance of the whole organization.

Esprit de Corps Managers should encourage the development of shared feelings of comradeship, enthusiasm, or devotion to a common cause.

process.[22] We discuss these principles in detail here because, although they were developed at the turn of the 20th century, they remain the bedrock on which much of recent management theory and research is based. In fact, as the "Management Insight" following this discussion suggests, modern writers such as well-known management guru Tom Peters continue to extol these principles.

DIVISION OF LABOR A champion of job specialization and the division of labor for reasons already mentioned, Fayol was nevertheless among the first to point out the downside of too much specialization: boredom—a state of mind likely to cause a fall in product quality, worker initiative, and flexibility. As a result, Fayol advocated that workers be given more job duties to perform or be encouraged to assume more responsibility for work outcomes, a principle increasingly applied today in organizations that empower their workers.

AUTHORITY AND RESPONSIBILITY Like Weber, Fayol emphasized the importance of authority and responsibility. Fayol, however, went beyond Weber's formal authority, which derives from a manager's position in the hierarchy, to recognize the *informal* authority that derives from personal expertise, technical knowledge, moral worth, and the ability to lead and to generate commitment from subordinates. (The study of authority is the subject of recent research into leadership, discussed in Chapter 12.)

Henri Fayol, who maintained Weber's principles of formal organization but added recognition of the pivotal role played by informal authority.

unity of command
A reporting relationship in which an employee receives orders from, and reports to, only one superior.

line of authority The chain of command extending from the top to the bottom of an organization.

centralization The concentration of authority at the top of the managerial hierarchy.

unity of direction The singleness of purpose that makes possible the creation of one plan of action to guide managers and workers as they use organizational resources.

UNITY OF COMMAND   The principle of **unity of command** specifies that an employee should receive orders from, and report to, only one superior. Fayol believed that *dual command,* the reporting relationship that exists when two supervisors give orders to the same subordinate, should be avoided except in exceptional circumstances. Dual command confuses subordinates, undermines order and discipline, and creates havoc within the formal hierarchy of authority. Assessing any manager's authority and responsibility in a system of dual command is difficult, and the manager who is bypassed feels slighted and angry and may be uncooperative in the future.

LINE OF AUTHORITY   The **line of authority** is the chain of command extending from the top to the bottom of an organization. Fayol was one of the first management theorists to point out the importance of limiting the length of the chain of command by controlling the number of levels in the managerial hierarchy. The greater the number of levels in the hierarchy, the longer the communication between managers at the top and bottom takes and the slower the pace of planning and organizing. Restricting the number of hierarchical levels to lessen these communication problems enables an organization to act quickly and flexibly; this is one reason for the recent trend toward restructuring (discussed in Chapter 1).

Fayol also pointed out that when organizations are split into different departments or functions, each with its own hierarchy, it is important to allow middle and first-line managers in each department to interact with managers at similar levels in other departments. This interaction helps to speed decision making, because managers know each other and know whom to go to when problems arise. For cross-departmental integration to work, Fayol noted the importance of keeping one's superiors informed about what is taking place so that lower-level decisions do not harm activities taking place in other parts of the organization. One alternative to cross-departmental integration is to create cross-departmental teams controlled by a team leader (see Chapter 1).

CENTRALIZATION   Fayol also was one of the first management writers to focus on **centralization,** the concentration of authority at the top of the managerial hierarchy. Fayol believed that authority should not be concentrated at the top of the chain of command. One of the most significant issues that top managers face is how much authority to centralize at the top of the organization and what authority to decentralize to managers and workers at lower hierarchical levels. This is an important issue because it affects the behavior of people at all levels in the organization.

If authority is very centralized, only managers at the top make important decisions, and subordinates simply follow orders. This arrangement gives top managers great control over organizational activities and helps ensure that the organization is pursuing its strategy, but it makes it difficult for the people who are closest to problems and issues to respond to them in a timely manner. It also can lower the motivation of middle and first-line managers and make them less flexible and adaptable because they become reluctant to make decisions on their own, even when doing so is necessary. They get used to passing the buck. As we saw in Chapter 1, the pendulum is now swinging toward decentralization, as organizations seek to empower middle managers and create self-managed teams that monitor and control their own activities both to increase organizational flexibility and to reduce operating costs and increase efficiency.

UNITY OF DIRECTION   Just as there is a need for unity of command, there is also a need for **unity of direction,** the singleness of purpose that makes possible the creation of one plan of action to guide managers and workers as they use organizational resources. An organization without a single guiding plan becomes inefficient and ineffective; its activities become unfocused, and individuals and groups work at cross-purposes. Successful planning starts with top managers working as a team to craft the organization's strategy, which they communicate to middle managers, who decide how to use organizational resources to implement the strategy.

EQUITY As Fayol wrote, "For personnel to be encouraged to carry out their duties with all the devotion and loyalty of which they are capable, they must be treated with respect for their own sense of integrity, and equity results from the combination of respect and justice."[23] **Equity**—the justice, impartiality, and fairness to which all organizational members are entitled—is receiving much attention today; the desire to treat employees fairly is a primary concern for many managers. (Equity theory is discussed in Chapter 12).

equity The justice, impartiality, and fairness to which all organizational members are entitled.

ORDER Like Taylor and the Gilbreths, Fayol was interested in analyzing jobs, positions, and individuals to ensure that the organization was using resources as efficiently as possible. To Fayol, **order** meant the methodical arrangement of positions to provide the organization with the greatest benefit and to provide employees with career opportunities that satisfy their needs. Thus, Fayol recommended the use of organizational charts to show the position and duties of each employee and to indicate which positions an employee might move to or be promoted into in the future. He also advocated that managers engage in extensive career planning to help ensure orderly career paths. Career planning is of primary interest today as organizations increase the resources they are willing to devote to training and developing their workforces.

order The methodical arrangement of positions to provide the organization with the greatest benefit and to provide employees with career opportunities.

INITIATIVE Although order and equity are important means to fostering commitment and loyalty among employees, Fayol believed that managers must also encourage employees to exercise **initiative,** the ability to act on their own, without direction from a superior. Used properly, initiative can be a major source of strength for an organization because it leads to creativity and innovation. Managers need skill and tact to achieve the difficult balance between the organization's need for order and employees' desire for initiative. Fayol believed that the ability to strike this balance was a key indicator of a superior manager.

initiative The ability to act on one's own, without direction from a superior.

DISCIPLINE In focusing on the importance of **discipline** obedience, energy, application, and other outward marks of respect for a superior's authority—Fayol was addressing the concern of many early managers: how to create a workforce that was reliable and hardworking and would strive to achieve organizational goals. According to Fayol, discipline results in respectful relations between organizational members and reflects the quality of an organization's leadership and a manager's ability to act fairly and equitably.

discipline Obedience, energy, application, and other outward marks of respect for a superior's authority.

focus on future

REMUNERATION OF PERSONNEL Fayol proposed reward systems including bonuses and profit-sharing plans, which are increasingly utilized today as organizations seek improved ways to motivate employees. Convinced from his own experience that an organization's payment system has important implications for organizational success, Fayol believed that effective reward systems should be equitable for both employees and the organization, encourage productivity by rewarding well-directed effort, not be subject to abuse, and be uniformly applied to employees.

STABILITY OF TENURE OF PERSONNEL Fayol also recognized the importance of long-term employment, and the idea has been echoed by contemporary management gurus such as Tom Peters, Jeff Pfeffer, and William Ouchi. When employees stay with an organization for extended periods of time, they develop skills that improve the organization's ability to utilize its resources.

SUBORDINATION OF INDIVIDUAL INTERESTS TO THE COMMON INTEREST The interests of the organization as a whole must take precedence over the interests of any one individual or group if the organization is to survive. Equitable agreements must be established between the organization and its members to ensure that employees are treated fairly and rewarded for their performance and to maintain the disciplined organizational relationships so vital to an efficient system of administration.

ESPRIT DE CORPS As this discussion of Fayol's ideas suggests, the appropriate design of an organization's hierarchy of authority and the right mix of order and discipline foster cooperation and commitment. Likewise, a key element in a successful organization is the development of **esprit de corps,** a French expression that refers to shared feelings of comradeship, enthusiasm, or devotion to a common cause among members of a group. Esprit de corps can result when managers encourage personal, verbal contact between managers and workers and encourage communication to solve problems and implement solutions. (Today, the term *organizational culture* is used to refer to these shared feelings; this concept is discussed at length in Chapter 3.)

esprit de corps Shared feelings of comradeship, enthusiasm, or devotion to a common cause among members of a group.

Some of the principles that Fayol outlined have faded from contemporary management practices, but most have endured. The characteristics of organizations that Tom Peters and Robert Waterman identified as being "excellently managed" in their best-selling book *In Search of Excellence* (1982) are discussed in the following "Management Insight."[24]

Management Insight

Peters and Waterman's Excellent Companies

In the early 1980s, Tom Peters and Robert Waterman identified 62 organizations that they considered to be the best-performing organizations in the United States. They asked, "Why do these companies perform better than their rivals?" and discovered that successful organizations have managers who manage according to three sets of related principles. Those principles have a great deal in common with Fayol's principles.

First, Peters and Waterman argued, top managers of successful companies create principles and guidelines that emphasize managerial autonomy and entrepreneurship and encourage risk taking and *initiative.* For example, they allow middle managers to develop new products, even though there is no assurance that these products will be winners. In high-performing organizations, top managers are closely involved in the day-to-day operations of the company, provide *unity of command* and *unity of direction,* and do not simply make decisions in an isolated ivory tower. Top managers *decentralize authority* to lower-level managers and nonmanagerial employees and give them the freedom to get involved and the motivation to get things done.

The second approach that managers of excellent organizations use to increase performance is to create one central plan that puts organizational goals at center stage. In high-performing organizations, managers focus attention on what the organization does best, and the emphasis is on continuously improving the goods and services the organization provides to its customers. Managers of top-performing companies resist the temptation to get sidetracked into pursuing ventures outside their area of expertise just because they seem to promise a quick return. These managers also focus on customers and establish close relationships with them to learn their needs, for responsiveness to customers increases competitive advantage.

The third set of management principles pertains to organizing and controlling the organization. Excellent companies establish a *division of work* and a *division of authority and responsibility* that will motivate employees to *subordinate their individual interests to the common interest.* Inherent in this approach is the belief that high performance derives from individual skills and abilities and that *equity, order, initiative,* and other indications of respect for the individual create the *esprit de corps* that fosters productive behavior. An emphasis on entrepreneurship and respect for every employee leads the best managers to create a structure that gives employees room to exercise *initiative* and motivates them to succeed. Because a simple, streamlined managerial hierarchy is best suited to achieve this outcome, top managers keep the *line of authority* as short as possible. They also decentralize authority to permit employee participation, but they keep enough control to maintain *unity of direction.*

As this insight into contemporary management suggests, the basic concerns that motivated Fayol continue to motivate management theorists.[25] The principles that Fayol and Weber set forth still provide a clear and appropriate set of guidelines that managers can use to create a work setting that makes efficient and effective use of organizational resources. These principles remain the bedrock of modern management theory; recent researchers have refined or developed them to suit modern conditions. For example, Weber's and Fayol's concerns for equity and for establishing appropriate links between performance and reward are central themes in contemporary theories of motivation and leadership.

Behavioral Management Theory

behavioral management
The study of how managers should behave to motivate employees and encourage them to perform at high levels and be committed to the achievement of organizational goals.

Because the writings of Weber and Fayol were not translated into English and published in the United States until the late 1940s, American management theorists in the first half of the 20th century were unaware of the contributions of these European pioneers. American management theorists began where Taylor and his followers left off. Although their writings were all very different, these theorists all espoused a theme that focused on **behavioral management,** the study of how managers should personally behave to motivate employees and encourage them to perform at high levels and be committed to achieving organizational goals.

The Work of Mary Parker Follett

LO4 Trace the changes in theories about how managers should behave to motivate and control employees.

If F. W. Taylor is considered the father of management thought, Mary Parker Follett (1868–1933) serves as its mother.[26] Much of her writing about management and about the way managers should behave toward workers was a response to her concern that Taylor was ignoring the human side of the organization. She pointed out that management often overlooks the multitude of ways in which employees can contribute to the organization when managers allow them to participate and exercise initiative in their everyday work lives.[27] Taylor, for example, never proposed that managers should involve workers in analyzing their jobs to identify better ways to perform tasks or should even ask workers how they felt about their jobs. Instead, he used time-and-motion experts to analyze workers' jobs for them. Follett, in contrast, argued that because workers know the most about their jobs, they should be involved in job analysis and managers should allow them to participate in the work development process.

Mary Parker Follett, an early management thinker who advocated that "Authority should go with knowledge . . . whether it is up the line or down."

Follett proposed that "authority should go with knowledge . . . whether it is up the line or down." In other words, if workers have the relevant knowledge, then workers, rather than managers, should be in control of the work process itself, and managers should behave as coaches and facilitators—not as monitors and supervisors. In making this statement, Follett anticipated the current interest in self-managed teams and empowerment. She also recognized the importance of having managers in different departments communicate directly with each other to speed decision making. She advocated what she called "cross-functioning": members of different departments working together in cross-departmental teams to accomplish projects—an approach that is increasingly utilized today.[28]

Fayol also mentioned expertise and knowledge as important sources of managers' authority, but Follett went further. She proposed that knowledge and expertise, and not managers' formal authority deriving from their position in the hierarchy, should decide who will lead at any particular moment. She believed, as do many management theorists today, that power is fluid and should flow to the person who can best help the organization achieve its goals. Follett took a horizontal view of power and authority, in contrast to Fayol, who saw the formal line of authority and vertical chain of command as being most essential to effective management. Follett's behavioral approach to management was very radical for its time.

The Hawthorne Studies and Human Relations

Probably because of its radical nature, Follett's work was unappreciated by managers and researchers until quite recently. Most continued to follow in the footsteps of Taylor and the Gilbreths. To increase efficiency, they studied ways to improve various characteristics of the work setting, such as job specialization or the kinds of tools workers used. One series of studies was conducted from 1924 to 1932 at the Hawthorne Works of the Western Electric Company.[29] This research, now known as the *Hawthorne studies,* began as an attempt to investigate how characteristics of the work setting—specifically the level of lighting or illumination—affect worker fatigue and performance. The researchers conducted an experiment in which they systematically measured worker productivity at various levels of illumination.

The experiment produced some unexpected results. The researchers found that regardless of whether they raised or lowered the level of illumination, productivity increased. In fact, productivity began to fall only when the level of illumination dropped to the level of moonlight, a level at which, presumably, workers could no longer see well enough to do their work efficiently.

The researchers found these results puzzling and invited a noted Harvard psychologist, Elton Mayo, to help them. Mayo proposed another series of experiments to solve the mystery. These experiments, known as the *relay assembly test experiments,* were designed to investigate the effects of other aspects of the work context on job performance, such as the effect of the number and length of rest periods and hours of work on fatigue and monotony.[30] The goal was to raise productivity.

During a two-year study of a small group of female workers, the researchers again observed that productivity

Workers in a telephone manufacturing plant, in 1931. Around this time, researchers at the Hawthorne Works of the Western Electric Company began to study the effects of work setting characteristics—such as lighting and rest periods—on productivity. To their surprise, they discovered that workers' productivity was affected more by the attention they received from researchers than by the characteristics of the work setting—a phenomenon that became known as the Hawthorne Effect.

increased over time, but the increases could not be solely attributed to the effects of changes in the work setting. Gradually, the researchers discovered that, to some degree, the results they were obtaining were influenced by the fact that the researchers themselves had become part of the experiment. In other words, the presence of the researchers was affecting the results because the workers enjoyed receiving attention and being the subject of study and were willing to cooperate with the researchers to produce the results they believed the researchers desired.

Subsequently, it was found that many other factors also influence worker behavior, and it was not clear what was actually influencing the Hawthorne workers' behavior. However, this particular effect—which became known as the **Hawthorne effect**—seemed to suggest that workers' attitudes toward their managers affect the level of workers' performance. In particular, the significant finding was that each manager's personal behavior or leadership approach can affect performance. This finding led many researchers to turn their attention to managerial behavior and leadership. If supervisors could be trained to behave in ways that would elicit cooperative behavior from their subordinates, then productivity could be increased. From this view emerged the **human relations movement,** which advocates that supervisors be behaviorally trained to manage subordinates in ways that elicit their cooperation and increase their productivity.

The importance of behavioral or human relations training became even clearer to its supporters after another series of experiments—the *bank wiring room experiments.* In a study of workers making telephone switching equipment, researchers Elton Mayo and F. J. Roethlisberger discovered that the workers, as a group, had deliberately adopted a norm of output restriction to protect their jobs. Workers who violated this informal production norm were subjected to sanctions by other group members. Those who violated group performance norms and performed above the norm were called "ratebusters"; those who performed below the norm were called "chiselers."

The experimenters concluded that both types of workers threatened the group as a whole. Ratebusters threatened group members because they revealed to managers how fast the work could be done. Chiselers were looked down on because they were not doing their share of the work. Work-group members disciplined both ratebusters and chiselers to create a pace of work that the workers (not the managers) thought was fair. Thus, a work group's influence over output can be as great as the supervisors' influence. Since the work group can influence the behavior of its members, some management theorists argue that supervisors should be trained to behave in ways that gain the goodwill and cooperation of workers so that supervisors, not workers, control the level of work-group performance.

One of the main implications of the Hawthorne studies was that the behavior of managers and workers in the work setting is as important in explaining the level of performance as the technical aspects of the task. Managers must understand the workings of the **informal organization,** the system of behavioral rules and norms that emerge in a group, when they try to manage or change behavior in organizations. Many studies have found that, as time passes, groups often develop elaborate procedures and norms that bond members together, allowing unified action either to cooperate with management to raise performance or to restrict output and thwart the attainment of organizational goals.[31] The Hawthorne studies demonstrated the importance of understanding how the feelings, thoughts, and behavior of work-group members and managers affect performance. It was becoming increasingly clear to researchers that understanding behavior in organizations is a complex process that is critical to increasing performance.[32] Indeed, the increasing interest in the area of management known as **organizational behavior,** the study of the factors that have an impact on how individuals and groups respond to and act in organizations, dates from these early studies.

Theory X and Theory Y

Several studies after World War II revealed how assumptions about workers' attitudes and behavior affect managers' behavior. Perhaps the most influential approach was developed by Douglas McGregor. He proposed two sets of assumptions about how work attitudes and behaviors not only dominate the way managers think but also

Hawthorne effect The finding that a manager's behavior or leadership approach can affect workers' level of performance.

human relations movement A management approach that advocates the idea that supervisors should receive behavioral training to manage subordinates in ways that elicit their cooperation and increase their productivity.

informal organization The system of behavioral rules and norms that emerge in a group.

organizational behavior The study of the factors that have an impact on how individuals and groups respond to and act in organizations.

Figure 2.3
Theory X versus Theory Y

THEORY X	THEORY Y
The average employee is lazy, dislikes work, and will try to do as little as possible.	Employees are not inherently lazy. Given the chance, employees will do what is good for the organization.
To ensure that employees work hard, managers should closely supervise employees.	To allow employees to work in the organization's interest, managers must create a work setting that provides opportunities for workers to exercise initiative and self-direction.
Managers should create strict work rules and implement a well-defined system of rewards and punishments to control employees.	Managers should decentralize authority to employees and make sure employees have the resources necessary to achieve organizational goals.

Source: D. McGregor, *The Human Side of Enterprise,* © 1960 by The McGraw–Hill Companies, Inc. Used with permission.

affect how they behave in organizations. McGregor named these two contrasting sets of assumptions *Theory X* and *Theory Y* (see Figure 2.3).[33]

Theory X A set of negative assumptions about workers that lead to the conclusion that a manager's task is to supervise workers closely and control their behavior.

THEORY X   According to the assumptions of **Theory X,** the average worker is lazy, dislikes work, and will try to do as little as possible. Moreover, workers have little ambition and wish to avoid responsibility. Thus, the manager's task is to counteract workers' natural tendencies to avoid work. To keep workers' performance at a high level, the manager must supervise workers closely and control their behavior by means of "the carrot and stick"—rewards and punishments.

Managers who accept the assumptions of Theory X design and shape the work setting to maximize their control over workers' behaviors and minimize workers' control over the pace of work. These managers believe that workers must be made to do what is necessary for the success of the organization, and they focus on developing rules, SOPs, and a well-defined system of rewards and punishments to control behavior. They see little point in giving workers autonomy to solve their own problems because they think that the workforce neither expects nor desires cooperation. Theory X managers see their role as closely monitoring workers to ensure that they contribute to the production process and do not threaten product quality. Henry Ford, who closely supervised and managed his workforce, fits McGregor's description of a manager who holds Theory X assumptions.

Theory Y A set of positive assumptions about workers that lead to the conclusion that a manager's task is to create a work setting that encourages commitment to organizational goals and provides opportunities for workers to be imaginative and to exercise initiative and self-direction.

THEORY Y   In contrast, **Theory Y** assumes that workers are not inherently lazy, do not naturally dislike work, and, if given the opportunity, will do what is good for the organization. According to Theory Y, the characteristics of the work setting determine whether workers consider work to be a source of satisfaction or punishment, and managers do not need to closely control workers' behavior to make them perform at a high level because workers exercise self-control when they are committed to organizational goals. The implication of Theory Y, according to McGregor, is that "the limits of collaboration in the organizational setting are not limits of human nature but of management's ingenuity in discovering how to realize the potential represented by its human resources."[34] It is the manager's task to create a work setting that encourages commitment to organizational goals and provides opportunities for workers to be imaginative and to exercise initiative and self-direction.

When managers design the organizational setting to reflect the assumptions about attitudes and behavior suggested by Theory Y, the characteristics of the organization are quite different from those of an organizational setting based on Theory X. Managers who believe that workers are motivated to help the organization reach its goals can decentralize authority and give more control over the job to workers, both as individuals and in groups. In this setting, individuals and groups are still accountable for their activities, but the manager's role is not to control employees but to provide support and advice, to make sure employees have the resources they need to perform their jobs, and to evaluate them on their ability to help the organization meet its goals. Henri Fayol's approach to administration more closely reflects the assumptions of Theory Y, rather than Theory X.

One company that was founded on the type of management philosophy inherent in Theory Y is the electronics company Hewlett-Packard (HP), which from its founding consistently put into practice principles derived from Theory Y. (Go to the company's Web site at www.hp.com for additional information.) Founders William Hewlett and David Packard—Bill and Dave, as they are still known throughout the organization—established a philosophy of management known as the "HP Way" that is people-oriented, stresses the importance of treating every person with consideration and respect, and offers recognition for achievements.[35]

From the time that Dave Packard and Bill Hewlett first set up shop in a garage in 1938, they established a new people-oriented approach to management, known as the "HP Way."

The HP Way was based on several guiding principles. One was a policy of long-term employment, and in the past HP went to great lengths not to lay off workers. At times when fewer people were needed, rather than lay off workers, management would cut pay and shorten the workday until demand for HP products picked up. This policy strengthened employees' loyalty to the organization. Another guiding principle in the HP Way concerned how to treat members of the organization so that they feel free to be innovative and creative. HP managers believed that every employee of the company was a member of the HP team. They emphasized the need to increase the level of communication among employees, believing that horizontal communication between peers, not just vertical communication up and down the hierarchy, is essential for creating a positive climate for innovation. So, to promote communication between employees at different levels of the hierarchy, HP encouraged informality. And managers and workers were on a first-name basis with each other and with the founders, Bill and Dave. In addition, Bill and Dave pioneered the technique known as "managing by wandering around": People were expected to wander around learning what others were doing so that they could tap into opportunities to develop new products or find new avenues for cooperation. Bill and Dave also pioneered the principle that employees should spend 15% of their time working on projects of their own choosing, and HP's product design engineers were told to leave their current work out in the open on their desks so that anybody could see what they were doing, learn from it, or suggest ways to improve it. Bill and Dave promoted managers because of their ability to engender excitement and enthusiasm for innovation in their subordinates.[36]

The results of HP's practices helped it become one of the leading electronics companies in the world. In 2001, however, HP, like most other high-tech companies, was experiencing major problems because of the collapse of the telecommunications industry, and the company announced that it was searching for ways to reduce costs. At first, its new CEO, Carly Fiorino, did not lay off employees but asked them to accept lower salaries to help the company through this rough spot.[37] It soon became clear, however, that HP's very survival was at stake as it battled with efficient global competitors such as Dell and Canon. Fiorino was forced to begin layoffs, and by 2004 HP had laid off over 40% of its employees and outsourced thousands of jobs abroad to remain competitive.

These cuts were still not enough, and in 2005 Fiorino lost her job as investors became concerned she was not doing enough.[38] The HP Way seemed to have disappeared, and she was replaced as CEO by Mark Hurd, a manager known for his cost-cutting skills. By 2006 HP had turned the corner and it was profitable once more; by 2008 it overtook Dell to become the largest global PC maker. Whether the company will once again choose to pursue the HP Way is open to question, however, although research remains the backbone of the company.[39] Today, Google exemplifies a company that follows Theory Y and the HP Way, and its organizational culture and leadership are discussed in later chapters of the book.

Management Science Theory

LO5 Explain the contributions of management science to the efficient use of organizational resources.

management science theory An approach to management that uses rigorous quantitative techniques to help managers make maximum use of organizational resources.

Management science theory is a contemporary approach to management that focuses on the use of rigorous quantitative techniques to help managers make maximum use of organizational resources to produce goods and services. In essence, management science theory is a contemporary extension of scientific management, which, as developed by Taylor, also took a quantitative approach to measuring the worker-task mix to raise efficiency. There are many branches of management science, and once again IT, which is having a significant impact on all kinds of management practices, is affecting the tools managers use to make decisions.[40] Each branch of management science deals with a specific set of concerns:

- *Quantitative management* utilizes mathematical techniques—such as linear and non-linear programming, modeling, simulation, queuing theory, and chaos theory—to help managers decide, for example, how much inventory to hold at different times of the year, where to locate a new factory, and how best to invest an organization's financial capital. IT offers managers new and improved ways of handling information so that they can make more accurate assessments of the situation and better decisions.

- *Operations management* provides managers with a set of techniques that they can use to analyze any aspect of an organization's production system to increase efficiency. IT, through the Internet and through growing B2B networks, is transforming the way managers handle the acquisition of inputs and the disposal of finished products.

- *Total quality management (TQM)* focuses on analyzing an organization's input, conversion, and output activities to increase product quality.[41] Once again, through sophisticated software packages and computer-controlled production, IT is changing the way managers and employees think about the work process and ways of improving it.

- *Management information systems (MISs)* help managers design systems that provide information about events occurring inside the organization as well as in its external environment—information that is vital for effective decision making. Once again, IT gives managers access to more and better information and allows more managers at all levels to participate in the decision-making process.

All these subfields of management science, enhanced by sophisticated IT, provide tools and techniques that managers can use to help improve the quality of their decision making and increase efficiency and effectiveness. We discuss many of the important developments in management science theory thoroughly in this book. In particular, Chapter 9, "Value-Chain Management: Functional Strategies for Competitive Advantage," focuses on how to use operations management and TQM to improve quality, efficiency, and responsiveness to customers. And, Chapter 18, "Using Advanced Information Technology to Increase Performance," describes the many ways managers use information systems and technologies to improve their planning, organizing, and controlling functions.

Organizational Environment Theory

An important milestone in the history of management thought occurred when researchers went beyond the study of how managers can influence behavior within organizations to consider how managers control the organization's relationship with its external environment, or **organizational environment**–the set of forces and conditions that operate beyond an organization's boundaries but affect a manager's ability to acquire and utilize resources. Resources in the organizational environment include the raw materials and skilled people that an organization requires to produce goods and services, as well as the support of groups, including customers who buy these goods and services and provide the organization with financial resources. One way of determining the relative success of an organization is to consider how effective its managers are at obtaining scarce and valuable resources.[42] The importance of studying the environment became clear after the development of open-systems theory and contingency theory during the 1960s.

LO6 Explain why the study of the external environment and its impact on an organization has become a central issue in management thought.

organizational environment The set of forces and conditions that operate beyond an organization's boundaries but affect a manager's ability to acquire and utilize resources.

open system A system that takes in resources from its external environment and converts them into goods and services that are then sent back to that environment for purchase by customers.

The Open-Systems View

One of the most influential views of how an organization is affected by its external environment was developed by Daniel Katz, Robert Kahn, and James Thompson in the 1960s.[43] These theorists viewed the organization as an **open system**–a system that takes in resources from its external environment and converts or transforms them into goods and services that are sent back to that environment, where they are bought by customers (see Figure 2.4).

At the *input stage* an organization acquires resources such as raw materials, money, and skilled workers to produce goods and services. Once the organization has gathered the necessary resources, *conversion* begins. At the *conversion stage* the organization's workforce, using appropriate tools, techniques, and machinery, transforms the inputs into outputs of finished goods and services such as cars, hamburgers, or flights to Hawaii. At the *output stage* the organization releases finished

Figure 2.4
The Organization as an Open System

goods and services to its external environment, where customers purchase and use them to satisfy their needs. The money the organization obtains from the sales of its outputs allows the organization to acquire more resources so that the cycle can begin again.

The system just described is said to be open because the organization draws from and interacts with the external environment in order to survive; in other words, the organization is open to its environment. A **closed system,** in contrast, is a self-contained system that is not affected by changes in its external environment. Organizations that operate as closed systems, that ignore the external environment, and that fail to acquire inputs are likely to experience **entropy,** the tendency of a closed system to lose its ability to control itself and thus to dissolve and disintegrate.

Management theorists can model the activities of most organizations by using the open-systems view. Manufacturing companies like Ford and General Electric, for example, buy inputs such as component parts, skilled and semiskilled labor, and robots and computer-controlled manufacturing equipment; then at the conversion stage they use their manufacturing skills to assemble inputs into outputs of cars and appliances. As we discuss in later chapters, competition between organizations for resources is one of several major challenges to managing the organizational environment.

Researchers using the open-systems view are also interested in how the various parts of a system work together to promote efficiency and effectiveness. Systems theorists like to argue that the whole is greater than the sum of its parts; they mean that an organization performs at a higher level when its departments work together rather than separately. **Synergy,** the performance gains that result from the *combined* actions of individuals and departments, is possible only in an organized system. The recent interest in using teams combined or composed of people from different departments reflects systems theorists' interest in designing organizational systems to create synergy and thus increase efficiency and effectiveness.

Contingency Theory

Another milestone in management theory was the development of **contingency theory** in the 1960s by Tom Burns and G. M. Stalker in Britain and Paul Lawrence and Jay Lorsch in the United States.[44] The crucial message of contingency theory is that *there is no one best way to organize:* The organizational structures and the control systems that managers choose depend on—are contingent on—characteristics of the external environment in which the organization operates. According to contingency theory, the characteristics of the environment affect an organization's ability to obtain resources; and to maximize the likelihood of gaining access to resources, managers must allow an organization's departments to organize and control their activities in ways most likely to allow them to obtain resources, given the constraints of the particular environment they face. In other words, how managers design the organizational hierarchy, choose a control system, and lead and motivate their employees is contingent on the characteristics of the organizational environment (see Figure 2.5).

An important characteristic of the external environment that affects an organization's ability to obtain resources is the degree to which the environment is changing. Changes in the organizational environment include changes in technology, which can lead to the creation of new products (such as compact discs) and result in the obsolescence of existing products (eight-track tapes); the entry of new competitors (such as foreign organizations that compete for available resources); and unstable economic conditions. In general, the more quickly the organizational environment is changing, the greater are the problems associated with gaining access to resources and the greater is managers' need to find ways to coordinate the

closed system A system that is self-contained and thus not affected by changes occurring in its external environment.

entropy The tendency of a closed system to lose its ability to control itself and thus to dissolve and disintegrate.

synergy Performance gains that result when individuals and departments coordinate their actions.

contingency theory The idea that the organizational structures and control systems managers choose depend on—are contingent on—characteristics of the external environment in which the organization operates.

Figure 2.5

Contingency Theory of Organizational Design

There is no one best way to organize; organizational structure depends on the environment in which an organization operates.

activities of people in different departments to respond to the environment quickly and effectively.

MECHANISTIC AND ORGANIC STRUCTURES Drawing on Weber's and Fayol's principles of organization and management, Burns and Stalker proposed two basic ways in which managers can organize and control an organization's activities to respond to characteristics of its external environment: They can use a *mechanistic structure* or an *organic structure.*[45] As you will see, a mechanistic structure typically rests on Theory X assumptions, and an organic structure typically rests on Theory Y assumptions.

When the environment surrounding an organization is stable, managers tend to choose a mechanistic structure to organize and control activities and make employee behavior predictable. In a **mechanistic structure,** authority is centralized at the top of the managerial hierarchy, and the vertical hierarchy of authority is the main means used to control subordinates' behavior. Tasks and roles are clearly specified, subordinates are closely supervised, and the emphasis is on strict discipline and order. Everyone knows his or her place, and there is a place for everyone. A mechanistic structure provides the most efficient way to operate in a stable environment because it allows managers to obtain inputs at the lowest cost, giving an organization the most control over its conversion processes and enabling the most efficient production of goods and services with the smallest expenditure of resources. McDonald's restaurants operate with a mechanistic structure. Supervisors make all important decisions; employees are closely supervised and follow well-defined rules and standard operating procedures.

In contrast, when the environment is changing rapidly, it is difficult to obtain access to resources, and managers need to organize their activities in a way that allows them to cooperate, to act quickly to acquire resources (such as new types of inputs to produce new kinds of products), and to respond effectively to the unexpected. In an **organic structure,** authority is decentralized to middle and first-line managers to encourage them to take responsibility and act quickly to pursue scarce resources. Departments are encouraged to take a cross-departmental or functional perspective and cross-functional teams composed of people from different departments are formed. As in Mary Parker Follett's model, the organization operates in an organic way because authority rests with the individuals, departments, and teams best positioned to control the current problems the organization is facing, as the story of Nokia suggests.

mechanistic structure
An organizational structure in which authority is centralized, tasks and rules are clearly specified, and employees are closely supervised.

organic structure
An organizational structure in which authority is decentralized to middle and first-line managers and tasks and roles are left ambiguous to encourage employees to cooperate and respond quickly to the unexpected.

Managing Globally

Teams, Teams, and More Teams at Nokia

Nokia Corporation, headquartered in Espoo, Finland, employs 60,000 people around the world and is the market leader in the global wireless communications industry.[46] Nokia has research and development (R&D) units in 14 countries, to which it dedicates one-third of its workforce.[47] The company's success and competitive advantage is the result of its use of teams throughout the organization. In fact, it has been said that any task or project that is of any significance in the company is assigned to a team. This commitment to teams starts at the top of the organization, where managers work together as a team to make all of Nokia's important business decisions.[48] The number of teams cascades down through the organization, with almost all its employees mirroring the model set by the company's top managers.

Why does Nokia get good results from its teams? Teams are given high levels of autonomy and encouraged to be creative. High emphasis is placed on letting those people who are most knowledgeable about a problem or opportunity make decisions concerning it regardless of their position in the hierarchy (which by nature is very flat at Nokia).[49] Teams and their members take personal responsibility for decisions and believe that their efforts and contributions are important for Nokia's continued success. Good communication, mutual respect, and a high regard for the members of one's team are its central values and norms. Annual meetings, referred to as the "Nokia Way," help keep teams on track as well as enable teams throughout the organization to help actualize Nokia's vision for the future.[50] Through these means, Nokia ensures that team goals are aligned with organizational goals and that its cohesive groups work to benefit the organization as a whole.

As Nokia's organic approach to operating suggests, control is much looser and decentralized in an organic structure than it is in a mechanistic structure, and reliance on shared norms and common expectations to guide organizational activities is greater. As a result, managers in an organic structure can react more quickly to a changing environment than can managers in a mechanistic structure. However, an organic structure is generally more expensive to operate because it requires that more managerial time, money, and effort be spent on coordination. So it is used only when needed—when the organizational environment is unstable and rapidly changing.[51]

Summary and Review

In this chapter we examined the evolution of management theory and research over the last century. Much of the material in the rest of this book stems from developments and refinements of this work. Indeed, the results of the extensive research in management that has been conducted in the time since the theories discussed here were developed are incorporated in the chapters in the rest of this book.

LO 1, 2   SCIENTIFIC MANAGEMENT THEORY   The search for efficiency started with the study of how managers could improve person-task relationships to increase efficiency. The concept of job specialization and division of labor remains the basis for the design of work settings in modern organizations. New developments such as lean production and total quality management are often viewed as advances on the early scientific management principles developed by Taylor and the Gilbreths.

LO3 **ADMINISTRATIVE MANAGEMENT THEORY** Max Weber and Henri Fayol outlined principles of bureaucracy and administration that are as relevant to managers today as they were when developed at the turn of the 20th century. Much of modern management research refines these principles to suit contemporary conditions. For example, the increasing interest in the use of cross-departmental teams and the empowerment of workers are issues that managers also faced a century ago.

LO4 **BEHAVIORAL MANAGEMENT THEORY** Researchers have described many different approaches to managerial behavior, including Theories X and Y. Often, the managerial behavior that researchers suggest reflects the context of their own historical era and culture. Mary Parker Follett advocated managerial behaviors that did not reflect accepted modes of managerial behavior at the time, and her work was largely ignored until conditions changed.

LO5 **MANAGEMENT SCIENCE THEORY** The various branches of management science theory provide rigorous quantitative techniques that give managers more control over each organization's use of resources to produce goods and services.

LO6 **ORGANIZATIONAL ENVIRONMENT THEORY** The importance of studying the organization's external environment became clear after the development of open-systems theory and contingency theory during the 1960s. A main focus of contemporary management research is to find methods to help managers improve the ways they utilize organizational resources and compete successfully in the global environment. Strategic management and total quality management are two important approaches intended to help managers make better use of organizational resources.

Management in Action

Topics for Discussion and Action

DISCUSSION

1. Choose a fast-food restaurant, a department store, or some other organization with which you are familiar, and describe the division of labor and job specialization it uses to produce goods and services. How might this division of labor be improved? **[LO 1, 2]**

2. Apply Taylor's principles of scientific management to improve the performance of the organization you chose in item 1. **[LO2]**

3. In what ways are Weber's and Fayol's ideas about bureaucracy and administration similar? In what ways do they differ? **[LO3]**

4. Which of Weber's and Fayol's principles seem most relevant to the creation of an ethical organization? **[LO 4, 6]**

5. Why was the work of Mary Parker Follett ahead of its time? To what degree do you think it is appropriate today? **[LO 4, 5]**

6. What is contingency theory? What kinds of organizations familiar to you have been successful or unsuccessful in dealing with contingencies from the external environment? **[LO6]**

7. Why are mechanistic and organic structures suited to different organizational environments? **[LO 4, 6]**

ACTION

8. Question a manager about his or her views of the relative importance of Fayol's 14 principles of management. **[LO 3, 4]**

9. Visit at least two organizations in your community, and identify those that seem to operate with a Theory X or a Theory Y approach to management. **[LO4]**

Building Management Skills
Managing Your Own Business [LO 2, 4]

Now that you understand the concerns addressed by management thinkers over the last century, use this exercise to apply your knowledge to developing your management skills.

Imagine that you are the founding entrepreneur of a software company that specializes in developing games for home computers. Customer demand for your games has increased so much that over the last year your company has grown from a busy one-person operation to one with 16 employees. In addition to yourself, you employ six software developers to produce the software, three graphic artists, two computer technicians, two marketing and sales personnel, and two secretaries. In the next year you expect to hire 30 new employees, and you are wondering how best to manage your growing company.

1. Use the principles of Weber and Fayol to decide on the system of organization and management that you think will be most effective for your growing organization. How many levels will the managerial hierarchy of your organization have? How much authority will you decentralize to your subordinates? How will you establish the division of labor between subordinates? Will your subordinates work alone and report to you or work in teams?

2. Which management approach (for example, Theory X or Y) do you propose to use to run your organization? In 50 words or less write a statement describing the management approach you believe will motivate and coordinate your subordinates, and tell why you think this style will be best.

Managing Ethically [LO 3, 4]

Mr. Edens Profits from Watching His Workers' Every Move

Read the case below, "Mr. Edens Profits from Watching His Workers' Every Move," and think about the following issues.

Small Business

Control is one of Ron Edens's favorite words. "This is a controlled environment," he says of the blank brick building that houses his company, Electronic Banking System Inc.

Inside, long lines of women sit at spartan desks, slitting envelopes, sorting contents and filling out "control cards" that record how many letters they have opened and how long it has taken them. Workers here, in "the cage," must process three envelopes a minute. Nearby, other women tap keyboards, keeping pace with a quota that demands 8,500 strokes an hour.

The room is silent. Talking is forbidden. The windows are covered. Coffee mugs, religious pictures and other adornments are barred from workers' desks.

In his office upstairs, Mr. Edens sits before a TV monitor that flashes images from eight cameras posted throughout the plant. "There's a little bit of Sneaky Pete to it," he says, using a remote control to zoom in on a document atop a worker's desk. "I can basically read that and figure out how someone's day is going."

This day, like most others, is going smoothly, and Mr. Edens's business has boomed as a result. "We maintain a lot of control," he says. "Order and control are everything in this business."

Mr. Edens's business belongs to a small but expanding financial service known as "lockbox processing." Many companies and charities that once did their paperwork in-house now "out-source" clerical tasks to firms like EBS, which processes donations to groups such as Mothers Against Drunk Driving, the Doris Day Animal League, Greenpeace and the National Organization for Women.

More broadly, EBS reflects the explosive growth of jobs in which workers perform low-wage and limited tasks in white-collar settings.

This has transformed towns like Hagerstown—a blue-collar community hit hard by industrial layoffs in the 1970s—into sites for thousands of jobs in factory-sized offices.

Many of these jobs, though, are part time and most pay far less than the manufacturing occupations they replaced. Some workers at EBS start at the minimum wage of $4.25 an hour and most earn about $6 an hour. The growth of such jobs—which often cluster outside major cities—also completes a curious historic circle. During the Industrial Revolution, farmers' daughters went to work in textile towns like Lowell, Mass. In post-industrial America, many women of modest means and skills are entering clerical mills where they process paper instead of cloth (coincidentally, EBS occupies a former garment factory).

"The office of the future can look a lot like the factory of the past," says Barbara Garson, author of *The Electronic Sweatshop* and other books on the modern workplace. "Modern tools are being used to bring 19th-century working conditions into the white-collar world."

The time-motion philosophies of Frederick Taylor, for instance, have found a 1990s correlate in the phone, computer and camera, which can be used to monitor workers more closely than a foreman with a stopwatch ever could. Also, the nature of the work often justifies a vigilant eye. In EBS workers handle thousands of dollars in checks and cash, and Mr. Edens says cameras help deter would-be thieves. Tight security also reassures visiting clients. "If you're disorderly, they'll think we're out of control and that things could get lost," says Mr. Edens, who worked as a financial controller for the National Rifle Association before founding EBS in 1983.

But tight observation also helps EBS monitor productivity and weed out workers who don't keep up. "There's multiple uses," Mr. Edens says of surveillance. His desk is covered with computer printouts recording the precise toll of keystrokes tapped by each data-entry worker. He also keeps a day-to-day tally of errors. The work floor itself resembles an enormous classroom in the throes of exam period. Desks point toward the front, where a manager keeps watch from a raised platform that workers call "the pedestal" or "the birdhouse." Other supervisors are positioned toward the back of the room. "If you want to watch someone," Mr. Edens explains, "it's easier from behind because they don't know you're watching." There also is a black globe hanging from the ceiling, in which cameras are positioned.

Mr. Edens sees nothing Orwellian about this omniscience. "It's not a Big Brother attitude," he says. "It's more of a calming attitude."

But studies of workplace monitoring suggest otherwise. Experts say that surveillance can create a hostile environment in which workers feel pressured, paranoid and prone to stress-related illness. Surveillance also can be used punitively, to intimidate workers or to justify their firing.

Following a failed union drive at EBS, the National Labor Relations Board filed a series of complaints against the company, including charges that EBS threatened, interrogated, and spied on workers. As part of an out-of-court settlement, EBS reinstated a fired worker and posted a notice that it would refrain from illegal practices during a second union vote, which also failed.

"It's all noise," Mr. Edens says of the unfair labor charges. As to the pressure that surveillance creates, Mr. Edens sees that simply as "the nature of the beast." He adds: "It's got to add stress when everyone knows their production is being monitored. I don't apologize for that."

Mr. Edens also is unapologetic about the Draconian work rules he maintains, including one that forbids all talk unrelated to the completion of each task. "I'm not paying people to chat. I'm paying them to open envelopes," he says. Of the blocked windows. Mr. Edens adds: "I don't want them looking out—it's distracting. They'll make mistakes."

This total focus boosts productivity but it makes many workers feel lonely and trapped. Some try to circumvent the silence rule, like kids in a school library. "If you don't turn your head and sort of mumble out of the side of your mouth, supervisors won't hear you most of the time," Cindy Kesselring explains during her lunch break. Even so, she feels isolated and often longs for her former job as a waitress. "Work is your social life, particularly if you've got kids," says the 27-year-old mother. "Here it's hard to get to know people because you can't talk."

During lunch, workers crowd in the parking lot outside, chatting nonstop. "Some of us don't eat much because the more you chew the less you can talk," Ms. Kesselring says. There aren't other breaks and workers aren't allowed to sip coffee or eat at their desks during the long stretches before and after lunch. Hard candy is the only permitted desk snack.

New technology, and the breaking down of labor into discrete, repetitive tasks, also have effectively stripped jobs such as those at EBS of whatever variety and skills clerical work once possessed. Workers in the cage (an antiquated banking term for a money-handling area) only open envelopes and sort contents; those

in the audit department compute figures; and data-entry clerks punch in the information that the others have collected. If they make a mistake, the computer buzzes and a message such as "check digit error" flashes on the screen.

"We don't ask these people to think—the machines think for them," Mr. Edens says. "They don't have to make any decisions." This makes the work simpler but also deepens its monotony. In the cage, Carol Smith says she looks forward to envelopes that contain anything out of the ordinary, such as letters reporting that the donor is deceased. Or she plays mental games. "I think to myself, A goes in this pile, B goes here and C goes there—sort of like Bingo." She says she sometimes feels "like a machine," particularly when she fills out the "control card" on which she lists "time in" and "time out" for each tray of envelopes. In a slot marked "cage operator" Ms. Smith writes her code number, 3173. "That's me," she says.

Barbara Ann Wiles, a keyboard operator, also plays mind games to break up the boredom. Tapping in the names and addresses of new donors, she tries to imagine the faces behind the names, particularly the odd ones. "Like this one, Mrs. Fittizzi," she chuckles. "I can picture her as a very stout lady with a strong accent, hollering on a street corner." She picks out another: "Doris Angelroth—she's very sophisticated, a monocle maybe, drinking tea on an overstuffed mohair couch."

It is a world remote from the one Ms. Wiles inhabits. Like most EBS employees, she must juggle her low-paying job with child care. On this Friday, for instance, Ms. Wiles will finish her eight-hour shift at about 4

p.m., go home for a few hours, then return for a second shift from midnight to 8 a.m. Otherwise, she would have to come in on Saturday to finish the week's work.

"This way I can be home on the weekend to look after my kids," she says.

Others find the work harder to leave behind at the end of the day. In the cage, Ms. Smith says her husband used to complain because she often woke him in the middle of the night. "I'd be shuffling my hands in my sleep," she says, mimicking the motion of opening envelopes.

Her cage colleague, Ms. Kesselring, says her fiancé has a different gripe. "He dodges me for a couple of hours after work because I don't shut up—I need to talk, talk, talk," she says. And there is one household task she can no longer abide.

"I won't pay bills because I can't stand to open another envelope," she says. "I'll leave letters sitting in the mailbox for days."

Questions

1. Which of the management theories described in the chapter does Ron Edens make most use of?

2. What do you think are the effects of this approach on (a) workers and (b) supervisors?

3. Do you regard Ron Eden's approach to management as ethical and acceptable or unethical and unacceptable in the 2000s? Why?

Source: Tony Horwitz, "Mr. Edens Profits from Watching His Workers' Every Move," *The Wall Street Journal,* December 1, 1994. Reproduced with permission of Dow Jones & Company Inc.

Form groups of three to five people, and appoint one group member as the spokesperson who will communicate your findings to the class when called on by the instructor. Then discuss the following scenario.

Think of an organization with which you are all familiar, such as a local restaurant, store, or bank. After choosing an organization, model it from an open-systems perspective. Identify its input, conversion, and output processes; and identify forces in the external environment that help or hurt the organization's ability to obtain resources and dispose of its goods or services.

Exploring the World Wide Web [LO 3, 6]

Research Ford's Web site (www.ford.com), and locate and read the material on Ford's history and evolution over time. What have been the significant stages in the company's development? What problems and issues confronted managers at these stages? What are the challenges facing Ford's managers now?

Be the Manager [LO 2, 4]

How to Manage a Hotel

You have been called in to advise the owners of an exclusive new luxury hotel. For the venture to succeed, hotel employees must focus on providing customers with the highest-quality customer service possible. The challenge is to devise a way of organizing and controlling employees that will promote high-quality service, that will encourage employees to be committed to the hotel, and that will reduce the level of employee turnover and absenteeism—which are typically high in the hotel business.

Questions

1. How do the various theories of management discussed in this chapter offer clues for organizing and controlling hotel employees?

2. Which parts would be the most important for an effective system to organize and control employees?

BusinessWeek Case in the News [LO 3, 6]

Netflix: Flex to the Max

I had the great fortune of doing a mediocre job at my first company," says Netflix Inc. (NFLX) founder Reed Hastings. He's talking about his 1990s startup Pure Software, a wildly successful maker of debugging programs that, through a series of mergers, became part of IBM (IBM). Hastings says Pure, like many other outfits, went from being a heat-filled, everybody-wants-to-be-here place to a dronish, when-does-the-day-end sausage factory. "We got more bureaucratic as we grew," says Hastings.

After Pure, the Stanford-trained engineer spent two years thinking about how to ensure his next endeavor wouldn't suffer the same big-company creep.

The resulting sequel is Netflix, where Hastings is trying to revolutionize not only the way people rent movies but also how his managers work. Hastings pays his people lavishly, gives them unlimited vacations, and lets them structure their own compensation packages. In return, he expects ultra-high performance. His 400 salaried employees are expected to do the jobs of three or four people. Netflix is no frat party with beer bashes and foosball tables. Nor does the company want to play cruise director to its employees. Rather, Netflix is a tough, fulfilling, "fully formed adult" culture, says marketing manager Heather McIlhany. "There's no place to hide at Netflix."

Hastings calls his approach "freedom and responsibility." And as one might expect, employees get all cinematic when describing the vibe. Netflix is the workplace equivalent of *Ocean's 11,* says Todd S. Yellin, hired to perfect the site's movie-rating system. Hastings is Danny Ocean, the bright, charismatic leader who recruits the best in class, gives them a generous cut, and provides the flexibility to do what they do best, all while uniting them on a focused goal. The near-impossible mission, in this case, is trying to outmaneuver Blockbuster (BBI), Amazon (AMZN), the cable companies, and Apple (AAPL) in the race to become the leading purveyor of online movies.

The tension has never been higher. Last quarter, for the first time in Netflix's history, the company lost customers in its bloody, fight-to-the-death battle with Blockbuster Inc. Netflix shares cratered and have yet to recover. Some analysts are talking doom.

Netflix executives like to point out, though, that the company has been pronounced dead more than once before. When Wal-Mart (WMT) started offering online movie rentals in 2002, for example, analysts started referring to Netflix as *The Last Picture Show.* But by 2005, Wal-Mart had closed shop. It referred all its customers to Netflix.

Today, Netflix is embroiled in an even tougher, two-front war: competing with Blockbuster for online supremacy in DVD rentals while also inaugurating a digital streaming service to compete with the likes of Apple. That's one mighty gang of entrenched competitors. "There's usually room in a marketplace for more than one," says Wedbush Morgan Securities analyst Michael Pachter. "But in this case there really isn't."

Hastings is betting on Netflix's culture to get the company out of this corner. The plan includes continuing to increase what Hastings calls "talent density." Most companies go to great scientific lengths to ensure they are paying just enough to attract talent but not a dollar more than they need

to. Netflix, which hands out salaries that are typically much higher than what is customary in Silicon Valley, is unabashed in its we-pay-above-market swagger. "We're unafraid to pay high," says Hastings.

To ensure that the company is constantly nabbing A players, company talent hunters are told that money is no object. Each business group has what amounts to an internal boutique headhunting firm. Employees often recommend people they bonded with at work before (that *Ocean's 11* effect again).

Gibson Biddle, who runs the Web site, knew that Yelling, who had both deep tech and film expertise, was the perfect guy to help Netflix improve how it recommends movies to customers on its site. Yellin had worked for Biddle at a family entertainment site during the boom. The snag was that Yellin, also a filmmaker, was finishing up his first feature film, *Brother's Shadow,* in Los Angeles. He also was allergic to anything corporate or publicly traded.

Impossible sell, right? But Netflix threw so much cash and flexibility at Yellin that he couldn't turn it down. During his first three months he flew back and forth between L.A. and San Francisco doing his Netflix job and finishing his movie. "This company is *über*-flexible," says Yellin. "I'm given the freedom to do what I do well without being micromanaged."

No Golden Handcuffs

Pay is not tied to performance reviews, nor to some predetermined raise pool, but to the job market. Netflix bosses are constantly gleaning market compensation data from new hires and then amping up salaries when needed. And what happens when someone doesn't live up to expectations? "At most companies, average performers get an average raise," says Hastings. "At Netflix, they get a generous severance package." Why? Because Hastings believes that otherwise managers feel too guilty to let someone go.

When it comes to paychecks, Netflix is arguably going where no public company has gone before. Employees are free to choose annually how

much of their compensation they want in cash vs. stock. Unlike the case at most companies, options vest immediately. Netflix doesn't want golden-handcuffs types. One engineer got so excited that he told human resources head Patty McCord to give him half his pay in stock. When McCord saw him drive away in an old minivan, she wasn't surprised when he popped into her office the next day and told her he wanted to make it more cash: 80–20.

Good thing for him. With great choice comes great risk. Netflix employees who loaded up on stock this year have gotten hammered, leaving some to pine for the paternalism that has long shielded employees from the vagaries of stock market volatility. But great risk also means great freedom, as in: "Take as much vacation as you want." Last year, engineering manager Aroon Ramadoss took off five weeks to go to Europe with his girlfriend. He plans on taking another extended vacation next year in Brazil. "I like to travel in bigger chunks rather than take five days off and rush right back," says Ramadoss.

Despite the luxe perks and killer culture, Hastings still has the battle of his career ahead. The Netflix people have "a huge competitive advantage because they are smart and they hire really well," says Pachter. "But that doesn't help you in the long run if your business model is flawed."

Questions for Discussion

1. What are the main principles behind Reed Hastings's approach to managing? How do they affect Netflix's organizational culture?

2. Compare these principles to those developed by Henry Fayol. In what ways are they similar or different? And, what different effects do they have on employee motivation and Netflix's culture and "esprit de corps"?

Source: Michelle Conlin, "Netflix: Flex to the Max." Reprinted from the September 23, 2007, issue of *BusinessWeek* Online by special permission. Copyright © 2007 by The McGraw-Hill Companies, Inc.

BusinessWeek Case in the News [LO 4, 5]

Oticon's No-Cubicle Culture

It sounds like the corporate paradise of the future. Workers organize themselves, coalescing around natural leaders and gravitating to the most exciting projects. There are no middle managers, no hierarchies, no fixed assignments.

At Oticon, a midsize Danish maker of hearing aids, the future started back in 1991. That's when its chief executive, Lars Kolind, turned traditional notions of the workplace upside down. Kolind, a corporate renegade trained as a mathematician, swept away old structures. Workers were suddenly free to concentrate on any project and join any team.

Kolind's radical idea was to transform the company's once-stodgy culture into a free marketplace of ideas. He moved headquarters to a new location where none of the 150 employees had a permanent desk or office, only filing cabinets on wheels that they pushed from project to project. Meeting areas had no tables or chairs. He called it the spaghetti organization, because the place had no fixed structure yet somehow

held together. Ideas bubbled up and turned into hits such as a new hearing aid that required less adjustment. Sales and profits soared. The company became a model for management creativity. Even CNN showed up to tape a segment. Yet as the company grew and went public, many of the old structures crept back.

Kolind eventually left, and these days there's not much talk about his spaghetti revolution. Still, its spirit survives. None of the 500 head-office employees at Oticon has even a cubicle. The latest headquarters features few interior walls. Workers sit around the perimeter of the building at simple desks. They attend meetings on sofas in the middle of each floor.

The relaxed atmosphere helps retain top engineers, keeping Oticon at the forefront of innovation. Its unobtrusive Delta hearing aid has been a success. Sales of parent William Demant Holding Group, of which Oticon is the largest business, have grown 36% since 2002, to $927 million, while operating profit has risen 57%, to $232 million.

But some things have clearly changed. Everyone has a boss to whom they report and they no longer

have total freedom to choose projects. That seems to suit people fine. A degree of freedom sparks creativity, but workers also crave leadership. The trick is striking the right balance. Says Mads Kamp, Oticon's director of human resources: "People want to be led."

Questions for Discussion

1. How and why did Lars Kolind change the way Oticon organized and controlled its employees?

2. What new kinds of skills and ways of working are managers and employees having to learn to perform well in Oticon's new culture?

3. How do these new ways of working relate to those talked about in the chapter, such as those suggested by Fayol and Follett?

Source: Jack Ewing, "No-Cubicle Culture." Reprinted from the August 20, 2007, issue of *BusinessWeek* Online by special permission. Copyright © 2007 by The McGraw-Hill Companies, Inc.

CHAPTER 3

Values, Attitudes, Emotions, and Culture: The Manager as a Person

After studying this chapter, you should be able to:

LO1 Describe the various personality traits that affect how managers think, feel, and behave.

LO2 Explain what values and attitudes are and describe their impact on managerial action.

LO3 Appreciate how moods and emotions influence all members of an organization.

LO4 Describe the nature of emotional intelligence and its role in management.

LO5 Define organizational culture and explain how managers both create and are influenced by organizational culture.

A MANAGER'S CHALLENGE

Ryla Stands Out Among Telemarketers

www.ryla.com

How can managers create and sustain a caring culture and instill loyalty in employees in an industry known for dead-end jobs and inferior working conditions? Ryla Inc., founded by Mark Wilson in 2001, is a customer-contact and business-process outsourcing firm headquartered in Kennesaw, Georgia.[1] Wilson had years of experience managing call centers as an executive at Dun & Bradstreet, the financial information publisher, when his openness to new approaches and ideas led him to recognize a potential opportunity.[2] Telemarketing and customer-contact organizations are notorious for high levels of turnover, dismal working conditions, and employees who are eager to abandon what they see as dead-end jobs as soon as a better opportunity comes along. Wilson imagined a different kind of customer-contact business, one in which his employees would feel "like it's the best job they've ever had."[3]

Having the idea and being open to the possibility and potential benefits of operating a customer-contact business in a dramatically different way was one thing. Securing the financing to start such a business was another. Wilson hired a consultant to help him approach venture capital firms for financing to start his business and over a dozen of them were unwilling to invest in his idea. Despite this setback, Wilson persisted and his determination paid off when he contacted SJF Ventures, a venture capital firm in Durham, North Carolina, which invests in start-ups that are likely to have good financial returns while at the same time providing jobs for those with low incomes. SJF Ventures invested $700,000 in return for equity in the company and Ryla was born.[4]

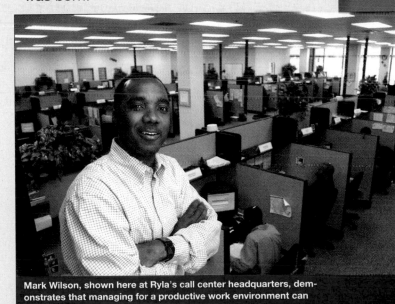

Mark Wilson, shown here at Ryla's call center headquarters, demonstrates that managing for a productive work environment can also include managing for employees' well-being.

From the start and to this day, Wilson has strived to create and sustain a work environment and company culture that are true to his own personal values. Treating employees with respect, fostering open communication, providing opportunities for training, growth, and development, and demonstrating a real commitment to the well-being of employees as well as the local community have helped Ryla to grow and prosper. Today, Ryla has nearly 400 full-time employees, less than 30% turnover in an industry with average turnover rates over 40% and as high as 75%, very high client retention rates, and revenue growth of at least 10% per year.[5] Ryla has over a 1,500 telemarketing seat capacity and thus hires many people who are not full-time employees, as is not uncommon in this industry.[6]

While call center work tends to be relatively routine and boring, Wilson's emphasis on both creating a caring culture and providing employees with opportunities for training and advancement go a long way toward building employee loyalty.[7] Wilson maintains an open-door policy and keeps employees informed about how the business is doing.[8] He not only solicits employee suggestions for improvements but also acts on them. In the company's early days, for example, during an employee training session, the trainer happened to hear one of the new trainees grumbling about having to go to work the Friday after Thanksgiving. The trainer told Wilson, who then addressed the trainees and asked them if anyone had a concern with the Thanksgiving holiday schedule. One of the trainees made the point that she had never had to work the day after Thanksgiving before and Wilson, eager to demonstrate that his open-door policy was more than just window dressing and could

yield real changes, changed the schedule and made that Friday a holiday.[9]

Ryla employees have access to a variety of benefits ranging from medical and life insurance to 401K plans, employee assistance programs, and aerobics classes.[10] Employees who remain with Ryla for three years and attain performance and attendance goals become eligible for stock options in the company.[11] Based on employee feedback about areas in which employees would like to develop and improve their skills, Ryla provides training and development seminars on both professional and personal topics (e.g., financial planning). Ryla also provides employees with the opportunity to advance within the company by promoting from within, so telemarketing is no longer viewed as a dead-end job with no opportunities for advancement. Eighty percent of the managers in Ryla once manned the telephones.[12] During "Ryla Huddles," employees celebrate team accomplishments as well as individual achievements.[13]

Ryla also engages in charity events, which have the dual benefit of giving back to the community while at the same time fostering a sense of camaraderie among employees. For example, on a Spirit Day commemorating Ryla's fifth anniversary, employees were grouped into teams based on the clients they served. Teams created and performed their own cheers for the anniversary celebration and winning teams were given $500 to donate to a charity of their choosing.[14]

Never one to rest on his laurels, Wilson continues to seek out new approaches and ways for his business to better serve customers. Recently, for example, Ryla started a new practice area of short-term projects requiring quick ramp-up and ramp-down, such as crisis response for product recalls and data breaches.[15] For example, natural emergencies, confidential personal data breaches, and other crisis situations often require organizations to have a response system up and running within a day, and now Ryla provides such services.[16]

Wilson's efforts to create a new and different kind of call center that provides excellent service to clients and a caring and supportive environment for employees have not gone unnoticed in the business community. For example, in 2007, Ryla was one of 35 finalists in *The Wall Street Journal*—Winning Workplace's Top Small Workplaces competition.[17] And it is not surprising that loyal employees like Denise Burdick, who never imagined working in telemarketing, are satisfied with their jobs and committed to Ryla.[18]

Overview

Like people everywhere, Mark Wilson has his own distinctive personality, values, ways of viewing things, and personal challenges and disappointments. In this chapter, we focus on the manager as a feeling, thinking human being. We start by describing enduring characteristics that influence how managers "manage," as well as how they view other people, their organizations, and the world around them. We discuss as well how managers' values, attitudes, and moods play out in organizations, shaping organizational culture. By the end of this chapter, you will have a good appreciation of how the personal characteristics of managers influence the process of management in general, and organizational culture in particular.

Enduring Characteristics: Personality Traits

All people, including managers, have certain enduring characteristics that influence how they think, feel, and behave both on and off the job. These characteristics are **personality traits,** particular tendencies to feel, think, and act in certain ways that can be used to describe the personality of every individual. It is important to understand the personalities of managers because their personalities influence their behavior and their approach to managing people and resources.

Some managers are demanding, difficult to get along with, and highly critical of other people. Other managers may be as concerned about effectiveness and efficiency as highly critical managers but are easier to get along with, are likable, and frequently praise the people around them. Both styles of management may produce excellent results, but their effects on employees are quite different. Do managers deliberately decide to adopt one or the other of these approaches to management? Although they may do so part of the time, in all likelihood their personalities also account for their different approaches. Indeed, research suggests that the way people react to different conditions depends, in part, on their personalities.[19]

LO1 Describe the various personality traits that affect how managers think, feel, and behave.

personality traits Enduring tendencies to feel, think, and act in certain ways.

The Big Five Personality Traits

We can think of an individual's personality as being composed of five general traits or characteristics: extraversion, negative affectivity, agreeableness, conscientiousness, and openness to experience.[20] Researchers often consider these the Big Five personality traits.[21] Each of them can be viewed as a continuum along which every individual or, more specifically, every manager falls (see Figure 3.1).

Some managers may be at the high end of one trait continuum, others at the low end, and still others somewhere in between. An easy way to understand how these traits can affect a person's approach to management is to describe what people are like at the high and low ends of each trait continuum. As will become evident as you read about each trait, no single trait is right or wrong for being an effective manager. Rather, effectiveness is determined by a complex interaction between the characteristics of managers (including personality traits) and the nature of the job and organization in

Figure 3.1

The Big Five Personality Traits

Manager's personalities can be described by determining which point on each of the following dimensions best characterizes the manager in question:

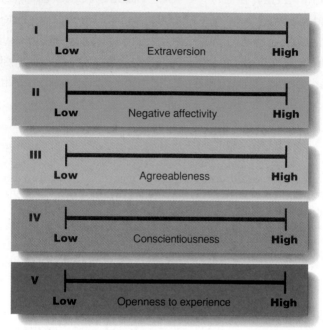

which they are working. Moreover, personality traits that enhance managerial effectiveness in one situation may actually impair it in another situation.

EXTRAVERSION   **Extraversion** is the tendency to experience positive emotions and moods and feel good about oneself and the rest of the world. Managers who are high on extraversion (often called *extraverts*) tend to be sociable, affectionate, outgoing, and friendly. Managers who are low on extraversion (often called *introverts*) tend to be less inclined toward social interactions and to have a less positive outlook. Being high on extraversion may be an asset for managers whose jobs entail especially high levels of social interaction. Managers who are low on extraversion may nevertheless be highly effective and efficient, especially when their jobs do not require excessive social interaction. Their more "quiet" approach may enable them to accomplish quite a bit of work in limited time. See Figure 3.2 for an example of a scale that can be used to measure a person's level of extraversion.

extraversion The tendency to experience positive emotions and moods and to feel good about oneself and the rest of the world.

NEGATIVE AFFECTIVITY   **Negative affectivity** is the tendency to experience negative emotions and moods, feel distressed, and be critical of oneself and others. Managers high on this trait may often feel angry and dissatisfied and complain about their own and others' lack of progress. Managers who are low on negative affectivity do not tend to experience many negative emotions and moods and are less pessimistic and critical of themselves and others. On the plus side, the critical approach of a manager high on negative affectivity may sometimes be effective if it spurs both the manager and others to improve their performance. Nevertheless, it is probably more pleasant to work with a manager who is low on negative affectivity; the better working relationships that such a manager is likely to cultivate also can be an important asset. Figure 3.3 is an example of a scale developed to measure a person's level of negative affectivity.

negative affectivity The tendency to experience negative emotions and moods, to feel distressed, and to be critical of oneself and others.

AGREEABLENESS   **Agreeableness** is the tendency to get along well with others. Managers who are high on the agreeableness continuum are likable, tend to be affectionate, and care about other people. Managers who are low on agreeableness may

agreeableness The tendency to get along well with other people.

Figure 3.2

Measures of Extraversion, Agreeableness, Conscientiousness, and Openness to Experience

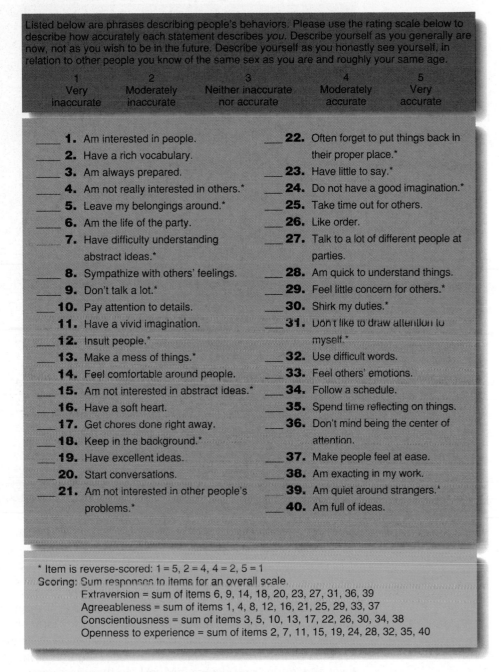

Listed below are phrases describing people's behaviors. Please use the rating scale below to describe how accurately each statement describes *you*. Describe yourself as you generally are now, not as you wish to be in the future. Describe yourself as you honestly see yourself, in relation to other people you know of the same sex as you are and roughly your same age.

1 Very inaccurate	2 Moderately inaccurate	3 Neither inaccurate nor accurate	4 Moderately accurate	5 Very accurate

____ **1.** Am interested in people.	____ **22.** Often forget to put things back in their proper place.*
____ **2.** Have a rich vocabulary.	
____ **3.** Am always prepared.	____ **23.** Have little to say.*
____ **4.** Am not really interested in others.*	____ **24.** Do not have a good imagination.*
____ **5.** Leave my belongings around.*	____ **25.** Take time out for others.
____ **6.** Am the life of the party.	____ **26.** Like order.
____ **7.** Have difficulty understanding abstract ideas.*	____ **27.** Talk to a lot of different people at parties.
____ **8.** Sympathize with others' feelings.	____ **28.** Am quick to understand things.
____ **9.** Don't talk a lot.*	____ **29.** Feel little concern for others.*
____ **10.** Pay attention to details.	____ **30.** Shirk my duties.*
____ **11.** Have a vivid imagination.	____ **31.** Don't like to draw attention to myself.*
____ **12.** Insult people.*	
____ **13.** Make a mess of things.*	____ **32.** Use difficult words.
____ **14.** Feel comfortable around people.	____ **33.** Feel others' emotions.
____ **15.** Am not interested in abstract ideas.*	____ **34.** Follow a schedule.
____ **16.** Have a soft heart.	____ **35.** Spend time reflecting on things.
____ **17.** Get chores done right away.	____ **36.** Don't mind being the center of attention.
____ **18.** Keep in the background.*	
____ **19.** Have excellent ideas.	____ **37.** Make people feel at ease.
____ **20.** Start conversations.	____ **38.** Am exacting in my work.
____ **21.** Am not interested in other people's problems.*	____ **39.** Am quiet around strangers.*
	____ **40.** Am full of ideas.

* Item is reverse-scored: 1 = 5, 2 = 4, 4 = 2, 5 = 1
Scoring: Sum responses to items for an overall scale.
   Extraversion = sum of items 6, 9, 14, 18, 20, 23, 27, 31, 36, 39
   Agreeableness = sum of items 1, 4, 8, 12, 16, 21, 25, 29, 33, 37
   Conscientiousness = sum of items 3, 5, 10, 13, 17, 22, 26, 30, 34, 38
   Openness to experience = sum of items 2, 7, 11, 15, 19, 24, 28, 32, 35, 40

Source: Lewis R. Goldberg, Oregon Research Institute, http://ipip.ori.org/ipip/. Reprinted with permission.

be somewhat distrustful of others, unsympathetic, uncooperative, and even at times antagonistic. Being high on agreeableness may be especially important for managers whose responsibilities require that they develop good, close relationships with others. Nevertheless, a low level of agreeableness may be an asset in managerial jobs that actually require that managers be antagonistic, such as drill sergeants, and some other kinds of military managers. See Figure 3.2 for an example of a scale that measures a person's level of agreeableness.

conscientiousness The tendency to be careful, scrupulous, and persevering.

CONSCIENTIOUSNESS **Conscientiousness** is the tendency to be careful, scrupulous, and persevering.[22] Managers who are high on the conscientiousness continuum

Figure 3.3
A Measure of Negative Affectivity

Instructions: Listed below are a series of statements a person might use to describe her/his attitudes, opinions, interests, and other characteristics. If a statement is true or largely true, put a "T" in the space next to the item. Or if the statement is false or largely false, mark an "F" in the space.

Please answer every statement, even if you are not completely sure of the answer. Read each statement carefully, but don't spend too much time deciding on the answer.

_____ **1.** I worry about things a lot.

_____ **2.** My feelings are often hurt.

_____ **3.** Small problems often irritate me.

_____ **4.** I am often nervous.

_____ **5.** My moods often change.

_____ **6.** Sometimes I feel bad for no apparent reason.

_____ **7.** I often have very strong emotions such as anger or anxiety without really knowing why.

_____ **8.** The unexpected can easily startle me.

_____ **9.** Sometimes, when I am thinking about the day ahead of me, I feel anxious and tense.

_____ **10.** Small setbacks sometimes bother me too much.

_____ **11.** My worries often cause me to lose sleep.

_____ **12.** Some days I seem to be always "on edge."

_____ **13.** I am more sensitive than I should be.

_____ **14.** Sometimes I go from feeling happy to sad, and vice versa, for no good reason.

Scoring: Level of negative affectivity is equal to the number of items answered "True."

Source: Auke Tellegen, *Brief Manual for the Differential Personality Questionnaire,* Copyright © 1982. Paraphrased version reproduced by permission of University of Minnesota Press.

are organized and self-disciplined; those who are low on this trait might sometimes appear to lack direction and self-discipline. Conscientiousness has been found to be a good predictor of performance in many kinds of jobs, including managerial jobs in a variety of organizations.[23] Entrepreneurs who found their own companies, like Mark Wilson profiled in "A Manager's Challenge," often are high on conscientiousness and their persistence and determination help them to overcome obstacles and turn their ideas into successful new ventures. Figure 3.2 provides an example of a scale that measures conscientiousness.

openness to experience The tendency to be original, have broad interests, be open to a wide range of stimuli, be daring, and take risks.

OPENNESS TO EXPERIENCE Openness to experience is the tendency to be original, have broad interests; be open to a wide range of stimuli, be daring, and take risks.[24] Managers who are high on this trait continuum may be especially likely to take risks and be innovative in their planning and decision making. Entrepreneurs who start their own businesses—like Bill Gates of Microsoft, Jeff Bezos of Amazon.com, and Anita Roddick of The Body Shop—are, in all likelihood, high on openness to experience, which has contributed to their success as entrepreneurs and managers. Mark Wilson, discussed in this chapter's "A Manager's Challenge," founded his own company and continues to explore new ways for it to grow—a testament to his high level of openness to experience. Managers who are low on openness to experience may be less prone to take risks and more conservative in their planning and decision making. In certain organizations and positions, this tendency might be an asset. The manager of the fiscal office in a public university, for example, must ensure that all university departments and units follow the university's rules and regulations pertaining to budgets, spending accounts, and reimbursements of expenses. Figure 3.2 provides an example of a measure of openness to experience.

Managers who come up with and implement radically new ideas are often high on openness to experience, as is true of Mike Rowe, creator of the hit Discovery Channel TV show *Dirty Jobs*.

Manager as a Person

Who Would Have Thought *Dirty Jobs* Would Be a Hit?

Mike Rowe is hardly the person you would have thought would have created a hit TV show like the Discovery Channel's *Dirty Jobs*.[25] Not the most ambitious of types, and as an actor in the business for over two decades who never made it big, his work experiences have ranged from performing with the Baltimore Opera to selling fake simulated diamonds on QVC on TV to appearing in Tylenol commercials.[26] While cohosting a local TV show on CBS-5 in San Francisco, Rowe hit upon the idea behind *Dirty Jobs*. Rowe did a segment on the show called "Somebody's Gotta Do It," viewers liked it, and it really struck a cord with him personally.[27]

His openness to experience led him to try to develop a TV show featuring him working as an apprentice to men and women performing the kinds of hard, dirty work we all depend on and no one wants to do (think bat cave scavenger, worm dung farmer, roadkill cleaner, sewer inspector, pig farmer . . .).[28] As he puts it, his show features "men and women who do the kinds of jobs that make civilized life possible for the rest of us."[29] While he originally had a hard time finding a home for *Dirty Jobs* (the Discovery Channel turned him down twice before agreeing to air a pilot series in 2003), the show has become a bona fide hit, aired 700 times in 2007, and is the Discovery Channel's number-one show, according to David Zaslav, the CEO of Discovery Communications.[30]

Mike Rowe's openness to experience has given him a real appreciation of all kinds of work and jobs.

Rowe's openness to experience enables him to get down and dirty with the best of them, try his hand at all sorts of dirty jobs, and thoroughly enjoy it. As would be expected, all sorts of mishaps occur and that is part of the fun. And, Rowe has come to appreciate the earnestness of the workers he profiles—"the celebration of work, and the mixing of pain and fun."[31] Interestingly enough, as one who never had embraced the value of too much hard work in the past, *Dirty Jobs* has instilled in Rowe a healthy respect and admiration for the people who perform all sorts of dirty jobs, work hard at them, and are happy when the work is done.[32]

Successful managers occupy a variety of positions on the Big Five personality-trait continua. One highly effective manager may be high on extraversion and negative affectivity, another equally effective manager may be low on both these traits, and still another may be somewhere in between. Members of an organization must understand these differences among managers because they can shed light on how managers behave and on their approach to planning, leading, organizing, or controlling. If subordinates realize, for example, that their manager is low on extraversion, they will not feel slighted when their manager seems to be aloof because they will realize that by nature he or she is simply not outgoing.

Managers themselves also need to be aware of their own personality traits and the traits of others, including their subordinates and fellow managers. A manager who knows that he has a tendency to be highly critical of other people might try to tone down his negative approach. Similarly, a manager who realizes that her chronically complaining subordinate tends to be so negative because of his personality may take all his complaints with a grain of salt and realize that things probably are not as bad as this subordinate says they are.

In order for all members of an organization to work well together and with people outside the organization, such as customers and suppliers, they must understand each other. Such understanding comes, in part, from an appreciation of some of the fundamental ways in which people differ from one another—that is, an appreciation of personality traits.

Other Personality Traits That Affect Managerial Behavior

Many other specific traits in addition to the Big Five describe people's personalities. Here we look at traits that are particularly important for understanding managerial effectiveness: locus of control; self-esteem; and the needs for achievement, affiliation, and power.

LOCUS OF CONTROL   People differ in their views about how much control they have over what happens to and around them. The locus-of-control trait captures these beliefs.[33] People with an **internal locus of control** believe that they themselves are responsible for their own fate; they see their own actions and behaviors as being major and decisive determinants of important outcomes such as attaining levels of job performance, being promoted, or being turned down for a choice job assignment. Some managers with an internal locus of control see the success of a whole organization resting on their shoulders. One example is Mark Wilson in "A Manager's Challenge." An internal locus of control also helps to ensure ethical behavior and decision making in an organization because people feel accountable and responsible for their own actions.

People with an **external locus of control** believe that outside forces are responsible for what happens to and around them; they do not think that their own actions make much of a difference. As such, they tend not to intervene to try to change a situation or solve a problem, leaving it to someone else.

Managers need to have an internal locus of control because they *are* responsible for what happens in organizations; they need to believe that they can and do make a difference, as does Mark Wilson at Ryla. Moreover, managers are responsible for ensuring that organizations and their members behave in an ethical fashion, and for this as well they need to have an internal locus of control—they need to know and feel they can make a difference.

SELF-ESTEEM   **Self-esteem** is the degree to which individuals feel good about themselves and their capabilities. People with high self-esteem believe that they are competent, deserving, and capable of handling most situations, as does Mark Wilson. People with low self-esteem have poor opinions of themselves, are unsure about their capabilities, and question their ability to succeed at different endeavors.[34]

internal locus of control The tendency to locate responsibility for one's fate within oneself.

external locus of control The tendency to locate responsibility for one's fate in outside forces and to believe that one's own behavior has little impact on outcomes.

self-esteem The degree to which individuals feel good about themselves and their capabilities.

Research suggests that people tend to choose activities and goals consistent with their levels of self-esteem. High self-esteem is desirable for managers because it facilitates their setting and keeping high standards for themselves, pushes them ahead on difficult projects, and gives them the confidence they need to make and carry out important decisions.

need for achievement The extent to which an individual has a strong desire to perform challenging tasks well and to meet personal standards for excellence.

need for affiliation The extent to which an individual is concerned about establishing and maintaining good interpersonal relations, being liked, and having other people get along.

need for power The extent to which an individual desires to control or influence others.

NEEDS FOR ACHIEVEMENT, AFFILIATION, AND POWER   Psychologist David McClelland has extensively researched the needs for achievement, affiliation, and power.[35] The **need for achievement** is the extent to which an individual has a strong desire to perform challenging tasks well and to meet personal standards for excellence. People with a high need for achievement often set clear goals for themselves and like to receive performance feedback. The **need for affiliation** is the extent to which an individual is concerned about establishing and maintaining good interpersonal relations, being liked, and having the people around him or her get along with one another. The **need for power** is the extent to which an individual desires to control or influence others.[36]

Research suggests that high needs for achievement and for power are assets for first-line and middle managers and that a high need for power is especially important for upper-level managers.[37] One study found that U.S. presidents with a relatively high need for power tended to be especially effective during their terms of office.[38] A high need for affiliation may not always be desirable in managers because it might lead them to try too hard to be liked by others (including subordinates) rather than doing all they can to ensure that performance is as high as it can and should be. Although most research on these needs has been done in the United States, some studies suggest that these findings may also be applicable to people in other countries such as India and New Zealand.[39]

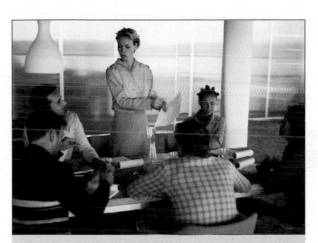

Research suggests that the needs for achievement and power are desirable personality traits in first-line and middle managers, while the need for power is especially important for upper-level managers.

Taken together, these desirable personality traits for managers—an internal locus of control, high self-esteem, and high needs for achievement and power—suggest that managers need to be take-charge people who not only believe that their own actions are decisive in determining their own and their organizations' fates but also believe in their own capabilities. Such managers have a personal desire for accomplishment and influence over others.

Values, Attitudes, and Moods and Emotions

LO2 Explain what values and attitudes are and describe their impact on managerial action.

What are managers striving to achieve? How do they think they should behave? What do they think about their jobs and organizations? And how do they actually feel at work? Some answers to these questions can be found by exploring managers' values, attitudes, and moods.

Values, attitudes, and moods and emotions capture how managers experience their jobs as individuals. *Values* describe what managers are trying to achieve through work and how they think they should behave. *Attitudes* capture their thoughts and feelings about their specific jobs and organizations. *Moods and emotions* encompass how managers actually feel when they are managing. Although these three aspects of managers' work experience are highly personal, they also have important implications for understanding how managers behave, how they treat and respond to others, and how, through their efforts, they help contribute to organizational effectiveness through planning, leading, organizing, and controlling.

Values: Terminal and Instrumental

The two kinds of personal values are *terminal* and *instrumental*. A **terminal value** is a personal conviction about lifelong goals or objectives; an **instrumental value** is a personal conviction about desired modes of conduct or ways of behaving.[40] Terminal values often lead to the formation of **norms,** or unwritten, informal codes of conduct that prescribe how people should act in particular situations and are considered important by most members of a group or organization, such as behaving honestly or courteously.

Milton Rokeach, one of the leading researchers in the area of human values, identified 18 terminal values and 18 instrumental values that describe each person's value system (see Figure 3.4).[41] By rank ordering the terminal values from 1 (most important as a guiding principle in one's life) to 18 (least important as a guiding principle in one's life) and then rank ordering the instrumental values from 1 to 18, people can give good pictures of their **value systems**—what they are striving to achieve in life and how they want to behave.[42] (You can gain a good understanding of your own values by rank ordering first the terminal values and then the instrumental values listed in Figure 3.4.)

Several of the terminal values listed in Figure 3.4 seem to be especially important for managers—such as *a sense of accomplishment (a lasting contribution), equality (brotherhood, equal opportunity for all),* and *self-respect (self-esteem).* A manager who thinks a

Figure 3.4
Terminal and Instrumental Values

Terminal Values	Instrumental Values
A comfortable life (a prosperous life)	Ambitious (hardworking, aspiring)
An exciting life (a stimulating, active life)	Broad-minded (open-minded)
A sense of accomplishment (lasting contribution)	Capable (competent, effective)
A world at peace (free of war and conflict)	Cheerful (lighthearted, joyful)
A world of beauty (beauty of nature and the arts)	Clean (neat, tidy)
Equality (brotherhood, equal opportunity for all)	Courageous (standing up for your beliefs)
Family security (taking care of loved ones)	Forgiving (willing to pardon others)
Freedom (independence, free choice)	Helpful (working for the welfare of others)
Happiness (contentedness)	Honest (sincere, truthful)
Inner harmony (freedom from inner conflict)	Imaginative (daring, creative)
Mature love (sexual and spiritual intimacy)	Independent (self-reliant, self-sufficient)
National security (protection from attack)	Intellectual (intelligent, reflective)
Pleasure (an enjoyable, leisurely life)	Logical (consistent, rational)
Salvation (saved, eternal life)	Loving (affectionate, tender)
Self-respect (self-esteem)	Obedient (dutiful, respectful)
Social recognition (respect, admiration)	Polite (courteous, well-mannered)
True friendship (close companionship)	Responsible (dependable, reliable)
Wisdom (a mature understanding of life)	Self-controlled (restrained, self-disciplined)

sense of accomplishment is of paramount importance might focus on making a lasting contribution to an organization by developing a new product that can save or prolong lives, as is true of managers at Medtronic (a company that makes medical devices such as cardiac pacemakers), or by opening a new foreign subsidiary. A manager who places equality at the top of his or her list of terminal values may be at the forefront of an organization's efforts to support, provide equal opportunities to, and capitalize on the many talents of an increasingly diverse workforce.

Other values are likely to be considered important by many managers, such *as a comfortable life (a prosperous life), an exciting life (a stimulating, active life), freedom (independence, free choice),* and *social recognition (respect, admiration).* The relative importance that managers place on each terminal value helps explain what they are striving to achieve in their organizations and what they will focus their efforts on.

Several of the instrumental values listed in Figure 3.4 seem to be important modes of conduct for managers, such as being *ambitious (hardworking, aspiring), broad-minded (open-minded), capable (competent, effective), responsible (dependable, reliable),* and *self-controlled (restrained, self-disciplined).* Moreover, the relative importance a manager places on these and other instrumental values may be a significant determinant of actual behaviors on the job. A manager who considers being *imaginative (daring, creative)* to be highly important, for example, is more likely to be innovative and take risks than is a manager who considers this to be less important (all else being equal). A manager who considers being *honest (sincere, truthful)* to be of paramount importance may be a driving force for taking steps to ensure that all members of a unit or organization behave ethically, as indicated in the following "Ethics in Action."

Ethics in Action

Telling the Truth at Gentle Giant Moving

Gentle Giant Moving Company, based in Somerville, Massachusetts, was founded by Larry O'Toole in 1980 and now has over $28 million in revenues and offices in multiple states.[43] While moving is undoubtedly hard work and many people would never think about having a career in this industry, Gentle Giant's unique culture and approach to managing people have not only contributed to the company's success but also provided its employees with satisfying careers. For example, when Ryan Libby was in college, he worked for Gentle Giant during one of his summer vacations to make some extra money. Now the Assistant Manager for the Providence, Rhode Island, Gentle Giant Office, Libby is contemplating opening an office of his own. As he puts it, "First it was just a paycheck, and it kind of turned into a long-term career."[44]

Libby is just the kind of employee O'Toole seeks to hire—employees who start out driving moving trucks and eventually move into management positions running offices. While some moving companies hire a lot of temporary help in the summer to meet seasonal demand, 60% of Gentle Giant employees are employed full time.[45] Since the demand for moving services is lower in the winter, Gentle Giant uses this time to provide employees with training

At Gentle Giant Moving Co., employees are given leadership training, access to company outings, and the opportunity to advance to management positions.

Small Business

and leadership development activities. Of course, new employees receive training in the basics of moving: packing, lifting, and carrying household goods in a safe manner. However, employees looking to advance in the company receive training in a host of other areas ranging from project management, communication, problem solving, and customer relations to leadership. An overarching goal of Gentle Giant's training efforts is inculcating in employees the importance of honesty. According to O'Toole, "We really emphasize that what matters most to us is telling the truth."[46]

Training benefits Gentle Giant's employees, customers, and the company as a whole. About one-third of the company's office and management employees started out driving moving trucks. Customers are satisfied because employees are capable, honest, and professional. And the company has continued to grow, prosper, and receive recognition in the business press. For example, in 2007, Gentle Giant was named one of the fifteen Top Small Workplaces by *The Wall Street Journal* in collaboration with Winning Workplaces (a nonprofit organization that focuses on helping small- and medium-size companies improve their work environments).[47]

Having fun and getting to know each other as people is also important at Gentle Giant.[48] The company holds parties and arranges for outings for employees to sporting events, amusement parks, and other local attractions. Most workdays, O'Toole takes an employee out to lunch. Some college athletes are attracted to work for Gentle Giant because they see moving as a way to keep fit while at the same time having the opportunity to grow and develop on the job and move into a managerial position if they desire.[49]

All in all, managers' value systems signify what managers as individuals are trying to accomplish and become in their personal lives and at work. Thus, managers' value systems are fundamental guides to their behavior and efforts at planning, leading, organizing, and controlling.

Attitudes

attitude A collection of feelings and beliefs.

An **attitude** is a collection of feelings and beliefs. Like everyone else, managers have attitudes about their jobs and organizations, and these attitudes affect how they approach their jobs. Two of the most important attitudes in this context are job satisfaction and organizational commitment.

job satisfaction The collection of feelings and beliefs that managers have about their current jobs.

JOB SATISFACTION Job satisfaction is the collection of feelings and beliefs that managers have about their current jobs.[50] Managers who have high levels of job satisfaction generally like their jobs, feel that they are being fairly treated, and believe that their jobs have many desirable features or characteristics (such as interesting work, good pay and job security, autonomy, or nice coworkers). Figure 3.5 shows sample items from two scales that managers can use to measure job satisfaction. Levels of job satisfaction tend to increase as one moves up the hierarchy in an organization. Upper managers, in general, tend to be more satisfied with their jobs than entry-level employees. Managers' levels of job satisfaction can range from very low to very high and anywhere in between.

According to a recent survey, job satisfaction levels in the United States have declined over the past 20 years or so.[51] In particular, some workers report being dissatisfied with opportunities for growth and advancement on their jobs, heavy workloads and work/life balance issues, performance reviews and bonus plans, and communication in their organizations.[52]

Figure 3.5

Sample Items from Two Measures of Job Satisfaction

Sample items from the Minnesota Satisfaction Questionnaire:
People respond to each of the items in the scale by checking whether they are:

[ ] Very dissatisfied   [ ] Satisfied
[ ] Dissatisfied   [ ] Very satisfied
[ ] Can't decide whether satisfied or not

On my present job, this is how I feel about . . .

_____ **1.** Being able to do things that don't go against my conscience.

_____ **2.** The way my job provides for steady employment.

_____ **3.** The chance to do things for other people.

_____ **4.** The chance to do something that makes use of my abilities.

_____ **5.** The way company policies are put into practice.

_____ **6.** My pay and the amount of work I do.

_____ **7.** The chances for advancement on this job.

_____ **8.** The freedom to use my own judgment.

_____ **9.** The working conditions.

_____ **10.** The way my coworkers get along with each other.

_____ **11.** The praise I get for doing a good job.

_____ **12.** The feeling of accomplishment I get from tho job.

The Faces Scale
Workers select the face which best expresses how they feel about their job in general.

| 11 | 10 | 9 | 8 | 7 | 6 | 5 | 4 | 3 | 2 | 1 |

Source: D. J. Weiss et al., *Manual for the Minnesota Satisfaction Questionnaire,* 1967, Minnesota Studies in Vocational Rehabilitation: XXII. Copyright © 1967 University of Minnesota. Copyright © 1975 by the American Psychological Association. Adapted by permission of Randall B. Dunham and J. B. Brett.

Focus on Diversity

Changing Attitudes

An interesting trend in job attitudes has been observed among some managers in their 20s and 30s.[53] For example, after Sandi Garcia graduated from the University of Wyoming with a degree in marketing, she landed a good job in Florida and was soon promoted into the managerial ranks. By all counts, Garcia should have been satisfied with her job–she was advancing in the company, making good money, and doing the kind of work she had hoped for. Ironically, Garcia found herself becoming increasingly dissatisfied with her job. Putting in 12-hour workdays was not unusual for Garcia, nor was it unusual for her to work during the weekends. Living a hectic, fast-paced life revolving around work soon made Garcia dream of a simpler life where she would have time to do things she enjoyed such as skiing, being with family and friends, and doing volunteer work.

Garcia acted on her dream: She moved back to Wyoming, and is now more satisfied with a less demanding job at the Wyoming Business Council.[54]

Gregg Steiner was a high-tech manager on the West Coast who seemed to have everything, including a Malibu beach house. However, he was dissatisfied with a job that left him no free time to enjoy the beach or much else. Steiner quit the high-tech world and works at his now more modest home, handling customer service for his family's diaper rash ointment business (Pinxav).[55]

Young managers like Garcia and Steiner are not lazy, nor do they lack ambition. Rather, they have lived through changes in the corporate landscape that cause them to question what work should be and should mean to them. Some of these young managers have seen their parents slaving away at their jobs in corporate America year after year, only to be laid off in tough times. While their parents might never have questioned their commitment to their organizations, the need to work long hours, and the lack of time for much else other than work and raising a family, Garcia and Steiner desire the flexibility and time to live lives that are simpler but also richer in terms of meaningful activities. And they want to be in charge of their own lives rather than having their lives dictated by persons higher up the corporate hierarchy.[56]

Of course, for every young manager like Garcia and Steiner who voluntarily leaves the fast track for a more balanced life, there are other young prospective managers eager to take their place in the corporate world. And a job that is dissatisfying for one manager might be satisfying for another. In any case, in an era when trust in corporations has come under question (e.g., due to ethical lapses and fraud at companies like Enron and WorldCom), some young managers are seeking to invest themselves in things they can really trust.[57]

organizational citizenship behaviors (OCBs) Behaviors that are not required of organizational members but that contribute to and are necessary for organizational efficiency, effectiveness, and competitive advantage.

In general, it is desirable for managers to be satisfied with their jobs, for at least two reasons. First, satisfied managers may be more likely to go the extra mile for their organization or perform **organizational citizenship behaviors (OCBs),** behaviors that are not required of organizational members but that contribute to and are necessary for organizational efficiency, effectiveness, and competitive advantage.[58] Managers who are satisfied with their jobs are more likely to perform these "above and beyond the call of duty" behaviors, which can range from putting in extra-long hours when needed to coming up with truly creative ideas and overcoming obstacles to implement them (even when doing so is not part of the manager's job), or to going out of one's way to help a coworker, subordinate, or superior (even when doing so entails considerable personal sacrifice).[59]

A second reason why it is desirable for managers to be satisfied with their jobs is that satisfied managers may be less likely to quit.[60] A manager who is highly satisfied may never even think about looking for another position; a dissatisfied manager may always be on the lookout for new opportunities. Turnover can hurt an organization because it results in the loss of the experience and knowledge that managers have gained about the company, industry, and business environment.

A growing source of dissatisfaction for many lower- and middle-level managers, as well as for nonmanagerial employees, is the threat of unemployment and increased workloads from organizational downsizings and layoffs. Organizations that try to improve their efficiency through restructuring and layoffs often eliminate a sizable number of first-line and middle management positions. This decision obviously hurts the managers who are laid off, and it also can reduce the job satisfaction levels of managers who remain. They might fear that they may be the next to be let go. In addition, the workloads of remaining employees often are dramatically increased as a result of restructuring, and this can contribute to dissatisfaction.

Managers and employees who are very committed to their organizations may be more inclined to go above and beyond the call of duty by, for example, working long hours when need be.

organizational commitment The collection of feelings and beliefs that managers have about their organization as a whole.

The ways in which managers and organizations handle layoffs is of paramount importance, not only for the layoff victims but also for those employees who survive the layoff and keep their jobs.[61] Showing compassion and empathy for layoff victims, providing them with as much advance notice as possible about the layoff, providing clear information about severance benefits, and also helping layoff victims in their job search efforts are a few of the ways in which managers can humanely manage a layoff.[62] For example, when Ron Thomas, vice president of organizational development for Martha Stewart Living Omnimedia, had to lay off employees as a result of closing the organization's catalogue business, he personally called all the catalogue businesses he knew to find out about potential positions for laid-off employees.[63] Efforts such as Thomas's to help layoff victims find new jobs can contribute to the job satisfaction of those who survive the layoff. As Thomas puts it, "If you handle a restructuring well, the word gets out that you're a good place to work . . . if we post a job opening today, we'll get 1,500 resumes tomorrow."[64]

ORGANIZATIONAL COMMITMENT Organizational commitment is the collection of feelings and beliefs that managers have about their organization as a whole.[65] Managers who are committed to their organizations believe in what their organizations are doing, are proud of what these organizations stand for, and feel a high degree of loyalty toward their organizations. Committed managers are more likely to go above and beyond the call of duty to help their company and are less likely to quit.[66] Organizational commitment can be especially strong when employees and managers truly believe in organizational values; it also leads to a strong organizational culture, as found in Ryla.

Organizational commitment is likely to help managers perform some of their figurehead and spokesperson roles (see Chapter 1). It is much easier for a manager to persuade others both inside and outside the organization of the merits of what the organization has done and is seeking to accomplish if the manager truly believes in and is committed to the organization. Figure 3.6 is an example of a scale that managers can use to measure a person's level of organizational commitment.

Do managers in different countries have similar or different attitudes? Differences in the levels of job satisfaction and organizational commitment among managers in different countries are likely because these managers have different kinds of opportunities and rewards and because they face different economic, political, or sociocultural forces in their organizations' general environments. In countries with relatively high unemployment rates, such as France, levels of job satisfaction may be higher among employed managers because they may be happy simply to have a job.

Levels of organizational commitment from one country to another may depend on the extent to which countries have legislation affecting firings and layoffs and the extent to which citizens of a country are geographically mobile. In both France and Germany legislation protects workers (including managers) from being fired or laid off. U.S. workers, in contrast, have very little protection. In addition, managers in the United States are more willing to relocate than managers in France and Germany. In France citizens have relatively strong family and community ties; and in Germany housing is expensive and difficult to find. For those reasons citizens in both countries tend to be less geographically mobile than Americans.[67] Managers who know that their jobs are secure and who are reluctant to relocate (such as those in Germany and France) may be more committed to their organizations than managers who know that their organizations could lay them off any day and who would not mind geographic relocations.

Figure 3.6
A Measure of Organizational Commitment

People respond to each of the items in the scale by checking whether they:
[ ] Strongly disagree   [ ] Slightly agree
[ ] Moderately disagree   [ ] Moderately agree
[ ] Slightly disagree   [ ] Strongly agree
[ ] Neither disagree nor agree

_____ 1. I am willing to put in a great deal of effort beyond that normally expected in order to help this organization be successful.

_____ 2. I talk up this organization to my friends as a great organization to work for.

_____ 3. I feel very little loyalty to this organization.*

_____ 4. I would accept almost any type of job assignment in order to keep working for this organization.

_____ 5. I find that my values and the organization's values are very similar.

_____ 6. I am proud to tell others that I am part of this organization.

_____ 7. I could just as well be working for a different organization as long as the type of work was similar.*

_____ 8. This organization really inspires the very best in me in the way of job performance.

_____ 9. It would take very little change in my present circumstances to cause me to leave this organization.*

_____ 10. I am extremely glad that I chose this organization to work for over others I was considering at the time I joined.

_____ 11. There's not too much to be gained by sticking with this organization indefinitely.*

_____ 12. Often, I find it difficult to agree with this organization's policies on important matters relating to its employees.*

_____ 13. I really care about the fate of this organization.

_____ 14. For me this is the best of all possible organizations for which to work.

_____ 15. Deciding to work for this organization was a definite mistake on my part.*

Scoring: Responses to items 1, 2, 4, 5, 6, 8, 10, 13, and 14 are scored such that 1 = strongly disagree; 2 = moderately disagree; 3 = slightly disagree; 4 = neither disagree nor agree; 5 = slightly agree; 6 = moderately agree; and 7 = strongly agree. Responses to "*" items 3, 7, 9, 11, 12, and 15 are scored 7 = strongly disagree; 6 = moderately disagree; 5 = slightly disagree; 4 = neither disagree nor agree; 3 = slightly agree; 2 = moderately agree; and 1 = strongly agree. Responses to the 15 items are averaged for an overall score from 1 to 7; the higher the score, the higher the level of organizational commitment.

Source: L. W. Porter and F. J. Smith, "Organizational Commitment Questionnaire," in J. D. Cook, S. J. Hepworth, T. D. Wall, and P. B. Warr, eds., *The Experience of Work: A Compendium and Review of 249 Measures and Their Use* (New York: Academic Press, 1981), 84–86.

Moods and Emotions

LO3 Appreciate how moods and emotions influence all members of an organization.

mood A feeling or state of mind.

Just as you sometimes are in a bad mood and at other times are in a good mood, so too are managers. A **mood** is a feeling or state of mind. When people are in a positive mood, they feel excited, enthusiastic, active, or elated.[68] When people are in a negative mood, they feel distressed, fearful, scornful, hostile, jittery, or nervous.[69] People who are high on extraversion are especially likely to experience positive moods; people who are high on negative affectivity are especially likely to experience negative moods. People's situations or circumstances also determine their moods; however, receiving a raise is likely to put most people in a good mood regardless of their personality traits. People who are high on negative affectivity are not always in a bad mood, and people who are low on extraversion still experience positive moods.[70]

emotions Intense, relatively short-lived feelings.

Emotions are more intense feelings than moods, are often directly linked to whatever caused the emotion, and are more short-lived.[71] However, once whatever has triggered the emotion has been dealt with, the feelings may linger in the form of a less intense mood.[72] For example, a manager who gets very angry when one of his subordinates has engaged in an unethical behavior may find his anger decreasing in intensity once he has decided how to address the problem. Yet he continues to be in a bad mood the rest of the day, even though he is not directly thinking about the unfortunate incident.[73]

Research has found that moods and emotions affect the behavior of managers and all members of an organization. For example, research suggests that the subordinates of managers who experience positive moods at work may perform at somewhat higher levels and be less likely to resign and leave the organization than the subordinates of managers who do not tend to be in a positive mood at work.[74] Other research suggests that under certain conditions creativity might be enhanced by positive moods, whereas under other conditions negative moods might push people to work harder to come up with truly creative ideas.[75] Recognizing that both mood states have the potential to contribute to creativity in different ways, recent research suggests that employees may be especially likely to be creative to the extent that they experience both mood states (at different times) on the job and the work environment is supportive of creativity.[76]

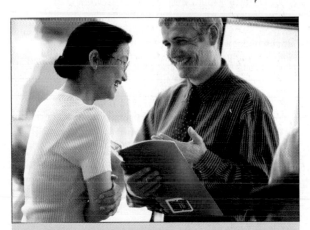

As might be expected, research has shown that a manager's positive moods may contribute to employees' job performance and job satisfaction.

Other research suggests that moods and emotions may play an important role in ethical decision making. For example, researchers at Princeton University found that when people are trying to solve difficult personal moral dilemmas, the parts of their brains that are responsible for emotions and moods are especially active.[77]

Recognizing the benefits of positive moods, the Northbrook, Illinois, accounting firm of Lipschultz, Levin, & Gray[78] has gone to great lengths to promote positive feelings among its employees. Chief executive Steven Siegel claims that positive feelings promote relaxation and alleviate stress, increase revenues and attract clients, and reduce turnover. Positive moods are promoted in a variety of ways at Lipschultz, Levin, & Gray. Siegel has been known to put on a gorilla mask at especially busy times; clerks sometimes don chicken costumes; a foghorn announces the signing of a new client; employees can take a break and play miniature golf in the office, play darts, or exercise with a hula-hoop (even during tax time). A casual dress code also lightens things up at the firm. By all counts, positive moods seem to be paying off for this group of accountants, whose good feelings seem to be attracting new clients.

Patrick Corboy, president and chief executive of Austin Chemical, switched his account from a bigger firm to Lipschultz, Levin, & Gray because he found the people at the bigger firm to be "too stuffy and dour for us." Of the accountant William Finestone, who now manages the Austin Chemical account, Corboy says the following: "[He] is a barrel of laughs . . . Bill not only solves our problems more quickly but he puts us at ease, too."[79]

Nevertheless, sometimes negative moods can have their advantages. Some studies suggest that critical thinking and devil's advocacy may be promoted by a negative mood, and sometimes especially accurate judgments may be made by managers in negative moods.[80]

Managers and other members of an organization need to realize that how they feel affects how they treat others and how others respond to them, including their subordinates. For example, a subordinate may be more likely to approach a manager

Figure 3.7

A Measure of Positive and Negative Mood at Work

People respond to each item by indicating the extent to which the item descibes how they felt at work during the past week on the following scale:

1 = Very slightly or not at all   4 = Quite a bit
2 = A little   5 = Very much
3 = Moderately

____ **1.** Active   ____ **7.** Enthusiastic

____ **2.** Distressed   ____ **8.** Fearful

____ **3.** Strong   ____ **9.** Peppy

____ **4.** Excited   ____**10.** Nervous

____ **5.** Scornful   ____**11.** Elated

____ **6.** Hostile   ____**12.** Jittery

Scoring: Responses to items 1, 3, 4, 7, 9, and 11 are summed for a positive mood score; the higher the score, the more positive mood is experienced at work. Responses to items 2, 5, 6, 8, 10, and 12 are summed for a negative mood score; the higher the score, the more negative mood is experienced at work.

Source: A. P. Brief, M. J. Burke, J. M. George, B. Robinson, and J. Webster, "Should Negative Affectivity Remain an Unmeasured Variable in the Study of Job Stress?" *Journal of Applied Psychology* 73 (1988), 193–98; M. J. Burke, A. P. Brief, J. M. George, L. Robinson, and J. Webster, "Measuring Affect at Work: Confirmatory Analyses of Competing Mood Structures with Conceptual Linkage in Cortical Regulatory Systems," *Journal of Personality and Social Psychology* 57 (1989), 1091–102.

with a somewhat far-out but potentially useful idea if the subordinate thinks the manager is in a good mood. Likewise, when managers are in very bad moods, their subordinates might try to avoid them at all costs. Figure 3.7 is an example of a scale that managers can use to measure the extent to which a person experiences positive and negative moods at work.

Emotional Intelligence

In understanding the effects of managers' and all employees' moods and emotions, it is important to take into account their levels of emotional intelligence. **Emotional intelligence** is the ability to understand and manage one's own moods and emotions and the moods and emotions of other people.[81] Managers with a high level of emotional intelligence are more likely to understand how they are feeling and why, and they are more able to effectively manage their feelings. When managers are experiencing stressful feelings and emotions such as fear or anxiety, emotional intelligence enables them to understand why and manage these feelings so that they do not get in the way of effective decision making.[82]

Emotional intelligence also can help managers perform their important roles such as their interpersonal roles (figurehead, leader, and liaison).[83] Understanding how your subordinates feel, why they feel that way, and how to manage these feelings is central to developing strong interpersonal bonds with them.[84] Moreover, emotional intelligence has the potential to contribute to effective leadership in multiple ways[85] and can help managers make lasting contributions to society. For example, Bernard (Bernie) Goldhirsh founded *INC.* magazine back in 1979, when entrepreneurs received more notoriety than respect, if they were paid attention to at all.[86] Goldhirsh

LO4 Describe the nature of emotional intelligence and its role in management.

emotional intelligence The ability to understand and manage one's own moods and emotions and the moods and emotions of other people.

was an entrepreneur himself at the time, with his own publishing company. He recognized the vast contributions entrepreneurs could make to society, creating something out of nothing, and also realized firsthand what a tough task entrepreneurs faced.[87] His emotional intelligence helped him to understand the challenges and frustrations entrepreneurs like himself faced and their need for support.

When Goldhirsh founded *INC.*, entrepreneurs had little they could turn to for advice, guidance, and solutions to management problems. *INC.* was born to fill this gap and provide entrepreneurs with information and support by profiling successful and unsuccessful entrepreneurial ventures, highlighting management techniques that work, and providing readers with firsthand accounts of how successful entrepreneurs developed and managed their businesses.[88]

Goldhirsh's emotional intelligence helped him recognize the many barriers entrepreneurs face and the emotional roller coaster of staking all one has on an idea that may or may not work. Goldhirsh believed that helping society understand the entrepreneurial process through *INC.* magazine not only helped entrepreneurs but also enlightened bankers, lawmakers, and the public at large about the role these visionaries play, the challenges they face, and the support their ventures depend on.[89]

Emotional intelligence helps managers understand and relate well to other people.[90] It also helps managers maintain their enthusiasm and confidence and energize subordinates to help the organization attain its goals.[91] Recent theorizing and research suggest that emotional intelligence may be especially important in awakening employee creativity.[92] Managers themselves are increasingly recognizing the importance of emotional intelligence. As Andrea Jung, CEO of Avon Products, indicates, "Emotional intelligence is in our DNA here at Avon because relationships are critical at every stage of our business."[93] An example of a scale that measures emotional intelligence is provided in Figure 3.8.

Organizational Culture

LO5 Define organizational culture and explain how managers both create and are influenced by organizational culture.

organizational culture The shared set of beliefs, expectations, values, norms, and work routines that influence the ways in which individuals, groups, and teams interact with one another and cooperate to achieve organizational goals.

Personality is a way of understanding why all managers and employees, as individuals, characteristically think and behave in different ways. However, when people belong to the same organization, they often tend to share certain beliefs and values that lead them to act in similar ways.[94] **Organizational culture** comprises the shared set of beliefs, expectations, values, norms, and work routines that influence how members of an organization relate to one another and work together to achieve organizational goals. In essence, organizational culture reflects the distinctive ways organizational members go about performing their jobs and relating to others inside and outside the organization. It may, for example, be a distinctive way in which customers in a particular hotel chain are treated from the time they are greeted at check-in until their stay is completed; or it may be the shared work routines that research teams use to guide new product development. When organizational members share an intense commitment to cultural values, beliefs, and routines and use them to achieve their goals, a *strong* organizational culture exists.[95] When organizational members are not strongly committed to a shared system of values, beliefs, and routines, organizational culture is weak.

The stronger the culture of an organization, the more one can think about it as being the "personality" of an organization because it influences the way its members behave.[96] Organizations that possess strong cultures may differ on a wide variety of dimensions that determine how their members behave toward one another and perform their jobs. For example, organizations differ in terms of how members relate to each other (e.g., formally or informally), how important decisions are made (e.g., top-down or bottom-up), willingness to change (e.g., flexible or unyielding), innovation (e.g., creative or predictable), and playfulness (e.g., serious or serendipitous). In an innovative design firm like IDEO Product Development in Silicon Valley, employees are encouraged to adopt a playful attitude to their work, look outside the organization

Figure 3.8

A Measure of Emotional Intelligence

Please indicate the extent to which you agree or disagree with each of the following items using the 1–7 scale below:

1	2	3	4	5	6	7
Totally disagree	Disagree	Somewhat disagree	Neither agree nor disagree	Somewhat agree	Agree	Totally agree

____ **1.** I have a good sense of why I have certain feelings most of the time.

____ **2.** I always know my friends' emotions from their behavior.

____ **3.** I always set goals for myself and then try my best to achieve them.

____ **4.** I am able to control my temper so that I can handle difficulties rationally.

____ **5.** I have a good understanding of my own emotions.

____ **6.** I am a good observer of others' emotions.

____ **7.** I always tell myself I am a competent person.

____ **8.** I am quite capable of controlling my own emotions.

____ **9.** I really understand what I feel.

___ **10.** I am sensitive to the feelings and emotions of others.

___ **11.** I am a self-motivating person.

___ **12.** I can always calm down quickly when I am very angry.

___ **13.** I always know whether or not I am happy.

___ **14.** I have good understanding of the emotions of people around me.

___ **15.** I would always encourage myself to try my best.

___ **16.** I have good control of my own emotions.

Scoring: Self-emotions appraisal = sum of items 1, 5, 9, 13
Others-emotions appraisal = sum of items 2, 6, 10, 14
Use of emotion = sum of items 3, 7, 11, 15
Regulation of emotion = sum of items 4, 8, 12, 16

Source: K. Law, C. Wong, and L. Song, "The Construct and Criterion Validity of Emotional Intelligence and its Potential Utility for Management Studies," *Journal of Applied Psychology* 89, no. 3 (June 2004), 496; C. S. Wong and K. S. Law, "The Effects of Leader and Follower Emotional Intelligence on Performance and Attitude: An Exploratory Study," *Leadership Quarterly* 13 (2002), 243–74.

to find inspiration, and adopt a flexible approach toward product design that uses multiple perspectives.[97] IDEO's culture is vastly different from that of companies such as Citibank and ExxonMobil, in which employees treat each other in a more formal or deferential way, employees are expected to adopt a serious approach to their work, and decision making is constrained by the hierarchy of authority.

Managers and Organizational Culture

While all members of an organization can contribute to the development and maintenance of organizational culture, managers play a particularly important part in influencing organizational culture,[98] given their multiple and important roles (see Chapter 1). How managers create culture is most vividly evident in start-ups of new companies. Entrepreneurs who start their own companies are typically also the start-ups' top

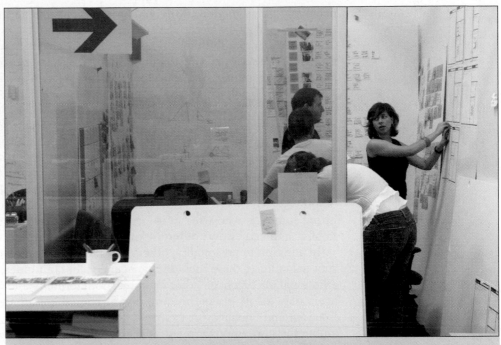

IDEO employees brainstorming—informal communication, casual attire, and flexibility are all hallmarks of this organization.

managers until the companies grow and/or become profitable. Often referred to as the firms' founders, these managers literally create their organizations' cultures.

Often, the founders' personal characteristics play an important role in the creation of organizational culture. Benjamin Schneider, a well-known management researcher, developed a model that helps to explain the role that founders' personal characteristics play in determining organizational culture.[99] His model, called the **attraction-selection-attrition (ASA) framework,** posits that when founders hire employees for their new ventures, they tend to be attracted to and choose employees whose personalities are similar to their own.[100] These similar employees are more likely to stay with the organization. While employees who are dissimilar in personality might be hired, they are more likely to leave the organization over time.[101] As a result of these attraction, selection, and attrition processes, people in the organization tend to have similar personalities, and the typical or dominant personality profile of organizational members determines and shapes organizational culture.[102]

For example, when David Kelley became interested in engineering and product design challenges in the late 1970s, he realized that who he was as a person meant that he would not be happy working in the typical corporate environment. Kelley is high on openness to experience, driven to go where his interests take him, and not content to follow others' directives. Kelley recognized that he needed to start his own business and, with the help of other Stanford-schooled engineers and design experts, IDEO was born.[103]

From the start, IDEO's culture has embodied Kelley's spirited, freewheeling approach to work and design—from colorful and informal work spaces to an emphasis on networking and communicating with as many people as possible to understand a design problem. No project or problem is too big or too small for IDEO: The company designed the Apple Lisa computer and mouse (the precursor of the Mac) and the Palm as well as the Crest Neat Squeeze toothpaste dispenser and the Racer's Edge water bottle.[104] Kelley hates rules, job titles, big corner offices, and all the other trappings of large traditional organizations that stifle creativity. Employees who are attracted to, selected by, and remain with IDEO value creativity and innovation and embrace one of IDEO's mottos: "Fail often to succeed sooner."[105]

While ASA processes are most evident in small firms such as IDEO, they also can operate in large companies.[106] According to the ASA model, this is a naturally

attraction-selection-attrition (ASA) framework A model that explains how personality may influence organizational culture.

occurring phenomenon to the extent that managers and new hires are free to make the kinds of choices the model specifies. While people tend to get along well with others who are similar to themselves, too much similarity in an organization can actually impair organizational effectiveness. That is, similar people tend to view conditions and events in similar ways and thus can be resistant to change. Moreover, organizations benefit from a diversity of perspectives rather than similarity in perspectives (see Chapter 4). At IDEO, Kelley recognized early on how important it is to take advantage of the diverse talents and perspectives that people with different personalities, backgrounds, experiences, and education can bring to a design team. Hence, IDEO's design teams include not only engineers but others who might have a unique insight into a problem, such as anthropologists, communications experts, doctors, and users of a product. When new employees are hired at IDEO, they meet with many employees who have different backgrounds and characteristics—the focus is not on hiring someone who will "fit in" but, rather, on hiring someone who has something to offer and can "wow" different kinds of people with his or her insights.[107]

In addition to personality, other personal characteristics of managers shape organizational culture; these include managers' values, attitudes, moods and emotions, and emotional intelligence.[108] For example, both terminal and instrumental values of managers play a role in determining organizational culture. Managers who highly value freedom and equality, for example, might be more likely to stress the importance of autonomy and empowerment in their organizations, as well as fair treatment for all. As another example, managers who highly value being helpful and forgiving may not only be tolerant of mistakes but also be prone to emphasize the importance of organizational members' being kind and helpful to one another.

Managers who are satisfied with their jobs, are committed to their organizations, and experience positive moods and emotions might also encourage these attitudes and feelings in others. The result would be an organizational culture emphasizing positive attitudes and feelings. Research suggests that attitudes like job satisfaction and organizational commitment can be affected by the influence of others. Managers are in a particularly strong position to engage in social influence given their multiple roles. Moreover, research suggests that moods and emotions can be "contagious" and that spending time with people who are excited and enthusiastic can increase one's own levels of excitement and enthusiasm.

The Role of Values and Norms in Organizational Culture

Shared terminal and instrumental values play a particularly important role in organizational culture. *Terminal values* signify what an organization and its employees are trying to accomplish, and *instrumental values* guide the ways in which the organization and its members achieve organizational goals. In addition to values, shared norms also are a key aspect of organizational culture. Recall that norms are unwritten, informal rules or guidelines that prescribe appropriate behavior in particular situations. For example, norms at IDEO include not being critical of others' ideas, coming up with multiple ideas before settling on one, and developing prototypes of new products.[109]

Managers determine and shape organizational culture through the kinds of values and norms they promote in an organization. Some managers, like David Kelley of IDEO, cultivate values and norms that encourage risk taking, creative responses to problems and opportunities, experimentation, tolerance of failure in order to succeed, and autonomy.[110] Top managers at organizations such as Microsoft and Google encourage employees to adopt such values to support their commitment to innovation as a source of competitive advantage.

Other managers, however, might cultivate values and norms that indicate to employees that they should always be conservative and cautious in their dealings with others and should try to consult with their superiors before making important decisions or any changes to the status quo. Accountability for actions and decisions is stressed, and detailed records are kept to ensure that policies and procedures are followed. In settings where caution is needed—nuclear power stations, large oil refineries, chemical

Figure 3.9
Factors that Maintain and Transmit Organizational Culture

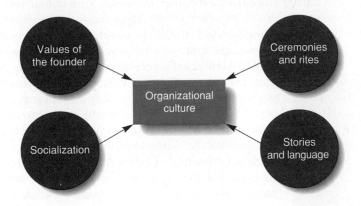

plants, financial institutions, insurance companies—a conservative, cautious approach to making decisions might be highly appropriate.[111] In a nuclear power plant, for example, the catastrophic consequences of a mistake make a high level of supervision vital. Similarly, in a bank or mutual fund company, the risk of losing investors' money makes a cautious approach to investing highly appropriate.

Managers of different kinds of organizations deliberately cultivate and develop the organizational values and norms that are best suited to their task and general environments, strategy, or technology. Organizational culture is maintained and transmitted to organizational members through the values of the founder, the process of socialization, ceremonies and rites, and stories and language (see Figure 3.9).

VALUES OF THE FOUNDER   From the ASA model discussed above, it is clear that founders of an organization can have profound and long-lasting effects on organizational culture. Founders' values inspire the founders to start their own companies and, in turn, drive the nature of these new companies and their defining characteristics. Thus, an organization's founder and his or her terminal and instrumental values have a substantial influence on the values, norms, and standards of behavior that develop over time within the organization.[112] Founders set the scene for the way cultural values and norms develop because their own values guide the building of the company and they hire other managers and employees who they believe will share these values and help the organization to attain them. Moreover, new managers quickly learn from the founder what values and norms are appropriate in the organization and thus what is desired of them. Subordinates imitate the style of the founder and, in turn, transmit their values and norms to their subordinates. Gradually, over time, the founder's values and norms permeate the organization, as has been the case at PAETEC Communications profiled in the following "Manager as a Person."[113]

**Manager as
a Person**

PAETEC's Caring Culture

PAETEC Communications is a broadband telecommunications company that provides local, long distance, and Internet services in 52 markets across the United States.[114] Founded in 1998, PAETEC's growth and ongoing success are a tribute to the values of its five founders and the culture they created.[115] In particular, Arunas Chesonis, one of the founders and its current chairman and

CEO, ensures that PAETEC's values are upheld by using them to guide the way he manages on a day-to-day basis. The four core values of PAETEC are "a caring culture, open communication, unmatched service, and personalized solutions."[116] The ways in which these values are enacted on a daily basis result in a satisfied, motivated, and loyal workforce whose members have developed a unique and distinct approach to the way they perform their jobs.[117]

PAETEC founder and current CEO Arunas Chesonis believes that when a company takes good care of its employees, they will take good care of their customers.

An overarching principle at PAETEC is that people—employees and customers—come first.[118] Chesonis believes that when a company takes good care of its employees, they will take good care of their customers.[119] Chesonis believes in helping employees attain a well-balanced and prosperous work and family life, providing them with deserved recognition and admiration, and fostering open communication and helping behavior.[120] Chesonis also believes that all employees should be treated with respect and as equals. Managers at PAETEC do not receive special perks, and pay differentials between managers and nonmanagers are deliberately kept relatively low. In recognition of its commitment to its employees and ethical action, PAETEC received the American Business Ethics Award for midsize companies in 2005.[121]

Chesonis also nurtures a culture of care, cooperation, and open communication in which every employee voluntarily offers help when it is needed.[122] Employees are expected to share their knowledge, and Chesonis strives to eliminate boundaries between departments and units. True to this culture, Chesonis has a companywide conference call every two weeks in which he shares up-to-date information with employees and solicits and answers their questions. More often than not, the information he conveys is the kind that managers in other companies rarely, if ever, would share with their employees.[123]

He also recognizes that employees at the front line are often in the best position to make suggestions for improvements and develop new services and ways to deliver them. For example, Mike Meath, an employee in the Network Operations Center, came up with the idea of a managed router service whereby companies (i.e., PAETEC's customers) could remotely maintain their customers' voice and data services. Meath presented his idea to his team, the team implemented the idea, and the new service increased revenues by $50,000 in its first six months.[124]

Chesonis's values and PAETEC's culture emphasize putting employees first; this employee-centered approach makes good business sense. Employees at PAETEC really want the company to continue to grow and succeed; they are highly motivated and committed to providing the best service they can to their customers.[125]

A founder who requires a great display of respect from subordinates and insists on proprieties such as formal job titles and formal modes of dress encourages subordinates to act in this way toward their subordinates. Often, a founder's personal values affect an organization's competitive advantage. For example, McDonald's founder Ray Kroc insisted from the beginning on high standards of customer service and cleanliness at McDonald's restaurants; these became core sources of McDonald's competitive advantage. Similarly, Bill Gates, the founder of Microsoft, pioneered certain cultural values in Microsoft. Employees are expected to be creative and to work hard, but they are encouraged to dress informally and to personalize their offices. Gates also established a host of company events such as cookouts, picnics, and sports events to emphasize to employees the importance of being both an individual and a team player.

organizational socialization The process by which newcomers learn an organization's values and norms and acquire the work behaviors necessary to perform jobs effectively.

SOCIALIZATION Over time, organizational members learn from each other which values are important in an organization and the norms that specify appropriate and inappropriate behaviors. Eventually, organizational members behave in accordance with the organization's values and norms—often without realizing they are doing so. **Organizational socialization** is the process by which newcomers learn an organization's values and norms and acquire the work behaviors necessary to perform jobs effectively.[126] As a result of their socialization experiences, organizational members internalize an organization's values and norms and behave in accordance with them not only because they think they have to but because they think that these values and norms describe the right and proper way to behave.[127]

At Texas A&M University, for example, all new students are encouraged to go to "Fish Camp" to learn how to be an "Aggie" (the traditional nickname of students at the university). They learn about the ceremonies that have developed over time to commemorate significant events or people in A&M's history. In addition, they learn how to behave at football games and in class and what it means to be an Aggie. As a result of this highly organized socialization program, by the time new students arrive on campus and start their first semester, they have been socialized into what a Texas A&M student is supposed to do, and they have relatively few problems adjusting to the college environment.

Most organizations have some kind of socialization program to help new employees learn the ropes—the values, norms, and culture of the organization. The military, for example, is well known for the rigorous socialization process it uses to turn raw recruits into trained soldiers. Organizations such as the Walt Disney Company also put new recruits through a rigorous training program to provide them with the knowledge they need not only to perform well in their jobs but also to ensure that each employee plays his or her part in helping visitors to Disneyland have fun in a wholesome theme park. New recruits at Disney are called "cast members" and attend Disney University to learn the Disney culture and their part in it. Disney's culture emphasizes the values of safety, courtesy, entertainment, and efficiency, and these values are brought to life for newcomers at Disney University. Newcomers also learn about the attraction area they will be joining (e.g., Adventureland or Fantasyland) at Disney University and then receive on-the-job socialization in the area itself from experienced cast members.[128] Through organizational socialization, founders and managers of an organization transmit to employees the cultural values and norms that shape the behavior of organizational members. Thus, the values and norms of founder Walt Disney live on today at Disneyland as newcomers are socialized into the Disney way.

The Walt Disney Company sends new 'cast members' through Disney University in order to train them in living out and maintaining the Disney culture in whatever their new roles might be, whether that's Pinocchio or Cinderella.

CEREMONIES AND RITES Another way in which managers can create or influence organizational culture is by developing organizational ceremonies and rites—formal events that recognize incidents of importance to the organization as a whole and to specific employees.[129] The most common rites that organizations use to transmit cultural norms and values to their members are rites of passage, of integration, and of enhancement (see Table 3.1).[130]

Rites of passage determine how individuals enter, advance within, or leave the organization. The socialization programs developed by military organizations (such as the U.S. Army) or by large accountancy and law firms are rites of passage. Likewise, the ways in which an organization prepares people for promotion or retirement are rites of passage.

Table 3.1

Organizational Rites

Type of Rite	Example of Rite	Purpose of Rite
Rite of passage	Induction and basic training	Learn and internalize norms and values
Rite of integration	Office Christmas party	Build common norms and values
Rite of enhancement	Presentation of annual award	Motivate commitment to norms and values

Rites of integration, such as shared announcements of organizational successes, office parties, and company cookouts, build and reinforce common bonds among organizational members. IDEO uses many rites of integration to make its employees feel connected to one another and special. In addition to having wild "end-of-year" celebratory bashes, groups of IDEO employees periodically take time off to go to a sporting event, movie, or meal, or sometimes on a long bike ride or for a sail. These kinds of shared activities not only reinforce IDEO's culture but also can be a source of inspiration on the job (e.g., IDEO has been involved in the making of movies such as *The Abyss* and *Free Willy*). One 35-member design studio at IDEO led by Dennis Boyle has bimonthly lunch fests with no set agenda–anything goes. While enjoying great food, jokes, and camaraderie, studio members often end up sharing ideas for their latest great products, and the freely flowing conversation that results often leads to creative insights.[131]

A company's annual meeting also may be used as a ritual of integration, offering an opportunity to communicate organizational values to managers, other employees, and shareholders. Wal-Mart, for example, makes its annual stockholders' meeting an extravagant ceremony that celebrates the company's success. The company often flies thousands of its highest-performing employees to its annual meeting at its Bentonville, Arkansas, headquarters for a huge weekend entertainment festival complete with performances by country and western stars. Wal-Mart believes that rewarding its supporters with entertainment reinforces the company's high-performance values and culture. The proceedings are shown live over closed-circuit television in all Wal-Mart stores so that all employees can join in the rites celebrating the company's achievements.[132]

Rites of enhancement, such as awards dinners, newspaper releases, and employee promotions, let organizations publicly recognize and reward employees' contributions and thus strengthen their commitment to organizational values. By bonding members within the organization, rites of enhancement reinforce an organization's values and norms.

Stories and language also communicate organizational culture. Stories (whether fact or fiction) about organizational heroes and villains and their actions provide important clues about values and norms. Such stories can reveal the kinds of behaviors that are valued by the organization and the kinds of practices that are frowned on.[133] At the heart of McDonald's rich culture are hundreds of stories that organizational members tell about founder Ray Kroc. Most of these stories focus on how Kroc established the strict operating values and norms that are at the heart of McDonald's culture. Kroc was dedicated to achieving perfection in McDonald's quality, service, cleanliness, and value for money (QSC&V), and these four central values permeate McDonald's culture. For example, an often retold story describes what happened when Kroc and a group of managers from the Houston region were touring various restaurants. One of the restaurants was having a bad day operationally. Kroc was incensed about the long lines of customers, and he was furious when he realized that the product customers were receiving that day was not up to his high standards. To address the problem, he jumped up and stood on the front counter and got the attention of all customers and operating crew personnel. He introduced himself, apologized for the long wait and cold food, and told the customers that they could have freshly cooked food or their money back–whichever they wanted. As a result, the customers left happy, and when

Kroc checked on the restaurant later, he found that his message had gotten through to its managers and crew—performance had improved. Other stories describe Kroc scrubbing dirty toilets and picking up litter inside or outside a restaurant. These and similar stories are spread around the organization by McDonald's employees. They are the stories that have helped establish Kroc as McDonald's "hero."

Because spoken language is a principal medium of communication in organizations, the characteristic slang or jargon—that is, organization-specific words or phrases—that people use to frame and describe events provides important clues about norms and values. "McLanguage," for example, is prevalent at all levels of McDonald's. A McDonald's employee described as having "ketchup in his (or her) blood" is someone who is truly dedicated to the McDonald's way—someone who has been completely socialized to its culture. McDonald's has an extensive training program that teaches new employees "McDonald's speak," and new employees are welcomed into the family with a formal orientation that illustrates Kroc's dedication to QSC&V.

The concept of organizational language encompasses not only spoken language but how people dress, the offices they occupy, the cars they drive, and the degree of formality they use when they address one another. Casual dress reflects and reinforces Microsoft's entrepreneurial culture and values. Formal business attire supports the conservative culture found in many banks, which emphasize the importance of conforming to organizational norms such as respect for authority and staying within one's prescribed role. Traders in the Chicago futures and options trading pits frequently wear garish and flamboyant ties and jackets to make their presence known in a sea of faces. The demand for magenta, lime green, and silver lamé jackets featuring bold images such as the Power Rangers—anything that helps the traders stand out and attract customers—is enormous.[134] When employees speak and understand the language of their organization's culture, they know how to behave in the organization and what is expected of them.

At IDEO, language, dress, the physical work environment, and extreme informality all underscore a culture that is adventuresome, playful, risk taking, egalitarian, and innovative. For example, at IDEO, employees refer to taking the consumers' perspective when designing products as "being left-handed." Employees dress in T-shirts and jeans, the physical work environment is continually evolving and changing depending upon how employees wish to personalize their workspace, no one "owns" a fancy office with a window, and rules are nonexistent.[135]

Culture and Managerial Action

While founders and managers play a critical role in the development, maintenance, and communication of organizational culture, this same culture shapes and controls the behavior of all employees, including managers themselves. For example, culture influences the way managers perform their four main functions: planning, organizing, leading, and controlling. As we consider these functions, we continue to distinguish between top managers who create organizational values and norms that encourage creative, innovative behavior and top managers who encourage a conservative, cautious approach by their subordinates. We noted earlier that both kinds of values and norms can be appropriate depending upon the situation and type of organization.

PLANNING Top managers in an organization with an innovative culture are likely to encourage lower-level managers to participate in the planning process and develop a flexible approach to planning. They are likely to be willing to listen to new ideas and to take risks involving the development of new products. In contrast, top managers in an organization with conservative values are likely to emphasize formal top-down planning. Suggestions from lower-level managers are likely to be subjected to a formal review process, which can significantly slow decision making. Although this deliberate approach may improve the quality of decision making in a nuclear power plant, it can have unintended consequences. In the past, at conservative IBM, the planning process became so formalized that managers spent most of their time assembling complex slide shows and overheads to defend their current positions rather than thinking about what they should be doing to keep IBM abreast of the changes taking place in the computer industry. When former CEO Lou Gerstner took over, he used every means at his disposal to abolish this culture, even building a brand-new campus-style headquarters to change managers' mind-sets. IBM's culture is undergoing further changes initiated by its current CEO, Samuel Palmisano.[136]

ORGANIZING What kinds of organizing will managers in innovative and in conservative cultures encourage? Valuing creativity, managers in innovative cultures are likely to try to create an organic structure, one that is flat, with few levels in the hierarchy, and one in which authority is decentralized so that employees are encouraged to work together to find solutions to ongoing problems. A product team structure may be very suitable for an organization with an innovative culture. In contrast, managers in a conservative culture are likely to create a well-defined hierarchy of authority and establish clear reporting relationships so that employees know exactly whom to report to and how to react to any problems that arise.

LEADING In an innovative culture, managers are likely to lead by example, encouraging employees to take risks and experiment. They are supportive regardless of whether employees succeed or fail. In contrast, managers in a conservative culture are likely to use management by objectives and to constantly monitor subordinates' progress toward goals, overseeing their every move. We examine leadership in detail in Chapter 13 when we consider the leadership styles that managers can adopt to influence and shape employee behavior.

CONTROLLING The ways in which managers evaluate, and take actions to improve, performance differ depending upon whether the organizational culture emphasizes formality and caution or innovation and change. Managers who want to encourage risk taking, creativity, and innovation recognize that there are multiple potential paths to success and that failure must be accepted in order for creativity to thrive. Thus, they are less concerned about employees' performing their jobs in a specific, predetermined manner and in strict adherence to preset goals and more concerned about employees' being flexible and taking the initiative to come up with ideas for improving performance. Managers in innovative cultures are also more concerned about long-run performance than short-term targets because they recognize that real innovation entails much uncertainty that necessitates flexibility. In contrast, managers in cultures that emphasize caution and maintenance of the status quo often set specific, difficult goals for employees, frequently monitor progress toward these goals, and develop a clear set of rules that employees are expected to adhere to.

The values and norms of an organization's culture strongly affect the way managers perform their management functions. The extent to which managers buy into the values and norms of their organization shapes their view of the world and their actions and decisions in particular circumstances.[137] In turn, the actions that managers take can have an impact on the performance of the organization. Thus, organizational culture, managerial action, and organizational performance are all linked together.

This linkage is apparent at Hewlett-Packard (HP), a leader in the electronic instrumentation and computer industries. Established in the 1940s, HP developed a culture that is an outgrowth of the strong personal beliefs of the company's founders, William Hewlett and David Packard. As discussed in Chapter 2, Bill and Dave, as they are known within the company, formalized HP's culture in 1957 in a statement of corporate objectives known as the "HP Way." The basic values informing the HP Way stress serving everyone who has a stake in the company with integrity and fairness, including customers, suppliers, employees, stockholders, and society in general. Bill and Dave helped build this culture within HP by hiring like-minded people and by letting the HP Way guide their own actions as managers.

Although the Hewlett-Packard example and our earlier example of IDEO illustrate how organizational culture can give rise to managerial actions that ultimately benefit the organization, this is not always the case. The cultures of some organizations become dysfunctional, encouraging managerial actions that harm the organization and discouraging actions that might lead to an improvement in performance.[138] Recent corporate scandals at large companies like Enron, Tyco, and WorldCom show how damaging a dysfunctional culture can be to an organization and its members. For example, Enron's arrogant, "success-at-all costs" culture led to fraudulent behavior on the part of its top managers.[139] Unfortunately, hundreds of Enron employees have paid a heavy price for the unethical behavior of these top managers and the dysfunctional organizational culture. Not only have these employees lost their jobs, but many also have lost their life savings in Enron stock and pension funds, which became worth just a fraction of their former value before the wrongdoing at Enron came to light. We discuss ethics and ethical cultures in depth in the next chapter.

Summary and Review

LO1 **ENDURING CHARACTERISTICS: PERSONALITY TRAITS** Personality traits are enduring tendencies to feel, think, and act in certain ways. The Big Five general traits are extraversion, negative affectivity, agreeableness, conscientiousness, and openness to experience. Other personality traits that affect managerial behavior are locus of control, self-esteem, and the needs for achievement, affiliation, and power.

LO 2, 3, 4 **VALUES, ATTITUDES, AND MOODS AND EMOTIONS** A terminal value is a personal conviction about lifelong goals or objectives; an instrumental value is a personal conviction about modes of conduct. Terminal and instrumental values have an impact on what managers try to achieve in their organizations and the kinds of behaviors they engage in. An attitude is a collection of feelings and beliefs. Two attitudes important for understanding managerial behaviors include job satisfaction (the collection of feelings and beliefs that managers have about their jobs) and organizational commitment (the collection of feelings and beliefs that managers have about their organizations). A mood is a feeling or state of mind; emotions are intense feelings that are short-lived and directly linked to their causes. Managers' moods and emotions, or how they feel at work on a day-to-day basis, have the potential to impact not only their own behavior and effectiveness but also those of their subordinates. Emotional intelligence is the ability to understand and manage one's own and other people's moods and emotions.

LO5 **ORGANIZATIONAL CULTURE** Organizational culture is the shared set of beliefs, expectations, values, norms, and work routines that influence how members of an organization relate to one another and work together to achieve organizational goals. Founders of new organizations and managers play an important role in creating and maintaining organizational culture. Organizational socialization is the process by which newcomers learn an organization's values and norms and acquire the work behaviors necessary to perform jobs effectively.

Management in Action

Topics for Discussion and Action

DISCUSSION

1. Discuss why managers who have different types of personalities can be equally effective and successful. [LO1]

2. Can managers be too satisfied with their jobs? Can they be too committed to their organizations? Why or why not? [LO2]

3. Assume that you are a manager of a restaurant. Describe what it is like to work for you when you are in a negative mood. [LO3]

4. Why might managers be disadvantaged by low levels of emotional intelligence? [LO4]

ACTION

5. Interview a manager in a local organization. Ask the manager to describe situations in which he or she is especially likely to act in accordance with his or her values. Ask the manager to describe situations in which he or she is less likely to act in accordance with his or her values. [LO2]

6. Watch a popular television show, and as you watch it, try to determine the emotional intelligence levels of the characters the actors in the show portray. Rank the characters from highest to lowest in terms of emotional intelligence. As you watched the show, what factors influenced your assessments of emotional intelligence levels? [LO4]

7. Go to an upscale clothing store in your neighborhood, and go to a clothing store that is definitely not upscale. Observe the behavior of employees in each store as well as the store's environment. In what ways are the organizational cultures in each store similar? In what ways are they different? [LO5]

Building Management Skills [LO5]
Diagnosing Culture

Think about the culture of the last organization you worked for, your current university, or another organization or club to which you belong. Then, answer the following questions:

1. What values are emphasized in this culture?

2. What norms do members of this organization follow?

3. Who seems to have played an important role in creating the culture?

4. In what ways is the organizational culture communicated to organizational members.

Managing Ethically [LO 1, 2]

Some organizations rely on personality and interest inventories to screen potential employees. Other organizations attempt to screen employees by using paper-and-pencil honesty tests.

Questions

1. Either individually or in a group, think about the ethical implications of using personality and interest inventories to screen potential employees. How might this practice be unfair to potential applicants? How might organizational members who are in charge of hiring misuse it?

2. Because of measurement error and validity problems, some relatively trustworthy people may "fail" an honesty test given by an employer. What are the ethical implications of trustworthy people "failing" honesty tests, and what obligations do you think employers should have when relying on honesty tests for screening purposes?

Small Group Breakout Exercise [LO 2, 3, 4, 5]
Making Difficult Decisions in Hard Times

Form groups of three or four people, and appoint one member as the spokesperson who will communicate your findings to the whole class when called on by the instructor. Then discuss the following scenario:

You are on the top-management team of a medium-size company that manufactures cardboard boxes, containers, and other cardboard packaging materials. Your company is facing increasing levels of competition for major corporate customer accounts, and profits have declined significantly. You have tried everything you can to cut costs and remain competitive, with the exception of laying off employees. Your company has had a no-layoff policy for the past 20 years, and you believe it is an important part of the organization's culture. However, you are experiencing mounting pressure to increase your firm's performance, and your no-layoff policy has been questioned by shareholders. Even though you haven't decided whether to lay off employees and thus break with a 20-year tradition for your company, rumors are rampant in your organization that something is afoot, and employees are worried. You are meeting today to address this problem.

1. Develop a list of options and potential courses of action to address the heightened competition and decline in profitability that your company has been experiencing.

2. Choose your preferred course of action, and justify why you will take this route.

3. Describe how you will communicate your decision to employees.

4. If your preferred option involves a layoff, justify why. If it doesn't involve a layoff, explain why.

Exploring the World Wide Web [LO 1, 2, 5]

Go to IDEO's Web site (www.ideo.com) and read about this company. Try to find indicators of IDEO's culture that are provided on the Web site. How does the design of the Web site itself, and the pictures and words it contains, communicate the nature of IDEO's organizational culture? What kinds of people do you think would be attracted to IDEO? What kinds of people do you think would be likely to be dissatisfied with a job at IDEO?

Be the Manager [LO 1, 2, 3, 4, 5]

You have recently been hired as the vice president for human resources in an advertising agency. One of the problems that has been brought to your attention is the fact that in the creative departments at the agency, there are dysfunctionally high levels of conflict. You have spoken with members of each of these departments, and in each one it seems that there are a few members of the department who are creating all the problems. All of these individuals are valued contributors who have many creative ad campaigns to their credit. The very high levels of conflict are creating problems in the departments, and negative moods and emotions are much more prevalent than positive feelings. What are you going to do to both retain valued employees and alleviate the excessive conflict and negative feelings in these departments?

BusinessWeek Case in the News [LO 1, 2, 3, 4]

The Blogging Czar of Moscow

Andrew Paulson has a knack for spinning chance encounters with the rich and famous into business opportunities. In the late '80s the New Haven native carved out a career as a fashion photographer after rubbing elbows with designers and models at parties in Paris. In 1993, Paulson was invited to Moscow for a shindig put on by Russian baritone Dmitri Hvorostovsky, where he met the editor of a local business magazine. Shortly thereafter he moved to Moscow to run the monthly for its French publisher. Then, in 2005, Paulson ran into reclusive Russian banker Alexander Mamut at a Moscow dinner. The two got to talking over the meal, and soon Mamut agreed to bankroll an Internet venture Paulson was hoping to launch.

Together the pair founded a company called SUP-Fabrik with an eye toward assembling a network of online businesses. In December, SUP scored a coup when it bought LiveJournal, a blogging and social networking Web site owned by Six Apart, a San Francisco software developer—the largest-ever takeover of a U.S. Net outfit by a Russian company. Moscow media reports say SUP paid about $30 million for LiveJournal, although Paulson declines to disclose the figures.

Why the interest? LiveJournal is a bit player in the U.S., with about 3 million users there, compared with industry leader Blogger's 35 million. But in Russia it was the No. 4 Web site overall and tops in blogging, with 8 million unique visitors monthly. Today, the term *"zhe-zhe"* (short for *"Zhivoy Zhurnal,"* or *"LiveJournal"* in Russian) is a synonym for blog. "The fourth-largest site in Russia belonged to a company in San Francisco that had done nothing to bring this level of prominence," says Paulson, 49. "They really had no idea how it got there."

Paulson discovered LiveJournal's Russian popularity in 2006. That October, he signed a licensing agreement to manage the site's Russian-language pages. Under Paulson and SUP, visitors in Russia jumped by 80% last year. This year, he predicts, they will climb an additional 60%. Paulson doesn't rule out more acquisitions, but he hopes to use LiveJournal to attract users to SUP's other ventures, such as sports site Championat.ru.

First, though, SUP's president will have to quell an uprising in Russia's blogosphere. The LiveJournal deal sparked outrage among many Russian users, who thought they smelled a Kremlin plot to silence debate in advance of presidential elections on Mar. 2. With LiveJournal headquartered in Moscow, bloggers say, it will be easier for the security services to keep tabs on political malcontents. "LiveJournal. . .is the only platform for free speech in Russia," so the Kremlin "had something to fear," a blogger who uses the handle "halph" wrote. But Paulson brushes aside such concerns. "Judge us by our actions," he says. Since SUP took over the Russian pages, "we've had no problems."

Paulson oversees his growing empire from a penthouse office with panoramic views in Moscow's Smolenskaya district. Stepping out of the elevator into the 15th-floor lobby, the first thing you see is an Andy Warhol print of a Campbell's soup can, a play on the company's name. (SUP, which stands for Single User Portal, is also the Russian word for "soup.") The son of a Johns Hopkins University literature professor, Paulson graduated from Yale with a degree in French literature in 1981. "Everybody started going to business school and law school chasing vast fortunes in various stock market ups and downs," he says disdainfully. That wasn't the life for Paulson, who instead escaped to Paris to write novels. (He was "far too shy" to publish them.) He paid the bills by returning to New York for three months a year to work 100-hour weeks as a typist at law firms.

After breaking into the fashion world, taking photos for the likes of Yves Saint Laurent and Paco Rabanne, in 1992 he founded an ad agency that he called Pourriture Noble, or Noble Rot. Then in 1994, after moving to Moscow to run *Deloviye Ludi,* Russia's first full-color business magazine, he launched business and entertainment publications of his own that all quickly failed. It wasn't until 1999 that he got the formula right with *Afisha (Notice),* a biweekly guide to Moscow's cultural life. The timing was perfect. Nightlife in Moscow was taking off as the country emerged from an economic crisis, and *Afisha* quickly became the best-selling magazine in Russia. Paulson sold *Afisha* in 2005 to Prof-Media, a publisher owned by metals magnate Vladimir Potanin.

With the proceeds, he decided to start some sort of online venture. He didn't know exactly what he wanted to do but saw that the Russian Internet was "growing at an incredible rate based on two things: broadband penetration and the possibility to make real money, a solid business." But why gobble up the rest of LiveJournal, as SUP did, including its U.S. portion? In part, Paulson was worried that Six Apart might sell LiveJournal. A new owner, he figured, could complicate the lucrative deal SUP had managing the site's Russian pages. But just as important, Paulson believed, SUP had a global perspective that would help it expand the site into other countries. "Silicon Valley," he says, "is ignoring the rest of the world."

Questions for Discussion

1. What personality traits do you think Andrew Paulson is high on? Why?

2. What personality traits do you think he is low on? Why?

3. What terminal values do you think are relatively important to him? Why?

4. What instrumental values do you think are relatively important to him? Why?

Source: Jason Bush, "The Blogging Czar Of Moscow." Reprinted from the February 25, 2008, issue of *BusinessWeek* by special permission. Copyright © 2008 by The McGraw-Hill Companies, Inc.

BusinessWeek **Case in the News** [LO 2, 5]

Young and Impatient in India

Ravikiran's parents took the safe route. In post-colonial India, even though they had college degrees, they chose low-paying but secure government jobs. Today, they live with their three sons in a modest concrete house in a working-class section of Bangalore. While colorful paintings of Hindu gods adorn their walls, the furniture is mostly plastic chairs and steel cots. For Ravikiran M.S., their oldest son, security and stability simply aren't enough. The 24-year-old programmer is brimming with ambition. He rides a motorbike to work and hopes to buy a car. And he expects quick promotions, dreaming of becoming a CEO. "I want the posh life," he declares.

Ravikiran is typical of India's in-a-hurry younger generation. With the tech-services boom, the country's college grads are coming of age in a time of economic optimism, and unlike their parents and grandparents, this group has vibrant job prospects and high hopes. The challenge for companies is to harness their energy while reining in inflated expectations. If these young people feel they're being short-changed in terms of either salary or advancement, the best and brightest will find work elsewhere, shift careers, or leave the country. "It's a very different generation," says S. Gopalakrishnan, chief executive of Indian tech giant Infosys Technologies. "They want immediate rewards."

Proving Ground

This pattern will be repeated in other emerging nations as prosperity spreads. So India is becoming a proving ground for managing the global workforce, with companies developing new schemes to keep the younger generation engaged. The likes of MindTree Consulting, Infosys, and IBM have revamped their orientation programs to better engage young people, tapped men and women under 30 to serve on management committees, and launched mini-MBA programs for eager young managers. "India is going to be a lab for lessons that we'll apply to other countries," says Lyndon Rego, manager of innovation at the Center for Creative Leadership in Greensboro, N.C., which develops leadership training programs in emerging markets.

The challenge for companies is to address both the desires and frustrations of the younger generation. These become abundantly evident in the cafés and bars of Bangalore. As the city has developed into India's Silicon Valley, it also has become the country's bar-hopping capital. "We need capitalism with a human face," says P.B. Devaiah, a 20-year-old industrial engineering major at a local college. Sitting with friends at Java City, a crowded coffee shop, he complains that much of the programming in India is the equivalent of sweatshop labor, where new hires are expected to spend as much as 12 hours a day writing code. "We're being used as machines," Devaiah says.

When the conversation turns to social issues, India's young people are likely to erupt in grousing about arranged marriage, the caste system, and interactions with Westerners—all of which should concern employers. Caste attitudes, for instance, clash with merit-based corporate values, and young techies sometimes feel they're treated poorly by American and European clients. "We're not Martians. We're human beings," says a young woman engineer at a Bangalore tech firm.

One of the biggest concerns is the changing role of women. The tech industry was once almost exclusively male, but by last year about 35% of employees were women. Nasscom, the software industry trade group, says that will rise to 45% by 2010. The rise of women in tech has taken companies by surprise, and they're scrambling to react. At software and research outfit MindTree, for instance, 40% of new hires last fall were female, compared with just 23% of the company's overall workforce of 5,500. And these young women tend to be more outspoken than their male counterparts. At MindTree, a council run by a top female scientist now addresses gender issues.

"They Have To Learn To Adjust"
Veena Parashuram is one of this new generation of Indian women. The 26-year-old engineer grew up in a village so primitive that she never used a spoon, fork, or napkin until she went away to boarding school at age 10. When a teacher told her girls could become anything they wanted, "my mind opened up," she says. Although her parents wanted her to submit to an arranged marriage and settle in their village, she went to engineering school in Bangalore and the Netherlands, where she met a German man. The couple married to ease the difficulties of getting work permits, but Parashuram says "the concept of marriage is pretty weird." While she's planning a traditional Indian wedding, she says, she doesn't "like to follow rules that were set down hundreds of years ago."

Companies are starting to coddle this new generation from Day One, helping to smooth the transition between school and work. MindTree, for instance, revamped its initiation process because young hires felt "they

got lost in a sea of people," says HR chief Puneet Jetli. Under the new program, called Orchard, each new hire is placed in one of three groups called "houses" and assigned to a manager called a PAL, or "parent, anchor, and leader." The company redesigned an entire floor of a Bangalore building to give each house an assembly space, lockers, and classrooms. On a recent visit, a small group clustered around a young man strumming a guitar and singing *Hotel California*. The houses begin and end their days in these rooms with meetings and the occasional Q&A with a top MindTree executive. "The senior people at MindTree are very caring," says Deepthi R. Halbhavi, a young woman who completed the eight-week induction program last fall. "They treat us like we're their children."

Still, there are plenty of tensions between companies and young employees. Many Indian engineers are fascinated with cutting-edge technologies, yet much of the work for clients calls for tried-and-true techniques. And while young people are eager to get promotions and overseas assignments, there are practical limits to how quickly they can advance. "They have to learn to adjust," says T.V. Mohandas Pai, director of human resources at Infosys. "It's almost like growing up."

It's also a two-way street. Infosys executives understand that they can't simply empathize with their young employees, but must also learn from them. So Infosys set up something called the Voice of Youth Council: a dozen people under 30 who sit on the executive management committee, which deals with business strategy and HR policies. The youth contingent was instrumental in establishing a program for spotting and nurturing innovation. Being in the group is "very empowering," says Bela Gupta, 24, the council's youngest member.

While not every ambitious young Indian will sit on a management coun-

cil or become a boss, there's huge pressure on companies to identify and train those with leadership potential. Facing a shortage of competent managers, IBM last year devised an in-house mini-MBA, called ProPel, aimed at keeping hungry recruits on board and giving them the training they need to oversee a growing staff. The program consists of testing, seminars, on-the-job training, databases for sharing the tricks of the trade, and e-mail quizzes about the appropriate response to workplace problems.

The program might be a good match for the likes of Ravikiran, the Bangalore programmer who wants a "posh life" as an executive. He got a master's degree in computer applications before going to work a year ago at software shop Torry Harris Business Solutions. When Ravikiran's father landed a job in the government engineering office, he stuck around for 37 years. Ravikiran, by contrast, is already plotting his next career move. "I don't want to be lost in the crowd," he vows. "I envision a path, and I go for it."

Questions for Discussion

1. What values are especially important to young professionals in India?

2. How are companies and managers in India attempting to help young professionals achieve their values?

3. What factors are likely to contribute to job satisfaction and organizational commitment among young professionals in India?

4. What kinds of organizational cultures are likely to be especially appealing to them?

CHAPTER 4

Ethics and Social Responsibility

After studying this chapter, you should be able to:

LO1 Explain the relationship between ethics and the law.

LO2 Differentiate between the claims of the different stakeholder groups that are affected by managers and their companies' actions.

LO3 Describe four rules that can be used to help companies and their managers act in ethical ways.

LO4 Discuss why it is important for managers to behave ethically.

LO5 Identify the four main sources of managerial ethics.

LO6 Distinguish between the four main approaches toward social responsibility that a company can take.

A MANAGER'S CHALLENGE

The Ethics of the Global Flower-Growing Business

How do ethics guide managers decisions? Every year on Valentine's Day tens of millions of roses are delivered to sweethearts and loved ones in the United States, and anyone who has bought roses knows that their price has been dropping. One of the main reasons for this is that global rose growing is now concentrated in poorer countries in Central and South America and Africa. Rose growing has been a boon to poor countries, where the extra income women earn can mean the difference between starving or eating for their families. Ecuador, for example, is the fourth-biggest rose-growing nation in the world, and the industry employs over 50,000 women who tend, pick, and package roses for wages above the nation's national minimum. Most of these women are employed by Rosas del Ecuador, the company that controls the rose business in that country.

The hidden side of the global rose-growing business is that poorer countries tend to have lax or unenforced health and safety laws—a major reason why they have lower rose-growing costs. And, industry-watchers argue, many rose-growing companies and countries are *not* considering the well-being of their workers; neither are

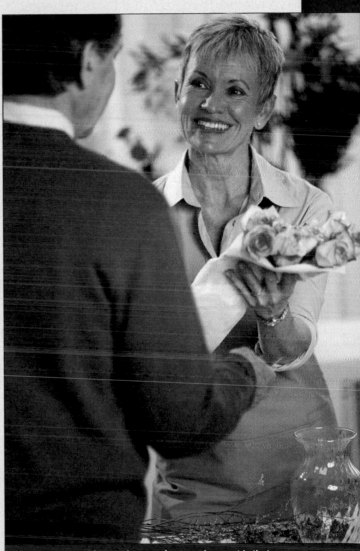

What you may not know when purchasing a bouquet is that many workers on flower-growing farms in poorer countries are often subjected to unsafe working conditions that may harm their health. However, a new generation of florists is putting pressure on these companies to act fairly, refrain from retaliation, and allow third-party inspections to improve working conditions.

the companies around the world that distribute and sell roses to customers. For example, the CEO of Rosas del Ecuador, Erwin Pazmino, denies that workers are subjected to unsafe working conditions. Almost 60% of his workers have reported blurred vision, nausea, headaches, asthma, and other symptoms of pesticide poisoning, however.[1] Workers labor in hot, poorly ventilated greenhouses in which roses have been sprayed with pesticides and herbicides. Safety equipment such as masks and ventilators is scarce, and the long hours women work adds to chemical overexposure. If workers complain, they may be fired and blacklisted, which makes it very hard for them to find other jobs. So, to protect their families' well-being, workers rarely complain and thus their health remains at risk. Given the lack of protest, companies that buy the roses it produces are therefore often unaware of the conditions under which they are produced.

Increasingly in the 2000s, however, government agencies and ethical consumer "watchdogs" in Europe, Japan, and the United States have been reporting the working conditions under which roses are grown, and the possible health risks for both workers and consumers from flowers that have been treated with herbicides. As a result, rose buyers the world over are becoming increasingly aware of the need to know about the conditions under which roses are grown when deciding what brand of roses to buy—which company and country they come from, for example. As a result, the managers who run the companies that are the main buyers and distributors of flowers in countries such as the United States have become increasingly concerned with regulating the conditions under which roses are grown and the well-being of the workers who grow them.

In the United States one result of this concern has been the creation of VeriFlora, managed by Scientific Certification Systems, which has developed a highly regarded certification system for sustainable flowers, based on various environmental and social responsibility categories.[2] Some large companies such as Sierra Flower Trading, Canada's largest floral distributor, have adopted VeriFlora's standards, as have some small U.S. companies such as California Organic Flowers, Diamond Organics, and Flowerbud.com. Large U.S. flower distributors such as FTD and flowers.com have been slower to adopt these standards, however, because of increasing competition between bricks and mortar and virtual flower companies for U.S. customers' business, which is often based on which seller has the lowest price.[3]

However, the increasing global attention to the conditions under which flowers are grown around the world has encouraged more and more major flower growers in countries such as Eucador, Columbia, and Kenya to adopt social and environmental standards that comply with the demands of consumers in countries around the world for flowers that are grown "ethically" with a concern for the health and well-being of all people concerned. For example, Colombia's flower industry earns $1 billion a year from its flower exports to countries such as the United States. To protect its exports major Columbian flower companies have adopted Florverde®, a national program that guarantees that flowers grown in Columbia comply with 165 social and environmental criteria, including commitments to seal off growing areas recently sprayed by pesticides and to avoid the use of pesticides in the future, and that impose a maximum working week of 48 hours with no more than 12 hours overtime for workers. Since 2003, 25% of Colombian flower farms have received a Florverde certificate and a further 17% are on track to receive one; the result has been that in 2008, 300 million of the billion stems exported to U.S. supermarkets and other buyers for Valentine's Day have met Florverde standards. Florverde's success has inspired similar programs in other countries such as Ecuador and Kenya.[4] Clearly, when nations and their citizens use ethical and "green" environmental standards to guide their behavior, they can influence the ethics of other countries around the globe.

Overview

As the story of global rose growing and selling suggests, an ethical dimension is present in most kinds of management decision making that involve the production and sale of products—be they flowers, cars, or fast food—because their decisions affect people's well-being. But globally, nations, companies, and managers often differ enormously in their commitment to these people, or *stakeholders*—various groups of people who may benefit or be harmed by the way managers make decisions that affect them. Managers of some companies make the need to behave ethically toward stakeholders their main priority. Managers of other companies pursue their own self-interest at the expense of their stakeholders and do harm to them—such as the harm done to the millions of people around the world who work in dangerous, unsanitary conditions, or who do so for a pittance.

In this chapter, we examine the nature of the obligations and responsibilities of managers and the companies they work for toward the people and society that are affected by their actions. First, we examine the nature of ethics and the sources of ethical problems. Second, we discuss the major stakeholder groups that are affected by the way companies operate. Third, we look at four rules or guidelines that managers can use to decide whether a specific business decision is ethical or unethical. Finally, we consider the sources of managerial ethics and the reasons why it is important for a company to behave in a socially responsible manner. By the end of this chapter you will understand the central role that ethics plays in shaping the practice of management and the life of a people, society, and nation.

The Nature of Ethics

Suppose you see a person being mugged in the street. How will you behave? Will you act in some way to help, even though you risk being hurt? Will you walk away? Perhaps you might adopt a "middle way" and not intervene but call the police? Does the way you act depend on whether the person being mugged is a fit male, an elderly person, or even a street person? Does it depend on whether there are other people around, so you can tell yourself, "Oh well, someone else will help or call the police. I don't need to"?

Ethical Dilemmas

ethical dilemma The quandary people find themselves in when they have to decide if they should act in a way that might help another person or group even though doing so might go against their own self-interest.

The situation described above is an example of an **ethical dilemma,** the quandary people find themselves in when they have to decide if they should act in a way that might help another person or group, and is the "right" thing to do, even though doing so might go against their own self-interest.[5] A dilemma may also arise when a person has to decide between two different courses of action, knowing that whichever course he or she chooses will result in harm to one person or group even while it may benefit another. The ethical dilemma here is to decide which course of action is the "lesser of two evils."

People often know they are confronting an ethical dilemma when their moral scruples come into play and cause them to hesitate, debate, and reflect upon the "rightness" or "goodness" of a course of action. Moral scruples are thoughts and feelings that tell a person what is right or wrong; they are a part of a person's ethics. **Ethics** are the inner-guiding moral principles, values, and beliefs that people use to analyze or interpret a situation and then decide what is the "right" or appropriate way to behave. At the same time, ethics also indicate what is inappropriate behavior and how a person should behave to avoid doing harm to another person.

The essential problem in dealing with ethical issues, and thus solving moral dilemmas, is that there are no absolute or indisputable rules or principles that can be developed to decide if an action is ethical or unethical. Put simply, different people or groups may dispute which actions are ethical or unethical depending on their own personal self-interest and specific attitudes, beliefs, and values—concepts we discussed in Chapter 3. How, therefore, are we and companies and their managers and employees to decide what is ethical and so act appropriately toward other people and groups?

Ethics and the Law

The first answer to this question is that society as a whole, using the political and legal process, can lobby for and pass laws that specify what people can and cannot do. Many different kinds of laws exist to govern business, for example, laws against fraud and deception and laws governing how companies can treat their employees and customers. Laws also specify what sanctions or punishments will follow if those laws are broken. Different groups in society lobby for which laws should be passed based on their own personal interests and beliefs with regard to what is right or wrong. The group that can summon most support is able to pass the laws that most closely align with its interests and beliefs. Once a law is passed, a decision about what the appropriate behavior is with regard to a person or situation is taken from the personally determined ethical realm to the societally determined legal realm. If you do not conform to the law, you can be prosecuted; and if you are found guilty of breaking the law, you can be punished. You have little say in the matter; your fate is in the hands of the court and its lawyers.

In studying the relationship between ethics and law, it is important to understand that *neither laws nor ethics are fixed principles,* cast in stone, which do not change over time. Ethical beliefs alter and change as time passes, and as they do so, laws change to reflect the changing ethical beliefs of a society. It was seen as ethical, and it was legal, for example, to acquire and possess slaves in ancient Rome and Greece and in the United States until the late 19th century. Ethical views regarding whether slavery was morally right or appropriate changed, however. Slavery was made illegal in the United States when those in power decided that slavery degraded the very meaning of being human. Slavery is a statement about the value or worth of human beings and about their right to life, liberty, and the pursuit of happiness. And if I deny these rights to other people, how then can I claim to have any natural or "god-given" rights to these things myself?

Moreover, what is to stop any person or group that becomes powerful enough to take control of the political and legal process from enslaving me and denying me the right to be free and to own property? In denying freedom to others, one risks losing it oneself, just as stealing from others opens the door for them to steal from me in return. "Do unto others as you would have them do unto you" is a commonly used ethical or moral rule that people apply in such situations to decide what is the right thing to do. This moral rule is discussed in detail below.

ethics The inner-guiding moral principles, values, and beliefs that people use to analyze or interpret a situation and then decide what is the "right" or appropriate way to behave.

LO1 Explain the relationship between ethics and the law.

Changes in Ethics over Time

There are many types of behavior—such as murder, theft, slavery, rape, driving while intoxicated—that most, if not all, people currently believe are totally unacceptable and unethical and should therefore be illegal. There are also, however, many other kinds of actions and behaviors whose ethical nature is open to dispute. Some people might believe that a particular behavior—for example, smoking tobacco or possessing guns—is unethical and so should be made illegal. Others might argue that it is up to the individual or a group to decide if such behaviors are ethical or not and thus whether a particular behavior should remain legal.

Coldbath Fields Prison, London, circa 1810. The British criminal justice system around this time was quite severe: There were over 350 different crimes for which a person could be executed, including sheep stealing. Thankfully in this case, as ethical beliefs change over time, so do laws.

As ethical beliefs change over time, some people may begin to question whether existing laws that make specific behaviors illegal are still appropriate today. They might argue that although a specific behavior is deemed illegal, this does not make it unethical and thus the law should be changed. In the United States, for example, it is illegal to possess or use marijuana (cannabis). To justify this law, it is commonly argued that smoking marijuana leads people to try more dangerous drugs. Once the habit of taking drugs has been acquired, people can get hooked on them. More powerful drugs such as the murderous heroin are fearfully addictive, and most people cannot stop using them without help from others. Thus, the use of marijuana, because it might lead to further harm, is an unethical practice.

It has been documented medically, however, that the use of marijuana has many medical benefits for people with certain illnesses. For example, for cancer sufferers who are undergoing chemotherapy and for those with AIDS who are on potent medications, marijuana offers relief from many of the treatment's side effects, such as nausea and lack of appetite. Yet, in the United States, it is illegal in many states for doctors to prescribe marijuana for these patients, so their suffering goes on. Since 1996, however, 35 states have made it legal to prescribe marijuana for medical purposes; nevertheless, the federal government has sought to stop such state legislation. The U.S. Supreme Court ruled in 2005 that only Congress or the states could decide whether the medical use of the drug should be made legal, and people in many states are currently lobbying for a relaxation of state laws against its use for medical purposes.[6] In Canada there has been a widespread movement to decriminalize marijuana. While not making the drug legal, decriminalization removes the threat of prosecution even for uses that are not medically related. A major ethical debate is currently raging over this issue in many countries.

The important point to note is that while ethical beliefs lead to the development of laws and regulations to prevent certain behaviors or encourage others, laws themselves can and do change or even disappear as ethical beliefs change. In Britain in 1830 there were over 350 different crimes for which a person could be executed, including sheep stealing. Today there are none; capital punishment and the death penalty are no longer legal in Britain. Thus, both ethical and legal rules are relative: No absolute or unvarying standards exist to determine how we should behave, and people are caught up in moral dilemmas all the time. Because of this we have to make ethical choices.

The previous discussion highlights an important issue in understanding the relationship between ethics, law, and business. Throughout the 2000s many scandals have plagued major companies such as Enron, Arthur Andersen, WorldCom, Tyco, Adelphia, and others. Managers in some of these companies clearly broke the law and used illegal means to defraud investors. At Enron, former chief financial officer Andrew Fastow, and his wife, pleaded guilty to falsifying the company's books so that they could siphon off tens of millions of dollars of Enron's money for their own use.

In other cases, some managers took advantage of loopholes in the law to divert hundreds of millions of dollars of company capital into their own personal fortunes. At WorldCom, for example, former CEO Bernie Ebbers used his position to place six personal, long-time friends on its 13-member board of directors. While this is not illegal, obviously these people would vote in his favor at board meetings. As a result of their support Ebbers received huge stock options and a personal loan of over $150 million from WorldCom. In return, his supporters were well rewarded for being directors; for example, Ebbers allowed them to use WorldCom's corporate jets for a minimal cost—something that saved them hundreds of thousands of dollars a year.[7]

In the light of these events some people said, "Well, what these people did was not illegal," implying that because such behavior was not illegal it was also not unethical. However, not being illegal does *not* make it ethical; such behavior is clearly unethical.[8] In many cases laws are passed *later* to close the loopholes and prevent unethical people, such as Fastow and Ebbers, from taking advantage of them to pursue their own self-interest at the expense of others. Like ordinary people, managers must confront the need to decide what is appropriate and inappropriate as they use a company's resources to produce goods and services for customers.[9]

Stakeholders and Ethics

Just as people have to work out the right and wrong ways to act, so do companies. When the law does not specify how companies should behave, their managers must decide what is the right or ethical way to behave toward the people and groups affected by their actions. Who are the people or groups that are affected by a company's business decisions? If a company behaves in an ethical way, how does this benefit people and society? Conversely, how are people harmed by a company's unethical actions?

The people and groups affected by the way a company and its managers behave are called its stakeholders. **Stakeholders** supply a company with its productive resources; as a result, they have a claim on and stake in the company.[10] Since stakeholders can directly benefit or be harmed by its actions, the ethics of a company and its managers are important to them. Who are a company's major stakeholders? What do they contribute to a company, and what do they claim in return? Below we examine the claims of these stakeholders—stockholders; managers; employees; suppliers and distributors; customers; and community, society, and nation-state (Figure 4.1).

stakeholders The people and groups that supply a company with its productive resources and so have a claim on and stake in the company.

Stockholders

LO2 Differentiate between the claims of the different stakeholder groups that are affected by managers and their companies' actions.

Stockholders have a claim on a company because when they buy its stock or shares they become its owners. Whenever the founder of a company decides to publicly incorporate the business to raise capital, shares of the stock of that company are issued. This stock grants its buyers ownership of a certain percentage of the company and the right to receive any future stock dividends. For example, in December 2004 Microsoft decided to pay the owners of its 5 billion shares a record dividend payout of $32 billion! Bill Gates received $3.3 billion in dividends based on his stockholding, and he donated this money to the Bill and Melinda Gates Foundation, to which he has reportedly donated over $30 billion to date, with the promise of much more to come—so has Warren Buffet who committed in 2006 to donate at least $30 billion to the Gates Foundation over the next decade. The two richest people in the world have decided to give away a large part of their wealth to serve global ethical causes—in particular to address global health concerns such as malnutrition, malaria, tuberculosis, and AIDS.

Stockholders are interested in the way a company operates because they want to maximize the return on their investment. Thus, they watch the company and its

Figure 4.1

Types of Company Stakeholders

managers closely to ensure that management is working diligently to increase the company's profitability.[11] Stockholders also want to ensure that managers are behaving ethically and not risking investors' capital by engaging in actions that could hurt the company's reputation. Managers of companies such as WorldCom, Brocade Communications, and Enron pursued their own self-interest at the expense of their stakeholders. As a result of their managers' unethical actions, in 2006 WorldCom's ex-CEO Bernie Ebbers was sentenced to a long jail term as was Enron's former top manager Jeffrey Skilling. And, in 2008, the first of a long line of top managers from many companies who have been accused of backdating stock options to inflate their personal wealth at the expense of stockholders was convicted. Ex-CEO of Brocade Communications, Gregory Reyes, was found guilty of illegally backdating stock options that resulted in he and his top managers receiving tens of millions of dollars of extra unearned income. He was sentenced to 21 months in jail and fined $15 million.[12]

Managers

Managers are a vital stakeholder group because they are responsible for using a company's financial capital and human resources to increase its performance and thus its stock price.[13] Managers have a claim on an organization because they bring to it their skills, expertise, and experience. They have the right to expect a good return or reward by investing their human capital to improve a company's performance. Such rewards include good salaries and benefits, the prospect of promotion and a career, and stock options and bonuses tied to company performance.

Managers are the stakeholder group that bears the responsibility to decide which goals an organization should pursue to most benefit stakeholders and how to make the most efficient use of resources to achieve those goals. In making such decisions, managers are frequently in the position of having to juggle the interests of different stakeholders, including themselves.[14] These decisions are sometimes very difficult and challenge managers to uphold ethical values because in some cases decisions that benefit some stakeholder groups (managers and stockholders) harm other groups (individual workers and local communities). For example, in economic downturns or when a company experiences performance shortfalls, layoffs may help to cut costs

Top executives, including Angelo Mizilo of Countryside Mortgage and Stanley O'Neal of Merrill Lynch testify before Senator Henry Waxman in 2008 on the issue of exorbitant CEO compensation packages that remain in full effect even though these companies lost billions of dollars.

(thus benefiting shareholders) at the expense of the employees laid off. Many U.S. managers have recently been faced with this very difficult decision. On average about 1.6 million employees out of a total labor force of 140 million are affected by mass layoffs each year in the United States;[15] a million jobs from the United States, Europe, and Japan were outsourced to Asia in 2006, and a million since.[16] Layoff decisions are always difficult, as they not only take a heavy toll on workers, their families, and local communities but also mean the loss of the contributions of valued employees to an organization. Whenever decisions such as these are made—benefiting some groups at the expense of others—ethics come into play.

As we discussed in Chapter 1, managers must be motivated and given incentives to work hard in the interests of stockholders. Their behavior must also be scrutinized to ensure they do not behave illegally or unethically, pursuing goals that threaten stockholders and the company's interests.[17] Unfortunately, we have seen in the 2000s how easy it is for top managers to find ways to ruthlessly pursue their self-interest at the expense of stockholders and employees because laws and regulations were not strong enough to force them to behave ethically.

In a nutshell, the problem has been that in many companies corrupt managers focus not on building the company's capital and stockholders' wealth but on maximizing their own *personal capital and wealth*. In an effort to prevent future scandals the Securities and Exchange Commission (SEC), the government's top business watchdog, began to rework the rules governing a company's relationship with its auditor, as well as regulations concerning stock options, and to increase the power of outside directors to scrutinize a CEO. The SEC's goal is to turn many actions that were previously classified as only unethical into illegal behavior in the near future. For example, companies are now forced to reveal to stockholders the value of the stock options they give their top executives and directors, and when they give them these options, and this shows how much such payments reduce company profits. Managers and directors can now be prosecuted if they disguise or try to hide these payments. In 2007, SEC chairman Christopher Cox announced new rules that would require that companies disclose myriad details of executive compensation packages to investors; already the boards of directors of many companies have stopped giving CEOs perks such as free personal jet travel, membership in exclusive country clubs, and luxury accommodations on "business trips."

Indeed, many experts are arguing that the rewards given to top managers, particularly the CEO and COO, have grown out of control in the 2000s. Top managers are today's "aristocrats," and through their ability to influence the board of directors and raise their own pay, they have amassed personal fortunes worth hundreds of millions of dollars. For example, according to a study by the Federal Reserve, U.S. CEOs now get paid about 600 times what the average worker earns, compared to about 40 times in 1980—a staggering increase. Michael Eisner, ex-CEO of Disney, received over $1 billion in Disney stock options. Jack Welch, the former CEO of General Electric and one of the most admired managers in the United States, received more than $500 million in GE stock options as a reward for his services. And Bob Nardelli, ex-CEO of Home Depot, received over $200 million in salary, bonus, stock, stock options, and other perks during the period when Home Depot's stock plunged by 13%. When he was forced out of the company in 2007 he also received a $150 million early-termination payment that had been agreed on in advance.

Is it ethical for top managers to receive such vast amounts of money from their companies? Do they really earn it? Remember, this money could have gone to shareholders in the form of dividends. It could also have gone to reduce the huge salary gap between those at the top and those at the bottom of the hierarchy. Many people argue that the growing disparity between the rewards given to CEOs and to other employees is unethical and should be regulated. CEO pay has become too high because CEOs are the people who set and control one another's salaries and bonuses! They can do this because they sit on the boards of other companies, as outside directors, and thus can control the salaries and stock options paid to other CEOs. As the example of Bernie Ebbers at WorldCom, discussed earlier, suggests, when a CEO can control and select many of the outside directors, the CEO can abuse his or her power. Others argue that because top managers play an important role in building a company's capital and wealth, they deserve a significant share of its profits. Jack Welch, for example, deserved stock options worth $500 million because he created hundreds of billions of dollars in stockholder wealth. Some recent research has suggested that the companies whose CEOs compensation includes a large percentage of stock options tend to experience big share losses more often than big gains, and that on average, company performance improves as stock option use declines![18]

The debate over how much money CEOs and other top managers should be paid is currently raging, especially because the subprime mortgage crisis that began in 2007 showed how much money the CEOs of troubled financial companies earned even as their companies' performance and stock price collapsed. A U.S. House Oversight and Government Reform Committee chaired by Senator Henry Waxman that was convened to examine the issue of high executive pay first noted that *Forbes* magazine estimated the average CEO of the largest 500 companies earned $15.2 million in 2006, an increase of 38 percent over 2005.[19] Then, Waxman went on to question the CEOs of financial giants Countrywide Mortgage and Merrill Lynch about how they could justify their high salaries while their companies were losing billions of dollars and their stock values were plunging. He noted, for example, that Countrywide suffered losses of over $1.7 billion in 2007 and that the company's stock had fallen 80%. Yet, during the same period, its CEO Angelo Mozilo received a $1.9 million salary, $20 million more in stock awards contingent upon performance, and sold $121 million in stock he had already been given before the price fall. Similarly, during 2007 Merrill Lynch reported $18 billion in write-downs related to risky subprime mortgages but its ex-CEO Stanley O'Neal received a retirement package of $161 million when he was forced out of office in 2007. The committee noted that if the company had terminated O'Neal for poor performance as a manager, rather than letting him retire, he would not have been entitled to $131 million of the package in unvested stock and options.[20] The issue of what is fair compensation for top managers is not just limited to for-profit companies, however; it is one of the many issues facing nonprofits as well, as discussed in the following "Ethics in Action."

The Ethics of Some Nonprofits Are Not So Good

The many ethics scandals that have plagued companies in the 2000s might suggest that the issue of ethics is important only for profit-seeking companies, but this would be untrue. There are 1.8 million private nonprofit charitable and philanthropic organizations in the United States, and charges that their managers have acted in unethical and even illegal ways have grown in the 2000s. For example, many states and the federal government are investigating the huge salaries that the top executives of charitable institutions earn. One impetus for this was the revelation that the NYSE, which is classified as a charitable organization, paid its disgraced top executive Richard A. Grasso over $187 million in pension benefits. It turns out that over 200 nonprofits pay their top executives more than $1 million a year in salary and that the boards of trustees or directors of many of these organizations also enjoy lavish perks and compensation for attendance at board meetings. And, unlike for-profit companies, which are required by law to provide detailed reports of their operations to their shareholders, nonprofits do not have shareholders, so the laws governing disclosure are far weaker. As a result, the board and its top managers have considerable latitude to decide how they will spend a nonprofit's resources, and little oversight exists. To remedy this situation, many states and the federal government are considering new laws that would subject nonprofits to strict Sarbanes-Oxley-type regulations that force the disclosure of issues related to managerial compensation and financial integrity. There are also efforts in progress to strengthen the legal power of the IRS to oversee nonprofits' expenditures so that it has more scope to examine the way these organizations spend their resources on managerial and director compensation and perks.

Experts hope that the introduction of new rules and regulations to monitor and oversee how nonprofits spend their funds will result in much more value being created from the funds given by donors. After all, every cent that is spent just administering a nonprofit is a cent not being used to help the people (or cause) for whom the money was intended. Major ethical issues are involved because some badly run charities spend 70 cents of every dollar on administration costs! And charges have been leveled against charities such as the Red Cross for mishandling the hundreds of millions of dollars they received in donations after Hurricane Katrina struck. Major changes have been made in the Red Cross to address these issues, as we discuss in Chapter 9. Clearly, the directors and managers of all organizations need to carefully consider the ethical issues involved in their decision making.

Employees

A company's employees are the hundreds of thousands of people who work in its various departments and functions, such as research, sales, and manufacturing. Employees expect that they will receive rewards consistent with their performance. One principle way that a company can act ethically toward employees and meet their expectations is by creating an occupational structure that fairly and equitably rewards employees for their contributions. Companies, for example, need to develop recruitment, training, performance appraisal, and reward systems that do not discriminate between employees and that employees believe are fair.

Suppliers and Distributors

No company operates alone. Every company is in a network of relationships with other companies that supply it with the inputs (e.g., raw materials, components, contract labor, and clients) that it needs to operate. It also depends on intermediaries such as wholesalers and retailers to distribute its products to the final customer. Suppliers expect to be paid fairly and promptly for their inputs; distributors expect to receive quality products at agreed-upon prices.

Once again, many ethical issues arise in the way companies contract and interact with their suppliers and distributors. Important issues concerning how and when payments are to be made or product quality specifications are governed by the terms of the legal contracts a company signs with its suppliers and distributors. Many other issues are dependent on business ethics. For example, numerous products sold in U.S. stores have been outsourced to countries that do not have U.S.-style regulations and laws to protect the workers who make these products. All companies must take an ethical position on the way they obtain and make the products they sell. Commonly this stance is published on the company's Web site. Table 4.1 presents part of the Gap's statement on its approach to global ethics (www.gapinc.com).

Table 4.1
Some Principles from the Gap's Code of Vendor Conduct

As a condition of doing business with Gap Inc., each and every factory must comply with this Code of Vendor Conduct. Gap Inc. will continue to develop monitoring systems to assess and ensure compliance. If Gap Inc. determines that any factory has violated this Code, Gap Inc. may either terminate its business relationship or require the factory to implement a corrective action plan. If corrective action is advised but not taken, Gap Inc. will suspend placement of future orders and may terminate current production.

I. General Principles

Factories that produce goods for Gap Inc. shall operate in full compliance with the laws of their respective countries and with all other applicable laws, rules and regulations.

II. Environment

Factories must comply with all applicable environmental laws and regulations. Where such requirements are less stringent than Gap Inc.'s own, factories are encouraged to meet the standards outlined in Gap Inc.'s statement of environmental principles.

III. Discrimination

Factories shall employ workers on the basis of their ability to do the job, without regard to race, color, gender, nationality, religion, age, maternity or marital status.

IV. Forced Labor

Factories shall not use any prison, indentured or forced labor.

V. Child Labor

Factories shall employ only workers who meet the applicable minimum legal age requirement or are at least 14 years of age, whichever is greater. Factories must also comply with all other applicable child labor laws. Factories are encouraged to develop lawful workplace apprenticeship programs for the educational benefit of their workers, provided that all participants meet both Gap Inc.'s minimum age standard of 14 and the minimum legal age requirement.

VI. Wages & Hours

Factories shall set working hours, wages and overtime pay in compliance with all applicable laws. Workers shall be paid at least the minimum legal wage or a wage that meets local industry standards, whichever is greater. While it is understood that overtime is often required in garment production, factories shall carry out operations in ways that limit overtime to a level that ensures humane and productive working conditions.

Customers

Customers are often regarded as the most critical stakeholder group since if a company cannot attract them to buy its products, it cannot stay in business. Thus, managers and employees must work to increase efficiency and effectiveness in order to create loyal customers and attract new ones. They do so by selling customers quality products at a fair price and providing good after-sales service. They can also strive to improve their products over time and provide guarantees to customers about the integrity of their products as Whole Foods Markets, profiled in the following "Ethics in Action," does.

Ethics in Action

Whole Foods Market Practices What It Preaches

The Whole Foods Market supermarket chain was founded by two hippies in Austin, Texas, in 1978 as a natural counterculture food store. Today, it is the world's leading retailer of natural and organic foods, with over 270 stores in North America and the United Kingdom. Whole Foods specializes in the sale of chemical- and drug-free meat, poultry, and produce; its products are the "purest" possible, meaning it selects the ones least adulterated by artificial additives, sweeteners, colorings, and preservatives. Despite the fact that it charges high prices for its pure produce, sales per store are growing fast and the company plans to double both the number of its stores and its $5 billion revenue by 2010.[21] Why has Whole Foods been so successful? Because, says founder and CEO John Mackey, of the principles he established to manage his company since its beginning—principles founded on the need to behave in an ethical and socially responsible way toward everybody affected by its business. The way in which Whole Food views its responsibilities to stakeholders and its approach to ethical business is depicted in Figure 4.2.

Mackey says he started his business for three reasons—to have fun, to make money, and to contribute to the well-being of other people.[22] The company's mission is based on its members' collective responsibility to the well-being of the people and groups it affects, its *stakeholders;* in order of priority, at Whole Foods these are customers, team members, investors, suppliers, the community, and the natural environment. Mackey measures his company's success on how well it satisfies the needs of these stakeholders. His ethical stance toward customers is that they are guaranteed that Whole Foods products are 100% organic, hormone-free, or as represented. To help achieve this promise, Whole Foods insists that its suppliers also behave in an ethical way so that it knows, for example, that the beef it sells comes from cows pastured on grass, not corn-fed in feed lots, and the chicken it sells is from free-range hens and not from hens that have been confined in tiny cages that prevent even movement.

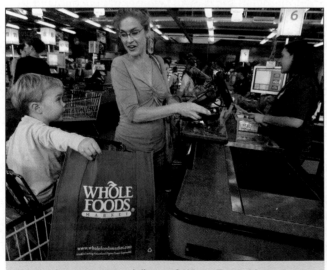

Where do your grocery dollars go? Whole Foods Market's goal is to make shopping fun and socially responsible. Customers' money supports an organization that monitors its suppliers, rewards its employees, and seeks to reduce its impact on the environment.

His management approach toward "team members," as Whole Foods employees are called, is also based on a well-defined ethical position. Mackey says, "We put great emphasis at Whole Foods on the 'Whole People' part of the company mission. We believe in helping support our team members to grow as individuals–to become 'Whole People.' We allow tremendous individual initiative at Whole Foods and that's why our company is so innovative and creative."[23] Mackey claims that each supermarket in the chain is unique because in each one team members are constantly experimenting with new and better ways to serve customers and improve their well-being. As team members learn, they become "self-actualized" or self-fulfilled, and this increase in their well-being translates into a desire to increase the well-being of other stakeholders.

Finally, Mackey's strong views on ethics and social responsibility also serve shareholders. Mackey does not believe the object of being in business is to primarily maximize profits for shareholders; he puts customers first. He believes, however, that companies that behave ethically, and strive to satisfy the needs of customers and employees, simultaneously satisfy the needs of investors because high profits are the result of loyal customers and committed employees. Indeed, since Whole Foods issued shares to the public in 1992, the value of those shares has increased 25 times.[24] Clearly, taking a strong position on ethics and social responsibility has worked so far at Whole Foods.

Many laws exist that protect customers from companies that attempt to provide dangerous or shoddy products. Laws exist that allow customers to sue a company whose product causes them injury or harm, such as a defective tire or vehicle. Other laws force companies to clearly disclose the interest rates they charge on purchases–an

Figure 4.2
Whole Food Market's Stakeholder Approach to Ethical Business

Source: www.wholefoodsmarket.com.

important hidden cost that customers frequently do not factor into their purchase decisions. Every year thousands of companies are prosecuted for breaking these laws, so "buyer beware" is an important rule customers must follow when buying goods and services.

Community, Society, and Nation

The effects of the decisions made by companies and their managers permeate all aspects of the communities, societies, and nations in which they operate. *Community* refers to physical locations like towns or cities or to social milieus like ethnic neighborhoods in which companies are located. A community provides a company with the physical and social infrastructure that allows it to operate; its utilities and labor force; the homes in which its managers and employees live; the schools, colleges, and hospitals that service their needs; and so on.

Through the salaries, wages, and taxes it pays, a company contributes to the economy of the town or region and often determines whether the community prospers or declines. Similarly, a company affects the prosperity of a society and a nation and, to the degree that a company is involved in global trade, all the countries it operates in and thus the prosperity of the global economy. We have already discussed the many issues surrounding global outsourcing and the loss of jobs in the United States, for example.

Although the individual effects of the way each McDonald's restaurant operates might be small, for instance, the combined effects of the way all McDonald's and other fast-food companies do business are enormous. In the United States alone, over 500,000 people work in the fast-food industry, and many thousands of suppliers like farmers, paper cup manufacturers, builders, and so on, depend on it for their livelihood. Small wonder then that the ethics of the fast-food business are scrutinized closely. The industry is the major lobbyer against attempts to raise the national minimum wage (which will be raised to $7.25 an hour by 2009, up from $5.15–a figure that had not changed since 1997), for example, because a higher minimum wage would substantially increase its operating costs. However, responding to protests about chickens raised in cages where they cannot move their wings, McDonald's–the largest egg buyer in the United States–issued new ethical guidelines concerning cage size and related matters that its egg suppliers must abide by if they are to retain its business. What ethical rules does McDonald's use to decide its stance toward minimum pay or minimum cage size?

Business ethics are also important because the failure of companies can have catastrophic effects on a community; a general decline in business activity affects a whole nation. The decision of a large company to pull out of a community, for example, can seriously threaten the community's future. Some companies may attempt to improve their profits by engaging in actions that, although not illegal, can hurt communities and nations. One of these actions is pollution. For example, many U.S. companies reduce costs by trucking their waste to Mexico, where it is legal to dump waste in the Rio Grande. The dumping pollutes the river from the Mexican side, and the effects are increasingly being felt on the U.S. side too.

Rules for Ethical Decision Making

When a stakeholder perspective is taken, questions on company ethics abound.[25] What is the appropriate way to manage the claims of all stakeholders? Company decisions that favor one group of stakeholders, for example, are likely to harm the interests of others.[26] High prices to customers may lead to high returns to shareholders and high salaries for managers in the short run. If in the long run customers turn to companies that offer lower-cost products, however, the result may be declining sales, laid-off employees, and the decline of the communities that support the high-price company's business activity.

When companies act ethically, their stakeholders support them. For example, banks are willing to supply them with new capital, they attract highly qualified job applicants, and new customers are drawn to their products. Thus ethical companies grow and expand over time, and all their stakeholders benefit. The result of unethical behavior is the loss of reputation and resources, shareholders who sell their shares, skilled managers and employees who leave the company, and customers who turn to the products of more reputable companies.

When making business decisions, managers must take the claims of all stakeholders into consideration.[27] To help themselves and employees make ethical decisions and behave in ways that benefit their stakeholders, managers can use four ethical rules or principles to analyze the effects of their business decisions on stakeholders: the *utilitarian, moral rights, justice,* and *practical* rules (Figure 4.3).[28] These rules are useful guidelines that help managers decide on the appropriate way to behave in situations where it is necessary to balance a company's self-interest against the interests of its stakeholders. Remember, the right choices will lead resources to be used where they can create the most value. If all companies make the right choices, all stakeholders will benefit in the long run.[29]

utilitarian rule An ethical decision is a decision that produces the greatest good for the greatest number of people.

UTILITARIAN RULE   The **utilitarian rule** is that an ethical decision is a decision that produces the greatest good for the greatest number of people. To decide which is the most ethical course of business action, managers should first consider how different possible courses of business action would benefit or harm different stakeholders. They should then choose the course of action that provides the most benefits, or conversely the one that does the least harm, to stakeholders.[30]

The ethical dilemma for managers is, How do you measure the benefits and harms that will be done to each stakeholder group? Moreover, how do you evaluate the rights of different stakeholder groups, and the relative importance of each group, in coming to a decision? Since stockholders are the owners of the company, shouldn't their claims be held above those of employees? For example, managers might be

Figure 4.3
Four Ethical Rules

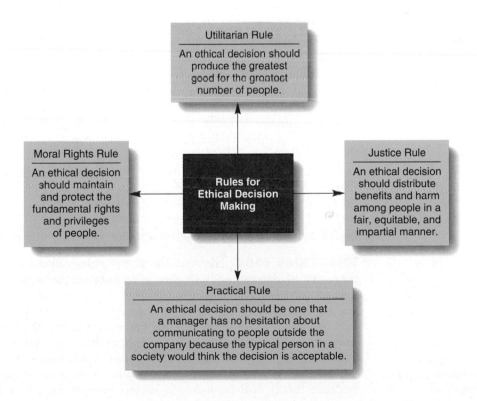

faced with a choice of using global outsourcing to reduce costs and lower prices to customers or continuing with high-cost production at home. A decision to use global outsourcing benefits shareholders and customers but will result in major layoffs that will harm employees and the communities in which they live. Typically, in a capitalist society such as the United States, the interests of shareholders are put above those of employees, so production will move abroad. This is commonly regarded as being an ethical choice because in the long run the alternative, home production, might cause the business to collapse and go bankrupt, in which case greater harm will be done to all stakeholders.

LO3 Describe four rules that can be used to help companies and their managers act in ethical ways.

moral rights rule An ethical decision is one that best maintains and protects the fundamental or inalienable rights and privileges of the people affected by it.

MORAL RIGHTS RULE   Under the **moral rights rule,** an ethical decision is a decision that best maintains and protects the fundamental or inalienable rights and privileges of the people affected by it. For example, ethical decisions protect people's rights to freedom, life and safety, property, privacy, free speech, and freedom of conscience. The adage "Do unto others as you would have them do unto you" is a moral rights principle that managers should use to decide which rights to uphold. Customers must also consider the rights of the companies and people who create the products they wish to consume (see "Ethics in Action" box "Digital Piracy, Ethics, and Napster").

From a moral rights perspective, managers should compare and contrast different courses of business action on the basis of how each course will affect the rights of the company's different stakeholders. Managers should then choose the course of action that best protects and upholds the rights of *all* the stakeholders. For example, decisions that might result in significant harm to the safety or health of employees or customers would clearly be unethical choices.

The ethical dilemma for managers is that decisions that will protect the rights of some stakeholders often will hurt the rights of others. How should they choose which group to protect? For example, in deciding whether it is ethical to snoop on employees, or search them when they leave work to prevent theft, does an employee's right to privacy outweigh an organization's right to protect its property? Suppose a coworker is having personal problems and is coming in late and leaving early, placing you in the position of being forced to pick up the person's workload. Do you tell your boss even though you know this will probably get that person fired?

justice rule An ethical decision is a decision that distributes benefits and harms among people and groups in a fair, equitable, or impartial way.

JUSTICE RULE   The **justice rule** is that an ethical decision is a decision that distributes benefits and harms among people and groups in a fair, equitable, or impartial way. Managers should compare and contrast alternative courses of action based on the degree to which they will result in a fair or equitable distribution of outcomes for stakeholders. For example, employees who are similar in their level of skill, performance, or responsibility should receive the same kind of pay. The allocation of outcomes should not be based on differences such as gender, race, or religion.

The ethical dilemma for managers is to determine the fair rules and procedures for distributing outcomes to stakeholders. Managers must not give people they like bigger raises than they give to people they do not like, for example, or bend the rules to help their favorites. On the other hand, if employees want managers to act fairly toward them, then employees need to act fairly toward their companies and work hard and be loyal. Similarly, customers need to act fairly toward a company if they expect it to be fair to them—something people who illegally copy digital media should consider.

practical rule An ethical decision is one that a manager has no reluctance about communicating to people outside the company because the typical person in a society would think it is acceptable.

PRACTICAL RULE   Each of the above rules offers a different and complementary way of determining whether a decision or behavior is ethical, and all three rules should be used to sort out the ethics of a particular course of action. Ethical issues, as we just discussed, are seldom clear-cut, however, because the rights, interests, goals, and incentives of different stakeholders often conflict. For this reason many experts on ethics add a fourth rule to determine whether a business decision is ethical: The **practical rule** is that an ethical decision is one that a manager has no hesitation or reluctance about communicating to people outside the company because the typical person in a society would think it is acceptable. A business decision is probably acceptable on ethical grounds if a manager can answer yes to each of these questions:

1. Does my decision fall within the accepted *values* or *standards* that typically apply in business activity today?

2. Am I willing to see the decision *communicated* to all people and groups *affected* by it—for example, by having it reported in newspapers or on television?

3. Would the people with whom I have a *significant* personal relationship, such as family members, friends, or even managers in other organizations, *approve* of the decision?

Applying the practical rule to analyze a business decision ensures that managers are taking into account the interests of all stakeholders.[31] After applying this rule managers can judge if they have chosen to act in an ethical or unethical way and they must abide by the consequences. The following "Ethics in Action," which describes the issues surrounding individuals copying digital content from the Internet, provides a good example to test these different ethical issues—what is the right or ethical thing to do in this situation?

Ethics in Action

Digital Piracy, Ethics, and Napster

Today, almost all written text, music, movies, and software are recorded in digital form and can be easily copied electronically and sent between personal computers through the Internet. Many sites on the Internet contain illegal copies of music, movies, and so on, that can be easily accessed and downloaded. Millions of people and companies have taken advantage of this to make illegal copies of music CDs, software programs, and DVDs. As a result, it has been estimated that over one-third of all CDs and cassettes recorded around the world were illegally produced and sold in the 2000s, and the music industry has lost tens of billions in sales revenues.[32]

As you can imagine, the managers of music and movie companies have been doing all they can to reduce illegal recording because it decreases their sales and profits. One enterprise that music company CEOs went after with a vengeance was Napster.[33] Shawn Fanning created Napster while he was an undergraduate student at Northeastern University. His roommate downloaded music from Internet sites using the MP3 format, which compresses digital files, making them faster to transmit and easier to store. As Fanning watched his roommate search the Internet for new material, he realized that it would be easy to create a software platform to help people easily locate and download digital music files stored in any PC that was logged into this platform. Fanning created the necessary software, and word of mouth did the rest; soon Napster was a phenomenon, and millions of people were swapping and downloading music.[34]

Managers in the music industry became desperate to stop this practice. The value of their companies' copyrights to songs and contracts with artists was being destroyed by this new technology that allowed pirating of their products. They sought legal injunctions against Napster to shut the company down, and since it was clearly violating copyright laws, the courts stopped Napster's operations. However, many other Internet sites then sprung up from which people can still download music and other digital media.

Shawn Fanning created both a company and an ethical controversy when he took Napster's copying platform public. Was it a work of genius or just promotion of selfishness? What about Google's similar book-scanning operations today?

The copying of digital material is illegal because it infringes on copyright laws that protect the rights of artists, authors, composers, and the companies that produce and distribute their work. Is this copying unethical? Is it an unacceptable or acceptable way to behave? Why are so many people doing it if it is illegal? The obvious answer is that people are doing it to pursue their own self-interest. Paying nothing for valuable digital media is attractive, and who, goes the argument, suffers anyway? Music companies have been making billions of dollars of profit out of music sales for decades. Songs may be the property of music stars like the Rolling Stones and Eminem, but these people are fabulously wealthy. Why shouldn't the average person benefit from digital technology? After all, the pleasure gained by hundreds of millions of people is more important than the harm done to only a few thousand musicians and a handful of music companies, so copying is not "really" unethical. It may be illegal, but it's not actually such a bad thing to do, is it?

Arguments like these may make people feel that their copying is doing no real harm to others. But what about the rights of artists and companies to profit from their property—the songs, books, and movies that result from their creative endeavors? The average person would not like it if a "poorer" person came along and said, "You don't need all those appliances, cars, and jewelry? I'll just help myself; you'll never miss it." Those who steal digital media not only are weakening the rights of musicians and writers to own property but also are weakening *their* rights to own property. Digital piracy is not a fair or equitable practice. And, although each person may argue that engaging in it doesn't have much of an effect since he or she is "only one person," if many people do it a major problem emerges.

To illustrate the problem, suppose that by 2010 about 80% of all music and movies are illegally copied rather than bought. What will musicians and music companies and movie stars and movie studios do? If these people and companies cannot protect their property and profit from it, then they are not going to make or sell digital products. Over time, music and movie companies will cease to operate. Creative people will find new ways to make money, or musicians will make music only for their own pleasure or in live concerts (where recording devices are not permitted!). The result will be a loss to everyone because no new music or movies will be made, and the world will become a less interesting place to live in.

It is no easy matter to determine what is a fair or equitable division of the value and profit in a particular business activity. Music companies have no desire to see their revenues fall because potential customers are "profiting" from their ability to make illegal copies of CDs. Music companies have a responsibility to make profits so that they can reward their stockholders, pay the musicians who receive royalties on their record sales, and pay their employees salaries. Of course, they also have a responsibility toward customers—they should charge only a fair price for their CDs. In fact, since Apple opened its iTunes store in 2001 and other online music stores followed suit, tens of millions of songs have been legally downloaded and paid for, something that indicates that millions of customers do accept their obligation to pay a fair price for the products they receive. At the same time, artists and companies also recognize they have to provide first-class content if customers are going to continue to purchase, rather than copy, digital content.

Why Should Managers Behave Ethically?

LO4 Discuss why it is important for managers to behave ethically.

Why is it so important that managers, and people in general, should act ethically and temper their pursuit of self-interest by considering the effects of their actions on others? The answer is that the relentless pursuit of self-interest can lead to a collective disaster when one or more people start to profit from being unethical because this encourages other people to act in the same way.[35] Quickly, more and more people jump onto the bandwagon, and soon everybody is trying to manipulate the situation in the way that best serves their personal ends with no regard for the effects of their action on others. The situation brought about by Napster is an example of how what is called the "tragedy of the commons" works.

Suppose that in an agricultural community there is common land that everybody has an equal right to use. Pursuing self-interest, each farmer acts to make the maximum use of the free resource by grazing his or her own cattle and sheep. Collectively, all the farmers overgraze the land, which quickly becomes worn out. Then a strong wind blows away the exposed topsoil so tragically, the common land is destroyed. The pursuit of individual self-interest with no consideration for societal interests leads to disaster for each individual and for the whole society because scarce resources are destroyed.[36] In the Napster case the tragedy that would result if all people were to steal digital media would be the disappearance of music, movie, and book companies as creative people decided there was no point in their working hard to produce original songs, stories, and so on.

We can look at the effects of unethical behavior on business activity in another way. Suppose companies and their managers operate in an unethical society, meaning one in which stakeholders routinely try to cheat and defraud one another. If stakeholders expect each other to cheat, how long will it take them to negotiate the purchase and shipment of products? When they do not trust each other, stakeholders will probably spend hours bargaining over fair prices, and this is a largely unproductive activity that reduces efficiency and effectiveness.[37] All the time and effort that could be spent improving product quality or customer service is being lost because it is spent on negotiating and bargaining. Thus, unethical behavior ruins business commerce, and society has a lower standard of living because fewer goods and services are produced, as Figure 4.4 illustrates.

On the other hand, suppose companies and their managers operate in an ethical society, meaning that stakeholders believe they are dealing with others who are basically moral and honest. In this society stakeholders have a greater reason to trust others. **Trust** is the willingness of one person or group to have faith or confidence in the goodwill of another person, even though this puts them at risk (because the other might act in a deceitful way). When trust exists, stakeholders are more likely to signal their good intentions by cooperating and providing information that makes it easier to exchange and price goods and services. When one person acts in a trustworthy way, this encourages others to act in the same way. Over time, as greater trust between stakeholders develops, they can work together more efficiently and effectively and this raises company performance (see Figure 4.4). As people see the positive results of acting in an honest way, ethical behavior becomes a valued social norm and society in general becomes increasingly ethical.

As noted in Chapter 1, a major responsibility of managers is to protect and nurture the resources under their control. Any organizational stakeholders—managers, workers, stockholders, suppliers—who advance their own interests by behaving unethically toward other stakeholders, either by taking resources or by denying resources to others, waste collective resources. If other individuals or groups copy the behavior of the unethical stakeholder ("If he can do it, we can do it, too"), the rate at which collective resources are misused increases, and eventually there are few resources available to produce goods and services. Unethical behavior that goes unpunished creates incentives for people to put their unbridled self-interests above the rights of others.[38] When this happens, the benefits that people reap from joining together in organizations disappear very quickly.

An important safeguard against unethical behavior is the potential for loss of reputation.[39] **Reputation,** the esteem or high repute that people or organizations gain when they behave ethically, is an important asset. Stakeholders have valuable reputations that they must protect because their ability to earn a living and obtain resources in the long run depends on the way they behave on a day-to-day, week-to-week, and month-to-month basis.

trust The willingness of one person or group to have faith or confidence in the goodwill of another person, even though this puts them at risk.

reputation The esteem or high repute that individuals or organizations gain when they behave ethically.

Figure 4.4
Some Effects of Ethical and Unethical Behavior

If a manager misuses resources and other parties regard that behavior as being at odds with acceptable standards, the manager's reputation will suffer. Behaving unethically in the short run can have serious long-term consequences. A manager who has a poor reputation will have difficulty finding employment with other companies. Stockholders who see managers behaving unethically may refuse to invest in their companies, and this will decrease the stock price, undermine the companies' reputations, and ultimately put the managers' jobs at risk.[40]

All stakeholders have reputations to lose. Suppliers who provide shoddy inputs find that organizations learn over time not to deal with them, and eventually they go out of business. Powerful customers who demand ridiculously low prices find that their suppliers become less willing to deal with them, and resources ultimately become harder for them to obtain. Workers who shirk responsibilities on the job find it hard to get new jobs when they are fired. In general, if a manager or company is known for being unethical, other stakeholders are likely to view that individual or organization with suspicion and hostility, and the reputation of each will be poor. But if a manager or company is known for ethical business practices, each will develop a good reputation.[41]

In summary, in a complex, diverse society, stakeholders, and people in general, need to recognize they are all part of a larger social group. The way in which they make decisions and act not only affects them personally but also affects the lives of many other people. The problem is that for some people their daily struggle to survive and succeed or their total disregard for the rights of others can lead them to lose that "bigger" connection to other people. We can see our relationships to our families and friends, to our school, church, and so on. But we always need to go further and keep in mind the effects of our actions on other people—people who will be judging our actions and whom we might harm by acting unethically. Our moral scruples are like that "other person" but are inside our heads.

Ethics and Social Responsibility

Some companies, like GlaxoSmithKlein, Bristol Myers Squib, Prudential Insurance, Whole Foods, and Blue Cross–Blue Shield, are well-known for their ethical business practices.[42] Other companies, such as Arthur Andersen and Enron, which are now out of business, or WorldCom, Tyco, Qwest, and Adelphia, which have been totally restructured, repeatedly engaged in unethical and illegal business activities. What explains such differences between the ethics of these companies and their managers?

There are four main determinants of differences in ethics between people, employees, companies, and countries: *societal* ethics, *occupational* ethics, *individual* ethics, and *organizational* ethics, especially the ethics of a company's top managers.[43] (See Figure 4.5.)

Societal Ethics

societal ethics Standards that govern how members of a society should deal with one another in matters involving issues such as fairness, justice, poverty, and the rights of the individual.

Societal ethics are standards that govern how members of a society should deal with one another in matters involving issues such as fairness, justice, poverty, and the rights of the individual. Societal ethics emanate from a society's laws, customs, and practices and from the unwritten values and norms that influence how people interact with each other. People in a particular country may automatically behave ethically because they have *internalized* (i.e., made a part of their morals) certain values, beliefs, and norms that specify how they should behave when confronted with an ethical dilemma.

Societal ethics vary among societies. Countries like Germany, Japan, Sweden, and Switzerland are well known as being some of the most ethical countries in the world, with strong values about social order and the need to create a society that protects

Figure 4.5
Sources of Ethics

the welfare of all groups of their citizens. In other countries the situation is very different. In many economically poor countries bribery is standard practice to get things done—such as getting a telephone installed or a contract awarded. In the United States and other economically advanced countries, bribery is considered unethical and has been made illegal.

IBM experienced the problem of differences in ethical standards in its Argentinean division. Managers there became involved in an unethical scheme to secure a $250 million contract for IBM to provide and service the computers of one of Argentina's largest state-owned banks. After $6 million was paid to bribe the bank executives who agreed to give IBM the contract, IBM announced that it had fired the three top managers of its Argentine division. According to IBM, transactions like this, though unethical by IBM's standards, are not necessarily illegal under Argentine law. The Argentine managers were fired, however, for failing to follow IBM's organizational rules, which preclude the payment of bribes to obtain contracts in foreign countries. Moreover, the payment of bribes violates the U.S. *Foreign Corrupt Practices Act,* which forbids payment of bribes by U.S. companies to secure contracts abroad, makes companies liable for the actions of their foreign managers, and allows companies found in violation to be prosecuted in the United States. By firing the managers, IBM signaled that it would not tolerate unethical behavior by any of its employees, and it continues today to take a rigorous stance toward ethical issues.

Countries also differ widely in their beliefs about appropriate treatment for their employees. In general, the poorer a country is, the more likely employees are to be treated with little regard. One issue of particular concern on a global level is whether it is ethical to use child labor, as discussed in the following "Ethics in Action."

Ethics in Action

Is It Right to Use Child Labor?

In recent years, the number of U.S. companies that buy their products from low-cost foreign suppliers has been growing, and concern about the ethics associated with employing young children in factories has been increasing. In Pakistan, children as young as age six work long hours in deplorable conditions to make rugs and carpets for export to Western countries. Children in poor countries throughout Africa, Asia, and South America work in similar conditions. Is it ethical to employ children in factories, and should U.S. companies buy and sell products made by these children?

Opinions about the ethics of child labor vary widely. Robert Reich, an economist and secretary of labor in the first Clinton administration, believes that the practice is totally reprehensible and should be outlawed on a global level. Another view, championed by *The Economist* magazine, is that, while nobody wants to see children employed in

Afghan boys weave a rug while their father stands nearby inside their home in Kabul, Afghanistan. Afghan rug makers contract children to make rugs, paying their families roughly 8 U.S. dollars a yard. To make one 18-foot rug takes approximately one month, and the children often work in shifts around their schooling or other household duties.

factories, citizens of rich countries need to recognize that in poor countries children are often a family's only breadwinners. Thus, denying children employment would cause whole families to suffer, and one wrong (child labor) might produce a greater wrong (poverty). Instead, *The Economist* favors regulating the conditions under which children are employed and hopes that over time, as poor countries become richer, the need for child employment will disappear.

Many U.S. retailers typically buy their clothing from low-cost foreign suppliers, and managers in these companies have had to take their own ethical stance on child labor. Managers in Wal-Mart, Target, JCPenney, and Gap Inc. (Table 4.1) have followed U.S. standards and rules and have policies dictating that their foreign suppliers not employ child labor. They also vow to sever ties with any foreign supplier found to be in violation of this standard.

Apparently, however, retailers differ widely in the way they choose to enforce such policies. It has been estimated that more than 300,000 children under age 14 are being employed in garment factories in Guatemala, a popular low-cost location for clothing manufacturers that supply the U.S. market. These children frequently work more than 60 hours a week and often are paid less than $3 a day, close to the minimum wage in Guatemala. Many U.S. retailers do not check up on their foreign suppliers. Clearly, if U.S. retailers are to be true to their ethical stance on this troubling issue, they cannot ignore the fact that they are buying clothing made by children and they must do more to regulate the conditions under which these children work.

One recent attempt to do this is through the Fair Factories Clearinghouse, a joint effort launched in 2006 by companies such as L.L. Bean, Reebok, and Timberland to pool the information they collect about the work practices of the factories with which they have contracted to make their products. The aim is to create a single set of labor code standards that plants the world over must comply with if they are to be certified as ethical suppliers—or else they will be axed by all reputable companies.[44] The way in which Columbian flower growers have adopted uniform labor code practices to meet global demands for the ethical treatment of employees, described in the opening case, is another example of the spread of ethical standards throughout the world.

occupational ethics
Standards that govern how members of a profession, trade, or craft should conduct themselves when performing work-related activities.

Occupational Ethics

Occupational ethics are standards that govern how members of a profession, trade, or craft should conduct themselves when performing work-related activities.[45] For example, medical ethics govern the way doctors and nurses should treat their patients. Doctors are expected to perform only necessary medical procedures and to act in the patient's interest and not in their own self-interest. The ethics of scientific research require that scientists conduct their experiments and present their findings in ways that ensure the validity of their conclusions. Like society at large, most professional groups can impose punishments for violations of ethical standards.[46] Doctors and lawyers can be prevented from practicing their professions if they disregard professional ethics and put their own interests first.

Within an organization, occupational rules and norms often govern how employees such as lawyers, researchers, and accountants should make decisions to

Former Enron Corp Chief Financial Officer Andrew Fastow (center) is escorted by U.S. marshals as Fastow leaves court in Houston March 7, 2006, after his first day of testimony against former bosses Ken Lay and Jeff Skilling.

further stakeholder interests. Employees internalize the rules and norms of their occupational group (just as they do those of society) and often follow them automatically when deciding how to behave. Because most people tend to follow established rules of behavior, people often take ethics for granted. However, when occupational ethics are violated, such as when scientists fabricate data to disguise the harmful effects of products, ethical issues come to the forefront. In 2006, for example, Merck scientists were accused of playing down evidence that Vioxx, one of its best-selling drugs, increased the risk of heart attacks and the drug was pulled from the market. Top researchers in pharmaceutical companies have been accused of deliberately hiding research evidence that revealed the harmful effects of products such as Merck's Vioxx heart drug and Guidant's heart pacemaker, so doctors and patients could not make informed medical treatment decisions. Table 4.2 lists some failures or lapses in professional ethics according to type of functional manager.

Individual Ethics

individual ethics Personal standards and values that determine how people view their responsibilities to others and how they should act in situations when their own self-interests are at stake.

Individual ethics are personal standards and values that determine how people view their responsibilities to other people and groups and thus how they should act in situations when their own self-interests are at stake.[47] Sources of individual ethics include the influence of one's family, peers, and upbringing in general. The

Table 4.2
Some Failures in Professional Ethics

For manufacturing and materials management managers:

- Releasing products that are not of a consistent quality because of defective inputs.
- Producing batches of the product that may be dangerous or defective and harm customers.
- Compromising workplace health and safety to reduce costs (e.g., to maximize output, employees are not given adequate training to maintain and service machinery and equipment).

For sales and marketing managers:

- Knowingly making unsubstantiated product claims.
- Engaging in sales campaigns that use covert persuasive or subliminal advertising to create customer need for the product.
- Marketing to target groups such as the elderly, minorities, or children to build demand for a product.
- Having ongoing campaigns of unsolicited junk mail, spam, door-to-door, or telephone selling.

For accounting and finance managers:

- Engaging in misleading financial analysis involving creative accounting or "cooking the books" to hide salient facts.
- Authorizing excessive expenses and perks to managers, customers, and suppliers.
- Hiding the level and amount of top-management and director compensation.

For human resource managers:

- Failing to act fairly, objectively, and in a uniform way toward different employees or kinds of employees because of personal factors such as personality and beliefs.
- Excessively encroaching on employee privacy through non-job-related surveillance or personality, ability, and drug testing.
- Failing to respond to employee observations and concerns surrounding health and safety violations, hostile workplace issues, or inappropriate or even illegal behavior by managers or employees.

experiences gained over a lifetime—through membership in social institutions such as schools and religions, for example—also contribute to the development of the personal standards and values that a person uses to evaluate a situation and decide what is the morally right or wrong way to behave. However, suppose you are the son or daughter of a mobster and your upbringing and education take place in an organized-crime context; this affects the way you evaluate a situation. You may come to believe that it is ethical to do anything and perform any act, up to and including murder, if it benefits your family or friends. These are your ethics. They are obviously not the ethics of the wider society and so are subject to sanction. In a similar way, managers and employees in an organization may come to believe that actions they take to promote or protect their organization are more important than any harm these actions may cause to other stakeholders. So they behave unethically or illegally, and when this is discovered, they also are sanctioned.

In general, many decisions or behaviors that one person finds unethical, such as using animals for cosmetics testing, may be acceptable to another person. If decisions or behaviors are not illegal, individuals may agree to disagree about their ethical beliefs, or they may try to impose their own beliefs on other people and make those ethical beliefs the law. In all cases, however, people should develop and follow the ethical criteria described earlier to balance their self-interests against those of others when determining how they should behave in a particular situation.

Organizational Ethics

organizational ethics The guiding practices and beliefs through which a particular company and its managers view their responsibility toward their stakeholders.

Organizational ethics are the guiding practices and beliefs through which a particular company and its managers view their responsibility toward their stakeholders. The individual ethics of a company's founders and top managers are especially important in shaping the organization's code of ethics. Organizations whose founders had a vital role in creating a highly ethical code of organizational behavior include UPS, Procter & Gamble, Johnson & Johnson, and the Prudential Insurance Company. Johnson & Johnson's code of ethics—its credo—reflects a well-developed concern for its stakeholders (see Figure 4.7 on page 139). Company credos, such as that of Johnson & Johnson, are meant to deter self-interested, unethical behavior; to demonstrate to managers and employees that a company will not tolerate people who, because of their own poor ethics, put their personal interests above the interests of other organizational stakeholders and ignore the harm that they are inflicting on others; and to demonstrate that those who act unethically will be punished.

Managers or workers may behave unethically if they feel pressured to do so by the situation they are in and by unethical top managers. People typically confront ethical issues when weighing their personal interests against the effects of their actions on others. Suppose a manager knows that promotion to vice president is likely if she can secure a $100 million contract, but getting the contract requires bribing the contract giver with $1 million. The manager reasons that performing this act will ensure her career and future, and what harm would it do anyway? Bribery is common, and she knows that even if she decides not to pay the million, somebody else surely will. So what to do? Research seems to suggest that people who realize they have the most at stake in a career sense or a monetary sense are the ones most likely to act unethically. And it is exactly in this situation that a strong code of organizational ethics can help people behave in the right or appropriate way. *The New York Times's* detailed code of ethics (see nytco.com/corporate_governance/code_of_ethics/business_ethics.html), for example, was crafted by its editors to ensure the integrity and honesty of its journalists as they report sensitive information.

If a company's top managers consistently endorse the ethical principles in its corporate credo, they can prevent employees from going astray. Employees are much more likely to act unethically when a credo does not exist or is disregarded. Arthur Andersen, for example, did not follow its credo at all; its unscrupulous partners ordered middle managers to shred records that showed evidence of their wrongdoing. Although the middle managers knew this was wrong, they followed the orders because they responded to the personal power and status of the partners and not the company's code of ethics. They were afraid they would lose their jobs if they did not behave unethically, but their actions still cost them their jobs.

Top managers play a crucial role in determining a company's ethics. It is clearly important, then, that when making appointment decisions, the board of directors should scrutinize the reputations and ethical records of top managers. It is the responsibility of the board to decide whether a prospective CEO has the maturity, experience, and integrity needed to head a company and be entrusted with the capital and wealth of the organization, on which the fate of all its stakeholders depends. In the 2000s it was disclosed that the top managers of several major companies did not have the kinds of degrees or experience they had claimed on their résumés and that they had acted unethically to get their current jobs. For example, the ex-CEO of RadioShack claimed degrees he had not received.

Clearly, a track record of success is not enough to decide whether a top manager is capable of moral decision making, for a manager might have achieved this success through unethical or illegal means. It is important to investigate prospective top managers and examine their credentials. While the best predictor of future behavior is often past behavior, the board of directors needs to be on guard against unprincipled executives who use unethical means to rise to the top of the organizational hierarchy. For this reason it is necessary that a company's directors continuously monitor the behavior of top executives. In the 2000s this increased scrutiny has led to the dismissal of many top executives for breaking ethical rules concerning issues such as excessive personal loans, stock options, inflated expense accounts, and even sexual misconduct as the following "Ethics in Action" discusses.

Ethics in Action

Jonathan Reckford Rebuilds Goodwill at Habitat for Humanity

Habitat for Humanity is the 17th-largest U.S. nonprofit, and its mission is to build or renovate cost-effective, modest homes in partnership with families in need, who repay the organization by helping to build their own home or the homes of others and by repaying a no-profit mortgage. Founded decades ago by Millard and Linda Fuller, it receives more than $1 billion in donations a year for its work in more than 90 countries around the world. In 2004, a scandal struck the nonprofit when Millard Fuller was accused of sexually harassing a female employee. The board brought in an investigator to review the complaint. As the investigation unfolded, it was the Fullers' behavior and ongoing comments about the matter, however, that was deemed divisive to the organization's work and led to their dismissal. In the 2000s the efficiency and effectiveness of nonprofits have been questioned, and many analysts believe that nonprofits need to introduce new management techniques in order to improve their level of performance. Indeed, one study estimated that nonprofits could save $100 billion by using such techniques as total quality management and benchmarking, which involve an organization's imitating a company that excels in performing some functional activity.

So Habitat's board of directors searched for a new CEO who could simultaneously help the organization continue its work and improve its performance. The person they chose was Jonathan Reckford, an ex-Walt Disney, Best Buy executive and Presbyterian pastor. Reckford relished the challenge of using his management skills to find better ways to use Habitat's $1 billion in donations and to attract more donors. Quickly Reckford began to introduce best-practice techniques. For example, modeling companies like Dell and Wal-Mart that use

When Habitat for Humanity needed a new CEO, they looked to Jonathan Reckford, a Presbyterian pastor and former executive at Walt Disney and Best Buy. Reckford, pictured here with Habitat founder Jimmy Carter, quickly implemented best-practice techniques in order to help Habitat perform more effectively.

their huge buying power to lower the costs of their inputs, he emphasized the need for "scale" or volume purchasing of building products to lower costs. He introduced new kinds of output controls to provide detailed feedback on vital aspects of Habitat's performance, such as the number of new houses it built in different regions and countries and the time and cost of construction involved per house. He also introduced better human resource management practices, including creating a promotion ladder in Habitat and raising salaries to competitive levels found in other nonprofits. He decided to move a portion of Habitat's headquarters from the small city in which it had been founded to Atlanta, Georgia, to make it easier to hire skilled functional managers. Finally, he established a new set of goals and priorities for the company, and given that Reckford took over only a month after Hurricane Katrina struck, one obvious priority was to rebuild homes along the Gulf Coast. Habitat's goal was to begin construction or complete 1,000 permanent homes by the end of 2007, a feat it achieved by May 2007 upon which Reckford announced that it had a new goal–to build 1,000 more.[48]

Approaches to Social Responsibility

A company's ethics are the result of differences in societal, organizational, occupational, and individual ethics. In turn, a company's ethics determine its stance or position on social responsibility. A company's stance on **social responsibility** is the way its managers and employees view their duty or obligation to make decisions that protect, enhance, and promote the welfare and well-being of stakeholders and society as a whole.[49] As we noted earlier, when no laws exist that specify how a company should act toward stakeholders, managers must decide what the right, ethical, and socially responsible thing to do is. Differences in business ethics can lead companies to take very different positions or views on what their responsibility is toward their stakeholders.

Many kinds of decisions signal a company's beliefs about its obligations to make socially responsible business decisions. (See Table 4.3.) The decision to spend money on training and educating employees–investing in them–is one such decision; so is the decision to minimize or avoid layoffs whenever possible. The decision to act promptly and warn customers when a batch of defective merchandise has been accidentally sold is another one. Companies that try to hide such problems show little regard for social responsibility. In the 1990s, both GM and Ford tried to hide the fact that several of their vehicles had defects that rendered them dangerous to drive; the companies were penalized with hundreds of millions of dollars in damages for their unethical behavior. In the 2000s they have been quick to announce recalls to fix problems. On the other hand, in 2006, when HP discovered one of its most popular cameras could catch fire if users attempted to recharge ordinary batteries, it quickly announced a software fix for the problem; informing the public was the right thing to do.[50] The way a company announces business problems or admits its mistakes provides strong clues about its stance on social responsibility.

Four Different Approaches

The strength of companies' commitment to social responsibility can range from low to high (see Figure 4.6). At the low end of the range is an **obstructionist approach,** in which companies and their managers choose *not* to behave in a socially responsible

LO6 Distinguish between the four main approaches toward social responsibility that a company can take.

social responsibility The way a company's managers and employees view their duty or obligation to make decisions that protect, enhance, and promote the welfare and well-being of stakeholders and society as a whole.

obstructionist approach Companies and their managers choose *not* to behave in a socially responsible way and instead behave unethically and illegally.

Table 4.3
Forms of Socially Responsible Behavior

Managers are being socially responsible and showing their support for their stakeholders when they:

- Provide severance payments to help laid-off workers make ends meet until they can find another job.

- Provide workers with opportunities to enhance their skills and acquire additional education so that they can remain productive and do not become obsolete because of changes in technology.

- Allow employees to take time off when they need to and provide health care and pension benefits for employees.

- Contribute to charities or support various civic-minded activities in the cities or towns in which they are located. (Target and Levi Strauss both contribute 5% of their profits to support schools, charities, the arts, and other good works.)

- Decide to keep open a factory whose closure would devastate the local community.

- Decide to keep a company's operations in the United States to protect the jobs of American workers rather than move abroad.

- Decide to spend money to improve a new factory so that it will not pollute the environment.

- Decline to invest in countries that have poor human rights records.

- Choose to help poor countries develop an economic base to improve living standards.

way. Instead, they behave unethically and illegally and do all they can to prevent knowledge of their behavior from reaching other organizational stakeholders and society at large. Managers at the Mansville Corporation adopted this approach when they sought to hide evidence that asbestos causes lung damage; so, too, did tobacco companies when they sought to hide evidence that cigarette smoking causes lung cancer.

Top managers at Enron also acted in an obstructionist way when they prevented employees from selling Enron shares in their pension funds even before employees knew the company was in trouble. At the same time, top managers sold hundreds of millions of dollars' worth of their own Enron stock. Senior partners at Arthur Andersen who instructed their subordinates to shred files chose, like the managers of all these organizations, an obstructionist approach. The result was not only a loss of reputation but devastation for the organization and for all stakeholders involved. All these companies are no longer in business. The unethical behavior characteristic of the obstructionist approach is exemplified in the way Beech-Nut's management team in the 1980s put personal interests before customers' health and above the law.

Figure 4.6
Four Approaches to Social Responsibility

Ethics in Action

Apple Juice or Sugar Water?

In the early 1980s Beech-Nut, a maker of baby foods, was in grave financial trouble as it strove to compete with Gerber Products, the market leader. Threatened with the bankruptcy of the company if it could not lower its operating costs, Beech-Nut entered into an agreement with a low-cost supplier of apple juice concentrate. The agreement would save the company over $250,000 annually at a time when every dollar counted. Soon, one of Beech-Nut's food scientists became concerned about the quality of the concentrate. He believed that it was not made from apples alone but contained large quantities of corn syrup and cane sugar. He brought this information to the attention of top managers at Beech-Nut, but they were obsessed with the need to keep costs down and chose to ignore his concerns. The company continued to produce and sell its product as pure apple juice.[51]

Eventually investigators from the U.S. Food and Drug Administration (FDA) confronted Beech-Nut with evidence that the concentrate was adulterated. The top managers issued denials and quickly shipped the remaining stock of apple juice to the market before their inventory could be seized. The scientist who had questioned the purity of the apple juice had resigned from Beech-Nut, but he decided to blow the whistle on the company. He told the FDA that Beech-Nut's top management had known of the problem with the concentrate and had acted to maximize company profits rather than to inform customers about the additives in the apple juice. In 1987, the company pleaded guilty to charges that it had deliberately sold adulterated juice and was fined over $2 million. Its top managers were also found guilty and were sentenced to prison terms.

Consumer trust in Beech-Nut products plummeted, as did the value of Beech Nut stock. The company's reputation was ruined, and it was eventually sold to Ralston Purina, now owned by Nestlé, which installed a new management team and a new ethical code of values to guide future business decisions.

defensive approach Companies and their managers behave ethically to the degree that they stay within the law and abide strictly with legal requirements.

A **defensive approach** indicates at least a commitment to ethical behavior.[52] Defensive companies and managers stay within the law and abide strictly with legal requirements but make no attempt to exercise social responsibility beyond what the law dictates—thus they can and often do act unethically. These are the kinds of companies, like Computer Associates and WorldCom, that give their managers large stock options and bonuses even when company performance is declining. The managers are the kind who sell their stock in advance of other stockholders because they know that their company's performance is about to fall. Although acting on inside information is illegal, it is often very hard to prove since top managers have the right to sell their shares whenever they choose. The founders of most dot-com companies took advantage of this legal loophole to sell hundreds of millions of dollars of their dot-com shares before their stock prices collapsed. When making ethical decisions, such managers put their own interests first and commonly harm other stakeholders.

accommodative approach Companies and their managers behave legally and ethically and try to balance the interests of different stakeholders as the need arises.

An **accommodative approach** is an acknowledgment of the need to support social responsibility. Accommodative companies and managers agree that organizational members ought to behave legally and ethically, and they try to balance the interests of different stakeholders against one another so that the claims of stockholders are seen in relation to the claims of other stakeholders. Managers adopting this approach want to make choices that are reasonable in the eyes of society and want to do the right thing when called on to do so.

This approach is the one taken by the typical large U.S. company, which has the most to lose from unethical or illegal behavior. Generally, the older and more reputable a company, the more likely are its managers to curb attempts by their subordinates to act unethically. Large companies like GM, Intel, Du Pont, and Dell seek every way to build their companies' competitive advantages. Nevertheless, they reign in attempts by their managers to behave unethically or illegally, knowing the grave consequences such behavior can have on future profitability.

proactive approach
Companies and their managers actively embrace socially responsible behavior, going out of their way to learn about the needs of different stakeholder groups and utilizing organizational resources to promote the interests of all stakeholders.

Companies and managers taking a **proactive approach** actively embrace the need to behave in socially responsible ways. They go out of their way to learn about the needs of different stakeholder groups and are willing to utilize organizational resources to promote the interests not only of stockholders but also of the other stakeholders. Such companies are at the forefront of campaigns for causes such as a pollution-free environment; recycling and conservation of resources; the minimization or elimination of the use of animals in drug and cosmetics testing; and the reduction of crime, illiteracy, and poverty. For example, companies like McDonald's, Green Mountain Coffee, Ben and Jerry's, Whole Foods, and Target all have a reputation for being proactive in the support of stakeholders such as their suppliers or the community in which they operate.

Why Be Socially Responsible?

Several advantages result when companies and their managers behave in a socially responsible manner. First, demonstrating its social responsibility helps a company build a good reputation. Reputation is the trust, goodwill, and confidence others have in a company that leads them to want to do business with it. The reward for a good company reputation is increased business and improved ability to obtain resources from stakeholders.[53] Reputation thus can enhance profitability and build stockholder wealth. Therefore, behaving socially responsibly is the economically right thing to do because companies that do so benefit from increasing business and rising profits.

A second major reason for companies to act socially responsibly toward employees, customers, and society is that in a capitalist system companies, as well as the government, have to bear the costs of protecting their stakeholders, providing health care and income, paying taxes, and so on. So if all companies in a society act socially responsibly, the quality of life as a whole increases.

Moreover, the way companies behave toward their employees determines many of a society's values and norms and the ethics of its citizens, as noted above. It has been suggested that if all organizations adopted a caring approach and agreed that their responsibility is to promote the interests of their employees, a climate of caring would pervade the wider society. Experts point to Japan, Sweden, Germany, the Netherlands, and Switzerland as countries where organizations are highly socially responsible and where, as a result, crime, poverty, and unemployment rates are relatively low, literacy rates are relatively high, and sociocultural values promote harmony between different groups of people. Business activity affects all aspects of people's lives, so the way business behaves toward stakeholders affects how stakeholders will behave toward business. You "reap what you sow," as the adage goes.

Google employees Yadi Arewal, right, and Harpreet Arewal, left, dance during the annual Google Dance at its headquarters in Mountain View, California. Google is one of many companies known for having a culture that promotes employee well-being.

The Role of Organizational Culture

While an organization's code of ethics guides decision making when ethical questions arise, managers can go one step further by ensuring that important ethical values and norms are key features of an organization's culture. For example, Herb Kelleher and Coleen Barrett created Southwest Airlines' culture in which promoting employee well-being is a main company priority; this translates into organizational values and norms dictating that layoffs should be avoided and employees should share in the profits the company makes.[54] Google, UPS, and Toyota, are among the many companies

Figure 4.7
Johnson & Johnson's Credo

Our Credo

We believe our first responsibility is to the doctors, nurses and patients,
to mothers and fathers and all others who use our products and services.
In meeting their needs everything we do must be of high quality.
We must constantly strive to reduce our costs
in order to maintain reasonable prices.
Customers' orders must be serviced promptly and accurately.
Our suppliers and distributors must have an opportunity
to make a fair profit.

We are responsible to our employees,
the men and women who work with us throughout the world.
Everyone must be considered as an individual.
We must respect their dignity and recognize their merit.
They must have a sense of security in their jobs.
Compensation must be fair and adequate,
and working conditions clean, orderly and safe.
We must be mindful of ways to help our employees fulfill
their family responsibilities.
Employees must feel free to make suggestions and complaints.
There must be equal opportunity for employment, development
and advancement for those qualified.
We must provide competent management,
and their actions must be just and ethical.

We are responsible to the communities in which we live and work
and to the world community as well.
We must be good citizens—support good works and charities
and bear our fair share of taxes.
We must encourage civic improvements and better health and education.
We must maintain in good order
the property we are privileged to use,
protecting the environment and natural resources.

Our final responsibility is to our stockholders.
Business must make a sound profit.
We must experiment with new ideas.
Research must be carried on, innovative programs developed
and mistakes paid for.
New equipment must be purchased, new facilities provided
and new products launched.
Reserves must be created to provide for adverse times.
When we operate according to these principles,
the stockholders should realize a fair return.

Johnson & Johnson

Source: © Johnson & Johnson. Used with permission.

who espouse similar values. When ethical values and norms such as these are part of an organization's culture, they help organizational members resist self-interested action because they recognize that they are part of something bigger than themselves.[55]

Managers' roles in developing ethical values and standards in other employees are very important. Employees naturally look to those in authority to provide leadership, just as a country's citizens look to its political leaders, and managers become ethical role models whose behavior is scrutinized by subordinates. If top managers are perceived as being self-interested, and not ethical, their subordinates are not likely to behave in an ethical manner. Employees may think that if it's all right for a top manager to engage in dubious behavior, it's all right for them too, and for employees this might mean slacking off, reducing customer support, and not taking supportive kinds of actions to help their company. The actions of top managers such as CEOs and the president of the United States are scrutinized so closely for ethical improprieties because their actions represent the values of their organizations and, in the case of the president, the values of the nation.

Managers can also provide a visible means of support to develop an ethical culture. Increasingly, organizations are creating the role of ethics officer, or **ethics ombudsman,** to monitor their ethical practices and procedures. The ethics ombudsman is responsible for communicating ethical standards to all employees, for designing systems to monitor employees' conformity to those standards, and for teaching managers and employees at all levels of the organization how to respond to ethical dilemmas appropriately.[56] Because the ethics ombudsman has organizationwide authority, organizational members in any department can communicate instances of unethical behavior by their managers or coworkers without fear of retribution. This arrangement makes it easier for everyone to behave ethically. In addition, ethics ombudsmen can provide guidance when organizational members are uncertain about whether an action is ethical. Some organizations have an organizationwide ethics committee to provide guidance on ethical issues and help write and update the company code of ethics.

Ethical organizational cultures encourage organizational members to behave in a socially responsible manner. In fact, managers at Johnson & Johnson take social responsibility so seriously that their organization is often held up as an example of a socially responsible firm. The Johnson & Johnson Credo (see Figure 4.7) is one of the many ways in which social responsibility is emphasized at the company. As discussed in the "Ethics in Action" below, Johnson & Johnson's ethical organizational culture provides the company and its various stakeholder groups with numerous benefits.

ethics ombudsman

A manager responsible for communicating and teaching ethical standards to all employees and monitoring their conformity to those standards.

Ethics in Action

Johnson & Johnson's Ethical Culture

Johnson & Johnson is so well known for its ethical culture that it has been judged as having the best corporate reputation for two years in a row, based on a survey of over 26,000 consumers conducted by Harris Interactive and the Reputation Institute at New York University.[57] Johnson & Johnson grew from a family business led by General Robert Wood Johnson in the 1930s to a major maker of pharmaceutical and medical products. Attesting to the role of managers in creating ethical organizational cultures, Johnson emphasized the importance of ethics and responsibility to stakeholders and wrote the first Johnson & Johnson Credo in 1943.[58]

The credo continues to guide employees at Johnson & Johnson today and outlines the company's commitments to its different stakeholder groups. It emphasizes that the organization's first responsibility is to doctors, nurses, patients, and consumers. Following this group are suppliers and distributors, employees, communities, and, lastly, stockholders.[59] This credo has served managers and employees at Johnson & Johnson well and guided some difficult decision making, such as the decision to recall all Tylenol capsules in the U.S. market after cyanide-laced capsules were responsible for seven deaths in Chicago.

True to its ethical culture and outstanding reputation, consumer well-being always comes before profit considerations at Johnson & Johnson. For example, around 20 years ago, Johnson & Johnson's baby oil was used as a tanning product at a time when the harmful effects of sun exposure were not well known by the public.[60] The product manager for baby oil at the time, Carl Spalding, was making a presentation to top management about marketing plans when the company's president, David Clare, mentioned that tanning might not be healthy.[61] Before launching his planned marketing campaign, Spalding looked into the health-related concerns connected with tanning and discovered some evidence suggesting that health problems could arise from too much exposure to the sun. Even though the evidence was not definitive, Spalding recommended that baby oil no longer be marketed as a tanning aid, a decision that resulted in a 50% decrease in sales of baby oil, to the tune of $5 million.[62]

The ethical values and norms in Johnson & Johnson's culture, along with its credo, guide managers such as Spalding to make the right decision in difficult situations. Hence, it is understandable why Johnson & Johnson is renowned for its corporate reputation. An ethical culture and outstanding reputation have other benefits in addition to helping employees make the right decisions in questionable situations. Jeanne Hamway, vice president for recruiting, finds that Johnson & Johnson's reputation helps the company recruit and attract a diverse workforce.[63] Moreover, when organizations develop an outstanding reputation, their employees often are less tempted to act in a self-interested or unethical manner. For example, managers at Johnson & Johnson suggest that since employees in the company never accept bribes, the company is known as one in which bribes should not be offered in the first place.[64] All in all, ethical cultures such as Johnson & Johnson's benefit various stakeholder groups in multiple ways.

Summary and Review

THE NATURE OF ETHICS   Ethical issues are central to the way companies and their managers make decisions, and they affect not only the efficiency and effectiveness of the way companies operate but also the prosperity of a nation. The result of ethical behavior is a general increase in company performance and in a nation's standard of living, well-being, and wealth.

An ethical dilemma is the quandary people find themselves in when they have to decide if they should act in a way that might help another person or group, and is the "right" thing to do, even though it might go against their own self-interest. Ethics are the inner-guiding moral principles, values, and beliefs that people use to analyze or interpret a situation and then decide what is the "right" or appropriate way to behave.

LO1   Ethical beliefs alter and change as time passes, and as they do so laws change to reflect the changing ethical beliefs of a society.

LO 2, 4   **STAKEHOLDERS AND ETHICS**   Stakeholders are people and groups who have a claim on and a stake in a company. The main stakeholder groups are stockholders, managers, employees, suppliers and distributors, customers, and a community, society, and nation. Companies and their managers need to make ethical business decisions that promote the well-being of their stakeholders and avoid doing them harm.

LO 3, 5   To determine if a business decision is ethical, managers can use four ethical rules to analyze it: the utilitarian, moral rights, justice, and practical rules. Managers should behave ethically because this avoids the tragedy of the commons and results in a general increase in efficiency, effectiveness, and company performance. The main determinants of differences in a manager's, company's, and country's business ethics are societal, occupational, individual, and organizational.

LO6   **ETHICS AND SOCIAL RESPONSIBILITY**   A company's stance on social responsibility is the way its managers and employees view their duty or obligation to make decisions that protect, enhance, and promote the welfare and well-being of stakeholders and society as a whole.

LO6   **APPROACHES TO SOCIAL RESPONSIBILITY**   There are four main approaches to social responsibility: obstructionist, defensive, accommodative, and proactive. The rewards from behaving in a socially responsible way are a good reputation, the support of all organizational stakeholders, and thus superior company performance.

Management in Action

Topics for Discussion and Action

DISCUSSION

1. What is the relationship between ethics and the law? **[LO1]**

2. Why do the claims and interests of stakeholders sometimes conflict? **[LO2]**

3. Why should managers use ethical criteria to guide their decision making? **[LO3]**

4. As an employee of a company, what are some of the most unethical business practices that you have encountered in its dealings with stakeholders? **[LO4]**

5. What are the main determinants of business ethics? **[LO5]**

ACTION

6. Find a manager and ask about the most important ethical rules that he or she uses to make the right decisions. **[LO3]**

7. Find an example of (a) a company that has an obstructionist approach to social responsibility and (b) one that has an accommodative approach. **[LO6]**

Building Management Skills
Dealing with Ethical Dilemmas [LO 1, 4]

Use the chapter material to decide how you, as a manager, should respond to each of the following ethical dilemmas.

1. You are planning to leave your job to go work for a competitor; your boss invites you to an important meeting where you will learn about new products your company will be bringing out next year. Do you go to the meeting?

2. You're the manager of sales in an expensive sports-car dealership. A young executive who has just received a promotion comes in and wants to buy a car that you know is out of her price range. Do you encourage the executive to buy it so that you can receive a big commission on the sale?

3. You sign a contract to manage a young rock band, and that group agrees to let you produce their next seven records, for which they will receive royalties of 5%. Their first record is a smash hit and sells millions. Do you increase their royalty rate on their future records?

Managing Ethically [LO 3, 5]

As the chapter discussed, Arthur Andersen's culture had become so strong that some of the company's partners and their subordinates acted unethically and pursued their own interests at the expense of other stakeholders. Many employees knew they were doing wrong but were afraid to refuse to follow orders. At Beech-Nut, the company's ethical values completely broke down; some managers joked about the harm being done to stakeholders.

Questions

1. Why is it that an organization's values and norms can become too strong and lead to unethical behavior?

2. What steps can a company take to prevent this problem—to stop its values and norms from becoming so inwardly focused that managers and employees lose sight of their responsibility to their stakeholders?

Small Group Breakout Exercise

Is Chewing Gum the "Right" Thing to Do? [LO 1, 3]

Read the paragraph below. Then break up into groups of three or four people and answer the discussion questions.

In the United States the right to chew gum is taken for granted. Although it is often against the rules to chew gum in a high school classroom, church, and so on, it is legal to do so on the street. If you possess or chew gum on a street in Singapore, you can be arrested. Chewing gum has been made illegal in Singapore because those in power believe that it creates a disgusting mess on pavements and feel that people cannot be trusted to dispose of their gum properly and thus should have no right to use it.

1. What makes chewing gum acceptable in the United States and unacceptable in Singapore?

2. Why can you chew gum on the street but not in a church?

3. How can you use ethical principles to decide when gum chewing is ethical or unethical and if and when it should be made illegal?

Exploring the World Wide Web [LO 2, 5]

Go to Wal-Mart's Web site (www.walmart.com) and read the information there about the company's stance on the ethics of global outsourcing and the treatment of workers in countries abroad. Then search the Web for some recent stories about Wal-Mart's global purchasing practices and reports on the enforcement of its code of conduct.

1. What ethical principles guide Wal-Mart's approach to global purchasing?

2. Does Wal-Mart appear to be doing a good job of enforcing its global code of conduct?

Be the Manager [LO3]

Creating an Ethical Code

You are an entrepreneur who has decided to go into business and open a steak and chicken restaurant. Your business plan requires that you hire at least 20 people as chefs, waiters, and so on. As the owner, you are drawing up a list of ethical principles that each of these people will receive and must agree to when he or she accepts a job offer. These principles outline your view of what is right or acceptable behavior and what will be expected both from you and from your employees.

Create a list of the five main ethical rules or principles you will use to govern the way your business operates. Be sure to spell out how these principles relate to your stakeholders; for example, state the rules you intend to follow in dealing with your employees and customers.

BusinessWeek ## Case in the News [LO 1, 3, 5]

Cleaning Up Boeing

When W. James McNerney Jr. decided that Boeing Co.'s top managers needed a loud wake-up call, the new chief executive chose the obvious place to sound the alarm: the company's annual executive retreat. A year earlier, the event had been held at the posh Mission Hills Country Club in Palm Springs, CA, and nobody apparently had a better time than McNerney's predecessor, Harry Stonecipher. After a day devoted largely to socializing and playing golf, the former CEO, surrounded by Boeing's elite, closed down the bar and then fired up a cigar. It was at the same event that the married Stonecipher began a relationship with a female vice-president at Boeing—a misjudgment that ultimately paved the way for his humiliating ouster, and for McNerney's appointment as CEO.

The "Palm Springs fling," as it became known at Boeing, marked an all-time low for the company. It followed a three-year binge of widely publicized corporate misbehavior highlighted by the jailing of Boeing's former chief financial officer for holding illegal job negotiations with a senior Pentagon official, the indictment of a manager for allegedly stealing some 25,000 pages of proprietary documents from his former employer, Lockheed Martin Corp.,

and the judicial finding that Boeing had abused attorney-client privilege to help cover up internal studies showing that female employees were paid less than men. Scandals involving multiple forms of misconduct in geographically scattered locations enveloped nearly every division at Boeing, leaving little doubt that the legendary company, even as it began to enjoy a cyclical boom, was plagued by a poisonous culture.

Given that backdrop, nobody was particularly shocked when the 2006 annual retreat was moved to the more quotidian Hyatt Regency in Orlando and pared from three days to one and a half. The real surprises began during a breakfast speech when the normally upbeat McNerney launched into the sharpest critique of the company he had ever aired before such a large audience. Speaking without notes, McNerney said that "management had gotten carried away with itself," that too many executives had become used to "hiding in the bureaucracy," that the company had failed to "develop the best leadership." The next day, McNerney introduced General Counsel Douglas G. Bain, who really lowered the boom, railing against Boeing's pervasive "culture of silence." To grab the group's attention, Bain rattled off the federal prison numbers of two jailed former employees. "These are not ZIP Codes," Bain snapped. With

McNerney looking on in clear support, Bain warned the audience that many prosecutors "believe that Boeing is rotten to the core."

The challenge of cleaning out the rot at the heart of Boeing is one for which McNerney, 56, has spent his entire professional life preparing. Since earning his master's degree from Harvard Business School in 1975, he has uprooted his family every two or three years in search of the next professional test. He started in brand marketing at Procter & Gamble Co., jumped to McKinsey & Co., and then climbed the ranks through General Electric Co. for 18 years, where he topped out as CEO of GE's aircraft engine business, one of Boeing's most important business partners. After losing in a three-way race to replace Jack Welch as CEO of GE, McNerney was snapped up by 3M Co. in 2001 to turn around the struggling manufacturer. A short time later, he joined Boeing's board.

Straight Arrow

McNerney is a leader who both understands and cares about the aerospace giant. The series of ethical violations that surfaced at Boeing grated on the arrow-straight McNerney when he was a director, as did the fact that in 2003 the iconic company lost its status as the world's No. 1 commercial aircraft company to Airbus. Now McNerney has what he has always wanted: a chance to seal his legacy at one of America's most important companies. But to do so, he'll have to reinvent the 153,000-employee, $55 billion colossus, which, besides losing its moral compass, has not yet reached its profit-making potential. "I think the culture had morphed in dysfunctional ways in some places," the polished, soft-spoken McNerney said in a recent conversation with *BusinessWeek,* his first extensive interview since taking the job. "There are elements of our culture that I think we all would like to change."

Specifically, McNerney wants to unite a balkanized management team that has been at war ever since Boeing merged with McDonnell Douglas Corp. in 1997. The distinct cultures of the two companies never meshed, and the differences calcified into bitter rivalries. Having spent his first six months on the job in a "deep dive" learning about the company, McNerney believes that internal rivalry not only is at the root of the company's ethical scandals but also has prevented managers from cutting costs and sharing good ideas effectively. His prescription includes some predictable elements, including exerting more effective central leadership over Boeing's three divisions, changing the way executives are paid, and encouraging managers to exploit the giant manufacturer's cost-cutting leverage. But it also includes some unusual ones, such as encouraging

managers to talk more openly about Boeing's severe ethical lapses. "I want to try to make it OK to have that dialogue," says McNerney. The scandals at Boeing aren't "something that happened in a separate part of the company that half of us aren't responsible for."

Relentless ethical scandals and bitter infighting, he believes, have dampened the aerospace giant's performance. "If we can get the values lined up with performance, then this is an absolutely unbeatable company," says McNerney. Rather than simply giving speeches about management virtue, insiders say that McNerney is trying to lead by example. He wins praise from coworkers for paying attention to the small things like remembering people's names, listening closely to their presentations, and not embarrassing underlings in public. That marks a sharp distinction from the blunt Stonecipher and the remote Philip M. Condit, who stepped down as CEO in 2003 in the wake of the Pentagon scandals.

More important, McNerney asks different types of questions than Stonecipher and Condit. "Phil or Harry would get into the weeds on the technical stuff," says this executive. "But Jim is more interested in the human side. He is interested in how to . . . create a culture where people speak up and take the risk and stop a production line because something is wrong."

Revamping pay is another powerful tool McNerney is using to reform Boeing's culture. In the old days, no points were awarded for collaborating with other units or following ethics rules. Now pay and bonuses are directly linked to how well executives embrace a set of six leadership attributes such as "Living Boeing Values." That includes new criteria such as promoting integrity and avoiding abusive behavior. McNerney is also giving managers financial incentives that better reflect the cyclical nature of the aerospace industry. Boeing's past long-term incentive system, called Performance Shares, paid out based on a higher stock price. But that system failed to consider management's performance during the down cycles inherent in the industry, thus offering managers few incentives to find a way to improve performance during a downturn.

Questions for Discussion

1. What kinds of factors resulted in Boeing's unethical culture?

2. What steps is its new CEO taking to change Boeing's culture and make ethical behavior the center of attention?

Source: Stanley Holmes, "Cleaning Up Boeing." Reprinted from the March 13, 2006, issue of *BusinessWeek* by special permission. Copyright © 2006 by The McGraw-Hill Companies, Inc.

BusinessWeek Case in the News

Fixing Apple's "Sweatshop" Woes

As workers in the United States and elsewhere commanded ever higher wages, manufacturers shifted operations elsewhere, including such places as Mexico and Japan, and later Taiwan and China. Many companies, Apple among them, get outside companies to handle the manufacturing

entirely, often in places where labor costs are low and workplace regulations differ from those in the United States and Europe.

On June 25, it was reported that Apple Computer's iPod portable media players are made in what was portrayed as sweatshop conditions. The plant specified in the report is operated in Longhua, China, by an outfit called Foxconn, the trade name

given to Hon Hai Precision Industry. Known as a contract electronics manufacturer—a company whose sole purpose is to manufacture products for other companies—it is said to employ some 200,000 people who live in dormitories crammed with up to 100 people at a time, for wages that appear to Western eyes shockingly low—about $50 a month.

Last year, Hon Hai eclipsed Flextronics, the Singapore-based electronics giant, as the world's biggest contract manufacturer. Hon Hai's other clients include Hewlett-Packard, Nokia, and Sony. Hon Hai executives initially took issue with the report, pointing out what they said were inconsistencies: Its entire corporate workforce is only 160,000 people, and so how could a single plant employ 200,000? A later report appeared on ChinaCSR.com, a Web site devoted to promoting corporate responsibility in China. In that account, Hon Hai admitted to breaking some local laws regarding overtime. It also said its salary structure had been misinterpreted in media reports and that it complies with minimum-wage laws.

Walking the Walk?

Apple, clearly wanting to avoid unpleasant appearances, had sent a team to investigate. Some reports have suggested the investigation was complete, but at the time of printing, it was not. "We are still investigating the working conditions at Foxconn's manufacturing plant in Longhua," says Apple spokesman Steve Dowling. "This is a thorough audit, which includes employee working and living conditions, interviews of employees and managers, compliance with overtime and wage regulations, and other areas as necessary to insure adherence to Apple's supplier code of conduct. Apple's supplier code of conduct sets the bar higher than accepted industry standards and we take allegations of noncompliance very seriously."

Clearly, much about this situation is not yet known, and Apple is to be commended for springing into action when the allegations surfaced. Steve Jobs is a socially conscious person, and he associates with people of the same ilk. Former Vice President Al Gore is on the Apple board of directors. Apple makes a special U2-branded version of the iPod whose front man is global activist Bono,

the band's lead singer. Such high-profile folks linked with Apple—and more importantly for Apple, a lot of its customers—will eagerly await the investigation's outcome.

What are the possible scenarios, starting with the worst-case? For the sake of argument, let's assume that the allegations are true, and that working conditions at the plant are horrible. In this case, it would be incumbent on Apple to either demand rapid and sweeping changes at Hon Hai's plant, or to take its business elsewhere. Certainly, other companies could build iPods, but such a change wouldn't happen without major disruption to Apple's business. Products could be delayed or go in short supply. This would anger shareholders, and could cause serious damage to Apple's reputation.

No Hiding

But Apple would clearly want to avoid the kind of public-relations problems that for so long plagued Nike about sweatshops in Vietnam. Stigmas like the one in that case don't go away fast. Decisive, corrective action would be the order of the day, even if it hurts business.

Consider the opposite scenario. Let's say that Apple's investigation finds nothing amiss or improper with the way iPods are made by Hon Hai and the conditions under which its employees work. Apple and Hon Hai jointly brand the story as fiction and go their merry way, making iPods and money.

Both scenarios call for transparency. If the findings are bad, people will wonder if the whole story has been told. If the findings are good, questions may linger, nevertheless, and doubt will fester. Some will wonder if it's really humane to buy an iPod. Regardless of the findings, Apple should make every effort to disclose whatever it finds—good or bad—immediately. And it should ask for help from an independent authority to verify whatever the company

finds and to help oversee whatever corrective action is taken—if any is ultimately needed.

Be a Model

I'd suggest the U.K.-based Catholic Agency for Overseas Development. In 2003, the agency reported on working conditions in the PC industry—again at contract manufacturers—and spurred changes from companies such as Dell, HP, and IBM, which were targeted in the first report. They've since updated their supplier codes of conduct to address issues the agency raised.

Apple has a Supplier Code of Conduct as well, which can be read at this site. Among the actions it forbids are corporal punishment of workers. Working hours are to be no more than 60 hours in a single week, including overtime. Plus, workers must be allowed one day off each week. Dowling says Apple's code of conduct is intended to exceed standards established by the International Labor Organization. "We set the bar high," he says.

But is it enough to demand that another company do things in a manner you prefer? High-profile companies like Apple are often held to higher standards because they lead in what they do. The industry follows Apple in how computers are made and personal electronics are designed. Apple should also set an example for how their products are made.

Controlling its Destiny

One way to do that: build a factory in China. Rather than hire a Chinese company to build iPods, why couldn't Apple build them in China in its own factory? It has $8.2 billion in cash and would be in good corporate company. I can think of at least two electronics companies, Motorola and Plantronics, that both build products at wholly owned facilities in China. Plantronics spent $23 million to build a 270,000 square-foot plant for wireless-phone headsets. It employs 425 now, and expects the headcount there to grow to 2,000.

An Apple factory built to accommodate good working standards in China would give the company total control over conditions, environmental practices, and all the other things that manufacturers like to brag about these days. It would erase any concerns—warranted or not—about worker exploitation there.

It would be no small undertaking: Expensive, complicated, fraught with bureaucracy. But it could be done. No one said running the world's most influential technology company would be easy.

Questions for Discussion

1. What kinds of ethical criteria could Apple use to decide if it should continue to buy from Foxcomm, or establish its own factory in China?

2. If it decides to continue to buy its components, what kinds of safeguard could it put in place?

CHAPTER 5

Managing Diverse Employees in a Multicultural Environment

Learning Objectives

After studying this chapter, you should be able to:

LO1 Discuss the increasing diversity of the workforce and of the organizational environment.

LO2 Explain the central role that managers play in the effective management of diversity.

LO3 Explain why the effective management of diversity is both an ethical and a business imperative.

LO4 Discuss how perception and the use of schemas can result in unfair treatment.

LO5 List the steps managers can take to effectively manage diversity.

LO6 Identify the two major forms of sexual harassment and how they can be eliminated.

A Manager's Challenge

Reaping the Benefits of Diversity

How can managers reap the benefits of an increasingly diverse workforce?
By all counts, the diversity of the workforce is increasing. Effectively managing diversity is more than just ensuring that diverse members of organizations are treated fairly (in and of itself, a very challenging task). When diversity is effectively managed, organizations are able to benefit from the diverse perspectives, points of view, experiences, and knowledge bases of their diverse members to produce better goods and services and be responsive to their increasingly diverse customer bases.

Extolling the benefits of effectively managing diversity is one thing, taking real and tangible steps to ensure that an organization continuously improves in this regard is another. Both organizationwide initiatives and the steps that each individual manager takes to effectively manage diversity have the potential for substantial payoffs both in terms of improved organizational effectiveness and maintaining a satisfied, committed, and motivated workforce.

Consider the steps that Sodexo, Inc., a major food and facilities management company serving over ten million customers per day in businesses, health care facilities, schools and universities, and government agencies, takes to ensure that diversity is effectively managed.[1] Sodexo encourages managers like Ron Bond, in his late 50s, to interact with diverse groups to gain a better appreciation and understanding of their experiences. When Bond attended a meeting of the Women's Food Service Forum with some of his female coworkers, he stood out as one of the very few men in attendance among around 1,500 women. Thinking back on his own experiences when,

Managers at Sodexo, which supplies and manages cafeterias like this one, have taken numerous steps to effectively manage diversity.

for example, he started out his career and women were very rare in the management ranks, Bond gained a deeper appreciation of what it means to be different in a group or organization. As he suggests, "That's a profound experience . . . I can begin to feel what it must have felt like to be different."[2]

Sodexo provides employees and managers with extensive diversity training, encourages managers to mentor and coach employees who are different from themselves, and bases 25% of top managers' bonuses on their performance on diversity initiatives including hiring and training diverse employees.[3] Managers are encouraged to sponsor affinity groups for employees that differ from themselves. For example, Bond sponsored the women's affinity group, which provides a forum for female employees to connect with each other and address their mutual concerns (e.g., a lactation room so that new mothers can pump breast milk). Sponsoring such groups helps managers become aware of and address concerns of some employee groups that they might never have thought of otherwise. Bond realized that having a lactation room was ". . . just one of those things I'd never thought about."[4]

Lorna Donatone manages a unit of Sodexo that provides food services for cruise companies. Of Swedish-German ancestry and raised in Nebraska, sponsoring Sodexo's Latino affinity group helped her to discover a better way to serve her unit's customers. Donatone now relies on more bilingual materials to promote the services she provides to cruise companies and their customers. As senior vice president and chief diversity officer for Sodexo, Dr. Rohini Anand indicates, "To really engage people, you have to create a series of epiphanies and take leaders through

those epiphanies."[5] Raytheon joins Sodexo and a growing number of companies aiming to provide managers with just these kinds of epiphanies through sponsoring affinity groups that provide a means for employees of different races, genders, religions, or sexual orientations to interact with each other and address mutual concerns as well other initiatives. For example, at Raytheon's missile-systems division, managers spent a day at work in a wheelchair so that they could better appreciate the issues disabled employees face on the job.[6]

Sodexo's effective management of diversity has not gone unnoticed in the business community, and the company and its diverse employees have received numerous awards and recognition for their diversity initiatives.[7] Frequently ranked as a best place to work for diverse employees by magazines such as *DiversityInc., Working Mother, and Latina Style,* Sodexo recently received the DiversityFirst Leadership Award from the Texas Diversity Council.[8] Dr. Anand recently was named one of the Top 20 Diversity Champions by *Diversity Edge* magazine, and Ivan Gutierrez, who heads up Sodexo's supply management unit, was recently named one of 28 Young Hispanic Corporate Achievers by the Hispanic Association on Corporate Responsibility.[9]

Other organizations taking real and concrete steps to effectively manage diversity include Coca-Cola, Johnson & Johnson, Merrill Lynch, and General Mills.[10] At General Mills, for example, top managers' pay is tied to their effective management of diversity, and achieving diversity goals is taken into account in determining their bonuses. With specific diversity goals in place, initiatives such as General Mills' have the potential to have real payoffs. General Mills reports that the percentage of its top managers who are women and minorities has about doubled over the past 10 years and, thus, it appears that the company is better able to utilize the talents of its diverse members.[11]

As these and many other companies and their managers realize, effectively managing diversity is much more than ensuring that diverse applicants are hired. It also means ensuring that they have the same opportunities to advance and succeed in an organization as other employees do and are retained. Merrill Lynch, for example, bases about 20% of its branch managers' bonuses on the hiring, development, success, and retention of diverse employees.[12] Holding top managers accountable for effectively managing diversity and providing all employees with the kinds of experiences that foster understanding of those who are different from them helps to ensure that organizations do reap the benefits from an increasingly diverse workforce.[13]

Overview

As indicated in "A Manager's Challenge," the effective management of diversity means much more than hiring diverse employees. It means learning to appreciate and respond appropriately to the needs, attitudes, beliefs, and values that diverse people bring to an organization. It also means correcting misconceptions about why and how different kinds of employee groups are different from one another and finding the most effective way to utilize the skills and talents of diverse employees.

In this chapter, we focus on the effective management of diversity in an environment that is becoming increasingly diverse in all respects. Not only is the diversity of the global workforce increasing, but suppliers and customers are also becoming increasingly diverse. Managers need to proactively manage diversity to be able to attract and retain the best employees and effectively compete in a diverse global environment. For example, managers at the audit and consulting firm Deloitte & Touche have instituted a program to encourage minority suppliers to compete for its business, and the firm sponsors schools and colleges that supply a stream of well-trained recruits.[14]

Sometimes well-intentioned managers inadvertently treat one group of employees differently from another group, even though there are no performance-based differences between the two groups. This chapter explores why differential treatment occurs and the steps managers and organizations can take to ensure that diversity, in all respects, is effectively managed for the good of all organizational stakeholders.

LO1 Discuss the increasing diversity of the workforce and of the organizational environment.

The Increasing Diversity of the Workforce and the Environment

One of the most important management issues to emerge over the last 30 years has been the increasing diversity of the workforce. **Diversity** is dissimilarities—differences—among people due to age, gender, race, ethnicity, religion, sexual orientation, socioeconomic background, education, experience, physical appearance, capabilities/disabilities, and any other characteristic that is used to distinguish between people (see Figure 5.1).

Diversity raises important ethical issues and social responsibility issues (see Chapter 4). It is also a critical issue for organizations, one that if not handled well can bring an organization to its knees, especially in our increasingly global environment. There are several reasons why diversity is such a pressing concern and issue both in the popular press and for managers and organizations:

diversity Differences among people in age, gender, race, ethnicity, religion, sexual orientation, socioeconomic background, and capabilities/disabilities.

• There is a strong ethical imperative in many societies that diverse people receive equal opportunities and be treated fairly and justly. Unfair treatment is also illegal.

Figure 5.1
Sources of Diversity in the Workplace

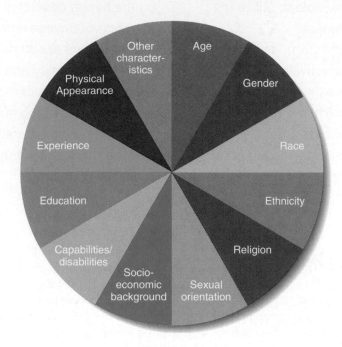

- Effectively managing diversity can improve organizational effectiveness.[15] When managers effectively manage diversity, they not only encourage other managers to treat diverse members of an organization fairly and justly but also realize that diversity is an important organizational resource that can help an organization gain a competitive advantage.

- There is substantial evidence that diverse individuals continue to experience unfair treatment in the workplace as a result of biases, stereotypes, and overt discrimination.[16] In one study, résumés of equally qualified men and women were sent to high-priced Philadelphia restaurants (where potential earnings are high). Though equally qualified, men were more than twice as likely as women to be called for a job interview and more than five times as likely to receive a job offer.[17] Findings from another study suggest that both women and men tend to believe that women will accept lower pay than men; this is a possible explanation for the continuing gap in pay between men and women.[18]

Other kinds of diverse employees may face even greater barriers. For example, the federal Glass Ceiling Commission Report indicated that African-Americans have the hardest time being promoted and climbing the corporate ladder, that Asians are often stereotyped into technical jobs, and that Hispanics are assumed to be less well educated than other minority groups.[19] (The term **glass ceiling** alludes to the invisible barriers that prevent minorities and women from being promoted to top corporate positions.)[20]

Before we can discuss the multitude of issues surrounding the effective management of diversity, we must document just how diverse the U.S. workforce is becoming.

glass ceiling A metaphor alluding to the invisible barriers that prevent minorities and women from being promoted to top corporate positions.

Age

According to data from the U.S. Census Bureau, the median age of a person in the United States is the highest it has ever been, 36.2 years.[21] Moreover, by 2030, it is projected that 20% of the population will be over 65.[22] Title VII of the Civil Rights Act of 1964 and the Age Discrimination in Employment Act of 1967 are the major federal laws prohibiting age discrimination.[23] While we discuss federal employment legislation in more depth in Chapter 12, major equal employment opportunity legislation that prohibits discrimination among diverse groups is summarized in Table 5.1.

The aging of the population suggests managers need to be vigilant that employees are not discriminated against because of age. Moreover, managers need to ensure that the policies and procedures they have in place treat all workers fairly, regardless of their ages. Additionally, effectively managing diversity means that employees of diverse ages are able to learn from each other, work well together, and take advantage of the different perspectives each has to offer.

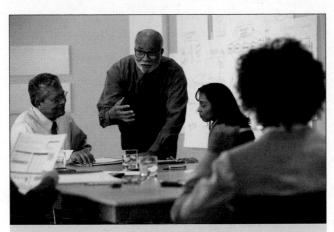

As the workforce ages, more companies are facing age discrimination lawsuits. Managers need to ensure that all policies and procedures treat workers fairly, regardless of their ages.

Gender

Women and men are almost equally represented in the U.S. workforce (approximately 53.5% of the U.S. workforce is male and 46.5% female),[24] yet women's median weekly earnings are estimated to be $572 compared to $714 for men.[25] Thus, the gender pay gap appears to be as alive and well as the glass ceiling. According to the nonprofit organization Catalyst, which studies women in business, while women comprise about 50.5% of the employees in managerial and professional positions, only around 15.4% of corporate officers in the 500 largest U.S. companies (i.e., Fortune 500) are women, and only 6.7% of the top earners are women.[26] These women, such as Andrea Jung, CEO of Avon Products, and Indra Nooyi, CEO of Pepsico, stand out among their male peers and often receive a disparate amount of attention in the media. (We address this issue later, when we discuss the effects of being salient.) Women are also very underrepresented on boards of directors—they currently hold 14.8% of the board seats

Table 5.1

Major Equal Employment Opportunity Laws Affecting Human Resources Management

Year	Law	Description
1963	Equal Pay Act	Requires that men and women be paid equally if they are performing equal work.
1964	Title VII of the Civil Rights Act	Prohibits discrimination in employment decisions on the basis of race, religion, sex, color, or national origin; covers a wide range of employment decisions, including hiring, firing, pay, promotion, and working conditions.
1967	Age Discrimination in Employment Act	Prohibits discrimination against workers over the age of 40 and restricts mandatory retirement.
1978	Pregnancy Discrimination Act	Prohibits discrimination against women in employment decisions on the basis of pregnancy, childbirth, and related medical decisions.
1990	Americans with Disabilities Act	Prohibits discrimination against disabled individuals in employment decisions and requires that employers make accommodations for disabled workers to enable them to perform their jobs.
1991	Civil Rights Act	Prohibits discrimination (as does Title VII) and allows for the awarding of punitive and compensatory damages, in addition to back pay, in cases of intentional discrimination.
1993	Family and Medical Leave Act	Requires that employers provide 12 weeks of unpaid leave for medical and family reasons, including paternity and illness of a family member.

of Fortune 500 companies.[27] However, as Sheila Wellington, president of Catalyst, indicates, "Women either control or influence nearly all consumer purchases, so it's important to have their perspective represented on boards."[28]

Additionally, research conducted by consulting firms suggests that female executives outperform their male colleagues on skills such as motivating others, promoting good communication, turning out high-quality work, and being a good listener.[29] For example, the Hagberg Group performed in-depth evaluations of 425 top executives in a variety of industries, with each executive rated by approximately 25 people. Of the 52 skills assessed, women received higher ratings than men on 42 skills, although at times the differences were small.[30] Results of a recent study conducted by Catalyst found that organizations with higher proportions of women in top-management positions had significantly better financial performance than organizations with lower proportions of female top managers.[31] Another study conducted by Catalyst found that companies with three or more women on their boards of directors performed better in terms of returns on equity, sales, and invested capital than companies with fewer women on their boards or no women.[32] All in all, studies such as these make one wonder why the glass ceiling continues to hamper the progress of women in business (a topic we address later in the chapter).

Race and Ethnicity

The U.S. Census Bureau typically distinguishes between the following races: American Indian or Alaska Native (native Americans of origins in North, Central, or South America), Asian (origins in the Far East, Southeast Asia, or India), African-American (origins in Africa), Native Hawaiian or Pacific Islander (origins in the Pacific Islands such as Hawaii, Guam, and Somoa), and white (origins in Europe, the Middle East, or North Africa). While ethnicity refers to a grouping of people based on some shared characteristic such as national origin, language, or culture, the U.S. Census Bureau treats ethnicity in terms of whether a person is Hispanic or not Hispanic. Hispanics, also referred to as Latinos, are people whose origins are in Spanish cultures such as those of Cuba, Mexico, Puerto Rico, and South and Central America. Hispanics can be of different races.[33] According to a recent poll, most Hispanics prefer to be identified by their country of origin (e.g., Mexican, Cuban, or Salvadoran) rather than by the overarching term *Hispanic*.[34]

The racial and ethnic diversity of the U.S. population is increasing at an exponential rate, as is the composition of the workforce.[35] According to the U.S. Census Bureau, approximately one of every three U.S. residents belongs to a minority group (i.e., is not a non-Hispanic white); approximately 67% of the population is white, 13.4% is African-American, 14.4% is Hispanic, and 4.8% is Asian.[36] According to projections released by the U.S. Census Bureau, the composition of the U.S. population in 2050 will be quite different from its composition in 2000. It is estimated that the Hispanic and Asian populations will triple during this 50-year period.[37]

The increasing racial and ethnic diversity of the workforce and the population as a whole underscores the importance of effectively managing diversity. Statistics compiled by the National Urban League suggest that much needs to be done in terms of ensuring that diverse employees are provided with equal opportunities. For example, African-Americans' earnings are approximately 73% of the earnings of whites,[38] and of 10,092 corporate officers in Fortune 500 companies, only 106 are African-American women.[39] In the remainder of this chapter, we focus on the fair treatment of diverse employees and explore why this is such an important challenge and what managers can do to meet it. We begin by taking a broader perspective and considering how increasing racial and ethnic diversity in an organization's environment (e.g., customers and suppliers) affects decision making and organizational effectiveness.

At a general level, managers and organizations are increasingly being reminded that stakeholders in the environment are diverse and expect organizational decisions and actions to reflect this diversity. For example, the NAACP (National Association for the Advancement of Colored People) and Children Now (an advocacy group) have lobbied the entertainment industry to increase the diversity in television programming, writing, and producing.[40] The need for such increased diversity is more than apparent. For example, while Hispanics make up 12.5% of the U.S. population (or 35 million potential TV viewers), only about 2% of the characters in prime-time TV shows are Hispanics (i.e., of the 2,251 characters in prime-time shows, only 47 are Hispanic), according to a study conducted by Children Now.[41] Moreover, only about 1.3% of the evening network TV news stories are reported by Hispanic correspondents, according to the Center for Media and Public Affairs.[42]

Pressure is mounting on networks to increase diversity for a variety of reasons revolving around the diversity of the population as a whole, TV viewers, and consumers. For example, home and automobile buyers are increasingly diverse, reflecting the increasing diversity of the population as a whole.[43] Moreover, managers have to be especially sensitive to avoid stereotyping different groups when they communicate with potential customers. For example, Toyota Motor Sales USA made a public apology to the Reverend Jesse Jackson and his Rainbow Coalition for using a print advertisement depicting an African-American man with a Toyota RAV4 sport utility image embossed on his gold front tooth.[44]

Religion

Title VII of the Civil Rights Act prohibits discrimination based on religion (as well as based on race/ethnicity, country of origin, and sex; see Table 5.1 and Chapter 12). In addition to enacting Title VII, in 1997 the federal government issued "The White House Guidelines on Religious Exercise and Expression in the Federal Workplace."[45] These guidelines, while technically applicable only in federal offices, also are frequently relied on by large corporations. The guidelines require that employers make reasonable accommodations for religious practices, such as observances of holidays, as long as doing so does not entail major costs or hardships.[46]

A key issue for managers when it comes to religious diversity is recognizing and being aware of different religions and their beliefs, with particular attention being paid to when religious holidays fall. For example, critical meetings should not be scheduled during a holy day for members of a certain faith, and managers should be flexible in allowing people to have time off for religious observances. According to Lobna Ismail, director of a diversity training company in Silver Spring, Maryland, when managers acknowledge, respect, and make even small accommodations for religious diversity, employee loyalty is often enhanced. For example, allowing employees to leave work early on certain days instead of taking a lunch break or posting holidays for different religions on the company calendar can go a long way toward making individuals of diverse religions feel respected and valued as well as enable them to practice their faith.[47] According to research conducted by the Tanenbaum Center for Interreligious Understanding in New York, while only about 23% of employees who feel they are victims of religious discrimination actually file complaints, about 45% of these employees start looking for other jobs.[48]

Capabilities/Disabilities

The Americans with Disabilities Act (ADA) of 1990 prohibits discrimination against persons with disabilities and also requires that employers make reasonable accommodations to enable these people to effectively perform their jobs. In force for more than a decade, the ADA is not uncontroversial. On the surface, few would argue with the intent of this legislation. However, as managers attempt to implement policies and procedures to comply with the ADA, they face a number of interpretation and fairness challenges.

On the one hand, some people with real disabilities warranting workplace accommodations are hesitant to reveal their disabilities to their employers and claim the accommodations they deserve.[49] On the other hand, some employees abuse the ADA by seeking unnecessary accommodations for disabilities that may or may not exist.[50]

Thus, it is perhaps not surprising that the passage of the ADA does not appear to have increased employment rates significantly for those with disabilities.[51] A key challenge for managers is to promote an environment in which employees needing accommodations feel comfortable disclosing their need and, at the same time, to ensure that the accommodations not only enable those with disabilities to effectively perform their jobs but also are perceived to be fair by those not disabled.[52]

In addressing this challenge, often managers must educate both themselves and their employees about the disabilities, as well as the very real capabilities, of those who are disabled. For example, during Disability Awareness Week, administrators at the University of Notre Dame sought to increase the public's knowledge of disabilities while also heightening awareness of the abilities of persons who are disabled.[53] The University of Houston conducted a similar program called "Think Ability."[54] According to Cheryl Amoruso, director of the University of Houston's Center for Students with Disabilities, many people are unaware of the prevalence of disabilities as well as misinformed about their consequences. She suggests, for example, that although students may not be able to see, they can still excel in their coursework and have very successful careers.[55] Accommodations enabling such students to perform up to their capabilities are covered under the ADA.

The ADA also protects employees with acquired immune deficiency syndrome (AIDS) from being discriminated against in the workplace. AIDS is caused by the human immunodeficiency virus (HIV) and is transmitted through sexual contact, infected needles, and contaminated blood products. HIV is not spread through casual, nonsexual contact. Yet, out of ignorance, fear, or prejudice, some people wish to avoid all contact with anyone infected with HIV. Infected individuals may not necessarily develop AIDS, and some individuals with HIV are able to remain effective performers of their jobs, while not putting others at risk.[56]

AIDS awareness training can help people overcome their fears and also provide managers with a tool to prevent illegal discrimination against HIV-infected employees. Such training focuses on educating employees about HIV and AIDS, dispelling myths, communicating relevant organizational policies, and emphasizing the rights of HIV-positive employees to privacy and an environment that allows them to be productive.[57] The need for AIDS awareness training is underscored by some of the problems HIV-positive employees experience once others in their workplace become aware of their condition.[58] Moreover, organizations are required to make reasonable accommodations to enable people with AIDS to effectively perform their jobs.

Thus, managers have an obligation to educate employees about HIV and AIDS, dispel myths and the stigma of AIDS, and ensure that HIV-related discrimination is not occurring in the workplace. For example, Home Depot has provided HIV training and education to its store managers; such training was sorely needed given that over half of the managers indicated it was the first time they had the opportunity to talk about AIDS.[59] Moreover, advances in medication and treatment mean that more infected individuals are able to continue working or are able to return to work after their condition improves.[60] Thus, managers need to ensure that these employees are fairly treated by all members of their organizations. And managers and organizations that do not treat HIV-positive employees in a fair manner, as well as provide reasonable accommodations (e.g., allowing time off for doctor visits or to take medicine), risk costly lawsuits.

Socioeconomic Background

The term *socioeconomic background* typically refers to a combination of social class and income-related factors. From a management perspective, socioeconomic diversity (and, in particular, diversity in income levels) requires that managers be sensitive and responsive to the needs and concerns of individuals who might not be as well off as others. U.S. welfare reform in the mid- to late 1990s emphasized the need for single mothers and others receiving public assistance to join or return to the workforce. In conjunction with a strong economy, this led to record declines in the number of families, households, and children living below the poverty level, according to the 2000 U.S. census.[61] However, the economic downturn in the early 2000s, along with increased terrorism and the tragic collapse of the World Trade Center in New York City, resulted in domestic and international repercussions. These suggest that some past gains, which lifted families out of poverty, have been reversed. In a very strong economy, it is much easier for poor people with few skills to find jobs; in a weak economy, when companies lay off employees in hard times, people who need their incomes the most are unfortunately often the first to lose their jobs.[62]

Even with all the gains from the 1990s, the U.S. Census Bureau estimates that 6,825,399 families had incomes below the poverty level in 2000, with 3,581,475 of these families being headed by single women.[63] The Census Bureau relies on predetermined threshold income figures, based on family size and composition, adjusted annually for inflation, to determine the poverty level. Families whose income falls below the threshold level are considered poor.[64] For example, in 2000 a family of four with two children under 18 was considered poor if their annual income fell below $17,463.[65] When workers earn less than $10 or $15 per hour, it is often difficult, if not impossible, for them to meet their families' needs.[66] Moreover, increasing numbers of families are facing the challenge of finding suitable child care arrangements that enable the adults to work long hours and/or through the night to maintain an adequate income level. New information technology has led to more and more businesses operating 24 hours a day, creating real challenges for workers on the night shift, especially those with children.[67]

Hundreds of thousands of parents across the country are scrambling to find someone to care for their children while they are working the night shift, commuting several hours a day, working weekends and holidays, or putting in long hours on one or more jobs. This has led to the opening of day care facilities that operate around the clock as well as to managers seeking ways to provide such care for children of their employees. For example, the Children's Choice Learning Center in Las Vegas, Nevada, operates around the clock to accommodate employees working nights in neighboring casinos, hospitals, and call centers. Randy Donahue, a security guard who works until midnight, picks his children up from the center when he gets off work; his wife is a nurse on the night shift. There currently are five Children's Choice Learning Centers in the United States operating 24 hours a day, and plans are under way to add seven more.[68]

Judy Harden, who focuses on families and child care issues for the United Workers Union, indicates that the demands families are facing necessitate around-the-clock and odd-hour child care options. Many parents simply do not have the choice of working at hours that allow them to take care of their children at night and/or on weekends, never mind when the children are sick.[69] In 1993, Ford Motor Company built an around-the-clock child care facility for 175 children of employees in Livonia, Michigan. However, a recent survey of child care needs indicates that many employees in other locations require such a facility. Some parents and psychologists feel uneasy having children separated from their families for so much time and particularly at night. Most agree that, unfortunately for many families, this is not a choice but a necessity.[70]

Socioeconomic diversity suggests that managers need to be sensitive and responsive to the needs and concerns of workers who may be less fortunate than themselves in terms of income and financial resources, child care and elder care options, housing opportunities, and existence of sources of social and family support. Moreover—and equally important—managers should try to provide such individuals with opportunities to learn, advance, and make meaningful contributions to their organizations while improving their economic well-being.

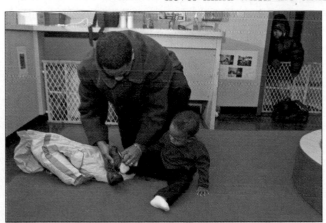

A father drops his children off at a day care facility before going to work. Managers need to be aware that many employees deal with challenging socioeconomic factors such as long commutes and finding suitable child care arrangements.

Sexual Orientation

Approximately 2% to 10% of the U.S. population is gay or lesbian.[71] While no federal law prohibits discrimination based on sexual orientation, 20 states have such laws, and a 1998 executive order prohibits sexual orientation discrimination in civilian federal offices.[72] Moreover, an increasing number of organizations recognize the minority status of gay and lesbian employees, affirm their rights to fair and equal treatment, and provide benefits to same-sex partners of gay and lesbian employees.[73] For example, 95% of Fortune 500 companies prohibit discrimination based on sexual orientation, and 70% of the Fortune 500 provide domestic-partner benefits.[74] As indicated in the following "Focus on Diversity," there are many steps that managers can take to ensure that sexual orientation is not used to unfairly discriminate among employees.

Preventing Discrimination Based on Sexual Orientation

Focus on Diversity

While gays and lesbians have made great strides in terms of attaining fair treatment in the workplace, much more needs to be done. In a recent study conducted by Harris Interactive Inc. (a research firm) and Witeck Communications Inc. (a marketing firm), over 40% of gay and lesbian employees indicated that they had been unfairly treated, denied a promotion, or pushed to quit their jobs because of their sexual orientation.[75] Given continued harassment and discrimination despite the progress that has been made,[76] many gay and lesbian employees fear disclosing their sexual orientation in the workplace and thus live a life of secrecy. While there are a few openly gay top managers, such as David Geffen, cofounder of DreamWorks SKG, and Allan Gilmour, former vice chairman and CFO of Ford and currently a member of the board of directors of Whirlpool and DTE Energy Company, many others choose not to disclose or discuss their personal lives, including long-term partners.[77]

Thus, it is not surprising that many managers are taking active steps to educate and train their employees in regard to issues of sexual orientation. S. C. Johnson & Sons, Inc., maker of Raid insecticide and Glade air fresheners in Racine, Wisconsin, provides mandatory training to its plant managers to overturn stereotypes, and Eastman Kodak, Lehman Brothers Holdings Inc., Merck & Co., Ernst & Young, and Toronto-Dominion Bank all provide training to managers on ways to prevent sexual orientation discrimination.[78] Other organizations such as Lucent Technologies, Microsoft, and Southern California Edison send employees to seminars conducted at prominent business schools. And many companies such as Raytheon, IBM, Eastman Kodak, and Lockheed Martin provide assistance to their gay and lesbian employees through gay and lesbian support groups.[79]

The Chubb Group of Insurance Companies, a property and casualty insurance company, provides its managers with a two-hour training session to help create work environments that are safe and welcoming for lesbian, gay, bisexual, and transgender (LGBT) people.[80] The sessions are conducted by two Chubb employees; usually one of the trainers is straight and the other is gay. The sessions focus on issues that affect

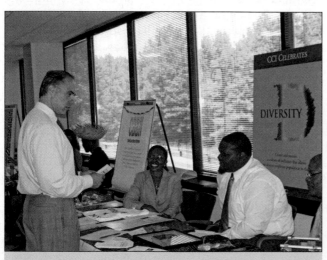

Chubb Corporation takes diversity awareness seriously, as is evidenced by this LGBT sensitivity training session.

a manager's ability to lead diverse teams, such as assessing how safe and welcoming the workplace is for LGBT people, how to refer to gay employees' significant others, and how to respond if employees or customers use inappropriate language or behavior. The idea for the program originated from one of Chubb's employee resource groups. Managers rate the program highly and say that they are better able to respond to the concerns of their LGBT employees while creating a safe and productive work environment for all.[81]

Other Kinds of Diversity

There are other kinds of diversity that are important in organizations, critical for managers to deal with effectively, and also potential sources of unfair treatment. For example, organizations and teams need members with diverse backgrounds and experiences. This is clearly illustrated by the prevalence of cross-functional teams in organizations whose members might come from various departments such as marketing, production, finance, and sales (teams are covered in depth in Chapter 15). A team responsible for developing and introducing a new product, for example, often will need the expertise of employees not only from R&D and engineering but also from marketing, sales, production, and finance.

Other types of diversity can also affect how employees are treated in the workplace. For example, employees differ from each other in how attractive they are [based on the standards of the culture(s) in which an organization operates] and in terms of body weight. Whether individuals are attractive or unattractive, thin or overweight, in most cases, has no bearing on their job performance unless they have jobs in which physical appearance plays a role, such as modeling. Yet sometimes these physical sources of diversity end up influencing advancement rates and salaries. For example, a recent study published in the *American Journal of Public Health* found that highly educated obese women earned approximately 30% less per year than women who were not obese and men (regardless of whether or not the men were obese).[82] Clearly, managers need to ensure that all employees are treated fairly, regardless of their physical appearance.

LO2 Explain the central role that managers play in the effective management of diversity.

Managers and the Effective Management of Diversity

The increasing diversity of the environment—which, in turn, increases the diversity of an organization's workforce—increases the challenges managers face in effectively managing diversity. Each of the kinds of diversity discussed above presents managers with a particular set of issues they need to appreciate before they can respond to them effectively. Understanding these issues is not always a simple matter, as many informed managers have discovered. Research on how different groups are currently treated and the unconscious biases that might adversely affect them is critical because it helps managers become aware of the many subtle and unobtrusive ways in which diverse employee groups can come to be treated unfairly over time. There are many more steps managers can take to become sensitive to the ongoing effects of diversity in their organizations, take advantage of all the contributions diverse employees can make, and prevent diverse employees from being unfairly treated.

Critical Managerial Roles

In each of their managerial roles (see Chapter 1), managers can either promote the effective management of diversity or derail such efforts; thus, they are critical to this process. For example, in their interpersonal roles, managers can convey that the effective management of diversity is a valued goal and objective (figurehead role), can

Table 5.2

Managerial Roles and the Effective Management of Diversity

Type of Role	Specific Role	Example
Interpersonal	Figurehead	Convey that the effective management of diversity is a valued goal and objective.
	Leader	Serve as a role model and institute policies and procedures to ensure that diverse members are treated fairly.
	Liaison	Enable diverse individuals to coordinate their efforts and cooperate with one another.
Informational	Monitor	Evaluate the extent to which diverse employees are being treated fairly.
	Disseminator	Inform employees about diversity policies and initiatives and the intolerance of discrimination.
	Spokesperson	Support diversity initiatives in the wider community and speak to diverse groups to interest them in career opportunities.
Decisional	Entrepreneur	Commit resources to develop new ways to effectively manage diversity and eliminate biases and discrimination.
	Disturbance handler	Take quick action to correct inequalities and curtail discriminatory behavior.
	Resource allocator	Allocate resources to support and encourage the effective management of diversity.
	Negotiator	Work with organizations (e.g., suppliers) and groups (e.g., labor unions) to support and encourage the effective management of diversity.

serve as a role model and institute policies and procedures to ensure that diverse organizational members are treated fairly (leader role), and can enable diverse individuals and groups to coordinate their efforts and cooperate with each other both inside the organization and at the organization's boundaries (liaison role). In Table 5.2 we summarize some of the ways in which managers can ensure that diversity is effectively managed as they perform their different roles.

Given the formal authority that managers have in organizations, they typically have more influence than rank-and-file employees. When managers commit to supporting diversity as managers at Sodexo do in "A Manager's Challenge," their authority and positions of power and status influence other members of an organization to make a similar commitment.[83] Research on social influence supports such a link, as people are more likely to be influenced and persuaded by others who have high status.[84]

Moreover, when managers commit to diversity, their commitment legitimizes the diversity management efforts of others.[85] In addition, resources are devoted to such efforts, and all members of an organization believe that their diversity-related efforts are supported and valued. Consistent with this reasoning, top-management commitment and rewards for the support of diversity are often cited as critical ingredients for the success of diversity management initiatives.[86] Additionally, seeing managers express confidence in the abilities and talents of diverse employees causes other organizational members to be similarly confident and helps to reduce any misconceived misgivings they may have as a result of ignorance or stereotypes.[87]

Two other important factors emphasize why managers are so central to the effective management of diversity. The first factor is that women, African-Americans, Hispanics, and other minorities often start out at a slight disadvantage due to the ways in which they are perceived by others in organizations, particularly in work settings where they are a numerical minority. As Virginia Valian, a psychologist at Hunter College who studies gender, indicates, "In most organizations women begin at a slight disadvantage. A woman does not walk into the room with the same status as an equivalent man, because she is less likely than a man to be viewed as a serious professional."[88]

The second factor is that research suggests that slight differences in treatment can cumulate and result in major disparities over time. Even small differences—such as a very slight favorable bias toward men for promotions—can lead to major differences in the number of male and female managers over time.[89] Thus, while women and other minorities are sometimes advised not to make "a mountain out of a molehill" when they perceive they have been unfairly treated, research conducted by Valian and others suggests that molehills (i.e., slight differences in treatment based on irrelevant distinctions such as race, gender, or ethnicity) can turn into mountains over time (i.e., major disparities in important outcomes such as promotions) if they are ignored.[90] Once again, managers have the obligation, from both an ethical and business perspective, to ensure that neither large nor small disparities in treatment and outcomes due to irrelevant distinctions such as race or ethnicity occur in organizations.

The Ethical Imperative to Manage Diversity Effectively

Effectively managing diversity not only makes good business sense (which is discussed in the next section) but also is an ethical imperative in U.S. society. Two moral principles provide managers with guidance in their efforts to meet this imperative: distributive justice and procedural justice.

DISTRIBUTIVE JUSTICE   The principle of **distributive justice** dictates that the distribution of pay raises, promotions, job titles, interesting job assignments, office space, and other organizational resources among members of an organization should be fair. The distribution of these outcomes should be based on the meaningful contributions that individuals have made to the organization (such as time, effort, education, skills, abilities, and performance levels) and not on irrelevant personal characteristics over which individuals have no control (such as gender, race, or age).[91] Managers have an obligation to ensure that distributive justice exists in their organizations. This does not mean that all members of an organization receive identical or similar outcomes; rather, it means that members who receive more outcomes than others have made substantially higher or more significant contributions to the organization.

Is distributive justice common in organizations in corporate America? Probably the best way to answer this question is by saying that things are getting better. Fifty years ago, overt discrimination against women and minorities was not uncommon; today, organizations are inching closer toward the ideal of distributive justice. Statistics comparing the treatment of women and minorities with the treatment of other employees suggest that most managers would need to take a proactive approach to achieve distributive justice in their organizations.[92] For example, across occupations, women consistently earn less than men (see Table 5.3) according to data collected by the U.S. Bureau of Labor Statistics.[93] Even in occupations dominated by women, such as teacher assistants and elementary and secondary school teachers, men tend to earn more than women.[94]

In many countries, managers have not only an ethical obligation to strive to achieve distributive justice in their organizations but also a legal obligation to treat all employees fairly. They risk being sued by employees who believe that they are not being fairly treated. That is precisely what six African-American employees at Texaco did when they experienced racial bias and discrimination.[95]

PROCEDURAL JUSTICE   The principle of **procedural justice** requires that managers use fair procedures to determine how to distribute outcomes to organizational members.[96] This principle applies to typical procedures such as appraising subordinates' performance, deciding who should receive a raise or a promotion, and

Margin notes

LO3   Explain why the effective management of diversity is both an ethical and a business imperative.

distributive justice
A moral principle calling for the distribution of pay raises, promotions, and other organizational resources to be based on meaningful contributions that individuals have made and not on personal characteristics over which they have no control.

procedural justice   A moral principle calling for the use of fair procedures to determine how to distribute outcomes to organizational members.

Table 5.3
Weekly Salaries by Sex and Occupation

Median Weekly Salaries

Occupation	Men	Women	Women's Salaries as a Percentage of Men's
Management	$1,172	$849	72
Business and finance	1,014	744	73
Computer and mathematics	1,130	906	80
Architecture and engineering	1,094	827	76
Life, physical, and social science	970	773	80
Community and social service	746	655	88
Law	1,480	796	54
Education, training, library	904	708	78
Art, entertainment, sports, media	837	648	77
Health care	1,002	770	77
Service	463	366	79
Sales and office work	658	502	76
Resources and construction	613	449	73
Production and transportation	570	407	71

Source: "Median Weekly Earnings of Full-Time Wage and Salary Workers by Selected Characteristics," www.bls.gov, May 1, 2004.

deciding whom to lay off when an organization is forced to downsize. Procedural justice exists, for example, when managers (1) carefully appraise a subordinate's performance, (2) take into account any environmental obstacles to high performance beyond the subordinate's control, such as lack of supplies, machine breakdowns, or dwindling customer demand for a product, and (3) ignore irrelevant personal characteristics such as the subordinate's age or ethnicity. Like distributive justice, procedural justice is necessary not only to ensure ethical conduct but also to avoid costly lawsuits.

Effectively Managing Diversity Makes Good Business Sense

The diversity of organizational members can be a source of competitive advantage, helping an organization provide customers with better goods and services.[97] The variety of points of view and approaches to problems and opportunities that diverse employees provide can improve managerial decision making. Suppose the Budget Gourmet frozen-food company is trying to come up with some creative ideas for new frozen meals that will appeal to health-conscious, time-conscious customers tired of the same old frozen-food fare. Which group do you think is likely to come up with the most creative ideas: a group of white women with master's degrees in marketing from Yale University who grew up in upper-middle-class families in the Northeast or a racially mixed group of men and women who grew up in families with varying income levels in different parts of the country and attended a mix of business schools (New York University, Oklahoma State, University of Michigan, UCLA, Cornell University, Texas A&M University, and Iowa State)? Most people would agree that the diverse group is likely to come up with a wider range of creative ideas. Although this example is simplistic, it underscores one way in which diversity can lead to a competitive advantage.

Just as the workforce is becoming increasingly diverse, so too are the customers who buy an organization's goods or services. In an attempt to suit local customers' needs and tastes, organizations like Target often vary the selection of products available in stores in different cities and regions to appeal to local customers.[98]

Diverse members of an organization are likely to be attuned to what goods and services diverse segments of the market want and do not want. Major car companies, for example, are increasingly assigning women to their design teams to ensure that the needs and desires of female customers (a growing segment of the market) are taken into account in new car design.

For Darden Restaurants, the business case for diversity rests on market share and growth. Darden seeks to satisfy the needs and tastes of diverse customers by providing menus in Spanish in communities with large Hispanic populations.[99] Similarly, market share and growth and the identification of niche markets led Tracey Campbell to cater to travelers with disabilities.[100] She heads InnSeekers, a telephone and online listing resource for bed and breakfasts. Nikki Daruwala works for the Calvert Group in Bethesda, Maryland, a mutual fund that emphasizes social responsibility and diversity. She indicates that profit alone is more than enough of an incentive to effectively manage diversity. As she puts it, "You can look at an automaker. There are more women making decisions about car buying or home buying . . . $3.72 trillion per year are spent by women."[101]

Another way in which the effective management of diversity can positively affect profitability is that it increases retention of valued employees, which decreases the costs of hiring replacements for those who quit as well as ensures that all employees are highly motivated. In terms of retention, given the current legal environment, more and more organizations are attuned to the need to emphasize the importance of diversity in hiring. Once hired, if diverse employees think they are being unfairly treated, however, they will be likely to seek opportunities elsewhere. Thus, the recruiting of diverse employees has to be followed up by the ongoing effective management of diversity to retain these valued organizational members.

If diversity is not effectively managed and results in turnover rates being higher for members of certain groups who are not treated fairly, profitability will suffer on several counts. Not only are the future contributions of diverse employees lost when they quit, but the organization also has to bear the costs of hiring replacement workers. According to the Employment Management Association, on average it costs more than $10,000 to hire a new employee; other estimates are significantly higher. For example, Ernst & Young estimates it costs about $1,200,000 to replace 10 professionals, and the diversity consulting firm Hubbard & Hubbard estimates replacement costs average one-and-a-half times an employee's annual salary.[102] Moreover, additional costs from failing to effectively manage diversity stem from time lost due to the barriers diverse members of an organization perceive as thwarting their progress and advancement.[103]

Effectively managing diversity makes good business sense for another reason. More and more, managers and organizations concerned about diversity are insisting that their suppliers also support diversity.[104]

Finally, from both a business and an ethical perspective, the effective management of diversity is necessary to avoid costly lawsuits such as those settled by Advantica (owner of the Denny's chain) and the Coca-Cola Company. In 2000, Coca-Cola settled a class-action suit brought by African-American employees, at a cost of $192 million. The damage such lawsuits cause goes beyond the monetary awards to the injured parties; it can tarnish a company's image. One positive outcome of Coca-Cola's 2000 settlement is the company's recognition of the need to commit additional resources to diversity management initiatives. In this regard, Coca-Cola is increasing its use of minority suppliers, instituting a formal mentoring program, and instituting days to celebrate diversity with its workforce.[105]

LO4 Discuss how perception and the use of schemas can result in unfair treatment.

By now, it should be clear that effectively managing diversity is a necessity on both ethical and business grounds. This brings us to the question of why diversity presents managers and all of us with so many challenges—a question we address in the next section, on perception.

Perception

Most people tend to think that the decisions managers make in organizations and the actions they take are the result of some objective determination of the issues involved and the surrounding situation. However, each manager's interpretation of a situation or even of another person is precisely that—an interpretation. Nowhere are the effects of perception more likely to lead to different interpretations than in the area of diversity. This is because each person's interpretation of a situation, and subsequent response to it, is affected by his or her own age, race, gender, religion, socioeconomic status, capabilities, and sexual orientation. For example, different managers may see the same 21-year-old, black, male, gay, gifted and talented subordinate in different ways: One may see a creative maverick with a great future in the organization, while another may see a potential troublemaker who needs to be watched closely.

perception The process through which people select, organize, and interpret what they see, hear, touch, smell, and taste to give meaning and order to the world around them.

Perception is the process through which people select, organize, and interpret sensory input—what they see, hear, touch, smell, and taste—to give meaning and order to the world around them.[106] All decisions and actions that managers take are based on their subjective perceptions. When these perceptions are relatively accurate—close to the true nature of what is actually being perceived—good decisions are likely to be made and appropriate actions taken. Managers of fast-food restaurant chains such as McDonald's, Pizza Hut, and Wendy's accurately perceived that their customers were becoming more health-conscious in the 1980s and 1990s and added salad bars and low-fat entries to their menus. Managers at Kentucky Fried Chicken, Jack-in-the-Box, and Burger King took much longer to perceive this change in what customers wanted.

One reason why McDonald's is so successful is that its managers go to great lengths to make sure that their perceptions of what customers want are accurate. McDonald's has 4,700 restaurants outside the United States (including 1,070 in Japan, 694 in Canada, 550 in Britain, 535 in Germany, 411 in Australia, 314 in France, 23 in China, and 3 in Russia) that generate approximately $3.4 billion in annual revenues. Key to McDonald's success in these diverse markets are managers' efforts to perceive accurately a country's culture and taste in food and then to act on these perceptions. For instance, McDonald's serves veggie burgers in Holland and black currant shakes in Poland.[107]

When managers' perceptions are relatively inaccurate, managers are likely to make bad decisions and take inappropriate actions, which hurt organizational effectiveness. Bad decisions concerning diversity for reasons of age, ethnicity, or sexual orientation include (1) not hiring qualified people, (2) failing to promote top-performing subordinates, who subsequently decide to take their skills to competing organizations, and (3) promoting poorly performing managers because they have the same "diversity profile" as the manager or managers making the decision.

Factors That Influence Managerial Perception

Several managers' perceptions of the same person, event, or situation are likely to differ because managers differ in personality, values, attitudes, and moods (see Chapter 3). Each of these factors can influence the way someone perceives a person or situation. An older middle manager who is high on openness to experience is likely to perceive the recruitment of able young managers as a positive learning opportunity; a similar middle manager who is low on openness to experience may perceive able younger subordinates as a threat. A manager who has high levels of job satisfaction and organizational commitment may perceive a job transfer to another department or geographic location that has very different employees (age, ethnicity, and so on) as an opportunity to learn and develop new skills. A dissatisfied, uncommitted manager may perceive the same transfer as a demotion.

Managers' and all organizational members' perceptions about one another also are affected by their past experience and acquired knowledge about people, events, and situations—information that is organized into preexisting schemas. **Schemas** are abstract knowledge structures stored in memory that allow people to organize and interpret information about a person, an event, or a situation.[108] Once a person develops a schema for a kind of person or event, any newly encountered person or situation that is related to the schema activates it and information is processed in ways consistent with the information stored in the schema. Thus, people tend to perceive others by using the expectations or preconceived notions contained in their schemas.[109] Once again, these expectations are derived from past experience and knowledge.

People tend to pay attention to information that is consistent with their schemas and to ignore or discount inconsistent information. Thus, schemas tend to be reinforced and strengthened over time because the information attended to is seen as confirming the schemas. This also results in schemas being resistant to change.[110] This does not mean that schemas never change; if that were the case, people could never adapt to changing conditions and learn from their mistakes. Rather, it suggests that schemas are slow to change and that a considerable amount of contradictory information needs to be encountered for people to change their schemas.

Schemas, when they are relatively accurate depictions of the true nature of a person or situation, are functional because they help people make sense of the world around them. People are typically confronted with so much information that it is not possible to make sense of it without relying on schemas. Schemas are dysfunctional when they are inaccurate because they cause managers and all members of an organization to perceive people and situations inaccurately and assume certain things that are not necessarily true.

Psychologist Virginia Valian refers to inaccurate preconceived notions of men and women as gender schemas. **Gender schemas** are a person's preconceived notions about the nature of men and women, their traits, attitudes, behaviors, and preferences.[111] Research suggests that among white, middle-class Americans, the following gender schemas are prevalent: Men are action-oriented, assertive, independent, and task-focused; women are expressive, nurturing, and oriented toward and caring of other people.[112] Any schemas such as these—which assume a single visible characteristic such as one's sex causes a person to possess specific traits and tendencies—are bound to be inaccurate. For example, not all women are alike and not all men are alike, and there are many women who are more independent and task-focused than men. Gender schemas can be learned in childhood and are reinforced in a number of ways in society. For instance, while young girls may be encouraged by their parents to play with toy trucks and tools (stereotypically masculine toys), boys generally are not encouraged, and sometimes are actively discouraged, from playing with dolls (stereotypically feminine toys).[113] As children grow up, they learn that occupations dominated by men have higher status than occupations dominated by women.

schema An abstract knowledge structure that is stored in memory and makes possible the interpretation and organization of information about a person, event, or situation.

gender schemas Preconceived beliefs or ideas about the nature of men and women, their traits, attitudes, behaviors, and preferences.

Perception as a Determinant of Unfair Treatment

Even though most people would agree that distributive justice and procedural justice are desirable goals, diverse organizational members are sometimes treated unfairly, as previous examples illustrate. Why is this problem occurring? One important overarching reason is inaccurate perceptions. To the extent that managers and other members of an organization rely on inaccurate schemas such as gender schemas to guide their perceptions of each other, unfair treatment is likely to occur.

stereotype Simplistic and often inaccurate beliefs about the typical characteristics of particular groups of people.

Gender schemas are a kind of **stereotype,** simplistic and often inaccurate beliefs about the typical characteristics of particular groups of people. Stereotypes are usually based on a highly visible characteristic such as a person's age, gender, or race.[114] Managers who allow stereotypes to influence their perceptions assume erroneously that a person possesses a whole host of characteristics simply because the person happens to be an Asian woman, a white man, or a lesbian, for example. African-American men are often stereotyped as good athletes, Hispanic women as subservient.[115] Obviously, there is no reason to assume that every African-American man is a good athlete or that every Hispanic woman is subservient. Stereotypes, however, lead people to make such erroneous assumptions. A manager who accepts stereotypes might, for example, decide not to promote a highly capable Hispanic woman into a management position because the manager is certain that she will not be assertive enough to supervise others.

A recent study suggests that stereotypes might hamper the progress of mothers in their organizations when they are seeking to advance in positions that are traditionally held by men. According to the study, based on gender stereotypes, people tend to view mothers as less competent in terms of skills and capabilities related to advancing in such positions.[116]

People with disabilities might also be unfairly treated due to stereotypes.[117] While, as mentioned previously, the ADA requires that organizations provide disabled employees with accommodations, employment rates of people with disabilities have declined in recent years. As profiled in the following "Ethics in Action," a number of organizations have not only provided employment opportunities for disabled adults but also have benefited from their valuable contributions.[118]

Ethics in Action

Disabled Employees Make Valuable Contributions

Some large organizations like McDonald's, Wal-Mart, Home Depot, and Walgreens actively recruit disabled employees to work in positions as cashiers, maintenance workers, greeters, shelf stockers, and floor workers that help customers find items. Home Depot, for example, works with a nonprofit agency called Ken's Kids, founded by parents of disabled adults, to recruit and place disabled employees in its stores. Thus far, working with Ken's Kids has enabled Home Depot to recruit and place around 100 disabled adults in over 50 of its stores.[119]

Often, when given the opportunity, disabled employees make valuable contributions to their organizations. Walgreen Co. recently opened an automated distribution center in Anderson, South Carolina, in which more than 40% of its 264 employees are disabled.[120] For disabled employees like 18-year old Harrison Mullinax who has autism and checks in merchandise to be distributed to drugstores with a bar-code scanner, having a regular job is a godsend. Randy Lewis, senior vice president of distribution and logistics at Walgreens, thought about hiring workers with disabilities when Walgreens was considering using technology to increase levels of automation in a distribution center. Lewis, the father of a young adult son who has autism, was aware of how difficult it can be for young adults like his son to find employment. Various accommodations were made like redesigning workstations and computer displays to suit employees' needs, and employees received appropriate training in how to do their jobs. Some days, disabled employees are actually the most productive in the center. As Lewis puts it, "One thing we found is they can all do the job. . . . What surprised us is the environment that it's created. It's a building where everybody helps each other out."[121]

Small Business

While Walgreens is a large organization, small organizations also have benefited from the valuable contributions of disabled employees. Habitat International, founded by current CEO David Morris and his father Saul over 20 years ago, is a manufacturer and contractor of indoor–outdoor carpet and artificial grass and a supplier to home improvement companies like Lowe's and Home Depot.[122] Habitat's profits have steadily increased over the years and the factory's defect rate is less than 0.5%.[123]

The first clue that Habitat isn't your run-of-the mill factory may be the gigantic animal sculptures at the plant entrance in Chattanooga, Tennessee. The Habitat team produces the sculptures, which can also be seen at restaurants, parks, garden centers, medical centers, museums, and other sites.

Morris attributes Habitat's success to its employees, 75% of whom have either a physical or a mental disability or both.[124] Habitat has consistently provided employment opportunities to people with disabilities such as Down syndrome, schizophrenia, or cerebral palsy.[125] The company has also hired the homeless, recovering alcoholics, and non-English-speaking refugees from other countries. And these very same employees were relied on by plant manager Connie Presnell when she needed to fill a rush order by assigning it to a team of her fastest workers.[126] Habitat pays its employees regionally competitive wages and has very low absence and turnover rates. Employees who need accommodations to perform their jobs are provided them, and Habitat has a highly motivated, satisfied, and committed workforce.[127]

While Habitat has actually gained some business from clients who applaud its commitment to diversity, Habitat's ethical values and social responsibility have also led the company to forgo a major account when stereotypes reared their ugly head. A few years ago, CEO Morris dropped the account of a distribution company because its representatives had made derogatory comments about his employees. Although it took Habitat two years to regain the lost revenues from this major account, Morris had absolutely no regrets.[128] Habitat's commitment to diversity and fair treatment is a win–win situation; the company is thriving, and so too are its employees.[129]

bias The systematic tendency to use information about others in ways that result in inaccurate perceptions.

Inaccurate perceptions leading to unfair treatment of diverse members of an organization also can be due to biases. **Biases** are systematic tendencies to use information about others in ways that result in inaccurate perceptions. Because of the way biases operate, people often are unaware that their perceptions of others are inaccurate. There are several types of biases.

The *similar-to-me effect* is the tendency to perceive others who are similar to ourselves more positively than we perceive people who are different.[130] The similar-to-me effect is summed up by the saying, "Birds of a feather flock together." It can lead to unfair treatment of diverse employees simply because they are different from the managers who are perceiving them, evaluating them, and making decisions that affect their future in the organization.

Managers (particularly top managers) are likely to be white men. Although these managers may endorse the principles of distributive and procedural justice, they may unintentionally fall into the trap of perceiving other white men more positively than they perceive women and minorities. This is the similar-to-me effect. Being aware of this bias as well as using objective information about employees' capabilities and performance as much as possible in decision making about job assignments, pay raises, promotions, and other outcomes can help managers avoid the similar-to-me effect.

Social status, a person's real or perceived position in a society or an organization, can be the source of another bias. The *social status effect* is the tendency to perceive individuals with high social status more positively than we perceive those with low

The salience effect is operating during this group meeting in which the only man is receiving excess attention.

social status. A high-status person may be perceived as smarter and more believable, capable, knowledgeable, and responsible than a low-status person, even in the absence of objective information about either person.

Imagine being introduced to two people at a company Christmas party. Both are white men in their late 30s, and you learn that one is a member of the company's top-management team and the other is a supervisor in the mailroom. From this information alone, you might assume that the top manager is smarter, more capable, more responsible, and even more interesting than the mailroom supervisor. Because women and minorities have traditionally had lower social status than white men, the social status effect may lead some people to perceive women and minorities less positively than they perceive white men.

Have you ever stood out in a crowd? Maybe you were the only man in a group of women; or maybe you were dressed formally for a social gathering, and everyone else was in jeans. Salience (i.e., conspicuousness) is another source of bias. The *salience effect* is the tendency to focus attention on individuals who are conspicuously different from us. When people are salient, they often feel as though all eyes are watching them, and this perception is not too far off the mark. Salient individuals are more often the object of attention than are other members of a work group, for example. A manager who has six white subordinates and one Hispanic subordinate reporting to her may inadvertently pay more attention to the Hispanic in group meetings because of the salience effect. In "A Manager's Challenge," Rod Bond of Sodexo experienced salience firsthand when he attended the Women's Food Service Forum.

Individuals who are salient are often perceived to be primarily responsible for outcomes and operations and are evaluated more extremely, in either a positive or a negative direction.[131] Thus, when the Hispanic subordinate does a good job on a project, she receives excessive praise, and when she misses a deadline, she is excessively chastised.

Overt Discrimination

overt discrimination
Knowingly and willingly denying diverse individuals access to opportunities and outcomes in an organization.

Inaccurate schemas and perceptual biases can lead well-meaning managers and organizational members to unintentionally discriminate against others due to their inaccurate perceptions. On the other hand, **overt discrimination,** or knowingly and willingly denying diverse individuals access to opportunities and outcomes in an organization, is intentional and deliberate. Overt discrimination is not only unethical but also illegal. Unfortunately, just as some managers steal from their organizations, others engage in overt discrimination.

Overt discrimination is a clear violation of the principles of distributive and procedural justice. Moreover, when managers are charged with overt discrimination, costly lawsuits can ensue. Organizations ranging from the Adam's Mark chain of luxury hotels, Texaco, and Ford Motor Company to Johnson & Johnson, BellSouth, the National Football League, General Electric, Wal-Mart, and Nike either have settled or face pending lawsuits alleging overt workplace discrimination.[132] While in the past, lawsuits due to overt workplace discrimination focused on unfair treatment of women and minority group members, given the aging of the U.S. workforce, increasing numbers of discrimination cases are being brought by older workers who believe they were unfairly dismissed from their jobs due to their age.[133]

Despite all the advances that have been made, allegations of overt discrimination based on gender, race, age, and other forms of diversity continue to occur in the United States. For example, Nike recently settled a class-action lawsuit filed on behalf of 400 African-American employees of its Chicago Niketown store.[134] Employees claimed that managers used racial slurs when referring to African-American employees and customers, gave African-American employees lower-paying jobs, made unwarranted accusations of theft, and had security personnel monitor employees and customers based on race.[135] While Nike denied the allegations, as part of the settlement, Nike agreed to pay current and former employees $7.6 million and also agreed to undertake a number of initiatives to promote the effective management of diversity, including providing diversity training to all managers and supervisors in the store.[136]

Overt discrimination continues to be a problem in many other countries as well. As profiled in the following "Managing Globally," the combination of discrimination and corporate cultures stressing long working hours has made it difficult for women to advance in their careers in Japan.

Managing Globally

Women Struggle to Advance in Their Careers in Japan

Japan passed its first Equal Employment Opportunity Law in 1985 and since then, Japanese women are increasingly being found in jobs once dominated by men such as factory jobs, construction work, and driving taxis.[137] However, professional Japanese women have continued to find it difficult to advance in their careers and assume managerial positions. While women make up almost one-half of the Japanese workforce, only around 10% of managerial positions in business and government are occupied by women, according to the International Labor Organization agency of the United Nations.[138]

According to the United Nations Development Program's gender empowerment measure, which assesses the participation of women in a country's politics and economy, Japan is the most unequal of the world's wealthy nations when it comes to women.[139] Takako Ariishi has witnessed women's struggle in Japan firsthand. As an employee of a family-owned manufacturing business that supplies parts to Nissan,[140] Ariishi was fired by her own father (who was then president of the company) when she had a son 10 years ago (her father claimed that her son would be his successor as president). Nonetheless, when Ariishi's father died, she took over as president of the company. Her company is one of 160 Nissan suppliers in Japan, and the heads of these companies meet twice a year; Arrishi is the only woman among the 160 presidents and the first time the group met, she was asked to wait in a separate room with the secretaries. Miiko Tsuda, an employee of a tutoring company, indicates that she is paid less than her male coworkers, and that she is often asked to push elevator buttons and make tea for male coworkers. Only 5 of the company's 300 management employees are women.[141]

Expectations for very long working hours compound problems for women who want to advance in their careers while at the same time have children and raise a family.[142] Ariishi goes home from work every night at 7 p.m. to put her son to bed and then returns to work. Tsuda works until 10 or 11 p.m. every evening and is single. Many Japanese companies expect employees to work very long hours (e.g., from the morning until midnight), which causes some women to leave the workforce or take less demanding jobs when they have children. When Yukako Kurose, an employee in the

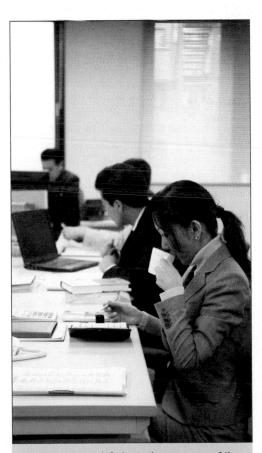

Assignments to inferior tasks are some of the components of the work environment some Japanese women have encountered as they have struggled to advance in their careers.

corporate office of a department store, had a baby and started to leave work before 6:30 p.m. to pick up her child from daycare, she stopped receiving promotions, was eventually reassigned to a low-level clerical job, and ended up quitting the company. As Kurose, who took another job at a polyester company suggests, "Japanese work customs make it almost impossible for women to have both a family and a career."[143] This not only hurts Japanese women but also hurts companies as they fail to reap the benefits of the contributions of many talented women.

How to Manage Diversity Effectively

Various kinds of barriers arise to managing diversity effectively in organizations. Some barriers have their origins in the person doing the perceiving; some, in the information and schemas that have built up over time concerning the person being perceived. To overcome these barriers and effectively manage diversity, managers (and other organizational members) must possess or develop certain attitudes and values and the skills needed to change other people's attitudes and values.

LO5 List the steps managers can take to effectively manage diversity.

Steps in Managing Diversity Effectively

Managers can take a number of steps to change attitudes and values and promote the effective management of diversity. Here, we describe these steps, some of which we have referred to previously (see Table 5.4).

SECURE TOP-MANAGEMENT COMMITMENT   As we mentioned earlier in the chapter, top management's commitment to diversity is crucial for the success of any diversity-related initiatives. Top managers need to develop the correct ethical values and performance or business-oriented attitudes that allow them to make appropriate use of their human resources.

STRIVE TO INCREASE THE ACCURACY OF PERCEPTIONS   One aspect of developing the appropriate values and attitudes is to take steps to increase the accuracy of perceptions. Managers should consciously attempt to be open to other points of view and perspectives, seek them out, and encourage their subordinates to do the same.[144] Organizational members who are open to other perspectives put their own beliefs and knowledge to an important reality test and will be more inclined to modify or change them when necessary. Managers should not be afraid to change their views about a person, issue, or event; moreover, they should encourage their subordinates to be open to changing their views in the light of disconfirming evidence. Additionally,

Table 5.4
Promoting the Effective Management of Diversity

- Secure top management commitment.
- Increase the accuracy of perceptions.
- Increase diversity awareness.
- Increase diversity skills.
- Encourage flexibility.
- Pay close attention to how employees are evaluated.
- Consider the numbers.
- Empower employees to challenge discriminatory behaviors, actions, and remarks.
- Reward employees for effectively managing diversity.
- Provide training utilizing a multipronged, ongoing approach.
- Encourage mentoring of diverse employees.

managers and all members of an organization should strive to avoid making snap judgments about people; rather, judgments should be made only when sufficient and relevant information has been gathered.[145]

INCREASE DIVERSITY AWARENESS It is natural for managers and other members of an organization to view other people from their own perspective, because their own feelings, thoughts, attitudes, and experiences guide their perceptions and interactions. The ability to appreciate diversity, however, requires that people become aware of other perspectives and the various attitudes and experiences of others. Many diversity awareness programs in organizations strive to increase managers' and workers' awareness of (1) their own attitudes, biases, and stereotypes and (2) the differing perspectives of diverse managers, subordinates, coworkers, and customers. Diversity awareness programs often have these goals:[146]

- Providing organizational members with accurate information about diversity.
- Uncovering personal biases and stereotypes.
- Assessing personal beliefs, attitudes, and values and learning about other points of view.
- Overturning inaccurate stereotypes and beliefs about different groups.
- Developing an atmosphere in which people feel free to share their differing perspectives and points of view.
- Improving understanding of others who are different from oneself.

Sometimes, simply taking the time to interact with someone who is different on some dimension can help to increase awareness. When employees and managers are at social functions or just having lunch with a coworker, often the people they interact with are those they feel most comfortable with. If all members of an organization make an effort to interact with people they ordinarily would not, mutual understanding is likely to be enhanced.[147]

In large organizations, top managers are often far removed from entry-level employees—they may lack a real understanding and appreciation for what these employees do day in and day out, the challenges and obstacles they face, and the steps that can be taken to improve effectiveness. Recognizing this fact, some managers have taken concrete steps to improve their understanding of the experiences, attitudes, and perspectives of frontline employees, as indicated in the following "Management Insight."

Top Execs Improve Their Understanding of the Front Line

Management Insight

A growing number of organizations are implementing programs whereby top managers spend time performing the jobs of frontline employees to improve their understanding of the challenges these employees face and ways to improve their working conditions.[148] For example, DaVita Inc.,[149] a major provider of kidney dialysis services in the United States, has a program called "Reality 101" through which senior executives who have never worked in a dialysis clinic before spend three days working as a clinic technician. Dialysis helps patients whose kidneys are not working properly to eliminate waste from their bloodstream. Treatments last around four hours and patients often require multiple treatments per week.[150]

Carolyn Kibler, a senior executive at DaVita who oversees 48 clinics and around 750 employees, gained a much better understanding of the challenges

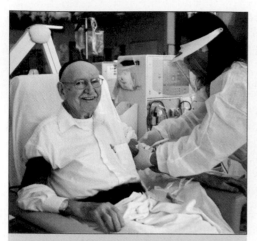

Spending some time working in dialysis clinics helps DaVita executives gain a better understanding of how best to manage them.

technicians face, the nature of their jobs, and how best to manage them, as a result of her participation in Reality 101. A former nurse, Kibler was surprised at how physically and emotionally demanding the job was and the high levels of stress it entailed. She also gained a real appreciation of the high levels of empathy technicians have for their patients—trying to make them as comfortable as possible, helping them deal with their frustrations, and mourning the loss of those who die as a results of their often multiple medical problems.[151]

Realizing how hard technicians work and how hectic and stressful the clinics can be, Kibler is now more understanding when paperwork is submitted late due to shortages of staff, gives positive feedback to those who might have to miss meetings or conference calls to treat patients, tries to avoid giving clinics last minute requests and deadlines for reports, and is more forthcoming with praise for clinic staff. More fully appreciating how patient care is the very top priority and the nature of work on the clinic floor, Kibler is also more sensitive to how her own initiatives might impact these frontline employees and the patients they serve. As she indicates, "I am more conscious of the power of my words and my actions and the impact they have down in the organization."[152]

As part of its "Now Who's Boss Day," senior executives at Loews Hotels perform entry-level jobs one day per year to appreciate and understand the challenges in these jobs and ways to make performing them easier while improving customer service.[153] This program originated when Loews CEO Jonathan Tisch took part in a reality TV show called "Now Who's Boss?" and performed the jobs of pool attendant, housekeeper, and bellman at a Florida hotel. He perspired so much in the polyester uniform people in these jobs were required to wear that he made changes in the uniform as a result of his experience. As a result of another manager's experience in the trenches, handle bars were installed on room service carts so that they weren't as difficult to push.[154]

Clearly, the jobs frontline employees perform are essential for organizational functioning. When top managers, who are very far removed from these jobs, gain a better understanding of these jobs and the employees who perform them, they are in a better position to manage them effectively.

INCREASE DIVERSITY SKILLS Efforts to increase diversity skills focus on improving the way managers and their subordinates interact with each other and on improving their ability to work with different kinds of people.[155] An important issue here is being able to communicate with diverse employees. Diverse organizational members may have different styles of communication, may differ in their language fluency, may use words differently, may differ in the nonverbal signals they send through facial expression and body language, and may differ in the way they perceive and interpret information. Managers and their subordinates must learn to communicate effectively with one another if an organization is to take advantage of the skills and abilities of its diverse workforce. Educating organizational members about differences in ways of communicating is often a good starting point.

Organizational members should also feel comfortable enough to "clear the air" and solve communication difficulties and misunderstandings as they occur rather than letting problems grow and fester without acknowledgment.

Diversity education can help managers and subordinates gain a better understanding of how people may interpret certain kinds of comments. Diversity education also can help employees learn how to resolve misunderstandings.

ENCOURAGE FLEXIBILITY Managers and their subordinates must learn how to be open to different approaches and ways of doing things. This does not mean that organizational members have to suppress their personal styles. Rather, it means that they must be open to, and not feel threatened by, different approaches and perspectives and must have the patience and flexibility needed to understand and appreciate diverse perspectives.[156]

To the extent it is feasible, managers should also be flexible enough to incorporate the differing needs of diverse employees. Earlier we mentioned that religious diversity suggests that people of certain religions might need time off for holidays that are traditionally workdays in the United States; managers need to anticipate and respond to such needs with flexibility (e.g., letting people skip the lunch hour so that they can leave work early). Moreover, flexible work hours, the option to work from home, and cafeteria-style benefit plans (see Chapter 11) are just a few of the many ways in which managers can be responsive to the differing needs of diverse employees while enabling those employees to be effective contributors to an organization.

PAY CLOSE ATTENTION TO HOW ORGANIZATIONAL MEMBERS ARE EVALUATED Whenever feasible, it is desirable to rely on objective performance indicators (see Chapter 11) as they are less subject to bias. When objective indicators are not available or are inappropriate, managers should ensure that adequate time and attention are focused on the evaluation of employees' performance and that evaluators are held accountable for their evaluations.[157] Vague performance standards should be avoided.[158]

CONSIDER THE NUMBERS Looking at the numbers of members of different minority groups and women in various positions, at various levels in the hierarchy, in locations that differ in their desirability, and in any other relevant categorizations in an organization can provide managers with important information about potential problems and ways to rectify them.[159] If members of certain groups are very underrepresented in particular kinds of jobs or units, managers need to understand why this is the case and resolve any problems they might uncover.

EMPOWER EMPLOYEES TO CHALLENGE DISCRIMINATORY BEHAVIORS, ACTIONS, AND REMARKS When managers or employees witness another organizational member being unfairly treated, they should be encouraged to speak up and rectify the situation. Top managers can make this happen by creating an organizational culture (see Chapter 3) that has zero tolerance for discrimination. As part of such a culture, organizational members should feel empowered to challenge discriminatory behavior, whether the behavior is directed at them or they witness it being directed at another employee.[160]

REWARD EMPLOYEES FOR EFFECTIVELY MANAGING DIVERSITY If the effective management of diversity is a valued organizational objective, then employees should be rewarded for their contributions to this objective, as is true at Sodexo in "A Manager's Challenge."[161] For example, after settling a major race discrimination lawsuit, Coca-Cola Company now ties managers' pay to their achievement of diversity goals. Examples of other organizations that do so include American Express and Bayer Corporation.[162]

PROVIDE TRAINING UTILIZING A MULTIPRONGED, ONGOING APPROACH Many managers use a multipronged approach to increase diversity awareness and skills in their organizations; they use films and printed materials supplemented by experiential exercises to uncover hidden biases and stereotypes. Sometimes simply providing a forum for people to learn about and discuss their differing attitudes, values, and experiences can be a powerful means for increasing awareness. Also useful are role-plays that enact problems resulting from lack of awareness and indicate the increased understanding that comes from appreciating others' viewpoints. Accurate information and training experiences can debunk stereotypes. Group exercises, role-plays, and diversity-related experiences can help organizational members develop the skills they need to work effectively with a variety of people. Many organizations hire outside consultants to provide diversity training, in addition to utilizing their own in-house diversity experts.[163]

United Parcel Service (UPS), a package delivery company, developed an innovative community internship program to increase the diversity awareness and skills of its managers and, at the same time, benefit the wider community. Upper and middle managers participating in the program take one month off the job to be community interns. They work in community organizations helping people who in many instances are very different from themselves—such organizations include a detention center in McAllen, Texas, for Mexican immigrants; homeless shelters; AIDS centers; Head Start programs; migrant-farmworker assistance groups; and groups aiming to halt the spread of drug abuse in inner cities. Approximately 40 managers a year are community interns at an annual cost to UPS of $400,000.

Since the program began in 1968, 800 managers have been community interns. Interacting with and helping diverse people enhances the interns' awareness of diversity because they experience it firsthand. Bill Cox, a UPS division manager who spent a month in the McAllen detention center, summed up his experience of diversity: "You've got these [thousands of] migrant workers down in McAllen . . . and they don't want what you have. All they want is an opportunity to earn what you have. That's a fundamental change in understanding that only comes from spending time with these people."[164]

Many managers who complete the UPS community internship program have superior diversity skills as a result of their experiences. During their internships, they learn about different cultures and approaches to work and life; they learn to interact effectively with people with whom they ordinarily do not come into contact; and they are forced to learn flexibility because of the dramatic difference between their role at the internship sites and their role as managers at UPS.

mentoring A process by which an experienced member of an organization (the mentor) provides advice and guidance to a less experienced member (the protégé) and helps the less experienced member learn how to advance in the organization and in his or her career.

ENCOURAGE MENTORING OF DIVERSE EMPLOYEES   Unfortunately, African-Americans and other minorities continue to be less likely to attain high-level positions in their organizations, and for those who do attain them, the climb up the corporate ladder typically takes longer than it does for white men. David Thomas, a professor at the Harvard Business School, has studied the careers of minorities in corporate America. One of his major conclusions is that mentoring is very important for minorities, most of whom have reached high levels in their organizations by having a solid network of mentors and contacts.[165] **Mentoring** is a process by which an experienced member of an organization (the mentor) provides advice and guidance to a less experienced member (the protégé) and helps the less experienced member learn how to advance in the organization and in his or her career.

According to Thomas, effective mentoring is more than providing instruction, offering advice, helping build skills, and sharing technical expertise. Of course, these aspects of mentoring are important and necessary. However, equally important is developing a high-quality, close, and supportive relationship with the protégé. Emotional bonds between a mentor and a protégé can enable a protégé, for example, to express fears and concerns, and sometimes even reluctance to follow a mentor's advice. The mentor can then help the protégé build his or her confidence and feel comfortable engaging in unfamiliar work behaviors.[166]

Pat Carmichael, a senior vice president at JPMorgan Chase, has mentored hundreds of protégés throughout her career and exemplifies effective mentoring.[167] She encourages her protégés to seek out difficult assignments and feedback from their supervisors. She also helps her protégés build networks of contacts and has a very extensive network herself. She serves as both a coach and a counselor to her protégés and encourages them to seek out opportunities to address their weaknesses and broaden their horizons.[168]

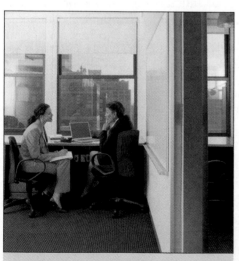

Mentoring helps less experienced employees learn how to advance in an organization and in their careers.

Sexual harassment

Sexual harassment seriously damages both the people who are harassed and the reputation of the organization in which it occurs. It also can cost organizations large amounts of money. In 1995, for example, Chevron Corporation agreed to pay $2.2 million to settle a sexual harassment lawsuit filed by four women who worked at the Chevron Information Technology Company in San Ramon, California. One woman involved in the suit said that she had received violent pornographic material through the company mail. Another, an electrical engineer, said that she had been asked to bring pornographic videos to Chevron workers at an Alaska drill site.[169] More recently, in 2001 TWA settled a lawsuit to the tune of $2.6 million that alleged that female employees were sexually harassed at JFK International Airport in New York. According to the EEOC, not only was sexual harassment tolerated at TWA, but also company officials did little to curtail it when it was brought to their attention.[170]

Unfortunately, the events at Chevron and TWA are not isolated incidents.[171] Of the 607 women surveyed by the National Association for Female Executives, 60% indicated that they had experienced some form of sexual harassment.[172] Sexual harassment victims can be women or men, and their harassers do not necessarily have to be of the opposite sex.[173] However, women are the most frequent victims of sexual harassment, particularly those in male-dominated occupations or those who occupy positions stereotypically associated with certain gender relationships, such as a female secretary reporting to a male boss. Though it occurs less frequently, men can also be victims of sexual harassment. For instance, several male employees at Jenny Craig filed a lawsuit claiming that they were subject to lewd and inappropriate comments from female coworkers and managers.[174] Sexual harassment is not only unethical; it is also illegal. Managers have an ethical obligation to ensure that they, their coworkers, and their subordinates never engage in sexual harassment, even unintentionally.

LO6 Identify the two major forms of sexual harassment and how they can be eliminated.

Forms of Sexual Harassment

There are two basic forms of sexual harassment: quid pro quo sexual harassment and hostile work environment sexual harassment. **Quid pro quo sexual harassment** occurs when a harasser asks or forces an employee to perform sexual favors to keep a job, receive a promotion, receive a raise, obtain some other work-related opportunity, or avoid receiving negative consequences such as demotion or dismissal.[175] This "Sleep with me, honey, or you're fired" form of harassment is the more extreme type and leaves no doubt in anyone's mind that sexual harassment has taken place.[176]

Hostile work environment sexual harassment is more subtle. It occurs when organizational members are faced with an intimidating, hostile, or offensive work environment because of their sex.[177] Lewd jokes, sexually oriented comments or innuendos, vulgar language, displays of pornography, displays or distribution of sexually oriented objects, and sexually oriented remarks about one's physical appearance are examples of hostile work environment sexual harassment.[178] A hostile work environment interferes with organizational members' ability to perform their jobs effectively and has been deemed illegal by the courts. Managers who engage in hostile work environment harassment or allow others to do so risk costly lawsuits for their organizations. For example, in February 2004, a federal jury awarded Marion Schwab $3.24 million after deliberating on her sexual harassment case against Federal Express.[179] Schwab was the only female tractor-trailer driver at the FedEx facility serving the Harrisburg International Airport vicinity in Middletown, Pennsylvania, from 1997 to 2000. During that period, she was the target of sexual innuendos, was given inferior work assignments, and was the brunt of derogatory comments about her appearance and the role of women in society. On five occasions, the brakes on her truck were tampered with. The federal EEOC sued FedEx, and Schwab was part of the suit. FedEx plans to appeal the decision.[180]

The courts have recently recognized other forms of hostile work environment harassment, in addition to sexual harassment. For example, in June 2006, a California jury awarded $61 million in punitive and compensatory damages to two FedEx

quid pro quo sexual harassment Asking for or forcing an employee to perform sexual favors in exchange for receiving some reward or avoiding negative consequences.

hostile work environment sexual harassment Telling lewd jokes, displaying pornography, making sexually oriented remarks about someone's personal appearance, and other sex-related actions that make the work environment unpleasant.

Ground drivers. The drivers, who are of Lebanese descent, indicated that they faced a hostile work environment and high levels of stress because a manager harassed them with racial slurs for two years.[181] FedEx plans to appeal the decision.[182]

Steps Managers Can Take to Eradicate Sexual Harassment

Managers have an ethical obligation to eradicate sexual harassment in their organizations. There are many ways to accomplish this objective. Here are four initial steps that managers can take to deal with the problem:[183]

- *Develop and clearly communicate a sexual harassment policy endorsed by top management.* This policy should include prohibitions against both quid pro quo and hostile work environment sexual harassment. It should contain (1) examples of types of behavior that are unacceptable, (2) a procedure for employees to use to report instances of harassment, (3) a discussion of the disciplinary actions that will be taken when harassment has taken place, and (4) a commitment to educate and train organizational members about sexual harassment.

- *Use a fair complaint procedure to investigate charges of sexual harassment.* Such a procedure should (1) be managed by a neutral third party, (2) ensure that complaints are dealt with promptly and thoroughly, (3) protect and fairly treat victims, and (4) ensure that alleged harassers are fairly treated.

- *When it has been determined that sexual harassment has taken place, take corrective actions as soon as possible.* These actions can vary depending on the severity of the harassment. When harassment is extensive, prolonged over a period of time, of a quid pro quo nature, or severely objectionable in some other manner, corrective action may include firing the harasser.

- *Provide sexual harassment education and training to all organizational members, including managers.* The majority of Fortune 500 firms currently provide this education and training for their employees. Managers at Du Pont, for example, developed Du Pont's "A Matter of Respect" program to help educate employees about sexual harassment and eliminate its occurrence. The program includes a four-hour workshop in which participants are given information that defines sexual harassment, sets forth the company's policy against it, and explains how to report complaints and access a 24-hour hotline. Participants watch video clips showing actual instances of harassment. One clip shows a saleswoman having dinner with a male client who, after much negotiating, seems about to give her company his business when he suddenly suggests that they continue their conversation in his hotel room. The saleswoman is confused about what to do. Will she be reprimanded if she says no and the deal is lost? After watching a video, participants discuss what they have seen, why the behavior is inappropriate, and what organizations can do to alleviate the problem.[184] Throughout the program, managers stress to employees that they do not have to tolerate sexual harassment or get involved in situations in which harassment is likely to occur.

Barry S. Roberts and Richard A. Mann, experts on business law and authors of several books on the topic, suggest a number of additional factors that managers and all members of an organization need to keep in mind about sexual harassment:[185]

- Every sexual harassment charge should be taken very seriously.

- Employees who go along with unwanted sexual attention in the workplace can be sexual harassment victims.

- Employees sometimes wait before they file complaints of sexual harassment.

- An organization's sexual harassment policy should be communicated to each new employee and reviewed with current employees on a periodic basis.

- Suppliers and customers need to be familiar with an organization's sexual harassment policy.

- Managers should provide employees with alternative ways to report incidents of sexual harassment.

- Employees who report sexual harassment must have their rights protected; this includes being protected from any potential retaliation.

- Allegations of sexual harassment should be kept confidential; those accused of harassment should have their rights protected.

- Investigations of harassment charges and any resultant disciplinary actions need to proceed in a very timely manner.

- Managers must protect employees from sexual harassment from any third-party employees they may interact with in the course of performing their jobs, such as suppliers or customers.[186]

Summary and Review

THE INCREASING DIVERSITY OF THE WORKFORCE AND THE ENVIRONMENT Diversity is dissimilarity or differences among people. Diversity is a pressing concern for managers and organizations for business and ethical reasons. There are multiple forms of diversity such as age, gender, race and ethnicity, religion, capabilities/disabilities, socioeconomic background, sexual orientation, and physical appearance.

LO1

LO 2, 3 **MANAGERS AND THE EFFECTIVE MANAGEMENT OF DIVERSITY** Both the workforce and the organizational environment are increasingly diverse, and effectively managing this diversity is an essential component of management. In each of their managerial roles, managers can encourage the effective management of diversity, which is both an ethical and a business imperative.

LO4 **PERCEPTION** Perception is the process through which people select, organize, and interpret sensory input to give meaning and order to the world around them. It is inherently subjective. Schemas guide perception; when schemas are based on a single visible characteristic such as race or gender, they are stereotypes and highly inaccurate, leading to unfair treatment. Unfair treatment also can result from biases and overt discrimination.

LO5 **HOW TO MANAGE DIVERSITY EFFECTIVELY** There are a number of steps that managers can take to effectively manage diversity. The effective management of diversity is an ongoing process that requires frequent monitoring.

LO6 **SEXUAL HARASSMENT** Two forms of sexual harassment are quid pro quo sexual harassment and hostile work environment sexual harassment. Steps that managers can take to eradicate sexual harassment include development and communication of a sexual harassment policy endorsed by top management, use of fair complaint procedures, prompt corrective action when harassment occurs, and sexual harassment training and education.

Management in Action

Topics for Discussion and Action

DISCUSSION

1. Discuss why violations of the principles of distributive and procedural justice continue to occur in modern organizations. What can managers do to uphold these principles in their organizations? **[LO 2, 3, 4, 5]**

2. Why do workers who test positive for HIV sometimes get discriminated against? **[LO 1, 4]**

3. Why would some employees resent accommodations made for employees with disabilities that are dictated by the Americans with Disabilities Act? **[LO 1, 4]**

4. Discuss the ways in which schemas can be functional and dysfunctional. **[LO4]**

5. Discuss an occasion when you may have been treated unfairly because of stereotypical thinking. What stereotypes were applied to you? How did they result in your being treated unfairly? **[LO4]**

6. How does the similar-to-me effect influence your own behavior and decisions? **[LO4]**

7. Why is mentoring particularly important for minorities? **[LO5]**

8. Why is it important to consider the numbers of different groups of employees at various levels in an organization's hierarchy? **[LO5]**

9. Think about a situation in which you would have benefited from mentoring but a mentor was not available. What could you have done to try to get the help of a mentor in this situation? **[LO5]**

ACTION

10. Choose a Fortune 500 company not mentioned in the chapter. Conduct research to determine what steps this organization has taken to effectively manage diversity and eliminate sexual harassment. **[LO 2, 5, 6]**

Building Management Skills [LO 1, 2, 3, 4, 5, 6]
Solving Diversity-Related Problems

Think about the last time that you (1) were treated unfairly because you differed from a decision maker on a particular dimension of diversity or (2) observed someone else being treated unfairly because that person differed from a decision maker on a particular dimension of diversity. Then answer these questions:

1. Why do you think the decision maker acted unfairly in this situation?

2. In what ways, if any, were biases, stereotypes, or overt discrimination involved in this situation?

3. Was the decision maker aware that he or she was acting unfairly?

4. What could you or the person who was treated unfairly have done to improve matters and rectify the injustice on the spot?

5. Was any sexual harassment involved in this situation? If so, what kind was it?

6. If you had authority over the decision maker (e.g., if you were his or her manager or supervisor), what steps would you take to ensure that the decision maker no longer treated diverse individuals unfairly?

Managing Ethically [LO 1, 2, 3, 5]

Some companies require that their employees work very long hours and travel extensively. Employees with young children, employees taking care of elderly relatives, and employees who have interests outside the workplace sometimes find that their careers are jeopardized if they try to work more reasonable hours or limit their work-related travel. Some of these employees feel that it is unethical for their manager to expect so much of them in the workplace and not understand their needs as parents and caregivers.

Questions

1. Either individually or in a group, think about the ethical implications of requiring long hours and extensive amounts of travel for some jobs.

2. What obligations do you think managers and companies have to enable employees to have a balanced life and meet nonwork needs and demands?

Small Group Breakout Exercise [LO 1, 2, 3, 4, 5]
Determining If a Problem Exists

Form groups of three or four people, and appoint one member as the spokesperson who will communicate your findings to the whole class when called on by the instructor. Then discuss the following scenario.

You and your partners own and manage a local chain of restaurants, with moderate to expensive prices, that are open for lunch and dinner during the week and for dinner on weekends. Your staff is diverse, and you believe that you are effectively managing diversity. Yet on visits to the different restaurants you have noticed that your African-American employees tend to congregate together and communicate mainly with each other. The same is true for your Hispanic employees and your white employees. You are meeting with your partners today to discuss this observation.

1. Discuss why the patterns of communication that you observed might be occurring in your restaurants.

2. Discuss whether your observation reflects an underlying problem. If so, why? If not, why not?

3. Discuss whether you should address this issue with your staff and in your restaurants. If so, how and why? If not, why not?

Exploring the World Wide Web [LO 1, 2, 3, 5, 6]

Go to the U.S. government Web sites that deal with employment issues, diversity, and sexual harassment, such as the Web sites of the Equal Employment Opportunity Commission (EEOC) and the Bureau of Labor Statistics. After reviewing these Web sites, develop a list of tips to help managers effectively manage diversity and avoid costly lawsuits.

Be the Manager [LO 1, 2, 3, 4, 5]

You are Maria Herrera and have been recently promoted to the position of director of financial analysis for a medium-size consumer goods firm. During your first few weeks on the job, you took the time to have lunch with each of your subordinates to try to get to know them better. You have 12 direct reports who are junior and senior financial analysts who support different product lines. Susan Epstein, one of the female financial analysts you had lunch with, made the following statement, "I'm so glad we finally have a woman in charge. Now, hopefully things will get better around here." You pressed Epstein to elaborate, but she clammed up. She indicated that she didn't want to unnecessarily bias you and that the problems were pretty self-evident. In fact, Epstein was surprised that you didn't know what she was talking about and jokingly mentioned that perhaps you should spend some time undercover, observing her group and their interactions with others.

You spoke with your supervisor and the former director, who had been promoted and had volunteered to be on call if you had any questions. Neither man knew of any diversity-related issues in your group. In fact, your supervisor's response was, "We've got a lot of problems, but fortunately that's not one of them."

What are you going to do to address this issue?

BusinessWeek Case in the News [LO 1, 2, 3, 4, 5]

What Works in Women's Networks

Corporate women's networks frequently get a bad rap—for good reason. The groups frequently toil on the fringes, hosting "lunch and learns" and book clubs that rarely provide the skills or exposure women need to rise in the ranks. Often, "these initiatives are run by people who don't really have much power," notes Claudia Peus, a visiting scholar at Massachusetts Institute of Technology's Sloan School of Management. When she interviewed more than 900 female executives about critical factors in their success, they ranked programs for the promotion of women last. "The spontaneous reaction was, 'They don't work.'"

Yet such initiatives are flourishing. One reason is an eagerness on the part of talent-hungry employers to appear more female-friendly. Networks are cheap, usually relying on female volunteers and garnering little corporate funding. The groups may become little more than social gatherings, and have trouble attracting heavy hitters.

But networks need not be feeble. They can be a magnet for recruiting and retaining top achievers. They may go beyond mentoring and networking to draw in clients, as General Electric Co.'s does, or let members work on key business issues, as they do at Best Buy Co. For companies like Deloitte & Touche USA, the network helps address the needs of all employees, male and female. Here's a look at some practices that work:

GET CUSTOMERS IN ON THE ACT

Formed 10 years ago after a handful of senior female employees had dinner with Jack Welch, the GE Women's Network has since grown to 40,000 active members worldwide. Its focus on leadership, advancement, and career-broadening opportunities has helped GE get to the point where women now run businesses generating some $40 billion in sales, more than 20% of total revenues. One distinguishing feature of the network: Its annual Leading & Learning summit that brings together about 150 top-level women, two-thirds of whom are customers or suppliers, to discuss a wide range of ideas and issues. "We did it, thinking it would be a one-off," says Susan Peters, GE's vice-president of executive development and chief learning officer.

Five years later, the Leading & Learning summit has become a coveted invitation both inside and outside the company. Susan Phillips, vice-president of marketing at PayPal Inc., says she came because "the agenda topics and speakers looked amazing and compelling, and I knew there would be a networking opportunity with senior women." The fact that it was an all-female gathering just made for a richer experience, adds Phillips, as she "felt the ability to relate with other participants." Among the speakers at the May 15–16 event this year: eBay Inc. CEO Meg Whitman, author Karenna Gore Schiff, playwright Sarah Jones, Atlanta Mayor Shirley Franklin, and *Today* co-anchor Meredith Vieira. CEO Jeffrey R. Immelt also came, as he always does, to speak and spend a few hours with the participants.

Within GE, the benefits of linking the company network to outsiders are many. One big positive is the exposure. "I don't get an awful lot of opportunities to interact with customers in my job," notes Tracie Winbigler, an executive vice-president at NBC Universal and co-chair of the network. "This gives me a chance to have more external focus." Another payoff to hosting such events is having customers form "a favorable impression of GE," adds co-chair Julie DeWane, who works as a general manager at GE Transportation.

That's one reason why each geographic network "hub"—there are 140 of them around the world—is asked to participate in a range of community activities, from philanthropic ventures to other customer-oriented events. Network members in Europe now plan to hold a similar high-level summit there, and others are looking to extend the concept elsewhere. The buzz is already mounting. "I heard from past participants that it is an incredible opportunity to meet people doing fascinating things," says Michelle McMurry of the Aspen Institute, a GE partner, who went to the May summit. "They were right."

TACKLE REAL BUSINESS PROBLEMS

Julie Gilbert doesn't mind admitting that the women's network at Best Buy started with some hugs. Three and a half years ago, Gilbert, who launched the company's store-within-a-store concept for home theater buffs, noticed that during store visits the few female staffers she'd see would come up and hug her. When she asked a store greeter about it, the young woman told her: "Every day when we have people in from the corporate office, they're all guys. When we see you, we realize if we just keep working hard, one day we'll [get there], too."

Such chummy beginnings belie the pragmatic nature of the network Gilbert would go on to create. Inspired by the encounter with the greeter, Gilbert typed up a business plan for a new women's initiative that night. Unlike the women's network that existed at the time—a 25-person shell of a program at Best Buy's Minneapolis headquarters—Gilbert designed the program as a way for employees, from top executives to cashiers, to get more deeply involved in core business issues. "The frame on it is leadership," she says, "but you don't go to a course to build a leader. You learn by doing actual business issues, by solving business problems."

One problem was coming up with better ways to recruit and retain women in Best Buy's male-dominated, techie culture. In the home theater department, for example, the rate of female turnover was double that of their male colleagues. But just as important, Gilbert wanted the network to be an innovation engine for the company's woefully underserved female customers. At the time, Best Buy was grappling with how to better appeal to women, who influence 89% of consumer electronics purchases and spend $68 billion on them each year.

Gilbert's program, known as WOLF (Women's Leadership Forum), includes a web of regional "WOLF packs" and innovation teams, which are based in Minneapolis. Each of the innovation teams chooses a project, such as finding ways to attract more female customers, and then has to get the ideas into a few stores in three months and into a large number of stores in six. Next month, for example, one WOLF group will launch designer iPod holders and laptop cases in 100 of Best Buy's stores. Another WOLF team is revamping the online gift registry; yet another is working with designers to make stores more woman-friendly.

The efforts are paying off. Recruitment of female sales managers is up 100% over the past year, and the company has a greater share of female customers than before the network started. Internally, the network has found fans among executives like Midwest regional manager Shawn Score, who has attracted more than 300 new female employees and seen turnover among women managers in his territory drop almost 10 percentage points in the last year thanks to the WOLF program. He has also tapped the network to help him better serve women customers. One WOLF team suggested switching signs on washing machines to promote how many loads they hold instead of measuring the machine's volume in cubic feet, leading to more pertinent, mom-friendly signage. "We think that's going to be an absolute home run," says Score.

BRIDGE THE GENDER DIVIDE

Few women's networks can boast of a track record like that of Deloitte. Now in its 14th year, Deloitte's Initiative for the Retention and Advancement of Women, known as WIN, has been lauded for its success in promoting women to the most senior ranks: 19.3% of partners are women, the highest percentage among the Big Four public accounting firms. That's up from 7% since WIN was started in 1993.

One reason for its success? Many of the programs born out of Deloitte's women's initiative are geared toward both women and men. For instance, the firm is piloting a "mass career customization" program that will give every employee a framework for dialing up and down their hours, travel demands, and responsibilities as their personal needs change over the course of their careers. Unlike flextime or job-sharing policies, which men often avoid because of the stigma still associated with opting into them, everyone in the pilot locations will be enrolled in the program.

Still, such initiatives have little direct impact on hard-charging audit partners whose idea of work-life balance is a three-day weekend after tax season. When asked, says Cathy Benko, the national managing director in charge of WIN, men almost always say that the women's initiative is important. "But then they'll stop, and if they continue, they'll say 'but it hasn't done anything for me.'"

To help change that thinking, Benko came up with a new program two years ago called Women as Buyers. It would specifically help men with what mattered to them—winning more clients—while improving understanding between men and women at the firm. Noticing a dearth of research on how executive women make decisions, the WIN team sponsored a yearlong study on the topic. It has been presenting its findings in four-hour workshops made up of two-thirds men and one-third women.

The sessions remind men of simple differences such as client entertaining (women prefer breakfast to dinner, since they often have more evening responsibilities at home) and communication styles (just because a woman is nodding doesn't mean she agrees with you). While male executives may prefer consultants or accountants to sit by their side, women are more visual than men, the research found, and partners should face women executives in client meetings.

And because women tend to see leadership roles as positions of responsibility rather than power, partners should think carefully about whom they parachute in to help sell services. "If it's a guy, you might want to bring your big mucky-muck in," says Paul Silverglate, an audit partner who went through the training.

"Women partners are more focused on who's going to do the work with their team day-to-day. That was very interesting to me."

The feedback from men has been overwhelmingly positive: More than 90% say the workshops were useful. Silverglate, who's also a leader in WIN, says he's even had male colleagues tell him they've used the tips in their personal lives. "If you really want to make a difference for women," says Silverglate, "it has to make sense for all the partners."

Questions for Discussion

1. In what ways can women's networks contribute to the effective management of diversity?

2. What kinds of networks and network practices are especially likely to be beneficial?

3. How might these networks help organizations to be more responsive to customers?

4. How might all employees and organizations benefit from effective women's networks?

Source: Diane Brady and Jena McGregor, "What Works In Women's Networks." Reprinted from the June 18, 2007, issue of *BusinessWeek* by special permission. Copyright © 2007 by The McGraw-Hill Companies, Inc.

BusinessWeek   ## Case in the News [LO 1, 2, 3, 4, 5]

The Best Places to Launch a Career

Accountants used to be spoofed as bean counters—dutiful, middle-aged, gray-suited men with considerable analytical expertise but little charisma. That was during the good times. After their uninspiring performances in the corporate scandals of recent years, accounting seemed like a profession without much of a future, and the firms certainly no place to launch a career. Scratch that. This year accountants became sexy.

Accounting firms dominated *BusinessWeek*'s second annual ranking of the best companies for new college graduates: Deloitte & Touche is No. 1, followed by PricewaterhouseCoopers and Ernst & Young. The last of the Big Four, KPMG, moved up four spots, to No. 11.

Why did the accounting firms do so well? Enormous demand. Across industries, there is a mad scramble to recruit the best and brightest of a new generation, the much-maligned, heavily scrutinized Gen Y. Nowhere is the pressure more intense than in the Big Four. The Sarbanes-Oxley Act has so greatly increased the need for their services that the firms are facing an epic talent shortage.

That has put them in an unusual position: They are among the first to rethink how to recruit college grads, keep them happy on the job, or just keep them at all. Ernst & Young uses Facebook to let prospective employees talk freely with real ones. Deloitte will show a rap video about office life—made by interns—to give students a realistic view of the company. And PwC requires some bosses to get a second opinion on their evaluations of new hires to make sure the feedback is clear enough, the goals ambitious enough for kids who are uncomfortable with ambiguity. Welcome to the post-millennial world.

THE GOOGLE EFFECT

Our ranking is based on three extensive surveys: of career services directors at U.S. colleges, the employers they identify as the best for new graduates, and college students themselves. This year we were able to examine the records of many more companies, which allowed us to expand our list of employers from 55 to 95 and broaden our view of the corporate landscape. Several newcomers, including PwC, IBM, and Microsoft, eclipsed last year's favorites. Walt Disney had been No. 1; this year it fell to No. 7. Last year's No. 2, Lockheed Martin, slipped to No. 9.

There were a number of surprises beyond the rise of the accounting firms. Only nine companies in the top 50 last year offered starting salaries of at least $55,000. This year twice that many pay big money; among them are the brand-name tech companies, where, thanks to the Google effect, first-year salaries now average $60,000 to $65,000 (and that's before bonuses). We also saw the three pharmaceutical companies surveyed last year fall in the rankings. Merck & Co. (No. 49), which was in the news because of its problems with Vioxx, did poorly in the student poll.

Our survey shows how some of the smartest employers are starting to deal with a new generation that expects a very different workplace from the one of their parents. The intense desire to hire young graduates is prompted by the retirement of the boomers, of course, but also the dead certainty among executives that their success marketing to youthful consumers depends on the insights of IM-ing, YouTube-watching twentysomethings who are often heralded for their tech savvy, if not much else.

The employers that did best in our ranking recognize that they have to accommodate this new generation. Many of them are trying to appeal to Gen Y by making themselves more transparent, flexible, responsive, even nurturing. Their initiatives range from the conventional (more vacation) to the questionable (a faux sitcom about office life).

So who are these people? Officially, this generation comprises the 78 million born between 1982 and 2000 who began entering the workforce three years ago. They are supposed to be the hothouse kids: praised and coddled from infancy and watched over by their parents well into adulthood. As employees, they are said to have high expectations and demand meaningful work, constructive feedback, and positions of influence within their organizations. In other words, they want a seat at the table, or they'll walk. "It is crucial for us to meet the students partway," says Ernst & Young's director of campus recruitment, Dan Black. "If you don't make an effort to provide an environment in which this generation can do their best, they're going to find one where they can."

Naturally, there are managers who don't think the special treatment is necessary. At Microsoft Corp. (No. 6), for example, interviewees visiting its headquarters are offered concierge services. A few lucky interns at Ernst & Young get to fly with the chief executive on the corporate jet to a conference in Orlando. And there are experts who believe companies are making empty promises about how much a 22-year-old can really contribute. "I don't care how brilliant you are, when you start out in a job, you're not going to run things," says Courtney E. Anderson, founder of Courtney Anderson & Associates, a firm that provides workplace consulting.

You won't hear that note of skepticism at the accounting firms. Indeed, few are trying harder to connect with Gen Y than they are. Deloitte alone estimates it will need to hire as many as 50,000 employees in the next five years. Luckily for them, the Enron era left an impression on some Gen Yers that few expected: Accountants don't have to labor thanklessly and out of sight; they can be vital to the fortunes of a company. "I thought those occurrences would cause people to shy away from the discipline. Instead it's done the opposite," says John J. Fernandes, the president of the Association to Advance Collegiate Schools of Business International. "I think that people want to be in an important position that's visible."

Indeed, the number of U.S. students graduating from college with accounting degrees has risen almost 29% since 2002. But accounting firms are also competing with high-paying, bonus-giving investment banks as well as major corporations. So the Big Four are falling over themselves to win the favor of Generation Y. "The ability to recruit and retain younger workers will become critical," says Barry Salzberg, CEO of Deloitte & Touche USA. "In many ways, Gen Y is our future."

And in facing that future, one of the most important lessons the accounting firms and others have learned is that Gen Yers appreciate straight talk about what they can expect from the workplace. "It's all about authenticity," says Andrea S. Hershatter, the director of the undergraduate business program at Emory University. As consumers, these twentysomethings expect that the promise of the brand will match the reality. If it doesn't, they'll try something else. Same goes for the workplace.

New York Life Insurance (No. 47) is one of those experimenting with a real-world introduction to corporate life. Last year it faced up to a dismal reality: Only 3% of corporate interns accepted full-time positions, one of the worst rates in the industry. So instead of showering this year's interns with frivolous perks and other goodies, it did the exact opposite—it took away their Friday afternoons off, ordered them into classes on business etiquette, and put them to work brainstorming about how to make the company's products more appealing to Gen Y. The company says it may use elements of the winning marketing campaign, which targeted young people during critical periods in their lives.

New York Life doesn't know if its new approach worked, but more than 90% of the interns said they would like to receive an offer. "They want a challenge," says program head Elizabeth King. "We don't treat them as kids, we treat them as employees." Employees, that is, who in their first weeks on the job get to make suggestions about how to improve operations.

Other companies are taking more risks, wandering way out of their comfort zones to meet Gen Yers on their own turf. At Ernst & Young, the recruiter, Black, launched a Facebook campaign in July, 2006, which now brings together some 10,000 employees and job seekers in an open forum to discuss the application process and prospective workplace. "This lack of control is something that is very new and makes a lot of larger organizations uncomfortable," he says with considerable understatement. He has received calls from other recruiters asking how he persuaded management to go along with the idea. "It was difficult for that group because clearly FaceBook was a new concept, but they thought the reward of reaching Gen Y in a meaningful way would be worth the risk."

The message board is generally full of serious questions and enthusiastic responses. There is, however, the occasional skeptic about the forum: "This is the lamest thing I have ever seen," wrote one student. Black can live with that. "We knew going in we would get feedback that wasn't exactly positive," he says.

JPMorgan Chase & Co.'s investment bank (No. 17) might be tempted to use as its recruiting pitch the $68,000 average bonus it handed out in 2006 to first-year employees. Instead, it is actually trying to give Gen Yers a realistic sense of what they have to do to earn that money. It allowed a New York University film grad to shadow three young employees for a documentary-style film that will be posted online this month. After, that is, company officials approve it.

Deloitte has also opened up a bit in an effort to present a real picture of working life to potential recruits. It asked employees to create short videos describing what the company means to them. Nearly 400 videos were judged by a group of interns and employees of all ages. The dozen or so best will be part of Deloitte's campus recruiting efforts. One of them is a rap video. If the head of the selection panel, a partner at the firm, no less, had any reservations about rap, he kept them to himself. Instead, ever so gently, he expressed concern about the video's references to long hours and difficult work assignments: Wouldn't that dissuade students? A few interns didn't hesitate to set him straight. "You want to be busy," said Cindy Quintanilla, an intern in Dallas. Steve Mai, an intern in New York, added: "If all they did was talk about the good stuff, then I'd be skeptical."

But when it comes to asking older managers to set aside their doubts and get involved, PwC has gone even further than Deloitte. It has just launched an online recruiting campaign that includes a faux sitcom. Called *The Firm,* it features real employees acting out scenarios in which the female Gen Y star has awkward interactions with older employees. That's right, real, older employees. Senior partner Bob is "kinda scary," and Blake, a senior associate, apparently smells. "We hear all the time that students

are interested in what it's like in the workplace," says Amy Thompson, PwC's national director of campus recruiting. "This is a funny way to talk about a serious subject."

Aside from giving up control, putting themselves in uncomfortable positions, and in general spending an awful lot of time thinking about how to please kids who would like nothing more than to have their jobs, managers are also expected to relearn how to manage. Specifically, they are supposed to deal with young employees who have lived in a constant feedback loop.

It has been said that Gen Y needs buckets of praise. In fact, in many cases these folks are looking for honest appraisals of their work. Boeing Co. (No. 14) is starting to move in that direction. The aerospace giant has one of the lowest retention rates in its industry (59%), and one way it hopes to improve upon this is by teaching managers how to deliver criticism—harsh, if necessary—along with praise. "We're starting to tell our managers that we want them to have very clear and candid conversations with their employees," says Julie-Ellen Acosta, vice-president for leadership development. And that's for employees of all ages. The company is retooling its training to reflect the new philosophy. The goal: more ongoing and personalized feedback and more honesty. "The managers are worried about hurting people's feelings," says Richard Stephens, senior vice-president for human resources. "We want to let them know it's O.K. to have those conversations."

Here's another thing about Gen Y that managers are starting to figure out: Twentysomethings want not just honest feedback but also routine conversations about their progress and their career paths. This generation, says Emory's Hershatter, feels "entitled to have others support them in their efforts to accomplish and achieve." And that means right from the start. Abbott Laboratories

(No. 15) recently began an extended orientation that includes goals for the first, second, and third months on the job, as well as the promise of consistent dialogue with managers. "People have the expectation of a more planned and deliberate approach," says Ann Johnston, director of learning and development.

PwC is taking this approach even further. A few years ago the company resolved to let employees themselves decide when during their first 90 days they would sit down with their boss for a performance review. (After that, they could do so every month if they choose to.) And, get this, a second reader is supposed to review the initial written evaluation to make sure it is sufficiently clear.

Some companies are even giving employees more say over how their careers will unfold. In the first two months after KPMG launched a Web-based training program to better prepare young employees and their managers to talk about career building, more than 9,300 employees logged on. Some 2,500 created their own (ideal) career paths.

As a concession to the expressed desire of some millennials to do good before they do well, 15 companies and investment banks are allowing new hires to defer employment for two years. During that time they teach at troubled high schools around the country through Teach for America (No. 10).

Some companies have decided it makes more sense, and is less costly, to test their new programs on a few lucky souls first. At DHL (No. 78), executives weren't sure about training people "so new you had to tell them how to tie their shoelaces," says Paul Read, the director of sales training. The company, which usually hires experienced salespeople, decided to offer an 11-week program to recent college grads—but only to nine. Pooja Shambhu, a 24-year-old Purdue University grad who went through the intensive course, says: "The first time

I went out on my own, the feeling was unbelievable. Within two weeks, I won my first account."

DHL executives aren't complaining anymore. They say the new hires generate more revenue and more shipments per sale. This year the company expanded the program to 19 people. "They were hungrier and more easily moldable than the other reps," says Read. Now he just hopes these well-trained salespeople stay for a while.

Of course, some companies are establishing policies that everyone can take advantage of. IBM (No. 4) introduced ThinkPlace, an online suggestion box to help it cull the best ideas from its global workforce. And over at that other tech company, Google Inc. (No. 5), there are free lunches and on-site massages. But perhaps the most popular perk is that employees, all of them, are allowed to devote one day a week to developing new ideas.

And the accounting firms, for all of their out-there experiments, are making use of some more traditional incentives, too. PwC has instituted an extra 11-day firmwide vacation. Ernst & Young offers four-day weekends several times during the summer. And KPMG declared that every summer weekend starts at 3 p.m. Friday. You don't have to be under 25 to qualify.

Questions for Discussion

1. How are companies and managers trying to attract and retain Generation Y workers?

2. Why are they so concerned about doing this?

3. How might the changes managers are making, in response to Generation Y workers, contribute to organizational effectiveness?

4. How might these changes increase responsiveness to customers?

Source: Lindsey Gerdes, "The Best Places to Launch a Career," Reprinted from the September 24, 2007, issue of *BusinessWeek* by special permission. Copyright © 2007 by The McGraw-Hill Companies, Inc.

CHAPTER 6

Managing in the Global Environment

After studying this chapter, you should be able to:

LO1 Explain why the ability to perceive, interpret, and respond appropriately to the global environment is crucial for managerial success.

LO2 Differentiate between the global task and global general environments.

LO3 Identify the main forces in both the global task and general environments and describe the challenges that each force presents to managers.

LO4 Explain why the global environment is becoming more open and competitive and identify the forces behind the process of globalization that increase the opportunities, complexities, challenges, and threats that managers face.

LO5 Discuss why national cultures differ and why it is important that managers be sensitive to the effects of falling trade barriers and regional trade associations on the political and social systems of nations around the world.

A Manager's Challenge

Nestlé's Global Food Empire

www.nestle.com

Why is managing the global environment so complex today? Nestlé is the world's largest food company, it enjoyed record profits on sales of over $100 billion in 2007, and globally it has over 200,000 employees and 600 factories in 83 countries. It makes and sells over 8,000 food products, including such popular brands as Kit-Kat chocolate bars, Taster's Choice coffee, Carnation Instant milk, and Stouffer's Foods. At its corporate headquarters in Vevey, Switzerland, CEO Peter Brabeck-Latmathe, who has been in charge since 1997, is the person responsible for Nestlé's improving global performance. And, by 2008 he has faced and managed many global challenges.[1]

From the beginning Brabeck worked to increase Nestlé's revenues and profits by entering new attractive national markets in both developed and emerging nations as trade barriers fell. He continued the ambitious global expansion that Nestlé began in the 1990s, when, for example, it bought the U.S. food companies Carnation and Buitoni Pasta, the British chocolate maker Rowntree, the French bottled-water company Perrier, and the Mexican food maker Ortega.

Under Brabeck, Nestlé spent $18 billion to acquire U.S. companies Ralston Purina, Dreyer's Ice-cream, and Chef America. Brabeck's intention was not only to develop these food brands in the United States but also to customize their products to suit the tastes of customers in countries around the world. He is particularly anxious to enter emerging markets such as those in eastern Europe, India, and Asia to take advantage of the enormous numbers of potential new customers in these regions. In this way Nestlé can leverage its well-known brand

A serious caffeine fix! Nestlé's South Korea marketing staff make a huge cup of coffee at a sales event, using the company's new Latte Creamer.

image and products around the world to drive up its performance.

Increasing global revenues from increased product sales was only the first part of Brabeck's global business model, however. He was also anxious to increase Nestlé's operating efficiency and reduce the cost of managing its global operations. As you can imagine, with over 200,000 employees and 600 factories the costs of organizing Nestlé's global activities are enormous. Brabeck benchmarked its operating costs to those of competitors such as Kraft Foods and Unilever and found Nestlé's costs were significantly higher than theirs. Brabeck cut the workforce by 20%, closed 150 factories, and reduced operating costs by over 12%. Nestlé is also using advanced IT both to reduce the number of its global suppliers and to negotiate more favorable supply contracts with them—moves that have and will result in a significant drop in purchasing costs. Brabeck also designed Nestlé's new streamlined operating structure and IT to increase the flow of information between its food products units and all the countries in which it

sells its products. His goal is to capitalize on a prime source of its competitive advantage: superior innovation.

Thus, Brabeck's global strategy for Nestlé was driven by three main goals: (1) Expand Nestlé's range of products, and offer them to new and existing customers in countries throughout the world; (2) find lower-cost ways to make and sell these products; and (3) speed up Nestlé's product innovation by leveraging its expertise across its food businesses to create more attractive food products that will increase its global market share. In addition, customers around the world today are demanding healthier and more nutritious food products. So, Brabeck has adopted a new approach to developing Nestlé's products that he calls an "organic approach." Brabeck claims his company is engaged in a "transformation" that will lead it to become the "world's leading nutrition, health, and wellness" food company that makes consumer health and safety its prime concern.[2] He claims that Nestlé's record 2007 sales are proof of its commitment to make foods that better meet the needs of global customers.

Overview

Top managers of a global company like Nestlé are always operating in an environment where they are competing with other companies for scarce and valuable resources. Managers of companies large and small have concluded that to survive and prosper in the 21st century, most organizations must become **global organizations,** organizations that operate and compete not only domestically, at home, but also globally, in countries around the world. Operating in the global environment is uncertain and unpredictable because it is complex and constantly changing.

If organizations are to adapt to this changing environment, their managers must learn to understand the forces that operate in it and how these forces give rise to opportunities and threats. In this chapter, we examine why the environment, both domestically and globally, has become more open, vibrant, and competitive. We examine how forces in the task and general environments affect global organizations and their managers. By the end of this chapter, you will appreciate the changes that have been taking place in the environment and understand why it is important for managers to develop a global perspective as they strive to increase organizational efficiency and effectiveness.

global organization An organization that operates and competes in more than one country.

global environment The set of global forces and conditions that operate beyond an organization's boundaries but affect a manager's ability to acquire and utilize resources.

What Is the Global Environment?

The **global environment** is a set of forces and conditions in the world outside an organization's boundary that affect the way it operates and shape its behavior.[3] These forces change over time and thus present managers with *opportunities* and *threats.* Changes in the global environment, such as the development of efficient new production technology, the availability of lower-cost components, or the opening of new global markets, create opportunities for managers to make and sell more products, obtain more resources and capital, and thereby strengthen their organization. In contrast, the rise of new global competitors, a global economic recession, or an oil shortage poses threats that can devastate an organization if managers are unable to sell its products and revenues and profits plunge. The quality of managers' understanding of forces in the global environment and their ability to respond appropriately to those forces, such as Nestlé's managers' ability to make and sell the food products customers around the world want to buy, are critical factors affecting organizational performance.

In this chapter we explore the nature of these forces and consider how managers can respond to them. To identify opportunities and threats caused by forces in the environment, it is helpful for managers to distinguish between the *task environment* and the more encompassing *general environment* (see Figure 6.1, page 190).

The **task environment** is the set of forces and conditions that originate with global suppliers, distributors, customers, and competitors; these forces and conditions affect an organization's ability to obtain inputs and dispose of its outputs. The task environment contains the forces that have the most *immediate* and *direct* effect on managers because they pressure and influence managers on a daily basis. When managers turn on the radio or television, arrive at their offices in the morning, open their mail, or look at their computer screens, they are likely to learn about problems facing them because of changing conditions in their organization's task environment.

The **general environment** includes the wide-ranging global, economic, technological, sociocultural, demographic, political, and legal forces that affect the organization and its task environment. For the individual manager, opportunities and threats resulting from changes in the general environment are often more difficult to identify and respond to than are events in the task environment. However, changes in these forces can have major impacts on managers and their organizations.

LO1 Explain why the ability to perceive, interpret, and respond appropriately to the global environment is crucial for managerial success.

task environment The set of forces and conditions that originate with suppliers, distributors, customers, and competitors and affect an organization's ability to obtain inputs and dispose of its outputs because they influence managers on a daily basis.

LO2 Differentiate between the global task and global general environments.

general environment The wide-ranging global, economic, technological, sociocultural, demographic, political, and legal forces that affect an organization and its task environment.

The Task Environment

Forces in the task environment result from the actions of suppliers, distributors, customers, and competitors both at home and abroad (see Figure 6.1). These four groups affect a manager's ability to obtain resources and dispose of outputs on a daily, weekly, and monthly basis and thus have a significant impact on short-term decision making.

LO3 Identify the main forces in both the global task and general environments and describe the challenges that each force presents to managers.

Suppliers

Suppliers are the individuals and companies that provide an organization with the input resources (such as raw materials, component parts, or employees) that it needs to produce goods and services. In return, the supplier receives payment for those goods and services. An important aspect of a manager's job is to ensure a reliable supply of input resources.

Take Dell Computer, for example, the company we focused on in Chapter 1. Dell has many suppliers of component parts such as microprocessors (Intel and AMD) and disk drives (Quantum and Seagate Technologies). It also has suppliers of preinstalled software, including the operating system (Microsoft) and specific applications software (IBM, Oracle, and America Online). Dell's providers of capital, such as banks and financial institutions, are also important suppliers. Cisco Systems and Oracle are important providers of Internet hardware and software for dot-coms.

suppliers Individuals and organizations that provide an organization with the input resources that it needs to produce goods and services.

Figure 6.1
Forces in the Global Environment

Dell has several suppliers of labor. One source is the educational institutions that train future Dell employees and therefore provide the company with skilled workers. Another is trade unions, organizations that represent employee interests and can control the supply of labor by exercising the right of unionized workers to strike. Unions also can influence the terms and conditions under which labor is employed. Dell's workers are not unionized; when layoffs became necessary due to an economic slowdown in the early 2000s, Dell had few problems in laying off workers to reduce costs. In organizations and industries where unions are very strong, however, an important part of a manager's job is negotiating and administering agreements with unions and their representatives.

Changes in the nature, number, or type of suppliers results in forces that produce opportunities and threats to which managers must respond if their organizations are to prosper. For example, a major supplier-related threat that confronts managers arises when suppliers' bargaining position is so strong that they can raise the prices of the inputs they supply to the organization. A supplier's bargaining position is especially strong when (1) the supplier is the sole source of an input and (2) the input is vital to the organization.[4] For example, for 17 years G. D. Searle was the sole supplier of Nutra-Sweet, the artificial sweetener used in most diet soft drinks. Not only was NutraSweet an important ingredient in diet soft drinks, but it also was one for which there was no acceptable substitute (saccharin and other artificial sweeteners raised health concerns). Searle earned its privileged position because it invented and held the patent for NutraSweet. Patents prohibit other organizations from introducing competing products for 17 years. In 1992, Searle's patent expired, and many companies began to produce products similar to NutraSweet. Prior to 1992, Searle was able to demand a high price for NutraSweet, charging twice as much as the price of an equivalent amount of sugar. Paying that price raised the costs of soft-drink manufacturers, including Coca-Cola and PepsiCo, which had no alternative but to buy the product.[5] In the 2000s Splenda, made by McNeil Nutritionals owned by Tate & Lyle, a British company, has replaced NutraSweet as the artificial sweetener of choice, and NutraSweet's price has fallen while Splenda now commands a high price from soft-drink companies.[6]

In contrast, when an organization has many suppliers for a particular input, it is in a relatively strong bargaining position with those suppliers and can demand low-cost, high-quality inputs from them. Often, an organization can use its power with suppliers to force them to reduce their prices, as Dell frequently does. Dell, for example, is constantly searching for low-cost suppliers abroad to keep its PC prices competitive. At a global level, organizations have the opportunity to buy products from suppliers overseas or to become their own suppliers and manufacture their own products abroad.

It is important that managers recognize the opportunities and threats associated with managing the global supply chain. On the one hand, gaining access to low-cost products made abroad represents an opportunity for U.S. companies to lower their input costs. On the other hand, managers who fail to utilize low-cost overseas suppliers create a threat and put their organizations at a competitive disadvantage.[7] Levi Strauss, for example, was slow to realize that it could not compete with the low-priced jeans sold by Wal-Mart and other retailers, and it was eventually forced to close almost all of its U.S. jean factories and utilize low-cost overseas suppliers to keep the price of its jeans competitive. Now it sells its low-priced jeans in Wal-Mart! The downside to global outsourcing is, of course, the loss of millions of U.S. jobs, an issue we have discussed in previous chapters.

The purchasing activities of global companies have become increasingly complicated in recent years. More than 500 suppliers around the world produce parts for Boeing's popular 777 and even more will be needed for the new Dreamliner.

A common problem facing managers of large global companies such as Ford, Procter & Gamble, and IBM is managing the development of a global network of suppliers that will allow their companies to keep costs down and quality high. For example, Boeing's popular 777 jet airline requires 132,500 engineered parts produced around the world by 545 suppliers.[8] While Boeing makes the majority of these parts, eight Japanese suppliers make parts for the 777's fuselage, doors, and wings; a Singapore supplier makes the doors for the plane's forward landing gear; and three Italian suppliers manufacture wing flaps. Boeing's rationale for buying so many inputs from overseas suppliers is that these suppliers are the best in the world at performing their particular activity and doing business with them helps Boeing to produce a high-quality final product, a vital requirement given the need for aircraft safety and reliability.[9] Its new plane, the Dreamliner, uses even more parts made by overseas suppliers, and Boeing has outsourced some of the plane's assembly to companies' abroad—something that has led to the charge that it is giving away the source of its competitive advantage!

The purchasing activities of global companies have become increasingly complicated as a result of the development of a whole range of skills and competencies in different countries around the world. It is clearly in their interests to search out the lowest-cost, best-quality suppliers no matter where they may be. Also, the Internet makes it possible for companies to coordinate complicated, arm's-length exchanges involving the purchasing of inputs and the disposal of outputs.

global outsourcing The purchase of inputs from overseas suppliers or the production of inputs abroad to lower production costs and improve product quality or design.

Global outsourcing is the process by which organizations purchase inputs from other companies or produce inputs themselves throughout the world to lower their production costs and improve the quality or design of their products.[10] To take advantage of national differences in the cost and quality of resources such as labor or raw materials, GM might build its own engines in one country, transmissions in another, and brakes in a third and buy other components from hundreds of global suppliers. Trade expert Robert Reich once calculated that of the $20,000 that customers pay

GM for a Pontiac Le Mans, about $6,000 goes to South Korea, where the Le Mans is assembled; $3,500, to Japan for advanced components such as engines, transaxles, and electronics; $1,500, to Germany, where the Le Mans was designed; $800, to Taiwan, Singapore, and Japan for small components; $500, to Britain for advertising and marketing services; and about $100, to Ireland for data-processing services. The remaining $7,000 goes to GM–and to the lawyers, bankers, and insurance agents that GM retains in the United States.[11]

Is the Le Mans a U.S. product? Yes, but it is also a Korean product, a Japanese product, and a German product. Today, such global exchanges are becoming so complex that specialized organizations are emerging to help manage global organizations' supply chains, that is, the flow of inputs necessary to produce a product. One example is Li & Fung, profiled below in "Managing Globally."

Managing Globally

Global Supply Chain Management

Finding the overseas suppliers that offer the lowest-priced and highest-quality products is an important task facing the managers of global organizations. Since these suppliers are located in thousands of cities in many countries around the world, finding them is a difficult business. Often, global companies use the services of overseas intermediaries or brokers, located near these suppliers, to find the one that best meets their input requirements. Li & Fung, now run by brothers Victor and William Fung, is one of the brokers that has helped hundreds of global companies to locate suitable overseas suppliers, especially suppliers in mainland China.[12]

In the 2000s, however, managing global companies' supply chains became a more complicated task. To reduce costs, overseas suppliers were increasingly *specializing* in just one part of the task of producing a product. For example, in the past, a company such as Target might have negotiated with an overseas supplier to manufacture 1 million units of some particular shirt at a certain cost per unit. But with specialization, Target might find it can reduce the costs of producing the shirt even further by splitting apart the operations involved in its production and having *different* overseas suppliers, often in *different* countries, perform each operation. For example, to get the lowest cost per unit, rather than negotiating with a single overseas supplier over the price of making a particular shirt, Target might first negotiate with a yarn manufacturer in Vietnam to make the yarn; then ship the yarn to a Chinese supplier to weave it into cloth; and then ship the cloth to several different factories in Malaysia and the Philippines to cut the fabric and sew the shirts. Then, another overseas company might take responsibility for packaging and shipping the shirts to wherever in the world they are required. Because a company such as Target has thousands of different clothing products under production, and they change all the time, the problems of managing such a supply chain to get the full cost savings from global expansion are clearly difficult and costly.

Li & Fung capitalized on this opportunity. Realizing that many global companies do not have the time or expertise to find such specialized low-price suppliers, its founders moved quickly to provide such a service. Li & Fung employs 3,600 agents who travel across 37 countries to locate new suppliers and inspect existing suppliers to find new ways to help its global clients get lower prices or higher-quality products. Global companies are happy to outsource their supply chain management to Li & Fung because they realize significant cost savings. Even though they pay a hefty fee to Li & Fung, they avoid the costs of employing their own agents. As the complexity of supply chain management continues to increase, more and more companies like Li & Fung are appearing.

Distributors

distributors
Organizations that help other organizations sell their goods or services to customers.

Distributors are organizations that help other organizations sell their goods or services to customers. The decisions that managers make about how to distribute products to customers can have important effects on organizational performance. For example, package delivery companies such as Federal Express, UPS, and the U.S. Postal Service became vital distributors for the millions of items bought online and shipped to customers by dot-com companies.

The changing nature of distributors and distribution methods can bring opportunities and threats for managers. If distributors become so large and powerful that they can control customers' access to a particular organization's goods and services, they can threaten the organization by demanding that it reduce the prices of its goods and services.[13] For example, the huge retail distributor Wal-Mart controls its suppliers' access to a great number of customers and thus often demands that its suppliers reduce their prices. If an organization such as Procter & Gamble refuses to reduce its prices, Wal-Mart might respond by buying products only from Procter & Gamble's competitors—companies such as Unilever and Dial. In 2004, Wal-Mart announced that by 2006 all its suppliers must adopt a new wireless scanning technology that will reduce its cost of distributing products to its stores or it would stop doing business with them.[14]

In contrast, the power of a distributor may be weakened if there are many options. This has been the experience of the three broadcast television networks—ABC, NBC, and CBS—which "distribute" TV programs. Their ability to demand lower prices from the producers of television programs has been weakened because today hundreds of new cable television channels exist that have reduced the three networks' share of the viewing audience to less than 40%, down from more than 90% a decade ago. Similarly, because there are at least four major package delivery companies—USPS, FedEx, UPS, and DHL—dot-coms and other companies would not really be threatened if one delivery firm tried to increase its prices; they could simply switch delivery companies.

It is illegal for distributors to collaborate or collude to keep prices high and thus maintain their power over buyers; however, this frequently happens. In the early 2000s, several European drug companies conspired to keep the price of vitamins artificially high. In 2005 the three largest global makers of flash memory, including Samsung, were also found guilty of price fixing (they collaborated to keep prices high). All these companies paid hundreds of millions of dollars in fines, and many of their top executives were sentenced to jail terms. Sometimes even government regulation can hurt customers because it confers monopoly power on distributors as the following "Ethics in Action" suggests.

Ethics in Action

Why Is Beer and Wine So Expensive: Powerful Distributors

One of the reasons Prohibition came into being in the United States was that many bars were owned by the brewers of alcoholic beverages and it was thought by many that this could lead to abuse. To keep the makers of alcoholic drinks such as beer and wine away from alcohol sellers most states adopted a three-tier distribution system that required manufacturers to sell to large distributors or wholesalers, and then wholesalers would sell to retailers—bars, liquor stores, and increasingly to supermarkets and chain stores over time. It is estimated that the result of this three-tier distribution system results in wholesalers adding a markup of about 25%, which means customers are paying 25% more than they need to pay and wholesalers are making huge profits.

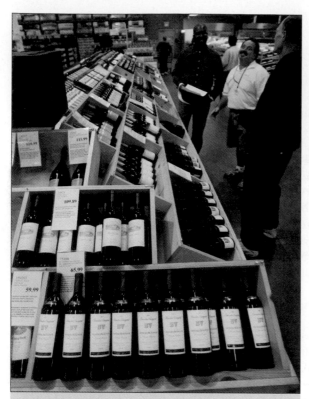

Costco's recent lawsuit means that lawmakers in the United States will be rethinking the regulation of alcohol sales in order to recoup the greatest profit for the states and to avoid wholesalers gobbling it up.

In 2006, Costco, the large warehouse store chain, won an antitrust lawsuit challenging its home state's three-tier system. As its CEO James Sinegal said of alcohol wholesalers, "I would like to have a business where everybody had to buy from me," and he estimated Costco could sell beer and wine for at least 10–20% less if retailers like Costco or Wal-Mart or Kroger's could buy directly from the makers of alcoholic products. Their great buying power would allow them to demand large price discounts from sellers, just as has happened for other products such as soap and detergent.

The state of Washington sued, however, arguing that the 21st Amendment ending prohibition gave states the authority to control alcohol regulation, including distribution. The state was supported by 30 other states for one important reason—sales of alcohol generate billions of dollars in state revenues and it is much easier for states to collect that money when wholesalers are used to distribute it. In 2008 the U.S. Ninth Circuit Court of Appeals ruled largely in favor of Washington state, agreeing it had the right to decide if the three-tier system was appropriate. However, it also agreed with Costco that an important distribution rule, called a post-and-hold requirement, that requires every beer or wine distributor to file with the Liquor Control Board its wholesale prices and then maintain those prices for at least 30 days, was illegal and anticompetitive because it gives large wholesalers the information they need to keep prices high.[15]

Despite the fact that Costco lost the case (and it may still appeal) the lawsuit showed how much profit is going to wholesalers, and so it has led many lawmakers to think about how to change the whole distribution system so that each state—and not the wholesalers—receives the high profits or taxes that the sale of alcohol brings. Thus, while consumers might gain some relief if prices were lowered, each state would receive billions of dollars more in revenue, and moreover, could decide how high to set the sales taxes on alcohol to discourage its use. In Sweden, for example, taxes on alcohol are often on the order of 300–400%, so that the cheapest bottle of liquor costs over $100 since that country wishes to reduce the amount of alcohol its citizens consume.

Customers

customers Individuals and groups that buy the goods and services that an organization produces.

Customers are the individuals and groups that buy the goods and services that an organization produces. For example, Dell's customers can be segmented into several distinct groups: (1) individuals who purchase PCs for home use, (2) small companies, (3) large companies, (4) government agencies, and (5) educational institutions. Changes in the number and types of customers or in customers' tastes and needs result in opportunities and threats. An organization's success depends on its response to customers.[16] In the PC industry, customers are demanding lower prices and increased multimedia capability, and PC companies must respond to the changing types and needs of customers. A school, too, must adapt to the changing needs of its customers. For example, if more Spanish-speaking students enroll, additional classes in English as a second language may need to be scheduled. A manager's ability to identify an organization's main customers and produce the goods and services they want is a crucial factor affecting organizational and managerial success.

The most obvious opportunity associated with expanding into the global environment is the prospect of selling goods and services to new customers, as Amazon.com's CEO Jeff Bezos discovered when he began to start operating in many countries abroad. Similarly, Accenture and Cap Gemini, two large consulting companies, have established operations throughout the world and recruit and train thousands of overseas consultants to serve the needs of customers in a wide variety of countries.

Today, many products are becoming global products and have gained wide acceptance from customers in countries around the globe. This consolidation is occurring both for consumer goods and for business products and has created enormous opportunities for managers. The global acceptance of Coca-Cola, Apple iPods, McDonald's hamburgers, Doc Martin boots, and Nokia cell phones is a sign that the tastes and preferences of consumers in different countries may not be so different after all.[17] Likewise, large global markets currently exist for business products such as telecommunications equipment, electronic components, computer services, and financial services. Thus, Motorola sells its telecommunications equipment, Intel its microprocessors, and SAP its business systems management software to customers throughout the world.

Competitors

competitors Organizations that produce goods and services that are similar to a particular organization's goods and services.

One of the most important forces that an organization confronts in its task environment is competitors. **Competitors** are organizations that produce goods and services similar to a particular organization's goods and services. In other words, competitors are organizations vying for the same customers. Dell's competitors include other domestic manufacturers of PCs (such as Apple, HP, and Gateway) as well as overseas competitors (such as Sony and Toshiba in Japan and Lenovo, the Chinese company that bought IBM's PC division in 2005). Dot-com stockbroker E*Trade has other dot-com competitors, like Ameritrade and Scottrade, as well as bricks-and-clicks competitors, such as Merrill Lynch and Charles Schwab.

Rivalry between competitors is potentially the most threatening force that managers must deal with. A high level of rivalry often results in price competition, and falling prices reduce access to resources and lower profits. In the 2000s, competition in the PC industry became intense not only because of an economic slowdown but also because Dell was aggressively cutting costs and prices to increase its global market share.[18] IBM exited the PC business because it was losing millions in its battle against low-cost rivals, and Gateway and HP also suffered, while Dell's profits soared. By 2006, however, HP's fortunes had recovered as it lowered its costs and offered new PCs with AMD's popular chips, while Dell's profit margins had shrunk.

Dell grew quickly to become the biggest global maker of PCs by 2000 as it took advantage of low-cost PC components made abroad and outsourced its PC manufacturing to companies in many Asian countries. In the 2000s, however, it began to experience intense competition from HP, the second-largest PC maker, whose managers were striving to develop a low-cost global network of suppliers and distributors that would allow it to match Dell's low costs. At the same time, PC makers based in Asia, such as Acer, also worked to create a global network that would allow it to sell PCs for prices similar to Dell's, and after Acer bought struggling Gateway Computer in 2006, it became the third-largest PC maker.

Dell's managers, used to being the industry leader, failed to appreciate how fast its global competitors were catching up; they were shocked in 2006 when HPs new low-cost skills allowed it to overtake Dell to became the biggest global PC maker in 2006, although Dell still retained its lead in the United States. Realizing the growing threat to his company, Michael Dell once again became CEO and with his top managers he began to develop a new global plan to increase Dell's global sales.

The two fastest-growing markets in Asia are China and India and, to regain its position as global leader, Dell had to expand sales in these countries. Since India imposes high tariffs on imported PCs Dell rushed to open new manufacturing facilities inside the country, where sales in both the consumer and business segments of the PC market are expected to increase 30% each year. It opened a major facility in Chennai, in Southern India, to produce low-price machines tailored for the local market; it expects sales of $500 million from this venture in 2007. However, HP has also been working to expand its presence in India, and opened a second plant in 2007 to help it to expand its market share, which is already 20% making it the second-largest PC maker in India.

In China, Dell is competing with domestic market leader Lenovo Group, the Chinese PC maker that bought IBM's PC division and its popular ThinkPad. To compete with Lenovo, which has costs as low as Dell, it has focused on expanding its manufacturing facilities in China to produce PCs customized to the Chinese market. The Dell brand name is popular in China and in the attempt to reach more Chinese customers and rapidly increase sales of its PCs in 2007 Dell decided to sell its PCs through Gome, China's largest retail electronics chain. This new strategy worked, and in 2008 Dell doubled to 900 the number of Gome stores that sell its PCs. In 2008, it also decided to sell desktop and notebook computers at Suning, China's second-largest electronics chain; it also plans to increase spending for online marketing and in-store promotions at Gome and Suning to attract the over one billion potential Chinese customers.

With these moves, and its decision to branch out from its phone and Internet sales strategy and to retail its PCs directly through stores such as Wal-Mart and Best Buy in the United States will put its PCs in more than 12,000 stores worldwide. By 2008 its new global strategy seemed to be working; its attempts to regain the lead in worldwide PC shipments seemed to be paying off as sales in the Asia-Pacific and Japan region rose 28%.[19] But HP, Lenovo, Acer, and all its other global competitors have not been idle. Indeed, HP, which has always retailed its PCs, claims they are available in 81,000 stores around the world, so Dell has much more to do to catch up. The race is on not just to provide low price PCs to consumers in poorer nations, but to develop new, smaller, sleeker machines, and PCs with state-of-the-art graphics and processing speed for gaming, as well as luxury PCs aimed at capturing market share from Apple, whose high-priced Macs are also attracting increasing numbers of well-heeled customers around the globe.

Because fierce competition drives down prices and profits, unethical companies often try to find ways to collude with competitors to keep prices high. Boeing adopted a different, very unsavory, method to gain market share and beat its rivals. In 2006 Boeing agreed to pay $615 million in fines to end a three-year Justice Department investigation into contracting scandals involving Boeing, thereby avoiding criminal charges or admission of wrongdoing. Boeing had been under investigation for improperly acquiring proprietary competitive information about Lockheed Martin's bidding intentions for government rocket-launching contracts. Once it knew how much Lockheed was willing to bid, it could then simply undercut its price by a few million to win the billion dollar auction! The government stripped Boeing of $1 billion worth of the contracts it had won through its improper use of the Lockheed documents. Additionally, Boeing illegally recruited senior U.S. Air Force procurement officer Darleen Druyun while she still had authority over billions of dollars in other Boeing contracts. Druyun served nine months in prison for violating federal conflict-of-interest laws. Michael Sears, formerly chief financial officer at Boeing, was fired in 2003 and spent four months in federal prison for illegally recruiting her. The scandals also led to the resignation of Boeing Chairman Phil Condit. Clearly, Boeing went to "enormous" lengths to beat its rivals, and supposedly it had a strong code of ethics that should have prevented such illegal actions!

potential competitors
Organizations that presently are not in a task environment but could enter if they so choose.

Although extensive rivalry between existing competitors is a major threat to profitability, so is the potential for new competitors to enter the task environment. **Potential competitors** are organizations that are not presently in a task environment but could enter if they so choose. Amazon.com, for example, is not currently in the retail furniture or appliance business, but it could enter these businesses if its managers decided it could profitably sell such products online. When new competitors enter an industry, competition increases and prices and profits decrease.

Figure 6.2
Barriers to Entry and Competition

BARRIERS TO ENTRY   In general, the potential for new competitors to enter a task environment (and thus increase competition) is a function of barriers to entry.[20] **Barriers to entry** are factors that make it difficult and costly for a company to enter a particular task environment or industry.[21] In other words, the more difficult and costly it is to enter the task environment, the higher are the barriers to entry. The higher the barriers to entry, the fewer the competitors in an organization's task environment and thus the lower the threat of competition. With fewer competitors, it is easier to obtain customers and keep prices high.

Barriers to entry result from three main sources: Economies of scale, brand loyalty, and government regulations that impede entry (see Figure 6.2). **Economies of scale** are the cost advantages associated with large operations. Economies of scale result from factors such as manufacturing products in very large quantities, buying inputs in bulk, or making more effective use of organizational resources than do competitors by fully utilizing employees' skills and knowledge. If organizations already in the task environment are large and enjoy significant economies of scale, then their costs are lower than the costs that potential entrants will be, and newcomers will find it very expensive to enter the industry. Amazon.com, for example, enjoys significant economies of scale relative to most other dot-com companies.[22]

Brand loyalty is customers' preference for the products of organizations currently existing in the task environment. If established organizations enjoy significant brand loyalty, then a new entrant will find it extremely difficult and costly to obtain a share of the market. Newcomers must bear huge advertising costs to build customer awareness of the goods or services they intend to provide.[23] Both Amazon.com and Yahoo, for example, two of the first dot-coms to go online, enjoy a high level of brand loyalty and have some of the highest Web site hit rates of all dot-coms (the latter also allows them to increase their advertising revenues).

In some cases, *government regulations* function as a barrier to entry at both the industry and the country levels. Many industries that were deregulated, such as air transport, trucking, utilities, and telecommunications, experienced a high level of new entry after deregulation; this forced existing companies in those industries to operate more efficiently or risk being put out of business.

At the national and global level, administrative barriers are government policies that create a barrier to entry and limit imports of goods by overseas companies. Japan is well known for the many ways in which it attempts to restrict the entry of overseas competitors or lessen their impact on Japanese firms. For example, why do Dutch companies export tulip bulbs to almost every country in the world except Japan? Japanese customs inspectors insist on checking every tulip bulb by cutting the stems vertically down the middle, and even Japanese ingenuity cannot put them back together.[24] Japan has come under intense pressure to relax and abolish such regulations, as the following "Managing Globally" suggests.

barriers to entry Factors that make it difficult and costly for an organization to enter a particular task environment or industry.

economies of scale Cost advantages associated with large operations.

brand loyalty Customers' preference for the products of organizations currently existing in the task environment.

American Rice Invades Japan

The Japanese rice market, similar to many other Japanese markets, was closed to overseas competitors until 1993 to protect Japan's thousands of high-cost, low-output rice farmers. Rice cultivation is expensive in Japan because of the country's mountainous terrain, so Japanese consumers have always paid high prices for rice. Under overseas pressure, the Japanese government opened the market, and overseas competitors are now allowed to export to Japan 8% of its annual rice consumption. Despite the still-present hefty overseas tariff on rice–$2.33 per 2.2 pounds–U.S. rice sells for $14 dollars per pound bag, while Japanese rice sells for about $19. With the recession affecting Japan, price-conscious consumers are turning to overseas rice, which has hurt domestic farmers.

In the 2000s, however, an alliance between organic rice grower Lundberg Family Farms of California and the Nippon Restaurant Enterprise Co. found a new way to break into the Japanese rice market. Because there is no tariff on rice used in processed foods, Nippon takes the U.S. organic rice and converts it into "O-bento," an organic hot boxed lunch packed with rice, vegetables, chicken, beef, and salmon, all imported from the United States. The new lunches, which cost about $4 compared to a Japanese rice bento that costs about $9, are sold at railway stations and other outlets throughout Japan.[25] They are proving to be very popular and are creating a storm of protest from Japanese rice farmers, who already have been forced to leave 37% of their rice fields idle and grow less profitable crops because of the entry of U.S. rice growers. Japanese and overseas companies are increasingly forming alliances to find new ways to break into the high-price Japanese market, and, little by little, Japan's restrictive trade practices are being whittled away.

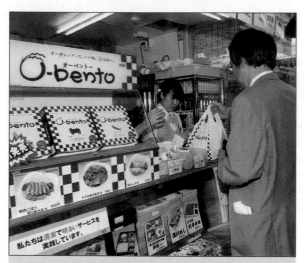

The tyranny of the lower price. A Japanese businessman purchases a pre-frozen, U.S.-sourced rice O-bento lunch at a Nippon Tokyo restaurant. Nippon's importing practices have angered Japanese rice farmers.

In summary, intense rivalry among competitors creates a task environment that is highly threatening and causes difficulty for managers trying to gain access to the resources an organization needs. Conversely, low rivalry results in a task environment where competitive pressures are more moderate and managers have greater opportunities to acquire the resources they need for their organizations to be effective.

The General Environment

Economic, technological, sociocultural, demographic, political, and legal forces in the general environment can have profound effects on forces in the task environment, effects that may not be evident to managers. For example, the sudden, dramatic upheavals in the Internet and dot-com industry environment in the early 2000s were brought about by a combination of changing Internet and digital technology, the softening U.S. stock market and economy, and increasing fears about global recession. These changes triggered intense competition between dot-com companies that further worsened the industry situation.

The implication is clear: Managers must constantly analyze forces in the general environment because these forces affect ongoing decision making and planning. Next, we discuss the major forces in the general environment, and examine their impact on an organization's task environment.

Economic Forces

economic forces Interest rates, inflation, unemployment, economic growth, and other factors that affect the general health and well-being of a nation or the regional economy of an organization.

Economic forces affect the general health and well-being of a country or world region. They include interest rates, inflation, unemployment, and economic growth. Economic forces produce many opportunities and threats for managers. Low levels of unemployment and falling interest rates give more people more money to spend, and as a result organizations have an opportunity to sell more goods and services. Good economic times affect supplies: Resources become easier to acquire, and organizations have an opportunity to flourish, as high-tech companies did throughout the 1990s. The high-techs made record profits as the economy boomed in large part because of advances in information technology and growing global trade.

In contrast, worsening macroeconomic conditions, as in the 2000s, pose a major threat because they limit managers' ability to gain access to the resources their organizations need. Profit-seeking organizations such as retail stores and hotels have fewer customers for their goods and services during economic downturns. Nonprofits such as charities and colleges receive fewer donations during economic downturns. Even a moderate deterioration in national or regional economic conditions can seriously reduce performance. A relatively mild recession was a major factor in the staggering collapse of dot-com companies in the early 2000s.

Poor economic conditions make the environment more complex and managers' jobs more difficult and demanding. Managers may need to reduce the number of individuals in their departments and increase the motivation of remaining employees, and managers and workers alike may need to identify ways to acquire and utilize resources more efficiently. Successful managers realize the important effects that economic forces have on their organizations, and they pay close attention to what is occurring in the national and regional economies to respond appropriately.

Technological Forces

technology The combination of skills and equipment that managers use in the design, production, and distribution of goods and services.

technological forces Outcomes of changes in the technology that managers use to design, produce, or distribute goods and services.

Technology is the combination of tools, machines, computers, skills, information, and knowledge that managers use in the design, production, and distribution of goods and services. **Technological forces** are outcomes of changes in the technology that managers use to design, produce, or distribute goods and services. The overall pace of technological change has accelerated greatly in the last decade because of advances in microprocessors and computer hardware and software, and technological forces have increased in magnitude.[26]

Technological forces can have profound implications for managers and organizations. Technological change can make established products obsolete—for example, typewriters, black-and-white televisions, bound sets of encyclopedias—forcing managers to find new ways to satisfy customer needs. Although technological change can threaten an organization, it also can create a host of new opportunities for designing, making, or distributing new and better kinds of goods and services. More powerful microprocessors developed by Intel caused a revolution in IT that spurred demand for PCs, contributed to the success of companies such as Dell and HP, but led to the decline of mainframe computer makers such as IBM.[27] However, IBM responded in the last decade by changing its emphasis from providing computer hardware to providing advanced computer services and consulting, and it has regained its strong global position. Managers must move quickly to respond to such changes if their organizations are to survive and prosper. Today Intel is being pressured by chip maker AMD, which was first to develop a powerful 64-bit PC chip, the Athlon, and has moved quickly to develop its own 64-bit chips.[28]

Changes in IT are altering the very nature of work itself within organizations, including that of the manager's job. Telecommuting along the information superhighway, videoconferencing, and text messaging are now everyday activities that provide opportunities for managers to supervise and coordinate geographically dispersed employees. Salespeople in many companies work from home offices and commute electronically to work. They communicate with other employees through company-wide electronic mail networks and use video cameras attached to PCs for "face-to-face" meetings with coworkers who may be across the country.

Sociocultural Forces

sociocultural forces Pressures emanating from the social structure of a country or society or from the national culture.

Sociocultural forces are pressures emanating from the social structure of a country or society or from the national culture, pressures that were discussed at length in the previous chapter. Pressures from both sources can either constrain or facilitate the way organizations operate and managers behave. **Social structure** is the arrangement of relationships between individuals and groups in a society. Societies differ substantially in social structure. In societies that have a high degree of social stratification, there are many distinctions among individuals and groups. Caste systems in India and Tibet and the recognition of numerous social classes in Great Britain and France produce a multilayered social structure in each of those countries. In contrast, social stratification is lower in relatively egalitarian New Zealand and in the United States, where the social structure reveals few distinctions among people. Most top managers in France come from the upper classes of French society, but top managers in the United States come from all strata of American society.

social structure The arrangement of relationships between individuals and groups in a society.

Societies also differ in the extent to which they emphasize the individual over the group. For example, the United States emphasizes the primacy of the individual, and Japan emphasizes the primacy of the group. This difference may dictate the methods managers need to use to motivate and lead employees. **National culture** is the set of values that a society considers important and the norms of behavior that are approved or sanctioned in that society. Societies differ substantially in the values and norms that they emphasize. For example, in the United States individualism is highly valued, and in Korea and Japan individuals are expected to conform to group expectations.[29] National culture, discussed at length later in this chapter, also affects the way managers motivate and coordinate employees and the way organizations do business. Ethics, an important aspect of national culture, was discussed in detail in Chapter 4.

national culture The set of values that a society considers important and the norms of behavior that are approved or sanctioned in that society.

Social structure and national culture not only differ across societies but also change within societies over time. In the United States, attitudes toward the roles of women, love, sex, and marriage changed in each past decade. Many people in Asian countries such as Hong Kong, Singapore, Korea, and Japan think that the younger generation is far more individualistic and "American-like" than previous generations. Currently, throughout much of eastern Europe, new values that emphasize individualism and entrepreneurship are replacing communist values based on collectivism and obedience to the state. The pace of change is accelerating.

Individual managers and organizations must be responsive to changes in, and differences among, the social structures and national cultures of all the countries in which they operate. In today's increasingly integrated global economy, managers are likely to interact with people from several countries, and many managers live and work abroad. Effective managers are sensitive to differences between societies and adjust their behaviors accordingly.

Managers and organizations also must respond to social changes within a society. In the last few decades, for example, Americans have become increasingly interested in their personal health and fitness. Managers who recognized this trend early and exploited the opportunities that resulted

Olive oil gets a boost for today's health trends. Notice the bottle boasting Omega-3 content—and the higher price as a result!

from it were able to reap significant gains for their organizations. PepsiCo used the opportunity presented by the fitness trend and took market share from archrival Coca-Cola by being the first to introduce diet colas and fruit-based soft drinks. Quaker Oats made Gatorade the most popular sports drink and brought out a whole host of low-fat food products. The health trend, however, did not offer opportunities to all companies; to some it posed a threat. Tobacco companies came under intense pressure due to consumers' greater awareness of negative health impacts from smoking. Hershey Foods and other manufacturers of candy bars have been threatened by customers' desires for low-fat, healthy foods. The rage for "low-carb" foods in the 2000s led to a huge increase in demand for meat and hurt bread and doughnut companies such as Kraft and Krispy Kreme.

Demographic Forces

demographic forces
Outcomes of changes in, or changing attitudes toward, the characteristics of a population, such as age, gender, ethnic origin, race, sexual orientation, and social class.

Demographic forces are outcomes of changes in, or changing attitudes toward, the characteristics of a population, such as age, gender, ethnic origin, race, sexual orientation, and social class. Like the other forces in the general environment, demographic forces present managers with opportunities and threats and can have major implications for organizations. We examined the nature of these challenges in depth in our discussion of diversity in Chapter 5, so we will not discuss these forces again here.

We will just note one important change occurring today: Most industrialized nations are experiencing the aging of their populations as a consequence of falling birth and death rates and the aging of the baby-boom generation. In Germany, for example, the percentage of the population over age 65 is expected to rise to 20.7% by 2010 from 15.4% in 1990. Comparable figures for Canada are 14.4% and 11.4%; for Japan, 19.5% and 11.7%; and for the United States, 13.5% and 12.6%.[30] In the United States the percentage increase is far smaller because of the huge wave of immigration during the 1990s and the large families that new immigrants typically have. However, the absolute number of older people has increased substantially and is increasing opportunities for organizations that cater to older people; the home health care and recreation industries, for example, are seeing an upswing in demand for their services.

The aging of the population also has several implications for the workplace. Most significant are a relative decline in the young people joining the workforce and an increase in the number of active employees willing to postpone retirement past the traditional retirement age of 65. These changes suggest that organizations need to find ways to motivate and utilize the skills and knowledge of older employees, an issue that many Western societies have yet to tackle.

Political and Legal Forces

political and legal forces
Outcomes of changes in laws and regulations, such as the deregulation of industries, the privatization of organizations, and the increased emphasis on environmental protection.

Political and legal forces are outcomes of changes in laws and regulations. They result from political and legal developments that take place within a nation, within a world region, or across the world and significantly affect managers and organizations everywhere. Political processes shape a nation's laws and the international laws that govern the relationships between nations. Laws constrain the operations of organizations and managers, and thus create both opportunities and threats.[31] For example, throughout much of the industrialized world there has been a strong trend toward deregulation of industries previously controlled by the state and privatization of organizations once owned by the state.

In the United States, deregulation of the airline industry in 1978 ushered into the task environment of commercial airlines major changes that are still working themselves out. Deregulation allowed 29 new airlines to enter the industry between 1978 and 1993. The increase in airline-passenger carrying capacity after deregulation led to excess capacity on many routes, intense competition, and fare wars. To respond to this more competitive task environment, in the 1980s airlines looked for ways to reduce operating costs. The development of hub-and-spoke systems, the rise of non-union airlines, and the introduction of no-frills discount service are all responses to increased competition in the airlines' task environment. By the 1990s, once again in control of their environments, airlines were making record profits. However, soaring oil prices in the 2000s wiped out these profits, and airlines found themselves once again under pressure. In April 2008, for example, United Airlines and Delta reported losses that amounted to $10.6 billion due to high fuel costs; they also announced that they wanted to merge to help reduce costs and protect their future. While this proposal was being reviewed by the SEC's antitrust agency, American and Continental airlines also announced they were negotiating a merger. Clearly, the shape of the airline industry is changing because of economic and political forces.

Another important political and legal force affecting managers and organizations is the political integration of countries that has been taking place during the past decades.[32] Increasingly, nations are joining together into political unions that allow for the free exchange of resources and capital. The growth of the European Union (EU) is one example: Common laws govern trade and commerce between EU member countries, and the European Court has the right to examine the business of global organizations and to approve any proposed mergers between overseas companies that operate inside the EU. For example, Microsoft's anticompetitive business practices have come under scrutiny, and the court refused to approve a proposed merger between GE and Honeywell that had been approved by U.S. regulators. The North American Free Trade Agreement (NAFTA), discussed later in the chapter, has more modest political goals, but as with the EU, it has changed the laws that affect international commerce by lowering the barriers to the free flow of goods and services between member nations.[33]

Indeed, international agreements to abolish laws and regulations that restrict and reduce trade between countries have been having profound effects on global organizations. The fall in legal trade barriers creates enormous opportunities for companies in one country to sell goods and services in other countries. But, by allowing nondomestic companies to compete in a nation's domestic market for customers, falling trade barriers also pose a serious threat because they increase competition in the task environment. Between 1973 and 2006, for example, Japanese competitors increased their share of the U.S. car market from 3% to 30%.[34] This growth would not have been possible without relatively low trade barriers, which allowed producers in Japan to export cars to the United States. However, competition from Toyota, Honda, and other Japanese companies has forced U.S. car companies to improve their operations. Finding new ways to design and make cars is an ongoing process as they fight to protect their market share, which was continuing to fall in 2006–Japanese carmakers' market share had grown to over 33%. In essence, the removal of legal restrictions to global trade has the same effect as deregulating industries and removing restrictions against competition: It increases the intensity of competition in the task environment and forces conservative, slow-moving companies to become more efficient, improve product quality, and learn new values and norms to compete in the global environment.

Deregulation, privatization, and the removal of legal barriers to trade are just a few of the many ways in which changing political and legal forces can challenge organizations and managers. Others include increased emphasis on environmental protection and the preservation of endangered species, increased emphasis on safety in the workplace, and legal constraints against discrimination on the basis of race, gender, or age. Managers face major challenges when they seek to take advantage of the opportunities created by changing political, legal, and economic forces.

The Changing Global Environment

In the 21st century, any idea that the world is composed of a set of distinct national countries and markets that are separated physically, economically, and culturally from one another has vanished. Managers now recognize that companies exist and compete in a truly global market. Today, managers regard the global environment as a source of important opportunities and threats that they

Figure 6.3
The Global Environment

must respond to. Managers constantly confront the challenges of global competition—establishing operations in a country abroad or obtaining inputs from suppliers abroad—or the challenges of managing in a different national culture.[35] (See Figure 6.3.)

In essence, as a result of falling trade barriers, managers view the global environment as open, that is, as an environment in which companies are free to buy goods and services from, and sell goods and services to, whichever companies and countries they choose. They also are free to compete against each other to attract customers around the world. They must establish an international network of operations and subsidiaries to build global competitive advantage. Coca-Cola and PepsiCo, for example, have competed aggressively for 20 years to develop the strongest global soft-drink empire, just as Toyota and Honda have built hundreds of car plants around the world to provide the vehicles that global customers like. This is also becoming increasingly true in the food processing industry as the following "Managing Globally" suggests.

LO4 Explain why the global environment is becoming more open and competitive and identify the forces behind the process of globalization that increase the opportunities, complexities, challenges, and threats that managers face.

Managing Globally

Customizing Food to the Tastes of Different Cultures

India is a good example of the challenges faced by global food makers, such as Kellogg's and Nestlé, in seeking to expand their global operations and revenues. India's processed food market is worth $90 billion a year and growing. And, to compete with domestic food processors, large global food makers have to go to great lengths to make sure their products meet the cultural preferences of Indian consumers. In particular, they have to invest heavily in building food-making

Kellogg's in India has learned to offer more than just the standard cornflakes. In recent years, the company has appealed to customers by offering basmati rice and mango-flavored cereal.

plants in the nations in which they do business, often to avoid tariff problems, and they must learn how to customize products extensively to meet the needs of local customers.

When Kellogg's, for example, launched its breakfast cereals in India in the 1990s it failed to understand that most Indians eat cooked breakfasts because milk is normally not pasteurized. Now, with the growing availability of pasteurized or canned milk, it offers exotic cornflakes made from basmati rice and flavored with mango to appeal to customers. Similarly, Nestlé pushed its Milkmaid condensed milk as being ideal for traditional Indian sweets but with limited success since many local brands are available. Then it took its Maggi noodles brand and once it was given the ethnic "marsala" or mixed curry spice flavor this became a staple in school lunch boxes. It recently launched packaged yogurt.

Today Indian consumers, like those in many Asian nations, are more willing to pay higher prices for convenient packaged foods because of rising incomes and a growing middle class, estimated at some 50 million households. Clearly, given the billions of potential new customers in Asia, as well as in many other developing countries around the world, many challenges remain for global food makers.

In this section, we first explain how this open global environment is the result of globalization and the flow of capital around the world. Next, we examine how specific economic, political, and legal changes, such as the lowering of barriers to trade and investment, have increased globalization and led to greater interaction and exchanges between organizations and countries. Then we discuss how declining barriers of distance and culture have also increased the pace of globalization, and we consider the specific implications of these changes for managers and organizations. Finally, we note that nations still differ widely from each other because they have distinct cultural values and norms and that managers must appreciate these differences if they are to compete successfully across countries.

The Process of Globalization

globalization The set of specific and general forces that work together to integrate and connect economic, political, and social systems *across* countries, cultures, or geographical regions so that nations become increasingly interdependent and similar.

Perhaps the most important reason why the global environment has become more open and competitive is the increase in globalization. **Globalization** is the set of specific and general forces that work together to integrate and connect economic, political, and social systems *across* countries, cultures, or geographic regions. The result of globalization is that nations and peoples become increasingly *interdependent* because the same forces affect them in similar ways. The fates of peoples in different countries become interlinked as the world's markets and businesses become increasingly interconnected. And, as nations become more interdependent, they become more similar to one another in the sense that people develop a similar liking for products as diverse as cell phones, iPods, blue jeans, coke, Manchester United, curry, green tea, Japanese cars, and Columbian coffee. One outcome of globalization is that the world is becoming a "global village": Products, services, or people can become well known throughout the world—something IKEA, with its range of furniture designed to appeal to customers around the world, is taking advantage of, as the following "Managing Globally" describes.

IKEA Is on Top of the Furniture World

IKEA is the largest furniture chain in the world, and in 2008 the Swedish company operated over 231 stores in 24 countries. In 2007 IKEA sales had soared to over $30 billion, or over 20% of the global furniture market, but to its managers and employees this is just the tip of the iceberg. They believe IKEA is poised for massive growth throughout the world in the coming decade because it can provide what the average customer wants: well-designed and well-made contemporary furniture at an affordable price. IKEA's ability to provide customers with affordable furniture is very much the result of its approach to globalization, to the way it treats its global employees and operates its global store empire. In a nutshell, IKEA's global approach revolves around simplicity, attention to detail, cost-consciousness, and responsiveness in every aspect of its operations and behavior.

IKEA's global approach derives from the personal values and beliefs of its founder, Ingvar Kamprad, about how companies should treat their employees and customers. Kamprad, who is in his early 80s, was born in Smaland, a poor Swedish province whose citizens are well known for being entrepreneurial, frugal, and hardworking. Kamprad definitely absorbed these values, for when he entered the furniture business, he made them the core of his management approach. He teaches store managers and employees his values; his beliefs about the need to operate in a no-frills, cost-conscious way; and his view that they are all in business "together," by which he means that every person who works in his global empire plays an essential role and has an obligation to everyone else.

What does Kamprad's approach mean in practice? It means that all IKEA's members fly coach class on business trips, stay in inexpensive hotels, and keep traveling expenses to a minimum. It also means that IKEA stores operate on the simplest set of rules and procedures possible and that employees are expected to cooperate to solve problems and get the job done. Many famous stories exist about the frugal Kamprad, such as that even he always flies coach class and that when he takes a coke can from the mini-bar in a hotel room, he replaces it with one bought in a store—despite the fact that he is a multibillionaire ranked in the top 20 on the *Forbes* list of the world's richest people!

IKEA's employees see what his global approach means as soon as they are recruited to work in a store in one of the many countries in which the company operates. They start learning about IKEA's global corporate culture by performing jobs at the bottom of the ladder, and they are quickly trained to perform all the various jobs involved in store operations. During this process they internalize IKEA's global values and norms, which center on the importance the company attaches to their taking the initiative and responsibility for solving problems and for focusing on the customer. Employees are rotated between departments and sometimes stores, and rapid promotion is possible for those who demonstrate the enthusiasm and togetherness that signifies they have bought into IKEA's global culture.

Most of IKEA's top managers rose from its ranks, and the company holds "breaking the bureaucracy weeks" in which they are required to work in stores and warehouses for a week each year to make sure they and all employees stay committed to IKEA's global values. No matter which country they operate in, all employees wear informal clothes to work at IKEA—Kamprad has always worn an open-neck shirt—and there are no marks of status such as executive dining rooms or private parking places. Employees believe that if they buy into IKEA's work values, behave in ways that keep its growing global operations streamlined and efficient, and focus on being one step ahead of potential problems, they will share in its success. Promotion, training, above-average pay, a generous store bonus system, and the personal well-being that comes from working in a company where people feel valued are some of the rewards that Kamprad pioneered to build and strengthen IKEA's global approach.

Whenever IKEA enters a new country, it sends its most experienced store managers to establish its global approach in its new stores. When IKEA first entered the United States, the attitude of U.S. employees puzzled its managers. Despite their obvious drive to succeed and good education, employees seemed reluctant to take the initiative and assume responsibility. IKEA's managers discovered that their U.S. employees were afraid mistakes would result in the loss of their jobs, so the managers strove to teach employees the "IKEA way." The approach paid off: The United States has become the company's second-best country market, and IKEA plans to open many more U.S. stores, as well as stores around the world, over the next decade.

But what drives or spurs globalization? What makes people and companies like Nestlé, Toyota, or Microsoft want to venture into an uncertain global environment that puts into motion the complex set of forces that result in globalization? The answer is that the path of globalization is shaped by the ebb and flow of *capital,* that is, valuable wealth-generating assets, as it moves through companies, countries, and world regions seeking its most highly valued use, that is, the investment through which capital can earn the greatest returns (wealth). Managers, employees, and companies like IKEA and Nestlé are motivated to try to profit or benefit by using their skills to make products customers around the world want to buy. The four principal forms of capital that flow between countries are:

- *Human capital:* the flow of people around the world through immigration, migration, and emigration.

- *Financial capital:* the flow of money capital across world markets through overseas investment, credit, lending, and aid.

- *Resource capital:* the flow of natural resources and semifinished products between companies and countries such as metals, minerals, lumber, energy, food products, microprocessors, and auto parts.

- *Political capital:* the flow of power and influence around the world using diplomacy, persuasion, aggression, and force of arms to protect a country's or world region or political bloc's access to the other forms of capital.

Most of the changes associated with globalization are the result of these four capital flows and the interactions between them, as nations compete on the world stage to protect and increase their standards of living and to further the political goals and social causes that are espoused by their societies' cultures. The next sections look at the factors that have increased the rate at which capital flows between companies and countries. In a positive sense the faster the flow, the more capital is being utilized where it can create the most value, in the sense of people moving to where their skills earn them more money, or investors switching to the stocks or bonds that give them higher dividends or interest, or companies finding lower-cost sources of inputs. In a negative sense, however, a fast flow of capital also means that individual countries or world regions can find themselves in trouble when companies and investors move their capital to invest it in more productive ways in other countries or world regions, often those with lower labor costs or rapidly expanding markets. When capital leaves a country, the result is higher unemployment, recession, and a lower standard of living for its people.

Declining Barriers to Trade and Investment

One of the main factors that has speeded globalization by freeing the movement of capital has been the decline in barriers to trade and investment, discussed earlier. During the 1920s and 1930s, many countries erected formidable barriers to international trade and investment in the belief that this was the best way to promote their economic well-being. Many of these barriers were high tariffs on imports of manufactured goods. A **tariff** is a tax that a government imposes on imported or, occasionally, on exported goods. The aim of import tariffs is to protect domestic industries and jobs, such as those in the auto or steel industry, from overseas competition by raising the price of goods from abroad. In 2001, for example, the U.S. government increased the tariffs on the import of overseas steel to protect U.S. steelmakers; however, under pressure from the European Union, these tariffs were significantly reduced in 2003.

The reason for removing tariffs is that, very often, when one country imposes an import tariff, others follow suit and the result is a series of retaliatory moves as countries progressively raise tariff barriers against each other. In the 1920s this behavior depressed world demand and helped usher in the Great Depression of the 1930s and massive unemployment. It was to avoid tariffs on U.S. goods entering Europe that the steel tariffs were reduced. In short, rather than protecting jobs and promoting economic well-being, governments of countries that resort to raising high tariff barriers ultimately reduce employment and undermine economic growth.[36]

GATT AND THE RISE OF FREE TRADE   After World War II, advanced Western industrial countries, having learned from the Great Depression, committed themselves to the goal of removing barriers to the free flow of resources and capital between countries. This commitment was reinforced by acceptance of the principle that free trade, rather than tariff barriers, was the best way to foster a healthy domestic economy and low unemployment.[37]

The **free-trade doctrine** predicts that if each country agrees to specialize in the production of the goods and services that it can produce most efficiently, this will make the best use of global capital resources and will result in lower prices.[38] For example, if Indian companies are highly efficient in the production of textiles and U.S. companies are highly efficient in the production of computer software, then under a free-trade agreement capital would move to India and be invested there to produce textiles, while capital from around the world would flow to the United States and be invested in its innovative computer software companies. Consequently, prices of both textiles and software should fall because each good is being produced in the location where it can be made at the lowest cost, benefiting consumers and making the best use of scarce capital. This doctrine is, of course, responsible for the increase in global outsourcing and the loss of millions of U.S. jobs in textiles and manufacturing as capital is invested in factories in China and Malaysia. However, millions of jobs have also been created because of new capital investments in high-tech, IT, and the service sector that in theory should offset manufacturing job losses in the long run.

Historically, countries that accepted this free-trade doctrine set as their goal the removal of barriers to the free flow of goods, services, and capital between countries. They attempted to achieve this through an international treaty known as the General Agreement on Tariffs and Trade (GATT). In the half-century since World War II, there have been eight rounds of GATT negotiations aimed at lowering tariff barriers. The last round, the Uruguay Round, involved 117 countries and was completed in December 1993. This round succeeded in lowering tariffs by over 30% from the previous level. It also led to the dissolving of GATT and its replacement by the World Trade Organization (WTO), which today, in 2006, continues the struggle to reduce tariffs and has more power to sanction countries that break global agreements.[39] On average, the tariff barriers among the governments of developed countries declined from over 40% in 1948 to about 3% in 2000, causing a dramatic increase in world trade.[40]

tariff A tax that a government imposes on imported or, occasionally, exported goods.

free-trade doctrine The idea that if each country specializes in the production of the goods and services that it can produce most efficiently, this will make the best use of global resources.

Declining Barriers of Distance and Culture

Historically, barriers of distance and culture also closed the global environment and kept managers focused on their domestic market. The management problems Unilever, the huge British-based, global soap and detergent maker, experienced at the turn of the 20th century illustrate the effect of these barriers.

Founded in London during the 1880s by William Lever, a Quaker, Unilever had a worldwide reach by the early 1900s and operated subsidiaries in most major countries of the British Empire, including India, Canada, and Australia. Lever had a very hands-on, autocratic management style and found his far-flung business empire difficult to control. The reason for Lever's control problems was that communication over great distances was difficult. It took six weeks to reach India by ship from England, and international telephone and telegraph services were very unreliable.

Another problem that Unilever encountered was the difficulty of doing business in societies that were separated from Britain by barriers of language and culture. Different countries have different sets of national beliefs, values, and norms, and Lever found that a management approach that worked in Britain did not necessarily work in India or Persia (now Iran). As a result, management practices had to be tailored to suit each unique national culture. After Lever's death in 1925, top management at Unilever lowered or *decentralized* (see Chapter 10) decision-making authority to the managers of the various national subsidiaries so that they could develop a management approach that suited the country in which they were operating. One result of this strategy was that the subsidiaries grew distant and remote from one another—something that reduced Unilever's performance.[41]

Since the end of World War II, a continuing stream of advances in communications and transportation technology have worked to reduce the barriers of distance and culture that affected Unilever and all global organizations. Over the last 30 years, global communication has been revolutionized by developments in satellites, digital technology, the Internet and global computer networks, and video teleconferencing that allow for the transmission of vast amounts of information and make reliable, secure, and instantaneous communication possible between people and companies anywhere in the world.[42] This revolution has made it possible for a global organization—a tiny garment factory in Li & Fung's network or a huge company such as Nestlé or Unilever—to do business anywhere, anytime, and to search for customers and suppliers around the world.

One of the most important innovations in transportation technology that has made the global environment more open has been the growth of commercial jet travel, which reduced the time it takes to get from one location to another. Because of jet travel, New York is now closer to Tokyo than it was to Philadelphia in the days of the 13 colonies—a fact that makes control of far-flung international businesses much easier today than in William Lever's era. In addition to making travel faster, modern communications and transportation technologies have also helped reduce the cultural distance between countries. The Internet and its millions of Web sites facilitate the development of global communications networks and media that are helping to create a worldwide culture above and beyond unique national cultures. Moreover, television networks such as CNN, MTV, ESPN, BBC, and HBO can now be received in many countries, and Hollywood films are shown throughout the world.

Effects of Free Trade on Managers

The lowering of barriers to trade and investment and the decline of distance and culture barriers has created enormous opportunities for companies to expand the market for their goods and services through exports and investments in overseas countries. Although managers at some organizations, like Barnes & Noble, have shied away from trying to sell their goods and services overseas, the situation of Wal-Mart and Lands' End, which have developed profitable global operations, is more typical. The shift toward a more open global economy has created not only more opportunities to sell goods and services in markets abroad but also the opportunity to buy more from other countries. Indeed, the success in the United States of Lands' End has been based in part on its managers' willingness to import low-cost clothes and bedding from overseas manufacturers. Lands' End purchases clothing from manufacturers in Hong Kong, Malaysia, Taiwan, and China because U.S. textile makers often do not offer the same quality, styling, flexibility, or price.[43] Indeed, most clothing companies, such as Levi Strauss, Wal-Mart, and Target, are major players in the global environment by virtue of their purchasing activities, even if like Target or Dillard's they sell only in the United States.

The manager's job is more challenging in a dynamic global environment because of the increased intensity of competition that goes hand in hand with the lowering of barriers to trade and investment. Thus, as discussed above, the job of the average manager in a U.S. car company became a lot harder from the mid-1970s as a result of the penetration of the U.S. market by efficient Japanese competitors. Recall that Levi Strauss closed its last U.S. clothing factory in 2001 because it could not match the prices of low-cost overseas jeans manufacturers that compete with Levi's to sell to clothing chains such as Wal-Mart, Dillard's, and Target.

REGIONAL TRADE AGREEMENTS The growth of regional trade agreements such as the North American Free Trade Agreement (NAFTA), and most recently the Central American Free Trade Agreement (CAFTA), also presents opportunities and threats for managers and their organizations. Table 6.1 outlines some of the most

Table 6.1

Most Active Regional Global Free-Trade Associations

Regional Associations	Area (km^2)	Population	GDP ($US) in Millions	Per Capita	Member states
European Union (EU)	3,977,487	460,124,266	11,723,816	25,480	25
Caribbean Community and Common Market (CARICOM)	462,344	14,565,083	64,219	4,409	15
Economic Community of West African States (ECOWAS)	5,112,903	251,646,263	342,519	1,361	15
Economic and Monetary Community of Central Africa (CEMAC)	3,020,142	34,970,529	85,136	2,435	6
East African Community (EAC)	1,763,777	97,865,428	104,239	1,065	3
South American Community of Nations (CSN)	17,339,153	370,158,470	2,868,430	7,749	10
Cooperation Council of the Arab States of the Gulf (GCC)	2,285,844	35,869,438	536,223	14,949	6
Southern African Customs Union (SACU)	2,693,418	51,055,878	541,433	10,605	5
Common Market for Eastern and Southern Africa (COMESA)	3,779,427	118,950,321	141,962	1,193	5
North American Free Trade Agreement (NAFTA)	21,588,638	430,495,039	12,889,900	29,942	3
Association of Southeast Asian Nations (ASEAN)	4,400,000	553,900,000	2,172,000	4,044	10
South Asian Association for Regional Cooperation (SAARC)	5,136,740	1,467,255,669	4,074,031	2,777	8
Euro-Mediterranean Free Trade Area (Agadir)	1,703,910	126,066,286	513,674	4,075	4
Eurasian Economic Community (EurAsEC)	20,789,100	208,067,618	1,689,137	8,118	6
Central American Common Market (CACM)	422,614	37,816,598	159,536	4,219	5
Pacific Islands Forum (PARTA)	528,151	7,810,905	23,074	2,954	14

Source: *CIA World Factbook 2005*, IMF WEO database.

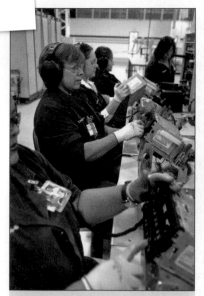

Mexican workers at CyOptics in Matamoros, Mexico, a high-tech manufacturing facility just across the U.S. border from Brownsville, Texas. CyOptics, a U.S-owned company, designs, develops, and markets a range of optical chips and components for communications systems. The more competitive environment brought about by NAFTA poses both opportunities and threats for managers.

active regional trade associations; they have been formed between countries in most continents or world regions.

In North America, NAFTA, which became effective on January 1, 1994, had the aim of abolishing the tariffs on 99% of the goods traded between Mexico, Canada, and the United States by 2004. Although it has not achieved this lofty goal, NAFTA has removed most barriers on the cross-border flow of resources, giving, for example, financial institutions and retail businesses in Canada and the United States unrestricted access to the Mexican marketplace. After NAFTA was signed, there was a flood of investment into Mexico from the United States, as well as many other countries such as Japan. Wal-Mart, Costco, Radio Shack, and other major U.S. retail chains have expanded their operations in Mexico; Wal-Mart, for example, is stocking many more products from Mexico in its U.S. stores, and its Mexican store chain is also expanding rapidly.

The establishment of free-trade areas creates an opportunity for manufacturing organizations because it allows them to reduce their costs. They can do this either by shifting production to the lowest-cost location within the free-trade area (for example, U.S. auto and textile companies shifting production to Mexico) or by serving the whole region from one location, rather than establishing separate operations in each country. Some managers, however, view regional free-trade agreements as a threat because they expose a company based in one member country to increased competition from companies based in the other member countries. NAFTA has had this effect; today Mexican managers find themselves facing the threat of head-to-head competition in some industries against efficient U.S. and Canadian companies. But the opposite is true as well: U.S. and Canadian managers are experiencing threats in labor-intensive industries, such as the flooring tile and textile industries, where Mexican businesses have a cost advantage.

In July 2005 the U.S. House of Representatives approved the formation of CAFTA, a regional trade agreement designed to eliminate tariffs on products between the United States and all countries in Central America. By 2006, the Dominican Republic, El Salvador, Guatemala, Nicaragua, and Honduras had also approved and implemented the agreement, but Costa Rica has not. CAFTA is seen as a stepping-stone toward establishing the Free Trade Area of the Americas (FTAA), an ambitious attempt to establish a free-trade agreement that would increase economic prosperity throughout the Americas. FTAA would include all South American and Caribbean nations, except Cuba, as well as those of North and Central America. However, the economic problems many countries have been experiencing, together with major political and ideological differences—such as the political resistance within the United States because of jobs lost to Mexico and Canada—have slowed down the process of integration and globalization. The more competitive environment NAFTA has brought about has increased both the opportunities that managers can take advantage of and the threats they must respond to in performing their jobs effectively.

The Role of National Culture

Despite evidence that countries are becoming more similar to one another because of globalization, and that the world is on the verge of becoming a global village, the cultures of different countries still vary widely because of critical differences in their values, norms, and attitudes. As noted earlier, national culture includes the values, norms, knowledge, beliefs, moral principles, laws, customs, and other practices that unite the citizens of a country.[44] National culture shapes individual behavior by specifying appropriate and inappropriate behavior and interaction with others. People learn national culture in their everyday lives by interacting with those around them. This learning starts at an early age and continues throughout their lives.

Cultural Values and Norms

values Ideas about what a society believes to be good, right, desirable, or beautiful.

The basic building blocks of national culture are values and norms. **Values** are ideas about what a society believes to be good, right, desirable, or beautiful. They provide the basic underpinnings for notions of individual freedom, democracy, truth, justice, honesty, loyalty, social obligation, collective responsibility, the appropriate roles for men and women, love, sex, marriage, and so on. Values are more than merely abstract concepts; they are invested with considerable emotional significance. People argue, fight, and even die over values such as freedom.

Although deeply embedded in society, values are not static; however, change in a country's values is likely to be slow and painful. For example, the value systems of many formerly communist states, such as Russia, are undergoing significant changes as those countries move away from a value system that emphasizes the state and toward one that emphasizes individual freedom. Social turmoil often results when countries undergo major changes in their values.

norms Unwritten, informal codes of conduct that prescribe how people should act in particular situations and are considered important by most members of a group or organization.

Norms are unwritten, informal codes of conduct that prescribe appropriate behavior in particular situations and are considered important by most members of a group or organization. They shape the behavior of people toward one another. Two types of norms play a major role in national culture: Folkways and mores. **Folkways** are the routine social conventions of everyday life. They concern customs and practices such as dressing appropriately for particular situations, good social manners, eating with the correct utensils, and neighborly behavior. Although folkways define the way people are expected to behave, violation of folkways is not a serious or moral matter. People who violate folkways are often thought to be eccentric or ill-mannered, but they are not usually considered to be evil or bad. In many countries, initially foreigners may be excused for violating folkways because they are unaccustomed to local behavior, but repeated violations are not excused because foreigners are expected to learn appropriate behavior.

folkways The routine social conventions of everyday life.

mores Norms that are considered to be central to the functioning of society and to social life.

Mores are norms that are considered to be central to the functioning of society and to social life. They have much greater significance than folkways. Accordingly, the violation of mores can be expected to bring serious retribution. Mores include proscriptions against theft, adultery, and incest. In many societies mores have been enacted into law. Thus, all advanced societies have laws against theft and incest. However, there are many differences in mores from one society to another.[45] In the United States, for example, drinking alcohol is widely accepted; but in Saudi Arabia, the consumption of alcohol is viewed as a violation of social norms and is punishable by imprisonment (as many U.S. citizens working in Saudi Arabia have discovered).

LO5 Discuss why national cultures differ and why it is important that managers be sensitive to the effects of falling trade barriers and regional trade associations on the political and social systems of nations around the world.

Hofstede's Model of National Culture

Researchers have spent considerable time and effort identifying similarities and differences in the values and norms of different countries. One model of national culture was developed by Geert Hofstede.[46] As a psychologist for IBM, Hofstede collected data on employee values and norms from more than 100,000 IBM employees in 64 countries. Based on his research, Hofstede developed five dimensions along which national cultures can be placed (see Figure 6.4).[47]

individualism A worldview that values individual freedom and self-expression and adherence to the principle that people should be judged by their individual achievements rather than by their social background.

INDIVIDUALISM VERSUS COLLECTIVISM   The first dimension, which Hofstede labeled "individualism versus collectivism," has a long history in human thought. **Individualism** is a worldview that values individual freedom and self-expression and adherence to the principle that people should be judged by their individual achievements rather than by their social background. In Western countries, individualism usually includes admiration for personal success, a strong belief in individual rights, and high regard for individual entrepreneurs.[48]

collectivism A worldview that values subordination of the individual to the goals of the group and adherence to the principle that people should be judged by their contribution to the group.

In contrast, **collectivism** is a worldview that values subordination of the individual to the goals of the group and adherence to the principle that people should be judged by their contribution to the group. Collectivism was widespread in communist

Figure 6.4
Hofstede's Model of National Culture

Source: Geert Hofstede, Bram Nevijen, Denise Daval Ohayv, and Geert Sanders, "Measuring Organizational Cultures: A Qualitative and Quantitative Study Across Twenty Cases," *Administrative Science Quarterly,* volume 35, Number 2 (June 1990), pp. 286–316. Approval of request for permission to reprint. © Johnson Graduate School of Management, Cornell University.

countries but has become less prevalent since the collapse of communism in most of those countries. Japan is a noncommunist country where collectivism is highly valued.

Collectivism in Japan traces its roots to the fusion of Confucian, Buddhist, and Shinto thought that occurred during the Tokugawa period in Japanese history (1600–1870s).[49] One of the central values that emerged during this period was strong attachment to the group—whether a village, a work group, or a company. Strong identification with the group is said to create pressures for collective action in Japan, as well as strong pressure for conformity to group norms and a relative lack of individualism.[50]

Managers must realize that organizations and organizational members reflect their national culture's emphasis on individualism or collectivism. Indeed, one of the major reasons why Japanese and American management practices differ is that Japanese culture values collectivism and U.S. culture values individualism, as the following "Managing Globally" suggests.[51]

Managing Globally

A *Gaijin* Works to Turn Around Sony

Sony, the Japanese electronics maker, used to be renowned for using its innovation and engineering prowess to turn out blockbuster new products such as the Walkman and Trinitron TV. In the 1990s product engineers at Sony turned out an average of four new product ideas every day. Why? A large part of the answer was Sony's culture, called the "Sony Way," which emphasized communication, cooperation, and harmony between groups of engineers across the company to foster innovation and change. Engineers were given considerable freedom to pursue their own ideas, and the managers of different product groups championed their own innovations, but problems arose with Sony's approach in the 2000s.

Companies in Korea, Taiwan, and China began to innovate new technologies like digital LCD screens and flash memory that made Sony's technologies

Sony's new CEO, Sir Howard Stringer, shakes hands with Sony President and COO Ryoji Chubachi at a news conference in Tokyo in 2006. In his effort to revamp the company, Stringer is confronting difficult, challenging cultural differences while bringing his cost-cutting expertise to bear on Sony's deteriorating situation. In 2008, Sony is still struggling to regain its former leadership position.

obsolete. Companies such as Apple and Nokia came out with the iPod, smart phones, and tablet computers that better fitted customer needs than Sony's "old-generation" products such as the Walkman. One reason that Sony experienced major problems responding to these changes was that its culture had changed with its success. The top managers of its many divisions had become used to acting as if they had control of a fiefdom, and, protected by the Japanese tradition of lifetime employment, they worked to promote their own division's interests, not their company's. This competition had increased Sony's bureaucracy and slowed its decision making, making it much harder for Sony to take advantage of its pipeline of new product innovations! At the same time, its research was becoming enormously expensive, as divisions demanded more and more funds to create innovative new products.

Sensing this was a crucial turning point in their company's history, Sony's Japanese top managers turned to a *gaijin,* or non-Japanese, executive to lead their company. Their choice was Sir Howard Stringer, a Welshman, who headed Sony's North American operations and had been instrumental in cutting costs and increasing the profits of Sony's U.S. division. Stringer cannot speak Japanese, but luckily for him many of Sony's top executives speak English.

Now that he is in command, he faces the problem of reducing costs in Japan, where many Japanese companies have a policy of lifetime employment. He has made it clear that layoffs will be forthcoming, as Sony must reduce its high operating costs. He has also made it clear that the politicking going on between Sony's different product groups must stop and that managers must prioritize new products, investing only in those that have the highest chance of success, for Sony must reduce its huge R&D budget. Indeed, he wants to make engineering, not management, the focus once again at Sony and eliminate the tall, bloated hierarchy that has developed over time—by, for example, downsizing corporate headquarters. In Stringer's own words, the culture or "business of Sony has been management, not making products." However, he has to accomplish this in Japan, which has a national culture known for its collectivist, long-term orientation and for its distrust of *gaijin* or overseas values. And, these same values operate inside Sony, so Stringer will have to be hardheaded and push Sony to make the best use of its resources.

power distance The degree to which societies accept the idea that inequalities in the power and well-being of their citizens are due to differences in individuals' physical and intellectual capabilities and heritage.

POWER DISTANCE By **power distance** Hofstede meant the degree to which societies accept the idea that inequalities in the power and well-being of their citizens are due to differences in individuals' physical and intellectual capabilities and heritage. This concept also encompasses the degree to which societies accept the economic and social differences in wealth, status, and well-being that result from differences in individual capabilities.

Societies in which inequalities are allowed to persist or grow over time have *high power distance.* In high-power-distance societies, workers who are professionally successful amass wealth and pass it on to their children, and, as a result, inequalities may grow over time. In such societies, the gap between rich and poor, with all the attendant political and social consequences, grows very large. In contrast, in societies with *low power distance,* large inequalities between citizens are not allowed to develop. In low-power-distance countries, the government uses taxation and social welfare programs to reduce inequality and improve the welfare of the least fortunate. These societies are more attuned to preventing a large gap between rich and poor and minimizing discord between different classes of citizens.

Advanced Western countries such as the United States, Germany, the Netherlands, and the United Kingdom have relatively low power distance and high individualism. Economically poor Latin American countries such as Guatemala and Panama, and Asian countries such as Malaysia and the Philippines, have high power distance and low individualism.[52] These findings suggest that the cultural values of richer countries emphasize protecting the rights of individuals and, at the same time, provide a fair chance of success to every member of society.

ACHIEVEMENT VERSUS NURTURING ORIENTATION   Societies that have an **achievement orientation** value assertiveness, performance, success, competition, and results. Societies that have a **nurturing orientation** value the quality of life, warm personal relationships, and services and care for the weak. Japan and the United States tend to be achievement-oriented; the Netherlands, Sweden, and Denmark are more nurturing-oriented.

UNCERTAINTY AVOIDANCE   Societies as well as individuals differ in their tolerance for uncertainty and risk. Societies low on **uncertainty avoidance** (such as the United States and Hong Kong) are easygoing, value diversity, and tolerate differences in personal beliefs and actions. Societies high on uncertainty avoidance (such as Japan and France) are more rigid and skeptical about people whose behaviors or beliefs differ from the norm. In these societies, conformity to the values of the social and work groups to which a person belongs is the norm, and structured situations are preferred because they provide a sense of security.

LONG-TERM VERSUS SHORT-TERM ORIENTATION   The last dimension that Hofstede described is orientation toward life and work.[53] A national culture with a **long-term orientation** rests on values such as thrift (saving) and persistence in achieving goals. A national culture with a **short-term orientation** is concerned with maintaining personal stability or happiness and living for the present. Societies with a long-term orientation include Taiwan and Hong Kong, well known for their high rate of per capita savings. The United States and France have a short-term orientation, and their citizens tend to spend more and save less.

National Culture and Global Management

Differences among national cultures have important implications for managers. First, because of cultural differences, management practices that are effective in one country might be troublesome in another. General Electric's managers learned this while trying to manage Tungsram, a Hungarian lighting products company GE acquired for $150 million. GE was attracted to Tungsram, widely regarded as one of Hungary's best companies, because of Hungary's low wage rates and the possibility of using the company as a base from which to export lighting products to western Europe. GE transferred some of its best managers to Tungsram and hoped it would soon become a leader in Europe. Unfortunately, many problems arose.

One of the problems resulted from major misunderstandings between the American managers and the Hungarian workers. The Americans complained that the Hungarians were lazy; the Hungarians thought the Americans were pushy. The Americans wanted strong sales and marketing functions that would pamper customers. In the prior command economy, sales and marketing activities were unnecessary. In addition, Hungarians expected GE to deliver Western-style wages, but GE came to Hungary to take advantage of the country's low-wage structure.[54] As Tungsram's losses mounted, GE managers had to admit that, because of differences in basic attitudes between countries, they had underestimated the difficulties they would face in turning Tungsram around. Nevertheless, by 2001, these problems had been solved, and the increased efficiency of GE's Hungarian operations made General Electric a major player in the European lighting market, causing it to invest another $1 billion.[55]

achievement orientation
A worldview that values assertiveness, performance, success, and competition.

nurturing orientation
A worldview that values the quality of life, warm personal friendships, and services and care for the weak.

uncertainty avoidance
The degree to which societies are willing to tolerate uncertainty and risk.

long-term orientation
A worldview that values thrift and persistence in achieving goals.

short-term orientation
A worldview that values personal stability or happiness and living for the present.

Often, management practices must be tailored to suit the cultural contexts within which an organization operates. An approach effective in the United States might not work in Japan, Hungary, or Mexico because of differences in national culture. For example, U.S.-style pay-for-performance systems that emphasize the performance of individuals alone might not work well in Japan, where individual performance in pursuit of group goals is the value that receives emphasis.

Managers doing business with individuals from another country must be sensitive to the value systems and norms of that country and behave accordingly. For example, Friday is the Islamic Sabbath. Thus, it would be impolite and inappropriate for a U.S. manager to schedule a busy day of activities for Saudi Arabian managers on a Friday.

A culturally diverse management team can be a source of strength for an organization participating in the global marketplace. Compared to organizations with culturally homogeneous management teams, organizations that employ managers from a variety of cultures have a better appreciation of how national cultures differ, and they tailor their management systems and behaviors to the differences. Indeed, one of the advantages that many Western companies have over their Japanese competitors is greater willingness to build an international team of senior managers.[56]

Managing Globally

Nokia Makes a Big Bet on Romania

Nokia is the world's largest cell-phone maker and it took a commanding lead in 2007 when it achieved a 38% global market share compared to number two Samsung's 14.5%. One reason for its dominance in cell phones is its skills in global supply-chain management. Nokia's global strategy is to make its phones in the world region in which they are to be sold, even if this means building several factories around the world, as opposed to Samsung or Motorola which outsource most of their manufacturing to factories in China. Nokia has plants in Germany, Brazil, China, and India and in 2008 it will open a new plant in Romania in Eastern Europe to make phones for the expanding European/Russian market.

A major reason for beginning operations in Romania is low labor costs. Skilled Romanian engineers can be hired for one-quarter of what they would earn in Finland or Germany and production line employees can expect to earn about $450 a month—a fraction of what their German employees currently earn. Indeed, once its new Romanian factory is up and running Nokia plans to close down its Bochum, Germany, factory which it claims is simply too expensive to operate in today's competitive global environment.

Opening a new factory in a new country is a complex process. To increase the chances that its new factory will operate at the high level of efficiency Nokia expects, its managers have adopted several strategies. First, they have worked to create a culture in the factory that will prove attractive to its new Romanian employees and encourage them to stay with the company and learn the skills required to make it operate more and more efficiently over time. For example, despite the relatively low monthly wage, the factory's cafeteria will offer free food, and there will be gyms, sports facilities, and (of course) a Finnish sauna. In addition, although managers from other countries will run the plant at first, Nokia hopes that within four years all the new factory's managers and supervisors will be Romanian. Its goal is to create a "career ladder" that will motivate employees to perform at a high level and so be promoted. In addition, its managers from abroad are required to take Romanian language classes so that

Nokia's new plant in Romania seeks to take advantage of lower labor costs and create a supply hub for its Eastern European/Russian market. But will the Romanians be on board? While the signpost suggests that Nokia's offer of free food and career training will be enticing, the horse-drawn cart suggests that new recruits may have very different needs and desires.

they can better interact with new employees and build a cooperative, efficiency-driven factory culture.

At the same time, Nokia is hardheaded about how efficient it expects its new factory to be. All its factories are required to operate at the same level of efficiency that its most efficient global factory has achieved. To achieve this Nokia has created a compensation plan for factory managers based upon the *collective* performance of all its factories. This means that the managers in all the countries in which its factories are located will find their bonuses are reduced if just one factory in any country performs below expectations. This is a very tough approach but its purpose is to encourage all managers to develop more efficient manufacturing techniques, which, when learned in one factory, must be shared with all other factories around the world if managers are to obtain their bonuses. Nokia's goal is that efficiency will therefore improve constantly over time as managers are encouraged to find better ways to operate and then share this knowledge across the company.

The plant will open with 500 workers in the summer of 2008 and the number of employees will grow to 2,500 by 2010. Nokia's attempts to develop a productive work culture that motivates its new Romanian employees to perform well will be an important determinant of its ability to maintain and increase its market share and performance—and establish a new home in the business world.

Summary and Review

LO1

WHAT IS THE GLOBAL ENVIRONMENT? The global environment is the set of forces and conditions that operate beyond an organization's boundaries but affect a manager's ability to acquire and utilize resources. The global environment has two components, the task environment and the general environment.

LO 2, 3 THE TASK ENVIRONMENT The task environment is the set of forces and conditions that originate with global suppliers, distributors, customers, and competitors that influence managers on a daily basis. The opportunities and threats associated with forces in the task environment become more and more complex as a company expands globally.

LO 2, 3 THE GENERAL ENVIRONMENT The general environment comprises wider-ranging global economic, technological, sociocultural, demographic, political, and legal forces that affect an organization and its task environment.

LO 4, 5 THE CHANGING GLOBAL ENVIRONMENT In recent years there has been a marked shift toward a more open global environment in which capital flows more freely as people and companies search for new opportunities to create profit and wealth. This has hastened the process of globalization. Globalization is the set of specific and general forces that work together to integrate and connect economic, political, and social systems across countries, cultures, or geographic regions so that nations become increasingly interdependent and similar. The process of globalization has been furthered by declining barriers to international trade and investment and declining barriers of distance and culture.

Management in Action

Topics for Discussion and Action

DISCUSSION

1. Why is it important for managers to understand the nature of the forces in the global environment that are acting on them and their organizations? **[LO1]**

2. Which organization is likely to face the most complex task environment, a biotechnology company trying to develop a new cure for cancer or a large retailer like The Gap or Macy's? Why? **[LO 2, 3]**

3. The population is aging because of declining birth rates, declining death rates, and the aging of the baby-boom generation. What might some of the implications of this demographic trend be for

(a) a pharmaceutical company and (b) the home construction industry? **[LO 1, 2, 3]**

4. How do political, legal, and economic forces shape national culture? What characteristics of national culture do you think have the most important effect on how successful a country is in doing business abroad? **[LO 3, 5]**

5. After the passage of NAFTA, many U.S. companies shifted production operations to Mexico to take advantage of lower labor costs and lower standards for environmental and worker protection. As a result, they cut their costs and were better able

to survive in an increasingly competitive global environment. Was their behavior ethical—that is, did the ends justify the means? **[LO4]**

ACTION

6. Choose an organization, and ask a manager in that organization to list the number and strengths of forces in the organization's task environment. Ask the manager to pay particular attention to identifying opportunities and threats that result from pressures and changes in customers, competitors, and suppliers. **[LO 1, 2, 3]**

Building Management Skills
Analyzing an Organization's Environment [LO 1, 2, 3]

Pick an organization with which you are familiar. It can be an organization in which you have worked or currently work or one that you interact with regularly as a customer (such as the college that you are currently attending). For this organization do the following:

1. Describe the main forces in the global task environment that are affecting the organization.

2. Describe the main forces in the global general environment that are affecting the organization.

3. Explain how environmental forces affect the job of an individual manager within this organization. How do they determine the opportunities and threats that its managers must confront?

Managing Ethically [LO 4, 5]

In recent years, the number of U.S. companies that buy their inputs from low-cost overseas suppliers has

been growing, and concern about the ethics associated with employing young children in factories has been

increasing. In Pakistan and India, children as young as six years old work long hours to make rugs and carpets for export to Western countries or clay bricks for local use. In countries like Malaysia and in Central America, children and teenagers routinely work long hours in factories and sweatshops to produce the clothing that is found in most U.S. discount and department stores.

1. Either by yourself or in a group, discuss whether it is ethical to employ children in factories and whether U.S. companies should buy and sell products made by these children? What are some arguments for and against child labor?

2. If child labor is an economic necessity, what ways could be employed to make it as ethical a practice as possible? Or is it simply unethical?

Small Group Breakout Exercise
How to Enter the Copying Business [LO 1, 2]

Form groups of three to five people, and appoint one group member as the spokesperson who will communicate your findings to the whole class when called on by the instructor. Then discuss the following scenario.

You and your partners have decided to open a small printing and copying business in a college town of 100,000 people. Your business will compete with companies like FedEx Kinko's. You know that over 50% of small businesses fail in their first year, so to increase your chances of success, you have decided to do a detailed analysis of the task environment of the copying business to discover what opportunities and threats you will encounter. As a group:

1. Decide what you must know about (a) your future customers, (b) your future competitors, and (c) other critical forces in the task environment if you are to be successful.

2. Evaluate the main barriers to entry into the copying business.

3. Based on this analysis, list some of the steps you would take to help your new copying business succeed.

Exploring the World Wide Web [LO 2, 3, 4]

Go to Fuji Films' Web site (http://home.fujifilm.com), and then click on "corporate," "profile," and "global operations" and read about Fuji's global activities.

1. How would you characterize the way Fuji manages the global environment? For example, how has Fuji responded to the needs of customers in different countries?

2. How have increasing global competition and declining barriers of distance and culture been affecting Fuji's operations?

Be the Manager [LO 1, 2]

The Changing Environment of Retailing

You are the new manager of a major clothing store that is facing a crisis. This clothing store has been the leader in its market for the last 15 years. In the last three years, however, two other major clothing store chains have opened up, and they have steadily been attracting customers away from your store—your sales are down 30%. To find out why, your store surveyed former customers and learned that they perceive the store as not keeping up with changing fashion trends and new forms of customer service. In examining the way the store operates, you found out that the 10 purchasing managers who buy the clothing and accessories for the store have been buying increasingly from the same clothing suppliers and have become reluctant to try new ones. Moreover, salespeople rarely, if ever, make suggestions for changing the way the store operates, they don't respond to customer requests, and the culture of the store has become conservative and risk-averse.

Questions

1. Analyze the major forces in the task environment of a retail clothing store.

2. Devise a program that will help other managers and employees to better understand and respond to their store's task environment.

BusinessWeek Case in the News [LO 1, 4, 5]

A Guide for Multinationals

Willy Chiu was parked outside a Palo Alto (Calif.) convenience store early one evening in January with his notebook PC switched on. Suddenly he heard the ping of an instant message arriving. It was the Tokyo-based head of IBM's Asia operations with urgent news: A major competitor was homing in on a pivotal project IBM had been chasing. The job, to develop a new IT system for a Korean bank, could be worth up to $100 million. Chiu, who runs IBM's worldwide network of elite labs, was needed to help develop a pilot product.

That plea ignited a flurry of online, BlackBerry, and cell-phone conversations across four continents. Within minutes, Chiu had 18 chat windows open simultaneously on his laptop. "How do we mobilize resources worldwide?" he typed in one message to the head of worldwide operations in San Jose. "I'll take the lead," responded IBM's country manager in Seoul. Chiu dashed off a note asking a team in Beijing to free up staff and quickly received confirmation that they were on the case. Then a banking specialist from England chimed in: "Our team can provide reference cases from Spain." Chiu to his administrative assistant: "Stella, please change my flight to a later time tonight. Also, looks like I may go to Korea again in a few weeks." Chiu to his wife: "Will be working late."

For global corporations, the borderless world of Willy Chiu offers a glimpse of what's to come. International success once meant having bodies and factories on the ground from São Paulo to Silicon Valley to Shanghai. Coordinating their activities was a deliberately planned effort handled by headquarters.

The challenge now is to weld these vast, globally dispersed workforces into superfast, efficient organizations. Given the conflicting needs of multinational staff and the swiftly shifting nature of competition brought about by the Internet, that's an almost impossible task. And getting workers to collaborate instantly—not tomorrow or next week, but now—requires nothing less than a management revolution.

Complicating matters is the fact that the very idea of a company is shifting away from a single outfit with full-time employees and a recognizable hierarchy. It is something much more fluid, with a classic corporation at the center of an ever-shifting network of suppliers and outsourcers, some of whom only join the team for the duration of a single project.

To adapt, multinationals are hiring sociologists to unlock the secrets of teamwork among colleagues who have never met. They're arming staff with an arsenal of new tech tools to keep them perpetually connected. They include software that helps engineers co-develop 3D prototypes in virtual worlds and services that promote social networking and that track employees and outsiders who have the skills needed to nail a job. Corporations are investing lavishly in posh campuses, crafting leadership training centers, and offering thousands of online courses to develop pipelines of talent.

To function in this Age of Diffusion, businesses are rethinking traditional practices. In human resources, the era of standardized benefits and work requirements is vanishing. Instead, to keep prized talent, companies need to accommodate a wide range of cultural and generational idiosyncrasies. In China, where personal relationships are paramount, employers have to tread carefully with hard-edged practices such as management reshuffles and 360-degree performance reviews. To keep valued Indian workers from jumping ship, companies are offering one-on-one career planning and reaching out to parents and spouses. Multinationals that viewed Eastern Europe as a terrific low-cost engineering shop are finding that if they don't give the local scientists a crack at real innovation, they soon are coping with a brain drain.

Dow Chemical is trying to navigate this complex new territory. Dow expects 30% of its 20,000 workers to retire in the next five years. Meanwhile, enrollment in U.S. chemical engineering schools is declining, forcing Dow to fight against deep-pocketed oil and gas companies for scarce talent. To persuade veterans to stay as long as possible, Dow is offering flexible hours, three-day workweeks, and reminders that the door is always open should they want to come back after retirement. But when recruiting college grads, says Dow human resources manager Deborah Borg, the company stresses its efforts to develop green technologies and improve living standards in developing nations.

The hard part for multinationals is getting people to work well together, especially given that day-and-night collaboration across the globe is growing. Over the past decade many companies rushed to spread key functions, such as product development, to the far corners of the earth. The idea was to save time and money. But corporations are finding that running these new operations requires much more effort than connecting staff by phone and e-mail. "One problem with distributing work is that you lose the intimacy of talking things through at a local café," says Forrester Research network innovation expert Navi Radjou. London Business School management professor Lynda Gratton, who led a study of 52 global teams in 15 leading multinationals, spotted the same problem. "Complex teams really struggle to be productive," says Gratton.

Such pressures put a premium on recruiting staff who are globally minded from the outset rather than being mere technicians. Gratton found that global marketing and product development teams at Nokia were especially effective, even though they involve scores of people working in several countries. She says Nokia is careful to select people who have a "collaborative mindset" and carefully includes in task forces a range of nationalities, ages, and education levels. Teams also are made up of people who have worked together in the past and others who have never met, Gratton adds. Members are encouraged to network online and share their photographs and personal biographies.

Training is essential to making staffers globally minded. Accenture, which spent $700 million on education last year, says its 38,000 consultants and most of its services workers take courses on collaborating with offshore colleagues. And each year, Accenture puts up to 400 of its most promising managers through a special leadership development program. They are assigned to groups that can include Irish, Chinese, Belgians, and Filipinos, and specialists in fields such as finance, marketing,

and technology. Over 10 months, teams meet in different international locations. As part of the program, they pick a project—developing a new Web page, say—and learn how to tap the company's worldwide talent pool to complete it.

IBM aims to set itself apart with a spate of Web-based services that make it easier for its 360,000-member staff to "work as one virtual team," says Lab chief Chiu. Big Blue has launched what it calls an innovation portal, where any employee with a product idea can use online chat boxes to organize a team, line up resources, and gain access to market research. Developers in IBM labs around the world then can collaborate on prototypes and testing. This way, enterprising staff can build a global team in as little as half an hour and cut the time to start a business from at least six months to around 30 days.

An example: For a major U.S. telecom client that needed a Web-based tool to launch new services such as video streaming for cell phones, IBM organized a 20-member group including staff from Japan, Brazil, and

Britain. These IBMers built a working prototype in two weeks and delivered a finished product in two months.

Since IBM introduced the portal, in early 2006, 93,000 workers have logged on, leading to 70 businesses and 10 new products.

Creating a seamless global workforce is hard. But certain multinationals are slowly figuring out how to do it.

Questions for Discussion

1. What kinds of factors in the social and cultural environment must global organizations be aware of in recruiting employees and building global teams?

2. In what ways can organizations increase the performance of their global employees and teams?

Source: Pete Engardio, "A Guide for Multinationals: How to Build a Productive Global Team." Reprinted from the August 20, 2007, issue of *BusinessWeek* by special permission. Copyright © 2007 by The McGraw-Hill Companies, Inc.

BusinessWeek ## Case in the News [LO 2, 5]

Remade in the USA— Sony Global

Sony Corp.'s design center in suburban Los Angeles is the very picture of Japanese minimalist chic. The stark white walls are imprinted with a concave eggshell pattern, and the boxy, blond-wood work spaces are inspired by *masu,* or sake cups made from cypress. Despite the decor, though, the Santa Monica (Calif.) facility is taking Sony far from its Japanese roots. The center's dozen or so designers are doing work that in the past was reserved for headquarters, creating high-margin products, from Internet TV devices to stereo systems, that are helping shore up the bottom line.

Once little more than a sales and marketing arm, the U.S. consumer

electronics unit has become key to Sony's worldwide turnaround efforts. At the same time, Sony's U.S. chiefs are increasingly empowered to reject products conceived in Japan that they believe won't fly stateside, including a recently introduced Walkman whose screen they deemed too small to make a dent in the U.S. against Apple Inc.'s dominant iPod.

Sure, Japan remains the center of Sony's creative universe. More than 80% of the company's 225 designers are based there. And many products that become hits in the U.S. are still dreamed up in Sony labs across the Pacific. Yet executives in the U.S. now enjoy an unprecedented degree of influence in shaping everything from a gadget's styling to the software that makes it tick. "What

you're seeing is a fairly dramatic shift in which communication and collaboration on ideas and projects go both ways," says Stan Glasgow, Sony Electronics Inc.'s chief operating officer.

Local Flavor

The American-made gizmos may prove critical to the hoped-for turnaround. The company appears to be pulling out of a nearly decade-long sales and profit slump. Consumer electronics either conceived or improved in the U.S. have helped stanch losses in other divisions, such as film and music. For the company as a whole, sales for the fiscal year that began on Apr. 1 could reach an all-time high of $75 billion, say analysts at JPMorgan Chase, yielding an operating profit of $3.4 billion. Similarly rosy forecasts by other analysts have helped buoy the stock by 25% since the start of the year.

Credit Chairman Howard K. Stringer. The former chief of Sony Corp. of America—and the first Westerner to lead the entire company—is two years into a push to revitalize Sony and restore its reputation as the leader of the cutthroat consumer electronics business, which still accounts for nearly 70% of the company's revenues. One big element of his strategy is tailoring products to differing tastes across the globe. "Putting regional divisions more in charge of their own destiny ensures that . . . local conditions are better accounted for," says analyst David Gibson at Macquarie Securities in Tokyo. "It's Management 101."

Basic, perhaps, but the change has been a long time coming. Sony has endured a string of commercial flops in recent years, from its online music store to movie disks for the PlayStation Portable handheld. And while researcher NPD Group Inc. pegs Sony as the 2006 sales leader in HDTVs, videocameras, and home audio, the company that gave the world the Walkman—and as a result owned the personal audio business for years—boasts no real category-killers today. Sony's portable digital audio and video players haven't come close to the iconic ubiquity of the iPod. And the PlayStation 3 video-game console has yet to match the buzz or sales of rival machines from Microsoft Corp. and Nintendo. Indeed, at the design center, Nintendo's Wii sat ready for play alongside a giant Sony HDTV, while Sony's own PS3 was nowhere to be seen.

Since Stringer's appointment, Sony's U.S. unit has become an important incubator for new products and services. And the early success of U.S. initiatives has prompted the company to start offering similar products elsewhere. In France and Britain, Sony is now marketing VAIO PCs with built-in cellular broadband access. That strategy, initiated in the U.S., helps boost razor-thin PC margins because Sony collects a fee from cellular carriers every time a user activates the wireless service. The Mylo, a handheld Web-browsing and text-messaging gadget aimed at teens that was designed jointly in Japan and the U.S., was recently introduced in Japan after initial American sales exceeded expectations. Now the company is mulling whether to offer the Portable Reader for digital books—a gizmo revamped extensively in the U.S.—in Europe later this year.

Big American ideas are also showing up on big TVs. Engineers in the U.S. developed a $299 box called the Bravia Internet Video Link that lets TV viewers download video clips from America Online and Yahoo! Inc., as well as films and tunes from Sony Pictures and BMG Music, all with a click of their remote. The device will go on sale this summer at Best Buy Co., Circuit City Stores Inc., and other U.S. outlets. Sony TV executives in Japan were so enthusiastic about it that they're planning to build the technology into TVs they sell there as well.

In the old days, instead of embracing an innovative product such as the Bravia Link, Sony's warring factions might have deep-sixed it. That's because the technology could easily be adapted to deliver games and other content, which might cannibalize sales of Sony PCs, audio receivers, and even the PlayStation 3. But in Stringer's eyes, the Bravia could become a potent weapon against Apple, Microsoft, and other rivals seeking to dominate Web-connected homes. "If we don't do it, someone else will," Stringer said in January.

A Better Book

The U.S. center is also tweaking designs to boost the appeal of Sony products to American buyers. For retailer Target Corp. the Santa Monica design center created the $99 Liv music system whose wood-like trim and environment-friendly packaging is a nod to American design trends. Tim Schaaf, a 15-year Apple veteran who defected to Sony in late 2005, replaced the clunky keyboard on the $350 Portable Reader for digital books with easy-to-understand buttons and added an MP3 player. And when rivals last year began introducing sleek new high-definition TVs that made the entry-level Bravia look dated after just five months on the market, Sony's U.S. team worked with Japan to spiff up the design. They quickly introduced the new model, boosting sales by 10% in just a few weeks. "In Japan they have a lot of innovative ideas," says the center's director, Alex Arie. "But that doesn't mean every idea fits into the U.S. market and consumer lifestyle."

Questions for Discussion

1. How and why has Howard Stringer changed the way Sony organizes its global design engineers and activities?

2. In what ways has this improved Sony's ability to innovate new kinds of products global customers desire?

BusinessWeek Case in the News [LO 2, 3, 5]

Nokia Connects

It wasn't hard for Wang Ninie to decide on a mobile phone. In early March the twentysomething Beijing entrepreneur saw a golden Nokia handset with a flower pattern etched into the trim, one of the company's "L'Amour" line of high-end designer phones. "I fell in love with it," she says. At $470, the phone wasn't cheap. No matter. "I didn't even look at other phones," says Wang. Jeevanlal Pitodia is equally smitten with Nokia. The 27-year-old Bombay fruit vendor used to spend his days pounding the pavement in the city's alleys, hawking oranges, apples, and bananas. Last September, Pitodia ponied up $56 for his first handset, a simple but sturdy Nokia 1100. Now he sits under a colorful beach umbrella, earning as much as $10 a day taking orders by phone for both himself and nearby vendors. "I tried many phones, but Nokia is the most user-friendly," says Pitodia.

More than any other handset maker, Nokia Corp. has connected with the likes of Wang and Pitodia and their billions of countrymen. In both China and India, the Finnish company is the top brand. In China last year, it had nearly 31% of a crowded market, well ahead of the 10% controlled by No. 2 Motorola Inc. In India, Nokia has a 60% share, with sales last year of about $1 billion.

Nokia isn't letting up: On March 11 it opened its first Indian factory, a $150 million facility near the southern city of Madras that will turn out as many as 20 million inexpensive phones annually both for the local market and for export. And the company is doubling the size of its plant in the Chinese city of Dongguan, near Hong Kong. The two Asian giants are of fundamental importance for Nokia. The Finnish company has played catch-up in the U.S., where Motorola has beaten it with hot-selling models such as the ultra-thin RAZR. But the U.S. market is nearly saturated. The company that can control Asia's Big Two will have a lead in the global handset wars.

Caught Off Guard

Just a few years ago, Nokia faced big troubles in both countries. In India, growth was sluggish. In China, Nokia not only trailed Motorola but was threatened by domestic players such as TCL and Ningbo Bird, newcomers to the business that had quickly gobbled up almost half of the market with their inexpensive but well-designed handsets. The local upstarts flooded stores nationwide with armies of sales assistants flogging their brands. "Our people would put up posters, and within 30 minutes they would be torn down," recalls Colin Giles, manager of Nokia's China handset business.

To fight back, Giles pushed through big changes. Nokia decentralized, going from three Chinese sales offices in 2003 to 70 today. Instead of eight national distributors, Nokia now has 50 provincial ones. And since rivals were having great success with handsets designed for local users, Nokia introduced its own China-specific models with software that lets them write Chinese characters with a stylus. The result: Nokia sold 27.5 million handsets in China last year, triple what it sold in 2003. Since 2002, when India's cellular market took off, Nokia has drawn on its China experience to consolidate its lead. In 2004 the company launched two India-specific models, which included a flashlight, dust cover, and slip-free grip (handy during India's scorching, sweaty summers). Nokia introduced software in seven Indian regional languages and the company's marketers pitched the phones through ads tailored to India, with one early campaign showing burly truck drivers calling home on Nokia handsets.

Fierce Rivals

Nokia has also reaped the fruits of rivals' missteps. Motorola was slower in reacting to the threat from the Chinese locals and has had a tougher time bouncing back because it didn't change its strategy for a long time. The Chinese upstarts, meanwhile, suffered from sharp reversals due to disappointing quality.

Rivals say the time is right to eat into Nokia's lead. Samsung in the past focused solely on the middle to high end of the market in India but began selling lower-cost phones last year Aad opened a new factory in Gurgaon, near Delhi. Motorola revamped its structure in China, expanding its sales force and strengthening its distribution network to cover 300 cities. By February, Motorola had boosted its market share by several percentage points. And in India, Motorola is planning to market phones costing as little as $35. Motorola Vice President Allen Burnes calls India "pivotal" and says the company will open its first factory there in 18 months.

Questions for Discussion

1. What are the opportunities associated with being first into a major new country market?

2. What are the threats associated with being late in entering a major new country market?

3. How can a company help its products compete effectively in a growing market?

Source: Bruce Einhorn, Nandini Lakshman, Manjeet Kripalani, and Jack Ewing, "Nokia Connects." Reprinted from the March 27, 2006, issue of *BusinessWeek* by special permission. Copyright © 2006 by The McGraw-Hill Companies, Inc.

CHAPTER 7

Decision Making, Learning, Creativity, and Entrepreneurship

Learning Objectives

After studying this chapter, you should be able to:

LO1 Understand the nature of managerial decision making, differentiate between programmed and nonprogrammed decisions, and explain why nonprogrammed decision making is a complex, uncertain process.

LO2 Describe the six steps that managers should take to make the best decisions, and explain how cognitive biases can lead managers to make poor decisions.

LO3 Identify the advantages and disadvantages of group decision making, and describe techniques that can improve it.

LO4 Explain the role that organizational learning and creativity play in helping managers to improve their decisions.

LO5 Describe how managers can encourage and promote entrepreneurship to create a learning organization, and differentiate between entrepreneurs and intrapreneurs.

A MANAGER'S CHALLENGE

Making Good Decisions at PUMA

www.puma.com

Why is decision making of a paramount importance in organizations?
When Jochen Zeitz took over as CEO of PUMA AG in 1993 at the age of 30, the company was facing major threats.[1] PUMA AG, based in the small German sneaker-producing town of Herzogenaurach,[2] had lost money for the past eight years and PUMA North America was facing imminent bankruptcy. The company's cash levels were very low and it was no match for major industry leaders like Adidas (Adidas and PUMA were both founded in Herzogenaurach by two brothers who have long competed with each other), Reebok, and Nike.[3]

Facing tough decisions about how to turnaround the company's fortunes, Zeitz decided that rather than trying to compete based on the performance capabilities of its athletic shoes and equipment, PUMA would focus more on style, colors, and lines of shoes. Essentially, Zeitz saw a potential opportunity in trying to start up a new division focus on experimental fashion and sport as lifestyle. Of course, Zeitz also made difficult decisions to respond to the threats the company was facing by, for example, dramatically reducing costs of production and taking back control over distribution of PUMA

The decisions CEO Jochen Zeitz has made at PUMA and the decisions he and other managers continue to make on a day-to-day basis are key contributors to PUMA's success today.

products in the United States.[4] And PUMA continues to produce high-performance athletic shoes and gear for serious sport. In 2008, for example, PUMA sponsored 9 teams participating in the African Nations Cup soccer tournament and 5 teams in the soccer championships in Europe; 17 teams competing in the summer Olympics in Beijing were outfitted with PUMA products.[5]

Nonetheless, Zeitz's bold decision to pursue the world of fashion and style was a major contributor to PUMA becoming the fourth biggest athletic apparel company worldwide. Recognizing the importance of coming up with creative designs and products, he decided to create a new division called "sport lifestyle" lead by Antonio Bertone, a then 21-year-old skateboarder.[6] The division was tasked to create experimental fashion products. In 1998, Bertone partnered with German fashion designer Jil Sander to turn PUMA's traditional 1960's style cleated soccer shoe into a trendy fashion sneaker using funky colors and suede. At first, this new experimental product line received a lot of skepticism from industry experts and retailers alike; famed soccer player Pelé had worn PUMA cleats and it was unthinkable to many that PUMA would succeed in the world of fashion. As Zeitz indicates, "It took a while—and from my perspective, a lot of energy—to protect this new little child [the lifestyle group] of PUMA from getting killed . . . Eventually, it became the entire company."[7]

Customers loved the retro look and edgy colors of the new line of sneakers, which are now sold in a variety of venues ranging from the Foot Locker to high-end stores like Barneys to upscale department stores. PUMA has its own showcase boutique in the Meatpacking District of Manhattan and 74 stores around the world.[8]

Zeitz continues to pursue new opportunities at PUMA—reinventing traditional products to combine performance with style—and continues to partner with creative thinkers such as Zuly Bet, born in Mali and now a Paris fashion designer, and Yasuhiro Mihara of Japan to create new products.[9] Designers Philippe Starck and Alexander McQueen have both created product lines for PUMA. PUMA partnered with the BMW Mini to make a new driving shoe. The Mostro shoe PUMA created continues to be a top seller.[10]

Former skateboarder Bertone is now based in Boston as PUMA's global director of brand management. Now a top manager, Bertone continues to make decisions to seize opportunities for creative and innovative product lines such as the limited-edition line called Thrift (products made from vintage clothing) and Mongolian Shoe BBQ (shoes that can be customized online).

Zeitz continues to make decisions in response to opportunities and, in the process, has expanded PUMA's range of products in far-reaching directions. The company's 24 Hour Tubism is an aluminum covered wardrobe carrier designed for business travelers. Teaming up with Danish bicycle maker Biomega and the London design group Vexed Generation, PUMA created a foldable "unstealable" bicycle that retails for around $775. When they first started working on the project, the team decided that they wanted to develop a truly creative bike—one that had never been built before. The "unstealable" bicycle met the bill—its lock is integrated into the frame of the bike and once broken, renders the bike unusable.[11]

Clearly, the decisions Zeitz and other managers made at PUMA, and continue to make on a day-to-day basis, are key contributors to the success of PUMA today.[12] And while much uncertainty and ambiguity surrounds these decisions at the time they are made, and they are sometimes met with skepticism, they have propelled PUMA to be a powerhouse of innovation.[13]

Overview

The "Manager's Challenge" illustrates how decision making can have a profound influence on organizational effectiveness. The decisions that managers make at all levels in companies large and small can have a dramatic impact on the growth and prosperity of these companies and the well-being of their employees, customers, and other stakeholders. Yet such decisions can be very difficult to make because they are fraught with uncertainty.

In this chapter, we examine how managers make decisions, and we explore how individual, group, and organizational factors affect the quality of the decisions they make and ultimately determine organizational performance. We discuss the nature of managerial decision making and examine some models of the decision-making process that help reveal the complexities of successful decision making. Then we outline the main steps of the decision-making process; in addition, we explore the biases that may cause capable managers to make poor decisions both as individuals and as members of a group. Next, we examine how managers can promote organizational learning and creativity and improve the quality of decision making throughout an organization. Finally, we discuss the important role of entrepreneurship in promoting organizational creativity, and we differentiate between entrepreneurs and intrapreneurs. By the end of this chapter, you will appreciate the critical role of management decision making in creating a high-performing organization.

The Nature of Managerial Decision Making

Every time managers act to plan, organize, direct, or control organizational activities, they make a stream of decisions. In opening a new restaurant, for example, managers have to decide where to locate it, what kinds of food to provide to customers, which people to employ, and so on. Decision making is a basic part of every task managers perform. In this chapter we study how these decisions are made.

As we discussed in the last three chapters, one of the main tasks facing a manager is to manage the organizational environment. Forces in the external environment give rise to many opportunities and threats for managers and their organizations. In addition, inside an organization managers must address many opportunities and threats that may arise during the course of utilizing organizational resources. To deal with these opportunities and threats, managers must make decisions—that is, they must select one solution from a set of alternatives. **Decision making** is the process by which managers respond to the opportunities and threats that confront them by analyzing the options and making determinations, or *decisions,* about specific organizational goals and courses of action. Good decisions result in the selection of appropriate goals and courses of action that increase organizational performance; bad decisions result in lower performance.

Decision making in response to opportunities occurs when managers search for ways to improve organizational performance to benefit customers, employees, and other stakeholder groups. In "A Manager's Challenge," Jochen Zeitz turned around PUMA's fortunes by the decisions he made in response to opportunities and he continues to engage in decision making in response to opportunities to this day. *Decision making in response to threats* occurs when events inside or outside the organization are adversely affecting organizational performance and managers are searching for ways to increase performance.[14] When Zeitz become CEO of PUMA, high production costs and an ineffective distribution system were threats that prompted Zeitz to make a number of decisions to

LO1 Understand the nature of managerial decision making, differentiate between programmed and nonprogrammed decisions, and explain why nonprogrammed decision making is a complex, uncertain process.

decision making The process by which managers respond to opportunities and threats by analyzing options and making determinations about specific organizational goals and courses of action.

improve the performance and viability of the company.[15] Decision making is central to being a manager, and whenever managers engage in planning, organizing, leading, and controlling–their four principal tasks–they are constantly making decisions.

Managers are always searching for ways to make better decisions to improve organizational performance. At the same time, they do their best to avoid costly mistakes that will hurt organizational performance. Examples of spectacularly good decisions include Liz Claiborne's decision in the 1980s to focus on producing clothes for the growing number of women entering the workforce–a decision that contributed to making her company one of the largest clothing manufacturers. Also, Bill Gates's decision to buy a computer operating system for $50,000 from a small company in Seattle and sell it to IBM for the new IBM personal computer turned Gates and Microsoft, respectively, into the richest man and richest software company in the United States. Examples of spectacularly bad decisions include the decision by managers at NASA and Morton Thiokol to launch the *Challenger* space shuttle–a decision that resulted in the deaths of six astronauts in 1986. Also, the decision of Ken Olsen, founder of Digital Equipment Corporation, to stay with mainframe computers in the 1980s and not allow his engineers to spend the company's resources on creating new kinds of personal computers because of his belief that "personal computers are just toys" was a decision that cost Olsen his job as CEO and almost ruined his company.

Programmed and Nonprogrammed Decision Making

Regardless of the specific decisions that a manager makes, the decision-making process is either programmed or nonprogrammed.[16]

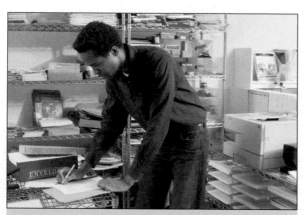

An employee takes inventory of office supplies. The decision-making process involved in such a routine, repetitive task is an example of programmed decision making.

programmed decision making Routine, virtually automatic decision making that follows established rules or guidelines.

PROGRAMMED DECISION MAKING **Programmed decision making** is a *routine,* virtually automatic process. Programmed decisions are decisions that have been made so many times in the past that managers have developed rules or guidelines to be applied when certain situations inevitably occur. Programmed decision making takes place when a school principal asks the school board to hire a new teacher whenever student enrollment increases by 40 students; when a manufacturing supervisor hires new workers whenever existing workers' overtime increases by more than 10%; and when an office manager orders basic office supplies, such as paper and pens, whenever the inventory of supplies on hand drops below a certain level. Furthermore, in the last example, the office manager probably orders the same amount of supplies each time.

This decision making is called *programmed* because office managers, for example, do not need to repeatedly make new judgments about what should be done. They can rely on long-established decision rules such as these:

- *Rule 1:* When the storage shelves are three-quarters empty, order more copy paper.
- *Rule 2:* When ordering paper, order enough to fill the shelves.

Managers can develop rules and guidelines to regulate all routine organizational activities. For example, rules can specify how a worker should perform a certain task, and rules can specify the quality standards that raw materials must meet to be acceptable. Most decision making that relates to the day-to-day running of an organization is programmed decision making. Examples include decision making about how much inventory to hold, when to pay bills, when to bill customers, and when to order materials and supplies. Programmed decision making occurs when managers have the information they need to create rules that will guide decision making. There is little ambiguity involved in assessing when the stockroom is empty or counting the number of new students in class.

As profiled in the following "Focus on Diversity," effectively training new employees is essential to reap the benefits of programmed decision making.

Focus on Diversity

Programmed Decision Making at UPS

UPS is unrivaled in its use of programmed decision making. Practically all the motions, behaviors, and actions that its drivers perform day in and day out have been carefully honed to maximize efficiency and minimize strain and injuries while delivering high-quality customer service. For example, a 12-step process prescribes how drivers should park their trucks, locate the package they are about to deliver, and step off the truck in 15.5 seconds (a process called "selection" at UPS).[17] Rules and routines such as these are carefully detailed in UPS's "340 methods" manual (UPS actually has far more than 340 methods). Programmed decision making dictates where drivers should stop to get gas, how they should hold their keys in their hands, and how to lift and lower packages.[18]

When programmed decision making is so heavily relied on, ensuring that new employees learn tried and-true routines is essential. UPS has traditionally taught new employees with a two-week period of lectures followed by practice.[19] In the 2000s, however, managers began to wonder if they needed to alter their training methods to suit their new Generation Y (Generation Y typically refers to people born after 1980) trainees not so keen on memorization and drills.[20] Generation Y trainees seemed to require more training time to become effective drivers (90–180 days compared to a typical average of 30–45 days) and quit rates for new drivers had increased.[21]

Given the fundamental importance of performance programs for UPS operations, managers decided to try to alter the training new hires receive so it would be better received by Generation Y trainees. In September 2007, UPS opened a new pilot training center called Integrad in Landover, Maryland, which is over 11,000 square feet and cost over $30 million to build and equip. Integrad was developed over a three-year time period through a collaborative effort of over 170 people, including UPS top managers (many of whom started out their careers with UPS as drivers), teams from Virginia Tech and MIT, animators from the Indian company Brainvisa, and forecasters from the Institute for the Future with the support of a grant from the Department of Labor for $1.8 million.[22]

Training at Integrad emphasizes hands-on learning.[23] For example, in Integrad, a UPS truck with transparent sides is used to teach trainees selection so they can actually see the instructor performing the steps and then practice the steps themselves rather than trying to absorb the material in a lecture. Trainees can try out different movements and see, with the help of computer diagrams and simulations, how following UPS routines will help to protect them from injury and how debilitating work as a driver could be to their bodies if they do not follow routines. Video recorders track and document what trainees do correctly and incorrectly so they can see it for themselves rather relying on feedback from an instructor, which they might question. As Stephen Jones, who is in charge of training for UPS and manages Integrad indicates, "Tell them what they did incorrectly, and they'll tell you, 'I didn't do that. You saw wrong.' This way we've got it on tape and they can see it for themselves."[24]

At Integrad, trainees get practice driving in a pseudo town that has been constructed in a parking lot.[25] And they also watch animated demonstrations on computer screens, participate in simulations, take electronic quizzes, and receive scores on various components that are retained in a database to track learning and performance. Recognizing that Generation Y trainees have a lot of respect for expertise and reputation, older employees also are brought in to facilitate learning at Integrad. Long-time UPS employee Don Petersik who is about to retire, for example, trains facilitators at Integrad and shares stories with them to reinforce the UPS culture such as the time he was just starting out as a preloader and, unbeknownst to him, the founder of UPS, Jim Casey, approached him and said, "Hi, I'm Jim. I work for UPS."[26] As Petersik indicates, "What's new about the company now is that our teaching style matches your learning styles."[27] Clearly, when learning programmed decision making is of utmost importance, as it is at UPS, it is essential to take into account diversity in learning styles and approaches.

NONPROGRAMMED DECISION MAKING   Suppose, however, managers are not at all certain that a course of action will lead to a desired outcome. Or, in even more ambiguous terms, suppose managers are not even clear about what they are really trying to achieve. Obviously, rules cannot be developed to predict uncertain events.

nonprogrammed decision making Nonroutine decision making that occurs in response to unusual, unpredictable opportunities and threats.

   Nonprogrammed decision making is required for these *nonroutine* decisions. Nonprogrammed decisions are made in response to unusual or novel opportunities and threats. Nonprogrammed decision making occurs when there are no ready-made decision rules that managers can apply to a situation. Rules do not exist because the situation is unexpected or uncertain and managers lack the information they would need to develop rules to cover it. Examples of nonprogrammed decision making include decisions to invest in a new kind of technology, develop a new kind of product, as did Jochen Zeitz in "A Manager's Challenge," launch a new promotional campaign, enter a new market, expand internationally, or start a new business.

   How do managers make decisions in the absence of decision rules? They may rely on their **intuition**–feelings, beliefs, and hunches that come readily to mind, require little effort and information gathering, and result in on-the-spot decisions.[28] Or they may make **reasoned judgments**–decisions that take time and effort to make and result from careful information gathering, generation of alternatives, and evaluation of alternatives. "Exercising" one's judgment is a more rational process than "going with" one's intuition. For reasons that we examine later in this chapter, both intuition and judgment often are flawed and can result in poor decision making. Thus, the likelihood of error is much greater in nonprogrammed decision making than in programmed decision making.[29] In the remainder of this chapter, when we talk about decision making, we are referring to *nonprogrammed* decision making because it causes the most problems for managers and is inherently challenging.

intuition Feelings, beliefs, and hunches that come readily to mind, require little effort and information gathering, and result in on-the-spot decisions.

   Sometimes managers have to make rapid decisions and don't have the time for careful consideration of the issues involved. They must rely on their intuition to quickly respond to a pressing concern. For example, when fire chiefs, captains, and lieutenants manage firefighters battling dangerous, out-of-control fires, they often need to rely on their expert intuition to make on-the-spot decisions that will protect the lives of the firefighters and save the lives of others, contain the fires, and preserve property–decisions made in emergency situations entailing high uncertainty, high risk, and rapidly changing conditions.[30] Other times, managers do have the time available to make reasoned judgments but there are no established rules to guide their decisions, such as when deciding whether or not to proceed with a proposed merger.

reasoned judgment A decision that takes time and effort to make and results from careful information gathering, generation of alternatives, and evaluation of alternatives.

   Regardless of the circumstances, making nonprogrammed decisions can result in effective or ineffective decision making. As indicated in the following "Manager as a Person," managers have to be on their guard to avoid being overconfident in decisions that result from their intuition and reasoned judgment.

Manager as a Person

Curbing Overconfidence

Should managers be confident in their intuition and reasoned judgments?[31] Decades of research by Nobel Prize winner Daniel Kahneman, his long-time collaborator the late Amos Tversy, and other researchers suggests that managers (like all people) tend to be overconfident in the decisions they make (whether based on intuition or reasoned judgment). And with overconfidence comes the failure to evaluate and rethink the wisdom of the decisions one makes and to learn from mistakes.[32]

Kahneman distinguishes between the intuitions of managers who are truly expert in the content domain of a decision and the intuition of managers who have some knowledge and experience but are not true experts.[33] While the intuition of both types can be faulty, that of experts is less likely to be flawed. This is why fire captains can make good decisions and why expert chess players can make good moves, in both cases without spending much time or deliberating carefully on what, for nonexperts, is a very complicated set of circumstances. What distinguishes expert managers from those with "some" expertise is that the experts have extensive experience under conditions in which they receive quick and clear feedback about the outcomes of their decisions.[34]

Unfortunately, managers who have some experience in a content area but are not true experts tend to be overly confident in their intuition and their judgments.[35] As Kahneman puts it, "People jump to statistical conclusions on the basis of very weak evidence. We form powerful intuitions about trends and about the replicability of results on the basis of information that is truly inadequate."[36] Not only do managers, and all people, tend to be overconfident about their intuitions and judgments, but they also tend not to learn from mistakes. Compounding this undue optimism is a very human tendency to be overconfident in one's own abilities and influence over unpredictable events. Surveys have found that the majority of people think they are above average, make better decisions, and are less prone to making bad decisions than others (of course, it is impossible for most people to be above average on any dimension).[37]

A recent example of managerial overconfidence is particularly telling. Research has consistently found that mergers tend to turn out poorly—postmerger profitability declines, stock prices decline, and so forth. (For example, Chrysler had the biggest profits of the three largest automobile makers in the United States when it merged with Daimler; the merger has not worked out well, and Chrysler would have been better off if it never had happened.)[38] So one would imagine that top executives and boards of directors would learn from this research and from articles in the business press about the woes of merged companies (e.g., the AOL–Time Warner merger).[39] Evidently not. According to a recent study by Hewitt Associates, top executives and board members are, if anything, planning on increasing their involvement in mergers over the next few years. These top managers evidently overconfidently believe that they can succeed where others have failed.[40]

Jeffrey Pfeffer, a professor at Stanford University's Graduate School of Business, suggests that managers can avoid the perils of overconfidence by critically evaluating the decisions they have made and the outcomes of those decisions. They should admit to themselves when they have made a mistake and really learn from their mistakes (rather than dismissing them as flukes or situations out of their control). In addition, managers should be leery of too much agreement at the top. As Pfeffer puts it, "If two people agree all the time, one of them is redundant."[41]

Figure 7.1
The Classical Model of Decision Making

The classical and the administrative decision-making models reveal many of the assumptions, complexities, and pitfalls that affect decision making. These models help reveal the factors that managers and other decision makers must be aware of to improve the quality of their decision making. Keep in mind, however, that the classical and administrative models are just guides that can help managers understand the decision-making process. In real life, the process is typically not cut-and-dried, but these models can help guide a manager through it.

The Classical Model

classical decision-making model A prescriptive approach to decision making based on the assumption that the decision maker can identify and evaluate all possible alternatives and their consequences and rationally choose the most appropriate course of action.

One of the earliest models of decision making, the **classical model,** is *prescriptive,* which means that it specifies how decisions *should* be made. Managers using the classical model make a series of simplifying assumptions about the nature of the decision-making process (see Figure 7.1). The premise of the classical model is that once managers recognize the need to make a decision, they should be able to generate a complete list of *all* alternatives and consequences and make the best choice. In other words, the classical model assumes that managers have access to *all* the information they need to make the **optimum decision,** which is the most appropriate decision possible in light of what they believe to be the most desirable future consequences for the organization. Furthermore, the classical model assumes that managers can easily list their own preferences for each alternative and rank them from least to most preferred to make the optimum decision.

optimum decision The most appropriate decision in light of what managers believe to be the most desirable future consequences for the organization.

The Administrative Model

James March and Herbert Simon disagreed with the underlying assumptions of the classical model of decision making. In contrast, they proposed that managers in the real world do *not* have access to all the information they need to make a decision. Moreover, they pointed out that even if all information were readily available, many managers would lack the mental or psychological ability to absorb and evaluate it correctly. As a result, March and Simon developed the **administrative model** of decision making to explain why decision making is always an inherently uncertain and risky process—and why managers can rarely make decisions in the manner prescribed by the classical model. The administrative model is based on three important concepts: *bounded rationality, incomplete information,* and *satisficing.*

Figure 7.2

Why Information Is Incomplete

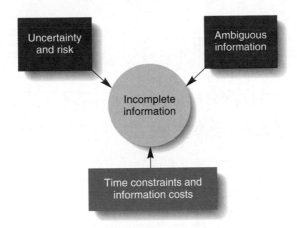

administrative model An approach to decision making that explains why decision making is inherently uncertain and risky and why managers usually make satisfactory rather than optimum decisions.

bounded rationality Cognitive limitations that constrain one's ability to interpret, process, and act on information.

BOUNDED RATIONALITY   March and Simon pointed out that human decision-making capabilities are bounded by people's cognitive limitations—that is, limitations in their ability to interpret, process, and act on information.[42] They argued that the limitations of human intelligence constrain the ability of decision makers to determine the optimum decision. March and Simon coined the term **bounded rationality** to describe the situation in which the number of alternatives a manager must identify is so great and the amount of information so vast that it is difficult for the manager to even come close to evaluating it all before making a decision.[43]

INCOMPLETE INFORMATION   Even if managers did have an unlimited ability to evaluate information, they still would not be able to arrive at the optimum decision because they would have incomplete information. Information is incomplete because the full range of decision-making alternatives is unknowable in most situations and the consequences associated with known alternatives are uncertain.[44] In other words, information is incomplete because of risk and uncertainty, ambiguity, and time constraints (see Figure 7.2).

risk The degree of probability that the possible outcomes of a particular course of action will occur.

uncertainty Unpredictability.

RISK AND UNCERTAINTY   As we saw in Chapter 6, forces in the organizational environment are constantly changing. **Risk** is present when managers know the possible outcomes of a particular course of action and can assign probabilities to them. For example, managers in the biotechnology industry know that new drugs have a 10% probability of successfully passing advanced clinical trials and a 90% probability of failing. These probabilities reflect the experiences of thousands of drugs that have gone through advanced clinical trials. Thus, when managers in the biotechnology industry decide to submit a drug for testing, they know that there is only a 10% chance that the drug will succeed, but at least they have some information on which to base their decision.

When **uncertainty** exists, the probabilities of alternative outcomes *cannot* be determined and future outcomes are *unknown*. Managers are working blind. Since the probability of a given outcome occurring is *not* known, managers have little information to use in making a decision. For example, in 1993, when Apple Computer introduced the Newton, its personal digital assistant (PDA), managers had no idea what the probability of a successful product launch for a PDA might be. Because Apple was the first to market this totally new product, there was no body of well-known data that Apple's managers could draw on to calculate the probability of a successful launch. Uncertainty plagues most managerial decision making.[45] Although Apple's initial launch of its PDA was a disaster due to technical problems, an improved version was more successful. In fact, Apple created the PDA market that has boomed during the 2000s as new and different wireless products have been introduced.

As indicated in the following "Information Technology Byte," a major source of uncertainty for top managers revolves around being unable to accurately predict future demand for products and services.

Information Technology Byte

Revising Plans at Associated Business Systems

Having a good business plan is essential for entrepreneurs to obtain funding from banks, venture capitalists, and other sources of funds. Once entrepreneurs have secured funding and their businesses are up and running, their business plans are typically reviewed only once a year as part of an annual planning process, unless, of course, the entrepreneurs are seeking to obtain additional funds. These business plans are inherently fraught with uncertainty, as is starting a new business and having it actually succeed. However, viewing a business plan as a work in progress that should be evolving on an almost continuous basis has turned out to be a blessing for Craig Knouf, founder, CEO, and majority owner of Associated Business Systems (ABS), a Portland, Oregon, supplier of office equipment.[46]

Knouf estimates that he has revised his business plan over 120 times since founding ABS in 1997; he makes a point of reviewing and, if necessary, revising ABS's business plan on a monthly basis after consulting with the firm's seven vice presidents. As Knouf puts it, "If you only looked at the plan every quarter, by the time you realize the mistake, you're five months off. . . . You're done. You're not going to get back on track."[47] Of course, the reason why managers like Knouf have to continually rethink their decisions is the inherent uncertainty in all that they do. As a case in point, in the early years Knouf never anticipated that scanners would be a significant part of his business. But during his monthly reviews of the business, he noticed that sales of office equipment with scanning capabilities were steadily increasing. Acting on what his sales data were telling him, Knouf quickly added products with scanning capabilities to his company's offerings.[48]

Knouf's ability to appreciate the inherent uncertainty of the best-made plans and decisions, and the benefit of frequently changing courses of action in response to feedback from customers and the market, has certainly paid off handsomely for his company. Since its founding in 1997, ABS's revenues have grown from $880,000 to over $32.5 million.[49] ABS appeared on *INC.* magazine's list of fastest-growing private companies, was on the *Portland Business Journal's* list of fastest-growing companies in Oregon, and has been one of 100 fastest growing companies in Oregon for six consecutive years.[50] Even suppliers have taken notice of ABS's ability to stay in touch with the market, provide excellent, timely service to customers, and actively respond to changing market conditions.[51] ABS currently represents four of the leading global technology producers (Hewlett Packard, Canon, Kyocera, and Ricoh).[52] Management experts agree that Knouf's approach to planning makes good business sense. As Eric Siegel, Wharton Business School lecturer and president of Siegel Management Consultants, puts it, "The world turns; things change. . . . What you commit to a document on Dec. 19 is not necessarily appropriate on Jan. 19."[53]

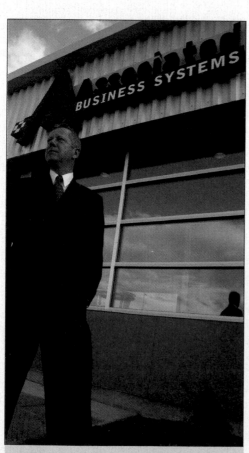

Craig Knouf appreciates the inherent uncertainty of the best-made plans and decisions.

AMBIGUOUS INFORMATION   A second reason why information is incomplete is that much of the information managers have at their disposal is **ambiguous information.** Its meaning is not clear—it can be interpreted in multiple and often conflicting ways.[54] Take a look at Figure 7.3. Do you see a young woman or an old woman? In a similar fashion, managers often interpret the same piece of information differently and make decisions based on their own interpretations.

TIME CONSTRAINTS AND INFORMATION COSTS   The third reason why information is incomplete is that managers have neither the time nor the money to search for all possible alternative solutions and evaluate all the potential consequences of those alternatives. Consider the situation confronting a Ford Motor Company purchasing manager who has one month to choose a supplier for a small engine part. Of the thousands of potential suppliers for this part, there are 20,000 in the United States alone. Given the time available, the purchasing manager cannot contact all potential suppliers and ask each for its terms (price, delivery schedules, and so on). Moreover, even if the time were available, the costs of obtaining the information, including the manager's own time, would be prohibitive.

SATISFICING   March and Simon argue that managers do not attempt to discover every alternative when faced with bounded rationality, an uncertain future, unquantifiable risks, considerable ambiguity, time constraints, and high information costs. Rather, they use a strategy known as **satisficing,** exploring a limited sample of all potential alternatives.[55] When managers satisfice, they search for and choose acceptable, or satisfactory, ways to respond to problems and opportunities rather than trying to make the optimal decision.[56] In the case of the Ford purchasing manager's search, for example, satisficing may involve asking a limited number of suppliers for their terms, trusting that they are representative of suppliers in general, and making a choice from that set. Although this course of action is reasonable from the perspective of the purchasing manager, it may mean that a potentially superior supplier is overlooked.

March and Simon pointed out that managerial decision making is often more art than science. In the real world, managers must rely on their intuition and judgment to make what seems to them to be the best decision in the face of uncertainty and ambiguity.[57] Moreover, managerial decision making is often fast-paced, as managers use their experience and judgment to make crucial decisions under conditions of incomplete

ambiguous information
Information that can be interpreted in multiple and often conflicting ways.

satisficing Searching for and choosing an acceptable, or satisfactory, response to problems and opportunities, rather than trying to make the best decision.

Figure 7.3

Ambiguous Information: Young Woman or Old Woman?

information. Although there is nothing wrong with this approach, decision makers should be aware that human judgment is often flawed. As a result, even the best managers sometimes end up making very poor decisions.[58]

Steps in the Decision-Making Process

LO2 Describe the six steps that managers should take to make the best decisions, and explain how cognitive biases can lead managers to make poor decisions.

Using the work of March and Simon as a basis, researchers have developed a step-by-step model of the decision-making process and the issues and problems that managers confront at each step. Perhaps the best way to introduce this model is to examine the real-world nonprogrammed decision making that Scott McNealy had to engage in at a crucial point in Sun Microsystems' history.

In early August 1985, Scott McNealy, CEO of Sun Microsystems[59] (a hardware and software computer workstation manufacturer focused on network solutions), had to decide whether to go ahead with the launch of the new Carrera workstation computer, scheduled for September 10. Sun's managers had chosen the date nine months earlier when the development plan for the Carrera was first proposed. McNealy knew that it would take at least a month to prepare for the September 10 launch and that the decision could not be put off.

Customers were waiting for the new machine, and McNealy wanted to be the first to provide a workstation that took advantage of Motorola's powerful 16-megahertz 68020 microprocessor. Capitalizing on this opportunity would give Sun a significant edge over Apollo, its main competitor in the workstation market. McNealy knew, however, that committing to the September 10 launch date was risky. Motorola was having production problems with the 16-megahertz 68020 microprocessor and could not guarantee Sun a steady supply of these chips. Moreover, the operating system software was not completely free of bugs.

If Sun launched the Carrera on September 10, the company might have to ship some machines with software that was not fully operational, was prone to crash the system, and utilized Motorola's less-powerful 12 megahertz 68020 microprocessor instead of the 16-megahertz version.[60] Of course, Sun could later upgrade the microprocessor and operating system software in any machines purchased by early customers, but the company's reputation would suffer as a result. If Sun did not go ahead with the September launch, the company would miss an important opportunity.[61] Rumors were circulating in the industry that Apollo would be launching a new machine of its own in December.

Scott McNealy clearly had a difficult decision to make. He had to decide quickly whether to launch the Carrera, but he was not in possession of all the facts. He did not know, for example, whether the microprocessor or operating system problems could be resolved by September 10; nor did he know whether Apollo was going to launch a competing machine in December. But he could not wait to find these things out—he had to make a decision. We'll see what he decided later in the chapter.

Many managers who must make important decisions with incomplete information face dilemmas similar to McNealy's. There are six steps that managers should consciously follow to make a good decision (see Figure 7.4).[62] We review them in the remainder of this section.

Recognize the Need for a Decision

The first step in the decision-making process is to recognize the need for a decision. Scott McNealy recognized this need, and he realized that a decision had to be made quickly.

Some stimuli usually spark the realization that there is a need to make a decision. These stimuli often become apparent because changes in the organizational environment result in new kinds of opportunities and threats. This happened at Sun Microsystems. The September 10 launch date had been set when it seemed that Motorola chips would be readily available. Later, with the supply of chips in doubt

Figure 7.4

Six Steps in Decision Making

and bugs remaining in the system software, Sun was in danger of failing to meet its launch date.

The stimuli that spark decision making are as likely to result from the actions of managers inside an organization as they are from changes in the external environment.[63] An organization possesses a set of skills, competencies, and resources in its employees and in departments such as marketing, manufacturing, and research and development. Managers who actively pursue opportunities to use these competencies create the need to make decisions. Managers thus can be proactive or reactive in recognizing the need to make a decision, but the important issue is that they must recognize this need and respond in a timely and appropriate way.[64]

Generate Alternatives

Having recognized the need to make a decision, a manager must generate a set of feasible alternative courses of action to take in response to the opportunity or threat. Management experts cite failure to properly generate and consider different alternatives as one reason why managers sometimes make bad decisions.[65] In the Sun Microsystems decision, the alternatives seem clear: to go ahead with the September 10 launch or to delay the launch until the Carrera was 100% ready for market introduction. Often, however, the alternatives are not so obvious or so clearly specified.

One major problem is that managers may find it difficult to come up with creative alternative solutions to specific problems. Perhaps some of them are used to seeing the world from a single perspective—they have a certain "managerial mind-set." In a manner similar to that of Digital's Olsen, many managers find it difficult to view problems from a fresh perspective. According to best-selling management author Peter Senge, we all are trapped within our personal mental models of the world—our ideas about what is important and how the world works.[66] Generating creative alternatives to solve problems and take advantage of opportunities may require that we abandon our existing mind-sets and develop new ones—something that usually is difficult to do.

The importance of getting managers to set aside their mental models of the world and generate creative alternatives is reflected in the growth of interest in the work of authors such as Peter Senge and Edward de Bono, who have popularized techniques for stimulating problem solving and creative thinking among managers.[67] Later in this chapter, we discuss the important issues of organizational learning and creativity in detail.

Assess Alternatives

Once managers have generated a set of alternatives, they must evaluate the advantages and disadvantages of each one.[68] The key to a good assessment of the alternatives is to define the opportunity or threat exactly and then specify the criteria that *should* influence the selection of alternatives for responding to the problem or opportunity. One reason for bad decisions is that managers often fail to specify the criteria that are important in reaching a decision.[69] In general, successful managers use four criteria to evaluate the pros and cons of alternative courses of action (see Figure 7.5):

1. *Legality:* Managers must ensure that a possible course of action is legal and will not violate any domestic and international laws or government regulations.
2. *Ethicalness:* Managers must ensure that a possible course of action is ethical and will not unnecessarily harm any stakeholder group. Many of the decisions that managers make may help some organizational stakeholders and harm others (see Chapter 3). When examining alternative courses of action, managers need to be very clear about the potential effects of their decisions.
3. *Economic feasibility:* Managers must decide whether the alternatives are economically feasible—that is, whether they can be accomplished given the organization's performance goals. Typically, managers perform a cost-benefit analysis of the various alternatives to determine which one will have the best net financial payoff.
4. *Practicality:* Managers must decide whether they have the capabilities and resources required to implement the alternative, and they must be sure that the alternative will not threaten the attainment of other organizational goals. At first glance, an alternative might seem to be economically superior to other alternatives, but if managers realize that it is likely to threaten other important projects, they might decide that it is not practical after all.

Figure 7.5

General Criteria for Evaluating Possible Courses of Action

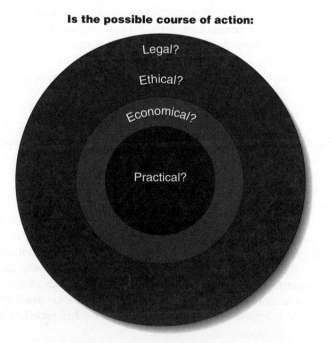

Very often, a manager must consider these four criteria simultaneously. Scott McNealy framed the problem at hand at Sun Microsystems quite well. The key question was whether to go ahead with the September 10 launch date. Two main criteria were influencing McNealy's choice: the need to ship a machine that was as "complete" as possible (the *practicality* criterion) and the need to beat Apollo to market with a new workstation (the *economic feasibility* criterion). These two criteria conflicted. The first suggested that the launch should be delayed; the second, that the launch should go ahead. McNealy's actual choice was based on the relative importance that he assigned to these two criteria. In fact, Sun Microsystems went ahead with the September 10 launch, which suggests that McNealy thought the need to beat Apollo to market was the more important criterion.

Some of the worst managerial decisions can be traced to poor assessment of the alternatives, such as the decision to launch the *Challenger* space shuttle, mentioned earlier. In that case, the desire of NASA and Morton Thiokol managers to demonstrate to the public the success of the U.S. space program in order to ensure future funding *(economic feasibility)* conflicted with the need to ensure the safety of the astronauts *(ethicalness)*. Managers deemed the economic criterion more important and decided to launch the space shuttle even though there were unanswered questions about safety. Tragically, some of the same decision-making problems that resulted in the *Challenger* tragedy led to the demise of the *Columbia* space shuttle in 2003, 17 years later, killing all seven astronauts on board.[70] In both the *Challenger* and the *Columbia* disasters, safety questions were raised before the shuttles were launched; safety concerns took second place to budgets, economic feasibility, and schedules; top decision makers seemed to ignore or downplay the inputs of those with relevant technical expertise; and speaking up was discouraged.[71] Rather than making safety a top priority, decision makers seemed overly concerned with keeping on schedule and within budget.[72]

Choose Among Alternatives

Once the set of alternative solutions has been carefully evaluated, the next task is to rank the various alternatives (using the criteria discussed in the previous section) and make a decision. When ranking alternatives, managers must be sure *all* the information available is brought to bear on the problem or issue at hand. As the Sun Microsystems case indicates, however, identifying all *relevant* information for a decision does not mean that the manager has *complete* information; in most instances, information is incomplete.

Perhaps more serious than the existence of incomplete information is the often-documented tendency of managers to ignore critical information, even when it is available. We discuss this tendency in detail below when we examine the operation of cognitive biases and groupthink.

Implement the Chosen Alternative

Once a decision has been made and an alternative has been selected, it must be implemented, and many subsequent and related decisions must be made. After a course of action has been decided—say, to develop a new line of women's clothing—thousands of subsequent decisions are necessary to implement it. These decisions would involve recruiting dress designers, obtaining fabrics, finding high-quality manufacturers, and signing contracts with clothing stores to sell the new line.

Although the need to make subsequent decisions to implement the chosen course of action may seem obvious, many managers make a decision and then fail to act on it. This is the same as not making a decision at all. To ensure that a decision is implemented, top managers must assign to middle managers the responsibility for making the follow-up decisions necessary to achieve the goal. They must give middle managers sufficient resources to achieve the goal, and they must hold the middle managers accountable for their performance. If the middle managers are successful at implementing the decision, they should be rewarded; if they fail, they should be subject to sanctions.

Learn from Feedback

The final step in the decision-making process is learning from feedback. Effective managers always conduct a retrospective analysis to see what they can learn from past successes or failures.[73] Managers who do not evaluate the results of their decisions do not learn from experience; instead, they stagnate and are likely to make the same mistakes again and again.[74] To avoid this problem, managers must establish a formal procedure with which they can learn from the results of past decisions. The procedure should include these steps:

1. Compare what actually happened to what was expected to happen as a result of the decision.
2. Explore why any expectations for the decision were not met.
3. Derive guidelines that will help in future decision making.

Managers who always strive to learn from past mistakes and successes are likely to continuously improve the decisions they make. A significant amount of learning can take place when the outcomes of decisions are evaluated, and this assessment can produce enormous benefits.

Management Insight

Decision Making and Learning from Feedback at GarageTek

Decision making has been an ongoing challenge for Marc Shuman, founder and president of GarageTek, headquartered in Syosset, New York.[75] Since founding his company less than 12 years ago, he has met this challenge time and time again, recognizing when decisions need to be made and learning from feedback about prior decisions.

Shuman was working with his father in a small business, designing and building interiors of department stores, when he created and installed a series of wall panels with flexible shelving for a store to display its merchandise. When he realized that some of his employees were using the same concept in their own homes to organize the clutter in their basements and garages, he recognized that he had a potential opportunity to start a new business, GarageTek, designing and installing custom garage systems to organize and maximize storage capacities and uses for home garage space.[76]

Schuman decided to franchise his idea, as he feared that other entrepreneurs were probably having similar thoughts and competition could be around the corner.[77] Within three years, GarageTek had 57 franchises in 33 states contributing revenues to the home office of around $12 million. While this would seem to be an enviable track record of success,

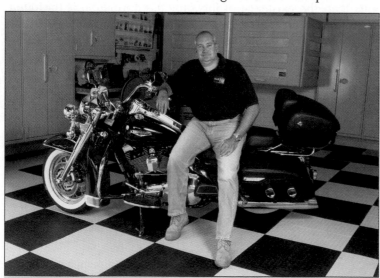

Marc Shuman, founder of GarageTek, recognizes when decisions need to be made and learns from feedback about prior decisions.

Shuman recognized that although many of the franchises were succeeding, some were having very serious problems. With the help of a consulting company, Shuman and home office managers set about trying to figure out why some of the franchises were failing. They gathered detailed information about each franchise, ranging from the market served, pricing strategies, costs, managerial talent, and franchisee investment. From this information, Shuman learned that the struggling franchises tended either to have lower levels of capital investment behind them or to be managed by nonowners.[78]

Shuman learned from this experience. He now has new decision criteria for accepting new franchisees to help ensure that their investments of time and money lead to a successful franchise.[79] Shuman also decided to give new franchisees much more training and support than he had in the past. Now, new franchises receive two weeks of training at the home office; on-site assistance in sales, marketing, and operations; a multivolume training manual; a sales and marketing kit; and access to databases and GarageTek's intranet. Franchisees learn from each other through monthly conference calls and regional and national meetings. For Shuman, however, making good decisions and learning from prior ones are still an ongoing challenge; in his words, "We're not, by any stretch, done."[80]

Cognitive Biases and Decision Making

heuristics Rules of thumb that simplify decision making.

systematic errors Errors that people make over and over and that result in poor decision making.

In the 1970s psychologists Daniel Kahneman and Amos Tversky suggested that because all decision makers are subject to bounded rationality, they tend to use **heuristics,** rules of thumb that simplify the process of making decisions.[81] Kahneman and Tversky argued that rules of thumb are often useful because they help decision makers make sense of complex, uncertain, and ambiguous information. Sometimes, however, the use of heuristics can lead to systematic errors in the way decision makers process information about alternatives and make decisions. **Systematic errors** are errors that people make over and over and that result in poor decision making. Because of cognitive biases, which are caused by systematic errors, otherwise-capable managers may end up making bad decisions.[82] Four sources of bias that can adversely affect the way managers make decisions are prior hypotheses, representativeness, the illusion of control, and escalating commitment (see Figure 7.6).

Prior-Hypothesis Bias

prior-hypothesis bias A cognitive bias resulting from the tendency to base decisions on strong prior beliefs even if evidence shows that those beliefs are wrong.

Decision makers who have strong prior beliefs about the relationship between two variables tend to make decisions based on those beliefs *even when presented with evidence that their beliefs are wrong.* In doing so, they are falling victim to **prior-hypothesis bias.** Moreover, decision makers tend to seek and use information that is consistent with their prior beliefs and to ignore information that contradicts those beliefs.

Figure 7.6
Sources of Cognitive Bias at the Individual and Group Levels

Representativeness Bias

representativeness bias
A cognitive bias resulting from the tendency to generalize inappropriately from a small sample or from a single vivid event or episode.

Many decision makers inappropriately generalize from a small sample or even from a single vivid case or episode. An interesting example of the **representativeness bias** occurred after World War II, when Sewell Avery, the CEO of Montgomery Ward, shelved plans for national expansion to meet competition from Sears because he believed there would be a depression after the war. The basis for Avery's belief was the occurrence of the Great Depression after World War I. However, there was no second Great Depression, and Avery's poor decision allowed Sears to establish itself as the number-one nationwide retailer. Avery's mistake was generalizing from the post-World War I experience and assuming that "depressions always follow wars."

Illusion of Control

illusion of control A source of cognitive bias resulting from the tendency to overestimate one's own ability to control activities and events.

Other errors in decision making result from the **illusion of control,** the tendency of decision makers to overestimate their ability to control activities and events. Top-level managers seem to be particularly prone to this bias. Having worked their way to the top of an organization, they tend to have an exaggerated sense of their own worth and are overconfident about their ability to succeed and to control events.[83] The illusion of control causes managers to overestimate the odds of a favorable outcome and, consequently, to make inappropriate decisions. For example, Nissan used to be controlled by Katsuji Kawamata, an autocratic CEO who thought he had the ability to run the car company single-handedly. He made all the decisions, some of which resulted in a series of spectacular mistakes, including changing the company's name from Datsun to Nissan.

escalating commitment
A source of cognitive bias resulting from the tendency to commit additional resources to a project even if evidence shows that the project is failing.

Escalating Commitment

Having already committed significant resources to a course of action, some managers commit more resources to the project *even if they receive feedback that the project is failing.*[84]

The 1986 disastrous take-off of the space shuttle *Challenger.*

Feelings of personal responsibility for a project apparently bias the analysis of decision makers and lead to this **escalating commitment.** The managers decide to increase their investment of time and money in a course of action and ignore evidence that it is illegal, unethical, uneconomical, or impractical (see Figure 7.5). Often, the more appropriate decision would be to cut their losses and run.

A tragic example of where escalating commitment can lead is the *Challenger* disaster. Apparently, managers at both NASA and Morton Thiokol were so anxious to keep the shuttle program on schedule that they ignored or discounted any evidence that would slow the program down. Thus, the information offered by two Thiokol engineers, who warned about O-ring failure in cold weather, was discounted, and the shuttle was launched on a chilly day in January 1986.

Another example of escalating commitment occurred during the 1960s and 1970s when large U.S. steelmakers responded to low-cost competition from minimills and foreign steelmakers by increasing their investments in the technologically obsolete steelmaking facilities they already possessed, rather than investing in new, cutting-edge technology.[85] This decision was irrational because investment in obsolete technology would never enable them to lower their costs and compete successfully. Similarly, overly optimistic top managers at Lucent Technologies escalated their commitment to growth, engaging in practices like discounting and vendor loans that ultimately may have hurt organizational performance.[86]

Be Aware of Your Biases

How can managers avoid the negative effects of cognitive biases and improve their decision-making and problem-solving abilities? Managers must become aware of biases and their effects, and they must identify their own personal style of making decisions.[87] One useful way for managers to analyze their decision-making style is to review two decisions that they made recently—one decision that turned out well and one that turned out poorly. Problem-solving experts recommend that managers start by determining how much time to spend on each of the decision-making steps, such as gathering information to identify the pros and cons of alternatives or ranking the alternatives, to make sure that they spend sufficient time on each step.[88]

Another recommended technique for examining decision-making style is for managers to list the criteria they typically use to assess and evaluate alternatives—the heuristics (rules of thumb) they typically employ, their personal biases, and so on—and then critically evaluate the appropriateness of these different factors.

Many individual managers are likely to have difficulty identifying their own biases, so it is often advisable for managers to scrutinize their own assumptions by working with other managers to help expose weaknesses in their decision-making style. In this context, the issue of group decision making becomes important.

Group Decision Making

LO3 Identify the advantages and disadvantages of group decision making, and describe techniques that can improve it.

Many, perhaps most, important organizational decisions are made by groups or teams of managers rather than by individuals. Group decision making is superior to individual decision making in several respects. When managers work as a team to make decisions and solve problems, their choices of alternatives are less likely to fall victim to the biases and errors discussed previously. They are able to draw on the combined skills, competencies, and accumulated knowledge of group members and thereby improve their ability to generate feasible alternatives and make good decisions. Group decision making also allows managers to process more information and to correct one another's errors. And in the implementation phase, all managers affected by the decisions agree to cooperate. When a group of managers makes a decision (as opposed to one top manager making a decision and imposing it on subordinate managers), the probability that the decision will be implemented successfully increases. (We discuss how to encourage employee participation in decision making in Chapter 13.)

There are some potential disadvantages associated with group decision making. Groups often take much longer than individuals to make decisions. Getting two or more managers to agree to the same solution can be difficult because managers' interests and preferences are often different. In addition, just like decision making by individual managers, group decision making can be undermined by biases. A major source of group bias is *groupthink*.

The Perils of Groupthink

groupthink A pattern of faulty and biased decision making that occurs in groups whose members strive for agreement among themselves at the expense of accurately assessing information relevant to a decision.

Groupthink is a pattern of faulty and biased decision making that occurs in groups whose members strive for agreement among themselves at the expense of accurately assessing information relevant to a decision.[89] When managers are subject to groupthink, they collectively embark on a course of action without developing appropriate criteria to evaluate alternatives. Typically, a group rallies around one central manager, such as the CEO, and the course of action that manager supports. Group members become blindly committed to that course of action without evaluating its merits.

Commitment is often based on an emotional, rather than an objective, assessment of the optimal course of action.

The decision President Kennedy and his advisers made to launch the unfortunate Bay of Pigs invasion in Cuba in 1962, the decisions made by President Johnson and his advisers from 1964 to 1967 to escalate the war in Vietnam, the decision made by President Nixon and his advisers in 1972 to cover up the Watergate break-in, and the decision made by NASA and Morton Thiokol in 1986 to launch the ill-fated *Challenger* shuttle—all were likely influenced by groupthink. After the fact, decision makers such as these who may fall victim to groupthink are often surprised that their decision-making process and outcomes were so flawed.

When groupthink occurs, pressures for agreement and harmony within a group have the unintended effect of discouraging individuals from raising issues that run counter to majority opinion. For example, when managers at NASA and Morton Thiokol fell victim to groupthink, they convinced each other that all was well and that there was no need to delay the launch of the *Challenger* space shuttle.

Devil's Advocacy and Dialectical Inquiry

The existence of cognitive biases and groupthink raises the question of how to improve the quality of group and individual decision making so that managers make decisions that are realistic and are based on a thorough evaluation of alternatives. Two techniques known to counteract groupthink and cognitive biases are devil's advocacy and dialectic inquiry (see Figure 7.7).[90]

Devil's advocacy is a critical analysis of a preferred alternative to ascertain its strengths and weaknesses before it is implemented.[91] Typically, one member of the decision-making group plays the role of devil's advocate. The devil's advocate critiques and challenges the way the group evaluated alternatives and chose one over the others. The purpose of devil's advocacy is to identify all the reasons that might make the preferred alternative unacceptable after all. In this way, decision makers can be made aware of the possible perils of recommended courses of action.

Dialectical inquiry goes one step further. Two groups of managers are assigned to a problem, and each group is responsible for evaluating alternatives and selecting one of them.[92] Top managers hear each group present its preferred alternative, and then each group critiques the other's position. During this debate, top managers challenge both groups' positions to uncover potential problems and perils associated with their solutions. The goal is to find an even better alternative course of action for the organization to adopt.

devil's advocacy Critical analysis of a preferred alternative, made in response to challenges raised by a group member who, playing the role of devil's advocate, defends unpopular or opposing alternatives for the sake of argument.

dialectical inquiry Critical analysis of two preferred alternatives in order to find an even better alternative for the organization to adopt.

Figure 7.7

Devil's Advocacy and Dialectical Inquiry

Both devil's advocacy and dialectical inquiry can help counter the effects of cognitive biases and groupthink.[93] In practice, devil's advocacy is probably the easier method to implement because it involves less commitment in managerial time and effort than does dialectical inquiry.

Diversity Among Decision Makers

Another way to improve group decision making is to promote diversity in decision-making groups (see Chapter 4).[94] Bringing together managers of both genders from various ethnic, national, and functional backgrounds broadens the range of life experiences and opinions that group members can draw on as they generate, assess, and choose among alternatives. Moreover, diverse groups are sometimes less prone to groupthink because group members already differ from each other and thus are less subject to pressures for uniformity.

Organizational Learning and Creativity

The quality of managerial decision making ultimately depends on innovative responses to opportunities and threats. How can managers increase their ability to make nonprogrammed decisions, decisions that will allow them to adapt to, modify, and even drastically alter their task environments so that they can continually increase organizational performance? The answer is by encouraging organizational learning.[95]

LO4 Explain the role that organizational learning and creativity play in helping managers to improve their decisions.

Organizational learning is the process through which managers seek to improve employees' desire and ability to understand and manage the organization and its task environment so that employees can make decisions that continuously raise organizational effectiveness.[96] A **learning organization** is one in which managers do everything possible to maximize the ability of individuals and groups to think and behave creatively and thus maximize the potential for organizational learning to take place. At the heart of organizational learning is **creativity,** the ability of a decision maker to discover original and novel ideas that lead to feasible alternative courses of action. Encouraging creativity among managers is such a pressing organizational concern that many organizations hire outside experts to help them develop programs to train their managers in the art of creative thinking and problem solving.

organizational learning The process through which managers seek to improve employees' desire and ability to understand and manage the organization and its task environment.

learning organization An organization in which managers try to maximize the ability of individuals and groups to think and behave creatively and thus maximize the potential for organizational learning to take place.

creativity A decision maker's ability to discover original and novel ideas that lead to feasible alternative courses of action.

Creating a Learning Organization

How do managers go about creating a learning organization? Learning theorist Peter Senge identified five principles for creating a learning organization (see Figure 7.8):[97]

1. For organizational learning to occur, top managers must allow every person in the organization to develop a sense of *personal mastery*. Managers must empower employees and allow them to experiment and create and explore what they want.

2. As part of attaining personal mastery, organizations need to encourage employees to develop and use *complex mental models*–sophisticated ways of thinking that challenge them to find new or better ways of performing a task–to deepen their understanding of what is involved in a particular activity. Here Senge is arguing that managers must encourage employees to develop a taste for experimenting and risk taking.[98]

3. Managers must do everything they can to promote group creativity. Senge thinks that *team learning* (learning that takes place in a group or team) is more important than individual learning in increasing organizational learning. He points out that most important decisions are made in subunits such as groups, functions, and divisions.

4. Managers must emphasize the importance of *building a shared vision*–a common mental model that all organizational members use to frame problems or opportunities.

Figure 7.8
Senge's Principles for Creating a Learning Organization

5. Managers must encourage *systems thinking* (a concept drawn from systems theory, discussed in Chapter 2). Senge emphasizes that to create a learning organization, managers must recognize the effects of one level of learning on another. Thus, for example, there is little point in creating teams to facilitate team learning if managers do not also take steps to give employees the freedom to develop a sense of personal mastery.

Building a learning organization requires that managers change their management assumptions radically. Developing a learning organization is neither a quick nor an easy process. Senge has been working with Ford Motor Company to help managers make Ford a learning organization. Why does Ford want this? Top management believes that to compete successfully, Ford must improve its members' ability to be creative and make the right decisions.

Increasingly, managers are being called on to promote global organizational learning. For example, managers at Wal-Mart use the lessons derived from its failures and successes in one country to promote global organizational learning across the many countries in which it now operates. For instance, when Wal-Mart entered Malaysia, it was convinced customers there would respond to its one-stop shopping format. It found, however, that Malaysians enjoy the social experience of shopping in a lively market or bazaar and thus did not like the impersonal efficiency of the typical Wal-Mart store. As a result, Wal-Mart has learned the importance of designing store layouts to appeal specifically to the customers of each country in which it operates.

When purchasing and operating a chain of stores in another country, such as the British ASDA chain, Wal-Mart now strives to retain what customers value in the local market while taking advantage of all of its own accumulated organizational learning. For example, Wal-Mart improved ASDA's information technology used for inventory and sales tracking in stores and enrolled ASDA in Wal-Mart's global purchasing operations, which has enabled the chain to pay less for certain products, sell them for less, and, overall, significantly increase sales. At the same time, Wal-Mart empowered local ASDA managers to run the stores; as the president of ASDA indicates, "This is still essentially a British business in the way it's run day to day."[99] Clearly, global organizational learning is essential for companies such as Wal-Mart that have significant operations in multiple countries.

Promoting Individual Creativity

Research suggests that when certain conditions are met, managers are more likely to be creative. People must be given the opportunity and freedom to generate new ideas.[100] Creativity declines when managers look over the shoulders of talented employees and try to "hurry up" a creative solution. How would you feel if your boss said you had one week to come up with a new product idea to beat the competition? Creativity results when employees have an opportunity to experiment, to take risks, and to make mistakes and learn from them. And employees must not fear that they will be looked down on or penalized for ideas that might at first seem outlandish, as it is sometimes those ideas that yield truly innovative products and services.[101] Highly innovative companies such as Google, Apple, and Facebook are well known for the wide degree of freedom they give their managers and employees to experiment and develop innovative goods and services.[102]

Once managers have generated alternatives, creativity can be fostered by providing them with constructive feedback so that they know how well they are doing. Ideas that seem to be going nowhere can be eliminated and creative energies refocused in other directions. Ideas that seem promising can be promoted, and help from other managers can be obtained as well.[103]

Top managers must stress the importance of looking for alternative solutions and should visibly reward employees who come up with creative ideas. Being creative can be demanding and stressful. Employees who believe that they are working on important, vital issues are motivated to put forth the high levels of effort that creativity demands. Creative people like to receive the acclaim of others, and innovative organizations have many kinds of ceremonies and rewards to recognize creative employees.

Promoting Group Creativity

To encourage creativity at the group level, organizations can make use of group problem-solving techniques that promote creative ideas and innovative solutions. These techniques can also be used to prevent groupthink and to help managers uncover biases. Here, we look at three group decision-making techniques: *brainstorming*, the *nominal group technique*, and the *Delphi technique*.

production blocking
A loss of productivity in brainstorming sessions due to the unstructured nature of brainstorming.

BRAINSTORMING *Brainstorming* is a group problem-solving technique in which managers meet face-to-face to generate and debate a wide variety of alternatives from which to make a decision.[104] Generally, from 5 to 15 managers meet in a closed-door session and proceed like this:

These ad agency employees are conducting a brainstorming session. Brainstorming can be used to generate multiple ideas and solutions for problems.

- One manager describes in broad outline the problem the group is to address.

- Group members then share their ideas and generate alternative courses of action.

- As each alternative is described, group members are not allowed to criticize it; everyone withholds judgment until all alternatives have been heard. One member of the group records the alternatives on a flip chart.

- Group members are encouraged to be as innovative and radical as possible. Anything goes; and the greater the number of ideas put forth, the better. Moreover, group members are encouraged to "piggyback" or build on each other's suggestions.

- When all alternatives have been generated, group members debate the pros and cons of each and develop a short list of the best alternatives.

Brainstorming is very useful in some problem-solving situations—for example, when managers are trying to find a new name for a perfume or for a model of car. But sometimes individuals working alone can generate more alternatives. The main reason for the loss of productivity in brainstorming appears to be **production blocking,** which occurs because group members cannot always simultaneously make sense of all the alternatives being generated, think up additional alternatives, and remember what they were thinking.[105]

nominal group technique
A decision-making technique in which group members write down ideas and solutions, read their suggestions to the whole group, and discuss and then rank the alternatives.

NOMINAL GROUP TECHNIQUE To avoid production blocking, the **nominal group technique** is often used. It provides a more structured way of generating alternatives in writing and gives each manager more time and opportunity to come up with potential solutions. The nominal group technique is especially useful when an issue is controversial and when different managers might be expected to champion different courses of action. Generally, a small group of managers meet in a closed-door session and adopt the following procedures:

- One manager outlines the problem to be addressed, and 30 or 40 minutes are allocated for group members, working individually, to write down their ideas and solutions. Group members are encouraged to be innovative.

- Managers take turns reading their suggestions to the group. One manager writes all the alternatives on a flip chart. No criticism or evaluation of alternatives is allowed until all alternatives have been read.

- The alternatives are then discussed, one by one, in the sequence in which they were first proposed. Group members can ask for clarifying information and critique each alternative to identify its pros and cons.

- When all alternatives have been discussed, each group member ranks all the alternatives from most preferred to least preferred, and the alternative that receives the highest ranking is chosen.[106]

delphi technique
A decision-making technique in which group members do not meet face-to-face but respond in writing to questions posed by the group leader.

entrepreneur An individual who notices opportunities and decides how to mobilize the resources necessary to produce new and improved goods and services.

social entrepreneur An individual who pursues initiatives and opportunities and mobilizes resources to address social problems and needs in order to improve society and well-being through creative solutions.

DELPHI TECHNIQUE Both the nominal group technique and brainstorming require that managers meet together to generate creative ideas and engage in joint problem solving. What happens if managers are in different cities or in different parts of the world and cannot meet face-to-face? Videoconferencing is one way to bring distant managers together to brainstorm. Another way is to use the **Delphi technique,** a written approach to creative problem solving.[107] The Delphi technique works like this:

- The group leader writes a statement of the problem and a series of questions to which participating managers are to respond.

- The questionnaire is sent to the managers and departmental experts who are most knowledgeable about the problem. They are asked to generate solutions and mail the questionnaire back to the group leader.

- A team of top managers records and summarizes the responses. The results are then sent back to the participants, with additional questions to be answered before a decision can be made.

- The process is repeated until a consensus is reached and the most suitable course of action is apparent.

Entrepreneurship and Creativity

LO5 Describe how managers can encourage and promote entrepreneurship to create a learning organization, and differentiate between entrepreneurs and intrapreneurs.

Entrepreneurs are individuals who notice opportunities and decide how to mobilize the resources necessary to produce new and improved goods and services. Entrepreneurs make all of the planning, organizing, leading, and controlling decisions necessary to start new business ventures. Thus, entrepreneurs are an important source of creativity in the organizational world. These people are the David Filo's and Jerry Yang's (founders of Yahoo!) of the world, who make vast fortunes when their businesses succeed. Or they are among the millions of people who start new business ventures only to lose their money when they fail. Despite the fact that an estimated 80% of small businesses fail in the first three to five years, by some estimates 38% of men and 50% of women in today's workforce want to start their own companies.[108]

Social entrepreneurs are individuals who pursue initiatives and opportunities to address social problems and needs in order to improve society and well-being, such as reducing poverty, increasing literacy, protecting the natural environment, or reducing substance abuse.[109] Social entrepreneurs seek to mobilize resources to solve social problems through creative solutions.[110]

As indicated in the following "Ethics in Action," while social entrepreneurs often face challenges in raising funds to support their initiatives, their options are increasing.

Ethics in Action

Small Business

Finding Funding to Do Good

Typically, venture capitalists who provide funding for entrepreneurs to start their businesses are concerned with getting a good return on their investment and not having to wait a long time to do so and banks expect entrepreneurs to have a prior track record of success. For social entrepreneurs, this can make raising funds to support their new ventures a real challenge as achieving their social goals are of paramount importance. Fortunately, an increasing number of social venture funds seek to invest in companies that are focused on social goals.[111]

World of Good is a San Francisco Bay Area start-up that creates opportunities for thousands of producers in the developing world by bringing their products to the mainstream consumer market. Through their network of more than 1,200 retail outlets, their signature product line (Original Good) and their new online marketplace for People-Positive and Eco-Positive products (www.worldofgood com), they seek to create a global network of entrepreneurs in the informal sector, uplifted by their direct access to large-scale markets and empowered through the use of ethical wage standards.

When Priya Haji, the company's cofounder and CEO, initially sought funding for her venture, she had to look beyond traditional banks, who weren't interested because she didn't have a three-year track record.[112] "For them, it didn't make sense," Haji says. "There is a consumer driven demand for this kind of ethical consumption, but the debt markets don't understand that." Instead, Haji turned to social lenders, and in 2006, reached a deal with three of them: RSF Social Finance, Root Capital, and Shared Interest, each of whom insist that portfolio companies maintain their social missions as they grow.[113] Their investment paid off – the company has doubled revenues every year since.

When Charlie Crystle sought funding for Mission Research, the new social enterprise he cofounded, which provides nonprofits with fundraising software, traditional investors questioned some of Mission's practices, such as giving the software away for free to nonprofits with annual budgets less than $25,000 and even the fact that he was starting a business focused on selling to nonprofits in the first place.[114] Crystle was able to secure $300,000 in funding from Underdog Ventures in return for a 5% share in the company. Unlike other venture capital firms that aim to sell their stake in new ventures within 5–7 years, Underdog is willing to wait 7–8 years and also requires that companies it invests in get prior approval from Underdog if they want to change their social mission.[115]

World of Good and Mission Research have both experienced substantial revenue growth since receiving funding from social investors.[116] Of equal importance, they also are achieving their social goals, which is a prime reason they were founded in the first place. As Crystle indicates, "I focus on building my business and building revenues. . . . But it's not the reason I get up every morning and go to work."[117]

Priya Haji, founder of World of Good, Inc.,

Many managers, scientists, and researchers employed by companies engage in entre-preneurial activity, and they are an important source of organizational creativity. They are involved in innovation, developing new and improved products and ways to make them, which we describe in detail in Chapter 9. Such employees notice oppor-tunities for either quantum or incremental product improvements and are respon-sible for managing the product development process. These individuals are known as **intrapreneurs,** to distinguish them from entrepreneurs who start their own busi-nesses. But, in general, entrepreneurship involves creative decision making that pro-vides customers with new or improved goods and services.

There is an interesting relationship between entrepreneurs and intrapreneurs. Many managers with intrapreneurial talents become dissatisfied if their superiors decide neither to support nor to fund new product ideas and development efforts that the managers think will succeed. What do intrapreneurial managers who feel that they are getting nowhere do? Very often they decide to leave their current organizations and start their own companies to take advantage of their new product ideas! In other words, intrapreneurs become entrepreneurs and found companies that often compete with the companies they left. To avoid losing these individuals, top managers must find ways to facilitate the entrepreneurial spirit of their most creative employees. In the remainder of this section we consider issues involved in promoting successful entrepreneurship in both new and existing organizations.

> **intrapreneur** A manager, scientist, or researcher who works inside an organization and notices opportunities to develop new or improved products and better ways to make them.

Entrepreneurship and New Ventures

The fact that a significant number of entrepreneurs were frustrated intrapreneurs pro-vides a clue about the personal characteristics of people who are likely to start a new venture and bear all the uncertainty and risk associated with being an entrepreneur.

CHARACTERISTICS OF ENTREPRENEURS   Entrepreneurs are likely to possess a particular set of the personality characteristics we discussed in Chapter 4. First, they are likely to be high on the personality trait of *openness to experience,* meaning that they are predisposed to be original, to be open to a wide range of stimuli, to be daring, and to take risks. Entrepreneurs also are likely to have an *internal locus of control,* believing that they are responsible for what happens to them and that their own actions deter-mine important outcomes such as the success or failure of a new business. People with an external locus of control, in contrast, would be very unlikely to leave a secure job in an organization and assume the risk associated with a new venture.

Entrepreneurs are likely to have a high level of *self-esteem* and feel competent and capable of handling most situations—including the stress and uncertainty surrounding a plunge into a risky new venture. Entrepreneurs are also likely to have a high *need for achievement* and have a strong desire to perform challenging tasks and meet high personal standards of excellence.

ENTREPRENEURSHIP AND MANAGEMENT   Given that entrepreneurs are predisposed to activities that are somewhat adventurous and risky, in what ways can people become involved in entrepreneurial ventures? One way is to start a business from scratch. Taking advantage of mod-ern IT, many people are starting solo ventures. The total number of small-office and home-office workers is more than 40 million, and each year more than a million new solo entrepreneurs join the ranks of the more than 29 million self-employed.

When people who go it alone succeed, they frequently need to hire other people to help them run the business. Michael Dell, for example, began his computer business as a college student and within weeks had hired several people to help him to assemble computers from the component

Intrapreneurs are an important source of organizational creativity.

parts he bought from suppliers. From his solo venture grew Dell Computer, one of the largest PC makers in the world today.

Some entrepreneurs who found a new business often have difficulty deciding how to manage the organization as it grows; **entrepreneurship** is *not* the same as management. Management encompasses all the decisions involved in planning, organizing, leading, and controlling resources. Entrepreneurship is noticing an opportunity to satisfy a customer need and then deciding how to find and use resources to make a product that satisfies that need. When an entrepreneur has produced something that customers want, entrepreneurship gives way to management, as the pressing need becomes providing the product both efficiently and effectively. Frequently, a founding entrepreneur lacks the skills, patience, and experience to engage in the difficult and challenging work of management. Some entrepreneurs find it very hard to delegate authority because they are afraid to risk their company by letting others manage it. As a result, they become overloaded, and the quality of their decision making declines. Other entrepreneurs lack the detailed knowledge necessary to establish state-of-the-art information systems and technology or to create the operations management procedures that are vital to increase the efficiency of their organizations' production systems. Thus, to succeed, it is necessary to do more than create a new product; an entrepreneur must hire managers who can create an operating system that will let a new venture survive and prosper.

entrepreneurship The mobilization of resources to take advantage of an opportunity to provide customers with new or improved goods and services.

Intrapreneurship and Organizational Learning

The intensity of competition today, particularly from agile, small companies, has made it increasingly important for large, established organizations to promote and encourage intrapreneurship to raise the level of innovation and organizational learning. As we discussed earlier, a learning organization encourages all employees to identify opportunities and solve problems, thus enabling the organization to continuously experiment, improve, and increase its ability to provide customers with new and improved goods and services. The higher the level of intrapreneurship, the higher will be the level of learning and innovation. How can organizations promote organizational learning and intrapreneurship?

PRODUCT CHAMPIONS One way to promote intrapreneurship is to encourage individuals to assume the role of **product champion,** a manager who takes "ownership" of a project and provides the leadership and vision that take a product from the idea stage to the final customer. 3M, a company well known for its attempts to promote intrapreneurship, encourages all its managers to become product champions and identify new product ideas. A product champion becomes responsible for developing a business plan for the product. Armed with this business plan, the champion appears before 3M's product development committee, a team of senior 3M managers who probe the strengths and weaknesses of the plan to decide whether it should be funded. If the plan is accepted, the product champion assumes responsibility for product development.

product champion A manager who takes "ownership" of a project and provides the leadership and vision that take a product from the idea stage to the final customer.

SKUNKWORKS The idea behind the product champion role is that employees who feel ownership for a project are inclined to act like outside entrepreneurs and go to great lengths to make the project succeed. Using skunkworks and new venture divisions can also strengthen this feeling of ownership. A **skunkworks** is a group of intrapreneurs who are deliberately separated from the normal operation of an organization—for example, from the normal chain of command—to encourage them to devote all their attention to developing new products. The idea is that if these people are isolated, they will become so intensely involved in a project that development time will be relatively brief and the quality of the final product will be enhanced. The term *skunkworks* was coined at the Lockheed Corporation, which formed a team of design engineers to develop special aircraft such as the U2 spy plane. The secrecy

skunkworks A group of intrapreneurs who are deliberately separated from the normal operation of an organization to encourage them to devote all their attention to developing new products.

with which this unit functioned and speculation about its goals led others to refer to it as "the skunkworks."

REWARDS FOR INNOVATION   To encourage managers to bear the uncertainty and risk associated with the hard work of entrepreneurship, it is necessary to link performance to rewards. Increasingly, companies are rewarding intrapreneurs on the basis of the outcome of the product development process. Intrapreneurs are granted large bonuses if their projects succeed, or they are granted stock options that can make them millionaires if the product sells well. Both Microsoft and Google, for example, have made hundreds of their employees multimillionaires as a result of the stock options they were granted as part of their reward packages. In addition to receiving money, successful intrapreneurs can expect to receive promotion to the ranks of top management. Most of 3M's top managers, for example, reached the executive suite because they had a track record of successful entrepreneurship. Organizations must reward intrapreneurs equitably if they wish to prevent them from leaving and becoming outside entrepreneurs who might form a competitive new venture. Nevertheless, intrapreneurs frequently do so.

Summary and Review

THE NATURE OF MANAGERIAL DECISION MAKING   Programmed decisions are routine decisions made so often that managers have developed decision rules to be followed automatically. Nonprogrammed decisions are made in response to situations that are unusual or novel; they are nonroutine decisions. The classical

LO1   model of decision making assumes that decision makers have complete information, are able to process that information in an objective, rational manner, and make optimum decisions. March and Simon argue that managers are boundedly rational, rarely have access to all the information they need to make optimum decisions, and consequently satisfice and rely on their intuition and judgment when making decisions.

LO2   **STEPS IN THE DECISION-MAKING PROCESS**   When making decisions, managers should take these six steps: recognize the need for a decision, generate alternatives, assess alternatives, choose among alternatives, implement the chosen alternative, and learn from feedback.

LO2   **COGNITIVE BIASES AND DECISION MAKING**   Most of the time, managers are fairly good decision makers. On occasion, however, problems can result because human judgment can be adversely affected by the operation of cognitive biases that result in poor decisions. Cognitive biases are caused by systematic errors in the way decision makers process information and make decisions. Sources of these errors include prior hypotheses, representativeness, the illusion of control, and escalating commitment. Managers should undertake a personal decision audit to become aware of their biases and thus improve their decision making.

LO3   **GROUP DECISION MAKING**   Many advantages are associated with group decision making, but there are also several disadvantages. One major source of poor decision making is groupthink. Afflicted decision makers collectively embark on a dubious course of action without questioning the assumptions that underlie their decision. Managers can improve the quality of group decision making by using techniques such as devil's advocacy and dialectical inquiry and by increasing diversity in the decision-making group.

LO4   **ORGANIZATIONAL LEARNING AND CREATIVITY**   Organizational learning is the process through which managers seek to improve employees' desire and ability to understand and manage the organization and its task environment so that employees can make decisions that continuously raise organizational effectiveness. Managers must take steps to promote organizational learning and creativity at the individual and group levels to improve the quality of decision making.

LO5   **ENTREPRENEURSHIP**   Entrepreneurship is the mobilization of resources to take advantage of an opportunity to provide customers with new or improved goods and services. Entrepreneurs find new ventures of their own. Intrapreneurs work inside organizations and manage the product development process. Organizations need to encourage intrapreneurship because it leads to organizational learning and innovation.

Management in Action

Topics for Discussion and Action

DISCUSSION

1. What are the main differences between programmed decision making and nonprogrammed decision making? **[LO1]**

2. In what ways do the classical and administrative models of decision making help managers appreciate the complexities of real-world decision making? **[LO1]**

3. Why do capable managers sometimes make bad decisions? What can individual managers do to improve their decision-making skills? **[LO 1, 2]**

4. In what kinds of groups is groupthink most likely to be a problem? When is it least likely to be a problem? What steps can group members take to ward off groupthink? **[LO3]**

5. What is organizational learning, and how can managers promote it? **[LO4]**

6. What is the difference between entrepreneurship and intrapreneurship? **[LO5]**

ACTION

7. Ask a manager to recall the best and the worst decisions he or she ever made. Try to determine why these decisions were so good or so bad. **[LO 1, 2, 3]**

8. Think about an organization in your local community, your university, or an organization that you are familiar with that is doing poorly. Now think of questions managers in the organization should ask stakeholders to elicit creative ideas for turning around the organization's fortunes. **[LO4]**

Building Management Skills [LO 1, 2, 4]
How Do You Make Decisions?

Pick a decision that you made recently and that has had important consequences for you. It may be your decision about which college to attend, which major to select, whether to take a part-time job, or which part-time job to take. Using the material in this chapter, analyze the way in which you made the decision. In particular:

1. Identify the criteria you used, either consciously or unconsciously, to guide your decision making.

2. List the alternatives you considered. Were they all possible alternatives? Did you unconsciously (or consciously) ignore some important alternatives?

3. How much information did you have about each alternative? Were you making the decision on the basis of complete or incomplete information?

4. Try to remember how you reached the decision. Did you sit down and consciously think through the implications of each alternative, or did you make the decision on the basis of intuition? Did you use any rules of thumb to help you make the decision?

5. In retrospect, do you think that your choice of alternative was shaped by any of the cognitive biases discussed in this chapter?

6. Having answered the previous five questions, do you think in retrospect that you made a reasonable decision? What, if anything, might you do to improve your ability to make good decisions in the future?

Managing Ethically [LO3]

Sometimes groups make extreme decisions—decisions that are either more risky or more conservative than they would have been if individuals acting alone had made them. One explanation for the tendency of groups to make extreme decisions is diffusion of responsibility. In a group, responsibility for the outcomes of a decision is spread among group members, so each person feels less than fully accountable. The group's decision is extreme because no individual has taken full responsibility for it.

Questions

1. Either alone or in a group, think about the ethical implications of extreme decision making by groups.

2. When group decision making takes place, should members of a group each feel fully accountable for outcomes of the decision? Why or why not?

Small Group Breakout Exercise [LO 3, 4]

Brainstorming

Form groups of three or four people, and appoint one member as the spokesperson who will communicate your findings to the class when called on by the instructor. Then discuss the following scenario.

You and your partners are trying to decide which kind of restaurant to open in a centrally located shopping center that has just been built in your city. The problem confronting you is that the city already has many restaurants that provide different kinds of food at all price ranges. You have the resources to open any type of restaurant. Your challenge is to decide which type is most likely to succeed.

Use the brainstorming technique to decide which type of restaurant to open. Follow these steps:

1. As a group, spend 5 or 10 minutes generating ideas about the alternative restaurants that the members think will be most likely to succeed. Each group member should be as innovative and creative as possible, and no suggestions should be criticized.

2. Appoint one group member to write down the alternatives as they are identified.

3. Spend the next 10 or 15 minutes debating the pros and cons of the alternatives. As a group, try to reach a consensus on which alternative is most likely to succeed.

After making your decision, discuss the pros and cons of the brainstorming method, and decide whether any production blocking occurred.

When called on by the instructor, the spokesperson should be prepared to share your group's decision with the class, as well as the reasons the group made its decision.

Exploring the World Wide Web [LO4]

Go to www.brainstorming.co.uk. This Web site contains "Training on Creativity Techniques" and "Creativity Puzzles." Spend at least 30 minutes on the training and/or puzzles. Think about what you have learned. Come up with specific ways in which you can be more creative in your thinking and decision making based on what you have learned.

Be the Manager [LO 1, 2, 3, 4, 5]

You are a top manager who was recently hired by an oil field services company in Oklahoma to help it respond more quickly and proactively to potential opportunities in its market. You report to the chief operating officer (COO), who reports to the CEO, and you have been on the job for eight months. Thus far, you have come up with three initiatives you carefully studied, thought were noteworthy, and proposed and justified to the COO. The COO seemed cautiously interested when you presented the proposals, and each time he indicated he would think about them and discuss them with the CEO as consider-able resources were involved. Each time, you never heard back from the COO, and after a few weeks elapsed, you casually asked the COO if there was any news on the proposal in question. For the first proposal, the COO said, "We think it's a good idea but the timing is off. Let's shelve it for the time being and reconsider it next year." For the second proposal, the COO said, "Mike [the CEO] reminded me that we tried that two years ago and it wasn't well received in the market. I am surprised I didn't remember it myself when you first described the proposal but it came right back to me once Mike mentioned it." For the third proposal, the COO simply said, "We're not convinced it will work."

You believe that your three proposed initiatives are viable ways to seize opportunities in the marketplace, yet you cannot proceed with any of them. Moreover, for each proposal, you invested considerable amounts of time and have even worked to bring others on board to support the proposal, only to have it shot down by the CEO. When you interviewed for the position, both the COO and the CEO claimed they wanted "an outsider to help them step out of the box and innovate." Yet your experience to date has been just the opposite. What are you going to do?

BusinessWeek Case in the News [LO 1, 2, 4]

The Icelander Who Wants Saks

With his crisply tailored black suit and collar-length blond hair, Jon Asgeir Johannesson doesn't look much like a savage Viking raider. But over the past decade the 40-year-old Icelander has carried out corporate conquests that would make his forebears proud, building his Baugur Group into Britain's biggest fashion retailing conglomerate. And lest anyone forget Johannesson's heritage, he has out-fitted Baugur's London offices with a 10-foot-tall statue of a Viking. (The effect is softened somewhat by the Fender Stratocaster guitar strapped to its back, a souvenir Johannesson picked up at the Hard Rock Café in his native Reykjavik.)

In just two decades, Johannesson has transformed the family-controlled Baugur Group from a single discount supermarket on the Reykjavik docks into an international empire. Baugur has stakes in 20 retailers, with more than 3,900 outlets in 35 countries and total sales topping $19 billion.

Johannesson's biggest play may be about to take place in the U.S. In the past seven months he has built up an 8.5% stake in luxury retailer Saks in a prelude to what many expect will soon be a full-scale takeover. Though securities regulations prohibit Johannesson from discussing specific plans regarding Saks, he says the U.S. market is attractive in spite of recession fears. "Even if spending slows by 10%, the [American] consumer is still spending a lot," he says.

For a sense of what Johannesson might do in the U.S., take a look at Britain's House of Fraser. Baugur in 2006 paid $703 million for the mid-market department store and made the 61-outlet chain more upscale by introducing mini-boutiques from Baugur-owned women's wear designers Karen Millen and Oasis and toy shop Hamley's. That helped boost Fraser's same-store sales by 2.4% over the holidays, the retailer says. Johannesson says the "house of brands" model is lacking in the U.S. "We think there is opportunity to bring something fresh to the market," he says.

It won't be the first time Johannesson has crossed the Atlantic. In 2001, Baugur took over Bill's Dollar Stores, a Mississippi budget chain emerging from bankruptcy. That project ended when Bill's went belly-up just two years later. "It seemed a bargain at the time, but it probably never should have come out of Chapter 11," Johannesson says. "Now we do a lot more due diligence."

Saks is a far better fit with Johannesson's typical game plan: buying into retailers with good management and international potential. Most of Baugur's deals are leveraged buyouts in which the company takes 40% to 70% but leaves management in place. "[Its] strategy isn't about asset-stripping and a quick sale," says Jonathan Moore, an analyst at retail consultancy EC Harris in London. "Unlike much of the private money chasing this sector, they take a long-term view."

Managers get plenty of leeway. Johannesson keeps tabs on his vast portfolio with what he calls a "traffic light" system, evaluating the brands using dozens of performance indicators. He gives each brand a color code: green if things are running smoothly, yellow for those with potential problems, and red for any that require special attention. And he's not into long-winded explanations, demanding that reports be one page or shorter. "Baugur has a remarkably hands-off approach," says Richard Hyman, managing director of retail adviser Verdict Consulting in London.

NEVER ON A MONDAY

Johannesson credits his father with pioneering that simple management style and for teaching him most of what he knows about retail. As a child, Johannesson loved following his father, Johannes Jonsson, around the supermarkets he managed for a Reykjavik cooperative. Along the way he picked up tidbits such as a prohibition on completing deals on a Monday. (It's bad luck, Jonsson says.)

When his father planned to trash a broken-down amusement ride for kids at a supermarket he managed, 13-year-old Jon asked if he could have it instead. He promptly fixed the ride—an oversized monkey with a saddle on its back—and placed it back outside the store. Three years later, Johannesson bought 20 more kiddie rides from Germany and launched his first business. "He set them up on Sunday, and on Monday, with the trunk of his Toyota Celica practically dragging on the ground from the weight, he took the coins to the bank," Jonsson says.

After losing his job at the cooperative in 1988, Jonsson spotted an opportunity to shake up Iceland's retail industry, which was dominated by a handful of players that charged cartel-like prices. So he recruited his 19-year-old son, who was just finishing up at Commercial College, something between high school and junior college in the U.S. Jonsson had expected sales of around $110,000 in the first month for Bonus, the discount grocery they launched in a rented warehouse. Bonus did more than that in its first week. With only five employees at the start, father and son found themselves unloading stock in the mornings, manning the tills in the afternoon, and tracking sales at night. "We worked pretty much around the clock," says Johannesson.

Ten years later, Bonus merged with Icelandic hypermarket chain Hagkaup, the company name was changed to Baugur ("ring of strength" in the Vikings' ancient tongue), and it went public on the Reykjavik bourse. "It was the father's vision that created the company, but it is Jon Asgeir's drive and ambition that has made it an international player," says Sigurjon Arnason, CEO of Landsbanki, one of Iceland's biggest banks. Late last year, the merger became personal as Johannesson married the daughter of Hagkaup's founder.

In 2001, Baugur snapped up 20% of Arcadia Group, Britain's largest clothing retailer. But his plans for a full-scale takeover of Arcadia were derailed when Icelandic authorities, acting on a tip from a disgruntled former business partner, hit Johannesson and the company's former CEO with charges of accounting irregularities. Johannesson quickly sold his Arcadia shares, netting Baugur a profit of $200 million, a tenfold return on its initial investment.

It took five years, but Johannesson's legal problems are largely behind him. By last year all charges had been dropped but one: that of giving an incorrect statement about Baugur's accounts to the stock exchange. "I will be cleared," says Johannesson. And in 2003, no longer needing cash, Johannesson took Baugur private again. "All that time talking to banks and investors about the share price is better spent running the business," he says.

Johannesson has three residences: a $24 million triplex apartment near Manhattan's Gramercy Park and homes in London and Reykjavik. But the self-described workaholic, who fielded numerous calls about Baugur on his recent two-day honeymoon in Paris, has little time to enjoy them. "Even when I'm not working," he says, "I'm always thinking about business."

Questions for Discussion

1. Are most decisions Jon Johannesson makes as CEO of Baugur Group programmed decisions or nonprogrammed decisions?

2. What are some of the ways in which he recognizes the need for a decision?

3. To what extent are the decisions he makes characterized by risk or uncertainty?

4. How has he learned from feedback?

Source: Kerry Capell, "The Icelander Who Wants Saks." Reprinted from the February 11, 2008, issue of *BusinessWeek* by special permission. Copyright © 2008 by The McGraw-Hill Companies, Inc.

BusinessWeek Case in the News [LO 1, 2, 3, 4]

Bridging the Generation Gap

For a pair of colleagues born four decades apart, Penelope Burns and Rinath Benjamin spend a lot of time together. Burns, 68, and Benjamin, 29, are sales agents at the Manhattan office of employment agency Randstad USA. They sit inches apart, facing each other. They hear every call the other makes. They read every e-mail the other sends or receives. Sometimes they finish each other's sentences.

This may seem a little strange, but the unconventional pairing is all part of Randstad's effort to ensure that its twentysomething employees—the flighty, praise-seeking Generation Y that we have read so much about—fit in and, more to the point, stick around. The Dutch company, which has been expanding in the U.S., is hoping to win the hearts, minds, and loyalty of its young employees by teaming them up with older, more experienced hands. Every new sales agent is assigned a partner to work with until their business has grown to a certain size, which usually takes a few years. Then they both start over again with someone who has just joined the company. "This makes the corporate world more personal, approachable," says Randstad USA Chief Executive Stef Witteveen. "It's easier for the Gen Yers to identify with their jobs. They don't drown in their cubicles."

Randstad has been pairing people up almost since it opened for business four decades ago. The founder's motto was "Nobody should be alone." The original aim was to boost productivity by having sales agents share one job and trade off responsibilities. The system has been refined over the years and now each week one person is out making sales calls, and the other is in the office interviewing potential workers and handling the paperwork. Then they switch.

Randstad brought its partnership program to the U.S. in the late 1990s. But it wasn't until two years ago, once Randstad had integrated the personnel from the various firms it had acquired, that it began recruiting new employees. Last year it hired about 600 people, 420 of whom are in their twenties. Knowing that these Gen Yers need lots of attention in the workplace, Randstad executives figured that if they shared a job with someone whose own success depended on theirs, they were certain to get all the nurturing they required. As Belle Rose Ragins, a professor of human resource management at the University of Wisconsin at Milwaukee, puts it: "Gen Y's psychological contract is with the relationships embedded within the organization, not the organization itself."

NO TOUCHDOWNS ALLOWED

Of course, Randstad doesn't simply put people together and hope it all works out. First it figures out who will play well with other people. To assess that, the human resources department conducts extensive interviews and requires candidates to shadow a sales agent for half a day. "We have certain questions that we look for them to answer with 'we' instead of 'I,'" says HR chief Genia Spencer. "Somebody who needs to be recognized as the star, who needs personal achievement and doesn't like to share that, won't work in a unit. Partners cannot compete with each other." One question Randstad asks is: What's your most memorable moment while being on a team? "If they answer: 'When I scored the winning touchdown,' that's a deal killer," says Spencer. "Everything about our organization is based on the team and group."

Before joining Randstad in January, 2006, Benjamin had worked for six years as a sales agent at Verizon. When she first heard about Randstad's partnering program she was a little apprehensive. "It was completely different. I was used to being responsible for everything," she says. "Here you are forced to be open, to tell everything." But Burns knew they could work together: "I tested her during the interview to see if she had a sense of humor, if I could tease her a little bit and she would know it was to relieve the tension." The older woman is feisty and competitive. She is distinguished by a big, raspy voice; in another era, she would have been called brassy. Burns has been an agent at Randstad since 1998 and in all, she has been in the business for some two decades. Benjamin is quick, direct, confident. She's big on e-mail, texting, and her BlackBerry.

One of the most compelling features of Randstad's partnering program is that neither person is "the boss." And both are expected to teach the other.

Burns: "People think I run the works. I don't. She trains me as much as I train her."

Benjamin: "We have a great rapport. She's like my grandmother."

Burns: "You can get cynical when you've been in the business as long as I have. She doesn't let me get that way."

Benjamin: "During our training, we learn that we are each other's boss. The biggest shock was to have someone asking what I'm doing all the time. Now I'm over that."

Soon after Benjamin started, she suggested they begin to use the electronic payroll system Randstad offers to save time and reduce their paperwork. Burns hesitated: She had been filling out time sheets for the talent (as the temporary employees are called) and wasn't sure how they would take to the new task. But Benjamin persuaded her it would ultimately be simpler for everyone. "You don't have to drag me into the future, just give me a little push," says Burns. Now, when someone hasn't logged on in time, Burns calls and says: "Rinath says you have to get your time sheet in."

Burns, who has had a couple of other partners, says the younger agents are often too impatient. "They want to tell clients about problems before we have a solution. Sometimes new people don't realize that's not a good idea." She says Benjamin wants to act quickly, but hasn't made that mistake. "She tells me to take a breath," says Benjamin.

These are relationships like any other, full of promise yet always vulnerable to dysfunction. And even the best ones require a lot of maintenance. As Lucille Santos, a 61-year-old senior agent in North Haven, Conn., says: "My antennae are always up." Her partner, Allison Kaplan, is 28, and this is her first office job. "We need to be sure that we're asking the right questions and saying the right things to the clients and talent," says Santos. "In the beginning, Allison might have been a little timid about telling applicants they weren't dressed appropriately. I gave her some explicit suggestions, and she learned from watching me."

GAINING PERSPECTIVE

Santos says Kaplan has taught her to relax a little bit more at work. "I'm from the old school," she says. "It's important that people take lunch, and I don't always look upon that type of thing so well. She put that into perspective for me."

Randstad encourages people to solve problems with their partners and breaks up teams only when the situation is fairly dire—when, say, one person is sabotaging the other or when productivity suffers because of constant bickering. In those cases, which the company says are rare, the uncooperative partner usually ends up leaving the company.

Even so, Randstad's ability to keep its employees has improved. The company used to have a retention rate of 50%, which is the industry standard.

In the past year, its rate has increased to 60%. "We have determined a clear connection between being in a unit and feeling more successful and productive," says Spencer.

CEO Witteveen, who is 44, acknowledges that some managers resist having to accommodate the idiosyncrasies of Gen Y. "It's natural to think: Why should I do all these kinds of things for them? No one did that for me. You have to get over that. You have to think beyond your own feelings of fairness. It's about improving the relationship with the employee." He says he, too, had to learn to appreciate the concerns of the younger generation even though he gets practice at home. "I have two Gen Y kids, and they come with all the features," he says.

Questions for Discussion

1. How might Randstad's partnership program contribute to effective decision making?

2. How might it help employees generate and evaluate alternatives?

3. How might it help employees choose alternatives and learn from feedback?

4. How might the program contribute to organizational learning?

CHAPTER 8

The Manager as a Planner and Strategist

Learning Objectives

After studying this chapter, you should be able to:

LO1 Identify the three main steps of the planning process and explain the relationship between planning and strategy.

LO2 Describe some techniques managers can use to improve the planning process so that they can better predict the future and mobilize organizational resources to meet future contingencies.

LO3 Differentiate between the main types of business-level strategies and explain how they give an organization a competitive advantage that may lead to superior performance.

LO4 Differentiate between the main types of corporate-level strategies and explain how they are used to strengthen a company's business-level strategy and competitive advantage.

LO5 Describe the vital role managers play in implementing strategies to achieve an organization's mission and goals.

A Manager's Challenge

Why Does Best Buy Outperform Circuit City?

What makes it hard to compete in an industry? In 2008, Best Buy, the largest electronics retailer in the United States, reported rising profits, while Circuit City, the second largest electronics retailer, announced increasing losses.[1] In fact, over the last decade Best Buy's sales and profits have steadily increased as it opened more and more new stores, while Circuit City's sales and profits have plunged. What kinds of planning and strategies have Best Buy's managers crafted that have made it the industry leader and highest-performing electronics retailer? Conversely, where did Circuit City's managers go wrong? What have been the mistakes in their planning and strategy that have led to its current problems?

First, over the last decade competition has been increasing in electronics retailing as companies such as Wal-Mart and Costco also began to sell electronics at low prices. With fierce price competition, the company that performs the highest is often the one that is best able to keep its store operating costs low, such as by turning over its inventory quickly and by stocking the range of products that customers most want to buy. Over the years, Best Buy's managers did

Planning pays off for Best Buy, whose larger stores (top photo) and more diverse offerings attract more customers than Circuit City, whose stores (bottom photo) are smaller and fewer in number, and who failed to anticipate customer interest in such items as Apple products and gaming computers.

the best job in stocking the range of PCs, flat screen TVs, appliances, and so on, that have best met customer needs, so customers tend to come to Best Buy first. It also made developing good relationships with electronics makers an important part of its strategy, and as it has grown it has used its steadily increasing buying power to obtain more favorable prices and payment terms from them; this has allowed it to continually reduce its prices and capture customers away from Circuit City.

It was not just on the low-cost side that Best Buy's managers developed strategies to give it a competitive advantage over Circuit City. From the beginning its managers used several strategies to differentiate Best Buy from Circuit City and so attract more customers. First, its managers engaged in extensive planning to decide where to best locate its stores—it had around 2000 in 2008—and its rising sales show that they did the best job. They also decided that its stores would be bigger and better designed than Circuit City's so that Best Buy could offer customers a wider range of electronics products. Second, managers decided to focus on training salespeople to provide customers with high-quality customer service to help them make better purchasing decisions.[2] This also resulted in increased sales, and especially sales of more expensive PCs and TVs because salespeople could clearly explain to customers what they were getting for the higher price.

Best Buy also started new initiatives to boost revenues and profits. Realizing that servicing and installing electronics has high profit margins, it acquired the Geek Squad that now provides in-store and home tech support service to help install, repair, or upgrade its products. Recognizing that high-priced products also have high profit margins, another strategy was to devote a section of its store to selling luxury products that cater to big-spending customers. In 2007, for example, it reached an agreement with Apple, to sell Apple's premium products like its Macs and new iPods in its stores; it also offers high-end gaming computers from Dell that have large profit margins. Finally, it was much quicker to establish international operations than was Circuit City. For example, it opened a new chain of "Five Star" retail stores in China that earned a billion dollars in sales in 2007, and it was quick to develop an efficient online storefront with bestbuy.com.[3]

The problems facing Circuit City today are largely the result of its managers' inferior planning; they were slow recognizing how quickly Best Buy was building competitive advantage and late to adopt similar strategies. The result has been it has steadily lost customers, and falling sales revenues also means Circuit City's costs rise because inventory stays longer on the shelves and declining sales mean it is more difficult to negotiate favorable prices from electronics makers. To fight back it recruited a new CEO, Phillip Schoonover, who has tried to restructure the company by adopting strategies to reduce costs. One of his most controversial moves was to fire 3,400 experienced salespeople and to replace them with new, lower-cost employees to save around $35 million in operating costs. While this was a major saving, it has also led to lower-quality customer-service. He also closed all the company's Canadian stores and, in the United States, moved to a new strategy to build hundreds of smaller, more streamlined "City Stores" that can be operated at lower cost. At the same time, he decided to copy the Geek Squad and expand its higher–margin home-installation service called "Firedog." This has generated $300 million revenue.

In making these moves Circuit City has been playing catch-up, and many investors think few benefits will result from Schoonover's new turnaround strategies since the company will always be one step behind Best Buy—whose competitive advantage is still increasing. So, with its stock price trading at record lows in 2008 investors were cheered when Blockbuster, which has been busy trying to fix its own movie-rental business, made a hostile takeover bid of just over $1 billion for Circuit City! Apparently, Blockbuster's strategy is to create a huge chain of 9,300 stores that would sell both electronic products and rent movies and games. However, analysts are wondering how

Blockbuster's plan will result in strategies that help it reduce costs or make electronic products more appealing to customers— especially because its own sales are falling in its fight with Netflix and because more and more music buying, and movie and video-game rental is taking place over the Internet rather than in bricks-and-mortar stores.

So, how the battle between Best Buy and Circuit City will shape out remains to be seen. Indeed, in April 2008 it was not certain that Blockbuster would be able to gain control of the company, although it was apparent that Schoonover had no intention of voluntarily giving up control of Circuit City unless forced to by unhappy shareholders.

Overview

As the opening case suggests, in a fast-changing competitive environment such as electronics retailing, managers must continually evaluate how well products are meeting customer needs, and they must engage in thorough, systematic planning to find new strategies to better meet those needs. This chapter explores the manager's role both as planner and as strategist. First, we discuss the nature and importance of planning, the kinds of plans managers develop, and the levels at which planning takes place. Second, we discuss the three major steps in the planning process: (1) determining an organization's mission and major goals, (2) choosing or formulating strategies to realize the mission and goals, and (3) selecting the most effective ways to implement and put these strategies into action. We also examine several techniques, such as scenario planning and SWOT analysis, that can help managers improve the quality of their planning; and we discuss a range of strategies that managers can use to give their companies a competitive advantage over their rivals. By the end of this chapter, you will understand the vital role managers carry out when they plan, develop, and implement strategies to create a high-performing organization.

planning Identifying and selecting appropriate goals and courses of action; one of the four principal tasks of management.

strategy A cluster of decisions about what goals to pursue, what actions to take, and how to use resources to achieve goals.

Planning and Strategy

Planning, as we note in Chapter 1, is a process that managers use to identify and select appropriate goals and courses of action for an organization.[4] The organizational plan that results from the planning process details the goals of the organization and the specific set of strategies that managers will implement to attain those goals. Recall, from Chapter 1, that a **strategy** is a cluster of related managerial decisions and actions to help an organization attain one of its goals. Thus, planning is both a goal-making and a strategy-making process.

In most organizations, planning is a three-step activity (see Figure 8.1). The first step is determining the organization's mission and goals. A **mission statement** is a broad declaration of an organization's overriding purpose, what it is seeking to achieve from its activities; this statement is also intended to identify what is *unique or important* about its products to its employees and customers as well as to *distinguish or*

LO1 Identify the three main steps of the planning process and explain the relationship between planning and strategy.

Figure 8.1
Three Steps in Planning

DETERMINING THE ORGANIZATION'S MISSION AND GOALS

Define the business
Establish major goals

FORMULATING STRATEGY

Analyze current situation and develop strategies

IMPLEMENTING STRATEGY

Allocate resources and responsibilities to achieve strategies

mission statement
A broad declaration of an organization's purpose that identifies the organization's products and customers and distinguishes the organization from its competitors.

differentiate the organization in some ways from its competitors. (Three examples of mission statements, those created by Cisco Systems, Wal-Mart, and AT&T, are illustrated later, in Figure 8.4.)

The second step is formulating strategy. Managers analyze the organization's current situation and then conceive and develop the strategies necessary to attain the organization's mission and goals. The third step is implementing strategy. Managers decide how to allocate the resources and responsibilities required to implement the strategies among people and groups within the organization.[5] In subsequent sections of this chapter we look in detail at the specifics of each of these steps. But first we examine the general nature and purpose of planning.

The Nature of the Planning Process

Essentially, to perform the planning task, managers (1) establish and discover where an organization is at the *present time;* (2) determine where it should be in the future, its *desired future state;* and (3) decide how to *move it forward* to reach that future state. When managers plan, they must forecast what may happen in the future in order to decide what to do in the present. The better their predictions, the more effective will be the strategies they formulate to take advantage of future opportunities and counter emerging competitive threats in the environment. As previous chapters noted, however, the external environment is uncertain and complex, and managers typically must deal with incomplete information and bounded rationality. This is why planning and strategy making is such a difficult and risky activity, and as at Best Buy and Circuit City, if managers' predictions are wrong and strategies fail, organizational performance falls.

Why Planning Is Important

Almost all managers participate in some kind of planning because they must try to predict future opportunities and threats and develop a plan and strategies that will result in a high-performing organization. Moreover, the absence of a plan often results in hesitations, false steps, and mistaken changes of direction that can hurt an organization or even lead to disaster. Planning is important for four main reasons:

1. *Planning is necessary to give the organization a sense of direction and purpose.*[6] A plan states what goals an organization is trying to achieve and what strategies it intends to use to achieve them. Without the sense of direction and purpose that a formal

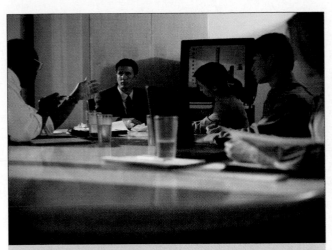

A group of managers meets to plot their company's strategy. Their ability to assess opportunities and challenges and to forecast the future doesn't just depend on brilliance. Such tools as SWOT Analysis can significantly bolster the accuracy of their predictions.

plan provides, managers may interpret their own specific tasks and jobs in ways that best suit themselves. The result will be an organization that is pursuing multiple and often conflicting goals and a set of managers who do not cooperate and work well together. By stating which organizational goals and strategies are important, a plan keeps managers on track so that they use the resources under their control efficiently and effectively.

2. *Planning is a useful way of getting managers to participate in decision making about the appropriate goals and strategies for an organization.* Effective planning gives all managers the opportunity to participate in decision making. At Intel, for example, top managers, as part of their annual planning process, regularly request input from lower-level managers to determine what the organization's goals and strategies should be.

3. *A plan helps coordinate managers of the different functions and divisions of an organization to ensure that they all pull in the same direction and work to achieve its desired future state.* Without a well-thought-out plan, for example, it is possible that the members of the manufacturing function will produce more products than the members of the sales function can sell, resulting in a mass of unsold inventory. This happened to high-flying Internet router supplier Cisco Systems in the early 2000s when manufacturing, which previously had been able to sell all the routers it produced, found it had over $2 billion of inventory that the sales force could not sell; customers now wanted new kinds of optical routers that Cisco had not planned to develop—even though sales had told manufacturing that customer needs were changing.

4. *A plan can be used as a device for controlling managers within an organization.* A good plan specifies not only which goals and strategies the organization is committed to but also *who* bears the responsibility for putting the strategies into action to attain the goals. When managers know that they will be held accountable for attaining a goal, they are motivated to do their best to make sure the goal is achieved.

Henri Fayol, the originator of the model of management we discussed in Chapter 1, said that effective plans should have four qualities: unity, continuity, accuracy, and flexibility.[7] *Unity* means that at any one time only one central, guiding plan is put into operation to achieve an organizational goal; more than one plan to achieve a goal would cause confusion and disorder. *Continuity* means that planning is an ongoing process in which managers build and refine previous plans and continually modify plans at all levels—corporate, business, and functional—so that they fit together into one broad framework. *Accuracy* means that managers need to make every attempt to collect and utilize all available information at their disposal in the planning process. Of course, managers must recognize the fact that uncertainty exists and that information is almost always incomplete (for reasons we discussed in Chapter 7). Despite the need for continuity and accuracy, however, Fayol emphasized that the planning process should be *flexible* enough so that plans can be altered and changed if the situation changes; managers must not be bound to a static plan.

Levels of Planning

In large organizations planning usually takes place at three levels of management: corporate, business or division, and department or functional. Consider how General Electric (GE) operates. One of the world's largest global organizations, GE competes in over 150 different businesses or industries.[8] GE has three main levels of management: corporate level, business or divisional level, and functional level (see Figure 8.2). At the corporate level are CEO and chairman Jeffrey Immelt, his top management

Figure 8.2
Levels of Planning at General Electric

team, and their corporate support staff. Together, they are responsible for planning and strategy making for the organization as a whole.

Below the corporate level is the business level. At the business level are the different *divisions* or *business units* of the company that compete in distinct industries; GE has over 150 divisions, including GE Aircraft Engines, GE Financial Services, GE Lighting, GE Motors, GE Plastics, and NBC. Each division or business unit has its own set of *divisional managers* who control planning and strategy for their particular division or unit. So, for example, GE Lighting's divisional managers plan how to operate globally to reduce costs while meeting the needs of customers in different countries.

Going down one more level, each division has its own set of *functions* or *departments,* such as manufacturing, marketing, human resource management (HRM), and research and development (R&D). For example, GE Aircraft has its own marketing function, as do GE Lighting, GE Motors, and NBC. Each division's *functional managers* are responsible for the planning and strategy making necessary to increase the efficiency and effectiveness of their particular function. So, for example, GE Lighting's marketing managers are responsible for increasing the effectiveness of its advertising and sales campaigns in different countries to improve light bulb sales.

Levels and Types of Planning

As just discussed, planning at GE, as at all other large organizations, takes place at each level. Figure 8.3 shows the link between these three levels and the three steps in the planning and strategy-making process illustrated in Figure 8.1.

The **corporate-level plan** contains top management's decisions concerning the organization's mission and goals, overall (corporate-level) strategy, and structure (see Figure 8.3). **Corporate-level strategy** specifies in which industries and national markets an organization intends to compete and why. One of the goals stated in GE's

corporate-level plan
Top management's decisions pertaining to the organization's mission, overall strategy, and structure.

corporate-level strategy
A plan that indicates in which industries and national markets an organization intends to compete.

Figure 8.3
Levels and Types of Planning

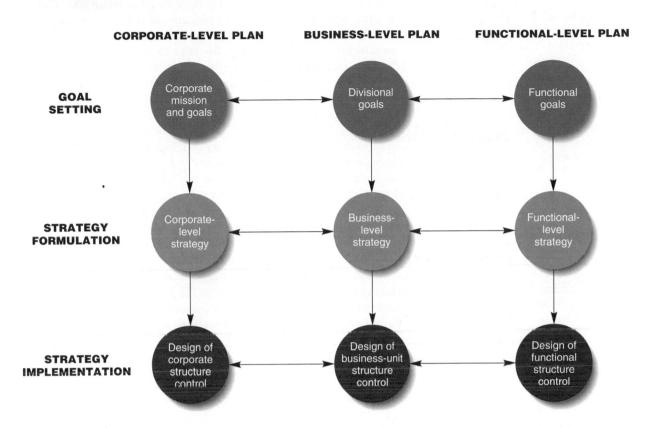

corporate-level plan is that GE should be first or second in market share in every industry in which it competes. A division that cannot attain this goal may be sold to another company. GE Medical Systems was sold to Thompson of France for this reason. Another GE goal is to acquire other companies that can help a division build its market share to reach its corporate goal of being first or second in an industry. Over the last decade, GE acquired several large financial services companies to meet this goal and has transformed the GE Financial Services Division into one of the largest financial services operations in the world.

In general, corporate-level planning and strategy is the primary responsibility of top or corporate managers.[9] The corporate-level goal that GE should be first or second in every industry in which it competes was first articulated by former CEO Jack Welch. Now, Welch's handpicked successor, Jeffrey Immelt, and his top-management team decide which industries GE should compete in.

The corporate-level plan provides the framework within which divisional managers create their business-level plans. At the business level, the managers of each division create a **business-level plan** that details (1) the long-term divisional goals that will allow the division to meet corporate goals and (2) the division's business-level strategy and structure necessary to achieve divisional goals. **Business-level strategy** outlines the specific methods a division, business unit, or organization will use to compete effectively against its rivals in an industry. Managers at GE's lighting division (currently number two in the global lighting industry, behind the Dutch company Philips NV) develop strategies designed to help their division take over the number-one spot and better contribute to GE's corporate goals. The lighting division's specific strategies might focus on ways to reduce costs in all departments to lower prices and so gain market share from Philips. For example, GE is currently expanding its European lighting operations in Hungary, which is a low-cost location.[10]

business-level plan
Divisional managers' decisions pertaining to divisions' long-term goals, overall strategy, and structure.

business-level strategy
A plan that indicates how a division intends to compete against its rivals in an industry.

At the functional level, the business-level plan provides the framework within which functional managers devise their plans. A **functional-level plan** states the goals that the managers of each function will pursue to help their division attain its business-level goals, which, in turn, will allow the entire company to achieve its corporate goals. **Functional-level strategy** is a plan of action that managers of individual functions (such as manufacturing or marketing) can take to improve the ability of each function to perform its task-specific activities in ways that add value to an organization's goods and services and thereby increase the value customers receive. Thus, for example, consistent with the lighting division's strategy of driving down costs, its manufacturing function might adopt the goal "To reduce production costs by 20% over the next three years," and functional strategies to achieve this goal might include (1) investing in state-of-the-art European production facilities and (2) developing an electronic global business-to-business network to reduce the costs of inputs and inventory holding. The many ways in which managers can use functional-level strategy to strengthen business-level strategy are discussed in detail in Chapter 9.

In the planning process, it is important to ensure that planning across the three different levels is *consistent*–functional goals and strategies should be consistent with divisional goals and strategies, which, in turn, should be consistent with corporate goals and strategies, and vice versa. When consistency is achieved, the whole company operates in harmony; activities at one level reinforce and strengthen those at the other levels, increasing efficiency and effectiveness. To help accomplish this, each function's plan is linked to its division's business-level plan, which, in turn, is linked to the corporate plan. Although few organizations are as large and complex as GE, most plan in the same way as GE and have written plans, which are frequently updated, to guide managerial decision making.

Time Horizons of Plans

Plans differ in their **time horizon,** the period of time over which they are intended to apply or endure. Managers usually distinguish among *long-term plans,* with a time horizon of five years or more; *intermediate-term plans,* with a horizon between one and five years; and *short-term plans,* with a horizon of one year or less.[11] Typically, corporate- and business-level goals and strategies require long- and intermediate-term plans, and functional-level goals and strategies require intermediate- and short-term plans.

Although most companies operate with planning horizons of five years or more, this does not mean that managers undertake major planning exercises only once every five years and then "lock in" a specific set of goals and strategies for that time period. Most organizations have an annual planning cycle that is usually linked to the annual financial budget (although a major planning effort may be undertaken only every few years). So, a corporate- or business-level plan that extends over several years is typically treated as a *rolling plan,* a plan that is updated and amended every year to take account of changing conditions in the external environment. Thus, the time horizon for an organization's 2009 corporate-level plan might be 2014; for the 2010 plan it might be 2015; and so on. The use of rolling plans is essential because of the high rate of change in the environment and the difficulty of predicting competitive conditions five years in the future. Rolling plans enable managers to make midcourse corrections if environmental changes warrant or to change the thrust of the plan altogether if it no longer seems appropriate. The use of rolling plans allows managers to plan flexibly, without losing sight of the need to plan for the long term.

Standing Plans and Single-Use Plans

Another distinction often made between plans is whether they are standing plans or single-use plans. Managers create standing and single-use plans to help achieve an organization's specific goals. *Standing plans* are used in situations in which programmed decision making is appropriate. When the same situations occur repeatedly, managers develop policies, rules, and standard operating procedures (SOPs) to control the way employees perform their tasks. A policy is a general guide to action; a rule is a formal, written guide to action; and a standing operating procedure is a written instruction describing the exact series of actions that should be followed in a specific situation. For example, an organization may have a standing plan about ethical behavior by employees. This plan includes a policy that all employees are expected to behave ethically in their dealings with suppliers and customers; a rule that requires any employee who receives from a supplier or customer a gift worth more than $10 to report the gift; and an SOP that obliges the recipient of the gift to make the disclosure in writing within 30 days.

In contrast, *single-use plans* are developed to handle nonprogrammed decision making in unusual or one-of-a-kind situations. Examples of single-use plans include *programs,* which are integrated sets of plans for achieving certain goals, and *projects,* which are specific action plans created to complete various aspects of a program. One of NASA's major programs was to reach the moon, and one project in this program was to develop a lunar module capable of landing on the moon and returning to the earth.

scenario planning The generation of multiple forecasts of future conditions followed by an analysis of how to respond effectively to each of those conditions.

LO2 Describe some techniques managers can use to improve the planning process so that they can better predict the future and mobilize organizational resources to meet future contingencies.

Scenario Planning

Earlier, we noted that effective plans have four qualities: unity, continuity, accuracy, and flexibility. One of the most widely used planning methods or techniques that can help managers create plans that have these qualities is scenario planning. **Scenario planning** (also known as *contingency planning*) is the generation of multiple forecasts of future conditions followed by an analysis of how to respond effectively to each of those conditions.

As we know all too well, oil and gas prices are unpredictable. Oil industry managers, therefore, sometimes use scenario planning to deal with this chaotic market.

As noted previously, planning is about trying to forecast and predict the future in order to be able to anticipate future opportunities and threats. The future, however, is inherently unpredictable. How can managers best deal with this unpredictability? This question preoccupied managers at Royal Dutch Shell, the third-largest global oil company, in the 1980s. In 1984, oil was $30 a barrel and most analysts and managers, including Shell's, believed that it would hit $50 per barrel by 1990. Although these high prices guaranteed high profits, Shell's top managers decided to conduct a scenario-planning exercise. Shell's corporate and divisional managers were told to use scenario planning to generate different future scenarios of conditions in the oil market and then to develop a set of plans that detailed how they would respond to these opportunities and threats if any such scenario occurred.

One scenario used the assumption that oil prices would fall to $15 per barrel, and managers had to decide what they should do in such a case. Managers went to work with the goal of creating a plan consisting of a series of recommendations. The final plan included proposals to cut oil exploration costs by investing in new technologies, to accelerate investments in cost-efficient oil-refining facilities, and to weed out unprofitable gas stations.[12] In reviewing these proposals, top management came to the conclusion that even if oil prices continued to rise, all of these actions would benefit Shell and increase its profit margin. So they decided to put the cost-cutting plan into action. As it happened, in the mid-1980s oil prices did not rise; they collapsed to $15 a barrel, but Shell, unlike its competitors, had already taken steps to be profitable in a low-oil-price world. Consequently, by 1990 the company was twice as profitable as its major competitors.

As this example suggests, because the future is unpredictable—the $30-a-barrel oil level was not reached again until the 2000s, for example—the best way to improve planning is first to generate "multiple futures," or scenarios of the future, based on different assumptions about conditions that *might prevail* in the future and then to develop different plans that detail what a company *should do* in the event that one of these scenarios actually occurs. Scenario planning is a learning tool that raises the quality of the planning process and can bring real benefits to an organization.[13] Shell's success with scenario planning influenced many other companies to adopt similar systems. By 1990, more than 50% of Fortune 500 companies were using some version of scenario planning, and the number has increased since then.

The great strength of scenario planning is its ability not only to anticipate the challenges of an uncertain future but also to educate managers to think about the future—*to think strategically*.[14] Unfortunately, as we described in the opening case, Circuit City's managers did not engage in a formal scenario planning exercise to forecast how Best Buy's strategies might impact the company over time and how it should change its own strategies to meet the growing threat. Circuit City's managers' failure to act allowed Best Buy to gain a competitive advantage that has made it the leading player in electronics retailing and now Circuit City has to play catch-up.

Determining the Organization's Mission and Goals

As we discussed earlier, determining the organization's mission and goals is the first step of the planning process. Once the mission and goals are agreed upon and formally stated in the corporate plan, they guide the next steps by defining which strategies are appropriate and which are inappropriate.[15] Figure 8.4 presents managers' vision of the mission and goals of three companies, Cisco, Wal-Mart, and AT&T.

Defining the Business

To determine an organization's *mission*—the overriding reason it exists to provide customers with goods or services they value—managers must first *define its business* so that they can identify what kind of value customers are receiving. To define the business, managers must ask three related questions about a company's products: (1) *Who* are our customers? (2) *What* customer needs are being satisfied? (3) *How* are we satisfying customer needs?[16] Managers ask these questions to identify the customer needs that

Figure 8.4
Three Mission Statements

COMPANY	MISSION STATEMENT
Cisco	Cisco solutions provide competitive advantage to our customers through more efficient and timely exchange of information, which in turn leads to cost savings, process efficiencies, and closer relationships with our customers, prospects, business partners, suppliers, and employees.
Wal-Mart	We work for you. We think of ourselves as buyers for our customers, and we apply our considerable strengths to get the best value for you. We've built Wal-Mart by acting on behalf of our customers, and that concept continues to propel us. We're working hard to make our customers' shopping easy.
AT&T	We are dedicated to being the world's best at bringing people together—giving them easy access to each other and to the information and services they want and need—anytime, anywhere.

the organization satisfies and the way the organization satisfies those needs. Answering these questions helps managers to identify not only the customer needs they are satisfying now, but the needs they should try to satisfy in the future and who their true competitors are. All of this information helps managers plan and establish appropriate goals. In the following "Management Insight," the case of Mattel shows the important role that defining the business has in the planning process.

Management Insight

Ups and Downs at Mattel

In the 1990s, Mattel Inc., the well-known maker of such classic toys as Barbie dolls and Hot Wheels, believed that the toy market and customer preferences for toys were changing rapidly. This was because of the growing popularity of electronic toys and computer games. Sales of computer games had increased dramatically as more and more parents saw the educational opportunities offered by games that children would enjoy playing. Moreover, many kinds of computer games could be played with other people over the Internet, so it seemed that in the future the magic of electronics and information technology would turn the toy world upside down. Mattel's managers feared that core products, such as its range of Barbie dolls, might lose their appeal and become passé given the future possibilities opened up by chips, computers, and the Internet. Mattel's managers believed that its customers' needs were changing and that the company needed to find new ways to satisfy those needs if it was to remain the biggest toy seller in the United States. Fearing they would lose their customers to the new computer-game companies, Mattel's managers decided that the quickest and easiest way to redefine its business and become a major player in the computer-game market would be to acquire one of these companies. So in 1998 Mattel paid $3.5 billion for The Learning Company, the maker of such popular games as "Thinking Things." Its goal was to use this company's expertise and knowledge both to build an array of new computer games and to take Mattel toys such as Barbie and create new games around them. In this way Mattel hoped to better meet the needs of its existing customers and cater to the needs of the new computer-game customers.[17]

Planning in and of itself does not always pay off—it must be realistic. With its diversion into buying a game company, Mattel failed to anticipate the rise of such competitors as these Bratz dolls, which have taken a big chunk out of Barbie's profitability.

In addition, while some classic toys like Barbie have the potential to satisfy customers' needs for generations, the popularity of many toys is temporary and is often linked to the introduction of a new movie from Disney, Pixar, or DreamWorks. To ensure that it could meet the changing needs of customers for these kinds of toys, Mattel contracted with the three film companies to become the supplier of the toys linked to their movies. For example, in 2001 it agreed to pay Warner Brothers 15% of the gross revenues, and a guaranteed $20 million, for the rights to produce toys linked to the *Harry Potter* movie, based on the books of the same name. It launched a line of toys, filled with electronics that allow them to move and make sounds, and also created Harry Potter computer games that satisfied its customers' needs.[18]

While Mattel's managers correctly sensed that customers' needs were changing, the way in which it decided to satisfy customers new needs—namely, by buying The Learning Company—was not the right decision. It turned out that the skills required to rapidly develop new games linked to Mattel's products were not present in The Learning Company, and few popular games were forthcoming. Moreover, Mattel had underestimated the need to promote and update its core toys, and the $3.5 billion could have been much better spent boosting and developing these toys. CEO Bob Eckert sold The Learning Company and decided that henceforth Mattel would hire independent specialist companies to develop new electronic toys and computer games, including many related to its well-known products.

In the fast-paced toy market where customers' needs change and evolve, and where new groups of customers emerge as new technologies result in new kinds of toys, toy companies like Mattel must learn to define and redefine their businesses to satisfy those needs. By 2001, Mattel had begun to turn out whole new ranges of electronic products linked to Barbie, a new Diva Starz doll line, and new electronic games, and its profits started to recover in the early 2000s. However, Barbie faced increasing competition from a new Bratz line of dolls, which, with their larger-than-life features and "personalities" were attracting more and more buyers. Barbie seemed to be out of date.

Beginning in 2004, sales of Barbie products faltered; international Barbie sales dipped by 11% and domestic sales by 15%. Eckert announced, "Our biggest challenge ahead is invigorating the fashion (doll) business. We're directing tremendous time, energy and resources to regain our momentum in the fashion doll category."[19] However, so far Mattel has not been successful and in March 2008 it announced yet further declines in doll sales that led its stock price to plunge.[20] The message is clear: Companies and their managers have to listen closely to their customers to decide how best to meet their changing needs and preferences.

Establishing Major Goals

Once the business is defined, managers must establish a set of primary goals to which the organization is committed. Developing these goals gives the organization a sense of direction or purpose. In most organizations, articulating major goals is the job of the CEO, although other managers have input into the process. Thus, at Mattel, CEO Eckert's primary goal is still to be the leader in every segment of the toy market in which the company competes, even though this is very challenging at present. However, the best statements of organizational goals are ambitious—that is, they stretch the organization and require that all its members work to improve its performance.[21] The role of **strategic leadership,** the ability of the CEO and top managers to convey a compelling vision of what they want to achieve to their subordinates, is important here. If subordinates buy into the vision, and model their behaviors on the leader, they develop a willingness to undertake the hard, stressful work that is necessary for creative, risk-taking strategy making.[22] Many popular books such as *Built to Last* provide lucid accounts of strategic leaders establishing "big, hairy, audacious goals (BHAGs)" that serve as rallying points for their subordinates.[23]

Although goals should be challenging, they should also be realistic. Challenging goals give managers at all levels an incentive to look for ways to improve organizational performance, but a goal that is clearly unrealistic and impossible to attain may prompt managers to give up.[24] Bob Eckert must be careful not to discourage Mattel's doll designers by setting unrealistic sales targets, for example.

Finally, the time period in which a goal is expected to be achieved should be stated. Time constraints are important because they emphasize that a goal must be attained within a reasonable period; they inject a sense of urgency into goal attainment and act as a motivator. Mattel's managers committed themselves to reviving the Barbie line and significantly increasing sales by 2008, but they have been unable to achieve this and their new plan has the goal of doing this by 2010.[25]

strategic leadership The ability of the CEO and top managers to convey a compelling vision of what they want the organization to achieve to their subordinates.

Formulating Strategy

strategy formulation The development of a set of corporate-, business-, and functional-level strategies that allow an organization to accomplish its mission and achieve its goals.

SWOT analysis A planning exercise in which managers identify organizational strengths (S) and weaknesses (W) and environmental opportunities (O) and threats (T).

In **strategy formulation** managers work to develop the set of strategies (corporate, divisional, and functional) that will allow an organization to accomplish its mission and achieve its goals.[26] Strategy formulation begins with managers' systematically analyzing the factors or forces inside an organization, and outside in the global environment, that affect the organization's ability to meet its goals now and in the future. SWOT analysis and the five forces model are two useful techniques managers can use to analyze these factors.

SWOT Analysis

SWOT analysis is a planning exercise in which managers identify *internal* organizational strengths (S) and weaknesses (W) and *external* environmental opportunities (O) and threats (T). Based on a SWOT analysis, managers at the different levels of the organization select the corporate-, business-, and functional-level strategies to best position the organization to achieve its mission and goals (see Figure 8.5). In Chapter 5 we discussed forces in the task and general environments that have the potential to affect an organization. We noted that changes in these forces can produce opportunities that an organization might take advantage of and threats that may harm its current situation.

The first step in SWOT analysis is to identify an organization's strengths and weaknesses. Table 8.1 (page 274) lists many important strengths (such as high-quality skills in marketing and in research and development) and weaknesses (such as rising manufacturing costs and outdated technology). The task facing managers is to identify the strengths and weaknesses that characterize the present state of their organization.

The second step in SWOT analysis begins when managers embark on a full-scale SWOT planning exercise to identify potential opportunities and threats in the environment that affect the organization at the present or may affect it in the future. Examples of possible opportunities and threats that must be anticipated (many of which were discussed in Chapter 6) are listed in Table 8.1. Scenario planning is often used to strengthen this analysis.

With the SWOT analysis completed, and strengths, weaknesses, opportunities, and threats identified, managers can continue the planning process and determine specific strategies for achieving the organization's mission and goals. The resulting strategies should enable the organization to attain its goals by taking advantage of opportunities, countering threats, building strengths, and correcting organizational weaknesses. To appreciate how managers use SWOT analysis to formulate strategy, consider how Douglas Conant, CEO of Campbell Soup, has used it to find strategies to turn around the performance of the troubled food products maker in the 2000s.

Figure 8.5

Planning and Strategy Formulation

Table 8.1

Questions for SWOT Analysis

Potential Strengths	Potential Opportunities	Potential Weaknesses	Potential Threats
Well-developed strategy? Strong product lines? Broad market coverage? Manufacturing competence? Good marketing skills? Good materials management systems? R&D skills and leadership? Human resource competencies? Brand-name reputation? Cost of differentiation advantage? Appropriate management style? Appropriate organizational structure? Appropriate control systems? Ability to manage strategic change? Others?	Expand core business(es)? Exploit new market segments? Widen product range? Extend cost or differentiation advantage? Diversify into new growth businesses? Expand into foreign markets? Apply R&D skills in new areas? Enter new related businesses? Vertically integrate forward? Vertically integrate backward? Overcome barriers to entry? Reduce rivalry among competitors? Apply brand-name capital in new areas? Seek fast market growth? Others?	Poorly developed strategy? Obsolete, narrow product lines? Rising manufacturing costs? Decline in R&D innovations? Poor marketing plan? Poor materials management systems? Loss of customer goodwill? Inadequate human resources? Loss of brand name? Growth without direction? Loss of corporate direction? Infighting among divisions? Loss of corporate control? Inappropriate organizational structure and control systems? High conflict and politics? Others?	Attacks on core business(es)? Increase in domestic competition? Increase in foreign competition? Change in consumer tastes? Fall in barriers to entry? Rise in new or substitute products? Increase in industry rivalry? New forms of industry competition? Potential for takeover? Changes in demographic factors? Changes in economic factors? Downturn in economy? Rising labor costs? Slower market growth? Others?

Manager as a Person

Douglas Conant Keeps Stirring Up Campbell Soup

Campbell Soup Co., one of the oldest and best-known global food companies, saw demand for its major product, condensed soup, plummet by 30% between 1998 and 2004 as customers switched from high-salt, processed soups to healthier low-fat, low-salt varieties. Campbell's profits and stock price plunged as its condensed soup business collapsed, and in 2001 its directors brought in a new CEO, Douglas Conant, to help the troubled company. Conant decided it was necessary to develop a three-year turnaround plan to help the company strengthen its market position against aggressive competitors such as General Mills, whose Progresso Soup division had attracted away many of Campbell's customers with its innovative new lines of healthier soup.

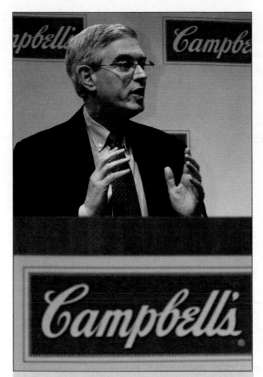

Douglas Conant, CEO of Campbell's, has revitalized the company through SWOT analysis. From SWOT analysis he has learned how to innovate successful new food products, and Campbell's has emerged as a leader in the low-carb, health-conscious, and luxury-food market segments.

One of Conant's first actions was to initiate a thorough SWOT planning exercise. *External analysis* of the environment identified the growth of the organic- and health-food segment of the food market and the increasing number of other kinds of convenience foods as a threat to Campbell's core soup business. It also revealed three growth opportunities: (1) the growing market for health and sports drinks, in which Campbell already was a competitor with its V8 juice; (2) the growing market for quality bread and cookies, in which Campbell competed with its Pepperidge Farm brand; and (3) chocolate products, where Campbell's Godiva brand had enjoyed increasing sales throughout the 1990s.

With the analysis of the environment complete, Conant turned his attention to his organization's resources and capabilities. His *internal analysis* of Campbell identified a number of major weaknesses. These included staffing levels that were too high relative to its competitors and high costs associated with manufacturing its soups because of the use of outdated machinery.

Also, Conant noted that Campbell had a very conservative culture in which people seemed to be afraid to take risks—something that was a real problem in an industry where customer tastes are always changing and new products must be developed constantly. At the same time, the SWOT analysis identified an enormous strength: Campbell enjoyed huge economies of scale because of the enormous quantity of food products that it makes, and it also had a first-rate R&D division capable of developing exciting new food products.

Using the information gained from this SWOT analysis, Conant and his managers decided that Campbell needed to use its product development skills to revitalize its core products and modify or reinvent them in ways that would appeal to increasingly health-conscious and busy consumers. Moreover, it needed to expand its franchise in the health- and sports-, snack-, and luxury-food segments of the market. Also, to increase sales, Campbell's needed to tap into new food outlets, such as corporate cafeterias, college dining halls, and other mass eateries, to expand consumers' access to its foods. Finally, Conant decided to decentralize authority to managers at lower levels in the organization and make them responsible for developing new soup, bread, and chocolate products that met customers changing needs. In this way he hoped to revitalize Campbell's slow-moving culture and speed the flow of improved and new products to the market.

Conant put his new plan into action, sales of new soup products increased, and he began to put more emphasis on sales of soup at outlets such as 7-11 and Subway and less on supermarket sales.[27] By 2004, analysts felt that he had made a significant difference in Campbell's performance but that there was still a lot to do, as Campbell's operating margins were still shrinking. Carrying on the SWOT analysis, Conant decided Campbell should produce more products to meet the needs of the "low-carb diet," such as new kinds of low-carb bread and cookies. He also decided to shrink the company's operations to lower costs. His goal was to raise profit margins to the level of his major competitors Kraft and General Mills by 2007 using a new three-year plan based on this SWOT analysis.[28]

By 2006 Conant had substantially achieved his goals: Sales of soup had recovered and the Pepperidge Farm and Godiva divisions were earning record sales and profits (sales of Goldfish crackers had increased by 100%!).[29] Campbell's stock price soared, and Conant and employees at all levels received bonuses that rewarded their intense efforts to turn around the company. However, Conant immediately set in motion a new round of SWOT analysis to find new opportunities to take advantage of for developing new kinds of products for new customers.[30]

On the threat side, it was clear that customers wanted more nutritious food and snack products so he set into motion research to make Campbell's food products more appealing to health-conscious customers. One major opportunity was to reformulate a number of its soups to reduce sodium content, and it introduced new kinds of low-salt soup in 2007. Another opportunity was to develop nutritious luxury soups that would command premium prices.[31] Both these initiatives worked well. On the other hand, pursuing his new goal of making Campbell's foods more nutritious led Conant to question if its highly profitable Godiva chocolate brand was still a good fit for the company. He decided it had become a weakness, and in 2007 he sold it for $850 million.[32] He then used some of the proceeds of this sale to build new company strengths. For example, he invested in R&D to develop the skills needed to customize Campbell's brands to the needs of customers in countries such as India and China, a move that spearheaded global expansion. Under Conant, Campbell's profits and stock price have continued to rise and with a culture of innovation permeating the organization, its future looks bright indeed.

The Five Forces Model

A well-known model that helps managers focus on the five most important competitive forces, or potential threats, in the external environment is Michael Porter's five forces model. We discussed the first four forces in the list below in Chapter 6. Porter identified these five factors as major threats because they affect how much profit organizations competing within the same industry can expect to make:

- *The level of rivalry among organizations in an industry:* The more that companies compete against one another for customers—for example, by lowering the prices of their products or by increasing advertising—the lower is the level of industry profits (low prices mean less profit).

- *The potential for entry into an industry:* The easier it is for companies to enter an industry—because, for example, barriers to entry, such as brand loyalty, are low—the more likely it is for industry prices and therefore industry profits to be low.

- *The power of large suppliers:* If there are only a few large suppliers of an important input, then suppliers can drive up the price of that input, and expensive inputs result in lower profits for companies in an industry.

- *The power of large customers:* If only a few large customers are available to buy an industry's output, they can bargain to drive down the price of that output. As a result, industry producers make lower profits.

- *The threat of substitute products:* Often, the output of one industry is a substitute for the output of another industry (plastic may be a substitute for steel in some applications, for example; similarly, bottled water is a substitute for cola). When a substitute for their product exists, companies cannot demand very high prices for it or customers will switch to the substitute, and this constraint keeps their profits low.

Porter argued that when managers analyze opportunities and threats, they should pay particular attention to these five forces because they are the major threats that an organization will encounter. It is the job of managers at the corporate, business, and functional levels to formulate strategies to counter these threats so that an organization can manage its task and general environments, perform at a high level, and generate high profits. At Campbell, Conant performs such an analysis to identify the opportunities and threats stemming from the actions of food industry rivals. For example, as noted earlier, General Mill's Progresso Soups division developed healthier kinds of soups, and this resulted in increased rivalry that lowered Campbell's sales and profits until Campbell succeeded at making new lines of healthy soups itself. Today, both companies are being affected by the threat of rising global food prices as the price of wheat, corn, rice, and dairy products soars. Both companies are striving to reduce operating costs to limit food price increases since the company with the lowest prices will attract the most customers and gain a competitive advantage.

Today, competition is tough in most industries, whether companies make cars, soup, computers, or dolls. The term **hypercompetition** applies to industries that are characterized by permanent, ongoing, intense competition brought about by advancing technology or changing customer tastes and fads and fashions.[33] Clearly, planning and strategy formulation is much more difficult and risky when hypercompetition prevails in an industry.

hypercompetition
Permanent, ongoing, intense competition brought about in an industry by advancing technology or changing customer tastes.

Formulating Business-Level Strategies

Michael Porter, the researcher who developed the five forces model, also developed a theory of how managers can select a business-level strategy, a plan to gain a competitive advantage in a particular market or industry.[34] Indeed, Porter argued that business-level strategy creates a competitive advantage because it allows an organization (or a division of a company) to *counter and reduce* the threat of the five industry forces. That is, successful business-level strategy reduces rivalry, prevents new competitors from entering the industry, reduces the power of suppliers or buyers, and lowers the threat of substitutes—and this raises prices and profits.

According to Porter, to obtain these higher profits managers must choose between two basic ways of increasing the value of an organization's products: *differentiating the product* to increase its value to customers or *lowering the costs* of making the product. Porter also argues that managers must choose between serving the whole market or serving just one segment or part of a market. Based on those choices, managers choose to pursue one of four business-level strategies: low cost, differentiation, focused low cost, or focused differentiation (see Table 8.2).

LO3 Differentiate between the main types of business-level strategies and explain how they give an organization a competitive advantage that may lead to superior performance.

Low-Cost Strategy

low-cost strategy Driving the organization's costs down below the costs of its rivals.

With a **low-cost strategy,** managers try to gain a competitive advantage by focusing the energy of all the organization's departments or functions on driving the company's costs down below the costs of its industry rivals. This strategy, for example, would require that manufacturing managers search for new ways to reduce production costs, R&D managers focus on developing new products that can be manufactured more cheaply, and marketing managers find ways to lower the costs of attracting customers. According to Porter, companies pursuing a low-cost strategy can sell a product for less than their rivals sell it and yet still make a good profit because of their lower costs.

Table 8.2
Porter's Business-Level Strategies

	Number of Market Segments Served	
Strategy	**Many**	**Few**
Low cost	✓	
Focused low cost		✓
Differentiation	✓	
Focused differentiation		✓

Thus, such organizations enjoy a competitive advantage based on their low prices. For example, BIC pursues a low-cost strategy; it offers customers razor blades priced lower than Gillette's and ball-point pens less expensive than those offered by Cross or Waterman. Also, when existing companies have low costs and can charge low prices, it is difficult for new companies to enter the industry because entering is always an expensive process.

Differentiation Strategy

differentiation strategy
Distinguishing an organization's products from the products of competitors on dimensions such as product design, quality, or after-sales service.

With a **differentiation strategy,** managers try to gain a competitive advantage by focusing all the energies of the organization's departments or functions on *distinguishing* the organization's products from those of competitors on one or more important dimensions, such as product design, quality, or after-sales service and support. Often, the process of making products unique and different is expensive. This strategy, for example, often requires that managers' increase spending on product design or R&D to differentiate the product, and costs rise as a result. Organizations that successfully pursue a differentiation strategy may be able to charge a *premium price* for their products, a price usually much higher than the price charged by a low-cost organization. The premium price allows organizations pursuing a differentiation strategy to recoup their higher costs. Coca-Cola, PepsiCo, and Procter & Gamble are some of the many well-known companies that pursue a strategy of differentiation. They spend enormous amounts of money on advertising to differentiate, and create a unique image for, their products. Also, differentiation makes industry entry difficult because new companies have no brand name to help them compete and customers don't perceive other products to be close substitutes, so this also allows for premium pricing and results in high profits.

"Stuck in the Middle"

According to Porter's theory, managers cannot simultaneously pursue both a low-cost strategy and a differentiation strategy. Porter identified a simple correlation: Differentiation raises costs and thus necessitates premium pricing to recoup those high costs. For example, if BIC suddenly began to advertise heavily to try to build a strong global brand image for its products, BIC's costs would rise. BIC then could no longer make a profit simply by pricing its blades or pens lower than Gillette or Cross. According to Porter, managers must choose between a low-cost strategy and a differentiation strategy. He refers to managers and organizations that have not made this choice as being "stuck in the middle."

Organizations stuck in the middle tend to have lower levels of performance than do those that pursue a low-cost or a differentiation strategy. To avoid being stuck in the middle, top managers must instruct departmental managers to take actions that will result in either low cost or differentiation.

However, exceptions to this rule can be found. In many organizations managers have been able to drive costs below those of rivals and simultaneously differentiate their products from those offered by rivals.[35] For example, Toyota's production system is the most efficient in the world, as we discuss in the next chapter. This efficiency gives Toyota a low-cost strategy vis-à-vis its rivals in the global car industry. At the same time, Toyota has differentiated its cars from those of rivals on the basis of superior design and quality. This superiority allows the company to charge a premium price for many of its popular models.[36] Thus, Toyota seems to be simultaneously pursuing both a low-cost and a differentiated business-level strategy. This example suggests that although Porter's ideas may be valid in most cases, very well managed companies such as Campbell, Toyota, McDonald's, and Dell may have both low costs and differentiated products—and so make the highest profits of any company in an industry.

Focused Low-Cost and Focused Differentiation Strategies

Both the differentiation strategy and the low-cost strategy are aimed at serving many or most segments of a particular market, such as for cars or computers. Porter identified two other business-level strategies that aim to serve the needs of customers in only one or a few market segments.[37] Managers pursuing a **focused low-cost strategy** serve one or a few segments of the overall market and aim to make their organization the lowest-cost company serving that segment. By contrast, managers pursuing a **focused differentiation strategy** serve just one or a few segments of the market and aim to make their organization the most differentiated company serving that segment.

Companies pursuing either of these strategies have chosen to *specialize* in some way by directing their efforts at a particular kind of customer (such as serving the needs of babies or affluent customers) or even the needs of customers in a specific geographic region (customers on the East or West Coast). BMW, for example, pursues a focused differentiation strategy, producing cars exclusively for higher-income customers. By contrast, Toyota pursues a differentiation strategy and produces cars that appeal to consumers in almost *all* segments of the car market, from basic transportation (Toyota Corolla) through the middle of the market (Toyota Camry), to the high-income end of the market (Lexus). An interesting example of how a company pursuing a focused low-cost strategy, by specializing on one market segment, can compete with powerful differentiators is profiled in the following "Management Insight."

focused low-cost strategy Serving only one segment of the overall market and trying to be the lowest-cost organization serving that segment.

focused differentiation strategy Serving only one segment of the overall market and trying to be the most differentiated organization serving that segment.

Management Insight

Different Ways to Compete in the Soft-Drink Business

"Coke" and "Pepsi" are household names worldwide. Together, Coca-Cola and PepsiCo control over 70% of the global soft-drink market and over 75% of the U.S. soft-drink market. Their success can be attributed to the differentiation strategies they developed to produce and promote their products—strategies that have made them two of the most profitable global organizations. There are several parts to their differentiation strategies. First, both companies built global brands by manufacturing the soft-drink concentrate that gives cola its flavor but then selling the concentrate in a syrup form to bottlers throughout the world. The bottlers are responsible for producing and distributing the actual cola. They add carbonated water to the syrup, package the resulting drink, and distribute it to vending machines, supermarkets, restaurants, and other retail outlets. The bottlers must also sign an exclusive agreement that prohibits them from bottling or distributing the products of competing soft-drink companies. This creates a barrier to entry that helps prevent new companies from entering the industry.

Second, Coca-Cola and PepsiCo charge the bottlers a *premium price* for the syrup; they then invest a large part of the profits in advertising to build and maintain brand awareness. The money they spend on advertising (in 2007 each company spent over $600 million) to develop a global brand name helps Coca-Cola and PepsiCo differentiate their products so that consumers are more likely to buy a Coke or a Pepsi than a lesser-known cola. Moreover, brand loyalty allows both companies to charge a premium or comparatively high price for what is, after all, merely colored water and flavoring.

SEIZING THE FUTURE: DRIVING RETAILER BRAND POWER

www.cott.com

Cott advertises the fact that any retailer can put its own company name, for example, "Sam's Cola" on its generic Cola.

In the last decade the global soft-drink environment has undergone a major change, however, because of Gerald Pencer, a Canadian entrepreneur who came up with a new strategy for competing against these powerful differentiators. Pencer's strategy was to produce a high-quality, low-priced cola, manufactured and bottled by the Cott Corporation, of which he was CEO at the time, but to sell it as the private-label house brand of major retail stores such as Wal-Mart (Sam's Cola brand) and supermarket chains such as Kroger's (Big K brand), thus bypassing the bottlers. Pencer could implement his *focused low-cost* strategy and charge a low price for his soft drinks because he did not need to spend any money on advertising (the retail stores did that) and because Cott's soft drinks are distributed by the store chains and retailers using their efficient national distribution systems, such as the nationwide trucking system developed by giant retailer Wal-Mart. Retailers are willing to do this because Cott's low-cost soft drinks allow them to make much more profit than they receive from selling Coke or Pepsi. At the same time, the products build their store-brand image.

Pencer implemented this plan first in Canada and then quickly expanded into the United States as retailers' demand for his products grew. He then went on to supply the international market by offering to sell soft-drink concentrate to global retailers at prices lower than Coca-Cola and PepsiCo. By 2004 Cott was the world's largest supplier of retailer-branded carbonated soft drinks.[38] It has manufacturing facilities in Canada, the United States, and the United Kingdom, and a syrup concentrate production plant in Columbus, Georgia, which supply most of the private-label grocery store, drugstore, mass-merchandising, and convenience store chains in these countries. However, note that while Cott is the leading supplier of retailer-branded sodas, it is still focusing on its low-cost strategy. It makes no attempt to compete with Coke and Pepsi, which pursue differentiation strategies and whose brand-name sodas dominate the global soda market.

Increasingly, smaller companies are finding it easier to pursue a focused strategy and compete successfully against large, powerful, low-cost and differentiated companies because of advances in IT that lower costs and enable them to reach and attract customers. By establishing a storefront on the Web, thousands of small, specialized companies have been able to carve out a profitable niche against large bricks-and-mortar competitors. Zara, a Spanish manufacturer of fashionable clothing whose sales have soared in recent years, provides an excellent example of the way even a small bricks-and-mortar company can use IT to pursue a focused strategy and compete globally.[39] Zara has managed to position itself as the low-price, low-cost leader in the fashion segment of the clothing market, against differentiators like Gucci, Dior, and Armani, because it has applied IT to its specific needs. Zara has created IT that allows it to manage its design and manufacturing process in a way that minimizes the inventory it has to carry—the major cost borne by a clothing retailer. However, its IT also gives its designers instantaneous feedback on which clothes are selling well and in which countries, and this gives Zara a competitive advantage from differentiation. Specifically, Zara can manufacture more of a particular kind of dress or suit to meet high customer demand, decide which clothing should be sold in its rapidly expanding network of global stores, and constantly change the mix of clothes it offers customers to keep up with fashion—at low cost.

Zara, whose stores are gaining popularity all over the world, uses a highly developed IT system to shorten production times and get clothing out faster and for lower prices than the offerings of high-end designers.

Zara's IT also allows it to manage the interface between its design and manufacturing operations more efficiently. Zara takes only five weeks to design a new collection and then a week to make it. Fashion houses like Channel and Armani, by contrast, can take six or more months to design the collection and then three more months before it is available in stores.[40] This short time to market gives Zara great flexibility and allows the company to respond quickly to the rapidly changing fashion market, in which fashions can change several times a year. Because of the quick manufacturing-to-sales cycle and just-in-time fashion, Zara offers its clothes collections at relatively low prices and still makes profits that are the envy of the fashion clothing industry.[41]

Zara has been able to pursue a focused strategy that is simultaneously low cost and differentiated because it has developed many kinds of strengths in functions such as clothing design, marketing, and IT that have given it a competitive advantage. Developing functional-level strategies that strengthen business-level strategy and increase competitive advantage is a vital managerial task. Discussion of this important issue is left until the next chapter. First, we need to go up one planning level and examine how corporate strategy helps an organization achieve its mission and goals.

Formulating Corporate-Level Strategies

Once managers have formulated the business-level strategies that will best position a company, or a division of a company, to compete in an industry and outperform its rivals, they must look to the future. If their planning has been successful the company will be generating high profits, and their task now is to plan how to invest these profits to increase performance over time.

Recall that *corporate-level strategy* is a plan of action that involves choosing in which industries and countries a company should invest its resources to achieve its mission and goals. In choosing a corporate-level strategy, managers ask: How should the growth and development of our company be managed to increase its ability to create value for customers (and thus increase its performance) over the long run? Managers of effective organizations actively seek out new opportunities to use a company's resources to create new and improved goods and services for customers. Examples of organizations whose product lines are growing rapidly are Google, chipmaker AMD, Apple, and Toyota, whose managers pursue any feasible opportunity to use their companies' skills to provide customers with new products.

LO4 Differentiate between the main types of corporate-level strategies and explain how they are used to strengthen a company's business-level strategy and competitive advantage.

In addition, some managers must help their organizations respond to threats due to changing forces in the task or general environment that have made their business-level strategies less effective and reduced profits. For example, customers may no longer be buying the kinds of goods and services a company is producing (high-salt soup, bulky computer monitors or televisions), or other organizations may have entered the market and attracted away customers (this happened to Intel in the 2000s after AMD began to produce more powerful chips). Top managers aim to find corporate strategies that can help the organization strengthen its business-level strategies and thus respond to these changes and improve performance.

The principal corporate-level strategies that managers use to help a company grow and keep it at the top of its industry, or to help it retrench and reorganize to stop its decline, are (1) concentration on a single industry, (2) vertical integration,

(3) diversification, and (4) international expansion. An organization will benefit from pursuing any one or more of these strategies only when the strategy helps further increase the value of the organization's goods and services so that more customers buy them. Specifically, to increase the value of goods and services, a corporate-level strategy must help a company, or one of its divisions, either (1) lower the costs of developing and making products or (2) increase product differentiation so that more customers want to buy the products even at high or premium prices. Both of these outcomes strengthen a company's competitive advantage and increase its performance.

Concentration on a Single Industry

concentration on a single industry Reinvesting a company's profits to strengthen its competitive position in its current industry.

Most growing companies reinvest their profits to strengthen their competitive position in the industry in which they are currently operating; in doing so, they pursue the corporate-level strategy of **concentration on a single industry.** Most commonly, an organization uses its functional skills to develop new kinds of products or it expands the number of locations in which it uses those skills. For example, Apple is expanding the range of its iPods and mobile wireless devices such as the iPhone, while McDonald's, which began as one restaurant in California, focused all its efforts on using its resources to quickly expand across the United States to become the biggest and most profitable U.S. fast-food company.

On the other hand, concentration on a single industry becomes an appropriate corporate-level strategy when managers see the need to *reduce* the size of their organizations to increase performance. Managers may decide to get out of certain industries when, for example, the business-level strategy pursued by a particular division no longer works and the division has lost its competitive advantage. To improve performance, managers now sell off low-performing divisions, concentrate remaining organizational resources in one industry, and try to develop new products customers want to buy. This happened to electronics maker Hitachi when customers were increasingly switching from bulky CRT monitors to newer, flat LCD monitors. Hitachi announced it would close its three CRT factories in Japan, Singapore, and Malaysia and would use its resources to invest in the new LCD technology.[42]

By contrast, when organizations are performing effectively, they often decide to enter new industries in which they can use their resources to create more valuable products. Thus, they begin to pursue vertical integration or diversification.

Vertical Integration

vertical integration Expanding a company's operations either backward into an industry that produces inputs for its products or forward into an industry that uses, distributes, or sells its products.

When an organization is performing well in its industry, managers often see new opportunities to create value by either producing the inputs it uses to make its products or distributing and selling its products to customers. Managers at E. & J. Gallo Winery, for example, realized that they could lower Gallo's costs if the company produced its own wine bottles rather than buying bottles from a glass company that was earning good profits from its bottle sales to Gallo. So Gallo established a new division to produce glass bottles more cheaply than buying them; it quickly found that it could also produce new-shaped bottles to help differentiate its wines. **Vertical integration** is a corporate-level strategy in which a company expands its business operations either backward into a new industry that produces inputs for the company's products *(backward vertical integration)* or forward into a new industry that uses, distributes, or sells the company's products *(forward vertical integration).*[43] A steel company that buys iron ore mines and enters the raw materials industry to supply the ore needed to make steel is engaging in backward vertical integration. A PC maker that decides to enter the retail industry and open a chain of company-owned retail outlets to sell its PCs is engaging in forward integration. For example, in 2001 Apple Computer entered the retail industry when it decided to set up a chain of Apple Stores to sell its computers.

Figure 8.6
Stages in a Vertical Value Chain

Figure 8.6 illustrates the four main stages in a typical raw material-to-customer value chain; value is added to the product at each stage by the activities involved in each industry. For a company based in the assembly stage, backward integration would involve establishing a new division in the intermediate manufacturing or raw material production industries; and forward integration would involve establishing a new division to distribute its products to wholesalers or a retail division to sell directly to customers. A division at one stage or one industry receives the product produced by the division in the previous stage or industry, transforms it in some way—adding value—and then transfers the output at a higher price to the division at the next stage in the chain.

As an example of how this industry value chain works, consider the cola segment of the soft-drink industry. In the raw material industry, suppliers include sugar companies and manufacturers of artificial sweeteners such as NutraSweet and Splenda, which are used in diet colas. These companies sell their products to companies in the soft-drink industry that make concentrate—such as Coca-Cola and PepsiCo, which mix these inputs with others to produce the cola concentrate. In the process, they add value to these inputs. The concentrate producers then sell the concentrate to companies in the bottling and distribution industry, which add carbonated water to the concentrate and package the resulting drink—again adding value to the concentrate. Next, the bottlers distribute and sell the soft drinks to retailers, including stores such as Costco and Wal-Mart and fast-food chains such as McDonald's. Companies in the retail industry add value by making the product accessible to customers, and they profit from direct sales to customers. Thus, value is added by companies at each stage in the raw material-to-consumer chain.

The reason managers pursue vertical integration is that it allows them either to add value to their products by making them special or unique or to lower the costs of making and selling them. An example of using forward vertical integration to increase differentiation is Apple's decision to open its own stores to make its unique products more accessible to customers who could try them out before they bought them. An example of using forward vertical integration to lower costs is Matsushita's decision to open company-owned stores to sell its Panasonic and JVC products and thus keep the profit that otherwise would be earned by independent retailers.[44]

Although vertical integration can strengthen an organization's competitive advantage and increase its performance, it can also reduce an organization's flexibility to respond to changing environmental conditions and create threats that must be countered by changing the organization's strategy. For example, IBM used to produce most of the components it used to make its own mainframe computers. While this made sense in the 1970s when IBM enjoyed a major competitive advantage, it became a major handicap for the company in the 1990s when the increasing use of organization-wide networks of PCs meant slumping demand for mainframes. IBM had lost its competitive advantage and found itself with an excess-capacity problem in its component operations. Closing down this capacity, and exiting the computer components industry, cost IBM over $5 billion.[45]

Thus, when considering vertical integration as a strategy to add value, managers must be careful because sometimes it may reduce a company's ability to create value when the environment changes. This is why so many companies now outsource the production of component parts to other companies and, like IBM, have exited the components industry—by vertically *disintegrating* backward. IBM, however, found a profitable new opportunity for forward vertical integration in the 1990s: It entered the IT consulting services industry to provide advice to large companies about how to install and manage their computer hardware and software.[46] Providing IT services has been a major source of IBM's profitability in the 2000s.

Diversification

diversification Expanding a company's business operations into a new industry in order to produce new kinds of valuable goods or services.

Diversification is the corporate-level strategy of expanding a company's business operations into a new industry in order to produce new kinds of valuable goods or services.[47] Examples include PepsiCo's diversification into the snack-food business with the purchase of Frito Lay, tobacco giant Philip Morris's diversification into the brewing industry with the acquisition of Miller Beer, and GE's move into broadcasting with its acquisition of NBC. There are two main kinds of diversification: related and unrelated.

related diversification Entering a new business or industry to create a competitive advantage in one or more of an organization's existing divisions or businesses.

synergy Performance gains that result when individuals and departments coordinate their actions.

RELATED DIVERSIFICATION **Related diversification** is the strategy of entering a new business or industry to create a competitive advantage in one or more of an organization's existing divisions or businesses. Related diversification can add value to an organization's products if managers can find ways for its various divisions or business units to share their valuable skills or resources so that synergy is created.[48] **Synergy** is obtained when the value created by two divisions cooperating is greater than the value that would be created if the two divisions operated separately and independently. For example, suppose two or more of the divisions of a diversified company can utilize the same manufacturing facilities, distribution channels, or advertising campaigns—that is, share functional activities. Each division has to invest fewer resources in a shared functional activity than it would have to invest if it performed the functional activity by itself. Related diversification can be a major source of cost savings when divisions share the costs of performing a functional activity.[49] Similarly, if one division's R&D skills can be used to improve another division's products and increase their differentiated appeal, this synergy can give the second division an important competitive advantage over its industry rivals—so the company as a whole benefits from diversification.

The way Procter & Gamble's disposable diaper and paper towel divisions cooperate is a good example of the successful production of synergies. These divisions share the costs of procuring inputs such as paper and packaging, a joint sales force sells both products to retail outlets, and both products are shipped using the same distribution system. This resource sharing has enabled both divisions to reduce their costs, and as a result, they can charge lower prices than their competitors and so attract more customers.[50] In addition, the divisions can share the research costs involved in developing new and improved products, such as finding more absorbent material, that increase both products' differentiated appeal. This is something that is also at the heart of 3M's corporate strategy, which is discussed in the following "Management Insight."

How to Make Related Diversification Work

3M is a 100-year-old industrial giant that in 2008 generated almost $25 billion in revenues and over $6 billion in profits from its more than 50,000 individual products, ranging from sandpaper and sticky tape to medical devices, office supplies, and electronic components.[51] From the beginning, 3M has pursued related diversification and created new businesses by leveraging its skills in research and development. Today, the company is composed of more than 40 separate divisions positioned in six major business groups: transportation, health care, industrial, consumer and office, electronics and communications, and specialty materials. The company currently operates with the goal of producing 40% of sales revenues from products introduced within the previous four years.[52] Its CEO George Buckley has "been on a mission to kick-start growth" and he plans to increase spending on R&D to $1.4 billion or almost 6% of sales to keep achieving this goal.

How does 3M do it? First, the company is a science-based enterprise with a strong tradition of innovation and risk taking. Risk taking is encouraged, and failure is not punished but seen as a natural part of the process of creating new products and business.[53] Second, 3M's management is relentlessly focused on the company's customers and the problems they face. Many of 3M's products have come from helping customers to solve difficult problems. Third, managers set stretch goals that require the company to create new products and businesses at a rapid rate. Fourth, employees are given considerable autonomy to pursue their own ideas; indeed, 15% of employees' time can be spent working on projects of their own choosing without management approval. Many products have resulted from this autonomy, including the ubiquitous Post-it Notes. Fifth, while products belong to business units and it is business units that are responsible for generating profits, the technologies belong to every unit within the company. Anyone at 3M is free to try to develop new applications for a technology developed by its business units. Finally, 3M organizes many companywide meetings where researchers from its different divisions are brought together to share the results of their work. It also implemented an IT system that promotes the sharing of technological knowledge between researchers so that new opportunities can be identified.

How did we ever survive without Post-It notes? 3M's intense focus on solving customer problems results in new products that sell very well, including countless variations of the original sticky note.

In sum, to pursue related diversification successfully, managers search for new businesses where they can use the existing skills and resources in their departments and divisions to create synergies, add value to new products and businesses, and improve their competitive position and that of the entire company. In addition, managers may try to acquire a company in a new industry because they believe it possesses skills and resources that will improve the performance of one or more of their existing divisions. If successful, such skill transfers can help an organization to lower its costs or better differentiate its products because they create synergies between divisions.

unrelated diversification Entering a new industry or buying a company in a new industry that is not related in any way to an organization's current businesses or industries.

UNRELATED DIVERSIFICATION Managers pursue **unrelated diversification** when they establish divisions or buy companies in new industries that are *not* linked in any way to their current businesses or industries. One main reason for pursuing unrelated diversification is that, sometimes, managers can buy a poorly performing company, transfer their management skills to that company, turn around its business, and increase its performance—all of which creates value.

Another reason for pursuing unrelated diversification is that purchasing businesses in different industries lets managers engage in *portfolio strategy,* which is apportioning financial resources among divisions to increase financial returns or spread risks among different businesses, much as individual investors do with their own portfolios. For example, managers may transfer funds from a rich division (a "cash cow") to a new and promising division (a "star") and, by appropriately allocating money between divisions, create value. Though used as a popular explanation in the 1980s for unrelated diversification, portfolio strategy ran into increasing criticism in the 1990s because it simply does not work.[54] Why? As managers expand the scope of their organization's operations and enter more and more industries, it becomes increasingly difficult for top managers to be knowledgeable about all of the organization's diverse businesses. Managers do not have the time to process all of the information required to adequately assess the strategy and performance of each division, and so the performance of the entire company often falls.

This problem arose at GE in the 1970s, as its former CEO Reg Jones commented: "I tried to review each business unit plan in great detail. This effort took untold hours and placed a tremendous burden on the corporate executive office. After a while I began to realize that no matter how hard we would work, we could not achieve the necessary in-depth understanding of the 40-odd business unit plans."[55] Unable to handle so much information, top managers are overwhelmed and eventually make important resource allocation decisions on the basis of only a superficial analysis of the competitive position of each division. This usually results in value being lost rather than created.[56]

Thus, although unrelated diversification can potentially create value for a company, research evidence suggests that *too much* diversification can cause managers to lose control of their organization's core business. As a result, diversification can reduce value rather than create it.[57] Because of this, during the last decade there has been an increasing trend for diversified companies to divest many of their unrelated, and sometimes related, divisions. Managers in companies like Tyco, Dial, and Textron sold off many or most of their divisions and focused on increasing the performance of the core division that remained—in other words, they went back to a strategy of concentrating on a single industry.[58] For example, in 2007 Tyco split into three different companies when it spun off its health care and electronics businesses and focused its activities on engineered and fire and security products, such as its ADT home security business.[59] By 2008, each of the different companies was performing at a higher level under its own team of top managers.[60]

International Expansion

As if planning whether or not to vertically integrate, diversify, or concentrate on the core business was not a difficult enough task, corporate-level managers also must decide on the appropriate way to compete internationally. A basic question confronts the managers of any organization that needs to sell its products abroad and compete in more than one national market: To what extent should the organization customize features of its products and marketing campaign to different national conditions?[61]

global strategy Selling the same standardized product and using the same basic marketing approach in each national market.

If managers decide that their organization should sell the same standardized product in each national market in which it competes, and use the same basic marketing approach, they adopt a **global strategy.**[62] Such companies undertake very little, if any, customization to suit the specific needs of customers in different countries. But if managers decide to customize products and marketing strategies to specific national conditions, they adopt a **multidomestic strategy.** Matsushita, with its Panasonic brand, has traditionally pursued a global strategy, selling the same basic TVs, camcorders, and DVD and MP3 players in every country in which it does business and often using the same basic marketing approach. Unilever, the European food and household products company, has pursued a multidomestic strategy. Thus, to appeal

multidomestic strategy Customizing products and marketing strategies to specific national conditions.

to German customers, Unilever's German division sells a different range of food products and uses a different marketing approach than its North American division.

Both global and multidomestic strategies have advantages and disadvantages. The major advantage of a global strategy is the significant cost savings associated with not having to customize products and marketing approaches to different national conditions. For example, Rolex watches, Ralph Lauren or Tommy Hilfiger clothing, Channel or Armani clothing or accessories or perfume, Dell computers, Chinese-made plastic toys and buckets, and U.S.-grown rice and wheat are all products that can be sold using the same marketing across many countries by simply changing the language. Thus, companies can save a significant amount of money. The major disadvantage of pursuing a global strategy is that, by ignoring national differences, managers may leave themselves vulnerable to local competitors that do differentiate their products to suit local tastes. This occurred in the British consumer electronics industry. Amstrad, a British computer and electronics company, got its start by recognizing and responding to local consumer needs. Amstrad captured a major share of the British audio market by ignoring the standardized inexpensive music centers marketed by companies pursuing a global strategy, such as Sony and Matsushita. Instead, Amstrad's product was encased in teak rather than metal and featured a control panel tailor-made to appeal to British consumers' preferences. To remain competitive in this market, Matsushita had to place more emphasis on local customization of its Panasonic and JVC brands.

The advantages and disadvantages of a multidomestic strategy are the opposite of those of a global strategy. The major advantage of a multidomestic strategy is that by customizing product offerings and marketing approaches to local conditions, managers may be able to gain market share or charge higher prices for their products. The major disadvantage is that customization raises production costs and puts the multidomestic company at a price disadvantage because it often has to charge prices higher than the prices charged by competitors pursuing a global strategy. Obviously, the choice between these two strategies calls for trade-offs.

Managers at Gillette, the well-known razor blade maker now part of Procter & Gamble, created a strategy that combined the best features of both international strategies. Like Procter & Gamble, Gillette has always been a global organization because its managers quickly saw the advantages of selling its core product, razor blades, in as many countries as possible. Gillette's strategy over the years has been pretty constant: Find a new country with a growing market for razor blades, form a strategic alliance with a local razor blade company and take a majority stake in it, invest in a large marketing campaign, and then build a modern factory to make razor blades and other products for the local market. For example, when Gillette entered Russia after the breakup of the Soviet Union, it saw a huge opportunity to increase sales. It formed a joint venture with a local company called Leninets Concern, which made a razor known as the Sputnik, and then with this base began to import its own brands into Russia. When sales growth rose sharply, Gillette decided to offer more products in the market and built a new plant in St. Petersburg.[63]

In establishing factories in countries where labor and other costs are low and then distributing and marketing its products to countries in that region of the world, Gillette pursued a global strategy. However, all of Gillette's research

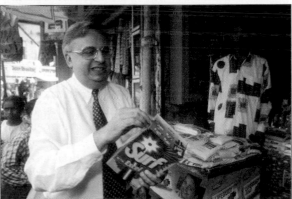

A study in contrasts. Matsushita, with its Panasonic brand (shown on the top), has largely pursued a global strategy, selling the same basic TVs and DVD players in every market and using a similar marketing message. Unilever, on the other hand, has pursued a multidomestic strategy, tailoring its product line and marketing approach to specific locations. On the bottom, the CEO of Hindustan Unilever, Keki Dadiseth, holds a box of Surf detergent designed for local customers.

and development and design activities are located in the United States. As it develops new kinds of razors, it equips its foreign factories to manufacture them when it decides that local customers are ready to trade up to the new product. So, for example, Gillette's latest razor may be introduced in a country abroad years later than in the United States. Thus, Gillette is customizing its product offering to the needs of different countries and so also pursues a multidomestic strategy.

By pursuing this kind of international strategy, Gillette achieves low costs and still differentiates and customizes its product range to suit the needs of each country or world region.[64] Procter & Gamble (P&G) pursues a similar international strategy, and the merger between them to create the world's largest consumer products company came about because of the value that could be realized by pursuing related diversification at a global level. For example, P&G's corporate managers realized that substantial global synergies could be obtained by combining their global manufacturing, distribution, and sales operations across countries and world regions. These synergies have resulted in billions of dollars in cost savings.[65] At the same time, by pooling their knowledge of the needs of customers in different countries, the combined company can better differentiate and position its products throughout the world. P&G's strategy is working; its principal competitors Colgate and Unilever have not performed well in the 2000s, and P&G is developing a commanding global position.

CHOOSING A WAY TO EXPAND INTERNATIONALLY   As we have discussed, a more competitive global environment has proved to be both an opportunity and a threat for organizations and managers. The opportunity is that organizations that expand globally are able to open new markets, reach more customers, and gain access to new sources of raw materials and to low-cost suppliers of inputs. The threat is that organizations that expand globally are likely to encounter new competitors in the foreign countries they enter and must respond to new political, economic, and cultural conditions.

Before setting up foreign operations, managers of companies such as Amazon.com, Lands' End, GE, P&G, Dell, and Boeing needed to analyze the forces in the environment of a particular country (such as Korea or Brazil) in order to choose the right method to expand and respond to those forces in the most appropriate way. In general, four basic ways to operate in the global environment are importing and exporting, licensing and franchising, strategic alliances, and wholly owned foreign subsidiaries, Gillette's preferred approach. We briefly discuss each one, moving from the lowest level of foreign involvement and investment required of a global organization and its managers, and the least amount of risk, to the high end of the spectrum (see Figure 8.7).[66]

IMPORTING AND EXPORTING   The least complex global operations are exporting and importing. A company engaged in **exporting** makes products at home and sells them abroad. An organization might sell its own products abroad or allow a local organization in the foreign country to distribute its products. Few risks are associated with exporting because a company does not have to invest in developing manufacturing

exporting Making products at home and selling them abroad.

Figure 8.7

Four Ways to Expand Internationally

Level of foreign involvement and investment
and degree of risk

facilities abroad. It can further reduce its investment abroad if it allows a local company to distribute its products.

A company engaged in **importing** sells products at home that are made abroad (products it makes itself or buys from other companies). For example, most of the products that Pier 1 Imports and The Limited sell to their customers are made abroad. In many cases the appeal of a product—Irish glass, French wine, Italian furniture, or Indian silk—is that it is made abroad. The Internet has made it much easier for companies to inform potential foreign buyers about their products; detailed product specifications and features are available online, and informed buyers can communicate easily with prospective sellers.

importing Selling products at home that are made abroad.

LICENSING AND FRANCHISING In **licensing,** a company (the licenser) allows a foreign organization (the licensee) to take charge of both manufacturing and distributing one or more of its products in the licensee's country or world region in return for a negotiated fee. Chemical maker DuPont might license a local factory in India to produce nylon or Teflon. The advantage of licensing is that the licenser does not have to bear the development costs associated with opening up in a foreign country; the licensee bears the costs. The risks associated with this strategy are that the company granting the license has to give its foreign partner access to its technological know-how and so risks losing control over its secrets.

licensing Allowing a foreign organization to take charge of manufacturing and distributing a product in its country or world region in return for a negotiated fee.

Whereas licensing is pursued primarily by manufacturing companies, franchising is pursued primarily by service organizations. In **franchising,** a company (the franchiser) sells to a foreign organization (the franchisee) the rights to use its brand name and operating know-how in return for a lump-sum payment and share of the franchiser's profits. Hilton Hotels might sell a franchise to a local company in Chile to operate hotels under the Hilton name in return for a franchise payment. The advantage of franchising is that the franchiser does not have to bear the development costs of overseas expansion and avoids the many problems associated with setting up foreign operations. The downside is that the organization that grants the franchise may lose control over the way in which the franchisee operates and product quality may fall. In this way, franchisers, such as Hilton, Avis, and McDonald's, risk losing their good names. American customers who buy McDonald's hamburgers in Korea may reasonably expect those burgers to be as good as the ones they get at home. If they are not, McDonald's reputation will suffer over time. Once again, the Internet facilitates communication between partners and allows them to better meet each other's expectations.

franchising Selling to foreign organization the rights to use a brand name and operating know-how in return for a lump-sum payment and a share of the profits.

STRATEGIC ALLIANCES One way to overcome the loss-of-control problems associated with exporting, licensing, and franchising is to expand globally by means of a strategic alliance. In a **strategic alliance,** managers pool or share their organization's resources and know-how with those of a foreign company, and the two organizations share the rewards or risks of starting a new venture in a foreign country. Sharing resources allows a U.S. company, for example, to take advantage of the high-quality skills of foreign manufacturers and the specialized knowledge of foreign managers about the needs of local customers and to reduce the risks involved in a venture. At the same time, the terms of the alliance give the U.S. company more control over how the good or service is produced or sold in the foreign country than it would have as a franchiser or licenser.

strategic alliance An agreement in which managers pool or share their organization's resources and know-how with a foreign company, and the two organizations share the rewards and risks of starting a new venture.

A strategic alliance can take the form of a written contract between two or more companies to exchange resources, or it can result in the creation of a new organization. A **joint venture** is a strategic alliance among two or more companies that agree to jointly establish and share the ownership of a new business.[67] An organization's level of involvement abroad increases in a joint venture because the alliance normally involves a capital investment in production facilities abroad in order to produce goods or services outside the home country. Risk, however, is reduced. The Internet and global teleconferencing provide the increased communication and coordination necessary for partners to work together on a global basis. For example, Coca-Cola and Nestlé formed a joint venture to market their teas, coffees, and health-oriented

joint venture A strategic alliance among two or more companies that agree to jointly establish and share the ownership of a new business.

beverages in more than 50 countries.[68] Similarly, BP Amoco and Italy's ENI formed a joint venture to build a $2.5 billion gas-liquefaction plant in Egypt.[69]

WHOLLY OWNED FOREIGN SUBSIDIARIES When managers decide to establish a **wholly owned foreign subsidiary,** they invest in establishing production operations in a foreign country independent of any local direct involvement. Many Japanese car component companies, for example, have established their own operations in the United States to supply U.S.-based Japanese carmakers such as Toyota and Honda with high-quality car components.

Operating alone, without any direct involvement from foreign companies, an organization receives all of the rewards and bears all of the risks associated with operating abroad.[70] This method of international expansion is much more expensive than the others because it requires a higher level of foreign investment and presents managers with many more threats. However, investment in a foreign subsidiary or division offers significant advantages: It gives an organization high potential returns because the organization does not have to share its profits with a foreign organization, and it reduces the level of risk because the organization's managers have full control over all aspects of their foreign subsidiary's operations. Moreover, this type of investment allows managers to protect their technology and know-how from foreign organizations. Large, well-known companies like DuPont, General Motors, and P&G, which have plenty of resources, make extensive use of wholly owned subsidiaries. Recall from Chapter 6 that Nokia establishes a wholly owned manufacturing subsidiary in each world region to make the mobile phones it sells in that region.

Obviously, global companies can use many of these different corporate strategies simultaneously to create the most value and strengthen their competitive position. We discussed above how P&G pursues related diversification at the global level, while it also pursues an international strategy that is a mixture of global and multidomestic. P&G also pursues vertical integration: It operates factories that make many of the specialized chemicals used in its products; it operates in the container industry and makes the thousands of different glass and plastic bottles and jars that contain its products; it prints its own product labels; and it distributes its products using its own fleet of trucks. Although P&G is highly diversified, it still puts the focus on its core individual product lines because it is famous for pursuing brand management—it concentrates resources around each brand, which is in effect is managed as a "separate company." So P&G is trying to add value in every way it can from its corporate- and business-level strategies. At the business-level, for example, P&G aggressively pursues differentiation and it charges premium prices for its products. However, it also strives to lower its costs and pursues the corporate-level strategies just discussed to achieve this. The way in which the largest global package delivery company chose to expand globally also illustrates the complex issues surrounding global expansion.

wholly owned foreign subsidiary Production operations established in a foreign country independent of any local direct involvement.

Managing Globally

How DHL Entered the U.S. Package Delivery Business

In 1971, Federal Express (FedEx) turned the package delivery world upside down when it began to offer overnight package delivery by air. Its founder, Fred Smith, had seen the opportunity for next-day delivery because both the U.S. Postal Service and United Parcel Service (UPS) were, at that time, taking several days to deliver packages. Smith was convinced there was pent-up demand for overnight delivery, and he was also convinced that customers would be willing

By expanding its international delivery operation by purchasing Airborne Express, DHL increased its presence in the U.S. small-package delivery business and so increased competition with its rivals UPS and FedEx.

to pay a high premium price to get such a unique new service, at least $15 a package at that time.[71] Smith was right; customers were willing to pay high prices for fast, reliable delivery. By discovering and tapping into an unmet customer need, he redefined the package delivery industry.

Several companies imitated FedEx's new strategy and introduced their own air overnight service. None, however, could match FedEx's state-of-the-art information system that allowed continuous tracking of all packages in transit. Several of its competitors went out of business. A few, like Airborne Express, managed to survive by focusing or specializing on serving the needs of one particular group of customers—corporate customers—and by offering lower prices than FedEx.

The well-known road delivery package company UPS initiated an overnight air delivery service of its own in 1998.[72] UPS managers realized that the future of package delivery lay both on the road and in the air because different customer groups, with different needs, were emerging. It began to aggressively imitate FedEx's state-of-the-art operating and information systems, especially its tracking system. Slowly and surely UPS increased the number of overnight packages that it was delivering. In 1999, UPS announced two major innovations. First, it introduced a new tracking and shipping information system that matched, and even exceeded, the sophistication of the FedEx tracking system because it could work with any IT system used by corporate customers. (By contrast, customers had to install and use FedEx's proprietary IT, an approach that caused more work and cost for them.) Second, UPS integrated its overnight air service into its nationwide delivery service and created a seamless interface between these two different aspects of its business. This gave it a differentiation advantage over FedEx because UPS can deliver short-range and mid-distance packages, those being shipped within about 500 miles, more quickly than FedEx, as well as match the speed and reliability of FedEx's long-range operations.

In the early 2000s competition between FedEx and UPS further increased, but in 2003 both companies received a major shock when the largest global package delivery company, DHL, announced that it was purchasing Airborne Express in order to enter the U.S. package delivery market.[73] Thus DHL bought the wholly owned subsidiary it needed to become a direct competitor of FedEx and UPS, and these companies went to court to try to block the purchase. They did not want DHL to enter the market because it is the world's largest package delivery company, and its entry would give it a differentiation advantage over them at the global level. They were unable to prevent DHL's entering the market, as U.S. regulators believed its entry would spur healthy competition in the industry.

Since 2003 all three companies have worked hard to find new ways to differentiate themselves. FedEx purchased Kinko's Copies and has made each of its new FedEx Kinko's stores a base for its global delivery operations. DHL began to promote and advertise its global delivery system as the most efficient in the world. Both UPS and FedEx formed strategic alliances with delivery companies in countries around the world to develop their own efficient global delivery systems. The fight is ongoing as each company strives to become the global leader in each world region in which it operates.

Planning and Implementing Strategy

After identifying appropriate business and corporate strategies to attain an organization's mission and goals, managers confront the challenge of putting those strategies into action. Strategy implementation is a five-step process:

1. Allocating responsibility for implementation to the appropriate individuals or groups.
2. Drafting detailed action plans that specify how a strategy is to be implemented.
3. Establishing a timetable for implementation that includes precise, measurable goals linked to the attainment of the action plan.
4. Allocating appropriate resources to the responsible individuals or groups.
5. Holding specific individuals or groups responsible for the attainment of corporate, divisional, and functional goals.

LO5   Describe the vital role managers play in implementing strategies to achieve an organization's mission and goals.

The planning process goes beyond just identifying effective strategies; it also includes plans to ensure that these strategies are put into action. Normally, the plan for implementing a new strategy requires the development of new functional strategies, the redesign of an organization's structure, and the development of new control systems; it might also require a new program to change an organization's culture. These are issues we address in the next three chapters.

Summary and Review

PLANNING   Planning is a three-step process: (1) determining an organization's mission and goals; (2) formulating strategy; and (3) implementing strategy. Managers use planning to identify and select appropriate goals and courses of action for an organization and to decide how to allocate the resources they need to attain those goals

LO 1, 2   and carry out those actions. A good plan builds commitment for the organization's goals, gives the organization a sense of direction and purpose, coordinates the different functions and divisions of the organization, and controls managers by making them accountable for specific goals. In large organizations planning takes place at three levels: corporate, business or divisional, and functional or departmental. Long-term plans have a time horizon of five years or more; intermediate-term plans, between one and five years; and short-term plans, one year or less.

LO 1, 2, 3, 4   **DETERMINING MISSION AND GOALS AND FORMULATING STRATEGY**   Determining the organization's mission requires that managers define the business of the organization and establish major goals. Strategy formulation requires that managers perform a SWOT analysis and then choose appropriate strategies at the corporate, business, and functional levels. At the business level, managers are responsible for developing a successful low-cost and/or differentiation strategy, either for the whole market or a particular segment of it. At the functional level, departmental managers develop strategies to help the organization either to add value to its products by differentiating them or to lower the costs of value creation. At the corporate level, organizations use strategies such as concentration on a single industry, vertical integration, related and unrelated diversification, and international expansion to strengthen their competitive advantage by increasing the value of the goods and services provided to customers.

LO5   **IMPLEMENTING STRATEGY**   Strategy implementation requires that managers allocate responsibilities to appropriate individuals or groups; draft detailed action plans that specify how a strategy is to be implemented; establish a timetable for implementation that includes precise, measurable goals linked to the attainment of the action plan; allocate appropriate resources to the responsible individuals or groups; and hold individuals or groups accountable for the attainment of goals.

Management in Action

Topics for Discussion and Action

DISCUSSION

1. Describe the three steps of planning. Explain how they are related. **[LO1]**

2. How can scenario planning help managers predict the future? **[LO2]**

3. What is the relationship among corporate-, business-, and functional-level strategies, and how do they create value for an organization? **[LO 3, 4]**

4. Pick an industry and identify four companies in the industry that pursue one of the four main business-level strategies (low-cost, focused low-cost, etc.) **[LO 2, 3]**

5. What is the difference between vertical integration and related diversification? **[LO4]**

ACTION

6. Ask a manager about the kinds of planning exercises he or she regularly uses. What are the purposes of these exercises, and what are their advantages or disadvantages? **[LO 1, 2]**

7. Ask a manager to identify the corporate- and business-level strategies used by his or her organization. **[LO 3, 4]**

Building Management Skills

How to Analyze a Company's Strategy [LO 3, 4]

Pick a well-known business organization that has received recent press coverage and that provides its annual reports at its Web site. From the information in the articles and annual reports:

1. What is (are) the main industry(ies) in which the company competes?

2. What business-level strategy does the company seem to be pursuing in this industry? Why?

3. What corporate-level strategies is the company pursuing? Why?

4. Have there been any major changes in its strategy recently? Why?

Managing Ethically [LO 2, 5]

A few years ago, IBM announced that it had fired the three top managers of its Argentine division because of their involvement in a scheme to secure a $250 million contract for IBM to provide and service the computers of one of Argentina's largest state-owned banks. The three executives paid $14 million of the contract money to a third company, CCR, which paid nearly $6 million to phantom companies. This $6 million was then used to bribe the bank

executives who agreed to give IBM the contract.

These bribes are not necessarily illegal under Argentine law. Moreover, the three managers argued that all companies have to pay bribes to get new business contracts and they were not doing anything that managers in other companies were not.

Questions

1. Either by yourself or in a group decide if the business practice

of paying bribes is ethical or unethical.

2. Should IBM allow its foreign divisions to pay bribes if all other companies are doing so?

3. If bribery is common in a particular country, what effect would this likely have on the nation's economy and culture?

Small Group Breakout Exercise

Low Cost or Differentiation? [LO 2, 3]

Form groups of three or four people, and appoint one member as spokesperson who will communicate your findings to the class when called on by the instructor. Then discuss the following scenario.

You are a team of managers of a major national clothing chain, and you have been charged with finding a way to restore your organization's competitive advantage. Recently, your organization has been experiencing increasing competition from two sources. First, discount stores such as Wal-Mart and Target have been undercutting your prices because they buy their clothes from low-cost foreign manufacturers while you buy most of yours from high-quality domestic suppliers. Discount stores have been

attracting your customers who buy at the low end of the price range. Second, small boutiques opening in malls provide high-price designer clothing and are attracting your customers at the high end of the market. Your company has become stuck in the middle, and you have to decide what to do: Should you start to buy abroad so that you can lower your prices and begin to pursue a low-cost strategy? Should you focus on the high end of the market and become more of a differentiator? Or should you try to pursue both

a low-cost strategy and a differentiation strategy?

1. Using scenario planning, analyze the pros and cons of each alternative.

2. Think about the various clothing retailers in your local malls and city, and analyze the choices they have made about how to compete with one another along the low-cost and differentiation dimensions.

Exploring the World Wide Web [LO 1, 3, 4]

Go to the corporate Web site of Google (www.google.com/corporate/execs.html), click on "corporate info," and explore this site; in particular, click on "Google's history" and

"The 10 Things" that guide Google's corporate philosophy.

1. How would you describe Google's mission and goals?

2. What is Google's business-level strategy?

3. What is Google's corporate-level strategy?

A group of investors in your city is considering opening a new upscale supermarket to compete with the major supermarket chains that are currently dominating the city's marketplace. They have called you in to help them determine what kind of upscale supermarket they should open. In other words, how can they best develop a competitive advantage against existing supermarket chains?

Questions

1. List the supermarket chains in your city, and identify their strengths and weaknesses.

2. What business-level strategies are these supermarkets currently pursuing?

3. What kind of supermarket would do best against the competition? What kind of business-level strategy should it pursue?

BusinessWeek Case in the News [LO 2, 3]

That Computer Is So You

With nearly 3,000 technology companies touting their wares at the annual International Consumer Electronics Show in Las Vegas from Jan. 7 to 10, it's a challenge to stand out from the crowd—even for an industry giant like Microsoft. So the software behemoth is staging a "fashion show" in which three top style mavens, including Nigel Barker from the TV show *America's Next Top Model,* will pick their favorites from among a dozen computers.

When it comes to design, rival Apple gets most of the ink, but Microsoft wants to demonstrate that PCs running Windows can turn heads, too. "There's a new bar being set," says Dave Fester, general manager of PC product marketing at Microsoft. "The market is pushing computer makers to do this."

Computers for the Fashion-Forward

PC makers are focusing as never before on turning utilitarian machines into fashion statements, and not just for the young and the hip. Lenovo Group, the world's No. 3 PC maker, is using the Vegas show to promote its expansion from commercial into consumer markets. The company is introducing three splashy notebooks—super-svelte and colorful, with textured covers that make them easy to grip. The lightest, at 2.3 pounds, is aimed at sophisticated, globe-trotting professionals.

Hewlett-Packard, the leading consumer PC brand, will hawk such new models as its Blackbird 002, a black-clad desktop gaming PC whose insides, with a copper-piped liquid cooling system, are as pleasing to the eye as the exterior via an easy-to-open side cover. And Netherlands-based Tulip Computers is showing off ultra-high-end notebooks that look like expensive purses and are pitched at wealthy, middle-age women.

Until recently, PCs were viewed by many in the industry as low-margin commodities. What changed? Apple proved with its flashy iPods, iPhones, and MacBook laptops that design really matters to consumers. The company's aura of cool, cultivated masterfully by Chief Executive Steve Jobs, helped increase its PC market share worldwide from 1.8% three years ago to 3.2% now, according to market researcher IDC. Thanks in part to its high-sheen brand, Apple's operating profit margins top 18%, compared with 6% for Dell. But other companies are riding the bandwagon successfully as well. HP's accent on design has helped it regain the title of the world's No. 1 PC maker from Dell, which concentrated on run-of-the-mill office machines.

So Long, White Box

Now even Dell has become style-conscious. Last year it brought out new consumer PCs that came in a choice of eight colors, including bubble-gum pink, yellow, green, and red. And it just introduced its XPS One—an elegant one-piece desktop. "We're in the fashion business. The products we sell increasingly make a statement about who you are," says CEO Michael S. Dell.

That perspective reflects a fundamental shift in who is buying computers today. Corporations and small businesses used to provide the lion's share of the demand. Now the consumer market is exerting a stronger pull on PC makers. Since 2002 the segment has been growing at a blistering pace. Last year consumer PC sales grew 19%, while commercial PC sales grew 11.7%, according to IDC. For much of the PC era, consumer machines made up about one-third of overall sales; today, consumer sales constitute 41% of the total PC market.

Just as the auto industry strives to create a car for every type of driver, PC models are being designed to appeal to specific kinds of people. Notable niches include young men with gaming machines, soccer moms with touch-screen models that sit shoulder-to-shoulder with kitchen appliances, and teenage girls with cute, pink, leather-clad laptops. "We're entering the age of style because we have multiple PCs in our households. So you no longer have one white box that serves every function for every person in the household," says J.P. Gownder, a Forrester Research analyst.

A few of the new machines hitting the market are clearly intended to capture some of Apple's design magic. But while most of Apple's designs seem aimed at that young, artsy slacker it features in its clever TV commercials, Apple's approach isn't about targeting hipsters, says Donald A. Norman, a professor at Northwestern University and author of *The Design of Future Things*. Rather, the company's design genius lies in its dedication to making simple, elegant

devices for specific activities, not demographic types, he says. Its early markets were learning and publishing; now they're creativity and entertainment. "The proper way to design is not to target an individual type of customer. You want 100 million customers," says Norman.

Questions for Discussion

1. What kinds of forces are changing the nature of industry competition in the PC industry?

2. How are PC companies changing their business-level strategies in response to these changes?

Source: Steve Hamm and Jay Greene, "That Computer Is So You." Reprinted from the January 2, 2008, issue of *BusinessWeek* by special permission. Copyright © 2008 by The McGraw-Hill Companies, Inc.

BusinessWeek Case in the News [LO 2, 3]

Is the Bloom Off at FTD?

With Valentine's Day nigh, the big flower merchants have slipped into marketing overdrive—creating bouquets with names like Petal Poetry, Love's First Bloom, and Butterfly Kisses. Behind the scenes, though, it's war.

FTD, burdened with debt following a stint in the hands of private equity, finds itself in a squeeze play between its two main rivals. Both 1-800-Flowers.com and Teleflora have entered retail and wholesale businesses FTD has long dominated. To make matters worse, the $19 billion industry is slowing along with the economy.

Four years ago, Los Angeles buyout shop Leonard Green & Partners paid $420 million for FTD Group. It's not hard to see what the private equity guys liked: FTD has an outstanding business model. It takes orders—say, for a dozen long-stemmed roses—and sends them to a network of 20,000 florists that, in exchange for the business, pay about $300 a month in membership dues. FTD doesn't pay for the flowers, arrange them, or deliver them but collects at least 7% of the purchase order. So the company throws off a lot of cash.

Plus, CEO Michael J. Soenen has kept a tight rein on expenses, lifting profits.

Trouble is, revenues are flat (thanks in part to discontinued products, says Soenen) and might be shrinking if, in 2006, it hadn't acquired a British floral network. Even worse, before relisting the company in 2005, Leonard Green loaded up FTD with $250 million in debt. Add $50 million borrowed for the acquisition, and you have a company that may be loath to spend at a time when its rivals are muscling in.

The biggest thorn in FTD's side is 1-800-Flowers.com. Founder James F. McCann transformed the industry by allowing people to order flowers by phone. Last year, 1-800-Flowers took in 11.6 million orders for flowers, candies, and gift baskets in the U.S., vs. FTD's 4.6 million.

For years, McCann used FTD's florist network to complete orders. Then, two years ago, he decided to take on FTD, forming his own network, called BloomNet. McCann has been offering florists rebates to persuade them to use his network. He says 9,000 have signed up so far. And though his network's revenues are a quarter the size of FTD's, BloomNet is growing much faster.

Presumably, Teleflora is also giving Soenen heartburn. For years the

privately held company mostly handled orders between florists. But now it's making a bigger play for FTD's (and 1-800-Flowers') consumer business, too. Teleflora says its online store, launched in 2004, is growing at a double-digit clip.

Big-name Bouquets

Given the competitive pressure, Brean Murray Carret analyst Eric Beder figures Soenen should do two things. One is cut florists' membership fees to prevent him from losing business to 1-800-Flowers.com. Beder also thinks Soenen should spend more on advertising. By contrast, Teleflora says it has stepped up ad spending. It is sponsoring NBC's America's Favorite Mom contest on Mother's Day and is offering Valentine's Day rose buyers a chance to win a $50,000 diamond necklace. Not to be left out, 1-800-Flowers has teamed up with Martha Stewart to create a line of bouquets that will debut this spring.

FTD isn't exactly sitting around watching the grass grow. The company has signed up Vera Wang and Todd Oldham to create bouquets. It is offering flowers grown sustainably and arranged in vases made from recycled glass. And Soenen says FTD can afford to spend more. But he is profit-obsessed—and handily beat Wall Street's expectations last quarter. Plus, since this is a cash-flow play, the stock, now at about 13, would probably suffer if he started throwing money around. Not that this will be Soenen's problem much longer. Sometime after Mother's Day, he is stepping down as CEO (though he will remain chairman). His successor won't inherit a bed of roses.

Questions for Discussion

1. How is competition changing in the flower delivery industry?

2. In what ways is FTD changing its business-level strategies to maintain its competitive position?

Source: "Is the Bloom Off at FTD?" Reprinted from the February 7, 2008, issue of *Business-Week* by special permission. Copyright © 2008 by The McGraw-Hill Companies, Inc.

BusinessWeek Case in the News [LO4]

Swords to Plowshares and Back Again at Rockwell Collins

It's the dream of every defense contractor: A product or service developed on the government's dime turns out to have broad appeal in the private sector. Think Hummer sport-utility vehicles. Night vision goggles. Tang.

Aerospace parts maker Rockwell Collins is a master at this particular form of technology transfer. Its head-up displays—transparent screens in the cockpit that tell pilots their speed, altitude, and direction—were originally developed for fighter jets and are now features of Bombardier's new Global Express aircraft and Boeing's new 787 Dreamliner.

By keeping his hands in both military and civilian work, Rockwell Collins CEO Clayton M. Jones has been able to double the company's sales and profits over the past five years, earning $585 million on sales of $4.4 billion in 2007. Those results helped the Cedar Rapids (Iowa) company soar to the No. 24 spot on *BusinessWeek*'s annual list of the 50 best-performing companies. A big part of the company's success comes from leveraging its $950 million a year in research and development spending, more than half of which comes from customers, including the Defense Dept. "He's probably one of the best at that, if not the best," says Cowen & Co. defense-industry analyst Cai von Rumohr.

Winnowing Down

Jones' company was once a part of the now-dismembered conglomerate Rockwell International. In 1996, Rockwell sold most of its space and defense businesses to Boeing but kept the units that made aircraft electronics. Back then, the defense and civilian sides of the company maintained separate design facilities, laboratories, and software. As a senior executive in the mid-1990s, Jones helped Rockwell reorganize the staff to focus on particular product lines, such as liquid-crystal displays for cockpits. "It was enormously difficult, because we completely changed the way our people did business," Jones says. "But it made us much more efficient."

Jones, a former U.S. Air Force pilot, flew F-15 fighters in the late 1970s and still has a top gun's instinct for maneuvering in tight situations. After Rockwell Collins was spun off as a public company in June 2001, the September 11 attacks all but devastated commercial aviation. But Jones was able to reassign many of the company's engineers to defense work. "As these markets go through cycles, we can shift resources and people and hold on to that intellectual capital," he says.

That capital is a valuable thing. Rockwell developed the satellites that created the global positioning system for the Defense Dept. in the 1970s. (These are the same satellites that consumer devices use today.) Rockwell still provides handheld GPS devices to troops in Iraq. The company also sells GPS systems to commercial carriers, such as Southwest Airlines, which is outfitting its fleet with them.

Sometimes the technology goes from commercial to military. One of the company's top products is Multi-Scan radar, which automatically checks different angles to get better readings of storms. It was developed in response to requests from commercial airlines, but Rockwell Collins is installing the devices on military helicopters and transport planes.

So what's in the lab these days? For one, Rockwell is designing sophisticated in-flight entertainment systems for private jets that include high-definition TV, iPod jacks, wireless Internet connections, and support for BlackBerry devices at 50,000 feet. If Jones has his way, in a few years some of that technology could find its way into commercial airliners, easing the journey for passengers riding in coach.

Questions for Discussion

1. Examine the ways in which Rockwell Collins is adding value to its existing products and entering new markets.

2. Given the way it is creating value, what kind of corporate-level strategy is the company pursuing?

Source: Christopher Palmeri, "Swords to Plowshares and Back Again at Rockwell Collins." Reprinted from the January 31, 2008, issue of *BusinessWeek* by special permission. Copyright © 2008 by The McGraw-Hill Companies, Inc.

APPENDIX

How to Develop a Business Plan

A **business plan** is a detailed, written statement that explains the purpose of creating a new venture—either a new company or a new project in an existing company—to provide new or improved products to customers. The purpose of a business plan is to guide the development, production, and marketing of a new and improved product and to accomplish this it must contain several important kinds of information: (1) It explains the purpose of the new venture, it outlines its mission and goals, and describes what kinds of product it will make and sell and why they will appeal to customers; (2) it explains why and how the new venture will be able to compete successfully against established competitors; and (3) it explains how the entrepreneur, business owner, or manager intends to obtain, use, and organize the resources the company will need to make and sell these products. The steps in the development of a business plan are listed in Table 8A.1.

If the assumptions in the business plan work out as intended, a company will have succeeded in creating a profitable new product. If the business plan does not work out because entrepreneurs and managers have made mistaken assumptions about customers' needs, or underestimated how much it will cost to make and sell the product, the new venture will be unprofitable and will probably be ended. To increase the chances of success it is therefore vital that the entrepreneur or managers do an accurate and thorough job of analyzing current industry conditions and formulating the right set of strategies.

Developing a Business Plan

Planning for a new business venture begins when an entrepreneur notices an opportunity to develop a new

Table 8A.1
Developing a Business Plan

1. Notice a Product Opportunity, and Develop a Basic Business Idea
    - Goods/services
    - Customers/markets
2. Conduct a Strategic (SWOT) Analysis
    - Identify opportunities
    - Identify threats
    - Identify strengths
    - Identify weaknesses
3. Decide Whether the Business Opportunity Is Feasible
4. Prepare a Detailed Business Plan
    - Executive summary: Statement of mission, goals, and financial objectives
    - Company background information
    - List of necessary functional and organizational strategies and resources
    - Organizational time line of events

or improved good or service. Similarly, planning for a new business venture or project *inside of* an established company begins when a manager notices an opportunity. On the one hand, an entrepreneur might notice an opportunity in the fast-food market to provide customers with healthy fast food such as rotisserie chicken served with fresh vegetables. This is what the founders of the Boston Market restaurant chain did. On the other hand, a manager at McDonald's might notice an opportunity to create a new kind of hamburger or fast-food product to attract more customers. And, in fact, the idea for the Big Mac and Egg McMuffin came from two of McDonald's franchisees who independently developed and tested these new products and then shared them with the whole McDonald's Company.

There is no formalized way in which a person can "come up" with a new idea for an attractive new product. Many successful new products result from continuous hard thinking and from intuition and luck. They can also result from a formal, in-house strategic planning process as product development and marketing managers brainstorm ideas for new products or new ways to package and deliver them to customers. Once a new product idea has been generated, the crucial next step in creating a business plan is to test the feasibility of the new idea and the strategies behind it.

To accomplish this, an entrepreneur or functional experts perform a detailed SWOT analysis, the strategic planning exercise discussed in Chapter 8 (see Table 8.1). For example, in the fast-food industry, to assess the viability of selling rotisserie chicken served with fresh vegetables, an entrepreneur needs to analyze opportunities and threats. One potential threat might be that if the new idea succeeds, McDonald's or KFC might decide to imitate the idea and rush to do so. If this happens, whatever competitive advantage the entrepreneur may have had will be short-lived. (KFC actually did this after Boston Market was successfully launched.) As the entrepreneur conducts a thorough analysis of the competitive environment, he or she must be willing to abandon an idea if it seems likely that industry threats will be difficult to counter so that the risks involved are too great to bear.

Entrepreneurs and managers must not become so committed to their ideas that they discount potential threats and forge ahead—only to lose all of the money they invested in their venture. Unfortunately, people make this mistake all the time in the restaurant business and the failure rate of new restaurants is very high.

If the environmental analysis suggests that the product idea is feasible, however, the next step is to examine the strengths and weaknesses of the idea. For a new company venture the main strength is likely to be the resources possessed by the entrepreneur. Does the entrepreneur have access to an adequate source of funds? Does the entrepreneur have any experience in the fast-food industry such as having been a chef or managed a restaurant? To identify weaknesses, the entrepreneur needs to assess what kinds of functional resources will be necessary to establish a viable new venture—such as a chain of chicken restaurants—and how much money will be required to fund it.

Thus, the first three steps in creating a business plan for a new venture are listed next. First, notice a product opportunity and develop a mission statement and goals that focuses on the product, customer needs, and potential markets. Second, conduct a SWOT analysis to identify opportunities, threats, strengths, and weaknesses. Third, make an initial assessment of whether the new venture is feasible and if it is, then write the detailed business plan.

Writing a Detailed Business Plan

Once these steps are completed, the hard work of writing up the detailed business plan begins. The business plan will be used (1) to continue the process of testing, assessing, and fine-tuning the proposed set of strategies, and (2) to attract the banks or investors who will provide the capital needed to launch the venture (or, in the case of an exiting company, get the buy-in of top managers). Business plans are formatted in many ways, but a typical format is as follows:

THE EXECUTIVE SUMMARY The executive summary is an opening, two-page statement of the organization's mission, goals, and financial objectives. The summary also contains a statement of the organization's strategic objectives, including an in-depth analysis of a new product's market potential based on the SWOT analysis that has already been conducted. Finally, it outlines the strategies needed to use an organization's resources to compete effectively in the industry. It is essential that these strategies should explain how the new venture will obtain a *sustainable competitive advantage,* one that will allow it to perform effectively over time and adapt to changing competitive conditions as needed.

COMPANY BACKGROUND INFORMATION The second part of the business plan provides a short biography of the entrepreneur or manager, and the new venture company that has been founded, or, in the case of a venture within an established company, specific details about a new project team's history. This should include:

- The age of the new venture, or company, and time of its founding.

- The number of people involved in the venture, including its owners, senior managers, scientists, researchers, and other functional experts, and what their background, experience, and competencies are.

- Existing and projected annual sales and costs figures.

- The current and future location of the facilities that will be used to make and sell the product.

- The current and future form of the legal ownership structure of the business, for example, whether it will be organized as a sole proprietorship, partnership, entrepreneurial startup, private corporate startup, publicly traded corporation, or not-for-profit organization.

FUNCTIONAL AND ORGANIZATIONAL STRATEGIES AND RESOURCES The third and very important section of a business plan contains a detailed account of the set of functional strategies that will be required to implement the chosen strategies and organize the new venture. Some of these functional plans are a marketing plan, production and materials management plan, financial plan, and human resource plan. A short description of each is as follows:

1. Marketing Plan *describes*

- The competitive industry environment.
- Customers' needs, priorities, and location.
- The product strategy.
- The pricing strategy.
- The promotion and advertising strategy.
- The distribution strategy.

2. Production and Material Management Plan *describes*

- All manufacturing and production processes.
- The requirements of the production facility, including the number of people that will be required to assemble products or deliver services, and the size, layout, capacity, and location of the facility.
- The inventory management plan for raw materials and finished goods inventory, and the warehouse space needed for each in the case of physical products. The number of functional specialists who will be required to provide a service, together with an assessment of when and where they will be needed to be responsive to customers.
- A full list of important and expensive production and computer equipment and service delivery requirements such as vehicles and transportation costs.

3. Human Resource Plan *describes*

- The allocation of authority and responsibility.
- The skills and training requirements personnel will need.
- The venture's recruitment and employee selection policies.
- The performance evaluation and compensation plans for the venture's members.

TIME LINE AND MAJOR MILESTONES Finally, a business plan contains a detailed description and roadmap of how and when a new venture intends to meet the overall goals and objectives set out in the other sections of the business plan. In particular, it contains a detailed timeline for purchasing resources, hiring new personnel, and creating the functional and organizational value chain that will be needed to implement the business venture. Examples include the target dates for the final design, construction, and opening of the first chicken restaurant. Such a roadmap allows the entrepreneur, employees, and investors to assess how much progress has been made in getting the new product to market. It also provides a way of assessing how new issues and problems may have emerged because of changing internal strengths and weaknesses and external opportunities, and threats.

Developing Your *Own* Business Plan

As you can see, developing a detailed business plan that provides an in-depth explanation of how entrepreneurs or managers can create profitable new products is a complex, creative, and time-consuming task. Yet it must be done to more accurately assess the potential risks and returns of a new venture. Unlike adventurous managers in established companies, many individual entrepreneurs do not have a team of expert functional managers to help them develop a detailed business plan. Also, they typically lack the in-house financial resources intrapreneurs can draw upon. This is one reason why franchising has become such a popular method of starting a new business in the United States. A prospective entrepreneur can purchase and draw upon the proven business plan of an already existing company, and, in this way, reduce the problems and risks associated with opening a new business. Of course, in return, a franchisee often pays a significant percentage of the franchise's revenues and profits to the franchising company. The founders of chains like Subway Sandwiches and Stanley Steamer have made a fortune by selling the rights to use their business plan.

A useful exercise to help you appreciate the amount of thought and effort that goes into opening a new business is to prepare a *simplified* business plan along the lines suggested above. But a good place to start—either by yourself or with others as a team—is to "brainstorm" about a novel product idea that you think might have commercial possibilities. Then test the idea by performing a SWOT analysis using some of the questions in Table 8.1.

Write down your responses to these questions, and after you have examined the strengths, weakness, opportunities, and threats associated with your new business idea, you can assess how viable it is. You may decide it is not, so then start another round of brainstorming. Once you have found a viable new product idea, write a simplified business plan. Start by describing your mission and goals. Then describe the series of subplans for marketing, materials management, production, HRM, sales, and the other value-creation functions that will be needed to develop and implement your idea.

A good way to test your detailed business plan is then to give copies of it to classmates or friends and have them assess its viability. Also, develop a slideshow presentation of your business plan, and then allow other people or teams to question and probe its details and assumptions. In this way you will gain an appreciation of the many complex issues involved in planning and strategy. You will gain a much better understanding of how much hard work and effort it takes for people to found, organize, and manage companies that provide customers with valuable goods and services.

CHAPTER 9

Value-Chain Management: Functional Strategies for Competitive Advantage

Learning Objectives

After studying this chapter, you should be able to:

LO1 Explain the role of functional strategy and value-chain management in achieving superior quality, efficiency, innovation, and responsiveness to customers.

LO2 Describe what customers want, and explain why it is so important for managers to be responsive to their needs.

LO3 Explain why achieving superior quality is so important, and understand the challenges facing managers and organizations that seek to implement total quality management.

LO4 Explain why achieving superior efficiency is so important, and understand the different kinds of techniques that need to be employed to increase efficiency.

LO5 Differentiate between two forms of innovation, and explain why innovation and product development is a crucial component of the search for competitive advantage.

A MANAGER'S CHALLENGE

Toyota's Approach to Building Competitive Advantage

www.toyota.com

How can managers increase operating performance? Toyota has long been known as a company that constantly strives to improve its car design and production systems to enhance efficiency, quality, innovation, and customer responsiveness. It pioneered the system of "lean production," a functional strategy that changes the way cars are assembled and results in dramatic improvements in vehicle reliability. And Toyota has always pursued total quality management, or *kaizen,* a functional strategy that makes production-line employees responsible for finding ways to continuously make incremental improvements to work procedures that drive down costs and drive up quality. Over time, the thousands of suggestions employees' make, individually and in quality groups or circles, result in innovations to the car assembly process that lead to major improvements in the final product. Employees receive cash bonuses and rewards for their contributions, which enable Toyota to continuously increase car quality and reduce manufacturing costs.

In the 2000s, however, under the leadership of Toyota's chairman, Jujio Cho, and president, Katsuaki Watanabe, the company sought new strategies to further improve

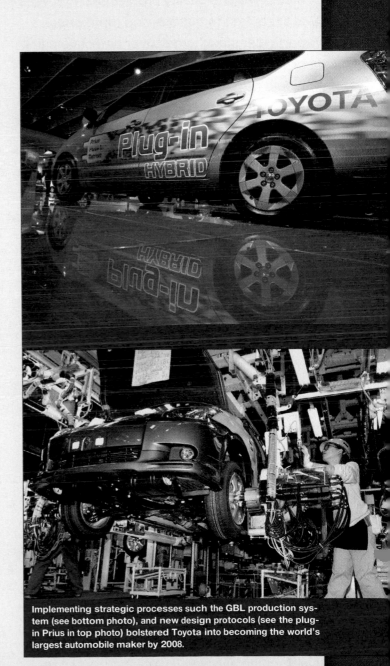

Implementing strategic processes such the GBL production system (see bottom photo), and new design protocols (see the plug-in Prius in top photo) bolstered Toyota into becoming the world's largest automobile maker by 2008.

efficiency and quality and strengthen its competitive advantage over rivals such as Volkswagen, Ford, and DaimlerChrysler.[1] It began to implement a series of new strategies, each directed at improving the way its various functions operate. One new manufacturing strategy to strengthen its kaizen program is "pokayoke," or mistake-proofing. This initiative concentrates on the stages of the assembly process that have led to most previous quality problems; employees are required to double- and triple-check a particular stage to discover defective parts or to fix improper assembly operations that would have led to subsequent customer complaints. Another strategy was "CCC21," which involves working with the company's suppliers to find ways to reduce the costs of Toyota's car components by 30%—this has succeeded so well that it has resulted in over $10 billion dollars in savings by 2007. Toyota also implemented a new manufacturing process called GBL that uses a sophisticated new assembly process to hold a car body firmly in place during production. This allows welding and assembly operations to be performed more accurately, resulting in better-quality cars. GBL has also enabled Toyota to build factories that can assemble several different car models on the same production line with no loss in efficiency or quality. This is a major competitive advantage. The company's global network of plants can now quickly switch among the kinds of cars they are making depending upon buyers' demands for various models at different points in time.

Other new functional strategies focus on revamping Toyota's development and design process to keep up with changing customer needs and demographics; for example, the age of the average Toyota car buyer has been steadily increasing, which is a major competitive problem. Despite Toyota's climbing global sales (which exceeded $220 billion in 2007), the company has often been criticized for failing to understand the needs of different kinds of customers. Analysts blamed the problem on centralized decision making at the company and a culture that had long been dominated by Toyota's cautious and frugal Japanese designers. Rather than designing innovative, flexible vehicles that customers were increasingly demanding, Toyota continued to focus on cutting costs and increasing quality. When the company's U.S. designers, for example, argued with designers in Tokyo that U.S. customers wanted an eight-cylinder pickup truck, and that Toyota needed to make such a vehicle to compete with GM and Ford, they were ignored. Headquarters also turned a deaf ear to the call to make innovative vehicles that would appeal to younger customers. Slow sales of its small pickups and compact cars soon showed that the company was not being responsive to customers and that design changes were necessary.

To speed innovation and the new product development process, Cho championed two new functional strategies that radically alter the way vehicles are designed: PDCA and Obeya. Obeya is based on frequent brainstorming sessions between product engineers, designers, production managers, and marketers and is designed to speed new-model cars to the market. PDCA, or "plan-do-check-action," is a strategy designed to empower the company's designers outside Japan to intervene in the product development process and champion vehicle designs that meet the needs of local customers. The results of promoting a flexible, decentralized car design process were the speedy introduction of the rugged eight-cylinder Tundra pickup truck and the angular ScionxB compact in the United States, as well as the Yaris, Toyota's best-selling European car. The Yaris was designed in Europe, and its success there led to its subsequent introduction in Japan, where it also sold well.

Toyota's mastery of value-chain management through implementing groundbreaking functional strategies has made it by far the most profitable of the major carmakers.[2] Its functional strategies strengthen its ability to pursue both low cost and differentiation business-level strategies and have given it a widening competitive advantage over its rivals. Toyota replaced Ford as the world's second-largest carmaker in 2004, and it replaced GM as the world's biggest carmaker in April 2008.

Overview

Toyota has developed many kinds of strategies to encourage managers in value-creating functions like manufacturing, materials management, and product development to improve the way functional activities are performed to promote the organization's competitive advantage. In this chapter we focus on the functional-level strategies managers can use to achieve superior efficiency, quality, innovation, and responsiveness to customers and so build competitive advantage. We also examine the nature of an organization's value chain and discuss how the combined or cooperative efforts of managers across the value chain are required if an organization is to achieve its mission and goal of maximizing the amount of value its products provide customers. By the end of this chapter, you will understand the vital role value-chain management plays in building competitive advantage and creating a high-performing organization.

Functional Strategies, the Value Chain, and Competitive Advantage

As we noted in Chapter 8, there are two basic business-level strategies managers can use to add value to an organization's products and achieve a competitive advantage over industry rivals. First, managers can pursue a *low-cost strategy* and lower the costs of creating value in order to attract customers by keeping product prices as low as or lower than competitors' prices. Second, managers can pursue a *differentiation strategy* and add value to a product by finding ways to make it superior in some way to the products of other companies. If they are successful, and customers see greater value in the product, then like Toyota they are able to charge a premium or higher price for the product. The four specific ways in which managers can lower costs and/or increase differentiation to obtain a competitive advantage were mentioned in Chapter 1 and are reviewed below; how organizations seek to achieve them is the topic of this chapter. (See Figure 9.1.)

LO1 Explain the role of functional strategy and value-chain management in achieving superior quality, efficiency, innovation, and responsiveness to customers.

1. *Achieve superior efficiency.* Efficiency is a measure of the amount of inputs required to produce a given amount of outputs. The fewer the inputs required to produce a given output, the higher is efficiency and the lower the cost of outputs. For example, in 1990 it took the average Japanese auto company 16.8 employee-hours to build a car, while the average American car company took 25.1 employee-hours. Japanese companies at that time were more efficient and had lower costs than their American rivals.[3] In the 2000s, U.S. companies have adopted more efficient manufacturing methods and narrowed the cost gap significantly; however, as the opening case suggests, Toyota continually works to reduce costs to maintain its position as the most efficient carmaker in the world.

Figure 9.1
Four Ways to Create a Competitive Advantage

2. *Achieve superior quality.* Quality means producing goods and services that have attributes—such as design, styling, performance, and reliability—that customers perceive as being superior to those found in competing products.[4] Providing high-quality products creates a brand-name reputation for an organization's products, and this enhanced reputation allows it to charge higher prices. In the car industry, for example, besides Toyota's efficiency-based cost advantage, the higher quality of Toyota's products also enables the company to outperform its rivals because customers are willing to pay a premium price for its cars.

3. *Achieve superior innovation, speed, and flexibility.* Anything new or better about the way an organization operates or the goods and services it produces is the result of innovation. Successful innovation gives an organization something *unique* or different about its products that rivals lack—more sophisticated products, production processes, or strategies and structures that strengthen its competitive advantage. Innovation adds value to products, and allows the organization to further differentiate itself from rivals and attract customers willing to pay a premium price for unique products. Toyota is widely credited with pioneering innovations in the way cars are built that have made them more reliable, quiet, and comfortable and allowed it to charge a premium price for them. For example, a Toyota Corolla or Camry is always priced a thousand or more dollars above its equivalent U.S. competitor such as the Ford Focus or Taurus or the Chevy Cobalt, Grand Prix, or Pontiac G6, and many customers are willing to pay the higher price.

4. *Attain superior responsiveness to customers.* An organization that is responsive to customers tries to satisfy their needs and give them *exactly* what they want. An organization that treats customers better than its rivals do also provides a valuable service some customers may be willing to pay a higher price for. Managers can increase responsiveness by providing excellent after-sales service and support and by working with customers to provide improved products or services in the future. Today, Toyota, like other carmakers, is always on the lookout for changing customer needs, and as "A Manager's Challenge" described, managers across its functions apply innovative strategies to design new cars to better meet those needs.

One way to measure how much managers are concerned with customer responsiveness is to look at the range of products a company makes and how fast it changes and improves them to better meet their needs. Figure 9.2 shows the range of vehicles that Toyota currently makes and the kinds of customers it is targeting according to the price they are willing or able to pay. As the figure illustrates, there are few major gaps in Toyota's product range; the company makes a variety of vehicles that are designed to be responsive to the needs of the largest possible range of customers.

Figure 9.2

Toyota's Product Lineup

Price	Sports Utility Vehicles	Passenger/ Sports Sedans	Passenger Vans	Personal Luxury Vehicles	Sporty Cars	Pickup Trucks
11–20K	RAV4 Scion XB	Corolla, Yaris Scion TC,XD			Matrix	Tacoma
21–30K	FJ Cruiser 4-Runner, Highlander	Prius, Camry	Sienna	Avalon	Camry Solara	Tundra
31–45K	Sequoia, Lexus RX	Lexus ES Lexus IS		Lexus ES ES 350	Camry Solara Conv	Tundra Double Cab
46–75K	Land Cruiser, Lexus EX Lexus LX	Lexus GS		Lexus LS	Lexus SC Lexus ISF	

☐ No vehicle in category

Functional Strategies and Value-Chain Management

functional-level strategy
A plan of action to improve the ability of each of an organization's functions to perform its task-specific activities in ways that add value to an organization's goods and services.

Functional-level strategy is a plan of action to improve the ability of each of an organization's functions or departments (such as manufacturing or marketing) to perform its task-specific activities in ways that add value to an organization's goods and services. A company's **value chain** is the coordinated series or sequence of functional activities necessary to transform inputs such as new product concepts, raw materials, component parts, or professional skills into the finished goods or services customers value and want to buy (see Figure 9.3). Each functional activity along the chain *adds value* to the product when it lowers costs or gives the product differentiated qualities that increase the price a company can charge for it.

Value-chain management is the development of a set of functional-level strategies that support a company's business-level strategy and strengthen its competitive

Figure 9.3

Functional Activities and the Value Chain

value chain The coordinated series or sequence of functional activities necessary to transform inputs such as new product concepts, raw materials, component parts, or professional skills into the finished goods or services customers value and want to buy.

value-chain management The development of a set of functional-level strategies that support a company's business-level strategy and strengthen its competitive advantage.

advantage. Functional managers develop the strategies that result in increased efficiency, quality, innovation, and/or responsiveness to customers and thus strengthen an organization's competitive advantage. So the better the fit between functional- and business-level strategies, the greater will be the organization's competitive advantage, and the better able the organization is to achieve its mission and goal of maximizing the amount of value it gives customers—something Toyota excels at. Each function along the value chain has an important role to play in the value-creation process.

As Figure 9.3 suggests, the starting point of the value chain is often the search for new and improved products that will better appeal to customers, so the activities of the product development and marketing functions become important. *Product development* is the engineering and scientific research activities involved in innovating new or improved products that add value to a product. For example, Toyota's engineers developed a hybrid gas-saving technology that has proved popular among car buyers; so popular it has been licensed by Ford and GM for use in their vehicles. Once a new product has been developed, then the *marketing function's* task is to persuade customers that the product meets their needs and convince them to buy it. Marketing can help create value through brand positioning and advertising that increases customer perceptions about the utility of a company's product. For example, in the 1980s the French company Perrier persuaded U.S. customers that carbonated bottled water was worth $1.50 per liter bottle rather than the 25 cents it cost to purchase a gallon of spring water. Perrier's marketing function had developed strategies that made customers want to buy the product, and major U.S. companies such as Coca-Cola and PepsiCo rushed to bring out their own bottled-water labels to capitalize on customers' growing appetite for bottled water.

Even the best-designed product can fail if the marketing function hasn't devised a careful plan to persuade people to buy it and try it out—or to make sure customers really want it. For this reason, marketing often conducts consumer research to discover unmet customer product needs and to find better ways to tailor existing products to satisfy customer needs. Marketing then presents its suggestions to product development, which performs its own research to discover how best to design and make the new or improved products.

At the next stage of the value chain, the *materials management function* controls the movement of physical materials from the procurement of inputs through production and to distribution and delivery to the customer. The efficiency with which this is carried out can significantly lower costs and create more value. Wal-Mart, the U.S. retailing giant, has the most efficient materials management function in the retail industry. By tightly controlling the flow of goods from its suppliers through its stores and into the hands of customers, Wal-Mart has eliminated the need to hold large inventories of goods. Lower inventories mean lower costs, and hence greater value creation. Similarly, Toyota insists that its suppliers establish car component plants close to its factories so that it does not have to bear the cost of holding a large inventory of car components—a significant cost savings.

The *production function* is responsible for the creation, assembly, or provision of a good or service—for transforming inputs into outputs. For physical products, when we talk about production, we generally mean manufacturing and assembly. For services such as banking or retailing, production takes place when the service is actually provided or delivered to the customer (for example, when a bank originates a loan for a customer, it is engaged in "production" of the loan). By performing its activities efficiently, the production function helps to lower costs. For example, the efficient production operations of Honda and Toyota have made them more profitable than competitors such as Renault, Volkswagen, and Ford. The production function can also perform its activities in a way that is consistent with high product quality, which leads to differentiation (and higher value) and to lower costs.

At the next stage in the value chain, the *sales function* plays a crucial role in locating customers and then informing and persuading them to buy the company's products. Personal selling, that is, direct face-to-face communication by salespeople with existing and potential customers to promote a company's products, is a crucial value-chain activity. Which products retailers choose to stock, for example, or which drugs doctors choose to prescribe often depend upon the salesperson's ability to inform and persuade customers that his or her company's product is superior and thus the best choice.

Finally, the role of the *customer service function* is to provide after-sales service and support. This function can create a perception of superior value in the minds of customers by solving customer problems and supporting customers after they have purchased the product. For example, FedEx can get its customers' parcels to any point in the world within 24 hours, thereby lowering the cost of its own value-creation activities. Finally, customer service controls the electronic systems for tracking sales and inventory, pricing products, selling products, dealing with customer inquires, and so on, all of which can greatly increase responsiveness to customers. Indeed, an important activity of sales and customer service is to inform product development and marketing about why a product is meeting or not meeting customers' needs so that the product can be redesigned or improved. Hence, the feedback loop links the end of the value chain to its beginning (see Figure 9.3).

In the rest of this chapter we examine the functional strategies used to manage the value chain to improve quality, efficiency, innovation, and responsiveness to customers. Notice, however, that achieving superior quality, efficiency, and innovation is *part* of attaining superior responsiveness to customers. Customers want value for their money, and managers who develop functional strategies that result in a value chain capable of creating innovative, high-quality, low-cost products best deliver this value to customers. For this reason, we begin by discussing how functional managers can increase responsiveness to customers.

Improving Responsiveness to Customers

All organizations produce outputs—goods or services—that are consumed by customers, who, in buying these products, provide the monetary resources most organizations need to survive. Since customers are vital to organizational survival, managers must correctly identify who their customers are and pursue strategies that result in products that best meet their needs. This is why the marketing function plays such an important part in the value chain, and good value-chain management requires that marketing managers focus on defining their company's business in terms of the customer *needs* it is satisfying and not by the *type of products* it makes—or the result can be disaster.[5] For example, Kodak's managers said "no thanks" when the company was offered the rights to "instant photography," which was later marketed by Polaroid. Why did they make this mistake? Because the managers adopted a product-oriented approach to their business which didn't put the needs of customers first. Kodak's managers believed their job was to sell high-quality, glossy photographs to people; why would they want to become involved in instant photography, which results in inferior-quality photographs? In reality, Kodak was not satisfying people's needs for high-quality photographs; it was satisfying the need customers had to *capture and record the images of their lives*—their birthday parties, weddings, graduations, and so on. And people wanted those images quickly so that they could share them right away with other people—which is why today digital photography has taken off. In the 2000s, Kodak is in serious trouble because its film-based photographic business has declined sharply, it has lost billions as it strives to position itself in the digital market to give customers what they want.

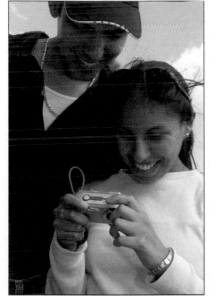

Kodak has fallen behind in the digital camera market by focusing more on products than on customers.

What Do Customers Want?

Given that satisfying customer demands is central to the survival of an organization, an important question is, "What do customers want?" Although specifying *exactly* what customers want is not possible because their needs vary from product to product, it is possible to identify some general product attributes or qualities that most customers desire:

1. A lower price to a higher price.
2. High-quality products to low-quality products.
3. Quick service and good after-sales service to slow service and poor after-sales support.
4. Products with many useful or valuable features to products with few features.
5. Products that are, as far as possible, customized or tailored to their unique needs.

Managers know that the more desired product attributes a company's value chain builds into its products, the higher the price that must be charged to cover the costs of developing and making the product. So what do managers of a customer-responsive organization try to do? They try to develop functional strategies that allow the organization's value chain to deliver to customers either *more* desired product attributes for the *same price* or the *same* product attributes for a *lower price*.[6] For example, by increasing the efficiency of its manufacturing process, and by finding new ways to design cars that are less expensive, Toyota has been able to increase the number of luxury features in its cars at very little or no extra cost, compared to its competitors. Similarly, Wal-Mart's "price rollbacks" or reductions are possible because it constantly searches for lower-cost suppliers or more efficient ways to manage its product inventory and deliver it to stores. It told its suppliers, for example, that if they did not put new radio frequency tags (that allow inventory to be monitored electronically as it moves around) on their products by 2006, it would cease to buy from them.[7] In general, new IT has allowed many organizations to offer new models of products with more attributes at a price similar to or even lower than that of earlier models, and so in the last decade customers have been able to choose from a wider variety of higher-quality products and receive quicker customer service.

Managing the Value Chain to Increase Responsiveness to Customers

Because satisfying customers is so important, managers try to design and improve the way their value chains operate so that they can supply products that have the desired attributes—quality, cost, and features. For example, the need to respond to customer demands for competitively priced, quality cars drove U.S. carmakers like Ford and GM to imitate Japanese companies and copy the way Toyota and Honda perform their value-chain activities. Today, the imperative of satisfying customer needs shapes the activities of GM's materials management and manufacturing functions. As an example of the link between responsiveness to customers and an organization's value chain, consider how Southwest Airlines, the most profitable U.S. airline, operates.[8]

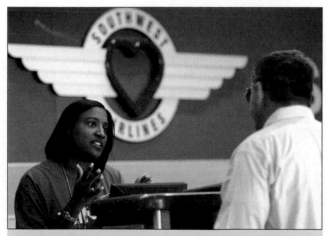

A Southwest ticket agent may assist a customer and then turn around to load his baggage as part of the organization's emphasis on cross-training workers for multiple tasks. Southwest's operating system is geared toward satisfying customer demands for low-priced, reliable, and convenient air travel, making it one of the most consistently successful airlines in recent years.

The major reason for Southwest's success is that it has striven to pursue functional strategies that improve the way its value chain operates to give customers what they want. Southwest commands high customer loyalty precisely because it can deliver products, such as flights from Houston to Dallas, which have all the desired attributes: reliability, convenience, and low price. In each one of its functions, Southwest's strategies revolve around finding ways to lower costs. For example, Southwest offers a no-frills approach to in-flight customer service; no meals are served onboard, and there are no first-class seats. Southwest does not subscribe to the big reservation computers used by travel agents because the booking fees are too costly. Also, the airline flies only one aircraft, the fuel-efficient Boeing 737, which keeps training and maintenance costs down. All this translates into low prices for customers.

Southwest's reliability derives from the fact that it has the quickest aircraft turnaround time in the industry. A Southwest ground crew needs only 15 minutes to turn around an incoming aircraft and prepare it for departure. This speedy operation helps to keep flights on time. Southwest has such a quick turnaround because it has a flexible workforce (as mentioned above) that has been cross-trained to perform multiple tasks. Thus, the person who checks tickets might also help with baggage loading if time is short.

Southwest's convenience comes from its scheduling multiple flights every day between its popular locations, such as Dallas and Houston, and its use of airports that are close to downtown areas (Hobby at Houston and Love Field at Dallas) instead of using more distant, major airports.[9] In sum, Southwest's excellent value-chain management has given it a competitive advantage in the airline industry.

Although managers must seek to improve their responsiveness to customers by improving the way the value chain operates, they should not offer a level of responsiveness to customers that results in costs becoming *too high*—something that threatens an organization's future performance and survival. For example, a company that customizes every product to the unique demands of individual customers is likely to find that its costs will get out of control. This happened to Toyota in the 1990s when its managers' push to offer customers many different choices of specifications for a particular model of car increased costs faster than it generated additional sales. At one point, Toyota factories were producing literally thousands of variations of Toyota's basic models, such as the Camry and Corolla! Toyota's managers decided that the costs of extreme customer responsiveness exceeded the benefits, and they reduced the number of models and specifications of its cars.[10] This is why today most models of Toyota vehicles listed in Figure 9.2 are assembled to three main levels of specifications—basic, sports, or luxury packages. Customers have less choice, but they also pay a lower price and still get more of the attributes they desire.

Customer Relationship Management

One functional strategy managers can use to get close to customers and understand their needs is **customer relationship management (CRM).** CRM is a technique that uses IT to develop an ongoing relationship with customers to maximize the value an organization can deliver to them over time. In the 2000s, most large companies have installed sophisticated CRM IT to track customers' changing demands for a company's products; it has become a vital tool used to maximize responsiveness to customers. CRM IT monitors, controls, and links each of the functional activities involved in marketing, selling, and delivering products to customers, such as monitoring the delivery of products through the distribution channel, monitoring salespeople's selling activities, setting product pricing, and coordinating after-sales service. CRM systems have three interconnected components, sales and selling, after-sales service and support, and marketing.

Suppose that a sales manager has access only to sales data that show the total sales revenue each salesperson had generated in the last 30 days. This information does not break down how much revenue came from sales to existing customers versus sales to new customers. What important knowledge is being lost? First, if most revenues are earned from sales to existing customers, this suggests that the money being spent by a company to advertise and promote its products is not attracting new customers and so is being wasted. Second, important dimensions involved in sales are pricing, financing, and order processing. In many companies, to close a deal, a salesperson has to send the paperwork to a central sales office that handles matters such as approving the customer for special financing and determining specific shipping and delivery dates. In some companies, different departments handle these activities, and it can take a long time to get a response from them; this keeps customers waiting—something that often leads to lost sales. Until CRM systems were introduced, these kinds of problems were widespread and resulted in missed sales and higher operating costs. Today, the sales and selling CRM software contains *best sales practices* that analyze this information and then recommend ways to improve the way the sales process operates. One company that has improved its sales, and after-sales, practices by implementing CRM is discussed in the following "Information Technology Byte."

Information Technology Byte

How CRM Helped Empire HealthChoice

Empire HealthChoice Inc., the largest health insurance provider in New York, sells its policies through 1,800 sales agents. For years, these agents were responsible for collecting all of the customer-specific information needed to determine the price of each policy. Once they had collected the necessary information, the agents called Empire to get their price quotes. After waiting days to get these quotes, the agents relayed them back to customers, who often then modified their requests to reduce the cost of their policies. When this occurred, the agent had to telephone Empire again to get a revised price quote. Because this frequently happened several times with each transaction, it often took more than 20 days to close a sale and another 10 days for customers to get their insurance cards.[11]

Recognizing these delays were resulting in lost sales, Empire decided to examine how a CRM system could help improve the sales process. Its managers chose a Web-based system so that agents themselves could calculate the insurance quotes online. Once an agent has entered a customer's data, a quote is generated in just a few seconds. The agent can continually modify a policy while sitting face-to-face with the customer until the policy and price are agreed upon. As a result, the sales process can now be completed in a few hours, and customers receive their insurance cards in 2 to 3 days rather than 10.[12]

When a company implements after-sales service and support CRM software, salespeople are required to input detailed information about their follow-up visits to customers. Because the system is now tracking and documenting every customer's case history, salespeople have instant access to a record of everything that occurred during previous phone calls or visits. They are now in a much better position to be responsive to customers' needs and build customer loyalty, so a company's after-sales service improves. Telephone providers like Sprint and MCI, for example, require that telephone sales reps collect information about all customers' inquiries, complaints, and requests, and this is recorded electronically in customer logs. The CRM module can analyze the information in these logs to evaluate whether the customer service reps are meeting or exceeding the company's required service standards.

The CRM system also identifies the top 10 reasons why customer complaints are arising. Sales managers can then work to eliminate the sources of these problems and improve after-sales support procedures. The CRM system also identifies the top 10 best service and support practices, which can then be taught to all sales reps.

Finally, as a CRM system processes information about changing customer needs, this improves the way marketing operates in many ways. Marketing managers, for example, now have access to detailed customer profiles, including data on purchases and the reasons why individuals were or were not attracted to a company's products. Armed with this knowledge, marketing can better identify customers and the specific product attributes they desire. It may become clear, for example, that a customer group that marketing had targeted has a specific need that is not being satisfied by a product—such as a need for a cell phone containing a 5-megapixel digital camera and an MP3 player. With real-time information, marketing can work with product development to redesign the product to better meet customer needs. In sum, a CRM system is a comprehensive method of gathering crucial information about the way customers respond to a company's products. It is a powerful functional strategy used to better align a company's products with customer needs.

Improving Quality

As noted earlier, high-quality products possess attributes such as superior design, features, reliability, and after-sales support; these products are designed to better meet customer requirements.[13] Quality is a concept that can be applied to the products of both manufacturing and service organizations—goods such as a Toyota car or services such as Southwest Airlines flight service or customer service in a Citibank branch. Why do managers seek to control and improve the quality of their organizations' products?[14] There are two reasons (see Figure 9.4).

First, customers usually prefer a higher-quality product to a lower-quality product. So an organization able to provide, *for the same price,* a product of higher quality than a competitor's product is serving its customers better—it is being more responsive to its customers. Often, providing high-quality products creates a brand-name reputation for an organization's products. In turn, this enhanced reputation may allow the organization to charge more for its products than its competitors are able to charge, and thus it makes even greater profits. In 2007 Lexus was ranked number one, as it has been for over a decade, on the J. D. Power list of the 10 most reliable carmakers, and Toyota was close behind.[15] The high quality of Toyota/Lexus vehicles enables the company to charge higher prices for its cars than the prices charged by rival carmakers.

The second reason for trying to boost product quality is that higher product quality can increase efficiency and thereby lower operating costs and boost profits. Achieving high product quality lowers operating costs because of the effect of quality on employee productivity: Higher product quality means less employee time is wasted in making defective products that must be discarded or in providing substandard services, and thus less time has to be spent fixing mistakes. This translates into higher employee productivity, which means lower costs.

LO3 Explain why achieving superior quality is so important, and understand the challenges facing managers and organizations that seek to implement total quality management.

Figure 9.4

The Impact of Increased Quality on Organizational Performance

Total Quality Management

total quality management (TQM) A management technique that focuses on improving the quality of an organization's products and services.

At the forefront of the drive to improve product quality is a functional strategy known as total quality management.[16] **Total quality management (TQM)** focuses on improving the quality of an organization's products and stresses that *all* of an organization's value-chain activities should be directed toward this goal. TQM requires the cooperation of managers in every function of an organization, and across functions, if it is to succeed.[17] To help understand how TQM works, we next describe the way that Citibank used the technique. Then, using Citibank as an example, we look at the 10 steps that are necessary for managers to implement a successful TQM program.

In the 2000s Citibank's top managers decided that the bank could only retain and expand its customer base if it could increase customer loyalty, so they decided to implement a TQM program to better satisfy customer needs. As the first step in its TQM effort, Citibank identified the factors that dissatisfy its customers. When analyzing the complaints, it found that most concerned the time it took to complete a customer's request, such as responding to an account problem or getting a loan. So Citibank's managers began to examine how they handled each kind of customer request. For each distinct request, they formed a cross-functional team that broke down the request into the steps required, between people and departments, to complete the response. In analyzing the steps, teams found that many of them were often unnecessary and could be replaced by using the right information systems. They also found that very often delays occurred because employees simply did not know how to handle a request. They were not being given the right kind of training, and when they couldn't handle a request, they simply put it aside until a supervisor could deal with it.

Citibank's second step to increase its responsiveness was to implement an organizationwide TQM program. Managers and supervisors were charged with reducing the complexity of the work process and finding the most effective way to process each particular request, such as a request for a loan. Managers were also charged with training employees to answer each specific request. The results were remarkable. For example, in the loan department the TQM program reduced the number of hand-offs necessary to process a request by 75%. The department's average response time dropped from several hours to 30 minutes. In the 2000s, almost all of its more than 100,000 employees worldwide have been trained in the new TQM processes, and Citibank can easily measure TQM's effectiveness by the increased speed with which it was handling an increased volume of customer requests. What are the 10 steps in TQM that made this possible?

1. *Build organizational commitment to quality.* TQM will do little to improve the performance of an organization unless all employees embrace it, and this often requires a change in an organization's culture.[18] At Citibank, the process of changing culture began at the top. First, a group of top managers, including the CEO, received training in TQM from consultants from Motorola. Each member of the top-management group was then given the responsibility of training a group at the next level in the hierarchy, and so on down through the organization until all 100,000 employees had received basic TQM training.
2. *Focus on the customer.* TQM practitioners see a focus on the customer as the starting point.[19] According to TQM philosophy, the customer, not managers in quality control or engineering, defines what quality is. The challenge is fourfold: (1) to identify what customers want from the good or service that the company provides; (2) to identify what the company actually provides to customers; (3) to identify the gap that exists between what customers want and what they actually get (the quality gap); and (4) to formulate a plan for closing the quality gap. The efforts of Citibank managers to increase responsiveness to customers illustrate this aspect of TQM well.
3. *Find ways to measure quality.* Another crucial element of TQM is the development of a measuring system that managers can use to evaluate quality. Devising

appropriate measures is relatively easy in manufacturing companies, where quality can be measured by criteria such as defects per million parts. It is more difficult in service companies, where outputs are less tangible. However, with a little creativity, suitable quality measures can be devised as they were by managers at Citibank. Similarly, at L. L. Bean, the mail-order retailer, managers use the percentage of orders that are correctly filled as one of their quality measures.

4. *Set goals and create incentives.* Once a measure has been devised, managers' next step is to set a challenging quality goal and to create incentives for reaching that goal. At Citibank, the CEO set an initial goal of reducing customer complaints by 50%. One way of creating incentives to attain a goal is to link rewards, such as bonus pay and promotional opportunities, to the goal.

5. *Solicit input from employees.* Employees are a major source of information about the causes of poor quality, so it is important that managers establish a system for soliciting employee suggestions about improvements that can be made. At most companies, like Citibank, this is an ongoing endeavor—the process never stops.

6. *Identify defects and trace them to their source.* A major source of product defects is the production system; a major source of service defects is poor customer service procedures. TQM preaches the need for managers to identify defects in the work process, trace those defects back to their source, find out why they occurred, and make corrections so that they do not occur again. Today, IT makes the measurement of quality much easier.

inventory The stock of raw materials, inputs, and component parts that an organization has on hand at a particular time.

just-in-time (JIT) inventory system A system in which parts or supplies arrive at an organization when they are needed, not before.

7. *Introduce just-in-time inventory systems.* **Inventory** is the stock of raw materials, inputs, and component parts that an organization has on hand at a particular time. When the materials management function designs a **just-in-time (JIT) inventory system,** parts or supplies arrive at the organization when they are needed, not before. Also, under a JIT inventory system, defective parts enter an organization's operating system immediately; they are not warehoused for months before use. This means that defective inputs can be quickly spotted. JIT is discussed more later in the chapter.

8. *Work closely with suppliers.* A major cause of poor-quality finished goods is poor-quality component parts. To decrease product defects, materials managers must work closely with suppliers to improve the quality of the parts they supply. Managers at Xerox worked closely with suppliers to get them to adopt TQM programs, and the result was a huge reduction in the defect rate of component parts. Managers also need to work closely with suppliers to get them to adopt a JIT inventory system, also required for high quality.

9. *Design for ease of production.* The more steps required to assemble a product or provide a service, the more opportunities there are for making a mistake. It follows that designing products that have fewer parts or finding ways to simplify providing a service should be linked to fewer defects or customer complaints. For example, Dell continually redesigns the way it assembles its computers to reduce the number of assembly steps required and it constantly searches for new ways to reduce the number of components that have to be linked together. The consequence of these redesign efforts was a continuous fall in assembly costs and marked improvement in product quality that led to Dell's becoming the number-one global PC maker—until it was overtaken by HP in 2007 as that company also put TQM to work.

10. *Break down barriers between functions.* Successful implementation of TQM requires substantial cooperation between the different value-chain functions. Materials managers have to cooperate with manufacturing managers to find high-quality inputs that reduce manufacturing costs; marketing managers have to cooperate with manufacturing so that customer problems identified by marketing can be acted on; information systems have to cooperate with all of the other functions of the company to devise suitable IT training programs; and so on.

In essence, to increase quality, all functional managers need to cooperate to develop goals and spell out exactly how they will be achieved. Managers should embrace the philosophy that mistakes, defects, and poor-quality materials are not acceptable and should be eliminated. Functional managers should spend more time working with employees and providing them with the tools they need to do the job. Managers should create an environment in which employees will not be afraid to report problems or recommend improvements. Output goals and targets need to include not only numbers or quotas but also some indicators of quality to promote the production of defect-free output. Functional managers also need to train employees in new skills to keep pace with changes in the workplace. Finally, achieving better quality requires that managers develop organizational values and norms centered on improving quality.

six sigma A technique used to improve quality by systematically improving the way value-chain activities are performed and then using statistical methods to measure how much improvement has been made.

SIX SIGMA   One TQM technique called **Six Sigma** has gained increasing popularity in the last decade, particularly because of the well-publicized success GE enjoyed as a result of implementing it across its operating divisions. The goal of Six Sigma is to improve a company's quality to only three defects per million by systematically altering the way all the processes involved in value-chain activities are performed, and then carefully measuring how much improvement has been made using statistical methods. Six Sigma shares with TQM its focus on improving value-chain processes to increase quality, but it differs because while TQM emphasizes top down organizationwide employee involvement, the Six Sigma approach is to create teams of expert change agents, known as "green belts and black belts," to take control of the problem-finding-solving process and then to train other employees how to implement solutions. The following "Management Insight" shows how Six Sigma works at the Starwood hotel chain.

Management Insight

Starwood Uses Six Sigma to Improve Hotel Performance

Starwood Hotels & Resorts, based in White Plains, New Jersey, is one of the largest global hotel chains and one of the most profitable—its profit margins are nearly 15% higher than rivals such as Hilton and Marriott. Why? Starwood attributes a significant part of its high performance to its use of Six Sigma, which it began to use in 2001 to improve the quality of service it provides its guests.[20]

The company's Six Sigma group is led by Brian Mayer, the vice president of "Six Sigma Operations Management & Room Support," whose father and grandfather both worked in the hospitality industry. Mayer, a Six Sigma expert, helped by a small group of other experts he recruited, implemented the program in 2001. Since then they have trained 150 Starwood employees as "black belts" and another 2,700 to be "green belts" in the practices of Six Sigma. Black belts are the lead change agent in each Starwood hotel who take responsibility for managing the change process to meet its main objectives—increasing quality customer service and responsiveness.[21] Green belts are the employees trained by Mayer's experts and each hotel's black belt to become the Six Sigma team in each hotel who work together to work to develop new ideas or programs that will improve customer responsiveness, and to find the work procedures and processes that will implement the new programs most effectively to improve customer service quality.

Almost all the new initiatives that have permeated across the thousands of individual hotels in the Starwood chain come from these Six Sigma teams—whose work has improved the company's performance by hundreds of millions of dollars. For example, the "Unwind Program" was an initiative developed to cater to the interests of the 34% of hotel guests that a study found felt lonely and

Guests and a bellhop share a laugh at a Starwoods Resort. The Starwoods company remains one of the most highly profitable in the entire industry based on its rigorous Six Sigma program, listening ear towards customers, and attention to employee needs.

isolated in overnight hotels stays. Its purpose was to make guests feel at home so that they would become return customers. The chain's Six Sigma teams began brainstorming ideas for new kinds of activities and services that would encourage nightly guests to leave their rooms and gather in the lobby, where they could meet and mingle with other guests and so feel more at home. They came up with hundreds of potential new programs. An initial concept was to offer guests short complimentary massages in the lobby that they hoped would then encourage them to book massage sessions that would boost hotel revenues. Teams at each hotel then dreamt up other programs that they felt would best meet guest needs. These ranged from fire-dancing in hotels in Fiji to Chinese watercolor painting in its hotels in Beijing.[22] These ideas are shared across all the individual hotels in the chain using Starwood's proprietary "E-Tool," which contains thousands of successful projects that have worked—and the specific work procedures needed to perform them successfully.

In another major project, Starwood's managers were was concerned about the number of injuries its hotel employees sustained during the course of their work, such as back-strain injuries common among the housekeepers who clean rooms. The black-green belt teams studied how housekeepers worked in the various hotels and, pooling their knowledge, they realized that several changes could reduce injuries. For example, they found a large number of back strains occurred early in each housekeeper's shift because they were not "warmed up," so one central coordinating team developed a series of job-related stretching exercises. This team also looked at the cleaning tools being used, and after experimenting with different sizes and types found that curved, longer-handled tools, which required less bending and stretching, could significantly help reduce injuries. To date the program has reduced the accident rate from 12 to 2 for every 200,000 work hours, a major achievement.

As Starwood has found, having teams of Six Sigma specialists trained to always be on the alert for opportunities to improve the tens of thousands of different work procedures that go to create high-quality customer service pays off. For guests and employees, the result is higher satisfaction and higher loyalty to the hotel chain both in the form of repeat guest visits and reduced employee turnover.

Improving Efficiency

The third goal of value-chain management is to increase the efficiency of the various functional activities. The fewer the input resources required to produce a given volume of output, the higher will be the efficiency of the operating system. So efficiency is a useful measure of how well an organization utilizes all of its resources—such as labor, capital, materials, or energy—to produce its outputs, or goods and services. Developing functional strategies to improve efficiency is an extremely important issue for managers because increased efficiency lowers production costs, which allows an organization to make a greater profit or to attract more customers by lowering its price. Several important functional strategies are discussed below.

LO4 Explain why achieving superior efficiency is so important, and understand the different kinds of techniques that need to be employed to increase efficiency.

Facilities Layout, Flexible Manufacturing, and Efficiency

The strategies managers use to lay out or design an organization's physical work facilities also determine its efficiency. First, the way in which machines and workers are organized or grouped together into workstations affects the efficiency of the operating system. Second, a major determinant of efficiency is the cost associated with setting up the equipment needed to make a particular product. **Facilities layout** is the strategy of designing the machine-worker interface to increase operating system efficiency. **Flexible manufacturing** is a strategy based on the use of IT to reduce the costs associated with the product assembly process or the way services are delivered to customers. For example, this might be the way computers are made on a production line or the way patients are routed through a hospital.

facilities layout
The strategy of designing the machine-worker interface to increase operating system efficiency.

flexible manufacturing
The set of techniques that attempt to reduce the costs associated with the product assembly process or the way services are delivered to customers.

FACILITIES LAYOUT   The way in which machines, robots, and people are grouped together affects how productive they can be. Figure 9.5 shows three basic ways of arranging workstations: product layout, process layout, and fixed-position layout.

Figure 9.5
Three Facilities Layouts

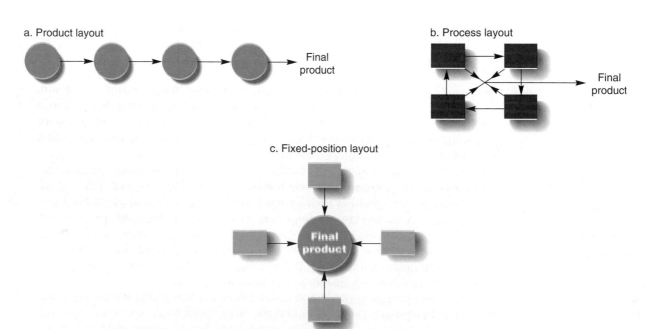

a. Product layout

Final product

b. Process layout

Final product

c. Fixed-position layout

Final product

In a *product layout,* machines are organized so that each operation needed to manufacture a product or process a patient is performed at workstations arranged in a fixed sequence. In manufacturing, workers are stationary in this arrangement, and a moving conveyor belt takes the product being worked on to the next workstation so that it is progressively assembled. Mass production is the familiar name for this layout; car assembly lines are probably the best-known example. It used to be that product layout was efficient only when products were created in large quantities; however, the introduction of modular assembly lines controlled by computers is making it efficient to make products in small batches.

In a *process layout,* workstations are not organized in a fixed sequence. Rather, each workstation is relatively self-contained, and a product goes to whichever workstation is needed to perform the next operation to complete the product. Process layout is often suited to manufacturing settings that produce a variety of custom-made products, each tailored to the needs of a different kind of customer. For example, a custom furniture manufacturer might use a process layout so that different teams of workers can produce different styles of chairs or tables made from different kinds of woods and finishes. Such a layout also describes how a patient might go through a hospital from emergency room, to X-ray room, to operating room, and so on. A process layout provides the flexibility needed to change a product, whether it is a PC or a patient. Such flexibility, however, often reduces efficiency because it is expensive.

In a *fixed-position layout,* the product stays in a fixed position. Its component parts are produced in remote workstations and brought to the production area for final assembly. Increasingly, self-managed teams are using fixed-position layouts. Different teams assemble each component part and then send the parts to the final assembly team, which makes the final product. A fixed-position layout is commonly used for products such as jet airliners, mainframe computers, and gas turbines—products that are complex and difficult to assemble or so large that moving them from one workstation to another would be difficult. The effects of moving from one facilities layout to another can be dramatic, as the following "Manager as a Person" suggests.

Manager as a Person

Paddy Hopkirk Improves Facilities Layout

Paddy Hopkirk established his car accessories business in Bedfordshire, England, shortly after he had shot to car-racing fame by winning the famous Monte Carlo Rally. Sales of Hopkirk's accessories, such as bicycle racks and axle stands, were always brisk, but Hopkirk was the first to admit that his operating system left a lot to be desired, so he invited consultants to help reorganize the system.

After analyzing his factory's operating system, the consultants realized that the source of the problem was the facilities layout Hopkirk had established. Over time, as sales grew, Hopkirk simply added new workstations to the operating system as they were needed. The result was a process layout in which the product being assembled moved in the irregular sequences shown in the "Before Change" half of Figure 9.6. The consultants suggested that to save time and effort, the workstations should be reorganized into the sequential product layout shown in the "After Change" illustration.

Once this change was made, the results were dramatic. One morning the factory was an untidy sprawl of workstations surrounded by piles of crates holding semifinished components. Two days later, when the 170-person workforce came

Figure 9.6

Changing a Facilities Layout

Axis-stand production line at Paddy Hopkirk Factory

Source: "The Application of Kaizen to Facilities Layout," *Financial Times* of January 4, 1994, p. 12. Reprinted by permission of Financial Times Syndication, London.

Small Business

back to work, the machines had been brought together into tightly grouped workstations arranged in the fixed sequence shown in the illustration. The piles of components had disappeared, and the newly cleared floor space was neatly marked with color-coded lines mapping out the new flow of materials between workstations.

In the first full day of production, efficiency increased by as much as 30%. The space needed for some operations had been cut in half, and work in progress had been cut considerably. Moreover, the improved layout allowed some jobs to be combined, freeing operators for deployment elsewhere in the factory. An amazed Hopkirk exclaimed, "I was expecting a change but nothing as dramatic as this . . . it is fantastic."[23]

FLEXIBLE MANUFACTURING In a manufacturing company, a major source of costs is the costs associated with setting up the equipment needed to make a particular product. One of these is the cost of production that is forgone because nothing is produced while the equipment is being set up. For example, components manufacturers often need as much as half a day to set up automated production equipment when switching from production of one component part (such as a washer ring for the steering column of a car) to another (such as a washer ring for the steering column of a truck). During this half-day, a manufacturing plant is not producing anything, but employees are paid for this "nonproductive" time.

It follows that if setup times for complex production equipment can be reduced, so can setup costs, and efficiency will rise, that is, the time that plant and employees spend in actually producing something will increase. This simple insight has been the driving force behind the development of flexible manufacturing techniques.

Housing units move on the production line as employees of Toyota Motor Corporation work during the installation process at the company's Kasugai Housing Works, one of the plants of Toyota home-brand houses on Kasugai, Aichi Prefecture, Japan. Toyota entered the housing industry 30 years ago where it applies the plant technology and experience it gained through producing cars.

Flexible manufacturing aims to reduce the time required to set up production equipment.[24] By redesigning the manufacturing process so that production equipment geared for manufacturing one product can be quickly replaced with equipment geared to make another product, setup times and costs can be reduced dramatically. Another favorable outcome from flexible manufacturing is that a company is able to produce many more varieties of a product than before in the same amount of time. Thus, flexible manufacturing increases a company's ability to be responsive to its customers.

Increasingly, organizations are experimenting with new designs for operating systems that not only allow workers to be more productive but also make the work process more flexible, thus reducing setup costs. Some Japanese companies are experimenting with facilities layouts arranged as a spiral, as the letter Y, and as the number 6, to see how these configurations affect setup costs and worker productivity. At a camcorder plant in Kohda, Japan, for example, Sony changed from a fixed-position layout in which 50 workers sequentially built a camcorder to a flexible spiral process design in which 4 workers perform all the operations necessary to produce the camcorder. This new layout allows the most efficient workers to work at the highest pace, and it reduces setup costs because workers can easily switch from one model to another, increasing efficiency by 10%.[25]

An interesting example of a company that built a new factory to obtain the benefits from flexible manufacturing is German company Igus Inc. Igus makes over 28,000 polymer bearings and energy supply cable products used in applications the world over. In the 1990s, Igus's managers realized they needed to build a new factory that could handle the company's rapidly growing product line. The product line was changing constantly as new products were innovated and old ones became obsolete. At Igus new products are often introduced on a daily basis, so this need for flexibility is the company's prime requirement. Moreover, because many of its products are highly customized, the specific and changing needs of its customers drive new product development.

Igus's new factory was designed with the need for flexibility in mind. As big as three football fields, nothing in the factory is tied down or bolted to the floor. All the machines, computers, and equipment can be moved and repositioned to suit changing product requirements. Moreover, all Igus employees are trained to be flexible and can perform many of the production tasks necessary. For example, when one new product line proved popular with customers, its employees and production operations were relocated four times as it grew into larger spaces. Igus can change its operating system at a moment's notice and with minimal disruption, and since the company operates seven days a week, 24 hours a day, these changes are occurring constantly.

To facilitate these changes, workers are equipped with power scooters to move around the plant quickly and reconfigure operations. This also allows them to move quickly to wherever in the factory their skills are most needed. Employees are also equipped with mobile phones so that they are always on call. Igus's decision to create a flexible factory of the future has paid off. In the last decade its global sales have tripled.

Just-in-Time Inventory and Efficiency

As noted earlier, a just-in-time inventory system gets components to the assembly line just as they are needed and thus drives down costs. Using a JIT inventory system, component parts travel from suppliers to the assembly line in a small-wheeled container known as a *kanban*. Assembly-line workers empty the kanbans and then the empty container is sent back to the supplier as the signal to produce another small batch of component parts, and so the process repeats itself. This system can be contrasted with a just-in-case view of inventory, which leads an organization to stockpile excess inputs in a warehouse just in case it needs them to meet sudden upturns in demand.

JIT inventory systems have major implications for efficiency. Major cost savings can result from increasing inventory turnover and reducing inventory holding costs, such as warehousing and storage costs and the cost of capital tied up in inventory. Although companies that manufacture and assemble products can obviously use JIT to great advantage, so can service organizations.[26] Wal-Mart, the biggest retailer in the United States, uses JIT systems to replenish the stock in its stores at least twice a week. Many Wal-Mart stores receive daily deliveries. Wal-Mart's main competitors, Kmart and Sears, typically replenish their stock every two weeks. Wal-Mart can maintain the same service levels as these competitors but at one-fourth the inventory holding cost, a major source of cost saving. Faster inventory turnover has helped Wal-Mart achieve an efficiency-based competitive advantage in the retailing industry.[27] Even a small company can benefit from a kanban, as the experience of United Electric suggests in the following "Management Insight."

United Electric's Kanban System

Management Insight

United Electric Controls, headquartered in Watertown, Massachusetts, is the market leader in the application of threshold detection and switching technology. At one time, the company simply warehoused its inputs and dispensed them as needed. Then it decided to reduce costs by storing these inputs at their point of use in the production system. However, this also caused problems because inventories of some inputs actually started to increase while other inputs were used up without anyone knowing which input caused a stoppage in production.

So managers decided to experiment with a supplier kanban system even though United Electric had fewer than 40 suppliers and they were totally up to date with its input requirements. Managers decided to store a three-week supply of parts in a central storeroom, a supply large enough to avoid unexpected shortages.[28] They began by asking their casting supplier to deliver inputs in kanbans and bins. Once a week, this supplier checks up on the bins to determine how much stock needs to be delivered the following week. Other suppliers were then asked to participate in this system, and now more than 35 of its major suppliers operate some form of the kanban system.

By all measures of performance, the results of using the kanban system have been successful. Inventory holding costs have fallen sharply. Products are delivered to all customers on time. And even new products' design-to-production cycles have dropped by 50% because suppliers are now involved much earlier in the design process so that they can supply new inputs as needed.

United Electric's kanban system involves suppliers in automatic checking and restocking, shortening production time and lowering costs.

Self-Managed Work Teams and Efficiency

Another functional strategy to increase efficiency is the use of self-managed work teams.[29] The typical team consists of 5 to 15 employees who produce an entire product instead of just parts of it.[30] Team members learn all team tasks and move from job to job. The result is a flexible workforce, because team members can fill in for absent coworkers. The members of each team also assume responsibility for scheduling work and vacations, ordering materials, and hiring new members—previously all responsibilities of first-line managers. Because people often respond well to being given greater autonomy and responsibility, the use of empowered self-managed teams can increase productivity and efficiency. Moreover, cost savings arise from eliminating supervisors and creating a flatter organizational hierarchy, which further increases efficiency.

The effect of introducing self-managed teams is often an increase in efficiency of 30% or more, sometimes much more. After the introduction of flexible manufacturing technology and self-managed teams, a GE plant in Salisbury, North Carolina, increased efficiency by 250% compared with other GE plants producing the same products.[31]

Process Reengineering and Efficiency

process reengineering
The fundamental rethinking and radical redesign of business processes to achieve dramatic improvement in critical measures of performance such as cost, quality, service, and speed.

The value chain is a collection of functional activities or business processes that take one or more kinds of inputs and transform them to create an output that is of value to the customer.[32] **Process reengineering** involves the fundamental rethinking and radical redesign of business processes (and thus the *value chain*) to achieve dramatic improvements in critical measures of performance such as cost, quality, service, and speed.[33] Order fulfillment, for example, can be thought of as a business process: When a customer's order is received (the input), many different functional tasks must be performed as necessary to process the order, and then the ordered goods are delivered to the customer (the output). Process reengineering boosts efficiency when it reduces the number of order-fulfillment tasks that must be performed, or reduces the time they take, and so reduces operating costs.

For an example of process reengineering in practice, consider how Ford used it. One day a manager from Ford was working at its Japanese partner Mazda and discovered quite by accident that Mazda had only five people in its accounts payable department. The Ford manager was shocked, since Ford's U.S. operation had 500 employees in accounts payable. He reported his discovery to Ford's U.S. managers, who decided to form a task force to figure out why the difference existed.

Ford managers discovered that procurement began when the purchasing department sent a purchase order to a supplier and sent a copy of the purchase order to Ford's accounts payable department. When the supplier shipped the goods and they arrived at Ford, a clerk at the receiving dock completed a form describing the goods and sent the form to accounts payable. The supplier, meanwhile, sent accounts payable an invoice. Thus, accounts payable received three documents relating to these goods: a copy of the original purchase order, the receiving document, and the invoice. If the information in all three was in agreement (most of the time it was), a clerk in accounts payable issued payment. Occasionally, however, all three documents did not agree. And Ford discovered that accounts payable clerks spent most of their time straightening out the 1% of instances in which the purchase order, receiving document, and invoice contained conflicting information.[34]

Ford managers decided to reengineer the procurement process to simplify it. Now when a buyer in the purchasing department issues a purchase order to a supplier, that buyer also enters the order into an online database. As before, suppliers send goods to the receiving dock. When the goods arrive, the clerk at the receiving dock checks a computer terminal to see whether the received shipment matches the description on the purchase order. If it does, the clerk accepts the goods and pushes a button on the terminal keyboard that tells the database the goods have arrived. Receipt of the goods is recorded in the database, and a computer automatically issues and sends a check to the supplier. If the goods do not correspond to the description on the purchase order in the database, the clerk at the dock refuses the shipment and sends it back to the supplier.

Payment authorization, which used to be performed by accounts payable, is now accomplished at the receiving dock. The new process has come close to eliminating the need for an accounts payable department. In some parts of Ford, the size of the accounts payable department has been cut by 95%. By reducing the head count in accounts payable, the reengineering effort reduced the amount of time wasted on unproductive activities, thereby increasing the efficiency of the total organization.

Information Systems, the Internet, and Efficiency

With the rapid spread of computers, the explosive growth of the Internet and corporate intranets, and high-speed digital Internet technology, the information systems function is moving to center stage in the quest for operating efficiencies and a lower cost structure. The impact of information systems on productivity is wide-ranging and potentially affects all other activities of a company. For example, Cisco Systems has been able to realize significant cost savings by moving its ordering and customer service functions online. The company has just 300 service agents handling all of its customer accounts, compared to the 900 it would need if sales were not handled online. The difference represents an annual saving of $20 million a year. Moreover, without automated customer service functions, Cisco calculates that it would need at least 1,000 additional service engineers, which would cost around $75 million.

Dell also makes extensive use of the Internet to lower its costs; by 2004 more than 90% of its PCs were sold online.[35] Dell's Web site allows customers to customize their orders to get the system that best suits their particular requirements. In this way, Dell increases its customer responsiveness. Dell has also put much of its customer service function online, reducing the need for telephone calls to customer service representatives and saving costs in the process. Each week, some 200,000 people access Dell's online troubleshooting tips. Each of these visits to Dell's Web site saves the company a potential $15, which is the average cost of a technical support call.[36] If just 10% of these online visitors were to call Dell by telephone instead, it would cost the company $15.6 million per year.

Dell, like most other large companies today, uses the Internet to manage its value chain, feeding real-time information about order flow to its suppliers, which use this information to schedule their own production, providing components to Dell on a just-in-time basis. This approach reduces the costs of coordination both between the company and its customers and between the company and its suppliers. By using Web-based programs to automate customer and supplier interactions, the number of people required to manage these interfaces can be substantially reduced, thereby reducing costs. This trend extends beyond high-tech companies. Banks and financial service companies are finding that they can substantially reduce costs by moving customer accounts and support functions online. Such a move reduces the need for customer service representatives, bank tellers, stockbrokers, insurance agents, and others. For example, it costs about $1 when a customers executes a transaction at a bank, such as shifting money from one account to another; over the Internet the same transaction costs about $0.01.

Improving Innovation

As discussed in Chapter 6, *technology* comprises the skills, know-how, experience, body of scientific knowledge, tools, machines, computers, and equipment used in the design, production, and distribution of goods and services. Technology is involved in all functional activities, and the rapid advance of technology today is a significant factor in managers' attempts to improve the way their value chains innovate new kinds of goods and services or ways to provide them.

Two Kinds of Innovation

LO5 Differentiate between two forms of innovation, and explain why innovation and product development is a crucial component of the search for competitive advantage.

Two principal kinds of innovation can be identified based on the nature of the technological change that brings them about. **Quantum product innovation** results in the development of new, often radically different, kinds of goods and services because of fundamental shifts in technology brought about by pioneering discoveries. Examples are the creation of the Internet and the World Wide Web, which have revolutionized the computer industry, and biotechnology, which has transformed the treatment of illness by creating new, genetically engineered medicines. McDonald's development of the principles behind the provision of fast food also qualifies as a quantum product innovation.

quantum product innovation The development of new, often radically different, kinds of goods and services because of fundamental shifts in technology brought about by pioneering discoveries.

incremental product innovation The gradual improvement and refinement to existing products that occurs over time as existing technologies are perfected.

Incremental product innovation results in gradual improvements and refinements to existing products over time as existing technologies are perfected and functional managers, like those at Toyota, learn how to perform value-chain activities in better ways—ways that add more value to products. For example, Google's staffers have made thousands of incremental improvements to the company's search engine itself since its debut, changes that have enhanced the engine's search capabilities, given the engine the ability to work on all kinds of mobile devices, and made it available to users who search in their native tongues.

Quantum product innovations are relatively rare; most managers' activities are focused on incremental product innovations that result from ongoing technological advances. For example, every time Dell or HP puts a new, faster Intel or AMD chip into a PC, or Google improves its search engine's capability, the company is making incremental product innovations. Similarly, every time auto engineers redesign a car model, and every time McDonald's managers work to improve the flavor and texture of burgers, fries, and salads, their product development efforts are intended to lead to incremental product innovations. Incremental innovation is frequently as important as or more important than quantum innovation in raising a company's performance. Indeed, as discussed below, it is often managers' ability to successfully manage incremental product development that results in success or failure in an industry.

The need to speed innovation and quickly develop new and improved products becomes especially important when the technology behind the product is advancing rapidly. This is because the first companies in an industry to adopt the new technology will be able to develop products that better meet customer needs and gain a "first-mover" advantage over their rivals. Indeed, managers who do not quickly adopt and apply new technologies to innovate products may soon find they have no customers for their products—and destroy their organizations.

Increasingly, to become more responsive to existing customers and attract new customers, managers are trying to outdo each other by being the first to market with a product that incorporates a new technology or that plays to a new fashion trend. In the car industry, for example, a particular car model used to be kept in production for five years, but today this has dropped to three years as car companies compete to attract new and existing customers to buy their newest models. In sum, the greater the rate of technological change in an industry, the more important it is for managers to innovate.

Strategies to Promote Innovation and Speed Product Development

product development The management of the value-chain activities involved in bringing new or improved goods and services to the market.

There are several ways in which managers can promote innovation and encourage the development of new products. **Product development** is the management of the value-chain activities involved in bringing new or improved goods and services to the market. The steps that Monte Peterson, former CEO of Thermos, took to develop a new barbecue grill show how good product development should proceed. Peterson had no doubt about how to increase Thermos's sales of barbecue grills: motivate Thermos's functional managers to create new and improved models. So

Peterson assembled a cross-functional product development team of five functional managers (from marketing, engineering, manufacturing, sales, and finance) and told them to develop a new barbecue grill within 18 months. To ensure that they were not spread too thin, he assigned them to this team only. Peterson also arranged for leadership of the team to rotate. Initially, to focus on what customers wanted, the marketing manager would take the lead; then, when technical developments became the main consideration, leadership would switch to engineering; and so on.

Team members christened the group the "Lifestyle team." To find out what people really wanted in a grill, the marketing manager and nine subordinates spent a month on the road, visiting customers. What they found surprised them. The stereotype of Dad slaving over a smoky barbecue grill was wrong: more women were barbecuing. Many cooks were tired of messy charcoal, and many homeowners did not like rusty grills that spoiled the appearance of their decks. Moreover, environmental and safety issues were increasing in importance. In California, charcoal starter fluid is considered a pollutant and is banned; in New Jersey, the use of charcoal and gas grills on the balconies of condos and apartments has been prohibited to avoid fires. Based on these findings, the team decided that Thermos had to produce a barbecue grill that not only made the food taste good but also looked attractive, used no pollutants, and was safe for balcony use (which meant it had to be electric).

Within one year the basic attributes of the product were defined, and leadership of the team moved to engineering. The critical task for engineering was to design a grill that gave food the cookout taste that conventional electric grills could not provide because they did not get hot enough. To raise the cooking temperature, Thermos's engineers designed a domed vacuum top that trapped heat inside the grill, and they built electric heat rods directly into the surface of the grill. These features made the grill hot enough to sear meat and give it brown barbecue lines and a barbecue taste.

Manufacturing had been active from the early days of the development process, making sure that any proposed design could be produced economically. Because manufacturing was involved from the beginning, the team avoided some costly mistakes. At one critical team meeting the engineers said they wanted tapered legs on the grill. Manufacturing explained that tapered legs would have to be custom-made—and would raise manufacturing costs—and persuaded the team to go with straight legs.

When the new grill was introduced on schedule, it was an immediate success. The study of many product development successes, such as that of Thermos's Lifestyle team, suggests three strategies managers can implement to increase the likelihood that their product development efforts will result in innovative, and successful, new products.

INVOLVE BOTH CUSTOMERS AND SUPPLIERS Many new products fail when they reach the marketplace because they were designed with scant attention to customer needs. Successful product development requires inputs from more than just an organization's members; also needed are inputs from customers and suppliers. At Thermos, team members spent a month on the road, visiting customers to identify their needs. The revolutionary electric barbecue grill was a direct result of this process. In other cases, companies have found it worthwhile to include customer representatives as peripheral members of their product development team. Boeing, for example, has included customers, the major airlines, in the design of its most recent commercial jet aircraft, the 777 and the new 787 Dreamliner. Boeing builds a mockup of the aircraft's cabin and then, over a period of months, allows each airline's representatives to experiment with repositioning the galleys, seating, aisles, and bathrooms to best meet the needs of their particular airline. Boeing has learned a great deal from this process.

ESTABLISH A STAGE-GATE DEVELOPMENT FUNNEL One of the most common mistakes that managers make in product development is trying to fund too many new projects at any one time. This approach spreads the activities of the different value-chain functions too thinly over too many different projects. As a consequence,

Figure 9.7
A Stage-Gate Development Funnel

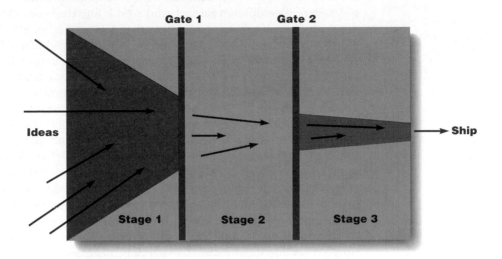

no single project is given the functional resources and attention that are required to make it succeed.

One strategy for solving this problem is for managers to develop a structured process for evaluating product development proposals and deciding which to support and which to reject. A common solution is to establish a **stage-gate development funnel,** a technique that forces managers to make choices among competing projects so that functional resources are not spread thinly over too many projects. The funnel gives functional managers control over product development and allows them to intervene and take corrective action quickly and appropriately (see Figure 9.7).

At stage 1, the development funnel has a wide mouth, so top managers initially can encourage employees to come up with as many new product ideas as possible. Managers can create incentives for employees to come up with ideas. Many organizations run "bright-idea programs" that reward employees whose ideas eventually make it through the development process. Other organizations allow research scientists to devote a certain amount of work time to their own projects. Top managers at 3M, for example, have a 15% rule: they expect a research scientist to spend 15% of the workweek working on a project of his or her own choosing. Ideas may be submitted by individuals or by groups. Brainstorming (see Chapter 7) is a technique that managers frequently use to encourage new ideas.

New product ideas are written up as brief proposals. The proposals are submitted to a cross-functional team of managers, who evaluate each proposal at gate1. The cross-functional team considers a proposal's fit with the organization's strategy and its technical feasibility. Proposals that are consistent with the strategy of the organization and are judged technically feasible pass through gate 1 and into stage 2. Other proposals are turned down (although the door is often left open for reconsidering a proposal at a later date).

The primary goal in stage 2 is to draft a detailed product development plan. The **product development plan** specifies all of the relevant information that managers need to make a decision about whether to go ahead with a full-blown product development

stage-gate development funnel A planning model that forces managers to make choices among competing projects so that organizational resources are not spread thinly over too many projects.

A cross-functional team at its best: employees work together and pool their skills to work on and solve all angles of a problem.

product development plan A plan that specifies all of the relevant information that managers need in order to decide whether to proceed with a full-blown product development effort.

contract book A written agreement that details product development factors such as responsibilities, resource commitments, budgets, time lines, and development milestones.

core members The members of a team who bear primary responsibility for the success of a project and who stay with a project from inception to completion.

effort. The product development plan should include strategic and financial objectives, an analysis of the product's market potential, a list of desired product features, a list of technological requirements, a list of financial and human resource requirements, a detailed development budget, and a time line that contains specific milestones (for example, dates for prototype completion and final launch).

A cross-functional team of managers normally drafts this plan. Good planning requires a good strategic analysis (see Chapter 8), and team members must be prepared to spend considerable time in the field with customers, trying to understand their needs. Drafting a product development plan generally takes about three months. Once completed, the plan is reviewed by a senior management committee at gate 2 (see Figure 9.7). These managers focus on the details of the plan to see whether the proposal is attractive (given its market potential) and viable (given the technological, financial, and human resources that would be needed to develop the product). Senior managers making this review keep in mind all other product development efforts currently being undertaken by the organization. One goal at this point is to ensure that limited organizational resources are used to their maximum effect.

At gate 2 projects are rejected, sent back for revision, or allowed to pass through to stage 3, the development phase. Product development starts with the formation of a cross-functional team that is given primary responsibility for developing the product. In some companies, at the beginning of stage 3 top managers and cross-functional team members sign a **contract book,** a written agreement that details factors such as responsibilities, resource commitments, budgets, time lines, and development milestones. Signing the contract book is viewed as the symbolic launch of a product development effort. The contract book is also a document against which actual development progress can be measured. At 3M, for example, team members and top management negotiate a contract and sign a contract book at the launch of a development effort, thereby signaling their commitment to the objectives contained in the contract.

The stage 3 development effort can last anywhere from 6 months to 10 years, depending on the industry and type of product. Some electronics products have development cycles of 6 months, but it takes from 3 to 5 years to develop a new car, about 5 years to develop a new jet aircraft, and as long as 10 years to develop a new medical drug.

ESTABLISH CROSS-FUNCTIONAL TEAMS   A smooth-running cross-functional team also seems to be a critical component of successful product development, as the experience of Thermos suggests. Marketing, engineering, and manufacturing personnel are **core members** of a successful product development team—the people who have primary responsibility for the product development effort. Other people besides core members work on the project as and when the need arises, but the core members (generally from three to six individuals) stay with the project from inception to completion of the development effort (see Figure 9.8).

The reason for using a cross-functional team is to ensure a high level of coordination and communication among managers in different functions. Input from both marketing and manufacturing members of Thermos's Lifestyle team determined the characteristics of the barbecue that the engineers on the team ended up designing.

If a cross-functional team is to succeed, it must have the right kind of leadership and it must be managed in an effective manner. To be successful, a product development team needs a team leader who can rise above a functional background and take a cross-functional view. In addition to having effective leadership, successful cross-functional product development teams have several other key characteristics. Often, core members of successful teams are located close to one another, in the same office space, to foster a sense of shared mission and commitment to a development program. Successful teams develop a clear sense of their objectives and how they will be achieved, the purpose again being to create a sense of shared mission. The way in which Philips used teams to develop its new razor is described in the closing *Business-Week* Case, but Google also uses many of these strategies to promote innovation as discussed in the following "Management Insight."

Figure 9.8
Members of a Cross-Functional Product Development Team

Management Insight

Google Encourages Innovation and Product Development

The history of Google, the Internet search engine company, began in 1995 when two Stanford graduate computer science students, Sergey Brin and Larry Page, decided to collaborate to develop a new kind of search engine technology.[37] They understood the limitations of existing search engines, and by 1998 they had developed a superior engine that they felt was ready to go online. They raised $1 million from family, friends, and risk-taking "angel" investors to buy the hardware necessary to connect Google to the Internet.

At first, Google answered 10,000 inquiries a day, but in a few months it was answering 500,000. By fall 1999, it was handling 3 million; by fall 2000, 60 million; and in spring 2001, 100 million per day. In the 2000s Google has become the dominant search engine, handling around 70% of inquiries by 2008; it is one of the top-five most used Internet companies, and rivals like Yahoo and Microsoft are working hard to catch up and beat Google at its own game. (In April 2008 Microsoft was seeking to takeover Yahoo and combine the two companies' resources to better compete against Google; however, Yahoo was resisting and had even formed an alliance with Google to try to stop the takeover).

Google's explosive growth is largely due to the culture of innovation its founders cultivated from the start. Although by 2008 Google had grown to 10,000 employees worldwide, its founders claim that Google still maintains a small-company feel because its culture empowers its employees, who are called staffers or "Googlers," to create the best software possible. Brin and Page created Google's innovative culture in several ways.

From the beginning, Google employees have always worked in "high-density clusters," which contributes to their comradarie and cooperative innovations—whether they're sitting on therapeutic bouncy balls or ergonomic office chairs.

From the beginning, lacking space and seeking to keep operating costs low, Google staffers worked in "high-density clusters." Three or four employees, each equipped with a high-powered Linux workstation, shared a desk, couch, and chairs that were large rubber balls, working together to improve the company's technology. Even when Google moved into more spacious surroundings at its "Googleplex" headquarters building, staffers continued to work in shared spaces. Google designed the building so that staffers are constantly meeting one another in its funky lobby; in its Google Café, where everyone eats together; in its state-of-the-art recreational facilities; and in its "snack rooms," equipped with bins packed with cereals, gummi bears, yogurt, carrots, and make-your-own cappuccino. Google also created many social gatherings of employees, such as a TGIF open meeting and a twice-weekly outdoor roller hockey game where staffers are encouraged to bring down the founders.[38]

All this attention to creating what might be the "grooviest" company headquarters in the world did not come about by chance. Brin and Page knew that Google's most important strength would be its ability to attract the best software engineers in the world and then motivate them to perform well. Common offices, lobbies, cafés, and so on, bring staffers into close contact with one another, develop collegiality, and encourage them to share their new ideas with their colleagues and to constantly improve Google's search engine technology and find new ways to expand the company. The freedom Google gives its staffers to pursue new ideas is a clear indication of its founders' desire to empower them to be innovative and to look off the beaten path for new ideas. Finally, recognizing that staffers who innovate important new software applications should be rewarded for their achievements, Google's founders give them stock in the company, effectively making staffers its owners as well.

Their focus on innovation did not blind Brin and Page to the need to build a viable competitive strategy so that Google could compete effectively in the cutthroat search engine market. They recognized, however, that they lacked business experience; they had never had to craft strategies to compete with giants like Microsoft and Yahoo. Moreover, they also had never been responsible for building a strong set of value-chain functions. So they recruited a team of talented and experienced functional managers to help them manage their company. They also decided to give responsibility for the company's value-chain management to a new CEO, Eric Schmidt, who came from Novell, where he had been in charge of strategic planning and technology development.

Brin and Page's understanding that successful product development requires building a strong organizational architecture has paid off. In August 2004, Google went public, and its shares, which were sold at $85 a share, were worth over $100 each by the end of the first day of trading, $500 by 2006, and reached a staggering $750 in late 2007 before falling back. This has made Brin and Page's stake in the company worth billions—clearly it can pay to focus on improving innovation.

Google prospers because of its founders' ability to create a culture that encourages staffers to be innovative and because of their willingness to delegate authority for product development to managers and staffers. Managing innovation is an increasingly important aspect of a manager's job in an era of dramatic changes in advanced IT. Promoting successful new product development is difficult and challenging, and some product development efforts are much more successful than others. Google is performing at a high level, while thousands of other dot-coms, including many search engine companies such as Magellan and Openfind, have gone out of business.

In sum, managers need to recognize that successful innovation and product development cuts across roles and functions and requires a high level of cooperation. They should recognize the importance of common values and norms in promoting the high levels of cooperation and cohesiveness necessary to build a culture for innovation. They also should reward successful innovators and make heroes of the employees and teams that develop successful new products. Finally, managers should fully utilize the product development techniques just discussed to guide the process.

Managing the Value Chain: Some Remaining Issues

Achieving improved quality, efficiency, and responsiveness to customers often requires a profound change in the way managers plan, lead, control, and organize a company's value-chain activities. For example, planning often involves managers at all levels, and customers are brought into the planning process. The use of self-managed teams and empowered workers changes the way managers lead and organize employees, and employees become responsible for controlling many more dimensions of their work activities.

Obtaining the information necessary to improve the value chain becomes an important and never-ending task for functional managers. It is their job to collect relevant information about the competitive environment, such as (1) the future intentions of competitors, (2) the identity of new customers for the organization's products, and (3) the identity of new suppliers of crucial or low-cost inputs. They also need to seek out new ways to use resources more efficiently to hold down costs or to get close to customers and learn what they want.

Two issues that arise from the constant need to improve a company's value chain are, first, the need to use boundary-spanning roles to obtain valuable functional information and, second, the need to consider the ethical implications of adopting advanced value-chain management techniques.

Boundary-Spanning Roles

The ability of functional managers to gain access to the information they need to improve value-chain management is critical. The history of business is littered with numerous once-great companies whose managers did not recognize, and adapt their value chains to respond to, significant changes taking place in the competitive environment. Examples include Digital Equipment, a former leading computer maker now defunct because its CEO believed that "personal computers are just toys," and Eastern Airlines and Pan Am, which were unable to survive because of their high operating costs in a competitive airline industry. History is also marked by companies whose managers made the wrong value-chain choices because they misinterpreted the competitive environment. Examples include Motorola managers who invested more than $3 billion in the Iridium satellite project that was abandoned in 2000 and the managers of thousands of dot-coms who underestimated the costs involved with delivering online products and services reliably to customers.

boundary spanning
Interacting with individuals and groups outside the organization to obtain valuable information from the environment.

Managers can learn to perceive, interpret, and appreciate better the competitive environments by practicing **boundary spanning**—interacting with individuals and groups outside the organization to obtain valuable information from the environment.[39] Managers who engage in boundary-spanning activities seek ways not only to respond to forces in the environment but also to directly influence and manage the perceptions of suppliers and customers in that environment to increase their organizations' access to resources.

To understand how boundary spanning works, see Figure 9.9. A functional manager in a boundary-spanning role in organization X establishes a personal or virtual link with a manager in a boundary-spanning role in organization Y. The two managers

Figure 9.9
The Nature of Boundary-Spanning Roles

ORGANIZATION X

ORGANIZATION Y

Managers in
boundary-spanning
roles feed back information
to managers inside their functional
areas and organizations

communicate and share information that helps both of them understand the changing forces and conditions in the environment. These managers then share this information with other functional managers in their respective organizations so that all managers become better informed about events outside their own organization's boundaries. As a result, the managers in both organizations can make value-chain decisions that lead to higher-performing operating systems.

For an example of a manager performing a boundary-spanning role, consider the situation of a purchasing manager for Taco Bell. The purchasing manager is charged with finding the lowest-cost supplier of low-fat cheese and sour cream. To perform this task, the manager could write to major food companies and ask for price quotes. Or the manager could phone food company managers personally, develop informal yet professional relationships with them, and, over time, learn from them which food companies are active in the low-fat-food area and what they envision for the future. By developing such relationships, the purchasing manager will be able to provide Taco Bell with valuable information that will allow its purchasing department to make well-informed choices. This flow of information from the environment may, in turn, allow marketing to develop more effective sales campaigns or allow product development to develop better-looking and better-tasting tacos. Note that personal communication is often necessary to supplement the information provided by IT.

What would happen if managers in all of an organization's functions performed boundary-spanning roles? The richness of the information available to managers throughout the organization probably would lead to an increase in the quality of managers' decision making and planning, enabling them to produce goods and services that customers prefer or to create advertising campaigns that attract new customers.

Searching for and collecting information to understand how changing trends and forces in the environment are affecting a company's operating system is an important boundary-spanning activity. Many organizations employ functional experts whose only job is to scan professional journals, trade association publications, and newspapers to identify changes in technology, government regulations, fashion trends, and so on, that will affect the way their organization operates. However, merely collecting information is not enough for the boundary-spanning manager. He or she must interpret what the information means and then practice **gatekeeping,** deciding what information to allow into the organization and what information to keep out. The nature of the information that the gatekeeper chooses to pass on to other managers will influence the decisions they make. Thus, accurate information processing is vital, and utilizing information technology can obviously help here.[40]

gatekeeping Deciding what information to allow into the organization and what information to keep out.

Value-Chain Management Over Time

The second issue in value-chain management is to make sure that a company keeps up its commitment to improving efficiency, quality, innovation, and responsiveness to customers over time. It is difficult, but necessary, for managers, supervisors, and employees to constantly scrutinize the way their companies are performing all the specific tasks necessary to ensure higher performance. Not only is it necessary that each person perform their specific job responsibilities to the best of their abilities, they are also expected at the same time to be thinking about ways to improve what they do. This puts an extra burden on members of an organization, and they must be rewarded for their commitment to achieving the lofty goals that initiatives such as TQM and innovation require. Many companies have failed in their attempts to continually increase performance because weary managers and overworked employees "give up" the quest to find better ways to operate, or mistakes creep in as they try to find shortcuts to achieve their goals, or simply because different functions fail to communicate because they become overloaded with work. Nothing is simple in value-chain management; everything has to be constantly worked at to achieve success and, as the following "Management Insight" suggests, Toyota, even though it is one of the best companies at managing the value chain, also has experienced many problems and failures over the years—but it never stops trying to solve them because this is part of its organizational culture.

Management Insight

Toyota Is Not Perfect, But It Continually Strives to Be

Although Toyota is regarded as a world leader in value-chain management, it would be a mistake to believe that its record is perfect—or anything close to it. Over the years it has made many mistakes and errors as it strives to find new methods to improve its value chain and increase innovation, quality, efficiency, and customer responsiveness. It always seeks to learn from its mistakes, however, and keeps on tackling a problem until it finds a solution.

On the innovation front for example, Toyota's Japanese engineers have often mistaken the needs of its global customers and the first generation of many of its new vehicles such as pickup trucks, minivans, and SUVs were flops. For example, its first pickup truck was too small for the U.S. market, its first minivan was clumsy compared to Chrysler's, and its first SUV was underpowered and lacked the comfort and features of competitors such as Ford and Land Rover. Nevertheless, Toyota's engineers have continually learned from their mistakes and today, using the skills of its U.S. and European designers, its new generation of pickup trucks, minivans, and SUVs are the market leaders.[41]

On the quality front it has also made mistakes; several times its engineers have designed parts such as air conditioning and brake systems that proved defective and led to many recalls. But they have learned from their mistakes and most problems have been corrected. Even so, it was only in 2007 that Toyota realized that it could improve quality even more if it started to collect repair information on what kinds of repair problems its vehicles suffered from *after* their warranty had expired. If it had taken such a long-term view earlier, then its engineers could have focused their attention on the specific problems that led to poor parts quality.[42]

On the efficiency front, cars have become more difficult to assemble because both components and work processes have become more complex. However, in the 2000s Toyota increasingly failed to realize the need to give employees more work training to prevent vehicle recalls because it has been expanding so quickly around the world.[43] Since 2004, for example, Toyota has recalled 9.3 million vehicles in the U.S. and Japan, almost three times the previous rate. To solve this problem Toyota has delayed the introduction of some of its new models by several months while it trains its workforce in the many intricate procedures that must be followed to achieve the high quality it demands. To help it regain its high quality standards it opened "global production centers" in Kentucky, England, and Thailand to allow its engineers to train production supervisors in the advanced techniques, such as in welding and painting, needed to maintain state-of-the-art production quality.

Toyota's president Katsuaki Watanabe in a cluster of Toyota employees and managers next to a new model Toyota Tundra—a successful pick-up truck which learned from the mistakes of previous models.

Its president, Katsuaki Watanabe, publicly apologized in 2007 for these increasing errors and affirmed that Toyota was now back on the right track—even though it is almost always at the top of the quality list of the best global carmakers.[44] Even the best companies have to strive to maintain—let alone exceed—their high standards.

Ethical Implications

Managers also need to understand the ethical implications of the adoption of many of the value-chain management techniques discussed in this chapter. Although TQM, JIT, flexible manufacturing, and reengineering can all increase quality, efficiency, and responsiveness to customers, they may do so at great cost to employees. Employees may see the demands of their jobs increase as the result of TQM or, worse, may see themselves reengineered out of a job. For example, Toyota is the most efficient car manufacturer in the world, but some of its gains have been achieved at a significant cost to its employees, as discussed in the following "Ethics in Action."

Ethics in Action

The Human Cost of Improving Productivity

Hisashi Tomiki is the leader of a four-man self-managed team in a Toyota production plant, 200 miles south of Tokyo, Japan. Tomiki and his team work at a grueling pace to build cowls (steel chambers onto which windshields and steering columns are attached). Consider this description of Tomiki at work:

> In two minutes Tomiki fits 24 metal pieces into designated slots on three welding machines; runs two large metal sheets through each of the machines, which weld on the parts; and fuses the two sheets together with two spot welds. There is little room for error. Once or twice an hour a mistake is made or a machine sticks, causing the next machine in line to stop. A yellow light flashes. Tomiki runs over. The squad must fix the part and work faster to catch up. A red button halts the production line if the problems are severe, but there is an unspoken rule against pushing it. Only once this day does Tomiki call in a special maintenance worker.[45]

The experience of workers like Tomiki has become increasingly common—especially in the 2000s when the threat of outsourcing has led workers to accept management demands for a faster work pace. Workers are heard to complain that constant attempts to increase quality and reduce costs really means continuous speedup and added job stress from the increase in the pressure put on employees to perform. Although some pressure is good, beyond a certain point it can seriously harm employees. Moreover, consider the following quote from Jerry Miller, a former employee of US West, whose team of billing clerks reengineered themselves out of a job:

> When we first formed our teams, the company came in talking teams and empowerment and promised that we wouldn't lose any jobs. It turns out all this was a big cover. The company had us all set up for reengineering. We showed them how to streamline the work, and now 9,000 people are gone. It was cut-your-own-throat. It makes you feel used.[46]

Is it ethical to continually increase the demands placed on employees, regardless of the human cost in terms of job stress? It is obvious that the answer is no. Employee support is vital if the organization is to function effectively. What kinds of work pressures are legitimate, and what pressures are excessive? There is no clear answer to this question. Ultimately, the issue comes down to the judgment of responsible managers seeking to act ethically.

Summary and Review

LO1 **VALUE-CHAIN MANAGEMENT AND COMPETITIVE ADVANTAGE** To achieve high performance, managers try to improve their responsiveness to customers, the quality of their products, and the efficiency of their organization. To achieve these goals, managers can use a number of value-chain management techniques to improve the way an organization's operating system operates.

LO2 **IMPROVING RESPONSIVENESS TO CUSTOMERS** To achieve high performance in a competitive environment, it is imperative that the organization's value chain is managed to produce outputs that have the attributes customers desire. One of the central tasks of value-chain management is to develop new and improved operating systems that enhance the ability of the organization to economically deliver more of the product attributes that customers desire for the same price. Techniques such as CRM and TQM, JIT, flexible manufacturing, and process reengineering are popular because they promise to do this. As important as responsiveness to customers is, however, managers need to recognize that there are limits to how responsive an organization can be and still cover its costs.

LO3 **IMPROVING QUALITY** Managers seek to improve the quality of their organization's output because doing so enables them to better serve customers, to raise prices, and to lower production costs. Total quality management focuses on improving the quality of an organization's products and services and stresses that all of an organization's operations should be directed toward this goal. Putting TQM into practice requires having an organizationwide commitment to TQM, having a strong customer focus, finding ways to measure quality, setting quality improvement goals, soliciting input from employees about how to improve product quality, identifying defects and tracing them to their source, introducing just-in-time inventory systems, getting suppliers to adopt TQM practices, designing products for ease of manufacture, and breaking down barriers between functional departments.

LO4   IMPROVING EFFICIENCY   Improving efficiency requires one or more of the following: the introduction of a TQM program, the adoption of flexible manufacturing technologies, the introduction of just-in-time inventory systems, the establishment of self-managed work teams, and the application of process reengineering. Top management is responsible for setting the context within which efficiency improvements can take place by, for example, emphasizing the need for continuous improvement. Functional-level managers bear prime responsibility for identifying and implementing efficiency-enhancing improvements in operating systems.

LO5   IMPROVING PRODUCT INNOVATION   When technology is changing, managers must quickly innovate new and improved products to protect their competitive advantage. Some value-chain strategies managers can use to help them achieve this are (1) involve both customers and suppliers in the development process; (1) establish a stage-gate development funnel for evaluating and controlling different product development efforts; and (3) establish cross-functional teams composed of individuals from different functional departments, and give each team a leader who can rise above his or her functional background.

Management in Action

Topics for Discussion and Action

DISCUSSION

1. What is CRM, and in what ways can it help improve responsiveness to customers? **[LO2]**

2. What are the main challenges to be overcome in implementing a successful total quality management program? **[LO3]**

3. What is efficiency, and what are some of the strategies that managers can use to increase it? **[LO4]**

4. Why is it important for managers to pay close attention to value-chain management if they wish to be responsive to their customers? **[LO 1, 2]**

5. What is innovation, and what are some of the strategies that managers can use to develop successful new products? **[LO5]**

ACTION

6. Ask a manager how responsiveness to customers, quality, efficiency, and innovation are defined and measured in his or her organization. **[LO 1, 2]**

7. Go to a local store, restaurant, or supermarket, observe how customers are treated, and list the ways in which you think the organization is being responsive or unresponsive to the needs of its customers. How could this business improve its responsiveness to customers? **[LO 1, 2]**

Building Management Skills
Managing the Value Chain [LO 1, 2]

Choose an organization with which you are familiar—one that you have worked in or patronized or one that has received extensive coverage in the popular press. The organization should be involved in only one industry or business. Answer these questions about the organization:

1. What is the output of the organization?

2. Describe the value-chain activities that the organization uses to produce this output.

3. What product attributes do customers of the organization desire?

4. Try to identify improvements that might be made to the organization's value chain to boost its responsiveness to customers, quality, efficiency, and innovation.

Managing Ethically [LO 1, 4]

Go back and review the "Ethics in Action" on the human costs of Toyota's production system. After implementing efficiency-improving techniques, many companies commonly lay off employees who are no longer needed. And, frequently, remaining employees must perform more tasks more quickly, a situation that can generate employee stress and other work-related problems.

Questions

1. Either by yourself or in a group, think through the ethical implications of using some new functional strategy to improve organizational performance.

2. What criteria would you use to decide which kind of strategy is ethical to adopt and/or how far to push employees to raise the level of their performance?

3. How big a layoff, if any, is acceptable? If layoffs are acceptable, what could be done to reduce their harm to employees?

Small Group Breakout Exercise
How to Compete in the Sandwich Business [LO 1, 2]

Form groups of three or four people, and appoint one member as the spokesperson who will communicate your findings to the class when called on by the instructor. Then discuss the following scenario.

You and your partners are thinking about opening a new kind of sandwich shop that will compete head-to-head with Subway and Thundercloud Subs. Because these chains have good brand-name recognition, it is vital that you find some source of competitive advantage for your new sandwich shop, and you are meeting to brainstorm ways of obtaining one.

1. Identify the product attributes that a typical sandwich shop customer wants the most.

2. In what ways do you think you will be able to improve on the operations and processes of existing sandwich shops and increase responsiveness to customers through better (a) product quality, (b) efficiency, or (c) innovation?

Exploring the World Wide Web [LO 3, 4]

Go to GM's Web site by typing the following address: http://media.gm.com/servlet/GatewayServlet?target=http://image.emerald.gm.com/gmnews/viewmonthlyreleasedetail.do?domain=3&docid=19989

This address leads to a page that discusses TQM at GM's Livonia engine plant. (If the link has changed, search for the 2004 press release containing the keyword "Livonia.")

Read the press release; then go back to the principles of TQM discussed in this chapter. How has GM used TQM to attain superior quality and efficiency at its Livonia plant?

Be the Manager [LO 1, 3, 4, 5]

How to Build Flat-Panel Displays

You are the top manager of a start-up company that will produce innovative new flat-screen displays for PC makers like Dell and HP. The flat-screen-display market is highly competitive, so there is also considerable pressure to reduce costs because prices fall rapidly. Also, PC makers are demanding ever-higher quality and better features to please customers.

In addition, they demand that delivery of your product meets their production schedule needs. Functional managers want your advice on how to best meet these requirements, especially as they are in the process of recruiting new workers and building a production facility.

Questions

1. What kinds of techniques discussed in the chapter can help your functional managers to increase efficiency?

2. In what ways can these managers go about developing a program to increase (1) quality? (2) innovation?

3. What critical lessons do these managers need to learn about value-chain management?

BusinessWeek Case in the News [LO 1, 5]

Philips' Norelco

The Problem

How do you dare redesign an icon? When the Dutch company Royal Philips Electronics pioneered the rotating blade electric razor in 1939 and sold it in 1947 in America as the Norelco shaver, it designed a brand as much as a product. "Norelco" stood for modern, industrial, technological. In the early 1960s, Norelco launched the first fully cordless razor and had 18% of the electric shaver market. By 1978, it controlled 60%.

But in more recent years, electric shavers have been overshadowed by the blade wars of the wet-shaving world. Gillette has captured the high-tech high ground with its multibladed razors. By 2004, though Philips held 50% of the electric market, only 18% of all men used solely electric shavers, according to the company's market research. Last year, Philips decided to talk to customers to figure out how to redesign the Norelco electric shaver to give as close a shave as possible.

The Research

Philips interviewed 5,000 men in the U.S., Europe, and China. Its target customer was between the ages of 35 and 54, an experienced shaver who is likely to spend more for a premium razor that will last six to seven years. The company searched for some undiscovered consumer need that might be met with a dynamite product—and found an opportunity in an unlikely place. It learned that one of the most common frustrations of shaving has nothing to do with the face: it's those pesky few flat-lying hairs on the neck under the chin. The men interviewed by the company had to shave over those hairs six or seven times, often irritating their skin and leaving welts or spawning in-grown hairs. Philips decided to develop a razor that closely shaves those neck hairs the first time. To do so, it needed to design an electric razor with much greater maneuverability to navigate the tricky area around the jugular vein. Its research also led the company to a name for the new model: the "Arcitec," a combination of "the arch of the neck" and "technology."

Prototyping

Philips' teams of engineers, designers, and business strategists, led by Nico Engelsman, a senior vice-president for business management, and senior design director Tammo de Ligny also studied consumer trends among potential customers. They learned from interviews that their customers wanted materials that radiated strength, like stainless steel in the razor head. The teams also looked in hundreds of magazines and ads showing cars, phones, and men's accessories. For color, they drew inspiration from the silver Motorola RAZR phone, the BMW Z4 Coupe, and the Volant silver series skis: they made the Arcitec models black, charcoal, and silver.

The designers began working up rough pictures of solutions to tackle the neck-shaving. Then they began prototyping and testing plastic models with consumers, iterating very quickly. To make the electric shaver more flexible and maneuverable than previous models, they created a bigger separation between the shaving head and the handle that men grasp as they shave. That allowed the head to pivot 360 degrees. Their testing also made clear they had to miniaturize the moving parts to make the grip easier as men moved the shaver under their chins along their necks. In the final testing in October, 2006, the designers tried out the razors in four sessions with four different panels of 50 participants each. In the first, the blades didn't protrude enough to give a close shave. The designers raised the blades, but went too far. The blades were too high, irritating the skin. On the third try, they got it right. They also tested the razors' performance using what they call a "paint-brush test." They shaved paintbrush bristles made of the thickest synthetic hair possible to evaluate how the shaver would perform on the toughest whiskers.

Marketing

Philips will start selling the Arcitec in the U.S. and Britain in July and in the rest of the world in September. Prices will range from $169 to $249, depending on the model. The company will not market it as aggressively in India or China yet. Why? In India people can get a shave at the corner stand for 20 rupees, or 50 cents, so that huge market is not yet primed for a premium product like the Arcitec, Philips learned.

Chinese men, the company found in its research, generally have less hair,

and Asian hair tends to be rounder in shape and thicker in diameter than Caucasian hair, making it stronger but slower-growing. So the Chinese don't necessarily need a razor with three rotating blades like the Arcitec. Electric shaving is growing in popularity with young men in China, however, so Philips will launch a double-headed razor there along with the Arcitec to give customers some options.

And what about female consumers? Philips' research shows nearly half of electric shaver purchases are gifts, and 75% of those are bought by women for men. Yet wives, girlfriends, and moms don't know much about men's razors and are terrified of choosing the wrong one, the company found. So Philips will create a specific marketing campaign for female shoppers, and will have video demos online through Amazon.com showing typical male shaving dilemmas, like getting at those nasty little neck hairs.

The Arcitec's packaging will represent Philips' broader attempt to unify all its products under one brand name worldwide. For decades, the company

sold its products in the U.S. under many brands, including Norelco. The Philips logo will now appear above the Norelco logo on the packaging. And in the future, Philips plans to phase out the name "Norelco."

Questions for Discussion

1. Discuss the steps Philips' teams took to develop its new razor in terms of the strategies for successful product development outlined in the chapter (e.g., involve customers and suppliers, use stage-gate development funnel, use cross-functional teams).

2. What other strategies did Philips adopt?

3. Go to the Internet to discover how successful Philips' new razor has been in the U.S. and global markets.

Source: Aili McConnon, "Philips' Norelco: How Neck Hairs Led to the Remaking of an Icon." Reprinted from the June 11, 2007, issue of *BusinessWeek* Online by special permission. Copyright © 2007 by The McGraw-Hill Companies, Inc.

BusinessWeek Case in the News [LO 3, 4]

No One Does Lean Like the Japanese

Two years ago, Matsushita Co.'s factory in Saga, on Japan's southern island of Kyushu, was looking mighty lean. The plant had doubled efficiency over the previous four years, and machinery stretching the length of the spotless facility could churn out cordless phones, fax machines, and security cameras in record time.

But Matsushita officials still saw fat that could be trimmed. So the plant's managers, Hitoshi Hirata and Hirofumi Tsuru, ripped out the conveyer belts and replaced them with clusters of robots. New software synchronizes production so each robot is ready to jump into action as soon as the previous step is completed. And if

one robot breaks down, the work flow can be shifted to others that do the same job. "It used to be 2 1/2 days into a production run before we had our first finished product. But now the first is done in 40 minutes," Hirata says. "Next year we'll try to shorten the cycle even more."

Japan, of course, has long been a global leader in lean production. Japanese companies invented just-in-time manufacturing, where parts arrive at the loading dock right when they're needed. But now, as these companies face increasing competition from low-cost rivals in Korea, China, and elsewhere in Asia, they're working double-time to stay ahead. And to ensure that they produce what consumers are actually buying, they're rearranging factories so

they can quickly shift gears to make gadgets that are hot, and ease up on those that are selling more slowly.

Network Hub

Matsushita's Saga plant is at the forefront of that effort. Kunio Nakamura, Matsushita's chairman, has often praised Saga as an example for the rest of the company as it seeks to cut plant inventories in half from 2004 levels by next March. "To get the most from our manufacturing strengths, we must lower inventories," Nakamura told employees last fall. In his speech, Nakamura cited Saga, which now makes a batch of 500 phones per eight-hour shift, vs. 1,500 phones in three days before the most recent changes. While that means Saga can make twice as many phones per week, the company is also trimming inventory costs because components such as chips, keypads, and circuit boards spend one-third as much time in the factory.

Those efficiency gains multiply when you look at the big picture. Saga is a "mother plant," or the hub of an overseas manufacturing network. Weeks after Hirata and Tsuru gave the green light to the new layout, six other Matsushita plants in China, Malaysia, Mexico, and Britain started copying the setup. Most have since been able to cut their inventories and have seen a similar boost in production, today churning out a total of 150,000 phones per shift.

That's just the kind of effort that has helped Matsushita bounce back from a $3.7 billion loss in 2002. The company on Apr. 29 announced its best earnings in more than a decade. And in the year ending next March, Matsushita expects net profit to increase by 23%, to $1.7 billion, on a 1% rise in sales, to $78 billion.

Matsushita has learned much from Hirata and Tsuru. They dress in factory-issued bamboo-green zip-up jackets and indoor-only shoes, and twice daily they join most of the 280 employees for calisthenics on the factory floor. But their real focus is on boosting efficiency. Their brainstorming began two years ago, when they discovered that a bottleneck on the assembly line meant that robots sat idle for longer than they were working. So they broke the line into stations, or "cells," that allowed them to double up on slower robots to make things flow more smoothly.

In test runs, the new setup worked, but with so many machines going at once it was tough to choreograph the production process. In the past, a person was assigned to schedule everything from deliveries of supplies to work shifts to maintenance. But that wouldn't fly in a factory that had to be prepared to shift gears for a sudden spike or dip in demand. Instead the managers found software that would do the trick.

The next step was figuring out how to apply the changes globally. With 75 markets to cater to, the seven factories in Saga's group make 35 million phones, faxes, printers, and other products annually. It was a logistical nightmare: there were 1,500 shape and color variations for phones alone, and engineers needed to rearrange as many as 77 circuit-board parts for each new model. Retooling the robots for every type of board was simply too time-consuming, so Matsushita engineers designed a circuit-board that would need only slight changes for each model. Despite the faster pace, Hirata says defects are at an all-time low: under 1% in every factory.

Questions for Discussion

1. What value-chain techniques has Matsushita been using to improve its performance lately?

2. Given its losses, Panasonic has been well behind Toyota in putting lean production into practice. Why is it difficult for all companies to implement lean production?

CHAPTER 10

Managing Organizational Structure and Culture

After studying this chapter, you should be able to:

LO1 Identify the factors that influence managers' choice of an organizational structure.

LO2 Explain how managers group tasks into jobs that are motivating and satisfying for employees.

LO3 Describe the types of organizational structures managers can design, and explain why they choose one structure over another.

LO4 Explain why managers must coordinate jobs, functions, and divisions using the hierarchy of authority and integrating mechanisms.

LO5 List the four sources of organizational culture, and explain why and how a company's culture can lead to competitive advantage.

A Manager's Challenge

Liz Claiborne Reorganizes Its Structure

How should managers organize to improve performance? Liz Claiborne, like other well-known apparel makers, embarked on a major product expansion strategy in the 1990s when it acquired many smaller branded clothing and accessory companies and started many new brands of its own. The company's goal was to achieve greater operating efficiencies so that rising sales would also result in rising profits. By 2005 it had grown to 36 different brands, but while revenues had soared from $2 billion to $5 billion its profits had not kept pace. In fact, by 2006 profits were falling because costs were rising as operational efficiency fell due to the enormous complexity and expense involved in managing so many brands.[1]

So, in 2006 Liz Claiborne recruited a new CEO, William McComb, to find a way to turnaround the troubled company. Within months he decided to reverse course, shrink the company, and move to a new form of organizational structure that would once again allow it to grow—but this time with increasing profitability. CEO McComb's problem was to find a new organizational structure that would reduce the problems associated with managing its 36 different brands. He believed the company had

developed a "culture of complexity" that had gotten out of control. Liz Claiborne's core merchandising culture that had made it so successful had been lost because of its rapid growth and overly complex organizational structure.

Lookin' good: William McComb's streamlining of Liz Claiborne Company's brands and organizational structure allowed the company to respond more quickly to changing fashion trends and so made it more competitive against brands such as Zara.

The company had created five different apparel divisions to manage its 36 brands; brands were grouped into different divisions according to nature of the clothing or accessories they made. For example, luxury designer lines such as Ellen Tracy were grouped into one division; clothes for working women such as its signature Liz Claiborne and Dana Buchman brands were in a second; trendy, hip clothing directed at young customers such as its Juicy Couture line were in a third division, and so on. Each division was controlled by a separate management team, and each division performed all the functional activities, such as marketing and design, needed to support its brands. The problem was that over time it had become increasingly difficult to differentiate between apparel brands in each division, as well as between the brands of different divisions, because fashion styles change quickly in response to changing customer tastes demands. Also, costs were rising because of the duplication of activities between divisions; and increasing competition was resulting in new pressure to lower prices to retail stores to protect sales.

McComb decided it was necessary to streamline and change Liz Claiborne's organizational structure to meet the changing needs of customers and increasing competition in retailing because of the growth of private-label brands. First, he decided that the company would either try to sell, license or close down 16 of its 36 brands and focus on the remaining 20 that had the best chance of generating good profits in the future.[2] To better manage these 20 brands he decided to change Liz Claiborne's organizational structure and to shrink from five different divisions to just two. This eliminated an entire level of top management, but it also allowed him to eliminate the duplication in marketing, distribution, and retail functions across the old five divisions, in which led to major cost savings.

The two remaining divisions are now Liz Claiborne's retail division called "direct brands" and its wholesale division called "partnered brands." Its new structure is intended to "bring focus, energy and clarity" to the way each division operates. The retail division, for example, is responsible for the brands that are sold primarily through Liz Claiborne's own retail store chains, such as its Kate Spade, Lucky Brand Jeans, and Juicy Couture chains. The goals of grouping together its fastest-growing brands is to allow divisional managers to make better marketing and distribution decisions to attract more customers. For example, Liz Claiborne plans to increase targeted marketing on direct labels to 3% to 5% of annual sales and to find ways to get new clothing designs more quickly to its store to compete with chains such as Zara that are able to innovate new clothing collections almost every month. The company also plans to open 300 more stores in the next few years to add to its 433 specialty stores and 350 outlet stores.[3]

On the other hand, the problem in the wholesale division, which sells branded apparel lines such as Liz Claiborne and Dana Buchman directly to department stores and other retailers, is to reduce costs to slow down the growing threat from private-labels. For example, sales of Macy's private-labels increased from 15% in 2005 to 18% in 2007. If managers of the wholesale division can find ways to improve operating efficiency, it can offer stores such as Macy's lower prices for its clothing to encourage them to stick with its brands. Similarly, if the division's managers can find ways to reduce costs, such as by turning inventory over more quickly, sharing marketing costs, and so forth, then even if the prices they can charge do fall they can still increase profits. Wholesale managers are also partnering with department stores to develop exclusive lines of branded clothing so both parties benefit. In 2007, for example, they reached an agreement with J.C. Penny to launch a line called Liz & Co. that will be sold only in Penny's stores; so far, sales have been good and both partners have enjoyed higher profits.

Thus, CEO McComb realized that to reduce complexity and allow each division to build the right merchandising culture it was necessary to change Liz Claiborne's organizational structure. From grouping clothing brands into divisions according to their quality or price, he changed to two market divisions where clothing brands are grouped according to the needs of each division's customers—either the people in its stores or the retail chains that buy its clothes to resell to individual customers. The real problem is that each division faces a quite different set of strategic and operational problems, and with its new structure managers in each division can now focus on solving the specific set of problems to achieve the best performance from their particular brands. McComb's hope is that in the next decade the company's sales will grow rapidly, but this time its new structure will lead to higher efficiency and effectiveness and so to rising profitability.

Overview

As the example of Liz Claiborne suggests, when the environment changes because, for example, customer tastes change, or because agile competitors have developed new strategies to outperform their rivals, a company often has to change its organizational structure and move to one better suited to its new environment. The way an organization is designed also has a major effect on the way employees behave and how well the organization operates; and, with competition heating up in the apparel industry, the challenge facing Liz Claiborne's CEO was to identify the best way to organize people and resources to increase efficiency and effectiveness.

In Part 4 of this book, we examine how managers can organize and control human and other resources to create high-performing organizations. To organize and control (two of the four tasks of management identified in Chapter 1), managers must design an organizational architecture that makes the best use of resources to produce the goods and services customers want. **Organizational architecture** is the combination of organizational structure, culture, control systems, and human resource management (HRM) systems that together determine how efficiently and effectively organizational resources are used.

By the end of this chapter, you will be familiar not only with various forms of organizational structures and cultures but also with various factors that determine the organizational design choices that managers make. Then, in Chapters 11 and 12, we examine issues surrounding the design of an organization's control systems and HRM systems.

organizational architecture The organizational structure, control systems, culture, and human resource management systems that together determine how efficiently and effectively organizational resources are used.

Designing Organizational Structure

Organizing is the process by which managers establish the structure of working relationships among employees to allow them to achieve organizational goals efficiently and effectively. **Organizational structure** is the formal system of task and job reporting relationships that determines how employees use resources to achieve organizational goals.[4] *Organizational culture,* discussed in Chapter 3, is the shared set of beliefs, values, and norms that influence the way people and groups work together to achieve organizational goals. **Organizational design** is the process by which managers create a specific type of

Figure 10.1
Factors Affecting Organizational Structure

organizational structure
A formal system of task and reporting relationships that coordinates and motivates organizational members so that they work together to achieve organizational goals.

organizational design
The process by which managers make specific organizing choices that result in a particular kind of organizational structure.

LO1 Identify the factors that influence managers' choice of an organizational structure.

organizational structure and culture so that a company can operate in the most efficient and effective way—just as William McComb did for Liz Claiborne.[5]

Once a company decides what kind of work attitudes and behaviors it wants from its employees, managers create a particular arrangement of task and authority relationships, and promote specific cultural values and norms, to obtain these desired attitudes and behaviors. The challenge facing all companies is to design a structure and culture that (1) *motivates* managers and employees to work hard and to develop supportive job behaviors and attitudes and (2) *coordinates* the actions of employees, groups, functions, and divisions to ensure they work together efficiently and effectively.

As noted in Chapter 2, according to contingency theory, managers design organizational structures to fit the factors or circumstances that are affecting the company the most and causing them the most uncertainty.[6] Thus, there is no one best way to design an organization: Design reflects each organization's specific situation, and researchers have argued that in some situations stable, mechanistic structures may be most appropriate while in others flexible, organic structures might be the most effective. Four factors are important determinants of the type of organizational structure or culture managers select: the nature of the organizational environment, the type of strategy the organization pursues, the technology (and particularly information technology) the organization uses, and the characteristics of the organization's human resources (see Figure 10.1).[7]

The Organizational Environment

In general, the more quickly the external environment is changing and the greater the uncertainty within it, the greater are the problems facing managers in trying to gain access to scarce resources. In this situation, to speed decision making and communication and make it easier to obtain resources, managers typically make organizing choices that result in more flexible structures and entrepreneurial cultures.[8] They are likely to decentralize authority, empower lower-level employees to make important operating decisions, and encourage values and norms that emphasize change and innovation—a more organic from of organizing.

In contrast, if the external environment is stable, resources are readily available, and uncertainty is low, then less coordination and communication among people and functions are needed to obtain resources. Managers can make organizing choices that bring more stability or formality to the organizational structure and can establish values and norms that emphasize obedience and being a team player. Managers in this situation prefer to make decisions within a clearly defined hierarchy of authority and to use detailed rules, standard operating procedures (SOPs), and restrictive norms to guide and govern employees' activities—a more mechanistic form of organizing.

As we discussed in Chapter 6, change is rapid in today's marketplace, and increasing competition both at home and abroad is putting greater pressure on managers to attract customers and increase efficiency and effectiveness. Consequently, interest in finding ways to structure organizations—such as through empowerment and self-managed teams—to allow people and departments to behave flexibly has been increasing.

Strategy

Chapter 8 suggests that once managers decide on a strategy, they must choose the right means to implement it. Different strategies often call for the use of different organizational structures and cultures. For example, a differentiation strategy aimed at increasing the value customers perceive in an organization's goods and services usually succeeds best in a flexible structure with a culture that values innovation; flexibility facilitates a differentiation strategy because managers can develop new or innovative products quickly—an activity that requires extensive cooperation among functions or departments. In contrast, a low-cost strategy that is aimed at driving down costs in all functions usually fares best in a more formal structure with more conservative norms, which gives managers greater control over the activities of an organization's various departments.[9]

In addition, at the corporate level, when managers decide to expand the scope of organizational activities by vertical integration or diversification, for example, they need to design a flexible structure to provide sufficient coordination among the different business divisions.[10] As discussed in Chapter 8, many companies have been divesting businesses because managers have been unable to create a competitive advantage to keep them up to speed in fast-changing industries. By moving to a more flexible structure, managers gain more control over their different businesses. Finally, expanding internationally and operating in many different countries challenges managers to create organizational structures that allow organizations to be flexible on a global level.[11] As we discuss later, managers can group their departments or divisions in several ways to allow them to effectively pursue an international strategy.

Technology

Recall that technology is the combination of skills, knowledge, machines, and computers that are used to design, make, and distribute goods and services. As a rule, the more complicated the technology that an organization uses, the more difficult it is to regulate or control it because more unexpected events can arise. Thus, the more complicated the technology, the greater is the need for a flexible structure and progressive culture to enhance managers' ability to respond to unexpected situations—and give them the freedom and desire to work out new solutions to the problems they encounter. In contrast, the more routine the technology, the more appropriate is a formal structure, because tasks are simple and the steps needed to produce goods and services have been worked out in advance.

What makes a technology routine or complicated? One researcher who investigated this issue, Charles Perrow, argued that two factors determine how complicated or nonroutine technology is: task variety and task analyzability.[12] *Task variety* is the number of new or unexpected problems or situations that a person or function encounters in performing tasks or jobs. *Task analyzability* is the degree to which programmed solutions are available to people or functions to solve the problems they encounter. Nonroutine or complicated technologies are characterized by high task variety and low task analyzability; this means that many varied problems occur and that solving these problems requires significant nonprogrammed decision making. In contrast, routine technologies are characterized by low task variety and high task analyzability; this means that the problems encountered do not vary much and are easily resolved through programmed decision making.

Examples of nonroutine technology are found in the work of scientists in an R&D laboratory who develop new products or discover new drugs, and they are seen in the planning exercises an organization's top-management team uses to chart the organization's future strategy. Examples of routine technology include typical mass-production or assembly operations, where workers perform the same task repeatedly and where managers have already identified the programmed solutions necessary to perform a task efficiently. Similarly, in service organizations such as fast-food restaurants, the tasks that crew members perform in making and serving fast food are very routine.

Human Resources

A final important factor affecting an organization's choice of structure and culture is the characteristics of the human resources it employs. In general, the more highly skilled its workforce, and the greater the number of employees who work together in groups or teams, the more likely an organization is to use a flexible, decentralized structure and a professional culture based on values and norms that foster employee autonomy and self-control. Highly skilled employees, or employees who have internalized strong professional values and norms of behavior as part of their training, usually desire greater freedom and autonomy and dislike close supervision.

Flexible structures, characterized by decentralized authority and empowered employees, are well suited to the needs of highly skilled people. Similarly, when people work in teams, they must be allowed to interact freely and develop norms to guide their own work interactions, which also is possible in a flexible organizational structure. Thus, when designing organizational structure and culture, managers must pay close attention to the needs of the workforce and to the complexity and kind of work employees perform.

In summary, an organization's external environment, strategy, technology, and human resources are the factors to be considered by managers in seeking to design the best structure and culture for an organization. The greater the level of uncertainty in the organization's environment, the more complex its strategy and technologies, and the more highly qualified and skilled its workforce, the more likely managers are to design a structure and a culture that are flexible, can change quickly, and allow employees to be innovative in their responses to problems, customer needs, and so on. The more stable the organization's environment, the less complex and more well understood its strategy or technology, and the less skilled its workforce, the more likely managers are to design an organizational structure that is formal and controlling and a culture whose values and norms prescribe how employees should act in particular situations.

LO2 Explain how managers group tasks into jobs that are motivating and satisfying for employees.

Later in the chapter we discuss how managers can create different kinds of organizational cultures. First, however, we discuss how managers can design flexible or formal organizational structures. The way an organization's structure works depends on the organizing choices managers make about three issues:

- How to group tasks into individual jobs.
- How to group jobs into functions and divisions.
- How to allocate authority and coordinate or integrate functions and divisions.

Grouping Tasks into Jobs: Job Design

The first step in organizational design is **job design,** the process by which managers decide how to divide into specific jobs the tasks that have to be performed to provide customers with goods and services. Managers at McDonald's, for example, have decided how best to divide the tasks required to provide customers with fast, cheap food in each McDonald's restaurant. After experimenting

job design The process by which managers decide how to divide tasks into specific jobs.

with different job arrangements, McDonald's managers decided on a basic division of labor among chefs and food servers. Managers allocated all the tasks involved in actually cooking the food (putting oil in the fat fryers, opening packages of frozen french fries, putting beef patties on the grill, making salads, and so on) to the job of chef. They allocated all the tasks involved in giving the food to customers (such as greeting customers, taking orders, putting fries and burgers into bags, adding salt, pepper, and napkins, and taking money) to food servers. In addition, they created other jobs—the job of dealing with drive-through customers, the job of keeping the restaurant clean, and the job of overseeing employees and responding to unexpected events. The result of the job design process is a *division of labor* among employees, one that McDonald's managers have discovered through experience is most efficient.

Establishing an appropriate division of labor among employees is a critical part of the organizing process, one that is vital to increasing efficiency and effectiveness. At McDonald's, the tasks associated with chef and food server were split into different jobs because managers found that, for the kind of food McDonald's serves, this approach was most efficient. It is efficient because when each employee is given fewer tasks to perform (so that each job becomes more specialized), employees become more productive at performing the tasks that constitute each job.

At Subway, the role of chef and server is combined into one, making the job "larger" than the jobs of McDonald's more specialized food servers. The idea behind job enlargement is that increasing the range of tasks performed by the worker will reduce boredom.

At Subway sandwich shops, however, managers chose a different kind of job design. At Subway, there is no division of labor among the people who make the sandwiches, wrap the sandwiches, give them to customers, and take the money. The roles of chef and food server are combined into one. This different division of tasks and jobs is efficient for Subway and not for McDonald's because Subway serves a limited menu of mostly submarine-style sandwiches that are prepared to order. Subway's production system is far simpler than McDonald's, because McDonald's menu is much more varied and its chefs must cook many different kinds of foods.

Managers of every organization must analyze the range of tasks to be performed and then create jobs that best allow the organization to give customers the goods and services they want. In deciding how to assign tasks to individual jobs, however, managers must be careful not to take **job simplification,** the process of reducing the number of tasks that each worker performs, too far.[13] Too much job simplification may reduce efficiency rather than increase it if workers find their simplified jobs boring and monotonous, become demotivated and unhappy, and, as a result, perform at a low level.

job simplification The process of reducing the number of tasks that each worker performs.

Job Enlargement and Job Enrichment

In an attempt to create a division of labor and design individual jobs to encourage workers to perform at a higher level and be more satisfied with their work, several researchers have proposed ways other than job simplification to group tasks into jobs: job enlargement and job enrichment.

job enlargement Increasing the number of different tasks in a given job by changing the division of labor.

Job enlargement is increasing the number of different tasks in a given job by changing the division of labor.[14] For example, because Subway food servers make the food as well as serve it, their jobs are "larger" than the jobs of McDonald's food servers. The idea behind job enlargement is that increasing the range of tasks performed by a worker will reduce boredom and fatigue and may increase motivation to perform at a high level—increasing both the quantity and the quality of goods and services provided.

job enrichment Increasing the degree of responsibility a worker has over his or her job.

Job enrichment is increasing the degree of responsibility a worker has over a job by, for example, (1) empowering workers to experiment to find new or better ways of doing the job, (2) encouraging workers to develop new skills, (3) allowing workers to decide how to do the work and giving them the responsibility for deciding how to respond to unexpected situations, and (4) allowing workers to monitor and measure their own performance.[15] The idea behind job enrichment is that increasing workers' responsibility increases their involvement in their jobs and thus increases their interest in the quality of the goods they make or the services they provide.

In general, managers who make design choices that increase job enrichment and job enlargement are likely to increase the degree to which people behave flexibly rather than rigidly or mechanically. Narrow, specialized jobs are likely to lead people to behave in predictable ways; workers who perform a variety of tasks and who are allowed and encouraged to discover new and better ways to perform their jobs are likely to act flexibly and creatively. Thus, managers who enlarge and enrich jobs create a flexible organizational structure, and those who simplify jobs create a more formal structure. If workers are grouped into self-managed work teams, the organization is likely to be flexible because team members provide support for each other and can learn from one another.

The Job Characteristics Model

J. R. Hackman and G. R. Oldham's job characteristics model is an influential model of job design that explains in detail how managers can make jobs more interesting and motivating.[16] Hackman and Oldham's model (see Figure 10.2) also describes the likely personal and organizational outcomes that will result from enriched and enlarged jobs.

According to Hackman and Oldham, every job has five characteristics that determine how motivating the job is. These characteristics determine how employees react to their work and lead to outcomes such as high performance and satisfaction and low absenteeism and turnover:

- *Skill variety:* The extent to which a job requires that an employee use a wide range of different skills, abilities, or knowledge. Example: The skill variety required by the job of a research scientist is higher than that called for by the job of a McDonald's food server.

- *Task identity:* The extent to which a job requires that a worker perform all the tasks necessary to complete the job, from the beginning to the end of the production process. Example: A craftsworker who takes a piece of wood and transforms it into

Figure 10.2
The Job Characteristics Model

a custom-made desk has higher task identity than does a worker who performs only one of the numerous operations required to assemble a flat screen TV.

- *Task significance:* The degree to which a worker feels his or her job is meaningful because of its effect on people inside the organization, such as coworkers, or on people outside the organization, such as customers. Example: A teacher who sees the effect of his or her efforts in a well-educated and well-adjusted student enjoys high task significance compared to a dishwasher who monotonously washes dishes as they come to the kitchen.

- *Autonomy:* The degree to which a job gives an employee the freedom and discretion needed to schedule different tasks and decide how to carry them out. Example: Salespeople who have to plan their schedules and decide how to allocate their time among different customers have relatively high autonomy compared to assembly-line workers, whose actions are determined by the speed of the production line.

- *Feedback:* The extent to which actually doing a job provides a worker with clear and direct information about how well he or she has performed the job. Example: An air traffic controller whose mistakes may result in a midair collision receives immediate feedback on job performance; a person who compiles statistics for a business magazine often has little idea of when he or she makes a mistake or does a particularly good job.

Hackman and Oldham argue that these five job characteristics affect an employee's motivation because they affect three critical psychological states (see Figure 10.2). The more employees feel that their work is *meaningful* and that they are *responsible for work outcomes and responsible for knowing how those outcomes affect others,* the more motivating work becomes and the more likely employees are to be satisfied and to perform at a high level. Moreover, employees who have jobs that are highly motivating are called on to use their skills more and to perform more tasks, and they are given more responsibility for doing the job. All of the foregoing are characteristic of jobs and employees in flexible structures where authority is decentralized and where employees commonly work with others and must learn new skills to complete the range of tasks for which their group is responsible.

LO3 Describe the types of organizational structures managers can design, and explain why they choose one structure over another.

Grouping Jobs into Functions and Divisions: Designing Organizational Structure

Once managers have decided which tasks to allocate to which jobs, they face the next organizing decision: how to group jobs together to best match the needs of the organization's environment, strategy, technology, and human resources. Typically, managers first decide to group jobs into departments and they design a *functional structure* to use organizational resources effectively. As an organization grows and becomes more difficult to control, managers must choose a more complex organizational design, such as a divisional structure or a matrix or product team structure. The different way in which managers can design organizational structure are discussed next. Selecting and designing an organizational structure to increase efficiency and effectiveness is a significant challenge. As noted in Chapter 7, managers reap the rewards of a well-thought-out strategy only if they choose the right type of structure to implement the strategy. The ability to make the right kinds of organizing choices is often what differentiates effective from ineffective managers and creates a high-performing organization.

Functional Structure

A *function* is a group of people, working together, who possess similar skills or use the same kind of knowledge, tools, or techniques to perform their jobs. Manufacturing,

Figure 10.3

The Functional Structure of Pier 1 Imports

functional structure An organizational structure composed of all the departments that an organization requires to produce its goods or services.

sales, and research and development are often organized into functional departments. A **functional structure** is an organizational structure composed of all the departments that an organization requires to produce its goods or services. Figure 10.3 shows the functional structure that Pier 1 Imports, the home furnishings company, uses to supply its customers with a range of goods from around the world to satisfy their desires for new and innovative products.

Pier 1's main functions are finance and administration, merchandising (purchasing the goods), stores (managing the retail outlets), planning and allocations (managing marketing, credit, and product distribution), and human resources. Each job inside a function exists because it helps the function perform the activities necessary for high organizational performance. Thus, within the planning and allocations function are all the jobs necessary to efficiently advertise Pier 1's products to increase their appeal to customers (such as promotion, photography, and visual communication) and then to distribute and transport the products to stores.

There are several advantages to grouping jobs according to function. First, when people who perform similar jobs are grouped together, they can learn from observing one another and thus become more specialized and can perform at a higher level. The tasks associated with one job often are related to the tasks associated with another job, which encourages cooperation within a function. In Pier 1's planning department, for example, the person designing the photography program for an ad campaign

Pier 1 organizes its operations by function, which means that employees can more easily learn from one another and improve the service they provide to its customers.

works closely with the person responsible for designing store layouts and with visual communication experts. As a result, Pier 1 is able to develop a strong, focused marketing campaign to differentiate its products.

Second, when people who perform similar jobs are grouped together, it is easier for managers to monitor and evaluate their performance.[17] Imagine if marketing experts, purchasing experts, and real-estate experts were grouped together in one function and supervised by a manager from merchandising. Obviously, the merchandising manager would not have the expertise to evaluate all these different people appropriately. However a functional structure allows workers to evaluate how well coworkers are performing their jobs, and if some workers are performing poorly, more experienced workers can help them develop new skills.

Finally, managers appreciate functional structure because it allows them to create the set of functions they need in order to scan and monitor the competitive environment and obtain information about the way it is changing.[18] With the right set of functions in place, managers are then in a good position to develop a strategy that allows the organization to respond to its changing situation. Employees in the marketing group can specialize in monitoring new marketing developments that will allow Pier 1 to better target its customers. Employees in merchandising can monitor all potential suppliers of home furnishings both at home and abroad to find the goods most likely to appeal to Pier 1's customers and manage Pier 1's global outsourcing supply chain.

As an organization grows, and particularly as its task environment and strategy change because it is beginning to produce a wider range of goods and services for different kinds of customers, several problems can make a functional structure less efficient and effective.[19] First, managers in different functions may find it more difficult to communicate and coordinate with one another when they are responsible for several different kinds of products, especially as the organization grows both domestically and internationally. Second, functional managers may become so preoccupied with supervising their own specific departments and achieving their departmental goals that they lose sight of organizational goals. If that happens, organizational effectiveness will suffer because managers will be viewing issues and problems facing the organization only from their own, relatively narrow, departmental perspectives.[20] Both of these problems can reduce efficiency and effectiveness.

Divisional Structures: Product, Market, and Geographic

divisional structure An organizational structure composed of separate business units within which are the functions that work together to produce a specific product for a specific customer.

As the problems associated with growth and diversification increase over time, managers must search for new ways to organize their activities to overcome the problems associated with a functional structure. Most managers of large organizations choose a **divisional structure** and create a series of business units to produce a specific kind of product for a specific kind of customer. Each *division* is a collection of functions or departments that work together to produce the product. The goal behind the change to a divisional structure is to create smaller, more manageable units within the organization. There are three forms of divisional structure (see Figure 10.4).[21] When managers organize divisions according to the *type of good or service* they provide, they adopt a product structure. When managers organize divisions according to the *area of the country or world* they operate in, they adopt a geographic structure. When managers

Figure 10.4
Product, Market, and Geographic Structures

organize divisions according to *the type of customer* they focus on, they adopt a market structure.

PRODUCT STRUCTURE   Imagine the problems that managers at Pier 1 would encounter if they decided to diversify into producing and selling cars, fast food, and health insurance—in addition to home furnishings—and tried to use their existing set of functional managers to oversee the production of all four kinds of products. No manager would have the necessary skills or abilities to oversee those four products. No individual marketing manager, for example, could effectively market cars, fast food, health insurance, and home furnishings at the same time. To perform a functional activity successfully, managers must have experience in specific markets or industries. Consequently, if managers decide to diversify into new industries or to expand their range of products, they commonly design a product structure to organize their operations (see Figure 10.4a).

product structure An organizational structure in which each product line or business is handled by a self-contained division.

Using a **product structure,** managers place each distinct product line or business in its own self-contained division and give divisional managers the responsibility for devising an appropriate business-level strategy to allow the division to compete effectively in its industry or market.[22] Each division is self-contained because it has a complete set of all the functions—marketing, R&D, finance, and so on—that it needs to produce or provide goods or services efficiently and effectively. Functional managers report to divisional managers, and divisional managers report to top or corporate managers.

Grouping functions into divisions focused on particular products has several advantages for managers at all levels in the organization. First, a product structure allows functional managers to specialize in only one product area, so they are able to build expertise and fine-tune their skills in this particular area. Second, each division's managers can become experts in their industry; this expertise helps them choose and develop a business-level strategy to differentiate their products or lower their costs while meeting the needs of customers. Third, a product structure frees corporate managers from the need to supervise directly each division's day-to-day operations; this latitude allows corporate managers to create the best corporate-level strategy to maximize the organization's future growth and ability to create value. Corporate managers are likely to make fewer mistakes about which businesses to diversify into or how to best expand internationally, for example, because they are able to take an organizationwide view.[23] Corporate managers also are likely to evaluate better how well divisional managers are doing, and they can intervene and take corrective action as needed.

The extra layer of management, the divisional management layer, can improve the use of organizational resources. Moreover, a product structure puts divisional managers close to their customers and lets them respond quickly and appropriately to the changing task environment. One pharmaceutical company that has recently adopted a new product structure to better organize its activities with great success is GlaxoSmithKline. The need to innovate new kinds of prescription drugs in order to boost performance is a continual battle for pharmaceutical companies. In the 2000s many of these companies have been merging to try to increase their research productivity, and one of them, GlaxoSmithKline, was created from the merger between Glaxo Wellcome and SmithKline Beecham.[24] Prior to the merger, both companies experienced a steep decline in the number of new prescription drugs their scientists were able to invent. The problem facing the new company's top managers was how to best use and combine the talents of the scientists and researchers from both of the former companies to allow them to quickly innovate exciting new drugs.

Top managers realized that after the merger there would be enormous problems associated with coordinating the activities of the thousands of research scientists

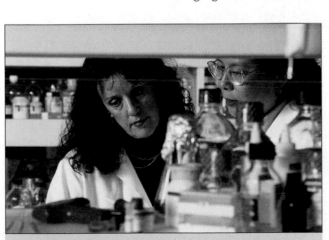

When Glaxo Wellcome and SmithKline Beecham merged, managers resolved the problem of how to coordinate the activities of thousands of research scientists by organizing them into product divisions focusing on clusters of diseases.

who were working on hundreds of different kinds of drug research programs. Understanding the problems associated with large size, the top managers decided to group the researchers into eight smaller product divisions to allow them to focus on particular clusters of diseases such as heart disease or viral infections. The members of each product division were told that they would be rewarded based on the number of new prescription drugs they were able to invent and the speed with which they could bring these new drugs to the market. To date, GlaxoSmithKline's new product structure has worked well. By 2008 research productivity had more than doubled since the reorganization and today a record number of new drugs are moving into clinical trials.[25]

GEOGRAPHIC STRUCTURE When organizations expand rapidly both at home and abroad, functional structures can create special problems because managers in one central location may find it increasingly difficult to deal with the different problems and issues that may arise in each region of a country or area of the world. In these cases, a **geographic structure,** in which divisions are broken down by geographic location, is often chosen (see Figure 10.4b). To achieve the corporate mission of providing next-day mail service, Fred Smith, CEO of FedEx, chose a geographic structure and divided up operations by creating a division in each region. Large retailers such as Macy's, Neiman Marcus, and Brooks Brothers also use a geographic structure. Since the needs of retail customers differ by region—for example, surfboards in California and down parkas in the Midwest—a geographic structure gives retail regional managers the flexibility they need to choose the range of products that best meets the needs of regional customers.

In adopting a *global geographic structure,* such as shown in Figure 10.5a, managers locate different divisions in each of the world regions where the organization operates.

geographic structure
An organizational structure in which each region of a country or area of the world is served by a self-contained division.

Figure 10.5

Global Geographic and Global Product Structures

Managers are most likely to do this when they pursue a multidomestic strategy, because customer needs vary widely by country or world region. For example, if products that appeal to U.S. customers do not sell in Europe, the Pacific Rim, or South America, then managers must customize the products to meet the needs of customers in those different world regions; a global geographic structure with global divisions will allow them to do this.

In contrast, to the degree that customers abroad are willing to buy the same kind of product, or slight variations thereof, managers are more likely to pursue a global strategy. In this case they are more likely to use a global product structure. In a *global product structure,* each product division, not the country and regional managers, takes responsibility for deciding where to manufacture its products and how to market them in countries worldwide (see Figure 10.5b). Product division managers manage their own global value chains and decide where to establish foreign subsidiaries to distribute and sell their products to customers in foreign countries. As we noted at the beginning of this chapter, an organization's strategy is a major determinant of its structure both at home and abroad and the way Nokia uses a global geographic structure to organize its worldwide operations is profiled in the following "Managing Globally."

Managing Globally

Nokia's Geographic Structure Helps It Conquer the World

In Chapter 8 we discussed how Nokia took a commanding lead in global cell phone sales over Motorola because of its strategy of customizing phones to the needs of local users and assembling the phones in a factory located in a country within the world region where the phones are to be sold. Nokia's most important function is its design and engineering function, which spearheads its global new product development efforts. And to allow this function, and so the company, to perform most effectively, Nokia adopted a global structure to organize its design activities.

Nokia was the first cell phone manufacturer to recognize that the needs of customers differ markedly in different countries of the world. In Western countries, for example, the style of the phone is paramount, as is its ability to offer users services like e-mail and video downloading, hence the popularity of Apple's iPhone, which Nokia is rushing to copy in 2008. In India, customers also value style, and they buy a cell phone as a status symbol and so are willing to pay a premium price for it. But in China customers want a bargain—the phone has to be at the right price point if customers are to buy the entry-level version or be enticed to spend more for premium features. How did Nokia discover how much customer needs diverge among customers in different countries?

Its top managers decided that the engineers in its vast central design studio in Finland should be in charge of basic cell phone R&D, and for monitoring changing global forces in technology and changing customer demand for services such as video downloads, touch screens, colors, and so forth. However, to get close to customers in different countries top managers decided to open nine different geographic design studios in various world regions and countries, such as India and China, where Nokia hopes to generate the most sales revenues. Engineers in these geographical studios, aided by marketing experts, determine the most important country-specific customer preferences.[26] The nature of these preferences are then transmitted back to Nokia's Finnish design headquarters, where they are incorporated into the studio's knowledge about changing global preferences for faster Internet service, touch screens, and so on. The result is a range of phones that share much in common but which are also highly customized to the needs of customers in different regions and countries. So, for example, in 2008 Nokia brought out eight different versions of a new entry-level cell phone to better meet global customer needs. One version of this phone is directed specifically at the poorest developing nations where it is common for a cell phone to be shared either among the members of a family—or even by a village.[27] Nokia made this version especially sturdy, and created several different phone directories, so each member of a family, for example, could have their own separate list.[28]

So, both in design and manufacturing Nokia has adopted a global divisional structure to spearhead its attempts to remain on top in the fiercely competitive global cell phone market and its success so far has been demonstrated by the increasing amount of its revenues that come from global sales.

Nokia maintains its central design studio in Finland, shown here, where its designers receive the ideas generated by its nine regional design centers scattered across the globe and use them to better customize its phones to the needs of global customers.

MARKET STRUCTURE   Sometimes the pressing issue facing managers is to group functions according to the type of customer buying the product, in order to tailor the products the organization offers to each customer's unique demands. A PC maker such as Dell, for example, has several kinds of customers, including large businesses (which might demand networks of computers linked to a mainframe computer), small companies (which may need just a few PCs linked together), educational users in schools and universities (which might want thousands of independent PCs for their students), and individual users (who may want a high-quality multimedia PC so that they can play the latest video games).

> **market structure** An organizational structure in which each kind of customer is served by a self-contained division; also called *customer structure.*

To satisfy the needs of diverse customers, a company might adopt a **market structure,** which groups divisions according to the particular kinds of customers they serve (see Figure 10.4c). A market structure allows managers to be responsive to the needs of their customers and allows them to act flexibly in making decisions in response to customers' changing needs. Dell, for example, moved from a functional to a market structure when it created four market divisions that are each focused on being responsive to a particular type of customer: corporate, small business, home computer users, and government and state agencies. Its new structure worked spectacularly well, as its sales soared through the 1990s.

Matrix and Product Team Designs

Moving to a product, market, or geographic divisional structure allows managers to respond more quickly and flexibly to the particular set of circumstances they confront. However, when customer needs or information technology are both changing rapidly and the environment is very uncertain, even a divisional structure may not provide managers with enough flexibility to respond to the environment quickly. To operate effectively under these conditions, managers must design the most flexible kind of organizational structure available: a matrix structure or a product team structure (see Figure 10.5).

> **matrix structure** An organizational structure that simultaneously groups people and resources by function and by product.

MATRIX STRUCTURE   In a **matrix structure,** managers group people and resources in two ways simultaneously: by function and by product.[29] Employees are grouped by *functions* to allow them to learn from one another and become more skilled and productive. In addition, employees are grouped into *product teams* in which members of different functions work together to develop a specific product. The result is a complex network of reporting relationships among product teams and functions that makes the matrix structure very flexible (see Figure 10.6a). Each person in a product team reports to two managers: (1) a functional boss, who assigns individuals to a team and evaluates their performance from a functional perspective, and (2) the boss of the product team, who evaluates their performance on the team. Thus, team members are known as *two-boss employees*. The functional employees assigned to product teams change over time as the specific skills that the team needs change. At the beginning of the product development process, for example, engineers and R&D specialists are assigned to a product team because their skills are needed to develop new products. When a provisional design has been established, marketing

Figure 10.6
Matrix and Product Team Structures

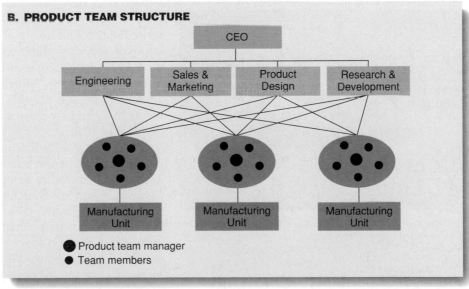

experts are assigned to the team to gauge how customers will respond to the new product. Manufacturing personnel join when it is time to find the most efficient way to produce the product. As their specific jobs are completed, team members leave and are reassigned to new teams. In this way the matrix structure makes the most use of human resources.

To keep the matrix structure flexible, product teams are empowered and team members are responsible for making most of the important decisions involved in product development.[30] The product team manager acts as a facilitator, controlling the financial resources and trying to keep the project on time and within budget. The functional managers try to ensure that the product is the best that it can be in order to maximize its differentiated appeal.

High-tech companies that operate in environments where new product development takes place monthly or yearly have used matrix structures successfully for many years, and the need to innovate quickly is vital to the organization's survival. The flexibility afforded by a matrix structure allows managers to keep pace with a changing and increasingly complex environment.[31]

PRODUCT TEAM STRUCTURE   The dual reporting relationships that are at the heart of a matrix structure have always been difficult for managers and employees to deal with. Often, the functional boss and the product boss make conflicting demands on team members, who do not know which boss to satisfy first. Also, functional and product team bosses may come into conflict over precisely who is in charge of which team members and for how long. To avoid these problems, managers have devised a way of organizing people and resources that still allows an organization to be flexible but makes its structure easier to operate: a product team structure.

The **product team structure** differs from a matrix structure in two ways: (1) It does away with dual reporting relationships and two-boss employees, and (2) functional employees are permanently assigned to a cross-functional team that is empowered to bring a new or redesigned product to market. A **cross-functional team** is a group of managers brought together from different departments to perform organizational tasks. When managers are grouped into cross-functional teams, the artificial boundaries between departments disappear, and a narrow focus on departmental goals is replaced with a general interest in working together to achieve organizational goals. The results of such changes have been dramatic: Chrysler can introduce a new model of car in two years, down from five; Black & Decker can innovate new products in months, not years; and Hallmark Cards can respond to changing customer demands for types of cards in weeks, not months.

product team structure
An organizational structure in which employees are permanently assigned to a cross-functional team and report only to the product team manager or to one of his or her direct subordinates.

cross-functional team
A group of managers brought together from different departments to perform organizational tasks.

Members of a cross-functional team report only to the product team manager or to one of his or her direct subordinates. The heads of the functions have only an informal, advisory relationship with members of the product teams–the role of functional managers is only to counsel and help team members, share knowledge among teams, and provide new technological developments that can help improve each team's performance (see Figure 10.6b).[32]

Increasingly, organizations are making empowered cross-functional teams an essential part of their organizational architecture to help them gain a competitive advantage in fast-changing organizational environments. For example, Newell Rubbermaid, the well-known maker of more than 5,000 household products, moved to a product team structure because its managers wanted to speed up the rate of product innovation. Managers created 20 cross-functional teams composed

A committee looks over an artist's work during a meeting at Hallmark in Kansas City. At Hallmark, cross-functional teams like this one can respond quickly to changing customer demands.

of five to seven people from marketing, manufacturing, R&D, and other functions.[33] Each team focuses its energies on a particular product line, such as garden products, bathroom products, or kitchen products. These teams develop more than 365 new products a year.

Hybrid Structure

A large organization that has many divisions and simultaneously uses many different structures has a **hybrid structure.** Most large organizations use product division structures and create self-contained divisions; then each division's managers select the structure that best meets the needs of the particular environment, strategy, and so on. Thus, one product division may choose to operate with a functional structure, a second may choose a geographic structure, and a third may choose a product team structure because of the nature of the division's products or the desire to be more responsive to customers' needs. Macy's, the largest U.S. department store company, uses a hybrid structure based on grouping by customer and by geography.

As shown in Figure 10.7, in 2008 Macy's organized its four main merchandising divisions, its bricks and mortar Bloomingdales and Macy's store chains, and its online Bloomingdales.com and Macys.com storefronts, as independent divisions in a product division structure. Beneath this organizational layer is another layer of structure because its flagship Macy's store chain operates with a geographic structure that groups stores by region. Macy's for example, has several different regional divisions that handle its over 800 stores. Each regional office is responsible for coordinating the market needs of the stores in its region and for responding to regional customer needs. The regional office feeds information back to divisional headquarters, where centralized merchandising functions make decisions for all stores.

Organizational structure may thus be likened to the layers of an onion. The outer layer provides the overarching organizational framework—most commonly a product or market division structure—and each inner layer is the structure that each division selects for itself in response to the contingencies it faces—such as a geographic or product team structure. The ability to break a large organization into smaller units or divisions makes it much easier for managers to change structure when the need arises—for example, when a change in technology or an increase in competition in the environment necessitates a change from a functional to a product team structure.

Figure 10.7
Macy's Hybrid Structure

Coordinating Functions and Divisions

The more complex the structure a company uses to group its activities, the greater are the problems of *linking and coordinating* its different functions and divisions. Coordination becomes a problem because each function or division develops a different orientation toward the other groups that affects the way it interacts with them. Each function or division comes to view the problems facing the company from its own particular perspective; for example, they may develop different views about the major goals, problems, or issues facing a company.

At the functional level, the manufacturing function typically has a very short-term view; its major goal is to keep costs under control and get the product out the factory door on time. By contrast, the product development function has a long-term viewpoint because developing a new product is a relatively slow process and high product quality is seen as more important than low costs. Such differences in viewpoint may make manufacturing and product development managers reluctant to cooperate and coordinate their activities to meet company goals. At the divisional level, in a company with a product structure, employees may become concerned more with making *their* division's products a success than with the profitability of the entire company. They may refuse, or simply not see, the need to cooperate and share information or knowledge with other divisions.

The problem of linking and coordinating the activities of different functions and divisions becomes more and more acute as the number of functions and divisions increases. We look first at how managers design the hierarchy of authority to coordinate functions and divisions so that they work together effectively. Then we focus on integration and examine the different integrating mechanisms that managers can use to coordinate functions and divisions.

Allocating Authority

authority The power to hold people accountable for their actions and to make decisions concerning the use of organizational resources.

hierarchy of authority An organization's chain of command, specifying the relative authority of each manager.

span of control The number of subordinates who report directly to a manager.

As organizations grow and produce a wider range of goods and services, the size and number of their functions and divisions increase. To coordinate the activities of people, functions, and divisions and to allow them to work together effectively, managers must develop a clear hierarchy of authority.[34] **Authority** is the power vested in a manager to make decisions and use resources to achieve organizational goals by virtue of his or her position in an organization. The **hierarchy of authority** is an organization's *chain of command*–the relative authority that each manager has–extending from the CEO at the top, down through the middle managers and first-line managers, to the nonmanagerial employees who actually make goods or provide services. Every manager, at every level of the hierarchy, supervises one or more subordinates. The term **span of control** refers to the number of subordinates who report directly to a manager.

Figure 10.8 shows a simplified picture of the hierarchy of authority and the span of control of managers in McDonald's in 2008. At the top of the hierarchy is Jim Skinner, CEO and vice chairman of McDonald's board of directors, who took control in 2004.[35] Skinner is the manager who has ultimate responsibility for McDonald's performance, and he has the authority to decide how to use organizational resources to benefit McDonald's stakeholders.[36] Ralph Alvarez is next in line, he is president and COO and is responsible for overseeing all of McDonald's U.S. restaurant operations. Roberts reports directly to Skinner, as does chief financial officer Peter Bensen. Unlike the other managers, Bensen is not a **line manager,** someone in the direct line or chain of command who has formal authority over people and resources. Rather, Bensen is a **staff manager,** responsible for one of McDonald's specialist functions, finance. Worldwide chief operations officer Jeff Stratton is responsible for overseeing all functional aspects of McDonald's overseas operations, which are headed by the presidents of world regions: Europe; Canada and Latin America; and Asia/Pacific, Middle East, and Africa. Of special mention is Donald Thompson, who is president of McDonald's U.S. operations and reports to Alvarez.

line manager Someone in the direct line or chain of command who has formal authority over people and resources at lower levels.

staff manager Someone responsible for managing a specialist function, such as finance or marketing.

Figure 10.8

The Hierarchy of Authority and Span of Control at McDonald's Corporation

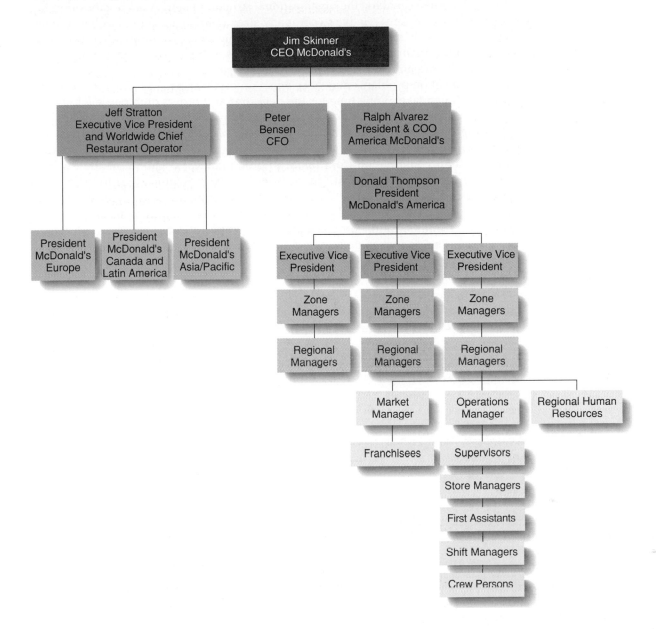

Managers at each level of the hierarchy confer on managers at the next level down the authority to make decisions about how to use organizational resources. Accepting this authority, those lower-level managers then become responsible for their decisions and are accountable for how well they make those decisions. Managers who make the right decisions are typically promoted, and organizations motivate managers with the prospects of promotion and increased responsibility within the chain of command.

Below Thompson are the other main levels or layers in the McDonald's domestic chain of command—executive vice presidents of its West, Central, and East regions, zone managers, regional managers, and supervisors. A hierarchy is also evident in each company-owned McDonald's restaurant. At the top is the store manager; at lower levels are the first assistant, shift managers, and crew personnel. McDonald's managers have decided that this hierarchy of authority best allows the company to pursue its business-level strategy of providing fast food at reasonable prices.

TALL AND FLAT ORGANIZATIONS As an organization grows in size (normally measured by the number of its managers and employees), its hierarchy of authority normally lengthens, making the organizational structure taller. A *tall* organization has many levels of authority relative to company size; a *flat* organization has fewer levels relative to company size (see Figure 10.9).[37] As a hierarchy becomes taller, problems that make the organization's structure less flexible and slow managers' response to changes in the organizational environment may result.

Communication problems may arise when an organization has many levels in the hierarchy. It can take a long time for the decisions and orders of upper-level managers to reach managers further down in the hierarchy, and it can take a long time for top managers to learn how well their decisions worked. Feeling out of touch, top managers may want to verify that lower-level managers are following orders and may require written confirmation from them. Middle managers, who know they will be held strictly accountable for their actions, start devoting too much time to the process of making decisions to improve their chances of being right. They might even try to avoid responsibility by making top managers decide what actions to take.

Another communication problem that can result is the distortion of commands and messages being transmitted up and down the hierarchy, which causes managers

Figure 10.9

Tall and Flat Organizations

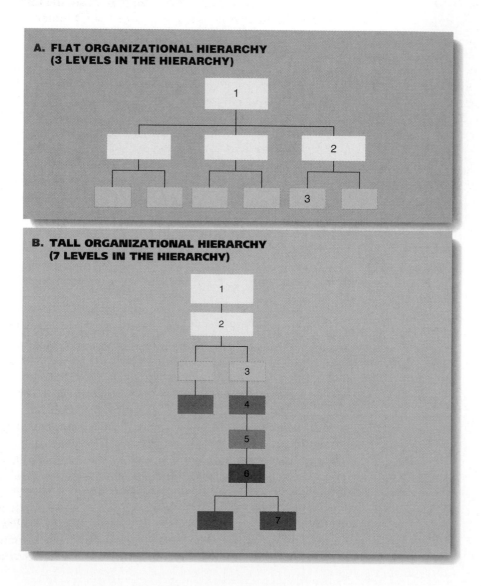

A. FLAT ORGANIZATIONAL HIERARCHY (3 LEVELS IN THE HIERARCHY)

B. TALL ORGANIZATIONAL HIERARCHY (7 LEVELS IN THE HIERARCHY) at different levels to interpret what is happening differently. Distortion of orders and messages can be accidental, occurring because different managers interpret messages from their own narrow, functional perspectives. Or distortion can be intentional, occurring because managers low in the hierarchy decide to interpret information in a way that increases their own personal advantage.

Another problem with tall hierarchies is that they usually indicate that an organization is employing many managers, and managers are expensive. Managerial salaries, benefits, offices, and secretaries are a huge expense for organizations. Large companies such as IBM and General Motors pay their managers billions of dollars a year. In the early 2000s, hundreds of thousands of middle managers were laid off as dot-coms collapsed and high-tech companies attempted to reduce costs by restructuring and downsizing their workforces. In 2008, as an economic downturn threatened, hundreds of companies also began to announce layoffs to reduce operating costs and to help them make better use of their resources in the future.

THE MINIMUM CHAIN OF COMMAND To ward off the problems that result when an organization becomes too tall and employs too many managers, top managers need to ascertain whether they are employing the right number of middle and first-line managers and whether they can redesign their organizational architecture to reduce the number of managers. Top managers might well follow a basic organizing principle—the principle of the minimum chain of command—which states that top managers should always construct a hierarchy with the fewest levels of authority necessary to efficiently and effectively use organizational resources.

Effective managers constantly scrutinize their hierarchies to see whether the number of levels can be reduced—for example, by eliminating one level and giving the responsibilities of managers at that level to managers above and by empowering employees below. One manager who is constantly trying to empower employees and keep the hierarchy flat is Colleen C. Barrett, the number-two executive of Southwest Airlines.[38] Barrett is the highest-ranking woman in the airline industry. At Southwest, she is well known for continually reaffirming Southwest's message that employees should feel free to go above and beyond their prescribed roles to provide better customer service. Her central message is that Southwest values and trusts its employees, who are empowered to take responsibility. Southwest employees are encouraged not to look to their superiors for guidance but, rather, to find ways on their own to do the job better. As a result, Southwest keeps the number of its middle managers to a minimum. The need to empower workers is increasing as companies battle low-cost foreign competitors by searching for new ways to reduce costs, as the following "Managing Globally" suggests.

Managing Globally

How to Use Empowered Self-Managed Teams

In the United States, over 5 million manufacturing jobs were lost to factories in low-cost countries abroad in the early 2000s. While many large U.S. manufacturing companies have given up the battle, some companies such as electronics maker Plexus Corp., based in Neenah, Wisconsin, have been able to find ways of organizing that allow them to survive and prosper in a low-cost manufacturing world. How have they done this? By creating empowered work teams.

In the late 1990s, Plexus saw the writing on the wall as more and more of its customers began to outsource the production of electronic components or even the whole product itself to manufacturers abroad. U.S. companies cannot match

Small Business

the efficiency of manufacturers abroad in producing high volumes of a single product, such as millions of a particular circuit board used in a laptop computer. So Plexus's managers decided to focus their efforts on developing a manufacturing technology called "low-high" that could efficiently produce low volumes of many different kinds of products.

Plexus's managers formed a team to design an organizational structure based on creating four "focused factories" in which control over production decisions is given to the workers, who perform all the operations involved in making a product. The managers cross-trained workers so that they can perform any particular operation in their "factory." With this approach, when work slows down at any point in the production of a particular product, a worker further along the production process can move back to help solve the problem that has arisen at the earlier stage.[39]

Furthermore, managers organized workers into self-managed teams that are empowered to make all the decisions necessary to make a particular product in one of the four factories. Since each product is different, these teams have to make their decisions quickly if they are to assemble the product in a cost-effective way. The ability of the teams to make rapid decisions and respond to unexpected contingencies is vital on a production line, where time is money—every minute a production line is not moving adds hundreds or thousands of dollars to production costs. Also, a second reason for empowering teams is that when a changeover takes place from making one product to making another, nothing is being produced, so it is vital that changeover time be kept to a minimum. At Plexus, managers, by allowing teams to experiment and by providing guidance, have reduced changeover time from hours to as little as 30 minutes, so the line is making products over 80% of the time.[40] This incredible flexibility, brought about by the way employees are organized, is the reason why Plexus is so efficient and can compete against low-cost manufacturers abroad.

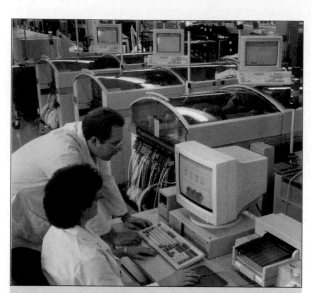

These two employees monitoring the progress of a circuit board production line embody cross-functional empowerment. If problems occur, they have the authority and expertise to make any changes necessary to keep the production line at full speed.

CENTRALIZATION AND DECENTRALIZATION OF AUTHORITY Another way in which managers can keep the organizational hierarchy flat is by **decentralizing authority,** that is, by giving lower-level managers and nonmanagerial employees the right to make important decisions about how to use organizational resources.[41] If managers at higher levels give lower-level employees the responsibility of making important decisions and only *manage by exception,* then the problems of slow and distorted communication noted previously are kept to a minimum. Moreover, fewer managers are needed because their role is not to make decisions but to act as coach and facilitator and to help other employees make the best decisions. In addition, when decision-making authority is low in the organization and near the customer, employees are better able to recognize and respond to customer needs.

Decentralizing authority allows an organization and its employees to behave in a flexible way even as the organization grows and becomes taller. This is why managers are so interested in empowering employees, creating self-managed work teams, establishing cross-functional teams, and even moving to a product team structure. These design innovations help keep the organizational architecture flexible and responsive to complex task and general environments, complex technologies, and complex strategies.

decentralizing authority Giving lower-level managers and nonmanagerial employees the right to make important decisions about how to use organizational resources.

Although more and more organizations are taking steps to decentralize authority, *too much* decentralization has certain disadvantages. If divisions, functions, or teams are given too much decision-making authority, they may begin to pursue their own goals at the expense of organizational goals. Managers in engineering design or R&D, for example, may become so focused on making the best possible product that they fail to realize that the best product may be so expensive that few people will be willing or able to buy it. Also, too much decentralization can result in a lack of communication among functions or divisions, and this prevents the synergies that result from cooperation ever materializing and organizational performance suffers.

Top managers must seek the balance between centralization and decentralization of authority that best meets the four major contingencies an organization faces (see Figure 10.1). If managers are in a stable environment, are using well-understood technology, and are producing staple kinds of products (such as cereal, canned soup, books, or televisions), then there is no pressing need to decentralize authority, and managers at the top can maintain control of much of organizational decision making.[42] However, in uncertain, changing environments where high-tech companies are producing state-of-the-art products, top managers must often empower employees and allow teams to make important strategic decisions so that the organization can keep up with the changes taking place. No matter what its environment, a company that fails to control the balance between centralization and decentralization will find its performance suffering as the example of Avon in the following "Manager as a Person" suggests.

Manager as a Person

Avon Is Calling for a New Structure

After a decade of profitable growth under its CEO Andrea Jung, Avon suddenly began to experience falling global sales in the mid-2000s both in developing markets in Central Europe, Russia, and China, a major source of its rising sales, as well as in the United States and Mexico. Avon's stock price plunged in 2006 and Jung was shocked by this turn of events; for the first time as CEO she found herself in the position of having to find strategies to solve its problems—rather than new ways to add to its success.[43]

After several months jetting around the globe to visit the managers of its worldwide divisions, she came to a surprising conclusion: Avon's rapid global expansion had given these managers too much autonomy. They had gained so much authority to control operations in their respective countries and world regions that they had made decisions to benefit their own divisions, and these decisions had hurt the performance of the whole company. Avon's country-level managers from Poland to Mexico ran their own factories, made their own product development decisions, and developed their own advertising campaigns. And, these decisions were often based on poor marketing knowledge and with little concern for operating costs—their goal was to increase sales as fast as possible. Also, when too much authority is decentralized to managers lower in an organization's hierarchy, these managers often recruit more and more managers to help them build their country "empires." The result was that Avon's global organizational hierarchy had exploded—it had risen from 7 levels to 15 levels of managers in a decade as tens of thousands of extra managers were hired around the globe![44] Because Avon's profits were rising fast, Jung and her top management team had not paid enough attention to the way Avon's organizational structure was becoming taller and taller—just as it was getting wider and wider as it entered more and more countries to expand cosmetics sales.

In 2006, Jung woke up from this nightmare; she had to confront the need to lay off thousands of managers and restructure the organizational hierarchy to reduce costs while maintaining profitability. She embarked on a program to take away the authority of Avon's country-level managers and to transfer authority to regional and corporate headquarters managers to streamline decision making and reduce costs. She cut out seven levels of management and laid off 25% of its global managers in its 114 worldwide markets. Then, using teams of expert managers from corporate headquarters, she embarked on a detailed examination of all Avon's functional activities, country by country, to find out why its costs had risen so quickly and what could be done to bring them under control. The duplication of marketing efforts in countries around the world was one source of these high costs. In Mexico, one team found that country managers' desire to expand their empires led to the development of a staggering 13,000 different products! Not only had this caused product development costs to soar, it had led to major marketing problems, for how could Avon's Mexican sales reps learn about the differences between 13,000 products—and then find an easy way to tell customers about them?

In Avon's new structure the focus was on centralizing all new major product development. Avon develops over 1,000 new products a year, but in the future while the input from different country managers would be used to customize products to country needs in terms of fragrance, packaging and soon, R&D would be performed in the United States. Similarly, in the future the goal was to develop marketing campaigns targeted toward the average "global" customer, but which could be easily customized to a country or world region by using the appropriate language or the nationality of the models used to market the product, for example. Other initiatives have been to increase the money spent on global marketing, which had not kept pace with Avon's rapid global expansion, and a major push to increase the number of Avon ladies in developing nations to attract more customers. In the last two years Avon has recruited another 399,000 reps in China alone![45]

Country-level managers now are responsible for managing this army of Avon reps, and for making sure that marketing dollars are being directed toward the right channels for maximum impact. However, they no longer have any authority to engage in major product development or build new manufacturing capacity—or to hire new managers without the agreement of regional or corporate level managers. The balance of control has changed at Avon, and Jung and all her managers are now firmly focused on making operational decisions in the best interests of the whole company and not just the country in which its cosmetics are sold.

Andrea Jung of Avon faced significant challenges in 2006, when the company woke up to the problems engendered by its extremely decentralized structure. Jung's changes mean that regional managers still supervise their own reps, but that the power to develop new products has shifted back to a leaner, more alert corporate headquarters.

Integrating and Coordinating Mechanisms

LO4 Explain why managers must coordinate jobs, functions, and divisions using the hierarchy of authority and integrating mechanisms.

Much coordination takes place through the hierarchy of authority. However, several problems are associated with establishing contact among managers in different functions or divisions. As discussed earlier, managers from different functions and divisions may have different views about what must be done to achieve organizational goals. But if the managers have equal authority (as functional managers typically do), the only manager who can tell them what to do is the CEO, who has the ultimate authority to resolve conflicts. The need to solve everyday conflicts, however, wastes top-management time and slows strategic decision making; indeed, one sign of a poorly performing structure is the number of problems sent up the hierarchy for top managers to solve.

Figure 10.10

Types and Examples of Integrating Mechanisms

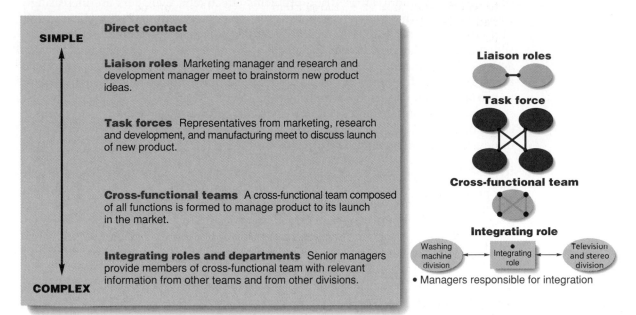

SIMPLE

Direct contact

Liaison roles Marketing manager and research and development manager meet to brainstorm new product ideas.

Task forces Representatives from marketing, research and development, and manufacturing meet to discuss launch of new product.

Cross-functional teams A cross-functional team composed of all functions is formed to manage product to its launch in the market.

Integrating roles and departments Senior managers provide members of cross-functional team with relevant information from other teams and from other divisions.

COMPLEX

Liaison roles

Task force

Cross-functional team

Integrating role

Washing machine division — Integrating role — Television and stereo division

• Managers responsible for integration

To increase communication and coordination among functions or between divisions and to prevent these problems from emerging, top managers incorporate various **integrating mechanisms** into their organizational architecture. The greater the complexity of an organization's structure, the greater is the need for coordination among people, functions, and divisions to make the organizational structure work efficiently and effectively.[46] Thus, when managers choose to adopt a divisional, matrix, or product team structure, they must use complex integrating mechanisms to achieve organizational goals. Several integrating mechanisms are available to managers to increase communication and coordination.[47] Figure 10.10 lists these mechanisms, as well as examples of the individuals or groups that might use them.

integrating mechanisms Organizing tools that managers can use to increase communication and coordination among functions and divisions.

LIAISON ROLES Managers can increase coordination among functions and divisions by establishing liaison roles. When the volume of contacts between two functions increases, one way to improve coordination is to give one manager in each function or division the responsibility for coordinating with the other. These managers may meet daily, weekly, monthly, or as needed. A liaison role is illustrated in Figure 10.10; the small dot represents the person within a function who has responsibility for coordinating with the other function. Coordinating is part of the liaison's full-time job, and usually an informal relationship develops between the people involved, greatly easing strains between functions. Furthermore, liaison roles provide a way of transmitting information across an organization, which is important in large organizations whose employees may know no one outside their immediate function or division.

task force A committee of managers from various functions or divisions who meet to solve a specific, mutual problem; also called *ad hoc committee.*

TASK FORCES When more than two functions or divisions share many common problems, direct contact and liaison roles may not provide sufficient coordination. In these cases, a more complex integrating mechanism, a **task force,** may be appropriate (see Figure 10.10). One manager from each relevant function or division is assigned to a task force that meets to solve a specific, mutual problem; members are responsible for reporting to their departments on the issues addressed and the solutions recommended. Task forces are often called *ad hoc committees* because they are temporary; they may meet on a regular basis or only a few times. When the problem or issue is solved, the task force is no longer needed; members return to their normal roles in their departments or are assigned to other task forces. Typically, task force members also perform many of their normal duties while serving on the task force.

CROSS-FUNCTIONAL TEAMS   In many cases, the issues addressed by a task force are recurring problems, such as the need to develop new products or find new kinds of customers. To address recurring problems effectively, managers are increasingly using permanent integrating mechanisms such as cross-functional teams. An example of a cross-functional team is a new product development committee that is responsible for the choice, design, manufacturing, and marketing of a new product. Such an activity obviously requires a great deal of integration among functions if new products are to be successfully introduced, and using a complex integrating mechanism such as a cross-functional team accomplishes this. As discussed earlier, in a product team structure people and resources are grouped into permanent cross-functional teams to speed products to market. These teams assume long-term responsibility for all aspects of development and making the product.

INTEGRATING ROLES   An integrating role is a role whose only function is to increase coordination and integration among functions or divisions to achieve performance gains from synergies. Usually, managers who perform integrating roles are experienced senior managers who can envisage how to use the resources of the functions or divisions to obtain new synergies. One study found that DuPont, the giant chemical company, had created 160 integrating roles to provide coordination among the different divisions of the company and improve corporate performance.[48] The more complex an organization and the greater the number of its divisions, the more important integrating roles are.

In summary, to keep an organization responsive to changes in its task and general environments as it grows and becomes more complex, managers must increase coordination among functions and divisions by using complex integrating mechanisms. Managers must decide on the best way to organize their structures, that is, choose the structure that allows them to make the best use of organizational resources.

Organizational Culture

The second principal issue in organizational design is to create, develop, and maintain an organization's culture. As we discussed in Chapter 3, **organizational culture** is the shared set of beliefs, expectations, values, and norms that influence how members of an organization relate to one another and cooperate to achieve organizational goals. Culture influences the work behaviors and attitudes of individuals and groups in an organization because its members adhere to shared values, norms, and expected standards of behavior. Employees *internalize* organizational values and norms and then let these values and norms guide their decisions and actions.[49]

A company's culture is a result of its pivotal or guiding values and norms. A company's *values* are the shared standards that its members use to evaluate whether or not they have helped the company achieve its vision and goals. The values a company might adopt include any or all of the following standards: excellence, stability, predictability, profitability, economy, creativeness, morality, and usefulness. A company's *norms* specify or prescribe the kinds of shared beliefs, attitudes, and behaviors that its members should observe and follow. Norms are informal, but powerful, rules about how employees should behave or conduct themselves in a company if they are to be accepted and help it to achieve its goals. Norms can be equally as constraining as the formal written rules contained in a company's handbook. Companies might encourage workers to adopt norms such as working hard, respecting traditions and authority, and being courteous to others; being conservative, cautious, and a "team player"; being creative and courageous and taking risks; being honest and frugal and maintaining high personal standards. Norms may also prescribe certain very specific behaviors such as keeping one's desk tidy, cleaning up at the end of the day, taking one's turn to bring doughnuts, and even wearing blue jeans and a t-shirt on Fridays.

Ideally, a company's norms help the company achieve its values. For example, a new computer company whose culture is based on values of excellence and innovation may try to attain this high standard by encouraging workers to adopt norms about being creative, taking risks, and working hard now and looking long-term for rewards (this combination of values and norms leads to an *entrepreneurial* culture in a company). On the other hand, a bank or insurance company that has values of stability and predictability may emphasize norms of cautiousness and obedience to authority (the result of adopting these values and norms would be a *stable, conservative* culture in a company).

Over time, members of a company learn from one another how to perceive and interpret various events that happen in the work setting and to respond to them in ways that reflect the company's guiding values and norms. This is why organizational culture is so important: When a strong and cohesive set of organizational values and norms is in place, employees focus on thinking about what is best for the organization in the long run—all their decisions and actions become oriented toward helping the organization perform well. For example, a teacher spends personal time after school coaching and counseling students; an R&D scientist works 80 hours a week, evenings, and weekends to help speed up a late project; a salesclerk at a department store runs after a customer who left a credit card at the cash register. An interesting example of a company founder who built a strong culture by focusing on values and norms is Sam Walton, profiled in the following "Manager as a Person."

Manager as a Person

Sam Walton and Wal-Mart's Culture

Wal-Mart, headquartered in Bentonville, Arkansas, is the largest retailer in the world. In 2007, it sold over $600 billion worth of products.[50] A large part of Wal-Mart's success is due to the nature of the culture that its founder, the late Sam Walton, established for the company. Walton wanted all his managers and workers to take a hands-on approach to their jobs and be totally committed to Wal-Mart's main goal, which he defined as total customer satisfaction. To motivate his employees, Walton created a culture that gave employees at all levels, who are called "associates," continuous feedback about their performance and the company's performance.

To involve his associates in the business and encourage them to develop work behaviors focused on providing quality customer service, Walton established strong cultural values and norms for his company. One of the norms associates are expected to follow is the "10-foot attitude." This norm encourages associates, in Walton's words, to "promise that whenever you come within 10 feet of a customer, you will look him in the eye, greet him, and ask him if you can help him." The "sundown rule" states that employees should strive to answer customer requests by sundown of the day they are made. The Wal-Mart cheer ("Give me a W, give me an A," and so on) is used in all its stores.[51]

The strong customer-oriented values that Walton created are exemplified in the stories Wal-Mart members tell one another about associates' concern for customers. They include stories like the one about Sheila, who risked her own safety when she jumped in front of a car to prevent a little boy from being struck; about Phyllis, who administered CPR to a customer who had suffered a heart attack in her store; and about Annette, who gave up the Power Ranger she had on layaway for her own son to fulfill the birthday wish of a customer's son.[52] The strong Wal-Mart culture helps to control and motivate employees to achieve the stringent output and financial targets the company has set for itself.[53]

A notable way Wal-Mart builds its culture is through its annual stockholders' meeting, an extravagant ceremony celebrating the

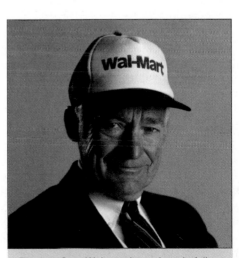

The late Sam Walton, shown here in full Wal-Mart regalia, wanted his stores to be marked by a can-do attitude and by constant attention to customer needs. As Wal-Mart faces increasing challenges, do you think Walton's culture can sustain it over the longer term?

company's success.[54] Every year Wal-Mart flies thousands of its highest performers to its annual meeting at corporate headquarters in Arkansas for a show featuring famous singers, rock bands, and comedians. Wal-Mart feels that expensive entertainment is a reward its employees deserve and that the event reinforces the company's high-performance values and culture. The proceedings are even broadcast live to all of Wal-Mart's stores so that employees can celebrate the company's achievements together.[55]

Since Sam Walton's death, however, Wal-Mart's increasing rise to prominence (it is the nation's largest private employer, with over 1 million employees) has brought attention to the "hidden side" of its culture. Critics have claimed that few ordinary Wal-Mart employees receive any reasonably priced health care or other benefits and that the company pays employees only the minimum wage or a little above it. They also contend that employees don't question these policies because managers have socialized them into believing that this has to be the case—that the only way Wal-Mart can keep its prices low is by keeping their pay and benefits low. In the 2000s, however, Wal-Mart's managers have responded to a barrage of criticism that it must do more to improve its human resource practices. While it still stresses the need to keep costs low, it has started to increase pay and health care benefits and has established new career ladders for its very loyal employees, who seem to be still following Sam Walton's 10-foot-attitude rule to the letter.

Where Does Organizational Culture Come From?

LO5 List the four sources of organizational culture, and explain why and how a company's culture can lead to competitive advantage.

In managing organizational architecture, an important question that arises is, Where does organizational culture come from? Why do different companies have different cultures? Why might a culture that for many years helped an organization achieve its goals suddenly harm the organization?

Figure 10.11
Sources of an Organization's Culture

Organizational culture is shaped by the interaction of four main factors: the personal and professional characteristics of people within the organization, organizational ethics, the nature of the employment relationship, and the design of its organizational structure (see Figure 10.11). These factors work together to produce different cultures in different organizations and cause changes in culture over time.

CHARACTERISTICS OF ORGANIZATIONAL MEMBERS   The ultimate source of organizational culture is the people who make up the organization. If you want to know why organizational cultures differ, look at the way the characteristics of their members differ. Organizations A, B, and C develop distinctly different cultures because they attract, select, and retain people who have different values, personalities, and ethics.[56] Recall the attraction-selection-attrition model from Chapter 3. People may be attracted to an organization whose values match theirs; similarly, an organization selects people who share its values. Over time, people who do not fit in leave. The result is that people inside the organization become more and more similar, the values of the organization become more and more pronounced and clear-cut, and the culture becomes more and more distinct from that of similar organizations.[57]

The fact that an organization's members become similar over time and come to share the same values may actually hinder their ability to adapt and respond to changes in the environment.[58] This happens when the organization's values and norms become *so* strong and promote *so* much cohesiveness in members' attitudes that the members begin to misperceive the environment.[59] To prevent this situation at Microsoft, which has strong, cohesive values that bond its members, Bill Gates worked hard to make it clear that employees should express their own personal views, even though they might differ from his and other top managers' views. One example of how Gates's understanding of culture worked to Microsoft's advantage occurred when the company started its Internet service, MSN. Microsoft believed the popularity of its Windows platform would allow it to control the future development of the Internet, even though Netscape had introduced a popular browser. Two concerned Microsoft programmers working in its Internet division wrote a memo to top managers arguing that Microsoft would end up with *no* control over the Internet, given the rapid pace at which the Internet was developing. They also argued that Netscape's browser would become the dominant means by which people would access the Internet. The programmers argued that to compete with Netscape, Microsoft should rush to develop its own Web browser. After reading their memo, Gates convened a major organizationwide meeting. Top managers listened while all of the issues were aired, and then they admitted they were wrong. The company then diverted most of its human talent to developing its own browser as quickly as possible. Within one year, the first version of Internet Explorer was ready, and Microsoft gave it away free to users.

Companies such as Microsoft need a strong set of values that emphasize innovation and hard work. However, they need to be careful that their success doesn't lead members to believe their company will always be the best in the business, or "invincible." Some companies have made this mistake. The old IBM of the 1980s believed its control of the mainframe market made it invincible; IBM employees laughed off the potential threat personal computers posed. The CEO of another dominant computer maker at that time, Digital Equipment, reportedly commented that "personal computers are just toys." Within a few years, Digital Equipment was experiencing huge losses. Today, Microsoft is facing the same problem in its battle with Google as the latter seeks to move PC operations, such as word processing and storage, online—a move that threatens Microsoft's power over the desktop PC world.

organizational ethics The moral values, beliefs, and rules that establish the appropriate way for an organization and its members to deal with each other and with people outside the organization.

ORGANIZATIONAL ETHICS   An organization can purposefully develop some kinds of cultural values to control the way its members behave. One important class of values in this category stems from **organizational ethics,** the moral values, beliefs, and rules that establish the appropriate way for an organization and its members to deal with each other and with people outside the organization. Recall from Chapter 4 that ethical values rest on principles stressing the importance of treating organizational stakeholders fairly and equitably. Managers and employees are constantly making choices about the right, or ethical, thing to do, and to help them make ethical decisions, top managers purposefully implant ethical values into an organization's culture.[60] Consequently, ethical values, and the rules and norms that embody them, become an integral part of an organization's culture and determine how its members will manage situations and make decisions.

THE EMPLOYMENT RELATIONSHIP   A third factor shaping organizational culture is the nature of the employment relationship a company establishes with its employees via its human resource policies and practices. Recall from Chapter 1 our discussion of the changing relationship between organizations and their employees due to the growth of outsourcing and employment of contingent workers. Like a company's hiring, promotion, and layoff policies, human resource policies, along with pay and benefits, can influence how hard employees will work to achieve the organization's goals, how attached they will be to the organization, and whether or not they will buy into its values and norms.[61] As we discuss in Chapter 12, an organization's human resource policies are a good indicator of the values in its culture concerning its responsibilities to employees. Consider the effects of a company's promotion policy, for example: A company with a policy of promoting from within will fill higher-level positions with employees who already work for the organization. On the other hand, a company with a policy of promotion from without will fill its open positions with qualified outsiders. What does this say about each organization's culture?

Promoting from within will bolster strong values and norms that build loyalty, align employees' goals with the organization, and encourage employees to work hard to advance within the organization. If employees see no prospect of being promoted from within, they are likely to look for better opportunities elsewhere, cultural values and norms result in self-interested behavior, and cooperation and cohesiveness fall. The tech sector has gone through great turmoil in recent years, and an estimated one million U.S. tech employees lost their jobs following the burst of the dot-com bubble. Apple, HP, and IBM–long well known for their strong employee-oriented values that emphasized long-term employment and respect for employees–were among the many companies forced to lay off employees, and their cultures have been changed forever as a result. To rebuild their cultures, and make their remaining employees feel like "owners," many companies have HRM pay policies that reward superior performance with bonuses and stock options.[62] For example, Southwest Airlines and Google established companywide stock option systems that encourage their employees to be innovative and responsive to customers.

ORGANIZATIONAL STRUCTURE   We have seen how the values and norms that shape employee work attitudes and behaviors derive from an organization's people, ethics, and HRM policies. A fourth source of cultural values comes from the organization's structure. *Different kinds of structure give rise to different kinds of culture,* so to create a certain culture, managers often need to design a particular type of structure. Tall and highly centralized structures give rise to totally different sets of norms, rules, and cultural values than do structures that are flat and decentralized. In a tall, centralized organization people have little personal autonomy, and norms that focus on being cautious, obeying authority, and respecting traditions emerge because predictability and stability are desired goals. In a flat, decentralized structure people have more freedom to choose and control their own activities, and norms that focus on being creative and courageous and taking risks appear, giving rise to a culture in which innovation and flexibility are desired goals.

Whether a company is centralized or decentralized also leads to the development of different kinds of cultural values. By decentralizing authority and empowering employees, an organization can establish values that encourage and reward creativity or innovation. In doing this, an organization signals employees that it's okay to be innovative and do things their own way–as long as their actions are consistent with the good of the organization. Conversely, in some organizations, it is important that employees do not make decisions on their own and that their actions be open to the scrutiny of superiors. In cases like this, centralization can be used to create cultural values that reinforce obedience and accountability. For example, in nuclear power plants, values that promote stability, predictability, and obedience to authority are deliberately fostered to prevent disasters.[63] Through norms and rules, employees are taught the importance of behaving consistently and honestly, and they learn that sharing information with supervisors, especially information about mistakes or errors, is the only acceptable form of behavior.[64]

An organization that seeks to manage and change its culture must take a hard look at all four factors that shape culture: the characteristics of its members, its ethical values, its human resource policies, and its organizational structure. However, changing a culture can be difficult because of the way these factors interact and affect one another.[65] Often, a major reorganization is necessary for a cultural change to occur, as we discuss in the next chapter.

Strong, Adaptive Cultures versus Weak, Inert Cultures

Many researchers and managers believe that employees of some organizations go out of their way to help the organization because it has a strong and cohesive organizational culture—an adaptive culture that controls employee attitudes and behaviors. *Adaptive cultures* are those whose values and norms help an organization to build momentum and to grow and change as needed to achieve its goals and be effective. By contrast, *inert cultures* are those whose values and norms fail to motivate or inspire employees; they lead to stagnation and, often, failure over time. What leads to a strong adaptive culture or one that is inert and hard to change?

Researchers have found that organizations with strong adaptive cultures, like 3M, UPS, Microsoft, and IBM, invest in their employees. They demonstrate their commitment to their members by, for example, emphasizing the long-term nature of the employment relationship and trying to avoid layoffs. These companies develop long-term career paths for their employees and spend a lot of money on training and development to increase employees' value to the organization. In these ways, terminal and instrumental values pertaining to the worth of human resources encourage the development of supportive work attitudes and behaviors.

In adaptive cultures employees often receive rewards linked directly to their performance and to the performance of the company as a whole. Sometimes, employee stock ownership plans (ESOPs) are developed in which workers as a group are allowed to buy a significant percentage of their company's stock. Workers who are owners of the company have additional incentive to develop skills that allow them to perform highly and search actively for ways to improve quality, efficiency, and performance. At Dell, for example, employees are able to buy Dell stock at a steep 15% discount, and this allows them to build a sizable stake in the company over time.

Some organizations, however, develop cultures with values that do not include protecting and increasing the worth of their human resources as a major goal. Their employment practices are based on short-term employment according to the needs of the organization and on minimal investment in employees who perform simple, routine tasks. Moreover, employees are not often rewarded on the basis of their performance and thus have little incentive to improve their skills or otherwise invest in the organization to help it to achieve goals. If a company has an inert culture, poor working relationships frequently develop between the organization and its employees, and instrumental values of noncooperation, laziness, and loafing and work norms of output restriction are common.

Moreover, an adaptive culture develops an emphasis on entrepreneurship and respect for the employee and allows the use of organizational structures, such as the cross-functional team structure, that empower employees to make decisions and motivate them to succeed. By contrast, in an inert culture, employees are content to be told what to do and have little incentive or motivation to perform beyond minimum work requirements. As you might expect, the emphasis is on close supervision and hierarchical authority, which result in a culture that makes it difficult to adapt to a changing environment.

Nokia, discussed earlier, is a good example of a company in which managers strive to create an adaptive culture.[66] Nokia's top managers, including its present CEO Jorma Ollila, have always believed that Nokia's cultural values are based on the Finnish character: Finns are down-to-earth, rational, straightforward people. They are also very friendly and democratic people who do not believe in a rigid hierarchy based either on a person's authority or on social class. Nokia's culture reflects these values because innovation and decision making are pushed right down to the bottom line, to teams of employees who take up the challenge of developing the ever-smaller and more sophisticated phones for which the company is known. Bureaucracy is kept to a minimum at Nokia; its adaptive culture is based on informal and personal relationships and norms of cooperation and teamwork.

To help strengthen its culture, Nokia built a futuristic open-plan steel and glass building just outside Helsinki. Here, in an open environment, its research and development people can work together to innovate new kinds of wireless phones. More than one out of every three of Nokia's 60,000 employees work in research; what keeps these people together and focused is Nokia's company mission to produce phones that are better, cheaper, smaller, and easier to use than competitor's phones.[67] This is the "Nokia Way," a system of cultural values and norms that can't be written down but is always present in the values that cement people together and in the language and stories that its members use to orient themselves to the company. Yet, as we noted before, Nokia is the cell phone company that is most sensitive to the need to appreciate the values, norms, and tastes of other nations. So the Nokia Way is not just confined to Finland; the company has taken it to every country around the globe in which it operates.

Another company with an adaptive culture is GlaxoSmithKline, the prescription drug maker. discussed earlier in the chapter. Much of GSK's success can be attributed to its ability to attract the very best research scientists, who come because its adaptive culture nurtures scientists and emphasizes values and norms of innovation. Scientists are given great freedom to pursue intriguing ideas even if the commercial payoff is questionable. Moreover, researchers are inspired to think of their work as a quest to alleviate human disease and suffering worldwide, and GSK has a reputation as an ethical company whose values put people above profits.

Although the experience of Nokia and GSK suggests that organizational culture can give rise to managerial actions that ultimately benefit the organization, this is not always the case. The cultures of some organizations become dysfunctional, encouraging managerial actions that harm the organization and discouraging actions that might lead to an improvement in performance.[68] For example, Sunflower Electric Power, a electricity generation and transmission cooperative, almost went bankrupt in the early 2000s. A state committee of inquiry that was set up to find the source of the problem put the blame on Sunflower's CEO. The committee decided that he had created an abusive culture based on fear and blame that encouraged managers to fight over and protect their turf—an inert culture. Managers were afraid to rock the boat or make suggestions since they could not predict what would happen to them.

The CEO was fired, and a new CEO, Chris Hauck, was appointed to change the cooperative's culture. He found it very hard to do so, as his senior managers were so used to the old values and norms. One top manager, for example, engaged so frequently in the practice of berating one supervisor that the man became physically sick.[69] Hauck fired this and other managers as a signal that such behavior would no longer be tolerated. With the help of consultants, he went about the process of changing values and norms to emphasize cooperation, teamwork, and respect for others. Clearly, managers can influence the way their organizational culture develops over time.[70]

Summary and Review

LO1

DESIGNING ORGANIZATIONAL STRUCTURE The four main determinants of organizational structure are the external environment, strategy, technology, and human resources. In general, the higher the level of uncertainty associated with these factors, the more appropriate is a flexible, adaptable structure as opposed to a formal, rigid one.

LO2 GROUPING TASKS INTO JOBS Job design is the process by which managers group tasks into jobs. To create more interesting jobs, and to get workers to act flexibly, managers can enlarge and enrich jobs. The job characteristics model is a tool that managers can use to measure how motivating or satisfying a particular job is.

LO3 ORGANIZATIONAL STRUCTURE: GROUPING JOBS INTO FUNCTIONS AND DIVISIONS Managers can choose from many kinds of organizational structures to make the best use of organizational resources. Depending on the specific organizing problems they face, managers can choose from functional, product, geographic, market, matrix, product team, and hybrid structures.

LO4 COORDINATING FUNCTIONS AND DIVISIONS No matter which structure managers choose, they must decide how to distribute authority in the organization, how many levels to have in the hierarchy of authority, and what balance to strike between centralization and decentralization to keep the number of levels in the hierarchy to a minimum. As organizations grow, managers must increase integration and coordination among functions and divisions. Four integrating mechanisms that facilitate this are liaison roles, task forces, cross-functional teams, and integrating roles.

LO5 ORGANIZATIONAL CULTURE Organizational culture is the set of values, norms, and standards of behavior that control the ways individuals and groups in an organization interact with one another and work to achieve organizational goals. The four main sources of organizational culture are the characteristics of its members, organizational ethics, the nature of the employment relationship, and the design of organizational structure. The way in which managers work to influence these four factors determines whether an organization's culture is strong and adaptive or is inert and difficult to change.

Management in Action

Topics for Discussion and Action

DISCUSSION

1. Would a flexible or a more formal structure be appropriate for these organizations: (a) a large department store, (b) a Big Five accountancy firm, (c) a biotechnology company? Explain your reasoning. **[LO 1, 2]**

2. Using the job characteristics model as a guide, discuss how a manager can enrich or enlarge subordinates' jobs. **[LO2]**

3. How might a salesperson's job or a secretary's job be enlarged or enriched to make it more motivating? **[LO 2, 3]**

4. When and under what conditions might managers change from a functional to (a) a product, (b) a geographic, or (c) a market structure? **[LO 1, 3]**

5. How do matrix structure and product team structure differ? Why is product team structure more widely used? **[LO 1, 3, 4]**

6. What is organizational culture, and how does it affect the way employees behave? **[LO5]**

ACTION

7. Find and interview a manager and identify the kind of organizational structure that his or her organization uses to coordinate its people and resources. Why is the organization using that structure? Do you think a different structure would be more appropriate? Which one? **[LO 1, 3, 4]**

8. With the same or another manager, discuss the distribution of authority in the organization. Does the manager think that decentralizing authority and empowering employees is appropriate? **[LO 1, 3]**

9. Interview some employees of an organization, and ask them about the organization's values and norms, the typical characteristics of employees, and the organization's ethical values and socialization practices. Using this information, try to describe the organization's culture and the way it affects the way people and groups behave. **[LO 1, 5]**

Building Management Skills
Understanding Organizing [LO 1, 2, 3]

Think of an organization with which you are familiar, perhaps one you have worked for—such as a store, restaurant, office, church, or school. Then answer the following questions:

1. Which contingencies are most important in explaining how the organization is organized? Do you think it is organized in the best way?

2. Using the job characteristics model, how motivating do you think the job of a typical employee in this organization is?

3. Can you think of any ways in which a typical job could be enlarged or enriched?

4. What kind of organizational structure does the organization use? If it is part of a chain, what kind of structure does the entire organization use? What other structures discussed in the chapter might allow the organization to operate more effectively? For example, would the move to a product team structure lead to greater efficiency or effectiveness? Why or why not?

5. How many levels are there in the organization's hierarchy? Is authority centralized or decentralized? Describe the span of control of the top manager and of middle or first-line managers.

6. Is the distribution of authority appropriate for the organization and its activities? Would it be possible to flatten the hierarchy by decentralizing authority and empowering employees?

7. What are the principal integrating mechanisms used in the organization? Do they provide sufficient coordination among individuals and functions? How might they be improved?

8. Now that you have analyzed the way this organization is structured, what advice would you give its managers to help them improve the way it operates?

Managing Ethically [LO 1, 3, 5]

Suppose an organization is downsizing and laying off many of its middle managers. Some top managers charged with deciding who to terminate might decide to keep the subordinates they like, and who are obedient to them, rather than the ones who are difficult or the best performers. They might also decide to lay off the most highly paid subordinates even if they are high performers. Think of the ethical issues involved in designing a hierarchy, and discuss the following issues.

Questions

1. What ethical rules (see Chapter 5) should managers use to decide which employees to terminate when redesigning their hierarchy?

2. Some people argue that employees who have worked for an organization for many years have a claim on the organization at least as strong as that of its shareholders. What do you think of the ethics of this position—can employees claim to "own" their jobs if they have contributed significantly to the organization's past success? How does a socially responsible organization behave in this situation?

Small Group Breakout Exercise

Bob's Appliances [LO 1, 3]

Form groups of three or four people, and appoint one member as the spokesperson who will communicate your findings to the class when called on by the instructor. Then discuss the following scenario.

Bob's Appliances sells and services household appliances such as washing machines, dishwashers, ranges, and refrigerators. Over the years, the company has developed a good reputation for the quality of its customer service, and many local builders patronize the store. Recently, some new appliance retailers, including Circuit City and Best Buy, have opened stores that also provide numerous appliances. To attract more customers, however, these stores also carry a complete range of consumer electronics

products—televisions, stereos, and computers. Bob Lange, the owner of Bob's Appliances, has decided that if he is to stay in business, he must widen his product range and compete directly with the chains.

In 2007, he decided to build a 20,000-square-foot store and service center, and he is now hiring new employees to sell and service the new line of consumer electronics. Because of his company's increased size, Lange is not sure of the best way to organize the employees. Currently, he uses a functional structure;

employees are divided into sales, purchasing and accounting, and repair. Bob is wondering whether selling and servicing consumer electronics is so different from selling and servicing appliances that he should move to a product structure (see figure) and create separate sets of functions for each of his two lines of business.[71]

You are a team of local consultants whom Bob has called in to advise him as he makes this crucial choice. Which structure do you recommend? Why?

FUNCTIONAL STRUCTURE

Bob Lange

- Sales
- Purchasing and Accounting
- Repair

PRODUCT STRUCTURE

Bob Lange

Appliances
- Sales
- Purchasing and Accounting
- Repair

Consumer Electronics
- Sales
- Purchasing and Accounting
- Repair

Exploring the World Wide Web [LO3]

Go to the Web site of Kraft, the food services company (www.kraft.com). Click on "brands," then answer the following questions:

1. Given the way it describes its brands, what kind of divisional structure do you think Kraft uses? Why do you think it uses this structure?

2. Click on featured brands, and look at products like its Oreo cookies. How is Kraft managing its different brands to grow global sales? What do you think are the main challenges Kraft faces in managing its global food business to improve performance?

Be the Manager [LO 1, 3, 5]

Speeding Up Web Site Design

You have been hired by a Web site design, production, and hosting company whose new animated Web site designs are attracting a lot of attention and a lot of customers. Currently, employees are organized into different functions such as hardware, software design, graphic art, and Web site hosting, as well as functions such as marketing and human resources. Each function takes its turn to work on a new project from initial customer request to final online Web site hosting.

The problem the company is experiencing is that it typically takes one year from the initial idea stage to the time that the Web site is up and running; the company wants to shorten this time by half to protect and expand its market niche. In talking to other managers, you discover that they believe the company's current functional structure is the source of the problem—it is not allowing employees to develop Web sites fast enough to satisfy customers' demands. They want you to design a better one.

Questions

1. Discuss ways in which you can improve the way the current functional structure operates so that it speeds Web site development.

2. Discuss the pros and cons of moving to a (a) multidivisional, (b) matrix, and (c) product team structure to reduce Web site development time.

3. Which of these structures do you think is most appropriate, and why?

4. What kind of culture would you help create to make the company's structure work more effectively?

BusinessWeek Case in the News [LO 3, 4]

Information Technology: Stopping the Sprawl at HP

When Randy Mott joined Wal-Mart fresh out of college in 1978, its in-house tech staff had only 30 members and company founder Sam Walton had not yet become a believer in the power of computing to revolutionize retailing. But Mott and his cohorts developed a network of computerized distribution centers that made it simple to open and run new stores with cookie-cutter efficiency.

Then in the early 1990s, Mott, by this time chief information officer, persuaded higher-ups to invest in a so-called data warehouse. That let the company collect and sift customer data to analyze buying trends as no company ever had—right down to which flavor of Pop-Tarts sells best at a given store.

By the time Mott took his latest job last summer, as CIO of HP, he had become a rock star of sorts among the corporate techie set—an executive who not only understood technology and how it could be used to improve a business but how to deliver those benefits. Besides his 22-year stint at Wal-Mart, Mott helped Dell hone its already huge IT advantage. By melding nearly 100 separate systems into a single data warehouse, Mott's team enabled Dell to quickly spot rising inventory for a particular chip, for instance, so the company could offer online promotions for devices containing that part before the price fell too steeply.

Now Mott, 49, is embarking on his boldest and most challenging project yet: a three-year, $1 billion-plus makeover of HP's internal tech systems that will replace 85 loosely connected data centers around the world with six cutting-edge facilities—two each in Austin, Atlanta, and Houston. Mott is pushing sweeping changes in the way HP operates, slashing thousands of smaller projects at the decentralized company to focus on a few corporatewide initiatives—including scrapping 784 isolated databases for one company-wide data warehouse. Says Mott: "We want to make HP the envy of the technology world." If it works, Mott's makeover could have more impact than any new HP advertising campaign, printer, or PC—and could turbocharge the company's already impressive turnaround. HP posted profits of $1.5 billion in its second quarter, up 51% from the year before, on a 5% increase in sales. If Mott is successful, HP's annual spending on tech should be cut in half in the years ahead, from $3.5 billion in 2005, say insiders.

More important, a Wal-Mart-style data warehouse could help HP make headway on its most vexing problem in recent years: how to capitalize on its vast product breadth. While HP sells everything from $10 ink cartridges to multimillion-dollar supercomputers, the company has operated more like a conglomerate of separate companies than a one-stop tech superstore. "We shipped 55 million printers, 30 million PCs, and 2 million servers last year," says CEO Hurd. "If we can integrate all that information, it would enable us to know exactly how we're doing in Chicago on a given day, or whether the CIO of a big customer also happens to own any of our products at home."

Mott's initiatives may well stir up a hornet's nest within HP. They will likely require thousands of layoffs, while requiring the support of remaining staffers in a company that has long resisted centralized control. Mott is testing the limits of the HP culture, taking away the right of thousands of IT workers to purchase their own tech equipment.

But Mott has the absolute backing of Hurd, who began recruiting him shortly after arriving at HP in February 2005. The pair have known each other for years. At both Wal-Mart and Dell, Mott bought data warehousing gear from Hurd, who was a leading evangelist for the technology during his years at NCR Corp. Hurd eventually wooed Mott in July on the strength of a $15 million pay package and a promise to support him if he'd sign on for the aggressive three-year transformation.

Still, Mott's greatest strength may be that while a technologist, he has the management skills to actually make IT take root in a company's culture. Linda M. Dillman, a onetime Wal-Mart CIO and now its executive vice president for risk management and benefits administration, recalls how Mott championed the deployment of IT by showing how it achieved Wal-Mart's business goals. Underlings say Mott's low-key Southern charm belies an intensity that typically brings him into the office by 6:15 a.m. He has no patience for quick summaries during grueling two-day-long business reviews he convenes once a month. That certainly jibes with Hurd's view of the world—which is why he's centralizing HP's balkanized information systems, even while working to decentralize operational control. The idea is to make sure all of HP's businesses are working off the same set of data, and to give them the tools to quickly make the best decisions for the entire company—say, a single customer management system, so executives can know the full breadth of what any account buys from HP.

Questions for Discussion

1. In what ways is Randy Mott trying to change HP's structure and the way it works?

2. In what ways has he been trying to change HP's culture?

3. Go to the Internet and find some articles on HP's recent performance? How have the changes he made affected HP's competitive advantage and performance?

BusinessWeek   Case in the News [LO 3, 5]

The Art of Motivation

It was about 2 p.m. on March 9 when three Nucor Corp. electricians got the call from their colleagues at the Hickman (Ark.) plant. It was bad news: Hickman's electrical grid had failed. For a minimill steelmaker like Nucor, which melts scrap steel from autos, dishwashers, mobile homes, and the like in an electric arc furnace to make new steel, there's little that could be worse. The trio immediately dropped what they were doing and headed out to the plant. Malcolm McDonald, an electrician from the Decatur (Ala.) mill, was in Indiana visiting another facility. He drove down, arriving at 9 o'clock that night. Les Hart and Bryson Trumble, from Nucor's facility in Hertford County, N.C., boarded a plane that landed in Memphis at 11 p.m. Then they drove two hours to the troubled plant.

No supervisor had asked them to make the trip, and no one had to. They went on their own. Camping out in the electrical substation with the Hickman staff, the team worked 20-hour shifts to get the plant up and running again in three days instead of the anticipated full week. There wasn't any direct financial incentive for them to blow their weekends, no extra money in their next paycheck, but for the company their contribution was huge. Hickman went on to post a first-quarter record for tons of steel shipped.

What's most amazing about this story is that at Nucor it's not considered particularly remarkable. Says Executive Vice President John J. Ferriola, who oversees the Hickman plant and seven others, "It happens daily." In an industry as Rust Belt as they come, Nucor has nurtured one of the most dynamic and engaged workforces around. The 11,300 nonunion employees at the Charlotte (N.C.) company don't see themselves as worker bees waiting for instructions from above. Nucor's flattened hierarchy and emphasis on pushing power to the front line lead its employees to adopt the mind-set of owner-operators. It's a profitable formula as Nucor's 387% return to shareholders suggests. Nucor gained renown in the late 1980s for its radical pay practices, which base the vast majority of most workers' income on their performance. An upstart nipping at the heels of the integrated steel giants, Nucor had a close-knit culture that was the natural outgrowth of its underdog identity. Legendary leader F. Kenneth Iverson's radical insight: that employees, even hourly clock-punchers, will make an extraordinary effort if you reward them richly, treat them with respect, and give them real power.

Nucor is an upstart no more, and the untold story of how it has clung to that core philosophy even as it has grown into the largest steel company in the U.S. is in many ways as compelling as the celebrated tale of its brash youth. Iverson retired in 1999. Under CEO Daniel R. DiMicco, a 23-year veteran, Nucor has snapped up 13 plants over the past five years while managing to instill its unique culture in all of the facilities it has bought, an achievement that makes him a more than worthy successor to Iverson.

At Nucor the art of motivation is about an unblinking focus on the people on the front line of the business. It's about talking to them, listening to them, taking a risk on their ideas, and accepting the occasional failure. It's a culture built in part with symbolic gestures. Every year, for example, every single employee's name goes on the cover of the annual report. And, like Iverson before him, DiMicco flies commercial, manages without an executive parking space, and really does make the coffee in the office when he takes the last cup.

Although he has an Ivy League pedigree, including degrees from Brown University and the University of Pennsylvania, DiMicco retains the plain-talking style of a guy raised in a middle-class family in Mt. Kisco, N.Y. Only 65 people—yes, 65—work alongside him at headquarters.

Money is where the rubber meets the road. Nucor's unusual pay system is the single most daring element of the company's model and the hardest for outsiders and acquired companies to embrace. An experienced steelworker at another company can easily earn $16 to $21 an hour. At Nucor the guarantee is closer to $10. A bonus tied to the production of defect-free steel by an employee's entire shift can triple the average steelworker's take-home pay.

With demand for steel scorching these days, payday has become a regular cause for celebration. Nucor gave out more than $220 million in profit sharing and bonuses to the rank and file in 2005. The average Nucor steelworker took home nearly $79,000 last year. Add to that a $2,000 one-time bonus to mark the company's record earnings and almost $18,000, on average, in profit sharing. Not only is good work rewarded, but bad work is penalized. Bonuses are calculated on every order and paid out every week. At the Berkeley mill in Huger, S.C., if workers make a bad batch of steel and catch it before it has moved on, they lose the bonus they otherwise would have made on that shipment. But if it gets to the customer, they lose three times that.

Managers don't just ask workers to put a big chunk of their pay at risk. Their own take-home depends heavily on results as well. Department managers typically get a base pay that's 75% to 90% of the market average. But in a great year that same manager might get a bonus of 75% or even 90%, based on the return on assets of the whole plant. "In average-to-bad years, we earn less than our peers in other companies. That's supposed to teach us that we don't want to be average or bad. We want to be good," says James M. Coblin, Nucor's vice president for human resources.

Compared with other U.S. companies, pay disparities are modest at Nucor. Today, the typical CEO makes more than 400 times what a factory worker takes home. Last year, Nucor's chief executive collected a salary and bonus precisely 23 times that of his average steelworker. DiMicco did well by any reasonable standard, making some $2.3 million in salary and bonus (plus long-term pay equaling $4.9 million), but that's because Nucor is doing well. When things are bad, DiMicco suffers, too.

Executive pay is geared toward team building. The bonus of a plant manager, a department manager's boss, depends on the entire corporation's return on equity.

So there's no glory in winning at your own plant if the others are failing. But to focus only on pay would be to miss something special about the culture Nucor has created. There's a healthy competition among facilities and even among shifts, balanced with a long history of cooperation and idea-sharing. Since there's always room for improvement, plant managers regularly set up contests for shifts to try to outdo one another on a set goal, generally related to safety, efficiency, or output. Ryan says Nucor's Utah plant is the benchmark these days. It is the most profitable, with the lowest costs per ton. "They've got everything down to a science," says Ryan admiringly. "It gives you something to shoot for."

Questions for Discussion

1. What is Nucor's managers' approach to organizing and controlling?

2. In what ways has this approach affected its organizational structure and culture?

Source: Nanette Byrnes and Michael Arndt, "The Art of Motivation." Reprinted from the May 1, 2006, issue of *BusinessWeek* by special permission. Copyright © 2006 by The McGraw-Hill Companies, Inc.

CHAPTER 11

Organizational Control and Change

Learning Objectives

After studying this chapter, you should be able to:

LO1 Define organizational control and explain how it increases organizational effectiveness.

LO2 Describe the four steps in the control process and the way it operates over time.

LO3 Identify the main output controls, and discuss their advantages and disadvantages as means of coordinating and motivating employees.

LO4 Identify the main behavior controls, and discuss their advantages and disadvantages as means of coordinating and motivating employees.

LO5 Discuss the relationship between organizational control and change, and explain why managing change is a vital management task.

A MANAGER'S CHALLENGE

What is the Best Way to Control People and Resources?

www.ford.com

Ford recorded a record loss of $13.3 billion in 2006, after which William Ford III, who had been CEO for the last five years, decided he was not the right person to turnaround the company's fortunes.[1] In fact, he was a part of the problem because it turned out that over the years Ford had developed a corporate culture based on empire-building, in which top managers had emulated Ford; they strived to build their own empires, and to protect those empires they would never admit that mistakes had occurred. Finally, Ford's board of directors realized they needed an outsider to change Ford's culture—and the way it was being controlled—and they recruited Alan Mulally in 2006 to become Ford's new CEO.

Mulally left Boeing, which had also recruited him to turnaround that company's unethical culture, to join Ford. After arriving at Ford he went to hundreds of meetings to meet his new managers, and at one executive meeting he became confused why one top division manager, who obviously did not know the answer to one of Mulally's questions concerning the performance of his car division, had rambled on for several minutes trying to disguise his ignorance. Mulally turned around to his second-in-command Mark Fields, and asked him why the manager had done that. Fields explained that "at Ford you never admit when you don't know something." He also told Mulally that when he arrived as a senior executive at Ford and wanted to ask his boss to lunch to gain information about divisional operations, he was told, "What rank are you at Ford? Don't you know that a subordinate never asks a superior to lunch?"[2]

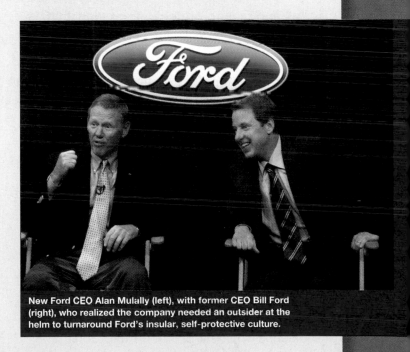

New Ford CEO Alan Mulally (left), with former CEO Bill Ford (right), who realized the company needed an outsider at the helm to turnaround Ford's insular, self-protective culture.

It turned out that over the years Ford had develop a tall hierarchy composed of managers whose main goal was to protect their turf and avoid any direct blame for its plunging car sales. So, when asked why car sales were falling they did not admit to bad design and poor quality issues in their divisions; instead, they hid in the details. They brought thick notebooks and binders to meetings, listing the high prices of components and high labor costs to explain why their own particular car models were not selling well or even why they had to be sold at a loss. Mulally wanted to know why Ford's top executives have this inward looking, destructive mind-set?

He soon realized that the problem was the values and norms in Ford's culture that had created a situation in which the managers of its different divisions and functions thought that the best way to maintain their jobs, salaries, and status was to hoard information and not share it. Thus, values and norms of secrecy and ambiguity, and of emphasizing status and rank to protect information, had developed. The reason only the boss could ask a subordinate to lunch was to enable superiors to hoard information and protect their positions. Ford's culture allowed managers to hide the extent of the problems they were facing and how badly they were performing. What could Mulally do?

He issued a direct order that the managers of every division should share with every other Ford division a detailed statement of the costs they incurred to build each of its vehicles. He insisted that each of Ford's divisional presidents should attend a weekly—rather than a monthly—meeting to discuss openly and share the problems all the company's division's faced. He also told them that they should bring a different subordinate with them to each meeting so that every manager in the hierarchy would learn of the problems that had been kept hidden.[3] Essentially, Mulally's goal was to demolish the dysfunctional inbred values and norms of Ford's culture that had focused managers' attention on their own empires at the expense of the whole company. No longer would they be allowed to protect their own careers at the expense of customers.

Mulally's goal is to create new values and norms that it is alright to admit mistakes, share information about all aspects of model design and costs, and of course find ways to speed development and reduce costs. He also wants to emphasize norms of cooperation within and across divisions to improve performance. When Mulally arrived he found that no two models shared even the most basic components, such as side mirrors or the hinges that hold up the hood—something that drives up costs. Now, all these kinds of problems are to be addressed through interdivisional openness and cooperation.

How could this situation have gone unchanged in a major car company that has been experiencing increased competition since the mid1970s? The answer is that the norms and values of an organization's culture are very hard to change; and despite Ford's major problems, no CEO had been able to change the mind-set of the top managers in the company. Ford had even become more hierarchical and bureaucratic over time as its problems increased because poor performance led managers to become even more defensive and concerned to defend their fiefdoms or empires. Can outsider Mulally succeed?

When Mulally, in one of his first meetings, was confronted by a Ford engineer about whether an outsider from Boeing could really cure Ford's problems, he told the engineer that a car has only ten thousand moving parts while an airplane has millions and it stays in the air. Obviously, Mulally believes Ford's problems can be solved if he can get its managers to adopt these new cultural values and norms. The mind-set of managers and employees, which determines how they control employees, goes a long way to determine a company's future success.[4]

Overview

As we discussed in Chapter 10, the first task facing managers is to establish a structure of task and job reporting relationships that allows organizational members to use resources most efficiently and effectively. Structure alone, however, does not provide the incentive or motivation for people to behave in ways that help achieve organizational goals. When managers make choices about how to influence, shape, and regulate the activities of organizational divisions, functions, and employees to achieve the organization's mission and goals, they establish the second foundation of organizational architecture: organizational control. An organization's structure provides the organization with a skeleton, but its control systems give it the muscles, sinews, nerves, and sensations that allow managers to regulate and govern its activities. The control systems also provide managers with specific feedback on how well the organization and its members are performing. The managerial functions of organizing and controlling are inseparable, and effective managers must learn to make them work together in a harmonious way.

In this chapter, we look in detail at the nature of organizational control and describe the main steps in the control process. We also discuss the different types of control systems that are available to managers to shape and influence organizational activities—*output control, behavior control,* and *clan control.*[5] Finally, we discuss the important issue of organizational change, change that is possible only when managers have put in place a control system that allows them to alter the way people and groups behave and alter or transform the way the organization operates—something Alan Mulally is trying to achieve at Ford. Control is the essential ingredient that is needed to bring about and manage organizational change efficiently and effectively. By the end of this chapter, you will appreciate the rich variety of control systems available to managers and understand why developing an appropriate control system is vital to increasing the performance of an organization and its members.

What Is Organizational Control?

As noted in Chapter 1, *controlling* is the process whereby managers monitor and regulate how efficiently and effectively an organization and its members are performing the activities necessary to achieve organizational goals. As discussed in previous chapters, when planning and organizing, managers develop the organizational strategy and structure that they hope will allow the organization to use resources most effectively to create value for customers. In controlling, managers monitor and evaluate whether the organization's strategy and structure are working as intended, how they could be improved, and how they might be changed if they are not working.

Control, however, does not mean just reacting to events after they have occurred. It also means keeping an organization on track, anticipating events that might occur, and then changing the organization to respond to whatever opportunities or threats have been identified. Control is concerned with keeping employees motivated, focused on the important problems confronting the organization, and working together to make the changes that will help an organization improve its performance over time.

LO1 Define organizational control and explain how it increases organizational effectiveness.

The Importance of Organizational Control

To understand the importance of organizational control, consider how it helps managers obtain superior efficiency, quality, responsiveness to customers, and innovation—the four building blocks of competitive advantage.

To determine how efficiently they are using their resources, managers must be able to accurately measure how many units of inputs (raw materials, human resources, and so on) are being used to produce a unit of output. Managers also must be able to measure how many units of outputs (goods and services) are being produced. A control system contains the measures or yardsticks that allow managers to assess how efficiently the organization is producing goods and services. Moreover, if managers experiment with changing the way the organization produces goods and services to find a more efficient way of producing them, these measures tell managers how successful they have been. For example, when managers at Ford decided to adopt a product team structure to design, engineer, and manufacture new car models, they used measures such as time taken to design a new car and cost savings per car produced to evaluate how well the new structure worked in comparison with the old structure. They found that the new one performed better. Without a control system in place, managers have no idea how well their organization is performing and how its performance can be improved—information that is becoming increasingly important in today's highly competitive environment.

Today, much of the competition among organizations revolves around increasing the quality of goods and services. In the car industry, for example, cars within each price range compete against one another in features, design, and reliability. Thus, whether a customer will buy a Ford Taurus, GM Grand Prix, Chrysler Sebring, Toyota Camry, or Honda Accord depends significantly on the quality of each product. Organizational control is important in determining the quality of goods and services because it gives managers feedback on product quality. If the managers of carmakers consistently measure the number of customer complaints and the number of new cars returned for repairs, or if school principals measure how many students drop out of school or how achievement scores on nationally based tests vary over time, they have a good indication of how much quality they have built into their product—be it an educated student or a car that does not break down. Effective managers create a control system that consistently monitors the quality of goods and services so that they can make continuous improvements to quality—an approach to change that gives them a competitive advantage.

Managers can help make their organizations more responsive to customers if they develop a control system, such as a CRM system, that allows them to evaluate how well customer-contact employees are performing their jobs. Monitoring employee behavior can help managers find ways to increase employees' performance levels, perhaps by revealing areas in which skill training can help employees or in which new procedures can allow employees to perform their jobs better. Also, when employees know that their behaviors are being monitored, they may have more incentive to be helpful and consistent in how they act toward customers. To improve customer service, for example, Ford regularly surveys customers about their experiences with particular Ford dealers. If a dealership receives too many customer complaints, Ford's managers investigate the dealership to uncover the sources of the problems and suggest solutions; if necessary, they might even threaten to reduce the number of cars a dealership receives to force the dealer to improve the quality of its customer service.

Finally, controlling can raise the level of innovation in an organization. Successful innovation takes place

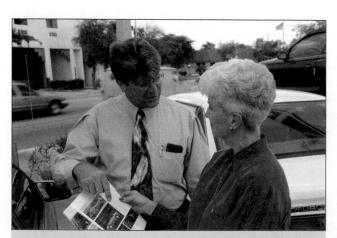

A Ford salesperson speaks with a prospective customer about her car-buying preferences, a measure the company has adopted in order to ensure quality customer service.

when managers create an organizational setting in which employees feel empowered to be creative and in which authority is decentralized to employees so that they feel free to experiment and take risks. Deciding on the appropriate control systems to encourage risk taking is an important management challenge; organizational culture becomes important in this regard. To encourage product teams at Ford to perform at a high level, top managers monitored the performance of each team separately—by examining how each team reduced costs or increased quality, for example—and used a bonus system related to performance to pay each team. The product team manager then evaluated each team member's individual performance, and the most innovative employees received promotions and rewards based on their superior performance.

Control Systems and IT

control systems Formal target-setting, monitoring, evaluation, and feedback systems that provide managers with information about how well the organization's strategy and structure are working.

Control systems are formal target-setting, monitoring, evaluation, and feedback systems that provide managers with information about whether the organization's strategy and structure are working efficiently and effectively.[6] Effective control systems alert managers when something is going wrong and give them time to respond to opportunities and threats. An effective control system has three characteristics: It is flexible enough to allow managers to respond as necessary to unexpected events; it provides accurate information and gives managers a true picture of organizational performance; and it provides managers with the information in a timely manner because making decisions on the basis of outdated information is a recipe for failure.

New forms of IT have revolutionized control systems because they facilitate the flow of accurate and timely information up and down the organizational hierarchy and between functions and divisions. Today, employees at all levels of the organization routinely feed information into a company's information system or network and start the chain of events that affect decision making at some other part of the organization. This could be the department store clerk whose scanning of purchased clothing tells merchandise managers what kinds of clothing need to be reordered or the salesperson in the field who feeds into a wireless laptop the CRM information necessary to inform marketing about customers' changing needs or problems.

feedforward control Control that allows managers to anticipate problems before they arise.

Control and information systems are developed to measure performance at each stage in the process of transforming inputs into finished goods and services (see Figure 11.1). At the input stage, managers use **feedforward control** to anticipate problems before they arise so that problems do not occur later, during the conversion process.[7] For example, by giving stringent product specifications to suppliers in advance (a form of performance target), an organization can control the quality of the inputs it receives from its suppliers and thus avoid potential problems during the conversion process. Also, IT can be used to keep in contact with suppliers and

Figure 11.1

Three Types of Control

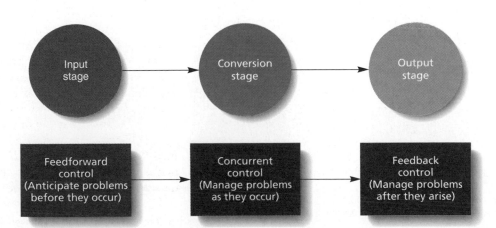

to monitor their progress. Similarly, by screening job applicants, often by viewing their résumés electronically, and using several interviews to select the most highly skilled people, managers can lessen the chance that they will hire people who lack the necessary skills or experience to perform effectively. In general, the development of management information systems promotes feedforward control that provides managers with timely information about changes in the task and general environments that may impact their organization later on. Effective managers always monitor trends and changes in the external environment to try to anticipate problems. (We discuss management information systems in detail in Chapter 18.)

concurrent control
Control that gives managers immediate feedback on how efficiently inputs are being transformed into outputs so that managers can correct problems as they arise.

At the conversion stage, **concurrent control** gives managers immediate feedback on how efficiently inputs are being transformed into outputs so that managers can correct problems as they arise. Concurrent control through IT alerts managers to the need to react quickly to whatever is the source of the problem, be it a defective batch of inputs, a machine that is out of alignment, or a worker who lacks the skills necessary to perform a task efficiently. Concurrent control is at the heart of total quality management programs (discussed in Chapter 9), in which workers are expected to constantly monitor the quality of the goods or services they provide at every step of the production process and inform managers as soon as they discover problems. One of the strengths of Toyota's production system, for example, is that individual workers are given the authority to push a button to stop the assembly line whenever they discover a quality problem. When all problems have been corrected, the result is a finished product that is much more reliable.

feedback control Control that gives managers information about customers' reactions to goods and services so that corrective action can be taken if necessary.

At the output stage, managers use **feedback control** to provide information about customers' reactions to goods and services so that corrective action can be taken if necessary. For example, a feedback control system that monitors the number of customer returns alerts managers when defective products are being produced, and a management information system (MIS) that measures increases or decreases in relative sales of different products alerts managers to changes in customer tastes so that they can increase or reduce the production of specific products.

The Control Process

LO2 Describe the four steps in the control process and the way it operates over time.

The control process, whether at the input, conversion, or output stage, can be broken down into four steps: establishing standards of performance, and then measuring, comparing, and evaluating actual performance (see Figure 11.2).[8]

* Step 1: *Establish the standards of performance, goals, or targets against which performance is to be evaluated.*

Figure 11.2

Four Steps in Organizational Control

Step 1	Establish the standards of performance, goals, or targets against which performance is to be evaluated
Step 2	Measure actual performance
Step 3	Compare actual performance against chosen standards of performance
Step 4	Evaluate the result and initiate corrective action if the standard is not being achieved

At step 1 in the control process managers decide on the standards of performance, goals, or targets that they will use in the future to evaluate the performance of the entire organization or part of it (such as a division, a function, or an individual). The standards of performance that managers select measure efficiency, quality, responsiveness to customers, and innovation.[9] If managers decide to pursue a low-cost strategy, for example, then they need to measure efficiency at all levels in the organization.

At the corporate level, a standard of performance that measures efficiency is operating costs, the actual costs associated with producing goods and services, including all employee-related costs. Top managers might set a corporate goal of "reducing operating costs by 10% for the next three years" to increase efficiency. Corporate managers might then evaluate divisional managers for their ability to reduce operating costs within their respective divisions, and divisional managers might set cost-saving targets for functional managers. Thus, performance standards selected at one level affect those at the other levels, and ultimately the performance of individual managers is evaluated in terms of their ability to reduce costs.

The number of standards or indicators of performance that an organization's managers use to evaluate efficiency, quality, and so on, can run into the thousands or hundreds of thousands. Managers at each level are responsible for selecting those standards that will best allow them to evaluate how well the part of the organization they are responsible for is performing.[10] Managers must be careful to choose the standards of performance that allow them to assess how well they are doing with all four of the building blocks of competitive advantage. If managers focus on just one standard (such as efficiency), and ignore others (such as determining what customers really want and innovating a new line of products to satisfy them), managers may end up hurting their organization's performance.

* Step 2: *Measure actual performance.*

Once managers have decided which standards or targets they will use to evaluate performance, the next step in the control process is to measure actual performance. In practice, managers can measure or evaluate two things: (1) the actual *outputs* that result from the behavior of their members and (2) the *behaviors* themselves (hence the terms *output control* and *behavior control* used below).[11]

Sometimes both outputs and behaviors can be easily measured. Measuring outputs and evaluating behavior is relatively easy in a fast-food restaurant, for example, because employees are performing routine tasks. Managers at Home Depot are rigorous in using output control to measure how fast inventory flows through its stores. Similarly, managers of a fast food restaurant can quite easily measure outputs by counting how many customers their employees serve, the time each transaction takes, and how much money each customer spends. Managers can easily observe each employee's behavior and quickly take action to solve any problems that may arise.

When an organization and its members perform complex, nonroutine activities that are intrinsically difficult to measure, it is much more difficult for managers to measure outputs or behavior.[12] It is very difficult, for example, for managers in charge of R&D departments at Intel or AMD, or at Microsoft or Google, to measure performance or to evaluate the performance of individual members because it can take several years to determine whether the new products that their engineers and scientists are developing are going to be profitable. Moreover, it is impossible for a manager to measure how creative an engineer or scientist is by watching his or her actions!

In general, the more nonroutine or complex organizational activities are, the harder it is for managers to measure outputs or behaviors.[13] Outputs, however, are usually easier to measure than behaviors because they are more tangible and objective. Therefore, the first kind of performance measures that managers tend to use are those that measure outputs. Then managers develop performance measures or standards that allow them to evaluate behaviors to determine whether employees at all levels are working toward organizational goals. Some simple behavior measures are (1) do employees come to work on time, and (2) do employees consistently follow the established rules for greeting and serving customers? Each type of output and behavior control and the way it is used at the different organizational levels–corporate, divisional, functional, and individual–is discussed in detail subsequently.

* Step 3: *Compare actual performance against chosen standards of performance.*

During step 3, managers evaluate whether–and to what extent–performance deviates from the standards of performance chosen in step 1. If performance is higher than expected, managers might decide that they set performance standards too low and may raise them for the next time period to challenge their subordinates.[14] Managers at Japanese companies are well known for the way they try to raise performance in manufacturing settings by constantly raising performance standards to motivate managers and workers to find new ways to reduce costs or increase quality–reread the Chapter 9 opening case on the way Toyota uses TQM from an organizational control perspective.

However, if performance is too low and standards were not reached, or if standards were set so high that employees could not achieve them, managers must decide whether to take corrective action.[15] It is easy to take corrective action when the reasons for poor performance can be identified–for instance, high labor costs. To reduce costs, managers can search for low-cost foreign sources of supply, invest more in technology, or implement cross-functional teams. More often, however, the reasons for poor performance are hard to identify. Changes in the environment, such as the emergence of a new global competitor, a recession, or an increase in interest rates, might be the source of the problem. Within an organization, perhaps the R&D function underestimated the problems it would encounter in developing a new product or the extra costs of doing unforeseen research. If managers are to take any form of corrective action, step 4 is necessary.

* Step 4: *Evaluate the result and initiate corrective action (that is, make changes) if the standard is not being achieved.*

The final step in the control process is to evaluate the results and bring about change as appropriate. Whether performance standards have been met or not, managers can learn a great deal during this step. If managers decide that the level of performance is unacceptable, they must try to change the way work activities are performed to solve the problem. Sometimes, performance problems occur because the work standard was too high–for example, a sales target was too optimistic and impossible to achieve. In this case, adopting more realistic standards can reduce the gap between actual performance and desired performance.

However, if managers determine that something in the situation is causing the problem, then to raise performance they will need to change the way resources are being utilized.[16] Perhaps the latest technology is not being used; perhaps workers lack the advanced training needed to perform at a higher level; perhaps the organization needs to buy its inputs or assemble its products abroad to compete against low-cost rivals; perhaps it needs to restructure itself or reengineer its work processes using Six Sigma to increase efficiency.

The simplest example of a control system is the thermostat in a home. By setting the thermostat, you establish the standard of performance with which actual temperature is to be compared. The thermostat contains a sensing or monitoring device, which measures the actual temperature against the desired temperature. Whenever there is a difference between them, the furnace or air-conditioning unit is activated to bring the temperature back to the standard. In other words, corrective action is initiated. This is a simple control system, for it is entirely self-contained and the target (temperature) is easy to measure.

Establishing targets and designing measurement systems are much more difficult for managers because the high level of uncertainty in the organizational environment causes managers to rarely know what might happen. Thus, it is vital for managers to design control systems to alert them to problems so that they can be dealt with before they become threatening. Another issue is that managers are not just concerned about bringing the organization's performance up to some predetermined standard; they want to push that standard forward, to encourage employees at all levels to find new ways to raise performance.

Figure 11.3

Three Organizational Control Systems

Type of control	Mechanisms of control
Output control	Financial measures of performance Organizational goals Operating budgets
Behavior control	Direct supervision Management by objectives Rules and standard operating procedures
Clan control	Values Norms Socialization

In the following sections, we consider three important types of control systems that managers use to coordinate and motivate employees to ensure they pursue superior efficiency, quality, innovation, and responsiveness to customers: output control, behavior control, and clan control (see Figure 11.3). Managers use all three to shape, regulate, and govern organizational activities, no matter what specific organizational structure is in place. However, as Figure 11.3 suggests, an important element of control is embedded in organizational culture, which is discussed later.

Output Control

All managers develop a system of output control for their organizations. First, they choose the goals or output performance standards or targets that they think will best measure efficiency, quality, innovation, and responsiveness to customers. Then they measure to see whether the performance goals and standards are being achieved at the corporate, divisional, functional, and individual employee levels of the organization. The three main mechanisms that managers use to assess output or performance are financial measures, organizational goals, and operating budgets.

LO3 Identify the main output controls, and discuss their advantages and disadvantages as means of coordinating and motivating employees.

Financial Measures of Performance

Top managers are most concerned with overall organizational performance and use various financial measures to evaluate it. The most common are profit ratios, liquidity ratios, leverage ratios, and activity ratios. They are discussed below and summarized in Table 11.1.[17]

- *Profit ratios* measure how efficiently managers are using the organization's resources to generate profits. *Return on investment (ROI),* an organization's net income before taxes divided by its total assets, is the most commonly used financial performance measure because it allows managers of one organization to compare performance with that of other organizations. ROI allows managers to assess an organization's competitive advantage. *Operating margin* is calculated by dividing a company's operating profit (the amount it has left after all the costs of making the product and running the business have been deducted) by sales revenues. This measure provides managers with information about how efficiently an organization is utilizing its resources; every attempt to reduce costs will be reflected in increased operating profit, for example. Also, operating margin is a means of comparing one year's performance to another; for example, if managers discover operating margin has improved by 5% from one year to the next, they know that their organization is building a competitive advantage.

Table 11.1

Four Measures of Financial Performance

Profit Ratios

Return on investment	=	$\dfrac{\text{net profit before taxes}}{\text{total assets}}$	Measures how well managers are using the organization's resources to generate profits.
Operating margin	=	$\dfrac{\text{total operating profit}}{\text{sales revenues}}$	A measure of how much percentage profit a company is earning on sales; the higher the percentage, the better a company is utilizing its resources to make and sell the product.

Liquidity Ratios

Current ratio	=	$\dfrac{\text{current assets}}{\text{current liabilities}}$	Do managers have resources available to meet claims of short-term creditors?
Quick ratio	=	$\dfrac{\text{current assets} - \text{inventory}}{\text{current liabilities}}$	Can managers pay off claims of short-term creditors without selling inventory?

Leverage Ratios

Debt-to-assets ratio	=	$\dfrac{\text{total debt}}{\text{total assets}}$	To what extent have managers used borrowed funds to finance investments?
Times-covered ratio	=	$\dfrac{\text{profit before interest and taxes}}{\text{total interest charges}}$	Measures how far profits can decline before managers cannot meet interest changes. If ratio declines to less than 1, the organization is technically insolvent.

Activity Ratios

Inventory turnover	=	$\dfrac{\text{cost of good sold}}{\text{inventory}}$	Measures how efficiently managers are turning inventory over so that excess inventory is not carried.
Days sales outstanding	=	$\dfrac{\text{current accounts receivable}}{\substack{\text{sales for period} \\ \text{divided by days in period}}}$	Measures how efficiently managers are collecting revenues from customers to pay expenses.

- *Liquidity ratios* measure how well managers have protected organizational resources to be able to meet short-term obligations. The *current ratio* (current assets divided by current liabilities) tells managers whether they have the resources available to meet the claims of short-term creditors. The *quick ratio* tells whether they can pay these claims without selling inventory.

- *Leverage ratios,* such as the *debt-to-assets ratio* and the *times-covered ratio,* measure the degree to which managers use debt (borrow money) or equity (issue new shares) to finance ongoing operations. An organization is highly leveraged if it uses more debt than equity. Debt can be very risky when net income or profit fail to cover the interest on the debt—as some people learn too late, when the size of their paychecks does not allow them to pay off their credit cards.

- *Activity ratios* provide measures of how well managers are creating value from organizational assets. *Inventory turnover* measures how efficiently managers are turning inventory over so that excess inventory is not carried. *Days sales outstanding* provides information on how efficiently managers are collecting revenue from customers to pay expenses.

The objectivity of financial measures of performance is the reason why so many managers use them to assess the efficiency and effectiveness of their organizations. When an organization fails to meet performance standards such as ROI, revenue, or stock price targets, managers know that they must take corrective action. Thus, financial controls tell managers when a corporate reorganization might be necessary, when they should sell off divisions and exit from businesses, or when they should rethink their corporate-level strategies.[18] Today, financial controls are being taught to all organizational employees, as the following "Management Insight" describes.

Management Insight

Making the Financial Figures Come Alive

You might think that financial control is the province of top managers and that employees lower in the organization don't need to worry about the numbers or about how their specific activities affect those numbers. However, some top managers make a point of showing employees exactly how their activities affect financial ratios, and they do so because employees' activities directly affect a company's costs and its sales revenues. One of those managers is Michael Dell.

Dell goes to enormous lengths to convince employees that they need to watch every dime spent in making the PCs that have made his company so prosperous, as well as in saying every word or making every phone call or service call that is needed to sell or repair them. Dell believes that all his managers need to have at their fingertips detailed information about Dell's cost structure, including assembly costs, selling costs, and after-sales costs, in order to squeeze out every cent of operating costs. And one good reason for this is that Dell puts a heavy emphasis on the operating-margin financial ratio in measuring his company's performance. Dell doesn't care about how much profits or sales are growing individually; he cares about how these two figures work together, because only if profits are growing faster than sales is the company increasing its long-run profitability by operating more efficiently and effectively.

So he insists that his managers search for every way possible to reduce costs or make customers happier and then help employees learn the new procedures to achieve these goals. At Dell's boot camp for new employees, in Austin, Texas, he has been known to bring financial charts that show employees how each minute spent on performing some job activity, or how each mistake made in assembling or packing a PC, affects bottom-line profitability. In the 2000s Dell's repeated efforts to slice costs while building customer loyalty have boosted efficiency and operating margins; it is much more efficient than HP or Gateway. However, these companies are applying Dell's principles and closing the performance gap, and in the 2000s all kinds of companies have begun training sessions in which employees at all levels are taught how their specific job activities, and the way their functions operate, affect the financial ratios used to judge how well an organization is performing.

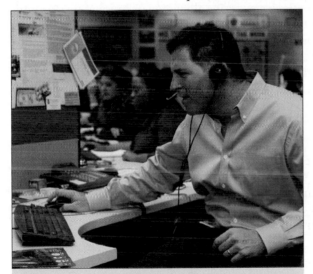

Michael Dell prepares to work the phone lines at Dell's U.S. customer service call center. Dell's emphasis on productivity everywhere means he has no qualms about sitting in an entry-level position for a day to both learn what his employees face and to better teach them.

Although financial information is an important output control, financial information by itself does not provide managers with all the information they need about the four building blocks of competitive advantage. Financial results inform managers about the results of decisions they have already made; they do not tell managers how to find new opportunities to build competitive advantage in the future. To encourage a future-oriented approach, top managers must establish organizational goals that encourage middle and first-line managers to achieve superior efficiency, quality, innovation, and responsiveness to customers.

Figure 11.4
Organizationwide Goal Setting

Organizational Goals

Once top managers consult with lower-level managers and set the organization's over-all goals, they establish performance standards for the divisions and functions. These standards specify for divisional and functional managers the level at which their units must perform if the organization is to achieve its overall goals.[19] Each division is given a set of specific goals to achieve (see Figure 11.4). We saw in Chapter 8, for example, that Jeffrey Immelt, CEO of GE, has established the goal of having each GE division be first or second in its industry in profit. Divisional managers then develop a business-level strategy (based on achieving superior efficiency or innovation) that they hope will allow them to achieve that goal.[20] In consultation with functional managers, they specify the functional goals that the managers of different functions need to achieve to allow the division to achieve its goals. For example, sales managers might be evaluated for their ability to increase sales; materials management managers, for their ability to increase the quality of inputs or lower their costs; R&D managers, for the number of products they innovate or the number of patents they receive. In turn, functional managers establish goals that first-line managers and nonmanagerial employees need to achieve to allow the function to achieve its goals.

Output control is used at every level of the organization, and it is vital that the goals set at each level harmonize with the goals set at other levels so that managers and other employees throughout the organization work together to attain the corporate goals that top managers have set.[21] It is also important that goals be set appropriately so that managers are motivated to accomplish them. If goals are set at an impossibly high level, managers might work only half-heartedly to achieve them because they are certain they will fail. In contrast, if goals are set so low that they are too easy to achieve, managers will not be motivated to use all their resources as efficiently and effectively as possible. Research suggests that the best goals are specific, difficult goals—goals that challenge and stretch managers' ability but are not out of reach and do not require an impossibly high expenditure of managerial time and energy. Such goals are often called *stretch goals*.

Deciding what is a specific, difficult goal and what is a goal that is too difficult or too easy is a skill that managers must develop. Based on their own judgment and work experience, managers at all levels must assess how difficult a certain task is, and they must assess the ability of a particular subordinate manager to achieve the goal. If they do so successfully, challenging, interrelated goals—goals that reinforce one another and focus on achieving overall corporate objectives—will energize the organization.

Operating Budgets

operating budget
A budget that states how managers intend to use organizational resources to achieve organizational goals.

Once managers at each level have been given a goal or target to achieve, the next step in developing an output control system is to establish operating budgets that regulate how managers and workers attain their goals. An **operating budget** is a blueprint that states how managers intend to use organizational resources to achieve organizational goals efficiently. Typically, managers at one level allocate to subordinate managers a specific amount of resources to use to produce goods and services. Once they have been given a budget, these lower-level managers must decide how to allocate money for different organizational activities. They are then evaluated for their ability to stay within the budget and to make the best use of available resources. For example, managers at GE's washing machine division might have a budget of $50 million to spend on developing and selling a new line of washing machines. They must decide how much money to allocate to the various functions such as R&D, engineering, and sales so that the division generates the most customer revenue and makes the biggest profit.

Large organizations often treat each division as a singular or stand-alone responsibility center. Corporate managers then evaluate each division's contribution to corporate performance. Managers of a division may be given a fixed budget for resources and be evaluated on the amount of goods or services they can produce using those resources (this is a cost or expense budget approach). Or managers may be asked to maximize the revenues from the sales of goods and services produced (a revenue budget approach). Or managers may be evaluated on the difference between the revenues generated by the sales of goods and services and the budgeted cost of making those goods and services (a profit budget approach). Japanese companies' use of operating budgets and challenging goals to increase efficiency is instructive in this context.

In summary, three components—objective financial measures, challenging goals and performance standards, and appropriate operating budgets—are the essence of effective output control. Most organizations develop sophisticated output control systems to allow managers at all levels to keep accurate account of the organization so that they can move quickly to take corrective action as needed.[22] Output control is an essential part of management. The way in which Wal-Mart is using output control to expand internationally is discussed in the following "Managing Globally."

Managing Globally

Wal-Mart Uses Output Control to Expand Internationally

Retailing giant Wal-Mart has been aggressively expanding internationally in recent years to raise its performance. After moving into Mexico and Europe in the last decade, it began to contemplate entering the Japanese market. An opportunity arose in 2004 when Japan's third-largest supermarket chain, Daiei, which had been losing money for years and was heavily in debt, was put up for sale. Why was a supermarket chain in one of the world's most lucrative markets struggling?

Unlike efficient Japanese carmakers, which employ state-of-the-art IT-based output control systems to collect the detailed information needed to increase their efficiency, Japan's retailers had lagged behind in adopting the new systems. A major reason for this was historical. Until the 1990s, Japan's Large Scale Retail Store Law allowed small Japanese retailers to block the opening of large, efficient new stores in their neighborhoods for 10 years or more. Although the Japanese government weakened the law so that local storeowners could delay a store opening for only 18 months, there was no history of low-cost competition in the Japanese retail market. So retailers, such as supermarket chains, had never been forced to develop output controls to become more efficient.

A second reason for Daiei's problems revolved around Japan's system of distributing Japanese products. Traditionally, Japanese manufacturers sold their products only by means of wholesalers with which they had developed long-term business relationships. Because the wholesalers added their own price markup and controlled distribution, this made it much more difficult for supermarkets to compete on price and lowered competition. Less competition reduced the incentive for Japanese retailers to invest in materials management output control systems to increase their efficiency.

In contrast, Wal-Mart's focus on developing sophisticated output controls to monitor all aspects of its purchasing and sales activities made it the most efficient U.S. discount retailer in the 1990s. In fact, its skills in materials management allowed it to enter the U.S. supermarket industry and become a major competitor there. So, in the 2000s, to further its global expansion, Wal-Mart bought a significant stake in Seiyu Ltd., Japan's fourth-largest supermarket. Then, in 2004, it tried to buy the troubled Japanese supermarket chain, Daiei, in order to combine it with its Seiyu division. Its managers believed that if Wal-Mart transplanted its proprietary IT-based output control systems into its expanded Japanese store operations, it could increase Seiyu's and Daiei's efficiency by so much that its supermarket chain would become highly profitable and eventually dominate the Japanese supermarket industry. Wal-Mart also planned to purchase lower-priced goods from abroad to sell in its Japanese stores, using its sophisticated global supply chain, which allows it to identify and purchase products efficiently from manufacturers throughout the world.

To Wal-Mart's annoyance, Japan's Industrial Revitalization Corp., which had the power to select the buyer for Daiei's 260 locations across Japan, decided it did not want Wal-Mart to become one of the largest retailers in Japan and thus threaten domestic Japanese companies. It rejected Wal-Mart Stores' bid for Daiei, but the world's largest retailer is still keeping its eyes peeled for other opportunities in the lucrative Japanese market, whose citizens pay some of the highest prices in the world for their food and other consumer products.

Although it has encountered success in China, as seen above, Wal-Mart's offer to buy Japan's struggling supermarket chain Daiei was refused.

Problems with Output Control

When designing an output control system, managers must be careful to avoid some pitfalls. For example, they must be sure that the output standards they create motivate managers at all levels and do not cause managers to behave in inappropriate ways to achieve organizational goals.

Suppose top managers give divisional managers the goal of doubling profits over a three-year period. This goal seems challenging and reachable when it is jointly agreed upon, and in the first two years profits go up by 70%. In the third year, however, an economic recession hits and sales plummet. Divisional managers think it is increasingly unlikely that they will meet their profit goal. Failure will mean losing the substantial monetary bonus tied to achieving the goal. How might managers behave to try to preserve their bonuses?

One course of action they might take is to find ways to reduce costs, since profit can be increased either by raising sales revenues or reducing costs. Thus, divisional managers might cut back on expensive research activities, delay maintenance on machinery, reduce marketing expenditures, and lay off middle managers and workers to reduce costs so that at the end of the year they will make their target of doubling profits and receive their bonuses. This tactic might help them achieve a short-run goal—doubling profits—but such actions could hurt long-term profitability or ROI (because a cutback in R&D can reduce the rate of product innovation, a cutback in marketing will lead to the loss of customers, and so on).

The message is clear: Although output control is a useful tool for keeping managers and employees at all levels motivated and the organization on track, it is only a guide to appropriate action. Managers must be sensitive to how they use output control and must constantly monitor its effects at all levels in the organization—and on customers and other stakeholders.

Behavior Control

Organizational structure by itself does not provide any mechanism that motivates managers and nonmanagerial employees to behave in ways that make the structure work—or even improve the way it works—hence the need for control. Put another way, managers can develop an organizational structure that has the right grouping of divisions and functions, and an effective chain of command, but it will work as designed *only* if managers also establish control systems that motivate and shape employee behavior in ways that *match* this structure.[23] Output control is one method of motivating employees; behavior control is another method. This section examines three mechanisms of behavior control that managers can use to keep subordinates on track and make organizational structures work as they are designed to work: direct supervision, management by objectives, and rules and standard operating procedures (see Figure 11.3).

Direct Supervision

The most immediate and potent form of behavior control is direct supervision by managers who actively monitor and observe the behavior of their subordinates, teach subordinates the behaviors that are appropriate and inappropriate, and intervene to take corrective action as needed. Moreover, when managers personally supervise subordinates, they lead by example and in this way can help subordinates develop and increase their own skill levels. (Leadership is the subject of Chapter 14.)

Direct supervision allows managers at all levels to become personally involved with their subordinates and allows them to mentor subordinates and develop their management skills. Thus, control through personal supervision can be a very effective way of motivating employees and promoting behaviors that increase efficiency and effectiveness.[24]

Nevertheless, certain problems are associated with direct supervision. First, it is very expensive because a manager can personally manage only a relatively small number of subordinates effectively. Therefore, if direct supervision is the main kind of control being used in an organization, a lot of managers will be needed and costs will increase. For this reason, output control is usually preferred to behavior control; indeed, output control tends to be the first type of control that managers at all levels use to evaluate performance. Second, direct supervision can *demotivate* subordinates. This occurs if employees feel that they are under such close scrutiny that they are not free to make their own decisions or if they feel that they are not being evaluated in an accurate and impartial way. Team members and other employees may start to pass the buck, avoid responsibility, and cease to cooperate with other team members if they feel that their manager is not accurately evaluating their performance and is favoring some people over others.

Third, as noted previously, for many jobs personal control through direct supervision is simply not feasible. The more complex a job is, the more difficult it is for a manager to evaluate how well a subordinate is performing. The performance of divisional and functional managers, for example, can be evaluated only over relatively long time periods (which is why an output control system is developed) so it makes little sense for top managers to continually monitor their performance. However, managers can still work to communicate the organization's mission and goals to their subordinates and reinforce the values and norms in the organization's culture through their own personal style.

Management by Objectives

management by objectives (MBO) A goal-setting process in which a manager and each of his or her subordinates negotiate specific goals and objectives for the subordinate to achieve and then periodically evaluate the extent to which the subordinate is achieving those goals.

To provide a framework within which to evaluate subordinates' behavior and, in particular, to allow managers to monitor progress toward achieving goals, many organizations implement some version of management by objectives. **Management by objectives (MBO)** is a formal system of evaluating subordinates on their ability to achieve specific organizational goals or performance standards and to meet operating budgets.[25] Most organizations use some form of MBO system because it is pointless to establish goals and then fail to evaluate whether or not they are being achieved. Management by objectives involves three specific steps:

- Step 1: *Specific goals and objectives are established at each level of the organization.*

MBO starts when top managers establish overall organizational objectives, such as specific financial performance goals or targets. Then objective setting cascades down throughout the organization as managers at the divisional and functional levels set their goals to achieve corporate objectives.[26] Finally, first-level managers and employees jointly set goals that will contribute to achieving functional objectives.

- Step 2: *Managers and their subordinates together determine the subordinates' goals.*

An important characteristic of management by objectives is its participatory nature. Managers at every level sit down with each of the subordinate managers who report directly to them, and together they determine appropriate and feasible goals for the subordinate and bargain over the budget that the subordinate will need to achieve his or her goals. The participation of subordinates in the objective-setting process is a way of strengthening their commitment to achieving their goals and meeting their budgets.[27] Another reason why it is so important for subordinates (both individuals and teams) to participate in goal setting is that doing so enables them to tell managers what they think they can realistically achieve.[28]

- Step 3: *Managers and their subordinates periodically review the subordinates' progress toward meeting goals.*

Once specific objectives have been agreed on for managers at each level, managers are accountable for meeting those objectives. Periodically, they sit down with their subordinates to evaluate their progress. Normally, salary raises and promotions are linked to the goal-setting process, and managers who achieve their goals receive greater rewards than those who fall short. (The issue of how to design reward systems to motivate managers and other organizational employees is discussed in Chapter 13.)

In the companies that have decentralized responsibility for the production of goods and services to empowered teams and cross-functional teams, management by objectives works somewhat differently. Managers ask each team to develop a set of goals and performance targets that the team hopes to achieve—goals that are consistent with organizational objectives. Managers then negotiate with each team to establish its final goals and the budget the team will need to achieve them. The reward system is linked to team performance, not to the performance of any one team member.

Cypress Semiconductor offers an interesting example of how IT can be used to manage the MBO process quickly and effectively. In the fast-moving semiconductor business a premium is placed on organizational adaptability. At Cypress, CEO T. J. Rodgers was facing a problem: How could he control his growing, 1,500-employee organization without developing a bureaucratic management hierarchy? Rodgers believed that a tall hierarchy hinders the ability of an organization to adapt to changing conditions. He was committed to maintaining a flat and decentralized organizational structure with a minimum of management layers. At the same time, he needed to control his employees to ensure that they perform in a manner consistent with the goals of the company.[29] How could he achieve this without resorting to direct supervision and the lengthy management hierarchy that it implies?

To solve this problem, Rodgers implemented an online information system through which he can monitor what every employee and team is doing in his fast-moving and decentralized organization. Each employee maintains a list of 10 to 15 goals, such as "Meet with marketing for new product launch" or "Make sure to check with customer X." Noted next to each goal are when it was agreed upon, when it is due to be finished, and whether it has been finished. All of this information is stored on a central computer. Rodgers claims that he can review the goals of all employees in about four hours and that he does so each week.[30] How is this possible? He *manages by exception* and looks only for employees who are falling behind. He then calls them, not to scold but to ask whether there is anything he can do to help them get the job done. It takes only about half an hour each week for employees to review and update their lists. This system allows Rodgers to exercise control over his organization without resorting to the expensive layers of a management hierarchy and direct supervision.

MBO does not always work out as planned, however. Managers and their subordinates at all levels must believe that performance evaluations are accurate and fair. Any suggestion that personal biases and political objectives play a part in the evaluation process can lower or even destroy MBO's effectiveness as a control system. This is why many organizations work so hard to protect the integrity of their systems. Jack Welsh, the former CEO of GE, was well known for his support of objective performance appraisal. Indeed, he systematically fired GE managers who worked the system to their own advantage and "smiled up but kicked down" to further their own goals at the expense of GE's. Currently, Ford is working hard to change the way its evaluation system is working and correct the biases and errors that can creep into any control system over time. Microsoft also has experienced problems with its performance evaluation system as the following "Management Insight" suggests.

Microsoft Has Problems Controlling and Evaluating Its Employees

Management Insight

From the beginning Microsoft organized its software engineers into small work groups and teams so that team members could cooperate, learning from and helping each other, and so speed the development of innovative software. Each team works on a subset of the thousands of programs that together make up its Windows operating system and applications software, which is loaded on over 90% of PCs today.[31] In the past, much of Microsoft's reward system was based on team performance; employees of successful teams that quickly developed innovative software received valuable stock options and other benefits. Microsoft's team-based reward system encouraged team members to work together intensively and cooperate to meet team goals. At the same time, the contributions of exceptional team members were recognized; these individuals received rewards such as promotion to become the managers or leaders of new teams as the company grew.

In 2006, however, Microsoft ran into serious problems with the development of Vista, its newest operating system. Vista had been scheduled to come out in the summer of 2006, but unforeseen delays had put the project six months behind schedule, delaying the planned launch until spring 2007. Many analysts blamed the delay on Microsoft's new performance evaluation system, which, because it is now primarily based on individual performance contributions, is hurting team performance. As Microsoft grew over time (it now employs over 60,000 people), it developed a more and more rigid performance evaluation system that became increasingly based on each engineer's individual performance. The manager of each team is expected to rate the performance of each team member on a scale of 2.5, 3.0, and so on to 5, the highest individual performance rating. Microsoft adopted this system to try to increase the perceived fairness of its evaluation system.

Employees still work principally in teams, however, and the new emphasis on individual performance negatively affects the relationships among team members because members are aware that they are in competition for the highest ratings. For example, when confronted with a situation in which they could help other team members but doing so might hurt their own personal performance evaluations, they behave self-interestedly and this hurts overall team performance. Moreover, Microsoft is highly secretive about employees' performance evaluations, current salaries, and raises. Indeed, employees are told *not* to share such information and can get fired if they do.[32] To make matters worse, the way these evaluations are made by team managers is also highly secretive. And employees believe that when the managers of different teams meet together to discuss which teams (as a unit) have achieved the highest level of team performance, these evaluations are distorted by favoritism. Specifically, leaders of the teams who are liked by *their* managers (often because the leaders actively support their managers) receive higher team evaluations than do leaders of teams who are not perceived as supportive by their managers. Because evaluations are biased by personal likes and dislikes, the performance evaluation system is now regarded as being highly political.

Increasingly, engineers and teams perceive they are being evaluated not objectively–by the results achieved–but subjectively, by the ability of an engineer or team leader to "make the right pitch" and curry favor with his or her direct superior. As a result, team members are increasingly pursuing their own interests at the expense of others, and so team performance is declining across the organization.[33] As you can imagine, when team members feel that their personal performance contributions are not being adequately recognized, and that even the performance of different teams is not being judged fairly, many performance problems arise.[34] And one of these problems is that many of Microsoft's best software engineers have left to join rivals such as Google and Yahoo as a result of their failure to achieve the recognition they think they deserved at Microsoft.[35]

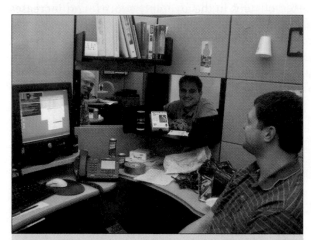

Microsoft employees revamped their work cubicles to allow for greater face-to-face contact and better communication, which improves their ability to cooperate with each other to achieve team goals.

Clearly, when people work in teams, both each member's contribution to the team and each team's contribution to the goals of the organization must be fairly evaluated. This is no easy thing to do. It depends on managers' ability to create an organizational control system that measures performance accurately and fairly and links performance evaluations to rewards so that employees stay motivated and coordinate their activities to achieve the organization's mission and goals. Microsoft's problem was that the changes it made to its control system (new performance evaluation measures) as the company grew hurt its ability to motivate its employees.

Bureaucratic Control

bureaucratic control
Control of behavior by means of a comprehensive system of rules and standard operating procedures.

When direct supervision is too expensive and management by objectives is inappropriate, managers might turn to another mechanism to shape and motivate employee behavior: bureaucratic control. **Bureaucratic control** is control by means of a comprehensive system of rules and standard operating procedures (SOPs) that shapes and regulates the behavior of divisions, functions, and individuals. In Chapter 2, we discussed Weber's theory of bureaucracy and noted that all organizations use bureaucratic rules and procedures but some use them more than others.[36] Recall that rules and SOPs are formal, written instructions that specify a series of actions to be taken to achieve a given end; for example, if *A* happens, then do *B*. A simple set of rules developed by the supervisor of some custodial workers (Crew G) at a Texas A&M University building clearly established task responsibilities and clarified expectations (see Table 11.2).

Rules and SOPs guide behavior and specify what employees are to do when they confront a problem that needs a solution. It is the responsibility of a manager to develop rules that allow employees to perform their activities efficiently and effectively. Rules and SOPs also clarify people's expectations about one another and prevent misunderstandings over responsibility or the use of power. Such guidelines can prevent a supervisor from arbitrarily increasing a subordinate's workload and prevent a subordinate from ignoring tasks that are a legitimate part of the job.

When employees follow the rules that managers have developed, their behavior is *standardized*—actions are performed the same way time and time again—and the outcomes of their work are predictable. And, to the degree that managers can make employees' behavior predictable, there is no need to monitor the outputs of behavior because *standardized behavior leads to standardized outputs,* such as goods and services of the same uniform quality. Suppose a worker at Toyota comes up with a way to attach exhaust pipes that reduces the number of steps in the assembly process and increases efficiency. Always on the lookout for ways to standardize and improve procedures, managers make this idea the basis of a new rule that says, "From now on, the procedure for attaching the exhaust pipe to the car is as follows." If all workers follow the rule to the letter, every car will come off the assembly line with its exhaust pipe attached in the new way and there will be no need to check exhaust pipes at the end of the line.

In practice, mistakes and lapses of attention do happen, so output control is used at the end of the line, and each car's exhaust system is given a routine inspection. However, the number of quality problems with the exhaust system is minimized because the rule (bureaucratic control) is being followed. Service organizations such as retail

Table 11.2
Team Rules of Conduct

---

1. All employees must call their supervisor or leader before 5:55 a.m. to notify of absence or tardiness.

2. Disciplinary action will be issued to any employee who abuses sick leave policy.

3. Disciplinary action will be issued to any employee whose assigned area is not up to custodial standards.

4. If a door is locked when you go in to clean an office, it's your responsibility to lock it back up.

5. Name tags and uniforms must be worn daily.

6. Each employee is responsible for buffing hallways and offices. Hallways must be buffed weekly, offices periodically.

7. All equipment must be put in closets during 9:00 a.m. and 11 a.m. breaks.

8. Do not use the elevator to move trash or equipment from 8:50 to 9:05, 9:50 to 10:05, 11:50 to 12:05, or 1:50 to 2:05, to avoid breaks between classes.

9. Try to mop hallways when students are in classrooms, or mop floors as you go down to each office.

10. Closets must be kept clean, and all equipment must be clean and operative.

11. Each employee is expected to greet building occupants with "Good morning."

12. Always knock before entering offices and conference rooms.

13. Loud talking, profanity, and horseplay will not be tolerated inside buildings.

14. All custodial carts must be kept uniform and cleaned daily.

15. You must have excellent "public relations" with occupants at all times.

Small Business

stores, fast-food restaurants, and home-improvement stores also attempt to standardize employee behavior, for example, customer-service quality, by instructing employees on the correct way to greet customers or the appropriate way to serve and bag food. Employees are trained to follow the rules that have proved to be most effective in a particular situation, and the better trained the employees are, the more standardized is their behavior and the more trust managers can have that outputs (such as food quality) will be consistent. An interesting example of how creating the wrong rules can reduce performance occurred at Gateway, the PC maker, which saw its customer satisfaction rating plummet as a result of its new rules. Managers at Gateway discovered that the reason for rising customer dissatisfaction was a series of new rules the company had instituted to reduce the increasing costs of after-sales service. As Gateway's product line had broadened, the complexity of its customer service procedures had increased. Employees had to have a great deal more information at their disposal to solve customer problems. These problems were often made more serious when customers installed additional software on their computers, which then caused problems with the software already installed on the Gateway machine. It often took customer reps considerable time to iron out the problems, and Gateway was spending millions of dollars in employee time to solve these problems and desired to reduce this cost.

So, Gateway told its service reps to inform customers that if they installed any other software on their machines, this would invalidate Gateway's warranty. This infuriated customers, who asked, why shouldn't they install other necessary software? Gateway also began to reward customer reps on the basis of how quickly they handled customer calls, meaning that the more calls they handled in an hour or day, the higher their bonuses. The joint effect of these changes was that customer reps were now motivated to minimize the length of a service call and, in particular, were unwilling to help solve customer problems that resulted from installation of "outlawed software" since doing so took a lot of time. Obviously, customers resented this treatment. Once Gateway's managers realized the source of the problem they went back to the old system and customer satisfaction soared. As Gateway's managers discovered, to prevent unexpected problems, it is necessary to carefully choose and evaluate the rules and policies used to control employees' behavior.

In contrast to the situation at Gateway, Dave Lilly, an ex-nuclear submarine commander, chose the right rules for siteROCK, whose business is hosting and managing other companies' Web sites to keep them up and running and error-free. A customer's site that goes down or runs haywire is the major enemy. To maximize the performance of his employees and to increase their ability to respond to unexpected online events, Lilly decided that they needed a comprehensive set of rules and SOPs to cover all the major known problems.[37] Lilly insisted that every problem-solving procedure should be written down and recorded. siteROCK's employees developed over 30 thick binders that list all the processes and checklists they need to follow when an unexpected event happens to solve a specific problem. Moreover, again drawing from his military experience, Lilly instituted a "two-man rule": Whenever the unexpected happens, each employee must immediately tell a coworker and the two together should attempt to solve the problem. The goal is simple: Use the rules to achieve a quick resolution of a complex issue. If the existing rules don't work, then employees must experiment; and when they find a solution, the solution is turned into a new rule to be included in the procedures book to aid the future decision making of all employees in the organization.

Problems with Bureaucratic Control

Like all organizations, Gateway and siteROCK make extensive use of bureaucratic control because rules and SOPs effectively control routine organizational activities. With a bureaucratic control system in place, managers can manage by exception and intervene and take corrective action only when necessary. However, managers need to be aware of a number of problems associated with bureaucratic control, because such problems can reduce organizational effectiveness.[38]

First, establishing rules is always easier than discarding them. Organizations tend to become overly bureaucratic over time as managers do everything according to the rule book. If the amount of red tape becomes too great, decision making slows and managers react slowly to changing conditions. This sluggishness can imperil an organization's survival if agile new competitors emerge. Once a siteROCK employee has found a better rule, the old one is discarded.

Second, because rules constrain and standardize behavior and lead people to behave in predictable ways, there is a danger that people become so used to automatically following rules that they stop thinking for themselves. Thus, too much standardization can actually *reduce* the level of learning taking place in an organization and get the organization off track if managers and workers focus on the wrong issues. An organization thrives when its members are constantly thinking of new ways to increase efficiency, quality, and customer responsiveness. By definition, new ideas do not come from blindly following standardized procedures. Similarly, the pursuit of innovation implies a commitment by managers to discover new ways of doing things; innovation, however, is incompatible with the use of extensive bureaucratic control. For example, consider what happened at Walt Disney when Bob Iger became its CEO, as presented in the following "Manager as a Person."

Manager as a Person

Bob Iger's Big Changes at Walt Disney

In 2006, Bob Iger, who had been COO of Disney under its then CEO Michael Eisner, took control of the troubled company. For several years Disney had been plagued by slow decision making, and analysts claimed it had made many mistakes in putting its new strategies into action. Its Disney stores were losing money, for example; its Internet properties were not getting many "hits"; and even its theme parks seemed to have lost their luster as few new rides or attractions had been introduced.

Iger believed that one of the main reasons for Disney's declining performance was that it had become too tall and bureaucratic and its top managers were following financial rules that did not lead to innovative strategies. So, one of Iger's first moves to turn around the performance of the poorly performing company was to dismantle Disney's central strategic planning office. In this office several levels of managers were responsible for sifting through all the new ideas and innovations send up by Disney's different business divisions, such as theme parks, movies, and gaming, and then deciding which ones to present to the CEO. Iger saw the strategic planning office as a bureaucratic bottleneck that actually reduced the number of ideas coming from below. So he dissolved the office and reassigned its managers back to the different business units.[39]

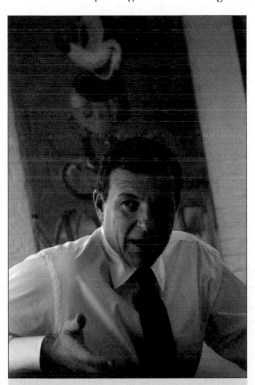

Bob Iger, Disney's CEO since 2006, breathed new life into Disney by removing a layer of management and returning creative power to its employees.

The result of cutting out an unnecessary layer in Disney's hierarchy has been that more new ideas are being generated by its different business units. The level of innovation has increased because managers are more willing to speak out and champion their ideas when they know they are dealing directly with the CEO and a top management team searching for innovative new ways to improve performance—rather than a layer of strategic planning "bureaucrats" only concerned with the bottom line.[40]

Managers must always be sensitive about the way they use bureaucratic control. It is most useful when organizational activities are routine and well understood and when employees are making programmed decisions—for example, in mass-production settings such as Ford or in routine service settings such as stores like Target or Midas Muffler. Bureaucratic control is much less useful in situations where nonprogrammed decisions have to be made and managers have to react quickly to changes in the task environment.

To use output control and behavior control, managers must be able to identify the outcomes they want to achieve and the behaviors they want employees to perform to achieve those outcomes. For many of the most important and significant organizational activities, however, output control and behavior control are inappropriate for several reasons:

- A manager cannot evaluate the performance of workers such as doctors, research scientists, or engineers by observing their behavior on a day-to-day basis.

- Rules and SOPs are of little use in telling a doctor how to respond to an emergency situation or a scientist how to discover something new.

- Output controls such as the amount of time a surgeon takes for each operation or the costs of making a discovery are very crude measures of the quality of performance.

How can managers attempt to control and regulate the behavior of their subordinates when personal supervision is of little use, when rules cannot be developed to tell employees what to do, and when outputs and goals cannot be measured at all or can be measured usefully only over long periods?

Clan Control

clan control The control exerted on individuals and groups in an organization by shared values, norms, standards of behavior, and expectations.

One source of control increasingly being used by organizations is **clan control,** which takes advantage of the power of internalized values and norms to guide and constrain employee attitudes and behavior in ways that increase organizational performance.[41] The first function of a control system is to shape the behavior of organizational members to ensure they are working toward organizational goals and to take corrective action if those goals are not being met. The second function of control, however, is to keep organizational members focused on thinking about what is best for their organization in the future and to keep them looking for new opportunities to use organizational resources to create value. Clan control serves this dual function of keeping organizational members goal-directed while open to new opportunities because it takes advantage of the power of organizational culture, discussed in the previous chapter.

Organizational culture functions as a kind of control system because managers can deliberately try to influence the kind of values and norms that develop in an organization—values and norms that specify appropriate and inappropriate behaviors and so determine the way its members behave.[42] We discussed the sources of organizational culture and the way managers can help create different kinds of cultures in Chapter 9, so there is no need to repeat this discussion here. Instead, the following "Management Insight" describes how one CEO created a very specific kind of company culture, one that survives until this day.

Management Insight

James Casey Creates a Culture for UPS

United Parcel Service (UPS) controls more than three-fourths of the U.S. ground and air parcel service, delivering over 10 million packages a day in its fleet of 150,000 trucks.[43] It is also the most profitable company in its industry. UPS employs over 250,000 people, and since its founding as a bicycle messenger service in 1907 by James E. Casey, UPS has developed a culture that has been a model for competitors such as FedEx and the U.S. Postal Service.

From the beginning, Casey made efficiency and economy the company's driving values and loyalty, humility, discipline, dependability, and intense effort the key norms and standards UPS employees should adopt. UPS has always gone to extraordinary lengths to develop and maintain these values and norms in its workforce.

First, its operating systems from the top of the company down to its trucking operations are the subject of intense scrutiny by the company's 3,000 industrial engineers. These engineers are constantly on the lookout for ways to measure outputs and behaviors to improve efficiency. They time every part of an employee's job. Truck drivers, for example, are instructed in extraordinary detail on how to perform their tasks: They must step from their truck with their right foot first, fold their money face-up, carry packages under their left arm, walk at a pace of 3 feet per second, and slip the key ring holding their truck keys over their third finger.[44] Employees are not allowed to have beards, must be carefully groomed, and are instructed in how to deal with customers. Drivers who perform below average receive visits from training supervisors who accompany them on their delivery routes and instruct them on how to raise their performance level. Not surprisingly, as a result of this intensive training and close behavior control, UPS employees internalize the company's strong norms about the appropriate ways to behave to help the organization achieve its values of economy and efficiency.

Its search to find the best set of output controls leads UPS to constantly develop and introduce the latest in IT into the company's operations, particularly its materials management operations. In fact, today UPS offers a consulting service to other companies in the area of global supply chain management. Its goal is to teach other companies how to pursue its values of efficiency and economy, values that the company has been pursuing for the last hundred years as a result of the values of its founder.

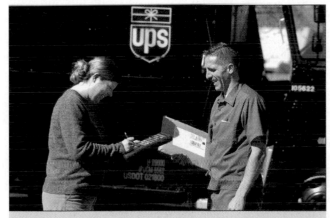

UPS drivers must follow strict guidelines regarding appearance, job performance, and customer interactions.

Organizational Change

organizational change The movement of an organization away from its present state and toward some desired future state to increase its efficiency and effectiveness.

As we have discussed above, many problems can arise if an organization's control systems are not designed correctly. One of these problems is that an organization cannot change or adapt in response to a changing environment unless it has effective control over its activities. Companies can lose this control over time as happened to Ford, which we discussed in the opening case, and too many other organizations such as Home Depot and Microsoft, or they can change in ways that make them more effective, as happened to UPS and Wal-Mart. **Organizational change** is the movement of an organization away from its present state and toward some desired future state to increase its efficiency and effectiveness.

Figure 11.5
Organizational Control and Change

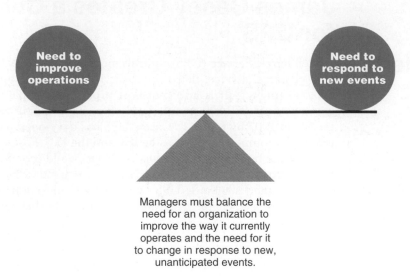

Managers must balance the
need for an organization to
improve the way it currently
operates and the need for it
to change in response to new,
unanticipated events.

LO5 Discuss the
relationship between
organizational control and
change, and explain why
managing change is a vital
management task.

Interestingly enough, there is a fundamental tension or need to balance two oppos-ing forces in the control process that influences the way organizations change. As just noted, organizations and their managers need to be able to control their activities and make their operations routine and predictable. At the same time, however, organi-zations have to be responsive to the need to change, and managers and employees have to "think on their feet" and realize when they need to depart from routines to be responsive to unpredictable events. In other words, even though adopting the right set of output and behavior controls is essential for improving efficiency, because the environment is dynamic and uncertain employees also need to feel that they have the autonomy to depart from routines as necessary to increase effectiveness. (See Figure 11.5.)

It is for this reason that many researchers believe that the highest-performing orga-nizations are those that are constantly changing—and thus become experienced at doing so—in their search to become more efficient and effective. And companies like UPS, Dell, and Home Depot are constantly changing the mix of their activities to move forward even as they are seeking to make their existing operations more effi-cient. For example, UPS entered the air express parcel market, bought a chain of mailbox stores, and began offering a consulting service. At the same time, it has been increasing the efficiency of its ground transport network.

Lewin's Force-Field Theory of Change

Researcher Kurt Lewin developed a theory about organizational change. According to his *force-field theory,* a wide variety of forces arise from the way an organization operates, from its structure, culture, and control systems, that make organizations resistant to change. At the same time, a wide variety of forces arise from changing task and general environments that push organizations toward change. These two sets of forces are always in opposition in an organization.[45] When the forces are evenly balanced, the organization is in a state of inertia and does not change. To get an orga-nization to change, managers must find a way to *increase* the forces for change, *reduce* resistance to change, or do *both* simultaneously. Any of these strategies will overcome inertia and cause an organization to change.

Figure 11.6 illustrates Lewin's theory. An organization at performance level P1 is in balance: Forces for change and resistance to change are equal. Management, however, decides that the organization should strive to achieve performance level P2. To get to level P2, managers must *increase* the forces for change (the increase

Figure 11.6
Lewin's Force-Field Model of Change

is represented by the lengthening of the up-arrows), *reduce* resistance to change (the reduction is represented by the shortening of the down-arrows), or both. If managers pursue any of the three strategies successfully, the organization will change and reach performance level P2. Before we look in more detail at the techniques that managers can use to overcome resistance and facilitate change, we need to look at the types of change they can implement to increase organizational effectiveness.

Evolutionary and Revolutionary Change

Managers continually face choices about how best to respond to the forces for change. There are several types of change that managers can adopt to help their organizations achieve desired future states.[46] In general, types of change fall into two broad categories: evolutionary change and revolutionary change.[47]

evolutionary change
Change that is gradual, incremental, and narrowly focused.

Evolutionary change is gradual, incremental, and narrowly focused. Evolutionary change is not drastic or sudden but, rather, is a constant attempt to improve, adapt, and adjust strategy and structure incrementally to accommodate to changes taking place in the environment.[48] Sociotechnical systems theory and total quality management, or kaizen, are two instruments of evolutionary change. Such improvements might entail utilizing technology in a better way or reorganizing the work process.

Some organizations, however, need to make major changes quickly. Faced with drastic, unexpected changes in the environment (for example, a new technological breakthrough) or with an impending disaster resulting from mismanagement, an organization might need to act quickly and decisively. In this case, revolutionary change is called for.

revolutionary change
Change that is rapid, dramatic, and broadly focused.

Revolutionary change is rapid, dramatic, and broadly focused. Revolutionary change involves a bold attempt to quickly find new ways to be effective. It is likely to result in a radical shift in ways of doing things, new goals, and a new structure for the organization. The process has repercussions at all levels in the organization—corporate, divisional, functional, group, and individual. Reengineering, restructuring, and innovation are three important instruments of revolutionary change.

Managing Change

The need to constantly search for ways to improve efficiency and effectiveness makes it vital that managers develop the skills necessary to manage change effectively. Several experts have proposed a model of change that managers can follow to implement

Figure 11.7

Four Steps in the Organizational Change Process

change successfully, that is, to move an organization away from its present state and toward some desired future state to increase its efficiency and effectiveness.[49] Figure 11.7 outlines the steps in this process. In the rest of this section we examine each one.

ASSESSING THE NEED FOR CHANGE Organizational change can affect practically all aspects of organizational functioning, including organizational structure, culture, strategies, control systems, and groups and teams, as well as the human resource management system and critical organizational processes such as communication, motivation, and leadership. Organizational change can bring alterations in the ways managers carry out the critical tasks of planning, organizing, leading, and controlling and the ways they perform their managerial roles.

Deciding how to change an organization is a complex matter because change disrupts the status quo and poses a threat, prompting employees to resist attempts to alter work relationships and procedures. Organizational learning, the process through which managers try to increase organizational members' abilities to understand and appropriately respond to changing conditions, can be an important impetus for change and can help all members of an organization, including managers, effectively make decisions about needed changes.

Assessing the need for change calls for two important activities: recognizing that there is a problem and identifying its source. Sometimes the need for change is obvious, such as when an organization's performance is suffering. Often, however, managers have trouble determining that something is going wrong because problems develop gradually; organizational performance may slip for a number of years before a problem becomes obvious. Thus, during the first step in the change process, managers need to recognize that there is a problem that requires change.

Often the problems that managers detect have produced a gap between desired performance and actual performance. To detect such a gap, managers need to look at performance measures—such as falling market share or profits, rising costs, or employees' failure to meet their established goals or stay within budgets—which indicate whether change is needed. These measures are provided by organizational control systems, discussed earlier in the chapter.

To discover the source of the problem, managers need to look both inside and outside the organization. Outside the organization, they must examine how changes in environmental forces may be creating opportunities and threats that are affecting internal work relationships. Perhaps the emergence of low-cost competitors abroad has led to conflict among different departments that are trying to find new ways to gain a competitive advantage. Managers also need to look within the organization to see whether its structure is causing problems between departments. Perhaps a company does not have integrating mechanisms in place to allow different departments to respond to low-cost competition.

DECIDING ON THE CHANGE TO MAKE Once managers have identified the source of the problem, they must decide what they think the organization's ideal future state would be. In other words, they must decide where they would like their organization to be in the future—what kinds of goods and services it should be making, what its business-level strategy should be, how the organizational structure should be changed, and so on. During this step, managers also must engage in planning how they are going to attain the organization's ideal future state.

This step in the change process also includes identifying obstacles or sources of resistance to change. Managers must analyze the factors that may prevent the company from reaching its ideal future state. Obstacles to change are found at the corporate, divisional, departmental, and individual levels of the organization.

Corporate-level changes in an organization's strategy or structure, even seemingly trivial changes, may significantly affect how divisional and departmental managers behave. Suppose that to compete with low-cost foreign competitors, top managers decide to increase the resources spent on state-of-the-art machinery and reduce the resources spent on marketing or R&D. The power of manufacturing managers would increase, and the power of marketing and R&D managers would fall. This decision would alter the balance of power among departments and might lead to increased conflict as departments start fighting to retain their status in the organization. An organization's present strategy and structure are powerful obstacles to change.

Whether a company's culture is adaptive or inert facilitates or obstructs change. Organizations with entrepreneurial, flexible cultures, such as high-tech companies, are much easier to change than are organizations with more rigid cultures, such as those sometimes found in large, bureaucratic organizations like the military or General Motors.

The same obstacles to change exist at the divisional and departmental levels as well. Division managers may differ in their attitudes toward the changes that top managers propose and, if their interests and power seem threatened, will resist those changes. Managers at all levels usually fight to protect their power and control over resources. Given that departments have different goals and time horizons, they may also react differently to the changes that other managers propose. When top managers are trying to reduce costs, for example, sales managers may resist attempts to cut back on sales expenditures if they believe that problems stem from manufacturing managers' inefficiencies.

At the individual level, too, people are often resistant to change because change brings uncertainty and uncertainty brings stress. For example, individuals may resist the introduction of a new technology because they are uncertain about their abilities to learn it and effectively use it.

These obstacles make organizational change a slow process. Managers must recognize the potential obstacles to change and take them into consideration. Some obstacles can be overcome by improving communication so that all organizational members are aware of the need for change and of the nature of the changes being made. Empowering employees and inviting them to participate in the planning for change also can help overcome resistance and allay employees' fears. In addition, managers can sometimes overcome resistance by emphasizing group or shared goals such as increased organizational efficiency and effectiveness. In Ford's case, the company's declining performance made many of its managers who had previously resisted change realize that the change was ultimately in everyone's best interests because it would increase organizational performance. However, many of its managers did leave the company because they didn't like its new culture and operating system. The larger and more complex an organization is, the more complex is the change process.

top-down change A fast, revolutionary approach to change in which top managers identify what needs to be changed and then move quickly to implement the changes throughout the organization.

IMPLEMENTING THE CHANGE Generally, managers implement—that is, introduce and manage—change from the top down or from the bottom up.[50] **Top-down change** is implemented quickly: Top managers identify the need for change, decide what to do, and then move quickly to implement the changes throughout the organization. For example, top managers may decide to restructure and downsize the organization and then give divisional and departmental managers specific goals to achieve. With top-down change, the emphasis is on making the changes quickly and dealing with problems as they arise; it is revolutionary in nature, such as the change that took place at Ford and Pfizer.

Bottom-up change is typically more gradual or evolutionary. Top managers consult with middle and first-line managers about the need for change. Then, over time, managers at all levels work to develop a detailed plan for change. A major advantage of bottom-up change is that it can co-opt resistance to change from employees. Because the emphasis in bottom-up change is on participation and on keeping people informed about what is going on, uncertainty and resistance are minimized. Pfizer's new chief of research did not have the luxury of adopting an evolutionary approach; he had to take swift action to turn around the company, as the following "Manager as a Person" describes.

bottom-up change
A gradual or evolutionary approach to change in which managers at all levels work together to develop a detailed plan for change.

Manager as a Person

Pfizer's Big Push to Create Blockbuster Drugs

Pfizer is the largest global pharmaceuticals company with sales of almost $50 billion in 2007. In the past, Pfizer's researchers have innovated some of the most successful and profitable drugs in the market, such as its leading cholesterol reducer Lipitor that earns $13 billion a year. In the 2000s, however, it has run into major roadblocks in innovating new blockbuster drugs. Although many of the drugs in its new product development seemed to be winners, when Pfizer's scientists tested them on groups of people they failed to work as planned; this was a major crisis for Pfizer. With no new drugs in its pipeline, and with blockbusters like Lipitor due to lose their patent protection in a few years, Pfizer desperately needed to find ways to make its product development pipeline work. And one manager, Martin Mackay, believed he knew how to do it.

In October 2007 Pfizer's long time R&D chief retired, and Mackay, his deputy, made it clear to CEO Jeffrey Kindler that he wanted the job. Kindler made it equally clear he thought the company could do with some fresh ideas and he began to bring in outsiders to interview for the job. So Mackay acted quickly and created a detailed plan for changing Pfizer's organizational structure and culture that he believed was what the company needed. Kindler reviewed the plan and was so impressed he promoted Mackay to the top R&D position. What was Mackay's plan?

Mackay had watched how Pfizer's organizational structure had become taller and taller over time as a result of huge mergers with pharmaceuticals companies Warner Lambert and Pharmacia. After every merger, with more managers and levels in the hierarchy, there was a much greater need for committees to integrate across all their activities. Mackay felt that too many managers and committees had resulted in Pfizer's R&D function developing a bureaucratic culture, in which scientists had to follow more and more rules and procedures to perform and report on their work. His plan was to change this situation.

Mackay slashed the number of management layers between top managers and scientists from 14 to 7. He then abolished the scores of product development committees that he felt hampered, not helped, the process of transforming innovative ideas into blockbuster drugs. After streamlining the hierarchy of authority, he then focused his efforts on reducing the number of bureaucratic rules scientists had to follow, many of which he thought unnecessary. He and his team examined all the types of reports that scientists were supposed to make to report the results of their work for evaluation. He then proceeded to eliminate every kind of report that he considered superfluous and that merely slowed down the innovation process. For example, scientists had been in the habit of submitting quarterly and monthly reports to executives explaining each drug's progress; Mackay told them to pick which one they wanted to keep and then the other would be eliminated.

So, Mackay's goal is to move the company to more of an organic structure, which as you recall from Chapter 2, is flat, decentralized, and in which teams of scientists can develop the norms and values that encourage a culture of innovation and entrepreneurship. Certainly Pfizer's scientists report that they feel "liberated" by the new structure and the indications in 2008 were that drugs were moving faster along the pipeline. However, new drugs can take seven to eight years from idea stage to the market, so only time will tell. In the meantime, to help it along Mackay is also looking outside the company and forming alliances and codevelopment deals with small drug startup companies to take advantage of opportunities to bring in new outside talent and open up the R&D function to new ideas and approaches. Very often, companies like Pfizer end up taking over these startups and integrating them into their structure, so this is one more avenue he is using to help create a new culture of innovation at the company.

EVALUATING THE CHANGE   The last step in the change process is to evaluate how successful the change effort has been in improving organizational performance.[51] Using measures such as changes in market share, in profits, or in Pfizer's case the ability of its scientists to innovate new drugs, managers compare how well an organization is performing after the change with how well it was performing before. Managers also can use **benchmarking,** comparing their performance on specific dimensions with the performance of high-performing organizations to decide how successful a change effort has been. For example, when Xerox was doing poorly in the 1980s, it benchmarked the efficiency of its distribution operations against that of L.L. Bean, the efficiency of its central computer operations against that of John Deere, and the efficiency of its marketing abilities against that of Procter & Gamble. Those three companies are renowned for their skills in these different areas, and by studying how they performed Xerox was able to dramatically increase its own performance. Benchmarking is a key tool in total quality management, an important change program discussed in Chapter 9.

benchmarking The process of comparing one company's performance on specific dimensions with the performance of other, high-performing organizations.

In summary, organizational control and change are closely linked because organizations operate in environments that are constantly changing and so managers must be alert to the need to change their strategies and structures. High-performing organizations are those whose managers are attuned to the need to continually modify the way they operate and which adopt techniques like empowered work groups and teams, benchmarking, and global outsourcing to remain competitive in a global world.

Summary and Review

WHAT IS ORGANIZATIONAL CONTROL?   Controlling is the process whereby managers monitor and regulate how efficiently and effectively an organization and its members are performing the activities necessary to achieve organizational goals. Controlling is a four-step process: (1) establishing performance standards, (2) measuring actual performance, (3) comparing actual performance against performance standards, and (4) evaluating the results and initiating corrective action if needed.

LO 1, 2

LO3   **OUTPUT CONTROL**   To monitor output or performance, managers choose goals or performance standards that they think will best measure efficiency, quality, innovation, and responsiveness to customers at the corporate, divisional, departmental or functional, and individual levels. The main mechanisms that managers use to monitor output are financial measures of performance, organizational goals, and operating budgets.

LO4 **BEHAVIOR CONTROL** In an attempt to shape behavior and induce employees to work toward achieving organizational goals, managers utilize direct supervision, management by objectives, and bureaucratic control by means of rules and standard operating procedures.

CLAN CONTROL Clan control is the control exerted on individuals and groups by shared values, norms, and prescribed standards of behavior. An organization's culture is deliberately fashioned to put emphasis on the values and norms top managers believe will lead to high performance.

LO5 **ORGANIZATIONAL CHANGE** There is a need to balance two opposing forces in the control process that influences the way organizations change. On the one hand, managers need to be able to control organizational activities and make their operations routine and predictable. On the other hand, organizations have to be responsive to the need to change, and managers must understand when they need to depart from routines to be responsive to unpredictable events. The four steps in managing change are (1) assessing the need for change, (2) deciding on the changes to make, (3) implementing change, and (4) evaluating the results of change.

Management in Action

Topics for Discussion and Action

DISCUSSION

1. What is the relationship between organizing and controlling? **[LO 1]**

2. How do output control and behavior control differ? **[LO 2, 3]**

3. Why is it important for managers to involve subordinates in the control process? **[LO 3, 4]**

4. What kind of controls would you expect to find most used in (a) a hospital, (b) the Navy, (c) a city police force? Why? **[LO 2, 3, 4]**

5. What are the main obstacles to organizational change? What techniques can managers use to overcome these obstacles? **[LO 1, 5]**

ACTION

6. Ask a manager to list the main performance measures that he or she uses to evaluate how well the organization is achieving its goals. **[LO 1, 3, 4]**

7. Ask the same or a different manager to list the main forms of output control and behavior control that he or she uses to monitor and evaluate employee behavior. **[LO 3, 4]**

Building Management Skills
Understanding Controlling [LO 1, 3, 4]

For this exercise you will analyze the control systems used by a real organization such as a department store, restaurant, hospital, police department, or small business. It can be the organization that you investigated in Chapter 10 or a different one. Your objective is to uncover all the different ways in which managers monitor and evaluate the performance of the organization and employees.

1. At what levels does control take place in this organization?

2. Which output performance standards (such as financial measures and organizational goals) do managers use most often to evaluate performance at each level?

3. Does the organization have a management-by-objectives system in place? If it does, describe it. If it does not, speculate about why not.

4. How important is behavior control in this organization? For example, how much of managers' time is spent directly supervising employees? How formalized is the organization? Do employees receive a book of rules to instruct them about how to perform their jobs?

5. What kind of culture does the organization have? What are the values and norms? What effect does the organizational culture have on the way employees behave or treat customers?

6. Based on this analysis, do you think there is a fit between the organization's control systems and its culture? What is the nature of this fit? How could it be improved?

Managing Ethically [LO 1, 5]

Some managers and organizations go to great lengths to monitor their employees' behavior, and they keep extensive records about employees' behavior and performance. Some organizations also seem to possess norms and values that cause their employees to behave in certain ways.

Questions

1. Either by yourself or in a group, think about the ethical implications of organizations' monitoring and collecting information about their employees. What kind of information is it ethical to collect or unethical to collect? Why? Should managers and organizations inform subordinates they are collecting such information?

2. Similarly, some organizations' cultures, like those of Arthur Andersen, the accounting firm, and of Enron, seemed to have developed norms and values that caused their members to behave in unethical ways. When and why does a strong norm that encourages high performance become one that can cause people to act unethically? How can organizations keep their values and norms from becoming "too strong"?

Small Group Breakout Exercise
How Best to Control the Sales Force? [LO 1, 3, 5]

Form groups of three or four people, and appoint one member as the spokesperson who will communicate your findings to the class when called on by the instructor. Then discuss the following scenario.

You are the regional sales managers of an organization that supplies high-quality windows and doors to building supply centers nationwide. Over the last three years, the rate of sales growth has slackened. There is increasing evidence that, to make their jobs easier, salespeople are primarily servicing large customer accounts and ignoring small accounts. In addition, the salespeople are not dealing promptly with customer questions and complaints, and this inattention has resulted in a drop in after-sales service. You have talked about these problems, and you are meeting to design a control system to increase both the amount of sales and the quality of customer service.

1. Design a control system that you think will best motivate salespeople to achieve these goals.

2. What relative importance do you put on (a) output control, (b) behavior control, and (c) organizational culture in this design?

Exploring the World Wide Web [LO 1, 5]

Go to the Web site of Google. Click on pages such as "Jobs at Google" and then on "Life at Google" and also click on "Company Overview" and then "Our Culture." And so on.

1. How would you expect Google's values and norms to affect its employees' behavior?

2. How does Google design its organizational structure and workspace to shape its culture?

You have been asked by your company's CEO to find a way to improve the performance of its teams of Web design and Web hosting specialists and programmers. Each team works on a different aspect of Web site production, and while each is responsible for the quality of its own performance, its performance also depends on how well the other teams perform. Your task is to create a control system that will help to increase the performance of each team separately and facilitate cooperation among the teams. This is necessary because the various projects are interlinked and affect one another just as the different parts of a car must fit together. Since competition in the Web site production market is intense, it is imperative that each Web site is up and running as quickly as possible and incorporates all the latest advances in Web site software technology.

Questions

1. What kind of output controls will best facilitate positive interactions both within the teams and among the teams?

2. What kind of behavior controls will best facilitate positive interactions both within the teams and among the teams?

3. How would you go about helping managers develop a culture to promote high team performance?

BusinessWeek Case in the News [LO 1, 3, 5]

Cracking the Whip at Wyeth

When Robert R. Ruffolo Jr. signed on at Wyeth in 2000, his mandate was simple: shake up the drugmaker's mediocre research and development operation. He has certainly succeeded. One of Ruffolo's first moves as executive vice president for R&D was conducting a top-to-bottom review of Wyeth's pipeline.

Shredding It Up

Since jumping ship at SmithKline Beecham in 2000, the 55-year-old Ruffolo has ripped apart and reassembled Wyeth's $2.7 billion research operation. Among his controversial changes: a series of quotas for how many compounds must be churned out by company scientists. For some of them, having to hit a hard-and-fast number seemed an anathema to the complex and at times serendipitous drug-development process.

But Ruffolo held bonuses hostage to managers' meeting that goal. More recently he began studying industries from aerospace to computer hardware manufacturing in a bid to better manage innovation. But don't expect him to steal from the playbooks of industry rivals. "Until recently, this industry didn't have to focus too much on productivity," he says. "The solutions to our problems aren't going to come from our competitors."

Wyeth's efforts to energize its labs reflect a major challenge in the drug business. In recent years the output from big-pharma R&D has been almost universally disappointing. According to the Tufts Center for the Study of Drug Development, only 58 new drugs were approved by the Food & Drug Administration from 2002 to 2004, down 47% from the peak of 110 from 1996 to 1998. The reasons are myriad, including a wealth of good treatments that are already available for many diseases and increased vigilance from regulators and physicians on safety. But with financial pressures building as more drugs go off-patent and as payers push back against rising drug costs, pharma companies can't afford to battle that problem by simply throwing bigger bucks at research.

That's why Ruffolo, who took over all of Wyeth R&D in mid-2002, is looking for ways to bring greater efficiency to the innovation process. His goal may not be unusual, but his hard-nosed approach to getting there is.

After signing on at Wyeth, Ruffolo followed Wyeth CEO Robert A. Essner's charge to "rattle the cage." Ruffolo moved quickly to instill discipline. With the help of outside consultants, 70 scientists at the company took a hard look at recent projects that had succeeded and failed. They came to a stunning conclusion: Often, drugs with the lowest chance of paying off ended up with the most resources. Why? Scientists continued to plow money and staff into troubled projects in an attempt to rescue them.

So Ruffolo instituted the review process that sent everyone scrambling. Under that system, a value is determined for every project in the pipeline based on a host of factors, including the cost of developing it, the likelihood of success, and expected future sales. That culminates in an annual review that determines which projects move forward, which get put on the back burner, and which are killed. That new rigor made people more willing to terminate troubled projects. That's critical in the drug business since late-stage human trials are so expensive.

Smart Decisions

Brenda Reis, an assistant vice president in Wyeth R&D, had to make one of those tough calls. In 2004 her group was developing a new oral contraceptive. As part of Ruffolo's portfolio-review process they determined what sort of safety and effectiveness they would need from the drug in order to make it a hit.

In late summer of 2004, Reis recalls, the group of 12 people leading the project sat in stunned silence as they digested disappointing data from midstage human testing of the drug. The product was triggering a side effect that would seriously limit its potential. A few weeks later the group recommended the development of the compound be dropped. Her team was given an internal company award for stopping the project—a move that sent a clear signal that the company would reward good decision making.

Ruffolo has set firm targets for how many compounds need to move forward at each stage of the development process. Take discovery scientists, the group that identifies new ways to attack diseases and creates compounds to be passed on to another group for more extensive testing. When Ruffolo came in, that group was moving just four drug candidates out of its labs every year. Ruffolo set the new target at 12—with no increase in resources or head count. The target has been met every year since its 2001 implementation. This year, the bar has been raised to 15.

Too Much Pressure?

Those targets forced big changes in the R&D operation. For one thing, scientists needed to standardize more

of what they did in an effort to move compounds more quickly through their shop. Case in point: At the old Wyeth, researchers could design the early human safety studies—known as Phase I trials—in almost any way they wanted. Under the new regime, researchers pick from four or five standardized formats. That helped cut the time for a Phase I trial from 18 months to six.

The approach has critics. Some former executives say he seemed out of touch with the anxiety his new demands created among scientists. Dr. Philip Frost, chief scientific officer at biotech ImClone Systems, describes Ruffolo as a "bully" at times. Ruffolo doesn't agree with that characterization, but he acknowledges that when it comes to the targets, "I forced it on them."

Critics also argue that Ruffolo went too far in trying to boost output. William J. Weiss, who left Wyeth in early 2004 and is now director of drug evaluation at biotech Cumbre in Dallas, says quotas like those set by Ruffolo can prompt scientists to "overlook problems with some compounds" in order to make their numbers. In fact, Wyeth has seen an increased failure rate for compounds in midstage testing recently. Ruffolo says that this has occurred throughout the industry. Still, even supporters such as C. Richard Lyttle, CEO at pharmaceutical company Radius Health in Cambridge, Mass., point out that those sorts of productivity pressures can also force

people to zero in on the projects that are the safest gambles. Ruffolo says he specifically put fewer controls in at the so-called exploratory phase, when scientists tend to have eureka moments of, say, spotting a new cellular target they want to hit with a drug. "I don't think you can manage creativity," he says. "But I think you can manage the outcome after you have that creative effort."

Has Ruffolo's prescription worked? UBS Investment Research analyst Carl Seiden says Wyeth's pipeline has shown major improvement, with a number of potentially hot-selling products likely to hit in the next few years. Among them: a new antidepressant based on its current blockbuster Effexor and a new schizophrenia treatment.

Questions for Discussion

1. What kinds of control systems tend to be used to measure the performance of R&D scientists?

2. What kind of control system did Ruffolo institute? What are the various parts or measures of the control system he instituted?

3. What are the pros and cons of his system? Does it seem to be working?

Source: Amy Barrett, "Cracking the Whip at Wyeth." Reprinted from the February 6, 2006, issue of *BusinessWeek* by special permission. Copyright © 2006 by The McGraw-Hill Companies, Inc.

BusinessWeek Case in the News [LO 1, 5]

How Failure Breeds Success

Ever heard of Choglit? How about OK Soda or Surge? Long after "New Coke" became nearly synonymous with innovation failure, these products joined Coca-Cola Co.'s graveyard of beverage busts. Given that history, failure hardly seems like a subject CEO E. Neville Isdell would want to trot out in front of investors. But Isdell did just that, deliberately airing the topic at

Coke's annual meeting in April. "You will see some failures," he told the crowd. "As we take more risks, this is something we must accept as part of the regeneration process."

Warning Coke investors that the company might experience some flops is a little like warning Atlantans they might experience afternoon thunderstorms in July. But Isdell thinks it's vital. He wants Coke to take bigger risks, and to do that, he knows he needs to convince employees

and shareholders that he will tolerate the failures that will inevitably result. That's the only way to change Coke's traditionally risk-averse culture. And given the importance of this goal, there's no podium too big for sending the signal.

While few CEOs are as candid about the potential for failure as Isdell, many are wrestling with the same problem, trying to get their organizations to cozy up to the risk-taking that innovation requires. A warning: It's not going to be an easy shift. After years of cost-cutting initiatives and growing job insecurity, most employees don't exactly feel like putting themselves on the line. Add to that the heightened expectations by management on individual performance, and it's easy to see why so many opt to play it safe.

Indeed, for a generation of managers weaned on the rigors of Six Sigma error-elimination programs, embracing failure—gasp!—is close to blasphemy. Stefan H. Thomke, a professor at Harvard Business School and author of *Experimentation Matters,* says that when he talks to business groups, "I try to be provocative and say: 'Failure is not a bad thing.' I always have lots of people staring at me, [thinking] 'Have you lost your mind?' That's O.K. It gets their attention. [Failure] is so important to the experimental process."

That it is. Crucial, in fact. After all, that's why true, breakthrough innovation—an imperative in today's globally competitive world, in which product cycles are shorter than ever—is so extraordinarily hard. It requires well-honed organizations built for efficiency and speed to do what feels unnatural: Explore. Experiment. Foul up, sometimes. Then repeat.

Granted, not all failures are praiseworthy. Some flops are just that: bad ideas. The eVilla, Sony Corp.'s $500 "Internet appliance." The Pontiac Aztek, GM's ugly duckling "crossover" SUV. But intelligent failures—those that happen early and inexpensively and that contribute new insights about your customers—should be more than just tolerable. They should be encouraged. "Figuring out how to master this process of failing fast and failing cheap and fumbling toward success is probably the most important thing companies have to get good at," says Scott Anthony, the managing director at consulting firm Innosight.

Perhaps most important, it means designing ways to measure performance that balance accountability with the freedom to make mistakes. People may fear failure, but they fear the consequences of it even more.

"The performance culture really is in deep conflict with the learning culture," says Paul J. H. Schoemaker, CEO of consulting firm Decision Strategies International Inc. "It's an unusual executive who can balance these."

Some organizations have tried to measure performance in a way that accounts for these opposing pressures. At IBM Research, engineers are evaluated on both one- and three-year time frames. The one-year term determines the bonus, while the three-year period decides rank and salary. The longer frame can help neutralize a year of setbacks. "A three-year evaluation cycle sends an important message to our researchers, demonstrating our commitment to investing in the early, risky stages of innovation," says Armando Garcia, vice president for technical strategy and worldwide operations at IBM Research.

In addition to making sure performance evaluations take a long-term view, managers should also think about celebrating smart failures. (Those who repeat their mistakes, of course, should hardly be rewarded.) Thomas D. Kuczmarski, a Chicago new-product development consultant, even proposes "failure parties" as a way of recognizing that it's part of the creative process. "What most companies do is put a wall around a failure as if it's radioactive," says Kuczmarski. Most companies don't spend enough time and resources looking backward. General Electric Co. (GE) is trying to do just that. The company, which is well-known for sharing best practices across its many units, has recently begun formally discussing failures, too. Last September the company set up a two-hour conference call for managers of eight "imagination breakthroughs" that didn't live up to expectations and were being shelved, or "retired," in GE's parlance. Such discussions can be nerve-racking, especially in companies where failure has traditionally been met with tough consequences. That was the case at GE, which is now three years into the effort spearheaded by Chairman and CEO Jeffrey R. Immelt to make innovation the new

mantra at the $150 billion behemoth.

Some companies have gone even further, taking a comprehensive look at all their previous failures. That was the case at Corning Inc., which found itself teetering on the brink of bankruptcy after the once red-hot market for its optical fiber collapsed during the telecom bust. Following that debacle, then-Corning CEO James R. Houghton asked Joseph A. Miller Jr., executive vice president and chief technology officer, to produce an in-depth review of the company's 150-year history of innovation, documenting both failures and successes.

That's why W.L. Gore & Associates Inc. in Newark, Del., makers of the waterproof fabric Gore-Tex, recognizes outsiders—people within Gore but not on the product development team—who make the call on projects that need to be pulled. When Brad Jones led Gore's Industrial Products Div., which makes sealants and filtration systems, he handed out "Sharp Shooter" trophies to these outside managers when a project was effectively killed. These marksmen, so to speak, freed from the trappings of familiarity, can identify potential snags that the team may have overlooked. "We're effusive in our thanks for that contribution," says Jones. "We ask them to write up what they learned from it, and how we could have made the decision [to kill the project] faster."

A company's reaction in the face of intelligent failures can send tremors or thrills through a culture. If top executives are accepting, people will embrace risk. But if managers react harshly, people will retreat from it.

Questions

1. Why can studying failure help managers to better manage the control process and improve performance?

2. What kind of specific changes in control systems would studying failure lead to?

Source: Jena McGregor, William C. Symonds, Dean Foust, Diane Brady, and Moira Herbst, "How Failure Breeds Success." Reprinted from the July 10, 2006, issue of *BusinessWeek* by special permission. Copyright © 2006 by The McGraw-Hill Companies, Inc.

CHAPTER 12

Human Resource Management

After studying this chapter, you should be able to:

LO1 Explain why strategic human resource management can help an organization gain a competitive advantage.

LO2 Describe the steps managers take to recruit and select organizational members.

LO3 Discuss the training and development options that ensure organizational members can effectively perform their jobs.

LO4 Explain why performance appraisal and feedback is such a crucial activity, and list the choices managers must make in designing effective performance appraisal and feedback procedures.

LO5 Explain the issues managers face in determining levels of pay and benefits.

LO6 Understand the role that labor relations play in the effective management of human resources.

A MANAGER'S CHALLENGE

Treating Employees Well Leads to Satisfied Customers

www.fourseasons.com

How can managers promote high levels of personalized customer service in an industry known for high employee turnover? Four Seasons Hotels and Resorts is one of only 14 companies to be ranked one of the "100 Best Companies to Work For" every year since *Fortune Magazine* started this annual ranking of companies over 10 years ago.[1] Robert Levering and Milton Moscowitz of the Great Place to Work Institute based in San Francisco compile the list based on employee responses to a survey (the "Great Place to Work Survey"). And the Four Seasons often receives other awards and recognition such as being named the "Best Hotel Group Worldwide" by Gallivanter's Guide and dominating *Travel + Leisure's* World's Best Awards Readers' Poll and Condé Nast Traveler Readers' Choice Awards based on customers' responses.[2] In an industry in which annual turnover rates are over 35%, the Four Seasons's is around 18%.[3] Evidently, employees and customers alike are very satisfied with the way they are treated at the Four Seasons. Understanding that the two are causally linked is perhaps the key to the Four Seasons's success. As the Four Seasons's founder, chairman of the board, and CEO, Isadore Sharp suggests, "How you treat your employees is how you expect them to treat the customer."[4]

The Four Seasons was founded by Sharp in 1961 when he opened his first hotel called the Four Seasons Motor Hotel in a less-than-desirable area outside of central downtown Toronto. While his first hotel had 125 inexpensively priced rooms appealing to the individual traveler, his fourth hotel was built to appeal to business travelers and conventions with 1,600 rooms, conference facilities, several restaurants, banquet halls,

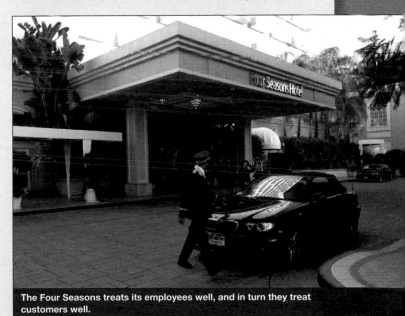

The Four Seasons treats its employees well, and in turn they treat customers well.

and shops in an arcade. While both these hotels were successful, Sharp decided that he could provide customers with a very different kind of hotel experience by trying to combine the best features of both kinds of hotel experiences—the sense of closeness and personal attention that a small hotel brings with the amenities of a big hotel to suit the needs of business travelers.[5]

Sharp sought to provide the kind of personal service that would really help business travelers on the road—providing them with the amenities they have at home and in the office and miss when traveling on business. Thus, the Four Seasons was the first hotel chain to provide bathrobes, shampoo, round-the-clock room service, laundry and dry cleaning services, large desks in every room, two-line phones, and round-the-clock secretarial assistance.[6] While these are relatively concrete ways of personalizing the hotel experience, Sharp realized that the ways in which employees treat customers are just as, or perhaps even more, important. When employees view each customer as an individual with his or her own needs and desires, and empathetically try to meet these needs and desires and help customers both overcome any problems or challenges they face and truly enjoy their hotel experience, a hotel can indeed serve the purposes of a home away from home (and an office away from office) and customers are likely to be both loyal and highly satisfied.[7]

Sharp has always realized that in order for employees to treat customers well, the Four Seasons needs to treat its employees well. Salaries are relatively high at the Four Seasons, by industry standards (i.e., between the 75th and 90th percentile), employees participate in a profit sharing plan, and the company contributes to their 401(k) plans. All employees are provided with free meals in the hotel cafeteria, have access to staff showers and a locker room, and are provided with an additional, highly attractive benefit. Once a new employee has worked for the Four Seasons for six months, he or she can stay for three nights free at any Four Seasons hotel or resort in the world. After a year of employment, this benefit increases to six free nights and it continues to increase as tenure with the company increases. Employees like waitress, Michelle De Rochemont, love this benefit. As she indicates, "You're never treated like just an employee. You're a guest. . . . You come back from those trips on fire. You want to do so much for the guest."[8]

All aspects of human resource management at the Four Seasons are oriented around ensuring that the guiding principle behind all Four Seasons operations is upheld. As Sharp indicates, all employees and managers should ". . . deal with others—partners, customers, coworkers, everyone—as we would want them to deal with us."[9]

All job applicants to the Four Seasons, regardless of level or area, have a minimum of four interviews, one of which is with the general manager of the property.[10] The human resources department interviews many of the applicants because the philosophy at the Four Seasons is that employees need to be helpful and have a positive approach or perspective; the specific requirements for each job can be taught but a helpful, positive attitude is something the Four Seasons looks for potential hires to bring with them to a new job. Given the reputation that the Four Seasons has for treating employees well and providing them with great benefits, it often has many applicants for job openings. For example, before the Doha, Qatar, hotel opened, 25,000 applicants applied for 600 positions that needed to be filled. The Four Seasons devotes so much attention to hiring the right people because of the importance of each and every employee providing a consistently high level of empathetic and responsive customer service.[11]

New hires participate in a three-month training program that includes improvisation activities to help new hires learn how to anticipate guests' needs, requirements, and actions and appropriately respond to them.[12] The aim of training is to help ensure that all employees, regardless of area or function, provide consistently high quality and highly responsive customer service. Since customer service is everyone's responsibility, the Four Seasons has no separate customer

service department per se. Training is an ongoing activity at the Four Seasons and never really stops.[13]

The Four Seasons also tends to promote from within.[14] For example, while recent college graduates may start out as assistant managers, those who do well and have high aspirations could potentially become general managers in less than 15 years. This helps to ensure that managers have empathy and respect for those in lower-level positions as well as the ingrained ethos of treating others (employees, subordinates, coworkers, and customers) the way they would like to be treated themselves. All in all, the ways in which the Four Seasons manages its human resources helps to ensure that customers are treated very well indeed.[15]

Overview

Managers are responsible for acquiring, developing, protecting, and utilizing the resources that an organization needs to be efficient and effective. One of the most important resources in all organizations is human resources—the people involved in the production and distribution of goods and services. Human resources include all members of an organization, ranging from top managers to entry-level employees. Effective managers like Isadore Sharp in "A Manager's Challenge" realize how valuable human resources are and take active steps to make sure that their organizations build and fully utilize their human resources to gain a competitive advantage.

This chapter examines how managers can tailor their human resource management system to their organization's strategy and structure. We discuss in particular the major components of human resource management: recruitment and selection, training and development, performance appraisal, pay and benefits, and labor relations. By the end of this chapter, you will understand the central role human resource management plays in creating a high-performing organization.

LO1 Explain why strategic human resource management can help an organization gain a competitive advantage.

Strategic Human Resource Management

Organizational architecture (see Part 4) is the combination of organizational structure, control systems, culture, and a human resource management system that managers develop to use resources efficiently and effectively. **Human resource management (HRM)** includes all the activities managers engage in to attract and retain employees and to ensure that they perform at a high level and contribute to the accomplishment of organizational goals. These activities make up an organization's human resource management system, which has five major components: recruitment and selection, training and development, performance appraisal and feedback, pay and benefits, and labor relations (see Figure 12.1).

Figure 12.1

Components of a Human Resource Management System

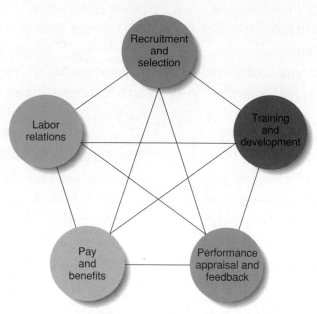

Each component of an HRM system influences
the others, and all five must fit together

**human resource
management
(HRM)** Activities that
managers engage in to attract
and retain employees and
to ensure that they perform
at a high level and contribute
to the accomplishment of
organizational goals.

Strategic human resource management is the process by which managers design the components of an HRM system to be consistent with each other, with other elements of organizational architecture, and with the organization's strategy and goals.[16] The objective of strategic HRM is the development of an HRM system that enhances an organization's efficiency, quality, innovation, and responsiveness to customers—the four building blocks of competitive advantage. At the Four Seasons in "A Manager's Challenge," HRM practices ensure that all employees provide excellent customer service.

As part of strategic human resource management, some managers have adopted "Six Sigma" quality improvement plans. These plans ensure that an organization's products and services are as free of error or defects as possible through a variety of human resource–related initiatives. Jack Welch, former CEO of General Electric Company, has indicated that these initiatives have saved his company millions of dollars, and other companies, such as Whirlpool and Motorola, also have implemented Six Sigma initiatives. In order for such initiatives to be effective, however, top managers have to be committed to Six Sigma, employees must be motivated, and there must be demand for the products or services of the organization in the first place. David Fitzpatrick, head of Deloitte Consulting's Lean Enterprise Practice, estimates that most Six Sigma plans are not effective because the conditions for effective Six Sigma are not in place. For example, if top managers are not committed to the quality initiative, they may not devote the necessary time and resources to make it work and may lose interest in it prematurely.[17]

**strategic human resource
management** The process
by which managers design
the components of an HRM
system to be consistent
with each other, with other
elements of organizational
architecture, and with the
organization's strategy and
goals.

Overview of the Components of HRM

Managers use *recruitment and selection,* the first component of an HRM system, to attract and hire new employees who have the abilities, skills, and experiences that will help an organization achieve its goals. Microsoft Corporation, for example, has the goal of remaining the premier computer software company in the world. To achieve this goal, managers at Microsoft realize the importance of hiring only the best software designers: hundreds of highly qualified candidates are interviewed and rigorously tested. This careful attention to selection has contributed to Microsoft's competitive advantage. Microsoft has little trouble recruiting top programmers because candidates know they will be at the forefront of the industry if they work for Microsoft.[18]

After recruiting and selecting employees, managers use the second component, *training and development,* to ensure that organizational members develop the skills and abilities that will enable them to perform their jobs effectively in the present and the future. Training and development is an ongoing process; changes in technology and the environment, as well as in an organization's goals and strategies, often require that organizational members learn new techniques and ways of working. At Microsoft Corporation, newly hired program designers receive on-the-job training by joining small teams that include experienced employees who serve as mentors or advisers. New recruits learn firsthand from team members how to go about developing computer systems that are responsive to customers' programming needs.[19]

The third component, *performance appraisal and feedback,* serves two different purposes in HRM. First, performance appraisal can provide managers with the information they need to make good human resources decisions—decisions about how to train, motivate, and reward organizational members.[20] Thus, the performance appraisal and feedback component is a kind of *control system* that can be used with management by objectives (discussed in Chapter 10). Second, feedback from performance appraisal serves a developmental purpose for members of an organization. When managers regularly evaluate their subordinates' performance, they can provide employees with valuable information about their strengths and weaknesses and the areas in which they need to concentrate.

On the basis of performance appraisals, managers distribute *pay* to employees, part of the fourth component of an HRM system. By rewarding high-performing organizational members with pay raises, bonuses, and the like, managers increase the likelihood that an organization's most valued human resources are motivated to continue their high levels of contribution to the organization. Moreover, by linking pay to performance, high-performing employees are more likely to stay with the organization, and managers are more likely to fill positions that become open with highly talented individuals. *Benefits* such as health insurance are important outcomes that employees receive by virtue of their membership in an organization.

Last, but not least, *labor relations* encompass the steps that managers take to develop and maintain good working relationships with the labor unions that may represent their employees' interests. For example, an organization's labor relations component can help managers establish safe working conditions and fair labor practices in their offices and plants.

Managers must ensure that all five of these components fit together and complement their company's structure and control systems.[21] For example, if managers decide to decentralize authority and empower employees, they need to invest in training and development to ensure that lower-level employees have the knowledge and expertise they need to make the decisions that top managers would make in a more centralized structure.

Each of the five components of HRM influences the others (see Figure 12.1).[22] The kinds of people that the organization attracts and hires through recruitment and selection, for example, determine (1) the kinds of training and development that are necessary, (2) the way performance is appraised, and (3) the appropriate levels of pay and benefits. Managers at Microsoft ensure that their organization has highly qualified program designers by (1) recruiting and selecting the best candidates, (2) providing new hires with the guidance of experienced team members, (3) appraising program designers' performance in terms of their individual contributions and their team's performance, and (4) basing programmers' pay on individual and team performance.

Effectively managing human resources helps to ensure that both customers and employees are satisfied and loyal, as illustrated in the following "Managing Globally."

Managing Globally

Managing Human Resources at Semco

Ricardo Semler was 21 years old (and one of the youngest graduates from the Harvard Business School MBA program) when he took his father's place as head of the family business, Semco, based in Sao Paolo, Brazil, in 1984.[23] His father, Antonio, had founded Semco in 1954 as a machine shop; the company went on to become a manufacturer of marine pumps for the shipbuilding industry, with $4 million a year in revenues when Ricardo Semler took over. Today, Semco's revenues are over $200 million a year from a diverse set of businesses ranging from industrial machinery, cooling towers, and facility management to environmental consulting and Web-based HRM outsourcing and inventory management services. Semco prides itself on being a premier provider of goods and services in its markets and has very loyal customers.[24]

Semler is the first to admit that Semco's track record of success is due to its human resources—its employees. In fact, Semler so firmly believes in Semco's employees that he and the other top managers are reluctant to tell employees what to do. Semco has no rules, regulations, or organizational charts; hierarchy is eschewed; and workplace democracy rules the day. Employees have levels of autonomy unheard of in other companies, and flexibility and trust are built into every aspect of human resource management at Semco.[25]

Human resource practices at Semco revolve around maximizing the contributions employees make to the company, and this begins by hiring individuals who want, can, and will contribute. Semco strives to ensure that all selection decisions are based on relevant and complete information. Job candidates are first interviewed as a group; the candidates meet many employees, receive a tour of the company, and interact with potential coworkers. This gives Semco a chance to size up candidates in ways more likely to reveal their true natures, and it gives the candidates a chance to learn about Semco. Once finalists are identified from the pool, multiple Semco employees interview each one five or six more times to choose the best person(s) to be hired. The result is that both Semco and new hires make very informed decisions and are mutually committed to making the relation a success.[26]

Once hired, entry-level employees participate in the Lost in Space program, in which they rotate through different positions and units of their own choosing for about a year.[27] In this way, the new hires learn about their options and can decide where their interests lie, and the units they work in learn about the new hires. At the end of the year, the new employees may be offered a job in one of the units in which they worked, or they may seek a position elsewhere in Semco. Seasoned Semco employees are also encouraged to rotate positions and work in different parts of the company to keep them fresh, energized, and motivated and to give them the opportunity to contribute in new ways as their interests change.[28]

Performance is appraised at Semco in terms of results; all employees and managers must demonstrate that they are making valuable contributions and deserve to be "rehired." For example, each manager's performance is anonymously appraised by all of the employees who report to him or her, and the appraisals are made publicly available in Semco. Employees also can choose how they are paid from a combination of 11 different compensation options, ranging from fixed salaries, bonuses, and profit sharing to royalties on sales or profits and arrangements

Ricardo Semler recognizes that Semco's success hinges on its employees.

based on meeting annual self-set goals. Flexibility in compensation promotes risk taking and innovation, according to Semler, and maximizes returns to employees in terms of their pay and to the company in terms of revenues and profitability.[29] Flexibility, autonomy, the ability to change jobs often, and control of working hours and even compensation are some of the ways by which Semler strives to ensure that employees are loyal and involved in their work because they *want* to be; turnover at Semco is less than 1% annually.[30] And with human resource practices geared toward maximizing contributions and performance, Semco is well poised to continue to provide value to its customers.

The Legal Environment of HRM

In the rest of this chapter we focus in detail on the choices managers must make in strategically managing human resources to attain organizational goals and gain a competitive advantage. Effectively managing human resources is a complex undertaking for managers, and we provide an overview of some of the major issues they face. First, however, we need to look at how the legal environment affects human resource management.

The local, state, and national laws and regulations that managers and organizations must abide by add to the complexity of HRM. For example, the U.S. government's commitment to **equal employment opportunity (EEO)** has resulted in the creation and enforcement of a number of laws that managers must abide by. The goal of EEO is to ensure that all citizens have an equal opportunity to obtain employment regardless of their gender, race, country of origin, religion, age, or disabilities. Table 12.1 summarizes some of the major EEO laws affecting HRM. Other laws, such as the Occupational Safety and Health Act of 1970, require that managers ensure that employees are protected from workplace hazards and safety standards are met.

equal employment opportunity (EEO) The equal right of all citizens to the opportunity to obtain employment regardless of their gender, age, race, country of origin, religion, or disabilities.

In Chapter 4, we explained how effectively managing diversity is an ethical and business imperative, and we discussed the many issues surrounding diversity. EEO laws and their enforcement make the effective management of diversity a legal imperative as well. The Equal Employment Opportunity Commission (EEOC) is the division of the Department of Justice that enforces most of the EEO laws and handles discrimination complaints. In addition, the EEOC issues guidelines for managers to follow to ensure that they are abiding by EEO laws. For example, the Uniform Guidelines on Employee Selection Procedures issued by the EEOC (in conjunction with the Departments of Labor and Justice and the Civil Service Commission) provide managers with guidance on how to ensure that the recruitment and selection component of human resource management complies with Title VII of the Civil Rights Act (which prohibits discrimination based on gender, race, color, religion, and national origin).[31]

Contemporary challenges that managers face related to the legal environment include how to eliminate sexual harassment (see Chapter 5 for an in-depth discussion of sexual harassment), how to make accommodations for employees with disabilities, how to deal with employees who have substance abuse problems, and how to manage HIV-positive employees and employees with AIDS.[32] HIV-positive employees are infected with the virus that causes AIDS but may show no AIDS symptoms and may not develop AIDS in the near future. Often, such employees are able to perform their jobs effectively, and managers must take steps to ensure that they are allowed to do so and are not discriminated against in the workplace.[33] Employees with AIDS may or may not be able to perform their jobs effectively, and, once again, managers need to ensure that they are not unfairly discriminated against.[34] Many organizations have instituted AIDS awareness training programs to educate organizational members

Table 12.1

Major Equal Employment Opportunity Laws Affecting HRM

Year	Law	Description
1963	Equal Pay Act	Requires that men and women be paid equally if they are performing equal work
1964	Title VII of the Civil Rights Act	Prohibits discrimination in employment decisions on the basis of race, religion, sex, color, or national origin; covers a wide range of employment decisions, including hiring, firing, pay, promotion, and working conditions
1967	Age Discrimination in Employment Act	Prohibits discrimination against workers over the age of 40 and restricts mandatory retirement
1978	Pregnancy Discrimination Act	Prohibits discrimination against women in employment decisions on the basis of pregnancy, childbirth, and related medical decisions
1990	Americans with Disabilities Act	Prohibits discrimination against individuals with disabilities in employment decisions and requires that employers make accommodations for such workers to enable them to perform their jobs
1991	Civil Rights Act	Prohibits discrimination (as does Title VII) and allows for the awarding of punitive and compensatory damages, in addition to back pay, in cases of intentional discrimination
1993	Family and Medical Leave Act	Requires that employers provide 12 weeks of unpaid leave for medical and family reasons including paternity and illness of a family member

about HIV and AIDS, dispel unfounded myths about how HIV is spread, and ensure that individuals infected with the HIV virus are treated fairly and are able to be productive as long as they can be while not putting others at risk.[35]

> **LO2**   Describe the steps managers take to recruit and select organizational members.

While the Age Discrimination in Employment Act prohibits discrimination against workers over 40, increasing numbers of older workers are finding themselves unemployed with few promising job prospects,[36] as discussed in the following "Focus on Diversity."

Focus on Diversity

Is It Age Discrimination?

There are approximately 77 million Americans classified as baby boomers, born in the post–World War II period of economic posterity between 1946 and 1964.[37] As baby boomers enter their 50s and 60s, some are finding their pre-retirement years to be fraught with anxiety and stress: After working hard to climb the corporate ladder for several decades, they are out of jobs and have few prospects.[38]

Take the case of Bob Miller, a top manager in the insurance and financial services industry, who lost his job at Zurich Financial a few years ago. Miller had a strong résumé, work history, and network of contacts in his field, as well as prior success at landing new jobs; he had been laid off from five positions during his career and always ended up with a new job that was better than the previous one. Not so today. Miller, now in his mid-50s, is still looking for work. And he has company. A member of the Marketing Executives Networking Group (MENG), Miller has realized that many of his 1,300 comembers are in the same boat as he is—former top managers in corporate marketing who can't find a job.[39]

Increasing numbers of older workers are filing age discrimination lawsuits. However, these can be hard to win and sometimes are dismissed by the courts before they even go to trial because of a failure to demonstrate deliberate bias. Occasionally, such cases are settled out of court, such as the case of a 48-year-old business analyst at GE Capital who was laid off seven months after receiving a raise for outstanding performance.[40]

Some older workers who once were at the very top of the corporate hierarchy are now hiring themselves out as temporary workers. Tatum Partners, a white-collar temp agency based in Atlanta, specializes in finding work for former top managers as temporary chief financial officers or chief information officers; the agency has around 400 clients. Sam Horgan, one of Tatum's clients, had changed jobs only once before he was 47; between 47 and 56, he had six different employers; and now, at 57, he finds that full-time employment opportunities have dried up. As he puts it, "If I'm between jobs and I'm getting well into my 50s, I'm a leper with executive recruiters."[41] For Tatum, temporary assignments help pay the bills, provide him with meaningful work that makes use of his skills and experience, and mean that he no longer has to sit through demoralizing job interviews that often seem pointless due to his age.[42]

Ironically, just as age discrimination seems to be on the minds of many an out-of-work baby boomer, some organizations are realizing they will have a shortage of skilled and experienced workers if they don't hold on to valuable employees.[43] There is a shortage of petroleum engineers in the United States (the average age of these employees is 50), and Georgia Pacific is trying to retain older researchers with PhD's by offering them a variety of incentives. Demographer Ken Bychtwald believes that organizations will need to roughly double their employment of older workers in the next 10 years. Bychtwald notes, "The managers trying to move everybody in their 50s out the door are taking their companies off a demographic cliff."[44] Clearly, some older workers who lost their jobs and can't find new ones might feel as if they are off a cliff. And their former employers might face age discrimination lawsuits.

Recruitment and Selection

Recruitment includes all the activities managers engage in to develop a pool of qualified candidates for open positions.[45] **Selection** is the process by which managers determine the relative qualifications of job applicants and their potential for performing well in a particular job. Prior to actually recruiting and selecting employees, managers need to engage in two important activities: human resource planning and job analysis (Figure 12.2).

Figure 12.2
The Recruitment and Selection System

Human Resource Planning

Human resource planning includes all the activities managers engage in to forecast their current and future human resource needs. Current human resources are the employees an organization needs today to provide high-quality goods and services to customers. Future human resource needs are the employees the organization will need at some later date to achieve its longer-term goals.

As part of human resource planning, managers must make both demand forecasts and supply forecasts. *Demand forecasts* estimate the qualifications and numbers of employees an organization will need given its goals and strategies. *Supply forecasts* estimate the availability and qualifications of current employees now and in the future, as well as the supply of qualified workers in the external labor market.

As a result of their human resource planning, managers sometimes decide to **outsource** to fill some of their human resource needs. Instead of recruiting and selecting employees to produce goods and services, managers contract with people who are not members of their organization to produce goods and services. Managers in publishing companies, for example, frequently contract with freelance editors to copyedit books that they intend to publish. Kelly Services is an organization that provides temporary typing, clerical, and secretarial workers to managers who want to use outsourcing to fill some of their human resource requirements in these areas.

Two reasons why human resource planning sometimes leads managers to outsource are flexibility and cost. First, outsourcing can give managers increased flexibility, especially when accurately forecasting human resource needs is difficult, human resource needs fluctuate over time, or finding skilled workers in a particular area is difficult. Second, outsourcing can sometimes allow managers to make use of human resources at a lower *cost*. When work is outsourced, costs can be lower for a number of reasons: The organization does not have to provide benefits to workers; managers are able to contract for work only when the work is needed; and managers do not have to invest in training. Outsourcing can be used for functional activities such as after-sales service on appliances and equipment, legal work, and the management of information systems. Roy Richie, general counsel for the Chrysler Corporation, uses temporary attorneys to write contracts and fill some of his department's human resource needs. As he says, "The math works. . . . Savings can be tremendous."[46]

Outsourcing does have its disadvantages, however.[47] When work is outsourced, managers may lose some control over the quality of goods and services. Also, individuals performing outsourced work may have less knowledge of organizational practices, procedures, and goals and less commitment to an organization than regular employees. In addition, unions resist outsourcing because it has the potential to eliminate some of their members. To gain some of the flexibility and cost savings of outsourcing and avoid some of its disadvantages, a number of organizations, such as Microsoft and IBM, rely on a pool of temporary employees to, for example, debug programs.

A major trend reflecting the increasing globalization of business is the outsourcing of office work, computer programming, and technical jobs from the United States and countries in Western Europe, with high labor costs, to countries like India and China, with low labor costs.[48] For example, computer programmers in India and China earn a fraction of what their U.S. counterparts earn. According to estimates by Gartner Inc., outsourcing (or *offshoring*, as it is also called when work is outsourced to other countries) of information technology and business process work is valued at over $34 billion per year.

As companies gain experience in outsourcing software and technological services, managers are learning what kinds of work can be effectively outsourced and what work should probably not be outsourced. In India, for example, the workforce is highly trained and motivated, and cities like Bangalore are bustling with high-tech jobs and companies like Infosys Technologies, providing software services to companies abroad. Managers who have outsourcing experience have found that outsourcing works best for tasks that can be rule-based, do not require closeness/familiarity with customers and/or the customs and culture of the country in which the company is based, and do not require creativity.[49] When the work requires the recognition and solution of problems rather than the application of preexisting algorithms, creativity in developing solutions, and independent thinking and judgment without the guidance of standard operating procedures, performance might suffer from outsourcing. Essentially, the more complex and uncertain the work and the more it depends on being close to customers and the company itself, the less advantageous outsourcing tends to be.[50]

Nonetheless, there are many kinds of tasks that can be effectively outsourced, and the cost savings for these tasks can be considerable.[51] And some managers believe that many tasks can be effectively outsourced, even those requiring creativity.

General Electric (GE) and McKinsey & Co. are two companies at the forefront of offshoring, seeing it as a way not only to cut costs but to grow (while boosting efficiency).[52] GE Capital first started off with an office in Delhi, India, because the company was having a difficult time filling positions in its growing business of mortgage refinancing. Called GE Capital Investment Services, the office had around 300 employees in the late 1990s. Today, Genpact (a company owned by GE and two private equity firms) has over 20,000 employees, offices in Mexico, Romania, Hungary, India, China, and the United States, and over $490 million in revenues.[53]

McKinsey and GE have such a legacy in offshoring that many current top managers of outsourcing companies were former McKinsey and GE employees. For example, the current president and CEO of Genpact, Pramod Bhasin, was a former GE employee.[54] As another example, Rizwan Koita, a former employee of McKinsey in London and New Delhi, has gone on to found two outsourcing companies, TransWork Information Services Ltd. (recently purchased by AV Birla Group) and Citius Tech. Inc.[55] Additionally, other former employees of GE and McKinsey have used their knowledge and experience of outsourcing in subsequent positions in other organizations.[56]

Job Analysis

job analysis Identifying the tasks, duties, and responsibilities that make up a job and the knowledge, skills, and abilities needed to perform the job.

Job analysis is a second important activity that managers need to undertake prior to recruitment and selection.[57] **Job analysis** is the process of identifying (1) the tasks, duties, and responsibilities that make up a job (the *job description*) and (2) the knowledge, skills, and abilities needed to perform the job (the *job specifications*).[58] For each job in an organization, a job analysis needs to be done.

A job analysis can be done in a number of ways, including observing current employees as they perform the job or interviewing them. Often, managers rely on questionnaires compiled by jobholders and their managers. The questionnaires ask about the skills and abilities needed to perform the job, job tasks and the amount of time spent on them, responsibilities, supervisory activities, equipment used, reports prepared, and decisions made.[59] The Position Analysis Questionnaire (PAQ) is a comprehensive standardized questionnaire that many managers rely on to conduct job analyses.[60] It focuses on behaviors jobholders perform, working conditions, and job characteristics and can be used for a variety of jobs.[61] The PAQ contains 194 items organized into six divisions: (1) information input (where and how the jobholder acquires information to perform the job), (2) mental processes (reasoning, decision making, planning, and information processing activities that are part of the job), (3) work output (physical activities performed on the job and machines and devices used), (4) relationships with others (interactions with other people that are necessary to perform the job), (5) job context (the physical and social environment of the job), and (6) other job characteristics (such as work pace).[62] A trend, in some organizations, is toward more flexible jobs in which tasks and responsibilities change and cannot be clearly specified in advance. For these kinds of jobs, job analysis focuses more on determining the skills and knowledge workers need to be effective and less on specific duties.

After managers have completed human resource planning and job analyses for all jobs in an organization, they will know their human resource needs and the jobs they need to fill. They will also know the knowledge, skills, and abilities that potential employees need to perform those jobs. At this point, recruitment and selection can begin.

External and Internal Recruitment

As noted earlier, recruitment is what managers do to develop a pool of qualified candidates for open positions.[63] They traditionally have used two main types of recruiting: external and internal, which is now supplemented by recruiting over the Internet.

EXTERNAL RECRUITING When managers recruit externally to fill open positions, they look outside the organization for people who have not worked for the organization previously. There are multiple means through which managers can recruit externally: advertisements in newspapers and magazines, open houses for students and career counselors at high schools and colleges or on-site at the organization, career fairs at colleges, and recruitment meetings with groups in the local community.

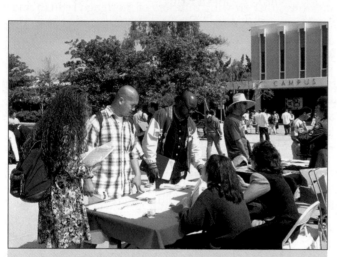

Many colleges and universities hold job fairs to connect employers with students looking for jobs.

Many large organizations send teams of interviewers to college campuses to recruit new employees. External recruitment can also take place through informal networks, as occurs when current employees inform friends about open positions in their companies or recommend people they know to fill vacant spots. Some organizations use employment agencies for external recruitment, and some external recruitment takes place simply through walk-ins—job hunters coming to an organization and inquiring about employment possibilities.

With all the downsizings and corporate layoffs that have taken place in recent years, you might think that external recruiting would be a relatively easy task for managers. However, it often is not, because even though many people may be looking for jobs, many of the jobs that are opening up require skills and abilities that these job hunters do not have. Managers needing to fill vacant positions and job hunters seeking employment opportunities are increasingly relying on the Internet to make connections with each other through employment Web sites such as Monster.com[64] and Jobline International. Jobline is Europe's largest electronic recruiting site, with operations in 12 countries.[65] Major corporations such as Coca-Cola, Cisco, Ernst & Young, Canon, and Telia have relied on Jobline to fill global positions.[66]

External recruiting has both advantages and disadvantages for managers. Advantages include having access to a potentially large applicant pool, being able to attract people who have the skills, knowledge, and abilities that an organization needs to achieve its goals, and being able to bring in newcomers who may have a fresh approach to problems and be up to date on the latest technology. These advantages have to be weighed against the disadvantages, including the relatively high costs of external recruitment. Employees recruited externally also lack knowledge about the inner workings of the organization and may need to receive more training than those recruited internally. Finally, when employees are recruited externally, there is always uncertainty concerning whether they will actually be good performers. Nonetheless, there are steps managers can take to reduce some of the uncertainty surrounding external recruitment, as profiled in the following "Information Technology Byte."

Fog Creek Software's Approach to Recruiting

Fog Creek Software is a small, privately owned software company founded in 2000 by Joel Spolsky and Michael Pryor in a renovated loft in the Fashion District of New York City.[67] Fog Creek has earned a profit and doubled in size each year since its founding.[68] Hiring great computer software developers is essential for a company like Fog Creek; according to Spolsky, the top 1% of software developers outperform average developers by a ratio of around 10:1. And the top 1% are the inventive types who can successfully develop new products while also being highly efficient.[69]

Finding, never mind recruiting, the top 1% is a real challenge for a small company like Fog Creek since many of these people already have great jobs and are not looking to switch employers. Realizing that the top 1% of developers might rarely apply for positions with Fog Creek (or any other company), over 50% of Fog Creek's developers were first recruited for a paid summer internship while still in college and then hired on full-time upon graduation.[70]

In the fall of every year, Spolsky sends personalized letters to computer science majors across the country who have the potential to be top developers in the future, contacts professors at leading computer science programs for recommendations, and also seeks applications through his blog.[71] This process yields hundreds of applicants for internships, the best of whom are then given a phone interview. During the interview, the candidates describe themselves and their classes, are asked how they would go about solving a software development problem or challenge, and then can ask Spolsky anything they want about the company or living in New York City.[72]

Those who do well in the phone interview are then flown to New York for an all-expense paid visit to Fog Creek—they are met at the airport in a limousine, stay in a hip hotel, receive welcoming gifts in their room, have a full day of interviews at Fog Creek, and then are given the option of staying 2 extra nights (at no cost to themselves) to get a feel for New York City. Typically, only one out of every three recruits who have an on-site visit receives an internship offer.[73]

Interns perform real software development work—several summers ago, a team of four interns developed a new successful technology support product called Fog Creek Copilot.[74] This is both motivating for the interns and also helps managers decide which interns they would like to offer full-time jobs to upon graduation. The interns are also treated very well—in addition to being paid, they receive free housing and are invited to outings, parties, and cultural events in New York City. At the conclusion of the internship, managers have a good sense of which interns are great programmers. These top programmers are offered jobs upon graduation with generous salaries, excellent working conditions, and great benefits. While Fog Creek's approach to external recruitment is somewhat lengthy and expensive, it more than pays for itself in terms of identifying and attracting top programmers. As Spolsky indicates, "An internship program creates a pipeline for great employees. It's a pretty long pipeline, so you need to have a long-term perspective, but it pays off in spades."[75]

Fog Creek Software uses paid summer internships to help identify and attract promising software developers.

INTERNAL RECRUITING   When recruiting is internal, managers turn to existing employees to fill open positions. Employees recruited internally are either seeking **lateral moves** (job changes that entail no major changes in responsibility or authority levels) or promotions. Internal recruiting has several advantages. First, internal applicants are already familiar with the organization (including its goals, structure, culture, rules, and norms). Second, managers already know the candidates; they have considerable information about their skills and abilities and actual behavior on the job. Third, internal recruiting can help boost levels of employee motivation and morale, both for the employee who gets the job and for other workers. Those who are not seeking a promotion or who may not be ready for one can see that promotion is a possibility in the future; or a lateral move can alleviate boredom once a job has been fully mastered and can also be a useful way to learn new skills. Finally, internal recruiting is normally less time-consuming and expensive than external recruiting.

Given the advantages of internal recruiting, why do managers rely on external recruiting as much as they do? The answer lies in the disadvantages of internal recruiting— among them, a limited pool of candidates and a tendency among those candidates to be set in the organization's ways. Often, the organization simply does not have suitable internal candidates. Sometimes, even when suitable internal applicants are available, managers may rely on external recruiting to find the very best candidate or to help bring new ideas and approaches into their organization. When organizations are in trouble and performing poorly, external recruiting is often relied on to bring in managerial talent with a fresh approach.

HONESTY IN RECRUITING   At times, when trying to recruit the most qualified applicants, managers may be tempted to paint overly rosy pictures of both the open positions and the organization as a whole. They may worry that if they are totally honest about advantages and disadvantages, they either will not be able to fill positions or will have fewer or less qualified applicants. A manager trying to fill a secretarial position, for example, may emphasize the high level of pay and benefits the job offers and fail to mention the fact that the position is usually a dead-end job offering few opportunities for promotion.

Research suggests that painting an overly rosy picture of a job and the organization is not a wise recruiting strategy. Recruitment is more likely to be effective when managers provide potential applicants with an honest assessment of both the advantages and the disadvantages of the job and organization. Such an assessment is called a **realistic job preview (RJP)**.[76] RJPs can reduce the number of new hires who quit when their jobs and organizations fail to meet their unrealistic expectations, and they help applicants decide for themselves whether the job is right for them.

Take the earlier example of the manager trying to recruit a secretary. The manager who paints a rosy picture of the job might have an easy time filling it but might end up with a secretary who expects to be promoted quickly to an administrative assistant position. After a few weeks on the job, the secretary may realize that a promotion is highly unlikely no matter how good his or her performance, become dissatisfied, and look for and accept another job. The manager then has to recruit, select, and train another new secretary. The manager could have avoided this waste of valuable organizational resources by using a realistic job preview. The RJP would have increased the likelihood of hiring a secretary who was comfortable with few promotional opportunities and subsequently would have been satisfied to remain on the job.

The Selection Process

Once managers develop a pool of applicants for open positions through the recruitment process, they need to find out whether each applicant is qualified for the position and likely to be a good performer. If more than one applicant meets these two conditions, managers must further determine which applicants are likely to be better performers than others. They have several selection tools to help them sort out the

lateral move A job change that entails no major changes in responsibility or authority levels.

realistic job preview (RJP) An honest assessment of the advantages and disadvantages of a job and organization.

Figure 12.3
Selection Tools

relative qualifications of job applicants and appraise their potential for being good performers in a particular job. These tools include background information, interviews, paper-and-pencil tests, physical ability tests, performance tests, and references (see Figure 12.3).[77]

BACKGROUND INFORMATION To aid in the selection process, managers obtain background information from job applications and from résumés. Such information might include the highest levels of education obtained, college majors and minors, type of college or university attended, years and type of work experience, and mastery of foreign languages. Background information can be helpful both to screen out applicants who are lacking key qualifications (such as a college degree) and to determine which qualified applicants are more promising than others. For example, applicants with a BS may be acceptable, but those who also have an MBA are preferable.

Increasing numbers of organizations are performing background checks to verify that the background information prospective employees provide is accurate (and also to uncover any negative information such as crime convictions).[78] According to ADP Employer Services, an outsourcing company that performs payroll and human resource functions for organizations, more and more companies are performing background checks on prospective employees and are uncovering inaccuracies, inconsistencies, and negative information such as prior convictions or driving violations.[79] According to a recent survey ADP conducted, about half of all background checks turn up an inconsistency between the education and credentials applicants list and the information other sources provide (e.g., universities or prior employers). And in some cases, background checks reveal convictions and driving violations.[80]

INTERVIEWS Virtually all organizations use interviews during the selection process, as is true at the Four Seasons in "A Manager's Challenge." Interviews may be structured or unstructured. In *a structured interview,* managers ask each applicant the same standard questions (e.g., "What are your unique qualifications for this position?" and "What characteristics of a job are most important to you?"). Particularly informative questions may be those that prompt an interviewee to demonstrate skills and abilities needed for the job by answering the question. Sometimes called *situational interview questions,* these often present interviewees with a scenario that they would likely encounter on the job and ask them to indicate how they would handle it.[81] For example, applicants for a sales job may be asked to indicate how they would respond to a customer who complains about waiting too long for service, a customer who is indecisive, and a customer whose order is lost.

An *unstructured interview* proceeds more like an ordinary conversation. The interviewer feels free to ask probing questions to discover what the applicant is like and does not ask a fixed set of questions determined in advance. In general, structured interviews are superior to unstructured interviews because they are more likely to yield information that will help identify qualified candidates, are less subjective, and may be less influenced by the interviewer's biases.

Even when structured interviews are used, however, the potential exists for the interviewer's biases to influence his or her judgment. Recall from Chapter 5 how the similar-to-me effect can cause people to perceive others who are similar to themselves more positively than those who are different and how stereotypes can result in inaccurate perceptions. Interviewers must be trained to avoid these biases and sources of inaccurate perceptions as much as possible. Many of the approaches to increasing diversity awareness and diversity skills described in Chapter 5 are used to train interviewers to avoid the effects of biases and stereotypes. In addition, using multiple interviewers can be advantageous as their individual biases and idiosyncrasies may cancel one another out.[82]

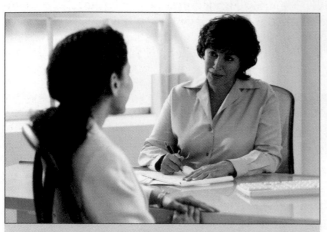

Practically all organizations use some kind of interview during the selection process.

When conducting interviews, managers cannot ask questions that are irrelevant to the job in question; otherwise, their organizations run the risk of costly lawsuits. It is inappropriate and illegal, for example, to inquire about an interviewee's spouse or to ask questions about whether an interviewee plans to have children. Because questions such as these are irrelevant to job performance, they are discriminatory and violate EEO laws (see Table 12.1). Thus, interviewers need to be instructed in EEO laws and informed about questions that may violate those laws.

Managers can use interviews at various stages in the selection process. Some use interviews as initial screening devices; others use them as a final hurdle that applicants must jump. Regardless of when they are used, managers typically use other selection tools in conjunction with interviews because of the potential for bias and for inaccurate assessments of interviewees. Even though training and structured interviews can eliminate the effects of some biases, interviewers can still come to erroneous conclusions about interviewees' qualifications. Interviewees, for example, who make a bad initial impression or are overly nervous in the first minute or two of an interview tend to be judged more harshly than other, less nervous candidates, even if the rest of the interview goes well.

PAPER-AND-PENCIL TESTS The two main kinds of paper-and-pencil tests used for selection purposes are ability tests and personality tests. *Ability tests* assess the extent to which applicants possess the skills necessary for job performance, such as verbal comprehension or numerical skills. Autoworkers hired by General Motors, Chrysler, and Ford, for example, are typically tested for their ability to read and to do mathematics.[83]

Personality tests measure personality traits and characteristics relevant to job performance. Some retail organizations, for example, give job applicants honesty tests to determine how trustworthy they are. The use of personality tests (including honesty tests) for hiring purposes is controversial. Some critics maintain that honesty tests do not really measure honesty (that is, they are not valid) and can be faked by job applicants. Before using any paper-and-pencil tests for selection purposes, managers must have sound evidence that the tests are actually good predictors of performance on the job in question. Managers who use tests without such evidence may be subject to costly discrimination lawsuits.

PHYSICAL ABILITY TESTS For jobs requiring physical abilities, such as firefighting, garbage collecting, and package delivery, managers use physical ability tests that measure physical strength and stamina as selection tools. Autoworkers are typically tested for mechanical dexterity because this physical ability is an important skill for high job performance in many auto plants.[84]

PERFORMANCE TESTS *Performance tests* measure job applicants' performance on actual job tasks. Applicants for secretarial positions, for example, typically are required to complete a keyboarding test that measures how quickly and accurately they type. Applicants for middle- and top-management positions are sometimes given short-term projects to complete—projects that mirror the kinds of situations that arise in the job being filled—to assess their knowledge and problem-solving capabilities.[85]

Assessment centers, first used by AT&T, take performance tests one step further. In a typical assessment center, about 10 to 15 candidates for managerial positions participate in a variety of activities over a few days. During this time they are assessed for the skills an effective manager needs—problem-solving, organizational, communication, and conflict resolution skills. Some of the activities are performed individually; others are performed in groups. Throughout the process, current managers observe the candidates' behavior and measure performance. Summary evaluations are then used as a selection tool.

REFERENCES Applicants for many jobs are required to provide references from former employers or other knowledgeable sources (such as a college instructor or adviser) who know the applicants' skills, abilities, and other personal characteristics. These individuals are asked to provide candid information about the applicant. References are often used at the end of the selection process to confirm a decision to hire. Yet the fact that many former employers are reluctant to provide negative information in references sometimes makes it difficult to interpret what a reference is really saying about an applicant.

In fact, several recent lawsuits filed by applicants who felt that they were unfairly denigrated or had their privacy invaded by unfavorable references from former employers have caused managers to be increasingly wary of providing any negative information in a reference, even if it is accurate. For jobs in which the jobholder is responsible for the safety and lives of other people, however, failing to provide accurate negative information in a reference does not just mean that the wrong person might get hired; it may also mean that other people's lives will be at stake.

THE IMPORTANCE OF RELIABILITY AND VALIDITY Whatever selection tools a manager uses, these tools need to be both reliable and valid. **Reliability** is the degree to which a tool or test measures the same thing each time it is administered. Scores on a selection test should be very similar if the same person is assessed with the same tool on two different days; if there is quite a bit of variability, the tool is unreliable. For interviews, determining reliability is more complex because the dynamic is personal interpretation. That is why the reliability of interviews can be increased if two or more different qualified interviewers interview the same candidate. If the interviews are reliable, the interviewers should come to similar conclusions about the interviewee's qualifications.

Validity is the degree to which a tool measures what it purports to measure—for selection tools, it is the degree to which the test predicts performance on the tasks or job in question. Does a physical ability test used to select firefighters, for example, actually predict on-the-job performance? Do assessment center ratings actually predict managerial performance? Do keyboarding tests predict secretarial performance? These are

reliability The degree to which a tool or test measures the same thing each time it is used.

validity The degree to which a tool or test measures what it purports to measure.

all questions of validity. Honesty tests, for example, are controversial because it is not clear that they validly predict honesty in such jobs as retailing and banking.

Managers have an ethical and legal obligation to use reliable and valid selection tools. Yet reliability and validity are matters of degree rather than all-or-nothing characteristics. Thus, managers should strive to use selection tools in such a way that they can achieve the greatest degree of reliability and validity. For ability tests of a particular skill, managers should keep up to date on the latest advances in the development of valid paper-and-pencil tests and use the test with the highest reliability and validity ratings for their purposes. Regarding interviews, managers can improve reliability by having more than one person interview job candidates.

LO3 Discuss the training and development options that ensure organizational members can effectively perform their jobs.

Training and Development

Training and development help to ensure that organizational members have the knowledge and skills needed to perform jobs effectively, take on new responsibilities, and adapt to changing conditions. **Training** primarily focuses on teaching organizational members how to perform their current jobs and helping them acquire the knowledge and skills they need to be effective performers. **Development** focuses on building the knowledge and skills of organizational members so that they are prepared to take on new responsibilities and challenges. Training tends to be used more frequently at lower levels of an organization; development tends to be used more frequently with professionals and managers.

Before creating training and development programs, managers should perform a **needs assessment** to determine which employees need training or development and what type of skills or knowledge they need to acquire (see Figure 12.4).[86]

training Teaching organizational members how to perform their current jobs and helping them acquire the knowledge and skills they need to be effective performers.

development Building the knowledge and skills of organizational members so that they are prepared to take on new responsibilities and challenges.

Types of Training

There are two types of training: classroom instruction and on-the-job training.

CLASSROOM INSTRUCTION Through classroom instruction, employees acquire knowledge and skills in a classroom setting. This instruction may take place within the organization or outside it, such as courses at local colleges and universities. Many

Figure 12.4
Training and Development

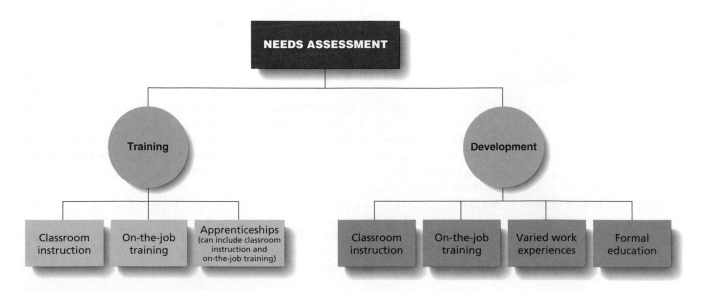

needs assessment
An assessment of which employees need training or development and what type of skills or knowledge they need to acquire.

organizations actually establish their own formal instructional divisions—some are even called "colleges"—to provide needed classroom instruction.

At Ethan Allen Interiors Inc., for example, employees from stores around the country attend Ethan Allen College at company headquarters in Danbury, Connecticut. During classes, employees acquire in-depth knowledge about the company's products and learn how to listen to customers and accurately assess their needs. In addition, the college provides instruction on such diverse topics as floor plans and window treatments. Training at Ethan Allen is an ongoing process. Veteran employees attend two- or three-day sessions at the college to brush up on their skills and keep abreast of the latest developments. M. Farooq Kathwari, chairman and CEO of Ethan Allen, believes that the classroom instruction that employees receive at Ethan Allen College has contributed significantly to his company's competitive advantage.[87]

Classroom instruction frequently includes the use of videos and role playing in addition to traditional written materials, lectures, and group discussions. *Videos* can be used to demonstrate appropriate and inappropriate job behaviors. For example, by watching an experienced salesperson effectively deal with a loud and angry customer in a video clip, inexperienced salespeople can develop skills in handling similar situations. During *role playing,* trainees either directly participate in or watch others perform actual job activities in a simulated setting. At McDonald's Hamburger University, for example, role playing helps franchisees acquire the knowledge and skills they need to manage their restaurants.

Simulations also can be part of classroom instruction, particularly for complicated jobs that require an extensive amount of learning and in which errors carry a high cost. In a simulation, key aspects of the work situation and job tasks are duplicated as closely as possible in an artificial setting. For example, air traffic controllers are trained by simulations because of the complicated nature of the work, the extensive amount of learning involved, and the very high costs of air traffic control errors.

on-the-job training
Training that takes place in the work setting as employees perform their job tasks.

ON-THE-JOB TRAINING   In **on-the-job training,** learning occurs in the work setting as employees perform their job tasks. On-the-job training can be provided by coworkers or supervisors or can occur simply as jobholders gain experience and knowledge from doing the work. Newly hired waiters and waitresses in chains such as Red Lobster or the Olive Garden often receive on-the-job training from experienced employees. The supervisor of a new bus driver for a campus bus system may ride the bus for a week to ensure that the driver has learned the routes and follows safety procedures. Chefs learn to create new and innovative dishes by experimenting with different combinations of ingredients and cooking techniques. For all on-the-job training, employees learn by doing.

Managers often use on-the-job training on a continuing basis to ensure that their subordinates keep up to date with changes in goals, technology, products, or customer needs and desires. For example, sales representatives at Mary Kay Cosmetics Inc. receive ongoing training so that they are not only knowledgeable about new cosmetic products and currently popular colors but also reminded of Mary Kay's guiding principles. Mary Kay's expansion into Russia has been very successful, in part because of the ongoing training that Mary Kay's Russian salespeople receive.[88]

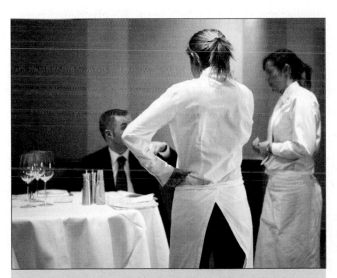
At many restaurants, new employees receive on-the-job training by shadowing more experienced waiters and waitresses as they go about their work.

Types of Development

Although both classroom instruction and on-the-job training can be used for development purposes as well as training, development often includes additional activities such as varied work experiences and formal education.

VARIED WORK EXPERIENCES Top managers need to develop an understanding of, and expertise in, a variety of functions, products and services, and markets. To develop executives who will have this expertise, managers frequently make sure that employees with high potential have a wide variety of different job experiences, some in line positions and some in staff positions. Varied work experiences broaden employees' horizons and help them think more about the big picture. For example, one- to three-year stints overseas are being used increasingly to provide managers with international work experiences. With organizations becoming more global, managers need to develop an understanding of the different values, beliefs, cultures, regions, and ways of doing business in different countries.

Another development approach is mentoring. (Recall from Chapter 5 that a *mentor* is an experienced member of an organization who provides advice and guidance to a less experienced member, called a *protégé*.) Having a mentor can help managers seek out work experiences and assignments that will contribute to their development and can enable them to gain the most possible from varied work experiences.[89] While some mentors and protégés hook up informally, organizations have found that formal mentorship programs can be valuable ways to contribute to the development of managers and all employees.

Formal mentoring programs ensure that mentoring takes place in an organization, structure the process, and make sure that diverse organizational members have equal access to mentors. Participants receive training, efforts are focused on matching up mentors and protégés so that meaningful developmental relationships ensue, and organizations can track reactions and assess the potential benefits of mentoring. Formal mentoring programs can also ensure that diverse members of an organization receive the benefits of mentoring. A study conducted by David A. Thomas, a professor at the Harvard Business School, found that members of racial minority groups at three large corporations who were very successful in their careers had the benefit of mentors. Formal mentorship programs help organizations make this valuable development tool available to all employees.[90]

When diverse members of an organization lack mentors, their progress in the organization and advancement to high-level positions can be hampered. Ida Abott, a lawyer and consultant on work-related issues, recently presented a paper to the Minority Corporate Counsel Association in which she concluded, "The lack of adequate mentoring has held women and minority lawyers back from achieving professional success and has led to high rates of career dissatisfaction and attrition."[91]

Mentoring can benefit all kinds of employees in all kinds of work.[92] John Washko, a manager at the Four Seasons hotel chain, benefited from the mentoring he received from Stan Bromley on interpersonal relations and how to deal with employees; mentor Bromley, in turn, found that participating in the Four Seasons's mentoring program helped him develop his own management style.[93] More generally, development is an ongoing process for all managers, and mentors often find that mentoring contributes to their own personal development.

FORMAL EDUCATION Many large corporations reimburse employees for tuition expenses they incur while taking college courses and obtaining advanced degrees. This is not just benevolence on the part of the employer or even a simple reward given to the employee; it is an effective way to develop employees who are able to take on new responsibilities and more challenging positions. For similar reasons, corporations spend thousands of dollars sending managers to executive development programs such as executive MBA programs. In these programs, experts teach managers the latest in business and management techniques and practices.

To save time and travel costs, managers are increasingly relying on *long-distance learning* to formally educate and develop employees. Using videoconferencing technologies, business schools such as the Harvard Business School, the University of Michigan, and Babson College are teaching courses on video screens in corporate conference rooms. Business schools are also customizing courses and degrees to fit the development needs of employees in a particular company. The University of Michigan uses long-distance learning, for example, to provide instruction for customized MBA degrees for employees of the Daewoo Corporation in Korea and Cathay Pacific Airways Ltd. in Hong Kong. In conjunction with Westcott Communications Inc., eight business schools have formed a new venture, Executive Education Network, to create and operate satellite classrooms in major corporations; almost 100 companies have already signed on, including Eastman Kodak Company, Walt Disney Company, and Texas Instruments.[94]

Transfer of Training and Development

Whenever training and development take place off the job or in a classroom setting, it is vital for managers to promote the transfer of the knowledge and skills acquired *to the actual work situation*. Trainees should be encouraged and expected to use their newfound expertise on the job.

LO4 Explain why performance appraisal and feedback is such a crucial activity, and list the choices managers must make in designing effective performance appraisal and feedback procedures.

Performance Appraisal and Feedback

performance appraisal
The evaluation of employees' job performance and contributions to their organization.

performance feedback
The process through which mangers share performance appraisal information with subordinates, give subordinates an opportunity to reflect on their own performance, and develop, with subordinates, plans for the future.

The recruitment/selection and training/development components of a human resource management system ensure that employees have the knowledge and skills needed to be effective now and in the future. Performance appraisal and feedback complement recruitment, selection, training, and development. **Performance appraisal** is the evaluation of employees' job performance and contributions to the organization. **Performance feedback** is the process through which managers share performance appraisal information with their subordinates, give subordinates an opportunity to reflect on their own performance, and develop, with subordinates, plans for the future. Before performance feedback, performance appraisal must take place. Performance appraisal could take place without providing performance feedback, but wise managers are careful to provide feedback because it can contribute to employee motivation and performance.

Performance appraisal and feedback contribute to the effective management of human resources in several ways. Performance appraisal gives managers important information on which to base human resource decisions.[95] Decisions about pay raises, bonuses, promotions, and job moves all hinge on the accurate appraisal of performance. Performance appraisal can also help managers determine which workers are candidates for training and development and in what areas. Performance feedback encourages high levels of employee motivation and performance. It lets good performers know that their efforts are valued and appreciated. It also lets poor performers know that their lackluster performance needs improvement. Performance feedback can provide both good and poor performers with insight on their strengths and weaknesses and ways in which they can improve their performance in the future.

Types of Performance Appraisal

Performance appraisal focuses on the evaluation of traits, behaviors, and results.[96]

TRAIT APPRAISALS   When trait appraisals are used, managers assess subordinates on personal characteristics that are relevant to job performance, such as skills, abilities, or personality. A factory worker, for example, may be evaluated based on her ability to use computerized equipment and perform numerical calculations. A social worker may be appraised based on his empathy and communication skills.

Three disadvantages of trait appraisals often lead managers to rely on other appraisal methods. First, possessing a certain personal characteristic does not ensure that the personal characteristic will actually be used on the job and result in high performance. For example, a factory worker may possess superior computer and numerical skills but be a poor performer due to low motivation. The second disadvantage of trait appraisals is linked to the first. Because traits do not always show a direct association with performance, workers and courts of law may view them as unfair and potentially discriminatory. The third disadvantage of trait appraisals is that they often do not enable managers to provide employees with feedback that they can use to improve performance. Because trait appraisals focus on relatively enduring human characteristics that change only over the long term, employees can do little to change their behavior in response to performance feedback from a trait appraisal. Telling a social worker that he lacks empathy provides him with little guidance about how to improve his interactions with clients, for example. These disadvantages suggest that managers should use trait appraisals only when they can demonstrate that the assessed traits are accurate and important indicators of job performance.

BEHAVIOR APPRAISALS Through behavior appraisals, managers assess how workers perform their jobs—the actual actions and behaviors that workers exhibit on the job. Whereas trait appraisals assess what workers are *like,* behavior appraisals assess what workers *do.* For example, with a behavior appraisal, a manager might evaluate a social worker on the extent to which he looks clients in the eye when talking with them, expresses sympathy when they are upset, and refers them to community counseling and support groups geared toward the specific problem they are encountering. Behavior appraisals are especially useful when *how* workers perform their jobs is important. In educational organizations such as high schools, for example, the number of classes and students taught is important, but also important is how they are taught or the methods teachers use to ensure that learning takes place.

Behavior appraisals have the advantage of providing employees with clear information about what they are doing right and wrong and how they can improve their performance. And because behaviors are much easier for employees to change than traits, performance feedback from behavior appraisals is more likely to lead to performance improvements.

RESULT APPRAISALS For some jobs, *how* people perform the job is not as important as *what* they accomplish or the results they obtain. With result appraisals, managers appraise performance by the results or the actual outcomes of work behaviors. Take the case of two new-car salespersons. One salesperson strives to develop personal relationships with her customers. She spends hours talking to them and frequently calls them up to see how their decision-making process is going. The other salesperson has a much more hands-off approach. He is very knowledgeable, answers customers' questions, and then waits for them to come to him. Both salespersons sell, on average, the same number of cars, and the customers of both are satisfied with the service they receive, according to postcards that the dealership mails to customers asking for an assessment of their satisfaction. The manager of the dealership appropriately uses result appraisals (sales and customer satisfaction) to evaluate the salespeople's performance because it does not matter which behavior salespeople use to sell cars as long as they sell the desired number and satisfy customers. If one salesperson sells too few cars, however, the manager can give that person performance feedback about his or her low sales.

OBJECTIVE AND SUBJECTIVE APPRAISALS Whether managers appraise performance in terms of traits, behaviors, or results, the information they assess is either *objective* or *subjective.* **Objective appraisals** are based on facts and are likely to be numerical—the number of cars sold, the number of meals prepared, the number of times late, the number of audits completed. Managers often use objective appraisals when results are being appraised because results tend to be easier to quantify than traits or behaviors. When *how* workers perform their jobs is important, however, subjective behavior appraisals are more appropriate than result appraisals.

Subjective appraisals are based on managers' perceptions of traits, behaviors, or results. Because subjective appraisals rest on managers' perceptions, there is always the chance that they are inaccurate (we discuss managerial perception in more detail

objective appraisal
An appraisal that is based on facts and is likely to be numerical.

subjective appraisal
An appraisal that is based on perceptions of traits, behaviors, or results.

Figure 12.5

Subjective Measures of Performance

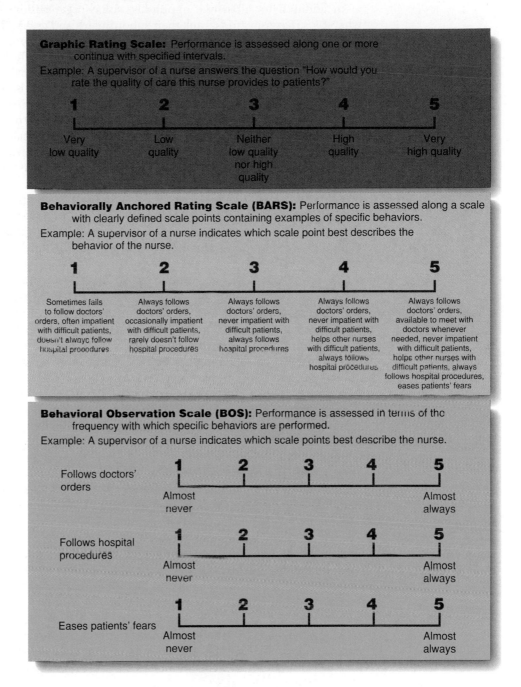

Graphic Rating Scale: Performance is assessed along one or more continua with specified intervals.

Example: A supervisor of a nurse answers the question "How would you rate the quality of care this nurse provides to patients?"

1	2	3	4	5
Very low quality	Low quality	Neither low quality nor high quality	High quality	Very high quality

Behaviorally Anchored Rating Scale (BARS): Performance is assessed along a scale with clearly defined scale points containing examples of specific behaviors.

Example: A supervisor of a nurse indicates which scale point best describes the behavior of the nurse.

1	2	3	4	5
Sometimes fails to follow doctors' orders, often impatient with difficult patients, doesn't always follow hospital procedures	Always follows doctors' orders, occasionally impatient with difficult patients, rarely doesn't follow hospital procedures	Always follows doctors' orders, never impatient with difficult patients, always follows hospital procedures	Always follows doctors' orders, never impatient with difficult patients, helps other nurses with difficult patients, always follows hospital procedures	Always follows doctors' orders, available to meet with doctors whenever needed, never impatient with difficult patients, helps other nurses with difficult patients, always follows hospital procedures, eases patients' fears

Behavioral Observation Scale (BOS): Performance is assessed in terms of the frequency with which specific behaviors are performed.

Example: A supervisor of a nurse indicates which scale points best describe the nurse.

Follows doctors' orders

1	2	3	4	5
Almost never				Almost always

Follows hospital procedures

1	2	3	4	5
Almost never				Almost always

Eases patients' fears

1	2	3	4	5
Almost never				Almost always

in the next chapter). This is why both researchers and managers have spent considerable time and effort on determining the best way to develop reliable and valid subjective measures of performance.

Some of the more popular subjective measures such as the graphic rating scale, the behaviorally anchored rating scale (BARS), and the behavior observation scale (BOS) are illustrated in Figure 12.5.[97] When graphic rating scales are used, performance is assessed along a continuum with specified intervals. With a BARS, performance is assessed along a scale with clearly defined scale points containing examples of specific behaviors. A BOS assesses performance by how often specific behaviors are performed. Many managers may use both objective and subjective appraisals. For example, a salesperson may be appraised both on the dollar value of sales (objective) and the quality of customer service (subjective).

In addition to subjective appraisals, some organizations employ *forced rankings* whereby supervisors must rank their subordinates and assign them to different categories according to their performance (which is subjectively appraised). For example, middle managers at Ford Motor Company are ranked by their supervisors in a forced distribution from A to C, with 10% of them receiving A's, 80% receiving B's, and 10% receiving C's.[98] The first year an employee receives a C, he or she does not receive a bonus, and after two years of C performance, a demotion or even firing is possible. Employees tend to not like these systems, as they believe they are unfair. For example, managers at Ford have filed a class-action lawsuit because they feel Ford's ranking system is unfair.[99] Relying on relative performance through ranking systems can force managers to rate some of their subordinates as unsatisfactory even if this might not be true and can also result in an employee's performance being downgraded not because of any change he or she has made but because coworkers have improved their performance. In other organizations that use ranking systems, employees tend to voice similar concerns. For example, forced-ranking systems can result in a zero-sum, competitive environment that can discourage cooperation and teamwork.[100]

Who Appraises Performance?

We have been assuming that managers or the supervisors of employees evaluate performance. This is a pretty reasonable assumption, for supervisors are the most common appraisers of performance; indeed, each year 70 million U.S. citizens have their job performance appraised by their managers or supervisors.[101] Performance appraisal is an important part of most managers' job duties. Managers are responsible for not only motivating their subordinates to perform at a high level but also making many decisions hinging on performance appraisals, such as pay raises or promotions. Appraisals by managers can be usefully augmented by appraisals from other sources (see Figure 12.6).

SELF, PEERS, SUBORDINATES, AND CLIENTS When self-appraisals are used, managers supplement their evaluations with an employee's assessment of his or her own performance. Peer appraisals are provided by an employee's coworkers.

Figure 12.6
Who Appraises Performance?

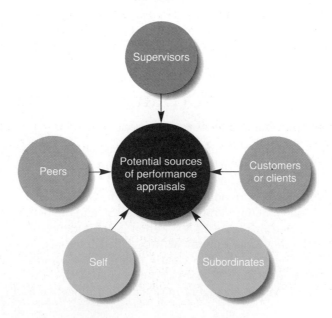

Especially when subordinates work in groups or teams, feedback from peer appraisals can motivate team members while providing managers with important information for decision making. A growing number of companies are having subordinates appraise their managers' performance and leadership as well. And sometimes customers or clients provide assessments of employee performance in terms of responsiveness to customers and quality of service. Although appraisals from each of these sources can be useful, managers need to be aware of potential issues that may arise when they are used. Subordinates sometimes may be inclined to inflate self-appraisals, especially if organizations are downsizing and they are worried about their job security. Managers who are appraised by their subordinates may fail to take needed but unpopular actions out of fear that their subordinates will appraise them negatively. Some of these potential issues can be mitigated to the extent that there are high levels of trust in an organization.

360-degree appraisal

A performance appraisal by peers, subordinates, superiors, and sometimes clients who are in a position to evaluate a manager's performance.

360-DEGREE PERFORMANCE APPRAISALS To improve motivation and performance, some organizations include 360-degree appraisals and feedback in their performance appraisal systems, especially for managers. In a **360-degree appraisal,** a variety of people, beginning with the manager and including peers or coworkers, subordinates, superiors, and sometimes even customers or clients, appraise a manager's performance. The manager receives feedback based on evaluations from these multiple sources.

The growing number of companies using 360-degree appraisals and feedback include AT&T Corp., Allied Signal Inc., Eastman Chemical Co., and Baxter International Inc.[102] For 360-degree appraisals and feedback to be effective, there has to be trust throughout an organization. More generally, trust is a critical ingredient in any performance appraisal and feedback procedure. In addition, research suggests that 360 degree appraisals should focus on behaviors rather than traits or results and that managers need to carefully select appropriate raters. Moreover, appraisals tend to be more honest when made anonymously and when raters have been trained in how to use 360-degree appraisal forms.[103] Additionally, managers need to think carefully about the extent to which 360-degree appraisals are appropriate for certain jobs and be willing to modify any appraisal system they implement if they become aware of unintended problems it creates.[104]

Even when 360-degree appraisals are used, it is sometimes difficult to design an effective process by which subordinates' feedback can be communicated to their managers. Advances in information technology provide organizations with a potential solution to this problem. For example, ImproveNow.com has online questionnaires that subordinates fill out to evaluate the performance of their managers and provide the managers with feedback. Each subordinate of a particular manager completes the questionnaire independently, all responses are tabulated, and the manager is given specific feedback on behaviors in a variety of areas, such as rewarding good performance, looking out for subordinates' best interest and being supportive, and having a vision for the future.[105]

Effective Performance Feedback

For the appraisal and feedback component of a human resource management system to encourage and motivate high performance, managers must provide their subordinates with feedback. To generate useful information to feed back to their subordinates, managers can use both formal and informal appraisals. **Formal appraisals** are conducted at set times during the year and are based on performance dimensions and measures that have been specified in advance. A salesperson, for example, may be evaluated by his or her manager twice a year on the performance dimensions of sales and customer service, sales being objectively measured from sales reports, and customer service being measured with a BARS (see Figure 12.5).

formal appraisal

An appraisal conducted at a set time during the year and based on performance dimensions and measures that were specified in advance.

Managers in most large organizations use formal performance appraisals on a fixed schedule dictated by company policy, such as every six months or every year. An integral part of a formal appraisal is a meeting between the manager and the subordinate in which the subordinate is given feedback on performance. Performance feedback lets subordinates know which areas they are excelling in and which areas need improvement; it also should provide them with guidance for improving performance.

Realizing the value of formal appraisals, managers in many large corporations have committed substantial resources to updating their performance appraisal procedures and training low-level managers in how to use them and provide accurate feedback to employees. Top managers at the pharmaceutical company Hoffmann-La Roche Inc., for example, spent $1.5 million updating and improving their performance appraisal procedures. Alan Rubino, vice president of human resources for Hoffmann-La Roche, believes that this was money well spent because "people need to know exactly where they stand and what's required of them." Before Hoffmann-La Roche's new system was implemented, managers attended a three-day training and development session to improve their performance appraisal skills. The new procedures call for every manager and subordinate to develop a performance plan for subordinates for the coming year—a plan that is linked to the company's strategy and goals and approved by the manager's own superiors. Formal performance appraisals are conducted every six months, during which actual performance is compared to planned performance.[106]

Formal performance appraisals supply both managers and subordinates with valuable information; but subordinates often want feedback on a more frequent basis, and managers often want to motivate subordinates as the need arises. For these reasons many companies, including Hoffman-La Roche, supplement formal performance appraisal with frequent **informal appraisals,** for which managers and their subordinates meet as the need arises to discuss ongoing progress and areas for improvement. Moreover, when job duties, assignments, or goals change, informal appraisals can provide workers with timely feedback concerning how they are handling their new responsibilities.

Managers often dislike providing performance feedback, especially when the feedback is negative, but doing so is an important managerial activity.[107] Here are some guidelines for giving effective performance feedback that contributes to employee motivation and performance:

- *Be specific and focus on behaviors or outcomes that are correctable and within a worker's ability to improve.* Example: Telling a salesperson that he is too shy when interacting with customers is likely to do nothing more than lower his self-confidence and prompt the salesperson to become defensive. A more effective approach would be to give the salesperson feedback about specific behaviors to engage in—greeting customers as soon as they enter the department, asking customers whether they need help, and volunteering to help customers find items.

- *Approach performance appraisal as an exercise in problem solving and solution finding, not criticizing.* Example: Rather than criticizing a financial analyst for turning in reports late, the manager helps the analyst determine why the reports are late and identify ways to better manage her time.

- *Express confidence in a subordinate's ability to improve.* Example: Instead of being skeptical, a first-level manager tells a subordinate that he is confident that the subordinate can increase quality levels.

- *Provide performance feedback both formally and informally.* Example: The staff of a preschool receives feedback from formal performance appraisals twice a year. The director of the school also provides frequent informal feedback such as complimenting staff members on creative ideas for special projects, noticing when they do a particularly good job handling a difficult child, and pointing out when they provide inadequate supervision.

- *Praise instances of high performance and areas of a job in which a worker excels.* Example: Rather than focusing on just the negative, a manager discusses the areas her subordinate excels in as well as the areas in need of improvement.

- *Avoid personal criticisms and treat subordinates with respect.* Example: An engineering manager acknowledges her subordinates' expertise and treats them as professionals.

informal appraisal An unscheduled appraisal of ongoing progress and areas for improvement.

Even when the manager points out performance problems to subordinates, she refrains from criticizing them personally.

* *Agree to a timetable for performance improvements.* Example: A first-level manager and his subordinate decide to meet again in one month to determine whether quality levels have improved.

LO5 Explain the issues managers face in determining levels of pay and benefits.

In following these guidelines, managers need to remember *why* they are giving performance feedback: to encourage high levels of motivation and performance. Moreover, the information that managers gather through performance appraisal and feedback helps them determine how to distribute pay raises and bonuses.

Pay and Benefits

Pay includes employees' base salaries, pay raises, and bonuses and is determined by a number of factors such as characteristics of the organization and the job and levels of performance. Employee *benefits* are based on membership in an organization (and not necessarily on the particular job held) and include sick days, vacation days, and medical and life insurance. In Chapter 13, we discuss the ways in which pay can motivate organizational members to perform at a high level, as well as the different kinds of pay plans managers can use to help an organization achieve its goals and gain a competitive advantage. As you will learn, it is important for pay to be linked to behaviors or results that contribute to organizational effectiveness. Next, we focus on establishing an organization's pay level and pay structure.

Pay Level

pay level The relative position of an organization's pay incentives in comparison with those of other organizations in the same industry employing similar kinds or workers.

Pay level is a broad comparative concept that refers to how an organization's pay incentives compare, in general, to those of other organizations in the same industry employing similar kinds of workers. Managers must decide if they want to offer relatively high wages, average wages, or relatively low wages. High wages help ensure that an organization is going to be able to recruit, select, and retain high performers, but high wages also raise costs. Low wages give an organization a cost advantage but may undermine the organization's ability to select and recruit high performers and to motivate current employees to perform at a high level. Either of these situations may lead to inferior quality or inadequate customer service.

In determining pay levels, managers should take into account their organization's strategy. A high pay level may prohibit managers from effectively pursuing a low cost strategy. But a high pay level may be well worth the added costs in an organization whose competitive advantage lies in superior quality and excellent customer service. As one might expect, hotel and motel chains with a low-cost strategy, such as Days Inn and Hampton Inns, have lower pay levels than chains striving to provide high-quality rooms and services, such as Four Seasons and Hyatt Regency.

Pay Structure

pay structures The arrangement of jobs into categories reflecting their relative importance to the organization and its goals, levels of skill required, and other characteristics.

After deciding on a pay level, managers have to establish a pay structure for the different jobs in the organization. A **pay structure** clusters jobs into categories reflecting their relative importance to the organization and its goals, levels of skill required, and other characteristics managers consider to be important. Pay ranges are established for each job category. Individual jobholders' pay within job categories is then determined by factors such as performance, seniority, and skill levels.

There are some interesting global differences in pay structures. Large corporations based in the United States tend to pay their CEOs and top managers higher salaries than do their European or Japanese counterparts. Also, the pay differential between employees at the bottom of the corporate hierarchy and those higher up is much greater in U.S. companies than in European or Japanese companies.[108]

Concerns have been raised over whether it is equitable or fair for CEOs of large companies in the United States to be making millions of dollars in years when their companies are restructuring and laying off a large portion of their workforces.[109] Additionally, the average CEO in the United States typically earns over 430 times what the average hourly worker earns.[110] Is a pay structure with such a huge pay differential ethical? Shareholders and the public are increasingly asking this very question and asking large corporations to rethink their pay structures.[111] Also troubling are the millions of dollars in severance packages that some CEOs receive when they leave their organizations. In an era in which many workers are struggling to find and keep jobs and make ends meet, more and more people are questioning whether it is ethical for some top managers to be making so much money.[112]

Benefits

Organizations are legally required to provide certain benefits to their employees, including workers' compensation, Social Security, and unemployment insurance. Workers' compensation provides employees with financial assistance if they become unable to work due to a work-related injury or illness. Social Security provides financial assistance to retirees and disabled former employees. Unemployment insurance provides financial assistance to workers who lose their jobs due to no fault of their own. The legal system in the United States views these three benefits as ethical requirements for organizations and thus mandates that they be provided.

Other benefits such as health insurance, dental insurance, vacation time, pension plans, life insurance, flexible working hours, company-provided day care, and employee assistance and wellness programs are provided at the option of employers. Recall how a very attractive benefit at the Four Seasons in "A Manager's Challenge" is being able to stay for free in any of the company's hotels and resorts. Benefits enabling workers to simultaneously balance the demands of their jobs and of their lives away from the office or factory are of growing importance for many workers who have competing demands on their all-too-scarce time and energy.

cafeteria-style benefit plan A plan from which employees can choose the benefits that they want.

In some organizations, top managers determine which benefits might best suit the employees and organization and offer the same benefit package to all employees. Other organizations, realizing that employees' needs and desires might differ, offer **cafeteria-style benefit plans** that let employees themselves choose the benefits they want. Cafeteria-style benefit plans sometimes assist managers in dealing with employees who feel unfairly treated because they are unable to take advantage of certain benefits available to other employees who, for example, have children. Some organizations have success with cafeteria-style benefit plans; others find them difficult to manage.

As health care costs are escalating and overstretched employees are finding it hard to take time out to exercise and take care of their health, more companies are providing benefits and incentives to promote employee wellness. AstraZeneca International offers its employees on-site counseling with a nutritionist and pays employees $125 for voluntarily taking a health risk assessment that covers wellness-related factors such as weight and nutrition.[113] Dole Food Company rewards employees with points toward gift certificates for participating in wellness activities provided on-site, such as yoga classes.[114]

Some organizations seek to promote employee wellness by providing on-site fitness centers.

For working parents and single mothers and fathers, family friendly benefits are especially attractive, as profiled in the following "Focus on Diversity."

Focus on Diversity

Family-Friendly Benefits at Guerra DeBerry Coody

Small Business

Guerra DeBerry Coody is a small public relations and advertising firm based in San Antonio, Texas.[115] Founded in 1995, the firm has 61 employees and over $50 million in annual revenues. Recently, Guerra DeBerry Coody was named a "Top Small Workplace" by *The Wall Street Journal* and Winning Workplaces, a nonprofit organization. Employees at Guerra DeBerry Coody nominated their employer for this award and given the family-friendly benefits this firm provides, it is easy to understand why.[116]

Guerra DeBerry Coody provides its employees with on-site child care up until employees' children enter kindergarten with the firm covering 85% of the cost and employees paying $20 per day per child.[117] Employees are able to spend time with their children during the workday–employees often eat with their children, play with them, and settle them down for naps. The on-site child care center has a ratio of 1 child care worker for every 2 children enrolled and around 11 children are currently enrolled. Employees with older children are able to bring their children to work after school if they wish. Senior account supervisor Patti Tanner sometimes has her two young teenage children come to the office after school. She indicates that "I don't even have any angst about having them here because I know it's completely and totally accepted."[118]

Guerra DeBerry Coody provides other benefits that help employees deal with the multiple demands and obligations in their lives. For example, employees who are having a major financial problem can apply for interest-free loans from the company. Employees also have the option of working from home and telecommuting and flexible work schedules. Guerra DeBerry Coody provides free health insurance for all its employees and those with dependents needing coverage can purchase it for around $125–$200 per month. The company also contributes to a 401(k) retirement plan for its employees.[119] As Frank Guerra, one of the founding partners of Guerra DeBerry Coody and its current CEO, indicated upon the firm being named a "Top Small Workplace," "With or without this recognition we are so proud that we have the ability to offer our employees a family-friendly work environment where everyone has a vested interest in each other and in the business, caring for one another like family."[120]

Guerra DeBerry Coody offers family-friendly benefits such as child care.

Same-sex domestic-partner benefits are also being used to attract and retain valued employees. Gay and lesbian workers are more and more reluctant to work for companies that do not provide them with the same kinds of benefits for their partners as those provided for partners of the opposite sex.[121]

Labor Relations

Labor relations are the activities that managers engage in to ensure that they have effective working relationships with the labor unions that represent their employees' interests. Although the U.S. government has responded to the potential for unethical and unfair treatment of workers by creating and enforcing laws regulating employment (including the EEO laws listed in Table 12.1), some workers believe that a union will ensure that their interests are fairly represented in their organizations.

LO6 Understand the role that labor relations play in the effective management of human resources.

labor relations The activities that managers engage in to ensure that they have effective working relationships with the labor unions that represent their employees' interests.

Before we describe unions in more detail, let's take a look at some examples of important employment legislation. In 1938 the government passed the Fair Labor Standards Act, which prohibited child labor and made provisions for minimum wages, overtime pay, and maximum working hours to protect workers' rights. In 1963 the Equal Pay Act mandated that men and women performing equal work (work requiring the same levels of skill, responsibility, and effort performed in the same kind of working conditions) receive equal pay (see Table 12.1). In 1970 the Occupational Safety and Health Act mandated procedures for managers to follow to ensure workplace safety. These are just a few of the U.S. government's efforts to protect workers' rights. State legislatures also have been active in promoting safe, ethical, and fair workplaces.

Unions

Unions exist to represent workers' interests in organizations. Given that managers have more power than rank-and-file workers and that organizations have multiple stakeholders, there is always the potential that managers might take steps that benefit one set of stakeholders such as shareholders while hurting another such as employees. For example, managers may decide to speed up a production line to lower costs and increase production in the hopes of increasing returns to shareholders. Speeding up the line, however, could hurt employees forced to work at a rapid pace and may increase the risk of injuries. Also, employees receive no additional pay for the extra work they are performing. Unions would represent workers' interests in a scenario such as this one.

Congress acknowledged the role that unions could play in ensuring safe and fair workplaces when it passed the National Labor Relations Act of 1935. This act made it legal for workers to organize into unions to protect their rights and interests and declared certain unfair or unethical organizational practices to be illegal. The act also established the National Labor Relations Board (NLRB) to oversee union activity. Currently, the NLRB conducts certification elections, which are held among the employees of an organization to determine whether they want a union to represent their interests. The NLRB also makes judgments concerning unfair labor practices and specifies practices that managers must refrain from.

Employees might vote to have a union represent them for any number of reasons.[122] They may think that their wages and working conditions are in need of improvement. They may believe that managers are not treating them with respect. They may think that their working hours are unfair or that they need more job security or a safer work environment. Or they may be dissatisfied with management and find it difficult to communicate their concerns to their bosses. Regardless of the specific reason, one overriding reason is power: A united group inevitably wields more power than an individual, and this type of power may be especially helpful to employees in some organizations.

Although these would seem to be potent forces for unionization, some workers are reluctant to join unions. Sometimes this reluctance is due to the perception that union leaders are corrupt. Some workers may simply believe that belonging to a union might not do them much good or may actually cause more harm than good while costing them money in membership dues. Employees also might not want to be forced into doing something they do not want to, such as striking because the union thinks it is in their best interest. Moreover, although unions can be a positive force in organizations, sometimes they also can be a negative force, impairing organizational effectiveness.

The recent Writer's Guild of America strike lasted for 100 days.

For example, when union leaders resist needed changes in an organization or are corrupt, organizational performance can suffer.

The percentage of U.S. workers represented by unions today is smaller than it was in the 1950s, an era when unions were especially strong.[123] The American Federation of Labor–Congress of Industrial Organizations (AFL-CIO) includes 64 voluntary member unions representing 13 million workers.[124] Union influence in manufacturing and heavy industries has been on the decline, presumably because their workers no longer see the need to be represented by unions. Recently, however, unions have made inroads in other segments of the workforce, particularly the low-wage end. Garbage collectors in New Jersey, poultry plant workers in North Carolina, and janitors in Baltimore are among the growing numbers of low-paid workers who are currently finding union membership attractive. North Carolina poultry workers voted in a union in part because they thought it was unfair that they had to buy their own gloves and hairnets used on the job and had to ask their supervisors' permission to go to the restroom.[125]

Union membership and leadership, traditionally dominated by white men, are becoming increasingly diverse. For example, Linda Chavez-Thompson was the executive vice president of the AFL-CIO from 1995–2007 and the first woman and Hispanic to hold a top-management position in the federation.[126] Labor officials in Washington, DC, also are becoming increasingly diverse. Elaine L. Chao, the 24th U.S. secretary of labor,[127] is the first Asian-American woman to hold an appointment in a U.S. president's cabinet. Chao, who has extensive management experience as a former CEO of the United Way of America and also as a former director of the Peace Corps, is committed to equal opportunity in the workplace, the well-being of workers and their families, and increased flexibility in the workplace.[128]

Collective Bargaining

collective bargaining
Negotiations between labor unions and managers to resolve conflicts and disputes about issues such as working hours, wages, benefits, working conditions, and job security.

Collective bargaining is negotiation between labor unions and managers to resolve conflicts and disputes about important issues such as working hours, wages, working conditions, and job security. Before sitting down with management to negotiate, union members sometimes go on strike to drive home their concerns to managers. Once an agreement that union members support has been reached (sometimes with the help of a neutral third party called a *mediator*), union leaders and managers sign a contract spelling out the terms of the collective bargaining agreement. We discuss conflict and negotiation in depth in Chapter 16, but some brief observations are in order here because collective bargaining is an ongoing consideration in labor relations.

The signing of a contract, for example, does not bring the collective bargaining process to a halt. Disagreement and conflicts can arise over the interpretation of the contract. In such cases, a neutral third party called an *arbitrator* is usually called in to resolve the conflict. An important component of a collective bargaining agreement is a *grievance procedure* through which workers who believe they are not being fairly treated are allowed to voice their concerns and have their interests represented by the union. Workers who think that they were unjustly fired in violation of a union contract, for example, may file a grievance, have the union represent them, and get their jobs back if an arbitrator agrees with them.

Union members sometimes go on strike when managers make decisions that the members think will hurt them and are not in their best interests. This is precisely what happened in 1996 when General Motors' North American assembly plants employing 177,000 workers were idled for 18 days. The strike originated in GM's Dayton, Ohio, brake assembly plants due to management's decision to buy some parts from other companies rather than make them in GM's own plants.[129] The United Auto Workers Union called a strike because outsourcing threatens union members' jobs. The agreement that the union and management, bargaining collectively, reached allowed the outsourcing to continue but contained provisions for the creation of hundreds of new jobs as well as for improvements in working conditions.[130]

Summary and Review

LO1 STRATEGIC HUMAN RESOURCE MANAGEMENT Human resource management (HRM) includes all the activities that managers engage in to ensure that their organizations are able to attract, retain, and effectively utilize human resources. Strategic HRM is the process by which managers design the components of a human resource management system to be consistent with each other, with other elements of organizational architecture, and with the organization's strategies and goals.

LO2 RECRUITMENT AND SELECTION Before recruiting and selecting employees, managers must engage in human resource planning and job analysis. Human resource planning includes all the activities managers engage in to forecast their current and future needs for human resources. Job analysis is the process of identifying (1) the tasks, duties, and responsibilities that make up a job and (2) the knowledge, skills, and abilities needed to perform the job. Recruitment includes all the activities that managers engage in to develop a pool of qualified applicants for open positions. Selection is the process by which managers determine the relative qualifications of job applicants and their potential for performing well in a particular job.

LO3 TRAINING AND DEVELOPMENT Training focuses on teaching organizational members how to perform effectively in their current jobs. Development focuses on broadening organizational members' knowledge and skills so that they will be prepared to take on new responsibilities and challenges.

LO4 PERFORMANCE APPRAISAL AND FEEDBACK Performance appraisal is the evaluation of employees' job performance and contributions to the organization. Performance feedback is the process through which managers share performance appraisal information with their subordinates, give them an opportunity to reflect on their own performance, and develop with them plans for the future. Performance appraisal provides managers with useful information for decision-making purposes. Performance feedback can encourage high levels of motivation and performance.

LO5   **PAY AND BENEFITS**   Pay level is the relative position of an organization's pay incentives in comparison with those of other organizations in the same industry employing similar workers. A pay structure clusters jobs into categories according to their relative importance to the organization and its goals, the levels of skill required, and other characteristics. Pay ranges are then established for each job category. Organizations are legally required to provide certain benefits to their employees; other benefits are provided at the discretion of employers.

LO6   **LABOR RELATIONS**   Labor relations include all the activities managers engage in to ensure that they have effective working relationships with the labor unions that represent their employees' interests. The National Labor Relations Board oversees union activity. Collective bargaining is the process through which labor unions and managers resolve conflicts and disputes and negotiate agreements.

Management in Action

Topics for Discussion and Action

DISCUSSION

1. Discuss why it is important for human resource management systems to be in sync with an organization's strategy and goals and with each other. **[LO1]**

2. Discuss why training and development are ongoing activities for all organizations. **[LO3]**

3. Describe the type of development activities you think middle managers are most in need of. **[LO3]**

4. Evaluate the pros and cons of 360-degree performance appraisals and feedback. Would you like your performance to be appraised in this manner? Why or why not? **[LO4]**

5. Discuss why two restaurants in the same community might have different pay levels. **[LO5]**

6. Explain why union membership is becoming more diverse. **[LO6]**

ACTION

7. Interview a manager in a local organization to determine how that organization recruits and selects employees. **[LO2]**

Building Management Skills [LO 1, 2, 3, 4, 5]
Analyzing Human Resource Systems

Think about your current job or a job that you have had in the past. If you have never had a job, then interview a friend or family member who is currently working. Answer the following questions about the job you have chosen:

1. How are people recruited and selected for this job? Are the recruitment and selection procedures that the organization uses effective or ineffective? Why?

2. What training and development do people who hold this job receive? Is it appropriate? Why or why not?

3. How is performance of this job appraised? Does performance feedback contribute to motivation and high performance on this job?

4. What levels of pay and benefits are provided on this job? Are these levels appropriate? Why or why not?

Managing Ethically [LO 4, 5]

Some managers do not want to become overly friendly with their subordinates because they are afraid that if they do so, their objectivity when conducting performance appraisals and making decisions about pay raises and promotions will be impaired. Some subordinates resent it when they see one or more of their coworkers being very friendly with the boss; they are concerned about the potential for favoritism.

Their reasoning runs something like this: If two subordinates are equally qualified for a promotion and one is a good friend of the boss and the other is a mere acquaintance, who is more likely to receive the promotion?

Questions

1. Either individually or in a group, think about the ethical implications of managers'

becoming friendly with their subordinates.

2. Do you think that managers should feel free to socialize and become good friends with their subordinates outside the workplace if they so desire? Why or why not?

Small Group Breakout Exercise [LO 1, 2, 3, 4, 5]
Building a Human Resource Management System

Form groups of three or four people, and appoint one group member as the spokesperson who will communicate your findings to the class when called on by the instructor. Then discuss the following scenario.

You and your three partners are engineers who minored in business at college and have decided to start a consulting business. Your goal is to provide manufacturing-process engineering and other engineering services to large and small organizations. You forecast that there will be an increased use of outsourcing for these activities. You discussed with managers in several large organizations the services you plan to offer, and they expressed considerable interest. You have secured

funding to start your business and now are building the HRM system. Your human resource planning suggests that you need to hire between five and eight experienced engineers with good communication skills, two clerical/secretarial workers, and two MBAs who between them have financial, accounting, and human resource skills. You are striving to develop your human resources in a way that will enable your new business to prosper.

1. Describe the steps you will take to recruit and select

(a) the engineers, (b) the clerical/secretarial workers, and (c) the MBAs.

2. Describe the training and development the engineers, the clerical/secretarial workers, and the MBAs will receive.

3. Describe how you will appraise the performance of each group of employees and how you will provide feedback.

4. Describe the pay level and pay structure of your consulting firm.

Exploring the World Wide Web [LO2]

Go to www.net-temps.com, a Web site geared toward temporary employment. Imagine that you have to take a year off from college and are seeking a one-year position. Guided

by your own interests, use this Web site to learn about your options and possible employment opportunities. What are the potential advantages of online job searching and recruiting?

What are the potential disadvantages? Would you ever rely on a Web site like this to help you find a position? Why, or why not?

Be the Manager [LO4]

You are Walter Michaels and have just received some disturbing feedback. You are the director of human resources for Maxi Vision Inc., a medium-size window and glass-door manufacturer. You recently initiated a 360-degree performance appraisal system for all middle and upper managers at Maxi Vision, including yourself but excluding the most senior executives and the top-management team.

You were eagerly awaiting the feedback you would receive from the managers who report to you; you had recently implemented several important initiatives that affected them and their subordinates, including a complete overhaul of the organization's performance appraisal system. While the managers who report to you were evaluated based on 360-degree appraisals, their own subordinates were evaluated using a 20-question BARS scale you recently created that focuses on behaviors. Conducted annually, appraisals are an important input into pay raise and bonus decisions.

You were so convinced that the new performance appraisal procedures were highly effective that you hoped your own subordinates would mention them in their feedback to you. And boy did they! You were amazed to learn that the managers *and* their subordinates thought the new BARS scales were unfair, inappropriate, and a waste of time. In fact, the managers' feedback to you was that their own performance was suffering, based on the 360-degree appraisals they received, because their subordinates hated the new appraisal system and partially blamed their bosses, who were part of management. Some managers even admitted giving all their subordinates approximately the same scores on the scales so that their pay raises and bonuses would not be affected by their performance appraisals.

You couldn't believe your eyes when you read these comments. You had spent so much time developing what you thought was the ideal rating scale for this group of employees. Evidently, for some unknown reason, they were being very closed-minded and wouldn't give it a chance. Your own supervisor was aware of these complaints and said that it was a top priority for you to fix "this mess" (with the implication that you were responsible for creating it). What are you going to do?

Case in the News [LO 1, 4, 5]

How to Make a Microserf Smile

Steven A. Ballmer had an epic morale problem on his hands. Microsoft Corp.'s stock had been drifting sideways for years, and Google envy was rampant on the Redmond (Wash.) campus. The chronically delayed Windows Vista was irking the Microserfs and blackening their outlook. So was the perception that their company was flabby, middle-aged, and unhip.

Ballmer decided he needed a new human resources chief, someone to help improve the mood. Rather than promoting an HR professional or looking outside, he turned to perhaps the most unlikely candidate on his staff, a veteran product manager named Lisa Brummel.

No one was more stunned than Brummel. The 47-year-old executive is about as un-HR as you can imagine. She shuns business books (her taste runs to historical nonfiction); she takes the bus to work (using the 20-minute ride to zone out); and her wardrobe (shorts and sneakers) is in flagrant violation of the HR fashion police.

When Ballmer floated the HR job in April, 2005, Brummel said: No way. But Ballmer wasn't about to take no for an answer. Picking up a traveling golf putter, the Microsoft chief started taking it apart as he barreled around Brummel's office, hammering home why she was the perfect candidate. As an outsider unsullied by HR dogma, he said, she'd bring a fresh approach. Besides, Ballmer argued, Brummel was hugely popular and had the people skills to get the job done. The two went back and forth, with Ballmer slapping Brummel's whiteboard for emphasis and Brummel parrying with: "But I love doing products." After more than two hours, Ballmer ended the meeting. By then the putter was in pieces. "Sorry about the golf club," he said.

Brummel was deeply conflicted. She had built a solid career developing software, getting customer feedback, launching it, and then making revisions. HR was foreign territory. Yet she loved Microsoft and recognized the internal challenges that the company was facing. By the next morning, she had relented. She called Ballmer and told him: "I'm in."

Over the next two years, Brummel tore up Microsoft's HR playbook. In the process, she has begun to sculpt a new HR that is junking a one-size-fits-all approach for a system tailored to the needs of individual employees. In Brummel's HR, her people are supposed to act less like cops and more like concierges.

With Microsoft's dormant stock, Brummel can do only so much to boost morale. But her approach seems to be resonating. She has made the annual performance review more equitable, introduced new perks, including a service that sends doctors to employees' homes in cases of emergency, and won plaudits for making HR—once widely considered a shadowy politburo—more transparent and consultative. "From the beginning," says Julie Madhusoodanan, a lead software tester in the Windows division, "Lisa was all about 'We're here to serve you.'"

Towel Tumult

Like many revolutions, the one at Microsoft began with a political miscalculation. One day in the summer of 2004 employees arrived to discover that the towels had vanished. Long provided in locker rooms adjoining the company's underground garages, they were a decidedly threadbare perk. But for the legions who cycled to work through the Seattle drizzle, the towels had become an entitlement. Now they were gone, yanked by some faceless HR functionary bent on saving, as one employee put it, "like, 0.000001% of earnings per share."

HR manager Anne Ensminger thought the towels' disappearance "wouldn't even be a blip." Instead, irate employees mobbed blogs and message boards. One post ranted: "It is a dark and dreary day at One Microsoft Way. Do yourself a favor and stay away." Inside HR, the rank-and-file rebellion was deemed ridiculously over the top. "It was like we were taking away 90% of their base salary," says Ensminger. But the vociferousness of the attacks shocked senior executives.

Management knew morale was bad. After all, many employees' options were under water. And Google Inc. was getting all the press as a paradise with free food and cushy perks. But Microsoft offered its own gold-plated bennies—free health care, for one—that actually put Google's largesse in the shade. Why was this not registering with employees? Why had turnover crept up from 6.7% in 2002 to 9.4% by 2004?

Ballmer needed to make a big statement. So he named Brummel HR chief and telegraphed to employees that she would be his consigliere of happiness.

Straight Shooter

With Brummel, Ballmer had the maverick he was looking for. From an early age, she was always giving things her own twist, like pairing yellow shoelaces with purple Converse sneakers in grade school. After earning a sociology degree from Yale University, Brummel also considered going to work for Hewlett-Packard, Tandem, and Ernst & Young.

She decided on Microsoft because on her interview she spotted a long-haired coder walking around with no shoes. "I knew I could be myself here," says Brummel, who has raised two twenty-something daughters with her partner. Brummel went on to earn a reputation as a superb leader in a company where software developers usually did the bossing and real managerial prowess was rare.

One of her first acts as HR chief typified her style: She cemented a reputation as a no-B.S., jargon-allergic truth-teller when she admitted in an interview on Microsoft's video blog, Channel 9, that she read the ultracritical Mini-Microsoft blog posted by an anonymous but influential insider. The admission gave her instant credibility among staffers, who were already glued to the site.

But in her first weeks as HR chief, Brummel felt as though she were flying at night without instruments. At first she was receiving about two e-mails a day from employees. "There was no communication with employees—none," she says. "It was a gulf." Internal surveys—which at most companies help inform HR policy—presented a picture of a happy, contented workforce. Brummel didn't buy the rosy findings. "People weren't connected to the company or our mission anymore," she says.

Brummel didn't want to follow the usual HR script: benchmarking best practices and imposing them on the company. "Before you go running off campus," she told herself, "you should know what's going on on campus."

So she launched a listening tour, holding town hall meetings from Redmond to Bangalore to London. Brummel half expected to be pelted with rotten tomatoes. In fact, employees were heartened that the Wizard was stepping out from behind the curtain.

Brummel started an internal blog to get people talking and created a portal on the intranet where people could suggest solutions to HR shortcomings. She held focus groups and mined her network of on-the-ground intelligence agents: the people, from managers to coders, she had come to know since joining the company in 1989.

Time and again, Brummel heard the same refrain: HR was a black box; it had to open up and get employee input. People loathed the forced curve in performance reviews. They wanted clarity on compensation, more direction on how to get promoted, and better managers.

They were fed up with the nickel-and-diming on creature comforts. How could a company headquartered near Seattle, home of all things barista, serve industrial-grade sludge in do-it-yourself makers that belonged in a mess hall? "The coffee was just really, really bad," says corporate Vice-President Chris Capossela.

In May, 2006, Brummel went live with a reimagined HR, dubbed my Microsoft 1.0. She signaled her intention to offer regularly timed software-style upgrades that she hoped would keep pace with a changing workplace. "It's the same way we talk to our customers," she says. "We don't let a product live for 10 years. We take feedback, we make improvements."

Nothing got people buzzing more than Brummel's overhaul of the performance review. Employees dreaded Microsoft's ranking system for all the usual reasons: It pitted coworkers against one another at a time when the company needed to be more collaborative; it was unfair; it made frank evaluations less likely.

Here Brummel faced a political third rail. Ballmer was the godfather of the forced curve, believing that differentiation—giving a few people the top grade, most a pass, and laggards failing marks—was the key to Microsoft's we-take-the-hills culture. And when Brummel broached ditching the curve, it was his turn to say "No way." More yelling ensued as they darted in and out of each other's adjacent offices.

Microsoft has always had two rankings: one measuring annual performance and one that captures long-term potential. A forced curve applied to both. To get Ballmer on board, Brummel created a new system that preserved the positive aspects— grades and the chance for stars to win bigger paychecks—while canceling out the negatives. No longer would the first ranking—employee's yearly performance—be subject to the curve. Raises and bonuses would be tied to that grade. Bosses would have freedom to pass out whatever grades they wanted, making less likely the excuse so many of us have heard: "I really wanted to give you a 4. But I had the curve, so I had to give you a 3."

The second, long-term potential ranking determines stock awards. A terrific manager who goes to a struggling division might get a lower grade on the first ranking but would get stock for his or her potential to turn things around. "We still have a weird system that celebrates the individual devoid of the team," says Mini-Microsoft. "But now it's not so much of a knife fight when you're doing your best to defend your people."

House Calls

Brummel won an easy PR victory by restoring the towels. But she knew she needed to offer more. One of her signature initiatives is Mobil Medicine, where the company dispatches doctors to an employee's home in case of emergency. The night before Real Estate and Facilities Director Susan Wagner was set to leave on a business trip, her toddler came down with a fever. A doctor was at her house within two hours and diagnosed the flu. "There was no way I could have gone on that trip," says Wagner, "if I'd been up all night waiting in the emergency room." Brummel estimates Mobil Medicine will save the company $1 million this year.

Sometimes it seemed as if Brummel were taking her cues from a certain Microsoft rival. Google gives discounts on hybrid cars. So does Microsoft. Google's restaurants use locally grown food. Microsoft employees can now get eats from some of their favorite restaurants—either in the cafeteria, where these eateries have set up shop, or delivered to their desks. Google has free shuttle bus service. Soon Microsoft will, too (with free Wi-Fi). Brummel also sorted out the coffee. Today 458 new Starbucks i-cup machines dot the Redmond campus. Some employees call the java "Brummel Brew" and circulate video recipes of favorite concoctions.

In May, Brummel released my Microsoft 2.0. Based on feedback from employees, she made a number of changes, including discontinuing desk-side delivery of groceries, since barely any employees were using it, and introducing new ways to hold managers accountable for how well they lead. She hopes to begin tailoring HR to individual work styles and life stages, using customized benefits and compensation as a way of differentiating between the needs of Gen Y-ers and their aging boomer colleagues. She's considering satellite offices so commuters don't have to waste time driving when they could be working. She's also a proponent of working remotely. "I'm home for dinner every day by 6:30," says Brummel. "The office is for meetings."

Brummel also wants to do a better job of recruiting fresh blood and has turned the formerly drab, taupe-and-brown recruiting center into what resembles a hip hotel lobby complete with an Xbox lounge and copious snacks.

So how's she doing so far? Attrition is down from 10% in 2005 to 8.3%. The new performance rating system has not yet led to grade inflation. And employees, who give Brummel rock-star positive reviews, describe a more buoyant mood. Then again, her Inside MS blog, intended as a marketplace of ideas, quickly turned into a rant-fest. Some employees say Microsoft needs to do a better job of recruiting internally. And, of course, Brummel can't do anything about the stock price.

Still, in two years Lisa Brummel has achieved much. In what may be the most personally satisfying response to her efforts, a memo has been popping up on Microsoft message boards recently. It's a manifesto listing all the ways Microsoft is superior to Google. Its author? A Microsoft engineer who fled to the search giant and returned. The title: "Just Say No To Google."

Questions for Discussion

1. How has Lisa Brummel changed the management of human resources at Microsoft?

2. How has she changed Microsoft's performance appraisal system?

3. How did she figure out what she should do to change Microsoft's human resource practices?

4. How has she altered benefits at Microsoft, and why are benefits important to employees?

Source: Michelle Conlin and Jay Greene, "How to Make a Microserf Smile." Reprinted from the September 10, 2007, issue of *BusinessWeek* by special permission. Copyright © 2007 by The McGraw-Hill Companies, Inc.

BusinessWeek Case in the News [LO 1, 2]

Guess Who's Hiring in America

Bennett Kalcevic's saga offers ample evidence of how the winds of globalization can unexpectedly shift. In the mid-1980s her parents lost their mill jobs when Pittsburgh's steel industry was hit by cheap imports. Now, with a business degree from Michigan State University, Kalcevic has just landed a plum position with Infosys Technologies Ltd., one of the low-cost Indian outfits that many blame for taking jobs from American programmers. After a six-month training stint in India, Kalcevic will return to the U.S. and write software for an Infosys customer. "Outsourcing has angered some people," she says. "It might be easier for clients to deal with Americans locally."

Think of it as offshoring in reverse. In the past, Indian companies almost always transferred Indians to work in the U.S. on temporary visas. But now Infosys and other Indian outfits are hiring aggressively in the U.S.

Wipro Ltd., for instance, is scouting U.S. locations for two big software writing centers that eventually could employ hundreds of programmers each. Cities on its short list include Austin, Tex., and Atlanta, because of their deep tech- talent pools and reasonable salary costs. "The work we're doing requires more and more knowledge of the customers' businesses, and you want local people to do that," says Wipro Chairman Azim H. Premji. Today only 2.5% of Wipro's global workforce is non-Indian, but the company wants to boost that to more than 10% in a few years.

The Indian outsourcers say their U.S. expansion plans predate the latest concerns over immigration and jobs. But they acknowledge the trend might ease tensions as the Senate mulls regulations that would require companies applying for H-1B visas—temporary working papers for foreigners—to try hiring Americans first. "If we can hire close to our clients, we don't have to bring in somebody from India on an H-1B," says S. Padmanabhan, human resources chief for Tata Consultancy Services Ltd. (TCS), India's largest outsourcing firm. About 1,000 of TCS's 10,000 U.S.-based workers are Americans (out of 90,000 total employees worldwide). And it plans to hire an additional 2,000 Americans within three years.

Surprisingly, it often costs more to ship in Indians on a temporary basis than it does to hire Americans. Base salaries are comparable, because Indian companies must by law pay market rates for people they bring in on work visas. But the companies typically have to provide the Indians with housing, and retirement benefits cost more because of India's social security contribution requirements. Also, as the Indian rupee has risen more than 10% against the dollar this year, hiring Americans has gotten cheaper. At the same time, fierce competition for tech talent in India is pushing salaries there up by 12% to 15% per year, although they remain less than a third of those in the U.S.

Allure On Campus

The Indians are recruiting a combination of fresh college grads and experienced vets who have worked at American companies. They're especially active at campus job fairs, and unlike a few years ago students know who these companies are and respect them. In fact, the Indian connection has become an attraction. "I thought this would be a fantastic opportunity, especially because they send you abroad for training," says Brian Oswald, a 23-year-old Rutgers University graduate with a 2006 degree in industrial engineering who joined TCS in February.

The U.S. hiring by the Indians echoes the strategy Japan's auto industry devised after soaring levels of imports sparked political outcry in Washington in December, 2000. "The Indians are doing to the world's IT processes what the Japanese did to manufacturing," says analyst John McCarthy of Forrester Research Inc. And now, like Japan's carmakers before them, the Indians are becoming major employers in the U.S. as well.

Questions for Discussion

1. Why are Indian companies like Infosys recruiting and hiring more workers in the United States?

2. What are the potential advantages of doing this?

3. Are these companies attractive to workers in the United States? Why, or why not?

4. How might the fact that Indian companies are recruiting and hiring more workers in the United States affect U.S. companies?

CHAPTER 13

Motivation and Performance

After studying this chapter, you should be able to:

LO1 Explain what motivation is and why managers need to be concerned about it.

LO2 Describe from the perspectives of expectancy theory and equity theory what managers should do to have a highly motivated workforce.

LO3 Explain how goals and needs motivate people and what kinds of goals are especially likely to result in high performance.

LO4 Identify the motivation lessons that managers can learn from operant conditioning theory and social learning theory.

LO5 Explain why and how managers can use pay as a major motivation tool.

A MANAGER'S CHALLENGE

Motivating Employees at Enterprise Rent-A-Car

www.enterprise.com

How can managers motivate employees at all levels to provide excellent customer service? Enterprise Rent-A-Car was founded by Jack Taylor in 1957 in St. Louis, Missouri, as a very small auto leasing business.[1] Today, Enterprise is the biggest car rental company in North America with over $9 billion in revenues and over 64,000 employees. Enterprise has over 6,900 locations in the United States, Canada, the United Kingdom, Ireland, and Germany.[2] One of the biggest employers of new college graduates in the United States, Enterprise typically hires over 7,000 entry-level employees each year.[3] While starting salaries tend to be on the low end and the work can be hard (e.g., a few years back, four assistant managers sued the company claiming that they should receive overtime pay), Enterprise has been ranked among the top 50 best companies for new college graduates to launch their careers by *BusinessWeek* magazine.[4]

A privately held company, Enterprise is very much a family business. In its entire history, Enterprise has had only two CEOs, founder Jack Taylor, who is now retired but still quite involved in the company, and his son Andrew Taylor, who became president in 1980 and CEO in 1994. Jack Taylor's daughter, Jo Ann Taylor Kindle, (Andrew's sister) manages much of Enterprise's and the Taylor family's philanthropic activities. Chrissy Taylor, Andrew's daughter, and Carolyn Kindle Payne, Jo Ann's daughter, are both managers at Enterprise who started out as management trainees (Andrew started out washing and moving around cars when he was 16 years old prior to obtaining his

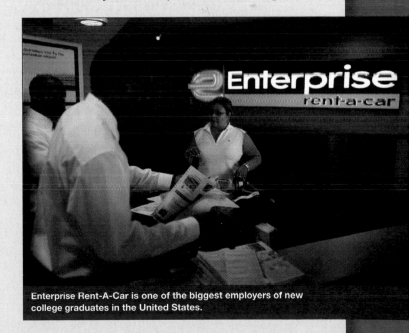

Enterprise Rent-A-Car is one of the biggest employers of new college graduates in the United States.

Bachelor's degree in business).[5] Nonetheless, Enterprise's policy of promoting from within ensures that all employees who perform well have the opportunity to advance in the company.[6]

One of the keys to Enterprise's success is the way it motivates its employees to provide excellent customer service.[7] Practically all entry-level hires participate in Enterprise's Management Training Program.[8] As part of the program, new hires learn all aspects of the company's business, and how to provide excellent customer service. Management trainees first have a four-day training session focused primarily on Enterprise's culture. They are then assigned to a branch office for around 8–12 months where they learn all aspects of the business from negotiating with body shops to helping customers to washing cars. As part of this training, they learn how important high-quality customer service is to Enterprise and how they can personally provide great service, increasing their confidence levels.[9]

All those who do well in the program are promoted after about a year to the position of management assistant. Management assistants who do well are promoted to become assistant branch managers with responsibility for mentoring and supervising employees. Assistant managers who do well can be promoted to become branch managers who are responsible for managing a branch's employees and provision of customer service, rental car fleet, and financial performance. Branch managers with about five years of experience in the position often move on to take up management positions at headquarters or assume the position of area manager overseeing all the branches in a certain geographic region.[10] By training all new hires in all aspects of the

business including the provision of excellent customer service, by providing them with valuable experience with increasing levels of responsibility and empowerment, and by providing all new hires who perform well with the opportunity to advance in the company, Enterprise has a highly motivated workforce. As Patrick Farrell, vice president of corporate communications indicated, "What's unique about our company is that everyone came up through the same system, from the CEOs on down . . . 100% of our operations personnel started as management trainees."[11]

In addition to motivating high performance and excellent customer service through training and promotional opportunities, Enterprise also uses financial incentives to motivate employees. Essentially, each branch is considered a profit center and the managers overseeing the branch and in charge of all aspects of its functioning have the autonomy and responsibility for the branch's profitability almost as if the branch was their own small business or franchise.[12] All branch employees at the rank of assistant manager and higher earn incentive compensation whereby their monthly pay depends upon the profitability of their branch. Managers at higher levels, such as area managers, have their monthly pay linked to the profitability of the region they oversee. Thus, managers at all levels know that their pay is linked to the profitability of the parts of Enterprise for which they are responsible. And they have the autonomy to make decisions ranging from buying and selling cars to even opening new branches.[13]

Providing high-quality customer service is essential at Enterprise.[14] One of the trademarks of this service is Enterprise's long-standing practice of picking up customers who need to rent cars from their homes or workplaces and then dropping them off where they need to go once they return their rental cars. To continuously keep track of how well branches are doing in providing high-quality customer service, Enterprise developed the Enterprise Service Quality index (ESQi).[15] The ESQi is based on phone calls that are made to one out of every 15 customers to follow-up on their experience renting a car from Enterprise. Customers are basically asked how satisfied they were with the experience and if they would rent a car from Enterprise again. Based on satisfaction scores, managers at each branch and unit of the company can see how well they are doing compared to the overall average for the company and take steps, when needed, to improve the quality of the service they provide.[16]

Another way in which Enterprise motivates its employees is through its philanthropic activities and initiatives to protect the natural environment.[17] For example, the Enterprise Rent-A-Car Foundation has committed $50 million to plant 50 million trees over a 50-year period in public forests. The Foundation also focuses on supporting and giving back to the communities in which Enterprise operates, whether it be donating $3,000 to an outreach center for troubled teens in Syracuse, New York, or donating $30 million to fund plant research around the world sponsored by the Missouri Botanical Garden.[18] Of all rental car companies, Enterprise has the biggest fleet of fuel-efficient cars, around 5,000 hybrid electric cars, and around 73,000 cars that can use fuel that is composed of 15% gasoline and 85% ethanol (E85).[19] As Andrew Taylor suggests, "We're not going to be able to save the world . . . but we think we can have an effect on the space where we play every day as a business. And we think that's what our customers and especially our employees want us to do."[20] All in all, the multiple ways in which Enterprise motivates its employees and satisfies its customers have contributed to its ongoing success story.[21]

Overview

Even with the best strategy in place and an appropriate organizational architecture, an organization will be effective only if its members are motivated to perform at a high level. Jack and Andrew Taylor clearly realize this. One reason why leading is such an important managerial activity is that it entails ensuring that each member of an organization is motivated to perform highly and help the organization achieve its goals. When managers are effective, the outcome of the leading process is a highly motivated workforce. A key challenge for managers of organizations both large and small is to encourage employees to perform at a high level.

In this chapter we describe what motivation is, where it comes from, and why managers need to promote high levels of it for an organization to be effective and achieve its goals. We examine important theories of motivation: expectancy theory, need theories, equity theory, goal-setting theory, and learning theories. Each provides managers with important insights about how to motivate organizational members. The theories are complementary in that each focuses on a somewhat different aspect of motivation. Considering all of the theories together helps managers gain a rich understanding of the many issues and problems involved in encouraging high levels of motivation throughout an organization. Last, we consider the use of pay as a motivation tool. By the end of this chapter, you will understand what it takes to have a highly motivated workforce.

The Nature of Motivation

motivation Psychological forces that determine the direction of a person's behavior in an organization, a person's level of effort, and a person's level of persistence.

LO1 Explain what motivation is and why managers need to be concerned about it.

intrinsically motivated behavior Behavior that is performed for its own sake.

extrinsically motivated behavior Behavior that is performed to acquire material or social rewards or to avoid punishment.

Motivation may be defined as psychological forces that determine the direction of a person's behavior in an organization, a person's level of effort, and a person's level of persistence in the face of obstacles.[22] The *direction of a person's behavior* refers to the many possible behaviors that a person could engage in. For example, employees at Enterprise Rent-A-Car know that they should do whatever is required to provide high-quality customer service such as giving customers rides to pick up and drop off rental cars. *Effort* refers to how hard people work. Employees at Enterprise Rent-A-Car exert high levels of effort to provide superior customer service. *Persistence* refers to whether, when faced with roadblocks and obstacles, people keep trying or give up. Branch managers at Enterprise Rent-A-Car persistently seek to improve the profitability of their branches while maintaining very high levels of customer service.

Motivation is central to management because it explains *why* people behave the way they do in organizations[23]—why employees at Enterprise Rent-A-Car provide excellent customer service. Motivation also explains why a waiter is polite or rude and why a kindergarten teacher really tries to get children to enjoy learning or just goes through the motions. It explains why some managers truly put their organizations' best interests first whereas others are more concerned with maximizing their salaries and why—more generally—some workers put forth twice as much effort as others.

Motivation can come from *intrinsic* or *extrinsic* sources. **Intrinsically motivated behavior** is behavior that is performed for its own sake; the source of motivation is actually performing the behavior, and motivation comes from doing the work itself. Many managers are intrinsically motivated; they derive a sense of accomplishment and achievement from helping the organization to achieve its goals and gain competitive advantages. Jobs that are interesting and challenging or high on the five characteristics described by the job characteristics model (see Chapter 9) are more likely to lead to intrinsic motivation than are jobs that are boring or do not make use of a person's skills and abilities. An elementary school teacher who really enjoys teaching children, a computer programmer who loves solving programming problems, and a commercial photographer who relishes taking creative photographs are all intrinsically motivated. For these individuals, motivation comes from performing their jobs whether it be teaching children, finding bugs in computer programs, or taking pictures.

Extrinsically motivated behavior is behavior that is performed to acquire material or social rewards or to avoid punishment; the source of motivation is the consequences of the behavior, not the behavior itself. A car salesperson who is motivated by receiving a commission on all cars sold, a lawyer who is motivated by the high salary and status that go along with the job, and a factory worker who is motivated by the opportunity to earn a secure income are all extrinsically motivated. Their motivation comes from the consequences they receive as a result of their work behaviors.

People can be intrinsically motivated, extrinsically motivated, or both intrinsically and extrinsically motivated.[24] A top manager who derives a sense of accomplishment and achievement from managing a large corporation and strives to reach year-end targets to obtain a hefty bonus is both intrinsically and extrinsically motivated. Similarly, a nurse who enjoys helping and taking care of patients and is motivated by having a secure job with good benefits is both intrinsically and extrinsically motivated. At Enterprise Rent-A-Car, employees are both extrinsically motivated, because of opportunities for promotions and having their pay linked to the performance of their branches or units, and intrinsically motivated, because they get a sense of satisfaction out of serving customers and learning new things. Whether workers are intrinsically motivated, extrinsically motivated, or both depends on a wide variety of factors: (1) workers' own personal characteristics (such as their personalities, abilities, values, attitudes, and needs), (2) the nature of their jobs (such as whether they have been enriched or where they are on the five core characteristics of the job characteristics model), and (3) the nature of the organization (such as its structure, its culture, its control systems, its human resource management system, and the ways in which rewards such as pay are distributed to employees).

prosocially motivated behavior Behavior that is performed to benefit or help others.

In addition to being intrinsically or extrinsically motivated, some people are prosocially motivated by their work.[25] **Prosocially motivated behavior** is behavior that is performed to benefit or help others.[26] Behavior can be prosocially motivated in addition to being extrinsically and/or intrinsically motivated. An elementary school teacher who not only enjoys the process of teaching young children (has high intrinsic motivation) but also has a strong desire to give children the best learning experience possible, help those with learning disabilities overcome their challenges, and keeps up with the latest research on child development and teaching methods in an effort to continually improve the effectiveness of his teaching has high prosocial motivation in addition to high intrinsic motivation. A surgeon who specializes in organ transplants and enjoys the challenge of performing complex operations, has a strong desire to help her patients regain their health and extend their lives through successful organ transplants, and also is motivated by the relatively high income she earns has high intrinsic, prosocial, and extrinsic motivation. Recent preliminary research suggests that when workers have high prosocial motivation, also having high intrinsic motivation can be especially beneficial for job performance.[27]

For some people, intrinsic and prosocial motivation comes from protecting the natural environment and encouraging others to do the same, as indicated in the following "Ethics in Action."

Ethics in Action

McDonough Protects the Planet

William McDonough's intrinsic and prosocial motivation comes from saving the natural environment from pollution and waste and encouraging large corporations and their managers to do the same.[28] McDonough, an environmental designer, is the founder and principal of Williman McDonough & Partners, an architecture and community design firm, and a cofounder of MBDC, a process and product design firm. MBDC, cofounded with Dr. Michael Braungart, focuses on developing ways for organizations to produce goods and services without producing waste and polluting the natural environment.[29] McDonough and Braungart helped the furniture manufacturer Herman Miller design a factory that, through its use of solar heating and cooling, has energy consumption savings of around 30%. They also helped create a new material for the soles of Nike athletic shoes that biodegrades without the customary release of toxic chemicals.[30]

McDonough is so intrinsically and prosocially motivated to protect our environment that for him, even recycling is not enough. Products made from recycled materials contain some of the toxic substances in the original products. Plastic bottles, for example, are often recycled, but the heavy metals and carcinogens in the bottles still find their ways into the new products made from them. And these new products eventually wind up in landfills, polluting the environment.[31]

McDonough and Braungart advocate that managers and organizations adopt "cradle-to-cradle design," which they introduced in their book *Cradle to Cradle: Remaking the Way We Make Things* (published by Northpoint Press; translated into Chinese, Korean, German, Spanish, and Italian).[32] Cradle-to-cradle design entails manufacturing products using biodegradable raw materials so that when a product is no longer useful, the materials it was made of either can be used over and over again in other products or will organically decompose. For example, McDonough recently designed a new carpet (called "A Walk in the Garden") for the Shaw Industries unit of Berkshire Hathaway that is

William McDonough's cradle-to-cradle philosophy revolutionizes the concept of recycling, eliminates waste, and promotes sustainability.

made of nylon pellets and polymers that can be reused again and again after the original carpet wears out.[33] This is in contrast to material from recyclable carpets being used to make other products which ultimately end up in landfills when they are discarded. Moreover, manufacturing costs for a Walk in the Garden are 10% lower than for some of Shaw's other carpet lines.[34]

Currently, McDonough is collaborating with the China Housing Industry Association to help it design sustainable housing in seven new Chinese cities using materials that contain no harmful chemicals and in ways that result in minimal energy costs for heating and cooling.[35] Clearly, McDonough's intrinsic and prosocial motivation to protect and preserve the natural environment is enabling other managers and organizations to proactively address this ethical concern in a socially responsible manner.

outcome Anything a person gets from a job or organization.

input Anything a person contributes to his or her job or organization.

Regardless of whether people are intrinsically, extrinsically, or prosocially motivated, they join and are motivated to work in organizations to obtain certain outcomes. An **outcome** is anything a person gets from a job or organization. Some outcomes, such as autonomy, responsibility, a feeling of accomplishment, and the pleasure of doing interesting or enjoyable work, result in intrinsically motivated behavior. Outcomes such as improving the lives or well-being of other people and doing good by helping others result in prosocially motivated behavior. Other outcomes, such as pay, job security, benefits, and vacation time, result in extrinsically motivated behavior.

Organizations hire people to obtain important inputs. An **input** is anything a person contributes to the job or organization, such as time, effort, education, experience, skills, knowledge, and actual work behaviors. Inputs such as these are necessary for an organization to achieve its goals. Managers strive to motivate members of an organization to contribute inputs—through their behavior, effort, and persistence—that help the organization achieve its goals. How do managers do this? They ensure that members of an organization obtain the outcomes they desire when they make valuable contributions to the organization. Managers use outcomes to motivate people to contribute their inputs to the organization. Giving people outcomes when they contribute inputs and perform well aligns the interests of employees with the goals of the organization as a whole because when employees do what is good for the organization, they personally benefit.

This alignment between employees and organizational goals as a whole can be described by the motivation equation depicted in Figure 13.1. Managers seek to

Figure 13.1
The Motivation Equation

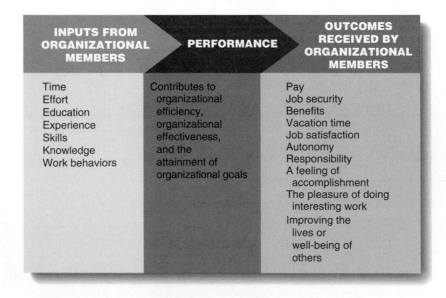

INPUTS FROM ORGANIZATIONAL MEMBERS	PERFORMANCE	OUTCOMES RECEIVED BY ORGANIZATIONAL MEMBERS
Time Effort Education Experience Skills Knowledge Work behaviors	Contributes to organizational efficiency, organizational effectiveness, and the attainment of organizational goals	Pay Job security Benefits Vacation time Job satisfaction Autonomy Responsibility A feeling of accomplishment The pleasure of doing interesting work Improving the lives or well-being of others

ensure that people are motivated to contribute important inputs to the organization, that these inputs are put to good use or focused in the direction of high performance, and that high performance results in workers' obtaining the outcomes they desire.

Each of the theories of motivation discussed in this chapter focuses on one or more aspects of this equation. Each theory focuses on a different set of issues that managers need to address to have a highly motivated workforce. Together, the theories provide a comprehensive set of guidelines for managers to follow to promote high levels of employee motivation. Effective managers, such as Jack and Andrew Taylor in "A Manager's Challenge," tend to follow many of these guidelines, whereas ineffective managers often fail to follow them and seem to have trouble motivating organizational members.

expectancy theory The theory that motivation will be high when workers believe that high levels of effort lead to high performance and high performance leads to the attainment of desired outcomes.

Expectancy Theory

Expectancy theory, formulated by Victor H. Vroom in the 1960s, posits that motivation is high when workers believe that high levels of effort lead to high performance and high performance leads to the attainment of desired outcomes. Expectancy theory is one of the most popular theories of work motivation because it focuses on all three parts of the motivation equation: inputs, performance, and outcomes. Expectancy theory identifies three major factors that determine a person's motivation: *expectancy, instrumentality,* and *valence* (see Figure 13.2).[36]

LO2 Describe from the perspectives of expectancy theory and equity theory what managers should do to have a highly motivated workforce.

Expectancy

expectancy In expectancy theory, a perception about the extent to which effort results in a certain level of performance.

Expectancy is a person's perception about the extent to which effort (an input) results in a certain level of performance. A person's level of expectancy determines whether he or she believes that a high level of effort results in a high level of performance. People are motivated to put forth a lot of effort on their jobs only if they think that their effort will pay off in high performance—that is, if they have high expectancy. Think about how motivated you would be to study for a test if you thought that no

Figure 13.2
Expectancy, Instrumentality, and Valence

matter how hard you tried, you would get a D. Think about how motivated a marketing manager would be who thought that no matter how hard he or she worked, there was no way to increase sales of an unpopular product. In these cases, expectancy is low, so overall motivation is also low.

Members of an organization are motivated to put forth a high level of effort only if they think that doing so leads to high performance.[37] In other words, in order for people's motivation to be high, expectancy must be high. Thus, in attempting to influence motivation, managers need to make sure that their subordinates believe that if they do try hard, they can actually succeed. One way managers can boost expectancies is through expressing confidence in their subordinates' capabilities. Managers at the Container Store, for example, express high levels of confidence in their subordinates. As Container Store co-founder Garrett Boone put it, "Everybody we hire, we hire as a leader. Anybody in our store can take an action that you might think of typically being a manager's action."[38]

In addition to expressing confidence in subordinates, other ways for managers to boost subordinates' expectancy levels and motivation is by providing training so that people have all the expertise needed for high performance and increasing their levels of autonomy and responsibility as they gain experience so that they have the freedom to do what it takes to perform at a high level. For example, the Best Buy chain of over 629 stores selling electronics, computers, music and movies, and gadgets of all sorts boosts salespeople's expectancies by providing them with extensive training in on-site meetings and online. Electronic learning terminals in each department not only help salespeople learn how different systems work and can be sold as an integrated package but also enable them to keep up to date with the latest advances in technology and products. Salespeople also receive extensive training in how to determine customers' needs.[39] At Enterprise Rent-A-Car in "A Manager's Challenge," the Management Training Program helps new hires develop high levels of expectancy and these high levels of expectancy are maintained as experienced employees are given more responsibility and autonomy to ensure that their branches' are profitable and provide excellent customer service.

Instrumentality

instrumentality In expectancy theory, a perception about the extent to which performance results in the attainment of outcomes.

Expectancy captures a person's perceptions about the relationship between effort and performance. **Instrumentality,** the second major concept in expectancy theory, is a person's perception about the extent to which performance at a certain level results in the attainment of outcomes (see Figure 13.2). According to expectancy theory, employees are motivated to perform at a high level only if they think that high performance will lead to (or is *instrumental* for attaining) outcomes such as pay, job security, interesting job assignments, bonuses, or a feeling of accomplishment. In other words, instrumentalities must be high for motivation to be high—people must perceive that because of their high performance they will receive outcomes.[40]

Managers promote high levels of instrumentality when they clearly link performance to desired outcomes. In addition, managers must clearly communicate this linkage to subordinates. By making sure that outcomes available in an organization are distributed to organizational members on the basis of their performance, managers promote high instrumentality and motivation. When outcomes are linked to performance in this way, high performers receive more outcomes than low performers. In "A Manager's Challenge," Andrew Taylor raises levels of instrumentality and motivation for Enterprise Rent-A-Car employees by linking opportunities for promotion and pay to performance.

Another example of high instrumentality contributing to high motivation can be found in the Cambodian immigrants who own, manage, and work in more than 80% of the doughnut shops in California.[41] These immigrants see high performance as leading to many important outcomes such as income, a comfortable existence, family security, and the autonomy provided by working in a small business. Their high instrumentality contributes to their high motivation to succeed.

Valence

valence In expectancy theory, how desirable each of the outcomes available from a job or organization is to a person.

Although all members of an organization must have high expectancies and instrumentalities, expectancy theory acknowledges that people differ in their preferences for outcomes. For many people, pay is the most important outcome of working. For others, a feeling of accomplishment or enjoying one's work is more important than pay. The term **valence** refers to how desirable each of the outcomes available from a job or organization is to a person. To motivate organizational members, managers need to determine which outcomes have high valence for them—are highly desired—and make sure that those outcomes are provided when members perform at a high level. From "A Manager's Challenge," it appears that not only pay but also autonomy, responsibility, and opportunities for promotions are highly valent outcomes for many employees at Enterprise Rent-A-Car.

Providing employees with highly valent outcomes can not only contribute to high levels of motivation, but also has the potential to reduce turnover, as indicated in the following "Management Insight."

Management Insight

Motivating and Retaining Employees at the Container Store

Kip Tindell and Garrett Boone founded the Container Store in Dallas, Texas, in 1978 and Tindell currently serves as CEO and chairman (Boone is chairman emeritus).[42] When they opened their first store, they were out on the floor trying to sell customers their storage and organization products that would economize on space and time and make purchasers' lives a little less complicated. The Container Store has grown to include 42 stores in 20 U.S. markets from coast to coast; although the original store in Dallas had only 1,600 square feet, the stores today average around 25,000 square feet.[43] The phenomenal growth in the size of the stores has been matched by impressive growth rates in sales and profits.[44] Surprisingly enough, Tindell and Boone can still be found on the shop floor tidying shelves and helping customers carry out their purchases.[45] And that, perhaps, is an important clue to the secret of their success. The Container Store has been consistently ranked among *Fortune* magazine's "100 Best Companies to Work For" for nine years running.[46] In 2008, the Container Store was 20th on this list.[47]

Early on, Tindell and Boone recognized that people are the Container Store's most valuable asset and that after hiring great people, one of the most important managerial tasks is motivating them. One would think that motivating employees might be especially challenging in the retail industry, which has an average annual turnover rate for full-time salespeople of more than 70% and an annual turnover rate for store managers of over 30%. The Container Store's comparable figures are fractions of these industry statistics, a testament to Tindell and Boone's ability to motivate.[48]

The Container Store's motivational approach means that each employee works as a leader—and that those in managerial positions still walk the floor to tidy up displays. Results are extremely positive, with the retail chain boasting significantly lower turnover rates than other chains in the industry.

Tindell and Boone have long recognized the importance of rewarding employees for a job well done with highly valent outcomes. For example, starting salaries for salespeople are around $40,000 which is significantly higher than retail averages and merit pay increases for superior sales performance are about 8% per year. To encourage high individual performance as well as teamwork and cooperation, both individual and team-based rewards are utilized at the Container Store. Some high-performing salespeople earn more than their store managers, which suits the store managers fine as long as equitable procedures are used and rewards are distributed fairly.[49]

Professional development is another valent outcome employees obtain from working at the Container Store. Full-time salespeople receive over 240 hours of training their first year and all employees have opportunities for additional training and development on an ongoing basis.[50] Employees also have flexible work options and flexible benefits; medical, dental, and 401(k) retirement plans; job security; a casual dress code; and access to a variety of wellness programs ranging from yoga classes and chair massages to a personalized, Web-based nutrition and exercise planner.[51] Another valent outcome is the opportunity to work with other highly motivated individuals in an environment that exudes enthusiasm and excitement. Not only are the Container Store's employees motivated, but they also look forward to coming to work and feel as if their coworkers and managers are part of their family. Employees feel pride in what they do—helping customers organize their lives, save space and time, and have a better sense of well-being. Hence, they not only personally benefit from high performance by receiving highly valent outcomes but also feel good about the products they sell and the help they give customers.[52] Tindell and Boone evidently have never lost sight of the importance of motivation for both organizations and their members.

Bringing It All Together

According to expectancy theory, high motivation results from high levels of expectancy, instrumentality, and valence (see Figure 13.3). If any one of these factors is low, motivation is likely to be low. No matter how tightly desired outcomes are linked to performance, if a person thinks it is practically impossible to perform at a high level, then motivation to perform at a high level is exceedingly low. Similarly, if a person does not think that outcomes are linked to high performance, or if a person does not desire the outcomes that are linked to high performance, then motivation to perform at a high level is low.

Figure 13.3
Expectancy Theory

Expectancy is high	Instrumentality is high	Valence is high
People perceive that if they try hard, they can perform at a high level.	People perceive that high performance leads to the receipt of certain outcomes.	People desire the outcomes that result from high performance.

HIGH MOTIVATION

For motivation to be high, managers must have good communication with employees so they know what is expected of them and what outcomes they will receive if they perform at a high level. As indicated in the following "Information Technology Byte," managers in small and growing companies need to be especially aware of the need for effective communication.

Information Technology Byte

Small Business

Boosting Motivation and Retention at Protus IP Solutions

Protus IP Solutions was founded in 1997 in Ottawa, Canada, and provides IT services to over 200,000 home users and business customers around the world centered on helping customers send and receive faxes via e-mail and the World Wide Web and effectively using voice and fax broadcasts.[53] A few years ago, turnover at Protus was as high as 60% per year. CEO Joseph Nour realized that something needed to be done to retain valuable employees, especially given that Protus is a small and growing company (Protus currently has 230 employees).[54]

Nour decided to hire Janice Vanderburg, who had experience in managing human resources at a larger company, to be the director of human resources at Protus.[55] Vanderburg soon realized that, similar to other young and growing small companies, Protus was lacking in terms of mechanisms to ensure effective communication with employees. Employees were not sure what was expected of them and what outcomes they could receive if they performed at a high level. For example, some employees had the option to participate in an incentive profit-sharing pay plan but the employees didn't know it.[56]

Vanderburg has since taken steps to encourage managers to effectively communicate with employees so that they know what is expected of them, they know about opportunities for promotions and lateral moves to other jobs in the company, and they know what outcomes they can and will receive if they perform at a high level. These steps are paying off—turnover has been reduced to around 15% per year and importantly, employees are motivated to perform at a high level.[57]

Need Theories

need A requirement or necessity for survival and well-being.

LO3 Explain how goals and needs motivate people and what kinds of goals are especially likely to result in high performance.

A **need** is a requirement or necessity for survival and well-being. The basic premise of **need theories** is that people are motivated to obtain outcomes at work that will satisfy their needs. Need theory complements expectancy theory by exploring in depth which outcomes motivate people to perform at a high level. Need theories suggest that to motivate a person to contribute valuable inputs to a job and perform at a high level, a manager must determine what needs the person is trying to satisfy at work and ensure that the person receives outcomes that help to satisfy those needs when the person performs at a high level and helps the organization achieve its goals.

There are several need theories. Here we discuss Abraham Maslow's hierarchy of needs, Clayton Alderfer's ERG theory, Frederick Herzberg's motivator-hygiene theory, and David McClelland's needs for achievement, affiliation, and power. These theories describe needs that people try to satisfy at work. In doing so, they provide managers with insights about what outcomes motivate members of an organization to perform at a high level and contribute inputs to help the organization achieve its goals.

Maslow's Hierarchy of Needs

need theories Theories of motivation that focus on what needs people are trying to satisfy at work and what outcomes will satisfy those needs.

Maslow's hierarchy of needs An arrangement of five basic needs that, according to Maslow, motivate behavior. Maslow proposed that the lowest level of unmet needs is the prime motivator and that only one level of needs is motivational at a time.

Psychologist Abraham Maslow proposed that all people seek to satisfy five basic kinds of needs: physiological needs, safety needs, belongingness needs, esteem needs, and self-actualization needs (see Table 13.1).[58] He suggested that these needs constitute a **hierarchy of needs,** with the most basic or compelling needs–physiological and safety needs–at the bottom. Maslow argued that these lowest-level needs must be met before a person strives to satisfy needs higher up in the hierarchy, such as self-esteem needs. Once a need is satisfied, Maslow proposed, it ceases to operate as a source of motivation. The lowest level of *unmet* needs in the hierarchy is the prime motivator of behavior; if and when this level is satisfied, needs at the next-highest level in the hierarchy motivate behavior.

Although this theory identifies needs that are likely to be important sources of motivation for many people, research does not support Maslow's contention that there is a need hierarchy or his notion that only one level of needs is motivational at a time.[59] Nevertheless, a key conclusion can be drawn from Maslow's theory: People try to satisfy different needs at work. To have a motivated workforce, managers must determine which needs employees are trying to satisfy in organizations and then make sure that individuals receive outcomes that satisfy their needs when they perform at a high level and contribute to organizational effectiveness. By doing this, managers align the interests of individual members with the interests of the organization as a whole. By doing what is good for the organization (that is, performing at a high level), employees receive outcomes that satisfy their needs.

In our increasingly global economy, managers must realize that citizens of different countries might differ in the needs they seek to satisfy through work.[60] Some research suggests, for example, that people in Greece and Japan are especially motivated by

Table 13.1
Maslow's Hierarchy of Needs

	Needs	Description	Examples of How Managers Can Help People Satisfy These Needs at Work
Highest-level needs	**Self-actualization needs**	The needs to realize one's full potential as a human being	By giving people the opportunity to use their skills and abilities to the fullest extent possible
	Esteem needs	The needs to feel good about oneself and one's capabilities, to be respected by others, and to receive recognition and appreciation	By granting promotions and recognizing accomplishments
	Belongingness needs	Needs for social interaction, friendship, affection, and love	By promoting good interpersonal relations and organizing social functions such as company picnics and holiday parties
	Safety needs	Needs for security, stability, and a safe environment	By providing job security, adequate medical benefits, and safe working conditions
Lowest-level needs (most basic or compelling)	**Physiological needs**	Basic needs for things such as food, water, and shelter that must be met in order for a person to survive	By providing a level of pay that enables a person to buy food and clothing and have adequate housing

The lowest level of unsatisfied needs motivates behavior; once this level of needs is satisfied, a person tries to satisfy the needs at the next level.

Jobs that involve artistic expression, such as dancing, can help people fulfill higher-level needs.

safety needs and that people in Sweden, Norway, and Denmark are motivated by belongingness needs.[61] In less-developed countries with low standards of living, physiological and safety needs are likely to be the prime motivators of behavior. As countries become wealthier and have higher standards of living, needs related to personal growth and accomplishment (such as esteem and self-actualization) become important as motivators of behavior.

Alderfer's ERG Theory

Clayton **Alderfer's ERG theory** collapses the five categories of needs in Maslow's hierarchy into three universal categories—existence, relatedness, and growth—also arranged in a hierarchy (see Table 13.2). Alderfer agrees with Maslow that as lower-level needs become satisfied, a person seeks to satisfy higher-level needs. Unlike Maslow, however, Alderfer believes that a person can be motivated by needs at more than one level at the same time. A cashier in a supermarket, for example, may be motivated both by existence needs and by relatedness needs. The existence needs motivate the cashier to come to work regularly and not make mistakes so that his job will be secure and he will be able to pay his rent and buy food. The relatedness needs motivate the cashier to become friends with some of the other cashiers and have a good relationship with the store manager. Alderfer also suggests that when people experience *need frustration* or are unable to satisfy needs at a certain level, they will focus all the more on satisfying the needs at the next-lowest level in the hierarchy.[62]

Alderfer's ERG theory
The theory that three universal needs—for existence, relatedness, and growth—constitute a hierarchy of needs and motivate behavior. Alderfer proposed that needs at more than one level can be motivational at the same time.

As with Maslow's theory, research does not support some of the specific ideas outlined in ERG theory, such as the existence of the three-level need hierarchy that Alderfer proposed.[63] However, for managers, the important message from ERG theory is the same as that from Maslow's theory: Determine what needs your subordinates are trying to satisfy at work, and make sure that they receive outcomes that satisfy these needs when they perform at a high level to help the organization achieve its goals.

Table 13.2

Alderfer's ERG Theory

	Needs	Description	Examples of How Managers Can Help People Satisfy These Needs at Work
Highest-level needs	**Growth needs**	The needs for self-development and creative and productive work	By allowing people to continually improve their skills and abilities and engage in meaningful work
↑	**Relatedness needs**	The needs to have good interpersonal relations, to share thoughts and feelings, and to have open two-way communication	By promoting good interpersonal relations and by providing accurate feedback
↓ **Lowest-level needs**	**Existence needs**	Basic needs for food, water, clothing, shelter, and a secure and safe environment	By promoting enough pay to provide for the basic necessities of life and safe working conditions

**As lower-level needs are satisfied, a person is motivated to satisfy higher-level needs.
When a person is unable to satisfy higher-level needs (or is frustrated),
motivation to satisfy lower-level needs increases.**

Herzberg's Motivator-Hygiene Theory

Adopting an approach different from Maslow's and Alderfer's, Frederick Herzberg focuses on two factors: (1) outcomes that can lead to high levels of motivation and job satisfaction and (2) outcomes that can prevent people from being dissatisfied. According to **Herzberg's motivator-hygiene theory,** people have two sets of needs or requirements: motivator needs and hygiene needs.[64] *Motivator needs* are related to the nature of the work itself and how challenging it is. Outcomes, such as interesting work, autonomy, responsibility, being able to grow and develop on the job, and a sense of accomplishment and achievement, help to satisfy motivator needs. To have a highly motivated and satisfied workforce, Herzberg suggested, managers should take steps to ensure that employees' motivator needs are being met.

Hygiene needs are related to the physical and psychological context in which the work is performed. Hygiene needs are satisfied by outcomes such as pleasant and comfortable working conditions, pay, job security, good relationships with coworkers, and effective supervision. According to Herzberg, when hygiene needs are not met, workers are dissatisfied, and when hygiene needs are met, workers are not dissatisfied. Satisfying hygiene needs, however, does not result in high levels of motivation or even high levels of job satisfaction. For motivation and job satisfaction to be high, motivator needs must be met.

Many research studies have tested Herzberg's propositions, and, by and large, the theory fails to receive support.[65] Nevertheless, Herzberg's formulations have contributed to our understanding of motivation in at least two ways. First, Herzberg helped to focus researchers' and managers' attention on the important distinction between intrinsic motivation (related to motivator needs) and extrinsic motivation (related to hygiene needs), covered earlier in the chapter. Second, his theory prompted researchers and managers to study how jobs could be designed or redesigned so that they are intrinsically motivating.

Herzberg's motivator-hygiene theory A need theory that distinguishes between motivator needs (related to the nature of the work itself) and hygiene needs (related to the physical and psychological context in which the work is performed) and proposes that motivator needs must be met for motivation and job satisfaction to be high.

McClelland's Needs for Achievement, Affiliation, and Power

Psychologist David McClelland has extensively researched the needs for achievement, affiliation, and power.[66] The **need for achievement** is the extent to which an individual has a strong desire to perform challenging tasks well and to meet personal standards for excellence. People with a high need for achievement often set clear goals for themselves and like to receive performance feedback. The **need for affiliation** is the extent to which an individual is concerned about establishing and maintaining good interpersonal relations, being liked, and having the people around him or her get along with each other. The **need for power** is the extent to which an individual desires to control or influence others.[67]

While each of these needs is present in each of us to some degree, their importance in the workplace depends upon the position one occupies. For example, research suggests that high needs for achievement and for power are assets for first-line and middle managers and that a high need for power is especially important for upper managers.[68] One study found that U.S. presidents with a relatively high need for power tended to be especially effective during their terms of office.[69] A high need for affiliation may not always be desirable in managers and other leaders because it might lead them to try too hard to be liked by others (including subordinates) rather than doing all they can to ensure that performance is as high as it can and should be. Although most research on these needs has been done in the United States, some studies suggest that the findings may be applicable to people in other countries as well, such as India and New Zealand.[70]

need for achievement The extent to which an individual has a strong desire to perform challenging tasks well and to meet personal standards for excellence.

need for affiliation The extent to which an individual is concerned about establishing and maintaining good interpersonal relations, being liked, and having the people around him or her get along with each other.

need for power The extent to which an individual desires to control or influence others.

Other Needs

Clearly more needs motivate workers than the needs described by the above four theories. For example, more and more workers are feeling the need for work-life balance and time to take care of their loved ones while simultaneously being highly motivated at work. Interestingly enough, recent research suggests that being exposed to nature (even just being able to see some trees from your office window) has many salutary effects and a lack of such exposure can actually impair well-being and performance.[71] Thus, having some time during the day when one can at least see nature may be another important need.

Managers of successful companies often strive to ensure that as many of their valued employees' needs as possible are satisfied in the workplace. This is illustrated by the following "Information Technology Byte" on the SAS Institute.

Information Technology Byte

High Motivation Rules at the SAS Institute

The SAS Institute is in the enviable position of being listed on *Fortune* magazine's annual ranking of the "100 Best Companies to Work For" for 11 years in a row; in 2008 the SAS Institute was ranked 29th.[72] The SAS Institute is the world's largest privately owned software company, with over 10,000 employees worldwide and approximately $1.9 billion in revenues.[73] Every indicator suggests that SAS employees are highly motivated and perform well while also working 35-hour weeks. How do managers at SAS do it? In large part, by ensuring that employees are highly motivated and the variety of needs they bring to the workplace are satisfied by doing a good job at SAS.[74]

Satisfying the need for intrinsically motivating work has also been a key priority at SAS. Managers strive to make sure that each employee is motivated by the work he or she performs, and employees are encouraged to change jobs to prevent becoming bored with their work (even if the job changes require that SAS provide additional training). Moreover, in contrast to the approach at some of the company's competitors, all new product development work at SAS is performed in-house, so employees have the opportunity to experience the excitement of developing a new product and seeing it succeed.[75]

The SAS Institute satisfies employees' needs for economic security by paying them fairly and providing them with secure jobs. Employees have their own offices, and the work environment is rich in pleasant vistas, whether they be artwork on the walls or views of the rolling hills of Cary, North Carolina, at company headquarters. Managers at SAS realize that needs for work–life balance are a top priority for many of their employees and seek to satisfy these needs in a variety of ways, including 35-hour workweeks, on-site day care and medical care, unlimited sick days, and high chairs in the company cafeteria so that employees can dine with their kids. Moreover, employees and their families are encouraged to use the 200 acres that surround company headquarters for family walks and picnics.[76]

Since the company was founded, CEO James Goodnight has been committed to motivating employees to develop creative and high-quality products that meet customers' needs. Today, 96% of the top 100 companies in the Fortune 500

Many employees at the SAS Institute's headquarters in Cary.North Carolina take advantage of an on-site recreation and fitness center.

list use SAS products for a wide variety of purposes including risk management, monitoring and measuring performance, managing relations with suppliers and customers, and detecting fraud.[77] SAS also provides educational software for schools and teachers through SAS in School.[78] Clearly, motivating employees and helping to satisfy their needs is a win–win situation for SAS.

Equity Theory

LO2 Describe from the perspectives of expectancy theory and equity theory what managers should do to have a highly motivated workforce.

equity theory A theory of motivation that focuses on people's perceptions of the fairness of their work outcomes relative to their work inputs.

equity The justice, impartiality, and fairness to which all organizational members are entitled.

Equity theory is a theory of motivation that concentrates on people's perceptions of the fairness of their work *outcomes* relative to, or in proportion to, their work *inputs*. Equity theory complements expectancy and need theories by focusing on how people perceive the relationship between the outcomes they receive from their jobs and organizations and the inputs they contribute. Equity theory was formulated in the 1960s by J. Stacy Adams, who stressed that what is important in determining motivation is the *relative* rather than the *absolute* levels of outcomes a person receives and inputs a person contributes. Specifically, motivation is influenced by the comparison of one's own outcome-input ratio with the outcome-input ratio of a referent.[79] The *referent* could be another person or a group of people who are perceived to be similar to oneself; the referent also could be oneself in a previous job or one's expectations about what outcome-input ratios should be. In a comparison of one's own outcome-input ratio to a referent's ratio, one's *perceptions* of outcomes and inputs (not any objective indicator of them) are key.

Equity

Equity exists when a person perceives his or her own outcome-input ratio to be equal to a referent's outcome-input ratio. Under conditions of equity (see Table 13.3), if a referent receives more outcomes than you receive, the referent contributes proportionally more inputs to the organization, so his or her outcome-input ratio still equals your

Table 13.3
Equity Theory

Condition	Person		Referent	Example
Equity	$\dfrac{\text{Outcomes}}{\text{Inputs}}$	=	$\dfrac{\text{Outcomes}}{\text{Inputs}}$	An engineer perceives that he contributes more inputs (time and effort) and receives proportionally more outcomes (a higher salary and choice job assignments) than his referent.
Underpayment inequity	$\dfrac{\text{Outcomes}}{\text{Inputs}}$	< (less than)	$\dfrac{\text{Outcomes}}{\text{Inputs}}$	An engineer perceives that he contributes more inputs but receives the same outcomes as his referent.
Overpayment inequity	$\dfrac{\text{Outcomes}}{\text{Inputs}}$	> (greater than)	$\dfrac{\text{Outcomes}}{\text{Inputs}}$	An engineer perceives that he contributes the same inputs but receives more outcomes than his referent.

ratio. Maria Sanchez and Claudia King, for example, both work in a shoe store in a large mall. Sanchez is paid more per hour than King but also contributes more inputs, including being responsible for some of the store's bookkeeping, closing the store, and periodically depositing cash in the bank. When King compares her outcome-input ratio to Sanchez's (her referent's), she perceives the ratios to be equitable because Sanchez's higher level of pay (an outcome) is proportional to her higher level of inputs (bookkeeping, closing the store, and going to the bank).

Similarly, under conditions of equity, if you receive more outcomes than a referent, then your inputs are perceived to be proportionally higher. Continuing with our example, when Sanchez compares her outcome-input ratio to King's (her referent's) ratio, she perceives them to be equitable because her higher level of pay is proportional to her higher level of inputs.

When equity exists, people are motivated to continue contributing their current levels of inputs to their organizations to receive their current levels of outcomes. If people wish to increase their outcomes under conditions of equity, they are motivated to increase their inputs.

Inequity

inequity Lack of fairness.

Inequity, lack of fairness, exists when a person's outcome-input ratio is not perceived to be equal to a referent's. Inequity creates pressure or tension inside people and motivates them to restore equity by bringing the two ratios back into balance.

There are two types of inequity: underpayment inequity and overpayment inequity (see Table 13.3). **Underpayment inequity** exists when a person's own outcome-input ratio is perceived to be *less* than that of a referent. In comparing yourself to a referent, you think that you are *not* receiving the outcomes you should be, given your inputs. **Overpayment inequity** exists when a person perceives that his or her own outcome-input ratio is *greater* than that of a referent. In comparing yourself to a referent, you think that you are receiving *more* outcomes than you should be, given your inputs.

underpayment inequity
The inequity that exists when a person perceives that his or her own outcome-input ratio is less than the ratio of a referent.

overpayment inequity
The inequity that exists when a person perceives that his or her own outcome-input ratio is greater than the ratio of a referent.

Ways to Restore Equity

According to equity theory, both underpayment inequity and overpayment inequity create tension that motivates most people to restore equity by bringing the ratios back into balance.[80] When people experience *underpayment* inequity, they may be motivated to lower their inputs by reducing their working hours, putting forth less effort on the job, or being absent or they may be motivated to increase their outcomes by asking for a raise or a promotion. Susan Richie, a financial analyst at a large corporation, noticed that she was working longer hours and getting more work accomplished than a coworker who had the same position, yet they both received the exact same pay and other outcomes. To restore equity, Richie decided to stop coming in early and staying late. Alternatively, she could have tried to restore equity by trying to increase her outcomes, say, by asking her boss for a raise.

When people experience *underpayment* inequity and other means of equity restoration fail, they can change their perceptions of their own or the referent's inputs or outcomes. For example, they may realize that their referent is really working on more difficult projects than they are or that they really take more time off from work than their referent does. Alternatively, if people who feel that they are underpaid have other employment options, they may leave the organization. As an example, John Steinberg, an assistant principal in a high school, experienced underpayment inequity when he realized that all of the other assistant principals of high schools in his school district had received promotions to the position of principal even though they had been in their jobs for a shorter time than he had been. Steinberg's performance had always been appraised as being high, so after his repeated requests for a promotion went unheeded, he found a job as a principal in a different school district.

When people experience *overpayment* inequity, they may try to restore equity by changing their perceptions of their own or their referent's inputs or outcomes. Equity can be restored when people realize that they are contributing more inputs than they originally thought. Equity also can be restored by perceiving the referent's inputs to be lower or the referent's outcomes to be higher than one originally thought. When equity is restored in this way, actual inputs and outcomes are unchanged and the person being overpaid takes no real action. What is changed is how people think about or view their or the referent's inputs and outcomes. For instance, Mary McMann experienced overpayment inequity when she realized that she was being paid $2 an hour more than a coworker who had the same job as she did in a record store and who contributed the same amount of inputs. McMann restored equity by changing her perceptions of her inputs. She realized that she worked harder than her coworker and solved more problems that came up in the store.

Experiencing either overpayment or underpayment inequity, you might decide that your referent is not appropriate because, for example, the referent is too different from yourself. Choosing a more appropriate referent may bring the ratios back into balance. Angela Martinez, a middle manager in the engineering department of a chemical company, experienced overpayment inequity when she realized that she was being paid quite a bit more than her friend, who was a middle manager in the marketing department of the same company. After thinking about the discrepancy for a while, Martinez decided that engineering and marketing were so different that she should not be comparing her job to her friend's job even though they were both middle managers. Martinez restored equity by changing her referent; she picked a middle manager in the engineering department as a new referent.

Motivation is highest when as many people as possible in an organization perceive that they are being equitably treated—their outcomes and inputs are in balance. Top contributors and performers are motivated to continue contributing a high level of inputs because they are receiving the outcomes they deserve. Mediocre contributors and performers realize that if they want to increase their outcomes, they have to increase their inputs. Managers of effective organizations, like Jack and Andrew Taylor at Enterprise Rent-A-Car, realize the importance of equity for motivation and performance and continually strive to ensure that employees believe they are being equitably treated.

The dot-com boom, its subsequent bust, and a recession, along with increased global competition, have resulted in some workers' putting in longer and longer working hours (i.e., increasing their inputs) without any kind of increase in their outcomes. For those whose referents are not experiencing a similar change, perceptions of inequity are likely. According to Jill Andresky Fraser, author of *White Collar Sweatshop,* over 25 million U.S. workers work more than 49 hours per week in the office, almost 11 million work more than 60 hours per week in the office, and many also put in additional work hours at home. Moreover, advances in information technology, such as e-mail and cell phones, have resulted in work intruding on home time, vacation time, and even special occasions.[81]

Goal-Setting Theory

goal-setting theory A theory that focuses on identifying the types of goals that are most effective in producing high levels of motivation and performance and explaining why goals have those effects.

Goal-setting theory focuses on motivating workers to contribute their inputs to their jobs and organizations; in this way it is similar to expectancy theory and equity theory. But goal-setting theory takes this focus a step further by considering as well how managers can ensure that organizational members focus their inputs in the direction of high performance and the achievement of organizational goals.

Ed Locke and Gary Latham, the leading researchers on goal-setting theory, suggest that the goals that organizational members strive to attain are prime determinants of their motivation and subsequent performance. A *goal* is what a person is trying to accomplish through his or her efforts and behaviors.[82] Just as you may have a goal to get a good grade in this course, so do members of an organization have goals that they strive to meet. For example, salespeople at Neiman Marcus strive to meet sales goals, while top managers pursue market share and profitability goals.

Goal-setting theory suggests that to stimulate high motivation and performance, goals must be *specific* and *difficult*.[83] Specific goals are often quantitative—a salesperson's goal to sell $200 worth of merchandise per day, a scientist's goal to finish a project in one year, a CEO's goal to reduce debt by 40% and increase revenues by 20%, a restaurant manager's goal to serve 150 customers per evening. In contrast to specific goals, vague goals such as "doing your best" or "selling as much as you can" do not have much motivational impact.

Difficult goals are hard but not impossible to attain. In contrast to difficult goals, easy goals are those that practically everyone can attain, and moderate goals are goals that about one-half of the people can attain. Both easy and moderate goals have less motivational power than difficult goals.

Regardless of whether specific, difficult goals are set by managers, workers, or teams of managers and workers, they lead to high levels of motivation and performance. When managers set goals for their subordinates, their subordinates must accept the goals or agree to work toward them; also, they should be committed to them or really want to attain them. Some managers find that having subordinates participate in the actual setting of goals boosts their acceptance of and commitment to the goals. In addition, organizational members need to receive *feedback* about how they are doing; feedback can often be provided by the performance appraisal and feedback component of an organization's human resource management system (see Chapter 12). More generally, goals and feedback are integral components of performance management systems such as management by objectives (see Chapter 11).

Specific, difficult goals can encourage people to exert high levels of effort and to focus efforts in the right direction.

Specific, difficult goals affect motivation in two ways. First, they motivate people to contribute more inputs to their jobs. Specific, difficult goals cause people to put forth high levels of effort, for example. Just as you would study harder if you were trying to get an A in a course instead of a C, so too will a salesperson work harder to reach a $200 sales goal instead of a $100 sales goal. Specific, difficult goals also cause people to be more persistent than easy, moderate, or vague goals when they run into difficulties. Salespeople who are told to sell as much as possible might stop trying on a slow day, whereas having a specific, difficult goal to reach causes them to keep trying.

A second way in which specific, difficult goals affect motivation is by helping people focus their inputs in the right direction. These goals let people know what they should be focusing their attention on, be it increasing the quality of customer service or sales or lowering new product development times. The fact that the goals are specific and difficult also frequently causes people to develop *action plans* for reaching them.[84] Action plans can include the strategies to attain the goals and timetables or schedules for the completion of different activities crucial to goal attainment. Like the goals themselves, action plans also help ensure that efforts are focused in the right direction and that people do not get sidetracked along the way.

Although specific, difficult goals have been found to increase motivation and performance in a wide variety of jobs and organizations both in the United States and abroad, recent research suggests that they may detract from performance under certain conditions. When people are performing complicated and very challenging tasks that require them to focus on a considerable amount of learning, specific, difficult goals may actually impair performance.[85] Striving to reach such goals may direct some of a person's attention away from learning about the task and toward trying to figure out how to achieve the goal. Once a person has learned the task and it no longer seems complicated or difficult, then the assignment of specific, difficult goals is likely to have its usual effects. Additionally, for work that is very creative and uncertain, specific, difficult goals may be detrimental.

learning theories Theories that focus on increasing employee motivation and performance by linking the outcomes that employees receive to the performance of desired behaviors and the attainment of goals.

Learning Theories

The basic premise of **learning theories** as applied to organizations is that managers can increase employee motivation and performance by the ways they link the outcomes that employees receive to the performance of desired behaviors and the attainment of goals. Thus, learning theory focuses on the linkage between performance and outcomes in the motivation equation (see Figure 13.1).

learning A relatively permanent change in knowledge or behavior that results from practice or experience.

Learning can be defined as a relatively permanent change in a person's knowledge or behavior that results from practice or experience.[86] Learning takes place in organizations when people learn to perform certain behaviors to receive certain outcomes. For example, a person learns to perform at a higher level than in the past or to come to work earlier because he or she is motivated to obtain the outcomes that result from these behaviors, such as a pay raise or praise from a supervisor. In "A Manager's Challenge," Enterprise Rent-a-Car's emphasis on training ensures that new hires learn how to provide excellent customer service and perform all the tasks necessary for successful branch operations.

LO4 Identify the motivation lessons that managers can learn from operant conditioning theory and social learning theory.

Of the different learning theories, operant conditioning theory and social learning theory provide the most guidance to managers in their efforts to have a highly motivated workforce.

Operant Conditioning Theory

operant conditioning theory The theory that people learn to perform behaviors that lead to desired consequences and learn not to perform behaviors that lead to undesired consequences.

According to **operant conditioning theory,** developed by psychologist B. F. Skinner, people learn to perform behaviors that lead to desired consequences and learn not to perform behaviors that lead to undesired consequences.[87] Translated into motivation terms, Skinner's theory means that people will be motivated to perform at a high level and attain their work goals to the extent that high performance and goal attainment allow them to obtain outcomes they desire. Similarly, people avoid performing behaviors that lead to outcomes they do not desire. By linking the performance of *specific behaviors* to the attainment of *specific outcomes,* managers can motivate organizational members to perform in ways that help an organization achieve its goals.

Operant conditioning theory provides four tools that managers can use to motivate high performance and prevent workers from engaging in absenteeism and other behaviors that detract from organizational effectiveness. These tools are positive reinforcement, negative reinforcement, extinction, and punishment.[88]

positive reinforcement
Giving people outcomes they desire when they perform organizationally functional behaviors.

POSITIVE REINFORCEMENT **Positive reinforcement** gives people outcomes they desire when they perform organizationally functional behaviors. These desired outcomes, called *positive reinforcers,* include any outcomes that a person desires, such as pay, praise, or a promotion. Organizationally functional behaviors are behaviors that contribute to organizational effectiveness; they can include producing high-quality goods and services, providing high-quality customer service, and meeting deadlines. By linking positive reinforcers to the performance of functional behaviors, managers motivate people to perform the desired behaviors.

negative reinforcement
Eliminating or removing undesired outcomes when people perform organizationally functional behaviors.

NEGATIVE REINFORCEMENT **Negative reinforcement** also can encourage members of an organization to perform desired or organizationally functional behaviors. Managers using negative reinforcement actually eliminate or remove undesired outcomes once the functional behavior is performed. These undesired outcomes, called *negative reinforcers,* can range from a manager's constant nagging or criticism to unpleasant assignments or the ever-present threat of losing one's job. When negative reinforcement is used, people are motivated to perform behaviors because they want to stop receiving or avoid undesired outcomes. Managers who try to encourage salespeople to sell more by threatening them with being fired are using negative reinforcement. In this case, the negative reinforcer is the threat of job loss, which is removed once the functional behavior is performed.

Whenever possible, managers should try to use positive reinforcement. Negative reinforcement can create a very unpleasant work environment and even a negative culture in an organization. No one likes to be nagged, threatened, or exposed to other kinds of negative outcomes. The use of negative reinforcement sometimes causes subordinates to resent managers and try to get back at them.

IDENTIFYING THE RIGHT BEHAVIORS FOR REINFORCEMENT
Even managers who use positive reinforcement (and refrain from using negative reinforcement) can get into trouble if they are not careful to identify the right behaviors to reinforce—behaviors that are truly functional for the organization. Doing this is not always as straightforward as it might seem. First, it is crucial for managers to choose behaviors over which subordinates have control; in other words, subordinates must have the freedom and opportunity to perform the behaviors that are being reinforced. Second, it is crucial that these behaviors contribute to organizational effectiveness.

extinction Curtailing the performance of dysfunctional behaviors by eliminating whatever is reinforcing them.

EXTINCTION Sometimes members of an organization are motivated to perform behaviors that actually detract from organizational effectiveness. According to operant conditioning theory, all behavior is controlled or determined by its consequences; one way for managers to curtail the performance of dysfunctional behaviors is to eliminate whatever is reinforcing the behaviors. This process is called **extinction.**

Suppose a manager has a subordinate who frequently stops by his office to chat—sometimes about work-related matters but at other times about various topics ranging from politics to last night's football game. The manager and the subordinate share certain interests and views, so these conversations can get quite involved, and both seem to enjoy them. The manager, however, realizes that these frequent and sometimes lengthy conversations are actually causing him to stay at work later in the evenings to make up for the time he loses during the day. The manager also realizes that he is actually reinforcing his subordinate's behavior by acting interested in the topics the subordinate brings up and responding at length to them. To extinguish this behavior, the manager stops acting interested in these non-work-related conversations and keeps his responses polite and friendly but brief. No longer being reinforced with a pleasurable conversation, the subordinate eventually ceases to be motivated to interrupt the manager during working hours to discuss non-work-related issues.

PUNISHMENT Sometimes managers cannot rely on extinction to eliminate dysfunctional behaviors because they do not have control over whatever is reinforcing the behavior or because they cannot afford the time needed for extinction to work.

punishment Administering an undesired or negative consequence when dysfunctional behavior occurs.

When employees are performing dangerous behaviors or behaviors that are illegal or unethical, the behavior needs to be eliminated immediately. Sexual harassment, for example, is an organizationally dysfunctional behavior that cannot be tolerated. In such cases managers often rely on **punishment,** administering an undesired or negative consequence to subordinates when they perform the dysfunctional behavior. Punishments used by organizations range from verbal reprimands to pay cuts, temporary suspensions, demotions, and firings. Punishment, however, can have some unintended side effects—resentment, loss of self-respect, a desire for retaliation—and should be used only when necessary.

To avoid the unintended side effects of punishment, managers should keep in mind these guidelines:

- Downplay the emotional element involved in punishment. Make it clear that you are punishing a person's performance of a dysfunctional behavior, not the person himself or herself.

- Try to punish dysfunctional behaviors as soon after they occur as possible, and make sure the negative consequence is a source of punishment for the individuals involved. Be certain that organizational members know exactly why they are being punished.

- Try to avoid punishing someone in front of others, for this can hurt a person's self-respect and lower esteem in the eyes of coworkers as well as make coworkers feel uncomfortable.[89] Even so, making organizational members aware that an individual who has committed a serious infraction has been punished can sometimes be effective in preventing future infractions and teaching all members of the organization that certain behaviors are unacceptable. For example, when organizational members are informed that a manager who has sexually harassed subordinates has been punished, they learn or are reminded of the fact that sexual harassment is not tolerated in the organization.

Managers and students alike often confuse negative reinforcement and punishment. To avoid such confusion, keep in mind the two major differences between them. First, negative reinforcement is used to promote the performance of functional behaviors in organizations; punishment is used to stop the performance of dysfunctional behaviors. Second, negative reinforcement entails the *removal* of a negative consequence when functional behaviors are performed; punishment entails the *administration* of negative consequences when dysfunctional behaviors are performed.

organizational behavior modification (OB MOD) The systematic application of operant conditioning techniques to promote the performance of organizationally functional behaviors and discourage the performance of dysfunctional behaviors.

ORGANIZATIONAL BEHAVIOR MODIFICATION When managers systematically apply operant conditioning techniques to promote the performance of organizationally functional behaviors and discourage the performance of dysfunctional behaviors, they are engaging in **organizational behavior modification (OB MOD).**[90] OB MOD has been successfully used to improve productivity, efficiency, attendance, punctuality, safe work practices, customer service, and other important behaviors in a wide variety of organizations such as banks, department stores, factories, hospitals, and construction sites.[91] The five basic steps in OB MOD are described in Figure 13.4.

OB MOD works best for behaviors that are specific, objective, and countable, such as attendance and punctuality, making sales, or putting telephones together, all of which lend themselves to careful scrutiny and control. OB MOD may be questioned because of its lack of relevance to certain work behaviors (for example, the many work behaviors that are not specific, objective, and countable). Some people also have questioned it on ethical grounds. Critics of OB MOD suggest that it is overly controlling and robs workers of their dignity, individuality, freedom of choice, and even creativity. Supporters counter that OB MOD is a highly effective means of promoting organizational efficiency. There is some merit to both sides of this argument. What is clear, however, is that when used appropriately, OB MOD provides managers with a technique to motivate the performance of at least some organizationally functional behaviors.[92]

Figure 13.4
Five Steps in OB MOD

Source: Adapted from *Organizational Behavior Modification and Beyond* by F. Luthans and R. Kreitner (Scott, Foresman, 1985). With permission of the authors.

Social Learning Theory

social learning theory
A theory that takes into account how learning and motivation are influenced by people's thoughts and beliefs and their observations of other people's behavior.

Social learning theory proposes that motivation results not only from direct experience of rewards and punishments but also from a person's thoughts and beliefs. Social learning theory extends operant conditioning's contribution to managers' understanding of motivation by explaining (1) how people can be motivated by observing other people perform a behavior and be reinforced for doing so *(vicarious learning)*, (2) how people can be motivated to control their behavior themselves *(self-reinforcement)*, and (3) how people's beliefs about their ability to successfully perform a behavior affect motivation *(self-efficacy)*.[93] We look briefly at each of these motivators.

vicarious learning Learning that occurs when the learner becomes motivated to perform a behavior by watching another person perform it and be reinforced for doing so; also called *observational learning*.

VICARIOUS LEARNING **Vicarious learning,** often called *observational learning,* occurs when a person (the learner) becomes motivated to perform a behavior by watching another person (the model) perform the behavior and be positively reinforced for doing so. Vicarious learning is a powerful source of motivation on many jobs in which people learn to perform functional behaviors by watching others. Salespeople learn how to be helpful to customers, medical school students learn how to treat patients, law clerks learn how to practice law, and nonmanagers learn how to be managers, in part, by observing experienced members of an organization perform these behaviors properly

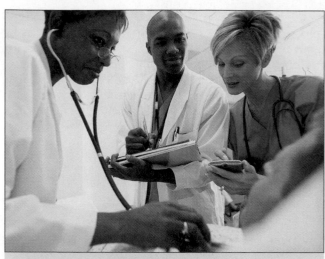

One of the ways in which aspiring physicians learn is by watching skilled physicians treat patients.

and be reinforced for them. In general, people are more likely to be motivated to imitate the behavior of models who are highly competent, are (to some extent) experts in the behavior, have high status, receive attractive reinforcers, and are friendly or approachable.[94]

To promote vicarious learning, managers should strive to have the learner meet the following conditions:

- The learner observes the model performing the behavior.

- The learner accurately perceives the model's behavior.

- The learner remembers the behavior.

- The learner has the skills and abilities needed to perform the behavior.

- The learner sees or knows that the model is positively reinforced for the behavior.[95]

self-reinforcer Any desired or attractive outcome or reward that a person gives to himself or herself for good performance.

SELF-REINFORCEMENT   Although managers are often the providers of reinforcement in organizations, sometimes people motivate themselves through self-reinforcement. People can control their own behavior by setting goals for themselves and then reinforcing themselves when they achieve the goals.[96] **Self-reinforcers** are any desired or attractive outcomes or rewards that people can give to themselves for good performance, such as a feeling of accomplishment, going to a movie, having dinner out, buying a new CD, or taking time out for a golf game. When members of an organization control their own behavior through self-reinforcement, managers do not need to spend as much time as they ordinarily would trying to motivate and control behavior through the administration of consequences because subordinates are controlling and motivating themselves. In fact, this self-control is often referred to as the *self-management of behavior.*

When employees are highly skilled and are responsible for creating new goods and services, managers typically rely on self-control and self-management of behavior, as is the case at Google. Employees at Google are given the flexibility and autonomy to experiment, take risks, and sometimes fail as they work on new projects. They are encouraged to learn from their failures and apply what they learn to subsequent projects.[97] Google's engineers are given one day a week to work on their own projects that they are highly involved with, and new products such as Google News often emerge from these projects.[98]

self-efficacy A person's belief about his or her ability to perform a behavior successfully.

SELF-EFFICACY   **Self-efficacy** is a person's belief about his or her ability to perform a behavior successfully.[99] Even with all the most attractive consequences or reinforcers hinging on high performance, people are not going to be motivated if they do not think that they can actually perform at a high level. Similarly, when people control their own behavior, they are likely to set for themselves difficult goals that will lead to outstanding accomplishments only if they think that they have the capability to reach those goals. Thus, self-efficacy influences motivation both when managers provide reinforcement and when workers themselves provide it.[100] The greater the self-efficacy, the greater is the motivation and performance. In "A Manager's Challenge," managers at Enterprise Rent-A-Car boost self-efficacy by providing employees with training, increasing their levels of autonomy and responsibility as they gain experience with the company, and expressing confidence in their ability to manage their own units. Such verbal persuasion, as well as a person's own past performance and accomplishments and the accomplishments of other people, plays a role in determining a person's self-efficacy.

Pay and Motivation

In Chapter 12, we discussed how managers establish a pay level and structure for an organization as a whole. Here we focus on how, once a pay level and structure are in place, managers can use pay to motivate employees to perform at a high level and attain their work goals. Pay is used to motivate entry-level workers, first-line and middle managers, and even top managers such as CEOs. Pay can be used to motivate people to perform behaviors that help an organization achieve its goals, and it can be used to motivate people to join and remain with an organization.

Each of the theories described in this chapter alludes to the importance of pay and suggests that pay should be based on performance:

- *Expectancy theory:* Instrumentality, the association between performance and outcomes such as pay, must be high for motivation to be high. In addition, pay is an outcome that has high valence for many people.

- *Need theories:* People should be able to satisfy their needs by performing at a high level; pay can be used to satisfy several different kinds of needs.

- *Equity theory:* Outcomes such as pay should be distributed in proportion to inputs (including performance levels).

- *Goal-setting theory:* Outcomes such as pay should be linked to the attainment of goals.

- *Learning theories:* The distribution of outcomes such as pay should be contingent on the performance of organizationally functional behaviors.

As these theories suggest, to promote high motivation, managers should base the distribution of pay to organizational members on performance levels so that high performers receive more pay than low performers (other things being equal).[101] At General Mills, for example, the pay of all employees, ranging from mailroom clerks to senior managers, is based, at least in part, on performance.[102] A compensation plan basing pay on performance is often called a **merit pay plan.** Once managers have decided to use a merit pay plan, they face two important choices: whether to base pay on individual, group, or organizational performance or to use salary increases or bonuses.

LO5 Explain why and how managers can use pay as a major motivation tool.

merit pay plan
A compensation plan that bases pay on performance.

Basing Merit Pay on Individual, Group, or Organizational Performance

Managers can base merit pay on individual, group, or organizational performance. When individual performance (such as the dollar value of merchandise a salesperson sells, the number of loudspeakers a factory worker assembles, and a lawyer's billable hours) can be accurately determined, individual motivation is likely to be highest when pay is based on individual performance.[103] When members of an organization work closely together and individual performance cannot be accurately determined (as in a team of computer programmers developing a single software package), pay cannot be based on individual performance, and a group- or organization-based plan must be used. When the attainment of organizational goals hinges on members' working closely together and cooperating with each other (as in a small construction company that builds custom homes), group- or organization-based plans may be more appropriate than individual-based plans.[104]

It is possible to combine elements of an individual-based plan with a group- or organization-based plan to motivate each individual to perform highly and, at the same time, motivate all individuals to work well together, cooperate with one another, and help one another as needed. Lincoln Electric, a very successful company and a leading manufacturer of welding machines, uses a combination individual- and organization-based plan.[105] Pay is based on individual performance. In addition, each year the size of a bonus fund depends on organizational performance. Money from the bonus fund is distributed to people on the basis of their contributions to the organization, attendance, levels of cooperation, and other indications of performance. Employees of Lincoln Electric are motivated to cooperate and help one another because when the firm as a whole performs well, everybody benefits by having a larger bonus fund. Employees also are motivated to contribute their inputs to the organization because their contributions determine their share of the bonus fund.

Salary Increase or Bonus?

Managers can distribute merit pay to people in the form of a salary increase or a bonus on top of regular salaries. Although the dollar amount of a salary increase or bonus might be identical, bonuses tend to have more motivational impact for at least three reasons. First, salary levels are typically based on performance levels, cost-of-living increases, and so forth, from the day people start working in an organization, which means that the absolute level of the salary is based largely on factors unrelated to *current* performance. A 5% merit increase in salary, for example, may seem relatively small in comparison to one's total salary. Second, a current salary increase may be affected by other factors in addition to performance, such as cost-of-living increases or across-the-board market adjustments. Third, because organizations rarely reduce salaries, salary levels tend to vary less than performance levels do. Related to this point is the fact that bonuses give managers more flexibility in distributing outcomes. If an organization is doing well, bonuses can be relatively high to reward employees for their contributions. However, unlike salary increases, bonus levels can be reduced when an organization's performance lags. All in all, bonus plans have more motivational impact than salary increases because the amount of the bonus can be directly and exclusively based on performance.[106]

Consistent with the lessons from motivation theories, bonuses can be linked directly to performance and vary from year to year and employee to employee, as at Gradient Corporation, a Cambridge, Massachusetts, environmental consulting firm.[107] Another organization that successfully uses bonuses is Nucor Corporation. Steelworkers at Nucor tend to be much more productive than steelworkers in other companies—probably because they can receive bonuses tied to performance and quality that are from 130% to 150% of their regular or base pay.[108]

In addition to receiving pay raises and bonuses, high-level managers and executives are sometimes granted employee stock options. **Employee stock options** are financial instruments that entitle the bearer to buy shares of an organization's stock at a certain price during a certain period of time or under certain conditions.[109] For example, in addition to salaries, stock options are sometimes used to attract high-level managers. The exercise price is the stock price at which the bearer can buy the stock, and the vesting conditions specify when the bearer can actually buy the stock at the exercise price. The option's exercise price is generally set equal to the market price of the stock on the date it is granted, and the vesting conditions might specify that the manager has to have worked at the organization for 12 months or perhaps met some performance target (increase in profits) before being able to exercise the option. In high-technology firms and start-ups, options are sometimes used in a similar fashion for employees at various levels in the organization.[110]

From a motivation standpoint, stock options are used not so much to reward past individual performance but, rather, to motivate employees to work in the future for the good of the company as a whole. This is true because stock options issued at current stock prices have value in the future only if an organization does well and its stock price appreciates; thus, giving employees stock options should encourage them to help the organization improve

employee stock option
A financial instrument that entitles the bearer to buy shares of an organization's stock at a certain price during a certain period of time or under certain conditions.

A steelworker at Nucor burns impurities from a tube used to pour molten steel in Decatur, Alabama. Nucor steelworkers can receive bonuses tied to performance and quality that are from 130 to 150 percent of their regular pay.

its performance over time.[111] At high-technology start-ups and dot-coms, stock options have often motivated potential employees to leave promising jobs in larger companies and work for the start-ups. In the late 1990s and early 2000s, many dot-commers were devastated to learn not only that their stock options were worthless, because their companies went out of business or were doing poorly, but also that they were unemployed. Unfortunately, stock options have also lead to unethical behavior; for example, sometimes individuals seek to artificially inflate the value of a company's stock to increase the value of stock options.

Examples of Merit Pay Plans

Managers can choose among several merit pay plans, depending on the work that employees perform and other considerations. Using *piece-rate pay,* an individual-based merit plan, managers base employees' pay on the number of units each employee produces, whether televisions, computer components, or welded auto parts. Managers at Lincoln Electric use piece-rate pay to determine individual pay levels. Advances in information technology are currently simplifying the administration of piece-rate pay in a variety of industries. For example, farmers typically allocated piece-rate pay to farmworkers through a laborious, time-consuming process. Now, they can rely on metal buttons the size of a dime that farmworkers clip to their shirts or put in their pockets. Made by Dallas Semiconductor Corporation, these buttons are customized for use in farming by Agricultural Data Systems, based in Laguna Niguel, California.[112] Each button contains a semiconductor linked to payroll computers by a wandlike probe in the field.[113] The wand relays the number of boxes of fruit or vegetables that each worker picks as well as the type and quality of the produce picked, the location it was picked in, and the time and the date. The buttons are activated by touching them with the probe; hence, they are called Touch Memory Buttons. Managers generally find that the buttons save time, improve accuracy, and provide valuable information about their crops and yields.[114]

Using *commission pay,* another individual-based merit pay plan, managers base pay on a percentage of sales. Managers at the successful real-estate company Re/Max International Inc. use commission pay for their agents, who are paid a percentage of their sales. Some department stores, such as Neiman Marcus, use commission pay for their salespeople.

Examples of organizational-based merit pay plans include the Scanlon plan and profit sharing. The *Scanlon plan* (developed by Joseph Scanlon, a union leader in a steel and tin plant in the 1920s) focuses on reducing expenses or cutting costs; members of an organization are motivated to come up with and implement cost-cutting strategies because a percentage of the cost savings achieved during a specified time is distributed to the employees.[115] Under *profit sharing,* employees receive a share of an organization's profits. Approximately 16% of the employees in medium or large firms receive profit sharing, and about 25% of small firms give their employees a share of the profits.[116] Regardless of the specific kind of plan that is used, managers should always strive to link pay to the performance of behaviors that help an organization achieve its goals.

Japanese managers in large corporations have long shunned merit pay plans in favor of plans that reward seniority. However, more and more Japanese companies are adopting merit-based pay due to its motivational benefits; among such companies are SiteDesign,[117] Tokio Marine and Fire Insurance, and Hissho Iwai, a trading organization.[118]

Summary and Review

THE NATURE OF MOTIVATION Motivation encompasses the psychological forces within a person that determine the direction of the person's behavior in an organization, the person's level of effort, and the person's level of persistence in the face of obstacles.

LO1   Managers strive to motivate people to contribute their inputs to an organization, to focus these inputs in the direction of high performance, and to ensure that people receive the outcomes they desire when they perform at a high level.

LO2   **EXPECTANCY THEORY**   According to expectancy theory, managers can promote high levels of motivation in their organizations by taking steps to ensure that expectancy is high (people think that if they try, they can perform at a high level), instrumentality is high (people think that if they perform at a high level, they will receive certain outcomes), and valence is high (people desire these outcomes).

LO3   **NEED THEORIES**   Need theories suggest that to motivate their workforces, managers should determine what needs people are trying to satisfy in organizations and then ensure that people receive outcomes that satisfy these needs when they perform at a high level and contribute to organizational effectiveness.

LO2   **EQUITY THEORY**   According to equity theory, managers can promote high levels of motivation by ensuring that people perceive that there is equity in the organization or that outcomes are distributed in proportion to inputs. Equity exists when a person perceives that his or her own outcome-input ratio equals the outcome-input ratio of a referent. Inequity motivates people to try to restore equity.

LO3   **GOAL-SETTING THEORY**   Goal-setting theory suggests that managers can promote high motivation and performance by ensuring that people are striving to achieve specific, difficult goals. It is important for people to accept the goals, be committed to them, and receive feedback about how they are doing.

LO4   **LEARNING THEORIES**   Operant conditioning theory suggests that managers can motivate people to perform highly by using positive reinforcement or negative reinforcement (positive reinforcement being the preferred strategy). Managers can motivate people to avoid performing dysfunctional behaviors by using extinction or punishment. Social learning theory suggests that people can also be motivated by observing how others perform behaviors and receive rewards, by engaging in self-reinforcement, and by having high levels of self-efficacy.

LO5   **PAY AND MOTIVATION**   Each of the motivation theories discussed in this chapter alludes to the importance of pay and suggests that pay should be based on performance. Merit pay plans can be individual-, group-, or organization-based and can entail the use of salary increases or bonuses.

Management in Action

Topics for Discussion and Action

DISCUSSION

1. Discuss why two people with similar abilities may have very different expectancies for performing at a high level. **[LO2]**

2. Describe why some people have low instrumentalities even when their managers distribute outcomes based on performance. **[LO2]**

3. Analyze how professors try to promote equity to motivate students. **[LO2]**

4. Describe three techniques or procedures that managers can use to determine whether a goal is difficult. **[LO3]**

5. Discuss why managers should always try to use positive reinforcement instead of negative reinforcement. **[LO4]**

ACTION

6. Interview three people who have the same kind of job (such as salesperson, waiter/waitress, or teacher), and determine what kinds of needs each is trying to satisfy at work. **[LO3]**

7. Interview a manager in an organization in your community to determine the extent to which the manager takes advantage of vicarious learning to promote high motivation among subordinates. **[LO3]**

Building Management Skills

Diagnosing Motivation [LO 1, 2, 3, 4]

Think about the ideal job that you would like to obtain upon graduation. Describe this job, the kind of manager you would like to report to, and the kind of organization you would be working in. Then answer the following questions:

1. What would be your levels of expectancy and instrumentality on this job? Which outcomes would have high valence for you on this job? What steps would your manager take to influence your levels of expectancy, instrumentality, and valence?

2. Whom would you choose as a referent on this job? What steps would your manager take to make you feel that you were being equitably treated? What would you do if, after a year on the job, you experienced underpayment inequity?

3. What goals would you strive to achieve on this job? Why? What role would your manager play in determining your goals?

4. What needs would you strive to satisfy on this job? Why? What role would your manager play in helping you satisfy these needs?

5. What behaviors would your manager positively reinforce on this job? Why? What positive reinforcers would your manager use?

6. Would there be any vicarious learning on this job? Why or why not?

7. To what extent would you be motivated by self-control on this job? Why?

8. What would be your level of self-efficacy on this job? Why would your self-efficacy be at this level? Should your manager take steps to boost your self-efficacy? If not, why not? If so, what would these steps be?

Managing Ethically [LO5]

Sometimes pay is so contingent upon performance that it creates stress for employees. Imagine a salesperson who knows that if sales targets are not met, she or he will not be able to make a house mortgage payment or pay the rent.

Questions

1. Either individually or in a group, think about the ethical implications of closely linking pay to performance.

2. Under what conditions might contingent pay be most stressful, and what steps can managers take to try to help their subordinates perform effectively and not experience excessive amounts of stress?

Small Group Breakout Exercise

Increasing Motivation [LO 1, 2, 3, 4, 5]

Form groups of three or four people, and appoint one member as the spokesperson who will communicate your findings to the class when called on by the instructor. Then discuss the following scenario.

You and your partners own a chain of 15 dry-cleaning stores in a medium-size town. All of you are concerned about a problem in customer service that has surfaced recently. When any one of you spends the day, or even part of the day, in a particular store, clerks seem to provide excellent customer service, spotters are making sure all stains are removed from garments, and pressers are doing a good job of pressing difficult items such as silk blouses. Yet during those same visits customers complain to you about such things as stains not being removed and items being poorly pressed in some of their previous orders; indeed, several customers have brought garments in to be redone. Customers also sometimes comment on having waited too long for service on previous visits. You and your partners are meeting today to address this problem.

1. Discuss the extent to which you believe that you have a motivation problem in your stores.

2. Given what you have learned in this chapter, design a plan to increase the motivation of clerks to provide prompt service to customers even when they are not being watched by a partner.

3. Design a plan to increase the motivation of spotters to remove as many stains as possible even when they are not being watched by a partner.

4. Design a plan to increase the motivation of pressers to do a top-notch job on all clothes they press, no matter how difficult.

Exploring the World Wide Web [LO 1, 2, 3, 4, 5]

If you had the chance to choose which well-known corporation you would work for, which would it be? Now go to the Web site of that company and find out as much as you can about how it motivates employees. Also, using *Google* and other search engines, try to find articles in the news about this company. Based upon what you have learned, would this company still be your top choice? Why or why not?

Be the Manager [LO 1, 2, 3, 4, 5]

You supervise a team of marketing analysts who work on different snack products in a large food products company. The marketing analysts have recently received undergraduate degrees in business or liberal arts and have been on the job between one and three years. Their responsibilities include analyzing the market for their respective products, including competitors; tracking current marketing initiatives; and planning future marketing campaigns. They also need to prepare quarterly sales and expense reports for their products and estimated budgets for the next three quarters; to prepare these reports, they need to obtain data from financial and accounting analysts assigned to their products.

When they first started on the job, you took each marketing analyst through the reporting cycle, explaining what needs to be done and how to accomplish it and emphasizing the need for timely reports. While preparing the reports can be tedious, you think the task is pretty straightforward and easily accomplished if the analysts plan ahead and allocate sufficient time for it. When reporting time approaches, you remind the analysts through e-mails and emphasize the need for accurate and timely reports in team meetings.

You believe that this element of the analysts' jobs couldn't be more straightforward. However, at the end of each quarter, the majority of the analysts turn their reports in a day or two late, and, worse yet, your own supervisor (whom the reports are eventually turned in to) has indicated that information is often missing and sometimes the reports contain errors. Once you started getting flak from your supervisor about this problem, you decided you better fix things, and quick. You met with the marketing analysts, explained the problem, told them to turn the reports in to you a day or two early so that you could look them over, and more generally emphasized that they really needed to get their act together. Unfortunately, things have not improved much, and you are spending more and more of your own time doing the reports. What are you going to do?

BusinessWeek Case in the News [LO 1, 3]

Why Settle for Just One Line of Work?

Macri Alboher gave up practicing law to write, teach, and speak about people who have made career transitions. To use a term she coined, she became a "slash" (as in writer/teacher/public speaker). The author of *One Person/Multiple Careers: A New Model for Work/Life Success,* Alboher spoke with Associate Editor Susan Berfield about how to juggle professions.

What's the difference between a slash and a career-changer?

Slashes are seeking a balance so they don't burn out or lose interest in their first job. I've met an art dealer/Pilates instructor and a theater director/computer programmer. A career-changer wants a divorce from the first career: The love is gone.

What's the main reason people don't pursue the slash interests full-time?

Financial security. It's hard to trash that when you are trying to learn something new and you're not sure if it will be more than a glorified hobby. Some people like what they do but want to do less of it. If they can find some way to add another dimension to their lives, it can rekindle interest in their main work.

How do you build a slash career?

In the corporate world, some people coast by at 80% and see if there's room to do something else with their time. Then there are people who test the flextime policy. The concept of going part-time to make room for something else is still new, but it is growing in acceptance. The third way is to take what you do in a corporate job and change it: Become

a consultant or sign up at one of the white-collar temp agencies.

Can people sustain life as a slash?

People who have these kinds of careers are never static. Six months later, they've shaken up the mix, evolved, gone deeper, dropped something. There is something inherently restless, endlessly curious about these people. Being a slash is a way to evolve without giving up the security of a job or losing the confidence in your expertise.

Do you see trends in what people are trying?

A lot of the people I talk to whose first vocation came after considerable education add a slash like massage therapy, or Pilates, or a certificate program of some kind. Adult and online education have exploded. It's easier than it has ever been to change careers. Leaving and reentering the corporate world is so much more accepted. Before it was like burning a bridge. Now you could have an entrepreneurial stint, then a corporate stint, and back again without any stigma.

What if you don't like being a Pilates instructor after all?

It's important to give yourself permission to not like something you are trying. It's like dating. You have to get out there, be unapologetic about sampling, and enjoy it.

How does this play out in different age groups?

Younger people don't find the slash concept at all unusual. They expect three-dimensional lives and careers,

and a lot of blurring. Older people need permission to live like this.

What do slashes give up?

You may not get to the highest rung on the corporate ladder if you want to follow other pursuits. To have more, you might have to have less. And a lot of idle time is lost. The most successful slashing occurs when activities serve more than one purpose. It's not multitasking—it's double time. It's the jogging stroller approach to life.

Questions for Discussion

1. Why are some people motivated to have "slash" careers?

2. How might "slash" careers help people maintain high levels of motivation over time?

3. How might motivation in any one pursuit suffer when a person has a "slash" career?

4. How might motivation in any one pursuit be enhanced when a person has a "slash" career?

Source: Q&A interview with Marci Alboher conducted by Associate Editor Susan Berfield, "Why Settle For Just One Line Of Work?" Reprinted from the December 3, 2007, issue of *BusinessWeek,* by special permission. Copyright © 2007 by The McGraw-Hill Companies, Inc.

BusinessWeek **Case in the News** [LO 1, 2, 3, 4, 5]

Nokia's New Home in Romania

The Transylvanian sheep pasture hadn't seen much action since the departure of the Roman whose ruined villa was recently unearthed nearby. But now, with handset maker Nokia tearing up the field to build a factory, the modern world is coming to this corner of Romania at a speed that amazes even John Guerry, the 36-year-old Texan in charge of the plant. "Every time I come it looks different," Guerry says, stooping to pet a stray dog the workers have named Nokia.

Wearing a bright green safety vest, Guerry leads visitors across muddy ground toward the gray, corrugated metal walls of the factory. Less than five months after work began, the plant's exterior is nearly complete. Inside, specialists have already installed a bank of computers to track the flow of phone parts. In March the factory outside the city of Cluj-Napoca will begin shipping handsets around Europe and Africa.

Nokia chose Cluj, home of a well-regarded technical university, in part because of its ample supply of engineering graduates willing to work for less than a quarter of what Western Europeans make. The plant will

come on line shortly before Nokia closes a factory in Bochum, Germany, which Nokia says has become too expensive. But low wages alone won't make the Romania plant competitive. To ensure that Nokia's $88 million investment pays off, Guerry will import the company's vaunted supply-chain expertise to a region linked to the outside world by a puny airport and a bumpy two-lane highway that snakes through the nearby Carpathian Mountains.

His challenge is to teach local workers to be as productive and exacting about quality as their counterparts in Brazil, China, and India. And he has to know enough about Romanian culture to create a workplace where skilled employees will want to stick around. Other multinationals such as St. Louis-based Emerson are also building factories in the region, so there is sure to be competition for the best people.

But if it all works, Nokia will extend its dominance of the global handset market. The company had a 38% global share in the third quarter of 2007, vs. 14.5% for No. 2 Samsung. Part of that commanding position, Nokia managers maintain, stems from the company's strategy of manufacturing closer to customers. Competitors

such as Motorola make most of their handsets in Asia—a disadvantage, Nokia believes. "When Motorola can't react as quickly as we can, we gain market share," says Guerry, who earlier in his career managed a Motorola plant in Texas.

Queuing Up At 6 A.M.

Finding willing workers for the new factory won't be a problem. Cluj, a city of 400,000, is still emerging from the poverty left behind by one of Eastern Europe's most repressive communist dictatorships. Sparkling dealerships offer BMWs and Audis to the newly rich, but on the streets, forlorn-looking young men peddle homemade wooden coat hangers. Although official unemployment was 3.1% in November, many people earn as little as $180 per month at local enterprises. They are eager to work for a multinational offering chances for training and advancement.

In fact, citizens are nearly euphoric at the prospect of joining the planet's biggest maker of handsets. "Everybody has been asking me: Do you have any contacts? Do you know where to apply?" says Bettina Binder, a 27-year-old regional manager for a cosmetics retailer in Cluj. At a Nokia-sponsored job fair in June, hopefuls from across Romania began queuing at 6 a.m. Eventually 8,000 applicants showed up, twice what Nokia expected and far more than it will ever employ. Early on, Nokia expects to hire about 500 people, a number that will gradually increase to 3,500 by the end of 2009.

Still, foreign companies in other emerging markets such as China and India have learned that finding and retaining skilled workers isn't easy. Wages rise quickly, and workers don't hesitate to sell new expertise to a higher bidder. One reason Nokia is setting up in Cluj is that its facility in Komarom, Hungary, has already tapped out the local workforce. Top-flight managers are especially scarce throughout the developing world. Nokia won't say what it will pay workers in Cluj, except that wages will be competitive with the region's average of about $450 a month.

Nokia hopes to hang on to its workers with perks that people in richer countries might envy. The factory will have a cafeteria with free food, a gym, playing fields, and—because Nokia is, after all, Finnish—a sauna. "The plant will be a place where people enjoy working," says Guerry. Nokia also offers international opportunities not available from Romanian companies. The crew setting up the Cluj plant, for instance, includes workers from Brazil, Hungary, India, and Poland. In a show of respect to local culture, Guerry is requiring foreign staffers to study Romanian. Nokia plans to turn the plant over to local managers within four years.

All In the Same Bonus Boat

But even as Guerry fits the plant into the Cluj environment, he has to make sure the factory fully exploits the worldwide knowhow that has strengthened Nokia. One way the company does that is by giving factory chiefs financial incentives to help each other rather than competing and hoarding information. Bonuses for Guerry and his peers at Nokia's 10 other factories around the world are tied to the performance of the overall manufacturing operation. If one plant isn't operating at top efficiency, all the managers feel it in their paychecks. That's unusual in a business where executives are typically rewarded only for the performance of their own factories, says Kevin O'Marah, chief strategy officer of Boston supply-chain specialists AMR Research. "Nokia's collective compensation plan is incredibly smart," he says.

Maximum productivity is everything in the mobile phone business. Growth is coming from emerging markets, where many customers live on just a few dollars a day and can't afford to spend a lot on a phone. Nokia reported a profit margin of 22.6% on handsets in the third quarter even as the cost of entry-level models fell below $40. To hit numbers like that, Nokia pays attention to every detail on the assembly line. One thing Guerry learned while visiting a Nokia plant in India, for example, is that the factory is more efficient if operators stand between two lines, allowing them to service both at once. "When you're making 12 phones a second, a minor thing can make a huge difference," Guerry says.

One of his biggest worries is getting supplies into Cluj smoothly. The city's connections to the outside world are primitive by European standards. Business-friendly officials are trying to help. The runway at Cluj's tiny airport is being lengthened to accommodate jumbo jets for delivery of components from Asia and other locations. And near Cluj, U.S. construction giant Bechtel is building the Transylvania Motorway, a $3.2 billion, four-lane road that will cut travel time to Hungary in half by 2011. Although it will be more costly to operate in Cluj before the region gets its infrastructure upgrade, Nokia wanted first crack at the best workers.

The local government also donated land for the factory and is building amenities such as a commuter rail station. So besides overseeing the plant, Guerry serves as a goodwill ambassador to the town. In late December he sat in a temporary office signing Christmas cards to local dignitaries, which he later delivered to City Hall—proof that operating comfortably in a strange culture is almost as important for a manager as, say, mastering logistics software. "You either get that," he says, "or you don't stay very long."

Questions for Discussion

1. Why are Romanians motivated to obtain a job at Nokia's new factory in Cluj?

2. For those hired, what factors are likely to contribute to their intrinsic motivation?

3. For those hired, what factors are likely to contribute to their extrinsic motivation?

4. How does Nokia motivate global managers to cooperate with each other and share their knowledge and expertise?

Source: Jack Ewing, "Nokia's New Home In Romania." Reprinted from the January 28, 2008, issue of *BusinessWeek* by special permission. Copyright © 2008 by The McGraw-Hill Companies, Inc.

CHAPTER 14

Leadership

Learning Objectives

After studying this chapter, you should be able to:

LO1 Explain what leadership is, when leaders are effective and ineffective, and the sources of power that enable managers to be effective leaders.

LO2 Identify the traits that show the strongest relationship to leadership, the behaviors leaders engage in, and the limitations of the trait and behavior models of leadership.

LO3 Explain how contingency models of leadership enhance our understanding of effective leadership and management in organizations.

LO4 Describe what transformational leadership is, and explain how managers can engage in it.

LO5 Characterize the relationship between gender and leadership and explain how emotional intelligence may contribute to leadership effectiveness.

A MANAGER'S CHALLENGE

Judy McGrath Leads MTV Networks

www.mtv.com

How can a manager continuously transform a hip company in a rapidly changing environment? As chairperson and CEO of MTV Networks, Judy McGrath has one of the most challenging and encompassing leadership positions in the media industry.[1] MTV Networks, a unit of Viacom, is home to the original MTV as well as Nickelodeon, VH1, Comedy Central, LOGO, MTV2, Nick at Nite, NOGGIN, TV Land, CMT, mtvU, the N, and Spike TV.[2] MTV Networks is accessed by more than 440 million households in over 165 viewing territories. Operating in an industry and markets whose rate of change is parallel to none, keeping MTV Networks hip and maintaining its appeal in an ever-changing digital landscape is a daunting task.[3]

McGrath certainly seems up to the challenge; in 2006, she received the Vanguard Award for Distinguished Leadership, and she was ranked 18th in *Fortune* magazine's list of the "50 Most Powerful Women" in 2007.[4] Interestingly enough, McGrath, who was born in Scranton, Pennsylvania, first came to New York City in the late 1970s with hopes of combining her love of rock music with her college degree in English literature to write for *Rolling Stone* magazine. Instead, McGrath started writing for *Mademoiselle* magazine and later for *Glamour*. In 1981, friends told her about the newly launched MTV, and she took a job there writing promotional pieces. And the rest has been history. With MTV from its earliest days, McGrath is now in the top post.[5]

McGrath is far from what comes to some people's minds when they think

Chairperson and CEO Judy McGrath successfully leads the complex organization that is MTV Networks.

of a traditional CEO. Widely read, she is very attuned to pop culture, is nurturing of employees and talent alike, and is a creative leader who encourages the same in others; she has been credited with creating a very inclusive culture at MTV, where all employees are listened to and heard. She is down to earth, as comfortable planning strategies with top managers as she is inter-acting with hip-hoppers or seeing live indie music acts. McGrath's confidence and high energy are matched by her knowledge of the industry, creativity, and integrity.[6]

Her personal leadership style emphasizes empowering all members of the MTV orga-nization as well as its viewers. According to McGrath, creativity and innovation stem from employees at all ranks, leaders and managers should listen to employees' ideas, and change must be the rule of the day in a dynamic environment.[7] She has also strived to empower the MTV viewing audience and raise viewers' awareness about impor-tant social concerns with award-winning programming such as the *Fight For Your Rights* series [e.g., "Take a Stand Against Violence," "Protect Yourself" (an AIDS aware-ness initiative), and "Take a Stand Against Discrimination"].[8]

McGrath networks with wide-ranging con-tacts on a daily basis, keeping up with the latest developments in the industry and pop culture and always on the lookout for new ideas and opportunities. She is visionary and can see possibilities and opportunities where others might see just risks or potential downsides. She works hard, perseveres, and believes that anything is possible. Under her leadership, MTV has launched scores of successful new programs, all of which were risky and could have failed. As she puts it, "Falling flat on your face is a great motivator. The smartest thing we can do when

confronted by something truly creative is to get out of the way."[9] That is what McGrath did when two producers came to her with the idea of filming people going through their day-to-day lives (with a soundtrack, of course, of new music); so started reality TV and MTV's *The Real World* series, which is in its 20th season.[10]

McGrath faces new challenges as she leads MTV forward. MTV's programming is now part of the media Establishment, and in an era of broadband, iPods, and online everything, she realizes that MTV cannot rest on its laurels: It must continually transform itself to maintain its hip and edgy focus and continue to appeal to its audience. Thus, McGrath is pushing MTV to deliver services from multiple digital platforms ranging from cell phones to new broadband channels to video games.[11]

In order to spearhead this digital transfor-mation, McGrath is expanding from MTV's tradition of developing its own offerings to seeking partnerships and acquisitions. For example, MTV Networks has partnered with Microsoft Corp. to offer a digital music download service called URGE.[12] MTV has purchased Web sites such as IFILM Corp., which is devoted to amateur short movies, and Neopets (popular with the younger set). McGrath is seeking synergies between digital acquisitions such as these and MTV's existing lineup. For example, IFILM debuted a show on VH1, and Nickelodeon is developing products for Neopets.[13]

Clearly, challenging times lie ahead for McGrath as she seeks to transform MTV in the digital era. Her vision and decisiveness, combined with her style of empowering employees, encouraging risk taking and creativity, and making sure that all enjoy the ride suggest that MTV is in good hands.[14]

Overview

Judy McGrath exemplifies the many facets of effective leadership. In Chapter 1 we explained that one of the four primary tasks of managers is leading. Thus, it should come as no surprise that leadership is a key ingredient in effective management. When leaders are effective, their subordinates or followers are highly motivated, committed, and high-performing. When leaders are ineffective, chances are good that their subordinates do not perform up to their capabilities, are demotivated, and may be dissatisfied as well. CEO Judy McGrath is a leader at the very top of an organization, but leadership is an important ingredient for managerial success at all levels of organizations: top management, middle management, and first-line management. Moreover, leadership is a key ingredient for managerial success for organizations large and small.

In this chapter we describe what leadership is and examine the major leadership models that shed light on the factors that contribute to a manager's being an effective leader. We look at trait and behavior models, which focus on what leaders are like and what they do, and contingency models—Fiedler's contingency model, path-goal theory, and the leader substitutes model—each of which takes into account the complexity surrounding leadership and the role of the situation in leader effectiveness. We also describe how managers can use transformational leadership to dramatically affect their organizations. By the end of this chapter, you will have a good appreciation of the many factors and issues that managers face in their quest to be effective leaders.

LO1 Explain what leadership is, when leaders are effective and ineffective, and the sources of power that enable managers to be effective leaders.

The Nature of Leadership

leadership The process by which an individual exerts influence over other people and inspires, motivates, and directs their activities to help achieve group or organizational goals.

leader An individual who is able to exert influence over other people to help achieve group or organizational goals.

Leadership is the process by which a person exerts influence over other people and inspires, motivates, and directs their activities to help achieve group or organizational goals.[15] The person who exerts such influence is a **leader.** When leaders are effective, the influence they exert over others helps a group or organization achieve its performance goals. When leaders are ineffective, their influence does not contribute to, and often detracts from, goal attainment. As "A Manager's Challenge" makes clear, Judy McGrath is taking multiple steps to inspire and motivate MTV's employees so that they help MTV achieve its goals.

Beyond facilitating the attainment of performance goals, effective leadership increases an organization's ability to meet all the contemporary challenges discussed throughout this book, including the need to obtain a competitive advantage, the need to foster ethical behavior, and the need to manage a diverse workforce fairly and equitably. Leaders who exert influence over organizational members to help meet these goals increase their organizations' chances of success.

In considering the nature of leadership, we first look at leadership styles and how they affect managerial tasks and at the influence of culture on leadership styles. We then focus on the key to leadership, *power,* which can come from a variety of sources. Finally, we consider the contemporary dynamic of empowerment and how it relates to effective leadership.

Personal Leadership Style and Managerial Tasks

A manager's *personal leadership style*—that is, the specific ways in which a manager chooses to influence other people—shapes the way that manager approaches planning, organizing, and controlling (the other principal tasks of managing). Consider Judy McGrath's personal leadership style in "A Manager's Challenge": She is down to earth, nurturing of employees and talent, and at the same time decisive and visionary. She empowers employees, encourages them to be creative and take risks, and fosters an inclusive culture at MTV Networks.[16]

Managers at all levels and in all kinds of organizations have their own personal leadership styles that determine not only how they lead their subordinates but also how they perform the other management tasks. Michael Kraus, owner and manager of a dry-cleaning store in the northeastern United States, for example, takes a hands-on approach to leadership. He has the sole authority for determining work schedules and job assignments for the 15 employees in his store (an organizing task), makes all important decisions by himself (a planning task), and closely monitors his employees' performance and rewards top performers with pay increases (a control task). Kraus's personal leadership style is effective in his organization. His employees are generally motivated, perform highly, and are satisfied, and his store is highly profitable.

Developing an effective personal leadership style often is a challenge for managers at all levels in an organization. This challenge is often exacerbated when times are tough, due, for example, to an economic downturn or a decline in customer demand. The dot-com bust and the slowing economy in the early 2000s provided many leaders with just such a challenge.

While leading is one of the four principal tasks of managing, a distinction is often made between managers and leaders. When this distinction is made, managers are thought of as those organizational members who establish and implement procedures and processes to ensure smooth functioning and who are accountable for goal accomplishment.[17] Leaders look to the future, chart the course for the organization, and attract, retain, motivate, inspire, and develop relationships with employees based on trust and mutual respect.[18] Leaders provide meaning and purpose, seek innovation rather than stability, and impassion employees to work together to achieve the leaders' vision.[19]

As part of their personal leadership style, some leaders strive to truly serve others. Robert Greenleaf, who was director of management research at AT&T and upon his retirement in 1964 embarked on a second career focused on writing, speaking, and consulting, came up with the term *servant leadership* to describe these leaders.[20] **Servant leaders,** above all else, have a strong desire to serve and work for the benefit of others.[21] Servant leaders share power with followers, strive to ensure that followers' most important needs are met, they are able to develop as individuals, and their well-being is enhanced, and that attention is paid to those who are least well-off in a society.[22] Greenleaf founded a nonprofit organization called the Greenleaf Center for Servant-Leadership (formerly called the Center for Applied Ethics) to foster leadership focused on service to others, power sharing, and a sense of community between organizations and their multiple stakeholders.[23] Some entrepreneurs strive to incorporate servant leadership into their personal leadership styles as profiled in the following "Ethics in Action."

servant leader A leader who has a strong desire to serve and work for the benefit of others.

Ethics in Action

Servant Leadership at Zingerman's

Ari Weinzweig and Paul Saginaw founded Zingerman's Delicatessen in Ann Arbor, Michigan, in 1982.[24] Food lovers at heart, Weinzweig and Saginaw delighted in finding both traditional and exotic foods from around the world, making delicious sandwiches to order, and having extensive selections of food items ranging from olives, oils, and vinegars to cheeses, smoked fish, and salami. As their business grew, and in order to maintain an intimate atmosphere with excellent customer service, Weinzweig and Saginaw expanded from their original deli into a community of related businesses called Zingerman's Community of Businesses. In addition to the original deli, Zingerman's Community of Businesses now includes a mail-order business, a bakery, a catering business, a creamery, a restaurant, a wholesale coffee business, and a training business and has combined annual revenues of about $30 million.[25] From the start, Weinzweig and Saginaw have been committed to excellent customer service, great food, and a commitment to people and community.[26]

Paul Saginaw (left) and Ari Weinzweig have incorporated servant leadership into their personal leadership styles at Zingerman's.

As part of their commitment to people and community, Weinzweig and Saginaw have incorporated servant leadership into their personal leadership styles. As their business has grown and prospered, they have realized that increasing success means increasing responsibility to serve others. They strive to treat their employees as well as they treat their customers and give their employees opportunities for growth and development on the job. They have also realized that when their own needs or desires differ from what is best for their company, they should do what is best for the company.[27]

To this day, the cofounders encourage their employees to let them know how they can help them and what they can do for them. And given Zingerman's culture of mutual respect and trust, employees do not hesitate to communicate how their leaders can serve them in many and varied ways. For example, when Weinzweig visits the Zingerman's Roadhouse restaurant and the staff is very busy, they may ask him to help out by serving customers or cleaning off tables. As he indicates, "People give me assignments all the time. Sometimes I'm the note taker. Sometimes I'm the cleaner-upper. . . . Sometimes I'm on my hands and knees wiping up what people spilled."[28]

Weinzweig and Saginaw also have a strong sense of commitment to serving the local community; Zingerman's founded the nonprofit organization, Food Gatherers, to eliminate hunger and distribute food to the needy, and Food Gatherers is now an independent nonprofit responsible for the Washtenaw County Food Bank with over 3,900 volunteers and a 15-member staff.[29] On Zingerman's 20th anniversary, 13 nonprofit community organizations in Ann Arbor erected a plaque next to Zingerman's Delicatessen with a dedication that read, "Thank you for feeding, sheltering, educating, uplifting, and inspiring an entire community."[30] Clearly, for Weinzweig and Saginaw, leadership does entail being of service to others.[31]

Leadership Styles Across Cultures

Some evidence suggests that leadership styles vary not only among individuals but also among countries or cultures. Some research indicates that European managers tend to be more humanistic or people-oriented than both Japanese and American managers. The collectivistic culture in Japan places prime emphasis on the group rather than the individual, so the importance of individuals' own personalities, needs, and desires is minimized. Organizations in the United States tend to be very profit-oriented and thus tend to downplay the importance of individual employees' needs and desires. Many countries in Europe have a more individualistic perspective than Japan and a more humanistic perspective than the United States, and this may result in some European managers' being more people-oriented than their Japanese or American counterparts. European managers, for example, tend to be reluctant to lay off employees, and when a layoff is absolutely necessary, they take careful steps to make it as painless as possible.[32]

Another cross-cultural difference occurs in time horizons. While managers in any one country often differ in their time horizons, there are also national differences. For example, U.S. organizations tend to have a short-run profit orientation, and thus U.S. managers' personal leadership styles emphasize short-run performance. Japanese organizations tend to have a long-run growth orientation, so Japanese managers' personal leadership styles emphasize long-run performance. Justus Mische, a personnel manager at the European organization Hoechst, suggests that "Europe, at least the big international firms in Europe, have a philosophy between the Japanese, long term, and the United States, short term."[33] Research on these and other global aspects of leadership is in its infancy; as it continues, more cultural differences in managers' personal leadership styles may be discovered.

Power: The Key to Leadership

No matter what one's leadership style, a key component of effective leadership is found in the *power* the leader has to affect other people's behavior and get them to act in certain ways.[34] There are several types of power: legitimate, reward, coercive, expert, and referent power (see Figure 14.1).[35] Effective leaders take steps to ensure that they have sufficient levels of each type and that they use the power they have in beneficial ways.

legitimate power The authority that a manager has by virtue of his or her position in an organization's hierarchy.

LEGITIMATE POWER   **Legitimate power** is the authority a manager has by virtue of his or her position in an organization's hierarchy. Personal leadership style

Figure 14.1
Source of Managerial Power

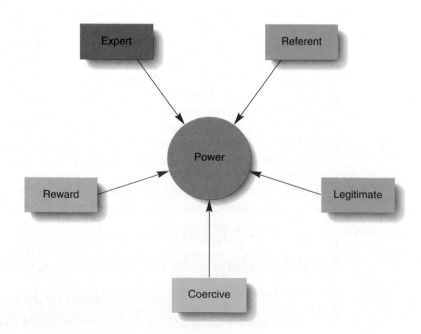

often influences how a manager exercises legitimate power. Take the case of Carol Loray, who is a first-line manager in a greeting card company and leads a group of 15 artists and designers. Loray has the legitimate power to hire new employees, assign projects to the artists and designers, monitor their work, and appraise their performance. She uses this power effectively. She always makes sure that her project assignments match the interests of her subordinates as much as possible so that they will enjoy their work. She monitors their work to make sure they are on track but does not engage in close supervision, which can hamper creativity. She makes sure her performance appraisals are developmental, providing concrete advice for areas where improvements could be made. Recently, Loray negotiated with her manager to increase her legitimate power so that now she can initiate and develop proposals for new card lines.

reward power The ability of a manager to give or withhold tangible and intangible rewards.

REWARD POWER Reward power is the ability of a manager to give or withhold tangible rewards (pay raises, bonuses, choice job assignments) and intangible rewards (verbal praise, a pat on the back, respect). As you learned in Chapter 12, members of an organization are motivated to perform at a high level by a variety of rewards. Being able to give or withhold rewards based on performance is a major source of power that allows managers to have a highly motivated workforce. Managers of salespeople in retail organizations like Neiman Marcus and Dillard's Department Stores, in car dealerships like General Motors and Ford, and in travel agencies like Liberty Travel and the Travel Company often use their reward power to motivate their subordinates. Subordinates in organizations such as these often receive commissions on whatever they sell and rewards for the quality of their customer service, which motivate them to do the best they can.

Effective managers use their reward power in such a way that subordinates feel that their rewards signal that they are doing a good job and their efforts are appreciated. Ineffective managers use rewards in a more controlling manner (wielding the "stick" instead of offering the "carrot") that signals to subordinates that the manager has the upper hand. Managers also can take steps to increase their reward power. Carol Loray had the legitimate power to appraise her subordinates' performance, but she lacked the reward power to distribute raises and end-of-year bonuses until she discussed with her own manager why this would be a valuable motivational tool for her to use. Loray now receives a pool of money each year for salary increases and bonuses and has the reward power to distribute them as she sees fit.

coercive power The ability of a manager to punish others.

COERCIVE POWER Coercive power is the ability of a manager to punish others. Punishment can range from verbal reprimands to reductions in pay or working hours to actual dismissal. In the previous chapter, we discussed how punishment can have negative side effects such as resentment and retaliation and should be used only when necessary (for example, to curtail a dangerous behavior). Managers who rely heavily on coercive power tend to be ineffective as leaders and sometimes even get fired themselves. William J. Fife is one example; he was fired from his position as CEO of Giddings and Lewis Inc., a manufacturer of factory equipment, because of his overreliance on coercive power. In meetings, Fife often verbally criticized, attacked, and embarrassed top managers. Realizing how destructive Fife's use of punishment was for them and the company, these managers complained to the board of directors, who, after a careful consideration of the issues, asked Fife to resign.[36]

Excessive use of coercive power seldom produces high performance and is questionable ethically. Sometimes it amounts to a form of mental abuse, robbing workers of their dignity and causing excessive levels of stress. Overuse of coercive power can even result in dangerous working conditions. Better results and, importantly, an ethical workplace that respects employee dignity can be obtained by using reward power.

EXPERT POWER Expert power is based on the special knowledge, skills, and expertise that a leader possesses. The nature of expert power varies, depending on the

expert power Power that is based on the special knowledge, skills, and expertise that a leader possesses.

leader's level in the hierarchy. First-level and middle managers often have technical expertise relevant to the tasks that their subordinates perform. Their expert power gives them considerable influence over subordinates. Carol Loray has expert power: She is an artist herself and has drawn and designed some of her company's top-selling greeting cards. Judy McGrath, in "A Manager's Challenge," has expert power from over 25 years' experience in the media industry, as well as from her efforts to stay attuned to pop culture through extensive networking, reading, and ever-ready openness for the new and the quirky. As indicated in the following "Manager as a Person," the kinds of positions that leaders with expert power assume depends upon who they are as individuals and the kinds of challenges that appeal to them.

Manager as a Person

Liane Pelletier Uses Her Expert Power in Alaska

Liane Pelletier was a senior vice president at Sprint when a recruiting firm called her to see if she was interested in becoming CEO of Alaska Communications Systems (ACS).[37] With over 15 years' experience in the telecommunications industry, she definitely had the skills, knowledge, and expertise to head ACS. Like many top managers, Connecticut-born Pelletier hesitated about making a move to Alaska—but she didn't hesitate for long.[38]

Pelletier loves adventure and new experiences; the opportunity to leverage her industry experience and take on the challenge of transforming ACS made her decision an easy one. For Pelletier, Alaska was not such a far-flung place to move to: She had traveled widely, on excursions ranging from hiking the Appalachian Trail to boating down the Amazon River. And now snowshoeing in Alaska is one of her new leisure activities.[39]

ACS is Alaska's largest local exchange carrier and the only in-state provider with its own local, long distance, wireless, and Internet infrastructure.[40] As an experienced top manager in telecommunications, Pelletier sees her role at ACS as an exciting opportunity.[41] When she came to ACS, she realized that the company was focused on products rather than customers: Different divisions would provide different kinds of services to customers without taking into account that the same customers might be using other services provided by other parts of the company. Pelletier restructured ACS around customers and how to better meet their needs through the multiple products and services ACS offers. Now, sales and service at ACS are integrated across product lines, and employees receive training so that they are knowledgeable about all of ACS's products and services.[42] Pelletier's vision for ACS revolves around customer-focused growth and improved wireless services. Already her efforts have paid off for the company in terms of increases in ACS's earnings and stock price.[43] Clearly, ACS is fortunate that Pelletier assumed the top post and is applying her expertise to enable the company to better serve its customers and expand its range of products.[44]

Liane Pelletier loves adventure, whether it's snowshoeing in Alaska or transforming the state's telecommunication systems.

Some top managers derive expert power from their technical expertise. Craig Barrett, chairman of the board of directors of Intel, has a PhD in materials science from Stanford University and is very knowledgeable about the ins and outs of Intel's business–producing semiconductors and microprocessors.[45] Similarly, Bill Gates, chairman of Microsoft, and CEO Steve Ballmer have expertise in software design; and Tachi Yamada, executive director of the Bill and Melinda Gates Foundation's Global Health Program has an MD and was previously chairman of research and development at GlaxoSmithKline.[46] Many top-level managers, however, lack technical expertise and derive their expert power from their abilities as decision makers, planners, and strategists. Jack Welch, the former, well-known leader and CEO of General Electric, summed it up this way: "The basic thing that we at the top of the company know is that we don't know the business. What we have, I hope, is the ability to allocate resources, people, and dollars."[47]

Effective leaders take steps to ensure that they have an adequate amount of expert power to perform their leadership roles. They may obtain additional training or education in their fields, make sure they keep up to date with the latest developments and changes in technology, stay abreast of changes in their fields through involvement in professional associations, and read widely to be aware of momentous changes in the organization's task and general environments. Expert power tends to be best used in a guiding or coaching manner rather than in an arrogant, high-handed manner.

referent power Power that comes from subordinates' and coworkers' respect, admiration, and loyalty.

REFERENT POWER **Referent power** is more informal than the other kinds of power. Referent power is a function of the personal characteristics of a leader; it is the power that comes from subordinates' and coworkers' respect, admiration, and loyalty. Leaders who are likable and whom subordinates wish to use as a role model are especially likely to possess referent power, as is true of Judy McGrath in "A Manager's Challenge."

In addition to being a valuable asset for top managers like McGrath, referent power can help first-line and middle managers be effective leaders as well. Sally Carruthers, for example, is the first-level manager of a group of secretaries in the finance department of a large state university. Carruthers's secretaries are known to be among the best in the university. Much of their willingness to go above and beyond the call of duty has been attributed to Carruthers's warm and caring nature, which makes each of them feel important and valued. Managers can take steps to increase their referent power, such as taking time to get to know their subordinates and showing interest in and concern for them.

Empowerment: An Ingredient in Modern Management

empowerment The expansion of employees' knowledge, tasks, and decision-making responsibilities.

More and more managers today are incorporating into their personal leadership styles an aspect that at first glance seems to be the opposite of being a leader. In Chapter 1, we described how **empowerment**–the process of giving employees at all levels the authority to make decisions, be responsible for their outcomes, improve quality, and cut costs–is becoming increasingly popular in organizations. When leaders empower their subordinates, the subordinates typically take over some of the responsibilities and authority that used to reside with the leader or manager, such as the right to reject parts that do not meet quality standards, the right to check one's own work, and the right to schedule work activities. Empowered subordinates are given the power to make some of the decisions that their leaders or supervisors used to make.

Empowerment might seem to be the opposite of effective leadership because managers are allowing subordinates to take a more active role in leading themselves. In actuality, however, empowerment can contribute to effective leadership for several reasons:

- Empowerment increases a manager's ability to get things done because the manager has the support and help of subordinates who may have special knowledge of work tasks.

- Empowerment often increases workers' involvement, motivation, and commitment, and this helps ensure that they are working toward organizational goals.

- Empowerment gives managers more time to concentrate on their pressing concerns because they spend less time on day-to-day supervisory activities.

Effective managers like Judy McGrath realize the benefits of empowerment. The personal leadership style of managers who empower subordinates often entails developing subordinates' ability to make good decisions as well as being their guide, coach, and source of inspiration. Empowerment is a popular trend in the United States at companies as diverse as United Parcel Service (a package delivery company) and Coram Healthcare Corporation (a provider of medical equipment and services) and is a part of servant leadership. Empowerment is also taking off around the world.[48] For instance, companies in South Korea (such as Samsung, Hyundai, and Daewoo), in which decision making typically was centralized with the founding families, are now empowering managers at lower levels to make decisions.[49]

LO2 Identify the traits that show the strongest relationship to leadership, the behaviors leaders engage in, and the limitations of the trait and behavior models of leadership.

Trait and Behavior Models of Leadership

Leading is such an important process in all organizations—nonprofit organizations, government agencies, and schools, as well as for-profit corporations—that it has been researched for decades. Early approaches to leadership, called the *trait model* and the *behavior model,* sought to determine what effective leaders are like as people and what they do that makes them so effective.

The Trait Model

The trait model of leadership focused on identifying the personal characteristics that cause effective leadership. Researchers thought effective leaders must have certain personal qualities that set them apart from ineffective leaders and from people who never become leaders. Decades of research (beginning in the 1930s) and hundreds of studies indicate that certain personal characteristics do appear to be associated with effective leadership. (See Table 14.1 for a list of these.)[50] Notice that although this

Table 14.1

Traits and Personal Characteristics Related to Effective Leadership

Trait	Description
Intelligence	Helps managers understand complex issues and solve problems
Knowledge and expertise	Helps managers make good decisions and discover ways to increase efficiency and effectiveness
Dominance	Helps managers influence their subordinates to achieve organizational goals
Self-confidence	Contributes to managers' effectively influencing subordinates and persisting when faced with obstacles or difficulties
High energy	Helps managers deal with the many demands they face
Tolerance for stress	Helps managers deal with uncertainty and make difficult decisions
Integrity and honesty	Helps managers behave ethically and earn their subordinates' trust and confidence
Maturity	Helps managers avoid acting selfishly, control their feelings, and admit when they have made a mistake

model is called the "trait" model, some of the personal characteristics that it identifies are not personality traits per se but, rather, are concerned with a leader's skills, abilities, knowledge, and expertise. As "A Manager's Challenge" shows, Judy McGrath certainly appears to possess many of these characteristics (such as intelligence, knowledge and expertise, self-confidence, high energy, and integrity and honesty). Leaders who do not possess these traits may be ineffective.

Traits alone are not the key to understanding leader effectiveness, however. Some effective leaders do not possess all of these traits, and some leaders who do possess them are not effective in their leadership roles. This lack of a consistent relationship between leader traits and leader effectiveness led researchers to shift their attention away from traits and to search for new explanations for effective leadership. Rather than focusing on what leaders are like (the traits they possess), researchers began looking at what effective leaders actually do—in other words, at the behaviors that allow effective leaders to influence their subordinates to achieve group and organizational goals.

The Behavior Model

After extensive study in the 1940s and 1950s, researchers at The Ohio State University identified two basic kinds of leader behaviors that many leaders in the United States, Germany, and other countries engaged in to influence their subordinates: *consideration* and *initiating structure*.[51]

consideration Behavior indicating that a manager trusts, respects, and cares about subordinates.

CONSIDERATION   Leaders engage in **consideration** when they show their subordinates that they trust, respect, and care about them. Managers who truly look out for the well-being of their subordinates, and do what they can to help subordinates feel good and enjoy their work, perform consideration behaviors. In "A Manager's Challenge," Judy McGrath engages in consideration when she listens to employees and fosters an inclusive, nurturing culture at MTV Networks.

At Costco Wholesale Corporation, CEO Jim Senegal believes that consideration not only is an ethical imperative but also makes good business sense,[52] as indicated in the following "Ethics in Action."

Ethics in Action

Consideration at Costco

Managers at Costco, including CEO Jim Senegal, believe that consideration is so important that one of the principles in Costco's Code of Ethics is "Take Care of Our Employees."[53] Costco Wholesale Corporation is the fifth-largest retailer, and the top warehouse retailer, in the United States.[54] Wages at Costco are an average of $17 per hour, over 40% higher than the average hourly wage at Wal-Mart, Costco's major competitor.[55] Costco pays the majority of health insurance costs for its employees (employees pay around 8% of health insurance costs compared to an industry average of around 25%), and part-time employees receive health insurance after they have been with the company six months. Overall, about 85% of Costco employees are covered by health insurance at any point in time, compared with less than 45% of employees at Target and Wal-Mart.[56]

Jim Senegal believes that caring about the well-being of his employees is a win–win proposition as Costco's employees are satisfied, committed, loyal, and motivated. Additionally, turnover and employee theft rates at Costco are much lower than industry averages.[57] In the retail industry, turnover tends to be very high and costly since for every employee who quits, a new hire needs to be recruited, tested, interviewed, and trained. Even though pay and benefits are higher at Costco than at rival Wal-Mart, Costco actually has lower labor costs as a percentage of sales and higher sales per square foot of store space than Wal-Mart.[58]

Additionally, treating employees well helps build customer loyalty at Costco. Surely, customers enjoy the bargains and low prices that come from shopping in a warehouse store, the relatively high quality of the goods Costco stocks, and Costco's policy of not marking up prices by more than 14% or 15% (relatively low markups for retail) even if the goods would sell with higher markups. However, customers are also very loyal to Costco because they know that the company treats its employees so well and that their bargains are not coming at the expense of employees' paychecks and benefits.[59]

Loyal Costco customers like these know that their bargains don't come at the expense of employees' paychecks and benefits.

Costco started out as a single warehouse store in Seattle, Washington, in 1983. Now, the company has 534 stores (including stores in South Korea, Taiwan, Japan, Canada, and Britain) and over 44 million members who pay $50 per year to shop at Costco stores.[60] Costco's growth and financial performance are enviable. For example, annual revenues for the 2007 fiscal year were $64.4 billion. Clearly, consideration has paid off for Costco and for its employees.[61]

initiating structure

Behavior that managers engage in to ensure that work gets done, subordinates perform their jobs acceptably, and the organization is efficient and effective.

INITIATING STRUCTURE   Leaders engage in **initiating structure** when they take steps to make sure that work gets done, subordinates perform their jobs acceptably, and the organization is efficient and effective. Assigning tasks to individuals or work groups, letting subordinates know what is expected of them, deciding how work should be done, making schedules, encouraging adherence to rules and regulations, and motivating subordinates to do a good job are all examples of initiating structure.[62] Michael Teckel, the manager of an upscale store selling imported men's and women's shoes in a midwestern city, engages in initiating structure when he establishes weekly work, lunch, and break schedules to ensure that the store has enough salespeople on the floor. Teckle also initiates structure when he discusses the latest shoe designs with his subordinates so that they are knowledgeable with customers, when he encourages adherence to the store's refund and exchange policies, and when he encourages his staff to provide high-quality customer service and to avoid a hard-sell approach.

Initiating structure and consideration are independent leader behaviors. Leaders can be high on both, low on both, or high on one and low on the other. Many effective leaders, like Judy McGrath of MTV Networks, engage in both of these behaviors.

Leadership researchers have identified leader behaviors similar to consideration and initiating structure. Researchers at the University of Michigan, for example, identified two categories of leadership behaviors, *employee-centered behaviors* and *job-oriented behaviors,* that correspond roughly to consideration and initiating structure, respectively.[63] Models of leadership popular with consultants also tend to zero in on these two kinds of behaviors. For example, Robert Blake and Jane Mouton's Managerial Grid focuses on *concern for people* (similar to consideration) and *concern for production* (similar to initiating structure). Blake and Mouton advise that effective leadership often requires both a high level of concern for people and a high level of concern for production.[64] As another example, Paul Hersey and Kenneth Blanchard's model focuses on *supportive behaviors* (similar to consideration) and *task-oriented behaviors* (similar to initiating structure). According to Hersey and Blanchard, leaders need to consider the nature of their subordinates when trying to determine the extent to which they should perform these two behaviors.[65]

You might expect that effective leaders and managers would perform both kinds of behaviors, but research has found that this is not necessarily the case. The relationship between performance of consideration and initiating-structure behaviors and leader effectiveness is not clear-cut. Some leaders are effective even when they do not perform consideration or initiating-structure behaviors, and some leaders are ineffective even when they do perform both kinds of behaviors. Like the trait model of leadership, the behavior model alone cannot explain leader effectiveness. Realizing this, researchers began building more complicated models of leadership, models focused not only on the leader and what he or she does but also on the situation or context in which leadership occurs.

LO3 Explain how contingency models of leadership enhance our understanding of effective leadership and management in organizations.

Contingency Models of Leadership

Simply possessing certain traits or performing certain behaviors does not ensure that a manager will be an effective leader in all situations calling for leadership. Some managers who seem to possess the "right" traits and perform the "right" behaviors turn out to be ineffective leaders. Managers lead in a wide variety of situations and organizations and have various kinds of subordinates performing diverse tasks in a multiplicity of environmental contexts. Given the wide variety of situations in which leadership occurs, what makes a manager an effective leader in one situation (such as certain traits or behaviors) is not necessarily what that manager needs to be equally effective in a different situation. An effective army general might not be an effective university president; an effective manager of a restaurant might not be an effective manager of a clothing store; an effective coach of a football team might not be an effective manager of a fitness center; and an effective first-line manager in a manufacturing company might not be an effective middle manager. The traits or behaviors that may contribute to a manager's being an effective leader in one situation might actually result in the same manager being an ineffective leader in another situation.

Contingency models of leadership take into account the situation or context within which leadership occurs. According to contingency models, whether or not a manager is an effective leader is the result of the interplay between what the manager is like, what he or she does, and the situation in which leadership takes place. Contingency models propose that whether a leader who possesses certain traits or performs certain behaviors is effective depends on, or is contingent on, the situation or context. In this section, we discuss three prominent contingency models developed to shed light on what makes managers effective leaders: Fred Fiedler's contingency model, Robert House's path-goal theory, and the leader substitutes model. As you will see, these leadership models are complementary; each focuses on a somewhat different aspect of effective leadership in organizations.

Fiedler's Contingency Model

Fred E. Fiedler was among the first leadership researchers to acknowledge that effective leadership is contingent on, or depends on, the characteristics of the leader *and* of the situation. Fiedler's contingency model helps explain why a manager may be an effective leader in one situation and ineffective in another; it also suggests which kinds of managers are likely to be most effective in which situations.[66]

LEADER STYLE   As with the trait approach, Fiedler hypothesized that personal characteristics can influence leader effectiveness. He used the term *leader style* to refer to a manager's characteristic approach to leadership and identified two basic leader styles: *relationship-oriented* and *task-oriented*. All managers can be described as having one style or the other.

Relationship-oriented leaders are primarily concerned with developing good relationships with their subordinates and being liked by them. Relationship-oriented

relationship-oriented leaders Leaders whose primary concern is to develop good relationships with their subordinates and to be liked by them.

managers focus on having high-quality interpersonal relationships with subordinates. This does not mean, however, that the job does not get done when such leaders are at the helm. But it does mean that the quality of interpersonal relationships with subordinates is a prime concern for relationship-oriented leaders. Lawrence Fish, for example, is the chairman of Citizens Financial Group Inc. of Providence, Rhode Island, which has tripled its assets in the last three years. As the top manager who helped to engineer this rapid growth, Fish has never lost sight of the importance of good relationships and personally writes a thank-you note to at least one of his subordinates each day.[67]

task-oriented leaders
Leaders whose primary concern is to ensure that subordinates perform at a high level.

Task-oriented leaders are primarily concerned with ensuring that subordinates perform at a high level and focus on task accomplishment. Some task-oriented leaders, like the top managers of the family-owned C. R. England Refrigerated Trucking Company based in Salt Lake City, Utah, go so far as to closely measure and evaluate performance on a weekly basis to ensure subordinates are performing as well as they can.[68]

In his research, Fiedler measured leader style by asking leaders to rate the coworker with whom they have had the most difficulty working (called the *least-preferred coworker* or *LPC*) on a number of dimensions, such as whether the person is boring or interesting, gloomy or cheerful, enthusiastic or unenthusiastic, cooperative or uncooperative. Relationship-oriented leaders tend to describe the LPC in relatively positive terms; their concern for good relationships leads them to think well of others. Task-oriented leaders tend to describe the LPC in negative terms; their concern for task accomplishment causes them to think badly about others who make getting the job done difficult. Thus, relationship-oriented and task-oriented leaders are sometimes referred to as *high*-LPC and *low*-LPC leaders, respectively.

leader–member relations
The extent to which followers like, trust, and are loyal to their leader; a determinant of how favorable a situation is for leading.

SITUATIONAL CHARACTERISTICS According to Fiedler, leadership style is an enduring characteristic; managers cannot change their style, nor can they adopt different styles in different kinds of situations. With this in mind, Fiedler identified three situational characteristics that are important determinants of how favorable a situation is for leading: leader–member relations, task structure, and position power. When a situation is favorable for leading, it is relatively easy for a manager to influence subordinates so that they perform at a high level and contribute to organizational efficiency and effectiveness. In a situation unfavorable for leading, it is much more difficult for a manager to exert influence.

task structure The extent to which the work to be performed is clear-cut so that a leader's subordinates know what needs to be accomplished and how to go about doing it; a determinant of how favorable a situation is for leading.

LEADER–MEMBER RELATIONS The first situational characteristic that Fiedler described, **leader–member relations,** is the extent to which followers like, trust, and are loyal to their leader. Situations are more favorable for leading when leader–member relations are good.

TASK STRUCTURE The second situational characteristic that Fiedler described, **task structure,** is the extent to which the work to be performed is clear-cut so that a leader's subordinates know what needs to be accomplished and how to go about doing it. When task structure is high, the situation is favorable for leading. When task structure is low, goals may be vague, subordinates may be unsure of what they should be doing or how they should do it, and the situation is unfavorable for leading.

Developing good relations with employees can make the "situation" more favorable for leading.

Task structure was low for Geraldine Laybourne when she was a top manager at Nickelodeon, the children's television network. It was never precisely clear what would appeal to her young viewers, whose tastes can change dramatically, or how to motivate her subordinates to come up with creative and novel ideas.[69] In contrast, Herman Mashaba, founder of Black Like Me, a hair care products company based in South Africa, seemed to have relatively high task structure when he started his company. His company's goals were to produce and sell inexpensive hair care products to native Africans, and managers accomplish these goals by using simple yet appealing packaging and distributing the products through neighborhood beauty salons.[70]

POSITION POWER The third situational characteristic that Fiedler described, **position power,** is the amount of legitimate, reward, and coercive power a leader has by virtue of his or her position in an organization. Leadership situations are more favorable for leading when position power is strong.

position power The amount of legitimate, reward, and coercive power that a leader has by virtue of his or her position in an organization; a determinant of how favorable a situation is for leading.

COMBINING LEADER STYLE AND THE SITUATION By taking all possible combinations of good and poor leader–member relations, high and low task structure, and strong and weak position power, Fiedler identified eight leadership situations, which vary in their favorability for leading (see Figure 14.2). After extensive research, he determined that relationship-oriented leaders are most effective in moderately favorable situations (IV, V, VI, and VII in Figure 14.2) and task-oriented leaders are most effective in situations that are either very favorable (I, II, and III) or very unfavorable (VIII).

PUTTING THE CONTINGENCY MODEL INTO PRACTICE Recall that, according to Fiedler, leader style is an enduring characteristic that managers cannot change. This suggests that to be effective, either managers need to be placed in leadership situations that fit their style or situations need to be changed to suit the managers. Situations can be changed, for example, by giving a manager more position power or taking steps to increase task structure, such as by clarifying goals.

Take the case of Mark Compton, a relationship-oriented leader employed by a small construction company, who was in a very unfavorable situation and having a rough time leading his construction crew. His subordinates did not trust him to look out for their well-being (poor leader–member relations); the construction jobs he supervised tended to be novel and complex (low task structure); and he had no control over the rewards and disciplinary actions his subordinates received (weak position power). Recognizing the need to improve matters, Compton's supervisor gave him the power to reward crew members with bonuses and overtime work as he saw fit and to discipline crew members for poor-quality work and unsafe on-the-job behavior. As his leadership situation improved to moderately favorable, so too did Compton's effectiveness as a leader and the performance of his crew.

Research studies tend to support some aspects of Fiedler's model but also suggest that, like most theories, it needs some modifications.[71] Some researchers have questioned

Figure 14.2
Fiedler's Contingency Theory of Leadership

what the LPC scale really measures. Others find fault with the model's premise that leaders cannot alter their styles. That is, it is likely that at least some leaders can diagnose the situation they are in and, when their style is inappropriate for the situation, modify their style so that it is more in line with what the leadership situation calls for.

House's Path-Goal Theory

path-goal theory
A contingency model of leadership proposing that leaders can motivate subordinates by identifying their desired outcomes, rewarding them for high performance and the attainment of work goals with these desired outcomes, and clarifying for them the paths leading to the attainment of work goals.

In what he called **path-goal theory,** leadership researcher Robert House focused on what leaders can do to motivate their subordinates to achieve group and organizational goals.[72] The premise of path-goal theory is that effective leaders motivate subordinates to achieve goals by (1) clearly identifying the outcomes that subordinates are trying to obtain from the workplace, (2) rewarding subordinates with these outcomes for high performance and the attainment of work goals, and (3) clarifying for subordinates the *paths* leading to the attainment of work *goals.* Path-goal theory is a contingency model because it proposes that the steps managers should take to motivate subordinates depend on both the nature of the subordinates and the type of work they do.

Based on the expectancy theory of motivation (see Chapter 12), path-goal theory provides managers with three guidelines to follow to be effective leaders:

1. *Find out what outcomes your subordinates are trying to obtain from their jobs and the organization.* These outcomes can range from satisfactory pay and job security to reasonable working hours and interesting and challenging job assignments. After identifying these outcomes, the manager should have the *reward power* needed to distribute or withhold the outcomes. Mark Crane, for example, is the vice principal of a large elementary school. Crane determined that the teachers he leads are trying to obtain the following outcomes from their jobs: pay raises, autonomy in the classroom, and the choice of which grades they teach. Crane had reward power for the latter two outcomes, but the school's principal determined how the pool of money for raises was to be distributed each year. Because Crane was the first-line manager who led the teachers and was most familiar with their performance, he asked the principal (his boss) to give him some say in determining pay raises. Realizing that this made a lot of sense, his principal gave Crane full power to distribute raises and requested only that Crane review his decisions with him prior to informing the teachers about them.

2. *Reward subordinates for high performance and goal attainment with the outcomes they desire.* The teachers and administrators at Crane's school considered several dimensions of teacher performance to be critical to achieving their goal of providing high-quality education: excellent in-class instruction, special programs to enhance student interest and learning (such as science and computer projects), and availability for meetings with parents to discuss their children's progress and special needs. Crane distributed pay raises to the teachers based on the extent to which they performed highly on each of these dimensions. The top-performing teachers were given first choice of grade assignments and also had practically complete autonomy in their classrooms.

3. *Clarify the paths to goal attainment for subordinates, remove any obstacles to high performance, and express confidence in subordinates' capabilities.* This does not mean that a manager needs to tell subordinates what to do. Rather, it means that a manager needs to make sure that subordinates are clear about what they should be trying to accomplish and have the capabilities, resources, and confidence levels needed to be successful. Crane made sure that all the teachers understood the importance of the three targeted goals and asked them whether, to reach them, they needed any special resources or supplies for their classes. Crane also gave additional coaching and guidance to teachers who seemed to be struggling. For example, Patrick Conolly, in his first year of teaching after graduate school, was unsure about how to use special projects in a third-grade class and how to react to parents who were critical. Conolly's actual teaching was excellent, but he even felt insecure about

how he was doing on this dimension. To help build Conolly's confidence, Crane told Conolly that he truly thought he could be one of the school's top teachers (which was true). He gave Conolly some ideas about special projects that worked particularly well with the third grade, such as a writing project. Crane also role-played teacher-parent interactions with Conolly. Conolly played the role of a particularly dissatisfied or troubled parent, while Crane played the role of a teacher trying to solve the underlying problem while making the parent feel that his or her child's needs were being met. Crane's efforts to clarify the paths to goal attainment for Conolly paid off: Within two years the local PTS voted Conolly teacher of the year.

Path-goal theory identifies four kinds of leadership behaviors that motivate subordinates:

- *Directive behaviors* are similar to initiating structure and include setting goals, assigning tasks, showing subordinates how to complete tasks, and taking concrete steps to improve performance.

- *Supportive behaviors* are similar to consideration and include expressing concern for subordinates and looking out for their best interests.

- *Participative behaviors* give subordinates a say in matters and decisions that affect them.

- *Achievement-oriented behaviors* motivate subordinates to perform at the highest level possible by, for example, setting very challenging goals, expecting that they be met, and believing in subordinates' capabilities.

Which of these behaviors should managers use to lead effectively? The answer to this question depends, or is contingent on, the nature of the subordinates and the kind of work they do.

Directive behaviors may be beneficial when subordinates are having difficulty completing assigned tasks, but they might be detrimental when subordinates are independent thinkers who work best when left alone. *Supportive* behaviors are often advisable when subordinates are experiencing high levels of stress. *Participative* behaviors can be particularly effective when subordinates' support of a decision is required. *Achievement-oriented* behaviors may increase motivation levels of highly capable subordinates who are bored from having too few challenges, but they might backfire if used with subordinates who are already pushed to their limit.

The Leader Substitutes Model

leadership substitute
A characteristic of a subordinate or of a situation or context that acts in place of the influence of a leader and makes leadership unnecessary.

The leader substitutes model suggests that leadership is sometimes unnecessary because substitutes for leadership are present. A **leadership substitute** is something that acts in place of the influence of a leader and makes leadership unnecessary. This model suggests that under certain conditions managers do not have to play a leadership role—that members of an organization sometimes can perform at a high level without a manager exerting influence over them.[73] The leader substitutes model is a contingency model because it suggests that in some situations leadership is unnecessary.

Take the case of David Cotsonas, who teaches English at a foreign-language school in Cyprus, an island in the Mediterranean Sea. Cotsonas is fluent in Greek, English, and French; is an excellent teacher; and is highly motivated. Many of his students are businesspeople who have some rudimentary English skills and wish to increase their fluency to be able to conduct more of their business in English. He enjoys not only teaching them English but also learning about the work they do, and he often keeps in touch with his students after they finish his classes. Cotsonas meets with the director of the school twice a year to discuss semiannual class schedules and enrollments.

With practically no influence from a leader, Cotsonas is a highly motivated top performer at the school. In his situation, leadership is unnecessary because substitutes for leadership are present. Cotsonas's teaching expertise, his motivation, and his enjoyment of his work all are substitutes for the influence of a leader—in this case, the school's director. If the school's director were to try to exert influence over the way Cotsonas goes about performing his job, Cotsonas would probably resent this infringement on his autonomy, and it is unlikely that his performance would improve because he is already one of the school's best teachers.

As in Cotsonas's case, *characteristics of subordinates*—such as their skills, abilities, experience, knowledge, and motivation—can be substitutes for leadership.[74] *Characteristics of the situation or context*—such as the extent to which the work is interesting and enjoyable—also can be substitutes. When work is interesting and enjoyable, as it is for Cotsonas, jobholders do not need to be coaxed into performing because performing is rewarding in its own right. Similarly, when managers *empower* their subordinates or use *self-managed work teams* (discussed in detail in Chapter 15), the need for leadership influence from a manager is decreased because team members manage themselves.

Substitutes for leadership can increase organizational efficiency and effectiveness because they free up some of managers' valuable time and allow managers to focus their efforts on discovering new ways to improve organizational effectiveness. The director of the language school, for example, was able to spend much of his time making arrangements to open a second school in Rhodes, an island in the Aegean Sea, because of the presence of leadership substitutes, not only in the case of Cotsonas but in that of most of the other teachers at the school as well.

Bringing It All Together

Effective leadership in organizations occurs when managers take steps to lead in a way that is appropriate for the situation or context in which leadership occurs and for the subordinates who are being led. The three contingency models of leadership discussed above help managers focus on the necessary ingredients for effective leadership. They are complementary in that each one looks at the leadership question from a different angle. Fiedler's contingency model explores how a manager's leadership style needs to be matched to that person's leadership situation for maximum effectiveness. House's path-goal theory focuses on how managers should motivate subordinates and describes the specific kinds of behaviors that managers can engage in to have a highly motivated workforce. The leadership substitutes model alerts managers to the fact that sometimes they do not need to exert influence over subordinates and thus can free up their time for other important activities. Table 14.2 recaps these three contingency models of leadership.

Table 14.2
Contingency Models of Leadership

Model	Focus	Key Contingencies
Fiedler's Contingency Model	Describes two leader styles, relationship-oriented and task-oriented, and the kinds of situations in which each kind of leader will be most effective	Whether or not a relationship-oriented or a task-oriented leader is effective is contingent on the situation
House's Path-Goal Theory	Describes how effective leaders motivate their followers	The behaviors that managers should engage in to be effective leaders are contingent on the nature of the subordinates and the work they do
Leader Substitutes Model	Describes when leadership is unnecessary	Whether or not leadership is necessary for subordinates to perform highly is contingent on characteristics of the subordinates and the situation

Transformational Leadership

LO4 Describe what transformational leadership is, and explain how managers can engage in it.

transformational leadership Leadership that makes subordinates aware of the importance of their jobs and performance to the organization and aware of their own needs for personal growth and that motivates subordinates to work for the good of the organization.

Time and time again, throughout business history, certain leaders seem to literally transform their organizations, making sweeping changes to revitalize and renew operations. For example, when Sue Nokes became senior vice president of sales and customer service at T-Mobile USA in 2002, the quality of T-Mobile's customer service was lower than that of its major competitors, on average; 12% of employees were absent on any day; and annual employee turnover was over 100%.[75] T-Mobile USA is a subsidiary of Deutsche Telekom, has 36,000 employees, and provides wireless voice, messaging, and data services.[76] When Nokes arrived at T-Mobile, valuable employees were quitting their jobs and customers weren't receiving high-quality service; neither employees nor customers were satisfied with their experience with the company.[77] By the late 2000s, T-Mobile was regularly receiving highest rankings for customer care and satisfaction in the wireless category by J. D. Power and Associates, absence and turnover rates substantially declined, and around 80% of employees indicated that they were satisfied with their jobs.[78] In fact, when Nokes visits call centers, it is not uncommon for employees to greet her with cheers and accolades.[79]

Nokes literally transformed T-Mobile into a company in which satisfied employees provide excellent service to customers.[80] When managers have such dramatic effects on their subordinates and on an organization as a whole, they are engaging in transformational leadership. **Transformational leadership** occurs when managers change (or transform) their subordinates in three important ways:[81]

1. *Transformational managers make subordinates aware of how important their jobs are for the organization and how necessary it is for them to perform those jobs as best they can so that the organization can attain its goals.* At T-Mobile, Nokes visited call centers, conducted focus groups, and had town hall meetings to find out what employees and customers were unhappy with and the steps she could take to improve matters.[82] Her philosophy is that when employees are satisfied with their jobs and view their work as important, they are much more likely to provide high-quality customer service. She made employees aware of how important their jobs were by the many steps she took to improve their working conditions, ranging from providing them with their own workspaces to substantially raising their salaries.[83] She emphasized the importance of providing excellent customer service by periodically asking employees what is working well and what is not working well, asking them what steps can be taken to improve problem areas, and taking actions to ensure that employees are able to provide excellent customer service. Nokes also instituted a performance measurement system to track performance in key areas such as quality of service and speed of problem resolution.[84] She sincerely tells employees that "You are No. 1, and the customer is why."[85]

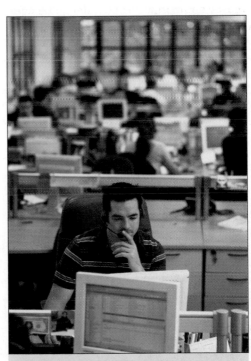

Sue Nokes transformed T-Mobile into a company in which satisfied employees provide excellent service to customers.

2. *Transformational managers make their subordinates aware of the subordinates' own needs for personal growth, development, and accomplishment.* Nokes made T-Mobile's employees aware of their own needs in this regard by transforming training and development at T-Mobile and increasing opportunities for promotions to more responsible positions. Employees now spend over 130 hours per year in training and development programs and team meetings. Nokes also instituted a promote-from-within policy, and around 80% of promotions are given to current employees.[86]

3. *Transformational managers motivate their subordinates to work for the good of the organization as a whole, not just for their own personal gain or benefit.* Nokes emphasizes that employees should be focused on what matters to customers, coworkers, and T-Mobile as a whole. She lets employees know that when they are unnecessarily absent from their jobs, they are not doing right by their coworkers. And she emphasizes the need to try to resolve customer problems in a single phone call so customers can get on with their busy lives.[87]

Table 14.3
Transformational Leadership

Transformational Managers

- Are charismatic
- Intellectually stimulate subordinates
- Engage in developmental consideration

Subordinates of Transformational Managers

- Have increased awareness of the importance of their jobs and high performance
- Are aware of their own needs for growth, development, and accomplishment
- Work for the good of the organization and not just their own personal benefit

When managers transform their subordinates in these three ways, subordinates trust the managers, are highly motivated, and help the organization achieve its goals. How do managers such as Nokes transform subordinates and produce dramatic effects in their organizations? There are at least three ways in which transformational leaders can influence their followers: by being a charismatic leader, by intellectually stimulating subordinates, and by engaging in developmental consideration (see Table 14.3).

Being a Charismatic Leader

charismatic leader An enthusiastic, self-confident leader who is able to clearly communicate his or her vision of how good things could be.

Transformational managers such as Nokes are **charismatic leaders.** They have a vision of how good things could be in their work groups and organizations that is in contrast with the status quo. Their vision usually entails dramatic improvements in group and organizational performance as a result of changes in the organization's structure, culture, strategy, decision making, and other critical processes and factors. This vision paves the way for gaining a competitive advantage. From "A Manager's Challenge," it is clear that part of Judy McGrath's vision for MTV Networks is increasing its digital offerings and transforming MTV into a truly digital company.

Charismatic leaders are excited and enthusiastic about their vision and clearly communicate it to their subordinates, as does Judy McGrath. The excitement, enthusiasm, and self-confidence of a charismatic leader contribute to the leader's being able to inspire followers to enthusiastically support his or her vision.[88] People often think of charismatic leaders or managers as being "larger than life." The essence of charisma, however, is having a vision and enthusiastically communicating it to others. Thus, managers who appear to be quiet and earnest can also be charismatic.

Stimulating Subordinates Intellectually

intellectual stimulation Behavior a leader engages in to make followers be aware of problems and view these problems in new ways, consistent with the leader's vision.

Transformational managers openly share information with their subordinates so that they are aware of problems and the need for change. The manager causes subordinates to view problems in their groups and throughout the organization from a different perspective, consistent with the manager's vision. Whereas in the past subordinates might not have been aware of some problems, may have viewed problems as a "management issue" beyond their concern, or may have viewed problems as insurmountable, the transformational manager's **intellectual stimulation** leads subordinates to view problems as challenges that they can and will meet and conquer. The manager engages and empowers subordinates to take personal responsibility for helping solve problems, as does Nokes at T-Mobile.[89]

Engaging in Developmental Consideration

developmental consideration Behavior a leader engages in to support and encourage followers and help them develop and grow on the job.

When managers engage in **developmental consideration,** they not only perform the consideration behaviors described earlier, such as demonstrating true concern for the well-being of subordinates, but go one step further. The manager goes out of his or her way to support and encourage subordinates, giving them opportunities to enhance their skills and capabilities and to grow and excel on the job.[90] As mentioned earlier, Nokes does this in numerous ways. In fact, after she had first met with employees in a call center in Albuquerque, New Mexico, Karen Viola, the manager of the call center, said: "Everyone came out crying. The people said that they had never felt so inspired in their lives, and that they had never met with any leader at that level who [they felt] cared."[91]

All organizations, no matter how large or small, successful or unsuccessful, can benefit when their managers engage in transformational leadership. Moreover, while the benefits of transformational leadership are often most apparent when an organization is in trouble, transformational leadership can be an enduring approach to leadership, leading to long-run organizational effectiveness.

The Distinction Between Transformational and Transactional Leadership

transactional leadership
Leadership that motivates subordinates by rewarding them for high performance and reprimanding them for low performance.

Transformational leadership is often contrasted with transactional leadership. In **transactional leadership,** managers use their reward and coercive powers to encourage high performance. When managers reward high performers, reprimand or otherwise punish low performers, and motivate subordinates by reinforcing desired behaviors and extinguishing or punishing undesired ones, they are engaging in transactional leadership.[92] Managers who effectively influence their subordinates to achieve goals, yet do not seem to be making the kind of dramatic changes that are part of transformational leadership, are engaging in transactional leadership.

Many transformational leaders engage in transactional leadership. They reward subordinates for a job well done and notice and respond to substandard performance. But they also have their eyes on the bigger picture of how much better things could be in their organizations, how much more their subordinates are capable of achieving, and how important it is to treat their subordinates with respect and to help them reach their full potential.

Research has found that when leaders engage in transformational leadership, their subordinates tend to have higher levels of job satisfaction and performance.[93] Additionally, subordinates of transformational leaders may be more likely to trust their leaders and their organizations and feel that they are being fairly treated, and this, in turn, may positively influence their work motivation (see Chapter 13).[94]

Gender and Leadership

LO5 Characterize the relationship between gender and leadership and explain how emotional intelligence may contribute to leadership effectiveness.

The increasing number of women entering the ranks of management, as well as the problems some women face in their efforts to be hired as managers or promoted into management positions, has prompted researchers to explore the relationship between gender and leadership. Although there are relatively more women in management positions today than there were 10 years ago, there are still relatively few women in top management and, in some organizations, even in middle management.

When women do advance to top-management positions, special attention often is focused on them and the fact that they are women. For example, women CEOs of large companies are still very rare; those who make it to the very top post, such as Meg Whitman former CEO of eBay, Judy McGrath of MTV Networks, and Andrea Jung of Avon, are very salient. As business writer Linda Tischler puts it, "In a workplace where women CEOs of major companies are so scarce . . . they can be identified, like rock stars, by first name only."[95] While women have certainly made inroads into leadership positions in organizations, they continue to be very underrepresented in top leadership posts. For example, as was indicated in Chapter 5, while around 50.5% of the employees in managerial and professional jobs in the United States are women, only about 15.4% of corporate officers in the Fortune 500 are women, and only 6.7% of the top earners are women.[96]

A widespread stereotype of women is that they are nurturing, supportive, and concerned with interpersonal relations. Men are stereotypically viewed as being directive and focused on task accomplishment. Such stereotypes suggest that women tend to be more relationship-oriented as managers and engage in more consideration behaviors, whereas men are more task-oriented and engage in more initiating-structure behaviors. Does the behavior of actual male and female managers bear out these stereotypes? Do women managers lead in different ways than men do? Are male or female managers more effective as leaders?

Research suggests that male and female managers who have leadership positions in organizations behave in similar ways.[97] Women do not engage in more consideration than men, and men do not engage in more initiating structure than women. Research does suggest, however, that leadership style may vary between women and men. Women tend to be somewhat more participative as leaders than are men, involving subordinates in decision making and seeking their input.[98] Male managers tend to be less participative than are female managers, making more decisions on their own and wanting to do things their own way. Moreover, research suggests that men tend to be harsher when they punish their subordinates than do women.[99]

There are at least two reasons why female managers may be more participative as leaders than are male managers.[100] First, subordinates may try to resist the influence of female managers more than they do the influence of male managers. Some subordinates may never have reported to a woman before; some may incorrectly see a management role as being more appropriate for a man than for a woman; and some may just resist being led by a woman. To overcome this resistance and encourage subordinates' trust and respect, women managers may adopt a participative approach.

A second reason why female managers may be more participative is that they sometimes have better interpersonal skills than male managers.[101] A participative approach to leadership requires high levels of interaction and involvement between a manager and his or her subordinates, sensitivity to subordinates' feelings, and the ability to make decisions that may be unpopular with subordinates but necessary for goal attainment. Good interpersonal skills may help female managers have the effective interactions with their subordinates that are crucial to a participative approach.[102] To the extent that male managers have more difficulty managing interpersonal relationships, they may shy away from the high levels of interaction with subordinates necessary for true participation.

The key finding from research on leader behaviors, however, is that male and female managers do *not* differ significantly in their propensities to perform different leader behaviors. Even though they may be more participative, female managers do not engage in more consideration or less initiating structure than male managers.

Perhaps a question even more important than whether male and female managers differ in the leadership behaviors they perform is whether they differ in effectiveness. Consistent with the findings for leader behaviors, research suggests that across different kinds of organizational settings, male and female managers tend to be *equally effective* as leaders.[103] Thus, there is no logical basis for stereotypes favoring male managers and leaders or for the existence of the "glass ceiling" (an invisible barrier that seems to prevent women from advancing as far as they should in some organizations). Because women and men are equally effective as leaders, the increasing number of women in the workforce should result in a larger pool of highly qualified candidates for management positions in organizations, ultimately enhancing organizational effectiveness.[104]

Emotional Intelligence and Leadership

Do the moods and emotions leaders experience on the job influence their behavior and effectiveness as leaders? Research suggests that this is likely to be the case. For example, one study found that when store managers experienced positive moods at work, salespeople in their stores provided high-quality customer service and were less likely to quit.[105] Another study found that groups whose leaders experienced positive moods had better coordination, while groups whose leaders experienced negative moods exerted more effort; members of groups with leaders in positive moods also tended to experience more positive moods themselves; and members of groups with leaders in negative moods tended to experience more negative moods.[106]

Moreover, a leader's level of emotional intelligence (see Chapter 3) may play a particularly important role in leadership effectiveness.[107] For example, emotional intelligence may help leaders develop a vision for their organizations, motivate their subordinates to commit to this vision, and energize them to enthusiastically work to achieve this vision. Moreover, emotional intelligence may enable leaders to develop a significant identity for their organization and instill high levels of trust and cooperation throughout the organization, while maintaining the flexibility needed to respond to changing conditions.[108]

Emotional intelligence also plays a crucial role in how leaders relate to and deal with their followers, particularly when it comes to encouraging followers to be creative.[109] Creativity in organizations is an emotion-laden process, as it often entails challenging the status quo, being willing to take risks and accept and learn from failures, and doing much hard work to bring creative ideas to fruition in terms of new products, services, or procedures and processes when uncertainty is bound to be high.[110] Leaders who are high on emotional intelligence are more likely to understand all the emotions surrounding creative endeavors, to be able to awaken and support the creative pursuits of their followers, and to provide the kind of support that enables creativity to flourish in organizations.[111]

Leaders, like people everywhere, sometimes make mistakes. Emotional intelligence may also help leaders respond appropriately when they realize that they have made a mistake. Recognizing, admitting, and learning from mistakes can be especially important for entrepreneurs who start their own businesses, as profiled in the following "Focus on Diversity."

Admitting a Mistake Helps Small-Business Leader

Focus on Diversity

Small Business

Things seemed to be going well for Maureen Borzacchiello, CEO of Creative Display Solutions, located in Garden City, New York.[112] She founded her small business in 2001 which provides displays, graphics, and exhibits for use in trade shows and at events for companies ranging from American Express, FedEx, and General Electric to JetBlue Airways, AIG, and The Weather Channel.[113] Her company was growing, and she had received an award from the nonprofit organization, Count Me In for Women's Economic Independence.[114]

However, in 2006 she realized that she had overextended her business financially. A large investment in inventory coupled with a sizable lease commitment, the need for office space renovations, the purchase of new furniture, and the addition of three new employees brought her to the point where she lacked the cash on hand to pay her employees their regular salaries. When she had made these decisions, she thought she and her husband (who also works in the company) would be able to generate the revenues to cover the expenditures. But her brother-in-law unexpectedly passed away and their involvement in family matters meant that they weren't able to get new accounts as quickly as she had thought they would.[115]

Still confident that if she could get through this tough period, she would be able to get her business back on track, Borzacchiello decided to be honest with her employees about the company's current financial problems, why they occurred, and how she would strive to prevent such problems in the future. She met with her employees and told them, "All I can tell you is that I apologize.... We were so focused on accelerating growth that I didn't see it coming."[116] She also admitted that she needed to have a better understanding of her company's financial situation and cash flow on a day-to-day basis, reassured employees that the company would be back on square footing in two to three months, and promised that she would pay much more attention to ongoing financial performance and cash flow in the future.[117]

Borzacchiello also told employees that she and her husband would take no money out of the business for their own salaries until the financial problems were resolved. By being honest and open with employees, Borzacchiello gained their commitment and support. All employees decided to work shorter hours, and two employees were willing to have their hourly pay rates cut.[118] True to her promise, within two months, all employees were able to return to their regular work hours and by the beginning of 2007, Creative Display Solutions had over $1 million in revenues (which was more than double its revenues at the time of the financial problems).[119] To this day, Creative Display Solutions remains a profitable business and by 2008, its list of clients included more than 500 companies.[120] Clearly, Borzacchiello effectively handled the temporary crisis her company faced by admitting and apologizing for her mistake and being open and honest with employees about her company's future prospects.[121]

By being honest and open with her employees, Maureen Borzacchiello has gained their commitment and support.

Summary and Review

THE NATURE OF LEADERSHIP Leadership is the process by which a person exerts influence over other people and inspires, motivates, and directs their activities to help achieve group or organizational goals. Leaders are able to influence others because they possess power. The five types of power available to managers are legitimate power, reward power, coercive power, expert power, and referent power. Many managers are using empowerment as a tool to increase their effectiveness as **LO1** leaders.

LO2 **TRAIT AND BEHAVIOR MODELS OF LEADERSHIP** The trait model of leadership describes personal characteristics or traits that contribute to effective leadership. However, some managers who possess these traits are not effective leaders, and some managers who do not possess all the traits are nevertheless effective leaders. The behavior model of leadership describes two kinds of behavior that most leaders engage in: consideration and initiating structure.

LO3 **CONTINGENCY MODELS OF LEADERSHIP** Contingency models take into account the complexity surrounding leadership and the role of the situation in determining whether a manager is an effective or ineffective leader. Fiedler's contingency model explains why managers may be effective leaders in one situation and ineffective in another. According to Fiedler's model, relationship-oriented leaders are most effective in situations that are moderately favorable for leading, and task-oriented leaders are most effective in situations that are very favorable or very unfavorable for leading.

House's path-goal theory describes how effective managers motivate their subordinates by determining what outcomes their subordinates want, rewarding subordinates with these outcomes when they achieve their goals and perform at a high level, and clarifying the paths to goal attainment. Managers can engage in four different kinds of behaviors to motivate subordinates: directive behaviors, supportive behaviors, participative behaviors, or achievement-oriented behaviors. The leader substitutes model suggests that sometimes managers do not have to play a leadership role because their subordinates perform at a high level without the manager having to exert influence over them.

LO4 **TRANSFORMATIONAL LEADERSHIP** Transformational leadership occurs when managers have dramatic effects on their subordinates and on the organization as a whole, and inspire and energize subordinates to solve problems and improve performance. These effects include making subordinates aware of the importance of their own jobs and high performance; making subordinates aware of their own needs for personal growth, development, and accomplishment; and motivating subordinates to work for the good of the organization and not just their own personal gain. Managers can engage in transformational leadership by being charismatic leaders, by intellectually stimulating subordinates, and by engaging in developmental consideration. Transformational managers also often engage in transactional leadership by using their reward and coercive powers to encourage high performance.

LO5 **GENDER AND LEADERSHIP** Female and male managers do not differ in the leadership behaviors that they perform, contrary to stereotypes suggesting that women are more relationship-oriented and men more task-oriented. Female managers sometimes are more participative than male managers, however. Research has found that women and men are equally effective as managers and leaders.

LO5 **EMOTIONAL INTELLIGENCE AND LEADERSHIP** The moods and emotions leaders experience on the job, and their ability to effectively manage these feelings, can influence their effectiveness as leaders. Moreover, emotional intelligence has the potential to contribute to leadership effectiveness in multiple ways, including encouraging and supporting creativity among followers.

Management in Action

Topics for Discussion and Action

DISCUSSION

1. Describe the steps managers can take to increase their power and ability to be effective leaders. **[LO1]**

2. Think of specific situations in which it might be especially important for a manager to engage in consideration and in initiating structure. **[LO2]**

3. For your current job or for a future job you expect to hold, describe what your supervisor could do to strongly motivate you to be a top performer. **[LO3]**

4. Discuss why managers might want to change the behaviors they engage in, given their situation, their subordinates, and the nature of the work being done. Do you think managers are able to readily change their leadership behaviors? Why or why not? **[LO3]**

5. Discuss why substitutes for leadership can contribute to organizational effectiveness. **[LO3]**

6. Describe what transformational leadership is, and explain how managers can engage in it. **[LO4]**

7. Discuss why some people still think that men make better managers than women even though research indicates that men and women are equally effective as managers and leaders. **[LO5]**

8. Imagine that you are working in an organization in an entry-level position after graduation and have come up with what you think is a great idea for improving a critical process in the organization that relates to your job. In what ways might your supervisor encourage you to actually implement your idea? How might your supervisor discourage you from even sharing your idea with others? **[LO 4, 5]**

ACTION

9. Interview a manager to find out how the three situational characteristics that Fiedler identified are affecting his or her ability to provide leadership. **[LO3]**

10. Find a company that has dramatically turned around its fortunes and improved its performance. Determine whether a transformational manager was behind the turnaround and, if one was, what this manager did. **[LO4]**

Building Management Skills

Analyzing Failures of Leadership [LO 1, 2, 3, 4]

Think about a situation you are familiar with in which a leader was very ineffective. Then answer the following questions:

1. What sources of power did this leader have? Did the leader have enough power to influence his or her followers?

2. What kinds of behaviors did this leader engage in? Were they appropriate for the situation? Why, or why not?

3. From what you know, do you think this leader was a task-oriented leader or a relationship-oriented leader? How favorable was this leader's situation for leading?

4. What steps did this leader take to motivate his or her followers? Were these steps appropriate or inappropriate? Why?

5. What signs, if any, did this leader show of being a transformational leader?

Managing Ethically [LO1]

Managers who verbally criticize their subordinates, put them down in front of their coworkers, or use the threat of job loss to influence behavior are exercising coercive power. Some employees subject to coercive power believe that using it is unethical.

Questions

1. Either alone or in a group, think about the ethical implications of the use of coercive power.

2. To what extent do managers and organizations have an ethical obligation to put limits on the amount of coercive power that is exercised?

Small Group Breakout Exercise
Improving Leadership Effectiveness [LO 1, 2, 3, 4]

Form groups of three to five people, and appoint one member as the spokesperson who will communicate your findings and conclusions to the class when called on by the instructor. Then discuss the following scenario.

You are a team of human resource consultants who have been hired by Carla Caruso, an entrepreneur who has started her own interior decorating business. A highly competent and creative interior decorator, Caruso established a working relationship with most of the major home builders in her community. At first, she worked on her own as an independent contractor. Then because of a dramatic increase in the number of new homes being built, she became swamped with requests for her services and decided to start her own company.

She hired a secretary-bookkeeper and four interior decorators, all of whom are highly competent. Caruso still does decorating jobs herself and has adopted a hands-off approach to leading the four decorators who report to her because she feels that interior design is a very personal, creative endeavor. Rather than pay the decorators on some kind of commission basis (such as a percentage of their customers' total billings), she pays them a premium salary, higher than average, so that they are motivated to do what's best for a customer's needs and not what will result in higher billings and commissions.

Caruso thought everything was going smoothly until customer complaints started coming in. The complaints ranged from the decorators' being hard to get hold of, promising unrealistic delivery times, and being late for or failing to keep appointments to their being impatient and rude when customers had trouble making up their minds. Caruso knows that her decorators are very competent and is concerned that she is not effectively leading and managing them. She wonders, in particular, if her hands-off approach is to blame and if she should change the manner in which she rewards or pays her decorators. She has asked for your advice.

1. Analyze the sources of power that Caruso has available to her to influence the decorators. What advice can you give her to either increase her power base or use her existing power more effectively?

2. Given what you have learned in this chapter (for example, from the behavior model and path-goal theory), does Caruso seem to be performing appropriate leader behaviors in this situation? What advice can you give her about the kinds of behaviors she should perform?

3. What steps would you advise Caruso to take to increase the decorators' motivation to deliver high-quality customer service?

4. Would you advise Caruso to try to engage in transformational leadership in this situation? If not, why not? If so, what steps would you advise her to take?

Exploring the World Wide Web [LO 1, 2, 3, 4, 5]

Go to the Web site of the Center for Creative Leadership (www.ccl.org). Spend some time browsing through the site to learn more about this organization, which specializes in leadership. Then click on "Services & Products" and then "Coaching Services." Read about the different coaching programs and options the center provides. How do you think leaders might benefit from coaching? What kinds of leaders/managers may find coaching especially beneficial? Do you think coaching services such as those provided by the Center for Creative Leadership can help leaders become more effective? Why, or why not?

Be the Manager [LO 1, 2, 3, 4, 5]

You are the CEO of a medium-size company that makes window coverings such as Hunter Douglas blinds and Douettes. Your company has a real cost advantage in terms of being able to make custom window coverings at costs that are relatively low in the industry. However, the performance of your company has been lackluster. In order to make needed changes and improve performance, you met with the eight other top managers in your company and charged them with identifying problems and missed opportunities in each of their areas and coming up with an action plan to address the problems and take advantage of opportunities.

Once you gave the managers the okay, they were charged with implementing their action plans in a timely fashion and monitoring the effects of their initiatives on a monthly basis for the next 8 to 12 months.

You approved each of the manager's action plans, and a year later most of the manager's were reporting that their initiatives had been successful in addressing the problems and opportunities they had identified a year ago. However, overall company performance continues to be lackluster and shows no signs of improvement. You are confused and starting to question your leadership capabilities and approach to change. What are you going to do to improve the performance and effectiveness of your company?

BusinessWeek Case in the News [LO 1, 2, 3, 4]

Big Blue Goes for the Big Win

It's a snowy February day at IBM's office in Yorktown Heights, N. Y., and John E. Kelly III drops by a cramped conference room to talk about his plans for IBM Research. The organization is already considered one of the world's best corporate research labs. Yet Kelly, a 27-year IBM veteran who took over as research director in July, is planning surprisingly dramatic changes. "We have to do bolder things, bigger things," he says, speaking about his plans publicly for the first time. "If we don't fail a third of the time, we're not stretching enough. On the other hand, when we win, we need to win big."

What does Kelly have in mind? For starters, he's focusing on four top research priorities, rather than spreading investments too thin. The four bets are enormous, though. Each of the projects will get $100 million over the next two to three years, in hopes of generating at least $1 billion, each, in new revenue. The projects: inventing a successor to today's semiconductor, designing computers that process data much more efficiently, using math to solve complex business problems, and building massive clusters of computers that operate like a single machine—an approach called "cloud" computing. Central to the effort will be even more emphasis on basic scientific research, such as physics, chemistry, and math.

The other major change Kelly has in the works is overhauling the way IBM does research. Today the tech giant has eight research facilities with 3,200 scientists, and it hasn't opened a new one in a decade. Kelly foresees creating dozens of new joint ventures for research, which he calls "collaboratories," with countries, companies, and independent research outfits. One venture with Saudi Arabia, focusing on nanotechnology, was unveiled on Feb. 26. Kelly believes IBM needs to leverage its resources and learn from others. "The nature of research itself is changing," he says. "Great ideas are springing up everywhere, and we need to shift from focusing on large brick-and-mortar operations to having a much more collaborative outreach program."

He'll try to do all this without a sharp increase in spending. IBM doesn't break out its research budget, but Kelly says it will rise at the rate of IBM's revenues, in the single digits. The company spends more than $6 billion a year overall on research and development of new products.

Kelly's moves will be closely watched. IBM has been one of the few old-line companies to continue investing in basic research, as others have cut back. The once-vaunted Bell Labs, now owned by Alcatel-Lucent, has become a shadow of its former self. "IBM has been the only one with the staying power," says Tim Studt, editor-in-chief of *R&D Magazine*, which last year ranked IBM as the country's top R&D company. IBM has been the leading recipient of U.S. patents for 14 years running.

But Kelly knows IBM can't be complacent. Both Microsoft and Google are investing heavily in research. For the first time, Microsoft broke the top 10 for U.S. patent awards last year, coming in at No.6. "It's a race," says Kelly. "While others are trying to emulate us, we're going to skate ahead."

Kelly, the seventh director since IBM established its labs in 1945, has research in his blood. His father worked as a technician at General Electric's lab in Niskayuna, N. Y., where Kelly would visit regularly as a boy and watch him work with vacuum tubes. Kelly got a PhD in materials engineering at Rensselaer Polytechnic Institute, just outside of Albany. At IBM, he ran one of the major research departments, in between stints in the chip division.

His collaborative research strategy emerged out of a dire situation he faced in 2003 as head of IBM's chip business. The company was suffering huge financial losses as the costs of

keeping up with the latest technology were soaring. Kelly took a gamble and set up research alliances with a handful of partners, including Sony Electronics and Advanced Micro Devices, to share expenses and brainpower. The approach eventually paid off, as IBM's chip business returned to profitability and remained on the cutting edge of technology. "This is a smart strategy," says Studt. "You can't be the leader all by yourself anymore. The technology is just too complicated and expensive."

The just-unveiled deal with Saudi Arabia is an example of where Kelly is headed. The two sides plan to develop technologies for solar energy and water desalinization. The Saudis chose IBM because of its expertise. IBM scientists won a Nobel Prize in 1986 for nanotech breakthroughs, and they're leaders in developing new nanotech materials. "We want to work with the best in the field," says Turki Saud Al-Saud, vice-president for Research Institutes in King Abdulaziz City for Science & Technology.

Kelly expects the basic research that IBM does with partners to feed back into its own four high-priority projects. Nanotechnology, for instance, will be critical to inventing the successor to today's chips. Performance improvements have been slowing down in the current chip technology, and scientists expect chips of the future to be made with tiny switches built with individual atoms. As part of its effort, IBM announced on Feb. 22 that it had calculated how much force it takes to move a single atom. "If they can come up with a true, game-changing technology, they'll have a clear first-mover

advantage and a huge business benefit," says Charles M. Vest, president of the National Academy of Engineering.

Another major research initiative with a big potential payoff is IBM's new computer reengineering project. IBM was at the forefront of redesigning microprocessors, the brains of computers, to include multiple parts, or cores, on a single piece of silicon. That makes it possible for the processors to run at lower power, with less heat. Now the company is designing chips with specialized cores that perform certain kinds of calculations more efficiently, plus software to take advantage of the new processing power. If the project works, it will help IBM strengthen its lead in high-margin server computers.

These are high-risk, high-reward ventures. "Big bets don't scare me at all," Kelly says. "I love this environment. I thrive on it."

Questions for Discussion

1. How would you describe John Kelly's personal leadership style?

2. What are his sources of power?

3. What behaviors does he appear to engage in?

4. Is he a transformational leader? Why, or why not?

Source: Steve Hamm, "Big Blue Goes for the Big Win." Reprinted from the March 10, 2008, issue of *BusinessWeek* by special permission. Copyright © 2008 by The McGraw-Hill Companies, Inc.

BusinessWeek **Case in the News** [LO 1, 2, 3, 4]

When CEOs Aren't Leaders

Blackstone Group CEO Stephen Schwarzman is only the latest high-profile poster boy in the furor over executive pay, reminding us that some of today's corner office occupants have very different motivations and values from other Americans. His "I'm worth every penny" jeering and other public comments make his narrow self-focus clear, relegating him to the gang of often piratical business executives who, sadly, have dominated the headlines in recent years.

Thanks to the lot of them and Enron, WorldCom, and other corporate scandals, the image of the corporate CEO has taken a pounding. While Americans generally strive for and celebrate achievement and success, they are increasingly sickened by the narcissism, greed, and other "me first" antics of such CEOs. Whether it is the imperious version (think Robert Nardelli or Hank Greenberg) or the self-dealing version (think Dennis Kozlowski or Jeffrey Skilling), much of the general public now believes CEOs are in the game only for themselves. The good of their employees, their customers, their communities, and even their investors are merely ancillary issues for them.

Rather than being shocked, amazed, or even entertained, we should be deeply concerned. The cumulative damage promises to make it harder for the business community to press its cases in the court of public opinion and government. Inevitably, all top U.S. corporate executives feel the impact and suffer at least some drop in personal effectiveness. And don't forget, a tarnished image is exceptionally hard to repair, both for CEOs and the companies that have hired them.

The problem's roots lie in the fact that the terms "CEO" and "leader" have mistakenly become synonymous. Nothing could be further from the truth. CEOs are measured by quantitative results. Leaders are shaped and defined by character. CEOs are expected to boost sales, improve profit margins, and make money for shareholders. Leaders inspire and enable others to do excellent work and realize their potential. As a result, they build successful, enduring organizations.

Neither PR spin campaigns nor stronger government regulations and accounting rules will fix today's CEO image crisis. Instead, the business community itself must recognize that finding CEOs who can generate business results is necessary but not sufficient. Those we elevate or hire to become CEOs must also possess the distinguishing qualities of great leaders: the ability to build trust, inspire dedicated and engaged followers, and make service to others their preeminent priority. In other words, the core values of CEOs should be examined just as closely as their drive, intellectual depth, financial acumen, or track record.

To accomplish that, why not start with three small but powerful changes. First, corporate board members and others who recruit CEOs must adopt disciplined approaches to investigate a candidate's character. For example, divide the interview process into two distinct components to vet candidates on both traditionally examined management talents, as well as on their lived—not just spoken—values. Those exploring the latter must, in addition to asking hard questions of the candidates, gather insights from their current and former employees, customers, and suppliers. This investigation should be pursued with the same level of rigor as a due diligence process prior to an acquisition.

Next, those who aspire to the CEO title need to understand that the ego-fired, command-and-control, "winning-at-all-costs" approach is no longer viable. Instead, by measuring success through the success of all those they serve, they will achieve superlative, sustainable results not only for their constituents but also for themselves.

Finally, the media and business need to do a better job spotlighting truly great leaders in Corporate America, such as Xerox's Anne Mulcahy or Southwest Airlines' Gary Kelly, to present a more accurate picture of today's chief executives.

Imagine the lubrication we could add to our business and economic engines if society recognized that the vast majority of CEOs are honorable leaders driven by more than the prospect of personal gain. That's why we must make sure that CEOs' values are considered on par with their business results. The alternative is to allow the bullies of business to define our world and ourselves, harming us all in the bargain.

Questions for Discussion

1. Do you agree or disagree with Givray's assertion that some CEOs are not leaders? Why, or why not?

2. How should the performance of CEOs be assessed to ensure that they are effective leaders?

3. Why are some CEOs very ineffective leaders?

4. Do you think all CEOs need to be transformational leaders? Why, or why not?

CHAPTER 15

Effective Groups and Teams

Learning Objectives

After studying this chapter, you should be able to:

LO1 Explain why groups and teams are key contributors to organizational effectiveness.

LO2 Identify the different types of groups and teams that help managers and organizations achieve their goals.

LO3 Explain how different elements of group dynamics influence the functioning and effectiveness of groups and teams.

LO4 Explain why it is important for groups and teams to have a balance of conformity and deviance and a moderate level of cohesiveness.

LO5 Describe how managers can motivate group members to achieve organizational goals and reduce social loafing in groups and teams.

A MANAGER'S CHALLENGE

Employees Form Teams at ICU Medical

How can an entrepreneur use teams to help manage a rapidly growing organization? Dr. George Lopez, an internal medicine physician, founded ICU Medical in San Clemente, California, in 1984 after a patient of his accidentally died when an intravenous (IV) line became inadvertently disconnected.[1] Lopez thought that there must be a better way to design components of IV lines so that these kinds of tragic accidents didn't happen. He developed a product called the Click Lock, which both has a locking mechanism for IV systems and also a protected needle so that health care workers are protected from accidental needle pricks.[2] Today, ICU Medical has approximately 1,480 employees and in 2007, net sales were over $180 million.[3] Lopez is CEO of the company, which is now publicly traded on the NASDAQ stock exchange.[4] ICU Medical continues to focus on the development and manufacture of products that improve the functioning of IV lines and systems while protecting health care workers from accidental needle pricks.[5] For example, the CLAVE NeedleFree Connector for IV lines is one of ICU Medical's top-selling products.[6]

In the early 1990s, Lopez experienced something not uncommon to successful entrepreneurs as their businesses grow. As the entrepreneur–CEO, he continued to make the majority of important decisions himself; yet, he had close to 100 employees, demand for the CLAVE was very high, and he was starting to feel overloaded to the point where he would often sleep at

George Lopez empowers ICU Medical employees to form teams to address problems and seize opportunities.

nights in the office.[7] After watching one of his son's hockey games, he realized that a well-functioning team could work wonders; in the case of the hockey game, while the opposing team had an outstanding player, his son's team really pulled together as a team and was able to win the game despite the rival team's outstanding member. Lopez decided to empower employees to form teams to work on a pressing goal for ICU Medical, increasing production.[8] While employees did form teams and spent a lot of time engaged in team interactions, the teams did not seem to come up with any real tangible results, perhaps because there were no team leaders in place and the teams had no guidelines or rules for behavior to follow to help them accomplish their goals.[9]

In an effort to improve team effectiveness, Lopez told employees that teams should elect team leaders. And together with Jim Reitz, who is currently ICU Medical's director of human resources, Lopez came up with rules or guidelines teams should follow such as "challenge the issue, not the person" and "stand up for your position, but never argue against the facts."[10] ICU Medical also started to reward team members for their team's contributions to organizational effectiveness. With these changes, Reitz and Lopez were striving to ensure that teams had leaders, had some guidelines for team member behavior, and were rewarded for their contributions to organizational effectiveness but, at the same time, were not bogged down by unnecessary constraints and structures and were truly self-managing.[11]

With these changes in place, teams at ICU Medical really did start to live up to their promise. For example, several years ago, Don Ramstead who was responsible for the planning of production schedules, noticed a significant process inefficiency whereby a forklift was used to move parts to and from

a molding site to a warehouse.[12] After discussing the issue with coworkers, he suggested that a team be formed to improve the production process for the CLAVE. The team was formed, included managers in charge of logistics and manufacturing, and within six months was able to reduce the number of steps in the process of producing the CLAVE from 27 to 9, for an annual cost savings of around $500,000.[13] Importantly, Ramstead and fellow team members were rewarded for their contributions to organizational effectiveness.[14]

Today, any ICU Medical employee can create a team to address a problem, seize an opportunity, or work on a project ranging from developing a new product to making improvements in the physical work environment.[15] The teams are self-managing, and team members divide up the work amongst themselves, assign roles and responsibilities, schedule meetings, and determine their own deadlines. Regardless of the extent of their involvement in teams, employees are still expected to perform all of the regular tasks and responsibilities that make up their individual jobs. On average, teams tend to have between five to seven members, meet once a week, and at the end of each quarter, around 12 to 15 teams have completed their projects. On a quarterly basis, ICU Medical makes available $75,000 to reward teams that successfully complete their projects.[16] Rewards to teams are based on the salaries of their members and the success and importance of their projects.[17]

While Lopez has retained the right to veto any decisions or initiatives teams come up with, he has not yet exercised that right.[18] He believes that teams have to be empowered to make decisions and those decisions should hold even if he or other top managers might have their own misgivings. For example, several years ago, a team proposed that ICU Medical provide employees with a 401(k) retirement plan. While Lopez was concerned about the cost and was not in favor of starting such a plan, he went along with the team and instituted a 401(k) plan, which he now realizes has been beneficial in terms of employee retention. According to Lopez, he would only exercise his veto power for a team recommendation he believed would put ICU Medical "on a pathway to destruction."[19]

Recognizing that self-managed teams still need rules, guidelines, leadership, and structure, a team of employees developed a 25-page guidebook for effective team functioning. And, in order to ensure that teams learn from each other as well as get feedback, teams are required to put up notes from each of their meetings on ICU Medical's intranet and any employee can provide feedback to any of the teams.[20]

Of course, sometimes teams have problems. For example, manager Colleen Wilder once worked on a team in which she felt some team members, including herself,

contributed much more than others who she felt just joined the team to get rewarded (without contributing). She suggested to the team that the team reward be split up among members based upon their contributions to the team project; her fellow team members agreed and those who did little to no work agreed to forego their share of the reward.[21]

Regardless of problems that might crop up with teams, Lopez believes that teams often make better decisions than would have been made by a single individual.[22] For example, a few years ago ICU Medical's information technology group purchased new laptops; many employees who travel a lot think the laptops weigh too much. As Lopez indicates, "That's what happens when you don't form a team. . . Top-down decisions are frequently wrong."[23] All in all, self-managed teams have helped Lopez manage his rapidly growing business and have substantially contributed to ICU Medical's overall effectiveness.[24]

Overview

ICU Medical is not alone in using groups and teams to improve organizational effectiveness. Managers in companies large and small are using groups and teams to enhance performance, increase responsiveness to customers, spur innovation, and motivate employees. In this chapter we look in detail at how groups and teams can contribute to organizational effectiveness and the types of groups and teams used in organizations. We discuss how different elements of group dynamics influence the functioning and effectiveness of groups, and we describe how managers can motivate group members to achieve organizational goals and reduce social loafing in groups and teams. By the end of this chapter, you will appreciate why the effective management of groups and teams is a key ingredient for organizational performance and effectiveness.

Groups, Teams, and Organizational Effectiveness

A **group** may be defined as two or more people who interact with each other to accomplish certain goals or meet certain needs.[25] A **team** is a group whose members work *intensely* with one another to achieve a specific common goal or objective. As these definitions imply, all teams are groups but not all groups are teams. The two characteristics that distinguish teams from groups are the *intensity* with which team members work together and the presence of a *specific, overriding team goal or objective*.

LO1 Explain why groups and teams are key contributors to organizational effectiveness.

group Two or more people who interact with each other to accomplish certain goals or meet certain needs.

team A group whose members work intensely with one another to achieve a specific common goal or objective.

synergy Performance gains that result when individuals and departments coordinate their actions.

Recall from "A Manager's Challenge" how the team Don Ramstead formed worked intensively together to achieve the goal of improving the production process for the CLAVE at ICU Medical; within six months, the team had reduced the number of steps in the production process from 27 to 9 for an annual costs savings of around $500,000.[26] In contrast, the accountants who work in a small CPA firm are a group: They may interact with one another to achieve goals such as keeping up to date on the latest changes in accounting rules and regulations, maintaining a smoothly functioning office, satisfying clients, and attracting new clients. But they are not a team because they do not work intensely with one another. Each accountant concentrates on serving the needs of his or her own clients.

Because all teams are also groups, whenever we use the term *group* in this chapter, we are referring to both groups *and* teams. As you might imagine, because members of teams work intensely together, teams can sometimes be difficult to form and it may take time for members to learn how to effectively work together. Groups and teams can help an organization gain a competitive advantage because they can (1) enhance its performance, (2) increase its responsiveness to customers, (3) increase innovation, and (4) increase employees' motivation and satisfaction (see Figure 15.1). In this section, we look at each of these contributions in turn.

Groups and Teams as Performance Enhancers

One of the main advantages of using groups is the opportunity to obtain a type of **synergy:** People working in a group are able to produce more or higher-quality outputs than would have been produced if each person had worked separately and all their individual efforts were later combined. The essence of synergy is captured in the saying "The whole is more than the sum of its parts." Factors that can contribute to synergy in groups include the ability of group members to bounce ideas off one another, to correct one another's mistakes, to solve problems immediately as they arise, to bring a diverse knowledge base to bear on a problem or goal, and to accomplish work that is too vast or all-encompassing for any one individual to achieve on his or her own.

To take advantage of the potential for synergy in groups, managers need to make sure that groups are composed of members who have complementary skills and knowledge relevant to the group's work. For example, at Hallmark Cards, synergies are created by bringing together all the different functions needed to create and produce a greeting card in a cross-functional team (a team composed of members from different

Figure 15.1

Groups' and Teams' Contributions to Organizational Effectiveness

departments or functions; see Chapter 10). For instance, artists, writers, designers, and marketing experts work together as members of a team to develop new cards.[27]

At Hallmark, the skills and expertise of the artists complement the contributions of the writers and vice versa. Managers also need to give groups enough autonomy so that the groups, rather than the manager, are solving problems and determining how to achieve goals and objectives, as is true in the cross-functional teams at Hallmark and the teams employees form at ICU Medical in "A Manager's Challenge." To promote synergy, managers need to empower their subordinates and be coaches, guides, and resources for groups while refraining from playing a more directive or supervisory role. The potential for synergy in groups may be the reason why more and more managers are incorporating empowerment into their personal leadership styles (see Chapter 14).

When tasks are complex and involve highly sophisticated and rapidly changing technologies, achieving synergies in teams often hinges on having the appropriate mix of backgrounds and areas of expertise represented on the team. In large organizations with operations in many states and countries, it is often difficult for managers to determine which employees might have the expertise needed on a particular team or for a certain project. As indicated in the following "Information Technology Byte," new software applications can help managers identify employees with the expertise needed to achieve real synergies.

Information Technology Byte

Technology Helps Teams Achieve Synergies by Identifying Expertise

Lockheed Martin Corporation has around 140,000 employees working in 939 different locations in over 450 cities in the United States and around the world.[28] These vast human resources provide Lockheed Martin with a tremendous amount of expertise to draw on to solve vexing problems and better meet customers' needs. However, it is a real challenge for managers to identify who in the company might actually have the expertise needed for a particular project or team.

Enter ActiveNet, a software application provided by Tacit Software.[29] ActiveNet scans documents in a company's computer systems, ranging from e-mails and instant messages to Word and PowerPoint documents, to identify areas of expertise based on what people write and the content of documents they produce;[30] the software creates searchable employee profiles based on this content.[31] For example, a Lockheed team of researchers in California was concerned about the potential for condensation to accumulate in missile canisters. Given all the work Lockheed does with missiles, it was likely that someone in the company had worked on this problem before. Through ActiveNet, the team was able to identify a researcher working in another California facility who had expertise in this area.[32]

Prototype development mechanic Stephen Moore, front, and others drill holes for fasteners on the fuselage of a prototype of an Unmanned Combat Air System (UCAS) aircraft at a Northrup Grumman plant. Moore and his crew at Grumman recognize the value of IT for fostering teamwork on complicated projects such as this one.

Northrop Grumman has 120,000 employees and faces similar challenges in identifying expertise needed to achieve synergies.[33] For example, when Werner Hinz, a Grumman engineer, was preparing a bid for the Pentagon to develop a new, unmanned airplane that could travel faster than the speed of sound, he needed someone with expertise in hypersonics on his team. Hinz couldn't think of any employees he knew with this expertise, so he used ActiveNet by typing in key phrases. ActiveNet provided Hinz with the name of an employee he had actually met and who worked in the same building as Hinz but whom Hinz did not know much about; after speaking to the employee on the phone, Hinz knew he had found the hypersonics expert he needed on his team to prepare the bid. (Hinz's team eventually was awarded a Pentagon contract of $1.5 million to design the new plane.)[34]

While an ActiveNet license is not inexpensive—it costs about $170 for each employee profile—it can help managers identify expertise needed for synergies in teams by allowing them to search employee profiles. ActiveNet also has privacy protections in place. For example, employees determine who can access which parts of their profiles, and the system does not keep copies of documents after they have been scanned for relevant content. And once ActiveNet identifies an individual in a content domain with regard to a particular query, that individual is contacted first, before his or her name is passed on to the person seeking expertise, to see if he or she wants to make contact with the person making the query, provide information anonymously, or ignore the query. After September 11, 2001, the CIA began using ActiveNet in its counterterrorist efforts.[35] To the extent that ActiveNet can help managers like Hinz find employees with needed expertise, it may help them achieve synergies in teams.

Groups, Teams, and Responsiveness to Customers

Being responsive to customers is not always easy. In manufacturing organizations, for example, customers' needs and desires for new and improved products have to be balanced against engineering constraints, production costs and feasibilities, government safety regulations, and marketing challenges. In service organizations such as health maintenance organizations (HMOs), being responsive to patients' needs and desires for prompt, high-quality medical care and treatment has to be balanced against meeting physicians' needs and desires and keeping health care costs under control. Being responsive to customers often requires the wide variety of skills and expertise found in different departments and at different levels in an organization's hierarchy. Sometimes, for example, employees at lower levels in an organization's hierarchy, such as sales representatives for a computer company, are closest to its customers and the most attuned to their needs. However, lower-level employees like salespeople often lack the technical expertise needed to come up with new product ideas; such expertise is found in the research and development department. Bringing salespeople, research and development experts, and members of other departments together in a group or cross-functional team can enhance responsiveness to customers. Consequently, when managers form a team, they need to make sure that the diversity of expertise and knowledge needed to be responsive to customers exists within the team; this is why cross-functional teams are so popular.

In a cross-functional team, the expertise and knowledge in different organizational departments are brought together in the skills and knowledge of the team members. Managers of high-performing organizations are careful to determine which types of expertise and knowledge are required for teams to be responsive to customers, and they use this information in forming teams.

Teams and Innovation

Innovation, the creative development of new products, new technologies, new services, or even new organizational structures, is a topic we discuss in detail in Chapter 18. Often, an individual working alone does not possess the extensive and diverse set of skills, knowledge, and expertise required for successful innovation. Managers can better encourage innovation by creating teams of diverse individuals who together have the knowledge relevant to a particular type of innovation rather than by relying on individuals working alone.

Using teams to innovate has other advantages as well. First, team members can often uncover one another's errors or false assumptions; an individual acting alone would not be able to do this. Second, team members can critique one another's approaches when need be and build off one another's strengths while compensating for weaknesses, one of the advantages of devil's advocacy and dialectical inquiry, discussed in Chapter 7.

To further promote innovation, managers are well advised to empower teams and make their members fully responsible and accountable for the innovation process. The manager's role is to provide guidance, assistance, coaching, and the resources team members need and *not* to closely direct or supervise their activities. To speed innovation, managers also need to form teams in which each member brings some unique resource to the team, such as engineering prowess, knowledge of production, marketing expertise, or financial savvy. Successful innovation sometimes requires that managers form teams with members from different countries and cultures.

Amazon uses teams to spur innovation, and many of the unique features on its Web site that enable it to be responsive to customers and meet their needs have been developed by teams, as indicated in the following "Information Technology Byte."

Information Technology Byte

Pizza Teams Innovate at Amazon

Jeff Bezos, founder, CEO, and chairman of the board of Amazon, is a firm believer in the power of teams to spur innovation.[36] At Amazon, teams have considerable autonomy to develop their ideas and experiment without interference from managers or other groups. And teams are kept deliberately small. According to Bezos, no team should need more than two pizzas to feed its members. If more than two pizzas are needed to nourish a team, the team is too large. Thus, teams at Amazon typically have no more than about five to seven members.[37]

"Pizza teams" have come up with unique and popular innovations that individuals working alone might never have thought of. A team developed the "Gold Box" icon that customers can click on to receive special offers that expire within an hour of opening the treasure chest. Another team developed "Search Inside the Book" that allows customers to search and read content from over 100,000 books.[38] And a team developed the Amazon Kindle, a wireless reader that weighs 10.3 ounces, can hold over 200 titles, can receive automatic delivery of major newspapers and blogs, and has a high-resolution screen that appears like and can be read like paper.[39]

While Bezos gives teams autonomy to develop and run with their ideas, he also believes in the careful analysis and testing of ideas. A great advocate of the power of facts, data, and analysis, Bezos feels that whenever an idea can be tested through analysis, analysis should rule the day. When an undertaking is just too large or too uncertain or when data are lacking and hard to come by, Bezos and other experienced top managers make the final call.[40] But in order to make such judgment calls about implementing new ideas (either by data analysis or expert judgment), what really is needed are truly creative ideas. To date, teams have played a very important role in generating ideas that have helped Amazon be responsive to its customers, have a widely known Internet brand name, and be the highly successful and innovative company it is today.[41]

At Amazon, teams adhere to the two-pizza rule; that is, no team should need more than two pizzas to feed its members.

Groups and Teams as Motivators

Managers often decide to form groups and teams to accomplish organizational goals and then find that using groups and teams brings additional benefits. Members of groups, and especially members of teams (because of the higher intensity of interaction in teams), are likely to be more satisfied than they would have been if they were working on their own. The experience of working alongside other highly charged and motivated people can be very stimulating. In addition, working on a team can be very motivating: Team members more readily see how their efforts and expertise directly contribute to the achievement of team and organizational goals, and they feel personally responsible for the outcomes or results of their work. This has been the case at Hallmark Cards.

The increased motivation and satisfaction that can accompany the use of teams can also lead to other outcomes, such as lower turnover. This has been Frank B. Day's experience as founder and chairman of the board of Rock Bottom Restaurants Inc.[42] To provide high-quality customer service, Day has organized the restaurants' employees into wait staff teams, whose members work together to refill beers, take orders, bring hot chicken enchiladas to the tables, or clear off the tables. Team members share the burden of undesirable activities and unpopular shift times, and customers no longer have to wait until a particular waitress or waiter is available. Motivation and satisfaction levels in Rock Bottom restaurants seem to be higher than in other restaurants, and turnover is about one-half of that experienced in other U.S. restaurant chains.[43]

Working in a group or team can also satisfy organizational members' needs for engaging in social interaction and feeling connected to other people. For workers who perform highly stressful jobs, such as hospital emergency and operating room staff, group membership can be an important source of social support and motivation. Family members or friends may not be able to fully understand or appreciate some sources of work stress that these group members experience firsthand. Moreover, group members may cope better with work stressors when they are able to share them with other members of their group. In addition, groups often devise techniques to relieve stress, such as the telling of jokes among hospital operating room staff.

Why do managers in all kinds of organizations rely so heavily on groups and teams? Effectively managed groups and teams can help managers in their quest for high performance, responsiveness to customers, and employee motivation. Before explaining how managers can effectively manage groups, however, we will describe the types of groups that are formed in organizations.

formal group A group that managers establish to achieve organizational goals.

Types of Groups and Teams

LO2 Identify the different types of groups and teams that help managers and organizations achieve their goals.

informal group A group that managers or nonmanagerial employees form to help achieve their own goals or meet their own needs.

To achieve their goals of high performance, responsiveness to customers, innovation, and employee motivation, managers can form various types of groups and teams (see Figure 15.2). **Formal groups** are those managers establish to achieve organizational goals. The formal work groups are *cross-functional* teams composed of members from different departments, such as those at Hallmark Cards, and *cross-cultural* teams composed of members from different cultures or countries, such as the teams at global carmakers. As you will see, some of the groups discussed in this section also can be considered to be cross-functional (if they are composed of members from different departments) or cross-cultural (if they are composed of members from different countries or cultures).

Sometimes organizational members, managers or nonmanagers, form groups because they feel that groups will help them achieve their own goals or meet their own needs (for example, the need for social interaction). Groups formed in this way are **informal groups.** Four nurses who work in a hospital and have lunch together twice a week constitute an informal group.

Figure 15.2

Types of Groups and Teams in Organizations

The Top-Management Team

top-management team A group composed of the CEO, the president, and the heads of the most important departments.

research and development team A team whose members have the expertise and experience needed to develop new products.

A central concern of the CEO and president of a company is to form a **top-management team** to help the organization achieve its mission and goals. Top-management teams are responsible for developing the strategies that result in an organization's competitive advantage; most have between five and seven members. In forming their top-management teams, CEOs are well advised to stress diversity—diversity in expertise, skills, knowledge, and experience. Thus, many top-management teams are also cross-functional teams: They are composed of members from different departments, such as finance, marketing, production, and engineering. Diversity helps ensure that the top-management team will have all the background and resources it needs to make good decisions. Diversity also helps guard against *groupthink,* faulty group decision making that results when group members strive for agreement at the expense of an accurate assessment of the situation (see Chapter 6).

Research and Development Teams

Managers in pharmaceuticals, computers, electronics, electronic imaging, and other high-tech industries often create **research and development teams** to develop new products. Managers select R&D team members on the basis of their expertise and experience in a certain area. Sometimes R&D teams are cross-functional teams with members from departments such as engineering, marketing, and production in addition to members from the research and development department.

Command Groups

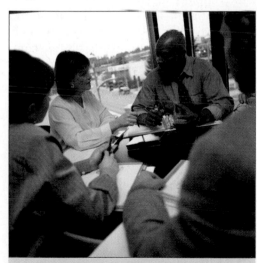

Top-management teams are responsible for developing the strategies that result in an organization's competitive advantage.

Subordinates who report to the same supervisor compose a **command group.** When top managers design an organization's structure and establish reporting relationships and a chain of command, they are essentially creating command groups. Command groups, often called *departments* or *units,* perform a significant amount of the work in many organizations. In order to have command groups that help an organization gain a competitive advantage, managers not only need to motivate group members to perform at a high level but also need to be effective leaders. Examples of command groups

command group A group composed of subordinates who report to the same supervisor; also called *department* or *unit*.

include the salespeople in a large department store in New York who report to the same supervisor, the employees of a small swimming pool sales and maintenance company in Florida who report to a general manager, the telephone operators at the MetLife insurance company who report to the same supervisor, and workers on an automobile assembly line in the Ford Motor Company who report to the same first-line manager.

Task Forces

task force A committee of managers or nonmanagerial employees from various departments or divisions who meet to solve a specific, mutual problem; also called *ad hoc committee*.

Managers form **task forces** to accomplish specific goals or solve problems in a certain time period; task forces are sometimes called *ad hoc committees*. For example, Michael Rider, owner and top manager of a chain of six gyms and fitness centers in the Midwest, created a task force composed of the general managers of each of the six gyms to determine whether the fitness centers should institute a separate fee schedule for customers who wanted to use the centers only for aerobics classes (and not use other facilities such as weights, steps, tracks, and swimming pools). The task force was given three months to prepare a report summarizing the pros and cons of the proposed change in fee schedules. Once the task force completed its report and reached the conclusion that the change in fee structure probably would reduce revenues rather than increase them and thus should not be implemented, it was disbanded. As in Rider's case, task forces can be a valuable tool for busy managers who do not have the time to personally explore an important issue in depth.

Sometimes managers need to form task forces whose work, so to speak, is never done. The task force may be addressing a long-term or enduring problem or issue facing an organization, such as how to most usefully contribute to the local community or how to make sure that the organization provides opportunities for potential employees with disabilities. Task forces that are relatively permanent are often referred to as *standing committees*. Membership in standing committees changes over time. Members may have, for example, a two- or three-year term on the committee, and memberships expire at varying times so that there are always some members with experience on the committee. Managers often form and maintain standing committees to make sure that important issues continue to be addressed.

Self-Managed Work Teams

self-managed work team A group of employees who supervise their own activities and monitor the quality of the goods and services they provide.

Self-managed work teams are teams in which team members are empowered and have the responsibility and autonomy to complete identifiable pieces of work. On a day-to-day basis, team members decide what the team will do, how it will do it, and which team members will perform which specific tasks.[44] Managers provide self-managed work teams with their overall goals (such as assembling defect-free computer keyboards) but let team members decide how to meet those goals. Managers usually form self-managed work teams to improve quality, increase motivation and satisfaction, and lower costs. Often, by creating self-managed work teams, they combine tasks that individuals working separately used to perform, so the team is responsible for the whole set of tasks that yields an identifiable output or end product.

Managers can take a number of steps to ensure that self-managed work teams are effective and help an organization achieve its goals:[45]

- Give teams enough responsibility and autonomy to be truly self-managing. Refrain from telling team members what to do or solving problems for them even if you (as a manager) know what should be done.

- Make sure that a team's work is sufficiently complex so that it entails a number of different steps or procedures that must be performed and results in some kind of finished end product.

- Carefully select members of self-managed work teams. Team members should have the diversity of skills needed to complete the team's work, have the ability to work with others, and want to be part of a team.

- As a manager, realize that your role vis-à-vis self-managed work teams calls for guidance, coaching, and supporting, not supervising. You are a resource for teams to turn to when needed.

- Analyze what type of training team members need, and provide it. Working in a self-managed work team often requires that employees have more extensive technical and interpersonal skills.

Managers in a wide variety of organizations have found that self-managed work teams help the organization achieve its goals,[46] as profiled in the following "Management Insight."

Management Insight

Self-Managed Teams at Louis Vuitton and Nucor Corporation

Managers at Louis Vuitton, the most profitable luxury brand in the world, and managers at Nucor Corporation, the largest producer of steel and biggest recycler in the United States, have succeeded in effectively using self-managed teams to produce luxury accessories and steel, respectively. Self-managed teams at both companies not only are effective but truly excel and have helped to make the companies leaders in their respective industries.[47]

Teams with between 20 and 30 members make Vuitton handbags and accessories. The teams work on only one particular product at a time; a team with 24 members might produce about 120 handbags per day. Team members are empowered to take ownership for the goods they produce, are encouraged to suggest improvements, and are kept up to date on key facts such as products' selling prices and popularity. As Thierry Nogues, a team leader at a Vuitton factory in Ducey, France, puts it, "Our goal is to make everyone as multiskilled and autonomous as possible."[48]

Production workers at Nucor are organized into teams ranging in size from 8 to 40 members based on the kind of work the team is responsible for, such as rolling steel or operating a furnace. Team members have considerable autonomy to make decisions and creatively respond to problems and opportunities, and there are relatively few layers in the corporate hierarchy, supporting the empowerment of teams.[49] Teams develop their own informal rules for behavior and make their own decisions. As long as team members follow organizational rules and policies (e.g., for safety) and meet quality standards, they are free to govern themselves. Managers act as coaches or advisers rather than supervisors, helping teams out when they need some additional outside assistance.[50]

To ensure that production teams are motivated to help Nucor achieve its goals, team members are eligible for weekly bonuses based on the team's performance. Essentially, these production workers receive base pay that does not vary and are eligible to receive weekly bonus pay that can average from 80% to 150% of their regular pay.[51] The bonus rate is predetermined

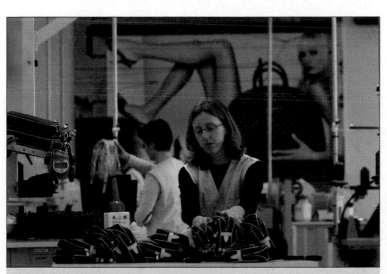

A team member assembles classic Louis Vuitton bags at the company's fine leather goods factory in the Normandy town of Ducey in France.

by the work a team performs and the capabilities of the machinery they use. Given the immediacy of the bonus and its potential magnitude, team members are highly motivated to perform at a high level, develop informal rules that support high performance, and strive to help Nucor reach its goals. Moreover, because all members of a team receive the same amount of weekly bonus money, they are motivated to do their best for the team, cooperate, and help one another out.[52]

Crafting a luxury handbag and making steel joists couldn't be more different from each other in certain ways. Yet the highly effective self-managed teams at Louis Vuitton and Nucor share some fundamental qualities. These teams really do take ownership of their work and are highly motivated to perform effectively. Team members have the skills and knowledge they need to be effective, they are empowered to make decisions about their work, and they know that their teams are making vital contributions to their organizations.[53]

Sometimes employees have their own individual jobs but also are part of a self-managed team that is formed to accomplish a specific goal or work on an important project. Employees need to perform their own individual job tasks and also actively contribute to the self-managed team that they are a member of so the team achieves its goal. Recall from "A Manager's Challenge" how employees at ICU Medical form their own self-managed teams to work on projects; at ICU Medical, employees have their own individual jobs and assigned responsibilities and also work in self-managed teams the employees form themselves to achieve specific goals such as reducing inefficiencies in a production process or developing a new product.[54]

Sometimes self-managed work teams can run into trouble. Members may be reluctant to discipline one another by withholding bonuses from members who are not performing up to par or by firing members.[55] Buster Jarrell, a manager who oversaw self-managed work teams in AES Corporation's Houston plant, found that although the self-managed work teams were highly effective, they had a very difficult time firing team members who were performing poorly.[56]

The Dallas office of the New York Life Insurance Co. experimented with having members of self-managed teams evaluate one another's performance and determine pay levels. Team members did not feel comfortable assuming this role, however, and managers ended up handling these tasks.[57] One reason for team members' discomfort may be the close personal relationships they sometimes develop with one another. In addition, members of self-managed work teams may sometimes take longer to accomplish tasks, such as when team members have difficulties coordinating their efforts.

Virtual Teams

virtual team A team whose members rarely or never meet face-to-face but, rather, interact by using various forms of information technology such as e-mail, computer networks, telephone, fax, and videoconferences.

Virtual teams are teams whose members rarely or never meet face-to-face but, rather, interact by using various forms of information technology such as e-mail, text messaging, computer networks, telephone, fax, and videoconferences. As organizations become increasingly global, and as the need for specialized knowledge increases due to advances in technology, managers can create virtual teams to solve problems or explore opportunities without being limited by the fact that team members need to be working in the same geographic location.[58]

Take the case of an organization that has manufacturing facilities in Australia, Canada, the United States, and Mexico and is encountering a quality problem in a complex manufacturing process. Each of its facilities has a quality control team headed by a quality control manager. The vice president for production does not try to solve the problem by forming and leading a team at one of the four manufacturing facilities; instead, she forms and leads a virtual team composed of the quality control managers of the four plants and the plants' general managers. When these team members communicate via e-mail, the company's networking site, and videoconferencing, a wide array of knowledge and experience is brought to bear to solve the problem.

The principal advantage of virtual teams is that they enable managers to disregard geographic distances and form teams whose members have the knowledge, expertise, and experience to tackle a particular problem or take advantage of a specific opportunity.[59] Virtual teams also can include members who are not actually employees of the organization itself; a virtual team might include members of a company that is used for outsourcing. More and more companies, including BP PLC, Nokia Corporation, and Ogilvy & Mather are using virtual teams.[60]

There are two forms of information technologies that members of virtual teams rely on, synchronous technologies and asynchronous technologies.[61] *Synchronous technologies* enable virtual team members to communicate and interact with one another in real time simultaneously and include videoconferencing, teleconferencing, and electronic meetings. *Asynchronous technologies* delay communication and include e-mail, electronic bulletin boards, and Internet Web sites. Many virtual teams use both kinds of technology depending on what projects they are working on.

Increasing globalization is likely to result in more organizations relying on virtual teams to a greater extent.[62] One of the major challenges members of virtual teams face is building a sense of camaraderie and trust among team members who rarely, if ever, meet face-to-face. To address this challenge, some organizations schedule recreational activities, such as ski trips, so that virtual team members can get together. Other organizations make sure that virtual team members have a chance to meet in person soon after the team is formed and then schedule periodic face-to-face meetings to promote trust, understanding, and cooperation in the teams.[63] The need for such meetings is underscored by research that suggests that while some virtual teams can be as effective as teams that meet face-to-face, virtual team members might be less satisfied with teamwork efforts and have fewer feelings of camaraderie or cohesion. (Group cohesiveness is discussed in more detail later in the chapter.)[64]

Research also suggests that it is important for managers to keep track of virtual teams and intervene when necessary by, for example, encouraging members of teams who do not communicate often enough to monitor their team's progress and make sure that team members actually have the time, and are recognized for, their virtual teamwork.[65] Additionally, when virtual teams are experiencing downtime or rough spots, managers might try to schedule face-to-face team time to bring team members together and help them focus on their goals.[66]

Researchers at the London Business School, including Professor Lynda Gratton, recently studied global virtual teams to try to identify factors that might help such teams be effective.[67] Based on their research, Gratton suggests that when forming virtual teams, it is helpful to include a few members who already know each other, other members who are very well connected to people outside of the team, and when possible, members who have volunteered to be a part of the team.[68] It is also advantageous for companies to have some kind of online site where team members can learn more about each other and the kinds of work they are engaged in, and in particular, a shared online workspace that team members can access around the clock.[69] Frequent communication is beneficial. Additionally, virtual team projects should be perceived as meaningful, interesting, and important by their members to promote and sustain their motivation.[70]

friendship group An informal group composed of employees who enjoy one another's company and socialize with one another.

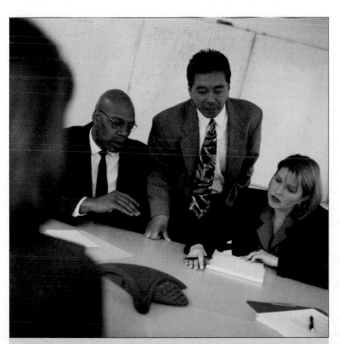

Some virtual teams periodically meet face-to-face to promote trust, understanding, and cooperation in the team.

Friendship Groups

The groups described so far are formal groups created by managers. **Friendship groups** are informal groups composed of employees who enjoy one another's company and socialize with one another. Members of friendship groups may have lunch together, take breaks together, or meet after work for meals, sports, or other activities. Friendship groups help satisfy employees' needs for interpersonal interaction, can provide needed social support in times of stress, and can contribute to people's feeling good at work and being satisfied with their jobs. Managers themselves often form friendship groups. The informal relationships that managers build in friendship groups can often help them solve work-related problems because members of these groups typically discuss work-related matters and offer advice.

Interest Groups

interest group An informal group composed of employees seeking to achieve a common goal related to their membership in an organization.

Employees form informal **interest groups** when they seek to achieve a common goal related to their membership in an organization. Employees may form interest groups, for example, to encourage managers to consider instituting flexible working hours, providing on-site child care, improving working conditions, or more proactively supporting environmental protection. Interest groups can provide managers with valuable insights into the issues and concerns that are foremost in employees' minds. They also can signal the need for change.

Group Dynamics

The ways in which groups function and, ultimately, their effectiveness hinge on group characteristics and processes known collectively as *group dynamics*. In this section, we discuss five key elements of group dynamics: group size, tasks, and roles; group leadership; group development; group norms; and group cohesiveness.

Group Size, Tasks, and Roles

LO3 Explain how different elements of group dynamics influence the functioning and effectiveness of groups and teams.

Managers need to take group size, group tasks, and group roles into account as they create and maintain high-performing groups and teams.

GROUP SIZE The number of members in a group can be an important determinant of members' motivation and commitment and group performance. There are several advantages to keeping a group relatively small—between two and nine members. Recall how the average size of self-managed teams at ICU Medical in "A Manager's Challenge" is around five to seven members.[71] Compared with members of large groups, members of small groups tend to (1) interact more with each other and find it easier to coordinate their efforts, (2) be more motivated, satisfied, and committed, (3) find it easier to share information, and (4) be better able to see the importance of their personal contributions for group success. A disadvantage of small rather than large groups is that members of small groups have fewer resources available to accomplish their goals.

Large groups—with 10 or more members—also offer some advantages. They have more resources at their disposal to achieve group goals than small groups do. These resources include the knowledge, experience, skills, and abilities of group members as well as their actual time and effort. Large groups also enable managers to obtain the advantages stemming from the **division of labor**—splitting the work to be performed into particular tasks and assigning tasks to individual workers. Workers who specialize in particular tasks are likely to become skilled at performing those tasks and contribute significantly to high group performance.

division of labor Splitting the work to be performed into particular tasks and assigning tasks to individual workers.

The disadvantages of large groups include the problems of communication and coordination and the lower levels of motivation, satisfaction, and commitment that members of large groups sometimes experience. It is clearly more difficult to share information with, and coordinate the activities of, 16 people rather than 8 people. Moreover, members of large groups might not think that their efforts are really needed and sometimes might not even feel a part of the group.

In deciding on the appropriate size for any group, managers attempt to gain the advantages of small-group size and, at the same time, form groups with sufficient resources to accomplish their goals and have a well-developed division of labor. As a general rule of thumb, groups should have no more members than necessary to achieve a division of labor and provide the resources needed to achieve group goals. In R&D teams, for example, group size is too large when (1) members spend more time communicating what they know to others than applying what they know to solve problems and create new products, (2) individual productivity decreases, and (3) group performance suffers.[72]

GROUP TASKS The appropriate size of a high-performing group is affected by the kind of tasks the group is to perform. An important characteristic of group tasks that affects performance is **task interdependence,** the degree to which the work performed by one member of a group influences the work performed by other members.[73] As task interdependence increases, group members need to interact more frequently and intensely with one another and their efforts have to be more closely coordinated if they are to perform at a high level. Management expert James D. Thompson identified three types of task interdependence: pooled, sequential, and reciprocal (see Figure 15.3).[74]

POOLED TASK INTERDEPENDENCE **Pooled task interdependence** exists when group members make separate and independent contributions to group performance; overall group performance is the sum of the performance of the individual members (see Figure 15.3a). Examples of groups that have pooled task interdependence include a group of teachers in an elementary school, a group of salespeople in a department store, a group of secretaries in an office, and a group of custodians in an office building. In these examples, group performance, whether it be the number of children who

task interdependence The degree to which the work performed by one member of a group influences the work performed by other members.

pooled task interdependence The task interdependence that exists when group members make separate and independent contributions to group performance.

Figure 15.3
Types of Task Interdependence

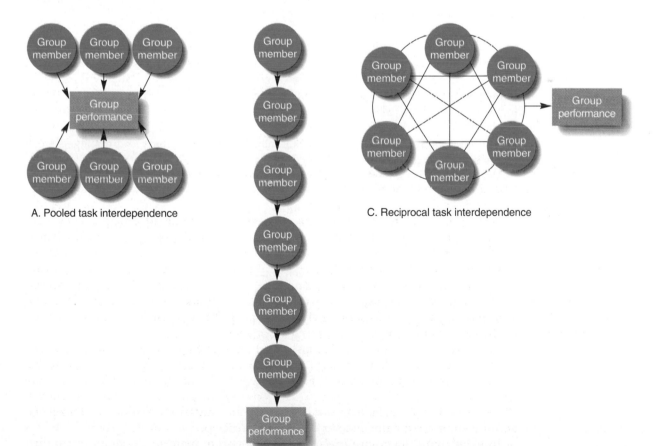

A. Pooled task interdependence

B. Sequential task interdependence

C. Reciprocal task interdependence

are taught and the quality of their education, the dollar value of sales, the amount of secretarial work completed, or the number of offices cleaned, is determined by summing the individual contributions of group members.

For groups with pooled interdependence, managers should determine the appropriate group size primarily from the amount of work to be accomplished. Large groups can be effective because group members work independently and do not have to interact frequently with one another. Motivation in groups with pooled interdependence will be highest when managers reward group members based on individual performance.

SEQUENTIAL TASK INTERDEPENDENCE **Sequential task interdependence** exists when group members must perform specific tasks in a predetermined order; certain tasks have to be performed before others, and what one worker does affects the work of others (see Figure 15.3b). Assembly lines and mass-production processes are characterized by sequential task interdependence.

When group members are sequentially interdependent, group size is usually dictated by the needs of the production process—for example, the number of steps needed in an assembly line to efficiently produce a CD player. With sequential interdependence, it is difficult to identify individual performance because one group member's performance depends on how well others perform their tasks. A slow worker at the start of an assembly line, for example, causes all workers further down to work slowly. Thus, managers are often advised to reward group members for group performance. Group members will be motivated to perform at a high level because if the group performs well, each member will benefit. In addition, group members may put pressure on poor performers to improve so that group performance and rewards do not suffer.

> **sequential task interdependence** The task interdependence that exists when group members must perform specific tasks in a predetermined order.

Sequential task interdependence characterizes this printing and binding assembly line.

> **reciprocal task interdependence** The task interdependence that exists when the work performed by each group member is fully dependent on the work performed by other group members.

RECIPROCAL TASK INTERDEPENDENCE **Reciprocal task interdependence** exists when the work performed by each group member is fully dependent on the work performed by other group members; group members have to share information, intensely interact with one another, and coordinate their efforts in order for the group to achieve its goals (see Figure 15.3c). In general, reciprocal task interdependence characterizes the operation of teams, rather than other kinds of groups. The task interdependence of R&D teams, top-management teams, and many self-managed work teams is reciprocal.

When group members are reciprocally interdependent, managers are advised to keep group size relatively small because of the necessity of coordinating team members' activities. Communication difficulties can arise in teams with reciprocally interdependent tasks because team members need to interact frequently with one another and be available when needed. As group size increases, communication difficulties increase and can impair team performance.

When a group's members are reciprocally interdependent, managers also are advised to reward group members on the basis of group performance. Individual levels of performance are often difficult for managers to identify, and group-based rewards help ensure that group members will be motivated to perform at a high level and make valuable contributions to the group. Of course, if a manager can identify instances of individual performance in such groups, they too can be rewarded to maintain high levels of motivation. Microsoft and many other companies reward group members for their individual performance as well as for the performance of their group.

> **group role** A set of behaviors and tasks that a member of a group is expected to perform because of his or her position in the group.

GROUP ROLES A **group role** is a set of behaviors and tasks that a member of a group is expected to perform because of his or her position in the group. Members of cross-functional teams, for example, are expected to perform roles relevant to their special areas of expertise. In our earlier example of cross-functional teams at Hallmark Cards, it is the role of writers on the teams to create verses for new cards, the role of artists to draw illustrations, and the role of designers to put verse and artwork together in an attractive and appealing card design. The roles of members of top-management teams are shaped primarily by their areas of expertise—production, marketing, finance, research and development—but members of top-management teams also typically draw on their broad-based expertise as planners and strategists.

In forming groups and teams, managers need to clearly communicate to group members the expectations for their roles in the group, what is required of them, and how the different roles in the group fit together to accomplish group goals. Managers also need to realize that group roles often change and evolve as a group's tasks and goals change and as group members gain experience and knowledge. Thus, to get the performance gains that come from experience or "learning by doing," managers should encourage group members to take the initiative to assume additional responsibilities as they see fit and modify their assigned roles. This process, called **role making,** can enhance individual and group performance.

In self-managed work teams and some other groups, group members themselves are responsible for creating and assigning roles. Many self-managed work teams also pick their own team leaders. When group members create their own roles, managers should be available to group members in an advisory capacity, helping them effectively settle conflicts and disagreements. At Johnsonville Foods, for example, the position titles of first-line managers have been changed to "advisory coach" to reflect the managers' new role vis-à-vis the self-managed work teams they oversee.[75]

role making Taking the initiative to modify an assigned role by assuming additional responsibilities.

Group Leadership

All groups and teams need leadership, as George Lopez learned at ICU Medical in "A Manager's Challenge."[76] Indeed, as we discussed in detail in Chapter 14, effective leadership is a key ingredient for high-performing groups, teams, and organizations. Sometimes managers assume the leadership role in groups and teams, as is the case in many command groups and top-management teams. Or a manager may appoint a member of a group who is not a manager to be group leader or chairperson, as is the case in a task force or standing committee. In other cases, group or team members may choose their own leaders, or a leader may emerge naturally as group members work together to achieve group goals. When managers empower members of self-managed work teams, they often let group members choose their own leaders. Some self-managed work teams find it effective to rotate the leadership role among their members. Whether leaders of groups and teams are managers or not, and whether they are appointed by managers (often referred to as *formal leaders*) or emerge naturally in a group (often referred to as *informal leaders*), they play an important role in ensuring that groups and teams perform up to their potential.

Group Development over Time

As many managers overseeing self-managed teams have learned, it sometimes takes a self-managed work team two or three years to perform up to its true capabilities.[77] As their experience suggests, what a group is capable of achieving depends in part on its stage of development. Knowing that it takes considerable time for self-managed work teams to get up and running has helped managers have realistic expectations for new teams and know that they need to provide new team members with considerable training and guidance.

Although every group's development over time is somewhat unique, researchers have identified five stages of group development that many groups seem to pass through (see Figure 15.4).[78] In the first stage, *forming,* members try to get to know one another and reach a common understanding of what the group is trying to accomplish and how group members should behave. During this stage, managers should strive to make each member feel that he or she is a valued part of the group.

Figure 15.4
Five Stages of Group Development

In the second stage, *storming,* group members experience conflict and disagreements because some members do not wish to submit to the demands of other group members. Disputes may arise over who should lead the group. Self-managed work teams can be particularly vulnerable during the storming stage. Managers need to keep an eye on groups at this stage to make sure that conflict does not get out of hand.

During the third stage, *norming,* close ties between group members develop, and feelings of friendship and camaraderie emerge. Group members arrive at a consensus about what goals they should be seeking to achieve and how group members should behave toward one another. In the fourth stage, *performing,* the real work of the group gets accomplished. Depending on the type of group in question, managers need to take different steps at this stage to help ensure that groups are effective. Managers of command groups need to make sure that group members are motivated and that they are effectively leading group members. Managers overseeing self-managed work teams have to empower team members and make sure that teams are given enough responsibility and autonomy at the performing stage.

The last stage, *adjourning,* applies only to groups that eventually are disbanded, such as task forces. During adjourning a group is dispersed. Sometimes, adjourning takes place when a group completes a finished product, such as when a task force evaluating the pros and cons of providing on-site child care produces a report supporting its recommendation.

Managers should have a flexible approach to group development and should keep attuned to the different needs and requirements of groups at the various stages.[79] Above all else, and regardless of the stage of development, managers need to think of themselves as *resources* for groups. Thus, managers always should be striving to find ways to help groups and teams function more effectively.

Group Norms

LO4 Explain why it is important for groups and teams to have a balance of conformity and deviance and a moderate level of cohesiveness.

group norms Shared guidelines or rules for behavior that most group members follow.

All groups, whether top-management teams, self-managed work teams, or command groups, need to control their members' behaviors to ensure that the group performs at a high level and meets its goals. Assigning roles to each group member is one way to control behavior in groups. Another important way in which groups influence members' behavior is through the development and enforcement of group norms.[80] **Group norms** are shared guidelines or rules for behavior that most group members follow. Groups develop norms concerning a wide variety of behaviors, including working hours, the sharing of information among group members, how certain group tasks should be performed, and even how members of a group should dress.

Managers should encourage members of a group to develop norms that contribute to group performance and the attainment of group goals. For example, group norms dictating that each member of a cross-functional team should always be available for the rest of the team when his or her input is needed, return phone calls as soon as possible, inform other team members of travel plans, and give team members a phone number at which he or she can be reached when traveling on business help to ensure that the team is efficient, performs at a high level, and achieves its goals. A norm in a command group of secretaries that dictates that secretaries who happen to have a light workload in any given week should help out secretaries with heavier workloads helps to ensure that the group completes all assignments in a timely and efficient manner.

And a norm in a top-management team that dictates that team members should always consult with one another before making major decisions helps to ensure that good decisions are made with a minimum of errors.

CONFORMITY AND DEVIANCE Group members conform to norms for three reasons: (1) They want to obtain rewards and avoid punishments. (2) They want to imitate group members whom they like and admire. (3) They have internalized the norm and believe it is the right and proper way to behave.[81] Consider the case of Robert King, who conformed to his department's norm of attending a fund-raiser for a community food bank. King's conformity could be due to (1) his desire to be a member of the group in good standing and to have friendly relationships with other group members (rewards), (2) his copying the behavior of other members of the department whom he respects and who always attend the fund-raiser (imitating other group members), or (3) his belief in the merits of supporting the activities of the food bank (believing that is the right and proper way to behave).

Failure to conform, or deviance, occurs when a member of a group violates a group norm. Deviance signals that a group is not controlling one of its member's behaviors. Groups generally respond to members who behave defiantly in one of three ways:[82]

1. The group might try to get the member to change his or her deviant ways and conform to the norm. Group members might try to convince the member of the need to conform, or they might ignore or even punish the deviant. For example, in a Jacksonville Foods plant Liz Senkbiel, a member of a self-managed work team responsible for weighing sausages, failed to conform to a group norm dictating that group members should periodically clean up an untidy interview room. Because Senkbiel refused to take part in the team's cleanup efforts, team members reduced her monthly bonus by about $225 for a two-month period.[83] Senkbiel clearly learned the costs of deviant behavior in her team.
2. The group might expel the member.
3. The group might change the norm to be consistent with the member's behavior.

That last alternative suggests that some deviant behavior can be functional for groups. Deviance is functional for a group when it causes group members to evaluate norms that may be dysfunctional but are taken for granted by the group. Often, group members do not think about why they behave in a certain way or why they follow certain norms. Deviance can cause group members to reflect on their norms and change them when appropriate.

Take the case of a group of receptionists in a beauty salon who followed the norm that all appointments would be handwritten in an appointment book and, at the end of each day, the receptionist on duty would enter the appointments into the salon's computer system, which printed out the hairdressers' daily schedules. One day, a receptionist decided to enter appointments directly into the computer system at the time they were being made, bypassing the appointment book. This deviant behavior caused the other receptionists to think about why they were using the appointment book in the first place, since all appointments could be entered into the computer directly. After consulting with the owner of the salon, the group changed its norm. Now appointments are entered directly into the computer, which saves time and cuts down on scheduling errors.

ENCOURAGING A BALANCE OF CONFORMITY AND DEVIANCE To effectively help an organization gain a competitive advantage, groups and teams need to have the right balance of conformity and deviance (see Figure 15.5). A group needs a certain level of conformity to ensure that it can control members' behavior and channel it in the direction of high performance and group goal accomplishment. A group also needs a certain level of deviance to ensure that dysfunctional norms are discarded and replaced with functional ones. Balancing conformity and deviance is a pressing concern for all groups, whether they are top-management teams, R&D teams, command groups, or self-managed work teams.

Figure 15.5

Balancing Conformity and Deviance in Groups

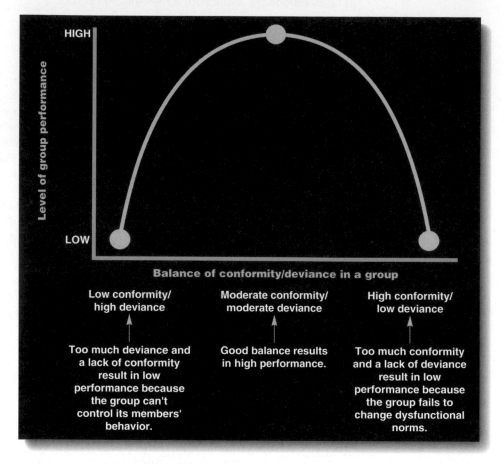

The extent of conformity and reactions to deviance within groups are determined by group members themselves. The three bases for conformity described above are powerful forces that more often than not result in group members' conforming to norms. Sometimes these forces are so strong that deviance rarely occurs in groups, and when it does, it is stamped out.

Managers can take several steps to ensure that there is enough tolerance of deviance in groups so that group members are willing to deviate from dysfunctional norms and, when deviance occurs in their group, reflect on the appropriateness of the violated norm and change the norm if necessary. First, managers can be role models for the groups and teams they oversee. When managers encourage and accept employees' suggestions for changes in procedures, do not rigidly insist that tasks be accomplished in a certain way, and admit when a norm that they once supported is no longer functional, they signal to group members that conformity should not come at the expense of needed changes and improvements. Second, managers should let employees know that there are always ways to improve group processes and performance levels and thus opportunities to replace existing norms with norms that will better enable a group to achieve its goals and perform at a high level. Third, managers should encourage members of groups and teams to periodically assess the appropriateness of their existing norms.

Managers in the innovative design firm IDEO, based in Palo Alto, California (IDEO's culture is described in Chapter 3), have excelled at ensuring that design teams have the right mix of conformity and deviance, resulting in IDEO's designing products in fields ranging from medicine to space travel to computing and personal hygiene, as indicated in the following "Management Insight."

Management Insight

Teams Benefit from Deviance and Conformity at IDEO

IDEO designed many products we now take for granted: the first Apple mouse, the Palm handheld organizer, stand-up toothpaste containers, flexible shelving for offices, self-sealing drink bottles for sports, blood analyzers, and even equipment used in space travel.[84] Managers and designers at IDEO pride themselves on being experts at the process of innovation in general, rather than in any particular domain. Of course, the company has technical design experts, such as mechanical and electrical engineers, who work on products requiring specialized knowledge, but on the same teams with the engineers might be an anthropologist, a biologist, and a social scientist.[85]

Essentially, a guiding principle at IDEO is that innovation comes in many shapes and sizes and it is only through diversity in thought that people can recognize opportunities for innovation. To promote such diversity in thought, new product development at IDEO is a team effort.[86] Moreover, both conformity and deviance are encouraged on IDEO teams.

Deviance, thinking differently, and not conforming to expected ways of doing things and mind-sets are encouraged at IDEO. In fact, innovative ideas often flow when designers try to see things as they really are and are not blinded by thoughts of what is appropriate, what is possible, or how things should be. Often, constraints on new product design are created by designers themselves conforming to a certain mind-set about the nature of a product or what a product can or should do and look like. IDEO designers are encouraged to actively break down these constraints in their design teams.[87]

Managers at IDEO realize the need for a certain amount of conformity so that members of design teams can work effectively together and achieve their goals. Thus, conformity to a few very central norms is emphasized in IDEO teams. These norms include understanding what the team is working on (e.g., the product,

New product design is a team effort at IDEO.

market, or client need), observing real people in their natural environments, visualizing how new products might work and be used, evaluating and refining product prototypes, encouraging wild ideas, and never rejecting an idea simply because it sounds too crazy.[88] As long as these norms are followed, diversity of thought and even deviance serve to promote innovation at IDEO. In fact, another norm at IDEO is to study "rule breakers"–people who don't follow instructions for products, for example, or who try to put products to different uses–as these individuals might help designers identify problems with existing products and unmet consumer needs.[89] All in all, IDEO's focus on encouraging both deviance and conformity in design teams has benefited all of us, as we use IDEO-designed products that seem so familiar we take them for granted. We forget these products weren't in existence until a design team at IDEO was called on by a client to develop a new product or improve an existing one.[90]

Group Cohesiveness

group cohesiveness The degree to which members are attracted to or loyal to their group.

Another important element of group dynamics that affects group performance and effectiveness is **group cohesiveness,** the degree to which members are attracted to or loyal to their group or team.[91] When group cohesiveness is high, individuals strongly value their group membership, find the group very appealing, and have strong desires to remain a part of the group. When group cohesiveness is low, group members do not find their group particularly appealing and have little desire to retain their group membership. Research suggests that managers should strive to have a moderate level of cohesiveness in the groups and teams they manage because that is most likely to contribute to an organization's competitive advantage.

CONSEQUENCES OF GROUP COHESIVENESS   There are three major consequences of group cohesiveness: level of participation within a group, level of conformity to group norms, and emphasis on group goal accomplishment (see Figure 15.6).[92]

LEVEL OF PARTICIPATION WITHIN A GROUP   As group cohesiveness increases, the extent of group members' participation within the group increases. Participation

Figure 15.6

Sources and Consequences of Group Cohesiveness

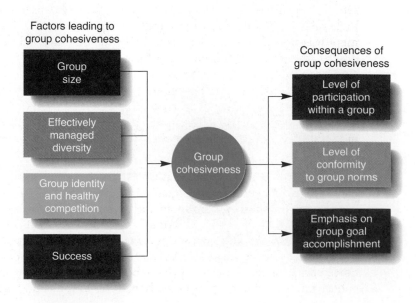

contributes to group effectiveness because group members are actively involved in the group, ensure that group tasks get accomplished, readily share information with each other, and have frequent and open communication (the important topic of communication is covered in depth in Chapter 16).

A moderate level of group cohesiveness helps to ensure that group members actively participate in the group and communicate effectively with one another. The reason why managers may not want to encourage high levels of cohesiveness is illustrated by the example of two cross-functional teams responsible for developing new toys. Members of the highly cohesive Team Alpha often have lengthy meetings that usually start with non-work-related conversations and jokes, meet more often than most of the other cross-functional teams in the company, and spend a good portion of their time communicating the ins and outs of their department's contribution to toy development to other team members. Members of the moderately cohesive Team Beta generally have efficient meetings in which ideas are communicated and discussed as needed, do not meet more often than necessary, and share the ins and outs of their expertise with one another to the extent needed for the development process. Teams Alpha and Beta have both developed some top-selling toys. However, it generally takes Team Alpha 30% longer to do so than Team Beta. This is why too much cohesiveness can be too much of a good thing.

LEVEL OF CONFORMITY TO GROUP NORMS   Increasing levels of group cohesiveness result in increasing levels of conformity to group norms, and when cohesiveness becomes high, there may be so little deviance in groups that group members conform to norms even when they are dysfunctional. In contrast, low cohesiveness can result in too much deviance and undermine the ability of a group to control its members' behaviors to get things done.

Teams Alpha and Beta in the toy company both had the same norm for toy development. It dictated that members of each team would discuss potential ideas for new toys, decide on a line of toys to pursue, and then have the team member from R&D design a prototype. Recently, a new animated movie featuring a family of rabbits produced by a small film company was an unexpected hit, and major toy companies were scrambling to reach licensing agreements to produce toy lines featuring the rabbits. The top-management team in the toy company assigned Teams Alpha and Beta to develop the new toy lines and to do so quickly to beat the competition.

Members of Team Alpha followed their usual toy development norm even though the marketing expert on the team believed that the process could have been streamlined to save time. The marketing expert on Team Beta urged the team to deviate from its toy development norm. She suggested that the team not have R&D develop prototypes but, instead, modify top-selling toys the company already made to feature rabbits and then reach a licensing agreement with the film company based on the high sales potential (given the company's prior success). Once the licensing agreement was signed, the company could take the time needed to develop innovative and unique rabbit toys with more input from R&D.

As a result of the willingness of the marketing expert on Team Beta to deviate from the norm for toy development, the toy company obtained an exclusive licensing agreement with the film company and had its first rabbit toys on the shelves of stores in a record three months. Groups need a balance of conformity and deviance, so a moderate level of cohesiveness often yields the best outcome, as it did in the case of Team Beta.

EMPHASIS ON GROUP GOAL ACCOMPLISHMENT   As group cohesiveness increases, the emphasis placed on group goal accomplishment also increases within a group. A very strong emphasis on group goal accomplishment, however, does not always lead to organizational effectiveness. For an organization to be effective and gain a competitive advantage, the different groups and teams in the organization must cooperate with one another and be motivated to achieve *organizational goals,* even if doing so sometimes comes at the expense of the achievement of group goals. A moderate level of cohesiveness motivates group members to accomplish both group and organizational goals. High levels of cohesiveness can cause group members to be so focused on group goal accomplishment that they may strive to achieve group goals no matter what–even when doing so jeopardizes organizational performance.

At the toy company, the major goal of the cross-functional teams was to develop new toy lines that were truly innovative, utilized the latest in technology, and were in some way fundamentally distinct from other toys on the market. When it came to the rabbit project, Team Alpha's high level of cohesiveness contributed to its continued emphasis on its group goal of developing an innovative line of toys; thus, the team stuck with its usual design process. Team Beta, in contrast, realized that developing the new line of toys quickly was an important organizational goal that should take precedence over the group's goal of developing groundbreaking new toys, at least in the short run. Team Beta's moderate level of cohesiveness contributed to team members' doing what was best for the toy company in this case.

FACTORS LEADING TO GROUP COHESIVENESS　　Four factors contribute to the level of group cohesiveness (see Figure 15.6).[93] By influencing these *determinants of group cohesiveness,* managers can raise or lower the level of cohesiveness to promote moderate levels of cohesiveness in groups and teams.

GROUP SIZE　　As we mentioned earlier, members of small groups tend to be more motivated and committed than members of large groups. Thus, to promote cohesiveness in groups, when feasible, managers should form groups that are small to medium in size (about 2 to 15 members). If a group is low in cohesiveness and large in size, managers might want to consider the feasibility of dividing the group in two and assigning different tasks and goals to the two newly formed groups.

EFFECTIVELY MANAGED DIVERSITY　　In general, people tend to like and get along with others who are similar to themselves. It is easier to communicate with someone, for example, who shares your values, has a similar background, and has had similar experiences. However, as discussed in Chapter 5, diversity in groups, teams, and organizations can help an organization gain a competitive advantage. Diverse groups often come up with more innovative and creative ideas. One reason why cross-functional teams are so popular in organizations like Hallmark Cards is that the diversity in expertise represented in the teams results in higher levels of team performance.

In forming groups and teams, managers need to make sure that the diversity in knowledge, experience, expertise, and other characteristics necessary for group goal accomplishment is represented in the new groups. Managers then have to make sure that this diversity in group membership is effectively managed so that groups will be cohesive (see Chapter 5).

GROUP IDENTITY AND HEALTHY COMPETITION　　When group cohesiveness is low, managers can often increase it by encouraging groups to develop their own identities or personalities and to engage in healthy competition. This is precisely what managers at Eaton Corporation's manufacturing facility in Lincoln, Illinois, did. Eaton's employees manufacture products such as engine valves, gears, truck axles, and circuit breakers. Managers at Eaton created self-managed work teams to cut costs and improve performance. They realized, however, that the teams would have to be cohesive to ensure that they would strive to achieve their goals. Managers promoted group identity by having the teams give themselves names such as "The Hoods," "The Worms," and "Scrap Attack" (a team striving to reduce costly scrap-metal waste by 50%). Healthy competition among groups was promoted by displaying measures of each team's performance and the extent to which teams met their goals on a large TV screen in the cafeteria and by rewarding team members for team performance.[94]

If groups are too cohesive, managers can try to decrease cohesiveness by promoting organizational (rather than group) identity and making the organization as a whole the focus of the group's efforts. Organizational identity can be promoted by making group members feel that they are valued members of the organization and by stressing cooperation across groups to promote the achievement of organizational goals. Excessive levels of cohesiveness also can be reduced by reducing or eliminating competition among groups and rewarding cooperation.

SUCCESS   When it comes to promoting group cohesiveness, there is more than a grain of truth to the saying "Nothing succeeds like success." As groups become more successful, they become increasingly attractive to their members, and their cohesiveness tends to increase. When cohesiveness is low, managers can increase cohesiveness by making sure that a group can achieve some noticeable and visible successes.

Take the case of a group of salespeople in the housewares department of a medium-size department store. The housewares department was recently moved to a corner of the store's basement. Its remote location resulted in low sales because of infrequent customer traffic in that part of the store. The salespeople, who were generally evaluated favorably by their supervisors and were valued members of the store, tried various initiatives to boost sales, but to no avail. As a result of this lack of success and the poor performance of their department, their cohesiveness started to plummet. To increase and preserve the cohesiveness of the group, the store manager implemented a group-based incentive across the store. In any month, members of the group with the best attendance and punctuality records would have their names and pictures posted on a bulletin board in the cafeteria and would each receive a $50 gift certificate. The housewares group frequently had the best records, and their success on this dimension helped to build and maintain their cohesiveness. Moreover, this initiative boosted attendance and discouraged lateness throughout the store.

Managing Groups and Teams for High Performance

Now that you have a good understanding of why groups and teams are so important for organizations, the types of groups that managers create, and group dynamics, we consider some additional steps that managers can take to make sure groups and teams perform at a high level and contribute to organizational effectiveness. Managers striving to have top-performing groups and teams need to (1) motivate group members to work toward the achievement of organizational goals, (2) reduce social loafing, and (3) help groups to manage conflict effectively.

LO5   Describe how managers can motivate group members to achieve organizational goals and reduce social loafing in groups and teams.

Motivating Group Members to Achieve Organizational Goals

When work is difficult, tedious, or requires a high level of commitment and energy, managers cannot assume that group members will always be motivated to work toward the achievement of organizational goals. Consider the case of a group of house painters who paint the interiors and exteriors of new homes for a construction company and are paid on an hourly basis. Why should they strive to complete painting jobs quickly and efficiently if doing so will just make them feel more tired at the end of the day and they will not receive any tangible benefits? It makes more sense for the painters to adopt a more relaxed approach, to take frequent breaks, and to work at a leisurely pace. This relaxed approach, however, impairs the construction company's ability to gain a competitive advantage because it raises costs and increases the time needed to complete a new home.

Managers can motivate members of groups and teams to achieve organizational goals by making sure that the members themselves benefit when the group or team performs highly. For example, if members of a self-managed work team know that they will receive a weekly bonus based on team performance, they will be highly motivated to perform at a high level. Recall from "A Manager's Challenge" how teams of employees formed at ICU Medical are rewarded when they successfully complete their projects.[95]

Managers often rely on some combination of individual and group-based incentives to motivate members of groups and teams to work toward the achievement of organizational goals. When individual performance within a group can be assessed, pay is often determined by individual performance or by both individual and group performance. When individual performance within a group cannot be accurately assessed, then group performance should be the key determinant of pay levels. Many companies that use self-managed work teams base team members' pay in part on team performance.[96] A major challenge for managers is to develop a fair pay system that will lead to both high individual motivation and high group or team performance.

Other benefits that managers can make available to high-performance group members—in addition to monetary rewards—include extra resources such as equipment and computer software, awards and other forms of recognition, and choice of future work assignments. For example, members of self-managed work teams that develop new software at companies such as Microsoft often value working on interesting and important projects; members of teams that have performed at a high level are rewarded by being assigned to interesting and important new projects.

At IDEO (profiled earlier in a "Management Insight"), managers motivate team members by making them feel important. As Tom Kelley, IDEO's general manager, puts it, "When people feel special, they'll perform beyond your wildest dreams."[97] To make IDEO team members feel special, IDEO managers plan unique and fun year-end parties, give teams the opportunity to take time off if they feel they need or want to, encourage teams to take field trips, and see pranks as a way to incorporate fun into the workplace.[98]

Valero Energy motivates groups and teams to achieve organizational goals by valuing its employees, looking out for their well-being, and standing by them in crisis situations.[99] For example, employees with medical emergencies can use Valero's corporate jet if they need to, and Valero covers the complete cost of employee's health insurance premiums.[100] In turn, group members put forth high levels of effort to help Valero achieve its goals. As former Valero CEO and chairman Bill Greehey put it, "The more you do for your employees, the more they do for shareholders and the more they do for the community."[101]

Valero Energy Corp. helped workers, like Ronald Lewis, get back on their feet in the wake of Hurricane Katrina, which damaged many homes and communities in Lousiana.

When Hurricane Katrina hit the Louisiana coastline in 2005, the way Valero stood by employees in its St. Charles oil refinery near New Orleans and the way employees stood by each other and the company brought plant manager Jonathan Stuart to tears as he was briefing Greehey and other top managers a few days after the hurricane hit.[102] Stuart led a 50-person crew that rode out the hurricane in the shut-down refinery. The day before the storm hit, a supervisor used his personal credit card to buy supplies and stayed up all night preparing meals for the crew. Crew members worked round the clock, putting up new power poles, repairing power lines, and replacing motors. The refinery was up and running within eight days (while a Shell refinery close by was still shut done) and the crew had located all of the plant's 570 employees.[103]

Valero's headquarters had supplies delivered to employees whose homes were damaged; trucks brought in food, water, generators, chain saws, refrigerators, shovels, and Nextel phones (the only cell phone system that was still working). Sixty mobile homes were brought in for employees whose houses were unlivable. Employees and law enforcement personnel were provided with free fuel, and employees were given up to $10,000 in aide from Valero's SAFE fund. Valero continued issuing paychecks to its employees, while other affected refineries did not.[104]

Reducing Social Loafing in Groups

We have been focusing on the steps that managers can take to encourage high levels of performance in groups. Managers, however, need to be aware of an important downside to group and team work: the potential for social loafing, which reduces group performance. **Social loafing** is the tendency of individuals to put forth less effort when they work in groups than when they work alone.[105] Have you ever worked on a group project in which one or two group members never seemed to be pulling their weight? Have you ever worked in a student club or committee in which some members always seemed to be missing meetings and never volunteered for activities? Have you ever had a job in which one or two of your coworkers seemed to be slacking off because they knew that you or other members of your work group would make up for their low levels of effort? If you have, you have witnessed social loafing in action.

social loafing The tendency of individuals to put forth less effort when they work in groups than when they work alone.

Social loafing can occur in all kinds of groups and teams and in all kinds of organizations. It can result in lower group performance and may even prevent a group from attaining its goals. Fortunately, there are steps managers can take to reduce social loafing and sometimes completely eliminate it; we will look at three (see Figure 15.7).

1. *Make individual contributions to a group identifiable.* Some people may engage in social loafing when they work in groups because they think that they can hide in the crowd—that no one will notice if they put forth less effort than they should. Other people may think that if they put forth high levels of effort and make substantial contributions to the group, their contributions will not be noticed and they will receive no rewards for their work so why bother.[106]

One way in which managers can effectively eliminate social loafing is by making individual contributions to a group identifiable so that group members perceive that low and high levels of effort will be noticed and individual contributions evaluated.[107] Managers can accomplish this by assigning specific tasks to group members and holding them accountable for their completion. Take the case of a group of eight employees responsible for reshelving returned books in a large public library in New York. The head librarian was concerned that there was always a backlog of seven or eight carts of books to be reshelved, even though the employees never seemed to be particularly busy and some even found time to sit down and read newspapers and

Figure 15.7

Three Ways to Reduce Social Loafing

Making individual contributions to a group identifiable when possible

Emphasizing the valuable contributions of individual members

Keeping group size at an appropriate level

Reduce

Social loafing

magazines. The librarian decided to try to eliminate the apparent social loafing by assigning each employee sole responsibility for reshelving a particular section of the library. Because the library's front-desk employees sorted the books by section on the carts as they were returned, holding the shelvers responsible for particular sections was easily accomplished. Once the shelvers knew that the librarian could identify their effort or lack of effort, there were rarely any backlogs of books to be reshelved.

Sometimes the members of a group can cooperate to eliminate social loafing by making individual contributions identifiable. For example, in a small security company, members of a self-managed work team who assemble control boxes for home alarm systems start each day by deciding who will perform which tasks that day and how much work each member and the group as a whole should strive to accomplish. Each team member knows that, at the end of the day, the other team members will know exactly how much he or she has accomplished. With this system in place, social loafing never occurs in the team. Remember, however, that in some teams, individual contributions cannot be made identifiable, as in teams whose members are reciprocally interdependent.

2. *Emphasize the valuable contributions of individual members.* Another reason why social loafing may occur is that people sometimes think that their efforts are unnecessary or unimportant when they work in a group. They feel the group will accomplish its goals and perform at an acceptable level whether or not they personally perform at a high level. To counteract this belief, when managers form groups, they should assign individuals to a group on the basis of the valuable contributions that *each* person can make to the group as a whole. Clearly communicating to group members why each person's contributions are valuable to the group is an effective means by which managers and group members themselves can reduce or eliminate social loafing.[108] This is most clearly illustrated in cross-functional teams, where each member's valuable contribution to the team derives from a personal area of expertise. By emphasizing why each member's skills are important, managers can reduce social loafing in such teams.

3. *Keep group size at an appropriate level.* Group size is related to the causes of social loafing we just described. As size increases, identifying individual contributions becomes increasingly difficult and members are increasingly likely to think that their individual contributions are not very important. To overcome this, managers should form groups with no more members than are needed to accomplish group goals and perform at a high level.[109]

Helping Groups to Manage Conflict Effectively

At some point or other, practically all groups experience conflict either within the group (*intragroup* conflict) or with other groups (*intergroup* conflict). In Chapter 16 we discuss conflict in depth and explore ways to manage it effectively. As you will learn there, managers can take several steps to help groups manage conflict and disagreements.

Summary and Review

GROUPS, TEAMS, AND ORGANIZATIONAL EFFECTIVENESS A group is two or more people who interact with each other to accomplish certain goals or meet certain needs. A team is a group whose members work intensely with one another to achieve a specific common goal or objective. Groups and teams can contribute to

LO1 organizational effectiveness by enhancing performance, increasing responsiveness to customers, increasing innovation, and being a source of motivation for their members.

LO2   TYPES OF GROUPS AND TEAMS   Formal groups are groups that managers establish to achieve organizational goals; they include cross-functional teams, cross-cultural teams, top-management teams, research and development teams, command groups, task forces, self-managed work teams, and virtual teams. Informal groups are groups that employees form because they believe that the groups will help them achieve their own goals or meet their needs; they include friendship groups and interest groups.

LO3   GROUP DYNAMICS   Key elements of group dynamics are group size, tasks, and roles; group leadership; group development; group norms; and group cohesiveness. The advantages and disadvantages of large and small groups suggest that managers should form groups with no more members than are needed to provide the group with the human resources it needs to achieve its goals and use a division of labor. The type of task interdependence that characterizes a group's work gives managers a clue about the appropriate size of the group. A group role is a set of behaviors and tasks that a member of a group is expected to perform because of his or her position in the group. All groups and teams need leadership.

LO 3, 4   Five stages of development that many groups pass through are forming, storming, norming, performing, and adjourning. Group norms are shared rules for behavior that most group members follow. To be effective, groups need a balance of conformity and deviance. Conformity allows a group to control its members' behavior to achieve group goals; deviance provides the impetus for needed change.

LO4   Group cohesiveness is the attractiveness of a group or team to its members. As group cohesiveness increases, so, too, does the level of participation and communication within a group, the level of conformity to group norms, and the emphasis on group goal accomplishment. Managers should strive to achieve a moderate level of group cohesiveness in the groups and teams they manage.

LO5   MANAGING GROUPS AND TEAMS FOR HIGH PERFORMANCE   To make sure that groups and teams perform at a high level, managers need to motivate group members to work toward the achievement of organizational goals, reduce social loafing, and help groups to effectively manage conflict. Managers can motivate members of groups and teams to work toward the achievement of organizational goals by making sure that members personally benefit when the group or team performs at a high level.

Management in Action

Topics for Discussion and Action

DISCUSSION

1. Why do all organizations need to rely on groups and teams to achieve their goals and gain a competitive advantage? **[LO1]**

2. What kinds of employees would prefer to work in a virtual team? What kinds of employees would prefer to work in a team that meets face-to-face? **[LO2]**

3. Think about a group that you are a member of, and describe that group's current stage of development. Does the development of this group seem to be following the forming, storming, norming, performing, and adjourning stages described in the chapter? **[LO3]**

4. Think about a group of employees who work in a McDonald's restaurant. What type of task interdependence characterizes this group? What potential problems in the group should the restaurant manager be aware of and take steps to avoid? **[LO3]**

5. Discuss the reasons why too much conformity can hurt groups and their organizations. **[LO4]**

6. Why do some groups have very low levels of cohesiveness? **[LO4]**

7. Imagine that you are the manager of a hotel. What steps will you take to reduce social loafing by members of the cleaning staff who are responsible for keeping all common areas and guest rooms spotless? **[LO5]**

ACTION

8. Interview one or more managers in an organization in your local community to identify the types of groups and teams that the organization uses to achieve its goals. What challenges do these groups and teams face? **[LO2]**

Building Management Skills
Diagnosing Group Failures [LO 1, 2, 3, 4, 5]

Think about the last dissatisfying or discouraging experience you had as a member of a group or team. Perhaps the group did not accomplish its goals, perhaps group members could agree about nothing, or perhaps there was too much social loafing. Now answer the following questions:

1. What type of group was this?

2. Were group members motivated to achieve group goals? Why or why not?

3. How large was the group, what type of task interdependence existed in the group, and what group roles did members play?

4. What were the group's norms? How much conformity and deviance existed in the group?

5. How cohesive was the group? Why do you think the group's cohesiveness was at this level? What consequences did this level of group cohesiveness have for the group and its members?

6. Was social loafing a problem in this group? Why or why not?

7. What could the group's leader or manager have done differently to increase group effectiveness?

8. What could group members have done differently to increase group effectiveness?

Managing Ethically [LO 1, 2, 3, 4, 5]

Some self-managed teams encounter a vexing problem: One or more members engage in social loafing, and other members are reluctant to try to rectify the situation. Social loafing can be especially troubling if team members' pay is based on team performance and social loafing reduces the team's performance and thus the pay of all members (even the highest performers). Even if managers are aware of the problem, they may be reluctant to take action because the team is supposedly self-managing.

Questions

1. Either individually or in a group, think about the ethical implications of social loafing in a self-managed team.

2. Do managers have an ethical obligation to step in when they are aware of social loafing in a self-managed team? Why, or why not? Do other team members have an obligation to try to curtail the social loafing? Why, or why not?

Small Group Breakout Exercise
Creating a Cross-Functional Team [LO 1, 2, 3, 4, 5]

Form groups of three or four people, and appoint one member as the spokesperson who will communicate your findings to the class when called on by the instructor. Then discuss the following scenario.

You are a group of managers in charge of food services for a large state university in the Midwest. Recently a survey of students, faculty, and staff was conducted to evaluate customer satisfaction with the food services provided by the university's eight cafeterias. The results were disappointing, to put it mildly. Complaints ranged from dissatisfaction with the type and range of meals and snacks provided, operating hours, and food temperature to frustration about unresponsiveness to current concerns about low-carbohydrate diets and the needs of vegetarians. You have decided to form a cross-functional team that will further evaluate reactions to the food services and will develop a proposal for changes to be made to increase customer satisfaction.

1. Indicate who should be on this important cross-functional team, and explain why.

2. Describe the goals the team should be striving to achieve.

3. Describe the different roles that will need to be performed on this team.

4. Describe the steps you will take to help ensure that the team has a good balance between conformity and deviance and has a moderate level of cohesiveness.

Exploring the World Wide Web [LO 1, 2, 3, 4, 5]

Many consultants and organizations provide team-building services to organizations. While some managers and teams have found these services to be helpful, others have found them to be a waste of time and money—another consulting fad that provides no real performance benefits. Search online for team-building services, and look at the Web sites of a few consultants/companies in depth. Based on what you have read, what might be some of the advantages and disadvantages of team-building services? For what kinds of problems/issues might these services be beneficial, and when might they have little benefit or perhaps even do more harm than good?

Be the Manager [LO 1, 2, 3, 4, 5]

You were recently hired in a boundary-spanning role for the global unit of an educational and professional publishing company. The company is headquartered in New York (where you work) and has divisions in multiple countries. Each division is responsible for translating, manufacturing, marketing, and selling a set of books in its country. Your responsibilities include interfacing with managers in each of the divisions in your region (Central and South America), overseeing their budgeting and financial reporting to headquarters, and leading a virtual team consisting of the top managers in charge of each of the divisions in your region. The virtual team's mission is to promote global learning,

explore new potential opportunities and markets, and address ongoing problems. You communicate directly with division managers via telephone and e-mail, as well as written reports, memos, and faxes. When virtual team meetings are convened, videoconferencing is often used.

After your first few virtual team meetings, you noticed that the managers seemed to be reticent about speaking up. Interestingly enough, when each manager communicates with you individually, primarily in telephone conversations and e-mails, she or he tends to be very forthcoming and frank and you feel you have a good rapport with each of them. However, getting the managers to communicate

with one another as a virtual team has been a real challenge. At the last meeting, you tried to prompt some of the managers to raise issues relevant to the agenda that you knew was on their minds from your individual conversations with them. Surprisingly, the managers skillfully avoided informing their teammates about the heart of the issues in question. You are confused and troubled. While you feel your other responsibilities are going well, you know that your virtual team is not operating like a team at all and, no matter what you try, discussions in virtual team meetings are forced and generally unproductive. What are you going to do to address this problem?

BusinessWeek Case in the News [LO 1, 2, 3, 4, 5]

Managing the New Workforce

Willy Chiu was parked outside a Palo Alto (Calif.) convenience store early one evening in January with his notebook PC switched on. Suddenly he heard the ping of an instant message arriving. It was the Tokyo-based head of IBM's Asia operations with urgent news: A major competitor was homing in on a pivotal project IBM had been chasing. The job, to develop a new IT system for a Korean bank, could be worth up to $100 million. Chiu, who runs IBM's worldwide network of elite labs, was needed to help develop a pilot product.

That plea ignited a flurry of online, BlackBerry, and cell-phone conversations across four continents. Within minutes, Chiu had 18 chat windows open simultaneously on his laptop. "How do we mobilize resources worldwide?" he typed in one message to the head of worldwide operations in San Jose. "I'll take the lead," responded IBM's country manager in Seoul. Chiu

dashed off a note asking a team in Beijing to free up staff and quickly received confirmation that they were on the case. Then a banking specialist from England chimed in: "Our team can provide reference cases from Spain." Chiu to his administrative assistant: "Stella, please change my flight to a later time tonight. Also, looks like I may go to Korea again in a few weeks." Chiu to his wife: "Will be working late."

For global corporations, the borderless world of Willy Chiu offers a glimpse of what's to come. International success once meant having bodies and factories on the ground from São Paulo to Silicon Valley to Shanghai. Coordinating their activities was a deliberately planned effort handled by headquarters.

The challenge now is to weld these vast, globally dispersed workforces into superfast, efficient organizations. Given the conflicting needs of multinational staff and the swiftly shifting nature of competition brought about by the Internet, that's an almost

impossible task. And getting workers to collaborate instantly—not tomorrow or next week, but now—requires nothing less than a management revolution.

Complicating matters is the fact that the very idea of a company is shifting away from a single outfit with full-time employees and a recognizable hierarchy. It is something much more fluid, with a classic corporation at the center of an ever-shifting network of suppliers and outsourcers, some of whom only join the team for the duration of a single project.

To adapt, multinationals are hiring sociologists to unlock the secrets of teamwork among colleagues who have never met. They're arming staff with an arsenal of new tech tools to keep them perpetually connected. They include software that helps engineers co-develop 3D prototypes in virtual worlds and services that promote social networking and that track employees and outsiders who have the skills needed to nail a job. Corporations are investing lavishly in posh campuses, crafting leadership training centers, and offering thousands of online courses to develop pipelines of talent.

To function in this Age of Diffusion, businesses are rethinking traditional practices. In human resources, the era of standardized benefits and work requirements is vanishing. Instead, to keep prized talent, companies need to accommodate a wide range of cultural and generational idiosyncrasies. In China, where personal relationships are paramount, employers have to tread carefully with hard-edged practices such as management reshuffles and 360-degree performance reviews. To keep valued Indian workers from jumping ship, companies are offering one-on-one career planning and reaching out to parents and spouses. Multinationals that viewed Eastern Europe as a terrific low-cost engineering shop are finding that if they don't give the local scientists a crack at real innovation, they soon are coping with a brain drain.

Dow Chemical is trying to navigate this complex new territory. Dow expects 30% of its 20,000 workers to retire in the next five years. Meanwhile, enrollment in U.S. chemical engineering schools is declining, forcing Dow to fight against deep-pocketed oil and gas companies for scarce talent. To persuade veterans to stay as long as possible, Dow is offering flexible hours, three-day workweeks, and reminders that the door is always open should they want to come back after retirement. But when recruiting college grads, says Dow human resources manager Deborah Borg, the company stresses its efforts to develop green technologies and improve living standards in developing nations.

The hard part for multinationals is getting people to work well together, especially given that day-and-night collaboration across the globe is growing. Over the past decade many companies rushed to spread key functions, such as product development, to the far corners of the earth. The idea was to save time and money.

But corporations are finding that running these new operations requires much more effort than connecting staff by phone and e-mail. "One problem with distributing work is that you lose the intimacy of talking things through at a local café," says Forrester Research network innovation expert Navi Radjou. London Business School management professor Lynda Gratton, who led a study of 52 global teams in 15 leading multinationals, spotted the same problem. "Complex teams really struggle to be productive," says Gratton.

Such pressures put a premium on recruiting staff who are globally minded from the outset rather than being mere technicians. Gratton found that global marketing and product development teams at Nokia were especially effective, even though they involve scores of people working in several countries. She says Nokia is careful to select people who have a "collaborative mindset" and carefully includes in task forces a range of nationalities, ages, and education levels. Teams also are made up of people who have worked together in the past and others who have never met, Gratton adds. Members are encouraged to network online and share their photographs and personal biographies.

Training is essential to making staffers globally minded. Accenture, which spent $700 million on education last year, says its 38,000 consultants and most of its services workers take courses on collaborating with offshore colleagues. And each year, Accenture puts up to 400 of its most promising managers through a special leadership development program. They are assigned to groups that can include Irish, Chinese, Belgians, and Filipinos, and specialists in fields such as finance, marketing, and technology. Over 10 months, teams meet in different international locations. As part of the program, they pick a project—developing a new Web page, say—and learn how to tap the company's worldwide talent pool to complete it.

IBM aims to set itself apart with a spate of Web-based services that make it easier for its 360,000-member staff to "work as one virtual team," says Lab chief Chiu. Big Blue has launched what it calls an innovation portal, where any employee with a product idea can use online chat boxes to organize a team, line up resources, and gain access to market research. Developers in IBM labs around the world then can collaborate on prototypes and testing. This way, enterprising staff can build a global team in as little as half an hour and cut the time to start a business from at least six months to around 30 days.

An example: For a major U.S. telecom client that needed a Web-based tool to launch new services such as video streaming for cell phones, IBM organized a 20-member group including staff from Japan, Brazil, and Britain. These IBMers built a working prototype in two weeks and delivered a finished product in two months.

Since IBM introduced the portal, in early 2006, 93,000 workers have logged on, leading to 70 businesses and 10 new products.

Creating a seamless global workforce is hard. But certain multinationals are slowly figuring out how to do it.

Questions for Discussion

1. Why are multinationals increasingly relying on global teams?

2. How can global teams contribute to innovation and responsiveness to customers?

3. What special challenges do global teams face?

4. Which aspects of group functioning and dynamics might be especially important in global teams? Why?

Source: Pete Engardio, "Managing the New Workforce: One of the Great Challenges for a Multinational Is Learning How to Build a Productive Global Team." Reprinted from the August 20 & 27, 2007, issue of *BusinessWeek* by special permission. Copyright © 2007 by The McGraw-Hill Companies, Inc.

BusinessWeek Case in the News [LO 1, 2, 3, 4, 5]

International Isn't Just IBM's First Name

When Rogerio Oliveira strolls through the vast IBM service delivery center in Hortolandia, Brazil, the contrast between the old and new IBM is stark. What was once a factory for mainframes is now crowded with hundreds of Brazilians on a different sort of assembly line. Their output is information, and they sit in rows of cubicles that stretch the length of a football field under a soaring, metal-trussed roof. A few years ago, the factory work performed here was just for Brazilian customers. Today, 100 clients for the facility's services, which range from software programming to financial accounting, come from 40 countries, including Canada, Mexico, South Africa, and the U.S.

Oliveira, a 35-year IBM veteran and general manager for Latin America, stands at the heart of IBM's effort to transform itself into what it calls a "globally integrated enterprise." IBM has talked about its new global vision for two years. But only recently have managers like Oliveira turned that vision into a practical and solidly profitable business.

This is not the IBM of the 20th century, when Big Blue defined what it meant to be a multinational. Back then, its subsidiaries in 160 countries behaved like mini-IBMs—essentially, standalone operations serving their local customers. But replicating itself became too costly for IBM. So now the company is reorganizing around the principle that it will perform work for customers where the jobs can best be done—tapping the right talent at the right price.

That philosophy has produced a monumental shift in how IBM operates. In the past three years, the company has hired some 90,000 people in low-cost countries including Brazil, China, and India. These people, working in so-called global service delivery centers, provide a wide array of services for clients. The work goes beyond software programming to include data center operations, help-desk call centers, financial accounting, and benefits management. Initially, cheap labor was the big attraction of this move, with pay in India 70% to 80% lower than in the U.S. But these days, tapping the abundant talent pools—and new ideas—in emerging markets such as India and China is important as well.

Many of those global service employees report both to local supervisors and to managers thousands of miles away. Pressure is most intense on those managers who run countries or regions, like Oliveira. "My worst day was the last day of the quarter," he says of his job as the Brazil country manager, which he held until he was promoted in late 2007. "I was measured for producing sales in Brazil, and at the same time, I had 6,000 global service delivery people with a different way of measuring. It was schizophrenic."

The task may be complex, but IBM is committed to it. "IBM is making real some new ideas about what it means to be global that were just a lot of talk before," says Rosabeth Moss Kanter, professor at Harvard Business School. The results are starting to come in. You can see them most clearly in the performance of IBM's $50 billion global services business, the focal point of the effort, which represents about half of IBM sales. In the third quarter of 2007, global services revenues grew 14%, to $13.7 billion, and pretax profit margins topped 10.7%, up from 8.2% three years earlier.

But there's still plenty of work to be done before IBM, with 375,000 people on six continents, is a smooth-running global machine. Says Chief Executive Samuel J. Palmisano: "The big issues for us are: Where do you put them? How do you retain them? How do you develop them? How do you move work to them or them to work?"

Palmisano began this journey almost three years ago. After getting the top job in 2003, he focused on innovation in high-end computers, chips, and software, and rapid expansion in emerging markets and services such as back-office information processing. Yet Palmisano's rise coincided with that of a handful of aggressive Indian tech services companies, which, thanks to their low-cost labor force, were able to undercut IBM's pricing. The result: Growth in services revenue slowed, and margins flattened out. IBM responded in 2005 by slashing more than 15,000 jobs in high-cost Western Europe, U.S., and Japan.

Cost-cutting alone wouldn't do the job: Palmisano had to transform how service work was done. He assigned Robert W. Moffat Jr., 51, a longtime IBMer, to the task. Moffat had already wrung $5 billion of annual costs out of IBM's manufacturing supply chain. For decades, IBM factories had focused primarily on one product and one geographic market. But by 2005 they made any number of products for a wide range of locales, so IBM was able to operate fewer plants and keep them running at higher capacity.

Moffat figured that the same approach could be taken with services. His team surveyed countries for costs, available talent, educational pipelines, languages spoken, proximity to markets, and political stability. They used this information to choose locations where IBM would serve clients anywhere around the world. Moffat set up finance and administration back-office centers, for example, in Bangalore, Buenos Aires, Krakow, Shanghai, and Tulsa.

Some longtime IBMers have found it difficult to accept the changes. When a bank in Spain asked IBM to provide financial services from two different delivery centers in order to reduce the risks of a major disruption, the first thought of IBM's Spanish staff was to set up a second facility within their country. Another executive pointed out that IBM's office in lower-cost Argentina could handle the bank's tasks. "Some people still think of themselves as being in separate companies," says Moffat.

Moffat and his colleagues also have used their manufacturing experience to keep track of IBM's far-flung employees. Just as every component used in an IBM computer is described in detail on inventory and planning documents, new databases contain profiles of employees that list their capabilities and their up-to-the-minute availability. Yet while a computer part doesn't change over time, people do. So the databases can be continuously updated by employees and their managers as employees gain skills and experience.

Before, project managers assembled teams largely made up of people they had worked with. But as IBM expanded around the globe, managers found it harder to pull teams together. Now project managers post detailed requests in one of the databases called Professional Marketplace that lists more than 170,000 employees along with their skills, pay rate, and availability. Other managers monitor the database and serve as matchmakers between jobs and people. The databases have shaved 20% from the average time it takes to assemble a team and have saved IBM $500 million overall.

Cross-border Hiring

By sifting through several personnel databases with sophisticated software, IBM's top managers can quantify the skills they have on hand worldwide and compare them with projections of what people they'll need in six to nine months. When they spot a coming shortfall, managers coordinate with colleagues in other countries to recruit or train people. In one case, IBM managers in Phoenix wanted to build a team in Brazil to test software for a large U.S. corporate client. After they put a request on Professional Marketplace, a manager in Brazil assembled a team in a week. Now IBM has 30 software testers working in Brazil.

IBM Brazil is a true microcosm of the enterprise. In five years the workforce has grown from 4,000 to 13,000 people, many of them based in Hortolandia, Brazil's Silicon Valley, about a 90-minute drive from São Paulo. Employees fly the national flags of their clients on their cubicles. Walk down the aisles and you'll hear English, French, Portuguese, and Spanish spoken. Salaries are about half of what IBM pays in the U.S. for similar work.

While most of the management team in Brazil is local, IBM mixes in people from other countries to hasten the global integration process. One such "assignee" is American Robert Payne, a 22-year IBM executive who runs part of the tech services organization in Brazil. Payne, 48, immerses himself in the cultures of the countries where he's assigned. He learned Japanese for his Tokyo gig. When he arrived in Brazil three years ago, he promised to conduct all of his meetings in Portuguese within nine months. And he did.

Yet at the start Payne found that when resources were tight, Brazilians favored local customers, while IBMers from other countries pushed for their clients. The rule of thumb, Payne advised them, was to "think as if you're the president of IBM. What's best for the company long-term?" That reduced the conflicts.

Payne and other senior executives know that operating globally requires a great deal of hands-on management. In the old days at IBM, projects often were born and died within a single office building in New York State. These days, they're broken into pieces and farmed out to small teams worldwide.

To understand how IBM choreographs this dance, consider Lotus Symphony, a package of PC software applications. Work on a new version of Symphony started last July. Teams in Beijing; Austin, Tex.; Raleigh, N.C.; and Boeblingen, Germany, are all contributing. Remarkably, it's the first time ever that the Beijing team is heading up a global project. Having an

important role is vital for attracting and keeping top Chinese programmers.

Troubled Waters

It didn't sink in with the Chinese that they were actually in charge until five days after a test version of the product was released. The programmers were getting complaints about the software from testers and knew they needed to make improvements. They realized that they were responsible for the success or failure of the product. "The team had a 'Holy crap!' moment. They were just terrified," recalls Michael Karasick, a 48-year-old Canadian who runs the Beijing lab. He and the local Chinese managers calmed the programmers by setting priorities. The project is now on schedule.

One of the major challenges in this setup is the difficulty of communicating by e-mail or even videoconferencing when programmers have never met one another. Strangers don't readily share knowledge. "A big problem is trust," says Dirk Wittkopp, director of IBM's Boeblingen lab. "It works better if you can go out to dinner with somebody and have a beer. But we can't put people on planes to visit each other all the time."

So Big Blue is trying to bridge the gap with software that borrows heavily from social networking. A new program called Beehive is essentially a corporate version of Facebook. IBM employees create profiles and post photos, list their interests, and comment about company events or happenings in their private lives. Klaus Rindtorff, an engineer who works for Wittkopp, lists his five favorite places to revisit, such as Death Valley, Calif., and includes photos of IBM colleagues in Germany, Italy, and the U.S.

Another program, called Small Blue, is a search engine for finding experts within the company. The software scans employees' blogs, e-mail, instant messages, and reports, then draws conclusions about each participant's skills and expertise. When other employees search by topic on Small Blue, the program scans its findings to get a list of experts. Currie Boyle, an IBM consultant in

Vancouver, used Small Blue to find a specialist for a Canadian client. His initial search turned up people in the U.S. and Europe, who in turn led him to an IBM staffer in Haifa, Israel, who had just the information he needed to help his customer.

Last month, IBM introduced a version of Small Blue called IBM Atlas for sale to customers. The company is positioning itself as a helping hand to other corporations who are taking similar paths to globalization. That puts extra pressure on IBM to succeed as

a new sort of organization. If it thrives, that's good marketing. If it stumbles, that would be a very poor advertisement for itself.

Questions for Discussion

1. How has IBM changed the ways it forms teams?

2. Why has it made these changes?

3. What are the benefits of IBM's new way of forming teams?

4. What challenges do global teams at IBM face and how is IBM helping them deal with these challenges?

CHAPTER 16

Promoting Effective Communication

After studying this chapter, you should be able to:

LO1 Explain why effective communication helps an organization gain a competitive advantage.

LO2 Describe the communication process, and explain the role of perception in communication.

LO3 Define information richness, and describe the information richness of communication media available to managers.

LO4 Describe the communication networks that exist in groups and teams.

LO5 Explain how advances in technology have given managers new options for managing communication.

LO6 Describe important communication skills that managers need as senders and as receivers of messages and why it is important to understand differences in linguistic styles.

A Manager's Challenge

Managers Need Feedback from Employees

How can managers ensure that they get needed feedback from employees? As managers advance in the corporate hierarchy and assume positions with increased responsibility, they often become removed from the day to day operations of their organizations. Thus, they are less likely to notice or become aware of problems with existing processes and procedures and sources of inefficiencies as well as how customers and clients are reacting to the goods and services the organization provides. Moreover, ideas for ways to improve goods and services sometimes occur to those who are most closely and immediately linked to producing and delivering products and services. Some of these ideas may rarely occur to upper-level managers who are not engaged in these activities on a day-to-day basis.[1]

Thus, it is crucial that managers receive and listen to feedback from employees. While this might seem pretty straightforward and easily accomplished, managers are sometimes the last ones to know about problems for a number of reasons. Employees sometimes fear that they will be blamed for problems that they make their bosses aware of, that they will be seen as "troublemakers," or that managers will perceive their well-intentioned feedback as a personal criticism or attack.[2] Moreover, if employees feel that their feedback, even suggestions for improvements or ways to seize new opportunities, will fall on deaf ears and be ignored, they will be reluctant to speak up.

Effective managers recognize the importance of receiving feedback from employees and take active steps to ensure that this

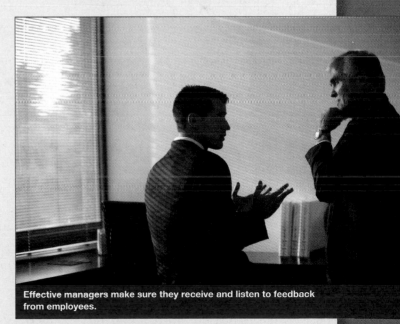

Effective managers make sure they receive and listen to feedback from employees.

happens. When Yogesh Gupta recently accepted the position of president and CEO of FatWire Software, one of his priorities was to ensure that his employees provided him with feedback on an ongoing basis.[3] FatWire Software, headquartered in Mineola, New York, is a privately owned Web content management company with around 200 employees, offices in over 10 countries, and over 450 customers ranging from 3M, *The New York Times*, and BestBuy to the Flemish Government, Dutch Railways, and TDC Cable TV.[4] An experienced manager who was senior vice president and chief technology strategist at CA, Inc., one of the largest information technology management software companies in world, prior to assuming the top position at FatWire Software, Gupta often witnessed managers inadvertently discouraging employees from providing them with feedback, even when the managers desired it.[5] As he indicates, "I've heard so many executives tell employees to be candid and then jump down their throats if they bring up a problem or ask a critical question."[6]

Gupta spends a lot of time talking with FatWire employees and its managers to get their perspectives and feedback about how the company is doing. He often has individual meetings with managers so they will feel more comfortable providing him with frank and honest feedback. And he explicitly asks them if he is doing anything wrong, if there is a better way for him to do things, and what kinds of obstacles interfere with their own performance. He also asks them how the company could be doing better. Early on, as a result of listening to the feedback he received, Gupta realized that FatWire might benefit from having more employees focused on product development and marketing and also that customer support services and processes could be enhanced.[7]

When Gupta receives valuable feedback, he makes it a point to positively reinforce the manager or employee who provided it in a public fashion, so other employees realize that he is open to, and really wants, their feedback. As he indicates, "I know I have to say 'You did the right thing to speak up' again and again, because employees fear they'll get blamed if they say anything negative."[8]

At Intuit Inc., a major provider of accounting and financial software, managers receive valuable feedback from employees in a number of ways. An annual employee survey is used to find out what employees they think about Intuit's practices and procedures.[9] Managers are advised to have what are called "skip level" meetings throughout the year whereby they meet with the subordinates of the managers who report to them to get their feedback on how things are going.[10] Managers also are encouraged to take part in what Intuit calls a "learn, teach, learn" process whereby employees provide managers with feedback about some issue, problem, or situation (the manager learns about the issue); the manager comes up with a course of action to deal with the issue and communicates it to the employees (the manager instructs or teaches the employees about the course of action); and then the employees provide the manager with more feedback (the manager learns if the course of action is viable or should be modified).[11] Jim Grenier, vice president for human resources at Intuit, suggests that obtaining employee feedback through this process leads to improved decision making. As he puts it, "You're looking for more input so you can make a better decision. Employees know that we are serious about asking for their feedback, and we listen and we do something about it."[12]

In order to obtain feedback from his employees, Jonathan McDaniel, manager of a Kentucky Fried Chicken restaurant in Houston, Texas, surveys them around four times a year.[13] More important, he listens to and acts on the feedback employees provide on the surveys. For example, from one of his periodic surveys, McDaniel learned that employees were unhappy about their working hours; some employees thought they should be working more hours per week while others thought they were working too many hours. Based on this feedback, McDaniel now communicates more frequently with employees to get their input on scheduling and working hours.[14] Clearly, and in organizations large and small, managers need to receive feedback from their employees in order to be effective, make good decisions, and help the organization achieve its goals.[15]

Overview

Even with all the advances in information technology that are available to managers, ineffective communication continues to take place in organizations. Ineffective communication is detrimental for managers, employees, and organizations; it can lead to poor performance, strained interpersonal relations, poor-quality service, and dissatisfied customers. For an organization to be effective and gain a competitive advantage, managers at all levels need to be good communicators. As illustrated in "A Manager's Challenge," an important part of being a good communicator is obtaining and listening to feedback from others; this is sometimes more challenging than it seems.

In this chapter, we describe the nature of communication and the communication process and explain why all managers and their subordinates need to be effective communicators. We describe the communication media available to managers and the factors they need to consider in selecting a communication medium for each message they send. We consider the communication networks that organizational members rely on, and we explore how advances in information technology have expanded managers' range of communication options. We describe the communication skills that help managers be effective senders and receivers of messages. By the end of this chapter, you will have a good appreciation of the nature of communication and the steps that managers can take to ensure that they are effective communicators.

LO1 Explain why effective communication helps an organization gain a competitive advantage.

Communication and Management

communication The sharing of information between two or more individuals or groups to reach a common understanding.

Communication is the sharing of information between two or more individuals or groups to reach a common understanding.[16] First and foremost, no matter how electronically based, communication is a human endeavor and involves individuals and groups. Second, communication does not take place unless a common understanding is reached. Thus, when you call a business to speak to a person in customer service or billing and are bounced back and forth between endless automated messages and menu options and eventually hang up in frustration, communication has not taken place.

The Importance of Good Communication

In Chapter 1, we described how an organization can gain a competitive advantage when managers strive to increase efficiency, quality, responsiveness to customers, and innovation. Good communication is essential for attaining each of these four goals and thus is a necessity for gaining a competitive advantage.

Managers can *increase efficiency* by updating the production process to take advantage of new and more efficient technologies and by training workers to operate the new technologies and expand their skills. Good communication is necessary for managers to learn about new technologies, implement them in their organizations, and train workers in how to use them. Similarly, *improving quality* hinges on effective communication. Managers need to communicate to all members of an organization the meaning and importance of high quality and the routes to attaining it. Subordinates need to communicate quality problems and suggestions for increasing quality to their superiors, and members of self-managed work teams need to share their ideas on improving quality with one another.

Good communication can also help to increase *responsiveness to customers*. When the organizational members who are closest to customers, such as department store salespeople and bank tellers, are empowered to communicate customers' needs and desires to managers, managers are better able to respond to these needs. Managers, in turn, must communicate with other organizational members to determine how best to respond to changing customer preferences.

Innovation, which often takes place in cross-functional teams, also requires effective communication. Members of a cross-functional team developing a new electronic game, for example, must effectively communicate with one another to develop a game that customers will want to play; that will be engaging, interesting, and fun; and that can potentially lead to sequels. Members of the team also must communicate with managers to secure the resources they need for developing the game and to keep managers informed of progress on the project. Innovation in organizations is increasingly taking place on a global level, making effective communication all the more important, as illustrated in the following "Managing Globally."

Global Communication for Global Innovation

Managing Globally

GE Healthcare Technologies, based in Waukesha, Wisconsin, is a unit of GE Healthcare (headquartered in the United Kingdom) that makes medical imaging, diagnostic, and monitoring systems such as CT scanners and has approximately $17 billion in revenues.[17] In order to make the best scanners that meet the needs of doctors and patients around the world with next-generation technology, new product development and manufacture is truly a global endeavor at GE Healthcare Technologies. Take the case of the new LightSpeed VCT scanner series (*VCT* stands for "volume controlled tomography"), which costs in the millions and is among the quickest and highest-resolution scanners available in the world.[18] The LightSpeed can perform a full-body scan in under 10 seconds and yields a three-dimensional picture of patients' hearts within five heartbeats.[19]

The LightSpeed was developed through true global collaboration. GE managers not only spoke with doctors (including cardiologists and radiologists) around the world to find out what their needs were and what kinds of tests they would perform with the LightSpeed but also gathered information about differences among patients in various countries. Engineers in Hino (Japan), Buc (France), and Waukesha developed the electronics for the Light-

The team responsible for GE's LightSpeed VCT scanner, which can perform a full-body scan in less than 10 seconds, was made up of individuals from at least six different countries.

Speed. Other parts, such as the automated table that patients lie on, are made in Beijing (China) and Hino. Software for the LightSpeed was written in Haifa (Israel), Bangalore (India), Buc, and Waukesha.[20]

Effective global communication was a challenge and a necessity to successfully develop the LightSpeed series. As Brian Duchinsky, GE's general manager for global CT, puts it, "If we sat around in this cornfield west of Milwaukee, we wouldn't come up with the same breadth of good ideas. But yet, getting six countries on the phone to make a decision can be a pain."[21]

GE managers facilitated effective communication in a number of ways—participating daily in conference calls, making sure that teams in different countries depended on one another, developing an internal Web site devoted to the LightSpeed, encouraging teams to ask one another for help, and holding face-to-face meetings in different locations. While much communication took place electronically, such as through conference calls, face-to-face meetings were also important. As Bob Armstrong, GE's general manager for engineering, indicates, "You need to get your people together in one place if you want them to really appreciate how good everyone is, and how good you are as a team."[22]

LO2 Describe the communication process, and explain the role of perception in communication.

sender The person or group wishing to share information.

message The information that a sender wants to share.

encoding Translating a message into understandable symbols or language.

noise Anything that hampers any stage of the communication process.

Effective communication is necessary for managers and all members of an organization to increase efficiency, quality, responsiveness to customers, and innovation and thus gain a competitive advantage for the organization. Managers therefore must have a good understanding of the communication process if they are to perform effectively.

The Communication Process

The communication process consists of two phases. In the *transmission phase*, information is shared between two or more individuals or groups. In the *feedback phase*, a common understanding is ensured. In both phases, a number of distinct stages must occur for communication to take place (see Figure 16.1).[23]

Starting the transmission phase, the **sender**, the person or group wishing to share information with some other person or group, decides on the **message**, what information to communicate. Then the sender translates the message into symbols or language, a process called **encoding**; often messages are encoded into words. **Noise** is a general term that refers to anything that hampers any stage of the communication process.

Figure 16.1
The Communication Process

receiver The person or group for which a message is intended.

medium The pathway through which an encoded message is transmitted to a receiver.

decoding Interpreting and trying to make sense of a message.

Once encoded, a message is transmitted through a medium to the **receiver,** the person or group for which the message is intended. A **medium** is simply the pathway, such as a phone call, a letter, a memo, or face-to-face communication in a meeting, through which an encoded message is transmitted to a receiver. At the next stage, the receiver interprets and tries to make sense of the message, a process called **decoding.** This is a critical point in communication.

The feedback phase is initiated by the receiver (who becomes a sender). The receiver decides what message to send to the original sender (who becomes a receiver), encodes it, and transmits it through a chosen medium (see Figure 16.1). The message might contain a confirmation that the original message was received and understood or a restatement of the original message to make sure that it has been correctly interpreted, or it might include a request for more information. The original sender decodes the message and makes sure that a common understanding has been reached. If the original sender determines that a common understanding has not been reached, sender and receiver cycle through the whole process as many times as needed to reach a common understanding. Feedback eliminates misunderstandings, ensures that messages are correctly interpreted, and enables senders and receivers to reach a common understanding.

verbal communication The encoding of messages into words, either written or spoken.

nonverbal communication The encoding of messages by means of facial expressions, body language, and styles of dress.

The encoding of messages into words, written or spoken, is **verbal communication.** We can also encode messages without using written or spoken language. **Nonverbal communication** shares information by means of facial expressions (smiling, raising an eyebrow, frowning, dropping one's jaw), body language (posture, gestures, nods, and shrugs), and even style of dress (casual, formal, conservative, trendy). For example, as they walk around GM plants, top managers in General Motors wear slacks and sports jackets rather than suits to communicate or signal that GM's old bureaucracy has been dismantled and that the company is decentralized and more informal than it used to be.[24] The trend toward increasing empowerment of the workforce has led some managers to dress informally to communicate that all employees of an organization are team members, working together to create value for customers.

Nonverbal communication can be used to back up or reinforce verbal communication. Just as a warm and genuine smile can back up words of appreciation for a job well done, a concerned facial expression can back up words of sympathy for a personal problem. In such cases, the congruence between the verbal and the nonverbal communication helps to ensure that a common understanding is reached.

Sometimes when members of an organization decide not to express a message verbally, they inadvertently do so nonverbally. People tend to have less control over nonverbal communication, and often a verbal message that is withheld gets expressed through body language or facial expressions. A manager who agrees to a proposal that she or he actually is not in favor of may unintentionally communicate her or his disfavor by grimacing.

Sometimes nonverbal communication is used to send messages that cannot be sent through verbal channels. Many lawyers are well aware of this communication tactic. Lawyers are often schooled in techniques of nonverbal communication, such as choosing where to stand in the courtroom for maximum effect and using eye contact during different stages of a trial. Lawyers sometimes get into trouble for using inappropriate nonverbal communication in an attempt to influence juries. In a Louisiana court, prosecuting attorney Thomas Pirtle was admonished and fined $2,500 by Judge Yada Magee for shaking his head in an expression of doubt, waving his arms indicating disfavor, and chuckling when the attorneys for the defense were stating their case.[25]

Nonverbal communication shares information by means of facial expressions, body language, and even style of dress.

The Role of Perception in Communication

Perception plays a central role in communication and affects both transmission and feedback. In Chapter 5, we defined *perception* as the process through which people select, organize, and interpret sensory input to give meaning and order to the world around them. We mentioned that perception is inherently subjective and is influenced by people's personalities, values, attitudes, and moods as well as by their experience and knowledge. When senders and receivers communicate with each other, they are doing so based on their own subjective perceptions. The encoding and decoding of messages and even the choice of a medium hinge on the perceptions of senders and receivers.

In addition, perceptual biases can hamper effective communication. Recall from Chapter 5 that *biases* are systematic tendencies to use information about others in ways that result in inaccurate perceptions. In Chapter 5, we described a number of biases that can result in the unfair treatment of diverse members of an organization. The same biases also can lead to ineffective communication. For example, *stereotypes*—simplified and often inaccurate beliefs about the characteristics of particular groups of people—can interfere with the encoding and decoding of messages.

Suppose a manager stereotypes older workers as being fearful of change. When this manager encodes a message to an older worker about an upcoming change in the organization, she may downplay the extent of the change so as not to make the older worker feel stressed. The older worker, however, fears change no more than his younger colleagues fear it and thus decodes the message to mean that only a minor change is going to be made. The older worker fails to adequately prepare for the change, and his performance subsequently suffers because of his lack of preparation for the change. Clearly, the ineffective communication was due to the manager's inaccurate assumptions about older workers. Instead of relying on stereotypes, effective managers strive to perceive other people accurately by focusing on their actual behaviors, knowledge, skills, and abilities. Accurate perceptions, in turn, contribute to effective communication.

The Dangers of Ineffective Communication

Because managers must communicate with others to perform their various roles and tasks, managers spend most of their time communicating, whether in meetings, in telephone conversations, through e-mail, or in face-to-face interactions. Indeed, some experts estimate that managers spend approximately 85% of their time engaged in some form of communication.[26]

Effective communication is so important that managers cannot just be concerned that they themselves are effective communicators; they also have to help their subordinates be effective communicators. When all members of an organization are able to communicate effectively with one another and with people outside the organization, the organization is much more likely to perform highly and gain a competitive advantage.

When managers and other members of an organization are ineffective communicators, organizational performance suffers and any competitive advantage the organization might have is likely to be lost. Moreover, poor communication sometimes can be downright dangerous and even lead to tragic and unnecessary loss of human life. For example, researchers from Harvard University recently studied the causes of mistakes, such as a patient receiving the wrong medication, in two large hospitals in the Boston area. They discovered that some mistakes in hospitals occur because of communication problems—physicians' not having the information they need to correctly order medications for their patients or nurses' not having the information they need to correctly administer medications. The researchers concluded that some of the responsibility for these mistakes lies with hospital management, which has not taken active steps to improve communication.[27]

Communication problems in the cockpit of airplanes and between flying crews and air traffic controllers are unfortunately all too common, sometimes with deadly consequences. In the late 1970s, two jets collided in Tenerife (one of the Canary Islands) because of miscommunication between a pilot and the control tower, and 600 people were killed. The tower radioed to the pilot, "Clipper 1736 report clear of runway." The pilot mistakenly interpreted this message to mean that he was cleared for takeoff.[28]

Unfortunately, errors like this one are not a thing of the past. A safety group at NASA tracked more than 6,000 unsafe flying incidents and found that communication difficulties caused approximately 529 of them.[29] And NASA has its own communication difficulties.[30] In 2004, NASA released a report detailing communication problems at the International Space Station jointly managed and staffed by NASA and the Russian space agency; the problems included inadequate record keeping, missing information, and failure to keep data current.[31]

Information Richness and Communication Media

To be effective communicators, managers (and other members of an organization) need to select an appropriate communication medium for *each* message they send. Should a change in procedures be communicated to subordinates in a memo sent through e-mail? Should a congratulatory message about a major accomplishment be communicated in a letter, in a phone call, or over lunch? Should a layoff announcement be made in a memo or at a plant meeting? Should the members of a purchasing team travel to Europe to cement a major agreement with a new supplier, or should they do so through faxes? Managers deal with these questions day in and day out.

There is no one best communication medium for managers to rely on. In choosing a communication medium for any message, managers need to consider three factors. The first and most important is the level of information richness that is needed. **Information richness** is the amount of information a communication medium can carry and the extent to which the medium enables the sender and receiver to reach a common understanding.[32] The communication media that managers use vary in their information richness (see Figure 16.2).[33] Media high in information richness are able to carry an extensive amount of information and generally enable receivers and senders to come to a common understanding.

The second factor that managers need to take into account in selecting a communication medium is the *time* needed for communication, because managers' and other organizational members' time is valuable. Managers at United Parcel Service,

information richness The amount of information that a communication medium can carry and the extent to which the medium enables the sender and receiver to reach a common understanding.

Figure 16.2
The Information Richness of Communication Media

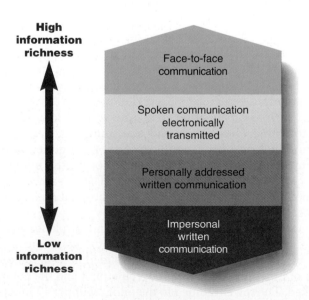

High information richness

Face-to-face communication

Spoken communication electronically transmitted

Personally addressed written communication

Impersonal written communication

Low information richness

for example, dramatically reduced the amount of time they spent on communicating by using videoconferences instead of face-to-face communication, which required that managers travel overseas.[34]

The third factor that affects the choice of a communication medium is the *need for a paper or electronic trail* or some kind of written documentation that a message was sent and received. A manager may wish to document in writing, for example, that a subordinate was given a formal warning about excessive lateness.

In the remainder of this section we examine four types of communication media that vary along these three dimensions (information richness, time, and paper or electronic trail).[35]

Face-to-Face Communication

Face-to-face communication is the medium that is highest in information richness. When managers communicate face-to-face, they not only can take advantage of verbal communication but also can interpret each other's nonverbal signals such as facial expressions and body language. A look of concern or puzzlement can sometimes say more than a thousand words, and managers can respond to such nonverbal signals on the spot. Face-to-face communication also enables managers to receive instant feedback. Points of confusion, ambiguity, or misunderstanding can be resolved, and managers can cycle through the communication process as many times as needed to reach a common understanding.

With the growing proliferation of electronic forms of communication, such as e-mail, some managers fear that face-to-face communication is being shortchanged to the detriment of building common understandings and rapport.[36] Moreover, some messages that really should be communicated face-to-face or at least in a phone conversation, and messages that are more efficiently communicated in this manner, are nonetheless sent electronically.[37] As indicated in the following "Management Insight," managers need to carefully consider whether face-to-face communication is being shortchanged in their organizations and, if it is, take steps to rectify the situation.

Management Insight

When Face-to-Face Communication Is Called For

Anyone who has participated in one of those frustrating e-mail exchanges where messages shoot back and forth and it seems to take forever to resolve a problem, reach a common understanding, or come to a resolution about an issue knows there must be a better way. In such cases, a face-to-face conversation (or if that is not possible, a phone conversation) often will lead to better outcomes all around.

According to Ron McMillan, a consultant to managers at all ranks and coauthor of best-selling books on communication, e-mail should not be relied on to communicate information that is complex, important, or sensitive.[38] In such cases, face-to-face communication (or even a phone conversation) can convey more information than e-mail can, and it is much more effective at reaching a common understanding. Research conducted by Professor Albert Mehrabian at UCLA suggests that more meaning is conveyed by nonverbal communication from facial expressions and body language and from tone of voice and vocal inflection than is conveyed by the actual words that are used when communicating.[39] And of course, nonverbal communication, tone of voice, and vocal inflection are all missing when e-mail is used. JoAnne Yates, a professor at the Sloan School of Management at MIT, suggests that e-mail is best for simple information that will be readily understood.[40]

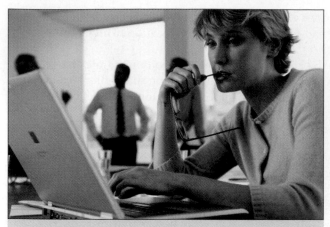

Sometimes, face-to-face communication is much more effective than relying on e-mail.

Sara Roberts, founder and president of Roberts Golden Consulting in San Francisco, recognizes the value of face-to-face communication. Although consultants in her firm regularly communicate with each other, clients, and suppliers via e-mail and this is often efficient and effective, Roberts believes that rapport and collaboration can suffer when e-mail is used extensively. So she instituted, "No E-mail Fridays" at her firm; on Fridays, employees are not to use e-mail unless it is clearly necessary (e.g., to reply to a client who wants an urgent e-mail response).[41] As Roberts puts it, "No E-mail Friday helps us to remember we really could go over to that person sitting right over there and collaborate more."[42] In fact, a growing number of organizations are experimenting with "no e-mail Fridays" to encourage more face-to-face communication and phone conversations.[43]

management by wandering around A face-to-face communication technique in which a manager walks around a work area and talks informally with employees about issues and concerns.

Management by wandering around is a face-to-face communication technique that is effective for many managers at all levels in an organization.[44] Rather than scheduling formal meetings with subordinates, managers walk around work areas and talk informally with employees about issues and concerns that both employees and managers may have. These informal conversations provide managers and subordinates with important information and at the same time foster the development of positive relationships. William Hewlett and David Packard, founders and former top managers of Hewlett-Packard, found management by wandering around to be a highly effective way of communicating with their employees.

Because face-to-face communication is highest in information richness, you might think that it should always be the medium of choice for managers. This is not the case, however, because of the amount of time it can take and the lack of a paper or electronic trail resulting from it. For messages that are important, personal, or likely to be misunderstood, it is often well worth managers' time to use face-to-face communication and, if need be, supplement it with some form of written communication documenting the message.

Advances in information technology are providing managers with new communication media that are close substitutes for face-to-face communication. Many organizations, such as American Greetings Corp. and Hewlett-Packard, are using *videoconferences* to capture some of the advantages of face-to-face communication (such as access to facial expressions) while saving time and money, since managers in different locations do not have to travel to meet with one another. During a videoconference, managers in two or more locations communicate with each other over large TV or video screens; they not only hear each other but also see each other throughout the meeting.

In addition to saving travel costs, videoconferences sometimes have other advantages. Managers at American Greetings have found that decisions get made more quickly when videoconferences are used, because more managers can be involved in the decision-making process and therefore fewer managers have to be consulted outside the meeting itself. Managers at Hewlett-Packard have found that videoconferences have shortened new product development time by 30% for similar reasons. Videoconferences also seem to lead to more efficient meetings. Some managers have found that their meetings are 20% to 30% shorter when videoconferences are used instead of face-to-face meetings.[45]

Taking videoconferences a leap forward, Cisco Systems has developed its Tele-Presence line of products, which enables individuals and teams in different locations to communicate live and in real time over the Internet with high definition and life-size video and excellent quality audio that makes it feel like everyone taking part, no matter where they are, are in the same room.[46] One morning, Cisco CEO John

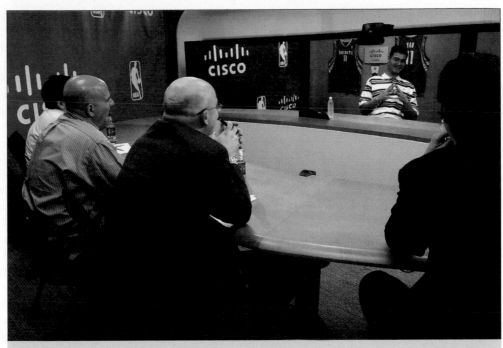

Cisco Systems conducts a press conference with Yao Ming using TelePresence's videoconferencing system with life-size imaging.

Chambers, was able to participate in meetings with employees and teams in India, Japan, Cleveland, and London in less than four hours by using TelePresence.[47] Other companies, such as HP, have developed similar products. What distinguishes these products from older videoconferencing systems is the fact that there are no delays in transmission and the video quality is sharp, clear, lifelike, and lifesize.[48]

Spoken Communication Electronically Transmitted

After face-to-face communication, spoken communication electronically transmitted over phone lines (and the World Wide Web) is second highest in information richness (see Figure 16.2). Although managers communicating over the telephone do not have access to body language and facial expressions, they do have access to the tone of voice in which a message is delivered, the parts of the message the sender emphasizes, and the general manner in which the message is spoken, in addition to the actual words themselves. Thus, telephone conversations have the capacity to convey extensive amounts of information. Managers can ensure that mutual understanding is reached because they can get quick feedback over the phone and answer questions.

Voice mail systems and answering machines also allow managers to send and receive verbal electronic messages over telephone lines. Voice mail systems are companywide systems that enable senders to record messages for members of an organization who are away from their desks and allow receivers to access their messages even when hundreds of miles away from the office. Such systems are obviously a necessity when managers are frequently out of the office, and managers on the road are well advised to periodically check their voice mail.

Personally Addressed Written Communication

Lower than electronically transmitted verbal communication in information richness is personally addressed written communication (see Figure 16.2). One of the advantages of face-to-face communication and verbal communication electronically transmitted is that they both tend to demand attention, which helps ensure that receivers pay attention. Personally addressed written communications, such as memos and letters, also have this advantage. Because they are addressed to a particular person, the chances are good that the person will actually pay attention to (and read) them. Moreover, the sender can write the message in a way that the receiver is most likely to understand. Like voice mail, written communication does not enable a receiver to have his or her questions answered immediately, but when messages are clearly written and feedback is provided, common understandings can still be reached.

Even if managers use face-to-face communication, sending a follow-up in writing is often necessary for messages that are important or complicated and need to be referred to later on. This is precisely what Karen Stracker, a hospital administrator, did when she needed to tell one of her subordinates about an important change in the way the hospital would be handling denials of insurance benefits. Stracker met with the subordinate and described the changes face-to-face. Once she was sure that the subordinate understood them, she handed her a sheet of instructions to follow, which essentially summarized the information they had discussed.

E-mail also fits into this category of communication media because senders and receivers are communicating through personally addressed written words. The words, however, are appearing on their computer screens rather than on pieces of paper. E-mail is so widespread in the business world that some managers are finding that they have to deliberately take time out from managing their e-mail to get their work done, think about pressing concerns, and come up with new and innovative ideas.[49] According to the Radacati Group, an independent market research firm, the average e-mail account in corporations today receives about 18 megabytes of e-mail and attachments per work day; the volume of e-mail is only expected to increase over time.[50] In order to help their employees effectively manage e-mail, a growing number of organizations are instituting training programs to help employees learn how to more effectively use e-mail by sending clearer messages, avoiding cc'ing multiple parties on an e-mail that do not really need to see it, and writing clear and informative subject lines.[51] For example, Capital One trains employees to write clear subject lines, so that recipients know why they are receiving a message and can easily search for it and retrieve it later on, and convey information clearly and effectively in the body of the e-mail.[52]

Ultimately, for messages that are sensitive, potentially misunderstood, or require the give-and-take of a face-to-face or telephone conversation, relying on e-mail can take considerably more time to reach a common understanding.[53] Additionally, given the lack of nonverbal cues, tone of voice, and intonation in e-mail, senders need to be aware of the potential for misunderstandings.[54] For example, Kristin Byron, a professor of management at Syracuse University, suggests that recipients may have a tendency to perceive some of the e-mails they receive as more negative than the senders intended, based on her research.[55] Senders who are very rushed, for example, may send short, curt messages lacking greeting and closing lines just because they are so busy.[56] Recipients, however, might read something more negative into messages like these.[57]

The growing popularity of e-mail has also enabled many workers and managers to become *telecommuters,* people who are employed by organizations and work out of offices in their own homes. There are over 45 million telecommuters in the United States.[58] Many telecommuters indicate that the flexibility of working at home enables them to be more productive and, at the same time, be closer to their families and not waste time traveling to and from the office.[59] In a study conducted by Georgetown University, 75% of the telecommuters surveyed said their productivity increased and 83% said their home life improved once they started telecommuting.[60]

Unfortunately, the widespread use of e-mail has been accompanied by growing abuse of e-mail. There have been cases of employees sexually harassing coworkers through e-mail, sending pornographic content via e-mail, and sending messages that disparage certain employees or groups.[61] To counter disparaging remarks making their way to employees' in-boxes (and being cc'd to coworkers), Mark Stevens, CEO of MSCO, a 40-person marketing firm in Purchase, New York, instituted a policy that forbids employees to use e-mail or Blackberrys to communicate messages that criticize someone else.[62]

Managers need to develop a clear, written policy specifying what company e-mail can and should be used for and what is out of bounds. Managers also should clearly communicate this policy to all members of the organization, as well as inform them of the procedures that will be used when e-mail abuse is suspected and the consequences that will result if the abuse is confirmed. According to a survey conducted by the ePolicy Institute, of the 79% of companies that have an e-mail policy, only about 54% are actually providing employees with training and education to ensure that they understand it.[63] Training and education are important to ensure that employees know not only what the policy is but also what it means for their own e-mail usage.

Additionally, e-mail policies should specify how much personal e-mail is appropriate and when the bounds of appropriateness have been overstepped. Just as employees make personal phone calls while on the job (and sometimes have to), so too do they send and receive personal e-mails. In fact, according to Waterford Technologies, a provider of e-mail management and archive services, based in Irvine, California, about one-third of e-mail to and from companies is personal or not work-related.[64] Clearly, banning all personal e-mails is impractical and likely to have negative consequences for employees and their organizations (e.g., lower levels of job satisfaction and increased personal phone conversations). Some companies limit personal e-mails to certain times of the day or a certain amount of time per day; others have employees create lists of contacts whom they want to receive e-mails from at work (e.g., family members, children, baby-sitters); while still others want personal e-mails to be sent and received through Web-based systems like Gmail and Hotmail rather than the corporate e-mail system.[65]

According to the American Management Association, while the majority of organizations have a written policy about e-mail usage, some do not have written guidelines for instant messaging.[66] *Instant messaging* allows people who are online and linked through a buddy or contact list to send instant messages back and forth through a small window on their computer screens without having to go through the steps of sending and receiving e-mails.[67]

What about surfing the Internet on company time? According to a study conducted by Websense, approximately half of the employees surveyed indicated that they surfed the Web at work, averaging about two hours per week.[68] Most visited news and travel sites, but about 22% of the male respondents and 12% of the female respondents indicated that they visited pornographic Web sites.[69] Of all those surveyed, 56% said that they sent personal e-mails at work. The majority of those surveyed felt that sending personal e-mails and surfing the Web had no effect on their performance, and 27% thought that doing so improved their productivity.[70] Other statistics suggest that while overall there is more Internet usage at home than at work, individuals who use the Internet at work spend more time on it and visit more sites than do those who use it at home.[71] As indicated in the following "Ethics in Action," personal e-mails and Internet surfing at work present managers with some challenging ethical dilemmas.

Ethics in Action

Monitoring E-mail and Internet Usage

A growing number of companies provide managers and organizations with tools to track the Web sites their employees visit and the e-mails they send. For example, Stellar Technologies Inc., based in Naples, Florida, sells software that managers can access anywhere to find out exactly how much time employees have spent at specific Web sites.[72] Currently, a majority of large corporations in the United States monitor their employees' e-mail; the percentage is higher among high-technology organizations. Most of the organizations that monitor e-mail let their employees know about the monitoring.[73] However, the means by which they let employees know are not necessarily that effective. For example, putting information about e-mail monitoring in an employee handbook might not be that effective if most employees do not read the handbook.[74]

Monitoring employees raises concerns about privacy.[75] Most employees would not like to have their bosses listening to their phone conversations; similarly, some believe that monitoring e-mails and tracking Internet usage are an invasion of privacy.[76] Given the increasingly long working hours many employees are clocking in, should personal e-mails and Internet usage be closely scrutinized? Clearly, when illegal and unethical e-mail usage is suspected, such as sexually harassing coworkers or divulging confidential company information to third parties, monitoring may be called for. But should it be a normal part of organizational life, even when there are no indications of a real problem?

Essentially, this dilemma revolves around issues of trust. Procter & Gamble does not monitor individuals unless there appears to be a need to do so. P&G has close to 140,000 employees working in 80 countries, and the different countries have different laws and different internal organizational rules and norms.[77] Rather than monitoring individuals to see if they are abiding by the particular standards at the location where they work, P&G monitors electronic communication at its work sites in the aggregate to spot patterns. As Sandy Hughes, head of P&G's Global Privacy Council, puts it, "At some level, you have to trust your employees are going to be doing the right things."[78] Interestingly enough, research suggests that people are less likely to lie in e-mail than they are in phone calls or face-to-face conversations.[79]

Monitoring employees' e-mail and Internet usage raises concerns about privacy.

Impersonal Written Communication

Impersonal written communication is lowest in information richness but is well suited for messages that need to reach a large number of receivers. Because such messages are not addressed to particular receivers, feedback is unlikely, so managers must make sure that messages sent by this medium are written clearly in language that all receivers will understand.

Managers often find company newsletters useful vehicles for reaching large numbers of employees. Many managers give their newsletters catchy names to spark employee interest and also to inject a bit of humor into the workplace.[80] Increasing numbers of companies are distributing their newsletters online. For example, IBM's employee newsletter w3, is distributed to employees online and is updated daily.[81]

Managers can use impersonal written communication for various messages, including announcements of rules, regulations, policies, newsworthy information, changes in procedures, and the arrival of new organizational members. Impersonal written communication also can convey instructions about how to use machinery or how to process work orders or customer requests. For these kinds of messages, the paper or electronic trail left by this communication medium can be invaluable for employees.

Just as with personal written communication, impersonal written communication can be delivered and retrieved electronically, and this is increasingly the case in companies large and small. Unfortunately, the ease with which electronic messages can be spread has led to their proliferation. Many managers' and workers' electronic inboxes are so backlogged that often they do not have time to read all the electronic work-related information available to them. The problem with such **information**

information overload The potential for important information to be ignored or overlooked while tangential information receives attention.

blog A Web site on which an individual, group, or organization posts information, commentary, and opinions and to which readers can often respond with their own commentary and opinions.

overload is the potential for important information to be ignored or overlooked (even that which is personally addressed) while tangential information receives attention. Moreover, information overload can result in thousands of hours and millions of dollars in lost productivity.

Some managers and organizations utilize blogs to communicate with employees, investors, customers, and the general public.[82] A **blog** is a Web site on which an individual, group, or organization posts information, commentary, and opinions and to which readers can often respond with their own commentary and opinions.[83] Some top managers such as Jonathan Schwartz, CEO of Sun Microsystems and Robert Lutz, a vice chairman of product development and chairman of GM North America have their own blogs, and some companies such as Cisco Systems and Oracle Corp. have corporate blogs.[84] Just as organizations have rules and guidelines about employee e-mail and Internet usage, a growing number of organizations are instituting employee guidelines for blogs.[85] At IBM, over 25,000 employees have blogs on IBM's internal computer network.[86] Guidelines for the use of blogs include following IBM's Code of Conduct (especially with regard to confidentiality, respect, and privacy), refraining from criticizing competitors, and refraining from mentioning customers' names without obtaining prior permission; bloggers must also reveal their own identity on their blogs (anonymous blogs are not permitted).[87]

LO4 Describe the communication networks that exist in groups and teams.

Communication Networks

communication networks The pathways along which information flows in groups and teams and throughout the organization.

Although various communication media are utilized, communication in organizations tends to flow in certain patterns. The pathways along which information flows in groups and teams and throughout an organization are called **communication networks.** The type of communication network that exists in a group depends on the nature of the group's tasks and the extent to which group members need to communicate with one another in order to achieve group goals.

Communication Networks in Groups and Teams

As you learned in Chapter 14, groups and teams, whether they are cross-functional teams, top-management teams, command groups, self-managed work teams, or task forces, are the building blocks of organizations. Four kinds of communication networks can develop in groups and teams: the wheel, the chain, the circle, and the all-channel network (see Figure 16.3).

WHEEL NETWORK   In a wheel network, information flows to and from one central member of the group. Other group members do not need to communicate with one another to perform at a high level, so the group can accomplish its goals by directing all communication to and from the central member. Wheel networks are often found in command groups with pooled task interdependence. Picture a group of taxi cab drivers who report to the same dispatcher, who is also their supervisor. Each driver needs to communicate with the dispatcher, but the drivers do not need to communicate with one another. In groups such as this, the wheel network results in efficient communication, saving time without compromising performance. Although found in groups, wheel networks are not found in teams because they do not allow for the intense interactions characteristic of teamwork.

CHAIN NETWORK   In a chain network, members communicate with one another in a predetermined sequence. Chain networks are found in groups with sequential task interdependence, such as in assembly-line groups. When group work has to be performed in a predetermined order, the chain network is often found because group members need to communicate with those whose work directly precedes and follows their own. Like wheel networks, chain networks tend not to exist in teams because of the limited amount of interaction among group members.

Figure 16.3
Communication Networks in Groups and Teams

Wheel network

Chain network

Circle network

All-channel network

CIRCLE NETWORK In a circle network, group members communicate with others who are similar to them in experiences, beliefs, areas of expertise, background, office location, or even where they sit when the group meets. Members of task forces and standing committees, for example, tend to communicate with others who have similar experiences or backgrounds. People also tend to communicate with people whose offices are next to their own. Like wheel and chain networks, circle networks are most often found in groups that are not teams.

ALL-CHANNEL NETWORK An all-channel network is found in teams. It is characterized by high levels of communication: Every team member communicates with every other team member. Top-management teams, cross-functional teams, and self-managed work teams frequently have all-channel networks. The reciprocal task interdependence often found in such teams requires information flows in all directions. Computer software specially designed for use by work groups can help maintain effective communication in teams with all-channel networks because it provides team members with an efficient way to share information with one another.

Organizational Communication Networks

An organization chart may seem to be a good summary of an organization's communication network, but often it is not. An organization chart summarizes the *formal* reporting relationships in an organization and the formal pathways along which communication takes place. Often, however, communication is *informal* and flows around issues, goals, projects, and ideas instead of moving up and down the organizational hierarchy in an orderly fashion. Thus, an organization's communication network includes

Figure 16.4
Formal and Informal Communication Networks in an Organization

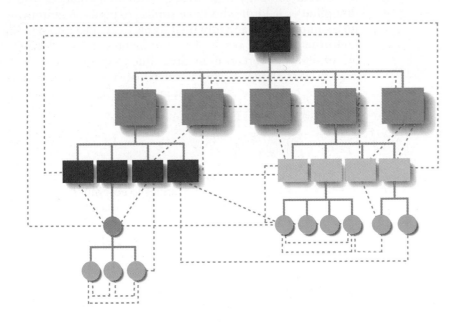

——— Formal pathways of communication summarized in an organization chart

- - - - - Informal pathways along which a great deal of communication takes place

not only the formal communication pathways summarized in an organization chart but also informal communication pathways along which a great deal of communication takes place (see Figure 16.4).

Communication can and should occur across departments and groups as well as within them and up and down and sideways in the corporate hierarchy. Communication up and down the corporate hierarchy is often called *vertical* communication. Communication among employees at the same level in the hierarchy, or sideways, is called *horizontal* communication. Managers obviously cannot determine in advance what an organization's communication network will be, nor should they try to. Instead, to accomplish goals and perform at a high level, organizational members should be free to communicate with whomever they need to contact. Because organizational goals change over time, so too do organizational communication networks. Informal communication networks can contribute to an organization's competitive advantage because they help ensure that organizational members have the information they need when they need it to accomplish their goals.

The **grapevine** is an informal organizational communication network along which unofficial information flows quickly, if not always accurately.[88] People in an organization who seem to know everything about everyone are prominent in the grapevine. Information spread over the grapevine can be on issues of either a business nature (an impending takeover) or a personal nature (the CEO's separation from his wife).

grapevine An informal communication network along which unofficial information flows.

External Networks

In addition to participating in networks within an organization, managers, professional employees, and those with work-related ties outside their employing organization often are part of external networks whose members span a variety of companies. For example, scientists working in universities and in corporations often communicate in networks formed around common underlying interests in a particular topic or subfield. As another example, physicians working throughout the country belong to specialty professional associations that help them keep up to date on the latest advances in their fields. For some managers and professionals, participation in such interest-oriented networks is just as important, or even more important, than participation in internal company networks. Networks of contacts who are working in the same discipline or field or who have similar expertise and knowledge can be very helpful, for example, when an individual wants to change jobs or even find a job after a layoff. Unfortunately, as a result of discrimination and stereotypes, some of these networks are off-limits to certain individuals due to gender or race. For example, the term *old boys' network* alludes to the fact that networks of contacts for job leads, government contracts, or venture capital funding have sometimes been dominated by men and less welcoming of women.[89]

Information Technology and Communication

Advances in information technology have dramatically increased managers' abilities to communicate with others as well as to quickly access information to make decisions. Advances that are having major impacts on managerial communication include the Internet, intranets, groupware, and collaboration software. However, managers must not lose sight of the fact that communication is essentially a human endeavor, no matter how much it may be facilitated by information technology.

LO5 Explain how advances in technology have given managers new options for managing communication.

The Internet

The **Internet** is a global system of computer networks that is easy to join and is used by employees of organizations around the world to communicate inside and outside their companies. Over 210 million people in the United States alone use the Internet, and the use of broadband connections (in place of dial-up service) has dramatically increased.[90] Table 16.1 lists the 20 countries with the most Internet users.[91]

Internet A global system of computer networks.

On the Internet, the World Wide Web is the "business district" with multimedia capabilities. Companies' home pages on the Web are like offices that potential customers can visit. In attractive graphic displays on home pages, managers communicate information about the goods and services they offer, why customers should want to purchase them, how to purchase them, and where to purchase them. By surfing the Web and visiting competitors' home pages, managers can see what their competitors are doing.[92] Each day, hundreds of new companies add themselves to the growing number of organizations on the World Wide Web.[93] According to one study, the six "Web-savviest" nations (taking into account usage of broadband connections) in descending order are Denmark, Great Britain, Sweden, Norway, Finland, and the United States.[94] By all counts, use of the Internet for communication is burgeoning.

Intranets

Growing numbers of managers are finding that the technology on which the World Wide Web and the Internet are based has enabled them to improve communication within their own companies. These managers are using the technology that allows information sharing over the Internet to share information within their own companies through company networks called **intranets.** Intranets are being used not just in high-tech companies such as Sun Microsystems and Digital Equipment but also in companies such as Chevron, Goodyear, Levi Strauss, Pfizer, Chrysler, Motorola, and Ford.[95]

intranet A companywide system of computer networks.

Intranets allow employees to have many kinds of information at their fingertips (or keyboards). Directories, phone books, manuals, inventory figures, product specifications, information about customers, biographies of top managers and the board of directors, global sales figures, minutes from meetings, annual reports, delivery schedules, and up-to-the-minute revenue, cost, and profit figures are just a few examples of the information that can be shared through intranets. Intranets can be accessed with different kinds of computers so that all members of an organization can be linked together. Intranets are protected from unwanted intrusions, by hackers or by competitors, by means of firewall security systems that ask users to provide passwords and other pieces of identification before they are allowed to access the intranet.[96]

The advantage of intranets lies in their versatility as a communication medium. They can be used for a number of different purposes by people who may have little expertise in computer software and programming. While some managers complain that the Internet is too crowded and the World Wide Web too glitzy, informed managers are realizing that using the Internet's technology to create their own computer network may be one of the Internet's biggest contributions to organizational effectiveness.

Groupware and Collaboration Software

groupware Computer software that enables members of groups and teams to share information with one another.

Groupware is computer software that enables members of groups and teams to share information with one another to improve their communication and performance. In some organizations, such as the Bank of Montreal, managers have had success in introducing groupware into the organization; in other organizations, such as the advertising agency Young & Rubicam, managers have encountered considerable resistance to groupware.[97] Even in companies where the introduction of groupware has been successful, some employees resist using it. Some clerical and secretarial workers at the Bank of Montreal, for example, were dismayed to find that their neat and accurate files were being consolidated into computer files that would be accessible to many of their coworkers.

Table 16.1

Top 20 Countries in Internet Usage

Country	Internet Users
United States	210,575,287
China	162,000,000
Japan	86,300,000
Germany	50,426,117
India	42,000,000
Brazil	39,140,000
United Kingdom	37,600,000
Korea (South)	34,120,000
France	32,925,953
Italy	31,481,928
Russia	28,000,000
Mexico	22,700,000
Canada	22,000,000
Indonesia	20,000,000
Spain	19,765,033
Vietnam	16,511,849
Turkey	16,000,000
Australia	15,085,600
Taiwan	14,500,000
Philippines	14,000,000

Source: "Top 20 Countries with the Highest Number of Internet Users," Internet World Stats and Population Statistics, www.internetworldstats.com/top20.htm, June 30, 2007. Used by permission.

Managers are most likely to be able to successfully use groupware in their organizations as a communication medium when certain conditions are met:[98]

1. The work is group- or team-based, and members are rewarded, at least in part, for group performance.
2. Groupware has the full support of top management.
3. The culture of the organization stresses flexibility and knowledge sharing, and the organization does not have a rigid hierarchy of authority.
4. Groupware is being used for a specific purpose and is viewed as a tool that enables group or team members to work more effectively together, not as a personal source of power or advantage.
5. Employees receive adequate training in the use of computers and groupware.[99]

Employees are likely to resist using groupware and managers are likely to have a difficult time implementing it when people are working primarily on their own and are rewarded for their own individual performances.[100] Under these circumstances, information is often viewed as a source of power, and people are reluctant to share information with others by means of groupware.

Take the case of three salespeople who sell insurance policies in the same geographic area; each is paid based on the number of policies he or she sells and on his or her retention of customers. Their supervisor invested in groupware and encouraged them to use it to share information about their sales, sales tactics, customers, insurance providers, and claim histories. The supervisor told the salespeople that having all this information at their fingertips would allow them to be more efficient as well as sell more policies and provide better service to customers.

Even though they received extensive training in how to use the groupware, the salespeople never got around to using it. Why? They all were afraid that giving away their secrets to their coworkers might reduce their own commissions. In this situation, the salespeople were essentially competing with one another and thus had no incentive to share information. Under such circumstances, a groupware system may not be a wise choice of communication medium. Conversely, had the salespeople been working as a team and had they received bonuses based on team performance, groupware might have been an effective communication medium.

For an organization to gain a competitive advantage, managers need to keep up to date on advances in information technology such as groupware. But managers should not adopt these or other advances without first considering carefully how the advance in question might improve communication and performance in their particular groups, teams, or whole organization. Moreover, managers need to keep in mind that all of these advances in IT are tools for people to use to facilitate effective communication; they are not replacements for face-to-face communication.

collaboration software
Groupware that promotes and facilitates collaborative, highly interdependent interactions and provides an electronic meeting site for communication among team members.

Collaboration software is groupware that aims to promote collaborative, highly interdependent interactions among members of a team and provide the team with an electronic meeting site for communication.[101] Collaboration software provides members of a team with an online work site where they can post, share, and save data, reports, sketches, and other documents; keep calendars; have team-based online conferences; and send and receive messages. The software can also keep and update progress reports, survey team members about different issues, forward documents to managers, and let users know which of their team members are also online and at the site.[102] Having an integrated online work area can help to organize and centralize the work of a team, help to ensure that information is readily available as needed, and also help team members to make sure that important information is not overlooked. Collaboration software can be much more efficient than e-mail or instant messaging for managing ongoing team collaboration and interaction that is not face-to-face. Moreover, when a team does meet face-to-face, all documents the team might need in the course of the meeting are just a click away.[103]

For work that is truly team-based, entails a number of highly interdependent yet distinct components, and involves team members with distinct areas of expertise who need to closely coordinate their efforts, collaboration software can be a powerful communication tool. The New York-based public relations company Ketchum Inc. uses collaboration software for some of its projects. For example, Ketchum is managing public relations, marketing, and advertising for a new charitable program that Fireman's Fund Insurance Co. has undertaken. By using the eRoom software provided by Documentum (a part of EMC Corporation), Ketchum employees working on the project at six different locations, employee representatives from Fireman's, and a graphics company that is designing a Web site for the program can share plans, documents, graphic designs, and calendars at an online work site.[104] Members of the Ketchum-Fireman team get e-mail alerts when something has been modified or added to the site. As Ketchum's chief information officer Andy Roach puts it, "The fact that everyone has access to the same document means Ketchum isn't going to waste time on the logistics and can focus on the creative side."[105]

Another company taking advantage of collaboration software is Honeywell International Inc. Managers at Honeywell decided to use the SharePoint collaboration software provided by Microsoft, in part because it can be integrated with other Microsoft software such as Outlook.[106] So, for example, if a team using SharePoint makes a change to the team's calendar, that change will be automatically made in team members' Outlook calendars.[107] Clearly, collaboration software has the potential to enhance communication efficiency and effectiveness in teams.

Wikis, a result of the open-source software movement, are a free or very low cost form of collaboration software that a growing number of organizations are using. Wikis enable the organizations not only to promote collaboration and better communication but also to cut back on the use of e-mail,[108] as indicated in the following "Information Technology Byte."

Information Technology Byte

Collaborating with Wikis

According to Postini Inc., an e-mail filtering company in Redwood, California, approximately 10% of all e-mails sent and received are legitimate.[109] And while many organizations have invested in filtering software to keep spam from flooding employees' in-boxes, according to the Gartner Group (an Internet research firm), 60% of messages that make their way into employees' in-boxes are spam.[110] Darren Lennard, a managing director at Dresdner Kleinwort Wasserstein, an investment bank in London, was receiving approximately 250 e-mails a day, of which only 15% were relevant to his job. Every day, Lennard's first and last activities were to clear out his inbox on his BlackBerry—until frustration got the better of him, after a long and grueling workday, and he smashed his BlackBerry on the kitchen countertop in his home.[111]

Lennard is not alone in his frustration. J. P. Rangaswani, global chief information officer at Dresdner, who particularly dislikes use of cc's and bcc's on e-mails, wants to reduce the reliance on e-mail communication at the bank. He is taking steps to implement the use of collaboration software and other electronic forms of communication such as instant messaging and RSS (really simple syndication, which enables users to subscribe for information they require). In fact, many organizations such as Yahoo, Eastman Kodak, Walt Disney, and the U.S. government are trying to reduce their reliance on e-mail by turning to other software tools that promote effective communication and collaboration.[112] While e-mail is likely to continue to be extensively used for one-on-one communication, for communication that involves collaboration within and between groups and teams, the use of other, more efficient and effective software tools is likely to dramatically increase in the coming years.[113]

In particular, wikis (in Hawaiian, the word *wiki* means "fast"), which are relatively easy to use and low cost or free, are becoming increasingly popular as collaborative communication tools.[114] A wiki uses server software to enable users to create and revise Web pages quickly on a company intranet or through a hosted Internet site. Users who are authorized to access a wiki can log on to it and edit and update data, as well as see what other authorized users have contributed. Wikis enable collaboration in real time, and they keep a history so that users can go back and see what changes were made to, for example, a spreadsheet or a proposal.[115]

Soar Technology Inc., an artificial intelligence company in Ann Arbor, Michigan, that does work for the U.S. Office of Naval Research, has found that relying on wikis for collaboration has reduced the time it takes to complete projects by 50%.[116] According to Jacob Crossman, an engineer at Soar, wikis save time because they do away with the need for multiple e-mails with attachments and eliminate the typical confusion that surrounds multiple iterations of the same document.[117] Dresdner has found that e-mail pertaining to projects that use wikis has been reduced by about 75% and even meeting times have been significantly lowered.[118] Lennard recently created a wiki to figure out how to increase profits on a certain kind of trade. In the past, he would send e-mails with attachments to multiple colleagues, have to integrate and make sense of all the responses he received back from them, and then perhaps follow-up with subsequent e-mails. Instead, on the wiki page he created, colleagues contributed ideas, commented on each others' ideas, and revised and edited in real time. Lennard estimates that what would have taken about two weeks to accomplish through e-mail took about two days using a wiki.[119]

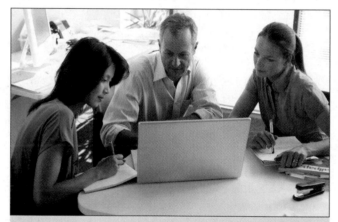

Wikis enable team members to collaborate on projects in real time.

Even though IBM has its own collaboration software, Lotus Notes, IBM employees rely on wikis for collaboration to such a great extent that IBM created Wiki Central, to manage the wikis. Wiki Central manages over 20,000 IBM wikis and has over 100,000 users.[120] For example, some teams use wikis to coordinate the development of computer software. Wiki Central also provides employees with tools to improve and enhance the functioning of their wikis, such as the "polling widget" (used for electronic voting) and the "rating widget" (used to evaluate proposals).[121] Clearly, managers have multiple options to ensure efficient, effective, and collaborative communication.[122]

Communication Skills for Managers

LO6 Describe important communication skills that managers need as senders and as receivers of messages and why it is important to understand differences in linguistic styles.

Some of the barriers to effective communication in organizations have their origins in senders. When messages are unclear, incomplete, or difficult to understand, when they are sent over an inappropriate medium, or when no provision for feedback is made, communication suffers. Other communication barriers have their origins in receivers. When receivers pay no attention to or do not listen to messages or when they make no effort to understand the meaning of a message, communication is likely to be ineffective. Sometimes advanced information technology, such as automated phone systems, can hamper effective communication to the extent that the human element is missing.

To overcome these barriers and effectively communicate with others, managers (as well as other organizational members) must possess or develop certain communication skills. Some of these skills are particularly important when managers *send* messages; others are critical when managers *receive* messages. These skills help ensure that managers will be able to share information, will have the information they need to make good decisions and take action, and will be able to reach a common understanding with others.

Communication Skills for Managers as Senders

Organizational effectiveness depends on the ability of managers (as well as other organizational members) to effectively send messages to people both inside and outside the organization. Table 16.2 summarizes seven communication skills that help ensure that when managers send messages, they are properly understood and the transmission phase of the communication process is effective. Let's see what each skill entails.

SEND CLEAR AND COMPLETE MESSAGES Managers need to learn how to send a message that is clear and complete. A message is clear when it is easy for the receiver to understand and interpret, and it is complete when it contains all the information that the sender and receiver need to reach a common understanding. In striving to send messages that are both clear and complete, managers must learn to anticipate how receivers will interpret messages and must adjust messages to eliminate sources of misunderstanding or confusion.

ENCODE MESSAGES IN SYMBOLS THE RECEIVER UNDERSTANDS Managers need to appreciate that when they encode messages, they should use symbols or language that the receiver understands. When sending messages in English to receivers whose native language is not English, for example, it is important to use commonplace vocabulary and to avoid using clichés that, when translated, may make little sense and sometimes are either comical or insulting. **Jargon,** specialized language that members of an occupation, group, or organization develop to facilitate communication among themselves, should never be used when communicating with people outside the occupation, group, or organization.

jargon Specialized language that members of an occupation, group, or organization develop to facilitate communication among themselves.

SELECT A MEDIUM APPROPRIATE FOR THE MESSAGE As you have learned, when relying on verbal communication, managers can choose from a variety of communication media, including face-to-face communication in person, written letters, memos, newsletters, phone conversations, e-mail, voice mail, faxes, and videoconferences. When choosing among these media, managers need to take into account the level of information richness required, time constraints, and the need for a paper or electronic trail. A primary concern in choosing an appropriate medium is the nature of the message. Is it personal, important, nonroutine, and likely to be misunderstood and in need of further clarification? If it is, face-to-face communication is likely to be in order.

Table 16.2
Seven Communication Skills for Managers as Senders of Messages

- Send messages that are clear and complete.
- Encode messages in symbols that the receiver understands.
- Select a medium that is appropriate for the message.
- Select a medium that the receiver monitors.
- Avoid filtering and information distortion.
- Ensure that a feedback mechanism is built into messages.
- Provide accurate information to ensure that misleading rumors are not spread.

SELECT A MEDIUM THE RECEIVER MONITORS Another factor that managers need to take into account when selecting a communication medium is whether the medium is one that the receiver monitors. Managers differ in the communication media they pay attention to. Many managers simply select the medium that they themselves use the most and are most comfortable with, but doing this can often lead to ineffective communication. Managers who dislike telephone conversations and too many face-to-face interactions may prefer to use e-mail, send many e-mail messages per day, and check their own e-mail very often. Managers who prefer to communicate with people in person or over the phone may have e-mail addresses but may be less likely to respond to e-mail messages. No matter how much a manager likes e-mail, sending e-mail to someone who does not respond to e-mail may be futile. Learning which managers like things in writing and which prefer face-to-face interactions and then using the appropriate medium enhances the chance that receivers will actually receive and pay attention to messages.

A related consideration is whether receivers have disabilities that hamper their ability to decode certain messages. A blind receiver, for example, cannot read a written message. Managers should ensure that employees with disabilities have resources available to communicate effectively with others. For example, deaf employees can effectively communicate over the telephone by using text-typewriters that have a screen and a keyboard on which senders can type messages. The message travels along the phone lines to special operators called *communication assistants*, who translate the typed message into words that the receiver can listen to. The receiver's spoken replies are translated into typewritten text by the communication assistants and appear on the sender's screen. The communication assistants relay messages back and forth to each sender and receiver.[123] Additionally, use of fax and e-mail instead of phone conversations can aid deaf employees.

filtering Withholding part of a message because of the mistaken belief that the receiver does not need or will not want the information.

AVOID FILTERING AND INFORMATION DISTORTION **Filtering** occurs when senders withhold part of a message because they (mistakenly) think that the receiver does not need the information or will not want to receive it. Filtering can occur at all levels in an organization and in both vertical and horizontal communication. Rank-and-file workers may filter messages they send to first-line managers, first-line managers may filter messages to middle managers, and middle managers may filter messages to top managers. Such filtering is most likely to take place when messages contain bad news or problems that subordinates are afraid they will be blamed for. As indicated in "A Manager's Challenge," managers need to hear bad news and be aware of problems as soon as they occur so that they can take swift steps to rectify the problem and limit the damage it may have caused.

Some filtering takes place because of internal competition in organizations or because organizational members fear that their power and influence will be diminished if others have access to some of their specialized knowledge. By increasing levels of trust in an organization, taking steps to motivate all employees (and the groups and teams they belong to) to work together to achieve organizational goals, and ensuring that employees realize that when the organization reaches its goals and performs effectively, they too will benefit, this kind of filtering can be reduced.

information distortion Changes in the meaning of a message as the message passes through a series of senders and receivers.

Information distortion occurs when the meaning of a message changes as the message passes through a series of senders and receivers. Some information distortion is accidental—due to faulty encoding and decoding or to a lack of feedback. Other information distortion is deliberate. Senders may alter a message to make themselves or their groups look good and to receive special treatment.

Managers themselves should avoid filtering and distorting information. But how can they eliminate these barriers to effective communication throughout their organization? They need to establish trust throughout the organization. Subordinates who trust their managers believe that they will not be blamed for things beyond their control and will be treated fairly. Managers who trust their subordinates provide them with clear and complete information and do not hold things back.

INCLUDE A FEEDBACK MECHANISM IN MESSAGES Because feedback is essential for effective communication, managers should build a feedback mechanism into the messages they send. They either should include a request for feedback or indicate when and how they will follow up on the message to make sure that it was received and understood. When managers write letters and memos or send faxes, they can request that the receiver respond with comments and suggestions in a letter, memo, or fax; schedule a meeting to discuss the issue; or follow up with a phone call. By building feedback mechanisms such as these into their messages, managers ensure that they get heard and are understood.

rumors Unofficial pieces of information of interest to organizational members but with no identifiable source.

PROVIDE ACCURATE INFORMATION **Rumors** are unofficial pieces of information of interest to organizational members but with no identifiable source. Rumors spread quickly once they are started, and usually they concern topics that organizational members think are important, interesting, or amusing. Rumors, however, can be misleading and can cause harm to individual employees and their organizations when they are false, malicious, or unfounded. Managers can halt the spread of misleading rumors by providing organizational members with accurate information on matters that concern them.

Table 16.3

Three Communication Skills for Managers as Receivers of Messages

- Pay attention.
- Be a good listener.
- Be empathetic.

Communication Skills for Managers as Receivers

Managers receive as many messages as they send. Thus, managers must possess or develop communication skills that allow them to be effective receivers of messages. Table 16.3 summarizes three of these important skills, which we examine here in greater detail.

PAY ATTENTION Because of their multiple roles and tasks, managers often are overloaded and forced to think about several things at once. Pulled in many different directions, they sometimes do not pay sufficient attention to the messages they receive. To be effective, however, managers should always pay attention to messages they receive, no matter how busy they are. When discussing a project with a subordinate, an effective manager focuses on the project and not on an upcoming meeting with his or her own boss. Similarly, when managers are reading written communications, they should focus their attention on understanding what they are reading; they should not be sidetracked into thinking about other issues.

BE A GOOD LISTENER Managers (and all other members of an organization) can do several things to be good listeners. First, managers should refrain from interrupting senders in the middle of a message so that senders do not lose their train of thought and managers do not jump to erroneous conclusions based on incomplete information. Second, managers should maintain good eye contact with senders so that senders feel their listeners are paying attention; doing this also helps managers focus on what they are hearing. Third, after receiving a message, managers should ask questions to clarify points of ambiguity or confusion. Fourth, managers should paraphrase, or restate in their own words, points senders make that are important, complex, or open to alternative interpretations; this is the feedback component so critical to successful communication.

Managers, like most people, often like to hear themselves talk rather than listen to others. Part of being a good communicator, however, is being a good listener, an

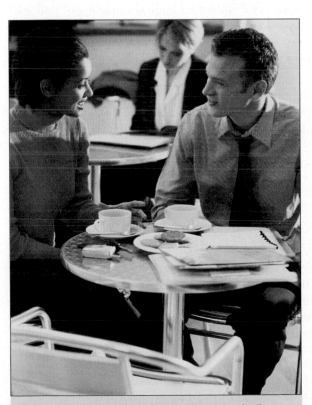

Being a good listener is an important communication skill for all members of an organization.

essential communication skill for managers as receivers of messages transmitted face-to-face and over the telephone.

BE EMPATHETIC Receivers are empathetic when they try to understand how the sender feels and try to interpret a message from the sender's perspective, rather than viewing the message from only their own point of view. Marcia Mazulo, the chief psychologist in a public school system in the Northwest, recently learned this lesson after interacting with Karen Sanchez, a new psychologist on her staff. Sanchez was distraught after meeting with the parent of a child she had been working with extensively. The parent was difficult to talk to and argumentative and was not supportive of her own child. Sanchez told Mazulo how upset she was, and Mazulo responded by reminding Sanchez that she was a professional and that dealing with such a situation was part of her job. This feedback upset Sanchez further and caused her to storm out of the room.

In hindsight, Mazulo realized that her response had been inappropriate. She had failed to empathize with Sanchez, who had spent so much time with the child and was deeply concerned about the child's well-being. Rather than dismissing Sanchez's concerns, Mazulo realized, she should have tried to understand how Sanchez felt and given her some support and advice for dealing positively with the situation.

Understanding Linguistic Styles

Consider the following scenarios:

- A manager from New York is having a conversation with a manager from Iowa City. The Iowa City manager never seems to get a chance to talk. He keeps waiting for a pause to signal his turn to talk, but the New York manager never pauses long enough. The New York manager wonders why the Iowa City manager does not say much. He feels uncomfortable when he pauses and the Iowa City manager says nothing, so he starts talking again.

- Elizabeth compliments Bob on his presentation to upper management and asks Bob what he thought of her presentation. Bob launches into a lengthy critique of Elizabeth's presentation and describes how he would have handled it differently. This is hardly the response Elizabeth expected.

- Catherine shares with co-members of a self-managed work team a new way to cut costs. Michael, another team member, thinks her idea is a good one and encourages the rest of the team to support it. Catherine is quietly pleased by Michael's support. The group implements "Michael's" suggestion, and it is written up as such in the company newsletter.

- Robert was recently promoted and transferred from his company's Oklahoma office to its headquarters in New Jersey. Robert is perplexed because he never seems to get a chance to talk in management meetings; someone else always seems to get the floor. Robert's new boss wonders whether Robert's new responsibilities are too much for him, although Robert's supervisor in Oklahoma rated him highly and said he is a real "go-getter." Robert is timid in management meetings and rarely says a word.

What do these scenarios have in common? Essentially, they all describe situations in which a misunderstanding of linguistic styles leads to a breakdown in communication. The scenarios are based on the research of linguist Deborah Tannen, who describes **linguistic style** as a person's characteristic way of speaking. Elements of linguistic style include tone of voice, speed, volume, use of pauses, directness or indirectness, choice of words, credit taking, and use of questions, jokes, and other manners of speech.[124] When people's linguistic styles differ and these differences are not understood, ineffective communication is likely.

The first and last scenarios illustrate regional differences in linguistic style.[125] The Iowa City manager and Robert from Oklahoma expect the pauses that signal turn taking in conversations to be longer than the pauses made by their colleagues in New

linguistic style A person's characteristic way of speaking.

York and New Jersey. This difference causes communication problems. The Iowan and transplanted Oklahoman think that their eastern colleagues never let them get a word in edgewise, and the easterners cannot figure out why their colleagues from the Midwest and South do not get more actively involved in conversations.

Differences in linguistic style can be a particularly insidious source of communication problems because linguistic style is often taken for granted. People rarely think about their own linguistic styles and often are unaware of how linguistic styles can differ. In the example above, Robert never realized that when dealing with his New Jersey colleagues, he could and should jump into conversations more quickly than he used to do in Oklahoma, and his boss never realized that Robert felt that he was not being given a chance to speak in meetings.

The aspect of linguistic style just described, length of pauses, differs by region in the United States. Much more dramatic differences in linguistic style occur cross-culturally.

CROSS-CULTURAL DIFFERENCES   Managers from Japan tend to be more formal in their conversations and more deferential toward upper-level managers and people with high status than are managers from the United States. Japanese managers do not mind extensive pauses in conversations when they are thinking things through or when they think that further conversation might be detrimental. In contrast, U.S. managers (even managers from regions of the United States where pauses tend to be long) find very lengthy pauses disconcerting and feel obligated to talk to fill the silence.[126]

Another cross-cultural difference in linguistic style concerns the appropriate physical distance separating speakers and listeners in business-oriented conversations.[127] The distance between speakers and listeners is greater in the United States, for example, than it is in Brazil or Saudi Arabia. Citizens of different countries also vary in how direct or indirect they are in conversations and the extent to which they take individual credit for accomplishments. Japanese culture, with its collectivist or group orientation, tends to encourage linguistic styles in which group rather than individual accomplishments are emphasized. The opposite tends to be true in the United States.

These and other cross-cultural differences in linguistic style can and often do lead to misunderstandings. For example, when a team of American managers presented

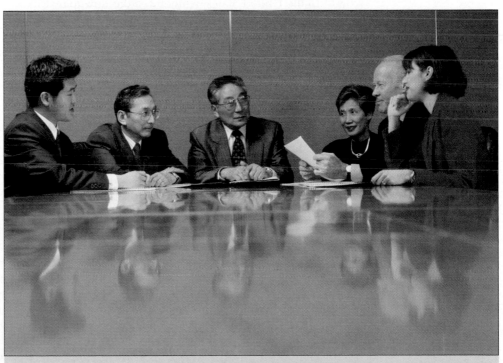

Cross-cultural differences in linguistic style can lead to misunderstandings.

a proposal for a joint venture to Japanese managers, the Japanese managers were silent as they thought about the implications of what they had just heard. The American managers took this silence as a sign that the Japanese managers wanted more information, so they went into more detail about the proposal. When they finished, the Japanese were silent again, not only frustrating the Americans but also making them wonder whether the Japanese were at all interested in the project. The American managers suggested that if the Japanese already had decided that they did not want to pursue the project, there was no reason for the meeting to continue. The Japanese were truly bewildered. They were trying to carefully think out the proposal, yet the Americans thought they were not interested!

Communication misunderstandings and problems like this can be overcome if managers make themselves familiar with cross-cultural differences in linguistic styles. If the American managers and the Japanese managers had realized that periods of silence are viewed differently in Japan and in the United States, their different linguistic styles might have been less troublesome barriers to communication. Before managers communicate with people from abroad, they should try to find out as much as they can about the aspects of linguistic style that are specific to the country or culture in question. Expatriate managers who have lived in the country in question for an extended period of time can be good sources of information about linguistic styles because they are likely to have experienced firsthand some of the differences that citizens of a country are not aware of. Finding out as much as possible about cultural differences also can help managers learn about differences in linguistic styles because the two are often closely linked.

GENDER DIFFERENCES   Referring again to the four scenarios that open this section, you may be wondering why Bob launched into a lengthy critique of Elizabeth's presentation after she paid him a routine compliment on his presentation, or you may be wondering why Michael got the credit for Catherine's idea in the self-managed work team. Research conducted by Tannen and other linguists has found that the linguistic styles of men and women differ in practically every culture or language.[128] Men and women take their own linguistic styles for granted and thus do not realize when they are talking with someone of a different gender that differences in their styles may lead to ineffective communication.

In the United States, women tend to downplay differences between people, are not overly concerned about receiving credit for their own accomplishments, and want to make everyone feel more or less on an equal footing so that even poor performers or low-status individuals feel valued. Men, in contrast, tend to emphasize their own superiority and are not reluctant to acknowledge differences in status. These differences in linguistic style led Elizabeth to routinely compliment Bob on his presentation even though she thought that he had not done a particularly good job. She asked him how her presentation was so that he could reciprocate and give her a routine compliment, putting them on an equal footing. Bob took Elizabeth's compliment and question about her own presentation as an opportunity to confirm his superiority, never realizing that all she was expecting was a routine compliment. Similarly, Michael's enthusiastic support for Catherine's cost-cutting idea and her apparent surrender of ownership of the idea after she described it led team members to assume incorrectly that the idea was Michael's.[129]

Do some women try to prove that they are better than everyone else, and are some men unconcerned about taking credit for ideas and accomplishments? Of course. The gender differences in linguistic style that Tannen and other linguists have uncovered are general tendencies evident in *many* women and men, not in *all* women and men.

Where do gender differences in linguistic style come from? Tannen suggests that they begin developing in early childhood. Girls and boys tend to play with children of their own gender, and the ways in which girls and boys play are quite different. Girls play in small groups, engage in a lot of close conversation, emphasize how similar they are to one another, and view boastfulness negatively. Boys play in large groups, emphasize status differences, expect leaders to emerge who boss others around, and give one another challenges to try to meet. These differences in styles of play and interaction result in differences in linguistic styles when boys and girls grow up and communicate as adults. The ways in which men communicate emphasize status differences and play up relative strengths; the ways in which women communicate emphasize similarities and downplay individual strengths.[130]

Interestingly, gender differences are also turning up in the ways that women and men use e-mail and electronic forms of communication. For example, Susan Herring, a researcher at Indiana University, has found that in public electronic forums such as message boards and chat rooms, men tend to make stronger assertions, be more sarcastic, and be more likely to use insults and profanity than women, while women are more likely to be supportive, agreeable, and polite.[131] David Silver, a researcher at the University of Washington, has found that women are more expressive electronic communicators and encourage others to express their thoughts and feelings, while men are briefer and more to the point.[132] Interestingly enough, some men are finding e-mail to be a welcome way to express their feelings to people they care about. For example, real estate broker Mike Murname finds it easier to communicate with, and express his love for, his grown children via e-mail.[133]

MANAGING DIFFERENCES IN LINGUISTIC STYLES Managers should not expect to change people's linguistic styles and should not try to. To be effective, managers need to understand differences in linguistic styles. Knowing, for example, that some women are reluctant to speak up in meetings not because they have nothing to contribute but because of their linguistic style should lead managers to ensure that these women have a chance to talk. And a manager who knows that certain people are reluctant to take credit for ideas can be extra careful to give credit where it is deserved. As Tannen points out, "Talk is the lifeblood of managerial work, and understanding that different people have different ways of saying what they mean will make it possible to take advantage of the talents of people with a broad range of linguistic styles."[134]

Summary and Review

LO 1, 2

COMMUNICATION AND MANAGEMENT Communication is the sharing of information between two or more individuals or groups to reach a common understanding. Good communication is necessary for an organization to gain a competitive advantage. Communication occurs in a cyclical process that entails two phases, transmission and feedback.

LO3 **INFORMATION RICHNESS AND COMMUNICATION MEDIA** Information richness is the amount of information a communication medium can carry and the extent to which the medium enables the sender and receiver to reach a common understanding. Four categories of communication media, in descending order of information richness, are face-to-face communication (includes videoconferences), spoken communication electronically transmitted (includes voice mail), personally addressed written communication (includes e-mail), and impersonal written communication.

LO4 **COMMUNICATION NETWORKS** Communication networks are the pathways along which information flows in an organization. Four communication networks found in groups and teams are the wheel, the chain, the circle, and the all-channel network. An organization chart summarizes formal pathways of communication, but communication in organizations is often informal, as is true of communication through the grapevine.

LO5 **INFORMATION TECHNOLOGY AND COMMUNICATION** The Internet is a global system of computer networks that managers around the world use to communicate within and outside their companies. The World Wide Web is the multimedia business district on the Internet. Intranets are internal communication networks that managers can create to improve communication, performance, and customer service. Intranets use the same technology that the Internet and World Wide Web are based on. Groupware is computer software that enables members of groups and teams to share information with one another to improve their communication and performance.

LO6 **COMMUNICATION SKILLS FOR MANAGERS** There are various barriers to effective communication in organizations. To overcome these barriers and effectively communicate with others, managers must possess or develop certain communication skills. As senders of messages, managers should send messages that are clear and complete, encode messages in symbols the receiver understands, choose a medium appropriate for the message and monitored by the receiver, avoid filtering and information distortion, include a feedback mechanism in the message, and provide accurate information to ensure that misleading rumors are not spread. Communication skills for managers as receivers of messages include paying attention, being a good listener, and being empathetic. Understanding linguistic styles is also an essential communication skill for managers. Linguistic styles can vary by geographic region, gender, and country or culture. When these differences are not understood, ineffective communication can occur.

Management in Action

Topics for Discussion and Action

DISCUSSION

1. Which medium (or media) do you think would be appropriate for each of the following kinds of messages that a subordinate could receive from his or her boss: (a) a raise, (b) not receiving a promotion, (c) an error in a report prepared by the subordinate, (d) additional job responsibilities, and (e) the schedule for company holidays for the upcoming year? Explain your choices. **[LO3]**

2. Discuss the pros and cons of using the Internet and World Wide Web for communication within and between organizations. **[LO 1, 2, 3, 5]**

3. Why do some organizational members resist using groupware? **[LO5]**

4. Why do some managers find it difficult to be good listeners? **[LO6]**

5. Explain why subordinates might filter and distort information about problems and performance shortfalls when communicating with their bosses. What steps can managers take to eliminate filtering and information distortion? **[LO6]**

6. Explain why differences in linguistic style, when not understood by senders and receivers of messages, can lead to ineffective communication. **[LO6]**

ACTION

7. Interview a manager in an organization in your community to determine with whom he or she communicates on a typical day, what communication media he or she uses, and which typical communication problems the manager experiences. **[LO 1, 2, 3, 4, 5, 6]**

Building Management Skills

Diagnosing Ineffective Communication [LO 1, 2, 3, 4, 5, 6]

Think about the last time you experienced very ineffective communication with another person—someone you work with, a classmate, a friend, a member of your family. Describe the incident. Then answer the following questions:

1. Why was your communication ineffective in this incident?

2. What stages of the communication process were particularly problematic and why?

3. Describe any filtering or information distortion that occurred.

4. Do you think differences in linguistic styles adversely affected the communication that took place? Why, or why not?

5. How could you have handled this situation differently so that communication would have been effective?

Managing Ethically [LO 3, 5]

Many employees use their company's Internet connections and e-mail systems to visit Web sites and send personal e-mails and instant messages.

Questions

1. Either individually or in a group, explore the ethics of using an organization's Internet connection and e-mail system for personal purposes at work and while away from the office. Should employees have some rights to use this resource? When does their behavior become unethical?

2. Some companies keep track of the way their employees use the company's Internet connection and e-mail system. Is it ethical for managers to read employees' personal e-mails or to record Web sites that employees visit? Why, or why not?

Small Group Breakout Exercise
Reducing Resistance to Advances in Information Technology [LO5]

Form groups of three or four people, and appoint one member as the spokesperson who will communicate your findings to the class when called on by the instructor. Then discuss the following scenario.

You are a team of managers in charge of information and communication in a large consumer products corporation. Your company has already implemented many advances in information technology. Managers and workers have access to e-mail, the Internet, your company's own intranet, groupware, and collaboration software.

Many employees use the technology, but the resistance of some is causing communication problems. A case in point is the use of groupware and collaboration software. Many teams in your organization have access to groupware and are encouraged to use it. While some teams welcome this communication tool and actually have made suggestions for improvements, others are highly resistant to sharing documents on their teams' online workspaces.

Although you do not want to force people to use the technology, you want them to at least try it and give it a chance. You are meeting today to develop strategies for reducing resistance to the new technologies.

1. One resistant group of employees is made up of top managers. Some of them seem computer-phobic and are highly resistant to sharing information online, even with sophisticated security precautions in place. What steps will you take to get these managers to have more confidence in electronic communication?

2. A second group of resistant employees consists of middle managers. Some middle managers resist using your company's intranet. Although these managers do not resist the technology per se and do use electronic communication for multiple purposes, including communication, they seem to distrust the intranet as a viable way to communicate and get things done. What steps will you take to get these managers to take advantage of the intranet?

3. A third group of resistant employees is made up of members of groups and teams who do not want to use the groupware that has been provided to them. You think that the groupware could improve their communication and performance, but they seem to think otherwise. What steps will you take to get these members of groups and teams to start using groupware?

Exploring the World Wide Web [LO5]

Atos Origin is a global information technology company that provides IT services to major corporations to improve, facilitate, integrate, and manage operations, information, and communication across multiple locations. Visit Atos Origin's Web site at www.atosorigin.com, and read about this company and the services it provides to improve communication. Then read the case studies on the Web site (listed under "Business Insights"). How can companies like Atos Origin help managers improve communication effectiveness in their organizations? What kinds of organizations and groups are most likely to benefit from services provided by Atos Origin? Why is it beneficial for some organizations to contract with firms like Atos Origin for their IT and communication needs rather than meet these needs internally with their own employees?

Be the Manager [LO 1, 2, 3, 6]

You supervise support staff for an Internet merchandising organization that sells furniture over the Internet. You always thought that you needed to expand your staff, and just when you were about to approach your boss with such a request, business slowed. Thus, your plan to try to add new employees to your staff is on hold.

However, you have noticed a troubling pattern of communication with your staff. Ordinarily, when you want one of your staff members to work on a task, you e-mail that subordinate the pertinent information. For the last few months, your e-mail requests have gone unheeded, and your subordinates seem to respond to your requests only after you visit them in person and give them a specific deadline. Each time, they apologize for not getting to the task sooner but say that they are so overloaded with requests that they sometimes even stop answering their phones. Unless someone asks for something more than once, your staff seems to feel the request is not that urgent and can be put on hold. You think this state of affairs is dysfunctional and could lead to serious problems down the road. Also, you are starting to realize that your subordinates seem to have no way of prioritizing tasks—hence, some very important projects you asked them to complete were put on hold until you followed up with them about the tasks. Knowing you can not add employees to your staff in the short term, what are you going to do to improve communication with your overloaded staff?

BusinessWeek Case in the News [LO 1, 2, 3, 4, 5, 6]

The Water Cooler Is Now on the Web

Like many twentysomethings, the workers at Starcom MediaVest Group spend a portion of their workday on a social network. So in April, executives of the ad-buying firm figured, why fight it? They launched a network of their own, for employees only, called SMG Connected. Today, a little more than a third of the company's workers, or 2,060 people, have signed up for their own pages where they can create profiles that outline their jobs, list the brands they admire (Nike? Starbucks?), and describe their values by choosing from words such as "creativity" and "humor."

The service even winks at how people use MySpace.com or Facebook to put themselves at the center of the universe: Search for someone—say, with digital experience in Mexico—and you show up as a pushpin in the center of a bull's eye, with surrounding pushpins representing people who fit the bill. Says Starcom Vice-President Pam Daniels: "Giving our employees a way to connect over the Internet around the globe made sense—because they're just doing it anyway."

Plenty of big, mainstream companies look at the fast-growing social network scene as a place to market their products. But many are also adopting the same Web technology to create internal networks. It turns out to be an efficient way to mine for in-house expertise, discover new recruits, and share information within their own walls. Setting up a corporate version of a social network has its own challenges, as well. Companies have to build in safeguards to ensure that they can track the discussions and document sharing, to be certain that employees comply with government regulations and don't tumble into legal hot water.

Corporations are being nudged along by employees, and not just the digital-savvy Generation Y that's now entering the workforce. More 30-plus employees are signing up with Facebook to trade daily updates with colleagues and friends. They're also building lists of contacts from among the 13 million professionals on LinkedIn. At Ernst & Young alone, 11,000 workers now have Facebook accounts.

That translates into a juicy new sales opportunity for tech companies that sell networking products. Everyone from IBM to Microsoft and on down to startups like introNetworks, Awareness Inc., and Jive Software, are offering applications and services. One company, SelectMinds, has created social networks for 60 companies, including Lockheed Martin and JPMorgan Chase. And SharePoint, the Microsoft software that lets companies set up MySpace-like profiles, blogs, and collaborative Web sites known as wikis within the confines of their firewalls, is one of the fastest-growing server products in the company's history. "At first people were slow to adopt this; they were nervous. But now we're seeing a bunch of adoption," says Rob Curry, director of the Microsoft Office SharePoint Server software. Both Microsoft and IBM are using their own offices as labs for their products.

Executives have legitimate concerns about spending time and money on something that could be just the latest techno flavor of the week. Remember knowledge management software? That product, designed to handle a lot of the same tasks as today's corporate social networks, was one of the hot buzzwords of the late 1990s. But the systems proved overly complicated and demanded hours to transfer information into databases.

Blocked Access

Executives also worry about losing control of information or opening up their networks to security breaches. The whole "open" ethos of the social Net—sharing pictures and music and letting "friends" know your every activity—goes against the instincts of big-company chief information officers. That has led some, especially financial institutions such as Citigroup and Lehman Brothers, simply to block employee access to those public social networks. In an online survey in July of 600 workers by security firm Sophos PLC, 50% said their companies block access to Facebook.

Regulatory or disclosure issues put a crimp on openness. Accounting firms, for instance, have to ensure that members don't provide tax or accounting advice through their networks. Some software lets management limit who can see what data, and tracks who looks at certain documents. Awareness, a company that creates networks and blogs for 100 companies, including Northwestern Mutual Financial Network, tracks network posts and sends any potentially inflammatory words into "moderation boxes" to be reviewed by a manager.

But companies also see a chance to harness the positive aspects of social networking—especially where it opens a door to a new demographic. Dow Chemical Co. faces a shrinking workforce as baby boomers start leaving the labor market en masse: About 40% of Dow's workers will be eligible for retirement in the next five years. So the 110-year-old company is pushing hard on hiring and retention. It plans to open four internal social networks in December for women, retired workers, current employees, and alumni who have left for other jobs. In an alumni network, for instance, current and former employees can create profiles and get information about full-time job openings. Another Dow social network is aimed solely at helping the company stay in contact with female employees as they leave the workforce for maternity leave or cut back their hours. "We want to keep in touch with the brainpower of past employees, and frankly, it's also a great group to consider for new hires," says Julie Fasone Holder, a corporate vice-president for human resources and marketing at Dow.

Reducing E-mails

Some of the new social networks look a lot like the old company Web sites.

KPMG set up an alumni network this spring, signing up around 10,000 former and current employees. The front page lists company news, networking events, and job openings. But look closer and you can see some social-network DNA: On the right-hand side, each member has a profile box, just like on Facebook, which they update with photos, information about their job or home life, and a list of contacts. Each member builds a contact list by searching on the service for people who are already signed up or eligible to join. KPMG credits the network with helping it hire 137 former employees, or around 14% of the company's total hires, since the service started, up from 72 people in the three months prior.

By luring employees into a network, companies hope to leverage their skills and contacts. But they also hope that all that collaboration will cut out time that's now spent mailing documents and e-mailing comments. In Los Angeles, the Film Foundation is using Lotus Connections, an IBM product, to help manage an educational film program. Workers can archive research documents, share calendars, chat, and blog. A team of 60 researchers, writers, teachers, and filmmakers is putting together a curriculum, distributed free to schools across the country, that teaches students how to understand the visual language of films. By having members brainstorm, review each other's work, and prepare budgets on the network, the Film Foundation believes it can cut by half the amount of time it takes to create the materials.

Questions for Discussion

1. Why are some companies starting their own in-house social networks?

2. What are the potential advantages of in-house social networks?

3. What are the potential disadvantages of in-house social networks?

4. Do you think employees should be able to access social networking sites such as MySpace.com and Facebook while they are at work? Why, or why not?

Source: Heather Green, "The Water Cooler Is Now on the Web." Reprinted from the October 1, 2007, issue of *BusinessWeek* by special permission. Copyright © 2007 by The McGraw-Hill Companies, Inc.

BusinessWeek Case in the News [LO 1, 2, 3, 5, 6]

It's All About the Face-to-Face

Some road warriors fly commercial. Others take the corporate jet. Some pack their own bags. Others keep complete wardrobes in major cities. Some work through the entire plane ride. Others sleep. But if there is one thing these globetrotters agree on, it's that there is no substitute for face time—with the Abu Dhabi moneyman who holds the key to the future; with the underling who is AWOL on e-mail; with the spouse and kids, who have been a little sullen and exasperated of late.

Schmoozing, humoring, hammering the table—all must be done in person. "I don't want to sound like a whirling dervish," says Paul Calello, Credit Suisse's investment banking chief. "But in a global world you have to get in front of your employees, spend time with your clients, and show commitment when it comes to joint ventures, mergers, and alliances. The key is thoughtful travel—traveling when necessary."

Yes, many predicted the end of face time. But, paradoxically, the great work diaspora unleashed by technology is making physical connection all the more important. As companies open more outposts in more emerging markets, the need to gather intensifies. That's why executives increasingly feel the inhuman pull of having to be in two, three, four places at one time. The road warrior's art is all about finessing the strategic calculation of where to be when; of what bets to make with one's time. How do road warriors do this? By knowing cultures, organizations, and who has the power. Their jobs may be global, but their understanding must be local. It's not just companies' operations that have gotten bigger. So have these jobs.

Not so long ago it seemed as though technology might make business travel, if not obsolete, then a whole lot rarer. We're not talking about teleporting—just simple things like smartphones, corporate wikis, and videoconferencing. Coca-Cola's president and CEO-designate, Muhtar Kent, has been flying around the globe for Coke since the late 1970s. "I thought 10 or 15 years ago when the concept of videoconferencing first came out that it's really going to take the place of travel," he recalls. Of course that didn't happen, and he now spends about 150 days a year in the corporate jet.

Outreach Pays

Kent considers travel key to meeting new people who might one day prove useful. Several years ago, he was eager to open a bottling plant in Albania but frustrated that Coke couldn't get the approvals it needed from the rudderless young government. A friend urged Kent to visit a doctor who was well-versed in local politics. He found the man's patients sitting on tangerine boxes because there were no chairs in the waiting room. "I'm interested in investing in your country," Kent recalls saying during the chat. Three years later, the doctor was Albania's first elected President, and 24 months after that Coke opened its first bottling plant in the country. The doctor-turned-President, Sali Berisha, cut the ribbon.

Kent has never forgotten the lesson. More recently, Coke was hoping to win the rights to the Vitaminwater brand from Glacéau, the U.S. beverage maker known for its so-called enhanced waters. Kent knew one of the company's minority owners was Ratan Tata of Tata Group. He'd never met Tata. So during a business trip to India, Kent requested a dinner with him—no agenda, just to get to know each other, he said. Oh, and by the way, was it O.K. to bring along a Glacéau executive? It was. "And 72 days later, we closed the deal."

Meeting the right people is all very well, but road warriors who haven't done their homework on the local potentate can run into big problems. Few understand this better than Bill Roedy, the chief of MTV Networks International. His job requires getting often risqué programming into as many countries as he can without offending local sensibilities. A history enthusiast, Roedy is pretty good at figuring out the local scene. Yet he found himself with a rare case of butterflies in mid-September as his flight from London was set to touch down in the Saudi Arabian city of Jiddah. Roedy was in town to persuade the mayor of Mecca to give his blessing to MTV Arabia, the network's biggest global launch, which had the potential to reach 200 million Arabs across the region. "Presidents and sheiks don't normally watch MTV, so we have to help them overcome stereotypical views they have," says Roedy. "Nobody was more important than the mayor of Mecca, the religious center of Islam. We had to get it right."

Despite a hectic schedule that included trips to Budapest (to launch MTV Hungary), Prague (to attend a sales meeting), and New York (to discuss 2008 budgets), Roedy carved out as much time in Saudi Arabia as he could. While there he attended recording sessions with the Arab rappers Jeddah Legends, where he learned that their lyrics tended to be about family and religion—themes that he would draw on during his meeting with the mayor of Mecca.

Finally the day arrived, and Roedy found himself providing assurances to a barrage of questions: Will there be opportunities to educate young people? (Yes.) Will there be a regular call to prayer? (Yes.) And, of course, there will be no skin, right, Mr. Roedy? (Correct.) To help seal the deal, Roedy attended an elaborate dinner in tents by the Red Sea. Ten days later, back at his London base, Roedy learned MTV Arabia could launch as scheduled in November. "Those meetings were crucial," he says.

Mark Sullivan, CEO of Whittman-Hart Consulting, which advises clients about information management, flies up to 300,000 miles a year and knows well the strain constant travel can put on a family. "My profession is riddled with failed marriages, broken families, and people who get swept up with the lifestyle," he says. Sullivan remains a road warrior for one reason: face time with his employees. About a year ago the firm's popular founder died. Sullivan, then president, knew voice messages, e-mail blasts, and memos wouldn't do. So he and two board members hopped on a plane and in two weeks traveled to nine offices around the U.S. to console bereft employees. "They needed a chance to swing away at you, to air concerns,"

says Sullivan. "If it's urgent, you've got to be physically there."

Ministering to clients, of course, is always urgent. Few know that better than Valerie E. Germain, a managing partner at global headhunting shop Heidrick & Struggles. Her job is recruiting executives for some of the world's biggest financial behemoths. Her clients often don't care if the person she is searching for hails from Hong Kong, Zürich, or London. The Thursday before Christmas, a client called to say he needed to meet with her for a few hours. In person. "They were like, 'Can you get to the side of a mountain in the Alps by Saturday at 6:00?' And the answer is 'Yes.' You travel round-trip for 31 hours to spend three hours with a client. If one wants to be global, you have to be willing to do that."

Recently, Germain was in London, only to find the candidate she wanted was in Zürich and wouldn't be back all week. Thinking he'd be perfect, she told him she'd meet him for dinner in five hours, rearranging seven scheduled interviews. "It's a risk-reward bet," says Germain. "You've got to figure out, do you risk pissing off seven other people for someone you think is the right candidate?" She bet right: The candidate took the job.

Even Masters of the Universe have little choice when called. In late November, Credit Suisse's Calello was in São Paulo, Brazil, attending a

party celebrating an investment in a local wealth management company. As his fellow revelers partied on into the night, the investment banking chief was on a red-eye to Manhattan—his third 12-hour plane ride in as many days. Calello had to be in New York because he and his executives had a meet-and-greet breakfast with a guy named Barack Obama.

Questions for Discussion

1. Why should some communication be conducted face-to-face?

2. What are the potential advantages of face-to-face communication?

3. What are the potential disadvantages of face-to-face communication?

4. How can managers and all employees determine if face-to-face communication is required in any given situation or if they can rely on other forms of communication such as a telephone conversation, e-mail, a videoconference, or a wiki?

CHAPTER 17

Managing Conflict, Politics, and Negotiation

Learning Objectives

After studying this chapter, you should be able to:

LO1 Explain why conflict arises, and identify the types and sources of conflict in organizations.

LO2 Describe conflict management strategies that managers can use to resolve conflict effectively.

LO3 Understand the nature of negotiation and why integrative bargaining is more effective than distributive negotiation.

LO4 Describe ways in which managers can promote integrative bargaining in organizations.

LO5 Explain why managers need to be attuned to organizational politics, and describe the political strategies that managers can use to become politically skilled.

A Manager's Challenge

Ravi Kant Effectively Manages Conflict

www.tata-daewoo.com

How can managers effectively handle conflict to achieve win–win situations?
Managers in all kinds of organizations, large and small, often face situations entailing conflict. How they manage the conflict can have dramatic effects on all parties involved. When conflict is effectively managed, there is much more potential for a win–win situation in which both parties to the conflict are better off as a result of collaboratively working together to achieve a resolution that is good for both parties.

Ravi Kant, who is currently the managing director of Tata Motors, approached a conflict situation he faced when he was executive director of Tata Motors' commercial vehicles unit, in precisely this manner.[1] The commercial vehicles unit of Tata Motors, the biggest automobile manufacturer in India, was interested in acquiring Daewoo's truck division based in Gunsan, South Korea, to increase its capabilities.[2] The Korean truck division was doing poorly, and an auction was being held in Korea to sell off the unit. When Kant traveled to Korea, he realized that there was resistance among some managers and employees at the Daewoo truck division to being potentially taken over by Tata Motors, who were concerned about what such a takeover would mean for the future of their company. Rather than trying to force the deal through, Kant grasped the fact that he needed to pave the way for mutual understanding.[3]

Kant arranged for Tata managers who were trying to negotiate the deal to take lessons in the Korean language so that they could better communicate with the Koreans.[4] He had brochures and other documents about Tata translated into Korean. Tata managers made presentations to multiple parties involved in the auction including Daewoo managers and employees, the head of the

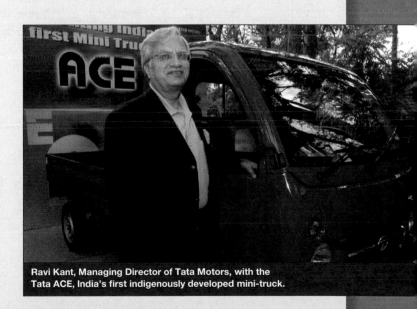

Ravi Kant, Managing Director of Tata Motors, with the Tata ACE, India's first indigenously developed mini-truck.

local auto association, Gunsun's mayor, and government decision makers in Seoul, Korea, including the prime minister. In these presentations, Tata managers indicated that if Tata were to win the auction, Daewoo employees would be able to keep their jobs and efforts would focus on building the Daewoo truck unit into a key exporter while integrating it into Tata Motors (and the larger Tata Group of which it is a part). Kant and Tata's efforts paid off and Tata purchased Daewoo's truck division for $102 million.[5] As Kwang-Ok Chae, CEO of Tata Daewoo who won the "CEO Korea Award 2007" from South Korea's *Economic Review* magazine,[6] indicates, "Tata had done its homework in everything needed to do business here."[7]

Throughout the process, Tata managers showed that they had respect for Daewoo employees and managers. In fact, whenever the Tata Group, a conglomerate of over 95 companies with combined revenues exceeding $28 billion,[8] has acquired a company outside of India, it has never laid off employees of the acquired company or closed down any of its operations.[9] It also tends to retain local top managers in key positions. A joint management board is typically formed to integrate the companies, overcome cultural misunderstandings, form mutual goals, and help make key decisions.[10]

At Tata Daewoo, a joint board of directors was created and Kwang-Ok Chae retained his top management position as CEO of the company.[11] When Kant requested that two Tata top managers advise him, Chae made them a part of his top management team. Together, Indian and Korean managers focused on ways to increase Tata Daewoo's product line and exports. While formerly, Daewoo focused predominantly on the Korean market, today Tata Daewoo is a major exporter of heavy trucks and its revenues have increased substantially since being bought by Tata.[12] Tata Daewoo is the second biggest manufacturer of heavy-duty trucks in Korea and now exports trucks to over 60 countries, including countries in the Middle East, South Africa, Eastern Europe, and Southeast Asia.[13]

Clearly, the process of acquiring a company can be fraught with the potential for conflict, which, if not effectively managed can lead both the acquiring company and the company being acquired worse off. The collaborative way in which the acquisition that cumulated in the creation of Tata Daewoo was handled enabled both parties to be better off as a result of the acquisition. Tata Daewoo is now a successful company, employees' and managers' jobs are secure, and the Tata Group as a whole is better off as a result of the acquisition. As Choi Jai Choon, a South Korean labor union leader, indicates, "It's turned out to be a win–win situation."[14]

Overview

Successful leaders such as Ravi Kant in "A Manager's Challenge" are able to effectively use their power to influence others and to manage conflict to achieve win–win solutions. In Chapter 14 we described how managers, as leaders, exert influence over other people to achieve group and organizational goals and how managers' sources of power enable them to exert such influence. In this chapter we describe why managers need to develop the skills necessary to manage organizational conflict, politics, and negotiation if they are going to be effective and achieve their goals, as does Ravi Kant.

We describe conflict and the strategies that managers can use to resolve it effectively. We discuss one major conflict resolution technique, negotiation, in detail, outlining the steps managers can take to be good negotiators. Lastly, we discuss the nature of organizational politics, and the political strategies that managers can use to maintain and expand their power and use it effectively. By the end of this chapter, you will appreciate why managers must develop the skills necessary to manage these important organizational processes if they are to be effective and achieve organizational goals.

Organizational Conflict

organizational conflict
The discord that arises when the goals, interests, or values of different individuals or groups are incompatible and those individuals or groups block or thwart one another's attempts to achieve their objectives.

Organizational conflict is the discord that arises when the goals, interests, or values of different individuals or groups are incompatible and those individuals or groups block or thwart one another's attempts to achieve their objectives.[15] Conflict is an inevitable part of organizational life because the goals of different stakeholders such as managers and workers are often incompatible. Organizational conflict also can exist between departments and divisions that compete for resources or even between managers who may be competing for promotion to the next level in the organizational hierarchy.

It is important for managers to develop the skills necessary to manage conflict effectively. In addition, the level of conflict present in an organization has important implications for organizational performance. Figure 17.1 illustrates the relationship between organizational conflict and performance. At point A, there is little or no conflict and organizational performance suffers. Lack of conflict in an organization often signals that managers emphasize conformity at the expense of new ideas, are resistant to change, and strive for agreement rather than effective decision making. As the level of conflict increases from point A to point B, organizational effectiveness is likely to increase. When an organization has an optimum level of conflict (point B), managers are likely to be open to, and encourage, a variety of perspectives; look for ways to improve organizational functioning and effectiveness; and view debates and disagreements as a necessary ingredient for effective decision making. As the level of conflict increases from point B to point C, conflict escalates to the point where organizational performance suffers. When an organization has a dysfunctionally high level of conflict, managers are likely to waste organizational resources to achieve their own ends, to be more concerned about winning political battles than about doing what will lead to a competitive advantage for their organization, and to try to get even with their opponents rather than make good decisions.

Conflict is a force that needs to be managed rather than eliminated.[16] Managers should never try to eliminate all conflict but, rather, should try to keep conflict at a moderate and functional level to promote change efforts that benefit the organization. Additionally, managers should strive to keep conflict focused on substantive, task-based issues, and minimize conflict based on personal disagreements and animosities. To manage conflict,[17] managers must understand the types and sources of conflict and be familiar with certain strategies that can be effective in dealing with it.

Types of Conflict

There are several types of conflict in organizations: interpersonal, intragroup, intergroup, and interorganizational (see Figure 17.2).[18] Understanding how these types differ can help managers to deal with conflict.

INTERPERSONAL CONFLICT Interpersonal conflict is conflict between individual members of an organization, occurring because of differences in their goals or values. Two managers may experience interpersonal conflict when their values concerning protection of the environment differ. One manager may argue that the organization should do only what is required by law. The other manager may counter that the

Tension starts to build during an office meeting. Since some degree of conflict is inevitable and desirable, conflict is a force that needs to be managed.

Figure 17.1

The Effect of Conflict on Organizational Performance

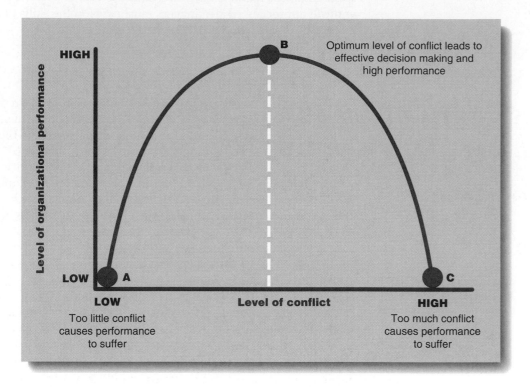

Figure 17.2

Types of Conflict in Organizations

organization should invest in equipment to reduce emissions even though the organization's current level of emissions is below the legal limit.

INTRAGROUP CONFLICT Intragroup conflict is conflict that arises within a group, team, or department. When members of the marketing department in a clothing company disagree about how they should spend budgeted advertising dollars for a new line of men's designer jeans, they are experiencing intragroup conflict. Some of the members want to spend all the money on advertisements in magazines. Others want to devote half of the money to billboards and ads in city buses and subways.

INTERGROUP CONFLICT Intergroup conflict is conflict that occurs between groups, teams, or departments. R&D departments, for example, sometimes experience intergroup conflict with production departments. Members of the R&D department may develop a new product that they think production can make inexpensively by using existing manufacturing capabilities. Members of the production department, however, may disagree and believe that the costs of making the product will be much higher. Managers of departments usually play a key role in managing intergroup conflicts such as this.

INTERORGANIZATIONAL CONFLICT   Interorganizational conflict is conflict that arises across organizations. Sometimes interorganizational conflict arises when managers in one organization feel that another organization is not behaving ethically and is threatening the well-being of certain stakeholder groups.

Sources of Conflict

Conflict in organizations springs from a variety of sources. The ones that we examine here are different goals and time horizons, overlapping authority, task interdependencies, different evaluation or reward systems, scarce resources, and status inconsistencies (see Figure 17.3).[19]

DIFFERENT GOALS AND TIME HORIZONS   Recall from Chapter 10 that an important managerial activity is organizing people and tasks into departments and divisions to accomplish an organization's goals. Almost inevitably, this grouping results in the creation of departments and divisions that have different goals and time horizons, and the result can be conflict. Production and production managers, for example, usually concentrate on efficiency and cost cutting; they have a relatively short time horizon and focus on producing quality goods or services in a timely and efficient manner. In contrast, marketing and marketing managers focus on sales and responsiveness to customers. Their time horizon is longer than that of production because they are trying to be responsive not only to customers' needs today but also to their changing needs in the future to build long-term customer loyalty. These fundamental differences between marketing and production are often breeding grounds for conflict.

Suppose production is behind schedule in its plan to produce a specialized product for a key customer. The marketing manager believes that the delay will reduce sales of the product and therefore insists that the product be delivered on time even if saving the production schedule means increasing costs by paying production workers overtime. The production manager says that she will happily schedule overtime if marketing will pay for it. Both managers' positions are reasonable from the perspective of their own departments, and conflict is likely.

Figure 17.3
Sources of Conflict in Organizations

OVERLAPPING AUTHORITY When two or more managers, departments, or functions claim authority for the same activities or tasks, conflict is likely.[20] This is precisely what happened when heirs of the Forman liquor distribution company, based in Washington, D.C., inherited the company from their parents. One of the heirs, Barry Forman, wanted to control the company and was reluctant to share power with the other heirs. Several of the heirs felt that they had authority over certain tasks crucial to Forman's success (such as maintaining good relationships with the top managers of liquor companies). What emerged was a battle of wills and considerable conflict, which escalated to the point of being dysfunctional, requiring that the family hire a consulting firm to help resolve it.[21]

TASK INTERDEPENDENCIES Have you ever been assigned a group project for one of your classes and had one group member who consistently failed to get things done on time? This probably created some conflict in your group because other group members were dependent on the late member's contributions to complete the project. Whenever individuals, groups, teams, or departments are interdependent, the potential for conflict exists.[22] With differing goals and time horizons, the managers of marketing and production come into conflict precisely because the departments are interdependent. Marketing is dependent on production for the goods it markets and sells, and production is dependent on marketing for creating demand for the things it makes.

DIFFERENT EVALUATION OR REWARD SYSTEMS The way in which interdependent groups, teams, or departments are evaluated and rewarded can be another source of conflict.[23] Production managers, for example, are evaluated and rewarded for their success in staying within budget or lowering costs while maintaining quality. So they are reluctant to take any steps that will increase costs, such as paying workers high overtime rates to finish a late order for an important customer. Marketing managers, in contrast, are evaluated and rewarded for their success in generating sales and satisfying customers. So they often think that overtime pay is a small price to pay for responsiveness to customers. Thus, conflict between production and marketing is rarely unexpected.

Whenever groups or teams are interdependent, the potential for conflict exists.

SCARCE RESOURCES Management is the process of acquiring, developing, protecting, and utilizing the resources that allow an organization to be efficient and effective (see Chapter 1). When resources are scarce, management is all the more difficult and conflict is likely.[24] For example, divisional managers may be in conflict over who has access to financial capital, and organizational members at all levels may be in conflict over who gets raises and promotions.

STATUS INCONSISTENCIES The fact that some individuals, groups, teams, or departments within an organization are more highly regarded than others in the organization can also create conflict. In some restaurants, for example, the chefs have relatively higher status than the people who wait on tables. Nevertheless, the chefs receive customers' orders from the wait staff, and the wait staff can return to the chefs food that their customers or they think is not acceptable. This status inconsistency—high-status chefs taking orders from low-status wait staff—can be the source of considerable conflict between chefs and the wait staff. For this reason, some restaurants require that the wait staff put orders on a spindle, thereby reducing the amount of direct order giving from the wait staff to the chefs.[25]

Conflict Management Strategies

LO2   Describe conflict management strategies that managers can use to resolve conflict effectively.

compromise A way of managing conflict in which each party is concerned about not only its own goal accomplishment but also the goal accomplishment of the other party and is willing to engage in a give-and-take exchange and make concessions.

collaboration A way of managing conflict in which both parties try to satisfy their goals by coming up with an approach that leaves them both better off and does not require concessions on issues that are important to either party.

accommodation An ineffective conflict-handling approach in which one party, typically with weaker power, gives in to the demands of the other, typically more powerful, party.

avoidance An ineffective conflict-handling approach in which the two parties try to ignore the problem and do nothing to resolve their differences.

competition An ineffective conflict-handling approach in which each party tries to maximize its own gain and has little interest in understanding the other party's position and arriving at a solution that will allow both parties to achieve their goals.

If an organization is to achieve its goals, managers must be able to resolve conflicts in a functional manner. *Functional conflict resolution* means that the conflict is settled by compromise or by collaboration between the parties in conflict (later in the chapter we discuss other, typically less functional ways in which conflicts are sometimes resolved).[26] **Compromise** is possible when each party is concerned about not only its own goal accomplishment but also the goal accomplishment of the other party and is willing to engage in a give-and-take exchange and to make concessions until a reasonable resolution of the conflict is reached. **Collaboration** is a way of handling conflict in which the parties try to satisfy their goals without making any concessions but, instead, come up with a way to resolve their differences that leaves them both better off.[27] In "A Manager's Challenge," collaboration was used to help resolve the potential conflict that existed when Ravi Kant and Tata Motors were in the process of trying to acquire Daewoo's truck division in Gunsan, South Korea.[28] Kant and Tata Motors wanted to acquire Daewoo's truck division as they viewed it as an opportunity to increase the overall capabilities of Tata Motors. Some employees and managers at the Daewoo truck division were resistant to having their company acquired by Tata Motors and were concerned about what the future would hold for them and their company if the acquisition took place. Through building mutual understanding, Kant and Tata Motors were able to successfully acquire the Daewoo truck division and achieve their goal and managers and employees at the Daewoo truck division were able to achieve their goal of having the future of their jobs and company secure.[29]

In addition to compromise and collaboration, there are three other ways in which conflicts are sometimes handled: accommodation, avoidance, and competition.[30] When **accommodation** takes place, one party to the conflict simply gives in to the demands of the other party. Accommodation typically takes place when one party has more power than the other and is able to pursue its goal attainment at the expense of the weaker party. From an organizational perspective, accommodation is often ineffective, as the two parties are not cooperating with each other, they are unlikely to want to cooperate in the future, and the weaker party who gives in or accommodates the more powerful party might look for ways to get back at the stronger party in the future.

When conflicts are handled by **avoidance,** the two parties to a conflict try to ignore the problem and do nothing to resolve the disagreement. Avoidance is often ineffective since the real source of the disagreement has not been addressed, conflict is likely to continue, and communication and cooperation are hindered.

Competition occurs when each party to a conflict tries to maximize its own gain and has little interest in understanding the other party's position and arriving at a solution that will allow both parties to achieve their goals. Competition can actually escalate levels of conflict as each party tries to outmaneuver the other. As a way of handling conflict, competition is ineffective for the organization since the two sides to a conflict are more concerned about "winning" the battle than cooperating to arrive at a solution that is best for the organization and acceptable to both sides. Handling conflicts through accommodation, avoidance, or competition is ineffective from an organizational point of view because the two parties do not cooperate with each other and work toward a mutually acceptable solution to their differences.

When the parties to a conflict are willing to cooperate with each other and, through compromise or collaboration, devise a solution that each finds acceptable, an organization is more likely to achieve its goals.[31] Conflict management strategies that managers can use to ensure that conflicts are resolved in a functional manner focus on individuals and on the organization as a whole. Below, we describe four strategies that focus on individuals: increasing awareness of the sources of conflict, increasing diversity awareness and skills, practicing job rotation or temporary assignments, and using permanent transfers or dismissals when necessary. We also describe two strategies that focus on the organization as a whole: changing an organization's structure or culture and directly altering the source of conflict.

STRATEGIES FOCUSED ON INDIVIDUALS

INCREASING AWARENESS OF THE SOURCES OF CONFLICT   Sometimes conflict arises because of communication problems and interpersonal misunderstandings. For example, differences in linguistic styles (see Chapter 16) may lead some men in work teams to talk more, and take more credit for ideas, than women in those teams. These communication differences can result in conflict when the men incorrectly assume that the women are uninterested or less capable because they participate less and the women incorrectly assume that the men are being bossy and are not interested in their ideas because they seem to do all the talking. By increasing people's awareness of this source of conflict, managers can help to resolve conflict functionally. Once men and women realize that the source of their conflict is differences in linguistic styles, they can take steps to interact with each other more effectively. The men can give the women more of a chance to provide input, and the women can be more proactive in providing this input.

Sometimes personalities clash in an organization. In these situations, too, managers can help resolve conflicts functionally by increasing organizational members' awareness of the source of their difficulties. For example, some people who are not inclined to take risks may come into conflict with those who are prone to taking risks. The non-risk takers might complain that those who welcome risk propose outlandish ideas without justification, while the risk takers might complain that their innovative ideas are always getting shot down. When both types of people are made aware that their conflicts are due to fundamental differences in their ways of approaching problems, they will likely be better able to cooperate in coming up with innovative ideas that entail only moderate levels of risk.

INCREASING DIVERSITY AWARENESS AND SKILLS   Interpersonal conflicts also can arise because of diversity. Older workers may feel uncomfortable or resentful about reporting to a younger supervisor, a Hispanic may feel singled out in a group of non-Hispanic workers, or a female top manager may feel that members of her predominantly male top-management team band together whenever one of them disagrees with one of her proposals. Whether these feelings are justified, they are likely to cause recurring conflicts. Many of the techniques we described in Chapter 5 for increasing diversity awareness and skills can help managers effectively manage diversity and resolve conflicts that have their origins in differences between organizational members.

Increasing diversity awareness and skills can be especially important when organizations expand globally and seek to successfully integrate operations in other countries, as illustrated in the following "Managing Globally."

Managing Globally

Xplane Integrates Operations in Spain

Xplane is a small consulting and design firm with offices in Portland, Oregon, and St. Louis, Missouri, and around 45 employees in the United States.[32] When Dave Gray, founder and chairman of the company, decided to expand operations by acquiring a small firm in Madrid, Spain, with around 6 employees, in the hopes of both expanding operations in Europe as well as building capabilities to provide services to companies in Spanish-speaking countries, he learned firsthand the importance of increasing diversity awareness and skills. Misunderstandings and conflict arose, ranging from a St. Louis employee inadvertently insulting Spanish employees during a dinner in Madrid to Spanish employees feeling excluded from communications and not integrated within Xplane's operations.[33] For example, Stephen O'Flynn, who is a project manager in the Madrid office and originally from Ireland, felt that some employees in the two U.S. offices almost seemed to forget that the company had a third office in Spain.[34]

Small Business

Gray realized that given cultural differences and the geographic distance between the U.S. and Spanish offices, it was vital to both improve communication across offices and provide more opportunities for employees in the different offices to interact with each other and establish a common understanding. E-mails of a company nature, for example, should not just be sent to U.S. employees but also to employees in Spain. The company changed to a Web-based phone system so that employees would only need to dial 4 numbers to make calls between Spain and the United States rather than 13.[35] Wikis were created with photos of all employees. O'Flynn made frequent phone calls to employees in Portland and St. Louis to discuss projects with them and encouraged other employees in the Madrid office to similarly reach out. As he indicates, "I did a lot of brokering to get people talking."[36]

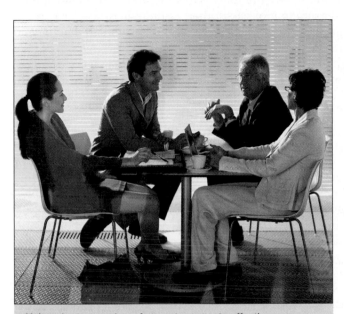

Xplane took a number of steps to promote effective communication among employees in different countries including an employee exchange program.

Gray also realized that it was important for U.S. and Spanish employees to have a chance to interact face-to-face and for more extended periods of time than a phone conversation, a dinner, or one-shot meeting in either country. To accomplish this, he created an exchange program for employees.[37] As part of the program, employees in each country have the opportunity to visit and work with their counterparts in the other country to build relationships, increase their diversity awareness and skills, and learn from each other. For example, a U.S. employee can stay in an apartment rented by Xplane in Madrid for a week and work with employees in the Spanish office. Similarly, a Spanish employee can stay in an apartment rented by Xplane in Portland and work with employees in Portland for a week.[38] As Wood indicates, "We tried to close the gap through technology, but ultimately we had to buy a lot of airline tickets."[39] By taking steps to increase diversity awareness and skills and foster effective communication, managers like Wood not only help to alleviate sources of misunderstanding and potential conflict but also increase their chances of reaping the benefits that different perspectives and points of view can bring.

PRACTICING JOB ROTATION OR TEMPORARY ASSIGNMENTS Sometimes conflicts arise because individual organizational members simply do not have a good understanding of the work activities and demands that others in an organization face. A financial analyst, for example, may be required to submit monthly reports to a member of the accounting department. These reports have a low priority for the analyst, who typically turns them in a couple of days late. On the due date, the accountant always calls up the financial analyst, and conflict ensues as the accountant describes in detail why she must have the reports on time and the financial analyst describes everything else he needs to do. In situations such as this, job rotation or temporary assignments, which expand organizational members' knowledge base and appreciation of other departments, can be a useful way of resolving the conflict. If the financial analyst spends some time working in the accounting department, he may appreciate better the need for timely reports. Similarly, a temporary assignment in the finance department may help the accountant realize the demands a financial analyst faces and the need to streamline unnecessary aspects of reporting.

USING PERMANENT TRANSFERS OR DISMISSALS WHEN NECESSARY   Sometimes when other conflict resolution strategies do not work, managers may need to take more drastic steps, including permanent transfers or dismissals.

Suppose two first-line managers who work in the same department are always at each other's throats; frequent bitter conflicts arise between them even though they both seem to get along well with the other employees. No matter what their supervisor does to increase their understanding of each other, the conflicts keep occurring. In this case, the supervisor may want to transfer one or both managers so that they do not have to interact as frequently.

When dysfunctionally high levels of conflict occur among top managers who cannot resolve their differences and understand each other, it may be necessary for one of them to leave the company. This is how Gerald Levin managed such conflict among top managers when he was chairman of Time Warner (later Levin was CEO of AOL Time Warner). Robert Daly and Terry Semel, one of the most respected management teams in Hollywood and top managers in the Warner Brothers film company, had been in conflict with Michael Fuchs, a long-time veteran of Time Warner and head of the music division, for two years. As Semel described it, the company "was running like a dysfunctional family, and it needed one management team to run it."[40] Levin realized that Time Warner's future success rested on resolving this conflict, that it was unlikely that Fuchs would ever be able to work effectively with Daly and Semel, and that he risked losing Daly and Semel to another company if he did not resolve the conflict. Faced with that scenario, Levin asked Fuchs to resign.[41]

STRATEGIES FOCUSED ON THE WHOLE ORGANIZATION

CHANGING AN ORGANIZATION'S STRUCTURE OR CULTURE   Conflict can signal the need for changes in an organization's structure or culture. Sometimes, managers can effectively resolve conflict by changing the organizational structure they use to group people and tasks.[42] As an organization grows, for example, the *functional structure* (composed of departments such as marketing, finance, and production) that was effective when the organization was small may cease to be effective, and a shift to a *product structure* might effectively resolve conflicts (see Chapter 10).

Managers also can effectively resolve conflicts by increasing levels of integration in an organization. Recall from Chapter 15 that Hallmark Cards increased integration by using cross-functional teams to produce new cards. The use of cross-functional teams speeded new card development and helped to resolve conflicts between different departments. Now, when a writer and an artist have a conflict over the appropriateness of the artist's illustrations, they do not pass criticisms back and forth from one department to another, because they are on the same team and can directly resolve the issue on the spot.

Sometimes managers may need to take steps to change an organization's culture to resolve conflict (see Chapter 3). Norms and values in an organizational culture might inadvertently promote dysfunctionally high levels of conflict that are difficult to resolve. For instance, norms that stress respect for formal authority may create conflict that is difficult to resolve when an organization creates self-managed work teams and managers' roles and the structure of authority in the organization change. Values stressing individual competition may make it difficult to resolve conflicts when organizational members need to put others' interests ahead of their own. In circumstances such as these, taking steps to change norms and values can be an effective conflict resolution strategy.

ALTERING THE SOURCE OF CONFLICT   When the source of conflict is overlapping authority, different evaluation or reward systems, or status inconsistencies, managers can sometimes effectively resolve the conflict by directly altering its source. For example, managers can clarify the chain of command and reassign tasks and responsibilities to resolve conflicts due to overlapping authority.

Negotiation

LO3 Understand the nature of negotiation and why integrative bargaining is more effective than distributive negotiation.

A particularly important conflict resolution technique for managers and other organizational members to use in situations where the parties to a conflict have approximately equal levels of power is negotiation. During **negotiation,** the parties to a conflict try to come up with a solution acceptable to themselves by considering various alternative ways to allocate resources to each other.[43] Sometimes the two sides involved in a conflict negotiate directly with each other. Other times, a **third-party negotiator** is relied on. Third-party negotiators are impartial individuals who are not directly involved in the conflict and have special expertise in handling conflicts and negotiations;[44] they are relied on to help the two negotiating parties reach an acceptable resolution of their conflict.[45] When a third-party negotiator acts as a **mediator,** his or her role in the negotiation process is to facilitate an effective negotiation between the two parties; mediators do not force either party to make concessions, nor can they force an agreement to resolve a conflict. **Arbitrators,** on the other hand, are third-party negotiators who can impose what they believe is a fair solution to a dispute that both parties are obligated to abide by.[46]

negotiation A method of conflict resolution in which the two parties consider various alternative ways to allocate resources to each other in order to come up with a solution acceptable to both of them.

third-party negotiator An impartial individual with expertise in handling conflicts and negotiations who helps parties in conflict reach an acceptable solution.

mediator A third-party negotiator who facilitates negotiations but has no authority to impose a solution.

arbitrator A third-party negotiator who can impose what he or she thinks is a fair solution to a conflict that both parties are obligated to abide by.

distributive negotiation Adversarial negotiation in which the parties in conflict compete to win the most resources while conceding as little as possible.

integrative bargaining Cooperative negotiation in which the parties in conflict work together to achieve a resolution that is good for them both.

LO4 Describe ways in which managers can promote integrative bargaining in organizations.

Distributive Negotiation and Integrative Bargaining

There are two major types of negotiation—distributive negotiation and integrative bargaining.[47] In **distributive negotiation,** the two parties perceive that they have a "fixed pie" of resources that they need to divide.[48] They take a competitive, adversarial stance. Each party realizes that he or she must concede something but is out to get the lion's share of the resources.[49] The parties see no need to interact with each other in the future and do not care if their interpersonal relationship is damaged or destroyed by their competitive negotiation.[50] In distributive negotiations, conflicts are handled by competition.

In **integrative bargaining,** the parties perceive that they might be able to increase the resource pie by trying to come up with a creative solution to the conflict. They do not view the conflict competitively, as a win-or-lose situation; instead, they view it cooperatively, as a win–win situation in which both parties can gain. Trust, information sharing, and the desire of both parties to achieve a good resolution of the conflict characterize integrative bargaining.[51] In integrative bargaining, conflicts are handled through collaboration and/or compromise.

Consider how Adrian Hofbeck and Joseph Steinberg, partners in a successful German restaurant in the Midwest, resolved their recent conflict. Hofbeck and Steinberg founded the restaurant 15 years ago, share management responsibilities, and share equally in the restaurant's profits. Hofbeck recently decided that he wanted to retire and sell the restaurant, but retirement was the last thing Steinberg had in mind; he wanted to continue to own and manage the restaurant. Distributive negotiation was out of the question, for Hofbeck and Steinberg were close friends and valued their friendship; neither wanted to do something that would hurt the other or their continuing relationship. So they opted for integrative bargaining, which they thought would help them resolve their conflict so that both could achieve their goals and maintain their friendship.

Strategies to Encourage Integrative Bargaining

There are five strategies that managers in all kinds of organizations can rely on to facilitate integrative bargaining and avoid distributive negotiation: emphasizing superordinate goals; focusing on the problem, not the people; focusing on interests, not demands; creating new options for joint gain; and focusing on what is fair (see Table 17.1).[52] Hofbeck and Steinberg used each of these strategies to resolve their conflict.

Table 17.1
Negotiation Strategies for Integrative Bargaining

- Empasize superordinate goals.
- Focus on the problem, not the people.
- Focus on interests, not demands.
- Create new options for joint gain.
- Focus on what is fair.

EMPHASIZING SUPERORDINATE GOALS *Superordinate goals* are goals that both parties agree to regardless of the source of their conflict. Increasing organizational effectiveness, increasing responsiveness to customers, and gaining a competitive advantage are just a few of the many superordinate goals that members of an organization can emphasize during integrative bargaining. Superordinate goals help parties in conflict to keep in mind the big picture and the fact that they are working together for a larger purpose or goal despite their disagreements. Hofbeck and Steinberg emphasized three superordinate goals during their bargaining: ensuring that the restaurant continued to survive and prosper, allowing Hofbeck to retire, and allowing Steinberg to remain an owner and manager as long as he wished.

FOCUSING ON THE PROBLEM, NOT THE PEOPLE People who are in conflict may not be able to resist the temptation to focus on the other party's shortcomings and weaknesses, thereby personalizing the conflict. Instead of attacking the problem, the parties to the conflict attack each other. This approach is inconsistent with integrative bargaining and can easily lead both parties into a distributive negotiation mode. All parties to a conflict need to keep focused on the problem or on the source of the conflict and avoid the temptation to discredit one another.

Given their strong friendship, this was not much of an issue for Hofbeck and Steinberg, but they still had to be on their guard to avoid personalizing the conflict. Steinberg recalls that when they were having a hard time coming up with a solution, he started thinking that Hofbeck, a healthy 57-year-old, was lazy to want to retire so young: "If only he wasn't so lazy, we would never be in the mess we're in right now." Steinberg never mentioned these thoughts to Hofbeck (who later admitted that sometimes he was annoyed with Steinberg for being such a workaholic), because he realized that doing so would hurt their chances for reaching an integrative solution.

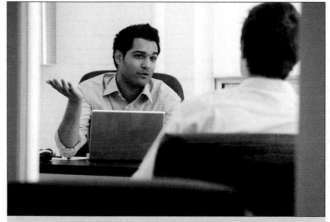

Remaining focused on superordinate goals and coming up with new options for joint gain can facilitate integrative bargaining.

FOCUSING ON INTERESTS, NOT DEMANDS Demands are *what* a person wants; interests are *why* the person wants them. When two people are in conflict, it is unlikely that the demands of both can be met. Their underlying interests, however, can be met, and meeting them is what integrative bargaining is all about.

Hofbeck's demand was that they sell the restaurant and split the proceeds. Steinberg's demand was that they keep the restaurant and maintain the status quo. Obviously, both demands could not be met, but perhaps their interests could be. Hofbeck wanted to be able to retire, invest his share of the money from the restaurant, and live off the returns on the investment. Steinberg wanted to continue managing, owning, and deriving income from the restaurant.

CREATING NEW OPTIONS FOR JOINT GAIN Once two parties to a conflict focus on their interests, they are on the road to achieving creative solutions to the conflict that will benefit them both. This win–win scenario means that rather than having a fixed set of alternatives from which to choose, the two parties can come up with new alternatives that might even expand the resource pie.

Hofbeck and Steinberg came up with three such alternatives. First, even though Steinberg did not have the capital, he could buy out Hofbeck's share of the restaurant. Hofbeck would provide the financing for the purchase, and in return Steinberg would pay him a reasonable return on his investment (the same kind of return he could have obtained had he taken his money out of the restaurant and invested it). Second, the partners could seek to sell Hofbeck's share in the restaurant to a third party under the stipulation that Steinberg would continue to manage the restaurant and receive income for his services. Third, the partners could continue to jointly own the restaurant. Steinberg would manage it and receive a proportionally greater share of its profits than Hofbeck, who would be an absentee owner not involved in day-to-day operations but would still receive a return on his investment in the restaurant.

FOCUSING ON WHAT IS FAIR Focusing on what is fair is consistent with the principle of distributive justice, which emphasizes the fair distribution of outcomes based on the meaningful contributions that people make to organizations (see Chapter 5). It is likely that two parties in conflict will disagree on certain points and prefer different alternatives that each party believes may better serve his or her own interests or maximize his or her own outcomes. Emphasizing fairness and distributive justice will help the two parties come to a mutual agreement about what the best solution is to the problem.

Steinberg and Hofbeck agreed that Hofbeck should be able to cut his ties with the restaurant if he chose to do so. They thus decided to pursue the second alternative described above and seek a suitable buyer for Hofbeck's share. They were successful in finding an investor who was willing to buy out Hofbeck's share and let Steinberg continue managing the restaurant. And they remained good friends.

When managers pursue these five strategies and encourage other organizational members to do so, they are more likely to be able to effectively resolve their conflicts through integrative bargaining. In addition, throughout the negotiation process, managers and other organizational members need to be aware of, and on their guard against, the biases that can lead to faulty decision making (see Chapter 7).[53]

organizational politics Activities that managers engage in to increase their power and to use power effectively to achieve their goals and overcome resistance or opposition.

Organizational Politics

Managers must develop the skills necessary to manage organizational conflict in order for an organization to be effective. Suppose, however, that top managers are in conflict over the best strategy for an organization to pursue or the best structure to adopt to utilize organizational resources efficiently. In such situations, resolving conflict is often difficult, and the parties to the conflict resort to organizational politics and political strategies to try to resolve the conflict in their favor.

Organizational politics are the activities that managers (and other members of an organization) engage in to increase their power and to use power effectively to achieve their goals and overcome resistance or opposition.[54] Managers often engage in organizational politics to resolve conflicts in their favor.

Political strategies are the specific tactics that managers (and other members of an organization) use to increase their power and to use power effectively to influence and gain the support of other people while overcoming resistance or opposition. Political strategies are especially important when managers are planning and implementing major changes in an organization: Managers need not only to gain support for their change initiatives and influence organizational members to behave in new ways but also to overcome often strong opposition from people who feel threatened by the change and prefer the status quo. By increasing their power, managers are better able to make needed changes. In addition to increasing their power, managers also must make sure that they use their power in a way that actually enables them to influence others.

LO5 Explain why managers need to be attuned to organizational politics, and describe the political strategies that managers can use to become politically skilled.

political strategies Tactics that managers use to increase their power and to use power effectively to influence and gain the support of other people while overcoming resistance or opposition.

The Importance of Organizational Politics

The term *politics* has a negative connotation for many people. Some may think that managers who are political have risen to the top not because of their own merit and capabilities but because of whom they know. Or people may think that political managers are self-interested and wield power to benefit themselves, not their organization. There is a grain of truth to this negative connotation. Some managers do appear to misuse their power for personal benefit at the expense of their organization's effectiveness.

Nevertheless, organizational politics are often a positive force. Managers striving to make needed changes often encounter resistance from individuals and groups who feel threatened and wish to preserve the status quo. Effective managers engage in politics to gain support for and implement needed changes. Similarly, managers often face resistance from other managers who disagree with their goals for a group or for the organization and with what they are trying to accomplish. Engaging in organizational politics can help managers overcome this resistance and achieve their goals.

Indeed, managers cannot afford to ignore organizational politics. Everyone engages in politics to a degree—other managers, coworkers, and subordinates, as well as people outside an organization, such as suppliers. Those who try to ignore politics might as well bury their heads in the sand because in all likelihood they will be unable to gain support for their initiatives and goals.

Political Strategies for Gaining and Maintaining Power

Managers who use political strategies to increase and maintain their power are better able to influence others to work toward the achievement of group and organizational goals. (Recall from Chapter 14 that legitimate, reward, coercive, expert, and referent powers help managers influence others as leaders.) By controlling uncertainty, making themselves irreplaceable, being in a central position, generating resources, and building alliances, managers can increase their power (see Figure 17.4).[55] We next look at each of these strategies.

CONTROLLING UNCERTAINTY   Uncertainty is a threat for individuals, groups, and whole organizations and can interfere with effective performance and goal attainment. For example, uncertainty about job security is threatening for many workers and may cause top performers (who have the best chance of finding another job) to quit and take a more secure position with another organization. When an R&D department faces uncertainty about customer preferences, its members may waste valuable resources to develop a product, such as smokeless cigarettes, that customers do not want. When top managers face uncertainty about global demand, they may fail to export products to countries that want them and thus may lose a source of competitive advantage.

Managers who are able to control and reduce uncertainty for other managers, teams, departments, and the organization as a whole are likely to see their power increase.[56] Managers of labor unions gain power when they can eliminate uncertainty over job security for workers. Marketing and sales managers gain power when they can eliminate uncertainty for other departments such as R&D by accurately forecasting customers' changing preferences. Top managers gain power when they are knowledgeable about global demand for an organization's products. Managers who are able to control uncertainty are likely to be in demand and be sought after by other organizations.

MAKING ONESELF IRREPLACEABLE   Managers gain power when they have valuable knowledge and expertise that allow them to perform activities that no one else can handle. This is the essence of being irreplaceable.[57] The more central these activities are to organizational effectiveness, the more power managers gain from being irreplaceable.

Figure 17.4
Political Strategies for Increasing Power

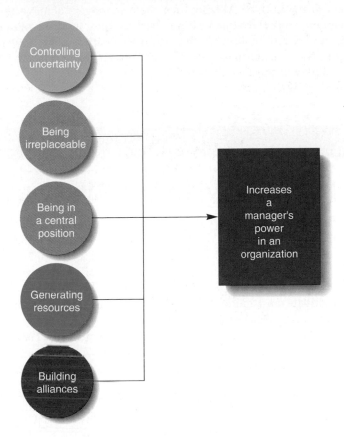

BEING IN A CENTRAL POSITION Managers in central positions are responsible for activities that are directly connected to an organization's goals and sources of competitive advantage and often are located in central positions in important communication networks in an organization.[58] Managers in key positions have control over crucial organizational activities and initiatives and have access to important information. Other organizational members are dependent on them for their knowledge, expertise, advice, and support, and the success of the organization as a whole is seen as riding on these managers. These consequences of being in a central position are likely to increase managers' power.

Managers who are outstanding performers, have a wide knowledge base, and have made important and visible contributions to their organizations are likely to be offered central positions that will increase their power.

GENERATING RESOURCES Organizations need three kinds of resources to be effective: (1) input resources such as raw materials, skilled workers, and financial capital; (2) technical resources such as machinery and computers; and (3) knowledge resources such as marketing, information technology, or engineering expertise. To the extent that a manager is able to generate one or more of these kinds of resources for an organization, that manager's power is likely to increase.[59] In universities, for example, professors who win large grants to fund their research, from associations such as the National Science Foundation and the Army Research Institute, gain power because of the financial resources they are generating for their departments and the university as a whole.

BUILDING ALLIANCES When managers build alliances, they develop mutually beneficial relationships with people both inside and outside the organization. The two parties to an alliance support one another because doing so is in their best interests, and both parties benefit from the alliance. Alliances provide managers with power because they provide the managers with support for their initiatives. Partners to alliances provide support because they know that the managers will reciprocate when their partners need support. Alliances can help managers achieve their goals and implement needed changes in organizations because they increase managers' levels of power. As illustrated in the following "Focus on Diversity," many powerful top managers such as Indra Nooyi, chairman and CEO of PepsiCo, are particularly skilled when it comes to building alliances.[60]

Focus on Diversity

Indra Nooyi Builds Alliances

By all counts, Indra Nooyi, is a powerful business leader.[61] As CEO and chairman of PepsiCo, she oversees a company with over $39 billion in revenues and over 185,000 employees; Pepsi-Cola, Lay's, Doritos, Tropicana, Mountain Dew, Gatorade, and Quaker are amongst Pepsi's many well-known brands.[62] She effectively uses her vision for PepsiCo, "Performance With Purpose," to both motivate and guide Pepsi employees and communicate PepsiCo's stance on important issues such as health, obesity, and protecting the natural environment around the world.[63] In 2008, she was included in *Time* magazine's list of "The World's Most Influential People";[64] in 2007, she was ranked the most powerful woman in business by *Fortune* magazine and ranked 22nd in *Fortune*'s "25 Most Powerful People in Business."[65]

Nooyi, born and raised in India, was senior vice president of strategic planning at PepsiCo before assuming the top post on October 1, 2006.[66] When the PepsiCo's board of directors was in the process of deciding who would be the next CEO of the company, two senior executives at PepsiCo were under consideration, Nooyi and Michael White, vice chairman.[67] When Nooyi found out that the board had chosen her, one of her top priorities was to ensure that White would stay at PepsiCo, the two would maintain the great relationship they had with each other that had evolved from years of working together, and she would have his support and advice.[68] At the time, White was on vacation at his beach house in Cape Cod, Massachusetts. Nooyi flew to Cape Cod and the two walked on the beach, had ice cream together, and even played a duet (Nooyi and White both are very fond of music and in this case, he played the piano and she sang). Prior to leaving Cape Cod, she told White, "Tell me whatever I need to do to keep you, and I will."[69] Ultimately, White decided to remain at PepsiCo and is currently CEO of PepsiCo International as well as vice chairman of PepsiCo.[70] At a meeting announcing Nooyi's appointment, Nooyi told employees, "I treat Mike as my partner. He could easily have been CEO." White said, "I play the piano and Indra sings."[71]

Nooyi excels at building alliances both inside and outside of PepsiCo. Given the breadth of her responsibilities, she decided to increase the team of top managers she works closely with to 29 (which is around double the size of the team before she became CEO). She has good relations with key decision makers around the world in both government and business. And she frequently consults with and seeks the advice of three former CEOs of PepsiCo, Stephen Reinemund, Roger Enrico, and Don Kendall, who she considers her friends.[72]

Indra Nooyi excels at building alliances both inside and outside of PepsiCo.

Nooyi also excels at gaining the support of PepsiCo's employees.[73] She is down-to-earth, sincere, and genuine in her interactions with employees and also comfortable just being herself; she has been known to walk barefoot in the halls of PepsiCo on occasion and sometimes sings at gatherings. Celebrations for employees' birthdays include a cake. Nooyi also recognizes how employees' families are affected by their work and what a great source of support families can be, as a mother of two daughters.[74]

Of course, Nooyi faces a number of challenges at PepsiCo as she strives to make the company more globally focused (and less focused on the United States), make healthier food products, protect the natural environment, and look out for the well-being of employees in a troubled economy with rising prices for ingredients in PepsiCo's products.[75] Her exceptional skills at building alliances and gaining support will only help. As she indicates, ". . . you give the team of people a set of objectives and goals and get them all to buy into it, and they can move mountains."[76]

Many powerful top managers focus on building alliances not only inside their organizations but also with individuals, groups, and organizations in the task and general environments on which their organizations are dependent for resources. These individuals, groups, and organizations enter into alliances with managers because doing so is in their best interests and they know that they can count on the managers' support when they need it. When managers build alliances, they need to be on their guard to ensure that everything is aboveboard, ethical, and legal.

Political Strategies for Exercising Power

Politically skilled managers not only have a good understanding of, and ability to use, the five strategies to increase their power; they also have a good appreciation of strategies for exercising their power. These strategies generally focus on how managers can use their power *unobtrusively*.[77] When managers exercise power unobtrusively, other members of an organization may not be aware that the managers are using their power to influence them. They may think that they support these managers for a variety of reasons: because they believe it is the rational or logical thing to do, because they believe that doing so is in their own best interests, or because they believe that the position or decision that the managers are advocating is legitimate or appropriate.

The unobtrusive use of power may sound devious, but managers typically use this strategy to bring about change and achieve organizational goals. Political strategies for exercising power to gain the support and concurrence of others include relying on objective information, bringing in an outside expert, controlling the agenda, and making everyone a winner (see Figure 17.5).[78]

RELYING ON OBJECTIVE INFORMATION Managers require the support of others to achieve their goals, implement changes, and overcome opposition. One way for a manager to gain this support and overcome opposition is to rely on objective information that supports the manager's initiatives. Reliance on objective information leads others to support the manager because of the facts; objective information causes others to believe that what the manager is proposing is the proper course of action. By relying on objective information, politically skilled managers unobtrusively exercise their power to influence others.

Take the case of Mary Callahan, vice president of Better Built Cabinets, a small cabinet company in the Southeast. Callahan is extremely influential in the company; practically every new initiative that she proposes to the president and owner of the company is implemented. Why is Callahan able to use her power in the company so effectively? Whenever she has an idea for a new initiative that she thinks the company might pursue, she and her subordinates begin by collecting objective information supporting the initiative. Recently, Callahan decided that Better Built should develop

Figure 17.5
Political Strategies for Exercising Power

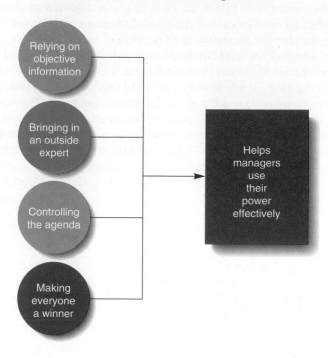

a line of high-priced European-style kitchen cabinets. Before presenting her proposal to Better Built's president, she compiled objective information showing that (1) there was strong unmet demand for these kinds of cabinets, (2) Better Built could manufacture them in its existing production facilities, and (3) the new line had the potential to increase Better Built's sales by 20% while not detracting from sales of the company's other cabinets. Presented with this information, the president agreed to Callahan's proposal. Moreover, the president and other members of Better Built whose cooperation was needed to implement the proposal supported it because they thought it would help Better Built gain a competitive advantage. Using objective information to support her position enabled Callahan to unobtrusively exercise her power and influence others to support her proposal.

BRINGING IN AN OUTSIDE EXPERT   Bringing in an outside expert to support a proposal or decision can, at times, provide managers with some of the same benefits that the use of objective information does. It lends credibility to a manager's initiatives and causes others to believe that what the manager is proposing is the appropriate or rational thing to do. Suppose Callahan had hired a consultant to evaluate whether her idea was a good one. The consultant reports back to the president that the new European-style cabinets are likely to fulfill Callahan's promises and increase Better Built's sales and profits. As with objective information, this information provided by an objective expert can lend a sense of legitimacy to Callahan's proposal and allow her to unobtrusively exercise power to influence others.

Although you might think that consultants and other outside experts are neutral or objective, they sometimes are hired by managers who want them to support a certain position or decision in an organization. For instance, when managers are facing strong opposition from others who fear that a decision will harm their or their departments' interests, the managers may bring in an outside expert. They hope this expert will be perceived as a neutral observer to lend credibility and "objectivity" to their point of view. The support of an outside expert may cause others to believe that a decision is indeed the right one. Of course, sometimes consultants and other outside experts actually are brought into organizations *to be* objective and provide managers with guidance on the appropriate course of action to take.

CONTROLLING THE AGENDA   Managers also can exercise power unobtrusively by controlling the agenda—influencing which alternatives are considered or even whether a decision is made.[79] When managers influence the alternatives that are considered, they can make sure that each considered alternative is acceptable to them and that undesirable alternatives are not in the feasible set. In a hiring context, for example, managers can exert their power unobtrusively by ensuring that job candidates whom they do not find acceptable do not make their way onto the list of finalists for an open position. They do this by making sure that these candidates' drawbacks or deficiencies are communicated to everyone involved in making the hiring decision. When three finalists for an open position are discussed and evaluated in a hiring meeting, a manager may seem to exert little power or influence and just go along with what the rest of the group wants. However, the manager may have exerted power in the hiring process unobtrusively, by controlling which candidates made it to the final stage.

Sometimes managers can prevent a decision from being made. A manager in charge of a community relations committee, for example, may not favor a proposal for the organization to become more involved in local youth groups such as the Boy Scouts and the Girl Scouts. The manager can exert influence in this situation by not including the proposal on the agenda for the committee's next meeting. Alternatively, the manager could place the proposal at the end of the agenda for the meeting and feel confident that the committee will run out of time and not get to the last items on the agenda because that is what always happens. Either approach enables the manager to unobtrusively exercise power. Committee members do not perceive this manager as trying to influence them to turn down the proposal. Rather, the manager has made the proposal into a nonissue that is not even considered.

MAKING EVERYONE A WINNER   Often, politically skilled managers are able to exercise their power unobtrusively because they make sure that everyone whose support they need benefits personally from providing that support. By making everyone a winner, a manager is able to influence other organizational members because these members see supporting the manager as being in their best interest.

When top managers turn around troubled companies, some organizational members and parts of the organization are bound to suffer due to restructurings that often entail painful layoffs. However, the power of the turnaround CEO often accelerates as it becomes clear that the future of the company is on surer footing and the organization and its stakeholders are winners as a result of the change effort.

Making everyone a winner not only is an effective way of exercising power but, when used consistently and forthrightly, can increase managers' power and influence over time. That is, when a manager actually does make everyone a winner, all stakeholders will see it as in their best interests to support the manager and his or her initiatives. When managers who make everyone a winner have strong ethical values, everyone really is a winner, as profiled in the following "Ethics in Action."

Ethics in Action

El Faro Benefits Multiple Stakeholders

When Estuardo Porras was taking business classes at Pepperdine University in Malibu, California, in the 1990s, he was surprised to see the high prices that Starbucks charged for coffee.[80] In his native country of Guatemala, coffee used to be the major export until prices declined in the 1980s due to a large influx of low-cost coffee beans coming on the market from countries like Vietnam. Porras had a vision of returning to Guatemala, resurrecting an old coffee plantation, and operating it in a socially responsible way that protected the natural environment, looked out for and contributed to the well-being of the workers who operated it and the local community, and produced high-quality coffee beans that a socially responsible organization like Starbucks would be interested in purchasing.[81]

Small Business

Porras returned to Guatemala, borrowed $1.25 million from his father, who had recently sold a Coca-Cola bottling company, and transformed an abandoned plantation called El Faro into a marvel of environmental sustainability, social responsibility, and effectiveness.[82] El Faro protects the natural environment, helps out a poor community, and produces high-quality arabica coffee used by specialty coffee companies like Starbucks. And, given Starbucks' commitment to purchasing coffee beans from growers that abide by ethical social and environmental values, El Faro is able to sell all the coffee beans it grows that meet Starbucks' standards for more than the beans would sell for on the general commodity export market.[83]

El Faro is located near a volcano, and the ash from the volcano provides excellent soil for growing coffee. Coffee beans are fermented in recycled water, and the casings from the beans are eaten by earthworms, yielding an excellent organic fertilizer. Much of the work on the plantation is done by hand.[84] El Faro supports a free elementary school for children in the local community and buses older children to a high school in the vicinity. Employees receive free health care after they have been with El Faro for three months; the care is provided in the plantation's medical office, staffed by a part-time doctor and full-time nurse. They also receive 15 days of paid vacation annually. Many of El Faro's full-time employees and their families live on the plantation; El Faro also has part-time employees.[85]

El Faro strives to maintain a healthy, sustainable, and fair work environment.

Porras initially sold El Faro's coffee beans on the commodity export market, while persistently trying to make inroads at Starbucks by sending letters and coffee samples to no avail. Eventually, an exporter who bought beans from El Faro persuaded two coffee buyers from Starbucks to visit the plantation. After a tour and coffee tasting, the buyers were so delighted with what they saw and tasted that they ordered coffee from El Faro that day and gave Porras the opportunity to participate in a program that gives long-terms contracts to growers who are socially responsible.[86]

Today, El Faro Estate Coffee is sold exclusively to Starbucks and Finca El Faro is a Starbucks's C.A.F.E. Practices supplier.[87] Clearly, Porras has made everyone a winner and, in the process, has created a sustainable and thriving business.[88]

Summary and Review

ORGANIZATIONAL CONFLICT Organizational conflict is the discord that arises when the goals, interests, or values of different individuals or groups are incompatible and those individuals or groups block or thwart each other's attempts to achieve their objectives. Four types of conflict arising in organizations are interpersonal conflict, intragroup conflict, intergroup conflict, and interorganizational conflict. Sources of conflict in organizations include different goals and time horizons, overlapping authority, task interdependencies, different evaluation or reward systems, scarce resources, and status inconsistencies. Conflict management strategies focused on individuals include increasing awareness of the sources of conflict, increasing diversity awareness and skills, practicing job rotation or temporary assignments, and using permanent transfers or dismissals when necessary. Strategies focused on the whole organization include changing an organization's structure or culture and altering the

LO 1, 2 source of conflict.

LO 3, 4 **NEGOTIATION** Negotiation is a conflict resolution technique used when parties to a conflict have approximately equal levels of power and try to come up with an acceptable way to allocate resources to each other. In distributive negotiation, the parties perceive that there is a fixed level of resources for them to allocate, and they compete to receive as much as possible at the expense of the other party, not caring about their relationship in the future. In integrative bargaining, both parties perceive that they may be able to increase the resource pie by coming up with a creative solution to the conflict, trusting each other, and cooperating with each other to achieve a win–win resolution. Five strategies that managers can use to facilitate integrative bargaining are to emphasize superordinate goals; focus on the problem, not the people; focus on interests, not demands; create new options for joint gain; and focus on what is fair.

LO5 **ORGANIZATIONAL POLITICS** Organizational politics are the activities that managers (and other members of an organization) engage in to increase their power and to use power effectively to achieve their goals and overcome resistance or opposition. Effective managers realize that politics can be a positive force that enables them to make needed changes in an organization. Five important political strategies for gaining and maintaining power are controlling uncertainty, making oneself irreplaceable, being in a central position, generating resources, and building alliances. Political strategies for effectively exercising power focus on how to use power unobtrusively and include relying on objective information, bringing in an outside expert, controlling the agenda, and making everyone a winner.

Management in Action

Topics for Discussion and Action

DISCUSSION

1. Discuss why too little conflict in an organization can be just as detrimental as too much conflict. **[LO1]**

2. Why are compromise and collaboration more effective ways of handling conflict than accommodation, avoidance, and competition? **[LO2]**

3. Why should managers promote integrative bargaining rather than distributive negotiation? **[LO3]**

4. How can managers promote integrative bargaining? **[LO4]**

5. Why do organizational politics affect practically every organization? **[LO5]**

6. Why do effective managers need good political skills? **[LO5]**

7. What steps can managers take to ensure that organizational politics are a positive force leading to a competitive advantage, not a negative force leading to personal advantage at the expense of organizational goal attainment? **[LO5]**

8. Think of a member of an organization whom you know

and who is particularly powerful. What political strategies does this person use to increase his or her power? **[LO5]**

9. Why is it best to use power unobtrusively? How are people likely to react to power that is exercised obtrusively? **[LO5]**

ACTION

10. Interview a manager in a local organization to determine the kinds of conflicts that occur in his or her organization and the strategies that are used to manage them. **[LO 1, 2]**

Building Management Skills [LO 1, 2]
Effective and Ineffective Conflict Resolution

Think about two recent conflicts that you had with other people, one conflict that you felt was effectively resolved (C1) and one that you felt was ineffectively resolved (C2). The other people involved could be coworkers, students, family members, friends, or members of an organization that you are a member of. Answer the following questions:

1. Briefly describe C1 and C2. What type of conflict was involved in each of these incidents?

2. What was the source of the conflict in C1 and in C2?

3. What conflict management strategies were used in C1 and in C2?

4. What could you have done differently to more effectively manage conflict in C2?

5. How was conflict resolved in C1 and in C2?

Managing Ethically [LO5]

One political strategy managers can engage in is controlling the agenda by subtly influencing which alternatives are considered or even whether a decision is up for discussion. Some employees believe that this can be unethical and prevent important issues from being raised and points of view from being expressed.

Questions

1. Either individually or in a group, think about the ethical implications of controlling the agenda as a political strategy.

2. What steps can managers and organizations take to ensure that this strategy does not result in important issues and differing points of view being suppressed in an organization?

Small Group Breakout Exercise [LO 3, 4]
Negotiating a Solution

Form groups of three or four people. One member of your group will play the role of Jane Rister, one member will play the role of Michael Schwartz, and one or two members will be observer(s) and spokesperson(s) for your group.

Jane Rister and Michael Schwartz are assistant managers in a large department store. They report directly to the store manager. Today they are meeting to discuss some important problems they need to solve but about which they disagree.

The first problem hinges on the fact that either Rister or Schwartz needs to be on duty whenever the store is open. For the last six months, Rister has taken most of the least desirable hours (nights and weekends). They are planning their schedules for the next six months. Rister thought Schwartz would take more of the undesirable times, but Schwartz has informed Rister that his wife has just gotten a nursing job which requires that she work weekends, so he needs to stay home weekends to take care of their infant daughter.

The second problem concerns a department manager who has had a hard time retaining salespeople in his department. The turnover rate in his department is twice that in the other store departments. Rister thinks the manager is ineffective and wants to fire him. Schwartz thinks the high turnover is just a fluke and the manager is effective.

The last problem concerns Rister's and Schwartz's vacation schedules. Both managers want to take off the week of July 4, but one of them needs to be in the store whenever it is open.

1. The group members playing Rister and Schwartz assume their roles and negotiate a solution to these three problems.

2. Observers take notes on how Rister and Schwartz negotiate solutions to their problems.

3. Observers determine the extent to which Rister and Schwartz use distributive negotiation or integrative bargaining to resolve their conflicts.

4. When called on by the instructor, observers communicate to the rest of the class how Rister and Schwartz resolved their conflicts, whether they used distributive negotiation or integrative bargaining, and their actual solutions.

Exploring the World Wide Web [LO 1, 2]

Think of a major conflict in the business world that you have read about in the newspaper in the past few weeks. Then search on the Web for magazine and newspaper articles presenting differing viewpoints and perspectives on the conflict. Based on what you have read, how are the parties to this conflict handling it? Is their approach functional or dysfunctional, and why?

Be the Manager [LO 1, 2, 3, 4, 5]

You are a middle manager in a large corporation and lately feel that you are being caught between a rock and a hard place. Times are tough, your unit has experienced layoffs, your surviving subordinates are overworked and demoralized, and you feel that you have no meaningful rewards, such as the chance for a pay raise, bonus, or promotion, to motivate them with. Your boss keeps increasing the demands on your unit as well as the unit's responsibilities. Moreover, you believe that you and your subordinates are being unfairly blamed for certain problems beyond your control. You believe that you have the expertise and skills to perform your job effectively and also that your subordinates are capable and effective in their jobs. Yet you feel that you are on shaky ground and powerless given the current state of affairs. What are you going to do?

BusinessWeek Case in the News [LO 1, 2]

My Way or the Highway at Hyundai

On the morning of Monday, Feb. 4, about 20 of the top executives at the Irvine (Calif.) headquarters of Kia Motors America left their warm offices to stand outside in near-freezing cold. They were awaiting the arrival of Byung Mo Ahn, the president of Kia Motors. The group organized itself into a receiving line and stayed in formation for more than 15 minutes until Ahn arrived in a chauffeur-driven Kia Amanti sedan.

Although some of the executives were shivering, it would have been bad form to return inside: Standing to greet top brass is customary at Hyundai Motor, Kia's Korean parent. After spending a full week in Irvine, Ahn performed another ritual that has become common at the company: sacking the American leadership team. On Feb. 8 he axed Len Hunt, president and CEO of Kia Motors America, and Ian Beavis, marketing vice-president.

It marked the fourth shakeup in three years for Kia's American operation. The U.S. unit of Hyundai, meanwhile, has churned through four top executives in five years. Many of the departures have come at awkward times. Hunt and Beavis got the news at the airport as they were about to fly from Irvine to an annual dealer meeting in San Francisco. According to several sources, Hunt's predecessor, Peter Butterfield, was dismissed during a dinner meeting with dealers

at the Bellagio Hotel in Las Vegas—between the entrée and dessert. The companies declined to comment on any of these executive departures.

The management shakeups at the American divisions of Hyundai and Kia—two once-separate manufacturers that are now essentially run as one company—come at a critical period. Both brands, which were originally marketed to American consumers as utilitarian econoboxes, are trying to move upscale and sell sedans that can compete with Cadillac and BMW. They are also banking on rapid growth in the U.S. Next year, for example, Kia is opening a plant in Georgia that was built on the optimistic assumption that the company could sell at least 370,000 cars in the U.S. annually. But sales momentum has been slowing. Kia sold 305,000 cars in America in 2007, 13% shy of its target of 350,000. Given their aggressive growth plans, both Hyundai and Kia "need North American auto expertise," says James N. Hall, president of 2953 Analytics, an auto industry consultancy near Detroit.

The problem is that the companies keep booting out American talent. And many of the American executives who do stay find parent Hyundai Motor's corporate culture to be suffocating. According to several current and former managers, Hyundai Chairman Chung Mong Koo, Kia's Ahn, and other top executives run the companies in a far more authoritarian style than do most American CEOs. The critics say

his team micromanages details, rarely listens to advice from local managers, and displays little tolerance for disagreement. "It's a very feudal approach to management," says Bob Martin, a former sales executive who left Hyundai in 2005 to become a consultant at CarLab, a Santa Ana (Calif.) consulting firm. "There's a king, he rules, and everyone curries his favor. It's very militaristic."

"Pushing All The Time"

While Chung's top-down management style might rub some Americans the wrong way, his long-term track record in the U.S. is impressive. Under his leadership, Hyundai has nearly doubled sales in the country since 2000, to 467,000 cars last year. Kia has posted almost identical growth.

Chung, who was convicted of embezzlement in Korea last year but had his prison sentence suspended, has won praise for creating a highly disciplined company. When quality complaints started to plague Hyundai during the 1990s, he ordered engineers to attack the problem. By 2004, Hyundai had soared up the rankings in quality surveys. Unlike Detroit's Big Three, Hyundai and Kia have fewer management layers to hold up decisions. "I can see where Americans would feel uncomfortable," says Alice Amsden, a professor of political economy at the Massachusetts Institute of Technology who has written books about Korea and other developing Asian economies. "American management is used to a different style. But Hyundai deserves a lot of credit."

Both Hyundai and Kia, speaking through representatives at their American units, said that all of the American managers who have left the companies in recent years were treated fairly. Even some of the executives who have departed praise the companies' management culture. "Being aggressive doesn't make them bad," says Robert Cosmai, who was CEO of Hyundai's American unit for two years before getting fired in January, 2006.

Boldness is part of Hyundai Motor's DNA. Like many of Korea's early corporate patriarchs, founder Chung Ju Yung had a simple strategy: Build factories first, worry about sales later. Starting with a small construction company in 1947, he moved into autos, shipbuilding, and other industries. Hyundai became one of the most successful Korean *chaebols,* family-controlled conglomerates with close ties to the government. But it was broken up into several pieces in the late 1990s in the wake of the Asian financial crisis. Last year, the global revenues of Hyundai and Kia grew 7%, to $63.5 billion.

Chung Ju Yung's heirs continue to run Hyundai Motor, and his business philosophy still prevails. In America, the two companies often establish sales targets based on what their auto plants can produce—a persistent source of tension with local managers. Several past executives say that Hyundai and Kia have set unhealthily aggressive sales goals that are causing inventory to pile up. Hyundai has about 32,000 Sonata sedans parked in lots around its Montgomery (Ala.) plant with no orders from dealers. "The production-oriented style of pushing all the time won't work anymore," says Kim Ki Chan, professor of auto economics at Catholic University of Korea.

One consequence of this philosophy is that both Hyundai and Kia have been forced to sell more cars to rental fleets—a practice that tends to make brands lose cachet with buyers. But consumer psychology is something

that Hyundai Motor has never mastered, says consultant Hall. At bottom, it has always had the mind-set of a manufacturer, not a marketer. Many of the products made by Chung Ju Yung's original conglomerate, such as locomotive engines and tanks, were sold to business. Hyundai Motor's leadership team "lacks marketing savvy," says Yoo Young Kwon, a Seoul-based auto analyst at Prudential Investment & Securities. "What they need in the U.S. is to let American executives implement marketing strategy in a sustainable way."

But handing over the reins to American marketers is not something that seems to come naturally to Hyundai Motor. After walking through the receiving line on that Monday morning in February, Kia CEO Ahn spent the day criticizing the company's advertising. The brand has marketed itself as sporty and fun as opposed to the more serious Hyundai. In one of the meetings, Ahn said he hated an ad depicting a Kia dealer doing an impression of the film *Flashdance,* dancing wildly as the jingle "He's a maniac, maniac, and he's selling like he's never sold before" plays. Ahn halted the spots and said Kia's message should lose the campy humor.

Heavy Handlers

Four days later, Kia America CEO Hunt and marketing vice-president Beavis lost their jobs. The firings came as a surprise to the Kia dealers gathered in San Francisco's Moscone Center. Some say they're worried that the brand's marketing message will become diffuse. "It doesn't inspire a lot of confidence," says Ed Tonkin, a Portland (Ore.) Kia dealer who opened one of the brand's original U.S. stores. "The danger is that every time you get a new person, they will go with different marketing and advertising."

Since the meeting, Ahn has taken over Hunt's old office and expanded it. He has tried to mollify dealers with offers of increased corporate support. Kia and Hyundai are also making a greater effort to improve the morale of disgruntled American executives. Kia spokesman Alex Fedorak says many

of them get training from a Korean culture coach.

Cross-cultural outreach is long overdue. Several Americans expressed resentment at the so-called coordinators, the Korean overseers whose job it is to keep an eye on American managers. Culled from the ranks of up-and-coming stars in Seoul, they sit alongside American managers, monitoring decision-making and results. Both Hyundai and Kia have about a dozen coordinators. They must agree to major decisions—and sometimes smaller ones, such as whether to award vacations to dealers who hit sales goals. Japanese automakers also have coordinators in their U.S. operations, but they play more of an advisory role while the American executives have free reign to make major decisions.

Mark Barnes, chief operating officer at Volkswagen Group of America, who worked as a sales executive at Hyundai Motor America until 2006, says the coordinators applied pressure to achieve targets. "If you were subpar, they would ask what you're going to do to get your numbers up," Barnes says. During some conference calls, he adds, the coordinators would speak Korean to managers in Seoul, all but shutting out the Americans.

Kia spokesman Fedorak says the coordinators serve a valuable purpose: bringing the corporate vision from Seoul to America, then relaying the needs of the local market back to headquarters. Since few American employees speak Korean, the coordinators also act as translators. While acknowledging that Kia has a Confucian-influenced corporate culture in which "father knows best," he said this was not the main source of conflict with American executives. Instead, he attributed the tension to Korean managers' greater comfort with "stretch goals."

At the moment, the stretch goal that is stressing out American executives at Hyundai Motor is the company's insistence on trying to move into the low end of the luxury business. For years, executives in the U.S. have been telling their counterparts in Seoul that the two brands are not strong enough to sell for much above the price range of $12,000 to $25,000. But their warnings have been ignored. Chung believes that going upscale is essential for Hyundai and Kia. The weak dollar has hurt profits, and concessions made to the Korean unions are eroding the company's cost advantage. So both Hyundai and Kia have launched a slate of vehicles priced near or above $30,000. In 2005, for example, Kia released the Amanti (Ahn's limo) with a mandate to sell 20,000 a year.

The company didn't come close to hitting that number, selling just 5,500 of the sedans, priced between $25,000 and $30,000, last year. Still, nobody expects Chung to heed the advice of some American managers

and pull back. "The top-down management style hasn't changed at Hyundai," says Lee Hang Koo, auto industry specialist at the Korea Institute for Industrial Economics & Trade. "This is bound to lead to cultural clashes with Americans. We've seen management churn in the past, and there's no reason to believe it will stop."

Questions for Discussion

1. What are the sources of conflict between Korean top executives at Hyundai and Kia and their North American counterparts?

2. How is the conflict (in question 1) being managed?

3. What are the sources of conflict between Korean executives and Hyundai and Kia dealers in the United States?

4. How is the conflict (in question 3) being managed?

Source: David Welch, David Kiley, and Moon Ihlwan, "My Way or the Highway at Hyundai." Reprinted from the March 17, 2008, issue of *BusinessWeek* by special permission. Copyright © 2008 by The McGraw-Hill Companies, Inc.

BusinessWeek Case in the News [LO 1, 2]

A Town Torn Apart by Nestlé

Tucked into the foothills of Mount Shasta, the Northern California town of McCloud has no stoplights and one grocery store. A former logger's El Dorado, McCloud fell on hard times in the 1980s when it started running out of trees to cut down. But with its drop-dead panoramas and crisp, clean air, the burg started to limp back in the 1990s. Today it is a world-renowned paradise for trout anglers, a respite for burned-out boomers looking to escape the status race, and a hotbed of New Age seekers, some of whom jet in from Japan to meditate and chant in what they regard as a spiritual vortex.

It is here that Nestlé Waters North America, a subsidiary of the Swiss food and beverage giant, plans to operate one of the largest spring-water bottling plants in the U.S. The 1 million-square-foot facility—picture five Wal-Mart supercenters strung together—is to rise on the site of McCloud's defunct lumber mill, a 250-acre swath of land that bends around the base of the mountain. Nestlé aims to draw 1,250 gallons

a minute of water from McCloud's glacier-fed springs. The company would then pack 300 semi-trailers a day full of Arrowhead brand water, truck it as far away as Los Angeles and Reno, and sell it at prices that are as much as 1,000 times more than the cost of tap water. In exchange, Nestlé has agreed to pay McCloud roughly $350,000 a year for the water and create up to 240 jobs in and around the town.

That contract was signed nearly five years ago. Nestlé had hoped to have the plant up and running by 2006. But the company has yet to break ground on the abandoned mill site.

Nestlé Waters has run into a wall of opposition, prompting it to delay construction and resubmit its environmental permit application. Since learning about the bottling plant, nearly half of McCloud's 1,300 residents have mobilized into a well-armed resistance force. Furious that their elected representatives inked the deal without consulting them and worried about the potential impact the plant could have on Mount Shasta's delicate local hydrology, they have ordered up studies, signed up wealthy backers, and lobbied politicians.

Nestlé, the largest bottled water company in America and purveyor of the Perrier, Poland Spring, and S. Pellegrino brands, has faced similar opposition in towns from Maine to Michigan. Time and again, it has used its clout and legal firepower to get the plants open. Nestlé is determined to prevail in McCloud, too. At a time when soda sales are soft, it hopes to improve on its 32% share of the U.S. bottled water market.

But this time the company seems to be taking its foes more seriously. "I want all the t's crossed, all the i's dotted," says Kim Jeffery, Nestlé Waters' CEO. "I don't want anyone to say we didn't do it right." It's not hard to see why Jeffery is proceeding cautiously. Amid rising concerns about the deteriorating condition of America's lakes, rivers, and springs, Congress late last year convened hearings about the potential threat posed by bottled spring water. Meanwhile, environmentalists say the stuff contributes to global warming because it takes oil to make the bottles and then truck them from source to supermarket. These critics have coalesced into the "tappening" movement, which is urging people to drink the water that comes out of your tap. Already, upscale restaurants are banning bottled water, while the mayors of San Francisco and New York are urging residents to use municipal supplies.

"WE NEEDED AN INSURANCE POLICY"

So far, Nestlé's foes in McCloud have managed to delay the plant, not kill it. But they have allied themselves with the international environmental movement and made their cause bigger than one town. "At some point you make enough people mad," says Debra Anderson, a fourth-generation McCloudite and real estate broker, whose understated and articulate manner makes her a powerful opponent. "If this plant gets built, it's going to be bad PR for Nestlé."

Nestlé employs 11 water hunters around the U.S. Besides monitoring water supplies, they search for new sources, typically in remote, pristine places like McCloud. A big part of their job is building relationships with locals, few of whom have dealt with a multinational. Dave Palais, 44, is one of the 11. Sturdy and upbeat, he's perpetually sunburned, a testament to the long weekend walks he takes with his wife and dogs. Palais holds a PhD in geology from Arizona State University and considers himself knowledgeable about watersheds.

Palais joined Nestlé Waters in 1996, about the time the bottled water business was starting to boom. He was managing the company's water supplies in Southern California near Palm Springs when drought hit the region. Going into 2003, Palais watched as the spring flows diminished. It was a wake-up call. "We were recognizing the vulnerability of our supplies in Southern California to things like drought [and] earthquakes," he recalls. "We needed to be in a position where we had an insurance policy, a backup source." In 2003, Palais' bosses in Greenwich, Conn., ordered him to set up a new bottling plant in McCloud. He sold his place in Corona, Calif., and moved to Redding, 70 miles outside town. Palais' gray Chevy Silverado pickup became a common

sight in McCloud as the water hunter went about educating himself on local politics and signing up allies.

On the face of it, McCloud seemed like the perfect spot to build a bottled water plant. For years, the five elected board members of the community services district had morosely contemplated the town's rickety infrastructure, 14.5% unemployment, and $100,000-plus deficit. McCloud sits in the southeastern corner of Siskiyou County, a ranching and agricultural area where local budgets are constantly stretched. In McCloud, things were so bleak that former mill workers who once took care of their families in middle-class comfort were now mowing lawns and showing up in the checkout line with food stamps.

Many old-timers longed for the glory days of "Mother McCloud," as the McCloud River Lumber Co. was known. They remember the logging behemoth as a ferociously paternalistic employer that supplied workers with freshly painted houses, groceries, a doctor, firewood, and a sumptuous Christmas party with a present for every child. When a faucet dripped or a light switch broke, employees called the Mother McCloud repairman. Get fired, though, and a truck rolled up to haul you and your family's belongings away.

The lumber industry was suffering, but McCloud resident Doris Dragseth knew the town possessed another valuable commodity: glacier-fed springs that gush crystal-clear, 41-degree water straight to the tap. So delicious is the water that Dragseth and her husband, Bill, still fill up old milk jugs and take a few weeks' supply to their son in nearby Orland. Some McCloud residents half-jokingly suggest they could market the town to Botox fanatics as a fountain of youth. The water, according to local lore, accounts for many McCloudites' freakishly young appearance.

TOO BROKE FOR A LAWYER

Throughout the late '90s, McCloud's district board members tried to lure a bottler to McCloud. Dragseth, who ran an auto parts store with her husband

before retiring, remembers thinking: "We need the jobs, we need the money." Various schemes came and went. Letters of intent were signed. But the deals went nowhere. McCloud even considered going into the bottled water business for itself. But trying to battle for shelf space was out of its league.

So from the moment Dave Palais arrived in town, the district board was susceptible to his ministrations. The mill, under new owners, was closing. What's more, Dragseth, by then a board member, and her colleagues considered Nestlé to be a classy company that might restore some of Mother McCloud's largesse. To cement the relationship, Palais invited Dragseth, another board member, and the town manager to two plants near Palm Springs. Nestlé offered to pick up the tab, but legally the town had to pay its own way.

Dragseth recalls a gorgeous, first-class operation. She couldn't believe how quiet and well-run the plants were. "I came back extremely impressed with this company," says Dragseth. "They had beautiful break rooms for their employees with microwaves and anything else they wanted. It was a beautiful plant." Dragseth's husband joked that he was thinking of junking retirement to work for Nestlé.

It wasn't long before the two sides were hammering out a contract for the five board members to vote on. McCloud's finances were so parlous it couldn't afford a lawyer. Nestlé covered the legal tab and all subsequent costs associated with the deal—including the time Pete Kampa, McCloud's town manager, and his staff worked on the project, fees for outside consultants, and all the preparations for the permitting process.

Few of McCloud's residents knew about the agreement. That is, not until September, 2003, when board members posted a notice in McCloud's post office announcing a town meeting to unveil the plan. Local business owner Richard McFarland did a double take when he saw the flyer. Like many in McCloud, he knew the town had long wanted to sell its water. But this was the first he'd heard about a contract or Nestlé. For McFarland, as for others, the name Nestlé raised a red flag. Wasn't this the company boycotted in the 1970s for promoting infant formula over breast milk to mothers in the Third World? Plus, Nestlé was the biggest food company in the world. How much water would they be sucking out of what many considered a sacred mountain with a world-class fishing river and a sensitive hydrology?

McFarland wasn't opposed to a new industry coming to town. But he had lots of questions, especially since his reclaimed-lumber business abuts the old mill. A few days later, on Sept. 29, he and 100 other residents piled into the elementary school gym for the Nestlé town meeting. As they waited for it to start, a TV beamed a continuous loop of CEO Jeffery extolling his company's environmental credentials. Many assumed a discussion would be had, questions fielded, and the community would then work together to assess options. They thought they were there to hear about a proposal. But after Kampa and Palais did their PowerPoints, the crowd was dumbfounded when the gavel struck and Dragseth and the other four board members voted unanimously to sign the contract right then and there. The deal was done.

McFarland and other residents were furious. "There was no public participation in the process," says McFarland. "That's where it falls apart for me." Dragseth concedes that the contract was done behind closed doors but counters: "You can't have a room full of people to negotiate. You'd have 50 different people wanting 50 different things."

When McFarland pored over the fine print of the contract, he felt sick. In his view, the town had practically given Nestlé exclusive rights to the water for 100 years. Town officials say they haggled and got the best deal they could. To McFarland, "the contract read like nobody on the services district knew what they were doing. It read like Nestlé's lawyers wrote it." The board members, for their part,

recall being stunned by the opposition. "I couldn't imagine for the life of me why anyone would be against this," says Dragseth.

In November, 2004, Nestlé's foes convened a water forum in the McCloud High School auditorium. The organizers brought in scientists and activists critical of the company's operations. One of the star attractions was a retired librarian named Terry Swier, who led the fight against Nestlé in Mecosta County, Mich. Palais, say several people who were there, sat silently, his arms folded, as Swier told the crowd what happened after Nestlé arrived in her town.

In 2000, Nestlé had begun negotiating a 99-year, renewable lease with private landowners to pump 400 gallons a minute from a deer-hunting preserve called Sanctuary Springs that eventually feeds into Lake Michigan. Swier was aghast. Water levels in the Great Lakes were at record lows. Water quality was declining, the result of a toxic brew of industrial runoff, pesticides, and sewage. Swier and other activists hired a scientist to examine what impact Nestlé's operation would have on water levels. His tests projected severe drop-offs in flow levels.

The residents decided to ask the courts to halt the plan, and threw bake sales and bingo tournaments to pay for the move. Despite the suit, Nestlé went forward and in 2002 opened the $150 million plant, cranking out Ice Mountain and Nestlé Pure Life water each day. A year later the Mecosta County circuit court ordered Nestlé to halt operations because the plant would deplete nearby wetlands, lakes, and streams. Nestlé appealed and continued pumping. (Eventually, the Court of Appeals upheld most of the lower court's findings about potential harm to the local watershed but ruled that jobs and the economy were more important. Still, Nestlé agreed to halve the amount of water it pumped to 218 gallons per minute.)

Swier's presentation had a profound impact on the people in the school auditorium that night. She told them: "Water is for life, not for profits." After the meeting the audience

ate a chicken-and-pasta dinner paid for by four Nestlé opponents. Palais went out to his truck and returned with several bottles of Arrowhead water for the pro-Nestlé people sitting at his table. Everyone else drank punch, coffee, and tap water.

SLASHED TIRES

McCloud had become two mutually hostile camps. And it wasn't long before things turned ugly. Former board member Ken Goates blames his two heart attacks on the rancor. Dragseth found herself denying rumors that Nestlé had bought her a condo in Switzerland. Debra Anderson's tires were slashed. Pro-Nestlé residents started boycotting her mother's grocery store, and sales fell by half, she says. After receiving crank calls, Kampa recalls standing in line to get fireworks with his daughter and hearing people behind him whisper that he was a Nestlé shill with bank accounts in Switzerland. Enough is enough, his wife said. Kampa took a job in another town.

The opposition was just getting going, however. The main anti-Nestlé citizens' group, the McCloud Watershed Council, banded together with other pro-watershed groups across the country. Funded by wealthy San Francisco-area families, including the Haas clan of Levi Strauss fame, Nestlé's opponents commissioned an independent economic analysis to study the Nestlé plan—both the benefits and the costs.

The much-anticipated study, conducted by Portland (Ore.) public policy consultancy EcoNorthwest, came out last October. The 63-page report found Nestlé would pay a fraction as much for McCloud's water as elsewhere; that the jobs and revenues promised by Nestlé in other communities never materialized; and that McCloud's board failed to factor in the costs the plant would exact in terms of wastewater, truck traffic, and air pollution. "There is a great risk that McCloud will be giving away too much for too little in return," the report stated. "We find that rather than provide an engine for economic growth,

Nestlé's proposed facility would impose costs and obligations on the community that would outweigh the benefits." Palais e-mailed the report back to Greenwich, where executives started working on their line-by-line rebuttal. They eventually disputed every one of the report's findings.

A pall of aggrievement hangs over Nestlé Waters' headquarters. There's an attitude that essentially asks: Why us? CEO Jeffery has been in bottled water since the late 1970s. He worked at Perrier until Nestlé bought it in 1992 and put him in charge of Nestlé's North American water business. And he has long seen his product as a healthy alternative to soda in a nation that is increasingly obese.

For several years now, Jeffery says, he has watched other companies win green cred for what he deems smoke-and-mirrors publicity stunts. A couple of years ago he recalls not being able to sleep, getting up and heading to his Greenwich study to write down the 10 things Nestlé was doing to reduce its carbon footprint. One of those things was designing the lightest-weight water bottle currently on the market. Jeffery also notes, correctly, that water bottlers use less H_2O than

makers of soda or beer. "It's a spit in the ocean," he says.

But soda and beer makers typically don't mine pristine springs; they use tap water. So, for that matter, do Nestlé Waters' main rivals, Coca-Cola's Dasani and PepsiCo's Aquafina. It's instructive that Nestlé Waters was the only company asked to attend Congress's first-ever hearings on the bottled water industry in December. "I had my trepidations about what to expect," says Nestlé Waters' corporate affairs chief Heidi Paul. She was right to be nervous; the hearings didn't go so well. Paul testified that there is no scientific proof that Nestlé's bottled water operations cause harm. But the panel of assembled experts pretty much drowned her out.

Congress continues to investigate the situation in McCloud as part of an overall probe into regulations governing groundwater. Meanwhile, McFarland and his allies vow they will keep making life hell for Jeffery & Co. So far they have won some concessions from Nestlé. The company has agreed to do more studies to understand McCloud's local hydrology better and to extract less water than originally planned. It also says it will

redo its environmental permit draft with the county. That will slow construction for at least an additional two years.

In the end, Jeffery will likely get his plant in McCloud. But the battle in Northern California—and the growing antipathy to bottled water—will only make it more difficult the next time the Nestlé Waters boss dispatches one of his water hunters to find a new spring.

Questions for Discussion

1. What are the sources of conflict surrounding Nestlé Waters North America's plans to build a bottled water plant in McCloud, California?

2. Why has the conflict divided the town?

3. Why were McCloud residents upset during and after the September 29th Nestlé town meeting?

4. How do you think this conflict should be resolved? Why?

Source: Michelle Conlin, "A Town Torn Apart by Nestlé." Reprinted from the April 14, 2008, issue of *BusinessWeek* by special permission. Copyright © 2008 by The McGraw-Hill Companies, Inc.

CHAPTER 18

Using Advanced Information Technology to Increase Performance

Learning Objectives

After studying this chapter, you should be able to:

LO1 Differentiate between data and information, and explain how the attributes of useful information allow managers to make better decisions.

LO2 Describe three reasons why managers must have access to information to perform their tasks and roles effectively.

LO3 Describe the computer hardware and software innovations that created the IT revolution and changed the way managers behave.

LO4 Differentiate among seven performance-enhancing kinds of management information systems.

LO5 Explain how IT is helping managers build strategic alliances and network structures to increase efficiency and effectiveness.

A Manager's Challenge

How B&M Retailers Use IT to Attract Customers

How can managers create competitive advantage through IT? The growing popularity of online shopping at Internet retailers such as Amazon.com, but also at the online stores of bricks-and-mortar (B&M) retailers such as Wal-Mart and Best Buy, is causing major changes in the way managers utilize IT in retail settings, and in the way they make use of the skills of retail employees.[1] Today, more and more potential buyers are taking advantage of the limitless information they can find on the World Wide Web (WWW) to become informed customers. Buyers can go online and search for information and reviews about the different qualities of competing products at shopping Web sites; they can then go to specific sites that specialize in providing up-to-date information about the current prices being charged for these products by different B&M and online retailers. The availability of so much information online poses huge challenges for all retailers, but especially B&M retailers, because their sales reps are now dealing with highly informed customers, and the ability to complete a sales often depends on the retailer being able to offer some kind of extra information or customer service compared to an online retailer.

With the availability of incredibly low prices from giants like amazon.com (bottom), B&M stores such as Wal-Mart (top) have to out-compete not just on pricing but also on customer service—the distinctive element that can win them an edge over another online order.

A main challenge confronting managers of B&M retailers is to use IT to improve the quality of the shopping experience and to better train their employees to provide higher-quality customer service. In the past, for example, one of the attractions of shopping at exclusive high-priced department stores was that their salespeople would go to great lengths to satisfy customers. For example, sales reps would phone other branches to locate the right size of a dress or comforter that a client wanted but was not in stock and have the item shipped overnight. But today, when customers are often as knowledgeable as employees because of their use of the WWW they may just say to a sales rep, "well why don't you look online," assuming that any retailer today would have IT that provides real-time information about where such items are located. In reality, many retail stores have not kept up with the need to use IT to improve customer service, nor have they thought about how they can improve employee training to make better use of their skills. The result has been falling store performance and the loss of customers to online stores.

So, how does a retailer attempt to catch up and use advanced retailing IT, combined with better customer relationship management (CRM) practices, to attract customers back to the B&M world? The first way is to invest in state-of-the-art retail IT such as touch-screen terminals, LCD monitors, and high-tech interactive TVs that (1) provide customers with detailed information about all the important features of the products that they have on hand, (2) help to speed up customer service and checkout, and (3) "involve" customers and help convince them they have made the best buying decisions. In one experiment to see what the future might hold, Bloomingdales linked up with a specialty IT company in 2007 to run a three-day experiment to use its IT to help

salespeople aid customers to make better purchasing decisions. As usual, salespeople help customers select new clothing choices, but then after the customer tries on the clothing, they parade in front of an interactive three-way mirror connected to the Internet via a broadband webcam linkup. This allows family members and friends who are online to see and comment on the different clothing selections, and the customer can then use all their extra input to make his or her final clothing choices.[2] In 2008 retailers are expected to spend over $1 billion on new in-store IT to improve the shopping experience and keep customers coming back to B&M stores.

Another way B&M stores can use IT to better serve customers is to find ways to link their store's online site to its B&M stores to encourage customers to think of both kinds of stores as two integrated parts of the same business. For example Circuit City has been a leader in guaranteeing online customers that if they buy a product at their online store they will be able to pick it up at their choice of B&M location within 24 minutes—they offer a guarantee that if it's not ready for pickup, customers will receive a $24 gift certificate. Customers like having a new product in their hands; they don't like waiting while it's shipped, so this increases sales. Bloom Supermarkets, owned by Food Lion, has adopted a novel approach to suit its food business: It has developed an interactive wireless shopping cart that records the nature and dollar value of the items customers put into their carts so they can keep track of their purchases.

The other main way B&M companies can better compete with online retailers is to make better use of their employees—especially to train employees so that they have more information at their disposal than IT-savvy customers. Also, to train them to provide other kinds of services that online stores cannot; for example, how to provide personalized in-store service, and to offer customers profitable extra services such as home setup, service, and repair. Best Buy, for example, decided that it would retrain 30% of its top salespeople so that they would not only possess detailed information about the products in their own store department (for example, PCs or flatscreen TVs) but also about how to match products across departments (for example, to help customers decide which printer is best for a PC that has a certain kind of graphics card). The goal it to provide customers with the "extra" or additional kinds of information that makes a difference and so encourages them to make their purchases in B&M stores as well as to believe it is worth their while to come back in the future.

Indeed, another advantage of investing in high-quality customer service is that using IT to bring customers into the store, either to pick up products or to gain better advice, is a major source of extra sales. Why? Customer reps are trained to inform customers about the accessories that will help them better enjoy their purchases (type of protective case for a laptop, or newest video games for a game console). And, in B&M stores that offer a wide array of products such as Best Buy or Wal-Mart, customers often explore its different departments and make extra purchases—such as a pack of $10 energy-efficient light bulbs or a $2,000 HDTV. These extra purchases contribute significantly to a store's performance, Wal-Mart, for example, which developed an online-to-B&M store program in select stores in 2007, found that it increased the number of customers by 20% and that they spent an extra $60 during their pick-up visit![3]

Overview

In an online world, retail managers must work to adopt the most effective IT solutions for their employees and their customers or else they risk being surpassed by rivals—either other retailers or the ones online who find ways to use IT to give customers what they want. The implication is clear: There are enormous opportunities for managers of all kinds of organizations to find new ways to use IT to utilize organizational resources more efficiently and effectively. However, IT will help an organization achieve high performance only if it can improve the way the organization operates relative to its rivals; in other words, in a way that gives it a competitive advantage.

In this chapter we begin by looking at the relationship between information and the manager's job and then examine the ongoing IT revolution. Then we discuss six types of specific management information systems, each of which is based on a different sort of IT, which can help managers perform their jobs more efficiently and effectively. Next, we examine the impact that rapidly evolving IT is having on managers' jobs and on an organization's competitive advantage. By the end of this chapter, you will understand the profound ways in which new developments in IT are shaping managers' tasks and roles and the way organizations operate.

Information and the Manager's Job

Managers cannot plan, organize, lead, and control effectively unless they have access to information. Information is the source of the knowledge and intelligence that they need to make the right decisions. Information, however, is not the same as data.[4] **Data** are raw, unsummarized, and unanalyzed facts such as volume of sales, level of costs, or number of customers. **Information** is data that are organized in a meaningful fashion, such as in a graph showing the change in sales

data Raw, unsummarized, and unanalyzed facts.

information Data that are organized in a meaningful fashion.

volume or costs over time. Data alone do not tell managers anything; information, in contrast, can communicate a great deal of useful knowledge to the person who receives it—such as a manager who sees sales falling or costs rising. The distinction between data and information is important because one of the purposes of IT is to help managers transform data into information in order to make better managerial decisions.

To further clarify the difference between data and information, consider the case of a manager in a supermarket who must decide how much shelf space to allocate to two breakfast cereal brands for children: Dentist's Delight and Sugar Supreme. Most supermarkets use checkout scanners to record individual sales and store the data on a computer. Accessing this computer, the manager might find that Dentist's Delight sells 50 boxes per day and Sugar Supreme sells 25 boxes per day. These raw data, however, are of little help in assisting the manager to decide about how to allocate shelf space. The manager also needs to know how much shelf space each cereal currently occupies and how much profit each cereal generates for the supermarket.

Suppose the manager discovers that Dentist's Delight occupies 10 feet of shelf space and Sugar Supreme occupies 4 feet and that Dentist's Delight generates 20 cents of profit a box while Sugar Supreme generates 40 cents of profit a box. By putting these three bits of data together (number of boxes sold, amount of shelf space, and profit per box), the manager gets some useful information on which to base a decision: Dentist's Delight generates $1 of profit per foot of shelf space per day [(50 boxes × $.20)/10 feet], and Sugar Supreme generates $2.50 of profit per foot of shelf space per day [(25 boxes ×$.40)/4 feet]. Armed with this information, the manager might decide to allocate less shelf space to Dentist's Delight and more to Sugar Supreme.

LO1 Differentiate between data and information, and explain how the attributes of useful information allow managers to make better decisions.

Attributes of Useful Information

Four factors determine the usefulness of information to a manager: quality, timeliness, completeness, and relevance (see Figure 18.1).

QUALITY Accuracy and reliability determine the quality of information.[5] The greater its accuracy and reliability, the higher is the quality of information. Modern IT gives managers much more access to high quality real-time information that they can use to improve long-term decision making and alter short-term operating decisions, such as how much of a particular product to make day-by-day or month-to-month. Supermarket managers, for example, use IT to monitor the way demand for particular products such

Figure 18.1

Factors Affecting the Usefulness of Information

as milk, chicken, or beer changes daily so that they know how to restock their shelves to ensure the product is always available.

TIMELINESS   Information that is timely is available when it is needed for managerial action, not after the decision has been made. In today's rapidly changing world, the need for timely information often means that information must be available on a real-time basis.[6] **Real-time information** is information that reflects current conditions. In an industry that experiences rapid changes, real-time information may need to be updated frequently.

Airlines use real-time information on the number of flight bookings and competitors' prices to adjust their prices on an hour-to-hour basis to maximize their revenues. Thus, for example, the fare for flights from New York to Seattle might change from one hour to the next as fares are reduced to fill empty seats and raised when most seats have been sold. Airlines use real-time information on reservations to adjust fares at the last possible moment to fill planes and maximize revenues. U.S. airlines make more than 100,000 fare changes each day.[7] Obviously, the managers who make such pricing decisions need real-time information about the current state of demand in the marketplace.

COMPLETENESS   Information that is complete gives managers all the information they need to exercise control, achieve coordination, or make an effective decision. Recall from Chapter 7, however, that managers rarely have access to complete information. Instead, because of uncertainty, ambiguity, and bounded rationality, they have to make do with incomplete information.[8] One of the functions of IT is to increase the completeness of the information that managers have at their disposal.

RELEVANCE   Information that is relevant is useful and suits a manager's particular needs and circumstances. Irrelevant information is useless and may actually hurt the performance of a busy manager who has to spend valuable time determining whether information is relevant. Given the massive amounts of information that managers are now exposed to and their limited information-processing capabilities, a company's IT engineers who design its information-processing systems need to ensure managers receive only relevant information.

What Is Information Technology?

Information technology (IT) is the set of methods or techniques for acquiring, organizing, storing, manipulating, and transmitting information.[9] A **management information system (MIS)** is a specific form of IT that managers select and utilize to generate the specific, detailed information they need to perform their roles effectively. Management information systems have existed for as long as there have been organizations—a long time indeed. Before the computer age, most systems were paper-based: Clerks recorded important information on documents (often in duplicate or triplicate) in the form of words and numbers; sent a copy of the document to superiors, customers, or suppliers, as the case might be; and stored other copies in files for future reference.

Rapid advances in the power of IT—specifically, through the development of more and more sophisticated computer hardware and software—are having a fundamental impact on organizations, managers, and their suppliers and customers, as suggested by developments discussed in "A Manager's Challenge."[10] Some new IT, such as inventory management and customer relationship management (CRM) systems, contributes so much to performance that organizations that do *not* adopt it, or that implement it ineffectively, become uncompetitive compared with organizations that do adopt it.[11] In the 2000s, much of the increasing productivity and efficiency of business in general has been attributed to advancing IT.

Managers need information for three reasons: to make effective decisions, to control the activities of the organization, and to coordinate the activities of the organization. Below we examine these uses of information in detail.

---

real-time information Frequently updated information that reflects current conditions.

information technology The set of methods or techniques for acquiring, organizing, storing, manipulating, and transmitting information.

management information system (MIS) A specific form of IT that managers utilize to generate the specific, detailed information they need to perform their roles effectively.

LO2   Describe three reasons why managers must have access to information to perform their tasks and roles effectively.

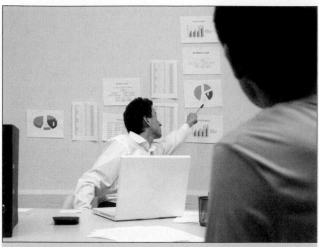

Charts and graphs may be the clichéd centerpieces of managerial meetings, but the data they represent is key for making informed decisions.

Information and Decisions

Much of management (planning, organizing, leading, and controlling) is about making decisions. For example, the marketing manager must decide what price to charge for a product, what distribution channels to use, and what promotional messages to emphasize. The manufacturing manager must decide how much of a product to make and how to make it. The purchasing manager must decide from whom to purchase inputs and what inventory of inputs to hold. The human relations manager must decide how much employees should be paid, how they should be trained, and what benefits they should be given. The engineering manager must make decisions about new product design. Top managers must decide how to allocate scarce financial resources among competing projects, how best to structure and control the organization, and what business-level strategy the organization should be pursuing. And, regardless of their functional orientation, all managers have to make decisions about matters such as what performance evaluation to give to a subordinate.

Decision making cannot be effective in an information vacuum. To make effective decisions, managers need information, both from inside the organization and from external stakeholders. When deciding how to price a product, for example, marketing managers need information about how consumers will react to different prices. They need information about unit costs because they do not want to set the price below the cost of production. And they need information about competitive strategy, since pricing strategy should be consistent with an organization's competitive strategy. Some of this information will come from outside the organization (for example, from consumer surveys) and some from inside the organization (information about production costs comes from manufacturing). As this example suggests, managers' ability to make effective decisions rests on their ability to acquire and process information.

Information and Control

As discussed in Chapter 11, controlling is the process whereby managers regulate how efficiently and effectively an organization and its members are performing the activities necessary to achieve organizational goals.[12] Managers achieve control over organizational activities by taking four steps (see Figure 11.2): (1) They establish measurable standards of performance or goals. (2) They measure actual performance. (3) They compare actual performance against established goals. (4) They evaluate the result and take corrective action if necessary.[13] The package delivery company DHL, for example, has a delivery goal: to deliver 95% of the packages it picks up by noon the next day.[14] Throughout the United States, DHL has thousands of ground stations (branch offices that coordinate the pickup and delivery of packages in a particular area) that are responsible for the physical pickup and delivery of packages. DHL managers monitor the delivery performance of these stations on a regular basis; if they find that the 95% goal is not being attained, they determine why and take corrective action if necessary.[15]

To achieve control over any organizational activity, managers must have information. To control ground-station activities, a DHL manager might need to know what percentage of packages each station delivers by noon. To obtain this information, the manager uses DHL's IT. All packages to be shipped to the stations have been scanned with handheld scanners by the DHL drivers who pick them up; then all this information is sent wirelessly to DHL's headquarters mainframe computer. When the packages are scanned again at delivery, this information is also transmitted to DHL's mainframe. Accessing the mainframe, the manager can quickly discover what percentage of packages were delivered by noon of the day after they were picked up and also how this information breaks down on a station-by-station basis.[16]

Management information systems are used to control all divisional and functional operations. In accounting, for example, information systems are used to monitor expenditures and compare them against budgets.[17] To track expenditures against budgets, managers need information on current expenditures, broken down by relevant organizational units; accounting IT is designed to provide managers with this information. An example of IT used to monitor and control the daily activities of employees is the online MBO information system used by T. J. Rodgers at Cypress Semiconductor, discussed in Chapter 11. Rodgers implemented IT that allows him to review the goals of all his employees in about four hours.[18] At first glance, it might seem that advances in IT would have a limited impact on the business of an office furniture maker; however, this assumption would be incorrect, as the following "Management Insight" suggests.

Management Insight

Herman Miller's Office of the Future

Managers at Herman Miller have been finding countless ways to use IT and the Internet to give their company a competitive advantage over rival office furniture makers (OFMs) such as Steelcase and Hon.[19] Early on, Miller's managers saw the potential of the Internet for selling its furniture to business customers. Other furniture companies' Web sites were online advertisements for their products, services, and other marketing information. However, Miller's managers quickly realized the true potential of using both the company's intranet and the Internet to reach customers.

First, Miller's managers developed IT that linked all the company's dealers and salespeople to its manufacturing hub so that sales orders could be coordinated with the custom design department and with manufacturing, enabling customers to receive pricing and scheduling information promptly. Then, with this customer delivery system in place, Miller developed IT to link its manufacturing operations with its network of suppliers so that its input supply chain would be coordinated with its customer needs.

When Miller's managers noticed that competitors were quickly imitating its IT, they began to search for new ways to use it to gain a competitive advantage. Soon they realized that IT could transform the office furniture business itself. When they began to define Herman Miller as a "digital" enterprise infused with e business, they realized IT could not only improve efficiency but also change the way the customer experienced "Herman Miller" and increase value for the customer. A major Web initiative was the establishment of an e-learning tool, Uknowit.com, which became Herman Miller's online university. Via the Web thousands of Miller's employees and dealers are currently enrolled in Uknowit.com, where they choose from 85 courses covering technology, products and services, product applications, consultative/selling skills, and industry competitive knowledge. The benefits to Miller, its dealers, and its customers from this IT initiative are improved speed to market and better ability to respond to competitors' tactics. That is, salespeople and dealers now have the information and tools they need to better compete for and keep customers.

Moreover, the office furniture business offers highly customized solutions to its customers. A main source of competitive advantage is the ability to give customers exactly what they want and at the right

Herman Miller's custom-made ergonomic office furniture arrives on time due to the company's use of IT that links its dealers with its manufacturing hub.

price. Using its new IT, Miller's salespeople are giving design and manufacturing more accurate and timely information, which has reduced the incidence of sales and specification errors during the selling process. Also, with the new systems time to market has been reduced, and Miller is committed to being able to offer customers highly customized furniture in 10 business days or less.

Of course, all these IT initiatives have been costly to Herman Miller. Thousands of hours of management time have been spent developing the IT and providing content, such as information on competitors for the company's online classes. Herman Miller's managers are looking at the long term; they believe they have created a real source of competitive advantage for their company that will sustain it in the years ahead.

Information and Coordination

Coordinating department and divisional activities to achieve organizational goals is another basic task of management. As an example of the size of the coordination task that managers face, consider the coordination effort involved in building Boeing's 787 Dreamliner jet aircraft, which is composed of over 3 million individual parts.[20] Managers at Boeing have to coordinate the production and delivery of all of these parts so that every part arrives at Boeing's Everett, Washington, facility exactly when it is needed (for example, the wings should arrive before the engines). To achieve this high level of coordination, managers need information about which global supplier is producing what part, and when it will be produced. To meet this need, managers at Boeing created global IT that links Boeing to all its suppliers and can track the flow of 3 million component parts through the production process around the world in real time—an immense task.

As we noted in previous chapters, the coordination problems that managers face in managing their global supply chains to take advantage of national differences in the costs of production are increasing. So managers have been adopting sophisticated IT that helps them coordinate the flow of materials, semifinished goods, and finished products throughout the world. Consider, for example, how Bose, which manufactures some of the world's best-known high-fidelity speakers, manages its global supply chain. Bose purchases almost all of the components for its speakers, and about 50% of its purchases are from foreign suppliers, the majority of which are in the Far East. The challenge for managers is to coordinate this globally dispersed supply chain to minimize Bose's inventory and transportation costs. Minimizing these costs requires that component parts arrive at Bose's assembly plant just in time to enter the production process and not before. Bose also has to remain responsive to customer demands, which means that the company and its suppliers have to be able to respond quickly to changes in the demand for certain kinds of speakers, increasing or decreasing production as needed.

The responsibility for coordinating the supply chain to simultaneously minimize inventory and transportation costs and respond quickly to changing customer demands belongs to Bose's logistics managers. They contracted with W. N. Procter, a Boston-based supply chain manager, to develop logistics IT that gives Bose the real-time information it needs to track parts as they move through the global supply chain. The IT is known as ProcterLink. When a shipment leaves a supplier, it is logged into ProcterLink.[21] From that point on, Bose can track the supplies as they move across the globe toward Massachusetts. This system allows Bose to fine-tune its production scheduling so that supplies enter the production process exactly when they are needed.

How well this system works was illustrated when one Japanese customer unexpectedly doubled its order for Bose speakers. Bose had to gear up its manufacturing in a hurry, but many of its components were stretched out across long distances. By using ProcterLink, Bose was able to locate the needed parts in its supply chain. It then broke them out of the normal delivery chain and moved them by air freight to get them to the assembly line in time for the accelerated schedule. As a result, Bose was able to meet the request of its customer.

The IT Revolution

Advances in IT have enabled managers to make gigantic leaps in the way they can collect more timely, complete, relevant, and high-quality information and use it in more effective ways. To better understand the ongoing revolution in IT that has transformed companies such as Herman Miller and Bose, and allowed them to improve their responsiveness to customers, minimize costs, and improve their competitive position, we need to examine several key aspects of advanced IT.

LO3 Describe the computer hardware and software innovations that created the IT revolution and changed the way managers behave.

The Effects of Advancing IT

The IT revolution began with the development of the first computers—the hardware of IT—in the 1950s. The language of computers is a digital language of zeros and ones. Words, numbers, images, and sound can all be expressed in zeros and ones. Each letter in the alphabet has its own unique code of zeros and ones, as does each number, each color, and each sound. For example, the digital code for the number 20 is 10100. In the language of computers it takes a lot of zeros and ones to express even a simple sentence, to say nothing of complex color graphics or moving video images. Nevertheless, modern computers can read, process, and store millions and billions of instructions per second (an *instruction* is a line of software code) and thus vast amounts of zeros and ones. This awesome "number-crunching" power forms the foundation of the ongoing IT revolution.

The products and services that result from advancing IT are all around us. Ever more powerful microprocessors and PCs, high-bandwith wireless smart phones, sophisticated word-processing software, ever-expanding computer networks, inexpensive digital cameras and camcorders, and more and more useful online information and retailing services that did not exist a generation ago. Now these products are commonplace and being continuously improved. Many of the managers and companies that helped develop the new IT have reaped enormous gains.

However, while many companies have benefited from advancing IT, others have been threatened. Traditional telephone companies the world over have seen their market dominance threatened by new companies offering Internet, broadband, and wireless telephone technology. For example, AT&T, Verizon, and other long-distance companies have been facing increased competition because of advances in telecommunications and have been forced to use new IT to compete. So, advancing IT is both an opportunity and a threat.[22]

On the one hand, IT helps create new product opportunities that managers and their organizations can take advantage of—such as online travel and vacation booking. On the other hand, IT creates new and improved products that reduce or destroy demand for older, established products—such as the services provided by bricks-and-mortar travel agents. Wal-Mart, by developing its own sophisticated proprietary IT, has been able to reduce retailing costs so much that it has put hundreds of thousands of small and medium-size stores out of business. Similarly, thousands of small, specialized bookstores have closed in the United States in the last decade as a result of advances in IT that made online bookselling possible.

IT and the Product Life Cycle

product life cycle The way demand for a product changes in a predictable pattern over time

When IT is advancing, organizational survival requires that managers quickly adopt and apply it. One reason for this is the way IT affects the length of the **product life cycle,** which is the way that the demand for a product changes in a predictable pattern over time.[23] In general, the product life cycle consists of four stages: the embryonic, growth, maturity, and decline stages (see Figure 18.2). In the *embryonic stage* a product

Figure 18.2
A Product Life Cycle

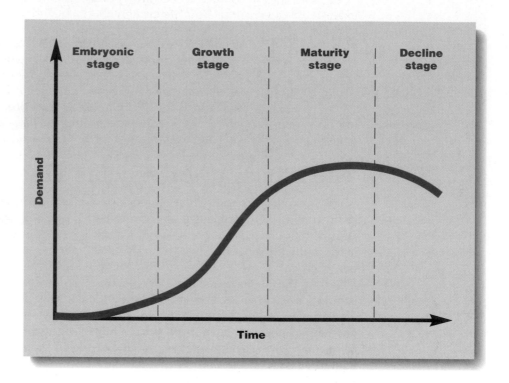

has yet to gain widespread acceptance; customers are unsure what a product, such as a new smart phone, has to offer, and demand for it is minimal. As a product, like Apple's iPod, becomes accepted by customers (although many products do *not,* like Dell's MP3 player), demand takes off and the product enters its growth stage. In the *growth stage* many consumers are entering the market and buying the product for the first time, and demand increases rapidly. This is the stage Apple iPods are in currently.

The growth stage ends and the *mature stage* begins when market demand peaks because most customers have already bought the product (there are relatively few first-time buyers left). At this stage, demand is typically replacement demand. In the PC market, for example, people who already have a PC are trading up to a more powerful model. Products such as PCs, wireless phones, and online information services are currently in this stage. If demand for a product starts to fall, then the *decline stage* begins; this frequently happens when advancing IT leads to the development of a more advanced product, making the old one obsolete. For example, demand for every generation of PC, wireless phone, or MP3 player falls off as the products are superseded by those that incorporate advances in IT, such as Apple iPods that have new video capabilities or 3G smart phones that have more powerful broadband capabilities.

Thus one reason the IT revolution has been so important for managers is that advances in IT are one of the most significant determinants of the length of a product's life cycle, and therefore of competition in an industry.[24] In some industries—such as PCs, semiconductors, and computer disk drives—technological advances are so rapid that product life cycles are very short. For example, in the disk-drive industry, a new model becomes technologically obsolete about 12 months after

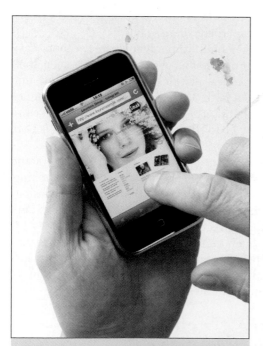

Apple's new iPhone 3G, with faster internet speed, fewer bugs, and new features, planted the phone solidly in a growth market as customers lined up in July 2008 to claim one.

its introduction; in the PC industry, product life cycles have shrunk from three years during the 1980s to a few months today because of advancing IT.

In other industries the product life cycle is often longer. In the car industry, for example, the average product life cycle is about three to five years. But even here the life cycle has been shortening because advancing IT has led to a continual stream of incremental innovations in car design. Today, a typical car has over 300 advanced electronic microcontrollers that run most of its operating functions, such as the hybrid engine in Toyota's Prius, which is powered by gas and an electric motor but controlled by chips.

The message for managers is clear: The shorter the length of a product's life cycle because of advancing IT, the more important it is to innovate products quickly and continuously. The PC company that cannot develop a new and improved product line every three to six months will soon find itself in trouble. Increasingly, managers are trying to outdo their rivals by being the first to market with a product that incorporates some advance in IT, such as advanced stability or steering control that prevents vehicle wrecks.[25] In sum, the tumbling price of information brought about by advances in IT is at the heart of the IT revolution. So the question is, How can managers use all this computing power to their advantage?

Computer Networks

networking The exchange of information through a group or network of interlinked computers.

The tumbling price of computing power and information has facilitated computer **networking,** the exchange of information through a group or network of interlinked computers. The most common arrangement now emerging is a four-tier network consisting of personal digital assistants (PDAs) and laptops, clients, servers, and a mainframe (see Figure 18.3). At the outer nodes of a typical four-tier system are laptops and PDAs, such as wireless smart phones and electronic organizers like the Palm

Figure 18.3

A Typical Four-Tier Information System

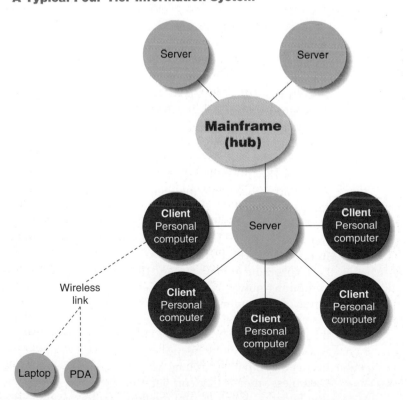

Pilot, which allow users to e-mail coworkers and which provide access to files on their PCs and on the company's intranet. Next in the network are the PCs that sit on the desks of individual users. These PCs, referred to as *clients,* are linked to a local server, a high-powered midrange computer that "serves" the client PCs. Servers often store power-hungry software programs that can be run more effectively on the server than on an individual's personal computer. Servers may also manage a network of printers that can be used by hundreds of clients, store data files, and handle e-mail communications between clients. The client computers linked directly to a server constitute a *local area network (LAN).* Within any organization there may be several LANs–for example, one in every division and function.

At the hub of a four-tier system are mainframe computers. *Mainframes* are large and powerful computers that can be used to store and process vast amounts of information. The mainframe can also be used to handle electronic communications between personal computers situated in different LANs. In addition, the mainframe may be connected to mainframes in other organizations and, through them, to LANs in other organizations. A manager with a laptop, PDA, or PC hooked into a four-tier system can access data and software stored in the local server, in the mainframe, or through the Internet in computers based in another organization. A manager can therefore communicate electronically with other individuals hooked into the system, whether they are in the manager's LAN, in another LAN within the manager's organization, or in another organization altogether. Moreover, with wireless communication an individual with the necessary IT can hook into the system from any location–at home, on a boat, on the beach, in the air–anywhere a wireless communication link can be established. Increasingly, the Internet, a worldwide network of interlinked computers, is used as the conduit for connecting the computer systems of different organizations, but specialist IT organizations such as IBM are also trying to provide this service, as the following "Management Insight" suggests.

Management Insight

IBM's "Business-on-Demand" IT

A company seeking to purchase new IT has to decide which components of computer hardware and software will result in the greatest gains in competitive advantage and profitability. Convincing a company to spend millions or billions of dollars to buy new kinds of software and hardware is a daunting task facing the sales force of a company that sells IT today. One company facing this challenge is IBM, which makes, sells, and services a vast array of computer hardware and software. To maintain its leading position in the highly competitive IT industry, Sam Palmisano, IBM's CEO, announced a bold new business strategy for IBM called "Business on Demand." Over the long run, he claims, companies that adopt IBM's new IT will generate millions or billions of dollars in savings in operating costs.

To promote its new strategy, IBM told its customers to think of information and computing power as being a fluid, like water, contained in the hundreds or thousands of computers that are the "reservoirs" or "lakes" of a large company's IT system. This water flows between computers in a company's computer network through the fiber-optic cables that connect them. Thus, computing power, like water, can potentially be moved between computers both inside a company and between companies, as long as all the computers are linked seamlessly together. "Seamless" means that computer hardware or software does not create information logjams, which disrupt the flow of information and computing power.

To allow the potential computing power of all a company's computers to be shared, IBM's software engineers developed new e-business software that enables computers to work seamlessly together. Among its other capabilities, this software allows computer operators to monitor hundreds of different computers at the same time and shift work from one machine to another to distribute a company's computing power to wherever it is most needed. This has several cost-saving advantages. First, companies can run their computers at a much higher level, close to capacity, thereby greatly improving IT productivity and reducing operating costs.

Second, to ensure that its customers never experience a "drought," IBM uses its own vast computer capacity as a kind of bank or reservoir that customers can tap into whenever their own systems become overloaded. For example, using IBM's e-business software, companies can shift any excess work to IBM's computers rather than investing tens of millions of dollars in extra computers—a huge cost saving. Third, when a company's computers are seamlessly networked together, they can function as a supercomputer, a computer with immense information processing power, which can easily cost upward of $50 million just to purchase and tens of millions more to maintain.

IBM decided to implement its new e-business IT in its own company to show customers the cost-saving potential of its new products. Previously, IBM had allowed its many different product divisions to choose whatever software they liked to manage their own purchasing and supply chain activities. Palmisano appointed star manager Linda Stanford to overhaul IBM's whole supply chain, which amounts to $44 billion in yearly purchases. She is responsible for developing software to link them all into a single e-business system. IBM expects this will result in a 5% productivity gain each year for the next 5 to 10 years—which translates into savings of $2 billion a year. IBM is telling its customers that they can expect to see similar savings if they purchase its software.

IBM's new e-business system also has many other performance-enhancing benefits. Its thousands of consultants are experts in particular industries, such as the car, financial services, or retail industries. They have a deep understanding of the particular problems facing companies in those industries and how to solve them. Palmisano asked IBM's consultants to work closely with its software engineers to find ways to incorporate their knowledge into advanced software that can be implanted into a customer's IT system. IBM has developed 17 industry-specific expert systems, which consist of problem-solving software managers can use to make better business decisions and control a company's operations. One expert system is being developed for the pharmaceutical industry. Using this new software, a pharmaceutical company's interlinked computers will be able to function as a supercomputer and simulate and model the potential success of new drugs under development. Currently, only 5% to 10% of new drugs make it to the market. IBM believes that its new IT could raise that rate to over 50%, which would lead to billions of dollars in cost savings.[26]

LO4 Differentiate among seven performance-enhancing kinds of management information systems.

Just as computer hardware has been advancing rapidly, so has computer software. *Operating system software* tells the computer hardware how to run. *Applications software,* such as programs for word processing, spreadsheets, graphics, and database management, is software developed for a specific task or use. The increase in the power of computer hardware has allowed software developers to write increasingly powerful programs that are, at the same time, increasingly user-friendly. By harnessing the rapidly growing power of microprocessors, applications software has vastly increased the ability of managers to acquire, organize, manipulate, and transmit information. In doing so, it also has increased the ability of managers to coordinate and control the activities of their organization and to make decisions, as discussed earlier.

Types of Management Information Systems

Advancing computer hardware and software has continuously increased managers' ability to obtain the information they need to make decisions and to coordinate and control organizational resources. Next, we discuss six types of management information systems that over time have been particularly helpful to managers as they go about the task of managing: transaction-processing systems, operations information systems, decision support systems, expert systems, enterprise resource planning systems, and e-commerce systems (see Figure 18.4). These systems are arranged along a continuum according to the sophistication of the IT they are based on—IT that determines their ability to provide managers with the information they need to make nonprogrammed decisions. (Recall from Chapter 7 that nonprogrammed decision making occurs in response to unusual, unpredictable opportunities and threats.) We examine each of these systems after focusing on the management information system that preceded them all: the organizational hierarchy.

The Organizational Hierarchy: The Traditional Information System

Traditionally, managers have used the organizational hierarchy as the main system for gathering the information necessary to make decisions and coordinate and control activities (see Chapter 10 for a detailed discussion of organizational structure and hierarchy). According to business historian Alfred Chandler, the use of the hierarchy as an information network was perfected by railroad companies in the United States during the 1850s.[27] At that time, the railroads were the largest industrial organizations in the United States. By virtue of their size and geographic spread, they faced unique problems of coordination and control. In the 1850s, railroad companies started to solve these problems by designing hierarchical management structures that provided senior managers with the information they needed to achieve coordination and control and to make decisions about the running of the railroads.

Daniel McCallum, superintendent of the Erie Railroad in the 1850s, realized that the lines of authority and responsibility defining the Erie's management hierarchy also represented channels of communication along which information traveled. McCallum established what was perhaps the first modern management information system. Regular daily and monthly reports were sent up the management chain so that top managers could make decisions about, for example, controlling costs and setting freight rates. Decisions were then relayed back down the hierarchy so that they could be carried out. Imitating the railroads, most other organizations used their hierarchies as systems for collecting and channeling information. This practice began to change only when computer-based IT became more reasonably priced in the 1960s.

Figure 18.4

Six Computer-Based Management Information Systems

Although hierarchy is a useful information system, it has several drawbacks. First, when an organization has many layers of managers, it takes a long time for information and requests to travel up the hierarchy and for decisions and answers to travel back down. This slow pace can reduce the timeliness and usefulness of the information and prevent an organization from responding quickly to changing market conditions.[28] Second, information can be distorted as it moves from one layer of management to another, and information distortion reduces the quality of information.[29] Third, because managers have only a limited span of control, as an organization grows larger, its hierarchy lengthens, and this tall structure can make the hierarchy a very expensive information system. The popular idea that companies with tall management hierarchies are bureaucratic and unresponsive to the needs of their customers arises from the inability of tall hierarchies to effectively process data and provide managers with timely, complete, relevant, and high-quality information. Until modern IT came along, however, the management hierarchy was the best information system available.

Transaction-Processing Systems

transaction-processing system A management information system designed to handle large volumes of routine, recurring transactions.

A **transaction-processing system** is an MIS designed to handle large volumes of routine, recurring transactions (see Figure 18.4). Transaction-processing systems began to appear in the early 1960s with the advent of commercially available mainframe computers. They were the first type of computer-based IT adopted by many organizations, and today they are commonplace. Bank managers use a transaction-processing system to record deposits into, and payments out of, bank accounts. Supermarket managers use a transaction-processing system to record the sale of items and to track inventory levels. More generally, most managers in large organizations use a transaction-processing system to handle tasks such as payroll preparation and payment, customer billing, and payment of suppliers.

Operations Information Systems

operations information system A management information system that gathers, organizes, and summarizes comprehensive data in a form that managers can use in their nonroutine coordinating, controlling, and decision-making tasks.

Many types of MIS followed hard on the heels of transaction-processing systems in the 1960s as companies like IBM advanced IT. An **operations information system** is an MIS that gathers comprehensive data, organizes them, and summarizes them in a form that is of value to managers. Whereas a transaction-processing system processes routine transactions, an operations information system provides managers with information that they can use in their nonroutine coordinating, controlling, and decision-making tasks. Most operations information systems are coupled with a transaction-processing system. An operations information system typically accesses data gathered by a transaction-processing system, processes those data into useful information, and organizes that information into a form accessible to managers. Managers often use an operations information system to get sales, inventory, accounting, and other performance-related information. For example, the information that T. J. Rodgers at Cypress Semiconductors gets on individual employee goals and performance is provided by an operations information system.

DHL uses an operations information system to track the performance of its 500 or so ground stations. Each ground station is evaluated according to four criteria: delivery (the goal is to deliver 95% of all packages by noon the day after they are picked up), productivity (measured by the number of packages shipped per employee-hour), controllable cost, and station profitability. Each ground station also has specific delivery, efficiency, cost, and profitability targets that it must attain. Every month DHL's operations information system is used to gather information on these four criteria and summarize it for top managers, who are then able to compare the performance of each station against its previously established targets. The system quickly alerts senior managers to underperforming ground stations, so they can intervene selectively to help solve any problems that may have given rise to the poor performance.[30]

Decision Support Systems

decision support system
An interactive computer-based management information system that managers can use to make nonroutine decisions.

A **decision support system** provides computer-built models that help managers make better nonprogrammed decisions.[31] Recall from Chapter 7 that nonprogrammed decisions are decisions that are relatively unusual or novel, such as decisions to invest in new productive capacity, develop a new product, launch a new promotional campaign, enter a new market, or expand internationally. Although an operations information system organizes important information for managers, a decision support system gives managers a model-building capability and so provides them with the ability to manipulate information in a variety of ways. Managers might use a decision support system to help them decide whether to cut prices for a product. The decision support system might contain models of how customers and competitors would respond to a price cut. Managers could run these models and use the results as an *aid* to decision making.

The stress on the word *aid* is important, for in the final analysis a decision support system is not meant to make decisions for managers. Rather, its function is to provide managers with valuable information that they can use to improve the quality of their decisions. A good example of a sophisticated decision support system, developed by Judy Lewent, chief financial officer of the U.S. pharmaceutical company Merck, is given in the following "Manager as a Person."

Manager as a Person

How Judy Lewent Became One of the Most Powerful Women in Corporate America

With annual sales of over $40 billion, Merck is one of the world's largest developers and marketers of advanced pharmaceuticals.[32] The company spent over $3 billion a year on R&D to develop new drugs—an expensive and difficult process that is fraught with risks. Most new drug ideas fail to make it through the development process. It takes an average of $300 million and 10 years to bring a new drug to market, and 7 out of 10 new drugs fail to make a profit for the developing company.

Given the costs, risks, and uncertainties involved in the new drug development process, Judy Lewent, the former director of capital analysis at Merck, decided to develop a decision support system that could help managers make more effective R&D investment decisions. Her aim was to give Merck's top managers the information they needed to evaluate proposed R&D projects on a case-by-case basis. The system that Lewent and her staff developed is referred to in Merck as the "Research Planning Model."[33] At the heart of this decision support system is a sophisticated model. The input variables to the model include data on R&D spending, manufacturing costs, selling costs, and demand conditions. The relationships among the input variables are modeled by means of several equations that factor in the probability of a drug's making it through the development process and to market. The outputs of this modeling process are the revenues, cash flows, and profits that a project might generate.

Judy Lewent's research planning model has allowed Merck to more strategically develop promising new drugs while avoiding pitfalls, thus sharpening the company's focus and allowing it to roll out such programs as an HIV/AIDS prevention initiative in China, pictured here.

The Merck model does not use a single value for an input variable, nor does it compute a single value for each output. Rather, a range is specified for each input variable (such as high, medium, and low R&D spending). The computer repeatedly samples at random from the range of values for each input variable and produces a probability distribution of values for each output. So, for example, instead of stating categorically that a proposed R&D project will yield a profit of $500 million, the decision support system produces a probability distribution. It might state that although $500 million is the most likely profit, there is a 25% chance that the profit will be less than $300 million and a 25% chance that it will be greater than $700 million.

Merck now uses Lewent's decision support system to evaluate all proposed R&D investment decisions. In addition, Lewent has developed other decision support system models that Merck's managers can use to help them decide, for example, whether to enter into joint ventures with other companies or how best to hedge foreign exchange risk. As for Lewent, her reward was promotion to the position of chief financial officer of Merck, and she became one of the most powerful women in corporate America.

Most decision support systems are geared toward aiding middle managers in the decision-making process. For example, a loan manager at a bank might use a decision support system to evaluate the credit risk involved in lending money to a particular client. Very rarely does a top manager use a decision support system. One reason for this may be that most electronic management information systems are not yet sophisticated enough to handle effectively the ambiguous types of problems facing top managers. To improve this situation, IT professionals have been developing a variant of the decision support system: an executive support system.

executive support system
A sophisticated version of a decision support system that is designed to meet the needs of top managers.

An **executive support system** is a sophisticated version of a decision support system that is designed to meet the needs of top managers. Lewent's Research Planning Model is actually an executive support system. One of the defining characteristics of executive support systems is user-friendliness. Many of them include simple pull-down menus to take a manager through a decision analysis problem. Moreover, they may contain stunning graphics and other visual features to encourage top managers to use them.[34] Increasingly, executive support systems are being used to link top managers so that they can function as a team; this type of executive support system is called a **group decision support system.**

group decision support system An executive support system that links top managers so that they can function as a team.

Artificial Intelligence and Expert Systems

artificial intelligence
Behavior performed by a machine that, if performed by a human being, would be called "intelligent."

Artificial intelligence is another interesting and potentially fruitful software development. **Artificial intelligence** has been defined as behavior by a machine that, if performed by a human being, would be called "intelligent."[35] Artificial intelligence has already made it possible to write programs that can solve problems and perform simple tasks. For example, software programs variously called *software agents, softbots,* or *knowbots* can be used to perform simple managerial tasks such as sorting through reams of data or incoming e-mail messages to look for the important ones. The interesting feature of these programs is that from "watching" a manager sort through such data they can "learn" what his or her preferences are. Having done this, they then can take over some of this work from the manager, freeing more time for the manager to work on other tasks. Most of these programs are still in the development stage, but they may be commonplace within a decade.[36]

expert system
A management information system that employs human knowledge, embedded in a computer, to solve problems that ordinarily require human expertise.

Expert systems, the most advanced management information systems available, incorporate artificial intelligence in their design.[37] An **expert system** is a system that employs human knowledge, embedded in computer software, to solve problems that ordinarily require human expertise.[38] Mimicking human expertise (and intelligence) requires IT that can at a minimum (1) recognize, formulate, and solve a problem; (2) explain the solution; and (3) learn from experience.

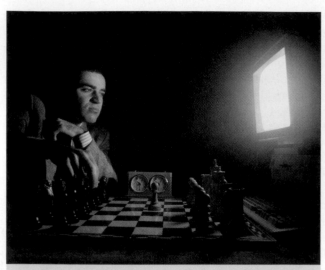

Artificial intelligence takes to the boards. Chess expert Garry Kasporov squares off against IBM's chess-playing computer Deep Blue. In 1997, Deep Blue and Garry traded wins, ending in a decisive victory for the computer—after it had been reprogrammed.

Recent developments in artificial intelligence that go by names such as "fuzzy logic" and "neural networks" have resulted in computer programs that, in a primitive way, try to mimic human thought processes. Although artificial intelligence is still at a fairly early stage of development, an increasing number of business applications are beginning to emerge in the form of expert systems. General Electric, for example, has developed an expert system to help troubleshoot problems in the diesel locomotive engines it manufactures. The expert system was originally based on knowledge collected from David Smith, GE's former top locomotive troubleshooter. A novice engineer or technician can use the system to uncover a fault by spending only a few minutes at a computer terminal. The system also can explain to the user the logic of its advice, thereby serving as a teacher as well as a problem solver. The system is based on a flexible, humanlike thought process, and it can be updated to incorporate new knowledge as it becomes available. GE has installed the system in every railroad repair shop that it serves, thus eliminating delays and boosting maintenance productivity.[39]

Enterprise Resource Planning Systems

To achieve high performance, it is not sufficient just to develop an MIS inside each of a company's functions or divisions to provide better information and knowledge. It is also vital that managers in the different functions and divisions have access to information about the activities of managers in other functions and divisions. The greater the flow of information and knowledge among functions and divisions, the more learning can take place, and this builds a company's stock of knowledge and expertise. This knowledge and expertise is the source of its competitive advantage and profitability.

In the last 25 years, another revolution has taken place in IT as software companies have worked to develop enterprise resource planning systems, which essentially incorporate most aspects of the MISs just discussed, as well as much more. **Enterprise resource planning (ERP) systems** are multimodule application software packages that allow a company to link and coordinate the entire set of functional activities and operations necessary to move products from the initial product design stage to the final customer stage. Essentially, ERP systems (1) help each individual function improve its functional-level skills and (2) improve integration among all functions so that they work together to build a competitive advantage for the company. Today, choosing and designing an ERP system to improve the way a company operates is the biggest challenge facing the IT function inside a company. To understand why almost every large global company has installed an ERP system in the last few decades, it is necessary to return to the concept of the value chain, introduced in Chapter 8.

Recall that a company's value chain is composed of the sequence of functional activities that are necessary to make and sell a product. The value-chain idea focuses attention on the fact that each function, in sequence, performs its activities to add or contribute value to a product. Once one function has made its contribution, it then hands the product over to the next function, which makes its own contribution, and so on down the line.

The primary activity of marketing, for example, is to uncover new or changing customer needs or new groups of customers and then decide what kinds of products should be developed to appeal to those customers. It then shares or "hands off" its information to product development, where engineers and scientists work to develop and design the new products. In turn, manufacturing and materials management then

enterprise resource planning (ERP) systems Multimodule application software packages that coordinate the functional activities necessary to move products from the product design stage to the final customer stage.

work to find ways to produce the new products as efficiently as possible. Then, sales is responsible for finding the best way to convince customers to buy these products.

The value chain is useful in demonstrating the sequence of activities necessary to bring products to the market successfully. In an IT context, however, it suggests the enormous amount of information and communication that needs to take place to link and coordinate the activities of all the various functions. Installing an ERP system for a large company can cost tens of millions of dollars. The following "Information Technology Byte" discusses the ERP system designed and sold by the German IT company SAP.

Information Technology Byte

SAP's ERP System

SAP is the world's leading supplier of ERP software; it introduced the world's first ERP system in 1973. So great was the demand for its software that it had to train thousands of consultants from companies like IBM, HP, Accenture, and Cap Gemini to install and customize its software to meet the needs of companies in different industries throughout the world.

The popularity of SAP's ERP is that it manages all the stages of a company's value chain, both individually and as a collection. SAP's software has modules specifically devoted to each of a company's core functional activities. Each module contains a set of "best practices," or the optimum way to perform specific activities, that SAP's IT experts have found results in the biggest increases in efficiency, quality, innovation, and responsiveness to customers. SAP's ERP is therefore "the expert system of expert systems." SAP claims that when a company reconfigures its IT system to make SAP's software work, it can achieve productivity gains of 30% to 50%, which amounts to many billions of dollars of savings for large companies.[40]

For each function in the value chain, SAP has a software module that it installs on a function's LAN. Each function then inputs its data into that module in the way specified by SAP. For example, the sales function inputs all the information about customer needs required by SAP's sales module, and the materials management function inputs information about the product specifications it requires from suppliers into SAP's materials management module. These modules give functional managers real-time feedback on the status of their particular functional activities. Essentially, each SAP module functions as an expert system that can reason through the information functional managers put into it. It then provides them with recommendations as to how they can improve functional operations. However, the magic of ERP does not stop there.

SAP's ERP software also connects across functions. Managers in all functions have access to the other functions' expert systems, and SAP's software is designed to alert managers when their functional activities will be affected by changes taking place in another function. Thus, SAP's ERP allows managers across the organization to better coordinate their activities, and this can be a major source of competitive advantage. Moreover, SAP software on corporate mainframe computers takes the information from all the different functional and divisional expert systems and creates a companywide ERP system that provides top managers with an overview of the operations of the whole company. In essence, SAP's ERP creates a sophisticated top-level expert system that can reason through the huge volume of information being provided by the company's functions. It can then recognize and diagnose common problems and issues in that information and develop and recommend organizationwide solutions for those problems and issues. Top managers armed with this information can then use it to improve the fit between their strategies and the changing environment.

As an example of how an ERP system works, let's examine how SAP's software allows managers to better coordinate their activities to speed product development. Suppose marketing has discovered some new unmet customer need, suggested what kind of product needs to be developed, and forecasted that the demand for the product will be 40,000 units a year. With SAP's IT, engineers in product development use their expert system to work out how to design the new product in a way that builds in quality at the lowest possible cost. Manufacturing managers, watching product development's progress, are working simultaneously to find the best way to make the product, and thus use their expert system to find out how to keep operating costs at a minimum.

Remember, SAP's IT gives all the other functions access to this information; they can tap into what is going on between marketing and manufacturing in real time. So materials management managers watching manufacturing make its plans can simultaneously plan how to order supplies of inputs or components from global suppliers or how and when to ship the final product to customers to keep costs at a minimum. At the same time, HRM is tied into the ERP system and uses its expert system to forecast the type and cost of the labor that will be required to carry out the activities in the other functions—for example, the number of manufacturing employees who will be required to make the product or the number of salespeople who will be needed to sell the product to achieve the 40,000 sales forecast.

How does this build competitive advantage and profitability? First, it speeds up the product development process; companies can bring products to market much more quickly, thereby generating higher sales revenues. Second, SAP's IT focuses on how to drive down operating costs while keeping quality high. Third, SAP's IT is oriented toward the final customer; its CRM module watches how customers respond to the new product and then feeds back this information quickly to the other functions.

To see what this means in practice, let's jump ahead three months and suppose that the CRM component of SAP's ERP software reports that actual sales are 20% below target. Further, the software has reasoned that the problem is due to the fact that the product lacks one crucial feature that customers want. The product is a smart phone, for example, and customers must have a built-in digital camera. Sales decides this issue deserves major priority and alerts managers in all the other functions about the problem. Now managers can begin to make decisions about how to manage this unexpected situation.

Engineers in product development, for example, use their expert system to work out how much it would cost, and how long it would take, to modify the product so that it includes the missing feature, the digital camera, that customers require. Managers in other functions watch the engineers' progress through the ERP system and can make suggestions for improvement. In the meantime, manufacturing managers know about the slow sales and have already cut back on production to avoid a buildup of the unsold product in the company's warehouse. They are also planning how to phase out this product and introduce the next version, with the digital camera, to keep costs as low as possible. Similarly, materials management managers are contacting digital-camera makers to find out how much such a camera will cost and when it can be supplied. In the meantime, marketing managers are researching how they came to miss this crucial product feature and are developing new sales forecasts to estimate demand for the modified product. They announce a revised sales forecast of 75,000 units of the modified product.

It takes the engineers one month to modify the product, but because SAP's IT has been providing information on the modified product to managers in manufacturing and materials management, the product hits the market only two months later. Within weeks, the sales function reports that early sales figures for the product have greatly exceeded even marketing's revised forecast. The company knows it has a winning product, and top managers give the go-ahead for manufacturing to build a second production line to double production of the product. All the other functions are expecting this decision; in fact, they have already been experimenting with their SAP modules to find out how long it will take them to respond to such a move. Each function provides the others with its latest information so that they can all adjust their functional activities accordingly.

All this quick and responsive action has been made possible because of the ERP system. Compare this situation to that of a company which relies only on a paper-based system, in which salespeople fill in paper sales reports. In such a company, it would take many times as long to find out about slow sales; it might take six months to a year for the company to find out that its sales projections were wrong. In the meantime, manufacturing, producing according to plan, will generate a huge stock of unsold products, which is a major source of operating costs. When the sales problem is finally uncovered, managers from the different functions will have to make frantic phone calls and hold face-to-face meetings to decide what to do. It might take another six months for the modified product to come into production, so more than one year of time, and huge potential profits, will have been lost.

In the ERP example, efficiency is promoted because a company has a better control of its manufacturing and materials management activities. Quality is increased because an increased flow of information between functions allows for a better-designed product. Innovation is speeded because a company can rapidly change its products to suit the changing needs of customers. Finally, responsiveness to customers improves because using its CRM software module, sales can better manage and react to customer's changing needs and provide better service and support to back up the sales of the product. ERP's ability to promote competitive advantage is the reason why managers in so many companies, large and small, are moving to find the best ERP "solution" for their particular companies.

E-Commerce Systems

e-commerce Trade that takes place between companies, and between companies and individual customers, using IT and the Internet.

E-commerce is trade that takes place between companies, and between companies and individual customers, using IT and the Internet. **Business-to-business (B2B) commerce** is trade that takes place between companies using IT and the Internet to link and coordinate the value chains of different companies. (See Figure 18.5.) The goal of B2B commerce is to increase the profitability of making and selling goods and services. B2B commerce increases profitability because it allows companies to reduce

Figure 18.5

Types of E-Commerce

their operating costs or because it may improve product quality. A principal B2B software application is **B2B marketplaces,** Internet-based trading platforms that have been set up in many industries to connect buyers and sellers. To participate in a B2B marketplace, companies adopt a common software standard that allows them to search for and share information with one another. Then companies can work together over time to find ways to reduce costs or improve quality.

Business-to-customer (B2C) commerce is trade that takes place between a company and individual customers using IT and the Internet. Using IT to connect directly to the customer means that companies can avoid having to use intermediaries, such as wholesalers and retailers, who capture a significant part of the profit being created in the value chain. The use of Web sites and online stores also allows companies to provide their customers with much more information about the value of their products. This often allows them to attract more customers and thus generate higher sales revenues. We discuss this important issue in depth in the chapters on marketing and sales.

In the last five years, computer software makers including Microsoft, Oracle, SAP, and IBM, have rushed to make their products work seamlessly with the Internet to respond to global companies' growing demand for e-commerce software. Previously, their software had been configured to work only on a particular company's intranet. Now, they have had to develop software that would network the computer systems of companies to their suppliers and customers.

Today, the challenge facing managers is to select the e-commerce software that allows the seamless exchange of information between companies anywhere in the world. The stakes are high; we discussed earlier how IBM's new thrust is toward on-demand software. SAP has also rushed to update its ERP modules to allow for transactions over the Internet. It calls its new B2B commerce software "mySAP," and today every one of its modules is Internet-compatible. Microsoft is promoting its .net Internet software, which is compatible with all its other Windows software, and is vigorously competing with IBM and SAP to raise its share of this growing software market.

LO5 Explain how IT is helping managers build strategic alliances and network structures to increase efficiency and effectiveness.

In summary, by using computer-based MISs, managers have more control over a company's activities and operations and can work to improve its competitive advantage and profitability. Today, the IT function is becoming increasingly important because IT managers select which kind of hardware and software a company will use and also train employees to use it.

The Impact and Limitations of Information Technology

The advances in IT and management information systems described in this chapter are having important effects on managers and organizations. By improving the ability of managers to coordinate and control the activities of the organization and by helping managers make more effective decisions, modern IT has become a central component of any organization's structure. And evidence that IT can be a source of competitive advantage is growing; organizations that do not adopt leading-edge IT are likely to be at a competitive disadvantage. In this section we examine how the rapid advances in IT are affecting organizational structure and competitive advantage. We also examine problems associated with implementing management information systems effectively, as well as the limitations of MISs.

Strategic Alliances, B2B Network Structures, and IT

Recently, increasing globalization and the use of new IT has brought about two innovations that are sweeping through U.S. and European companies: electronically managed strategic alliances and B2B network structures. A **strategic alliance** is a formal agreement that commits two or more companies to exchange or share their resources in order to produce and market a product.[41] Most commonly, strategic alliances are formed because the companies share similar interests and believe they can benefit from cooperating. For example, Japanese car companies such as Toyota and Honda have formed many strategic alliances with particular suppliers of inputs such as car axles, gearboxes, and air-conditioning systems. Over time, these car companies work closely with their suppliers to improve the efficiency and effectiveness of the inputs so that the final product—the car produced—is of higher quality and very often can be produced at lower cost. Toyota and Honda have also established alliances with suppliers throughout the United States and Mexico because both companies now build several models of cars in these countries.

Throughout the 1990s, the growing sophistication of IT with global intranets and teleconferencing has made it much easier to manage strategic alliances and allow managers to share information and cooperate. One outcome of this has been the growth of strategic alliances into an IT-based network structure. A **B2B network structure** is a formal series of global strategic alliances that one or several organizations create with suppliers, manufacturers, and/or distributors to produce and market a product. Network structures allow an organization to manage its global value chain in order to find new ways to reduce costs and increase the quality of products—without incurring the high costs of operating a complex organizational structure (such as the costs of employing many managers). More and more U.S. and European companies are relying on global network structures to gain access to low-cost foreign sources of inputs, as discussed in Chapter 6. Shoemakers such as Nike and Adidas are two companies that have used this approach extensively.

Nike is the largest and most profitable sports shoe manufacturer in the world. The key to Nike's success is the network structure that Nike founder and CEO Philip Knight created to allow his company to produce and market shoes. As noted in Chapter 8, the most successful companies today are trying to pursue simultaneously a low-cost and a differentiation strategy. Knight decided early that to do this at Nike he needed to focus his company's efforts on the most important functional activities, such as product design and engineering, and leave the others, such as manufacturing, to other organizations.

By far the largest function at Nike's Oregon headquarters is the design and engineering function, whose members pioneered innovations in sports shoe design such as the air pump and Air Jordans that Nike introduced so successfully. Designers use computer-aided design (CAD) to design Nike shoes, and they electronically store all new product information, including manufacturing instructions. When the designers have finished their work, they electronically transmit all the blueprints for the new products to a network of Southeast Asian suppliers and manufacturers with which Nike has formed strategic alliances.[42] Instructions for the design of a new sole may be sent to a supplier in Taiwan; instructions for the leather uppers, to a supplier in Malaysia. The suppliers produce the shoe parts and send them for final assembly to a manufacturer in China with which Nike has established another strategic alliance. From China the shoes are shipped to distributors throughout the world. Ninety-nine percent of the over 100 million pairs of shoes that Nike makes each year are made in Southeast Asia.

This network structure gives Nike two important advantages. First, Nike is able to respond to changes in sports shoe fashion very quickly. Using its global IT system, Nike literally can change the instructions it gives each of its suppliers overnight, so that within a few weeks its foreign manufacturers are producing new kinds of shoes.[43] Any alliance partners that fail to perform up to Nike's standards are replaced with new partners through the regular B2B marketplace.

Second, Nike's costs are very low because wages in Southeast Asia are a fraction of what they are in the United States, and this difference gives Nike a low-cost advantage. Also, Nike's ability to outsource and use foreign manufacturers to produce all its shoes abroad allows Knight to keep the organization's U.S. structure flat and flexible. Nike is able to use a relatively inexpensive functional structure to organize its activities.

B2B network structure
A series of global strategic alliances that an organization creates with suppliers, manufacturers, and/or distributors to produce and market a product.

The use of network structures is increasing rapidly as organizations recognize the many opportunities they offer to reduce costs and increase organizational flexibility. U.S. companies spent $300 billion on global supply chain management each year in the 2000s. The push to lower costs has led to the development of B2B marketplaces in which most or all of the companies in an industry (for example, carmakers) use the same software platform to link to each other and establish industry specifications and standards. Then these companies jointly list the quantity and specifications of the inputs they require and invite bids from the thousands of potential suppliers around the world. Suppliers also use the same software platform, so electronic bidding, auctions, and transactions are possible between buyers and sellers around the world. The idea is that high-volume standardized transactions can help drive down costs at the industry level. Also, quality will increase as these relationships become stable as a B2B network structure develops.

Flatter Structures and Horizontal Information Flows

Rapid advances in IT have been associated with a "delayering" (flattening) of the organizational hierarchy, a move toward greater decentralization and horizontal information flows within organizations, and the concept of the boundaryless organization.[44]

FLATTENING ORGANIZATIONS   By electronically providing managers with high-quality, timely, relevant, and relatively complete information, modern management information systems have reduced the need for tall management hierarchies. (See Figure 18.6). Consider again the computer-based operations information system that T. J. Rodgers uses at Cypress Semiconductor to review the performance of his 1,500 employees. Ten years ago, Rodgers might have needed 100 managers to conduct such performance reviews; now he can do them himself in four hours a week. Modern IT has reduced the need for a hierarchy to function as a means of coordinating and controlling organizational activities. Also, by reducing the need for hierarchy, modern IT can directly increase an organization's efficiency because fewer employees are required to perform organizational activities. At one time, for example, 13 layers of management separated Kodak's general manager of manufacturing and factory workers. With IT the number of layers has been cut to four. Similarly, Intel found that by increasing

Figure 18.6

How Computer-Based Information Systems Affect the Organizational Hierarchy

Before

Tall structure
primarily up-down
communication

After

Flat structure
both up-down
and lateral
communication

the sophistication of its own MIS, it could cut the number of hierarchical layers in the organization from 10 to 5.[45]

HORIZONTAL INFORMATION FLOWS   Fired by the growth of four-tier mainframe-server-client-laptop and PDA computing architecture (see Figure 18.3), expansion of organizationwide computer networks has been rapid in recent years. E-mail systems, the development of software programs for sharing documents electronically, and the development of intranets (see Chapter 16) have accelerated this trend. An important consequence has been the increase of horizontal information flows within organizations, something illustrated well by the experiences of Tel Co. and Soft Co., discussed in the following "Information Technology Byte."

Information Technology Byte

Small Business

Information Flows at Tel Co. and Soft Co.

Despite being part of a high-tech company, managers at Tel Co. were slow to adopt an internal electronic mail system (e-mail) to facilitate communication throughout the company. Soft Co., by contrast, is a software company in which managers virtually "live online" and most communication between them takes place by means of e-mail. Commenting on how the two companies differ, a manager who moved from Tel Co. to Soft Co. said:

At Tel Co. I would take two boxes of memos and company reports home with me each weekend to read. Then I had to go through all this stuff, most of which was irrelevant to my job, to find those pieces of paper that mattered to me. It was very time-consuming, very unproductive. At Soft Co. there is no paper to take home; most communication takes place via the company's e-mail system. I use a software agent to scan all my incoming e-mail and prioritize it [a software agent is a computer program that can perform certain tasks—such as sorting through and prioritizing incoming e-mail]. This saves a massive amount of time. The system alerts me instantly to e-mail that is relevant to my job.[46]

This manager also noted that the use of an e-mail system led to other communication differences between the two companies. At Tel Co. communication is primarily vertical; middle managers send information up the organizational hierarchy, and top managers send their responses back down. At Soft Co., however, communication between managers at different levels has become far less structured, and because of the e-mail system there is much less emphasis on formal channels of communication. E-mail allows managers at any level to communicate easily with one another, so managers at Soft Co. communicate directly with whomever they need to contact to get the job done. Also, e-mail has resulted in much more cross-functional, horizontal communication because it is so easy for managers in different functions to communicate.

The observations of this manager about communication flows at Tel Co. and Soft Co. were confirmed in a study undertaken by Alta Analytics, a management consulting company.[47] Figure 18.7 shows maps of the communication flows between managers based in different departments at Tel Co. and Soft Co. The boxes in these two maps are employees grouped by function. To make these maps, Alta asked employees to name every manager with whom they had communication in any form—phone, meeting, memo, e-mail—in the past week. If two people agreed that they had three or more important contacts, the mapmakers drew a line between their boxes, indicating a significant link.

Figure 18.7

Communication Flows at Tel Co. and Soft Co.

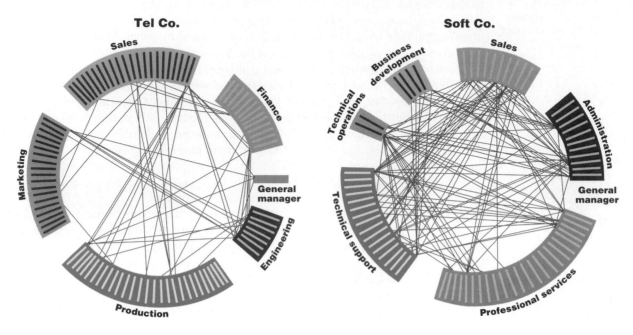

Source: T. A. Stewart, "Managing in a Wired Company," *Fortune,* July 11, 1994, 54. © 1994 Time, Inc. Reprinted with permission. NETMAP® is a registered trademark for the NETMAP Software Systems, Alta Analytics, Inc., Westerville, OH.

The differences between the two companies are immediately apparent. At Tel Co., the general manager communicated only with four senior functional managers, all of whom had a direct reporting relationship with him; there were hardly any links between the marketing and production departments; and a handful of functional managers accounted for most of the interfunctional communication. At Soft Co., there was a much richer flow of communication between managers in the different functions, as indicated by the number of lines connecting the different boxes. Clearly, boundaries between functions mean little at Soft Co., as do differences in rank. Almost everybody talks to everybody else because of Soft Co.'s e-mail system. At Soft Co. the development of organizationwide computer networks has broken down the barriers that have traditionally separated functional departments and divisions and the result has been improved performance.

THE BOUNDARYLESS ORGANIZATION The ability of IT to flatten structure and facilitate the flow of horizontal information between employees has led many researchers and consultants to popularize the idea of a **boundaryless organization.** Such an organization is composed of people linked by IT—computers, faxes, computer-aided design systems, and video teleconferencing—who may rarely, if ever, see one another face-to-face. People are utilized when their services are needed, much as in a matrix structure, but they are not formal members of an organization; they are functional experts who form an alliance with an organization, fulfill their contractual obligations, and then move on to the next project.

boundaryless organization
An organization whose members are linked by computers, faxes, computer-aided design systems, and video teleconferencing and who rarely, if ever, see one another face-to-face.

Large consulting companies, such as Accenture and McKinsey & Co., utilize their global consultants in this way. Consultants are connected by laptops to an organization's **knowledge management system,** its company-specific virtual information system that systematizes the knowledge of its employees and facilitates the sharing and integrating of expertise within and between functions and divisions through real-time, interconnected IT. Knowledge management systems enable employees to

knowledge management system A company-specific virtual information system that systematizes the knowledge of its employees and facilitates the sharing and integrating of their expertise.

share their knowledge and expertise and provide them with virtual access to other employees who have the expertise to solve the problems that they encounter as they perform their jobs.

Limitations of IT

For all of their usefulness, IT in general and management information systems in particular have some limitations. A serious potential problem is that in all of the enthusiasm for management information systems, electronic communication by means of a computer network, and the like, a vital *human element* of communication might be lost. Some kinds of information cannot be aggregated and summarized on an MIS report. Henry Mintzberg noted that *thick information* is often required to coordinate and control an enterprise and to make informed decisions; Mintzberg means information rich in meaning and significance, far beyond that which can be quantified and aggregated.[48] According to Mintzberg, such information must be dug out, on-site, by people closely involved in the events they wish to influence.

The importance of thick information is a strong argument in favor of using electronic communication to support face-to-face communication, not to replace it. For example, it would be wrong to make a judgment about an individual's performance merely by "reading the numbers" provided by an MIS. Instead, the numbers should be used to alert managers to individuals who may have a performance problem. The nature of this problem should then be explored in a face-to-face meeting, during which thick information can be gathered. As a top Boeing manager noted,

> *In our company, the use of e-mail and videoconferencing has not reduced the need to visit people at other sites; it has increased it. E-mail has facilitated the establishment of communications channels between people who previously would not communicate, which is good, but direct visits are still required to cement any working relationships that evolve out of these electronic meetings.[49]*

At Soft Co., discussed earlier, managers were heard to complain that one drawback of their internal e-mail system is that people spend a lot of time behind closed doors looking at computer screens and communicating electronically and very little time interacting directly with other managers.[50] When this is the case in an organization, management decisions may suffer because of a lack of thick information. As described in the following "Management Insight," the experience of George Lucas and his high-tech digital media company also illustrates how IT must be woven into the organization to get the most performance benefits from it—and the importance of personal face-to-face contact.

Management Insight

The *Star Wars* Studio Reorganizes

The *Star Wars* movies are some of the best known in the world and George Lucas, the director who writes and produces them, is famous for his pioneering special effects. But in the 2000s competition from other special effects companies has intensified, and there is a huge market for new videogames, so there is increasing pressure on all companies to make the best use of their resources. So, what do you do if you manage a special effects company that has many different units staffed by talented engineers who are so far apart and distant from each other that they have no incentive to cooperate and share their knowledge? This was the problem confronting CEO Lucas and Micheline Chua, the president and COO of Lucas Arts: how to make better use of the talents of their creative digital artists and engineers who worked in a very autonomous way—often working independently and connected to their coworkers mainly by video conferencing systems that allow them to share their ideas.[51]

By 2008 Lucas and Chau realized they were losing valuable synergies between their various groups. They especially needed to make more use of the Industrial Light & Magic (ILM) Group, the unit responsible for the special effects behind the *Star Wars* movies and many other movies whose directors rely on its services to make their state-of-the-art special effects. How do you make different groups cooperate, especially when they each contain hundreds of talented design artists who value their own autonomy and are proud of their own achievements?

George Lucas with a pair of storm troopers from *Star Wars*. Lucas' special effects studio faced very real challenges in getting his company's digital artists and special effects crews to work together in order to compete in the video game industry.

The answer for Lucas was to build a new state-of-the-art $250 million office complex in the Presidio, a former army base and now a national park that has spectacular views of San Francisco bay. In this modernistic, futuristic building everything—from its rooms, facilities, and recreational areas—has been designed to facilitate communication and cooperation between people, but especially between the different units.[52] Both the ILM and Lucas Arts units have been thrust together, for example, and their members who now work face-to-face have been told to build a common digital platform that will allow each unit to learn and take advantage of the skills and knowledge of the other. To increase its performance, Lucas Arts needs these experts to collaborate and share their expertise to develop the state-of-the-art new movies, and especially video games, on which its future profitability depends. Indeed, the gaming market is booming in the 2000s as the Nintendo Wii and its competitors compete to develop the games that customers want, and these often rely on the state-of-the-art graphics that only companies like Lucas can produce.

Apparently both units have learned to work together and take advantage of the open, inviting lounges and work areas where designers can meet personally to share their skills and knowledge. One recent result of their cooperation has been the videogame *Star Wars: The Force Unleashed*. The gaming group credits the ILM group with providing the technology for the incredible lighting, facial, and movement effects that have made the game so popular. Who knows what might be in store in the future as the members of these units develop the personal relationships and networks necessary to create the next generation digital technology for movies and gaming.

Another limitation of IT in organizations is that despite its many advantages there are still technological problems to be overcome.[53] One of these is the lack of consistent technological standards, since different manufacturers of computer and communication equipment use different standards. If a company uses different kinds of hardware or software systems, made by different IT companies, throughout its divisions or functions, the inconsistency can impede communication and decision making. For example, an IBM mainframe may be manufactured according to technical standards different from those of a Sun or Compaq server or an Apple personal computer. These different standards make it difficult to integrate various machines into a seamless computer network, and machines designed according to different standards may find it difficult to "talk" to one another. One reason for the growing popularity of SAP's ERP is that it solves these problems because it provides a common IT standard throughout a company.

Managers can take several steps to make it easier and quicker to implement an MIS. First, they have to develop a list of the organization's principal goals and then decide on the major types of information they need to collect to measure how well they are achieving those goals. Second, while making this analysis, managers should audit their current MISs to determine the degree to which the information they are currently collecting is accurate, reliable, timely, and relevant. Third, managers need to investigate what other sources of information might be available to measure and improve efficiency, quality, innovation, and responsiveness to customers. For example, are organizational members using state-of-the-art IT like wireless e-mail, computer-assisted design, and four-tier designs? It is useful to benchmark competitors to determine what kinds of systems they are using.

Fourth, when this analysis is complete, managers need to build support for the introduction of an advanced MIS and convince employees that the system will help raise job and organizational performance. Fifth, managers should create formal training programs, with appropriate backup support, to help train employees to use the new information system and technology, making sure that the system is as user-friendly as possible. Sixth, managers should emphasize that the MIS is not a substitute for face-to-face communication and that employees at all levels should be involved in a continuing discussion about how best to take advantage of ongoing developments in IT to create a competitive advantage.

Summary and Review

INFORMATION AND THE MANAGER'S JOB   Computer-based IT is central to the operation of most organizations. By providing managers with high-quality, timely, relevant, and relatively complete information, properly implemented IT can improve managers' ability to coordinate and control the operations of an organization and to make effective decisions. Moreover, IT can help the organization to attain a competitive advantage through its beneficial impact on productivity, quality, innovation, and responsiveness to customers. Thus, modern IT is an indispensable management tool.

LO 1,2

LO3   **THE IT REVOLUTION**   Over the last 30 years there have been rapid advances in the power, and rapid declines in the cost, of IT. Falling prices, wireless communication, computer networks, and software developments have all radically improved the power and efficacy of computer-based IT.

LO4   **TYPES OF MANAGEMENT INFORMATION SYSTEMS**   Traditionally, managers used the organizational hierarchy as the main system for gathering the information they needed to coordinate and control the organization and to make effective decisions. Today, managers use six main types of computer-based information systems. Listed in ascending order of sophistication, they are transaction-processing systems, operations information systems, decision support systems, expert systems, enterprise resource planning systems, and e-commerce systems.

LO5   **THE IMPACT AND LIMITATIONS OF IT**   Modern IT has changed organizational structure in many ways. Using IT, managers can create a series of electronic strategic alliances and form a B2B network structure. A network structure, based on some shared form of IT, can be formed around one company, or a number of companies can join together to create an industry B2B network. Modern IT also makes organizations flatter and encourages more horizontal cross-functional communication. As this increasingly happens across the organizational boundary, the term *boundaryless organizations* has been coined to refer to virtual organizations whose members are linked electronically together.

Management in Action

Topics for Discussion and Action

DISCUSSION

1. To be useful, information must be of high quality, be timely, be relevant, and be as complete as possible. Why does a tall management hierarchy, when used as a management information system, have negative effects on these desirable attributes? **[LO1]**

2. What is the relationship between IT and competitive advantage? **[LO2]**

3. Because of the growth of high-powered, low-cost wireless communications and IT such as videoconferencing, many managers soon may not need to come into the office to do their jobs. They will be able to work at home. What are the pros and cons of such an arrangement? **[LO 3, 4]**

4. Many companies have reported that it is difficult to implement advanced management information systems such as ERP systems. Why do you think this is so? How might the roadblocks to implementation be removed? **[LO4]**

5. How can IT help in the new product development process? **[LO4]**

6. Why is face-to-face communication between managers still important in an organization? **[LO 4, 5]**

ACTION

7. Ask a manager to describe the main kinds of IT that he or she uses on a routine basis at work. **[LO 1, 4]**

8. Compare the pros and cons of using a network structure to perform organizational activities versus performing all activities in-house or within one organizational hierarchy. **[LO 3, 4, 5]**

9. What are the advantages and disadvantages of business-to-business networks? **[LO5]**

Building Management Skills
Analyzing Management Information Systems [LO 3, 4]

Pick an organization about which you have some direct knowledge. It may be an organization that you worked for in the past or are in contact with now (such as the college or school that you attend). For this organization, answer the following questions:

1. Describe the management information systems that are used to coordinate and control organizational activities and to help make decisions.

2. Do you think that the organization's existing MISs provide managers with high-quality, timely, relevant, and relatively complete information? Why, or why not?

3. How might advanced IT be used to improve the competitive position of this organization? In particular, try to identify the impact that a new MIS might have on the organization's efficiency, quality, innovation, and responsiveness to customers.

Managing Ethically [LO 1, 2]

The use of management information systems, such as ERPs, often gives employees access to confidential information from all functions and levels of an organization. Employees have access to important information about the company's products that is of great value to competitors. As a result, many companies monitor employees' use of the intranet and Internet to prevent an employee from acting unethically, for example, by selling this information to competitors. On the other hand, with access to this information employees might discover that their company has been engaging in unethical or even illegal practices.

Questions

1. Ethically speaking, how far should a company go to protect its proprietary information, given that it needs to also protect the privacy of its employees? What steps can it take?

2. When is it ethical for employees to give information about a company's unethical or illegal practices to a third party, such as a newspaper or government agency?

Small Group Breakout Exercise
Using New Management Information Systems [LO 2, 4]

Form groups of three or four people, and appoint one member as the spokesperson who will communicate your findings to the class when called on by the instructor. Then discuss the following scenario.

You are a team of managing partners of a large management consultancy company. You are responsible for auditing your firm's MISs to determine whether they are appropriate and up to date. To your surprise, you find that although your organization does have a wireless e-mail system in place and consultants are connected into a powerful local area network (LAN) at all times, most of the consultants (including partners) are not using this technology. It seems that most important decision making still takes place through the organizational hierarchy.

Given this situation, you are concerned that your organization is not exploiting the opportunities offered by new IT to obtain a competitive advantage. You have discussed this issue and are meeting to develop an action plan to get consultants to appreciate the need to learn about and use the new IT.

1. What advantages can you tell consultants they will obtain when they use the new IT?

2. What problems do you think you may encounter in convincing consultants to use the new IT?

3. What steps might you take to motivate consultants to learn to use the new technology?

Exploring the World Wide Web [LO 2, 5]

Go to UPS's Web site (specific page is http://www.ups-scs.com/solutions/case_consumer.html). Download the case study "Addidas Goes for the Gold in Customer Service On Demand." Read about the way UPS used its IT and logistic systems to help Addidas. Then answer the following questions:

1. What are the main ways in which UPS used its IT and logistics skills to help Addidas?

2. In what specific ways did UPS's IT help Addidas improve its performance? (If the Addidas case study is no longer available, pick another.)

Be the Manager [LO4]

You are one of the managers of a small specialty furniture maker of custom-made tables, chairs, and cabinets. You've been charged with finding ways to use IT and the Internet to identify new business opportunities that can improve your company's competitive advantage, for example, ways to reduce costs or attract customers.

Questions

1. What are the various forces in a specialty furniture maker's task environment that have the most effect on its performance?

2. What kinds of IT or MISs can be used to help the company better manage these forces?

3. In what ways can the Internet be used to help this organization improve its competitive position?

BusinessWeek Case in the News [LO 2, 4, 5]

The Quickening at Nissan

Ever since Carlos Ghosn became president at Nissan Motor in 2000, Japan's second-largest auto maker has enjoyed the kind of recovery that bosses at strugglers like GM must dream about. Just as important, though, has been the way Nissan has spiced up its product offerings. Today a river of eye-catching autos—from the stylish Murano crossover and new Infiniti M luxury sedan to the boxy Cube minivan—streams out of Nissan's factories.

Just as impressive, under a program called V3P, Nissan is halving the time needed to take new cars from design to showroom. For the Japanese market, the Note subcompact was rolled out just 10.5 months after its design was finalized, vs. the 20.75 months that the process used to take. Key to the faster delivery has been wider use of the latest in computer-aided design software and a reliance on fewer prototypes.

To find out more about how Nissan aims to give customers what they want faster, *BusinessWeek* Tokyo correspondent Ian Rowley caught up with Nissan's Carlos Tavares, the executive vice-president who supervises design, product planning, and corporate strategy, at the company's Tokyo offices. Tavares, 47, joined Renault—44% owner of Nissan—in 1981 before moving to Nissan in 2004.

How does Nissan approach new vehicle development?
Ultimately, the process is about regularly creating exciting cars without disrupting the [production] process. We don't want a situation where we are putting so much pressure on the design teams that they have to keep using the existing parts and platforms and not be able to meet customer needs. This discussion between creativity on one side and disciplined, accurate implementation on the other is one of the most exciting things within this company.

But where does the process begin? Is it with a group of engineers?
Well, we actually put a lot of energy into trying to address the automotive answer as late as possible in the process. A lot of people in our organization are engineers and we tend to think about hardware answers or hardware solutions much too soon in the process. We need to first ask who will be our focus customers.

How do you do this?
We look at different groups and demographics and decide which people we will target.

So how big are the customer segments you focus on?
It can be quite a small number of people—you might think we'd only sell 50 cars—but this [partly explains] why most of our products are very strong. It might sound a little crazy to make a tailor-made car for a small number of people, but what we look for is to make a car for a very particular type of person.

We're not talking about a million people but small groups with the same kind of emotional needs, education, mind-set, and so forth. You then make a car for them. If you succeed and make the right car for these people, other people from outside the group will say they would also like to have one.

What about after you've identified the customers?
We then check that the designers and the product planners understand the concept in the same way. We listen to the designer and we listen to the product planner. We have a meeting where each one explains to us how he perceives the target customer, how he perceives the emotional values, the functional values, the mind-set. If they don't see things the same way, you can be sure there will be a mess.

How do you avoid that?
We tell them to go back to work and come back when they share the same vision of the target customer. If you have to postpone [moving on to the next stage] by two, three, or four months because people are not talking about the same target customer, it's no problem.

Is there any resistance to focusing so heavily on aspects other than engineering?

It's very important that you have a very strong [production] process that gives you the possibility to combine the talent of the designers, the product planners and the market intelligence people. But I'm convinced that automotive companies that are uniquely engineering-driven are in danger.

What about speed to market?

That's the strength of our engineering and manufacturing. If you put things in the pipeline properly—and you have to do this properly and with good design, planning, and features outlining performance targets—this company has huge strengths in terms of engineering and manufacturing.

But are you getting faster?

Yes. Our engineers have worked a lot at what we call V3P, a system which involves compressing the latter stages of development and manufacturing [from the moment the designs are fixed]. We're close to ten months in some Japanese products. This is very fast—it's half of what it was before.

How do you do this?

One example is that by using sophisticated [computer software] we can decrease the number of mistakes and increase quality. That helps save time. We've also reduced the number of prototypes from three to one for the Note [a subcompact sold in Japan].

Questions for Discussion

1. How does Nissan manage the relationship between its different value-chain functions to speed product development?

2. In what ways could Nissan use IT and the management information systems discussed in the chapter to speed the product development process?

Source: Cover story, "The Quickening at Nissan." Reprinted from the March 27, 2006, issue of *BusinessWeek* by special permission. Copyright © 2006 by The McGraw-Hill Companies, Inc.

BusinessWeek **Case in the News** [LO 2, 4, 5]

FedEx: Taking Off Like "a Rocket Ship"

As soon as Motion Computing Inc. in Austin, Tex., receives an order for one of its $2,200 tablet PCs, workers at a supplier's factory in Kunshan, China, begin assembling the product. When they've finished, they individually box each order and hand them to a driver from FedEx Corp., who trucks it 50 miles to Shanghai, where it's loaded on a jet bound for Anchorage before a series of flights and truck rides finally puts the product into the customer's hands.

Elapsed time: as little as five days. Motion's inventory costs? Nada. Zip. Zilch. "We have no inventory tied up in the process anywhere," marvels Scott Eckert, Motion's chief executive. "Frankly, our business is enabled by FedEx."

There are thousands of other Motion Computings that, without FedEx, would be crippled by warehouse and inventory costs. That value proposition has made the Memphis shipping giant an indispensable partner for companies whose products are made in China. In the past two years, the volume of goods that FedEx has shipped over its vast international network has soared 40%, with much of the growth from Asia. FedEx earnings leapt 21% last year, and its stock price has more than doubled since 2003, landing FedEx the No. 40 spot on the BusinessWeek 50. "FedEx has been a rocket ship," says Daniel Ortwerth, analyst at St. Louis brokerage Edward Jones.

That FedEx has become the preferred carrier out of China is no accident. As far back as the 1980s, FedEx founder and CEO Frederick W. Smith predicted that Asia would become an economic powerhouse. In 1989 he shelled out $895 million to buy Tiger International Inc., a struggling cargo hauler that nonetheless had assets Smith coveted: flying rights into most major Asian airports and a management team with a deep knowledge of the Pacific Rim. Wall Street roundly panned the move—many Asian economies were unstable at the time—but it was prescient, giving FedEx a 10-year jump on rivals.

These days, FedEx operates 120 flights weekly to and from Asia, including 26 out of China alone. As a result, FedEx now controls 39% of the China-to-U.S. air express market, vs. 32% for United Parcel Service Inc. and 27% for DHL International, according to Satish Jindel, president of SJ Consulting Group Inc. in Pittsburgh.

Now Smith is doubling his bets on China. FedEx plans to close its Asian hub in the Philippines by 2008 in favor of a new $150 million super-hub in Guangzhou, a city in the heart of one of China's fastest-growing manufacturing districts. Also in 2008, FedEx will take delivery of the first of up to 20 of Airbus' A380 cargo haulers, birds so massive that they hold twice the load of the Boeing MD-11. The A380 can fly nonstop from Asia to FedEx's U.S. hubs. Here again, Smith was ahead of the pack: By being the first American customer, he not only beat UPS to the punch but got to contribute to the configuration of the A380, too. "They played a pivotal role in the design," says Allan McArtor, chairman of Airbus North America Holdings Inc. and a former FedEx executive.

FedEx's ambitions in China may extend beyond exports. In January, it spent $400 million to buy out its

50–50 delivery partner in China, Datian Group. That gives FedEx full control over Datian's truck fleet and its 89 distribution hubs. Some analysts, such as Morgan Stanley's James Valentine, believe that the purchase is a step toward FedEx domestic service between China's largest cities, at least for large business customers. Some wonder, though, if China is ready for that, given the shabby state of its highways. "[FedEx] could run up against infrastructure problems," warns Ortwerth. Smith isn't worried. He's been right about China before.

Questions

1. How does FedEx use its IT to help other company's improve their performance?

2. Which kind of IT systems discussed in the chapter are most likely to increase FedEx's own level of performance?

Source: Dean Foust, "FedEx: Taking Off Like a Rocket Ship." Reprinted from the March 27, 2006, issue of *BusinessWeek* by special permission. Copyright © 2006 by The McGraw-Hill Companies, Inc.

Glossary

360-degree appraisal A performance appraisal by peers, subordinates, superiors, and sometimes clients who are in a position to evaluate a manager's performance.

A

accommodation An ineffective conflict-handling approach in which one party, typically with weaker power, gives in to the demands of the other, typically more powerful, party.

accommodative approach Companies and their managers behave legally and ethically and try to balance the interests of different stakeholders as the need arises.

achievement orientation A worldview that values assertiveness, performance, success, and competition.

administrative management The study of how to create an organizational structure and control system that leads to high efficiency and effectiveness.

administrative model An approach to decision making that explains why decision making is inherently uncertain and risky and why managers usually make satisfactory rather than optimum decisions.

agreeableness The tendency to get along well with other people.

alderfer's ERG theory The theory that three universal needs—for existence, relatedness, and growth—constitute a hierarchy of needs and motivate behavior. Alderfer proposed that needs at more than one level can be motivational at the same time.

ambiguous information Information that can be interpreted in multiple and often conflicting ways.

arbitrator A third-party negotiator who can impose what he or she thinks is a fair solution to a conflict that both parties are obligated to abide by.

artificial intelligence Behavior performed by a machine that, if performed by a human being, would be called "intelligent."

attitude A collection of feelings and beliefs.

attraction-selection-attrition (ASA) framework A model that explains how personality may influence organizational culture.

authority The power to hold people accountable for their actions and to make decisions concerning the use of organizational resources.

avoidance An ineffective conflict-handling approach in which the two parties try to ignore the problem and do nothing to resolve their differences.

B

B2B marketplace An Internet-based trading platform set up to connect buyers and sellers in an industry.

B2B network structure A series of global strategic alliances that an organization creates with suppliers, manufacturers, and/or distributors to produce and market a product.

barriers to entry Factors that make it difficult and costly for an organization to enter a particular task environment or industry.

behavioral management The study of how managers should behave to motivate employees and encourage them to perform at high levels and be committed to the achievement of organizational goals.

benchmarking The process of comparing one company's performance on specific dimensions with the performance of other, high-performing organizations.

bias The systematic tendency to use information about others in ways that result in inaccurate perceptions.

blog A Web site on which an individual, group, or organization posts information, commentary, and opinions and to which readers can often respond with their own commentary and opinions.

bottom-up change A gradual or evolutionary approach to change in which

managers at all levels work together to develop a detailed plan for change.

boundary spanning Interacting with individuals and groups outside the organization to obtain valuable information from the environment.

boundaryless organization An organization whose members are linked by computers, faxes, computer-aided design systems, and video teleconferencing and who rarely, if ever, see one another face-to-face.

bounded rationality Cognitive limitations that constrain one's ability to interpret, process, and act on information.

brand loyalty Customers' preference for the products of organizations currently existing in the task environment.

bureaucracy A formal system of organization and administration designed to ensure efficiency and effectiveness.

bureaucratic control Control of behavior by means of a comprehensive system of rules and standard operating procedures.

business-level plan Divisional managers' decisions pertaining to divisions' long-term goals, overall strategy, and structure.

business-level strategy A plan that indicates how a division intends to compete against its rivals in an industry.

business-to-business (B2B) commerce Trade that takes place between companies using IT and the Internet to link and coordinate the value chains of different companies.

business-to-customer (B2C) commerce Trade that takes place between a company and individual customers using IT and the Internet.

C

cafeteria-style benefit plan A plan from which employees can choose the benefits that they want.

centralization The concentration of authority at the top of the managerial hierarchy.

charismatic leader An enthusiastic, self-confident leader who is able to clearly communicate his or her vision of how good things could be.

clan control The control exerted on individuals and groups in an organization by shared values, norms, standards of behavior, and expectations.

classical decision-making model A prescriptive approach to decision making based on the assumption that the decision maker can identify and evaluate all possible alternatives and their consequences and rationally choose the most appropriate course of action.

closed system A system that is self-contained and thus not affected by changes occurring in its external environment.

coercive power The ability of a manager to punish others.

collaboration A way of managing conflict in which both parties try to satisfy their goals by coming up with an approach that leaves them both better off and does not require concessions on issues that are important to either party.

collaboration software Groupware that promotes and facilitates collaborative, highly interdependent interactions and provides an electronic meeting site for communication among team members.

collective bargaining Negotiations between labor unions and managers to resolve conflicts and disputes about issues such as working hours, wages, benefits, working conditions, and job security.

collectivism A worldview that values subordination of the individual to the goals of the group and adherence to the principle that people should be judged by their contribution to the group.

command group A group composed of subordinates who report to the same supervisor; also called *department* or *unit*.

communication The sharing of information between two or more individuals or groups to reach a common understanding.

communication networks The pathways along which information flows in groups and teams and throughout the organization.

competition An ineffective conflict-handling approach in which each party tries to maximize its own gain and has little interest in understanding the other party's position and arriving at a solution that will allow both parties to achieve their goals.

competitive advantage The ability of one organization to outperform other organizations because it produces desired goods or services more efficiently and effectively than they do.

competitors Organizations that produce goods and services that are similar to a particular organization's goods and services.

compromise A way of managing conflict in which each party is concerned about not only its own goal accomplishment but also the goal accomplishment of the other party and is willing to engage in a give-and-take exchange and make concessions.

concentration on a single industry Reinvesting a company's profits to strengthen its competitive position in its current industry.

conceptual skills The ability to analyze and diagnose a situation and to distinguish between cause and effect.

concurrent control Control that gives managers immediate feedback on how efficiently inputs are being transformed into outputs so that managers can correct problems as they arise.

conscientiousness The tendency to be careful, scrupulous, and persevering.

consideration Behavior indicating that a manager trusts, respects, and cares about subordinates.

contingency theory The idea that the organizational structures and control systems managers choose depend on—are contingent on—characteristics of the external environment in which the organization operates.

contract book A written agreement that details product development factors such as responsibilities, resource commitments, budgets, time lines, and development milestones.

control systems Formal target-setting, monitoring, evaluation, and feedback systems that provide managers with information about how well the organization's strategy and structure are working.

controlling Evaluating how well an organization is achieving its goals and taking action to maintain or improve performance; one of the four principal tasks of management.

core competency The specific set of departmental skills, knowledge, and experience that allows one organization to outperform another.

core members The members of a team who bear primary responsibility for the success of a project and who stay with a project from inception to completion.

corporate-level plan Top management's decisions pertaining to the organization's mission, overall strategy, and structure.

corporate-level strategy A plan that indicates in which industries and national markets an organization intends to compete.

creativity A decision maker's ability to discover original and novel ideas that lead to feasible alternative courses of action.

cross-functional team A group of managers brought together from different departments to perform organizational tasks.

customer relationship management (CRM) A technique that uses IT to develop an ongoing relationship with customers to maximize the value an organization can deliver to them over time.

customers Individuals and groups that buy the goods and services that an organization produces.

D

data Raw, unsummarized, and unanalyzed facts.

decentralizing authority Giving lower-level managers and nonmanagerial employees the right to make important decisions about how to use organizational resources.

decision making The process by which managers respond to opportunities and threats by analyzing options and making determinations about specific organizational goals and courses of action.

decision support system An interactive computer-based management information system that managers can use to make nonroutine decisions.

decoding Interpreting and trying to make sense of a message.

defensive approach Companies and their managers behave ethically to the degree that they stay within the law and abide strictly with legal requirements.

delphi technique A decision-making technique in which group members do not meet face-to-face but respond in writing to questions posed by the group leader.

demographic forces Outcomes of changes in, or changing attitudes toward, the characteristics of a population, such as age, gender, ethnic origin, race, sexual orientation, and social class.

department A group of people who work together and possess similar skills or use the same knowledge, tools, or techniques to perform their jobs.

development Building the knowledge and skills of organizational members so that they are prepared to take on new responsibilities and challenges.

developmental consideration Behavior a leader engages in to support and encourage followers and help them develop and grow on the job.

devil's advocacy Critical analysis of a preferred alternative, made in response to challenges raised by a group member who, playing the role of devil's advocate, defends unpopular or opposing alternatives for the sake of argument.

dialectical inquiry Critical analysis of two preferred alternatives in order to find an even better alternative for the organization to adopt.

differentiation strategy Distinguishing an organization's products from the products of competitors on dimensions such as product design, quality, or after-sales service.

discipline Obedience, energy, application, and other outward marks of respect for a superior's authority.

distributive justice A moral principle calling for the distribution of pay raises, promotions, and other organizational resources to be based on meaningful contributions that individuals have made and not on personal characteristics over which they have no control.

distributive negotiation Adversarial negotiation in which the parties in conflict compete to win the most resources while conceding as little as possible.

distributors Organizations that help other organizations sell their goods or services to customers.

diversification Expanding a company's business operations into a new industry in order to produce new kinds of valuable goods or services.

diversity Differences among people in age, gender, race, ethnicity, religion, sexual orientation, socioeconomic background, and capabilities/disabilities.

divisional structure An organizational structure composed of separate business units within which are the functions that work together to produce a specific product for a specific customer.

division of labor Splitting the work to be performed into particular tasks and assigning tasks to individual workers.

E

e-commerce Trade that takes place between companies, and between companies and individual customers, using IT and the Internet.

economic forces Interest rates, inflation, unemployment, economic growth, and other factors that affect the general health and well-being of a nation or the regional economy of an organization.

economies of scale Cost advantages associated with large operations.

effectiveness A measure of the appropriateness of the goals an organization is pursuing and of the degree to which the organization achieves those goals.

efficiency A measure of how well or how productively resources are used to achieve a goal.

emotional intelligence The ability to understand and manage one's own moods and emotions and the moods and emotions of other people.

emotions Intense, relatively short-lived feelings.

employee stock option A financial instrument that entitles the bearer to buy shares of an organization's stock at a certain price during a certain period of time or under certain conditions.

empowerment The expansion of employees' knowledge, tasks, and decision-making responsibilities.

encoding Translating a message into understandable symbols or language.

enterprise resource planning (ERP) systems Multimodule application software packages that coordinate the functional activities necessary to move products from the product design stage to the final customer stage.

entrepreneur An individual who notices opportunities and decides how to mobilize the resources necessary to produce new and improved goods and services.

entrepreneurship The mobilization of resources to take advantage of an opportunity to provide customers with new or improved goods and services.

entropy The tendency of a closed system to lose its ability to control itself and thus to dissolve and disintegrate.

equal employment opportunity (EEO) The equal right of all citizens to the opportunity to obtain employment regardless of their gender, age, race, country of origin, religion, or disabilities.

equity The justice, impartiality, and fairness to which all organizational members are entitled.

equity theory A theory of motivation that focuses on people's perceptions of the fairness of their work outcomes relative to their work inputs.

escalating commitment A source of cognitive bias resulting from the tendency to commit additional resources to a project even if evidence shows that the project is failing.

esprit de corps Shared feelings of comradeship, enthusiasm, or devotion to a common cause among members of a group.

ethical dilemma The quandary people find themselves in when they have to decide if they should act in a way that might help another person or group even though doing so might go against their own self-interest.

ethics The inner-guiding moral principles, values, and beliefs that people use to analyze or interpret a situation and then decide what is the "right" or appropriate way to behave.

ethics ombudsman A manager responsible for communicating and teaching ethical standards to all employees and monitoring their conformity to those standards.

evolutionary change Change that is gradual, incremental, and narrowly focused.

executive support system A sophisticated version of a decision support system that is designed to meet the needs of top managers.

expectancy In expectancy theory, a perception about the extent to which effort results in a certain level of performance.

expectancy theory The theory that motivation will be high when workers believe that high levels of effort lead to high performance and high performance leads to the attainment of desired outcomes.

expert power Power that is based on the special knowledge, skills, and expertise that a leader possesses.

expert system A management information system that employs human knowledge, embedded in a computer, to solve problems that ordinarily require human expertise.

exporting Making products at home and selling them abroad.

external locus of control The tendency to locate responsibility for one's fate in outside forces and to believe that one's own behavior has little impact on outcomes.

extinction Curtailing the performance of dysfunctional behaviors by eliminating whatever is reinforcing them.

extraversion The tendency to experience positive emotions and moods and to feel good about oneself and the rest of the world.

extrinsically motivated behavior Behavior that is performed to acquire material or social rewards or to avoid punishment.

F

facilities layout The strategy of designing the machine-worker interface to increase operating system efficiency.

feedback control Control that gives managers information about customers' reactions to goods and services so that corrective action can be taken if necessary.

feedforward control Control that allows managers to anticipate problems before they arise.

filtering Withholding part of a message because of the mistaken belief that the receiver does not need or will not want the information.

first-line manager A manager who is responsible for the daily supervision of nonmanagerial employees.

flexible manufacturing The set of techniques that attempt to reduce the costs associated with the product assembly process or the way services are delivered to customers.

focused differentiation strategy Serving only one segment of the overall market and trying to be the most differentiated organization serving that segment.

focused low-cost strategy Serving only one segment of the overall market and trying to be the lowest-cost organization serving that segment.

folkways The routine social conventions of everyday life.

formal appraisal An appraisal conducted at a set time during the year and based on performance dimensions and measures that were specified in advance.

formal group A group that managers establish to achieve organizational goals.

franchising Selling to a foreign organization the rights to use a brand name and operating know-how in return for a lump-sum payment and a share of the profits.

free-trade doctrine The idea that if each country specializes in the production of the goods and services that it can produce most efficiently, this will make the best use of global resources.

friendship group An informal group composed of employees who enjoy one another's company and socialize with one another.

functional structure An organizational structure composed of all the departments that an organization requires to produce its goods or services.

functional-level plan Functional managers' decisions pertaining to the goals that they propose to pursue to help the division attain its business-level goals.

functional-level strategy A plan of action to improve the ability of each of an organization's functions to perform its task-specific activities in ways that add value to an organization's goods and services.

G

gatekeeping Deciding what information to allow into the organization and what information to keep out.

gender schemas Preconceived beliefs or ideas about the nature of men and women, their traits, attitudes, behaviors, and preferences.

general environment The wide-ranging global, economic, technological, sociocultural, demographic, political, and legal forces that affect an organization and its task environment.

geographic structure An organizational structure in which each region of a country or area of the world is served by a self-contained division.

glass ceiling A metaphor alluding to the invisible barriers that prevent minorities and women from being promoted to top corporate positions.

global environment The set of global forces and conditions that operate beyond an organization's boundaries but affect a manager's ability to acquire and utilize resources.

global organization An organization that operates and competes in more than one country.

global outsourcing The purchase of inputs from overseas suppliers or the production of inputs abroad to lower production costs and improve product quality or design.

global strategy Selling the same standardized product and using the same basic marketing approach in each national market.

globalization The set of specific and general forces that work together to integrate and connect economic, political, and social systems *across* countries, cultures, or geographical regions so that nations become increasingly interdependent and similar.

goal-setting theory A theory that focuses on identifying the types of goals that are most effective in producing high levels of motivation and performance and explaining why goals have these effects.

grapevine An informal communication network along which unofficial information flows.

group Two or more people who interact with each other to accomplish certain goals or meet certain needs.

group cohesiveness The degree to which members are attracted to or loyal to their group.

group decision support system An executive support system that links top managers so that they can function as a team.

group norms Shared guidelines or rules for behavior that most group members follow.

group role A set of behaviors and tasks that a member of a group is expected to perform because of his or her position in the group.

groupthink A pattern of faulty and biased decision making that occurs in groups whose members strive for agreement among themselves at the expense of accurately assessing information relevant to a decision.

groupware Computer software that enables members of groups and teams to share information with one another.

H

hawthorne effect The finding that a manager's behavior or leadership approach can affect workers' level of performance.

herzberg's motivator-hygiene theory A need theory that distinguishes between motivator needs (related to the nature of the work itself) and hygiene needs (related to the physical and psychological context in which the work is performed) and proposes that motivator needs must be met for motivation and job satisfaction to be high.

heuristics Rules of thumb that simplify decision making.

hierarchy of authority An organization's chain of command, specifying the relative authority of each manager.

hostile work environment sexual harassment Telling lewd jokes, displaying pornography, making sexually oriented remarks about someone's personal appearance, and other sex-related actions that make the work environment unpleasant.

human relations movement A management approach that advocates the idea that supervisors should receive behavioral training to manage subordinates in ways that elicit their cooperation and increase their productivity.

human resource management (HRM) Activities that managers engage in to attract and retain employees and to ensure that they perform at a high level and contribute to the accomplishment of organizational goals.

human resource planning Activities that managers engage in to forecast their current and future needs for human resources.

human skills The ability to understand, alter, lead, and control the behavior of other individuals and groups.

hybrid structure The structure of a large organization that has many divisions and simultaneously uses many different organizational structures.

hypercompetition Permanent, ongoing, intense competition brought about in an industry by advancing technology or changing customer tastes.

I

illusion of control A source of cognitive bias resulting from the tendency to overestimate one's own ability to control activities and events.

importing Selling products at home that are made abroad.

incremental product innovation The gradual improvement and refinement to existing products that occurs over time as existing technologies are perfected.

individual ethics Personal standards and values that determine how people view their responsibilities to others and how they should act in situations when their own self-interests are at stake.

individualism A worldview that values individual freedom and self-expression and adherence to the principle that people should be judged by their individual achievements rather than by their social background.

inequity Lack of fairness.

informal appraisal An unscheduled appraisal of ongoing progress and areas for improvement.

informal group A group that managers or nonmanagerial employees form to help achieve their own goals or meet their own needs.

informal organization The system of behavioral rules and norms that emerge in a group.

information Data that are organized in a meaningful fashion.

information distortion Changes in the meaning of a message as the message passes through a series of senders and receivers.

information overload The potential for important information to be ignored or overlooked while tangential information receives attention.

information richness The amount of information that a communication medium can carry and the extent to which the medium enables the sender and receiver to reach a common understanding.

information technology The set of methods or techniques for acquiring, organizing, storing, manipulating, and transmitting information.

initiating structure Behavior that managers engage in to ensure that work gets done, subordinates perform their jobs acceptably, and the organization is efficient and effective.

initiative The ability to act on one's own, without direction from a superior.

innovation The process of creating new or improved goods and services or developing better ways to produce or provide them.

input Anything a person contributes to his or her job or organization.

instrumental value A mode of conduct that an individual seeks to follow.

instrumentality In expectancy theory, a perception about the extent to which performance results in the attainment of outcomes.

integrating mechanisms Organizing tools that managers can use to increase communication and coordination among functions and divisions.

integrative bargaining Cooperative negotiation in which the parties in conflict work together to achieve a resolution that is good for them both.

intellectual stimulation Behavior a leader engages in to make followers be aware of problems and view these problems in new ways, consistent with the leader's vision.

interest group An informal group composed of employees seeking to achieve a common goal related to their membership in an organization.

internal locus of control The tendency to locate responsibility for one's fate within oneself.

internet A global system of computer networks.

intranet A companywide system of computer networks.

intrapreneur A manager, scientist, or researcher who works inside an organization and notices opportunities to develop new or improved products and better ways to make them.

intrinsically motivated behavior Behavior that is performed for its own sake.

intuition Feelings, beliefs, and hunches that come readily to mind, require little effort and information gathering, and result in on-the-spot decisions.

inventory The stock of raw materials, inputs, and component parts that an organization has on hand at a particular time.

J

jargon Specialized language that members of an occupation, group, or organization develop to facilitate communication among themselves.

job analysis Identifying the tasks, duties, and responsibilities that make up a job and the knowledge, skills, and abilities needed to perform the job.

job design The process by which managers decide how to divide tasks into specific jobs.

job enlargement Increasing the number of different tasks in a given job by changing the division of labor.

job enrichment Increasing the degree of responsibility a worker has over his or her job.

job satisfaction The collection of feelings and beliefs that managers have about their current jobs.

job simplification The process of reducing the number of tasks that each worker performs.

job specialization The process by which a division of labor occurs as different workers specialize in different tasks over time.

joint venture A strategic alliance among two or more companies that agree to jointly establish and share the ownership of a new business.

just-in-time (JIT) inventory system A system in which parts or supplies arrive at an organization when they are needed, not before.

justice rule An ethical decision is a decision that distributes benefits and harms among people and groups in a fair, equitable, or impartial way.

K

knowledge management system A company-specific virtual information system that systematizes the knowledge of its employees and facilitates the sharing and integrating of their expertise.

L

labor relations The activities that managers engage in to ensure that they have effective working relationships with the labor unions that represent their employees' interests.

lateral move A job change that entails no major changes in responsibility or authority levels.

leader An individual who is able to exert influence over other people to help achieve group or organizational goals.

leader–member relations The extent to which followers like, trust, and are loyal to their leader; a determinant of how favorable a situation is for leading.

leadership The process by which an individual exerts influence over other people and inspires, motivates, and directs their activities to help achieve group or organizational goals.

leadership substitute A characteristic of a subordinate or of a situation or context that acts in place of the influence of a leader and makes leadership unnecessary.

leading Articulating a clear vision and energizing and enabling organizational members so that they understand the part they play in achieving organizational goals; one of the four principal tasks of management.

learning A relatively permanent change in knowledge or behavior that results from practice or experience.

learning organization An organization in which managers try to maximize the ability of individuals and groups to think and behave creatively and thus maximize the potential for organizational learning to take place.

learning theories Theories that focus on increasing employee motivation and performance by linking the outcomes that employees receive to the performance of desired behaviors and the attainment of goals.

legitimate power The authority that a manager has by virtue of his or her position in an organization's hierarchy.

licensing Allowing a foreign organization to take charge of manufacturing and distributing a product in its country or world region in return for a negotiated fee.

line manager Someone in the direct line or chain of command who has formal authority over people and resources at lower levels.

line of authority The chain of command extending from the top to the bottom of an organization.

linguistic style A person's characteristic way of speaking.

long-term orientation A worldview that values thrift and persistence in achieving goals.

low-cost strategy Driving the organization's costs down below the costs of its rivals.

M

management The planning, organizing, leading, and controlling of human and other resources to achieve organizational goals efficiently and effectively.

management by objectives (MBO) A goal-setting process in which a manager and each of his or her subordinates negotiate specific goals and objectives for the subordinate to achieve and then periodically evaluate the extent to which the subordinate is achieving those goals.

management by wandering around A face-to-face communication technique in which a manager walks around a work area and talks informally with employees about issues and concerns.

management information system (MIS) A specific form of IT that managers utilize to generate the specific, detailed information they need to perform their roles effectively.

management science theory An approach to management that uses rigorous quantitative techniques to help managers make maximum use of organizational resources.

market structure An organizational structure in which each kind of customer is served by a self-contained division; also called *customer structure.*

maslow's hierarchy of needs An arrangement of five basic needs that, according to Maslow, motivate behavior. Maslow proposed that the lowest level of unmet needs is the prime motivator and that only one level of needs is motivational at a time.

matrix structure An organizational structure that simultaneously groups people and resources by function and by product.

mechanistic structure An organizational structure in which authority is centralized, tasks and rules are clearly specified, and employees are closely supervised.

mediator A third-party negotiator who facilitates negotiations but has no authority to impose a solution.

medium The pathway through which an encoded message is transmitted to a receiver.

mentoring A process by which an experienced member of an organization (the mentor) provides advice and guidance to a less experienced member (the protégé) and helps the less experienced member learn how to advance in the organization and in his or her career.

merit pay plan A compensation plan that bases pay on performance.

message The information that a sender wants to share.

middle manager A manager who supervises first-line managers and is responsible for finding the best way to use resources to achieve organizational goals.

mission statement A broad declaration of an organization's purpose that identifies the organization's products and customers and distinguishes the organization from its competitors.

mood A feeling or state of mind.

moral rights rule An ethical decision is one that best maintains and protects the fundamental or inalienable rights and privileges of the people affected by it.

mores Norms that are considered to be central to the functioning of society and to social life.

motivation Psychological forces that determine the direction of a person's behavior in an organization, a person's level of effort, and a person's level of persistence.

multidomestic strategy Customizing products and marketing strategies to specific national conditions.

N

national culture The set of values that a society considers important and the norms of behavior that are approved or sanctioned in that society.

need A requirement or necessity for survival and well-being.

need for achievement The extent to which an individual has a strong desire to perform challenging tasks well and to meet personal standards for excellence.

need for affiliation The extent to which an individual is concerned about establishing and maintaining good interpersonal relations, being liked, and having other people get along.

need for power The extent to which an individual desires to control or influence others.

need theories Theories of motivation that focus on what needs people are trying to satisfy at work and what outcomes will satisfy those needs.

needs assessment An assessment of which employees need training or development and what type of skills or knowledge they need to acquire.

negative affectivity The tendency to experience negative emotions and moods, to feel distressed, and to be critical of oneself and others.

negative reinforcement Eliminating or removing undesired outcomes when people perform organizationally functional behaviors.

negotiation A method of conflict resolution in which the two parties consider various alternative ways to allocate

resources to each other in order to come up with a solution acceptable to both of them.

networking The exchange of information through a group or network of interlinked computers.

noise Anything that hampers any stage of the communication process.

nominal group technique A decision-making technique in which group members write down ideas and solutions, read their suggestions to the whole group, and discuss and then rank the alternatives.

nonprogrammed decision making Nonroutine decision making that occurs in response to unusual, unpredictable opportunities and threats.

nonverbal communication The encoding of messages by means of facial expressions, body language, and styles of dress.

norms Unwritten, informal codes of conduct that prescribe how people should act in particular situations and are considered important by most members of a group or organization.

nurturing orientation A worldview that values the quality of life, warm personal friendships, and services and care for the weak.

O

objective appraisal An appraisal that is based on facts and is likely to be numerical.

obstructionist approach Companies and their managers choose not to behave in a socially responsible way and instead behave unethically and illegally.

occupational ethics Standards that govern how members of a profession, trade, or craft should conduct themselves when performing work-related activities.

on-the-job training Training that takes place in the work setting as employees perform their job tasks.

open system A system that takes in resources from its external environment and converts them into goods and services that are then sent back to that environment for purchase by customers.

openness to experience The tendency to be original, have broad interests, be open to a wide range of stimuli, be daring, and take risks.

operant conditioning theory The theory that people learn to perform behaviors that lead to desired consequences and learn not to perform behaviors that lead to undesired consequences.

operating budget A budget that states how managers intend to use organizational resources to achieve organizational goals.

operations information system A management information system that gathers, organizes, and summarizes comprehensive data in a form that managers can use in their nonroutine coordinating, controlling, and decision-making tasks.

optimum decision The most appropriate decision in light of what managers believe to be the most desirable future consequences for the organization.

order The methodical arrangement of positions to provide the organization with the greatest benefit and to provide employees with career opportunities.

organic structure An organizational structure in which authority is decentralized to middle and first-line managers and tasks and roles are left ambiguous to encourage employees to cooperate and respond quickly to the unexpected.

organizational architecture The organizational structure, control systems, culture, and human resource management systems that together determine how efficiently and effectively organizational resources are used.

organizational behavior The study of the factors that have an impact on how individuals and groups respond to and act in organizations.

organizational behavior modification (OB MOD) The systematic application of operant conditioning techniques to promote the performance of organizationally functional behaviors and discourage the performance of dysfunctional behaviors.

organizational change The movement of an organization away from its present state and toward some desired future state to increase its efficiency and effectiveness.

organizational citizenship behaviors (OCBs) Behaviors that are not required of organizational members but that contribute to and are necessary for organizational efficiency, effectiveness, and competitive advantage.

organizational commitment The collection of feelings and beliefs that managers have about their organization as a whole.

organizational conflict The discord that arises when the goals, interests, or values of different individuals or groups are incompatible and those individuals or groups block or thwart one another's attempts to achieve their objectives.

organizational culture The shared set of beliefs, expectations, values, norms, and work routines that influence the ways in which individuals, groups, and teams interact with one another and cooperate to achieve organizational goals.

organizational design The process by which managers make specific organizing choices that result in a particular kind of organizational structure.

organizational environment The set of forces and conditions that operate beyond an organization's boundaries but affect a manager's ability to acquire and utilize resources.

organizational ethics The guiding practices and beliefs through which a particular company and its managers view their responsibility toward their stakeholders.

organizational ethics The moral values, beliefs, and rules that establish the appropriate way for an organization and its members to deal with each other and with people outside the organization.

organizational learning The process through which managers seek to improve employees' desire and ability to understand and manage the organization and its task environment.

organizational performance A measure of how efficiently and effectively a manager uses resources to satisfy customers and achieve organizational goals.

organizational politics Activities that managers engage in to increase their power and to use power effectively to achieve their goals and overcome resistance or opposition.

organizational socialization The process by which newcomers learn an organization's values and norms and acquire the work behaviors necessary to perform jobs effectively.

organizational structure A formal system of task and reporting relationships that coordinates and motivates organizational members so that they work together to achieve organizational goals.

organizations Collections of people who work together and coordinate their actions to achieve a wide variety of goals or desired future outcomes.

organizing Structuring working relationships in a way that allows organizational members to work together to achieve organizational goals; one of the four principal tasks of management.

outcome Anything a person gets from a job or organization.

outsource To use outside suppliers and manufacturers to produce goods and services.

outsourcing Contracting with another company, usually abroad, to have it perform an activity the organization previously performed itself.

overpayment inequity The inequity that exists when a person perceives that his or her own outcome-input ratio is greater than the ratio of a referent.

overt discrimination Knowingly and willingly denying diverse individuals access to opportunities and outcomes in an organization.

P

path-goal theory A contingency model of leadership proposing that leaders can motivate subordinates by identifying their desired outcomes, rewarding them for high performance and the attainment of work goals with these desired outcomes, and clarifying for them the paths leading to the attainment of work goals.

pay level The relative position of an organization's pay incentives in comparison with those of other organizations in the same industry employing similar kinds or workers.

pay structures The arrangement of jobs into categories reflecting their relative importance to the organization and its goals, levels of skill required, and other characteristics.

perception The process through which people select, organize, and interpret what they see, hear, touch, smell, and taste to give meaning and order to the world around them.

performance appraisal The evaluation of employees' job performance and contributions to their organization.

performance feedback The process through which mangers share performance appraisal information with subordinates, give subordinates an opportunity to reflect on their own performance, and develop, with subordinates, plans for the future.

personality traits Enduring tendencies to feel, think, and act in certain ways.

planning Identifying and selecting appropriate goals and courses of action; one of the four principal tasks of management.

political and legal forces Outcomes of changes in laws and regulations, such as the deregulation of industries, the privatization of organizations, and the increased emphasis on environmental protection.

political strategies Tactics that managers use to increase their power and to use power effectively to influence and gain the support of other people while overcoming resistance or opposition.

pooled task interdependence The task interdependence that exists when group members make separate and independent contributions to group performance.

position power The amount of legitimate, reward, and coercive power that a leader has by virtue of his or her position in an organization; a determinant of how favorable a situation is for leading.

positive reinforcement Giving people outcomes they desire when they perform organizationally functional behaviors.

potential competitors Organizations that presently are not in a task environment but could enter if they so choose.

power distance The degree to which societies accept the idea that inequalities in the power and well-being of their citizens are due to differences in individuals' physical and intellectual capabilities and heritage.

practical rule An ethical decision is one that a manager has no reluctance about communicating to people outside the company because the typical person in a society would think it is acceptable.

prior-hypothesis bias A cognitive bias resulting from the tendency to base decisions on strong prior beliefs even if evidence shows that those beliefs are wrong.

proactive approach Companies and their managers actively embrace

socially responsible behavior, going out of their way to learn about the needs of different stakeholder groups and utilizing organizational resources to promote the interests of all stakeholders.

procedural justice A moral principle calling for the use of fair procedures to determine how to distribute outcomes to organizational members.

process reengineering The fundamental rethinking and radical redesign of business processes to achieve dramatic improvement in critical measures of performance such as cost, quality, service, and speed.

product champion A manager who takes "ownership" of a project and provides the leadership and vision that take a product from the idea stage to the final customer.

product development The management of the value-chain activities involved in bringing new or improved goods and services to the market.

product development plan A plan that specifies all of the relevant information that managers need in order to decide whether to proceed with a full-blown product development effort.

product life cycle The way demand for a product changes in a predictable pattern over time.

product structure An organizational structure in which each product line or business is handled by a self-contained division.

product team structure An organizational structure in which employees are permanently assigned to a cross-functional team and report only to the product team manager or to one of his or her direct subordinates.

production blocking A loss of productivity in brainstorming sessions due to the unstructured nature of brainstorming.

programmed decision making Routine, virtually automatic decision making that follows established rules or guidelines.

prosocially motivated behavior Behavior that is performed to benefit or help others.

punishment Administering an undesired or negative consequence when dysfunctional behavior occurs.

Q

quantum product innovation The development of new, often radically different, kinds of goods and services because of fundamental shifts in technology brought about by pioneering discoveries.

quid pro quo sexual harassment Asking for or forcing an employee to perform sexual favors in exchange for receiving some reward or avoiding negative consequences.

R

real-time information Frequently updated information that reflects current conditions.

realistic job preview (RJP) An honest assessment of the advantages and disadvantages of a job and organization.

reasoned judgment A decision that takes time and effort to make and results from careful information gathering, generation of alternatives, and evaluation of alternatives.

receiver The person or group for which a message is intended.

reciprocal task interdependence The task interdependence that exists when the work performed by each group member is fully dependent on the work performed by other group members.

recruitment Activities that managers engage in to develop a pool of qualified candidates for open positions.

referent power Power that comes from subordinates' and coworkers' respect, admiration, and loyalty.

related diversification Entering a new business or industry to create a competitive advantage in one or more of an organization's existing divisions or businesses.

relationship-oriented leaders Leaders whose primary concern is to develop good relationships with their subordinates and to be liked by them.

reliability The degree to which a tool or test measures the same thing each time it is used.

representativeness bias A cognitive bias resulting from the tendency to generalize inappropriately from a small sample or from a single vivid event or episode.

reputation The esteem or high repute that individuals or organizations gain when they behave ethically.

research and development team A team whose members have the expertise and experience needed to develop new products.

restructuring Downsizing an organization by eliminating the jobs of large numbers of top, middle, and first-line managers and nonmanagerial employees.

revolutionary change Change that is rapid, dramatic, and broadly focused.

reward power The ability of a manager to give or withhold tangible and intangible rewards.

risk The degree of probability that the possible outcomes of a particular course of action will occur.

role making Taking the initiative to modify an assigned role by assuming additional responsibilities.

rules Formal written instructions that specify actions to be taken under different circumstances to achieve specific goals.

rumors Unofficial pieces of information of interest to organizational members but with no identifiable source.

S

satisficing Searching for and choosing an acceptable, or satisfactory, response to problems and opportunities, rather than trying to make the best decision.

scenario planning The generation of multiple forecasts of future conditions followed by an analysis of how to respond effectively to each of those conditions.

schema An abstract knowledge structure that is stored in memory and makes possible the interpretation and organization of information about a person, event, or situation.

scientific management The systematic study of relationships between people and tasks for the purpose of redesigning the work process to increase efficiency.

selection The process that mangers use to determine the relative qualifications of job applicants and their potential for performing well in a particular job.

self-efficacy A person's belief about his or her ability to perform a behavior successfully.

self-esteem The degree to which individuals feel good about themselves and their capabilities.

self-managed team A group of employees who assume responsibility for organizing, controlling, and supervising their own activities and monitoring the quality of the goods and services they provide.

self-managed work team A group of employees who supervise their own activities and monitor the quality of the goods and services they provide.

self-reinforcer Any desired or attractive outcome or reward that a person gives to himself or herself for good performance.

sender The person or group wishing to share information.

sequential task interdependence The task interdependence that exists when group members must perform specific tasks in a predetermined order.

servant leader A leader who has a strong desire to serve and work for the benefit of others.

short-term orientation A worldview that values personal stability or happiness and living for the present.

skunkworks A group of intrapreneurs who are deliberately separated from the normal operation of an organization to encourage them to devote all their attention to developing new products.

social entrepreneur An individual who pursues initiatives and opportunities and mobilizes resources to address social problems and needs in order to improve society and well-being through creative solutions.

social learning theory A theory that takes into account how learning and motivation are influenced by people's thoughts and beliefs and their observations of other people's behavior.

social loafing The tendency of individuals to put forth less effort when they work in groups than when they work alone.

social responsibility The way a company's managers and employees view their duty or obligation to make decisions that protect, enhance, and promote the welfare and well-being of stakeholders and society as a whole.

social structure The arrangement of relationships between individuals and groups in a society.

societal ethics Standards that govern how members of a society should deal with one another in matters involving issues such as fairness, justice, poverty, and the rights of the individual.

sociocultural forces Pressures emanating from the social structure of a country or society or from the national culture.

span of control The number of subordinates who report directly to a manager.

staff manager Someone responsible for managing a specialist function, such as finance or marketing.

stage-gate development funnel A planning model that forces managers to make choices among competing projects so that organizational resources are not spread thinly over too many projects.

stakeholders The people and groups that supply a company with its productive resources and so have a claim on and stake in the company.

standard operating procedures (SOPs) Specific sets of written instructions about how to perform a certain aspect of a task.

stereotype Simplistic and often inaccurate beliefs about the typical characteristics of particular groups of people.

strategic alliance An agreement in which managers pool or share their organization's resources and know-how with a foreign company, and the two organizations share the rewards and risks of starting a new venture.

strategic human resource management The process by which managers design the components of an HRM system to be consistent with each other, with other elements of organizational architecture, and with the organization's strategy and goals.

strategic leadership The ability of the CEO and top managers to convey a compelling vision of what they want the organization to achieve to their subordinates.

strategy A cluster of decisions about what goals to pursue, what actions to take, and how to use resources to achieve goals.

strategy formulation The development of a set of corporate-, business-, and functional-level strategies that allow an organization to accomplish its mission and achieve its goals.

subjective appraisal An appraisal that is based on perceptions of traits, behaviors, or results.

suppliers Individuals and organizations that provide an organization with the input resources that it needs to produce goods and services.

SWOT analysis A planning exercise in which managers identify organizational strengths (S) and weaknesses (W) and environmental opportunities (O) and threats (T).

synergy Performance gains that result when individuals and departments coordinate their actions.

systematic errors Errors that people make over and over and that result in poor decision making.

T

tariff A tax that a government imposes on imported or, occasionally, exported goods.

task environment The set of forces and conditions that originate with suppliers, distributors, customers, and competitors and affect an organization's ability to obtain inputs and dispose of its outputs because they influence managers on a daily basis.

task force A committee of managers or nonmanagerial employees from various departments or divisions who meet to solve a specific, mutual problem; also called *ad hoc committee.*

task force A committee of managers from various functions or divisions who meet to solve a specific, mutual problem; also called *ad hoc committee.*

task interdependence The degree to which the work performed by one member of a group influences the work performed by other members.

task structure The extent to which the work to be performed is clear-cut so that

a leader's subordinates know what needs to be accomplished and how to go about doing it; a determinant of how favorable a situation is for leading.

task-oriented leaders Leaders whose primary concern is to ensure that subordinates perform at a high level.

team A group whose members work intensely with one another to achieve a specific common goal or objective.

technical skills The job-specific knowledge and techniques required to perform an organizational role.

technological forces Outcomes of changes in the technology that managers use to design, produce, or distribute goods and services.

technology The combination of skills and equipment that managers use in the design, production, and distribution of goods and services.

terminal value A lifelong goal or objective that an individual seeks to achieve.

theory X A set of negative assumptions about workers that lead to the conclusion that a manager's task is to supervise workers closely and control their behavior.

theory Y A set of positive assumptions about workers that lead to the conclusion that a manager's task is to create a work setting that encourages commitment to organizational goals and provides opportunities for workers to be imaginative and to exercise initiative and self-direction.

third-party negotiator An impartial individual with expertise in handling conflicts and negotiations who helps parties in conflict reach an acceptable solution.

time horizon The intended duration of a plan.

top manager A manager who establishes organizational goals, decides how departments should interact, and monitors the performance of middle managers.

top-down change A fast, revolutionary approach to change in which top managers identify what needs to be changed and then move quickly to implement the changes throughout the organization.

top-management team A group composed of the CEO, the COO, the

president, and the heads of the most important departments.

total quality management (TQM) A management technique that focuses on improving the quality of an organization's products and services.

training Teaching organizational members how to perform their current jobs and helping them acquire the knowledge and skills they need to be effective performers.

transaction-processing system A management information system designed to handle large volumes of routine, recurring transactions.

transactional leadership Leadership that motivates subordinates by rewarding them for high performance and reprimanding them for low performance.

transformational leadership Leadership that makes subordinates aware of the importance of their jobs and performance to the organization and aware of their own needs for personal growth and that motivates subordinates to work for the good of the organization.

trust The willingness of one person or group to have faith or confidence in the goodwill of another person, even though this puts them at risk.

turnaround management The creation of a new vision for a struggling company based on a new approach to planning and organizing to make better use of a company's resources to allow it to survive and prosper.

U

uncertainty Unpredictability.

uncertainty avoidance The degree to which societies are willing to tolerate uncertainty and risk.

underpayment inequity The inequity that exists when a person perceives that his or her own outcome-input ratio is less than the ratio of a referent.

unity of command A reporting relationship in which an employee receives orders from, and reports to, only one superior.

unity of direction The singleness of purpose that makes possible the creation of one plan of action to guide managers and workers as they use organizational resources.

unrelated diversification Entering a new industry or buying a company in a new industry that is not related in any way to an organization's current businesses or industries.

utilitarian rule An ethical decision is a decision that produces the greatest good for the greatest number of people.

V

valence In expectancy theory, how desirable each of the outcomes available from a job or organization is to a person.

validity The degree to which a tool or test measures what it purports to measure.

value chain The coordinated series or sequence of functional activities necessary to transform inputs such as new product concepts, raw materials, component parts, or professional skills into the finished goods or services customers value and want to buy.

value-chain management The development of a set of functional-level strategies that support a company's business-level strategy and strengthen its competitive advantage.

value system The terminal and instrumental values that are guiding principles in an individual's life.

values Ideas about what a society believes to be good, right, desirable, or beautiful.

verbal communication The encoding of messages into words, either written or spoken.

vertical integration Expanding a company's operations either backward into an industry that produces inputs for its products or forward into an industry that uses, distributes, or sells its products.

vicarious learning Learning that occurs when the learner becomes motivated to perform a behavior by watching another person perform it and be reinforced for doing so; also called *observational learning*.

virtual team A team whose members rarely or never meet face-to-face but, rather, interact by using various forms of information technology such as e-mail, computer networks, telephone, fax, and videoconferences.

W

wholly owned foreign subsidiary Production operations established in a foreign country independent of any local direct involvement.

Credits

Notes

Chapter 1

1. www.xerox.com, 2008.

2. "She Put the Bounce Back into Xerox," www.businessweek.com, March 1, 2005.

3. F. Arner, "How Xerox Got Up to Speed," www.businessweek.com, March 2, 2006.

4. www.xerox.com, 2008.

5. Press release, www.xerox.com, January 24, 2008.

6. N. Byrnes, "Xerox's New Design Team: Customers," www.businessweek.com, May 7, 2007.

7. Press release, www.xerox.com, January 25, 2008.

8. G. R. Jones, *Organizational Theory, Design, and Change* (Upper Saddle River, NJ: Pearson, 2007).

9. www.xerox.com, 2008.

10. J. P. Campbell, "On the Nature of Organizational Effectiveness," in P. S. Goodman, J. M. Pennings, et al., *New Perspectives on Organizational Effectiveness* (San Francisco: Jossey-Bass, 1977).

11. M. J. Provitera, "What Management Is: How It Works and Why It's Everyone's Business," *Academy of Management Executive* 17 (August 2003), 152–54.

12. J. McGuire and E. Matta, "CEO Stock Options: The Silent Dimension of Ownership," *Academy of Management Journal* 46 (April 2003), 255–66.

13. www.apple.com, press releases, 2000, 2001, 2003, 2006, 2008.

14. J. G. Combs and M. S. Skill, "Managerialist and Human Capital Explanations for Key Executive Pay Premium: A Contingency Perspective," *Academy of Management Journal* 46 (February 2003), 63–74.

15. H. Fayol, *General and Industrial Management* (New York: IEEE Press, 1984). Fayol actually identified five different managerial tasks, but most scholars today believe these four capture the essence of Fayol's ideas.

16. P. F. Drucker, *Management Tasks, Responsibilities, and Practices* (New York: Harper & Row, 1974).

17. www.dell.com, 2008.

18. www.apple.com, press release, 2003.

19. G. McWilliams, "Lean Machine—How Dell Fine-Tunes Its PC Pricing to Gain Edge in a Slow Market," *The Wall Street Journal,* June 8, 2001, A1.

20. R. H. Guest, "Of Time and the Foreman," *Personnel* 32 (1955), 478–86.

21. L. Hill, *Becoming a Manager: Mastery of a New Identity* (Boston: Harvard Business School Press, 1992).

22. Ibid.

23. H. Mintzberg, "The Manager's Job: Folklore and Fact," *Harvard Business Review,* July–August 1975, 56–62.

24. H. Mintzberg, *The Nature of Managerial Work* (New York: Harper & Row, 1973).

25. J. Kotter, *The General Managers* (New York: Free Press, 1992).

26. C. P. Hales, "What Do Managers Do? A Critical Review of the Evidence," *Journal of Management Studies,* January 1986, 88–115; A. I. Kraul, P. R. Pedigo, D. D. McKenna, and M. D. Dunnette, "The Role of the Manager: What's Really Important in Different Management Jobs," *Academy of Management Executive,* November 1989, 286–93.

27. A. K. Gupta, "Contingency Perspectives on Strategic Leadership," in D. C. Hambrick, ed., *The Executive Effect: Concepts and Methods for Studying Top Managers* (Greenwich, CT: JAI Press, 1988), 147–78.

28. D. G. Ancona, "Top Management Teams: Preparing for the Revolution," in J. S. Carroll, ed., *Applied Social Psychology and Organizational Settings* (Hillsdale, NJ: Erlbaum, 1990); D. C. Hambrick and P. A. Mason, "Upper Echelons: The Organization as a Reflection of Its Top Managers," *Academy of Management Journal* 9 (1984), 193–206.

29. T. A. Mahony, T. H. Jerdee, and S. J. Carroll, "The Jobs of Management," *Industrial Relations* 4 (1965), 97–110; L. Gomez-Mejia, J. McCann, and R. C. Page, "The Structure of Managerial Behaviors and Rewards," *Industrial Relations* 24 (1985), 147–54.

30. W. R. Nord and M. J. Waller, "The Human Organization of Time: Temporal Realities and Experiences," *Academy of Management Review* 29 (January 2004), 137–40.

31. R. L. Katz, "Skills of an Effective Administrator," *Harvard Business Review,* September–October 1974, 90–102.

32. Ibid.

33. P. Tharenou, "Going Up? Do Traits and Informal Social Processes Predict Advancing in Management," *Academy of Management Journal* 44 (October 2001), 1005–18.

34. C. J. Collins and K. D. Clark, "Strategic Human Resource Practices, Top Management Team Social Networks, and Firm Performance: The Role of Human Resource Practices in Creating Organizational Competitive Advantage," *Academy of Management Journal* 46 (December 2003), 740–52.

35. R. Stewart, "Middle Managers: Their Jobs and Behaviors," in J. W. Lorsch, ed., *Handbook of Organizational Behavior* (Englewood Cliffs, NJ: Prentice-Hall, 1987), 385–91.

36. S. C. de Janasz, S. E. Sullivan, and V. Whiting, "Mentor Networks and Career Success: Lessons for Turbulent Times," *Academy of Management Executive* 17 (November 2003), 78–92.

37. K. Labich, "Making Over Middle Managers," *Fortune,* May 8, 1989, 58–64.

38. B. Wysocki, "Some Companies Cut Costs Too Far, Suffer from Corporate Anorexia," *The Wall Street Journal,* July 5, 1995, A1.

39. www.dell.com, 2008.

40. V. U. Druskat and J. V. Wheeler, "Managing from the Boundary: The Effective Leadership of Self-Managing Work Teams," *Academy of Management Journal* 46 (August 2003), 435–58.

41. S. R. Parker, T. D. Wall, and P. R. Jackson, "That's Not My Job: Developing Flexible Work Orientations," *Academy of Management Journal* 40 (1997), 899–929.

42. B. Dumaine, "The New Non-Manager," *Fortune,* February 22, 1993, 80–84.

43. H. G. Baum, A. C. Joel, and E. A. Mannix, "Management Challenges in a New Time," *Academy of Management Journal* 45 (October 2002), 916–31.

44. A. Shama, "Management Under Fire: The Transformation of Management in the Soviet Union and Eastern Europe," *Academy of Management Executive* 10 (1993), 22–35.

45. www.apple.com, 2006; www.nike.com, 2006.

46. K. Seiders and L. L. Berry, "Service Fairness: What It Is and Why It Matters," *Academy of Management Executive* 12 (1998), 8–20.

47. T. Donaldson, "Editor's Comments: Taking Ethics Seriously–A Mission Now More Possible," *Academy of Management Review* 28 (July 2003), 363–67.

48. C. Anderson, "Values-Based Management," *Academy of Management Executive* 11 (1997), 25–46.

49. W. H. Shaw and V. Barry, *Moral Issues in Business,* 6th ed. (Belmont, CA: Wadsworth, 1995); T. Donaldson, *Corporations and Morality* (Englewood Cliffs, NJ: Prentice-Hall, 1982).

50. www.consumerreports.com, 2003.

51. www.fda.com, 2004.

52. www.fda.org, press releases, 2004.

53. E. Werner, "Slaughterhouse Owner Acknowledges Abuse," www.pasadenastarnews.com, March 13, 2008.

54. D. Bunis and N. luna, "Sick Cows Never Made Food Supply, Meat Plant Owner Says," www.ocregister.com, March 12, 2008.

55. "Worker Sentenced in Slaughterhouse Abuse," www.yahoo.com, March 22, 2008.

56. S. Jackson et al., *Diversity in the Workplace: Human Resource Initiatives* (New York: Guilford Press, 1992).

57. G. Robinson and C. S. Daus, "Building a Case for Diversity," *Academy of Management Executive* 3 (1997), 21–31; S. J. Bunderson and K. M. Sutcliffe, "Comparing Alternative Conceptualizations of Functional Diversity in Management Teams: Process and Performance Effects," *Academy of Management Journal* 45 (October 2002), 875–94.

58. D. Jamieson and J. O'Mara, *Managing Workforce 2000: Gaining a Diversity Advantage* (San Francisco: Jossey-Bass, 1991).

59. www.uboc.com, 2008.

60. J. Hickman, C. Tkaczyk, E. Florian, and J. Stemple, "The 50 Best Companies for Minorities to Work For," *Fortune,* July 7, 2003, 55–58.

61. A. R. Randel and K. S. Jaussi, "Functional Background Identity, Diversity, and Individual Performance in Cross-Functional Teams," *Academy of Management Journal* 46 (December 2003), 763–75.

62. "Union Bank of California Honored by U.S. Labor Department for Employment Practices," press release, September 11, 2000.

63. Ibid.

64. Press release, "Dell CEO Kevin Rollins Cites Workforce Diversity as Key to Gaining Competitive Advantages in Business," www.dell.com, March 6, 2006.

65. D. R. Tobin, *The Knowledge Enabled Organization* (New York: AMACOM, 1998).

Chapter 2

1. H. Ford, "Progressive Manufacture," *Encyclopedia Britannica,* 13th ed. (New York: Encyclopedia Co., 1926).

2. R. Edwards, *Contested Terrain: The Transformation of the Workplace in the Twentieth Century* (New York: Basic Books, 1979).

3. A. Smith, *The Wealth of Nations* (London: Penguin, 1982).

4. Ibid., 110.

5. J. G. March and H. A. Simon, *Organizations* (New York: Wiley, 1958).

6. L. W. Fry, "The Maligned F. W. Taylor: A Reply to His Many Critics," *Academy of Management Review* 1 (1976), 124–29.

7. F. W. Taylor, *Shop Management* (New York: Harper, 1903); F. W. Taylor, *The Principles of Scientific Management* (New York: Harper, 1911).

8. J. A. Litterer, *The Emergence of Systematic Management as Shown by the Literature from 1870–1900* (New York: Garland, 1986).

9. H. R. Pollard, *Developments in Management Thought* (New York: Crane, 1974).

10. D. Wren, *The Evolution of Management Thought* (New York: Wiley, 1994), 134.

11. Edwards, *Contested Terrain.*

12. J. M. Staudenmaier, Jr., "Henry Ford's Big Flaw," *Invention and Technology* 10 (1994), 34–44.

13. H. Beynon, *Working for Ford* (London: Penguin, 1975).

14. Taylor, *Scientific Management.*

15. F. B. Gilbreth, *Primer of Scientific Management* (New York: Van Nostrand Reinhold, 1912).

16. F. B. Gilbreth, Jr., and E. G. Gilbreth, *Cheaper by the Dozen* (New York: Crowell, 1948).

17. D. Roy, "Efficiency and the Fix: Informal Intergroup Relations in a Piece Work Setting," *American Journal of Sociology* 60 (1954), 255–66.

18. M. Weber, *From Max Weber: Essays in Sociology,* ed. H. H. Gerth and C. W. Mills (New York: Oxford University Press, 1946); M. Weber, *Economy and Society,* ed. G. Roth and C. Wittich (Berkeley: University of California Press, 1978).

19. C. Perrow, *Complex Organizations,* 2d ed. (Glenview, IL: Scott, Foresman, 1979).

20. Weber, *From Max Weber,* 331.

21. See Perrow, *Complex Organizations,* chap. 1, for a detailed discussion of these issues.

22. H. Fayol, *General and Industrial Management* (New York: IEEE Press, 1984).

23. Ibid., 79.

24. T. J. Peters and R. H. Waterman, Jr., *In Search of Excellence: Lessons from America's Best-Run Companies* (New York: Harper & Row, 1982).

25. R. E. Eccles and N. Nohira, *Beyond the Hype: Rediscovering the Essence of Management* (Boston: Harvard Business School Press, 1992).

26. L. D. Parker, "Control in Organizational Life: The Contribution of Mary Parker Follett," *Academy of Management Review* 9 (1984), 736–45.

27. P. Graham, *M. P. Follett–Prophet of Management: A Celebration of Writings from the 1920s* (Boston: Harvard Business School Press, 1995).

28. M. P. Follett, *Creative Experience* (London: Longmans, 1924).

29. E. Mayo, *The Human Problems of Industrial Civilization* (New York: Macmillan, 1933); F. J. Roethlisberger and W. J. Dickson, *Management and the Worker* (Cambridge: Harvard University Press, 1947).

30. D. W. Organ, "Review of *Management and the Worker,* by F. J. Roethlisberger and W. J. Dickson," *Academy of Management Review* 13 (1986), 460–64.

31. D. Roy, "Banana Time: Job Satisfaction and Informal Interaction," *Human Organization* 18 (1960), 158–61.

32. For an analysis of the problems in determining cause from effect in the Hawthorne studies and in social settings in general, see A. Carey, "The Hawthorne Studies: A Radical Criticism," *American Sociological Review* 33 (1967), 403–16.

33. D. McGregor, *The Human Side of Enterprise* (New York: McGraw-Hill, 1960).

34. Ibid., 48.

35. Peters and Waterman, *In Search of Excellence.*

36. J. Pitta, "It Had to Be Done and We Did It," *Forbes,* April 26, 1993, 148–52.

37. Press release, www.hp.com, June 2001.

38. Press releases, www.hp.com, 2003–2004.

39. www.hp.com, 2006.

40. T. Dewett and G. R. Jones, "The Role of Information Technology in the Organization: A Review, Model, and Assessment," *Journal of Management* 27 (2001), 313–46.

41. W. E. Deming, *Out of the Crisis* (Cambridge: MIT Press, 1986).

42. J. D. Thompson, *Organizations in Action* (New York: McGraw-Hill, 1967).

43. D. Katz and R. L. Kahn, *The Social Psychology of Organizations* (New York: Wiley, 1966); Thompson, *Organizations in Action.*

44. T. Burns and G. M. Stalker, *The Management of Innovation* (London: Tavistock, 1961); P. R. Lawrence and J. R. Lorsch, *Organization and Environment*

(Boston: Graduate School of Business Administration, Harvard University, 1967).

45. Burns and Stalker, *The Management of Innovation.*

46. R. O. Crockett and S. Baker, "Suddenly, Mobile Phones Aren't Moving So Fast," *BusinessWeek Online,* November 6, 2000; S. Baker, I. Resch, and R. O. Crockett, "Commentary: Nokia's Costly Stumble," *BusinessWeek Online,* August 14, 2000.

47. www.nokia.com, 2008.

48. Ibid.

49. Ibid.

50. Ibid.

51. C. W. L. Hill and G. R. Jones, *Strategic Management: An Integrated Approach,* 6th ed. (Boston: Houghton Mifflin, 2007).

Chapter 3

1. S. Covel, "Telemarketer Bucks High Turnover Trend," *The Wall Street Journal,* November 19, 2007, B4; "Ryla History & Culture!" www.rylateleservices.com/print .asp?level=2&id=166, January 24, 2008.

2. L. Hall, "Call Center Bucks Overseas Outsourcing Trend," *Atlanta Business Chronicle,* http://atlanta.bizjournals .com/atlanta/stories/2005/12/12/smallb4 .html?t=printable, January 24, 2008.

3. Covel, "Telemarketer Bucks High Turnover Trend."

4. A. Field, "Capital for Companies That Aid Communities, *The New York Times,* October 16, 2003.

5. Covel, "Telemarketer Bucks High Turnover Trend."; "Ryla History & Culture!"

6. Covel, "Telemarketer Bucks High Turnover Trend."

7. "Company Culture," www. rylateleservices.com/print.asp? level=2&id=98, January 24, 2008.

8. Covel, "Telemarketer Bucks High Turnover Trend."

9. Ibid.

10. "A Great Career Is Waiting for You at Ryla," www.rylateleservices.com/print .asp?level=1&id=13, January 25, 2008.

11. Covel, "Telemarketer Bucks High Turnover Trend."

12. Ibid.

13. "Ryla Named by The Wall Street Journal and Winning Workplaces as a Top Small Workplace in US," October 1, 2007, www.rylateleservices.com/print .asp?level=2&id=168, January 24, 2008.

14. Covel, "Telemarketer Bucks High Turnover Trend."

15. "Ryla Launches Call Center Services for Crisis Response, Seasonal Retail and Political Solutions," Tuesday, November 20, 2007, www.rylateleservices.com/print .asp?level=2&id=171, January 24, 2008.

16. Ibid.

17. "Ryla Named by The Wall Street Journal and Winning Workplaces as a Top Small Workplace in US."

18. Covel, "Telemarketer Bucks High Turnover Trend."

19. S. Carpenter, "Different Dispositions, Different Brains," *Monitor on Psychology,* February 2001, 66–68.

20. J. M. Digman, "Personality Structure: Emergence of the Five-Factor Model," *Annual Review of Psychology* 41 (1990), 417–40; R. R. McCrae and P. T. Costa, "Validation of the Five-Factor Model of Personality Across Instruments and Observers," *Journal of Personality and Social Psychology* 52 (1987), 81–90; R. R. McCrae and P. T. Costa, "Discriminant Validity of NEO-PIR Facet Scales," *Educational and Psychological Measurement* 52 (1992), 229–37.

21. Digman, "Personality Structure"; McCrae and Costa, "Validation of the Five-Factor Model"; McCrae and Costa, "Discriminant Validity"; R. P. Tett and D. D. Burnett, "A Personality Trait-Based Interactionist Model of Job Performance," *Journal of Applied Psychology* 88, no. 3 (2003), 500–17; J. M. George, "Personality, Five-Factor Model," in S. Clegg and J. R. Bailey, eds., *International Encyclopedia of Organization Studies* (Thousand Oaks, CA: Sage, 2007).

22. L. A. Witt and G. R. Ferris, "Social Skills as Moderator of Conscientiousness-Performance Relationship: Convergent Results Across Four Studies," *Journal of Applied Psychology* 88, no.5 (2003), 809–20; M. J. Simmering, J. A. Colquitte, R. A. Noe, and C. O. L. H. Porter, "Conscientiousness, Autonomy Fit, and Development: A Longitudinal Study," *Journal of Applied Psychology* 88, no. 5 (2003), 954–63.

23. M. R. Barrick and M. K. Mount, "The Big Five Personality Dimensions and Job Performance: A Meta-Analysis," *Personnel Psychology* 44 (1991), 1–26; S. Komar, D. J. Brown, J. A. Komar, and C. Robie, "Faking and the Validity of Conscientiousness: A Monte Carlo Investigation," *Journal of Applied Psychology* 93 (2008), 140–54.

24. Digman, "Personality Structure"; McCrae and Costa, "Validation of the Five-Factor Model"; McCrae and Costa, "Discriminant Validity."

25. E. McGirt, "The Dirtiest Mind in Business: How Filth Met Opportunity and Created a Franchise," *Fast Company* 122 (February 2008), 64, www.fastcompany.com/ magazine/122/the-dirtiest-mind-in-business_ Printer_Friendl. . . , January 23, 2008.

26. "Mike Rowe's World: Mike's Bio: Discovery Channel," http://dsc.discovery .com/fansites/dirtyjobs/bio/bio-print.html, January 23, 2008.

27. McGirt, "The Dirtiest Mind in Business."

28. "Dirty Jobs: Season 1 DVD Set–Discovery Channel Store–754317," http:// shopping.discovery.com/product-60948 .html?jzid=40588004-66-0, January 25, 2008; "Mike Rowe's World: Mike's Bio: Discovery Channel."

29. McGirt, "The Dirtiest Mind in Business."

30. Ibid.

31. Ibid.

32. McGirt, "The Dirtiest Mind in Business."; M. Rowe, "Seven Dirty Habits of Highly Effluent People: Mike Rose's Seven Rules for Job Satisfaction," *Fast Company* 122 (February 2008), 69, www.fastcompany .com/magazine/122/seven-dirty-habits-of-highly-effluent-people_. . . , January 23, 2008.

33. J. B. Rotter, "Generalized Expectancies for Internal versus External Control of Reinforcement," *Psychological Monographs* 80 (1966), 1–28; P. Spector, "Behaviors in Organizations as a Function of Employees' Locus of Control," *Psychological Bulletin* 91 (1982), 482–97.

34. J. Brockner, *Self-Esteem at Work* (Lexington, MA: Lexington Books, 1988).

35. D. C. McClelland, *Human Motivation* (Glenview, IL: Scott, Foresman, 1985); D. C. McClelland, "How Motives, Skills, and Values Determine What People Do," *American Psychologist* 40 (1985), 812–25; D. C. McClelland, "Managing Motivation to Expand Human Freedom," *American Psychologist* 33 (1978), 201–10.

36. D. G. Winter, *The Power Motive* (New York: Free Press 1973).

37. M. J. Stahl, "Achievement, Power, and Managerial Motivation: Selecting Managerial Talent with the Job Choice Exercise," *Personnel Psychology* 36 (1983), 775–89; D. C. McClelland and D. H. Burnham, "Power Is the Great Motivator," *Harvard Business Review* 54 (1976), 100–10.

38. R. J. House, W. D. Spangler, and J. Woycke, "Personality and Charisma in the U.S. Presidency: A Psychological Theory of Leader Effectiveness," *Administrative Science Quarterly* 36 (1991), 364–96.

39. G. H. Hines, "Achievement, Motivation, Occupations and Labor Turnover in New Zealand," *Journal of Applied Psychology* 58 (1973), 313–17; P. S. Hundal, "A Study of Entrepreneurial Motivation: Comparison of Fast- and Slow-Progressing Small Scale Industrial Entrepreneurs in Punjab, India," *Journal of Applied Psychology* 55 (1971), 317–23.

40. M. Rokeach, *The Nature of Human Values* (New York: Free Press 1973).

41. Ibid.

42. Ibid.

43. K. K. Spors, "Top Small Workplaces 2007: Gentle Giant Moving," *The Wall Street Journal,* October 1, 2007, R4–R5; "Gentle

Giant Sees Revenue Boost, *Boston Business Journal,* January 15, 2008, www.gentlegiant.com/news-011508-1.htm, February 5, 2008.

44. Spors, "Top Small Workplaces 2007: Gentle Giant Moving."

45. Ibid.

46. Ibid.

47. Spors, "Top Small Workplaces 2007: Gentle Giant Moving."; "Gentle Giant Receives Top Small Workplace Award," www.gentlegiant.com/topsmallworkplace.htm, January 5, 2008.

48. Spors, "Top Small Workplaces 2007: Gentle Giant Moving."

49. Ibid.

50. A. P. Brief, *Attitudes In and Around Organizations* (Thousand Oaks, CA: Sage, 1998).

51. D. Stafford, "Job Satisfaction Takes a Tumble," *Houston Chronicle,* February 25, 2007, D6.

52. Ibid.

53. N. A. Hira, "You Raised Them, Now Manage Them," *Fortune,* May 28, 2007, 38–46.

54. M. Irvine, "In Search of the Simple Life," *Houston Chronicle,* February 1, 2004, 8A; M. Irvine, "Simple Life Holds Appeal for Young Professionals," http://the.honoluluandvertiser.com/article/2004/jan/26.bz/bz10a.html, January 26, 2004; "More Young People Pursuing Simpler Life," http://msnbc.msn.com/id/4062706, January 26, 2004; Wyoming Business Council, http://www.wyomingbusiness.org/txt_index.htm, February 5, 2008.

55. Irvine, "In Search of the Simple Life"; Irvine, "Simple Life Holds Appeal"; "More Young People Pursuing Simpler Life"; "Diaper Rash Cream and Ointment for Babies–PINXAV," www.pinxav.com, May 28, 2006; http://www.pinxav.com/, February 5, 2008.

56. Irvine, "In Search of the Simple Life"; Irvine, "Simple Life Holds Appeal"; "More Young People Pursuing Simpler Life."

57. Irvine, "In Search of the Simple Life"; Irvine, "Simple Life Holds Appeal"; "More Young People Pursuing Simpler Life."

58. D. W. Organ, *Organizational Citizenship Behavior: The Good Soldier Syndrome* (Lexington, MA: Lexington Books, 1988).

59. J. M. George and A. P. Brief, "Feeling Good–Doing Good: A Conceptual Analysis of the Mood at Work–Organizational Spontaneity Relationship," *Psychological Bulletin* 112 (1992), 310–29.

60. W. H. Mobley, "Intermediate Linkages in the Relationship Between Job Satisfaction and Employee Turnover," *Journal of Applied Psychology* 62 (1977), 237–40.

61. C. Hymowitz, "Though Now Routine, Bosses Still Stumble During Layoff Process," *The Wall Street Journal,* June 25, 2007, B1; J. Brockner, "The Effects of Work Layoffs on Survivors: Research, Theory and Practice ," in B. M. Staw and L. L. Cummings, eds., *Research in Organizational Behavior,* vol. 10 (Greenwich, CT: JAI Press, 1988), 213–55.

62. Hymowitz, "Though Now Routine, Bosses Still Stumble During Layoff Process."

63. Ibid.

64. Ibid.

65. N. Solinger, W. van Olffen, and R. A. Roe, "Beyond the Three-Component Model of Organizational Commitment," *Journal of Applied Psychology* 93 (2008), 70–83.

66. J. E. Mathieu and D. M. Zajac, "A Review and Meta-Analysis of the Antecedents, Correlates, and Consequences of Organizational Commitment," *Psychological Bulletin* 108 (1990), 171–94.

67. E. Slate, "Tips for Negotiations in Germany and France," *HR Focus,* July 1994, 18.

68. D. Watson and A. Tellegen, "Toward a Consensual Structure of Mood," *Psychological Bulletin* 98 (1985), 219–35.

69. Ibid.

70. J. M. George, "The Role of Personality in Organizational Life: Issues and Evidence," *Journal of Management* 18 (1992), 185–213.

71. H. A. Elfenbein, "Emotion in Organizations: A Review and Theoretical Integration," in J. P. Walsh and A. P. Brief eds., *The Academy of Management Annals,* vol. 1 (New York: Lawrence Erlbaum Associates, 2008), 315–86.

72. J. P. Forgas, "Affect in Social Judgments and Decisions: A Multi-Process Model," in M. Zanna, ed., *Advances in Experimental and Social Psychology,* vol. 25 (San Diego, CA: Academic Press, 1992), 227–75; J. P. Forgas and J. M. George, "Affective Influences on Judgments and Behavior in Organizations: An Information Processing Perspective," *Organizational Behavior and Human Decision Processes* 86 (2001), 3–34; J. M. George, "Emotions and Leadership: The Role of Emotional Intelligence," *Human Relations* 53 (2000), 1027–55; W. N. Morris, *Mood: The Frame of Mind* (New York: Springer-Verlag, 1989).

73. George, "Emotions and Leadership."

74. J. M. George and K. Bettenhausen, "Understanding Prosocial Behavior, Sales Performance, and Turnover: A Group Level Analysis in a Service Context," *Journal of Applied Psychology* 75 (1990), 698–709.

75. George and Brief, "Feeling Good–Doing Good"; J. M. George and J. Zhou, "Understanding When Bad Moods Foster Creativity and Good Ones Don't: The Role of Context and Clarity of Feelings," paper presented at the Academy of Management Annual Meeting, 2001; A. M. Isen and R. A. Baron, "Positive Affect as a Factor in Organizational Behavior," in B. M. Staw and L. L. Cummings, eds., *Research in Organizational Behavior,* vol. 13 (Greenwich, CT: JAI Press, 1991), 1–53.

76. J. M. George and J. Zhou, "Dual Tuning in a Supportive Context: Joint Contributions of Positive Mood, Negative Mood, and Supervisory Behaviors to Employee Creativity," *Academy of Management Journal,* 50 (2007), 605-622; J. M. George, "Creativity in Organizations," in J. P. Walsh and A. P. Brief eds., *The Academy of Management Annals,* vol. 1 (New York: Lawrence Erlbaum Associates, 2008),439–77.

77. J. D. Greene, R. B. Sommerville, L. E. Nystrom, J. M. Darley, and J. D. Cohen, "An FMRI Investigation of Emotional Engagement in Moral Judgment," *Science,* September 14, 2001, 2105–08; L. Neergaard, "Brain Scans Show Emotions Key to Resolving Ethical Dilemmas," *Houston Chronicle,* September 14, 2001, 13A.

78. www.thethinkers.com/homemain.cfm, February 5, 2008.

79. L. Berton, "It's Audit Time! Send in the Clowns," *The Wall Street Journal,* January 18, 1995, B1, B6.

80. R. C. Sinclair, "Mood, Categorization Breadth, and Performance Appraisal: The Effects of Order of Information Acquisition and Affective State on Halo, Accuracy, Informational Retrieval, and Evaluations," *Organizational Behavior and Human Decision Processes* 42 (1988), 22–46.

81. D. Goleman, *Emotional Intelligence* (New York: Bantam Books, 1994); J. D. Mayer and P. Salovey, "The Intelligence of Emotional Intelligence," *Intelligence* 17 (1993), 433–42; J. D. Mayer and P. Salovey, "What Is Emotional Intelligence?" in P. Salovey and D. Sluyter, eds., *Emotional Development and Emotional Intelligence: Implications for Education* (New York: Basic Books, 1997); P. Salovey and J. D. Mayer, "Emotional Intelligence," *Imagination, Cognition, and Personality* 9 (1989–1990), 185–211.

82. S. Epstein, *Constructive Thinking* (Westport, CT: Praeger, 1998).

83. "Leading by Feel," *Inside the Mind of the Leader,* January 2004, 27–37.

84. P. C. Early and R. S. Peterson, "The Elusive Cultural Chameleon: Cultural Intelligence as a New Approach to Intercultural Training for the Global Manger," *Academy of Management Learning and Education* 3, no. 1 (2004), 100–15.

85. George, "Emotions and Leadership"; S. Begley, "The Boss Feels Your Pain," *Newsweek,* October 12, 1998, 74; D. Goleman, *Working with Emotional Intelligence* (New York: Bantam Books, 1998).

86. J. Bercovici, "Remembering Bernie Goldhirsh," www.medialifemagazine.com/news2003/jun03/jun30/4_thurs/news1thursday.html, April 15, 2004.

87. B. Burlingham, "Legacy: The Creative Spirit," *INC.,* September 2003, 11–12.

88. Burlingham, "Legacy: The Creative Spirit"; "Inc. magazine," www.inc.com/magazine, May 28, 2006.

89. Burlingham, "Legacy: The Creative Spirit"; "Inc. magazine," www.inc.com/magazine, May 28, 2006; www.inc.com, February 5, 2008.

90. "Leading by Feel," *Inside the Mind of the Leader,* January 2004, 27–37.

91. George, "Emotions and Leadership."

92. J. Zhou and J. M. George, "Awakening Employee Creativity: The Role of Leader Emotional Intelligence," *Leadership Quarterly* 14 (2003), 545–68.

93. A. Jung, "Leading by Feel: Seek Frank Feedback," *Inside the Mind of the Leader,* January 2004, 31.

94. H. M. Trice and J. M. Beyer, *The Cultures of Work Organizations* (Englewood Cliffs, NJ: Prentice-Hall, 1993).

95. J. B. Sørensen, "The Strength of Corporate Culture and the Reliability of Firm Performance," *Administrative Science Quarterly* 47, (2002), 70–91.

96. "Personality and Organizational Culture," in B. Schneider and D. B. Smith, eds., *Personality and Organizations* (Mahway, NJ: Lawrence Erlbaum, 2004), 347–69; J. E. Slaughter, M. J. Zickar, S. Highhouse, and D. C. Mohr, "Personality Trait Inferences about Organizations: Development of a Measure and Assessment of Construct Validity," *Journal of Applied Psychology* 89, no. 1 (2004), 85–103.

97. T. Kelley, *The Art of Innovation: Lessons in Creativity from IDEO, America's Leading Design Firm* (New York: Random House, 2001).

98. "Personality and Organizational Culture."

99. B. Schneider, "The People Make the Place," *Personnel Psychology* 40 (1987), 437–53.

100. "Personality and Organizational Culture."

101. Ibid.

102. B. Schneider, H. B. Goldstein, and D. B. Smith, "The ASA Framework: An Update," *Personnel Psychology* 48 (1995), 747–73; J. Schaubroeck, D. C. Ganster, and J. R. Jones, "Organizational and Occupational Influences in the Attraction-Selection-Attrition Process," *Journal of Applied Psychology* 83 (1998), 869–91.

103. Kelley, *The Art of Innovation.*

104. www.ideo.com, February 5, 2008.

105. Kelley, *The Art of Innovation.*

106. "Personality and Organizational Culture."

107. Kelley, *The Art of Innovation.*

108. George, "Emotions and Leadership."

109. Kelley, *The Art of Innovation.*

110. Ibid.

111. D. C. Feldman, "The Development and Enforcement of Group Norms," *Academy of Management Review* 9 (1984), 47–53.

112. G. R. Jones, *Organizational Theory, Design, and Change* (Upper Saddle River, NJ: Prentice-Hall, 2003).

113. H. Schein, "The Role of the Founder in Creating Organizational Culture," *Organizational Dynamics* 12 (1983), 13–28.

114. "PAETEC Signs Exclusive Agreement with Los Angeles Area Hotel and Lodging Association," PAETEC News Current Press Releases, February 18, 2004; "Markets Served–PAETEC Communications, Inc.," www.paetec.com/2_1/2_1_5_2.html, May 27, 2006; "Media Center–2005 Press Releases–PAETEC Communications, Inc.," www.paetec.com/3/2005_news.html, May 27, 2006; "PAETEC SECURETEC MPLS Now Has a World–Reach," www.paetec.com, May 27, 2006; "Markets Served," http://www.paetec.com/strategic/markets_served.html, January 25, 2008.

115. "Company Profile," http://www.paetec.com/strategic/PAETEC_profile.html, January 25, 2008.

116. "PAETEC Communications, Inc.: 2005 Year in Review."; "Company Profile," http://www.paetec.com/strategic/PAETEC_profile.html, January 25, 2008

117. D. Dorsey, "Happiness Pays," *Inc. Magazine,* February 2004, 89–94.

118. "Company Profile about PAETEC," www.paetec.com, March 8, 2004; "Company Profile," http://www.paetec.com/strategic/PAETEC_profile.html, January 25, 2008.

119. "Company Profile," http://www.paetec.com/strategic/PAETEC_profile.html, January 25, 2008.

120. Dorsey, "Happiness Pays."

121. "PAETEC Receives 2005 American Business Ethics Award," www.paetec.com, May 27, 2006.

122. "PAETEC Communications, Inc.: 2005 Year in Review."

123. Dorsey, "Happiness Pays."

124. Ibid.

125. "Company Profile about PAETEC"; "Company Profile," http://www.paetec.com/strategic/PAETEC_profile.html, January 25, 2008.

126. J. M. George, "Personality, Affect, and Behavior in Groups," *Journal of Applied Psychology* 75 (1990), 107–16.

127. J. Van Maanen, "Police Socialization: A Longitudinal Examination of Job Attitudes in an Urban Police Department," *Administrative Science Quarterly* 20 (1975), 207–28.

128. www.intercotwest.com/Disney; M. N. Martinez, "Disney Training Works Magic," *HRMagazine,* May 1992, 53–57.

129. P. L. Berger and T. Luckman, *The Social Construction of Reality* (Garden City, NY: Anchor Books, 1967).

130. H. M. Trice and J. M. Beyer, "Studying Organizational Culture Through Rites and Ceremonials," *Academy of Management Review* 9 (1984), 653–69.

131. Kelley, *The Art of Innovation.*

132. H. M. Trice and J. M. Beyer, *The Cultures of Work Organizations* (Englewood Cliffs, NJ: Prentice-Hall, 1993).

133. B. Ortega, "Wal-Mart's Meeting Is a Reason to Party," *The Wall Street Journal,* June 3, 1994, A1.

134. Trice and Beyer, "Studying Organizational Culture."

135. Kelley, *The Art of Innovation.*

136. www.ibm.com.

137. S. McGee, "Garish Jackets Add to Clamor of Chicago Pits," *The Wall Street Journal,* July 31, 1995, C1.

138. K. E. Weick, *The Social Psychology of Organization* (Reading, MA: Addison-Wesley, 1979).

139. B. McLean and P. Elkind, *The Smartest Guys in the Room: The Amazing Rise and Scandalous Fall of Enron* (New York: Penguin Books, 2003); R. Smith and J. R. Emshwiller, *24 Days: How Two Wall Street Journal Reporters Uncovered the Lies That Destroyed Faith in Corporate America* (New York: HarperCollins, 2003); M. Swartz and S. Watkins, *Power Failure: The Inside Story of the Collapse of ENRON* (New York: Doubleday, 2003).

Chapter 4

1. J. Bohr, "Deadly Roses," *The Battalion,* February 13, 2006, 3.

2. www.veriflora.com, 2008.

3. "Valentine's Day Preparedness, Part 1: Flowers Whose Ethics Don't Stink," www.walletmouth.com, February 5, 2008.

4. H. Mance, "Behind Colombia's Flower Trade," www.news.bbc.uk, February 14, 2008.

5. A. E. Tenbrunsel, "Misrepresentation and Expectations of Misrepresentation in an Ethical Dilemma: The Role of Incentives and Temptation," *Academy of Management Journal* 41 (June 1998), 330–40.

6. D. Kravets, "Supreme Court to Hear Case on Medical Pot," www.yahoo.com, June 29, 2004; C. Lane "A Defeat for Users of Medical Marihuana," www.washingtonpost.com, June 7, 2005.

7. www.yahoo.com, 2003; www.mci.com, 2004.

8. J. Child, "The International Crisis of Confidence in Corporations," *Academy of Management Executive* 16 (August 2002), 145–48.

9. T. Donaldson, "Editor's Comments: Taking Ethics Seriously–A Mission Now More Possible," *Academy of Management Review* 28 (July 2003), 463–67.

10. R. E. Freeman, *Strategic Management: A Stakeholder Approach* (Marshfield, MA: Pitman, 1984).

11. J. A. Pearce, "The Company Mission as a Strategic Tool," *Sloan Management Review,* Spring 1982, 15–24.

12. J. Robertson, "Ex-Brocade CEO Sentenced to 21 Months, www.yahoo.com, January 16, 2008.

13. C. I. Barnard, *The Functions of the Executive* (Cambridge, MA: Harvard University Press, 1948).

14. Freeman, *Strategic Management.*

15. http://data.bls.gov/cgi-bin/surveymost, 2006.

16. G. Brown, "How to Embrace Change," *Newsweek,* June 12, 2006, 69.

17. P. S. Adler, "Corporate Scandals: It's Time for Reflection in Business Schools," *Academy of Management Executive* 16 (August 2002), 148–50.

18. W. G. Sanders, and D. C. Hambrick, "Swinging for the Fences: The Effects of CEO Stock Options on Company Risk-taking and Performance," *Academy of Management Journal* 53, no. 5 (2007), 1055–78.

19. House Oversight and Government Reform Committee Proceedings, February 2008, http://oversight.house.gov.

20. J. Abrams, "CEOs Involved in Mortgage Crisis Defend Their High Pay Before Congressional Panel," www.yahoo.com, March 7, 2008

21. www.wholefoodsmarket.com, 2008.

22. John Mackey's Blog: 20 Questions with Sunni's Salon," www.wholefoodsmarket.com, 2006.

23. Ibid.

24. "The Green Machine," *Newsweek,* March 21, 2005, E8–E10

25. T. L. Beauchamp and N. E. Bowie, eds., *Ethical Theory and Business* (Englewood Cliffs, NJ: Prentice-Hall, 1979); A. MacIntyre, *After Virtue* (South Bend, IN: University of Notre Dame Press, 1981).

26. R. E. Goodin, "How to Determine Who Should Get What," *Ethics,* July 1975, 310–21.

27. E. P. Kelly, "A Better Way to Think About Business" (book review), *Academy of Management Executive* 14 (May 2000), 127–29.

28. T. M. Jones, "Ethical Decision Making by Individuals in Organizations: An Issue Contingent Model," *Academy of Management Journal* 16 (1991), 366–95; G. F. Cavanaugh, D. J. Moberg, and M. Velasquez, "The Ethics of Organizational Politics," *Academy of Management Review* 6 (1981), 363–74.

29. L. K. Trevino, "Ethical Decision Making in Organizations: A Person-Situation Interactionist Model," *Academy of Management Review* 11 (1986), 601–17; W. H. Shaw and V. Barry, *Moral Issues in Business,* 6th ed. (Belmont, CA: Wadsworth, 1995).

30. T. M. Jones, "Instrumental Stakeholder Theory: A Synthesis of Ethics and Economics," *Academy of Management Review* 20 (1995), 404–37.

31. B. Victor and J. B. Cullen, "The Organizational Bases of Ethical Work Climates," *Administrative Science Quarterly* 33 (1988), 101–25.

32. www.yahoo.com, 2006.

33. www.napster.com, 2006.

34. C. W. L. Hill, "Napster," in C. W. L. Hill and G. R. Jones, *Strategic Management: An Integrated Approach* (Boston: Houghton Mifflin, 2007).

35. D. Collins, "Organizational Harm, Legal Consequences and Stakeholder Retaliation," *Journal of Business Ethics* 8 (1988), 1–13.

36. R. C. Soloman, *Ethics and Excellence* (New York: Oxford University Press, 1992).

37. T. E. Becker, "Integrity in Organizations: Beyond Honesty and Conscientiousness," *Academy of Management Review* 23 (January 1998), 154–62.

38. S. W. Gellerman, "Why Good Managers Make Bad Decisions," in K. R. Andrews, ed., *Ethics in Practice: Managing the Moral Corporation* (Boston: Harvard Business School Press, 1989).

39. J. Dobson, "Corporate Reputation: A Free Market Solution to Unethical Behavior," *Business and Society* 28 (1989), 1–5.

40. M. S. Baucus and J. P. Near, "Can Illegal Corporate Behavior Be Predicted? An Event History Analysis," *Academy of Management Journal* 34 (1991), 9–36.

41. Trevino, "Ethical Decision Making in Organizations."

42. "GSK, Merck and Bristol Myers Squibb Are the World's Most Ethical Companies, Across All Sectors, Swiss Study," www.medicalnewstoday.com, January 8, 2006.

43. A. S. Waterman, "On the Uses of Psychological Theory and Research in the Process of Ethical Inquiry," *Psychological Bulletin* 103, no. 3 (1988), 283–98.

44. P. Engardio and R. Dexter, "How to Makes Factories Play Fair, www.businessweek, November 27, 2006.

45. M. S. Frankel, "Professional Codes: Why, How, and with What Impact?" *Ethics* 8 (1989), 109–15.

46. J. Van Maanen and S. R. Barley, "Occupational Communities: Culture and Control in Organizations," in B. Staw and L. Cummings, eds., *Research in Organizational Behavior,* vol. 6 (Greenwich, CT: JAI Press, 1984), 287–365.

47. Jones, "Ethical Decision Making by Individuals in Organizations."

48. A. Soke, "Jimmy Carter Helps Build 1000th and 1001st Home," typepad.com May 22, 2007.

49. E. Gatewood and A. B. Carroll, "The Anatomy of Corporate Social Response," *Business Horizons,* September–October 1981, 9–16.

50. www.yahoo.com, June 7, 2006.

51. R. Johnson, "Ralston to Buy Beechnut, Gambling It Can Overcome Apple Juice Scandal," *The Wall Street Journal,* September 18, 1989, B11.

52. M. Friedman, "A Friedman Doctrine: The Social Responsibility of Business Is to Increase Its Profits," *New York Times Magazine,* September 13, 1970, 33.

53. P. Engardio and M. Arndt, "What Price Reputation?" www.businessweek.com, July 9, 2007.

54. Conlin, "Where Layoffs Are a Last Resort"; Southwest Airlines Fact Sheet, www.southwest.com, 2004.

55. G. R. Jones, *Organizational Theory: Text and Cases* (Englewood Cliffs, NJ: Prentice-Hall, 2006).

56. P. E. Murphy, "Creating Ethical Corporate Structure," *Sloan Management Review,* Winter 1989, 81–87.

57. C. Stavraka, "Strong Corporate Reputation at J&J Boosts Diversity Recruiting Efforts," DiversityInc.com, February 16, 2001.

58. "Our Credo," www.jj.com, 2008.

59. Ibid.

60. L. L. Nash, *Good Intentions Aside* (Boston: Harvard Business School Press, 1993).

61. Ibid.; L. L. Nash, "Johnson & Johnson's Credo," in *Corporate Ethics: A Prime Business Asset* (New York: Business Roundtable, February 1988).

62. Nash, *Good Intentions Aside.*

63. Stavraka, "Strong Corporate Reputation."

64. Nash, *Good Intentions Aside.*

Chapter 5

1. P. Dvorak, "Firms Push New Methods to Promote Diversity," *The Wall Street Journal,* December 18, 2006, B3; www.sodeshousa.com/, February 7, 2008.

2. Dvorak, "Firms Push New Methods to Promote Diversity."

3. Ibid.

4. Ibid.

5. Ibid.

6. Ibid.

7. "Sodexho Named Large Employer of the Year by Pike Area (Alabama) Committee," www.sodexhousa.com/press-releases/pr110907_2.asp, February 6, 2008.

8. "Corporate Diversity," www. sodexhousa.com/press-factsheets/press_fact_corporate.asp, February 6, 2008; "Sodexho Named to *Atlanta Tribune's* Top Companies for Minorities," www.sodexhousa.com/press-releases/pr111207_1.asp, February 6, 2008; "Sodexho Recognized as Leader in Corporate Social Responsibility by Montgomery County Chamber of Commerce," www.sodexhousa.com/press-releases/pr111507.asp, February 6, 2008.

9. "Sodexho Chief Diversity Officer Named Among Top 20 Diversity Champions," www.sodexhousa.com/press-releases/pr110907_3.asp, February 6, 2008; "Sodexho Receives Texas DiversityFirst Leadership Award," www.sodexhousa.com/press-releases/pr110907_1.asp, February 6, 2008; "Gutierrez Honored by the Hispanic Association on Corporate Responsibility," www.sodexhousa.com/press-releases/pr111207_2.asp, February 6, 2008.

10. D. Maxey, "Compensation Carrot," *The Wall Street Journal,* April 9, 2007, R4.

11. Ibid.

12. Ibid.

13. Dvorak, "Firms Push New Methods to Promote Diversity"; Maxey, "Compensation Carrot."

14. D. McCracken, "Winning the Talent War for Women," *Harvard Business Review,* November–December 2000, 159–67.

15. W. B. Swann, Jr., J. T. Polzer, D. C. Seyle, and S. J. Ko, "Finding Value in Diversity: Verification of Personal and Social Self-Views in Diverse Groups," *Academy of Management Review* 29, no. 1 (2004), 9–27.

16. "Usual Weekly Earnings Summary," *News: Bureau of Labor Statistics,* April 16, 2004 (www.bls.gov/news.release/whyeng.nr0.htm); "Facts on Affirmative Action in Employment and Contracting," *Americans for a Fair Chance,* January, 28, 2004 (fairchance.civilrights.org/research_center/details.cfm?id=18076); "Household Data Annual Averages," www.bls.gov, April 28, 2004.

17. "Prejudice: Still on the Menu," *BusinessWeek,* April 3, 1995, 42.

18. "She's a Woman, Offer Her Less," *BusinessWeek,* May 7, 2001, 34.

19. "Glass Ceiling Is a Heavy Barrier for Minorities, Blocking Them from Top Jobs," *The Wall Street Journal,* March 14, 1995, A1.

20. "Catalyst Report Outlines Unique Challenges Faced By African-American Women in Business," *Catalyst news release,* February 18, 2004.

21. C. Gibson, "Nation's Median Age Highest Ever, but 65-and-Over Population's Growth Lags, Census 2000 Shows," *U.S. Census Bureau News,* May 30, 2001 (www.census.gov); "U.S. Census Press Releases: Nation's Population One-Third Minority,"

U.S. Census Bureau News, May 10, 2006 (www.census.gov/Press-Release/www/releases/archives/population/ 006808.html).

22. "Table 2: United States Population Projections by Age and Sex: 2000–2050," *U.S. Census Board, International Data Base, 94,* April 28, 2004 (www.census.gov/ipc/www.idbprint.html).

23. U.S. Equal Employment Opportunity Commission, "Federal Laws Prohibiting Job Discrimination–Questions and Answers," www.eeoc.gov, June 20, 2001.

24. "Sex by Industry by Class of Worker for the Employed Civilian Population 16 Years and Over," *American FactFinder,* October 15, 2001 (factfinder.census.gov); "2002 Catalyst Census of Women Corporate Officers and Top Earners in the Fortune 500," www.catalystwomen.org, August 17, 2004.

25. "Profile of Selected Economic Characteristics: 2000," *American FactFinder,* October 15, 2001 (factfinder.census.gov); "Usual Weekly Earnings Summary," www.bls.gov/news.release, August 17, 2004.

26. "2000 Catalyst Census of Women Corporate Officers and Top Earners of the Fortune 500," www.catalystwomen.org, October 21, 2001; S. Wellington, M. Brumit Kropf, and P. R. Gerkovich, "What's Holding Women Back?" *Harvard Business Review,* June 2003, 18–19, D. Jones, "The Gender Factor," *USA Today.com,* December 30, 2003; "2002 Catalyst Census of Women Corporate Officers and Top Earners in the Fortune 500," www.catalystwomen.org, August 17, 2004; "2007 Catalyst Census of Women Corporate Officers and Top Earners of the *Fortune* 500," www.catalyst.org/knowledge/titles/title.php?page=cen_COTE_07, February 8, 2008.

27. T. Gutner, "Wanted: More Diverse Directors," *BusinessWeek,* April 30, 2001, 134; "2003 Catalyst Census of Women Board Directors," www.catalystwomen.org, August 17, 2004; "2007 Catalyst Census of Women Board Directors of the *Fortune* 500," www.catalyst.org/knowledge/titles/title.php?page+cen_WBD_07, February 8, 2008.

28. Gutner, "Wanted: More Diverse Directors"; "2003 Catalyst Census of Women Board Directors."

29. R. Sharpe, "As Leaders, Women Rule," *BusinessWeek,* November 20, 2000, 75–84.

30. Ibid.

31. "New Catalyst Study Reveals Financial Performance Is Higher for Companies with More Women at the Top," *Catalyst news release,* January 26, 2004.

32. P. Sellers, "Women on Boards (NOT!)," *Fortune,* October 15, 2007, 105.

33. B. Guzman, "The Hispanic Population," U.S. Census Bureau, May 2001; U.S. Census Bureau, "Profiles of General Demographic Characteristics," May 2001; U.S.

Census Bureau, "Revisions to the Standards for the Classification of Federal Data on Race and Ethnicity," November 2, 2000, 1–19.

34. L. Chavez, "Just Another Ethnic Group," *The Wall Street Journal,* May 14, 2001, A22.

35. Bureau of Labor Statistics, "Civilian Labor Force 16 and Older by Sex, Age, Race, and Hispanic Origin, 1978, 1988, 1998, and Projected 2008," stats.bls.gov/emp, October 16, 2001.

36. "U.S. Census Bureau, Profile of General Demographic Characteristics: 2000," *Census 2000,* www.census.gov; "U.S. Census Press Releases: Nation's Population One-Third Minority," *U.S. Census Bureau News,* May 10, 2006 (www.census.gov/Press-Release/www/releases/archives/population/006808.html).

37. *U.S. Census Bureau,* "Census Bureau Projects Tripling of Hispanic and Asian Populations in 50 Years; Non-Hispanic Whites May Drop to Half of Total Populations," www.census.gov/Press-Release/www/releases/archives/population/001720.html, March 18, 2004; "Asians Projected to Lead Next Population Growth Surge," *Houston Chronicle,* May 1, 2004, 3A.

38. "Report Says Disparities Abound Between Blacks, Whites," *Houston Chronicle,* March 24, 2004, 7A.

39. Ibid.

40. J. Flint, "NBC to Hire More Minorities on TV shows," *The Wall Street Journal,* January 6, 2000, B13.

41. J. Poniewozik, "What's Wrong with This Picture?" *Time,* June 1, 2001 (www.Time.com).

42. Ibid.

43. National Association of Realtors, "Real Estate Industry Adapting to Increasing Cultural Diversity," *PR Newswire,* May 16, 2001.

44. "Toyota Apologizes to African Americans over Controversial Ad," *Kyodo News Service,* Japan, May 23, 2001.

45. J. H. Coplan, "Putting a Little Faith in Diversity," *BusinessWeek Online,* December 21, 2000.

46. Ibid.

47. Ibid.

48. K. Holland, "When Religious Needs Test Company," *The New York Times,* February 25, 2007, BU17.

49. J. N. Cleveland, J. Barnes-Farrell, and J. M. Ratz, "Accommodation in the Workplace," *Human Resource Management Review* 7 (1997), 77–108; A. Colella, "Coworker Distributive Fairness Judgments of the Workplace Accommodations of Employees with Disabilities," *Academy of Management Review* 26 (2001), 100–16.

50. Colella, "Coworker Distributive Fairness Judgments"; D. Stamps, "Just How Scary Is the ADA," *Training* 32 (1995), 93–101;

M. S. West and R. L. Cardy, "Accommodating Claims of Disability: The Potential Impact of Abuses," *Human Resource Management Review* 7 (1997), 233–46.

51. G. Koretz, "How to Enable the Disabled," *BusinessWeek,* November 6, 2000 (BusinessWeek Archives).

52. Colella, "Coworker Distributive Fairness Judgments."

53. "Notre Dame Disability Awareness Week 2004 Events," www.nd.edu/~bbuddies/daw.html, April 30, 2004.

54. P. Hewitt, "UH Highlights Abilities, Issues of the Disabled," *Houston Chronicle,* October 22, 2001, 24A.

55. "Notre Dame Disability Awareness Week 2004 Events."Hewitt, "UH Highlights Abilities, Issues of the Disabled."

56. J. M. George, "AIDS/AIDS-Related Complex," in L. H. Peters, C. R. Greer, and S. A. Youngblood, eds., *The Blackwell Encyclopedic Dictionary of Human Resource Management* (Oxford, UK: Blackwell, 1997), 6–7.

57. J. M. George "AIDS Awareness Training," in L. H. Peters, C. R. Greer, and S. A. Youngblood, eds., *The Blackwell Encyclopedic Dictionary of Human Resource Management* (Oxford, UK: Blackwell, 1997), 6.

58. S. Armour, "Firms Juggle Stigma, Needs of More Workers with HIV," *USA Today,* September 7, 2000, B1.

59. Ibid.

60. Ibid; S. Vaughn, "Career Challenge; Companies' Work Not Over in HIV and AIDS Education," *Los Angeles Times,* July 8, 2001.

61. R. Brownstein, "Honoring Work Is Key to Ending Poverty," *Detroit News,* October 2, 2001, 9; G. Koretz, "How Welfare to Work Worked," *BusinessWeek,* September 24, 2001 (BusinessWeek Archives).

62. "As Ex-Welfare Recipients Lose Jobs, Offer Safety Net," *The Atlanta Constitution,* October 10, 2001, A18.

63. "Profile of Selected Economic Characteristics: 2000," *American FactFinder* (factfinder.census.gov).

64. U.S. Census Bureau, "Poverty–How the Census Bureau Measures Poverty," *Census 2000,* September 25, 2001.

65. U.S. Census Bureau, "Poverty 2000," www.census.gov, October 26, 2001.

66. I. Lelchuk, "Families Fear Hard Times Getting Worse/$30,000 in the Bay Area Won't Buy Necessities, Survey Says," *San Francisco Chronicle,* September 26, 2001, A13; S. R. Wheeler, "Activists: Welfare-to-Work Changes Needed," *Denver Post,* October 10, 2001, B6.

67. B. Carton, "Bedtime Stories: In 24-Hour Workplace, Day Care Is Moving to the Night Shift," *The Wall Street Journal,* July 6, 2001, A1, A4.

68. Ibid.

69. Ibid.

70. Ibid.

71. "Google View Question: Q: Homosexual Statistics," answers.google.com/answers/threadview?id= 271269, April 30, 2004; D. M. Smith and G. Gates, "Gay and Lesbian Families in the United States," *Urban Institute,* May 28, 2006 (www.urban.org/publications/1000491.html).

72. S. E. Needleman, "More Programs Move to Halt Bias against Gays," *The Wall Street Journal,* November 26, 2007, B3.

73. K. Fahim, "United Parcel Service Agrees to Benefits in Civil Unions," *The New York Times,* July 31, 2007, A19.

74. J. Hempel, "Coming Out in Corporate America," *BusinessWeek,* December 15, 2003, 64–72.

75. Ibid.

76. J. Files, "Study Says Discharges Continue Under 'Don't Ask, Don't Tell,'" *The New York Times,* March 24, 2004, A14; J. Files, "Gay Ex-Officers Say 'Don't Ask' Doesn't Work," *The New York Times,* December 10, 2003, A14.

77. Hempel, "Coming Out in Corporate America"; "DreamWorks Animation SKG Company History," www.dreamworksanimation.com/dwa/opencms/company/history/index.html, May 29, 2006; J. Chng, "Allan Gilmour: Former Vice-Chairman of Ford Speaks on Diversity," www.harbus.org/media/storage/paper343/news/2006/04/18/News/Allan.Gilmour.Former. ViceChairman.Of.Ford.Speaks.On.Diversity-1859600.shtml?norewrite200606021800& sourcedomain=www.harbus.org, April 18, 2006.

78. Needleman, "More Programs Move to Halt Bias against Gays."

79. Hempel, "Coming Out in Corporate America."

80. Needleman, "More Programs Move to Halt Bias against Gays."

81. Ibid.

82. "For Women, Weight May Affect Pay," *Houston Chronicle,* March 4, 2004, 12A.

83. V. Valian, *Why So Slow? The Advancement of Women* (Cambridge, MA: MIT Press, 2000).

84. S. T. Fiske and S. E. Taylor, *Social Cognition,* 2d ed. (New York: McGraw-Hill, 1991); Valian, *Why So Slow?*

85. Valian, *Why So Slow?*

86. S. Rynes and B. Rosen, "A Field Survey of Factors Affecting the Adoption and Perceived Success of Diversity Training," *Personnel Psychology* 48 (1995), 247–70; Valian, *Why So Slow?*

87. V. Brown and F. L. Geis, "Turning Lead into Gold: Leadership by Men and Women and the Alchemy of Social Consensus," *Journal of Personality and Social Psychology* 46 (1984), 811–24; Valian, *Why So Slow?*

88. Valian, *Why So Slow?*

89. J. Cole and B. Singer, "A Theory of Limited Differences: Explaining the Productivity Puzzle in Science," in H. Zuckerman, J. R. Cole, and J. T. Bruer, eds., *The Outer Circle: Women in the Scientific Community* (New York: Norton, 1991), 277–310; M. F. Fox, "Sex, Salary, and Achievement: Reward-Dualism in Academia," *Sociology of Education* 54 (1981), 71–84; J. S. Long, "The Origins of Sex Differences in Science," *Social Forces* 68 (1990), 1297–1315; R. F. Martell, D. M. Lane, and C. Emrich, "Male-Female Differences: A Computer Simulation," *American Psychologist* 51 (1996), 157–58; Valian, *Why So Slow?*

90. Cole and Singer, "A Theory of Limited Differences"; M. F. Fox, "Sex, Salary, and Achievement: Reward-Dualism in Academia," *Sociology of Education* 54 (1981), 71–84; Long, "The Origins of Sex Differences in Science"; R. F. Martell, D. M. Lane, and C. Emrich, "Male-Female Differences: A Computer Simulation," *American Psychologist* 51 (1996), 157–58; Valian, *Why So Slow?*

91. R. Folger and M. A. Konovsky, "Effects of Procedural and Distributive Justice on Reactions to Pay Raise Decisions," *Academy of Management Journal* 32 (1989), 115–30; J. Greenberg, "Organizational Justice: Yesterday, Today, and Tomorrow," *Journal of Management* 16 (1990), 399–402; "O. Janssen, "How Fairness Perceptions Make Innovative Behavior Much or Less Stressful," *Journal of Organizational Behavior* 25 (2004), 201–15.

92. Catalyst, "The Glass Ceiling in 2000: Where Are Women Now?" www.catalystwomen.org, October 21, 2001; Bureau of Labor Statistics, 1999, www.bls.gov; Catalyst, "1999 Census of Women Corporate Officers and Top Earners," www.catalystwomen.org; "1999 Census of Women Board Directors of the Fortune 1000," www.catalystwomen.org; Catalyst, "Women of Color in Corporate Management: Opportunities and Barriers, 1999," www.catalystwomen.org, October 21, 2001.

93. "Household Data Annual Averages," www.bls.gov, April 28, 2004.

94. Ibid.

95. A. M. Jaffe, "At Texaco, the Diversity Skeleton Still Stalks the Halls," *The New York Times,* December 11, 1994, sec. 3, p. 5.

96. Greenberg, "Organizational Justice"; M. G. Ehrhart, "Leadership and Procedural Justice Climate as Antecedents of Unit-Level Organizational Citizenship Behavior," *Personnel Psychology* 57 (2004), 61–94; A. Colella, R. L. Paetzold, and M. A. Belliveau, "Factors Affecting Coworkers' Procedural Justice Inferences of the Workplace Accommodations of Employees with Disabilities," *Personnel Psychology* 57 (2004), 1–23.

97. G. Robinson and K. Dechant, "Building a Case for Business Diversity," *Academy of Management Executive* 3 (1997), 32–47.

98. A. Patterson, "Target 'Micromarkets' Its Way to Success; No 2 Stores Are Alike," *The Wall Street Journal,* May 31, 1995, A1, A9.

99. "The Business Case for Diversity: Experts Tell What Counts, What Works," *DiversityInc.com,* October 23, 2001.

100. B. Hetzer, "Find a Niche—and Start Scratching," *BusinessWeek,* September 14, 1998 (BusinessWeek Archives).

101. K. Aaron, "Woman Laments Lack of Diversity on Boards of Major Companies," *The Times Union,* May 16, 2001 (www.timesunion.com).

102. "The Business Case for Diversity."

103. B. Frankel, "Measuring Diversity Is One Sure Way of Convincing CEOs of Its Value," *DiversityInc.com,* October 5, 2001.

104. A. Stevens, "Lawyers and Clients," *The Wall Street Journal,* June 19, 1995, B7.

105. J. Kahn, "Diversity Trumps the Downturn," *Fortune,* July 9, 2001, 114–16.

106. H. R. Schiffmann, *Sensation and Perception: An Integrated Approach* (New York: Wiley, 1990).

107. A. E. Serwer, "McDonald's Conquers the World," *Fortune,* October 17, 1994, 103–16.

108. S. T. Fiske and S. E. Taylor, *Social Cognition* (Reading, MA: Addison-Wesley, 1984).

109. J. S. Bruner, "Going Beyond the Information Given," in H. Gruber, G. Terrell, and M. Wertheimer, eds., *Contemporary Approaches to Cognition* (Cambridge, MA: Harvard University Press, 1957); Fiske and Taylor, *Social Cognition.*

110. Fiske and Taylor, *Social Cognition.*

111. Valian, *Why So Slow?*

112. D. Bakan, *The Duality of Human Existence* (Chicago: Rand McNally, 1966); J. T. Spence and R. L. Helmreich, *Masculinity and Femininity: Their Psychological Dimensions, Correlates, and Antecedents* (Austin: University of Texas Press, 1978); J. T. Spence and L. L. Sawin, "Images of Masculinity and Femininity: A Reconceptualization," in V. E. O'Leary, R. K. Unger, and B. B. Wallston, eds., *Women, Gender, and Social Psychology* (Hillsdale, NJ: Erlbaum, 1985), 35–66; Valian, *Why So Slow?*

113. Valian, *Why So Slow?*

114. Serwer, "McDonald's Conquers the World"; P. R. Sackett, C. M. Hardison, and M. J. Cullen, "On Interpreting Stereotype Threat as Accounting for African American–White Differences on Cognitive Tests," *American Psychologist* 59, no. 1 (January 2004), 7–13; C. M. Steele and J. A. Aronson, "Stereotype Threat Does Not Live by Steele and Aronson," *American Psychologist* 59, no. 1 (January 2004), 47–55; P. R. Sackett, C. M. Hardison, and M. J. Cullen, "On the Value of Correcting Mischaracterizations of Stereotype Threat Research," *American Psychologist* 59, no. 1 (January 2004), 47–49; D. M. Amodio, E. Harmon-Jones, P. G. Devine, J. J. Curtin, S. L. Hartley, and A. E. Covert, "Neural Signals for the Detection of Unintentional Race Bias," *Psychological Science* 15, no. 2 (2004), 88–93.

115. M. Loden and J. B. Rosener, *Workforce America! Managing Employee Diversity as a Vital Resource* (Burr Ridge, IL: Irwin, 1991).

116. M. E. Heilman and T. G. Okimoto, "Motherhood: A Potential Source of Bias in Employment Decisions," *Journal of Applied Psychology* 93, no. 1 (2008), 189–98.

117. L. Roberson, B. M. Galvin, and A. C. Charles, "Chapter 13, When Group Identities Matter: Bias in Performance Appraisal," in J. P. Walsh and A. P. Brief, eds., *The Academy of Management Annals* 1 (New York: Erlbaum, 2008, 617–50).

118. A. Stein Wellner, "The Disability Advantage," *Inc. Magazine,* October 2005, 29–31.

119. A. Merrick, "Erasing 'Un' from 'Unemployable,'" *The Wall Street Journal,* August 2, 2007, B6.

120. Ibid.

121. Ibid.

122. "Habitat International: Our Products," www.habitatint.com/products.htm, April 6, 2006; "Habitat International Home Page," www.habitatint.com, April 6, 2006.

123. Wellner, "The Disability Advantage."

124. "Habitat International: Our People."

125. Wellner, "The Disability Advantage."

126. "Habitat International: Our People." Wellner, "The Disability Advantage."

127. "Habitat International: Our People." Wellner, "The Disability Advantage."

128. "Habitat International: Our People." Wellner, "The Disability Advantage."

129. "Habitat International: Our People." Wellner, "The Disability Advantage."

130. E. D. Pulakos and K. N. Wexley, "The Relationship Among Perceptual Similarity, Sex, and Performance Ratings in Manager Subordinate Dyads," *Academy of Management Journal* 26 (1983), 129–39.

131. Fiske and Taylor, *Social Cognition.*

132. "Hotel to Pay $8 Million in Settlement," *The Houston Chronicle,* March 22, 2000, 3A; M. France and T. Smart, "The Ugly Talk on the Texaco Tape," *Business Week,* November 18, 1996, 58; J. S. Lublin, "Texaco Case Causes a Stir in Boardrooms," *The Wall Street Journal,* November 22, 1996, B1, B6; T. Smart, "Texaco: Lessons from a Crisis-in-Progress," *BusinessWeek,* December 2, 1996, 44; "Ford Settling Bias Case, Will Hire More Women, Minorities," *The Houston Chronicle,* February 19, 2000, 8C; C. Salter, "A Reformer Who Means Business," *Fast Company,* April 2003, 102–11; A. Zimmerman, "Wal-Mart Appeals Bias-Suit Ruling," *The Wall Street Journal,* August 8, 2005, B5; C. H. Deutsch, "Chief of Unit Files Lawsuit Accusing G.E. of Racial Bias," *The New York Times,* May 18, 2005, C3; "Nike Settles Discrimination Suit for $7.6 Million," *The Wall Street Journal,* July 31, 2007, B9; R. Parloff, "The War over Unconscious Bias," *Fortune,* October 15, 2007, 90–102.

133. N. Alster, "When Gray Heads Roll, Is Age Bias at Work?" *The New York Times,* January 30, 2005, BU3.

134. "Nike Settles Discrimination Suit for $7.6 Million," *The Wall Street Journal,* July 31, 2007, B9.

135. Ibid.

136. Ibid.

137. M. Fackler, "Career Women in Japan Find a Blocked Path," *The New York Times,* August 6, 2007, A6.

138. Ibid; www.un.org, February 11, 2008.

139. Ibid.

140. www.nissanusa.com.

141. Fackler, "Career Women in Japan Find a Blocked Path."

142. Ibid.

143. Ibid.

144. A. G. Greenwald and M. Banaji, "Implicit Social Cognition: Attitudes, Self-Esteem, and Stereotypes," *Psychological Review* 102 (1995), 4–27.

145. A. Fisher, "Ask Annie: Five Ways to Promote Diversity in the Workplace," *Fortune,* April 23, 2004 (www.fortune.com/fortune/subs/print/0,15935,455997,00.html); E. Bonabeau, "Don't Trust Your Gut," *Harvard Business Review,* May 2003, 116–23.

146. A. P. Carnevale and S. C. Stone, "Diversity: Beyond the Golden Rule," *Training & Development,* October 1994, 22–39.

147. Fisher, "Ask Annie."

148. J. S. Lublin, "Top Brass Try Life in the Trenches," *The Wall Street Journal,* June 25, 2007, B1, B3.

149. www.davita.com, February 11, 2008.

150. Lublin, "Top Brass Try Life in the Trenches."

151. Ibid.

152. Ibid.

153. Ibid; www.loews.com/loews.nsf/governance.htm, February 7, 2008.

154. Lublin, "Top Brass Try Life in the Trenches."

155. B. A. Battaglia, "Skills for Managing Multicultural Teams," *Cultural Diversity*

at Work 4 (1992); Carnevale and Stone, "Diversity: Beyond the Golden Rule."

156. Swann et al., "Finding Value in Diversity."

157. Valian, *Why So Slow?*

158. A. P. Brief, R. T. Buttram, R. M. Reizenstein, S. D. Pugh, J. D. Callahan, R. L. McCline, and J. B. Vaslow, "Beyond Good Intentions: The Next Steps Toward Racial Equality in the American Workplace," *Academy of Management Executive,* November 1997, 59–72.

159. A. P. Brief et al., "Beyond Good Intentions."

160. Ibid.

161. Ibid.

162. Y. Cole, "Linking Diversity to Executive Compensation," *Diversity Inc.,* August–September 2003, 58–62.

163. B. Mandell and S. Kohler-Gray, "Management Development That Values Diversity," *Personnel,* March 1990, 41–47.

164. B. Filipczak, "25 Years of Diversity at UPS," *Training,* August 1992, 42–46.

165. D. A. Thomas, "Race Matters: The Truth About Mentoring Minorities," *Harvard Business Review,* April 2001, 99–107.

166. Ibid.

167. S. N. Mehta, "Why Mentoring Works," *Fortune,* July 9, 2000.

168. Ibid; Thomas, "Race Matters."

169. "Chevron Settles Claims of 4 Women at Unit as Part of Sex Bias Suit," *The Wall Street Journal,* January 22, 1995, B12.

170. D. K. Berman, "TWA Settles Harassment Claims at JFK Airport for $2.6 Million," *The Wall Street Journal,* June 25, 2001, B6.

171. A. Lambert, "Insurers Help Clients Take Steps to Reduce Sexual Harassment," *Houston Business Journal,* March 19, 2004 (Houston.bizjournals.com/Houston/stories/2004/03/22/focus4.html).

172. T. Segal, "Getting Serious About Sexual Harassment," *BusinessWeek,* November 9, 1992, 78–82.

173. U.S. Equal Employment Opportunity Commission, "Facts About Sexual Harassment," www.eeoc.gov/facts/fs-sex.html, May 1, 2004.

174. B. Carton, "Muscled Out? At Jenny Craig, Men Are Ones Who Claim Sex Discrimination," *The Wall Street Journal,* November 29, 1994, A1, A7.

175. R. L. Paetzold and A. M. O'Leary-Kelly, "Organizational Communication and the Legal Dimensions of Hostile Work Environment Sexual Harassment," in G. L. Kreps, ed., *Sexual Harassment: Communication Implications* (Cresskill, NJ: Hampton Press, 1993).

176. M. Galen, J. Weber, and A. Z. Cuneo, "Sexual Harassment: Out of the Shadows," *Fortune,* October 28, 1991, 30–31.

177. A. M. O'Leary-Kelly, R. L. Paetzold, and R. W. Griffin, "Sexual Harassment as Aggressive Action: A Framework for Understanding Sexual Harassment," paper presented at the annual meeting of the Academy of Management, Vancouver, August 1995.

178. B. S. Roberts and R. A. Mann, "Sexual Harassment in the Workplace: A Primer," www3.uakron.edu/lawrev/robert1.html, May 1, 2004.

179. "Former FedEx Driver Wins EEOC Lawsuit," *Houston Chronicle,* February 26, 2004, 9B.

180. Ibid.

181. J. Robertson, "California Jury Awards $61M for Harassment," http://news.Yahoo.com, June 4, 2006.

182. "2 FedEx Drivers Win Slur Lawsuit," *Houston Chronicle,* June 4, 2006, p. A9.

183. S. J. Bresler and R. Thacker, "Four-Point Plan Helps Solve Harassment Problems," *HR Magazine,* May 1993, 117–24.

184. "Du Pont's Solution," *Training,* March 1992, 29.

185. Ibid.

186. Ibid.

Chapter 6

1. www.nestle.com, 2008.

2. 2007 Annual Report, www.nestle.com, 2008.

3. L. J. Bourgeois, "Strategy and Environment: A Conceptual Integration," *Academy of Management Review* 5 (1985), 25–39.

4. M. E. Porter, *Competitive Strategy* (New York: Free Press, 1980).

5. "Coca-Cola Versus Pepsi-Cola and the Soft Drink Industry," Harvard Business School Case 9-391–179.

6. www.splenda.com, 2008.

7. A. K. Gupta and V. Govindarajan, "Cultivating a Global Mind-set," *Academy of Management Executive* 16 (February 2002), 116–27.

8. "Boeing's Worldwide Supplier Network," *Seattle Post–Intelligencer,* April 9, 1994, 13.

9. I. Metthee, "Playing a Large Part," *Seattle Post-Intelligencer,* April 9, 1994, 13.

10. R. J. Trent and R. M. Monczke, "Pursuing Competitive Advantage Through Integrated Global Sourcing," *Academy of Management Executive* 16 (May 2002), 66–81.

11. R. B. Reich, *The Work of Nations* (New York: Knopf, 1991).

12. "Business: Link in the Global Chain," *The Economist,* June 2, 2001, 62–63.

13. M. E. Porter, *Competitive Advantage* (New York: Free Press, 1985).

14. www.walmart.com, 2008.

15. C. Harris, "Costco Loses State Case on Lowering Beer, Wine Prices," seattle post-intelligencer.com, January 29, 2008.

16. "The Tech Slump Doesn't Scare Michael Dell, *BusinessWeek,* April 16, 2001, 48.

17. T. Levitt, "The Globalization of Markets," *Harvard Business Review,* May–June 1983, 92–102.

18. "Dell CEO Would Like 40 Percent PC Market Share," www.daily news.yahoo.com, June 20, 2001.

19. "Dell Expanding China Presence via Large Retailers," www.yahoo.com, April 17, 2008.

20. For views on barriers to entry from an economics perspective, see Porter, *Competitive Strategy.* For the sociological perspective, see J. Pfeffer and G. R. Salancik, *The External Control of Organization: A Resource Dependence Perspective* (New York: Harper & Row, 1978).

21. Porter, *Competitive Strategy;* J. E. Bain, *Barriers to New Competition* (Cambridge, MA: Harvard University Press, 1956); R. J. Gilbert, "Mobility Barriers and the Value of Incumbency," in R. Schmalensee and R. D. Willig, eds., *Handbook of Industrial Organization,* vol. 1 (Amsterdam: North Holland, 1989).

22. Press release, www.amazon.com, May 2001.

23. C. W. L. Hill, "The Computer Industry: The New Industry of Industries," in Hill and Jones, *Strategic Management: An Integrated Approach* (Boston: Houghton Mifflin, 2003).

24. J. Bhagwati, *Protectionism* (Cambridge, MA; MIT Press, 1988).

25. www.yahoo.com, July 18, 2004.

26. J. Schumpeter, *Capitalism, Socialism and Democracy* (London: Macmillan, 1950), 68. Also see R. R. Winter and S. G. Winter, *An Evolutionary Theory of Economic Change* (Cambridge, MA: Harvard University Press, 1982).

27. "The Coming Clash of Logic," *The Economist,* July 3, 1993, 21–23.

28. S. Sherman, "The New Computer Revolution," *Fortune,* June 14, 1993, 56–84; www.amd.com, 2006.

29. N. Goodman, *An Introduction to Sociology* (New York: HarperCollins, 1991); C. Nakane, *Japanese Society* (Berkeley: University of California Press, 1970).

30. The Economist, *The Economist Book of Vital World Statistics* (New York: Random House, 1990).

31. For a detailed discussion of the importance of the structure of law as a factor explaining economic change and growth, see D. C. North, *Institutions, Institutional Change and Economic Performance* (Cambridge: Cambridge University Press, 1990).

32. R. B. Reich, *The Work of Nations* (New York: Knopf, 1991).

33. J. Bhagwati, *Protectionism*.

34. www.cnn.com, 2004.

35. M. A. Carpenter and J. W. Fredrickson, "Top Management Teams, Global Strategic Posture, and the Moderating Role of Uncertainty," *Academy of Management Journal* 44 (June 2001), 533–46.

36. Bhagwati, *Protectionism*.

37. For a summary of these theories, see P. Krugman and M. Obstfeld, *International Economics: Theory and Policy* (New York: HarperCollins, 1991). Also see C. W. L. Hill, *International Business* (New York: McGraw-Hill, 1997), chap. 4.

38. A. M. Rugman, "The Quest for Global Dominance," *Academy of Management Executive* 16 (August 2002), 157–60.

39. www.wto.org.com, 2004.

40. www.wto.org.com, 2001.

41. C. A. Bartlett and S. Ghoshal, *Managing Across Borders* (Boston: Harvard Business School Press, 1989).

42. C. Arnst and G. Edmondson, "The Global Free-for-All," *BusinessWeek*, September 26, 1994, 118–26.

43. W. Konrads, "Why Leslie Wexner Shops Overseas," *BusinessWeek*, February 3, 1992, 30.

44. E. B. Tylor, *Primitive Culture* (London: Murray, 1971).

45. For details on the forces that shape culture, see Hill, *International Business*, chap. 2.

46. G. Hofstede, B. Neuijen, D. D. Ohayv, and G. Sanders, "Measuring Organizational Cultures: A Qualitative and Quantitative Study Across Twenty Cases," *Administrative Science Quarterly* 35 (1990), 286–316.

47. M. H. Hoppe, "Introduction: Geert Hofstede's Culture's Consequences: International Differences in Work-Related Values," *Academy of Management Executive* 18 (February 2004), 73–75.

48. R. Bellah, *Habits of the Heart: Individualism and Commitment in American Life* (Berkeley: University of California Press, 1985).

49. R. Bellah, *The Tokugawa Religion* (New York: Free Press, 1957).

50. C. Nakane, *Japanese Society* (Berkeley: University of California Press, 1970).

51. Ibid.

52. G. Hofstede, "The Cultural Relativity of Organizational Practices and Theories," *Journal of International Business Studies*, Fall 1983, 75–89.

53. Hofstede et al., "Measuring Organizational Cultures."

54. J. Perlez, "GE Finds Tough Going in Hungary," *The New York Times*, July 25, 1994, C1, C3.

55. www.ge.com, 2004.

56. J. P. Fernandez and M. Barr, *The Diversity Advantage* (New York: Lexington Books, 1994).

Chapter 7

1. D. Sacks, "The Catalyst," *Fast Company* (October 2006), 59–61.

2. About PUMA, http://about.puma.com/EN/1/, February 13, 2008.

3. Sacks, "The Catalyst."

4. Ibid.

5. "Puma Expects 2008 Sales, Profits to Tise–PPR CFO, Thursday, January 24, 2008, www.reuters.com/articlePrint?articleId=USL2491288920080124, February 13, 2008.

6. Sacks, "The Catalyst."

7. Ibid.

8. Ibid.

9. Ibid; Fashion in Motion Africa 2005, Xuly Bet, www.vam.ac.uk/collections/fashion/fashion_motion/africa_05/index.html, February 14, 2008.

10. Sacks, "The Catalyst."

11. Ibid.

12. Company Structure, http://about.puma.com/EN/1/9/9/, February 13, 2008

13. Sacks, "The Catalyst."

14. G. P. Huber, *Managerial Decision Making* (Glenview, IL: Scott, Foresman, 1993).

15. Sacks, "The Catalyst."

16. H. A. Simon, *The New Science of Management* (Englewood Cliffs, NJ: Prentice-Hall, 1977).

17. N. A. Hira, "The Making of a UPS Driver," *Fortune*, November 12, 2007, 118–29.

18. Ibid; J. Lovell, "Left-Hand-Turn Elimination," *The New York Times*, nytimes.com, December 9, 2007, www.nytimes.com/2007/12/09/magazine/09left-handturn.html?_r=2&oref=slogin&r, February 20, 2008.

19. Hira, "The Making of a UPS Driver."

20. L. Osburn, "Expecting the World on a Silver Platter," *Houston Chronicle*, September 17, 2007, D1, D6.

21. Hira, "The Making of a UPS Driver."

22. Ibid; Welcome to UPS Careers, https://ups.managehr.com/Home.htm, February 20, 2008.

23. Hira, "The Making of a UPS Driver."

24. Ibid.

25. Ibid.

26. Ibid.

27. Ibid.

28. D. Kahneman, "Maps of Bounded Rationality: A Perspective on Intuitive Judgment and Choice," Prize Lecture, December 8, 2002; E. Jaffe, "What Was I Thinking? Kahneman Explains How Intuition Leads Us Astray," *American Psychological Society* 17, no. 5 (May 2004), 23–26; E. Dane and M. Pratt, "Exploring Intuition and Its Role in Managerial Decision-Making," *Academy of Management Review* 32 (2007), 33–54.

29. One should be careful not to generalize too much here, however; for as Peter Senge has shown, programmed decisions rely on the implicit assumption that the environment is in a steady state. If environmental conditions change, then sticking to a routine decision rule can produce disastrous results. See P. Senge, *The Fifth Discipline: The Art and Practice of the Learning Organization* (New York: Doubleday, 1990).

30. Kahneman, "Maps of Bounded Rationality"; Jaffe, "What Was I Thinking?"

31. Ibid.

32. J. Smutniak, "Freud, Finance and Folly: Human Intuition Is a Bad Guide to Handling Risk," *The Economist* 24 (January 2004), 5–6.

33. Kahneman, "Maps of Bounded Rationality"; Jaffe, "What Was I Thinking?"

34. Ibid.

35. J. Pfeffer, "Curbing the Urge to Merge," *Business 2.0,* July 2003, 58; Smutniak, "Freud, Finance and Folly."

36. Kahneman, "Maps of Bounded Rationality"; Jaffe, "What Was I Thinking?"

37. Pfeffer, "Curbing the Urge to Merge"; Smutniak, "Freud, Finance and Folly."

38. M. Landler, "New Austerity for German Car Industry," *The New York Times,* September 29, 2005, C3; E. Taylor and C. Rauwald, "DaimlerChrysler to Cut 8,500 Jobs at Mercedes," *The Wall Street Journal,* September 29, 2005, A6; G. Edmondson, "On the Hot Seat at Daimler," *BusinessWeek Online,* February 17, 2006 (www.businessweek.com/autos/content/feb2006/bw20060217_187348.htm?campaign_id=search).

39. "Hiring Freeze and Cost Cuts at Time Inc.," *The New York Times,* August 2005, B13.

40. Pfeffer, "Curbing the Urge to Merge."

41. Ibid.

42. H. A. Simon, *Administrative Behavior* (New York: Macmillan, 1947), 79.

43. H. A. Simon, *Models of Man* (New York: Wiley, 1957).

44. K. J. Arrow, *Aspects of the Theory of Risk Bearing* (Helsinki: Yrjo Johnssonis Saatio, 1965).

45. Ibid.

46. N. Gull, "Plan B (and C and D and . . .)," *Inc.,* March 2004, 40; C. Knouf, "Upgrading Your Office," *Oregon Business,* January 2006, 36–37; D. McMillan, "Printer, Copier Dealer Grows by Doing Business in a Markedly Different Way," *Portland Business Journal,* January 20, 2006; "Associated Business Systems: News & Events," www.associatedbusiness.com/sw/common/custom/internet/custompage/asp, May 30, 2006.

47. Gull, "Plan B."

48. Ibid.

49. B. Neill, "Nothing Sells a Printer Like the Promise of Good Service," *Business Journal of Portland,* January 5, 2004

(www.bizjournals.com/Portland/stories/ 2004/01/05/story4.html?t=printable); "Associated Business Systems Fact Sheet," www.associatedbusiness.com/news_detail .asp?id=6, May 11, 2004; McMillan, "Printer, Copier Dealer Grows."

50. "Associated Business Systems Ranks as One of America's Fastest Growing Private Companies," *Associated Business Systems News,* May 11, 2004 (www.associated business.com/ news_detail.asp?id=7); "About Us," *Associated Business Systems,* www.associatedbusiness.com/sw/common/ custom/internet/custompage.asp/SETSES, February 20, 2008.

51. "A Company Built on Service," *Associated Business Systems News,* May 11, 2004 (www.associatedbusiness.com/news_detail .asp?id=5); "Associated Business Systems Acquires Rik Metcalf Business Machines Inc.," *Associated Business Systems News,* May 11, 2004 (www.associatedbusiness. com/news_detail.asp?id=8); Associated Business Systems, "About ABS," www. associated business. com/about_abs.asp, May 11, 2004; "Associated Business Systems Financial Fact Sheet," www.hoovers.com/ associated-business-systems/–ID_106735–/ free-co-fin-factsheet.xhtml, May 11, 2004; "Associated Business Systems Company Profile," *Yahoo! Finance,* May 11, 2004 (biz .yahoo.com.ic/106/106735.html).

52. "About Us," *Associated Business Systems,* www.associatedbusiness.com/sw/common/ custom/internet/custompage.asp/SETSES, February 20, 2008.

53. Gull, "Plan B."

54. R. L. Daft and R. H. Lengel, "Organizational Information Requirements, Media Richness and Structural Design," *Management Science* 32 (1986), 554–71.

55. R. Cyert and J. March, *Behavioral Theory of the Firm* (Englewood Cliffs, NJ: Prentice-Hall, 1963).

56. J. G. March and H. A. Simon, *Organizations* (New York: Wiley, 1958).

57. H. A. Simon, "Making Management Decisions: The Role of Intuition and Emotion," *Academy of Management Executive* 1 (1987), 57–64.

58. M. H. Bazerman, *Judgment in Managerial Decision Making* (New York: Wiley, 1986). Also see Simon, *Administrative Behavior.*

59. "Sun Microsystems–Investor Relations: Officers and Directors," www.sun.com/ aboutsun/investor/sun_facts/officers_ directors.html, June 1, 2004; "How Sun Delivers Value to Customers," *Sun Microsystems–Investor Relations: Support & Training,* June 1, 2004 (www.sun.com/ aboutsun/investor/sun_facts/core_strategies .html); "Sun at a Glance," *Sun Microsystems– Investor Relations: Sun Facts,* June 1, 2004 (www.sun.com/aboutsun/ investor/

sun_facts/index.html); "Plug in the System, and Everything Just Works," *Sun Microsystems–Investor Relations: Product Portfolio,* June 1, 2004 (www.sun.com/aboutsun/ investor/sun_facts/portfolio/html).

60. N. J. Langowitz and S. C. Wheelright, "Sun Microsystems, Inc. (A)," Harvard Business School Case 686–133.

61. R. D. Hof, "How to Kick the Mainframe Habit," *BusinessWeek,* June 26, 1995, 102–04.

62. Bazerman, *Judgment in Managerial Decision Making;* Huber, *Managerial Decision Making;* J. E. Russo and P. J. Schoemaker, *Decision Traps* (New York: Simon & Schuster, 1989).

63. M. D. Cohen, J. G. March, and J. P. Olsen, "A Garbage Can Model of Organizational Choice," *Administrative Science Quarterly* 17 (1972), 1–25.

64. M. D. Cohen, J. G. March, and J. P. Olsen, "A Garbage Can Model of Organizational Choice," *Administrative Science Quarterly* 17 (1972), 1–25.

65. Bazerman, *Judgment in Managerial Decision Making.*

66. Senge, *The Fifth Discipline.*

67. E. de Bono, *Lateral Thinking* (London: Penguin, 1968); Senge, *The Fifth Discipline.*

68. Russo and Schoemaker, *Decision Traps.*

69. Bazerman, *Judgment in Managerial Decision Making.*

70. B. Berger, "NASA: One Year After *Columbia*–Bush's New Vision Changes Agency's Course Mid-stream," *Space News Business Report,* January 26, 2004 (www. space. com/spacenews/businessmonday_ 040126. html).

71. J. Glanz and J. Schwartz, "Dogged Engineer's Effort to Assess Shuttle Damage," *The New York Times,* September 26, 2003, A1.

72. M. L. Wald and J. Schwartz, "NASA Chief Promises a Shift in Attitude," *The New York Times,* August 28, 2003, A23.

73. S. Clifford, "Marc Shuman Was Determined to Expand Fast," *Inc.,* March 2006, 44–50

74. Russo and Schoemaker, *Decision Traps.*

75. Clifford, "Marc Shuman Was Determined to Expand Fast."; D. Kocieniewski, "After $12,000, There's Even Room to Park the Car," *The New York Times,* February 20, 2006; "The World's Cleanest Garage," www.garagetek.com, May 30, 2006 (www. garagetek.com/nav.asp); "What Is Garagetek?" www.garagetek.com, May 30, 2006 (www.garagetek. com/content_CNBC.asp); L. Christie, "7 Franchises: Riding the Housing Boom," CNNMoney.com, March 7, 2006 (http://money.cnn.com/2006/03/07/ smbusiness/homefranchises/index.htm); "745 Businesses to Start Now!" *Entrepreneur,* January 2005, 88, 192, 193.

76. Clifford, "Marc Shuman Was Determined to Expand Fast."

77. Ibid; "Franchise Opportunities," *Garage Tek,* www.garagetek.com/Franchise Opportunities/GarageTek-Opportunities .aspx, February 14, 2008

78. Clifford, "Marc Shuman Was Determined to Expand Fast."

79. Ibid

80. Ibid

81. D. Kahneman and A. Tversky, "Judgment Under Uncertainty: Heuristics and Biases," *Science* 185 (1974), 1124–31.

82. C. R. Schwenk, "Cognitive Simplification Processes in Strategic Decision Making," *Strategic Management Journal* 5 (1984), 111–28.

83. An interesting example of the illusion of control is Richard Roll's hubris hypothesis of takeovers. See R. Roll, "The Hubris Hypothesis of Corporate Takeovers," *Journal of Business* 59 (1986), 197–216.

84. B. M. Staw, "The Escalation of Commitment to a Course of Action," *Academy of Management Review* 6 (1981), 577–87.

85. M. J. Tang, "An Economic Perspective on Escalating Commitment," *Strategic Management Journal* 9 (1988), 79–92.

86. S. N. Mehta, "Lessons from the Lucent Debacle," *Fortune,* February 5, 2001, pp. 143–148.

87. Russo and Schoemaker, *Decision Traps.*

88. Russo and Schoemaker, *Decision Traps.*

89. I. L. Janis, *Groupthink: Psychological Studies of Policy Decisions and Disasters,* 2d ed. (Boston: Houghton Mifflin, 1982).

90. C. R. Schwenk, *The Essence of Strategic Decision Making* (Lexington, MA: Lexington Books, 1988).

91. See R. O. Mason, "A Dialectic Approach to Strategic Planning," *Management Science* 13 (1969) 403–14; R. A. Cosier and J. C. Aplin, "A Critical View of Dialectic Inquiry in Strategic Planning," *Strategic Management Journal* 1 (1980), 343–56; I. I. Mitroff and R. O. Mason, "Structuring III–Structured Policy Issues: Further Explorations in a Methodology for Messy Problems," *Strategic Management Journal* 1 (1980), 331–42.

92. Mason, "A Dialectic Approach to Strategic Planning."

93. D. M. Schweiger and P. A. Finger, "The Comparative Effectiveness of Dialectic Inquiry and Devil's Advocacy," *Strategic Management Journal* 5 (1984), 335–50.

94. Mary C. Gentile, *Differences That Work: Organizational Excellence Through Diversity* (Boston: Harvard Business School Press, 1994); F. Rice, "How to Make Diversity Pay," *Fortune,* August 8, 1994, 78–86.

95. B. Hedberg, "How Organizations Learn and Unlearn," in W. H. Starbuck

and P. C. Nystrom, eds., *Handbook of Organizational Design,* vol. 1 (New York: Oxford University Press, 1981), 1–27.

96. Senge, *The Fifth Discipline.*

97. Senge, *The Fifth Discipline.*

98. P. M. Senge, "The Leader's New Work: Building Learning Organizations," *Sloan Management Review,* Fall 1990, 7–23.

99. W. Zellner, K. A. Schmidt, M. Ihlwan, and H. Dawley, "How Well Does Wal-Mart Travel," *BusinessWeek,* September 3, 2001, 82-84.

100. J. P. Walsh and A. P. Brief (Eds.), "Creativity in Organizations," The Academy *of Management Annals,* Volume 1, New York: Erlbaum, 439-477.

101. Ibid.

102. C. Salter, "FAST 50: The World's Most Innovative Companies," *Fast Company,* March 2008, 73-117.

103. R. W. Woodman, J. E. Sawyer, and R. W. Griffin, "Towards a Theory of Organizational Creativity," *Academy of Management Review* 18 (1993), 293–321.

104. T. J. Bouchard, Jr., J. Barsaloux, and G. Drauden, "Brainstorming Procedure, Group Size, and Sex as Determinants of Problem Solving Effectiveness of Individuals and Groups," *Journal of Applied Psychology* 59 (1974), 135–38.

105. M. Diehl and W. Stroebe, "Productivity Loss in Brainstorming Groups: Towards the Solution of a Riddle," *Journal of Personality and Social Psychology* 53 (1987), 497–509.

106. D. H. Gustafson, R. K. Shulka, A. Delbecq, and W. G. Walster, "A Comparative Study of Differences in Subjective Likelihood Estimates Made by Individuals, Interacting Groups, Delphi Groups, and Nominal Groups," *Organizational Behavior and Human Performance* 9 (1973), 280–91.

107. N. Dalkey, *The Delphi Method: An Experimental Study of Group Decision Making* (Santa Monica, CA: Rand Corp., 1989).

108. T. Lonier, "Some Insights and Statistics on Working Solo," www.workingsolo.com.

109. I. N. Katsikis and L. P. Kyrgidou, "The Concept of Sustainable Entrepreneurship: A Conceptual Framework and Empirical Analysis," *Academy of Management Proceedings,* 2007, 1–6, 6p, web.ebscohost.com/ehost/delivery?vid=7&hid=102&sid=434afdf5-5ed9-45d4-993b-, January 24, 2008; "What is a Social Entrepreneur?" http://ashoka.org/social_entrepreneur, February 20, 2008; C. Hsu, "Entrepreneur for Social Change," October 31, 2005, *U.S.News.com,* www.usnews.com/usnews/news/articles/051031/31drayton.htm; D. M. Sullivan, "Stimulating Social Entrepreneurship: Can Support From Cities Make a Difference? *Academy of Management Perspectives,* February 2007, 78.

110. Ibid.

111. N. Tiku, "Do-Gooder Finance: How a New Crop of Investors is Helping Social Entrepreneurs," *Inc. Magazine,* February 2008.

112. Ibid; "About World of Good," *World of Good, Inc.,* www.worldofgoodinc.com/about/, February 20, 2008; "What Is Fair Trade?" *World of Good,* originalgood, www.originalgood.com/FT/, February 20, 2008.

113. Tiku, "Do-Gooder Finance."

114. Ibid.

115. Ibid.

116. Ibid.

117. Ibid.

Chapter 8

1. www.bestbuy.com, 2008; www.circuitcity.com, 2008.

2. J. Freed, "Tale of Two Tech Retailers," www.yahoo.com, February 13, 2008.

3. M. Felberbaum, "Circuit City Tries to Reinvent Itself," www.happynews.com, March 10, 2008.

4. A. Chandler, *Strategy and Structure: Chapters in the History of the American Enterprise* (Cambridge, MA: MIT Press, 1962).

5. Ibid.

6. H. Fayol, *General and Industrial Management* (1884; New York: IEEE Press, 1984).

7. Ibid., 18.

8. F. J. Aguilar, "General Electric: Reg Jones and Jack Welch," in *General Managers in Action* (Oxford: Oxford University Press, 1992).

9. Aguilar, *General Managers in Action.*

10. www.ge.com, 2008.

11. C. W. Hofer and D. Schendel, *Strategy Formulation: Analytical Concepts* (St. Paul, MN: West, 1978).

12. A. P. De Geus, "Planning as Learning," *Harvard Business Review,* March–April 1988, 70–74.

13. P. Wack, "Scenarios: Shooting the Rapids," *Harvard Business Review,* November–December 1985, 139–50.

14. R. Phelps, C. Chan, S. C. Kapsalis, "Does Scenario Planning Affect Firm Performance?" *Journal of Business Research,* March 2001, 223–32.

15. J. A. Pearce, "The Company Mission as a Strategic Tool," *Sloan Management Review,* Spring 1992, 15–24.

16. D. F. Abell, *Defining the Business: The Starting Point of Strategic Planning* (Englewood Cliffs, NJ: Prentice-Hall, 1980).

17. C. Palmeri, "Mattel: Up the Hill Minus Jill," *BusinessWeek,* April 9, 2001, 53–54.

18. www.mattel.com, 2004.

19. www.mattel.com, 2008.

20. Press release, www.mattel.com, March 24, 2008.

21. G. Hamel and C. K. Prahalad, "Strategic Intent," *Harvard Business Review,* May–June 1989, 63–73.

22. D. I. Jung and B. J. Avolio, "Opening the Black Box: An Experimental Investigation of the Mediating Effects of Trust and Value Congruence on Transformational and Transactional Leadership," *Journal of Organizational Behavior,* December 2000, 949–64; B. M. Bass and B. J. Avolio, "Transformational and Transactional Leadership: 1992 and Beyond," *Journal of European Industrial Training,* January 1990, 20–35.

23. J. Porras and J. Collins, *Built to Last: Successful Habits of Visionary Companies* (New York: HarperCollins, 1994).

24. E. A. Locke, G. P. Latham, and M. Erez, "The Determinants of Goal Commitment," *Academy of Management Review* 13 (1988), 23–39.

25. www.mattel.com, 2008.

26. K. R. Andrews, *The Concept of Corporate Strategy* (Homewood, IL: Irwin, 1971).

27. G. Mulvihill, "Campbell Is Really Cooking," *San Diego Tribune.com,* August 5, 2004.

28. W. D. Crotty, "Campbell Soup Is Not So Hot," www.MotleyFool.com, May 24, 2004.

29. A. Halperin, "Chicken Soup for the Investor's Soul," *BusinessWeek Online,* May 25, 2006 (www.businessweek.com).

30. A. Carter, "Lighting a Fire Under Campbell, www.businessweek.com, December 4, 2006.

31. www.campbellsoupcompany.com, 2008.

32. "Campbell Completes $850M Godiva Sale," www.yahoo.com, March 18, 2008.

33. R. D. Aveni, *Hypercompetition* (New York: Free Press, 1994).

34. M. E. Porter, *Competitive Strategy* (New York: Free Press, 1980).

35. C. W. L. Hill, "Differentiation Versus Low Cost or Differentiation and Low Cost: A Contingency Framework," *Academy of Management Review* 13 (1988), 401–12.

36. For details, see J. P. Womack, D. T. Jones, and D. Roos, *The Machine That Changed the World* (New York: Rawson Associates, 1990).

37. Porter, *Competitive Strategy.*

38. www.cott.com, 2008.

39. www.zara.com, 2008.

40. C. Vitzthum, "Just-in-Time-Fashion," *The Wall Street Journal,* May 18, 2001, B1, B4.

41. www.zara.com, 2008.

42. www.hitachi.com, 2008.

43. M. K. Perry, "Vertical Integration: Determinants and Effects," in R. Schmalensee and R. D. Willig, *Handbook of Industrial Organization,* vol. 1 (New York: Elsevier Science, 1989).

44. "Matsushita Electric Industrial (MEI) in 1987," Harvard Business School Case 388-144.

45. P. Ghemawat, *Commitment: The Dynamic of Strategy* (New York: Free Press, 1991).

46. www.ibm.com, 2008.

47. E. Penrose, *The Theory of the Growth of the Firm* (Oxford: Oxford University Press, 1959).

48. M. E. Porter, "From Competitive Advantage to Corporate Strategy," *Harvard Business Review* 65 (1987), 43–59.

49. D. J. Teece, "Economies of Scope and the Scope of the Enterprise," *Journal of Economic Behavior and Organization* 3 (1980), 223–47.

50. M. E. Porter, *Competitive Advantage: Creating and Sustaining Superior Performance* (New York: Free Press, 1985).

51. www.3M.com, 2008.

52. Ibid.

53. C. Wyant, "Minnesota Companies Make *BusinessWeek*'s 'Most Innovative' List," *Minneapolis/St. Paul Business Journal*, April 18, 2008.

54. For a review of the evidence, see C. W. L. Hill and G. R. Jones, *Strategic Management: An Integrated Approach*, 5th ed. (Boston: Houghton Mifflin, 2003), chap. 10.

55. C. R. Christensen et al., *Business Policy Text and Cases* (Homewood, IL: Irwin, 1987), 778.

56. C. W. L. Hill, "Conglomerate Performance over the Economic Cycle," *Journal of Industrial Economics* 32 (1983), 197–213.

57. V. Ramanujam and P. Varadarajan, "Research on Corporate Diversification: A Synthesis," *Strategic Management Journal* 10 (1989), 523–51. Also see A. Shleifer and R. W. Vishny, "Takeovers in the 1960s and 1980s: Evidence and Implications," in R. P. Rumelt, D. E. Schendel, and D. J. Teece, eds., *Fundamental Issues in Strategy* (Boston: Harvard Business School Press, 1994).

58. J. R. Williams, B. L. Paez, and L. Sanders, "Conglomerates Revisited," *Strategic Management Journal* 9 (1988), 403–14.

59. G. Marcial, "As Tyco Splits Into Three," www.businessweek.com, March 12, 2007.

60. www.tyco.com, 2008.

61. C. A. Bartlett and S. Ghoshal, *Managing Across Borders* (Boston: Harvard Business School Press, 1989).

62. C. K. Prahalad and Y. L. Doz, *The Multinational Mission* (New York: Free Press, 1987).

63. "Gillette Co.'s New $40 Million Razor Blade Factory in St. Petersburg Russia," *Boston Globe*, June 7, 2000, C6.

64. D. Sewell, "P&G Replaces Ex-Gillette CEO at Operations," www.yahoo.com, May 24, 2006.

65. www.pg.com, 2005, 2008.

66. R. E. Caves, *Multinational Enterprise and Economic Analysis* (Cambridge: Cambridge University Press, 1982).

67. B. Kogut, "Joint Ventures: Theoretical and Empirical Perspectives," *Strategic Management Journal* 9 (1988), 319–33.

68. "Venture with Nestlé SA Is Slated for Expansion," *The Wall Street Journal*, April 15, 2001, B2.

69. B. Bahree, "BP Amoco, Italy's ENI Plan $2.5 Billion Gas Plant," *The Wall Street Journal*, March 6, 2001, A16.

70. N. Hood and S. Young, *The Economics of the Multinational Enterprise* (London: Longman, 1979).

71. www.federalexpress.com, 2008.

72. www.ups.com, 2008.

73. www.dhl.com, 2008.

Chapter 9

1. www. Toyota.com, 2008.

2. "Quality is Major Concern of Toyota's Visiting Chief,' www.nytimes.com, January 15, 2008.

3. J. P. Womack, D. T. Jones, and D. Roos, *The Machine That Changed the World* (New York: Rawson Associates, 1990).

4. See D. Garvin, "What Does Product Quality Really Mean?" *Sloan Management Review* 26 (Fall 1984), 25–44; P. B. Crosby, *Quality Is Free* (New York: Mentor Books, 1980); A. Gabor, *The Man Who Discovered Quality* (New York: Times Books, 1990).

5. D. F. Abell, *Defining the Business: The Starting Point of Strategic Planning* (Englewood Cliffs, NJ: Prentice-Hall, 1980).

6. According to Richard D'Aveni, the process of pushing price-attribute curves to the right is a characteristic of the competitive process. See R. D'Aveni, *Hypercompetition* (New York: Free Press, 1994).

7. www.walmart.com, 2008.

8. www.southwest.com, 2008.

9. B. O'Brian, "Flying on the Cheap," *The Wall Street Journal*, October 26, 1992, A1; B. O'Reilly, "Where Service Flies Right," *Fortune*, August 24, 1992, 116–17; A. Salukis, "Hurt in Expansion, Airlines Cut Back and May Sell Hubs," *The Wall Street Journal*, April 1, 1993, A1, C8.

10. K. Done, "Toyota Warns of Continuing Decline," *Financial Times*, November 23, 1993, 23.

11. www.ciu.com, 2006.

12. www.crm.com, 2006.

13. The view of quality as reliability goes back to the work of Deming and Juran; see Gabor, *The Man Who Discovered Quality*.

14. See Garvin, "What Does Product Quality Really Mean?"; Crosby, *Quality Is Free;* Gabor, *The Man Who Discovered Quality*.

15. www.jdpa.com, 2006.

16. See J. W. Dean and D. E. Bowen, "Management Theory and Total Quality: Improving Research and Practice Through Theory Development," *Academy of Management Review* 19 (1994), 392–418.

17. For general background information, see J. C. Anderson, M. Rungtusanatham, and R. G. Schroeder, "A Theory of Quality Management Underlying the Deming Management Method," *Academy of Management Review* 19 (1994), 472–509; "How to Build Quality," *The Economist*, September 23, 1989, 91–92; Gabor, *The Man Who Discovered Quality;* Crosby, *Quality Is Free*.

18. Bowles, "Is American Management Really Committed to Quality?" *Management Review*, April 1992, 42–46.

19. Gabor, *The Man Who Discovered Quality*.

20. www.starwood.com, 2008.

21. S.E. Ante, "Six Sigma Kick-Starts Starwood," www.businessweek.com, August 30, 2007.

22. Ibid.

23. R. Gourlay, "Back to Basics on the Factory Floor," *Financial Times*, January 4, 1994, 12.

24. P. Nemetz and L. Fry, "Flexible Manufacturing Organizations: Implications for Strategy Formulation," *Academy of Management Review* 13 (1988), 627–38; N. Greenwood, *Implementing Flexible Manufacturing Systems* (New York: Halstead Press, 1986).

25. M. Williams, "Back to the Past," *The Wall Street Journal*, October 24, 1994, A1.

26. For an interesting discussion of some other drawbacks of JIT and other "Japanese" manufacturing techniques, see S. M. Young, "A Framework for Successful Adoption and Performance of Japanese Manufacturing Practices in the United States," *Academy of Management Review* 17 (1992), 677–701.

27. G. Stalk and T. M. Hout, *Competing Against Time* (New York: Free Press, 1990).

28. T. Stundza, "Massachusetts Switch Maker Switches to Kanban," *Purchasing*, November 16, 2000, 103.

29. B. Dumaine, "The Trouble with Teams," *Fortune*, September 5, 1994, 86–92.

30. See C. W. L. Hill, "Transaction Cost Economizing as a Source of National Competitive Advantage: The Case of Japan," *Organization Science*, 2 (1994); M. Aoki, *Information, Incentives, and Bargaining in the Japanese Economy* (Cambridge: Cambridge University Press, 1989).

31. J. Hoerr, "The Payoff from Teamwork," *BusinessWeek*, July 10, 1989, 56–62.

32. M. Hammer and J. Champy, *Re-engineering the Corporation* (New York: HarperBusiness, 1993), 35.

33. Ibid., 46.

34. Ibid.

35. www.dell.com, 2008.

36. Michael Dell, *Direct from Dell: Strategies That Revolutionized an Industry* (New York: HarperBusiness, 1999).

37. www.google.com, 2008.

38. Ibid.

39. J. S. Adams, "The Structure and Dynamics of Behavior in Boundary Spanning Roles," in M. D. Dunnette, ed., *The Handbook of Industrial and Organizational Psychology* (Chicago: Rand McNally, 1976).

40. For a discussion of sources of organizational inertia, see M. T. Hannah and J. Freeman, "Structural Inertia and Organizational Change," *American Sociological Review* 49 (1984), 149–64.

41. Press release, www.toyotausa.com, November 12, 2007.

42. I. Rowley, "Even Toyota Isn't Perfect," www.businessweek.com, January 22, 2007.

43. "Toyota Blames Rapid Growth for Quality Problems," www.iht.com, March 13, 2008.

44. I. Rowley, "Katsuaki Watanabe: Fighting to Stay Humble", www.businessweek.com, March 5, 2007.

45. L. Helm and M. Edid, "Life on the Line: Two Auto Workers Who Are Worlds Apart," *BusinessWeek*, September 30, 1994, 76–78.

46. Dumaine, "The Trouble with Teams."

Chapter 10

1. www.lizclaiborne.com, 2008.

2. R. Dodes, "Claiborne Seeks to Shed 16 Apparel Brands," www.businessweek.com, July 11, 2007.

3. www.lizclaiborne.com, 2008.

4. G. R. Jones, *Organizational Theory, Design and Change: Text and Cases* (Upper Saddle River: Prentice-Hall, 2003).

5. J. Child, *Organization: A Guide for Managers and Administrators* (New York: Harper & Row, 1977).

6. P. R. Lawrence and J. W. Lorsch, *Organization and Environment* (Boston: Graduate School of Business Administration, Harvard University, 1967).

7. R. Duncan, "What Is the Right Organizational Design?" *Organizational Dynamics,* Winter 1979, 59–80.

8. T. Burns and G. R. Stalker, *The Management of Innovation* (London: Tavistock, 1966).

9. D. Miller, "Strategy Making and Structure: Analysis and Implications for Performance," *Academy of Management Journal* 30 (1987), 7–32.

10. A. D. Chandler, *Strategy and Structure* (Cambridge, MA: MIT Press, 1962).

11. J. Stopford and L. Wells, *Managing the Multinational Enterprise* (London: Longman, 1972).

12. C. Perrow, *Organizational Analysis: A Sociological View* (Belmont, CA: Wadsworth, 1970).

13. F. W. Taylor, *The Principles of Scientific Management* (New York: Harper, 1911).

14. R. W. Griffin, *Task Design: An Integrative Approach* (Glenview, IL: Scott, Foresman, 1982).

15. Ibid.

16. J. R. Hackman and G. R. Oldham, *Work Redesign* (Reading, MA: Addison-Wesley, 1980).

17. J. R. Galbraith and R. K. Kazanjian, *Strategy Implementation: Structure, System, and Process,* 2d ed. (St. Paul, MN: West, 1986).

18. Lawrence and Lorsch, *Organization and Environment.*

19. Jones, *Organizational Theory.*

20. Lawrence and Lorsch, *Organization and Environment.*

21. R. H. Hall, *Organizations: Structure and Process* (Englewood Cliffs, NJ: Prentice-Hall, 1972); R. Miles, *Macro Organizational Behavior* (Santa Monica, CA: Goodyear, 1980).

22. Chandler, *Strategy and Structure.*

23. G. R. Jones and C. W. L. Hill, "Transaction Cost Analysis of Strategy-Structure Choice," *Strategic Management Journal* 9 (1988), 159–72.

24. www.gsk.com, 2006.

25. Ibid.

26. www.nokia.com, 2008

27. N. Lakshman, "Nokia's Global Design Sense," www.businessweek.com, August 10, 2007.

28. www.nokia.com, 2008.

29. S. M. Davis and P. R. Lawrence, *Matrix* (Reading, MA: Addison-Wesley, 1977); J. R. Galbraith, "Matrix Organization Designs: How to Combine Functional and Project Forms," *Business Horizons* 14 (1971), 29–40.

30. L. R. Burns, "Matrix Management in Hospitals: Testing Theories of Matrix Structure and Development," *Administrative Science Quarterly* 34 (1989), 349–68.

31. C. W. L. Hill, *International Business* (Homewood, IL: Irwin, 2003).

32. Jones, *Organizational Theory.*

33. A. Farnham, "America's Most Admired Company," *Fortune,* February 7, 1994, 50–54.

34. P. Blau, "A Formal Theory of Differentiation in Organizations," *American Sociological Review* 35 (1970), 684–95.

35. S. Grey, "McDonald's CEO Announces Shifts of Top Executives," *The Wall Street Journal,* July 16, 2004, A11.

36. www.mcdonalds.com, 2008.

37. Child, *Organization.*

38. S. McCartney, "Airline Industry's Top-Ranked Woman Keeps Southwest's Small-Fry Spirit Alive," *The Wall Street Journal,* November 30, 1995, B1.

39. www.plexus.com, 2006.

40. W. M. Bulkeley, "Plexus Strategy: Smaller Runs of More Things," *The Wall Street Journal,* October 8, 2003, B1, B12.

41. P. M. Blau and R. A. Schoenherr, *The Structure of Organizations* (New York: Basic Books, 1971).

42. Jones, *Organizational Theory.*

43. www.avon.com, 2008

44. N. Byrnes, "Avon: More Than Just Cosmetic Changes," www.businessweek.com, March 12, 2007.

45. www.avon.com, 2008.

46. Lawrence and Lorsch, *Organization and Environment,* 50–55.

47. J. R. Galbraith, *Designing Complex Organizations* (Reading, MA: Addison-Wesley, 1977), chap. 1; Galbraith and Kazanjian, *Strategy Implementation,* chap. 7.

48. Lawrence and Lorsch, *Organization and Environment,* 55.

49. S. D. N. Cook and D. Yanow, "Culture and Organizational Learning." *Journal of Management Inquiry* 2 (1993), 373–90.

50. www.walmart.com, 2006.

51. "Associates Keystone to Structure," *Chain Store Age,* December 1999, 17.

52. www.walmart.com, 2006.

53. M. Troy, "The Culture Remains the Constant," *Discount Store News,* June 8, 1998, 95–98.

54. S. Voros, "3D Management," *Management Review,* January 2000, 45–47.

55. "Neurosis, Arkansas-Style," *Fortune,* April 17, 2000, 36.

56. B. Schneider, "The People Make the Place," *Personnel Psychology* 40 (1987), 437–53.

57. J. E. Sheriden, "Organizational Culture and Employee Retention," *Academy of Management Journal* 35 (1992), 657–92.

58. M. Hannan and J. Freeman, "Structural Inertia and Organizational Change," *American Sociological Review* 49 (1984), 149–64.

59. C. A. O'Reilly, J. Chatman, and D. F. Caldwell, "People and Organizational Culture: Assessing Person-Organizational Fit," *Academy of Management Journal* 34 (1991), 487–517.

60. T. L. Beauchamp and N. E. Bowie, eds., *Ethical Theory and Business* (Englewood Cliffs, NJ: Prentice-Hall, 1979); A. MacIntyre, *After Virtue* (Notre Dame, IN: University of Notre Dame Press, 1981).

61. A. Sagie and D. Elizur, "Work Values: A Theoretical Overview and a Model of Their Affects," *Journal of Organizational Behavior* 17 (1996), 503–14.

62. G. R. Jones, "Transaction Costs, Property Rights, and Organizational Culture: An

Exchange Perspective," *Administrative Science Quarterly* 28 (1983), 454–67.

63.   C. Perrow, *Normal Accidents* (New York: Basic Books, 1984).

64.   H. Mintzberg, *The Structuring of Organizational Structures* (Englewood Cliffs, NJ: Prentice-Hall, 1979).

65.   G. Kunda, *Engineering Culture* (Philadelphia: Temple University Press, 1992).

66.   www.nokia.com, 2008.

67.   P. de Bendern, "Quirky Culture Paves Nokia's Road to Fortune," www.yahoo.com, 2000.

68.   K. E. Weick, *The Social Psychology of Organization* (Reading, MA: Addison-Wesley, 1979).

69.   J. W. Schulz, L. C. Hauck, and R. M. Hauck, "Using the Power of Corporate Culture to Achieve Results: A Case Study of Sunflower Electric Power Corporation," *Management Quarterly* 2 (2001), 2–19.

70.   J. P. Kotter and J. L. Heskett, *Corporate Culture and Performance* (New York: Free Press, 1992).

71.   Copyright © 2006, Gareth R. Jones.

Chapter 11

1.   www.ford.com, 2008.

2.   D. Kiley, "The New Heat On Ford," www.businessweek.com, June 4, 2007.

3.   Ibid.

4.   www.ford.com, 2008.

5.   W. G. Ouchi, "Markets, Bureaucracies, and Clans," *Administrative Science Quarterly* 25 (1980), 129–41.

6.   P. Lorange, M. Morton, and S. Ghoshal, *Strategic Control* (St. Paul, MN: West, 1986).

7.   H. Koontz and R. W. Bradspies, "Managing Through Feedforward Control," *Business Horizons,* June 1972, 25–36.

8.   E. E. Lawler III and J. G. Rhode, *Information and Control in Organizations* (Pacific Palisades, CA: Goodyear, 1976).

9.   C. W. L. Hill and G. R. Jones, *Strategic Management: An Integrated Approach,* 6th ed. (Boston: Houghton Mifflin, 2003).

10.   E. Flamholtz, "Organizational Control Systems as a Management Tool," *California Management Review,* Winter 1979, 50–58.

11.   W. G. Ouchi, "The Transmission of Control Through Organizational Hierarchy," *Academy of Management Journal* 21 (1978), 173–92.

12.   W. G. Ouchi, "The Relationship Between Organizational Structure and Organizational Control," *Administrative Science Quarterly* 22 (1977), 95–113.

13.   Ouchi, "Markets, Bureaucracies, and Clans."

14.   W. H. Newman, *Constructive Control* (Englewood Cliffs, NJ: Prentice-Hall, 1975).

15.   J. D. Thompson, *Organizations in Action* (New York: McGraw-Hill, 1967).

16.   R. N. Anthony, *The Management Control Function* (Boston: Harvard Business School Press, 1988).

17.   Ouchi, "Markets, Bureaucracies, and Clans."

18.   Hill and Jones, *Strategic Management.*

19.   R. Simons, "Strategic Orientation and Top Management Attention to Control Systems," *Strategic Management Journal* 12 (1991), 49–62.

20.   G. Schreyogg and H. Steinmann, "Strategic Control: A New Perspective," *Academy of Management Review* 12 (1987), 91–103.

21.   B. Woolridge and S. W. Floyd, "The Strategy Process, Middle Management Involvement, and Organizational Performance," *Strategic Management Journal* 11 (1990), 231–41.

22.   J. A. Alexander, "Adaptive Changes in Corporate Control Practices," *Academy of Management Journal* 34 (1991), 162–93.

23.   Hill and Jones, *Strategic Management.*

24.   G. H. B. Ross, "Revolution in Management Control," *Management Accounting* 72 (1992), 23–27.

25.   P. F. Drucker, *The Practice of Management* (New York: Harper & Row, 1954).

26.   S. J. Carroll and H. L. Tosi, *Management by Objectives: Applications and Research* (New York: Macmillan, 1973).

27.   R. Rodgers and J. E. Hunter, "Impact of Management by Objectives on Organizational Productivity," *Journal of Applied Psychology* 76 (1991), 322–26.

28.   M. B. Gavin, S. G. Green, and G. T. Fairhurst, "Managerial Control Strategies for Poor Performance over Time and the Impact on Subordinate Reactions," *Organizational Behavior and Human Decision Processes* 63 (1995), 207–21.

29.   www.cypress.com, 2001.

30.   B. Dumaine, "The Bureaucracy Busters," *Fortune,* June 17, 1991, 46.

31.   www.microsoft.com, 2006.

32.   O. Thomas, "Microsoft Employees Feel Maligned," www.money.cnn.com, March 10, 2006.

33.   J. Nightingale, "Rising Frustration with Microsoft's Compensation and Review System," www.washtech.org, March 10, 2006.

34.   Ibid.

35.   "Microsoft's Departing Employees," www.yahoo.news.com, May 6, 2006.

36.   D. S. Pugh, D. J. Hickson, C. R. Hinings, and C. Turner, "Dimensions of Organizational Structure," *Administrative Science Quarterly* 13 (1968), 65–91.

37.   B. Elgin, "Running the Tightest Ships on the Net," *BusinessWeek,* January 29, 2001, 125–26.

38.   P. M. Blau, *The Dynamics of Bureaucracy* (Chicago: University of Chicago Press, 1955).

39.   J. McGregor, "The World's Most Innovative Companies," www.businessweek.com, May 4, 2007.

40.   R. Nakashima, "Iger: Disney to reap $1 billion online," www.yahoo.com, March 11, 2008,

41.   Ouchi, "Markets, Bureaucracies, and Clans."

42.   Ibid.

43.   www.ups.com, 2004.

44.   J. Van Maanen, "Police Socialization: A Longitudinal Examination of Job Attitudes in an Urban Police Department," *Administrative Science Quarterly* 20 (1975), 207–28.

45.   This section draws heavily on K. Lewin, *Field Theory in Social Science* (New York: Harper & Row, 1951).

46.   L. Chung-Ming and R. W. Woodman, "Understanding Organizational Change: A Schematic Perspective," *Academy of Management Journal* 38, no. 2 (1995), 537–55.

47.   D. Miller, "Evolution and Revolution: A Quantum View of Structural Change in Organizations," *Journal of Management Studies* 19 (1982), 11–151; D. Miller, "Momentum and Revolution in Organizational Adaptation," *Academy of Management Journal* 2 (1980), 591–614.

48.   C. E. Lindblom, "The Science of Muddling Through," *Public Administration Review* 19 (1959), 79–88; P. C. Nystrom and W. H. Starbuck, "To Avoid Organizational Crises, Unlearn," *Organizational Dynamics* 12 (1984), 53–65.

49.   L. Brown, "Research Action: Organizational Feedback, Understanding and Change," *Journal of Applied Behavioral Research* 8 (1972), 697–711; P. A. Clark, *Action Research and Organizational Change* (New York: Harper & Row, 1972); N. Margulies and A. P. Raia, eds., *Conceptual Foundations of Organizational Development* (New York: McGraw-Hill, 1978).

50.   W. L. French and C. H. Bell, *Organizational Development* (Englewood Cliffs, NJ: Prentice-Hall, 1990).

51.   W. L. French, "A Checklist for Organizing and Implementing an OD Effort," in W. L. French, C. H. Bell, and R. A. Zawacki, eds., *Organizational Development and Transformation* (Homewood, IL: Irwin, 1994), 484–95.

Chapter 12

1.   J. M. O'Brien, "100 Best Companies to Work For–A Perfect Season," *Fortune,* February 4, 2008, 64–66; "Four Seasons Employees Name Company to Fortune '100 Best Companies to Work For' List," www.fourseasons.com/about_us/press_release_280.html, February 22, 2008.

2. "Four Seasons Employees Name Company to Fortune '100 Best Companies to Work For' List,"

3. O'Brien, "100 Best Companies to Work For–A Perfect Season."

4. Ibid.

5. Ibid; "Creating the Four Seasons Difference," www.businessweek.com/print/innovate/content/jan2008/id20080122_671354.htm, February 22, 2008.

6. O'Brien, "100 Best Companies to Work For–A Perfect Season."; "Creating the Four Seasons Difference."

7. Ibid; "Four Seasons Employees Name Company to Fortune '100 Best Companies to Work For' List."

8. O'Brien, "100 Best Companies to Work For–A Perfect Season."

9. "Creating the Four Seasons Difference."

10. O'Brien, "100 Best Companies to Work For–A Perfect Season."

11. Ibid.

12. Ibid.

13. Ibid.

14. Ibid.

15. Ibid; "Creating the Four Seasons Difference"; "Four Seasons Employees Name Company to Fortune '100 Best Companies to Work For' List."

16. J. E. Butler, G. R. Ferris, and N. K. Napier, *Strategy and Human Resource Management* (Cincinnati: Southwestern Publishing, 1991); P. M. Wright and G. C. McMahan, "Theoretical Perspectives for Strategic Human Resource Management," *Journal of Management* 18 (1992), 295–320.

17. L. Clifford, "Why You Can Safely Ignore Six Sigma," *Fortune,* January 22, 2001, 140.

18. J. B. Quinn, P. Anderson, and S. Finkelstein, "Managing Professional Intellect: Making the Most of the Best," *Harvard Business Review,* March–April 1996, 71–80.

19. Ibid.

20. C. D. Fisher, L. F. Schoenfeldt, and J. B. Shaw, *Human Resource Management* (Boston: Houghton Mifflin, 1990).

21. Wright and McMahan, "Theoretical Perspectives."

22. L. Baird and I. Meshoulam, "Managing Two Fits for Strategic Human Resource Management," *Academy of Management Review* 14, 116–28; J. Milliman, M. Von Glinow, and M. Nathan, "Organizational Life Cycles and Strategic International Human Resource Management in Multinational Companies: Implications for Congruence Theory," *Academy of Management Review* 16 (1991), 318–39; R. S. Schuler and S. E. Jackson, "Linking Competitive Strategies with Human Resource Management Practices," *Academy of Management Executive* 1 (1987), 207–19; P. M. Wright and S. A. Snell, "Toward an Integrative View of Strategic Human Resource Management," *Human Resource Management Review* 1 (1991), 203–225.

23. "Who's in Charge Here? No One," *The Observer,* April 27, 2003 (http://observer.guardian.co.uk/business/story/0,6903,944138,00.html); "Ricardo Semler, CEO, Semco SA," cnn.com, June 29, 2004 (http://cnn.worldnews.printthis.clickability.com/pt/cpt&title=cnn.com); D. Kirkpatrick, "The Future of Work: An 'Apprentice'-Style Office?" *Fortune,* April 14, 2004 (www.fortune.com/fortune/subs/print/0,15935,611068,00.html); A. Strutt and R. Van Der Beek, "Report from HR2004," www.mce.be/hr2004/reportd2.htm, July 2, 2004; R. Semler, "Seven-Day Weekend Returns Power to Employees," workopolis.com, May 26, 2004 (http://globeandmail.workopolis.com/servlet/content/qprinter/20040526/cabooks26); "SEMCO," http://semco.locaweb.com.br/ingles, May 31, 2006; "Ricardo Semler, Semco SA: What Are You Reading?" cnn.com, May 31, 2006. (www.cnn.com/2004/BUSINESS/06/29/semler.profile/index.html).

24. R. Semler, *The Seven-Day Weekend: Changing the Way Work Works* (New York: Penguin, 2003); "SEMCO."

25. Ibid.

26. A. Strutt, "Interview with Ricardo Semler," *Management Centre Europe,* April 2004 (www.mce.be/knowledge/392/35).

27. Semler, *The Seven-Day Weekend.*

28. Ibid.

29. R. Semler, "How We Went *Digital* Without a *Strategy,*" *Harvard Business Review* 78, no. 5 (September–October 2000), 51–56.

30. Semler, *The Seven-Day Weekend.*

31. Equal Employment Opportunity Commission, "Uniform Guidelines on Employee Selection Procedures," *Federal Register* 43 (1978), 38290–315.

32. R. Stogdill II, R. Mitchell, K. Thurston, and C. Del Valle, "Why AIDS Policy Must Be a Special Policy," *BusinessWeek,* February 1, 1993, 53–54.

33. J. M. George, "AIDS/AIDS-Related Complex," in L. Peters, B. Greer, and S. Youngblood, eds., *The Blackwell Encyclopedic Dictionary of Human Resource Management* (Oxford, England: Blackwell Publishers, 1997).

34. Ibid.

35. Ibid; Stogdill et al., "Why AIDS Policy Must Be a Special Policy"; K. Holland, "Out of Retirement and Into Uncertainty," *The New York Times,* May 27, 2007, BU17.

36. J. Helyar, "50 and Fired," *Fortune,* May 16, 2005, 78–90.

37. S. Clifford, "Saying No to Retirement," *Inc. Magazine,* September 2005, 27–29; "Demographic Profile of American Baby Boomers," www.metlife.com/Applications/Corporate/WPS/CDA/PageGenerator/0,P8895 AP,0. . . , May 5, 2006; "Baby Boomer," www.wikipedia.org, May 2, 2006 (http://en.wikipedia.org/wiki/Baby_boomer); "The Baby Boomer Generation–Trends, Research, Discussion and Comment," *Aging Hipsters: The Baby Boomer Generation,* May 2, 2006 (www.aginghipsters.com).

38. Helyar, "50 and Fired."

39. Ibid.

40. Ibid.

41. Ibid.

42. Ibid.

43. S. E. Needleman, "Speed Interviewing Grows as Skills Shortage Looms," The Wall Street Journal, November 6, 2007, B15.

44. Helyar, "50 and Fired."

45. S. L. Rynes, "Recruitment, Job Choice, and Post-Hire Consequences: A Call for New Research Directions," in M. D. Dunnette and L. M. Hough, eds., *Handbook of Industrial and Organizational Psychology,* vol. 2 (Palo Alto, CA: Consulting Psychologists Press, 1991), 399–444.

46. R. L. Sullivan, "Lawyers a la Carte," *Forbes,* September 11, 1995, 44.

47. E. Porter, "Send Jobs to India? U.S. Companies Say It's Not Always Best," *The New York Times,* April 28, 2004, A1, A7.

48. D. Wessel, "The Future of Jobs: New Ones Arise; Wage Gap Widens," *The Wall Street Journal,* April 2, 2004, A1, A5; "Relocating the Back Office," *The Economist,* December 13, 2003, 67–69.

49. Porter, "Send Jobs to India?"

50. Ibid.

51. "Learning to Live with Offshoring," *BusinessWeek,* January 30, 2006, 122.

52. "Offshoring: Spreading the Gospel," *BusinessWeek Online,* March 6, 2006 (www.businessweek.com/print/magazine/content/06_10/b3974074.htm?chan=gl).

53. "Offshoring: Spreading the Gospel"; "Genpact: Management Team," www.genpact.com/aboutus.asp?key=1&page=team.htm& submenu=0, April 25, 2006; "Genpact," www.genpact.com/genpact/aboutus?key=1, April 25, 2006; "Genpact: Growth History," www.genpact.com/genpact/aboutus.asp?key=1&page=growth.htm, April 25, 2006.

54. "Genpact: Management Team"; "Genpact."

55. "Offshoring: Spreading the Gospel."

56. Ibid.

57. R. J. Harvey, "Job Analysis," in Dunnette and Hough, *Handbook of Industrial and Organizational Psychology,* 71–163.

58. E. L. Levine, *Everything You Always Wanted to Know About Job Analysis: A Job Analysis Primer* (Tampa, FL: Mariner Publishing, 1983).

59. R. L. Mathis and J. H. Jackson, *Human Resource Management,* 7th ed. (Minneapolis: West, 1994).

60. E. J. McCormick, P. R. Jeannerette, and R. C. Mecham, *Position Analysis Questionnaire* (West Lafayette, IN: Occupational Research Center, Department of Psychological Sciences, Purdue University, 1969).

61. Fisher et al., *Human Resource Management;* Mathis and Jackson, *Human Resource Management;* R. A. Noe, J. R. Hollenbeck, B. Gerhart, and P. M. *Wright, Human Resource Management: Gaining a Competitive Advantage* (Burr Ridge, IL: Irwin, 1994).

62. Fisher et al., *Human Resource Management;* E. J. McCormick, *Job Analysis: Methods and Applications* (New York: American Management Association, 1979); E. J. McCormick and P. R. Jeannerette, "The Position Analysis Questionnaire," in S. Gael, ed., *The Job Analysis Handbook for Business, Industry, and Government* (New York: Wiley, 1988); Noe et al., *Human Resource Management.*

63. Rynes, "Recruitment, Job Choice, and Post-Hire Consequences."

64. R. Sharpe, "The Life of the Party? Can Jeff Taylor Keep the Good Times Rolling at Monster.com?" *BusinessWeek,* June 4, 2001 (*BusinessWeek* Archives); D. H. Freedman, "The Monster Dilemma," *Inc. Magazine,* May 2007, 77–78; P. Korkki, "So Easy to Apply, So Hard to Be Noticed," *The New York Times,* July 1, 2007, BU16.

65. www.monster.com, June 2001.

66. www.jobline.org, Jobline press releases, May 8, 2001, accessed June 20, 2001.

67. J. Spolsky, "There Is a Better Way to Find and Hire the Very Best Employees," *Inc. Magazine,* May 2007, 81–82; "About the Company," www.fogcreek.com/, March 5, 2008; "Fog Creek Software," www.fogcreek .com/, March 5, 2008.

68. Spolsky, "There Is a Better Way to Find and Hire the Very Best Employees"; "Fog Creek Software."

69. Spolsky, "There Is a Better Way to Find and Hire the Very Best Employees."

70. Ibid.

71. Ibid.

72. Ibid.

73. Ibid.

74. Ibid; "About the Company"; "Fog Creek Software."

75. Spolsky, "There Is a Better Way to Find and Hire the Very Best Employees."

76. S. L. Premack and J. P. Wanous, "A Meta-Analysis of Realistic Job Preview Experiments," *Journal of Applied Psychology* 70, (1985) 706–19; J. P. Wanous, "Realistic Job Previews: Can a Procedure to Reduce Turnover also Influence the Relationship Between Abilities and Performance?" *Personnel Psychology* 31, (1978) 249–58; J. P. Wanous, *Organizational Entry: Recruitment, Selection, and Socialization of Newcomers* (Reading, MA: Addison-Wesley, 1980).

77. R. M. Guion, "Personnel Assessment, Selection, and Placement," in Dunnette and Hough, *Handbook of Industrial and Organizational Psychology,* 327–97.

78. T. Joyner, "Job Background Checks Surge," *Houston Chronicle,* May 2, 2005, D6.

79. Joyner, "Job Background Checks Surge"; "ADP News Releases: Employer Services: ADP Hiring Index Reveals Background Checks Performed More than Tripled Since 1997," *Automatic Data Processing, Inc.,* June 3, 2006 (www.investquest.com/iq/a/aud/ne/news/adp042505background .htm).

80. "ADP News Releases."

81. Noe et al., *Human Resource Management;* J. A. Wheeler and J. A. Gier, "Reliability and Validity of the Situational Interview for a Sales Position," *Journal of Applied Psychology* 2 (1987), 484–87.

82. Noe et al., *Human Resource Management.*

83. J. Flint, "Can You Tell Applesauce from Pickles?" *Forbes,* October 9, 1995, 106–8.

84. Ibid.

85. "Wanted: Middle Managers, Audition Required," *The Wall Street Journal,* December 28, 1995, A1.

86. I. L. Goldstein, "Training in Work Organizations," in Dunnette and Hough, *Handbook of Industrial and Organizational Psychology,* 507–619.

87. S. Overman, "Ethan Allen's Secret Weapon," *HRMagazine,* May 1994, 61.

88. N. Banerjee, "For Mary Kay Sales Reps in Russia, Hottest Shade Is the Color of Money," *The Wall Street Journal,* August 30, 1995, A8.

89. T. D. Allen, L. T. Eby, M. L. Poteet, E. Lentz, and L. Lima, "Career Benefits Associated with Mentoring for Protégés: A Meta-Analysis," *Journal of Applied Psychology* 89, no. 1, (2004), 127–36.

90. P. Garfinkel, "Putting a Formal Stamp on Mentoring," *The New York Times,* January 18, 2004, BU10.

91. Ibid.

92. Allen et al., "Career Benefits Associated with Mentoring"; L. Levin, "Lesson Learned: Know Your Limits. Get Outside Help Sooner Rather than Later," *BusinessWeek Online,* July 5, 2004 (www.businessweek.com); "Family, Inc.," *BusinessWeek Online,* November 10, 2003 (www.businessweek.com); J. Salamon, "A Year with a Mentor. Now Comes the Test," *The New York Times,* September 30, 2003, B1, B5; E. White, "Making Mentorships Work," *The Wall Street Journal,* October 23, 2007, B11.

93. Garfinkel, "Putting a Formal Stamp on Mentoring."

94. J. A. Byrne, "Virtual B-Schools," *BusinessWeek,* October 23, 1995, 64–68.

95. Fisher et al., *Human Resource Management.*

96. Ibid; G. P. Latham and K. N. Wexley, *Increasing Productivity Through Performance Appraisal* (Reading, MA: Addison-Wesley, 1982).

97. T. A. DeCotiis, "An Analysis of the External Validity and Applied Relevance of Three Rating Formats," *Organizational Behavior and Human Performance* 19 (1977), 247–66; Fisher et al., *Human Resource Management.*

98. J. Muller, K. Kerwin, D. Welch, P. L. Moore, D. Brady, "Ford: It's Worse Than You Think," *BusinessWeek,* June 25, 2001 (*BusinessWeek* Archives).

99. Ibid.

100. L. M. Sixel, "Enron Rating Setup Irks Many Workers," *Houston Chronicle,* February 26, 2001, 1C.

101. J. S. Lublin, "It's Shape-Up Time for Performance Reviews," *The Wall Street Journal,* October 3, 1994, B1, B2.

102. J. S. Lublin, "Turning the Tables: Underlings Evaluate Bosses," *The Wall Street Journal,* October 4, 1994, B1, B14; S. Shellenbarger, "Reviews from Peers Instruct—and Sting," *The Wall Street Journal,* October 4, 1994, B1, B4.

103. C. Borman and D. W. Bracken, "360 Degree Appraisals," in C. L. Cooper and C. Argyris, eds., *The Concise Blackwell Encyclopedia of Management* (Oxford, England: Blackwell Publishers, 1998), 17; D. W. Bracken, "Straight Talk About Multi-Rater Feedback," *Training and Development* 48 (1994), 44–51; M. R. Edwards, W. C. Borman, and J. R. Sproul, "Solving the Double-Bind in Performance Appraisal: A Saga of Solves, Sloths, and Eagles," *Business Horizons* 85 (1985), 59–68.

104. M. A. Peiperl, "Getting 360 Degree Feedback Right," *Harvard Business Review,* January 2001, 142–47.

105. A. Harrington, "Workers of the World, Rate Your Boss!" *Fortune,* September 18, 2000, 340, 342; www.ImproveNow.com, June 2001.

106. Lublin, "It's Shape-Up Time for Performance Reviews."

107. S. E. Moss and J. I. Sanchez, "Are Your Employees Avoiding You? Managerial Strategies for Closing the Feedback Gap," *Academy of Management Executive* 18, no. 1 (2004), 32–46.

108. J. Flynn and F. Nayeri, "Continental Divide over Executive Pay," *BusinessWeek,* July 3, 1995, 40–41.

109. J. A. Byrne, "How High Can CEO Pay Go?" *BusinessWeek,* April 22, 1996, 100–06.

110. A. Borrus, "A Battle Royal Against Regal Paychecks," *BusinessWeek,* February 24, 2003, 127; "Too Many Turkeys," *The Economist,* November 26, 2005, 75–76; G. Morgenson, "How to Slow Runaway Executive Pay," *The New York Times,* October 23, 2005, 1, 4.

111. "Executive Pay."

112. "Home Depot Chief's Pay in 2007 Could Reach $8.9m.," *The New York Times,* Bloomberg News, January 25, 2007, C7; E. Carr, "The Stockpot," *The Economist, A Special Report on Executive Pay,* January 20, 2007, 6–10; E. Porter, "More than Ever, It Pays to BE the Top Executive,*" The New York Times,* May 25, 2007, A1, C7.

113. E. Tahmincioglu, "Paths to Better Health (On the Boss's Nickel)," *The New York Times,* May 23, 2004, BU7.

114. Ibid.

115. K. K. Spors, "Top Small Workplaces 2007," *The Wall Street Journal,* October 1, 2007, R1–R6; K. K. Spors, "Guerra DeBerry Coody," *The Wall Street Journal,* October 1, 2007, R5; "Guerra DeBerry Coody Named One of the Nation's 15 Top Small Workplaces of 2007," *Business Wire: Guerra DeBerry Coody Named One of the Nations 15 Top Small Workplaces,* http://findarticles.com/p/articles/mi_m0EIN/is_2007_Oct_1/ai_n20527510/print, March 6, 2008; "Guerra DeBerry Coody," www.gdc-co.com/, March 6, 2008; "Frank Guerra '83, Trish DeBerry-Mejia '87 and Tess Coody '93," *Trinity University, Alumni–Profiles,* www.trinity.edu/alumni/profiles/0503_guerra_deberry_coody.htm, March 6, 2008.

116. Spors, "Top Small Workplaces 2007"; Spors, "Guerra DeBerry Coody"; "Guerra DeBerry Coody Named One of the Nation's 15 Top Small Workplaces of 2007."

117. Spors, "Top Small Workplaces 2007"; Spors, "Guerra DeBerry Coody."

118. Ibid.

119. Ibid.

120. "Guerra DeBerry Coody Named One of the Nation's 15 Top Small Workplaces of 2007."

121. S. Shellenbarger, "Amid Gay Marriage Debate, Companies Offer More Benefits to Same-Sex Couples," *The Wall Street Journal,* March 18, 2004, D1.

122. S. Premack and J. E. Hunter, "Individual Unionization Decisions," *Psychological Bulletin* 103 (1988), 223–34.

123. M. B. Regan, "Shattering the AFL-CIO's Glass Ceiling," *BusinessWeek,* November 13, 1995, 46.

124. www.aflcio.org, June 2001.

125. G. P. Zachary, "Some Unions Step Up Organizing Campaigns and Get New Members," *The Wall Street Journal,* September 1, 1995, A1, A2.

126. Regan, "Shattering the AFL-CIO's Glass Ceiling"; www.aflcio.org, June 2001; R. S. Dunham, "Big Labor: So Out It's 'Off the Radar Screen,'" *BusinessWeek,* March 26, 2001 (*BusinessWeek* Archives); "Chavez-Thompson to Retire as Executive Vice President," *AFL-CIO Weblog,* http://blog.aflcio.org/2007/09/13/chavez-thompson-to-retire-as-executive-vice-president/print/, March 6, 2008.

127. "Secretary of Labor Elaine L. Chao, *U.S. Department of Labor–Office of the Secretary of Labor Elaine L. Chao (OSEC),* www.dol.gov/_sec/welcome.htm, March 6, 2008.

128. "The Honorable Elaine L. Chao United States Secretary of Labor," www.dol.gov/dol/sec/public/aboutosec/chao.htm, June 25, 2001.

129. R. Blumenstein, "Ohio Strike That Is Crippling GM Plants Is Tied to Plan to Outsource Brake Work," *The Wall Street Journal,* March 12, 1996, A3–A4.

130. J. Hannah, "GM Workers Agree to End Strike," *Bryan-College Station Eagle,* March 23, 1996, A12.

Chapter 13

1. C. J. Loomis, *Fortune* editor at large, "The Big Surprise Is Enterprise: Quietly beating out rivals Hertz and Avis, this privately held outfit reigns as the No. 1 car-rental company in America, and the Taylor family aims to keep it on top," *Fortune,* July 14, 2006, http://cnnmoney.printthis.clickability.com/pt/cpt?action=cpt&title=Fortune%3A+The+big . . ., March 31, 2008.

2. "Overview," *Enterprise Rent-A-Car Careers–Overview,* www.erac.com/recruit/about_enterprise.asp?navID=overview, March 27, 2008.

3. A. Fisher, *Fortune* senior writer, "Who's Hiring New College Grads Now," *CNNMoney.com,* http://cnnmoney.printthis.clickability.com/pt/cpt?action=cpt&title=Who%27s+hiring+coll . . ., March 31, 2008; Francesca Di Meglio, "A Transcript for Soft Skills, Wisconsin is considering a dual transcript – one for grades and one to assess critical areas such as leadership and communication," www.businessweek.com/print/bschools/content/feb2008/bs20080221_706663.htm, March 28, 2008.

4. "Enterprise Ranked in Top 10 of Business Week's 'Customer Service Champs,'" Thursday, February 22, 2007, *Enterprise Rent-A-Car Careers – Enterprise In The News,* www.erac.com/recruit/news_detail.asp?navID=frontpage&RID=211, March 27, 2008; L. Gerdes, "The Best Places to Launch a Career," *Business Week,* September 24, 2007, 49–60; P. Lehman, "A Clear Road to the Top," *Business Week,* September 18, 2006, 72–82.

5. Loomis, "The Big Surprise Is Enterprise."

6. "Enterprise Rent-A-Car's Pam Nicholson Named to FORTUNE's 50 Most Powerful Women in Business 2007," Monday, October 1, 2007, www.erac.com/recruit/news_details.asp?navID=frontpage&RID=234, March 27, 2008.

7. "Enterprise Ranked in Top 10 of Business Week's 'Customer Service Champs.'"; Gerdes, "The Best Places to Launch a Career."

8. "It's Running a Business . . . Not Doing a Job," *Enterprise Rent-A-Car Careers–Opportunities,* www.erac.com/recruit/opportunities.asp, March 27, 2008.

9. Loomis, "The Big Surprise Is Enterprise"; Lehman, "A Clear Road to the Top."

10. Loomis "The Big Surprise Is Enterprise; Lehman, "A Clear Road to the Top."

11. Lehman, "A Clear Road to the Top."

12. Loomis, "The Big Surprise is Enterprise."

13. Ibid; Lehman, "A Clear Road to the Top."

14. "Enterprise Ranked in Top 10 of Business Week's 'Customer Service Champs.'"

15. Loomis, "The Big Surprise Is Enterprise"; "Overview."

16. Ibid.

17. J. A. Taylor Kindle, "Enterprise: Why We Give Where We Give: For Enterprise Rent-A-Car, giving back is linked to the primary business. That means planting 50 million trees over 50 years, for starters," www.businessweek.com/print/investor/content/jun2007/pi20070628_339711.htm, March 28, 2008.

18. Ibid.

19. M. Gunther, senior writer, "Renting 'Green'? Not So Easy," *CNNMoney.com,* Enterprise-Rent-A-Car goes green, with limits, January 17, 2008, http://cnnmoney.printthis.clickability.com/pt/cpt?action=cpt&title=Enterprise-Rent-A-Car. . ., March 3, 2008; "Enterprise Rent-A-Car Announces Most Comprehensive Environmental Platform in Its Industry, Wednesday, June 06, 2007, *Enterprise Rent-A-Car Careers–Enterprise In The News,* www.erac.com/recruit/news_detail.asp?navID=frontpage&RID=221, March 27, 2008.

20. Gunther, "Renting 'Green'? Not So Easy."

21. Loomis, "The Big Surprise Is Enterprise"; Lehman, "A Clear Road to the Top."

22. R. Kanfer, "Motivation Theory and Industrial and Organizational Psychology," in M. D. Dunnette and L. M. Hough, eds., *Handbook of Industrial and Organizational Psychology,* 2d ed., vol. 1 (Palo Alto, CA: Consulting Psychologists Press, 1990), 75–170.

23. G. P. Latham & M. H. Budworth, "The Study of Work Motivation in the 20th Century," in L. L. Koppes, ed., *Historical Perspectives in Industrial and Organizational Psychology* (Hillsdale, NJ: Laurence Erlbaum, 2006).

24. N. Nicholson, "How to Motivate Your Problem People," *Harvard Business Review,* January 2003, 57–65.

25. A. M. Grant, "Does Intrinsic Motivation Fuel the Prosocial Fire? Motivational Synergy in Predicting Persistence, Performance, and Productivity," *Journal of Applied Psychology* 93, no. 1 (2008), 48–58.

26. Ibid.; C. D. Batson, "Prosocial Motiviation: Is It Ever Truly Altruistic?" in L. Berkowitz, ed., *Advances in Experimental Social Psychology,* vol. 20(New York: Academic Press, 1987), 65–122.

27. Grant, "Does Intrinsic Motivation Fuel the Prosocial Fire?"

28. L. Hales, "An Environmental Problem Slipping Through the Quacks," *washingtonpost.com,* August 27, 2005 (www. washingtonpost.com/wp-dyn/content/ article/2005/08/26/AR2005082601888).

29. "William McDonough, FAIA," www. mcdonough.com/full.htm, April 1, 2008.

30. M. Conlin and P. Raeburn, "Industrial Evolution," *Business Week,* April 8, 2002, 70–72.

31. Ibid.

32. "Masters of Design: William McDonough," *Fastcompany.com,* April 18, 2006 (www.fastcompany.com/magazine/ 83/mod_mcdonough.html); "William McDonough, FAIA."

33. "Masters of Design: William McDonough."

34. Ibid.

35. "Designing the Future," msnbc. com, April 18, 2006 (www.msnbc.com/id/ 7773650/site/newsweek/?artid=1130).

36. J. P. Campbell and R. D. Pritchard, "Motivation Theory in Industrial and Organizational Psychology," in M. D. Dunnette, ed., *Handbook of Industrial and Organizational Psychology* (Chicago: Rand McNally, 1976), 63–130; T. R. Mitchell, "Expectancy Value Models in Organizational Psychology," in N. T. Feather, ed., *Expectations and Actions: Expectancy Value Models in Psychology* (Hillsdale, NJ: Erlbaum, 1982), 293–312; V. H. Vroom, *Work and Motivation* (New York: Wiley, 1964).

37. N. Shope Griffin, "Personalize Your Management Development," *Harvard Business Review* 8, no. 10, 2003, 113–119.

38. T. A. Stewart, "Just Think: No Permission Needed," *Fortune,* January 8, 2001 (www.fortune.com, June 26, 2001).

39. M. Copeland, "Best Buy's Selling Machine," *Business 2.0,* July 2004, 91–102; L. Heller, "Best Buy Still Turning on the Fun," *DSN Retailing Today* 43, no. 13 (July 5, 2004), 3; S. Pounds, "Big-Box Retailers Cash In on South Florida Demand for Home Computer Repair," *Knight Ridder Tribune Business News,* July 5, 2004 (gateway .proquest.com); J. Bloom, "Best Buy Reaps the Rewards of Risking Marketing Failure," *Adverising Age* 75, no. 25 (June 21, 2004), 16;

L. Heller, "Discount Turns Up the Volume: PC Comeback, iPod Popularity Add Edge," *DSN Retailing Today* 43, no. 13 (July 5, 2004), 45; www.bestbuy.com, June 8, 2006.

40. T. J. Maurer, E. M. Weiss, and F. G. Barbeite, "A Model of Involvement in Work-Related Learning and Development Activity: The Effects of Individual, Situational, Motivational, and Age Variables," *Journal of Applied Psychology* 88, no. 4 (2003), 707–24.

41. J. Kaufman, "How Cambodians Came to Control California Doughnuts," *The Wall Street Journal,* February 22, 1995, A1, A8.

42. "Learn About Us," *The Container Store,* www.containerstore.com/learn/index.jhtml, April 1, 2008.

43. M. Duff, "Top-Shelf Employees Keep Container Store on Track," www.looksmart. com, www.findarticles.com, March 8, 2004; M. K. Ammenheuser, "The Container Store Helps People Think Inside the Box," www. icsc.org, May 2004; "The Container Store: Store Location," www.containerstore.com/ find/index/jhtml, June 5, 2006; "Store Locations," *The Container Store,* www.container- store.com/find/index.jhtml, April 1, 2008.

44. "Learn About Us," www.containerstore .com, June 26, 2001.

45. Ibid.

46. J. Schlosser and J. Sung, "The 100 Best Companies to Work For," *Fortune,* January 8, 2001, 148–68. "Fortune 100 Best Companies to Work For 2006," cnn.com, June 5, 2006, (http://money.cnn.com/magazines/fortune/ bestcompanies/snapshots/359.html); "Learn About Us," *The Container Store,* www. containerstore.com/learn/index.jhtml, April 1, 2008.

47. "The Container Store," www. careerbuilder.com, July 13, 2004; "Tom Takes Re-imagine to PBS," Case Studies, www.tompeters.com, March 15, 2004; "2004 Best Companies to Work For," www. fortune.com, July 12, 2004; "Fortune 100 Best Companies to Work For 2006," cnn .com, June 5, 2006, (http://money.cnn.com/ magazines/fortune/bestcompanies/ snapshots/359.html); R. Levering & M. Moskowitz, "100 Best Companies to Work For: The Rankings," *Fortune,* February 4, 2008, 75–94.

48. D. Roth, "My Job at the Container Store," *Fortune,* January 10, 2000 (www. fortune.com, June 26, 2001); "Fortune 2004: 100 Best Companies to Work For," www. containerstore.com/careers/FortunePR_2004 .jhtml?message=/repository/messages/ fortuneCareer.jhtml, January 12, 2004. R. Levering, M. Moskowitz, and S. Adams, "The 100 Best Companies to Work For," *Fortune* 149, no. 1 (2004), 56–78; www. containerstore.com/careers/FortunePR_ 2004.jhtml?message=/repository/messages/ fortuneCareer.jhtml, January 12, 2004.

49. Roth, "My Job at the Container Store."

50. "Learn About Us," *The Container Store,* http://www.containerstore.com/learn/index .jhtml, April 1, 2008.

51. R. Yu, "Some Texas Firms Start Wellness Programs to Encourage Healthier Workers," *Knight Ridder Tribune Business News,* July 7, 2004 (gateway.proquest.com); Levering et al., "The 100 Best Companies to Work For."

52. Roth, "My Job at the Container Store"; "The Foundation Is Organization."

53. "Company," *Protus IP Solutions,* www. protus.com/index.asp?pg=2, March 27, 2008; "News and Events," *Protus IP Solutions,* www.protus.com/news_release.asp? nr=148&yr=07, March 27, 2008; P. Serluco, managing editor, "Data–Document Management and the Raiders of the Lost Fax," *Homeland Defense Journal,* Data Section Feature Article, November 2007, 48.

54. S. Covel, "Tech Company Stems Departures by Listening to Employees' Needs," *The Wall Street Journal,* November 19, 2007, B4.

55. Ibid.

56. Ibid.

57. Ibid.

58. A. H. Maslow, *Motivation and Personality* (New York: Harper & Row, 1954); Campbell and Pritchard, "Motivation Theory in Industrial and Organizational Psychology."

59. Kanfer, "Motivation Theory and Industrial and Organizational Psychology."

60. S. Ronen, "An Underlying Structure of Motivational Need Taxonomies: A Cross-Cultural Confirmation," in H. C. Triandis, M. D. Dunnette, and L. M. Hough, eds., *Handbook of Industrial and Organizational Psychology,* vol. 4 (Palo Alto, CA: Consulting Psychologists Press, 1994), 241–69.

61. N. J. Adler, *International Dimensions of Organizational Behavior,* 2d ed. (Boston: P.W.S.-Kent, 1991); G. Hofstede, "Motivation, Leadership and Organization: Do American Theories Apply Abroad?" *Organizational Dynamics,* Summer 1980, 42–63.

62. C. P. Alderfer, "An Empirical Test of a New Theory of Human Needs," *Organizational Behavior and Human Performance* 4 (1969), 142–75; C. P. Alderfer, *Existence, Relatedness, and Growth: Human Needs in Organizational Settings* (New York: Free Press, 1972); Campbell and Pritchard, "Motivation Theory in Industrial and Organizational Psychology."

63. Kanfer, "Motivation Theory and Industrial and Organizational Psychology."

64. F. Herzberg, *Work and the Nature of Man* (Cleveland: World, 1966).

65. N. King, "Clarification and Evaluation of the Two-Factor Theory of Job Satisfaction," *Psychological Bulletin* 74 (1970), 18–31; E. A. Locke, "The Nature and Causes of Job Satisfaction," in Dunnette, *Handbook of Industrial and Organizational Psychology,* 1297–1349.

66. D. C. McClelland, *Human Motivation* (Glenview, IL: Scott, Foresman, 1985); D. C. McClelland, "How Motives, Skills, and Values Determine What People Do,"

American Psychologist 40 (1985), 812–25; D. C. McClelland, "Managing Motivation to Expand Human Freedom," *American Psychologist* 33 (1978), 201–10.

67.   D. G. Winter, *The Power Motive* (New York: Free Press, 1973).

68.   M. J. Stahl, "Achievement, Power, and Managerial Motivation: Selecting Managerial Talent with the Job Choice Exercise," *Personnel Psychology* 36 (1983), 775–89; D. C. McClelland and D. H. Burnham, "Power Is the Great Motivator," *Harvard Business Review* 54 (1976), 100–10.

69.   R. J. House, W. D. Spangler, and J. Woycke, "Personality and Charisma in the U.S. Presidency: A Psychological Theory of Leader Effectiveness," *Administrative Science Quarterly* 36 (1991), 364–96.

70.   G. H. Hines, "Achievement, Motivation, Occupations, and Labor Turnover in New Zealand," *Journal of Applied Psychology* 58 (1973), 313–17; P. S. Hundal, "A Study of Entrepreneurial Motivation: Comparison of Fast- and Slow-Progressing Small Scale Industrial Entrepreneurs in Punjab, India," *Journal of Applied Psychology* 55 (1971), 317–23.

71.   R. A. Clay, "Green Is Good for You," *Monitor on Psychology,* April 2001, 40–42.

72.   Schlosser and Sung, "The 100 Best Companies to Work For"; Levering et al., "The 100 Best Companies to Work For"; "Fortune 100 Best Companies to Work For 2006," CNNMoney.com, June 5, 2006 (www.money.cnn.com/magazines/fortune/bestcompanies/snapshots/1181.html); "Awards," *SAS,* www.sas.com/awards/index.html, April 1, 2008; Levering & Moskowitz, "100 Best Companies to Work For."

73.   E. P. Dalesio, "Quiet Giant Ready to Raise Its Profits," *Houston Chronicle,* May 6, 2001, 4D; Levering et al., "The 100 Best Companies to Work For"; J. Goodnight, "Welcome to SAS," www.sas.com/corporate/index.html, August 26, 2003; "SAS Press Center: SAS Corporate Statistics," www.sas.com/bin/pfp.pl?–fi, April 18, 2006; "SAS Continues Annual Revenue Growth Streak," www.sas.com/news/prelease/031003/news1.html, August 28, 2003; Levering & Moskowitz, "100 Best Companies to Work For."

74.   J. Pfeffer, "SAS Institute: A Different Approach to Incentives and People Management Practices in the Software Industry," Harvard Business School Case HR-6, January 1998; "Saluting the Global Awards Recipients of Arthur Andersen's Best Practices Awards 2000," www.fortune.com, September 6, 2000; N. Stein, "Winning the War to Keep Top Talent," www.fortune.com, September 6, 2000.

75.   Ibid.

76.   Ibid.

77.   Goodnight, "Welcome to SAS"; "By Solution," www.sas.com/success/solution.html, August 26, 2003; www.sas.com, June 8, 2006.

78.   S. H. Wildstrom, "Do Your Homework, Microsoft," *BusinessWeek Online,* August 8, 2005 (www.businessweek.com/print/magazine/content/05-b3946033-mz006.htm?chan); www.sas.com, June 8, 2006.

79.   J. S. Adams, "Toward an Understanding of Inequity," *Journal of Abnormal and Social Psychology* 67 (1963), 422–36.

80.   Ibid; J. Greenberg, "Approaching Equity and Avoiding Inequity in Groups and Organizations," in J. Greenberg and R. L. Cohen, eds., *Equity and Justice in Social Behavior* (New York: Academic Press, 1982), 389–435; J. Greenberg, "Equity and Workplace Status: A Field Experiment," *Journal of Applied Psychology* 73 (1988), 606–13; R. T. Mowday, "Equity Theory Predictions of Behavior in Organizations," in R. M. Steers and L. W. Porter, eds., *Motivation and Work Behavior* (New York: McGraw-Hill, 1987), 89–110.

81.   A. Goldwasser, "Inhuman Resources," *Ecompany.com,* March 2001, 154–55.

82.   E. A. Locke and G. P. Latham, *A Theory of Goal Setting and Task Performance* (Englewood Cliffs, NJ: Prentice-Hall, 1990).

83.   Ibid; J. J. Donovan and D. J. Radosevich, "The Moderating Role of Goal Commitment on the Goal Difficulty-Performance Relationship: A Meta-Analytic Review and Critical Analysis," *Journal of Applied Psychology* 83 (1998), 308–15; M. E. Tubbs, "Goal Setting: A Meta Analytic Examination of the Empirical Evidence," *Journal of Applied Psychology* 71 (1986), 474–83.

84.   E. A. Locke, K. N. Shaw, L. M. Saari, and G. P. Latham, "Goal Setting and Task Performance: 1969–1980," *Psychological Bulletin* 90 (1981), 125–52.

85.   P. C. Earley, T. Connolly, and G. Ekegren, "Goals, Strategy Development, and Task Performance: Some Limits on the Efficacy of Goal Setting," *Journal of Applied Psychology* 74 (1989), 24–33; R. Kanfer and P. L. Ackerman, "Motivation and Cognitive Abilities: An Integrative/Aptitude Treatment Interaction Approach to Skill Acquisition," *Journal of Applied Psychology* 74 (1989), 657–90.

86.   W. C. Hamner, "Reinforcement Theory and Contingency Management in Organizational Settings," in H. Tosi and W. C. Hamner, eds., *Organizational Behavior and Management: A Contingency Approach* (Chicago: St. Clair Press, 1974).

87.   B. F. Skinner, *Contingencies of Reinforcement* (New York: Appleton-Century-Crofts, 1969).

88.   H. W. Weiss, "Learning Theory and Industrial and Organizational Psychology," in Dunnette and Hough, *Handbook of Industrial and Organizational Psychology,* 171–221.

89.   Hamner, "Reinforcement Theory and Contingency Management."

90.   F. Luthans and R. Kreitner, *Organizational Behavior Modification and Beyond*

(Glenview, IL: Scott, Foresman, 1985); A. D. Stajkovic and F. Luthans, "A Meta-Analysis of the Effects of Organizational Behavior Modification on Task Performance, 1975–95," *Academy of Management Journal* 40 (1997), 1122–49.

91.   A. D. Stajkovic and F. Luthans, "Behavioral Management and Task Performance in Organizations: Conceptual Background, Meta Analysis, and Test of Alternative Models," *Personnel Psychology* 56 (2003), 155–94.

92.   Ibid; Luthans and A. D. Stajkovic, "Reinforce for Performance: The Need to Go Beyond Pay and Even Rewards," *Academy of Management Executive* 13, no. 2 (1999), 49–56; G. Billikopf Enciina and M. V. Norton, "Pay Method Affects Vineyard Pruner Performance," www.cnr.berkeley.edu/ucce50/ag-labor/7research/7calag05.htm.

93.   A. Bandura, *Principles of Behavior Modification* (New York: Holt, Rinehart and Winston, 1969); A. Bandura, *Social Learning Theory* (Englewood Cliffs, NJ: Prentice-Hall, 1977); T. R. V. Davis and F. Luthans, "A Social Learning Approach to Organizational Behavior," *Academy of Management Review* 5 (1980), 281–90.

94.   A. P. Goldstein and M. Sorcher, *Changing Supervisor Behaviors* (New York: Pergamon Press, 1974); Luthans and Kreitner, Organizational Behavior Modification and Beyond.

95.   Bandura, Social Learning Theory; Davis and Luthans, "A Social Learning Approach to Organizational Behavior"; Luthans and Kreitner, *Organizational Behavior Modification and Beyond.*

96.   A. Bandura, "Self-Reinforcement: Theoretical and Methodological Considerations," *Behaviorism* 4 (1976), 135–55.

97.   Hammonds, "Growth Search."

98.   B. Elgin, "Managing Google's Idea Factory," *Business Week,* October 3, 2005, 88–90.

99.   A. Bandura, Self-Efficacy: The Exercise of Control (New York: W.H. Freeman, 1997); J. B. Vancouver, K. M. More, and R. J. Yoder, "Self-Efficacy and Resource Allocation: Support for a Nonmonotonic, Discontinous Model," *Journal of Applied Psychology* 93, no. 1 (2008), 35–47.

100.   A. Bandura, "Self-Efficacy Mechanism in Human Agency," *American Psychologist* 37 (1982), 122–27; M. E. Gist and T. R. Mitchell, "Self-Efficacy: A Theoretical Analysis of Its Determinants and Malleability," *Academy of Management Review* 17 (1992), 183–211.

101.   E. E. Lawler III, *Pay and Organization Development* (Reading, MA: Addison-Wesley, 1981).

102.   "The Risky New Bonuses," *Newsweek,* January 16, 1995, 42.

103.   Lawler, *Pay and Organization Development.*

104. Ibid.

105. J. F. Lincoln, *Incentive Management* (Cleveland: Lincoln Electric Company, 1951); R. Zager, "Managing Guaranteed Employment," *Harvard Business Review* 56 (1978), 103–15.

106. Lawler, *Pay and Organization Development.*

107. M. Gendron, "Gradient Named 'Small Business of Year," *Boston Herald,* May 11, 1994, 35.

108. W. Zeller, R. D. Hof, R. Brandt, S. Baker, and D. Greising, "Go-Go Goliaths," *BusinessWeek,* February 13, 1995, 64–70.

109. "Stock Option," *Encarta World English Dictionary,* June 28, 2001 (www.dictionary .msn.com); personal interview with Professor Bala Dharan, Jones Graduate School of Business, Rice University, June 28, 2001.

110. Personal interview with Professor Bala Dharan.

111. Ibid.

112. A. J. Michels, "Dallas Semiconductor," *Fortune,* May 16, 1994, 81.

113. M. Betts, "Big Things Come in Small Buttons," *Computerworld,* August 3, 1992, 30.

114. M. Boslet, "Metal Buttons Toted by Crop Pickers Act as Mini Databases," *The Wall Street Journal,* June 1, 1994, B3.

115. C. D. Fisher, L. F. Schoenfeldt, and J. B. Shaw, *Human Resource Management* (Boston: Houghton Mifflin, 1990); B. E. Graham-Moore and T. L. Ross, *Productivity Gainsharing* (Englewood Cliffs, NJ: Prentice-Hall, 1983); A. J. Geare, "Productivity from Scanlon Type Plans," *Academy of Management Review* 1 (1976), 99–108.

116. J. Labate, "Deal Those Workers In," *Fortune,* April 19, 1993, 26.

117. K. Belson, "Japan's Net Generation," *BusinessWeek,* March 19, 2001 (*BusinessWeek* Archives, June 27, 2001).

118. K. Belson, "Taking a Hint from the Upstarts," *BusinessWeek,* March 19, 2001 (*BusinessWeek* Archives, June 27, 2001); "Going for the Gold," *BusinessWeek,* March 19, 2001 (*BusinessWeek* Archives, June 27, 2001); "What the Government Can Do to Promote a Flexible Workforce," *BusinessWeek,* March 19, 2001 (*BusinessWeek* Archives, June 27, 2001).

Chapter 14

1. T. Lowry, "Can MTV Stay Cool?" *Business Week,* February 20, 2006, 51–60; "Senior Management," *VIACOM,* www. viacom.com/aboutviacom/Pages/ seniormanagement.aspx, April 2, 2008.

2. www.viacom.com/2006/pdf/ Viacom_Fact_Sheet_4_5_06.pdf, June 9, 2006; M. Gunther, "Mr. MTV Grows Up," CNNMoney.com, April 13, 2006 (http://money.cnn.com/magazines/fortune/

fortune_archive/2006/04/17/8374305/ index.htm); "Viacom Completes Separation into CBS Corporation and 'New' Viacom," Viacom.com, January 1, 2006 (www. viacom.com/view_release.jhtml?inID= 10000040&inReleaseID=126683).

3. Lowry, "Can MTV Stay Cool?"; "VIACOM," *PULSE,* February 28, 2008, Fourth Quarter, 1, www.viacom.com/ investorrelations/investor_relations_docs/ pulse%20Q42007%20Final.pdf, April 2, 2008.

4. J. H. Higgins, "A Rockin' Role: McGrath Keeps MTV Networks Plugged In and Focused," www.broadcastingcable.com, April 10, 2006 (www.broadcastingcable .com/article/CA6323342.html?display= Search+Results&text=judy+mcgrath); "FORTUNE 50 Most Powerful Women in Business 2005," CNNMoney.com, November 14, 2005 (http://money.cnn.com/ magazines/fortune/ mostpowerfulwomen/ snapshots/10.html); E. Levenson, "Hall of Fame: Digging a Little Deeper into the List, We Salute the Highfliers and Share Some Facts to Inspire and Amuse," CNNMoney .com, November 14, 2005 (http:// money .cnn.com/magazines/fortune/fortune_ archive/2005/11/14/8360698/index.html); "50 Most Powerful Women 2007: The Power 50," *CNNMoney.com, Fortune,* The Power 50–Judy McGrath (18)–FORTUNE, http://money.cnn.com/galleries/2007/ fortune/0709/gallery.women_mostpowerful .fortune/18. . ., April 2, 2008.

5. Lowry, "Can MTV Stay Cool?"; "Welcome to Viacom–Senior Management," www.viacom.com/management .jhtml, June 9, 2006.

6. Lowry, "Can MTV Stay Cool?"

7. Ibid.

8. "The 2006 National Show Mobile Edition–Judy McGrath," www. thenationalshoe. com/Mobile/Speaker Detail.aspx?ID=199, June 9, 2006.

9. Lowry, "Can MTV Stay Cool?"

10. "Real World XX: Hollywood / Main," Real World XX: Hollywood / Show Cast, Episode Guides, Trailers, Aftershow & Preview. . ., www.mtv.com/ontv/dyn/real-world-season20/series.jhtml, April 2, 2008.

11. Lowry, "Can MTV Stay Cool?"; "Viacom's MTV Networks Completes Acquisition of Xfire, Inc.," www.viacom.com/ view_release.jhtml?inID= 10000040&in ReleaseID=227008, June 9, 2006.

12. "MTV Networks Unveils URGE Digital Music Service on Microsoft's New Windows Media Player 11 Platform," *Microsoft,* May 17, 2006 (www.microsoft.com/presspass/ press/ 2006/may06/05-17URGEPR.mspx).

13. Lowry, "Can MTV Stay Cool?"

14. Ibid.

15. G. Yukl, *Leadership in Organizations,* 2d ed. (New York: Academic Press, 1989);

R. M. Stogdill, *Handbook of Leadership: A Survey of the Literature* (New York: Free Press, 1974).

16. Lowry, "Can MTV Stay Cool?"

17. W. D. Spangler, R. J. House, and R. Palrecha, "Personality and Leadership," in B. Schneider and D. B. Smith, eds., *Personality and Organizations* (Mahwah, NJ: Lawrence Erlbaum, 2004), 251–90.

18. Ibid; "Leaders vs. Managers: Leaders Master the Context of Their Mission, Managers Surrender to It," www.msue. msu.edu/ msue/imp/modtd/visuals/tsld029.htm, July 28, 2004; *"Leadership,"* Leadership Center at Washington State University; M. Maccoby, "Understanding the Difference Between Management and Leadership," *Research Technology Mangement* 43, no. 1 (January–February 2000), 57–59 (www.maccoby.com/ articles/UtDBMaL.html); P. Coutts, "Leadership vs. Management," www.telusplanet. net/public/pdcoutts/leadership/LdrVsMgnt. htm, October 1, 2000; S. Robbins, "The Difference Between Managing and Leading," www.Entrepreneur.com/ article/ 0,4621,304743,00.html, November 18, 2002; W. Bennis, "The Leadership Advantage," *Leader to Leader* 12 (Spring 1999) (www.pfdf.org/leaderbooks/121/spring99/ bennis/html).

19. Spangler et al., "Personality and Leadership"; "Leaders vs. Managers"; "Leadership"; Maccoby, "Understanding the Difference Between Management and Leadership"; Coutts, "Leadership vs. Management"; Robbins, "The Difference Between Managing and Leading"; Bennis, "The Leadership Advantage."

20. "Greenleaf: Center for Servant-Leadership: History," *Greenleaf Center for Servant-Leadership,* www.greenleaf.org/ aboutus/history.html, April 7, 2008.

21. "What Is Servant Leadership?" *Greenleaf: Center for Servant-Leadership,* http:// www.greenleaf.org/whatissl/index.html, April 2, 2008.

22. Ibid; Review by F. Hamilton of L. Spears and M. Lawrence, *Practicing Servant Leadership: Succeeding Through Trust, Bravery, and Forgiveness,* (San Francisco: Jossey-Bass 2004), in *Academy of Management Review* 30 (October 2005), 875–87; R. R. Washington, "Empirical Relationships Between Theories of Servant, Transformational, and Transactional Leadership," *Academy of Management,* Best Paper Proceedings 2007, 1–6.

23. "Greenleaf: Center for Servant-Leadership: History"; "What is Servant Leadership?"; "Greenleaf: Center for Servant-Leadership: Our Mission," *Greenleaf Center for Servant-Leadership,* www.greenleaf. org/aboutus/mission.html, April 7, 2008.

24. B. Burlingham, "The Coolest Small Company in America," *Inc. Magazine,* January 2003, www.inc.com/magazine/

20030101/25036_Printer_Friendly.html, April 7, 2008.

25. Ibid; "Zingerman's Community of Businesses," *About Us,* www.zingermans. com/AboutUs.aspx, April 7, 2008; L. Buchanan, "In Praise of Selflessness," *Inc. Magazine,* May 2007, 33–35.

26. Burlingham, "The Coolest Small Company in America"; "Zingerman's Community of Businesses"; Buchanan, "In Praise of Selflessness."

27. Buchanan, "In Praise of Selflessness."

28. Ibid.

29. Burlingham, "The Coolest Small Company in America"; "In a Nutshell," *food gatherers,* www.foodgatherers.org/about.htm, April 7, 2008.

30. "In a Nutshell."

31. Buchanan, "In Praise of Selflessness."

32. R. Calori and B. Dufour, "Management European Style," *Academy of Management Executive* 9, no. 3 (1995), 61–70.

33. Ibid.

34. H. Mintzberg, *Power in and Around Organizations* (Englewood Cliffs, NJ: Prentice-Hall, 1983); J. Pfeffer, *Power in Organizations* (Marshfield, MA: Pitman, 1981).

35. R. P. French, Jr., and B. Raven, "The Bases of Social Power," in D. Cartwright and A. F. Zander, eds., *Group Dynamics* (Evanston, IL: Row, Peterson, 1960), 607–23.

36. R. L. Rose, "After Turning Around Giddings and Lewis, Fife Is Turned Out Himself," *The Wall Street Journal,* June 22, 1993, A1.

37. E. Olson, "Adventures as a Team Sport," *The New York Times,* October 23, 2005, 9; "Investor Relations–Alaska Communications System: Board of Directors," *ACS,* March 20, 2006 (www.acsalaska.com/ ALSK/en-US/Board+of+Directors/ Liane+Pelletier.htm).

38. Olson, "Adventures as a Team Sport."

39. Ibid.

40. "Alaska's Premier Telecommunications Provider," ACS, *Alaska Communications Systems Group, Inc.,* Corporate Fact Sheet, www.acsalaska.com/NR/ rdonlyres/47628010-7ADO-42BF-9484 0A7AE7E008AD/01ACSfactsheet031708 .pdf, April 8, 2008; "People–Technology–Potential," *Alaska Communications Systems,* www.acsalaska.com/cultures/en-us/ corporate%20information, April 8, 2008.

41. "Investor Relations–Alaska Communications System."

42. "Alaska Communications," *Corporate Spotlight,* March 21, 2006 (www. redcoatpub lishingcom/spotlights/s1_08_05_Alaska.asp).

43. G. G. Marcial, "Heading North To Alaska Communications," *BusinessWeek Online,* June 27, 2005 (www.businessweek .com).

44. Olson, "Adventures as a Team Sport;" "Management Team," ACS, Alaska Communications Systems, www.acsalaska.com/ ALSK/en-US/Management+Team/, April 8, 2008.

45. A. Grove, "How Intel Makes Spending Pay Off," *Fortune,* February 22, 1993, 56–61; "Craig R. Barrett, Chief Executive Officer: Intel Corporation," *Intel,* July 28, 2004 (www.intel.com/pressroom/kits/bios/ barrett/bio.htm).

46. Craig R. Barrett Bio, www.intel. com/pressroom/kits/bios/barrett.htm, April 8, 2008; Microsoft Press Pass–Microsoft Board of Directors, www.microsoft.com/ presspass/bod/default.mspx, April 8, 2008; "Tachi Yamada Selected to Lead Gates Foundation's Global Health Program," Announcements–Bill & Melinda Gates Foundation, February 6, 2006, www. gatesfoundation.org/GlobalHealth/ Announcements/Announce-060106.htm, April 8, 2008.

47. M. Loeb, "Jack Welch Lets Fly on Budgets, Bonuses, and Buddy Boards," *Fortune,* May 29, 1995, 146.

48. T. M. Burton, "Visionary's Reward: Combine 'Simple Ideas' and Some Failures; Result: Sweet Revenge," *The Wall Street Journal,* February 3, 1995, A1, A5.

49. L. Nakarmi, "A Flying Leap Toward the 21st Century? Pressure from Competitors and Seoul May Transform the Chaebol," *BusinessWeek,* March 20, 1995, 78–80.

50. B. M. Bass, *Bass and Stogdill's Handbook of Leadership: Theory, Research, and Managerial Applications,* 3d ed. (New York: Free Press, 1990); R. J. House and M. L. Baetz, "Leadership: Some Empirical Generalizations and New Research Directions," in B. M. Staw and L. L. Cummings, eds., *Research in Organizational Behavior,* vol. 1 (Greenwich, CT: JAI Press, 1979), 341–423; S. A. Kirpatrick and E. A. Locke, "Leadership: Do Traits Matter?" *Academy of Management Executive* 5, no. 2 (1991), 48–60; Yukl, *Leadership in Organizations;* G. Yukl and D. D. Van Fleet, "Theory and Research on Leadership in Organizations," in M. D. Dunnette and L. M. Hough, eds., *Handbook of Industrial and Organizational Psychology,* 2d ed., vol. 3 (Palo Alto, CA: Consulting Psychologists Press, 1992), 147–97.

51. E. A. Fleishman, "Performance Assessment Based on an Empirically Derived Task Taxonomy," *Human Factors* 9 (1967), 349–66; E. A. Fleishman, "The Description of Supervisory Behavior," *Personnel Psychology* 37 (1953), 1–6; A. W. Halpin and B. J. Winer, "A Factorial Study of the Leader Behavior Descriptions," in R. M. Stogdill and A. I. Coons, eds., *Leader Behavior: Its Description and Measurement* (Columbus Bureau of Business Research, Ohio State University, 1957); D. Tscheulin,

"Leader Behavior Measurement in German Industry," *Journal of Applied Psychology* 56 (1971), 28–31.

52. S. Greenhouse, "How Costco Became the Anti-Wal-Mart," *The New York Times,* July 17, 2005, BU1, BU8; "Directors," *Costco Wholesale, Investors Relations,* http://phx.corporate-ir.net/phoenix. zhtml?c=83830&p=irol-govBoard, April 8, 2008.

53. "Corporate Governance," *Costco Wholesale Investor Relations,* April 28, 2006, (http://phx.corporate-ir.net/phoenix. zhtml?c=83830&p=irol-govhighlights).

54. Greenhouse, "How Costco Became the Anti-Wal-Mart."

55. Ibid.

56. Ibid.

57. Ibid; S. Clifford, "Because Who Knew a Big-Box Chain Could Have a Generous Soul," *INC. Magazine,* April 2005, 88.

58. S. Holmes and W. Zellner, "Commentary: The Costco Way," *BusinessWeek Online,* April 12, 2004 (www.businessweek.com/ print/magazine/content/04_15/b3878084_ mz021.htm?chan . . .); M. Herbst, "The Costco Challenge: An Alternative to Wal-Martization?" *LRA Online,* July 5, 2005 (www. laborresearch.org/print .php?id=391).

59. Greenhouse, "How Costco Became the Anti-Wal-Mart."

60. Ibid; "Company Profile," *Costco Wholesale, Investor Relations,* http://phx.corporate-ir .net/phoenix.zhtml?c=83830&p=irol-home profile, April 8, 2008.

61. "Costco Wholesale Corporation Reports Second Quarter and Year-to-Date Operating Results Fiscal 2006 and February Sales Results," *Costco Wholesale Investor Relations: News Release,* April 28, 2006 (http://phx. corporate-ir.net/phoenix .zhtml?c=83830& p=irol-newsArticle& ID=824344&highlight–), "Costco Wholesale Corporation Reports March Sales Results and Plans for Membership Fee Increase," *Costco Wholesale Investor Relations: News Release,* April 28, 2006 (http://phx .corporate-ir.net/phoenix.zhtml?c=83830& p=irol-newsArticle& ID=839605& highlight=); "Wal-Mart Stores Post Higher January Sales," *BusinessWeek Online,* February 2, 2006 (www.businessweek.com/ print/investor/conent/feb2006/ pi2006022_ 0732_pi004.htm).

62. E. A. Fleishman and E. F. Harris, "Patterns of Leadership Behavior Related to Employee Grievances and Turnover," *Personnel Psychology* 15 (1962), 43–56.

63. R. Likert, *New Patterns of Management* (New York: McGraw-Hill, 1961); N. C. Morse and E. Reimer, "The Experimental Change of a Major Organizational Variable," *Journal of Abnormal and Social Psychology* 52 (1956), 120–29.

64. R. R. Blake and J. S. Mouton, *The New Managerial Grid* (Houston: Gulf, 1978).

65. P. Hersey and K. Blanchard, *Management of Organizational Behavior: Utilizing Human Resources* (Englewood Cliffs, NJ: Prentice-Hall, 1982).

66. F. E. Fiedler, *A Theory of Leadership Effectiveness* (New York: McGraw-Hill, 1967); F. E. Fiedler, "The Contingency Model and the Dynamics of the Leadership Process," in L. Berkowitz, ed., *Advances in Experimental Social Psychology* (New York: Academic Press, 1978).

67. J. Rebello, "Radical Ways of Its CEO Are a Boon to Bank," *The Wall Street Journal,* March 20, 1995, B1, B3.

68. J. Fierman, "Winning Ideas from Maverick Managers," *Fortune,* February 6, 1995, 66–80.

69. Ibid; "Laybourne, Geraldine, U.S. Media Executive," *Laybourne, Geraldine,* http://museum.tv/archives/etv/L/htmlL/laybournege/laybournege.htm, April 8, 2008.

70. M. Schuman, "Free to Be," *Forbes,* May 8, 1995, 78–80; "Profile–Herman Mashaba," *SAIE–Herman Mashaba,* www.entrepreneurship.co.za/page/herman_mashaba, April 8, 2008.

71. House and Baetz, "Leadership"; L. H. Peters, D. D. Hartke, and J. T. Pohlmann, "Fiedler's Contingency Theory of Leadership: An Application of the Meta-Analysis Procedures of Schmidt and Hunter," *Psychological Bulletin* 97 (1985), 274–85; C. A. Schriesheim, B. J. Tepper, and L. A. Tetrault, "Least Preferred Co-Worker Score, Situational Control, and Leadership Effectiveness: A Meta-Analysis of Contingency Model Performance Predictions," *Journal of Applied Psychology* 79 (1994), 561–73.

72. M. G. Evans, "The Effects of Supervisory Behavior on the Path-Goal Relationship," *Organizational Behavior and Human Performance* 5 (1970), 277–98; R. J. House, "A Path-Goal Theory of Leader Effectiveness," *Administrative Science Quarterly* 16 (1971), 321–38; J. C. Wofford and L. Z. Liska, "Path-Goal Theories of Leadership: A Meta-Analysis," *Journal of Management* 19 (1993), 857–76.

73. S. Kerr and J. M. Jermier, "Substitutes for Leadership: Their Meaning and Measurement," *Organizational Behavior and Human Performance* 22 (1978), 375–403; P. M. Podsakoff, B. P. Niehoff, S. B. MacKenzie, and M. L. Williams, "Do Substitutes for Leadership Really Substitute for Leadership? An Empirical Examination of Kerr and Jermier's Situational Leadership Model," *Organizational Behavior and Human Decision Processes* 54 (1993), 1–44.

74. Kerr and Jermier, "Substitutes for Leadership"; Podsakoff et al., "Do Substitutes for Leadership Really Substitute for Leadership?"

75. J. Reingold, "You Got Served," *Fortune,* October 1, 2007, 55–58; "News on Women," *News On Women: Sue Nokes SVP at T-Mobile,* http://newsonwomen.typepad.com/news_on_women/2007/09/sue-nokes-svp-a.html, April 8, 2008.

76. "Company Information," *T-Mobile Cell Phone Carrier Quick Facts,* http://www.t-mobile/Company/CompanyInfo.aspx?tp=Abt_Tab_CompanyOverview, April 8, 2008.

77. Reingold, "You Got Served."

78. Ibid; "Company Information," *Highest customer satisfaction & wireless call quality –J.D. Power Awards,* http://www.t-mobile.com/Company/CompanyInfo.aspx?tp=Abt_Tab_Awards, April 8, 2008.

79. Reingold, "You Got Served."

80. Ibid.

81. B. M. Bass, *Leadership and Performance Beyond Expectations* (New York: Free Press, 1985); Bass, *Bass and Stogdill's Handbook of Leadership;* Yukl and Van Fleet, "Theory and Research on Leadership."

82. Reingold, "You Got Served."

83. Ibid.

84. Ibid.

85. Ibid.

86. Ibid.

87. Ibid.

88. J. A. Conger and R. N. Kanungo, "Behavioral Dimensions of Charismatic Leadership," in J. A. Conger, R. N. Kanungo, and Associates, *Charismatic Leadership* (San Francisco: Jossey-Bass, 1988).

89. Bass, *Leadership and Performance Beyond Expectations;* Bass, *Bass and Stogdill's Handbook of Leadership;* Yukl and Van Fleet, "Theory and Research on Leadership;" Reingold, "You Got Served."

90. Bass, *Leadership and Performance Beyond Expectations;* Bass, *Bass and Stogdill's Handbook of Leadership;* Yukl and Van Fleet, "Theory and Research on Leadership."

91. Reingold, "You Got Served."

92. Bass, *Leadership and Performance Beyond Expectations.*

93. Bass, *Bass and Stogdill's Handbook of Leadership;* B. M. Bass and B. J. Avolio, "Transformational Leadership: A Response to Critiques," in M. M. Chemers and R. Ayman, eds., *Leadership Theory and Research: Perspectives and Directions* (San Diego: Academic Press, 1993), 49–80; B. M. Bass, B. J. Avolio, and L. Goodheim, "Biography and the Assessment of Transformational Leadership at the World Class Level," *Journal of Management* 13 (1987), 7–20; J. J. Hater and B. M. Bass, "Supervisors Evaluations and Subordinates' Perceptions of Transformational and Transactional Leadership," *Journal of Applied Psychology* 73, (1988), 695–702; R. Pillai, "Crisis and Emergence of Charismatic Leadership in Groups: An Experimental Investigation," *Journal of Applied Psychology* 26 (1996), 543–62; J. Seltzer and B. M. Bass, "Transformational Leadership: Beyond Initiation and Consideration," *Journal of Management* 16 (1990), 693–703; D. A. Waldman, B. M. Bass, and W. O. Einstein, "Effort, Performance, Transformational Leadership in Industrial and Military Service," *Journal of Occupation Psychology* 60 (1987), 1–10.

94. R. Pillai, C. A. Schriesheim, and E. S. Williams, "Fairness Perceptions and Trust as Mediators of Transformational and Transactional Leadership: A Two-Sample Study," *Journal of Management* 25 (1999), 897–933.

95. L. Tischler, "Where Are the Women?" *Fast Company,* February 2004, 52–60.

96. "2000 Catalyst Census of Women Corporate Officers and Top Earners of the Fortune 500," www.catalystwomen.org, October 21, 2001; S. Wellington, M. Brumit Kropf, and P. R. Gerkovich, "What's Holding Women Back?" *Harvard Business Review,* June 2003, 18–19; D. Jones, "The Gender Factor," *USA Today.com,* December 30, 2003; "2002 Catalyst Census of Women Corporate Officers and Top Earners in the Fortune 500," www.catalystwomen.org, August 17, 2004; "2007 Catalyst Census of Women Corporate Officers and Top Earners of the Fortune 500," www.catalyst.org/knowledge/titles/title/php?page=cen_COTE_07, February 8, 2008.

97. A. H. Eagly and B. T. Johnson, "Gender and Leadership Style: A Meta-Analysis," *Psychological Bulletin* 108 (1990), 233–56.

98. Ibid.

99. The Economist, "Workers Resent Scoldings from Female Bosses," *Houston Chronicle,* August 19, 2000, 1C.

100. Ibid.

101. Ibid.

102. Ibid.

103. A. H. Eagly, S. J. Karau, and M. G. Makhijani, "Gender and the Effectiveness of Leaders: A Meta-Analysis," *Psychological Bulletin* 117 (1995), 125–45.

104. Ibid.

105. J. M. George and K. Bettenhausen, "Understanding Prosocial Behavior, Sales Performance, and Turnover: A Group-Level Analysis in a Service Context," *Journal of Applied Psychology* 75 (1990), 698–709.

106. T. Sy, S. Cote, and R. Saavedra, "The Contagious Leader: Impact of the Leader's Mood on the Mood of Group Members, Group Affective Tone, and Group Processes," *Journal of Applied Psychology* 90(2), (2005), 295–305.

107. J. M. George, "Emotions and Leadership: The Role of Emotional Intelligence," *Human Relations* 53 (2000), 1027–55.

108. Ibid.

109. J. Zhou and J. M. George, "Awakening Employee Creativity: The Role of Leader Emotional Intelligence," *The Leadership Quarterly* 14, no. 45 (August–October 2003), 545–68.

110. Ibid.

111. Ibid.

112. D. Fenn, "My Bad," *Inc. Magazine,* October 2007, 37–38; "About Us," *Creative Display Solutions: About Us,* www.creative displaysolutions.com/pages/about/about .html, April 4, 2008.

113. Ibid.

114. Fenn, "My Bad."

115. Ibid.

116. Ibid.

117. Ibid.

118. Ibid.

119. Ibid; C. Mason-Draffen, "Inside Stories," "Feeling Like a Million," *Creative Display Solutions: CDS News,* www.creative displaysolutions.com/pages/about/news6 .html, April 4, 2008.

120. D. Sonnenberg, "Mother Load: How to Balance Career and Family," July 30, 2007, *Creative Display Solutions: CDS News,* www.creativedisplaysolutions.com/pages/ about/news8.html, April 4, 2008; C. Mason-Draffen, "Partnership at Work: Couples in Business Together Have Their Share of Sweet Rewards and Unique Challenges," February 13, 2007, *Creative Display Solutions, CDS News,* www.creative displaysolutions.com/pages/about/news7 .html, April 4, 2008; "Client List," *Creative Display Solutions: About Us,* www.creative displaysolutions.com/pages/about/clients .html, April 8, 2008; Fenn, "My Bad."

121. Fenn, "My Bad."

Chapter 15

1. "About ICU Medical, Inc.," www. icumed.com/about.asp, April 11, 2008.

2. Ibid.

3. "ICU Medical, Inc.–Fundamentals," http://phx.corporate-ir.net/phoenix. zhtml?c=86695&p=irol-fundamentals, April 11, 2008; "ICU Medical Inc. (ICUI): Stock Quote & Company Profile–Business Week, *Business Week,* http://investing .businessweek.com/research/stocks/ snapshot/snapshot_article.asp?symbol= . . . , April 11, 2008.

4. "ICU Medical, Inc.–Investor Relations Home," http://phx.corporate-ir.net/ phoenix.zhtml?c=86695&p=irol-IRHome, April 11, 2008.

5. "About ICU Medical, Inc.."

6. "Clave Connector," ICU Medical, Inc., www.icumend.com, April 11, 2008.

7. E. White, "How a Company Made Everyone a Team Player," *The Wall Street Journal,* August 13, 2007, B1, B7.

8. Ibid.

9. Ibid.

10. Ibid.

11. Ibid.

12. Ibid.

13. Ibid.

14. Ibid.

15. Ibid.

16. Ibid.

17. Ibid.

18. Ibid.

19. Ibid.

20. Ibid.

21. Ibid.

22. Ibid.

23. Ibid.

24. Ibid.

25. T. M. Mills, *The Sociology of Small Groups* (Englewood Cliffs, NJ: Prentice-Hall, 1967); M. E. Shaw, *Group Dynamics* (New York: McGraw-Hill, 1981).

26. White, "How a Company Made Everyone a Team Player,"

27. R. S. Buday, "Reengineering One Firm's Product Development and Another's Service Delivery," *Planning Review,* March–April 1993, 14–19; J. M. Burcke, "Hallmark's Quest for Quality Is a Job Never Done," *Business Insurance,* April 26, 1993, 122; M. Hammer and J. Champy, *Reengineering the Corporation* (New York: HarperBusiness, 1993); T. A. Stewart, "The Search for the Organization of Tomorrow," *Fortune,* May 18, 1992, 92–98.

28. T. Claburn, "Lockheed Finds a Way to Connect Questions with Answers," *InformationWeek,* June 14, 2004 (www. information-week.com/showArticle.jhtml?article ID=21700462); "About Us," www. lockheedmartin.com/wms/findPage.do? dsp=fec&ci=4&sc=400&prfr=true, June 19, 2006; "About Us," *Lockheed Martin,* www.lockheedmartin.com/cgi-bin/pfv.pl, April 17, 2008.

29. "Smart Organizations Choose Tacit," http://tacit.com/customers/index.html, June 19, 2006; "Tacit ActiveNet: A Powerful Way to Drive the Right Collaboration," http://tacit.com/products/index.html, June 19, 2006; "ActiveNet–Facilitating Real-Time Collaboration," *Software for Real-Time Collaboration,* www.tacit.com/products/ activenet/technology.html, April 17, 2008; "About Tacit," *Tacit Software–About Us,* www.tacit.com/company/about_tacit/index .html, April 17, 2008.

30. "Lockheed Martin Licenses Tacit to Network Space Systems Employees," www.

tacit.com/company/news/press/2004.05.24 .html. May, 24, 2004; "ActiveNet–Facilitating Real-Time Collaboration"; "About Tacit."

31. P. Kaihla, "The Matchmaker in the Machine," *Business 2.0,* February 2004, 52–55; "ActiveNet–Facilitating Real-Time Collaboration"; "About Tacit."

32. Claburn, "Lockheed Finds a Way to Connect Questions with Answers."

33. Kaihla, "The Matchmaker in the Machine"; "Northrop Grumman: About Us," www.northropgrumman.com/about_us/ about_us.html, June 19, 2006; "About Us," *Northrop Grumman,* www.northropgrumman .com/about_us/index.html, April 17, 2008.

34. Kaihla, "The Matchmaker in the Machine."

35. Ibid.

36. "Amazon.com Investor Relations: Officers & Directors," http://phx.corporate-ir .net/phoenix.zhtml?c=97664&p=irol-gov Manage, June 19, 2006; "Amazon.com Investor Relations: Press Release," http:// phx.corporate-ir.net/phoenix.zhtml? c=97664&p=irol-newsArticle&ID=110234 2&hi. . . , April 17, 2008.

37. A. Deutschman, "Inside the Mind of Jeff Bezos," *Fast Company,* August 2004, 50–58.

38. Ibid; "Amazon.com Digital Media Technology," http://media-server.amazon .com/jobs/jobs.html, June 19, 2006.

39. "Amazon.com: Kindle: Amazon's New Wireless Reading Device: Kindle Store," www.amazon.com/gp/product/ B000F173MA/ref=amb_link_6369712_2? pf_rd_m=A. . ., April 17, 2008.

40. Deutschman, "Inside the Mind of Jeff Bezos."

41. "Online Extra: Jeff Bezos on Word-of-Mouth Power," *BusinessWeek Online,* August 2, 2004 (www.businessweek.com); R. D. Hof, "Reprogramming Amazon," *BusinessWeek Online,* December 22, 2003 (www. businessweek.com); "About Amazon .com: Company Information," www.amazon .com/ exec/obidos/tg/browsw/-/574562/ 104-0138839-3693547, June 19, 2006; "Amazon.com Investor Relations: Press Release."

42. "RockBottom Restaurants," www. rockbottom.com/RockBottomWeb/RBR/ index.aspx?PageName=/RockBottom. . ., April 15, 2008.

43. S. Dallas, "Rock Bottom Restaurants: Brewing Up Solid Profits," *BusinessWeek,* May 22, 1995, 74.

44. J. A. Pearce II and E. C. Ravlin, "The Design and Activation of Self-Regulating Work Groups," *Human Relations* 11 (1987), 751–82.

45. B. Dumaine, "Who Needs a Boss?" *Fortune,* May 7, 1990, 52–60; Pearce and Ravlin, "The Design and Activation of Self-Regulating Work Groups."

46. Dumaine, "Who Needs a Boss"; A. R. Montebello and V. R. Buzzotta, "Work Teams That Work," *Training and Development,* March 1993, 59–64.

47. C. Matlack, R. Tiplady, D. Brady, R. Berner, and H. Tashiro, "The Vuitton Machine," *BusinessWeek,* March 22, 2004, 98–102; "America's Most Admired Companies," *Fortune.com,* August 18, 2004 (www.fortune.com/fortune/mostadmired/snapshot/0,15020,383,00.html); "Art Samberg's Ode to Steel," *Big Money Weekly,* June 29, 2004 (http://trading.sina/com/trading/rightside/bigmoney_weekly_040629.b5.shtml); "Nucor Reports Record Results for First Quarter of 2004," www.nucor.com/financials.asp?finpage=news releases, August 18, 2004; "Nucor Reports Results for First Half and Second Quarter of 2004," www.nucor.com/financials.asp?finpage=newsreleases; J. C. Cooper, "The Price of Efficiency," *BusinessWeek Online,* March 22, 2004 (www.businessweek.com/magazine/content/04_12/b3875603.htm); "LVHM–Fashion & Leather Goods," www.lvmh.com, June 18, 2006; C. Matlack, "Rich Times for the Luxury Sector," *BusinessWeek Online,* March 6, 2006 (www.businessweek.com/globalbiz/content/mar2006/gb20060306_296309.htm?campaign_id=search); N. Byrnes, "The Art of Motivation," *BusinessWeek,* May 1, 2006, 56–62; "Nucor Steel," http://www.nucor.com/indexinner.aspx?finpage=aboutus, April 16, 2008; "Annual General Meetings–Group Investor Relations–Corporate Governance," http://www.lvmh.com/comfi/pg_home.asp?rub=6&srub=0, March 16, 2008.

48. C. Matlack et al., "The Vuitton Machine."

49. M. Arndt, "Out of the Forge and into the Fire," *BusinessWeek,* June 18, 2001 (*BusinessWeek* Archives); N. Byrnes, "The Art of Motivation," *BusinessWeek,* May 1, 2006, 56–62.

50. S. Baker, "The Minimill That Acts like a Biggie," *BusinessWeek,* September 30, 1996, 101–104; S. Baker, "Nucor," *BusinessWeek* February 13, 1995, 70; S. Overman, "No-Frills at Nucor," *HRMagazine,* July 1994, 56–60.

51. www.nucor.com, November 21, 2001; "Nucor: About Us."

52. Baker, "The Minimill That Acts like a Biggie"; Baker, "Nucor"; Overman, "No-Frills at Nucor"; www.nucor.com; Byrnes, "The Art of Motivation"; "Nucor: About Us."

53. Matlack et al., "The Vuitton Machine"; "About Nucor"; "America's Most Admired Companies"; "Art Samberg's Ode to Steel"; "Nucor Reports Record Results for First Quarter of 2004"; "Nucor Reports Results for First Half and Second Quarter of 2004"; Byrnes, "The Art of Motivation."

54. White, "How a Company Made Everyone a Team Player."

55. T. D. Wall, N. J. Kemp, P. R. Jackson, and C. W. Clegg, "Outcomes of Autonomous Work Groups: A Long-Term Field Experiment," *Academy of Management Journal* 29 (1986): 280–304.

56. A. Markels, "A Power Producer Is Intent on Giving Power to Its People," *The Wall Street Journal,* July 3, 1995, A1, A12; "AES Corporation / The Power of Being Global," www.aes.com/aes/index?page=home, April 15, 2008.

57. J. S. Lublin, "My Colleague, My Boss," *The Wall Street Journal,* April 12, 1995, R4, R12.

58. W. R. Pape, "Group Insurance," *Inc. Magazine* (Technology Supplement), June 17, 1997, 29–31; A. M. Townsend, S. M. DeMarie, and A. R. Hendrickson, "Are You Ready for Virtual Teams?" *HRMagazine,* September 1996, 122–126; A. M. Townsend, S. M. DeMarie, and A. M. Hendrickson, "Virtual Teams: Technology and the Workplace of the Future," *Academy of Management Executive* (1998) 12, no. 3, 17–29.

59. Townsend et al., "Virtual Teams."

60. Pape, "Group Insurance"; Townsend et al., "Are You Ready for Virtual Teams?"; L. Gratton, "Working Together . . . When Apart," *The Wall Street Journal,* June 16–17, 2007, R4.

61. D. L. Duarte and N. T. Snyder, *Mastering Virtual Teams* (San Francisco: Jossey-Bass, 1999); K. A. Karl, "Book Reviews: *Mastering Virtual Teams,*" *Academy of Management Executive,* August 1999, 118–19.

62. B. Geber, "Virtual Teams," *Training* 32, no. 4 (August 1995), 36–40; T. Finholt and L. S. Sproull, "Electronic Groups at Work," *Organization Science* 1 (1990), 41–64.

63. Geber, "Virtual Teams."

64. E. J. Hill, B. C. Miller, S. P. Weiner, and J. Colihan, "Influences of the Virtual Office on Aspects of Work and Work/Life Balance," *Personnel Psychology* 31 (1998), 667–83; S. G. Strauss, "Technology, Group Process, and Group Outcomes: Testing the Connections in Computer-Mediated and Face-to-Face Groups," *Human Computer Interaction,* 12 (1997), 227–66; M. E. Warkentin, L. Sayeed, and R. Hightower, "Virtual Teams versus Face-to-Face Teams: An Exploratory Study of a Web-based Conference System," *Decision Sciences* 28, no. 4 (Fall 1997), 975–96.

65. S. A. Furst, M. Reeves, B. Rosen, and R. S. Blackburn, "Managing the Life Cycle of Virtual Teams," *Academy of Management Executive* 18, no. 2 (May 2004), 6–20.

66. Ibid.

67. Gratton, "Working Together . . . When Apart."

68. Ibid.

69. Ibid.

70. Ibid.

71. White, "How a Company Made Everyone a Team Player."

72. A. Deutschman, "The Managing Wisdom of High-Tech Superstars," *Fortune,* October 17, 1994, 197–206.

73. J. D. Thompson, *Organizations in Action* (New York: McGraw-Hill, 1967).

74. Ibid.

75. Lublin, "My Colleague, My Boss."

76. White, "How a Company Made Everyone a Team Player."

77. R. G. LeFauve and A. C. Hax, "Managerial and Technological Innovations at Saturn Corporation," *MIT Management,* Spring 1992, 8–19.

78. B. W. Tuckman, "Developmental Sequences in Small Groups," *Psychological Bulletin* 63 (1965), 384–99; B. W. Tuckman and M. C. Jensen, "Stages of Small Group Development," *Group and Organizational Studies* 2 (1977), 419–27.

79. C. J. G. Gersick, "Time and Transition in Work Teams: Toward a New Model of Group Development," *Academy of Management Journal* 31 (1988), 9–41; C. J. G. Gersick, "Marking Time: Predictable Transitions in Task Groups," *Academy of Management Journal* 32 (1989), 274–309.

80. J. R. Hackman, "Group Influences on Individuals in Organizations," in M. D. Dunnette and L. M. Hough, eds., *Handbook of Industrial and Organizational Psychology,* 2d ed., vol. 3 (Palo Alto, CA: Consulting Psychologists Press, 1992), 199–267.

81. Ibid.

82. Ibid.

83. Lublin, "My Colleague, My Boss."

84. T. Kelley and J. Littman, *The Art of Innovation* (New York: Doubleday, 2001); "ideo.com: Our Work," www.ideo.com/portfolio, June 19, 2006.

85. B. Nussbaum, "The Power of Design," *BusinessWeek,* May 17, 2004, 86–94; "ideo.com: About Us: Teams," www.ideo.com/about/index.asp?x=1&y=1, June 19, 2006.

86. Ibid; "ideo.com: About Us: Teams," www.ideo.com/about/index.asp?x=1&y=1, April 18, 2008;

87. Nussbaum, "The Power of Design."

88. Kelley and Littman, *The Art of Innovation.*

89. Ibid; www.ideo.com; "1999 Idea Winners," *BusinessWeek,* June 7, 1999 (*BusinessWeek* Archives).

90. Nussbaum, "The Power of Design; "ideo.com: About Us: Teams."

91. L. Festinger, "Informal Social Communication," *Psychological Review* 57 (1950), 271–82; Shaw, *Group Dynamics.*

92. Hackman, "Group Influences on Individuals in Organizations"; Shaw, *Group Dynamics.*

93. D. Cartwright, "The Nature of Group Cohesiveness," in D. Cartwright and A. Zander, eds., *Group Dynamics,* 3d ed. (New York: Harper & Row, 1968); L. Festinger, S. Schacter, and K. Black, *Social Pressures in Informal Groups* (New York: Harper & Row, 1950); Shaw, *Group Dynamics.*

94. T. F. O'Boyle, "A Manufacturer Grows Efficient by Soliciting Ideas from Employees," *The Wall Street Journal,* June 5, 1992, A1, A5.

95. White, "How a Company Made Everyone a Team Player."

96. Lublin, "My Colleague, My Boss."

97. Kelley and Littman, "The Art of Innovation," 93.

98. Kelley and Littman, "The Art of Innovation."

99. "Shared Commitment," www.valero .com/Work/SharedCommitment.htm, April 18, 2008.

100. R. Levering and M. Moskowitz, "100 Best Companies to Work For: The Rankings," *Fortune,* February 4, 2008, 75–94.

101. J. Guyon, "The Soul of a Moneymaking Machine," *Fortune,* October 3, 2005, 113–20.

102. Ibid.

103. Ibid.

104. Ibid.

105. P. C. Earley, "Social Loafing and Collectivism: A Comparison of the United States and the People's Republic of China," *Administrative Science Quarterly* 34 (1989), 565–81; J. M. George, "Extrinsic and Intrinsic Origins of Perceived Social Loafing in Organizations," *Academy of Management Journal* 35 (1992), 191–202; S. G. Harkins, B. Latane, and K. Williams, "Social Loafing: Allocating Effort or Taking It Easy," *Journal of Experimental Social Psychology* 16 (1980), 457–65; B. Latane, K. D. Williams, and S. Harkins, "Many Hands Make Light the Work: The Causes and Consequences of Social Loafing," *Journal of Personality and Social Psychology* 37 (1979), 822–32; J. A. Shepperd, "Productivity Loss in Performance Groups: A Motivation Analysis," *Psychological Bulletin* 113 (1993), 67–81.

106. George, "Extrinsic and Intrinsic Origins"; G. R. Jones, "Task Visibility, Free Riding, and Shirking: Explaining the Effect of Structure and Technology on Employee Behavior," *Academy of Management Review* 9 (1984), 684–95; K. Williams, S. Harkins, and B. Latane, "Identifiability as a Deterrent to Social Loafing: Two Cheering Experiments," *Journal of Personality and Social Psychology* 40 (1981), 303–11.

107. S. Harkins and J. Jackson, "The Role of Evaluation in Eliminating Social Loafing," *Personality and Social Psychology Bulletin* 11 (1985), 457–65; N. L. Kerr and S. E. Bruun, "Ringelman Revisited: Alternative Explanations for the Social Loafing Effect," *Personality and Social Psychology Bulletin* 7 (1981), 224–31; Williams et al., "Identifiability as a Deterrent to Social Loafing"; Harkins and Jackson, "The Role of Evaluation in Eliminating Social Loafing"; Kerr and Bruun, "Ringelman Revisited."

108. M. A. Brickner, S. G. Harkins, and T. M. Ostrom, "Effects of Personal Involvement: Thought-Provoking Implications for Social Loafing," *Journal of Personality and Social Psychology* 51 (1986), 763–69; S. G. Harkins and R. E. Petty, "The Effects of Task Difficulty and Task Uniqueness on Social Loafing," *Journal of Personality and Social Psychology* 43 (1982), 1214–29.

109. B. Latane, "Responsibility and Effort in Organizations," in P. S. Goodman, ed., *Designing Effective Work Groups* (San Francisco: Jossey-Bass, 1986); Latane et al., "Many Hands Make Light the Work"; I. D. Steiner, *Group Process and Productivity* (New York: Academic Press, 1972).

Chapter 16

1. C. Hymowitz, "Sometimes, Moving Up Makes It Harder to See What Goes On Below," *The Wall Street Journal,* October 15, 2007, B1.

2. Ibid; J. Sandberg, "Shooting Messengers Makes Us Feel Better but Work Dumber," *The Wall Street Journal,* September 11, 2007, B1.

3. Hymowitz, "Sometimes, Moving Up Makes It Harder to See What Goes On Below"; "FatWire Software Appoints Former CA Executive Yogesh Gupta President and CEO," http://news.manta.com/press/description/200708070500230_66132700_1-0304, April 23, 2008.

4. Hymowitz, "Sometimes, Moving Up Makes It Harder to See What Goes On Below"; "FatWire Corporation," *FatWire Corporation: Private Company Information–Business Week,* http://investing.business week.com/businessweek/research/stocks/private/snapshot.asp?priv. . . , April 23, 2008; "Customers," *FatWire US: Customers–Customer Overview,* www.fatwire.com/cs/Satellite/CustomerOverviewPage_US.html, April 24, 2008; "Case Studies," *FatWire US: Customers–Case Studies,* www.fatwire.com/cs/Satellite/CustomerCaseStudiesPage_US .html, April 24, 2008; "FatWire Software Reports Record Growth," March 3, 2008, *FatWire Software,* www.fatwire.com/cs/Satellite?c=FW_C&cid=1202240759097&pagename=FW%2F. . . , April 23, 2008; "Company Overview," *FatWire U.S.: Company–Company Overview,* www.fatwire .com/cs/Satellite/CompanyOVPage_US .html, April 23, 2008.

5. "Management," *FatWire US: Company–Management,* www.fatwire.com/cs/Satellite/ManagementPage_US.html, April 23, 2008; "Company Overview," *Company Overview–CA,* www.ca.com/us/ca .aspx, April 24, 2008.

6. Hymowitz, "Sometimes, Moving Up Makes It Harder to See What Goes On Below."

7. Ibid.

8. Ibid.

9. K. Holland, "The Silent May Have Something to Say," *The New York Times,* November 5, 2006, http://www.nytimes .com/2006/11/05/business/yourmoney/05mgmt.html, June 29, 2008.

10. Ibid.

11. Ibid.

12. Ibid.

13. E. White, "How Surveying Workers Can Pay Off," *The Wall Street Journal,* June 18, 2007, B3.

14. Ibid.

15. Hymowitz, "Sometimes, Moving Up Makes It Harder to See What Goes On Below."

16. C. A. O'Reilly and L. R. Pondy, "Organizational Communication," in S. Kerr, ed., *Organizational Behavior* (Columbus, OH: Grid, 1979).

17. "World's First Volume Computed Tomography (VCT) System, Developed by GE Healthcare, Scanning Patients at Froedtert," www.gehealthcare.com/company/pressroom/releases/pr_release_9722.html, June 18, 2004; "GE Healthcare Fact Sheet," *GE Healthcare Worldwide,* June 20, 2006 (www.gehealthcare.com/about/ge_factsheet.html); WTN News, "GE Healthcare Names New CEO," *Wisconsin Technology Network,* January 25, 2006 (http://wistechnology.com/printarticle.php?id=2639), June 20, 2006; "About GE Healthcare," *GE Healthcare-Brochure–About GE Healthcare,* www.gehealthcare.com/usen/about/about.html, April 25, 2008.

18. S. Kirsner, "Time [Zone] Travelers," *Fast Company,* August 2004, 60–66; "Light-Speed VCT Series," *GE Healthcare Worldwide,* June 20, 2006 (www.gehealthcare .com/usen/ct/products/vct.html).

19. "New CT Scanner by GE Healthcare Advances Imaging Technology," *Wisconsin Technology Network,* June 21, 2004 (www. wistechnology.com).

20. Kirsner, "Time [Zone] Travelers."

21. Ibid.

22. Ibid.

23. E. M. Rogers and R. Agarwala-Rogers, *Communication in Organizations* (New York: Free Press, 1976).

24. W. Nabers, "The New Corporate Uniforms," *Fortune,* November, 13, 1995, 132–56.

25. R. B. Schmitt, "Judges Try Curbing Lawyers' Body-Language Antics," *The Wall Street Journal,* September 11, 1997, B1, B7.

26. D. A. Adams, P. A. Todd, and R. R. Nelson, "A Comparative Evaluation of the Impact of Electronic and Voice Mail on Organizational Communication," *Information & Management* 24 (1993), 9–21.

27. R. Winslow, "Hospitals' Weak Systems Hurt Patients, Study Says," *The Wall Street Journal,* July 5, 1995, B1, B6.

28. B. Newman, "Global Chatter," *The Wall Street Journal,* March 22, 1995, A1, A15.

29. "Miscommunications Plague Pilots and Air-Traffic Controllers," *The Wall Street Journal,* August 22, 1995, A1.

30. P. Reinert, "Miscommunication Seen as Threat to Space Station," *Houston Chronicle,* September 24, 2003, 6A.

31. W. E. Leary, "NASA Report Says Problems Plague Space Station Program," *The New York Times,* February 28, 2004, A12.

32. R. L. Daft, R. H. Lengel, and L. K. Trevino, "Message Equivocality, Media Selection, and Manager Performance: Implications for Information Systems," *MIS Quarterly* 11 (1987), 355–66; R. L. Daft and R. H. Lengel, "Information Richness: A New Approach to Managerial Behavior and Organization Design," in B. M. Staw and L. L. Cummings, eds., *Research in Organizational Behavior* (Greenwich, CT: JAI Press, 1984).

33. R. L. Daft, *Organization Theory and Design* (St. Paul, MN: West, 1992).

34. "Lights, Camera, Meeting: Teleconferencing Becomes a Time-Saving Tool," *The Wall Street Journal,* February 21, 1995, A1.

35. Daft, *Organization Theory and Design.*

36. A. S. Wellner, "Lost in Translation", *Inc. Magazine,* September 2005, 37–38.

37. Ibid.

38. Ibid; R. McMillan, "Business Communication Expert and *New York Times* Bestselling Author," www.vitalsmarts.com, June 20, 2006.

39. Wellner, "Lost in Translation."

40. Ibid.

41. Ibid; S. Roberts, "Sara Roberts, President, Roberts Golden Consulting–Biographies," www.robertsgolden.com/bios.html, June 20, 2006; "Roberts Golden Consulting," www.robertsgolden.com, June 20, 2006.

42. Wellner, "Lost in Translation."

43. S. Shellenbarger, "A Day without Email is Like . . . ," *The Wall Street Journal,* October 11, 2007, D1, D2; D. Brady, "*!#?@ the E-Mail. Can we Talk?" *Business Week,* December 4, 2006, 109.

44. T. J. Peters and R. H. Waterman, Jr., *In Search of Excellence* (New York: Harper & Row, 1982); T. Peters and N. Austin, *A Passion for Excellence: The Leadership Difference* (New York: Random House, 1985).

45. "Lights, Camera, Meeting."

46. R. Kirkland, "Cisco's Display of Strength," *Fortune,* November 12, 2007, 90–100; "Cisco TelePresence Overview," *Overview (TelePresence)– Cisco Systems,* www.cisco.com/en/US/solutions/ns669/networking_solutions_products_generic-cont . . . , April 25, 2008.

47. R. Kirkland, "Cisco's Display of Strength."

48. Ibid; "Cisco TelePresence Overview."

49. Hymowitz, "Missing from Work."

50. D. Beizer, "Email Is Dead . . .," *Fast Company,* July–August 2007, 46; The Radicati Group, Inc., www.radicati.com, April 28, 2008.

51. J. Sandberg, "Employees Forsake Dreaded Email for the Beloved Phone," *The Wall Street Journal,* September 26, 2006, B1.

52. Beizer, "Email Is Dead . . ."

53. Sandberg, "Employees Forsake Dreaded Email for the Beloved Phone."

54. Ibid.

55. K. Byron, "Carrying Too Heavy a Load? The Communication and Miscommunication of Emotion by Email," *Academy of Management Review* 33, no. 2 (2008), 309–27.

56. "There's a Message in Every Email," *Fast Company,* September 2007, 43; Byron, "Carrying Too Heavy a Load? The Communication and Miscommunication of Emotion by Email."

57. Ibid.

58. "Telecommuters Bring Home Work and Broadband," www.emarketer.com/Article.aspx?1002943, July 20, 2004; "Annual Survey Shows Americans Are Working from Many Different Locations Outside Their Employer's Office," *International Telework Association & Council,* May 10, 2006 (www.workingfromanywhere.org/news); "Itac, the Telework Advisory Group for WorldatWork," www.workingfromanywhere. org, May 10, 2006; "Virtual Business Owners Community–FAQ Center: Telecommuting/ Telework," www.vsscyberoffice.com/vfaq/ 25.html, May 10, 2006.

59. E. Baig, "Taking Care of Business–Without Leaving the House," *BusinessWeek,* April 17, 1995, 106–07.

60. "Life Is Good for Telecommuters, but Some Problems Persist," *The Wall Street Journal,* August 3, 1995, A1.

61. "E-Mail Abuse: Workers Discover High-Tech Ways to Cause Trouble in the Office," *The Wall Street Journal,* November 22, 1994, A1; "E Mail Alert: Companies Lag in Devising Policies on How It Should Be Used," *The Wall Street Journal,* December 29, 1994, A1.

62. Wellner, "Lost in Translation."

63. "The Most Important Part of an E-mail System Isn't the Software. It's the Rules You Make About Using It," *Inc. Magazine,* October 2005, 119–22.

64. Ibid.

65. Ibid.

66. American Management Association and the ePolicy Institute's Nancy Flynn, "2004 Workplace E-Mail and Instant Messaging Survey Summary," www.amanet.org, 2004; "2007 Electronic Monitoring & Surveillance Survey," *AMA/ePolicy Institute Research, American Management Association,* 2008.

67. J. Tyson, "How Instant Messaging Works," computer.howstuffworks.com, August 23, 2004.

68. "Study: Workers Are Surfing on Company Time," www.medialifemagazine.com/news2004/may04/may03/3_wed/news8wednesday.html, May 5, 2004; "Company Profile," *Websense,* www.websense.com/global/en/AboutWebsense/, April 25, 2008.

69. "Study: Workers Are Surfing on Company Time."

70. Ibid.

71. ClikZ Stats staff, "U.S. Web Usage and Traffic, July 2004," www.clickz.com/stats/big_picture/traffic_patterns/article.php/3395351, August 23, 2004.

72. L. Conley, "The Privacy Arms Race," *Fast Company,* July 2004, 27–28; "Migrating to Microsoft Exchange . . . or Another Mail System?" www.stellarim.com, June 20, 2006; "About Stellar Technologies, Inc.," www.stellartechnologies.com/about_us.cfm, June 20, 2006.

73. Conley, "The Privacy Arms Race"; "2007 Electronic Monitoring & Surveillance Survey"; M. Villano, "The Risk Is All Yours in Office E-Mail," *The New York Times,* March 4, 2007, BU17.

74. "2007 Electronic Monitoring & Surveillance Survey."

75. J. Pfeffer, "It's Time to Start Trusting the Workforce," *Business 2.0,* December 2006, 68.

76. Conley, "The Privacy Arms Race."

77. "P & G Who We Are: Purpose, Values, and Principles," www.pg.com/company/ who_we_are/ppv.jhtml, August 25, 2004; L. Conley, "Refusing to Gamble on Privacy," *Fast Company,* July 2004 (http://pf.fastcompany.com/magazine/84.essay_hughes.html); "Who We Are," *P&G Global Operations,* June 20, 2006 (www.pg.com/company/ who_we_are/index.jhtml); "Company Who We Are," P&G, *PG.com–Who We Are,* www.pg.com/company/who_we_are/index.jhtml, April 28, 2008.

78. Conley, "The Privacy Arms Race."

79. J. O'Neil, "E-Mail Doesn't Lie (That Much)," *The New York Times,* March 2, 2004, D6.

80. "Employee-Newsletter Names Include the Good, the Bad, and the Boring," *The Wall Street Journal,* July 18, 1995, A1.

81. W. M. Bulkeley, "Playing Well with Others," *The Wall Street Journal,* June 18, 2007, R10.

82. E. White, J. S. Lublin, and D. Kesmodel, "Executives Get the Blogging Bug," *The Wall Street Journal,* July 13, 2007, B1, B2.

83. *Blog–Wikipedia, the free encyclopedia,* http://en.wikipedia.org/wiki/Blog, April 28, 2008; E. White et al., "Executives Get the Blogging Bug."

84. Ibid; GM FastLane Blog: Lutz Biography, http://fastlane.gmblogs.com/archives/2005/01/lutz_biography_1.html, April 28, 2008.

85. "2006 Workplace E-Mail, Instant Messaging & Blog Survey: Bosses Battle Risk by Firing E-Mail, IM & Blog Violators," New York, July 11, 2006, *AMA Press Room,* http://press.amanet.org/press-releases/28/2006-workpklace-e-mail-instant-messaging-blog-s . . . April 28, 2008.

86. Bulkeley, "Playing Well with Others."

87. Ibid.

88. O. W. Baskin and C. E. Aronoff, *Interpersonal Communication in Organizations* (Santa Monica, CA: Goodyear, 1989).

89. T. Gutner, "Move Over, Bohemian Grove," *BusinessWeek,* February 19, 2001, 102.

90. "We've All Got Mail," *Newsweek,* May 15, 2001, 73K; "Diversity Deficit," *BusinessWeek Online,* May 14, 2001; "Dial-Up Users Converting to Broadband in Droves," www.emarketer.com/Article.aspx?1003009, August 23, 2004; "Top 20 Countries with the Highest Number of Internet Users," *Internet World Stats,* June 20, 2006 (www.internetworldstats.com/top20.htm); "Top 20 Countries with the Highest Number of Internet Users," *Internet World Stats,* Usage and Population Statistics, www.internetworldstats.com/top20.htm April 29, 2008.

91. "Top 15 Countries in Internet Usage, 2002," www.infoplease.com/ipa/A0908185.html, August 25, 2004; "Top 20 Countries with the Highest Number of Internet Users;" "Top 20 Countries with the Highest Number of Internet Users," *Internet World Stats,* Usage and Population Statistics, http://www.internetworldstats.com/top20.htm April 29, 2008.

92. J. Sandberg, "Internet's Popularity in North America Appears to Be Soaring," *The Wall Street Journal,* October 30, 1995, B2.

93. "How to Research Companies," *Oxford Knowledge Company,* www.oxford-knowledge.co.uk, September, 16, 2004.

94. "Survey: Denmark Is Web-Savviest Nation," *MSNBC.com,* April 19, 2004 (www.msnbc.msn.com/id/4779944/1/displaymode/1098); L. Grinsven, "U.S. Drops on Lists of Internet Savvy," *Houston Chronicle,* April 20, 2004, 6B.

95. M. J. Cronin, "Ford's Intranet Success," *Fortune,* March 30, 1998, 158;

M. J. Cronin, "Intranets Reach the Factory Floor," *Fortune,* June 10, 1997; A. L. Sprout, "The Internet Inside Your Company," *Fortune,* November 27, 1995, 161–68; J. B. White, "Chrysler's Intranet: Promise vs. Reality," *The Wall Street Journal,* May 13, 1997, B1, B6.

96. Ibid.

97. G. Rifkin, "A Skeptic's Guide to Groupware," *Forbes ASAP,* 1995, 76–91.

98. Ibid.

99. Ibid.

100. "Groupware Requires a Group Effort," *BusinessWeek,* June 26, 1995, 154.

101. M. Totty, "The Path to Better Teamwork," *The Wall Street Journal,* May 20, 2004, R4; "Collaborative Software," *Wikipedia,* August 25, 2004 (en.wikipedia.org/wiki/Collaborative_software); "Collaborative Groupware Software," www.svpal.org/~grantbow/groupware.html, August 25, 2004.

102. Totty, "The Path to Better Teamwork"; "Collaborative Software."

103. Ibid; "Collaborative Groupware Software."

104. Totty, "The Path to Better Teamwork"; "Collaborative Software."

105. Ibid.

106. Microsoft Windows SharePoint Services Developer Center, "Windows SharePoint Service," http://msdn.microsoft.com/sharepoint, June 21, 2006.

107. Totty, "The Path to Better Teamwork"; "Collaborative Software."

108. M. Conlin, "E-mail Is So Five Minutes Ago," *BusinessWeek,* November 28, 2005, 111–12; D. Dahl, "The End of E-mail," *Inc. Magazine,* February 2006, 41–42; "Weaving a Secure Web Around Education: A Guide to Technology Standards and Security," http://nces.ed.gov/pubs2003/secureweb/glossary.asp, June 21, 2006; "Wikis Make Collaboration Easier," *InformationWeek,* June 20, 2006, (www.informationweek.com/shared/printableArticleSrc.jhtml?articleID=170100392).

109. "Postini," www.postini.com, April 28, 2008.

110. Conlin, "E-mail Is So Five Minutes Ago."

111. Ibid.

112. Ibid.

113. Ibid.

114. Dahl, "The End of E-mail"; "Wikis Make Collaboration Easier;" V. Vara, "Wikis at Work," *The Wall Street Journal,* June 18, 2007, R11.

115. Dahl, "The End of E-mail."

116. Conlin, "E-mail Is So Five Minutes Ago;" "Soar Technology, Thinking inside the box," *Soar Technology, Inc.,* www.soartech.com/home.php, April 28, 2008.

117. Conlin, "E-mail Is So Five Minutes Ago."

118. Ibid.

119. Ibid.

120. Bulkeley, "Playing Well with Others."

121. Ibid.

122. Conlin, "E-mail Is So Five Minutes Ago"; Dahl, "The End of E-mail"; "Weaving a Secure Web Around Education."

123. Wakizaka, "Faxes, E-Mail, Help the Deaf Get Office Jobs," *The Wall Street Journal,* October 3, 1995, B1, B5.

124. D. Tannen, "The Power of Talk," *Harvard Business Review,* September–October 1995, 138–48; D. Tannen, *Talking from 9 to 5* (New York: Avon Books, 1995).

125. Tannen, "The Power of Talk."

126. Ibid.

127. Ibid.

128. Ibid.

129. Ibid; Tannan, *Talking from 9 to 5.*

130. Ibid.

131. J. Cohen, "He Writes, She Writes," *Houston Chronicle,* July 7, 2001, C1–C2.

132. Ibid.

133. Ibid.

134. Tannen, "The Power of Talk," 148.

Chapter 17

1. M. Kripalana, "Tata: Master of The Gentle Approach," *BusinessWeek,* February 25, 2008; "Ravi Kant," *Tata Group,* www.tata.com/scripts/print.asp, May 2, 2008.

2. Kripalana, "Tata: Master of The Gentle Approach"; "Profile," TATA Motors, www.tatamotors.com/our_world/profile.php, May 2, 2008; "Our Companies: Tata Motors," www.tata.com/tata_motors/index.htm, May 2, 2008.

3. Kripalana, "Tata: Master of The Gentle Approach."

4. Ibid.

5. Ibid.

6. K. Chae, "CEO Message," *TATA Daewoo,* www.tata-daewoo.com/ver3/eng/03_company/01_ceo.html, May 7, 2008; "Events and Happenings," *TATA,* www.tata.com/scripts/print.asp, May 7, 2008.

7. Kripalana, "Tata: Master of The Gentle Approach."

8. "Tata Group Profile," *TATA Group,* www.tata.com/scripts/print.asp, May 2, 2008.

9. Kripalana, "Tata: Master of The Gentle Approach."

10. Ibid.

11. Ibid.

12. Ibid.

13. "Sales Activities," *TATA DAEWOO,* www.tata-daewoo.com/ver3/eng/08_center/01_faq.html, May 7, 2008;

"Company," *TATA DAEWOO,* www.tata-daewoo.com/ver3/eng/03_company/02_tata.html, May 7, 2008.

14. Kripalana, "Tata: Master of The Gentle Approach."

15. J. A. Litterer, "Conflict in Organizations: A Reexamination," *Academy of Management Journal* 9 (1966), 178–86; S. M. Schmidt and T. A. Kochan, "Conflict: Towards Conceptual Clarity," *Administrative Science Quarterly* 13 (1972), 359–70; R. H. Miles, *Macro Organizational Behavior* (Santa Monica, CA: Goodyear, 1980).

16. S. P. Robbins, *Managing Organizational Conflict: A Nontraditional Approach* (Englewood Cliffs, NJ: Prentice-Hall, 1974); L. Coser, *The Functions of Social Conflict* (New York: Free Press, 1956).

17. K. A. Jehn, "A Qualitative Analysis of Conflict Types and Dimensions in Organizational Groups," Cornell University, 1997; K. A. Jehn, "A Multimethod Examination of the Benefits and Detriments of Intragroup Conflict," Cornell University, 1995.

18. L. L. Putnam and M. S. Poole, "Conflict and Negotiation," in F. M. Jablin, L. L. Putnam, K. H. Roberts, and L. W. Porter, eds., *Handbook of Organizational Communication: An Interdisciplinary Perspective* (Newbury Park, CA: Sage, 1987), 549–99.

19. L. R. Pondy, "Organizational Conflict: Concepts and Models," *Administrative Science Quarterly* 2 (1967), 296–320; R. E. Walton and J. M. Dutton, "The Management of Interdepartmental Conflict: A Model and Review," *Administrative Science Quarterly* 14 (1969), 62–73.

20. G. R. Jones and J. E. Butler, "Managing Internal Corporate Entrepreneurship: An Agency Theory Perspective," *Journal of Management* 18 (1992), 733–49.

21. T. Petzinger, Jr., "All Happy Businesses Are Alike, but Heirs Bring Unique Conflicts," *The Wall Street Journal,* November 17, 1995, B1.

22. J. A. Wall, Jr., "Conflict and Its Management," *Journal of Management* 21 (1995), 515–58.

23. Walton and Dutton, "The Management of Interdepartmental Conflict."

24. Pondy, "Organizational Conflict."

25. W. F. White, *Human Relations in the Restaurant Industry* (New York: McGraw-Hill, 1948).

26. R. L. Pinkley and G. B. Northcraft, "Conflict Frames of Reference: Implications for Dispute Processes and Outcomes," *Academy of Management Journal* 37 (February 1994), 193–206.

27. K. W. Thomas, "Conflict and Negotiation Processes in Organizations," in M. D. Dunnette and L. M. Hough, eds., *Handbook of Industrial and Organizational Psychology,* 2d ed., vol. 3 (Palo Alto, CA:

Consulting Psychologists Press, 1992), 651–717.

28. Kripalana, "Tata: Master of The Gentle Approach."

29. Ibid.

30. Thomas, "Conflict and Negotiation Processes in Organizations."

31. Pinkley and Northcraft, "Conflict Frames of Reference."

32. N. Heintz, "In Spanish, It's *Un Equipo,*" *Inc. Magazine,* April 2008; S. McAdams, "Putting culture on the map," *Ragan Report,* June 11, 2007, www.xplane.com/#/news/; S. Powers, "12 Revolutionary Companies Transforming the City that Works (and Yes, They're Hiring.), *Portland Monthly,* October 2007, www.xplane.com/#/news/.

33. Heintz, "In Spanish, It's *Un Equipo.*"

34. Ibid.

35. Ibid.

36. Ibid.

37. Ibid.

38. Ibid.

39. Ibid.

40. E. Shapiro, J. A. Trachtenberg, and L. Landro, "Time Warner Settles Feud by Pushing Out Music Division's Fuchs," *The Wall Street Journal,* November 17, 1995, A1, A6.

41. Ibid.

42. P. R. Lawrence, L. B. Barnes, and J. W. Lorsch, *Organizational Behavior and Administration* (Homewood, IL: Irwin, 1976).

43. R. J. Lewicki and J. R. Litterer, *Negotiation* (Homewood, IL: Irwin, 1985); G. B. Northcraft and M. A. Neale, *Organizational Behavior* (Fort Worth, TX: Dryden, 1994); J. Z. Rubin and B. R. Brown, *The Social Psychology of Bargaining and Negotiation* (New York: Academic Press, 1975).

44. C. Bendersky, "Organizational Dispute Resolution Systems: A Complementarities Model," *Academy of Management Review* 28 (October 2003), 643–57.

45. R. E. Walton, "Third Party Roles in Interdepartmental Conflicts," *Industrial Relations* 7 (1967), 29–43.

46. "Meaning of Arbitrator," *hyperdictionary,* September 4, 2004 (www.hyperdictionary.com); "Definitions of Arbitrator on the Web," www.google.com, September 4, 2004.

47. L. Thompson and R. Hastie, "Social Perception in Negotiation," *Organizational Behavior and Human Decision Processes* 47 (1990), 98–123.

48. Thomas, "Conflict and Negotiation Processes in Organizations."

49. R. J. Lewicki, S. E. Weiss, and D. Lewin, "Models of Conflict, Negotiation and Third Party Intervention: A Review and Synthesis," *Journal of Organizational Behavior* 13 (1992) 209–52.

50. Northcraft and Neale, *Organizational Behavior.*

51. Lewicki et al., "Models of Conflict, Negotiation and Third Party Intervention"; Northcraft and Neale, *Organizational Behavior;* D. G. Pruitt, "Integrative Agreements: Nature and Consequences," in M. H. Bazerman and R. J. Lewicki, eds., *Negotiating in Organizations* (Beverly Hills, CA: Sage, 1983).

52. R. Fischer and W. Ury, *Getting to Yes* (Boston: Houghton Mifflin, 1981); Northcraft and Neale, *Organizational Behavior.*

53. P. J. Carnevale and D. G. Pruitt, "Negotiation and Mediation," *Annual Review of Psychology* 43 (1992), 531–82.

54. A. M. Pettigrew, *The Politics of Organizational Decision Making* (London: Tavistock, 1973); Miles, *Macro Organizational Behavior.*

55. D. J. Hickson, C. R. Hinings, C. A. Lee, R. E. Schneck, and D. J. Pennings, "A Strategic Contingencies Theory of Intraorganizational Power," *Administrative Science Quarterly* 16 (1971), 216–27; C. R. Hinings, D. J. Hickson, J. M. Pennings, and R. E. Schneck, "Structural Conditions of Interorganizational Power," *Administrative Science Quarterly* 19 (1974), 22–44; J. Pfeffer, *Power in Organizations* (Boston: Pitman, 1981).

56. Pfeffer, *Power in Organizations.*

57. Ibid.

58. M. Crozier, "Sources of Power of Lower Level Participants in Complex Organizations," *Administrative Science Quarterly* 7 (1962), 349–64; A. M. Pettigrew, "Information Control as a Power Resource," *Sociology* 6 (1972), 187–204.

59. Pfeffer, *Power in Organizations;* G. R. Salancik and J. Pfeffer, "The Bases and Uses of Power in Organizational Decision Making," *Administrative Science Quarterly* 19 (1974), 453–73; J. Pfeffer and G. R. Salancik, *The External Control of Organizations: A Resource Dependence View* (New York: Harper & Row, 1978).

60. B. Morris, Senior Editor, "The Pepsi Challenge," *Fortune Magazine,* What makes Pepsi great? – February 19, 2008, http://cnnmoney.printthis.clickability.com/pt/cpt?action=cpt&title=What+makes+Pepsi+gre . . . , April 8, 2008.

61. "The 100 Most Powerful Women #5 Indra K. Nooyi, Forbes.com, August 30, 2007, www.forbes.com/lists/2007/11/biz-07women_Indra-K-Nooyi_1S5D_print.html, April 23, 2008.

62. "PepsiCo–Investor Overview," http://phx.corporate-ir.net/phoenix.zhtml?c=78265&p=irol-irhome, May 2, 2008.

63. Morris, "The Pepsi Challenge"; D. Brady, "Indra Nooyi: Keeping Cool in Hot Water," *BusinessWeek,* June 11, 2007, www.businessweek.com/print/magazine/content/07_24/b4038067.htm?chan=gl, April 30, 2008; P. Maidment, "Re-Thinking

Social Responsibility," *Forbes.com,* January 25, 2008, www.forbes.com/2008/01/25/davos-corporate-responsibility-lead-cx_pm_0125notes. . . , April 23, 2008; B. Saporito, "Indra Nooyi," *TIME in partnership with CNN,* Monday, April 30, 2007, www.time.com/time/specials/2007/printout/0,29239,1595326_1615737_1615996,00. . . , April 23, 2008.

64. "The World's Most Influential People," *The 2008 TIME 100,* www.time.com/time/specials/2007/0,28757,1733748,00.html, May 2, 2008.

65. "25 Most Powerful People in Business," *Fortune,* http://money.cnn.com/galleries/2007/fortune/0711/gallery.power_25.fortune/22.html, April 30, 2008; "50 Most Powerful Women 2007, The Power 50," *CNNMoney.com, Fortune,* http://money.cnn.com/galleries/2007/fortune/0709/gallery.women_mostpowerful.fortune/i. . . , April 23, 2008.

66. Morris, "The Pepsi Challenge"; "PepsiCo's Board of Directors Appoints Indra K. Nooyi as Chief Executive Officer Effective October 1, 2006, Steve Reinemund to Retire as Chairman in May 2007, *PEPSICO,* News Release, http://phx.corporate-ir.net/phoenix.zhtml?c=78265&p=irol-newsArticle_print&ID=895346. . . , May 8, 2008.

67. Morris, "The Pepsi Challenge."

68. Ibid.

69. Ibid.

70. "PEPSICO Officers and Directors," *PepsiCo* http://www.pepsico.com/PEP_Company/OfficersDirectors/index.cfm, May 2, 2008.

71. Morris, Senior Editor, "The Pepsi Challenge."

72. Ibid.

73. A. Moore, MarketWatch, "Indra Nooyi's Pepsi challenge, CEO puts her own brand on new products and global goals," December 6, 2007, www.marketwatch.com/news/story/indra-nooyi-puts-her-brand/story.aspx?guid=%7. . . , April 23, 2008.

74. Morris, Senior Editor, "The Pepsi Challenge."

75. Ibid.

76. Ibid.

77. Pfeffer, *Power in Organizations.*

78. Ibid.

79. Ibid.

80. L. Kramer, "Doing Well and Good: How Social Responsibility Helped One Coffee Grower Land a Deal with Starbucks," *Inc. Magazine,* June 2006, 55–56.

81. Ibid; "Corporate Social Responsibility," www.starbucks.com/aboutus/csr.asp, June 25, 2006.

82. "The Exceptional Cup Participating Farms Finca El Faro," www.guatemalancoffees.com/GCContent/GCeng/auction_tec_fincas/FincaElFaro.asp, June 25, 2006.

83. Kramer, "Doing Well and Good."

84. Ibid.

85. Ibid.

86. Ibid.

87. "Welcome to El Faro Estate Website," *El Faro Estate Coffee,* www.elfaroestate.com/default.htm, May 7, 2008; "El Faro Today," El Faro Estate Coffee, www.elfaroestate.com/history/elFaro/ElFaroToday.htm, May 7, 2008; "C.A.F.E. practices (coffee and farmer equity practices)," *Starbucks Coffee,* The Business of Coffee, www.starbucks.com/aboutus/sourcingcoffee.asp, May 7, 2008.

88. Kramer, "Doing Well and Good."

Chapter 18

1. www.bestbuy.com, 2008; www.walmart.com, 2008.

2. N. Byrnes, "Clicks and Bricks Retailers," www.businessweek.com, December 6, 2007.

3. www.walmart.com, 2008.

4. N. B. Macintosh, *The Social Software of Accounting Information Systems* (New York: Wiley, 1995).

5. C. A. O'Reilly, "Variations in Decision Makers' Use of Information: The Impact of Quality and Accessibility," *Academy of Management Journal* 25 (1982), 756–71.

6. G. Stalk and T. H. Hout, *Competing Against Time* (New York: Free Press, 1990).

7. www.iata.com, 2008.

8. R. Cyert and J. March, *Behavioral Theory of the Firm* (Englewood Cliffs, NJ: Prentice-Hall, 1963).

9. E. Turban, *Decision Support and Expert Systems* (New York: Macmillan, 1988).

10. R. I. Benjamin and J. Blunt, "Critical IT Issues: The Next Ten Years," *Sloan Management Review,* Summer 1992, 7–19; W. H. Davidow and M. S. Malone, *The Virtual Corporation* (New York: HarperBusiness, 1992).

11. Davidow and Malone, *The Virtual Corporation;* M. E. Porter, *Competitive Advantage* (New York: Free Press, 1984).

12. S. M. Dornbusch and W. R. Scott, *Evaluation and the Exercise of Authority* (San Francisco: Jossey-Bass, 1975).

13. J. Child, *Organization: A Guide to Problems and Practice* (London: Harper & Row, 1984).

14. www.dhl.com, 2006.

15. Ibid.

16. Ibid.

17. Macintosh, *The Social Software of Accounting Information Systems.*

18. www.cypress.com, 2008.

19. www.hermanmiller.com, 2008.

20. www.boeing.com, 2008.

21. P. Bradley, "Global Souring Takes Split-Second Timing," *Purchasing,* July 20, 1989, 52–58.

22. J. A. Schumpeter, *Capitalism, Socialism and Democracy* (New York: Harper, 1942).

23. V. P. Buell, *Marketing Management* (New York: McGraw-Hill, 1985).

24. See M. M. J. Berry and J. H. Taggart, "Managing Technology and Innovation: A Review," *R & D Management* 24 (1994), 341–53; K. B. Clark and S. C. Wheelwright, *Managing New Product and Process Development* (New York: Free Press, 1993).

25. See Berry and Taggart, "Managing Technology and Innovation"; M. Gort and J. Klepper, "Time Paths in the Diffusion of Product Innovations," *Economic Journal,* September 1982, 630–53. Looking at the history of 46 products, Gort and Klepper found that the length of time before other companies entered the markets created by a few inventive companies declined from an average of 14.4 years for products introduced before 1930 to 4.9 years for those introduced after 1949–implying that product life cycles were being compressed. Also see A. Griffin, "Metrics for Measuring Product Development Cycle Time," *Journal of Production and Innovation Management* 10 (1993), 112–25.

26. www.ibm.com, 2008.

27. A. D. Chandler, *The Visible Hand* (Cambridge, MA: Harvard University Press, 1977).

28. C. W. L. Hill and J. F. Pickering, "Divisionalization, Decentralization, and Performance of Large United Kingdom Companies," *Journal of Management Studies* 23 (1986), 26–50.

29. O. E. Williamson, *Markets and Hierarchies: Analysis and Antitrust Implications* (New York: Free Press, 1975).

30. C. W. L. Hill, "Airborne Express," in C. W. L. Hill and G. R. Jones, *Strategic Management: An Integrated Approach* (Boston: Houghton-Mifflin, 2004).

31. Turban, *Decision Support and Expert Systems.*

32. www.merck.com, 2008.

33. N. A. Nichols, "Scientific Management at Merck: An Interview with CFO Judy Lewent," *Harvard Business Review,* January–February 1994, 88–91.

34. Turban, *Decision Support and Expert Systems.*

35. E. Rich, *Artificial Intelligence* (New York: McGraw-Hill, 1983).

36. Brandt, "Agents and Artificial Life."

37. Rich, *Artificial Intelligence.*

38. Ibid., 346.

39. P. P. Bonisson and H. E. Johnson, "Expert Systems for Diesel Electric

Locomotive Repair," *Human Systems Management* 4 (1985), 1–25.

40. G. R. Jones, "SAP and the Enterprise Resource Planning Industry," in C. W. L. Hill and G. R. Jones, *Strategic Management: An Integrated Approach,* 6th ed. (Boston: Houghton Mifflin, 2003).

41. B. Kogut, "Joint Ventures: Theoretical and Empirical Perspectives," *Strategic Management Journal* 9 (1988), 319–32.

42. G. S. Capowski, "Designing a Corporate Identity," *Management Review,* June 1993, 37–38.

43. J. Marcia, "Just Doing It," *Distribution,* January 1995, 36–40.

44. Davidow and Malone, *The Virtual Corporation.*

45. Ibid., 168.

46. The companies are real, but their names are fictitious. Information was obtained from a personal interview with a senior manager who had experience with both companies' information systems.

47. T. A. Stewart, "Managing in a Wired Company," *Fortune,* July 11, 1994, 54.

48. H. Mintzberg, *Mintzberg on Management: Inside Our Strange World of Organizations* (New York: Free Press, 1989).

49. From an interview conducted by C. W L Hill with a senior Boeing manager.

50. Stewart, "Managing in a Wired Company," 54.

51. www.lucasarts.com, 2008.

52. B. Hindo, " The Empire Strikes at Silos," www.businessweek.com, August 20, 2007.

53. See J. R. Meredith, "The Implementation of Computer Based Systems," *Journal of Operational Management,* October 1981; Turban, *Decision Support and Expert Systems;* R. J. Thierauf, *Effective Management and Evaluation of IT* (London: Quorum Books, 1994).

Photo Credits

Chapter 1

P1-1, page 3 © Stephen Hilger/Bloomberg News/Landov

P1-2, page 9 AP Images/Harry Cabluck

P1-3, page 10 © Michael Nagle/Getty Images

P1-4, page 12 © Mark Peterson/Redux Pictures

P1-5, page 21 © Tracy Hayes/ Bloomberg News/Landov

P1-6, page 25 © REUTERS/Brendan McDermid/Landov

P1-7, page 28 © Chuck Kennedy/MCT/Landov

P1-8, page 29 T © Bill Aron /PhotoEdit

P1-9, page 29 B © James Bergile/ZUMA Press

Chapter 2

P2-1, page 39 T © Austrian Archives/ Corbis

P2-2, page 39 B © Chad Ehlers/International Stock

P2-3, page 43 © Bettmann/Corbis

P2-4, page 44 © Bettmann/Corbis

P2-5, page 45 © Bettmann/Corbis

P2-6, page 46 20th Century Fox/Courtesy The Kobal Collection

P2-7, page 47 © Hulton Deutsch Collection/Corbis

P2-8, page 50 © The Granger Collection, New York

P2-9, page 51 © Jacques Boyer/Roger-Viollet/The Image Works

P2-10, page 56 T Courtesy Regina A. Greenwood and Henley Management College

P2-11, page 56 B © Fox Photos/Getty Images

P2-12, page 59 AP Images/HO/Hewlett Packard

Chapter 3

P3-1, page 73 © Ken Hawkins Photography

P3-2, page 79 Paul Drinkwater/NBCU Photo Bank via AP Images

P3-3, page 81 © PhotoDisc Green/Getty Images

P3-4, page 83 Courtesy of Gentle Giant Moving Company

P3-5, page 87 © Corbis

P3-6, page 89 Eric Audras/Photoalto/PictureQuest

P3-7, page 93 Courtesy of IDEO

P3-8, page 96 Courtesy of PAETEC Communications

P3-9, page 97 AP Images/Damian Dovarganes

Chapter 4

P4-1, page 109 © Tom Grill/Corbis

P4-2, page 113 © The Granger Collection, New York

P4-3, page 116 AP Images/Susan Walsh

P4-4, page 120 AP Images/Damian Dovarganes, file

P4-5, page 125 AP Images/Paul Sakuma

P4-6, page 130 © Darren McCollester/Getty Images

P4-7, page 131 © Richard Carson/Reuters/Corbis

P4-8, page 135 AP Images/John Todd

P4-9, page 138 © Charley Gallay/Getty Images

Chapter 5

P5-1, page 149 Courtesy of Sodexo

P5-2, page 153 © Blend Images/Alamy

P5-3, page 157 © Ellen B. Senisi/The Image Works

P5-4, page 158 Courtesy of Chubb Group of Insurance Companies

P5-5, page 167 © Habitat International, Inc. Photo by Jim Madden

P5-6, page 168 T © Digital Vision/Getty Images

P5-7, page 168 B © Corbis

P5-8, page 172 Copyright 2008 DaVita Inc. All rights reserved. Reprinted by permission. This material may not be published, reprinted or distributed without the express written consent of DaVita Inc.

P5-9, page 174 © Leland Bobbe/Getty Images/The Image Bank

Chapter 6

P6-1, page 187 © JUNG YEON-JE/AFP/Getty Images

P6-2, page 191 AP Images/The News Tribune, Lui Kit Wong

P6-3, page 194 AP Images/Paul Sakuma

P6-4, page 198 AP Images

P6-5, page 200 AP Images/Pat Wellenbach

P6-6, page 204 © REUTERS/Rupak De Chowdhuri/Landov

P6-7, page 210 © Bob Daemmrich/The Image Works

P6-8, page 213 © KAZUHIRO NOGI/AFP/Getty Images

P6-9, page 216 AP Images/Mircea Rosca

Chapter 7

P7-1, page 225 AP Images/Christof Stache

P7-2, page 228 © Christopher Robbins/Getty Images/Digital Vision

P7-3, page 234 Courtesy of ABS

P7-4, page 240 Courtesy of GarageTek

P7-5, page 242 © Corbis

P7-6, page 243 © Marc Romanelli/Getty Images/Workbook Stock

P7-7, page 249 Courtesy of World of Good, Inc.

P7-9, page 250 © Image 100/Corbis

Chapter 8

P8-1, page 261 T AP Images/ Damian Dovarganes

P8-2, page 261 B AP Images/Steve Helber

P8-3, page 265 © Ryan McVay/Getty Images

P8-4, page 269 AP Images/Tom Mihalek

P8-5, page 271 © Stephen Hird/Reuters/Corbis

P8-6, page 275 Mike Mergen/Bloomberg News/Landov

P8-7, page 280 Courtesy of Cott Corporation

P8-8, page 281 Courtesy of Inditex

P8-9, page 285 © Bill Varic/Corbis

P8-10, page 287 T AP Images/Katsumi Kasahara

P8-11, page 287 B © Pablo Bartholomew/Getty News/Liaison

P8-12, page 291 © Ramin Talaie/Corbis

Chapter 9

P9-1, page 303 T STAN HONDA/AFP/Getty Images

P9-2, page 303 B © TOSHIFUMI KITAMURA/AFP/Getty Images

P9-3, page 309 © Jeff Greenberg/PhotoEdit

P9-4, page 310 AP Images/Joseph Kaczmarek

P9-5, page 317 © Corbis

P9-6, page 321 © Junko Kimura/Getty Images

P9-7, page 322 Courtesy Toyota Motor Manufacturing, Kentucky, Inc.

P9-8, page 327 © Louis Psihoyos/Getty Images/Science Faction

P9-9, page 330 © Erin Siegal/Redux

P9-10, page 334 © Erich Schlegel/The New York Times/Redux

Chapter 10

P10-1, page 343 AP Images/Mark Lennihan

P10-2, page 349 © Jeffery Allan Salter/Corbis

P10-3, page 353 © Tim Boyle/Getty Images

P10-4, page 355 © Kim Steele/Photodisc Green/Getty Images

P10-5, page 358 © Nokia

P10-6, page 360 AP Images/Orlin Wagner

P10-7, page 366 © Tom Raymond/Getty Images/Stone

P10-8, page 368 AP Images/Jennifer Graylock

P10-9, page 371 © Louie Psihoyos/Corbis

Chapter 11

P11-1, page 385 © Fabrizio Costantini The New York Times/Redux

P11-2, page 388 © Willie Hill, Jr./The Image Works

P11-3, page 395 AP Images/Harry Cabluck

P11-4, page 398 © Claro Cortes IV/Reuters/Corbis

P11-5, page 402 AP Images/Alyssa Hurst

P11-6, page 405 © Felix Clay/Financial Times-REA/Redux

P11-7, page 407 © David Frazier/The Image Works

Chapter 12

P12-1, page 421 AP Images/Kevork Djansezian

P12-2, page 426 © James Leynse/Corbis

P12-3, page 432 © Amy Etra/PhotoEdit

P12-4, page 433 Courtesy Fog Creek Software

P12-5, page 436 © Chabruken/Getty Images/Taxi

P12-6, page 439 © Reza Estakhrian/Getty Images/Photographer's Choice

P12-7, page 448 AP Images/Ann Heisenfelt

P12-8, page 449 Photo by Jess Haessler/Courtesy Guerra DeBerry Coody

P12-9, page 451 AP Images/Reed Saxon

Chapter 13

P13-1, page 461 © Joe Raedle/Getty Images

P13-2, page 465 KIMBERLY WHITE/Reuters/Landov

P13-3, page 469 Courtesy of The Container Store

P13-4, page 471 Ottowa Business Journal

P13-5, page 473 © Mick Tsikas/epa/Corbis

P13-6, page 476 "Copyright © 2008. SAS Institute Inc. All rights reserved. Reproduced with permission of SAS Institute Inc., Cary, NC, USA"

P13-7, page 479 © Stockbyte/Punchstock Images

P13-8, page 484 © 2005 Comstock Images, JupiterImages Corporation

P13-9, page 486 AP Images/The Decatur Daily/John Godbey

Chapter 14

P14-1, page 495 © Frank Micelotta/Getty Images

P14-2, page 499 Courtesy of Zingerman's

P14-3, page 502 © Michael DeYoung/Corbis

P14-4, page 506 © Tim Boyle/Getty Images

P14-5, page 508 © Royalty-Free/Corbis

P14-6, page 513 © BananaStock, Ltd

P14-7, page 518 Courtesy of Creative Display Solutions, Inc.

Chapter 15

P15-1, page 527 Courtesy of ICU Medical, Inc. Photographer: Eric Glover

P15-2, page 531 AP Images/Reed Saxon

P15-3, page 533 © Ryan McVay/Photodisc Blue/Getty Images

P15-4, page 535 © Keith Brofsky/Getty Images

P15-5, page 537 AP Images/Alexandra Boulat/VII

P15-6, page 539 © Keith Brofsky/Getty Images/Photodisc

P15-7, page 542 © John A. Rizzo/Getty Images

P15-8, page 547 Courtesy of IDEO

P15-9, page 552 AP Images/Haraz Ghanbari

Chapter 16

P16-1, page 565 Comstock Images/Jupiter Images

P16-2, page 568 Courtesy of GE Healthcare

P16-3, page 570 © Jose Luis Pelaez Inc/Getty Images/Blend Images

P16-4, page 574 © David De Lossy/Getty Images/Photodisc Green

P16-5, page 575 Copyright 2008 NBAE (Photo by Jennifer Pottheiser/NBAE via Getty Images)

P16-6, page 578 © Thomas Jackson/Getty Images/Stone

P16-7, page 586 © Sam Roberts/Getty Images/Digital Vision

P16-8, page 589 © Digital Vision

P16-9, page 591 © Photodisc/Alamy

Chapter 17

P17-1, page 603 AP Images/Gautam Singh

P17-2, page 605 © Ryan McVay/PhotoDisc/Getty Images

P17-3, page 608 © BananaStock/JupiterImages

P17-4, page 611 © Cultura/Alamy

P17-5, page 614 © Jim Craigmyle/Corbis

P17-6, page 618 AP Images/Manish Swarup

P17-7, page 622 © Mike Goldwater/Alamy

Chapter 18

P18-1, page 633 T AP Images/Mark Lennihan

P18-2, page 633 B © Bill Freeman/PhotoEdit

P18-3, page 638 © Royalty-Free/Corbis

P18-4, page 639 Courtesy of Herman Miller, Inc.

P18-5, page 642 © Lourens Smak/Alamy

P18-6, page 648 © REUTERS/China Newsphoto/Landov

P18-7, page 650 © Louie Psihoyos/Corbis

P18-8, page 660 AP Images/Matt Sayles

Index

Names

A

Aaron, K., 687
Abell, D. F., 691, 692
Abott, Ida, 440
Abrams, J., 684
Acosta, Julie-Ellen, 184
Adams, D. A., 706
Adams, J. Stacy, 476, 693, 699
Adler, N. J., 698
Adler, P. S., 684
Agarwala-Rogers, R., 705
Aguilar, F. J., 691
Ahn, Byung Mo, 626
Al-Saud, Turki Saud, 523
Alboher, Marci, 491, 492
Alderfer, Clayton, 471, 473, 698
Alexander, J. A., 694
Allen, T. D., 696
Alster, N., 687
Alvarez, Ralph, 362
Anand, Rohini, 150
Ancona, D. G., 679
Anderson, C., 680
Anderson, Courtney E., 183
Anderson, Debra, 629
Anderson, J. C., 692
Anderson, P., 695
Andrews, K. R., 691
Anstice, David, 35
Ante, S. E., 692
Anthony, R. N., 694
Arewal, Harpreet, 138
Arewal, Yadi, 138
Arie, Alex, 222
Ariishi, Takako, 168, 169
Armour, S., 686
Armstrong, Bob, 569
Arndt, Michael, 383, 684, 704
Arner, F., 679
Arnst, C., 689
Aronoff, C. E., 707
Arrow, K. J., 689
Aveni, R. D., 691
Avery, Sewell, 242
Avolio, B. J., 691, 702
Ayman, R., 702

B

Bahree, B., 692
Baig, E., 706
Bain, Douglas G., 144
Baird, L., 695
Bakan, D., 687
Baker, S., 681, 700, 704
Balfour, Frederik, 600
Ballmer, Steven A., 456, 457, 503
Banaji, M., 687
Bandura, A., 699
Banerjee, N., 696
Barbeite, F. G., 698
Barley, S. R., 684
Barnard, C. I., 684
Barnes, L. B., 708
Barnes, Mark, 627
Barnes-Farrell, J., 685
Barr, M., 689
Barrett, Amy, 418
Barrett, Coleen, 138, 365
Barrett, Craig, 503, 701
Barrick, M. R., 681
Barry, V., 680
Barsaloux, J., 691
Bartlett, C. A., 689, 692
Baskin, O. W., 707
Bass, B. M., 691, 701, 702
Batson, C. D., 698
Battaglia, B. A., 687
Baucus, M. S., 684
Baum, H. G., 679
Bazerman, M. H., 690, 708
Beauchamp, T. L., 684, 693
Beavis, Ian, 626
Becker, T. E., 684
Beder, Eric, 296
Beizer, D., 706
Bell, C. H., 694
Bellah, R., 689
Belliveau, M. A., 686
Belson, K., 700
Bendersky, C., 708
Benjamin, Rinath, 257, 258, 709
Bensen, Peter, 362
Bercovici, J., 682
Berfield, Susan, 259, 491, 492

Berger, B., 690
Berger, P. L., 683
Berisha, Sali, 599
Berman, D. K., 688
Berner, R., 704
Berry, L. L., 680
Berry, M. M. J., 709
Berton, L., 682
Bertone, Antonio, 226
Bessemer, Sir Henry, 48
Bettenhausen, K., 682, 702
Beyer, J. M., 683
Beynon, H., 680
Bezos, Jeff, 78, 195, 533
Bhagwati, J., 688, 689
Bhasin, Pramod, 431
Black, Dan, 183
Blackburn, R. S., 704
Blake, R. R., 702
Blake, Robert, 506
Blanchard, Kenneth, 506, 702
Blau, P., 693, 694
Blumenstein, R., 697
Blunt, J., 709
Bohr, J., 683
Bond, Ron, 149
Bonisson, P. P., 709
Boone, Garrett, 468, 469
Borg, Deborah, 220
Borman, C., 696
Borzacchiello, Maureen, 517–518
Boslet, M., 700
Bouchard, T. J., Jr., 691
Bourgeois, L. J., 688
Bowen, D. E., 692
Bowie, N. E., 684, 693
Boyle, Currie, 561
Boyle, Dennis, 98
Brabeck-Latmathe, Peter, 187–188
Bracken, D. W., 696
Bradley, P., 709
Bradspies, R. W., 694
Brady, Diane, 182, 419, 696, 704, 708
Brandt, R., 700
Braungart, Michael, 465
Bresler, S. J., 688
Brett, J. B., 85
Brief, A. P., 90, 682, 688, 691

Brin, Sergey, 329–330
Brockner, J., 681
Brown, B. R., 708
Brown, G., 684
Brown, L., 694
Brown, V., 686
Brownstein, R., 686
Brummel, Lisa, 456–458
Bruner, J. S., 687
Bruun, S. E., 705
Buday, R. S., 703
Budworth, M. H., 697
Buell, V. P., 709
Buffet, Warren, 114
Bulkeley, W. M., 693, 707
Bunis, D., 680
Burcke, J. M., 703
Burke, M. J., 90
Burlingham, B., 683, 700, 701
Burnes, Allen, 223
Burns, L. R., 693
Burns, Penelope, 257, 258
Burns, Tom, 62, 63, 680, 681, 693
Burrows, Peter, 381
Burton, T. M., 701
Bush, Jason, 105
Butler, J. E., 695, 708
Buttram, R. T., 688
Buzzotta, V. R., 704
Bychtwald, Ken, 429
Byrne, J. A., 696, 697
Byrnes, N., 679, 693, 704, 709
Byrnes, Nanette, 383
Byron, Kristin, 576, 706

C

Caldwell, D. , 693
Calello, Paul, 599, 600
Callahan, J. D., 688
Callahan, Mary, 619–620
Calori, R., 701
Campbell, J. P., 679, 698
Campbell, Tracey, 163
Capell, Kerry, 257
Capossela, Chris, 457
Capowski, G. S., 710
Cardy, R. L., 686
Carey, A., 680
Carmichael, Pat, 174
Carnegie, Andrew, 46, 47–48
Carnevale, A. P., 687
Carnevale, P. J., 708
Carpenter, M. A., 689
Carpenter, S., 681
Carroll, A. B., 684
Carroll, S. J., 679, 694
Carter, A., 691
Carter, Jimmy, 135
Carton, B., 686, 688
Cartwright, D., 705
Casey, James, 407
Caves, R. E., 692

Chae, Kwang-Ok, 604, 707
Champy, J., 692, 703
Chan, C., 691
Chan, Kim Ki, 627
Chandler, Alfred, 646, 691, 693, 709
Chao, Elaine L., 451
Chaplin, Charlie, 44
Charles, A. C., 687
Chatman, J., 693
Chavez, L., 685
Chavez-Thompson, Linda, 451
Chemers, M. M., 702
Chenault, Ken, 12
Chesonis, Arunas, 95–96
Child, J., 683, 693, 709
Chiu, Willy, 220, 221, 558
Cho, Jujio, 303
Christensen, C. R., 692
Chua, Micheline, 659
Chung-Ming, L., 694
Claburn, T., 703
Claiborne, Liz, 228
Clare, David, 140
Clark, K. D., 679, 709
Clark, Richard T., 35
Clay, R. A., 699
Clegg, C. W., 704
Cleveland, J. N., 685
Clifford, L., 695
Clifford, S., 690, 695, 701
Coblin, James M., 382
Cohen, J. D., 682, 707
Cohen, M. D., 690
Cole, J., 686
Cole, Y., 688
Colella, A., 685, 686
Colihan, J., 704
Collins, C. J., 679
Collins, D., 684
Collins, J., 691
Combs, J. G., 679
Compton, Mark, 509
Conant, Douglas, 274–276
Condit, Philip M., 145, 196
Conger, J. A., 702
Conley, L., 706
Conlin, Michelle, 70, 458, 631,
    698, 707
Connolly, T., 699
Conolly, Patrick, 510–511
Conway, Ron, 26
Cook, J. D., 88
Cook, S. D. N., 693
Cooper, J. C., 704
Copeland, M., 698
Coplan, J. H., 685
Corboy, Patrick, 89
Coser, L., 708
Cote, S., 702
Cotsonas, David, 511–512
Coulombe, Joe, 10–11, 18, 21
Covel, S., 681

Cox, Bill, 174
Cox, Christopher, 116
Crane, Mark, 510–511
Crockett, R. O., 681
Cronin, M. J., 707
Crossman, Jacob, 586
Crotty, W. D., 691
Crozier, M., 708
Crystle, Charlie, 249
Cullen, J. B., 684
Cummings, L. L., 706
Cuneo, A. Z., 688
Curry, Rob, 598
Cyert, R., 690, 709

D

Daft, R. L., 690, 706
Dahl, D., 707
Dalesio, E. P., 699
Dalkey, N., 691
Dallas, S., 703
Daly, Robert, 612
Daniels, Pam, 597
Darley, J. M., 682
Daruwala, Nikki, 163
Daus, C. S., 680
D'Aveni, Richard, 692
Davidow, W. H., 709, 710
Davis, S. M., 693
Dawley, H., 691
de Bendern, P., 694
de Bono, Edward, 237, 690
De Geus, A. P., 691
de Janasz, S. C., 679
De Rochemont, Michelle, 422
Dean, J. W., 692
Dechant, K., 687
DeCotiis, 696
Del Valle, C., 695
Delbecq, A., 691
Dell, Michael, 9, 12, 15, 18, 24, 195,
    250–251, 295, 395, 693
DeMarie, S. M., 704
Deming, W. E., 680
Deutschman, A., 703, 704
Devaiah, P. B., 105
DeWane, Julie, 180
Dewett, T., 680
Dexter, R., 684
Diehl, M., 691
Digman, J. M., 681
Dillman, Linda M., 381
DiMicco, Daniel R., 382, 383
Dobson, J., 684
Dodes, R., 693
Donahue, Randy, 157
Donaldson, T., 680, 684
Donatone, Lorna, 150
Done, K., 692
Donovan, J. J., 699
Dornbusch, S. M., 709
Dorsey, D., 683

Dowling, Steve, 146
Doz, Y. L., 692
Dragseth, Doris, 629, 630
Drauden, G., 691
Drucker, P. F., 679, 694
Druskat, V. U., 679
Druyun, Darleen, 196
Duarte, D. L., 704
Duchinsky, Brian, 569
Duff, M., 698
Dufour, B., 701
Dumaine, B., 679, 692, 693, 694,
    703, 704
Duncan, R., 693
Dunham, Randall B., 85
Dunnette, M. D., 708
Dutton, J. M., 708
Dvorak, P., 684, 685

E

Eagly, A. H., 702
Earley, P. C., 682, 699, 705
Ebbers, Bernie, 114, 115
Eby, L. T., 696
Eccles, R. E., 680
Eckert, Bob, 272
Eckert, Scott, 665
Edid, M., 693
Edmondson, G., 689
Edwards, Cliff, 222
Edwards, R., 680
Ehrhart, M. G., 686
Einhorn, Bruce, 223
Eisner, Michael, 7, 117
Ekegren, G., 699
Elfenbein, H. A., 682
Elgin, B., 694, 699
Elizur, D., 693
Elkind, P., 683
Engardio, Pete, 221, 559, 684
Engelsman, Nico, 339
Ensminger, Anne, 457
Epstein, S., 682
Erez, M., 691
Essner, Robert A., 417
Evans, M. G., 702
Ewing, Jack, 71, 223, 493

F

Fackler, M., 687
Fahim, K., 686
Fairhurst, G. T., 694
Fanning, Shawn, 125
Farnham, A., 693
Farrell, Patrick, 462
Fastow, Andrew, 113, 131
Fayol, Henri, 8, 50, 265, 679, 680, 691
Felberbaum, M., 691
Feldman, D. C., 683
Fenn, D., 703
Fernandes, John J., 183

Fernandez, J. P., 689
Ferriola, John J., 382
Ferris, G. R., 681, 695
Fester, Dave, 295
Festinger, L., 704
Fiedler, Fred E., 507, 702
Field, A., 681
Fierman, J., 702
Fife, William J., 501
Files, J., 686
Filipczak, B., 688
Filo, David, 248
Finestone, William, 89
Finger, P. A., 690
Finkelstein, S., 695
Fiorino, Carly, 59–60
Fischer, R., 708
Fish, Lawrence, 508
Fisher, A., 687, 697
Fisher, C. D., 695, 700
Fiske, S. T., 686, 687
Fitzpatrick, David, 424
Flamholtz, E., 694
Fleishman, E. A., 701
Flint, J., 685, 696
Florian, E., 680
Floyd, S. W., 694
Flynn, J., 696
Folger, R., 686
Follett, Mary Parker, 55, 680
Ford, Henry, 39, 45, 680
Ford, William, III, 385–387
Forgas, J. P., 682
Forman, Barry, 608
Foust, Dean, 419, 666
Frankel, B., 687
Frankel, M. S., 684
Franklin, Shirley, 180
Fredrickson, J. W., 689
Freed, J., 691
Freeman, J., 693
Freeman, R. E., 684
French, R. P., Jr., 701
French, W. L., 694
Friedman, M., 684
Frost, Philip, 418
Fry, L. W., 680, 692
Fuchs, Michael, 612
Furst, S. A., 704

G

Galbraith, J. R., 693
Galen, M., 688
Galvin, B. M., 687
Garcia, Armando, 419
Garcia, Sandi, 85–86
Garfinkel, P., 696
Garvin, D., 692
Gates, Bill, 78, 96, 114, 228, 503
Gatewood, E., 684
Gavin, M. B., 694
Geber, B., 704

Geffen, David, 158
Geis, F. L., 686
Gellerman, S. W., 684
Gendron, M., 700
Gentile, Mary C., 690
George, J. M., 90, 682, 683, 686, 695,
    702, 703, 705
Gerdes, Lindsey, 185
Gerhart, B., 696
Germain, Valerie E., 600
Gersick, C. J. G., 704
Gerstner, Lou, 100
Ghemawat, P., 692
Ghoshal, S., 689, 692, 694
Ghosn, Carlos, 664
Gibson, C., 685
Gibson, David, 222
Gilbert, Julie, 181
Gilbreth, E. G., 680
Gilbreth, F. B., 680
Gilbreth, Frank, 46
Gilbreth, Lillian, 46
Giles, Colin, 223
Gilmour, Allan, 158
Givray, Henry S., 524
Glanz, J., 690
Glasgow, Stan, 221
Goates, Ken, 630
Golberg, Lewis R., 77
Goldhirsh, Bernard (Bernie), 90–91
Goldsein, A. P., 699
Goldstein, H. B., 683
Goldstein, I. L., 696
Goldwasser, A., 699
Goleman, D., 682
Goodin, R. E., 684
Goodman, N., 688
Goodnight, James, 475, 699
Gopalakrishnan, S., 105
Gore, Al, 146
Gort, M., 700
Gourlay, R., 692
Govindarajan, V., 688
Gowuder, J. P., 296
Graham, P., 680
Grant, A. M., 698
Grasso, Richard A., 118
Gratton, Lynda, 220, 539, 559
Gray, Dave, 610–611
Greehey, Bill, 552
Green, Heather, 599
Green, Leonard, 296
Green, S. G., 694
Greenberg, Hank, 524
Greenberg, J., 699
Greene, J. D., 682
Greene, Jay, 296, 458
Greenhouse, S., 701
Greenleaf, Robert, 498
Greenwald, A. G., 687
Greising, D., 700
Grenier, Jim, 566

Grey, S., 693
Griffin, A., 709
Griffin, N. Shope, 698
Griffin, R. W., 688, 691, 693
Grove, A., 701
Guerra, Frank, 449
Guerry, John, 492, 493
Guest, R. H., 679
Guion, R. M., 696
Gull, N., 689, 690
Gunther, M., 697, 700
Gupta, A. K., 679, 688
Gupta, Bela, 106
Gupta, Yogesh, 566
Gustafson, D. H., 691
Gutner, T., 685, 707
Guzman, B., 685

H

Hackman, J. R., 350, 351, 693, 704
Haji, Priya, 249
Hales, C. P., 679
Hales, L., 698
Hall, James N., 626
Hall, Kenji, 222, 341
Hall, L., 681
Hall, R. H., 693
Halperin, A., 691
Hambrick, D. C., 679, 684
Hamel, G., 691
Hamilton, F., 700
Hamm, Steve, 106, 296, 459, 523, 562
Hammer, M., 692, 703
Hamner, W. C., 699
Hannah, J., 697
Hannah, M. T., 693
Hannan, M., 693
Harkins, S. G., 705
Harrington, A., 696
Harris, C., 688
Harris, E. F., 701
Hartke, D. D., 702
Harvey, R. J., 695
Hastie, R., 708
Hastings, Reed, 69, 70
Hauck, Chris, 376
Hauck, L. C., 694
Hauck, R. M., 694
Hax, A. C., 704
Hedberg, B., 690
Heilman, M. E., 687
Heintz, N., 708
Helm, Burt, 35
Helm, L., 693
Helyar, J., 695
Hempel, J., 686
Hendrickson, A. R., 704
Hepworth, S. J., 88
Herbst, Moira, 419
Hersey, Paul, 506, 702
Hershatter, Andrea S., 183, 184
Herzberg, Frederick, 471, 474, 698

Heskett, J. L., 694
Hesseldahl, Arik, 147
Hetzer, B., 687
Hewitt, P., 686
Hewlett, William, 59, 100
Hickman, J., 680, 710
Hickson, D. J., 694, 708
Higgins, J. H., 700
Hill, C. W. L., 681, 684, 688, 689,
   691, 692, 693, 694, 709
Hill, E. J., 704
Hill, L., 679
Hindo, Brian, 35, 710
Hines, G. H., 681, 699
Hinings, C. R., 694, 708
Hinz, Werner, 531
Hira, N. A., 682, 689
Hirata, Hitoshi, 340
Hoerr, J., 692
Hof, R. D., 690, 700
Hofbeck, Adrian, 613–615
Hofer, C. W., 691
Hofstede, Geert, 211, 689
Holder, Julie Fasone, 598
Holland, K., 685, 705
Hollenbeck, J. R., 696
Holmes, Stanley, 145, 701
Hood, N., 692
Hopkirk, Paddy, 319–320
Hoppe, M. H., 689
Horgan, Sam, 429
Horwitz, Tony, 68
Hough, L. M., 708
Houghton, James R., 419
House, Robert, 510, 681, 699, 700, 702
Hout, T. M., 692, 709
Huber, G. P., 689
Hughes, Sandy, 578
Hunt, Len, 626
Hunter, J. E., 694, 697
Hurd, Mark, 60
Hvorostovsky, Dmitri, 104
Hyman, Richard, 257
Hymowitz, C., 682, 705, 706

I

Igger, Bob, 405
Ihlwan, Moon, 628, 691
Immelt, Jeffrey R., 180, 265, 267,
   396, 419
Irvine, M., 682
Isdell, E. Neville, 418
Ismail, Lobna, 155
Iuna, N., 680

J

Jablin, F. M., 708
Jackson, J. H., 696, 705
Jackson, P. R., 679, 704
Jackson, S., 680
Jaffe, A. M., 686

Jamieson, D., 680
Janis, I. L., 690
Jarrell, Buster, 538
Jaussi, K. S., 680
Jeannerette, P. R., 696
Jeffery, Kim, 628, 631
Jehn, K. A., 708
Jenner, Kris, 36
Jensen, M. C., 704
Jerdee, T. H., 679
Jermier, J. M., 702
Jetli, Puneet, 106
Jobs, Steve, 7, 17, 34, 295
Joel, A. C., 679
Johannesson, Jon Asgeir, 256–257
Johnson, B. T., 702
Johnson, H. E., 709
Johnson, Lyndon B., 244
Johnson, R., 684
Johnston, Ann, 184
Jones, Clayton M., 297
Jones, D. T., 691, 692
Jones, G. R., 679, 680, 681, 683, 684,
   692, 693, 694, 705, 708, 709, 710
Jones, Reg, 286
Jones, Sarah, 180
Jones, Stephen, 229
Jones, T. M., 684
Joyner, T., 696
Jung, Andrea, 91, 367–368, 515, 683
Jung, D. I., 691

K

Kahn, J., 687
Kahn, Robert, 61, 680
Kahneman, Daniel, 231, 241, 689, 690
Kaihla, P., 703
Kalcevic, Bennett, 459
Kamp, Mads, 71
Kamprad, Ingvar, 205
Kaner, R., 697
Kanfer, R., 699
Kant, Ravi, 603–604
Kanungo, R. N., 702
Kaplan, Allison, 258–259
Kapsalis, S. C., 691
Karau, S. J., 702
Kasparov, Gary, 650
Kathwari, M. Farooq, 439
Katsikis, I. N., 691
Katz, Daniel, 61, 680
Katz, R. L., 679
Kaufman, J., 698
Kawamata, Katsuji, 242
Kazanjian, R. K., 693
Kelleher, Herb, 138
Kelley, David, 93, 94
Kelley, T., 704, 705
Kelley, Tom, 552, 683
Kelly, E. P., 684
Kelly, Gary, 524
Kelly, John E., III, 522–523

Kemp, N. J., 704
Kennedy, John F., 244
Kent, Muhtar, 599
Kerr, N. L., 705
Kerr, S., 702, 705
Kerwin, K., 696
Kesmodel, D., 707
Kibler, Carolyn, 171–172
Kiley, David, 628, 694
Kindle, Jo Ann Taylor, 461, 697
Kindler, Jeffrey, 412
King, Elizabeth, 183
King, N., 698
King, Robert, 545
Kirkland, R., 706
Kirsner, S., 705
Klepper, J., 709
Knight, Philip, 655
Knouf, Craig, 234
Ko, S. J., 685
Kochan, T. A., 708
Kogut, B., 692, 710
Kohler-Gray, S., 688
Koita, Rizwan, 431
Kolind, Lars, 71
Konovsky, M. A., 686
Konrads, W., 689
Koo, Chung Mong, 626
Koontz, H., 694
Koretz, G., 686
Kotter, J., 679, 694
Kozlowski, Dennis, 524
Kramer, L., 709
Kraus, Michael, 498
Kravets, D., 683
Kreitner, R., 699
Kripalana, Manjeet, 223, 707, 708
Kroc, Ray, 96, 98–99
Krugman, P., 689
Kuczmarski, Thomas D., 419
Kunda, G., 694
Kurose, Yukako, 169–170
Kwon, Yoo Young, 627
Kyrgidou, L. K., 691

L

Labate, J., 700
Labich, K., 679
Lakshman, Nandini, 223, 693
Lambert, A., 688
Landler, M., 689
Landro, L., 708
Langowitz, N. J., 690
Latane, B., 705
Latham, Gary, 479, 691, 696, 697, 699
Law, K., 92
Lawler, E. E., III, 694, 699, 700
Lawrence, M., 700
Lawrence, Paul, 62, 693, 708
Laybourne, Geraldine, 508
Leary, W. E., 706
Lee, C. A., 708

LeFauve, R. G., 704
Lehman, P., 697
Lelchuk, I., 686
Lengel, R. H., 690, 706
Lennard, Dareen, 585
Lentz, E., 696
Lever, William, 208
Levering, R., 705
Levering, Robert, 421
Levin, Gerald, 612
Levine, E. L., 696
Levitt, T., 688
Lewent, Judy, 648–649
Lewicki, R. J., 708
Lewin, D., 708
Lewin, Kurt, 408
Lewis, Randy, 166
Libby, Ryan, 83
Lightman, Steven, 25
Likert, R., 701
Lilly, Dave, 404
Lima, L., 696
Lincoln, J. F., 700
Lindblom, C. E., 694
Litterer, J. A., 680, 708
Litterer, J. R., 708
Littman, J., 704, 705
Locke, Ed, 479, 691, 699
Loden, M., 687
Loeb, M., 701
Lonier, T., 691
Loomis, C. J., 697
Lopez, George, 527–529
Lorange, P., 694
Loray, Carol, 501
Lorsch, Jay, 62, 693, 708
Love, Lonnie, 21
Lovell, J., 689
Lowry, Tom, 600, 700
Lublin, J. S., 687, 696, 704, 707
Lucas, George, 659–660
Luckman, T., 683
Luthans, F., 699
Lutz, Robert, 579
Lyttle, C. Richard, 418

M

Macintosh, N. B., 709
Mackay, Martin, 412
Mackey, John, 120–121
Magee, Yada, 570
Mahony, T. A., 679
Mai, Steve, 184
Maidment, P., 708
Makhijani, M. G., 702
Malone, M. S., 709, 710
Mamut, Alexander, 104
Mance, H., 683
Mandell, B., 688
Mann, Richard A., 176, 688
Mannix, E. A., 679
March, James, 232–235, 680, 690, 709

Marcia, J., 710
Marcial, G., 692, 701
Markels, A., 704
Martin, Bob, 626
Martinez, Angela, 478
Martinez, M. N., 683
Mashaba, Herman, 508
Maslow, Abraham, 471, 472, 698
Mason, P. A., 679
Mason, R. O., 690
Mason-Draffen, C., 703
Mathieu, J. E., 682
Mathis, R. L., 696
Matlack, C., 704
Matta, E., 679
Maurer, T. J., 698
Maxey, D., 685
Mayer, Brian, 316
Mayo, Elton, 56, 680
McCallum, Daniel, 646
McCann, James F., 296
McCarthy, John, 459
McCartney, S., 693
McCauley, Jim, 29
McClelland, David, 81, 471, 474, 681, 698
McCline, R. L., 688
McComb, William, 343–345
McConnon, Aili, 340
McCormick, E. J., 696
McCracken, D., 685
McDaniel, Jonathan, 567
McDonald, Malcolm, 382
McDonough, William, 465–466
McFarland, Richard, 629, 630
McGee, S., 683
McGirt, E., 681
McGlynn, Margaret G., 35–36
McGrath, Judy, 495–496, 515
McGregor, Douglas, 57, 680
McGregor, J., 694
McGregor, Jena, 35, 182, 419
McGuire, J., 679
McLean, B., 683
McMahan, G. C., 695
McMann, Mary, 478
McMillan, Ron, 573, 706
McMurry, Michelle, 181
McNealy, Scott, 236–239
McNerney, W. James, Jr., 144–145
McQueen, Alexander, 226
McWilliams, G., 679
Mecham, R. C., 696
Mehrabian, Albert, 573
Mehta, S. N., 688
Mendell, Steven, 27–28
Meredith, J. R., 710
Merrick, A., 687
Meshoulam, I., 695
Metthee, I., 688
Michels, A. J., 700
Miles, R. H., 708

Miller, B. C., 704
Miller, Bob, 428
Miller, D., 693, 694
Miller, Jerry, 335
Miller, Joseph A., Jr., 419
Mills, T. M., 703
Mintzberg, Henry, 13, 659, 679, 694, 701, 710
Mische, Justus, 500
Mitchell, R., 695
Mobley, W. H., 682
Monczke, R. M., 688
Montebello, A. R., 704
Moore, A., 709
Moore, Jonathan, 256
Moore, P. L., 696
Moore, Stephen, 531
Moriguchi, Takahiro, 29
Morris, B., 708, 709
Morris, David, 167
Morton, M., 694
Moscowitz, Milton, 421
Moskowitz, M., 705
Moss, S. E., 696
Mott, Randy, 381
Mount, M. K., 681
Mouton, Jane, 506, 702
Mozilo, Angelo, 116, 117
Mulally, Alan, 385
Mulcahy, Anne, 3, 17, 18, 20, 24, 524
Muller, J., 696
Mullinax, Harrison, 166
Mulvihill, G., 691
Murphy, P. E., 684

N

Nabers, W., 705
Nakane, C., 689
Nakarmi, L., 701
Nakashima, R., 694
Napier, N. K., 695
Nardelli, Bob, 117, 524
Nash, L. L., 684
Nayeri, F., 696
Near, J. P., 684
Needleman, S. E., 686, 695
Neill, B., 689
Nelson, R. R., 706
Nelson, Scott, 21
Nemetz, P., 692
Neuijen, B., 689
Newman, B., 706
Newman, W. H., 694
Nichols, N. A., 709
Nicholson, N., 698
Nightingale, J., 694
Ninie, Wang, 223
Noe, R. A., 696
Nogues, Thierry, 537
Nohira, N., 680
Nokes, Sue, 513
Nooyi, Indra, 618–619

Nord, W. R., 679
Norman, Donald A., 296
North, D. C., 688
Northcraft, G. B., 708
Nour, Joseph, 471
Nussbaum, B., 704
Nystrom, L. E., 682

O

O'Boyle, T. F., 705
O'Brian, B., 692
O'Brien, J. M., 694, 695
Obstfeld, M., 689
O'Flynn, Stephen, 611
Ohayv, D. D., 689
Okimoto, T. G., 687
Oldham, G. R., 350, 351, 693
Oldham, Todd, 296
O'Leary-Kelly, A. M., 688
Oliveira, Rogerio, 560
Ollila, Jorma, 376
Olsen, J. P., 690
Olsen, Ken, 228
Olson, E., 701
O'Mara, J., 680
O'Neal, Stanley, 116, 117
O'Neil, J., 706
O'Reilly, C. A., 693, 705, 709
Organ, D. W., 680, 682
Ortega, B., 683
Osburn, L., 689
Oswald, Brian, 459
O'Toole, Larry, 83
Ouchi, W. G., 694
Overman, S., 696

P

Packard, David, 59, 100
Padmanabhan, S., 459
Paetzold, R. L., 686, 688
Paez, B. L., 692
Page, Larry, 329–330
Pai, T. V. Moandas, 106
Palais, Dave, 629
Palmeri, Christopher, 297, 691
Palmisano, Samuel, 100, 560, 644, 645
Palrecha, R., 700
Pape, W. R., 704
Parashuram, Veena, 106
Parker, L. D., 680
Parker, S. R., 679
Patterson, A., 687
Paulson, Andrew, 104–105
Payne, Carolyn Kindle, 461
Pazmino, Erwin, 110
Pearce, J. A., 684, 691, 703
Peiperl, M. A., 696
Pelletier, Liane, 502
Pencer, Gerald, 280
Pennings, D. J., 708
Penrose, E., 692

Perlez, J., 689
Perrow, Charles, 347, 680, 693, 694
Perry, M. K., 691
Peters, L. H., 702
Peters, Susan, 180
Peters, Tom, 54, 680, 706
Petersik, Don, 230
Peterson, Monte, 325–326
Peterson, R. S., 682
Pettigrew, A. M., 708
Petzinger, T., Jr., 708
Peus, Claudia, 180
Pfeffer, Jeffrey, 231, 689, 699, 706, 708
Phelps, R., 691
Pickering, J. F., 709
Pillai, R., 702
Pinkley, R. L., 708
Pirtle, Thomas, 570
Pitodia, Jeevanial, 223
Pitta, J., 680
Pleh, Muamer, 29
Pohlmann, J. T., 702
Pollard, H. R., 680
Polzer, J. T., 685
Pondy, L. R., 705, 708
Poniewozik, J., 685
Poole, M. S., 708
Porras, Estuardo, 621–622
Porras, J., 691
Porter, E., 695
Porter, L. W., 88, 708
Porter, Michael, 276, 688, 691, 692, 709
Potanin, Vladimir, 105
Poteet, M. L., 696
Powers, S., 708
Prahalad, C. K., 691, 692
Premack, S. L., 696, 697
Premji, Azim H., 459
Pritchard, R. D., 698
Provitera, M. J., 679
Pruitt, D. G., 708
Pryor, Michael, 433
Pugh, D. S., 694
Pugh, S. D., 688
Pulakos, E. D., 687
Putnam, L. L., 708

Q

Quinn, J. B., 695
Quintanilla, Cindy, 184

R

Radjou, Navi, 220, 559
Radosevich, D. J., 699
Raeburn, P., 698
Ragins, Belle Rose, 258
Ramadoss, Aroon, 70
Ramanujam, V., 692
Ramstead, Don, 528
Randel, A. R., 680

Rangaswani, J. P., 585
Ratz, J. M., 685
Raven, B., 701
Ravlin, E. C., 703
Read, Paul, 184, 185
Rebello, J., 702
Reckford, Jonathan, 134–135
Reeves, M., 704
Regan, M. B., 697
Rego, Lyndon, 105
Reich, Robert, 130, 191, 688
Reinert, P., 706
Reingold, J., 702
Reis, Brenda, 417
Reizenstein, R. M., 688
Reyes, Gregory, 115
Rhode, J. G., 694
Rich, E., 709
Richie, Roy, 430
Rider, Michael, 536
Roach, Andy, 585
Robbins, S. P., 708
Roberson, L., 687
Roberts, B. S., 688
Roberts, Barry S., 176
Roberts, K. H., 708
Roberts, Sara, 574, 706
Robertson, J., 684, 688
Robinson, B., 90
Robinson, G., 680, 687
Roddick, Anita, 78
Rodgers, R., 694
Rodgers, T. J., 400–401, 647, 656
Roe, R. A., 682
Roedy, Bill, 599–600
Roethlisberger, F. J., 57
Rogers, E. M., 705
Rokeach, Milton, 82, 681
Roll, R., 690
Rollins, Kevin, 29
Ronen, S., 698
Roos, D., 691, 692
Rose, R. L., 701
Rosen, B., 686, 704
Rosener, J. B., 687
Ross, G. H. B., 694
Roth, D., 698
Rotter, J. B., 681
Rowe, Mike, 79
Rowley, Ian, 664, 693
Roy, D., 680
Rubin, J. Z., 708
Ruffolo, Robert R., Jr., 417–418
Rugman, A. M., 689
Rungtusanatham, M., 692
Rynes, S., 686, 695

S

Saari, L. M., 699
Saavedra, R., 702
Sacks, D., 689
Sagie, A., 693

Saginaw, Paul, 498–499
Salancik, G. R., 708
Salter, C., 691
Salzberg, Barry, 183
Sanchez, J. I., 696
Sandberg, J., 705, 706, 707
Sanders, G., 689
Sanders, L., 692
Sanders, W. G., 684
Santos, Lucille, 258–259
Sawyer, J. E., 691
Scanlon, Joseph, 487
Schaaf, Tim, 222
Schein, H., 683
Schendel, D., 691
Schiff, Karenna Gore, 180
Schiffmann, H. R., 687
Schlosser, J., 698, 699
Schmidt, Eric, 330
Schmidt, K. A., 691
Schmidt, S. M., 708
Schmitt, R. B., 705
Schneck, R. E., 708
Schneider, Benjamin, 93, 683, 693
Schoemaker, Paul J. H., 419
Schoenfeldt, L. F., 695, 700
Schoenherr, R. A., 693
Schreyogg, G., 694
Schriesheim, C. A., 702
Schroeder, R. G., 692
Schultz, Howard, 34–35
Schulz, J. W., 694
Schuman, M., 702
Schumpeter, J., 688, 709
Schwab, Marion, 175
Schwartz, Jonathan, 579, 690
Schwarzman, Stephen, 523
Schweiger, D. M., 690
Schwenk, C. R., 690
Scott, Tom, 47
Scott, W. R., 709
Sears, Michael, 196
Segal, T., 688
Seiders, K., 680
Sellers, P., 685
Semel, Terry, 612
Semler, Ricardo, 426–427, 695
Senegal, Jim, 505
Senge, Peter, 237, 245, 246, 689, 691
Serwer, A. E., 687
Sewell, D., 692
Seyle, D. C., 685
Shama, A., 679
Shapiro, E., 708
Sharp, Isadore, 421–422
Sharpe, R., 685, 696
Shaw, J. B., 695, 700
Shaw, K.N., 699
Shaw, W. H., 680
Shellenbarger, S., 697, 706
Sheppard, J. A., 705
Sheriden, J. E., 693

Sherman, S., 688
Shulka, R. K., 691
Shuman, Marc, 240–241
Siegel, Eric, 234
Siegel, Steven, 89
Silver, David, 593
Silverglate, Paul, 182
Simon, Herbert, 232–235, 680,
  689, 690
Simons, R., 694
Sinclair, R. C., 682
Sinegal, James, 194
Singer, B., 686
Sixel, L. M., 696
Skill, M. S., 679
Skilling, Jeffrey, 115, 524
Skinner, B. F., 480, 699
Skinner, Jim, 362
Slate, E., 682
Smith, Adam, 42, 680
Smith, D. B., 683
Smith, David, 650
Smith, F. J., 88
Smith, Fred, 290, 356, 665
Smutniak, J., 689
Snyder, N. T., 704
Soenen, Michael J., 296
Soke, A., 684
Solinger, N., 682
Solomon, R. C., 684
Sommerville, R. B., 682
Song, L., 92
Sonnenberg, D., 703
Sorcher, M., 699
Sorensen, J. B., 683
Spalding, Carl, 140
Spangler, W. D., 681, 699, 700
Spears, L., 700
Spolsky, Joel, 433, 696
Spors, K. K., 681, 682, 697
Stafford, D., 682
Stahl, M. J., 681, 699
Stajkovic, A. D., 699
Stalk, G., 692, 709
Stalker, G. M., 62, 63, 680, 681
Stalker, G. R., 693
Stamps, D., 685
Stanford, Linda, 645
Starck, Philippe, 226
Staudenmaier, J. M., Jr., 680
Stavraka, C., 684
Staw, B. M., 690, 706
Steinberg, Joseph, 613–615
Steiner, Gregg, 86
Steinmann, H., 694
Stemple, J., 680
Stephens, Richard, 184
Stevens, A., 687
Stevens, Mark, 576
Stewart, R., 679
Stewart, T. A., 698, 710
Stogdill, R., II, 695, 700

Stone, S. C., 687
Stonecipher, Harry, 144
Stopford, J., 693
Stracker, Karen, 576
Stratton, Jeff, 362
Stringer, Sir Howard, 213, 222
Stroebe, W., 691
Stundza, T., 692
Sullivan, Mark, 600
Sullivan, R. L., 695
Sullivan, S. E., 679
Sung, J., 698, 699
Swann, W. B., Jr., 685
Sy, T., 702
Symonds, William C., 419

T

Taggart, J. H., 709
Tahmincioglu, E., 697
Taiichi, Ohno, 40
Tang, M. J., 690
Tannen, Deborah, 590, 592, 707
Tashiro, H., 704
Tata, Ratan, 599
Tavares, Carlos, 664
Taylor, Andrew, 461
Taylor, Frederick W., 43, 680, 693
Taylor, Jack, 461
Taylor, S. E., 686, 687
Teckel, Michael, 506
Teece, D. J., 692
Tellegen, A., 682
Tenbrunsel, A. E., 683
Thacker, R., 688
Thalheimer, Richard, 25
Tharenou, P., 679
Thierauf, R. J., 710
Thomas, David, 174, 688
Thomas, David A., 440
Thomas, K. W., 708
Thomas, O., 694
Thomke, Stefan H., 419
Thompson, Amy, 184
Thompson, Donald, 362
Thompson, J. D., 680, 694, 704
Thompson, James, 61, 541
Thompson, L., 708
Thurston, K., 695
Tiku, N., 691
Tindell, Kip, 469
Tiplady, R., 704
Tisch, Jonathan, 172
Tischler, Linda, 515, 702
Tkaczyk, C., 680
Tobin, D. R., 680
Todd, P. A., 706
Tomiki, Hisashi, 334
Tosi, H. L., 694
Totty, M., 707
Townsend, A. M., 704
Trachtenberg, J. A., 708
Trent, R. J., 688

Trevino, L. K., 684, 706
Trice, H. M., 683
Troy, M., 693
Tsuda, Miiko, 169
Tsuru, Hirofumi, 340
Tuckman, B. W., 704
Turban, E., 709
Turner, C., 694
Tversy, Amos, 231, 241, 690
Tylor, E. B., 689
Tyson, J., 706

U

Ury, W., 708

V

Valentine, James, 666
Valian, Virginia, 160, 686, 688
Van Maanen, J., 683, 684, 694
van Olffen, W., 682
Vanderburg, Janice, 471
Varadarajan, P., 692
Vaslow, J. B., 688
Vaughn, S., 686
Vest, Charles M., 523
Victor, B., 684
Vierira, Meredith, 180
Viola, Karen, 515
Vitzthum, C, 691
von Rumohr, Cai, 297
Voros, S., 693
Vroom, Victor H., 467

W

Wack, P., 691
Waitt, Ted, 34
Wald, M. L., 690
Wall, J. A., Jr., 708
Wall, T. D., 88, 679, 704
Waller, M. J., 679
Walsh, J. P., 691
Walster, W. G., 691
Walton, R. E., 708
Walton, Sam, 371–372
Wang, Vera, 296
Wanous, J. P., 696
Warr, P. B., 88
Washko, John, 440
Watanabe, Katsuaki, 303, 334
Waterman, A. S., 684
Waterman, Robert, 54, 680, 706
Watson, D., 682
Waxman, Henry, 116, 117
Weber, J., 688
Weber, Max, 49–50, 680
Webster, J., 90
Weick, K. E., 683, 694
Weiner, S. P., 704
Weintraub, Arlene, 36
Weinzweig, Ari, 498–499

Weiss, E. M., 698
Weiss, H. W., 699
Weiss, S. E., 708
Weiss, William J., 418
Welch, David, 628, 696
Welch, Jack, 117, 267, 401, 424, 503
Wellner, A. Stein, 687, 706
Wells, L., 693
Werner, E., 680
Wessel, D., 695
West, M. S., 686
Wexley, K. N., 687, 696
Wheeler, J. V., 679
Wheelright, S. C., 690, 709
White, E., 696, 703, 705, 707
White, J. B., 707
White, W. F., 708
Whiting, V., 679
Whitman, Meg, 180, 515
Wilder, Colleen, 529
Wildstrom, S. H., 699
Williams, E. S., 702
Williams, J. R., 692
Williams, K., 705
Williams, M., 692
Williamson, O. E., 709
Wilson, Mark, 73–75
Winslow, R., 706
Winter, D. G., 681, 698
Witt, L. A., 681
Witteveen, Stef, 258, 259
Womack, J. P., 691, 692
Wong, C., 92
Woodman, R. W., 691, 694
Woolridge, B., 694
Woycke, J., 681, 699
Wren, D., 680
Wright, P. M., 695, 696
Wyant, C., 692
Wysocki, B., 679

Y

Yamada, Tachi, 503
Yang, Jerry, 248
Yanow, D., 693
Yates, JoAnne, 573
Yellin, Todd S., 70
Young, S., 692
Yu, R., 698
Yukl, G., 700
Yung, Chung Ju, 627

Z

Zachary, G. P., 697
Zager, R., 700
Zajac, D. M., 682
Zander, A., 705
Zaslav, David, 79
Zeitz, Jochen, 225–227
Zellner, W., 691, 700, 701
Zhou, J., 682, 683, 703

Subjects

A

Ability tests, 436
Accommodation, 609
Accommodative approach, 137
Achievement orientation, 214
Achievement-oriented behavior, 511
ActiveNet, 531–532
Activity ratios, 394
Ad hoc committee, 369, 536
ADA (Americans with Disabilities Act), 153, 155–156, 428
Adaptive cultures, 375–376
Administrative management, 48
Administrative management theory, 48–55
Administrative model, 232–236
AFL-CIO, 451
Agadir, 209
Age, 152–153
Age discrimination, 428–429
Age Discrimination in Employment Act, 153, 428
Agreeableness, 76–77
AIDS, 156, 427–428
Alderfer's ERG theory, 473
All-channel network, 580
Ambiguous information, 235
Americans with Disabilities Act (ADA), 153, 155–156, 428
Annual meeting, 98
Answering machine, 575
Applications software, 645
Arbitrator, 452, 613
Artificial intelligence, 649–650
ASA (attention-selection-attrition) framework, 93
ASEAN, 209
Asynchronous technology, 539
Attention-selection-attrition (ASA) framework, 93
Attitude, 84–88
Authority, 49, 362
Autonomy, 351
Avoidance, 609

B

Background information, 435
Backward vertical integration, 282
Bank wiring room experiment, 57
Barriers to entry, 197
BARS (behaviorally anchored rating scale), 443
B2B (business-to-business) commerce, 653–654
B2B marketplace, 654
B2B network structure, 655–656

B2C (business-to-customer) commerce, 654
Behavior appraisals, 442
Behavior control, 399–401
Behavior observation scale (BOS), 443
Behavioral management, 55
Behavioral management theory, 55–60
Behaviorally anchored rating scale (BARS), 443
Benchmarking, 413
Bias, 167, 241–243
Big five personality traits, 75–79
Blog, 579
B&M retailers, 633–635
Bonus, 486
BOS (behavior observation scale), 443
Bottom-up change, 412
Boundary spanning, 331
Boundary-spanning roles, 331–332
Boundaryless organization, 658
Bounded rationality, 233
Brainstorming, 247
Brand loyalty, 197
Bricks-and-mortar (B&M) retailers, 633–635
Built to Last, 272
Bureaucracy, 49–50
Bureaucratic control, 402–406
Business-level plan, 267
Business-level strategy, 267, 277–281
Business-to-business (B2B) commerce, 653–654
Business-to-customer (B2C) commerce, 654

C

CACM, 209
Cafeteria-style benefit plans, 448
CAFTA, 210
Capabilities/disabilities, 155–156
CARICOM, 209
CEMAC, 209
Centralization, 52, 366
CEO (chief executive officer), 16
CEO compensation, 448
Ceremonies/rites, 97–99
Chain network, 579, 580
Chain of command, 362, 365
Challenger shuttle disaster, 242, 244
Change. *See* Organizational change
Charismatic leaders, 514
Cheaper by the Dozen, 46
Chief executive officer (CEO), 16
Chief operating officer (COO), 16
Child labor, 130–131
Circle network, 580
Civil Rights Act of 1991, 153, 428

Clan control, 406
Classical decision-making model, 232
Classroom instruction, 438–439
Client appraisal, 445
Clients, 644
Closed system, 62
Coercive power, 501
Collaboration, 609
Collaboration software, 584–585
Collective bargaining, 451–452
Collectivism, 211
COMESA, 209
Command group, 535–536
Commission pay, 487
Communication, 564–600
  collaboration software, 584–585
  communication networks, 579–580
  cross-cultural differences, 591–592
  dangers of ineffective, 571–572
  external networks, 581–582
  face-to-face, 573–575
  gender differences, 592–593
  groupware, 583–584
  impersonal written communication, 578–579
  importance, 567–568
  information richness, 572–573
  Internet, 582
  intranet, 582–583
  linguistic style, 590–593
  managers as receivers, 589–590
  managers as senders, 587–589
  monitoring e-mail and Internet usage, 577–578
  organizational communication networks, 580–581
  perception, 570–571
  personally addressed written communication, 575–577
  process, 569–570
  spoken communication electronically transmitted, 575
  verbal/nonverbal, 570
Communication assistant, 588
Communication networks, 579–580
Communication process, 569–570
Competition, 609
Competitive advantage, 23
Competitors, 195–198
Compromise, 609
Computer networks, 643–645
Concentration on a single industry, 282
Conceptual skills, 16
Concurrent control, 390
Conflict. *See* Organizational conflict
Conscientiousness, 77–78
Consideration, 505

Contingency models of leadership, 507–512
Contingency planning, 269
Contingency theory, 62
Contract book, 328
Control. *See* Organizational control
Control process, 390–393
Control systems, 389
Controlling, 12
COO (chief operating officer), 16
Core competency, 18
Core members, 328
Corporate culture. *See* Organizational culture
Corporate-level plan, 266–267
Corporate-level strategy, 266, 281
Cradle to Cradle: Remaking the Way We Make Things (McDonough/Braungart), 465
Creativity, 245–248
Crisis management, 30
CRM (customer relationship management), 311–313
Cross-functional team, 328, 360, 370
CSN, 209
Culture. *See* Organizational culture
Current ratio, 394
Customer relationship management (CRM), 311–313
Customer service function, 309
Customers, 194–195

D

Data, 635
Days sales outstanding, 394
Debt-to-assets ratio, 394
Decentralizing authority, 366
Decision making
  administrative model, 232–236
  bias, 241–243
  classical model, 232
  defined, 227
  group, 243–245
  nonprogrammed, 230
  programmed, 228–229
  steps in decision-making process, 236–240
Decision support system, 648–649
Decisional role, 14
Decoding, 570
Defensive approach, 137
Delphi technique, 248
Demand forecasts, 430
Demographic forces, 201
Department, 13, 535
Development, 438
Developmental consideration, 514
Devil's advocacy, 244
Dialectical inquiry, 244
Differentiation, 9
Differentiation strategy, 278
Digital piracy, 125–126

Direct supervision, 399
Directive behavior, 511
Dirty Jobs, 79
Disabilities, 155–156
Discipline, 53
Discrimination, 168–169
Disseminator, 14, 160
Distributive justice, 161
Distributive negotiation, 613
Distributors, 193
Disturbance handler, 14, 160
Diversification, 284–286
Diversity, 148–185
  age, 152–153
  business case for, 162–164
  capabilities/disabilities, 155–156
  defined, 151
  effective management, 170–174
  ethical imperative, 161–162
  gender, 153–154
  legislation, 153
  overt discrimination, 168–169
  perception, 164–168
  race and ethnicity, 154–155
  religion, 155
  sexual harassment, 175–177
  sexual orientation, 158–159
  socioeconomic background, 156–157
Division of labor, 51, 349, 540
Divisional structure, 354–358

E

E-commerce, 653
E-mail, 576–578
EAC, 209
Economic forces, 199
Economies of scale, 197
ECOWAS, 209
EEO (equal employment opportunity), 427
EEOC (Equal Employment Opportunity Commission), 427
Effectiveness, 6
Efficiency, 6, 318–324
Emotional intelligence, 90–91, 516–517
Employee stock option, 486
Employment interview, 435–436
Empowered self-managed team, 365–366
Empowerment, 503–504
Encoding, 569
Enterprise resource planning (ERP) system, 650–653
Entrepreneur, 14, 160, 248
Entrepreneurship, 251
Entropy, 62
Equal Employment Opportunity Commission (EEOC), 427
Equal employment opportunity (EEO), 427
Equal employment opportunity laws, 153, 428

Equal Pay Act, 153, 428
Equity, 53, 476
Equity theory, 476–479
ERG theory, 473
ERP (enterprise resource planning) system, 650–653
Escalating commitment, 242
Esprit de corps, 54
Ethics, 26–28, 108–147. *See also* Social responsibility
  changes over time, 113–114
  community, society, and nation, 122
  customers, 120–122
  defined, 112
  diversity, 161–162
  employees, 118
  ethical dilemma, 111–112
  failures in professional ethics, 132
  individual, 132–133
  law, and, 112
  managers, 115–117
  occupational, 131–132
  organizational, 133–134
  organizational culture, 373–374
  rules for ethical decision making, 122–125
  societal, 129–131
  stockholders, 114–115
  suppliers and distributors, 118–119
  value-chain management, 334–335
  why behave ethically?, 126–129
Ethics ombudsman, 140
EurAsEC, 209
European Union (EU), 209
Evolution of management theory, 39–71
  administrative management theory, 48–55
  behavioral management theory, 55–60
  bureaucracy, 49–50
  contingency theory, 62
  Fayol's 14 principles of management, 50–54
  Follett, 55–56
  Gilbreths, 46
  Hawthorne Studies, 56–57
  human relations movement, 57
  management science theory, 60
  mechanistic structure, 63
  open-systems view, 61–62
  organic structure, 63
  organizational environment theory, 61–64
  scientific management theory, 42–48
  Taylor, 43
  theory X and theory Y, 58
  Weber, 49–50
Evolutionary change, 409
Executive compensation, 448
Executive support system, 649
Exercise price, 486

Expectancy, 467
Expectancy theory, 467–471
Expert power, 501–503
Expert system, 649–650
Exporting, 288
External locus of control, 80
External networks, 581–582
External recruiting, 432
Extinction, 481
Extraversion, 76
Extrinsically motivated behavior, 464

F

Face-to-face communication, 573–575
Facilities layout, 318–320
Fair Factories Clearinghouse, 131
Family and Medical Leave Act,
    153, 428
Fayol's 14 principles of management,
    50–54
Feedback, 351
Feedback control, 390
Feedforward control, 389
Fiedler's contingency model, 507–510
Figurehead, 14, 160
Filtering, 588
Financial measures of performance,
    393–395
First-line manager, 15
Five forces model, 276
Fixed-position layout, 319
Flat organization, 364
Flatter organizations, 656
Flexible manufacturing, 318, 320–321
Flower industry, 109–111
Focused differentiation strategy, 279
Focused low-cost strategy, 279
Folkways, 211
Force-field theory, 408
Fordism, 45
Foreign Corrupt Practices Act, 130
Formal appraisal, 445
Formal leader, 543
Formulating strategy
    business-level strategies, 277–281
    corporate-level strategies, 281
    five forces model, 276
    SWOT analysis, 273–276
Forward vertical integration, 282
Franchising, 289
Free trade, 208–210
Free Trade Area of the Americas
    (FTAA), 210
Free-trade doctrine, 207
Friendship group, 539–540
FTAA (Free Trade Area of the
    Americas), 210
Functional-level plan, 268
Functional-level strategy, 268, 307
Functional strategies, 307–309
Functional structure, 351–354
Fuzzy logic, 650

G

Gatekeeping, 332
GATT (General Agreement on
    Tariffs and Trade), 207
GCC, 209
Gender, 153–154
Gender schema, 165
General Agreement on Tariffs and
    Trade (GATT), 207
General and Industrial Management
    (Fayol), 8
General environment, 189
Geographic structure, 356–357
Glass ceiling, 152
Global crisis management, 30
Global environment, 186–223
    barriers of distance and culture,
        207–208
    barriers to entry, 197
    barriers to trade and investment,
        206–207
    changes in the environment, 202–210
    competitors, 195–198
    customers, 194–195
    demographic forces, 201
    distributors, 193
    economic forces, 199
    free trade, 208–210
    general environment, 198–202
    national culture, 210–216
    political and legal forces, 201
    process of globalization, 204–206
    regional trade agreements, 209–210
    sociocultural forces, 200–201
    suppliers, 189–192
    task environment, 189–198
    technological forces, 199–200
Global geographic structure, 356
Global organization, 22, 188
Global outsourcing, 191
Global product structure, 357
Global strategy, 286
Global supply chain management, 192
Globalization, 204
Goal-setting theory, 479–480
Goals, 272, 396
Government regulations, 197
Grapevine, 581
Graphic rating scale, 443
Grievance procedure, 452
Group, 529
Group cohesiveness, 548–551
Group creativity, 247–248
Group decision making, 243–245
Group decision support system, 649
Group norms, 544–546
Group roles, 542–543
Groups and teams, 526–562
    conflict, 554
    conformity and deviance, 545–548
    defined, 529

group cohesiveness, 548–551
group development over time,
    543–544
group norms, 544–546
group roles, 542–543
group size, 540–541
group tasks, 541–542
innovation, 532–533
leadership, 543
motivation, 534
organizational goals, 551–552
performance enhancement, 530–531
responsiveness to customers, 532
social loafing, 553–554
types, 534–540
Groupthink, 243–244
Groupware, 583–584

H

Hawthorne effect, 57
Hawthorne Studies, 56–57
Herzberg's motivator-hygiene theory,
    474
Heuristics, 241
Hierarchy of authority, 362
Hierarchy of needs, 472
Historical overview. *See* Evolution of
    management theory
HIV/AIDS, 156, 427–428
Hofstede's model of national culture,
    211–214
Horizontal communication, 581
Horizontal information flows, 657
Hostile work environment sexual
    harassment, 175
House's path-goal theory, 510–511
HP Way, 59
HRM. *See* Human resource manage-
    ment (HRM)
Human relations movement, 57
Human resource management (HRM),
    420–459
    background information, 435
    classroom instruction, 438–439
    collective bargaining, 451–452
    defined, 423
    employment interview, 435–436
    external recruiting, 432
    formal education, 440–441
    internal recruiting, 434
    job analysis, 431
    labor relations, 450–452
    legal environment, 427–428
    on-the-job training, 439
    overview, 424–425
    paper-and-pencil tests, 436–437
    pay and benefits, 447–449
    performance appraisal and feedback,
        441–447
    performance tests, 437
    physical ability tests, 437
    planning, 430–431

recruitment, 429–434 – *Cont.*
references, 437
selection, 434–438
training and development, 438–441
varied work experiences, 440
Human skills, 18
Hybrid structure, 361
Hygiene needs, 474
Hypercompetition, 277

I

Illusion of control, 242
Impersonal written communication, 578–579
Importing, 289
In Search of Excellence (Peters/Waterman), 54
Incremental product innovation, 325
Individual ethics, 132–133
Individualism, 211
Inequity, 477
Inert cultures, 375
Informal appraisal, 446
Informal leader, 543
Informal organization, 57
Information, 635, 636–637
Information and control, 638–639
Information and coordination, 640
Information and decisions, 638
Information distortion, 588
Information overload, 578–579
Information richness, 572–573
Information systems, 324
Information technology (IT), 632–666
artificial intelligence, 649–650
B2B commerce, 653–654
B2B network structure, 655–656
B2C commerce, 654
boundaryless organization, 658
computer networks, 643–645
decision support system, 648–649
defined, 637
effects of advancing IT, 641
ERP system, 650–653
executive support system, 649
expert system, 649–650
flatter organizations, 656
horizontal information flows, 657
information and control, 638–639
information and coordination, 640
information and decisions, 638
limitations, 659–661
operations information system, 647
product life cycle, 641–643
strategic alliance, 654–655
transaction-processing system, 647
Informational role, 14
Initiating structure, 506
Initiative, 53
Innovation, 24, 324–331
Input, 466
Instant messaging, 577

Instrumental value, 82
Instrumentality, 468
Integrating mechanisms, 369
Integrative bargaining, 613
Intellectual stimulation, 514
Interest group, 540
Intergroup conflict, 606
Intermediate-term plans, 268
Internal locus of control, 80
Internal recruiting, 434
International expansion, 286–290
exporting, 288
franchising, 289
importing, 289
joint venture, 289
licensing, 289
strategic alliance, 289
wholly owned foreign subsidiary, 290
Internet, 324, 582
Interorganizational conflict, 607
Interpersonal conflict, 605
Interpersonal role, 14
Intragroup conflict, 606
Intranet, 582–583
Intrapreneur, 250
Intrapreneurship, 251
Intrinsically motivated behavior, 464
Intuition, 230
Inventory, 315
Inventory turnover, 394
IT. *See* Information technology (IT)

J

Jargon, 587
JIT (just-in-time) inventory system, 315, 321–322
Job analysis, 431
Job characteristics model, 350–351
Job design, 348–351
Job enlargement, 349
Job enrichment, 349
Job satisfaction, 84, 85
Job specialization, 42
Johnson & Johnson's credo, 139
Joint venture, 289
Just-in-time (JIT) inventory system, 315, 321–322
Justice rule, 124

K

Kanban, 322
Knowbot, 649
Knowledge management system, 658

L

Labor relations, 450–452
LAN (local area network), 644
Lateral moves, 434
Leader, 14, 160, 497
Leader-member relations, 508
Leader substitutes model, 511–512

Leadership, 494–524
behavior model, 505–507
charismatic leaders, 514
contingency models, 507
cultural diversity, 499–500
defined, 497
emotional intelligence, 516–517
empowerment, 503–504
Fiedler's contingency model, 507–510
gender, 515–516
House's path-goal theory, 510–511
leader substitutes model, 511–512
power, 500–503
trait model, 504–505
transactional, 515
transformational, 513–515
Leadership substitute, 511
Leading, 12
Lean manufacturing, 40
Learning, 480
Learning organization, 245
Learning theories, 480–484
Least-preferred coworker (LPC), 508
Legitimate power, 500–501
Leverage ratios, 394
Lewin's force-field theory of change, 408–409
Liaison, 14, 160
Liaison role, 369
Licensing, 289
Line manager, 362
Line of authority, 52
Linguistic style, 590–593
Liquidity ratios, 394
Local area network (LAN), 644
Locus of control, 80
Long-distance learning, 440
Long-term orientation, 214
Long-term plans, 268
Low-cost strategy, 277
LPC (least-preferred coworker), 508

M

Mainframe, 644
Management
defined, 5
levels of, 15–16
why studied, 7
Management by exception, 366
Management by objectives (MBO), 400–401
Management by wandering around, 574
Management information system (MIS), 60, 637, 646
Management science theory, 60
Managerial grid, 506
Managerial overconfidence, 231
Managerial skills, 16–19
Managerial tasks, 8–13
Market structure, 358

Marketing function, 308
Maslow's hierarchy of needs, 472–473
Materials management function, 308
Matrix structure, 358–360
MBO (management by objectives), 400–401
McClelland's needs for achievement, affiliation, and power, 474
McLanguage, 99
Mechanistic structure, 63
Mediator, 452, 613
Medium, 570
Mentoring, 174, 440
Merit pay, 485–487
Message, 569
Middle manager, 15
Mintzberg's typology of managerial tasks, 14
MIS (management information system), 60, 637, 646
Mission statement, 263, 270
Modern Times (Chaplin), 44
Monitor, 14, 160
Mood, 88–90
Moral rights rule, 124
Mores, 211
Motivation, 460–493
    Alderfer's ERG theory, 473
    defined, 464
    equity theory, 476–479
    expectancy theory, 467–471
    goal-setting theory, 479–480
    Herzberg's motivator hygiene theory, 474
    learning theories, 480–484
    Maslow's hierarchy of needs, 472–473
    McClelland's needs for achievement, affiliation, and power, 474
    nature of, 464–467
    need theories, 471–476
    OB MOD, 482
    operant conditioning theory, 480–482
    pay, 485–487
    social learning theory, 483–484
Motivation equation, 466
Motivator-hygiene theory, 474
Motivator needs, 474
Multicultural environment. See Diversity
Multidomestic strategy, 286

N

NAFTA, 209, 210
National culture, 200, 210–216
National Labor Relations Act, 450
National Labor Relations Board (NLRB), 450
Need, 471
Need for achievement, 81, 474
Need for affiliation, 81, 474

Need for power, 81, 474
Need theories, 471–476
Needs assessment, 438, 439
Negative affectivity, 76
Negative reinforcement, 481
Negotiation, 613–615
Negotiator, 14, 160
Networking, 643
Neural network, 650
Newsletters, 579
NLRB (National Labor Relations Board), 450
Noise, 569
Nominal group technique, 247–248
Nonprogrammed decision making, 230
Nonverbal communication, 570
Norms, 50, 82, 211
Nurturing orientation, 214

O

OB MOD (organizational behavior modification), 482
Objective appraisals, 442
Observational learning, 483
Obstructionist approach, 135–136
OCB (organizational citizenship behaviour), 86
Occupational ethics, 131–132
Offshoring, 430–431
Old boys' network, 582
On-the-job training, 439
Open system, 61
Open-systems view, 61–62
Openness to experience, 78–79
Operant conditioning theory, 480–482
Operating budget, 396–397
Operating margin, 393, 394
Operating system software, 645
Operations information system, 647
Operations management, 60
Optimum decision, 232
Order, 53
Organic structure, 63
Organization, 5
Organizational architecture, 345
Organizational behavior, 57
Organizational behavior modification (OB MOD), 482
Organizational change, 407–413
    assessing need for change, 410
    deciding on change to make, 410–411
    defined, 407
    evaluating the change, 413
    evolutionary change, 409
    implementing the change, 411–412
    Lewin's force-field theory of change, 408–409
    revolutionary change, 409
    top-down vs. bottom-up change, 412
Organizational citizenship behavior (OCB), 86

Organizational commitment, 87
Organizational communication networks, 580–581
Organizational conflict
    conflict management strategies, 609–612
    defined, 605
    sources of conflict, 607–608
    type of conflict, 605–607
Organizational control, 387–406
    behavior control, 399–401
    bureaucratic control, 402–406
    clan control, 406
    control process, 390–393
    control systems and IT, 389–390
    defined, 387
    direct supervision, 399
    financial measures of performance, 393–395
    importance, 388–389
    management by objectives (MBO), 400–401
    operating budget, 396–397
    organizational goals, 396
    output control, 393–399
    team rules of conduct, 403
Organizational culture, 370–376
    adaptive vs. inert cultures, 375–376
    ceremonies/rites, 97–99
    controlling, 100
    defined, 91
    employment relationship, 374
    leading, 100
    managers, 92–94
    organizational ethics, 373–374
    organizational members, 373
    organizational structure, 374–375
    organizing, 100
    planning, 99–100
    social responsibility, 138–140
    socialization, 97
    values/norms, 94–99
Organizational design, 345–346
Organizational environment, 61
Organizational environment theory, 61–64
Organizational ethics, 133–134
Organizational goals, 396
Organizational learning, 245, 251
Organizational performance, 6
Organizational politics, 615–621
Organizational socialization, 97
Organizational structure, 11, 345–370
    allocating authority, 362–368
    centralization/decentralization, 366–367
    chain of command, 365
    cross-functional team, 370
    defined, 346
    divisional structure, 354–358
    functional structure, 351–354
    geographic structure, 356–357

human resources, 348—*Cont.*
  hybrid structure, 361
  integrating/coordinating
      mechanisms, 368–370
  job characteristics model, 350–351
  job design, 348–351
  job enlargement, 349
  job enrichment, 349
  liaison role, 369
  market structure, 358
  matrix structure, 358–360
  organizational culture, 374–375
  product structure, 355–356
  product team structure, 360–361
  strategy, 347
  tall/flat organization, 364–365
  task force, 369
  technology, 347–348
Organizing, 11
Outcome, 466
Output control, 393–399
Outside expert, 620
Outsourcing, 20, 430
Overpayment inequity, 477, 478
Overt discrimination, 168–169

P

Paper-and-pencil tests, 436–437
PAQ (Position Analysis
    Questionnaire), 431
PARTA, 209
Participative behavior, 511
Path-goal theory, 510–511
Pay, 485–487
Pay and benefits, 447–449
Pay level, 447
Pay structure, 447
Peer appraisal, 444
Perception, 164
Performance appraisal, 441
Performance feedback, 441
Performance tests, 437
Personality tests, 436
Personality traits, 75–81
Personally addressed written
    communication, 575–577
Physical ability tests, 437
Piece-rate pay, 487
Planning, 8–10
  business-level plan, 267
  corporate-level plan, 266–267
  defined, 263
  functional-level plan, 268
  importance, 264–265
  levels of, 265–266
  scenario planning, 269–270
  single-use plans, 269
  standing plans, 268–269
  steps in planning process, 264
  time horizon, 268
Political and legal forces, 201

Political strategies, 615–621
Pooled task interdependence, 541
Portfolio strategy, 286
Position Analysis Questionnaire
    (PAQ), 431
Position power, 509
Positive reinforcement, 481
Positive reinforcers, 481
Potential competitors, 196
Power, 500–503
Power distance, 213–214
Practical rule, 124
Pregnancy Discrimination Act,
    153, 428
*Principles of Scientific Management,
    The* (Taylor), 46
Prior-hypothesis bias, 241
Proactive approach, 138
Procedural justice, 161–162
Process layout, 319
Process reengineering, 323–324
Product champion, 251
Product development, 308, 325–330
Product development plan, 327
Product layout, 319
Product life cycle, 641–643
Product structure, 355–356
Product team, 359
Product team structure, 360–361
Production function, 308
Profit ratios, 393, 394
Profit sharing, 487
Programmed decision making,
    228–229
Prosocially motivated behavior, 465
Protégé, 440
Punishment, 482

Q

Quality improvement, 313–317
Quantitative management, 60
Quantum product innovation, 325
Quick ratio, 394
Quid pro quo sexual harassment, 175

R

Race and ethnicity, 154–155
Real-time information, 637
Realistic job preview (RJP), 434
Reasoned judgment, 230
Receiver, 570
Reciprocal task interdependence,
    542
Recruitment, 429
References, 437
Referent power, 503
Regional trade agreements, 209–210
Related diversification, 284
Relationship-oriented leaders,
    507–508

Relay assembly test experiment, 56
Reliability, 437
Religion, 155
Representativeness bias, 242
Reputation, 127
Research and development team,
    535
Resource allocator, 14, 160
Responsiveness to customers,
    309–311
Restructuring, 20
Result appraisals, 442
Return on investment (ROI),
    393, 394
Revolutionary change, 409
Reward power, 501
Risk, 233
Rites of enhancement, 98
Rites of integration, 98
Rites of passage, 97
RJP (realistic job preview), 434
ROI (return on investment), 393, 394
Role making, 543
Role playing, 439
Rolling plan, 268
Rose growing, 109–110
Rules, 50

S

SAARC, 209
SACU, 209
Salary increase, 486
Sales function, 308
Salience effect, 168
Satisficing, 235
Scanlon plan, 487
Scenario planning, 269–270
Schema, 165
Scientific management, 43
Scientific management theory,
    42–48
Selection, 429, 434–438
Self-appraisal, 444
Self-efficacy, 484
Self-esteem, 80–81
Self-managed team, 21
Self-managed work teams, 323,
    536–538
Self-management of behavior, 484
Self-reinforcers, 484
Sender, 569
Sequential task interdependence,
    542
Servant leader, 498
Sexual harassment, 175–177
Sexual orientation, 158–159
Shop Management (Taylor), 46
Short-term orientation, 214
Short-term plans, 268
Similar-to-me effect, 167
Simulations, 439

Single-use plans, 269
Situational interview questions, 436
Six Sigma, 316–317, 424
Skill variety, 350
Skunkworks, 251
Social entrepreneur, 248
Social learning theory, 483–484
Social loafing, 553–554
Social responsibility. *See also* Ethics
  accommodative approach, 137
  defensive approach, 137
  defined, 135
  forms of socially responsible
    behavior, 136
  obstructionist approach, 135–136
  organizational culture, 138–140
  proactive approach, 138
  why be socially responsible?, 138
Social status effect, 167
Social structure, 200
Socialization, 97
Societal ethics, 129–131
Sociocultural forces, 200–201
Socioeconomic background, 156–157
Softbot, 649
Software agent, 649
SOP (standard operating procedure),
  50
Spam, 585
Span of control, 362
Spoken communication electronically
  transmitted, 575
Spokesperson, 14, 160
Staff manager, 362
Stage-gate development funnel, 327
Stakeholder, 114
Standard operating procedure (SOP),
  50
Standing committee, 536
Standing plans, 268–269
Star Wars studio, 659–660
Stereotype, 166
Stories and language, 98–99
Strategic alliance, 289, 654–655
Strategic human resource management,
  424
Strategic leadership, 272
Strategy, 9, 263
Strategy formulation, 273. *See also*
  Formulating strategy
Strategy implementation, 292
Stretch goals, 396
Structured interview, 435
Subjective appraisals, 442
Subordinate appraisal, 445
Superordinate goals, 614
Supervision, 399
Supervisor, 15
Suppliers, 189–192

Supply forecasts, 430
Supportive behavior, 511
SWOT analysis, 273–276
Synchronous technology, 539
Synergy, 62, 284, 530
Systematic errors, 241

T

Tall organization, 364–365
Tariff, 207
Task analyzability, 347
Task environment, 189
Task force, 369, 536
Task identity, 350–351
Task interdependence, 541
Task-oriented leaders, 508
Task significance, 351
Task structure, 508
Task variety, 347
Team, 529. *See also* Groups and teams
Team rules of conduct, 403
Technical skills, 18
Technological forces, 199–200
Technology, 199
Telecommuting, 576
Terminal value, 82
Theory X, 58
Theory Y, 58
Thick information, 659
Third-party negotiator, 613
360-degree appraisal, 445
Time horizon, 268
Times-covered ratio, 394
Title VII of the Civil Rights Act, 153,
  428
Top-down change, 411
Top-management team, 535
Top manager, 16
Total quality management (TQM),
  60, 314–316
Touch memory buttons, 487
TQM (total quality management),
  60, 314–316
Training, 438
Trait appraisals, 441–442
Transaction-processing system, 647
Transactional leadership, 515
Transformational leadership,
  513–515
Trust, 127
Turnaround management, 25
Two-boss employee, 359

U

Uncertainty, 233
Uncertainty avoidance, 214
Underpayment inequity, 477, 478
Unions, 450–451

Unity of command, 52, 535
Unity of direction, 52
Unrelated diversification, 285–286
Unstructured interview, 436
Utilitarian rule, 123

V

Valence, 469
Validity, 437
Value chain, 307
Value-chain management, 302–341
  boundary-spanning roles, 331–332
  cross-functional teams, 328
  customer relationship management
    (CRM), 311–313
  defined, 308
  efficiency, 318–324
  ethical implications, 334–335
  facilities layout, 318–320
  flexible manufacturing, 320–321
  functional strategies, 307–309
  improving efficiency, etc. over time,
    333
  information systems, 324
  innovation, 324–331
  Internet, 324
  JIT inventory, 321–322
  process reengineering, 323–324
  product development, 325–330
  quality improvement, 313–317
  responsiveness to customers,
    309–311
  self-managed work teams, 323
  Six Sigma, 316–317
  total quality management (TQM),
    314–316
Value system, 82
Values, 211
Verbal communication, 570
Vertical communication, 581
Vertical integration, 282–284
Vicarious learning, 483–484
Videoconference, 574
Virtual team, 538–539
Voice mail, 575

W

Wheel network, 579, 580
"White House Guidelines on Religious
  Exercise and Expression in the
  Federal Workplace, The," 155
Wholly owned foreign subsidiary, 290
Wikis, 585–586
WIN, 181
WOLF, 181
Women's networks, 180–182
World Trade Organization (WTO),
  207

Organizations

A

Abbott Laboratories, 184
ABC, 193
Accenture, 7, 195, 221, 559, 658
Acer, 9, 10, 196
Adam's Mark, 168
Adelphia, 113, 129
Advantica, 163
Afisha, 105
Agricultural Data Systems, 487
Airborne Express, 291
Airbus, 23
Alaska Communications
    Systems (ACS), 502
Amazon, 70, 195, 288, 533
AMD, 189, 199, 281, 391
America Greetings, 574
America Online, 189
American Airlines, 202
Ameritrade, 195
Amstrad, 287
Apple, 9, 24, 34, 70, 145–147, 195,
    213, 233, 281, 282, 283, 295,
    296, 374
Arthur Andersen, 113, 129
ASDA, 246
Associated Business Systems (ABS),
    234
AstraZeneca International, 448
AT&T, 20, 270, 437, 641
AV Birla Group, 431
Avis, 289
Avon, 367–368
Awareness, 598

B

Barnes & Noble, 208
Baugur Group, 256–257
BBC, 208
Beech-Nut, 137
BellSouth, 168
Ben and Jerry's, 138
Best Buy, 181, 196, 222, 261–263, 633,
    635
Better Built Cabinets, 619–620
BIC, 278
Black & Decker, 360
Black Like Me, 508
Blockbuster, 70, 263
Blue Cross-Blue Shield, 129
BMW, 279
Boeing, 144–145, 184, 191, 196, 288,
    326, 640, 659
Bose, 640
BP, 539
BP Amoco, 290
Bristol Myers Squib, 129

Brocade Communications, 115
Brooks Brothers, 356
Buitoni Pasta, 187
Burger King, 164

C

California Organic Flowers, 110
Calvert Group, 163
Campbell Soup, 274–276, 278
Canon, 59, 432
Cap Gemini, 195
Capital One, 576
Carnation, 187
Carnegie Steel Company, 48
Cathay Pacific, 441
CBS, 193
Charles Schwab, 195
Chef America, 187
Chevron, 175, 582
Children Now, 154
Chrysler, 40, 231, 360, 430, 436, 582
Chubb, 158
Circuit City, 222, 261–263, 270
Cisco Systems, 189, 265, 270, 324,
    432, 574–575, 579
Citibank, 92, 314–315
Citigroup, 598
Citius Tech, 431
CNN, 208
Coca-Cola, 150, 163, 191, 195, 201,
    203, 278, 279–280, 283, 289, 418,
    432, 599
Computer Associates, 137
Container Store, 469–470
Continental Airlines, 202
Coram Healthcare Corporation, 504
Corning, 419
Costco, 194, 283, 505–506
Countrywide Mortgage, 117
C. R. England Refrigerated Trucking,
    508
Creative Display Solutions, 517–518
CyOptics, 210
Cypress Semiconductor, 400–401, 647,
    656

D

Daewoo, 441, 504
Daiei, 397, 398
Dallas Semiconductor, 487
Darden Restaurants, 163
DaVita, 171
Days Inn, 447
Dell, 7, 9, 10, 15, 18, 20, 59, 137,
    189–190, 191, 194, 195–196, 199,
    278, 288, 295, 315, 324, 325, 358,
    375, 381, 395

Deloitte & Touche, 181, 182, 184
Deloviye Ludi, 105
Delta, 202
DHL, 184, 185, 291, 638, 647
Dial, 286
Diamond Organics, 110
Digital Equipment, 228, 331, 373, 582
Dillard's, 209, 501
Doc Martin, 195
Dole Food Company, 448
Dow Chemical, 220, 559, 598
Dreyer's Ice-cream, 187
DuPont, 20, 137, 176, 289, 290, 370

E

E. & J. Gallo, 282
Eastern Airlines, 331
Eastman Kodak, 158, 441, 585
Eaton, 550
El Faro, 622
Embraer, 23
Empire HealthChoice, 312
ENI, 290
Enron, 101, 113, 115, 129, 136
Enterprise Rent-A-Car, 461–463
Ernst & Young, 158, 182, 183, 185,
    432, 598
ESPN, 208
Ethan Allen Interiors, 439
E*Trade, 195
Executive Education Network, 441
ExxonMobil, 92

F

FatWire Software, 566
FedEx, 175–176, 193, 290–291, 309,
    356, 665–666
Film Foundation, 598
Finca El Faro, 622
Fireman's Fund Insurance, 585
Flowerbud.com, 110
flowers.com, 110
Fog Creek Software, 433
Ford, 20, 24, 40, 41, 157, 168, 191, 246,
    308, 310, 323, 385–387, 388, 401,
    406, 407, 411, 436, 444, 501, 582
Forman, 608
Four Seasons Hotels, 421–423, 447
Foxconn, 145
Franklin Motor Company, 44
FTD, 110, 296–297

G

G. D. Searle, 190
Gap Inc., 119, 131
GarageTek, 240–241
Gateway, 34, 195, 404

GE Capital, 429
GE Healthcare Technologies, 568–569
General Electric, 7, 19, 168, 180, 202, 214, 265–267, 286, 288, 323, 396, 401, 419, 424, 431, 650
General Mills, 150, 276
General Motors, 24, 25, 40, 41, 137, 290, 308, 310, 436, 452, 501, 570
Genpact, 431
Gentle Giant Moving Company, 83–84
Georgia Pacific, 429
Gillette, 287–288, 339
GlaxoSmithKlein, 129, 355–356, 376
Goodyear, 582
Google, 60, 138, 185, 252, 281, 325, 329–330, 391, 458
Gradient Corporation, 486
Green Mountain Coffee, 138
Greenleaf Center for Servant Leadership, 498
Guerra DeBerry Coody, 449

H

Habitat for Humanity, 7, 134–135
Habitat International, 167
Hallmark Cards, 360, 530, 543
Hampton Inns, 447
HBO, 208
Heidrick & Struggles, 600
Heinz, 24
Herman Miller, 639–640
Hershey Foods, 201
Hewlett-Packard, 9, 10, 20, 59, 100, 195, 196, 199, 295, 315, 325, 374, 381, 574, 575
Hilton Hotels, 289
Hissho Iwai, 487
Hoechst, 23
Hoffmann-La Roche, 446
Home Depot, 7, 156, 166, 391, 407
Hon Hai Precision Industry, 145–146
Honda, 40, 202, 203, 308, 310, 655
Honeywell, 202
House of Fraser, 256
Hyatt Regency, 447
Hyundai, 504
Hyundia, 626–628

I

IBM, 17, 19, 20, 22, 99, 105, 106, 130, 158, 182, 185, 189, 191, 195, 199, 220, 283–284, 373, 374, 375, 430, 522–523, 558–562, 578, 579, 586, 598, 644–645, 654
IBM Research, 419
ICU Medical, 527–529
IDEO Product Development, 91–94, 98, 99, 547–548, 552
Igus, 321
IKEA, 205

INC., 91
Infosys, 105, 106, 459
InnSeekers, 163
Intel, 137, 189, 195, 199, 265, 391, 656
IntroNetworks, 598
Intuit, 566

J

Jack-in-the-Box, 164
JCPenney, 131, 345
Jive Software, 598
Jobline International, 432
John Deere, 21, 413
Johnson & Johnson, 133, 139, 140–141, 150, 168
Johnsonville Foods, 543
JPMorgan Chase, 184

K

Kellogg's, 203–204
Kelly Services, 430
Kentucky Fried Chicken, 164, 567
Ketchum, 585
Kia, 626–628
Kinko's, 291
Kodak, 24, 25, 656
KPMG, 182, 184, 185, 598
Kraft, 201
Krispy Kreme, 201
Kroger's, 280

L

Lands' End, 208, 288
The Learning Company, 271–272
Lehman Brothers Holdings, 158, 598
Lenovo, 195, 196, 295
Leonard Green & Partners, 296
Levi Strauss, 24, 25, 191, 209, 582
LG, 23
Li & Fung, 192
Liberty Travel, 501
The Limited, 289
Lincoln Electric, 485–487
Lipschultz, Levin & Gray, 89
Liz Claiborne, 343–345
L. L. Bean, 131, 315, 413
Lockheed Martin, 158, 182, 251–252, 531
Loews Hotels, 172
Louis Vuitton, 537–538
Lucent, 158, 243
Lundberg Family Farms, 198

M

Macy's, 356, 361
Manville Corporation, 136
Mary Kay Cosmetics, 439
Matsushita, 283, 287, 340–341
Mattel, 271–272
Mazda, 323

MBDC, 465
McDonald's, 6–7, 96, 99, 122, 138, 164, 166, 195, 278, 282, 289, 325, 348–349, 362, 439
MCI, 312
McKinsey & Co., 431, 658
McNeil Nutritionals, 191
Merck, 35–36, 132, 158, 648–649
Merrill Lynch, 117, 150, 151, 195
Metabolife, 27
Microsoft, 17, 19, 96, 114, 158, 182, 183, 189, 252, 295, 373, 375, 391, 401–402, 407, 425, 430, 456–458, 496, 598, 654
Midas Muffler, 406
MindTree Consulting, 105
Mission Research, 249
Monster.com, 432
Morton Thiokol, 228, 242, 244
Motion Computing, 665
Motorola, 17, 146, 195, 223, 331, 424, 582
MTV, 208
MTV Networks, 495–496

N

NAACP, 154
Napster, 125
NASA, 242, 244, 572
National Football League, 168
Natuzzi, 23
NBC, 193
Neiman Marcus, 356, 487, 501
Nestlé, 137, 187, 203–204, 289
Nestlé Waters North America, 628–631
Netflix, 69
Netscape, 373
New York Life Insurance, 183, 538
New York Times, 133
Newell Rubbermaid, 360
Nike, 24, 26, 168, 169, 655
Nippon Restaurant Enterprise Co., 198
Nissan, 40, 242, 664–665
Nokia, 64, 195, 213, 215–216, 223, 357–358, 376, 492–493, 539
Northrop Grumman, 531
Nucor, 382–383, 486, 537–538
NUMMI, 40
NutraSweet, 283
NVE Pharmaceuticals, 27
NYSE, 118

O

Ogilvy & Mather, 539
Olive Garden, 439
1-800-Flowers, 296
Oracle, 189, 579, 654
Ortega, 187
Oticon, 71

P

PAETEC Communications, 95–96
Pan Am, 331
PepsiCo, 191, 201, 203, 278, 279–280, 283, 618–619
Perrier, 187, 308
Pfizer, 412–413, 582
Philips, 339–340
Pier 1 Imports, 289, 352–353
Pizza Hut, 164
Plantronics, 146
Plexus, 365–366
PricewaterhouseCoopers, 182, 184, 185
Procter & Gamble, 133, 191, 278, 284, 287, 288, 290, 413, 578
Prof-Media, 105
Protus, 471
Prudential Insurance, 129, 133
PUMA, 225–227

Q

Quaker Oats, 201
Quantum, 189
Qwest, 129

R

Ralston Purina, 137, 187
Randstad, 257–259
Raytheon, 158
Re/Max, 487
Red Cross, 118
Red Lobster, 439
Reebok, 131
Rockwell Collins, 297
Root Capital, 249
Rowntree, 187
RSF Social Finance, 249
Ryla, 73–75

S

Samsung, 23, 504
SAP, 195, 651–653, 654
SAS, 475–476
S. C. Johnson & Sons, 158
Schering, 23
Scottrade, 195
Seagate Technologies, 189
SelectMinds, 598
Semco, 426–427
Shared Interest, 249
Sharper Image, 25–26
Shell, 269

Sierra Flower Trading, 110
SiteDesign, 487
siteROCK, 404
SJF Ventures, 73
Soar Technology, 586
Sodexo, 149–150
Soft Co., 657–658, 659
Sony, 195, 212–213, 221–222, 287, 321, 419
Southern California Edison, 158
Southwest Airlines, 310–311, 365
Splenda, 283
Sprint, 312
Starbucks, 34–35
Starcom MediaVest, 597
Starwood Hotels & Resorts, 316–317
Stellar Technologies, 577
Subway, 349
Sun Microsystems, 236, 582
Sunflower Electric Power, 376
SUP-Fabrik, 104

T

T-Mobile, 513
Tacit Software, 531
Taco Bell, 332
Target, 131, 138, 209, 222, 406
Tata Consultancy Services (TCS), 459
Tata Daewoo, 604
Tata Motors, 603–604
Tate & Lyle, 191
Tatum Partners, 429
Teach for America, 184
Tel Co., 657–658
Telia, 432
Texaco, 161, 168
Texas A&M University, 97, 403
Texas Instruments, 441
Textron, 286
Thermos, 325–326
3M, 18, 19, 251, 252, 285, 327, 328, 375
Timberland, 131
Time Warner, 612
Tokio Marine and Fire Insurance, 487
Toronto-Dominion Bank, 158
Toshiba, 195
Toyota, 40, 138, 155, 202, 203, 278, 279, 281, 303–306, 308, 310, 311, 313, 333–334, 403, 655
Trader Joe's, 10
TransWork Information Services, 431

Travel Company, 501
TWA, 175
Tyco, 101, 113, 129, 286

U

Unilever, 208, 287
Union Bank, 28–29
United Airlines, 202
United Electric Controls, 322
U.S. Postal Service, 193
UPS, 29, 133, 138, 174, 193, 229–230, 291, 375, 407, 504

V

Valero, 552
Verizon, 641

W

W. N. Procter, 640
Wal-Mart, 7, 26, 70, 98, 131, 166, 168, 193, 196, 208, 209, 246, 270, 280, 283, 308, 310, 322, 371–372, 381, 397–398, 407, 633, 635, 641
Walgreens, 166
Walt Disney, 7, 97, 182, 405–406, 441, 585
Wendy's, 164
Westcott Communications, 441
Westland/Hallmark Meat Co., 27
Whirlpool, 424
Whittman-Hart Consulting, 600
Whole Foods, 120, 129, 138
William Demant Holding Group, 71
Wipro, 459
W. L. Gore & Associates, 419
World of Good, 249
WorldCom, 101, 113, 114, 115, 129, 137
Wyeth, 417–418

X

Xerox, 3–7, 24, 25, 315, 413
Xplane, 610–611

Y

Yahoo, 585

Z

Zara, 280–281
Zingerman, 498–499